UNDERSTANDING
SOCIAL PROBLEMS

Fifth Canadian Edition

M. Morgan Holmes
Wilfrid Laurier University

Linda A. Mooney
East Carolina University

David Knox
East Carolina University

Caroline Schacht
East Carolina University

NELSON
EDUCATION

NELSON EDUCATION

Understanding Social Problems, Fifth Canadian Edition

by Linda A. Mooney, M. Morgan Holmes, David Knox, and Caroline Schacht

Vice President, Editorial Higher Education:
Anne Williams

Publisher:
Maya Castle and Leanna MacLean

Marketing Manager:
Terry Fedorkiw

Developmental Editor:
Elke Price

Photo Researcher:
Jessie Coffey

Permissions Coordinator:
Jessie Coffey

Production Project Manager:
Jaime Smith

Production Service:
MPS Limited

Copy Editor:
Kelli Howey

Proofreader:
Kelli Howey

Indexer:
PJ Heim

Design Director:
Ken Phipps

Managing Designer:
Franca Amore

Interior Design:
Trinh Truong

Cover Design:
Trinh Truong

Cover Image:
oliv/Masterfile, © Pali Rao/iStockphoto

Compositor:
MPS Limited

Library and Archives Canada Cataloguing in Publication

Mooney, Linda A., author
Understanding social problems / M. Morgan Holmes (Wilfrid Laurier University), Linda A. Mooney (East Carolina University), David Knox (East Carolina University), Caroline Schacht (East Carolina University). — Fifth Canadian edition.

Revision of: Understanding social problems / Linda A. Mooney ... [et al.]. — 4th Canadian ed. — Toronto : Nelson Education, ©2012. Linda A. Mooney is lead author on all previous four editions. Includes bibliographical references and indexes.
ISBN 978-0-17-667524-0 (pbk.)

1. Social problems—Canada—Textbooks.
2. Canada—Social conditions—1991– —Textbooks.
3. Social problems—Textbooks.
4. Social history—Textbooks.
I. Holmes, M. Morgan, author
II. Knox, David, 1943–, author
III. Schacht, Caroline, author
IV. Title.

HN103.5.U65 2015
361.10971   C2014-905874-8

ISBN-13: 978-0-17-667524-0
ISBN-10: 0-17-667524-8

Section 3 Problems of Inequality and Power 316

PREFACE

Violence in the home, school, and street; global poverty made even worse in the face of globalization; increasing levels of environmental pollution and depletion of Earth's natural resources; persistent conflict between and within nations; ongoing oppression of minority groups; and the widening gap in health, well-being, and stability between those who hold economic power, prestige, and privilege and those who do not. In *A Guide for the Perplexed*, B. F. Schumacher questions whether a "turning around will be accomplished by enough people quickly enough to save the modern world" (quoted in Safransky 1990: 115). Schumacher notes, "This question is often asked, but whatever the answer given to it will mislead. The answer 'yes' would lead to complacency; the answer 'no' to despair. It is desirable to leave these perplexities behind us and get down to work."

In *Understanding Social Problems*, we "get down to work" by examining how the structure and culture of societies contributes to social problems and their consequences. Understanding the social forces that contribute to social problems is necessary for designing strategies for action—programs, policies, and other interventions intended to ameliorate the social problem.

Academic Features of *Understanding Social Problems*

Strong Integrative Theoretical Foundations

The three major sociological approaches—structural-functionalism, symbolic interactionism, and conflict theory—are introduced in the first chapter and discussed and applied, where appropriate, to various social problems throughout the text.

To foster the development of a nuanced understanding of contemporary problems, we have added significant discussion of the contributions of perspectives and research developed through feminist, postmodern, and queer theories.

With hundreds of contemporary sources drawn primarily from Canadian research and from the most recent Canadian census data analyses, this edition of *Understanding Social Problems* draws out a timely and thorough approach to problems that students will recognize. The inclusion of global perspectives on social problems will also help students to situate their understandings to contexts broader than the confines of their own local experiences.

Emphasis on the Structure and Culture of Society

As noted, the text emphasizes how the social structure and culture of society contribute to and maintain social problems, as well as provide the basis for alternative solutions.

Review of Basic Sociological Terms

An overview of basic sociological terms and concepts is presented in the first chapter. This overview is essential for students who have not taken an introductory course and is helpful, as a review, for those who have. The first chapter also addresses the relationship of theory to methods to show how specific theories can foster particular methods.

Unique Organization

The order of the 14 chapters reflects a progression from micro to macro levels of analysis, focusing first on problems of health care, drug use, and crime, and then broadening to the widening concerns of population health and welfare, science and technology, large-scale inequality, and environmental problems.

Three chapters merit special mention: "Sexualities" (Chapter 9), "Armed Conflict in Global Perspective" (Chapter 14), and "Environmental Problems" (Chapter 13). Whereas traditional texts approach sexualities through the lens of "deviance," we approach issues related to them as problems only insofar as they reflect dangerous prejudices and social structures and attitudes that have a negative impact on lesbian, gay, bisexual, and transgendered (LGBT) persons. Chapter 14 avoids the pitfalls of examining conflict in simple terms of "legitimate wars" and "illegitimate terrorism" and instead provides a context for understanding how and why armed conflicts occur, and what we might be able to do to reduce both the instance of such conflict and the damage that results when conflict does occur. Chapter 13, on environmental problems, departs from texts that usually pair population concerns with environmental ones to argue that a population explosion threatens world safety; here, we approach environmental problems by looking at how attitudes toward overconsumption of resources and the production of all types of waste threaten global well-being.

Consistent Chapter Format

Each chapter follows a similar format: the social problem is defined, the theoretical explanations are discussed, the consequences of the social problem are explored, and the alternative solutions and policies are examined. A concluding section assesses the current state of knowledge for each social problem. Every chapter opens by inviting students to reflect on the positions and knowledge—whether accurate or not—that they bring to the general social concern under discussion; the feature thus acknowledges the levels of preparation and awareness that students bring to the table, but also allows them an opportunity to reflect on shifts in their thinking that can result from exposure to new information presented in the text. Every chapter ends with reflective, developmental questions that encourage students to move through different learning stages developed in Bloom's taxonomy.

Changes in the Fifth Edition

In response to feedback from teachers, reviewers, and students who have read earlier Canadian editions of *Understanding Social Problems*, we have maintained our expanded inclusion of contemporary social theory, and we have added more studies by scholars whose work is focused on issues that affect people in the Canadian context. The majority of changes in this edition have been suggested by faculty reviewers and users of this book and have been made to coincide with the needs of instructors and to encourage critical reflection on learning and reading by students. In addition, by moving the majority of the boxed features out of the text and on to the book's companion Web site, we have been able to provide more in-depth discussion in every chapter and add new pedagogical features. The excised material remains available on the CourseMate site.

Recognizing that instructors will have their own goals and purposes for their courses, we have devised action-oriented learning outcomes based on the revised Bloom's taxonomy of the cognitive domain (Anderson and Krathwohl 2001) for each chapter that we hope will provide some guidance for readers. Alongside these intended learning outcomes, each chapter opens by inviting students to reflect on the conceptions and background experience that they bring to the general social concern under discussion. The "What do you already know?" feature acknowledges the levels of preparation and awareness that students bring to the table, but also allows them an opportunity to reflect on shifts in their thinking that can result from exposure to new information presented in the text. Each chapter ends with "What do you know now?"—critically reflective, developmental questions that encourage students to reflect metacognitively on their achievement of learning outcomes. These new features have been designed by one of Canada's most respected teaching and learning experts, Dr. Trevor Holmes.

In addition to problems that are typically addressed in social problems courses and texts, new and emerging topics are examined. Topics new to the fifth edition include sustained discussions of Aboriginal health in Canada and of changes to current health-care delivery and management affecting how Canadians access health care (Chapter 2), a critical introduction to how correlations between substance abuse and poor health are presented in "commonsense" views of Aboriginal communities in Canada; we also present proposals that seek to improve quality of life for Aboriginal peoples while avoiding racist stereotyping and blame of Canada's Native peoples (Chapter 3), and a feminist-oriented critical discussion of concerns related to "sex trafficking" in Canada and abroad (Chapter 4). Chapter 6 presents new critical thinking that challenges the normative demands for use to mature and age according to life stages meant to meet the economic interests of capitalism. Chapter 8 presents a contemporary debate among prominent Canadian sociologists Vic Satzewich, Frances Henry, and Carol Tator on a practice referred to as "racial profiling" in policing, and encourages students to consider the debate in consideration of Spector and Kitsuse's theorization of how we come to recognize social problems as such. Chapter 10 presents a new *Social Problems Research Up Close* feature on the relationship between family income and participation in postsecondary education in Canada. In many instances, we have introduced discussion of topics in which significant change is taking place in Canadian legislation, and instructors may wish to introduce news stories related to the current problems addressed in each chapter.

Other significant changes have been made in the fifth edition. For example, the text's interior design has been updated considerably for this edition and now appears in colour. We continue to have a marginal glossary in each of the 14 chapters so that students may readily locate definitions to useful key terms. In addition, the fifth edition of *Understanding Social Problems* uses the most recently available updates on Canadian and global statistics and provides updates in the research in each chapter, thus providing an up-to-date *and* long-term view of the social problems we face in Canada and around the globe.

Here are some further, specific changes to this edition presented by chapter:

Chapter 1—Thinking about Social Problems

- Chapter 1 has been enhanced with expanded coverage of feminist theories by Dorothy Smith and her "women's standpoint" theory—a view of knowledge and experience that begins from the position that women occupy in larger society.
- A new section called "An Analytic Toolkit for Reading Social Problems Research" has been added. This section provides a step-by-step approach to help students read more effectively, accurately, and with more purpose.

Chapter 2—Illness and Health Care

- In this chapter, the sections on patterns of morbidity and patterns of mortality have been thoroughly revised and data have been updated.
- The coverage of HIV/AIDS has been expanded and updated to include new regional figures on adults and children newly infected and living with HIV and AIDS-related deaths.
- New coverage of critical race theory and health in Canada has been added.

Chapter 3—Alcohol and Other Drugs

- The new term "social cost model" has been added.
- The discussion of the United Nations Office on Drugs and Crime (UNODC) and international data on drug use as it relates to health issues have been expanded.
- A new, comprehensive table called "Commonly Abused Drugs" has been added and the sections on tobacco and marijuana use have been expanded and revised.
- A new section on substance abuse and Canada's most vulnerable groups has been added, including coverage of fetal alcohol syndrome.

Chapter 4—Crime and Violence

- Data on homicide rates have been updated and new coverage of transnational crime, including human trafficking, has been added.
- A new *Social Problems Research Up Close* feature discusses the studies of homeless youth, social exclusion, and criminal victimization by York University professor and researcher Stephen Gaetz.

Chapter 5—Family Problems

- The section on intimate partner violence and abuse was expanded to include coverage of the Duluth Power and Control Wheel model.
- Coverage of a multinational study carried out at McMaster University's medical school in Hamilton as it relates to victims of intimate partner violence has been added.
- New information on advocacy and education groups supporting LGBT communities and education to prevent abuse within LGBT relationships (Northwest Network) has been included, as well as arguments by Nancy Berns (2004) outlining impediments of reducing the instance of intimate partner violence.

Chapter 6—Youth and Aging

- Chapter 6 has been enhanced with expanded coverage of childhood in the global context.
- The youth and aging section includes studies on adolescence as a life stage by Canadian Mary-Louise Adams's *The Trouble with Normal* and British scholar Nancy Lesko's *Act Your Age!*
- New coverage of queer theory perspectives by Halberstam has been included.
- The section on retirement income and poverty has been revised and updated to include coverage of Conference Board of Canada (2013) and how financial pressures are negatively affecting the well-being of elderly Canadians and negatively influencing those of working age from being able to save efficiently for the future.

Chapter 7—Gender Inequality

- In this chapter, current 2013 data and information from the United Nations Human Development Report (HDR) as it relates to the status of women and men in a global context has been included.
- A new term "heteronormativity" has been added along with new coverage of Australian scholar Nikki Sullivan's work and book *A Critical Introduction to Queer Theory*.

Chapter 8—Critical Studies in Race and Ethnicity

- This chapter includes an analysis of race and social construction of race by Robert Miles and Malcolm Brown (2003).
- The section on multiculturalism in Canada has been expanded to include coverage of power structure of class and ethnicity along with studies by John Porter and his book *The Vertical Mosaic*.
- New coverage, data, and figures related to the *Immigration and Refugee Protection Act (IRPA)* and permanent residents in Canada has been added.
- Critical race theories and coverage of racial profiling have been added in the sociological theories of race and ethnicity section.

Chapter 9—Sexualities

- In this chapter, coverage of bills as they relate to hate crime laws has been revised and updated.
- Global coverage and attitudes regarding same-sex relationships has been expanded to include Russia's current government and the rights of LGBT persons and Russia's ranking as the last of 49 countries in Europe for rights protections for LGBT persons by the International Lesbian Gay Association (ILGA).
- The discussion of strategies to reduce antigay prejudice and discrimination has been significantly expanded.

Chapter 10—Poverty: National and International Issues

- The coverage of international measures of poverty has been updated and revised and includes a new figure on world wealth levels.
- Additional information on Canadian measures of poverty with updated studies by Sarlo, economist David Macdonald, and former foreign diplomat Daniel Wilson has been added.
- Coverage of minimum wages in Canada has been updated and a new map has been added.

Chapter 11—Work and Unemployment

- In this chapter, the age of information technology section has been expanded to include telework studies as they relate to employee job satisfaction.
- The coverage of child prostitution and trafficking was expanded and includes a current report from child labour specialist Mary E. Miller for the Washington State Department of Labor and Industries explaining the root causes of child labour, exploitation, and trafficking. A critical analysis by Julia O'Connell Davidson has also been added.
- New coverage of industrial food production and agricultural workers, migrant workers, and the meat processing industry has been added.

Chapter 12—Problems in Education

- Chapter 12 has been enhanced with updated coverage of education trends and achievements using statistical measures for over 35 countries as published in *Education at a Glance*, a research publication from the OECD reports.
- New coverage and data on participation rates in postsecondary education for students from traditionally underrepresented and "minority" groups added as derived from the Canadian Youth in Transition Survey (YITS).
- The section on computers and technology has been expanded and updated, including new material on massive open online courses (MOOCs).
- New examples of alternative schooling such as SEED Alternative in Toronto and U-Turn Academy in Cambridge, Ontario have been added.

Chapter 13—Environmental Problems

- The discussion of the Kyoto accord has been expanded and updated.
- New content and diagrams have been included, for example on world energy production by source, CO_2 emissions per capita by region, and greenhouse gas emissions by province and territory.
- The section on destructive water and land use in Canada includes new coverage on the pipeline in the Athabasca, fracking, and the 13 objectives of Keepers of the Athabasca as they relate to oil sands development.
- Food waste studies by Gooch and colleagues and coverage of community supported agriculture (CSA) have been added.

Chapter 14—Armed Conflict in Global Perspective

- The discussion surrounding the sociological theories of armed conflict and war has been enhanced with new coverage of the costs associated with forming allegiances in Canada's role in post-9/11 relations with the United States.
- New key term and discussion surrounding primordial explanations has been added.
- Coverage of wars in Syria, Russia, and the Ukraine has been expanded and updated.

Pedagogical Features of the Fifth Edition

Student-Friendly Presentation

To enhance the book's appeal to students, the fifth edition includes streamlined information relevant to a current generation of students. The *Social Research Problems Up Close* features in every chapter provide students with relevant and timely research projects undertaken by sociologists in Canada and around the world. Chapter 2 presents research on how the HPV vaccine has been marketed in Canada, and problematized women's sexuality in particular; Chapter 4 presents Canadian research on the role of social exclusion in the lives of homeless youth, and their attendant risk for being victims of crime; and Chapter 5 presents a discourse analysis of health and parenting advice for breastfeeding and does so in a Canadian context.

These boxes demonstrate for students the sociological enterprise from theory and data collection to findings and conclusions, and potential for application in everyday life.

Ancillaries

About the Nelson Education Teaching Advantage (NETA)

The **Nelson Education Teaching Advantage (NETA)** program delivers research-based instructor resources that promote student engagement and higher-order thinking to enable the success of Canadian students and educators. To ensure the high quality of these materials, all Nelson ancillaries have been professionally copy-edited.

Planning Your Course: *NETA Engagement* presents materials that help instructors deliver engaging content and activities to their classes. **NETA Instructor's Manuals** not only identify the topics that cause students the most difficulty, but also describe techniques and resources to help students master these concepts. Dr. Roger Fisher's *Instructor's Guide to Classroom Engagement* accompanies every Instructor's Manual.

Assessing Your Students: *NETA Assessment* relates to testing materials. **NETA Test Bank** authors create multiple-choice questions that reflect research-based best practices for constructing effective questions and testing not just recall but also higher-order thinking. Our guidelines were developed by David DiBattista, psychology professor at Brock University and 3M National Teaching Fellow, whose research has focused on multiple-choice testing. All Test Bank authors receive training at workshops conducted by Prof. DiBattista, as do the copy-editors assigned to each Test Bank. A copy of *Multiple Choice Tests: Getting Beyond Remembering*, Prof. DiBattista's guide to writing effective tests, is included with every Nelson Test Bank.

Teaching Your Students: *NETA Presentation* has been developed to help instructors make the best use of Microsoft® PowerPoint® in their classrooms. With a clean and uncluttered design developed by Maureen Stone of StoneSoup Consulting, **NETA PowerPoints** features slides with improved readability, more multimedia and graphic materials, activities to use in class, and tips for instructors on the Notes page. A copy of *NETA Guidelines for Classroom Presentations* by Maureen Stone is included with each set of PowerPoint slides.

Instructor Resources

All NETA and other key instructor ancillaries are provided on the Instructor Companion Site at **www.nelson.com/socialproblems5e**, giving instructors the ultimate tool for customizing lectures and presentations.

NETA Test Bank: This resource was written by Thomas Groulx of St. Clair College. It includes over 800 multiple-choice questions written according to NETA guidelines for effective construction and development of higher-order questions. The Test Bank was copy-edited by a NETA-trained editor for adherence to NETA best practices. Also included are approximately 30 true/false questions, 70 short-answer questions, and 70 essay questions.

The NETA Test Bank is available in a new, cloud-based platform. **Testing Powered by Cognero®** is a secure online testing system that allows you to author, edit, and manage test bank content from any place you have Internet access. No special installations or downloads are needed, and the desktop-inspired interface, with its drop-down menus and familiar, intuitive tools, allows you to create and manage tests with ease. You can create multiple test versions in an instant, and import or export content into other systems. Tests can be delivered from your learning management system, your classroom, or wherever you want.

NETA PowerPoint: Microsoft® PowerPoint® lecture slides for every chapter have been created by Darlene Balandin, Western University. There is an average of 75 slides per chapter, many featuring key figures, tables, and photographs from *Understanding Social Problems*, Fifth Canadian Edition. NETA principles of clear design and engaging content have been incorporated throughout, making it simple for instructors to customize the deck for their courses.

Image Library: This resource consists of digital copies of figures, short tables, and photographs used in the book. Instructors may use these jpegs to customize the NETA PowerPoint or create their own PowerPoint presentations.

NETA Instructor's Manual: This resource was written by Darlene Balandin, Western University. It is organized according to the textbook chapters and addresses key educational concerns, such as typical stumbling blocks student face and how to address them. Other features include elements of a traditional Instructor's Manual, including learning outcomes and suggested resources to use in the classroom.

DayOne: Day One—Prof InClass is a PowerPoint presentation that instructors can customize to orient students to the class and their text at the beginning of the course.

CourseMate

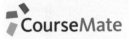

Nelson Education's Sociology CourseMate brings course concepts to life with interactive learning and exam preparation tools that integrate with the printed textbook. Students activate their knowledge through quizzes, games, and flashcards, among many other tools.

CourseMate provides immediate feedback that enables students to connect results to the work they have just produced, increasing their learning efficiency. It encourages contact between students and faculty: you can select to monitor your students' level of engagement with CourseMate, correlating their efforts to their outcomes. You can even use CourseMate's quizzes to practise "Just in Time" teaching by tracking results in the Engagement Tracker and customizing your lesson plans to address their learning needs.

Sociology CourseMate includes:

- an interactive eBook that includes note-taking and highlighting functionality
- interactive teaching and learning tools, including:

  - quizzes
  - flashcards
  - matching activities
  - Evaluate Social Problems in the Media boxed feature
  - Critically Reflect on Technology boxed feature
  - and more

- Engagement Tracker, a first-of-its-kind tool that monitors student engagement in the course

Acknowledgments

This text reflects the contributions of many people. I am especially grateful for the professionalism, patience, and support shown by my colleagues at Nelson Education Canada, especially to Laura McLeod for initially inviting my authorship on the third edition, and to Elke Price, senior developmental editor, and Maya Castle, publisher, for their support at all stages of the updates to the fifth edition; all have provided encouragement and patience that I have valued greatly. I also gratefully acknowledge the effort of the marketing team, including Terry Fedorkiw, marketing manager, and the assistance during the production stage provided by content production manager Jaime Smith, and Kelli Howey for her attentive work as copy editor.

My colleagues at Wilfrid Laurier University have been a tremendous support, but some deserve particular recognition. Pat Elliot aided in clearing the intellectual clutter from my own personal research specialization in sexuality, helping to distill it into a format that would be more accessible to students and non-specialist readers. Jeff Stepnisky generously shared his insights and helped with my research questions in areas concerned with mental health. Jasmin Zine and Glenda Wall were generously available to discuss their own current research. My former graduate student Lisa Dias was kind enough to allow her work to be included in the text, and I could not be more proud of her work or grateful for her generosity.

At all stages of writing I have been indebted to my partner, Trevor, whose patience, careful eye, thoughtful ear, and culinary prowess made completion of the work both possible and enjoyable, even when deadlines were tight.

Additionally, I would like to acknowledge many others who assisted in reviewing earlier editions of this textbook: Anne Charles, Conestoga College; Shanti Fernando, University of Ontario Institute of Technology; Loretta Gerlach, University of Regina; Lindsay Harris, Algonquin College; Uldis Kundrats, Nipissing University; Karen Moreau-Petti, Niagara College; Joseph O'Shea, Concordia University; Sharon Roberts, Western University; and Oliver R. Stoetzer, Fanshawe College.

For their useful suggestions and thoughtful comments, which helped to shape this edition, I am grateful to the following reviewers: Kenneth Caine, University of Alberta; Thomas Groulx, St. Clair College; Jo Gomes, Seneca College; Daniel Lett, University of Victoria; and Erin Steuter, Mount Allison University. Finally, I am always interested in ways to improve the text. I invite your feedback and suggestions for new ideas and material to be included in subsequent editions.

M. Morgan Holmes
Department of Sociology
Wilfrid Laurier University
Waterloo, ON N2L 3C5
mholmes@wlu.ca

1

Thinking about Social Problems

Student Reflection: What Do You Already Know?

Wherever you are in your life right now, your prior experience being a person in a society qualifies you to have some thoughts about social problems. Unless you were raised by space wolves on a distant planet, it's likely that you have had a lot of contact with the meaningful organization of our lives by medical, educational, family, religious, governmental, and legal systems (some of the structuring things that sociologists call "institutions"). So much so, in fact, that it's kind of like the saying "fish don't think about water." The analogy is that social elements of living are like the air we breathe. We stop noticing the air until something smells bad or it becomes hard to breathe. Same with social institutions. As you start to read this textbook, take some time to consider the kinds of things you think are socially important, and what happens when they don't go well. Not everything will be world-changing (though it is a good idea to consider what you *can* change). Some of it might even seem really mundane or insignificant in the big picture. Whether you're thinking of laws that restrict freedoms or the argument you had yesterday with an old acquaintance on social media, you're taking the first step toward thinking sociologically. Much of this textbook is devoted to considering those problems using sociological perspectives grounded in the six different classic and contemporary theoretical orientations introduced below. For now, you should think about what kinds of things you consider to be important social problems. Thinking about your own background or your own observations of the world around you, you might determine there is room for improvement in the lives of children, for example, or in the ways that medicine is delivered, how education is organized, or what the place of religion is in a secular society. Consider *how* you came to understand that these are problems worthy of attention. Where did you learn about the things you think are problems? What kinds of solutions do you think might make things better? What roles do your own family, educational experiences (in school or not), reading habits, religious beliefs, and community ties have in influencing your thinking? At the end of the chapter, you'll be asked to consider these questions again, taking into account the reading and lecture material that you cover in your class.

A Note on Learning Outcomes

Each chapter will list some intended learning outcomes that may be achieved as a result of your reading. Generally, your instructor will set course outcomes and this textbook will be one resource among many in your pursuit of their achievement.

You will also probably have your own learning goals for the topic or the textbook. Having said that, you may want to know a little more about why your textbook author updates the book as often as possible. The overall goals of the text can be found in Section 1.6, just before Chapter 2.

In the big picture we hope that, depending on how you use the textbook and in what context, you'll look at the world differently than if you hadn't read it. If you take the time to understand each chapter, by completing this book you should be able to:

- define the key terms bolded throughout each chapter
- distinguish among important classic sociological approaches to social problems as well as newer approaches
- identify different methods by which sociologists gather data and evidence
- recognize a sociological way of framing a problem differently than the other disciplines you'll encounter
- contemplate the many perspectives that can be brought to bear on a given problem
- identify the barriers and opportunities in social change in order to further develop your own hopes for change in the world and in your own context
- apply a relevant sociological approach to understanding social problems you have identified in a context that is meaningful for your own academic study and career
- imagine dimensions to problems that, like most of us, you may have missed at first glance

Along the way toward these outcomes, you'll be encouraged to develop critical skills and habits of mind that you can return to for a lifetime, not just for a term of school.

Understanding the persistence of such social problems as crime, unemployment, drug abuse, suicide, racism, sexism, and family violence tempers Canadians' optimism for the future. Consider that for the past three decades Canadian residents have consistently identified the economy, unemployment, and crime as primary areas of social concern (Bibby 1995: 94–95; Bibby 2001: 43). In addition, global political and economic shifts have domestic impacts; thus, "'we' are all some variation of the unsettled, some variation of transient subjectivities, more and more sutured into the 'time' of Global capitalism's networks and contingencies" (Miki 2000: 44). Such instability, argues Miki, feeds problems of racism, even while Canada claims to value cultural pluralism. Canada also faces unique internal stresses: regional economic instability forces migration and creates social upheaval for communities (Marshall and Foster 2002), and in health-care provision "there is concern that local community governance structures may lose some of their community-based authority and not be flexible enough to meet emerging and current needs" (Benoit et al. 2003: 831). These are only two examples of contemporary social problems facing Canadian society.

A global perspective on social problems is equally troubling. In 1990, the United Nations published its first annual "Human Development Report." The report focuses on measuring the well-being of world populations according to a "human development index" (HDI) measuring three basic dimensions of human development: longevity, educational attainment, and living standards. The 2010 HDI estimates that in spite of economic development over the last 20 years, 1.75 billion people around the globe continue to live with serious deprivations that include precarity in living conditions, health, child welfare, and economic and political environments. Of those, 1.44 billion live on less than $1.25 a day (Human Dev. Report 2010: 21).

This text provides a critical overview of social problems in Canada and around the world. Although the topics covered vary, all chapters share common objectives: to explain how social problems form and persist; to indicate how problems affect individuals, social groups, and societies as a whole; and to examine programs and policies for change. We begin by looking at what characterizes social problems.

1.1 What Is a Social Problem?

There is no universal, constant, or absolute definition of what constitutes a social problem. Rather, we define social problems through a combination of objective and subjective criteria. The criteria vary across societies, among individuals and groups within a society, and across historical periods.

Objective and Subjective Elements of Social Problems

Although social problems take many forms, all share two important elements: an objective social condition and its subjective interpretation. The **objective element** of a social problem refers to the existence of a social condition. Social conditions are objectively real; that is, they exist independently of our perception. Social conditions such as homelessness, financial crises, and joblessness can affect large numbers of people, and often in waves or patterns. Social conditions—such as illness and disease, or the loss of family members to crashes caused by drunk drivers—tend to be experienced at the personal level; however, as you will see, even "personal troubles" connect to larger social phenomena.

The **subjective element** of a social problem refers to beliefs that particular social conditions are harmful to society or to a segment of society, and that we should and can change them. We know, for example, that in addition to the problems mentioned above, crime, drug addiction, poverty, racism, violence, and pollution exist. These social conditions are not considered social problems, however, until a segment of society believes that these conditions diminish the quality of human life.

How a population comes to combine subjective and objective elements to identify some facts as problems is, in itself, an important research question. Spector and Kitsuse (2001) argue that **claims-making activities** are central to the development of the particular view of a social fact as a bona fide social problem; they explain:

> we define social problems as *the activities of individuals or groups making assertions of grievances and claims with respect to some putative conditions*. The emergence of a social problem is contingent upon the organization of activities asserting the need for eradicating, ameliorating, or otherwise changing some condition. (p. 76: emphasis in original)

Moreover, Spector and Kitsuse explain that there is little utility in trying to determine whether a condition actually exists if what we are trying to do is understand what people *perceive* as a social problem. We may see, for example, that hoaxes abound on the internet, forwarded from one person to the next. Such hoaxes often speak to larger social anxieties regarding rapid changes—in gender roles, for example—that many people experience as a threat to existing social structures and deeply held social mores. The hoaxes often warn women to stay in their "proper" social place lest they be robbed or assaulted while out in the public world of politics and commerce. That the warnings claim to be based on recent cases of assault or abductions (that, in fact, never actually happened) is entirely beside the point. Spector and Kitsuse use different examples, but as with the example presented here they "are not concerned whether or not the imputed condition exists" (p. 76). Rather, the point is to understand

objective element (of a social problem)
Awareness of social conditions through one's own life experience and through reports in the media.

subjective element (of a social problem)
The belief that a particular social condition is harmful to society, or to a segment of society, and that it should and can be changed.

claims-making activities
The strategies and actions that individuals or groups undertake to define social conditions as social problems that require remedy.

that defining conditions as problems is a social activity that assumes shared values and shared definitions regarding what counts as a social good: "The emergence of a social problem is contingent upon the organization of activities asserting the need for eradicating, ameliorating, or otherwise changing some condition" (p. 76). We pursue the development of the recognition of social problems *as such* later in this chapter in the discussion of how symbolic interactionist theory understands the process through which people begin to see certain phenomena—but not others—as social problems.

To the extent that sociologists are trained to recognize some conditions as social problems, this textbook begins with the explanation of conditions already recognized as social problems. The book also continues the *claims-making* work of arguing that these are problems precisely because the social conditions described *do* require amelioration, or even eradication (Figure 1.1). Past (and future) sociological assessments do not necessarily begin from the same shared definitions, and do not apprehend the same objective facts as obvious *problems*.

Figure 1.1 *Claims-Making Activities in Action*

"Ghost bicycles" are painted white and placed where a cyclist has been struck and killed in a motor-vehicle collision. Ghost bicycles draw attention to the vulnerabilities of cyclists on roadways, and aim to educate car drivers to be more attentive to the need to share the road with cyclists. The roadside markers identify a range of social facts as problems: absent cycling lanes; aggressive and/or hostile drivers; the hazards of inattentive or careless driving; loss of life that results from negative attitudes toward cyclists. Although criminal charges are rarely laid against drivers who hit cyclists, ghost bikes draw attention to the issue as a problem, and municipalities have taken note by improving cycling infrastructure. Improvements include the significant expansion of dedicated cycling lanes, pathways, and "wide berth" laws in cities across Canada.

AP Photo/Allen Breed

To sum up: a **social problem** is a social condition that a segment of society demonstrates to be significantly harmful to members of society and in need of remedy. The definition is relative, and is informed by larger social values that shape the way we understand and apprehend social facts. What we collectively agree are social problems changes over time as our society changes.

Variability in Definitions of Social Problems

Individuals and groups frequently disagree about what constitutes a social problem. For example, the use of physical punishment to discipline children is perceived differently by those who condone its use and those who condemn it. Those who condone it argue that the problem is not the use of corporal punishment, but the intrusion of courts and social agencies into private family matters. Those who condemn it argue that corporal punishment infringes on the right of children to protection of their bodies from harm. They point out that adult acceptance of physical harm as a "normal" part of discipline is a measure of just how damaging it is to the psyche. Such variations in views result from differences in values, beliefs, and life experiences.

Definitions of social problems vary not only within societies, but also across societies and historical periods. For example, prior to the nineteenth century it was a husband's legal right and marital obligation to discipline and control his wife through the use of physical force. Today, the use of physical force is regarded as a social problem and a criminal offence rather than a marital right.

Because social problems can be highly complex, it is helpful to have a framework to assess them. Sociology provides such a framework. Using a sociological perspective to examine social problems requires knowledge of the concepts and methods designed specifically for the purpose of accessing and analyzing social phenomena. In the remainder of this chapter, we discuss some of these concepts and methods.

1.2 Concepts

Social Structure and Culture

Although society surrounds us and permeates our lives, it is difficult to "see" society. A metaphor can help us visualize its two central features to understand it better. Imagine that society is a coin with two sides: on one side, social structure; on the other, culture. Although each "side" is distinct, each is inseparable from the whole. Analysis of the various elements of social structure and culture fosters understanding of the root causes of social problems.

Elements of Social Structure

The *structure* of a society refers to the organization of society into different parts: institutions, social groups, statuses, and roles.

Those who use structural analysis to assess and understand social regulation and change also understand that structures serve specific functions. For example, Durkheim's research demonstrated that suicide rates were **social facts**—that is, phenomena created by social organization rather than individual acts of desperation. Structural theorists have since argued that a society needs to have cohesion in its different parts, with complementary functions and values. Otherwise, as Durkheim demonstrated, social upheaval and poor institutional cohesion could have catastrophic outcomes.

Institutions

An **institution** is an established and enduring organization of social relationships. The five traditional institutions are family, religion, politics, economics, and education, but some sociologists argue that other social institutions, such as science and technology, mass media, medicine, sport, and the military, also play important roles in contemporary society.

Many social problems result from inadequacies in institutions or conflicts between institutions. For example, there is concern that unemployment may be influenced by the educational institution's inability to keep up with changing demands and instability in the structure of the economic institution. It is possible, though, that "closer links between education and economy might mean too much business influence over what is taught at all levels of the educational system" (Krahn and Lowe 2002: 46).

Social Groups

Institutions are made up of social groups—defined as two or more people who have a common identity, interact, and form a social relationship. For example, the family in which you were reared is a **social group** and part of the family institution.

social facts
Émile Durkheim refers to the phenomena that occur in the world as objectively identifiable facts. If the phenomena arise as a result of structural organization and functional needs, or dysfunctional problems, then those facts are not merely idiosyncrasies, but the result of social structures—they are part of the function of the society under consideration. Employment rates, morbidity, and mortality, as well as rates of population growth or decline, are all examples of "social facts."

institution
An established and enduring pattern of social relationships. The five traditional social institutions are family, religion, politics, economics, and education. Institutions are the largest elements of social structure.

social group
Two or more people who have a common identity and who interact and form a social relationship; institutions are made up of social groups.

primary group
A small group characterized by intimate and informal interaction.

secondary group
A group characterized by impersonal and formal interaction.

status
A position a person occupies within a social group.

ascribed status
A status that society assigns to an individual on the basis of factors over which the individual has no control.

achieved status
A status assigned on the basis of some characteristic or behaviour over which the individual has some control.

master status
The status that is considered the most significant in a person's social identity.

role
A set of rights, obligations, and expectations associated with a status.

beliefs
Definitions and explanations about what is assumed to be true.

A social group may be categorized as primary or secondary. **Primary groups**, which tend to involve a small number of individuals, are characterized by intimate and informal interaction. Families and friends are examples of primary groups. **Secondary groups**, which may involve a small or large number of individuals, are task-oriented and characterized by impersonal and formal interaction. Examples of secondary groups include employers and employees, and clerks and their customers. Because secondary groups are usually large, primary groups often form inside them, making large structures more manageable on a personal level.

Statuses

Just as an institution consists of social groups, a social group consists of statuses. A **status** is a position a person occupies within a social group. The statuses we occupy largely define our social identities. The statuses in a family may consist of mother, father, stepmother, stepfather, wife, husband, child, and so on. Statuses may be either ascribed or achieved. An **ascribed status** is one that society assigns to an individual on the basis of factors over which the individual has no control. For example, we have no control over the sex, race, ethnic background, and socio-economic status into which we are born. Similarly, we are assigned the status of "child," "teenager," "adult," or "senior citizen" on the basis of our age—something we do not choose or control.

An **achieved status** is assigned on the basis of characteristics or behaviour over which an individual has some control. For example, whether or not you achieve the status of university graduate depends partly on personal effort, behaviour, and choices. Critically, however, ascribed statuses may affect the likelihood of achieving other statuses. Canadian research shows that, of those who graduated in 1985, only 35 percent of those from low socio-economic status (SES) families had achieved a university degree by 1999; meanwhile, 62 percent of those from high SES families had achieved a university degree in the same time period (Krahn 2004: 197–98).

Everyone occupies numerous statuses simultaneously. You may simultaneously be a student, parent, tutor, community volunteer, female, and person with a disability. A person's **master status** is the one considered the most significant in a person's social identity. Typically, gender and race trump all other statuses, though occupation may operate as a master status that can change over time—for example from "full-time student" to "professor" or "lawyer."

Roles

Every status is associated with many **roles**—the rights, obligations, and expectations associated with a status. Roles guide our behaviour and allow us to predict the behaviour of others. Students are expected to attend class, listen and take notes, study for tests, and complete assignments. Because the status of professor has recognizable role expectations, you can predict that your teacher will lecture, give exams, and assign grades based on your performance.

A single status involves more than one role. For example, the status of nurse involves different roles for interacting with physicians, with patients, and with their families.

Elements of Culture

Whereas *social structure* refers to the organization of society, culture refers to the meanings and ways of life that characterize a society. The elements of culture include beliefs, values, norms, sanctions, and symbols.

Beliefs

Beliefs refer to definitions and explanations about what is assumed to be true. The beliefs of an individual or group influence whether that individual or group views a particular social condition as a social problem. For example, does violence in entertainment media lead to increased aggression in children? Our beliefs regarding social facts influence whether we view the issues as problems. Beliefs influence not only how a social condition is interpreted, but also the existence of the condition. It is important to remember that beliefs do not constitute sociological knowledge. Sociologists do not accept beliefs as true, but as sources of information about how social relations operate and how they influence the directions that social actors will take.

Values

Values are social agreements about what is considered good and bad, right and wrong, desirable and undesirable. Frequently, we apprehend social conditions as social problems when the conditions are incompatible with or contradict closely held values. For example, poverty and homelessness violate the value of human welfare; some types of crimes contradict values of honesty, private property, and nonviolence; racism, sexism, and heterosexism violate values of equality and fairness.

Values can also be central to the development of social problems. Sylvia Ann Hewlett (1992) explains how the values of freedom and individualism are at the root of many of our social problems:

> There are two sides to the coin of freedom. On the one hand, there is enormous potential for prosperity and personal fulfilment; on the other are all the hazards of untrammelled opportunity and unfettered choice. Free markets can produce grinding poverty as well as spectacular wealth; unregulated industry can create dangerous levels of pollution as well as rapid rates of growth; and an unfettered drive for personal fulfilment can have disastrous effects on families and children. Rampant individualism does not bring with it sweet freedom; rather, it explodes in our faces and limits life's potential. (pp. 350–51)

Absent or weak values may also contribute to social problems. For example, many industries do not value protection of the environment and thus contribute to environmental pollution.

Norms and Folkways

Norms are socially defined rules of behaviour. Norms serve as guidelines for personal behaviour and for our expectations of the behaviour of others.

There are three types of norms: folkways, laws, and mores. **Folkways** refer to the customs and manners of society. In many segments of our society, it is customary to shake hands when being introduced to a new acquaintance, to say "excuse me" after sneezing, and to give presents to family and friends on their birthdays. Although no laws require us to do these things, we are expected to do them because they are part of the cultural traditions, or folkways, of the society in which we live.

Laws, Mores, and Sanctions

Laws are formalized norms backed by political authority. A person who eats food out of a public garbage container is violating a folkway—no law prohibits this behaviour. However, throwing trash onto a public street is littering and is against the law.

Some norms, called **mores**, have a moral basis. Violations of mores may produce shock, horror, and moral indignation. Both littering and child sexual abuse are violations of law, but child sexual abuse is also a violation of our mores: we view such behaviour as immoral.

All norms are associated with **sanctions**: social consequences for conforming to or violating norms. When we conform, we may be rewarded by a positive sanction ranging from an approving smile to a public ceremony in our honour. When we violate

values
Social agreements about what is considered good and bad, right and wrong, desirable and undesirable.

norms
Socially defined rules of behaviour, including folkways, mores, and laws.

folkways
The customs and manners of society.

laws
Norms that are formalized and backed by political authority.

mores
Norms that have a moral basis.

sanctions
Social consequences for conforming to or violating norms. Types of sanctions include positive, negative, formal, and informal.

a social norm, we may be punished by a negative sanction, ranging from a disapproving look to execution. Most sanctions are spontaneous expressions of approval or disapproval by groups or individuals—referred to as informal sanctions. Sanctions carried out according to some recognized or formal procedure are formal sanctions. Types of sanctions, then, include positive informal sanctions, positive formal sanctions, negative informal sanctions, and negative formal sanctions (see Table 1.1).

Table 1.1 **Types and Examples of Sanctions**

	Positive	**Negative**
Informal	Praise from neighbours for organizing a neighbourhood recycling program.	Criticism from neighbours for refusing to participate in the neighbourhood recycling program.
Formal	Receiving a citizen's award for organizing a neighbourhood recycling program.	Fined by the city for failing to dispose of garbage properly.

Symbols

A **symbol** is something that represents something else. Without symbols, we could not communicate with one another or live as social beings.

The symbols of a culture include language, gestures, and objects whose meaning is commonly understood by the members of a society. In our society, a peace sign communicates the value of nonviolence; a police badge, the authority of law. Sometimes, people attach different meanings to the same symbol. The swastika is an ancient symbol that was supposed to bring good luck. However, its adoption as the official emblem of the Nazi Party and Nazi Germany has encouraged many to view it as a symbol of anti-Semitism, white supremacy, and bigotry.

The elements of social structure and culture just discussed play a central role in the creation, maintenance, and social response to various social problems. Taking a course in social problems helps develop an awareness of how the elements of social structure and culture contribute to social problems. Sociologists refer to this awareness as the "sociological imagination."

1.3 **The Sociological Imagination**

The **sociological imagination**, a term developed by C. Wright Mills (1959), refers to the ability to see the connections between our personal lives and the social world in which we live. Use of the sociological imagination enables distinction between "private troubles" and "public issues" and the seeing of connections between the events and conditions of our lives and the social and historical context in which we live.

For example, the fact that one person is unemployed constitutes a private trouble. The fact that thousands of people are unemployed in Canada constitutes a public issue. Once we understand that personal troubles such as HIV infection, criminal victimization, and poverty are shared by other segments of society, we can look for the elements of social structure and culture that contribute to these public issues and private troubles. If the various elements of social structure and culture contribute to private troubles and public issues, then society's social structure and culture must be changed in order to resolve these concerns.

symbol
Something that represents something else.

sociological imagination
A term coined by C. Wright Mills to refer to the ability to see the connections between our personal lives and the social world in which we live.

structural-functionalism
A sociological perspective that views society as a system of interconnected parts that work together in harmony to maintain a state of balance and social equilibrium for the whole; focuses on how each part of society influences and is influenced by other parts.

conflict theory
The theoretical framework that understands material inequalities to be a driving force behind many social problems. Some sociologists prefer to use "Marxist theory" to name this approach to thinking about social inequalities.

Rather than viewing the private trouble of being unemployed as the result of individual character flaws or lack of skills, we may understand unemployment as a public issue that results from the failure of the economic and political institutions of society to provide job opportunities to all citizens. For example, technological innovations in the steel industry threatened job security and altered the way of life for hundreds of Hamilton, Ontario, families in the 1970s (Leach 2005). During the economic recession of the 1980s, employers fired employees so the firms could stay in business or maximize profits, or both. In both cases, social forces rather than individual skills largely determined whether a person was employed or not.

1.4 Theoretical Perspectives

Theories in sociology provide different perspectives from which to view our social world. Sociological theories help us to explain and predict the social world in which we live.

Sociology includes four major theoretical perspectives. A perspective is simply a way of looking at the world. A theory is a set of interrelated propositions or principles designed to explain an observable phenomenon; a theory provides a perspective. **Structural-functionalism** assesses social structures and their functions or dysfunctions; it is often thought of principally as a historical perspective. **Conflict theory** understands differentials in power, well-being, and access to resources. **Symbolic interactionism** asks how people come to agree about the meaning and significance of what occurs between them, and how meanings fit into a society's sensibilities and practical strategies. **Feminist theory** demonstrates that women are marginalized by social structures, in symbolic operations, and in distribution of resources; it also shows that traditional sociological thinking has failed to account for these and other problems facing women. Feminists may use the tools of any combination of other theories, but all agree that the subordinate status of women constitutes a social problem.

In addition to the four central theoretical perspectives, two others—postmodern and "queer" theory—have gained prominence. **Postmodern theory** argues that the progressivist stance of modernism presupposes too easily that subjects and societies are stable and linear, moving toward their best possible manifestation. Postmodernists argue that we need to take account of the fluctuating and fractured aspects of social organization. By doing so we can listen to the shifting voices and needs of those overlooked by positivist assumptions and methods. **Queer theory** has strong ties to feminist work, but also corrects the pervasive assumption that heterosexuality is both natural and ahistorical. Queer theory offers more nuanced accounts of history, social organization, and sexual identity than those offered by the structural-functionalist perspective, for example. Structural-functionalists see the world divided neatly into male and female bodies that fulfill social roles, tasks, and institutional requirements based on heterosexual, prescriptive norms. In addition, queer theory has become a central conceptual model for those who study disability. Scholars who work on disability observe that many of the same prejudices and contestations regarding sexuality and family-based rights—such as the rights of gays, lesbians, and trans-persons to have children, to marry, to have bodily and sexual autonomy, to be seen as desirable and socially valuable—apply to persons with disabilities. Queer theory, thus, extends its utility well beyond the scope of questions focused on sexuality and into more general questions regarding the intersection of embodiment and social regulation.

Every theory offers a variety of explanations about the causes of and possible solutions for social problems, and each is subject to constant revision and refinement of both methods and interests. Sociologists never stop trying to improve on what we can know and to correct what we may have misapprehended before.

symbolic interactionism
A sociological perspective that emphasizes that human behaviour is influenced by definitions and meanings that are created and maintained through symbolic interaction with others.

feminist theory
A set of diverse perspectives joined by the focus on sex and gender as defining and important categories of oppression.

postmodern theory
A theory that rejects the positivist notion that societies are completely rational and that a single truth about social worlds can be identified. The theory takes account of the competing realities according to and through which people live their lives.

queer theory
A theory that developed largely out of the late 1980s response to public panics over HIV and to medical system failures to treat with respect and adequate priority the needs of HIV+ persons, especially gay men. Queer theory now asks how sexual identity relates to various problems rooted in oppression and prejudice. It provides an important analytic tool to understand the oppressive treatment of gay, lesbian, bisexual, and transgender persons in societal structures and in cultural representation.

Structural-Functionalist Theory

The structural-functionalist perspective is largely based on the works of Herbert Spencer, Émile Durkheim, Talcott Parsons, and Robert Merton. According to structural-functionalism, society is a system of interconnected parts that work together in harmony to maintain a state of balance and social equilibrium for the whole. For example, each social institution serves important functions for society: family provides a context for reproducing, nurturing, and socializing children; education offers a way to transmit a society's skills, knowledge, and culture to its youth; politics provides a means of governing members of society; economics provides for the production, distribution, and consumption of goods and services; and religion provides moral guidance and an outlet for worship of a higher power.

The structural-functionalist perspective emphasizes the interconnectedness of society by focusing on how each part influences and is influenced by other parts. For example, as a result of changes in technology, colleges and universities are offering more technical programs, and many adults are returning to school to learn new skills that are required in the workplace. The increasing number of women in the workforce has contributed to the formulation of policies against sexual harassment and job discrimination.

Structural-functionalists use the terms "functional" and "dysfunctional" to describe the effects of social elements on society. Elements of society are functional if they contribute to social stability and dysfunctional if they disrupt social stability. Some aspects of society may be both functional and dysfunctional for society. For example, crime is dysfunctional in that it is associated with physical violence, loss of property, and fear. But, according to Durkheim and other functionalists, crime is also functional for society because it leads to heightened awareness of shared moral bonds and increased social cohesion.

Sociologists have identified two types of functions: manifest and latent (Merton 1968). A manifest function is an intended, recognizable consequence or intent. A **latent function** is an unintended, commonly hidden consequence or denied intention. For example, the **manifest function** of education is to transmit knowledge and skills to society's youth. But public elementary schools also serve to stream populations into stratified jobs, and colleges and universities offer a place for young adults to meet potential mates. The job streaming and mate selection functions are not commonly recognized functions of education.

Structural-Functionalist Theories of Social Problems

Two dominant theories of social problems grew out of structural-functionalism: social pathology and social disorganization.

Social Pathology

According to the social pathology model, social problems result from some "sickness" in society. Just as the human body becomes ill when our systems, organs, and cells do not function normally, society becomes "ill" when its parts—elements of the structure and culture—no longer perform properly. For example, problems such as crime, violence, and poverty are often attributed to the breakdown of the family institution, the decline of the religious institution, and inadequacies in our economic, educational, and political institutions.

Social illness also results when members of a society are not adequately socialized to adopt its norms and values. Persons who do not value honesty, for example, are prone to dishonesties of all sorts. Early theorists attributed the failure in socialization to "sick" people who could not be socialized. Later theorists recognized that failure in the socialization process stemmed from "sick" social conditions, not "sick" people. To

latent function
Consequence that is unintended and often hidden or unrecognized; for example, a latent function of education is to provide schools that function as babysitters for employed parents.

manifest function
A consequence that is intended and commonly recognized; for example, a manifest function of education is to transmit knowledge and skills to youth.

prevent or solve social problems, members of society must receive proper socialization and moral education, which may be accomplished in the family, schools, churches, and workplace, and through the media.

Social Disorganization

According to the social disorganization view of social problems, rapid social change disrupts the norms in a society. When norms become weak or are in conflict with each other society is in a state of **anomie**, or normlessness. Hence, people may steal, physically abuse their partner or children, abuse drugs, commit sexual assault, or engage in other deviant behaviour because the norms regarding these behaviours are weak or conflicting. According to this view, the solution to social problems lies in slowing the pace of social change and strengthening social norms. For example, although the use of alcohol by teenagers is considered a violation of a social norm in our society, this norm is weak. The media portray young people drinking alcohol, teenagers teach one another to drink alcohol and buy fake identification cards to purchase alcohol, and parents model drinking behaviour by having a few drinks after work or at a social event. Solutions to teenage drinking may involve strengthening norms against it through public education, restricting media depictions of youth and alcohol, imposing stronger sanctions against the use of fake IDs to purchase alcohol, and educating parents to model moderate and responsible drinking behaviour.

anomie
A state of normlessness in which norms and values are weak or unclear; results from rapid social change and is linked to many social problems, including crime, drug addiction, and violence.

Conflict Theory

Whereas the structural-functionalists view society as a cooperation of different parts working together, conflict theory views society as a struggle among different groups and interests competing for power and resources. This perspective sees conflict and struggle as the central feature of our social world, in which some groups have power and benefit from hierarchical social arrangements.

Conflict theories originate with the classic works of Karl Marx. Marx argued that all societies go through stages of economic development. As societies shift from agricultural to industrial, a subsistence economy is replaced by a profit-making economy, the hallmark of capitalism. Industrialization leads to the development of two classes of people: the bourgeoisie, or the owners of the means of production (e.g., factories, farms, businesses), and the proletariat, or the workers who earn wages.

The division of society into two broad classes of people provides greater benefits to the owners of the means of production. The workers, who may earn only subsistence wages, cannot access the many resources available to wealthy owners. Marx argues that the bourgeoisie are able to control the institutions of society to their advantage. For example, Marx suggested that religion serves as an "opiate of the masses" that distracts attention from the suffering in working-class conditions and focuses the workers' attention on spirituality, God, and the afterlife. In essence, religion diverts workers' attention so that they accept their own exploitation.

Conflict Theories of Social Problems

There are two general types of conflict theories of social problems: Marxist and non-Marxist. Marxist conflict theories focus on economic inequalities; non-Marxist conflict theories focus on competing values and interests among social groups.

Marxist Conflict Theories

Contemporary Marxist theorists argue that social problems result from the class inequality inherent to capitalism. As we shall explore later, many social problems are linked to poverty.

corporate violence
The production of unsafe products and the failure of corporations to provide a safe working environment for their employees.

In addition to creating an impoverished class of people, capitalism also encourages "corporate violence." **Corporate violence** may be defined as actual harm or risk of harm inflicted on consumers, workers, and the general public as a result of decisions by corporate executives or managers. Corporate violence can result from corporate negligence, the quest for profits at any cost, and wilful violations of health, safety, and environmental laws (Hills 1987). Profit-motivated economies may encourage those who are otherwise good, kind, and law-abiding to participate knowingly in the manufacturing and marketing of defective brakes on jets, faulty fuel tanks on automobiles, and unsafe contraceptive devices such as some intrauterine devices (IUDs). As Eitzen and Baca Zinn (2000: 483) note, the "goal of profit is so central to capitalistic enterprises that many corporate decisions are made without consideration for the consequences."

alienation
The concept used by Karl Marx to describe the condition when workers feel powerlessness and meaninglessness as a result of performing repetitive, isolated work tasks. Alienation involves becoming estranged from one's work and/or education, the products one creates, other human beings, or one's self.

Marxist conflict theories also focus on **alienation**, or powerlessness and meaninglessness in people's lives. In industrialized societies, workers often have little power or control over their jobs, which fosters a sense of powerlessness. Furthermore, routinized work requires workers to perform limited, repetitive tasks; as a result, workers may perceive their lives as artless and meaningless.

Alienation is bred not only in the workplace, but also in the classroom. Students have little power over their education and often find their studies lack meaning. Like poverty, alienation is linked to other social problems, such as low educational achievement, violence, and suicide.

Marxist explanations of social problems imply that the solution lies in eliminating inequality among classes of people by creating a classless society, changing work to avoid alienation, and applying stronger controls to corporations to ensure that decisions and practices are based on safety rather than profit considerations.

Non-Marxist Conflict Theories

Neo-Marxist conflict theorists are concerned with conflict that arises when groups have opposing values and interests. For example, anti-abortion activists value the life of embryos and fetuses; pro-choice activists value the right of women to control their own lives, bodies, and reproductive decisions. These different value positions reflect different interpretations of what constitutes a social problem. For anti-abortionists, abortion is the social problem; for pro-choice advocates, restrictions on abortion are the social problem. Value conflicts may occur between different categories of people, generally between those who dominate and those who are marginalized based on statuses such as race, sexual identity, gender, age, and belief systems. Often, these are struggles not simply over meaning but also over basic recognition and access to full human rights. Moreover, outcomes of value conflicts are often influenced by power: the group with the most power may use its position to influence the outcome of value conflicts. Social change toward greater human rights can, therefore, be painfully slow; however as the social anthropologist Margaret Mead famously noted, we should "[n]ever doubt that a small group of thoughtful, committed people can change the world. Indeed, it is the only thing that ever has."

macro-sociology
The study of large aspects of society, such as institutions and large social groups.

Structural-functionalist and conflict perspectives both address how broad aspects of society, such as institutions and large social groups, influence the social world. This level of sociological analysis is called **macro-sociology**: it looks at the "big picture" of society and suggests how social problems are affected at the institutional level.

micro-sociology
The study of the social psychological dynamics of individuals interacting in small groups.

Symbolic Interactionism

Another level of sociological analysis, **micro-sociology** focuses on the psychological dynamics of individuals interacting in small groups. Symbolic interactionism reflects the micro-sociological perspective largely developed in the work of early sociologists and philosophers such as Max Weber, Georg Simmel, Charles Horton Cooley, G. H. Mead, W. I. Thomas, Erving Goffman, and Howard Becker. Symbolic interactionism emphasizes that human behaviour is influenced by definitions and meanings that are created and maintained through symbolic interaction with others.

Sociologist W. I. Thomas ([1931] 1966) emphasized the importance of definitions and meanings in social behaviour and in its consequences. He suggested that humans respond to their definition of a situation rather than to the objective situation. Hence, Thomas noted that situations we define as real become real in their consequences.

Symbolic interactionism also suggests that our identity or sense of self is shaped by social interaction. We develop our self-concept by observing how others interact with us and label us. By observing how others view us, we see a reflection of ourselves that Charles Horton Cooley calls the "looking-glass self."

Lastly, the symbolic interaction perspective has important implications for how social scientists conduct research. Max Weber (1864–1920) argued that to understand individual and group behaviour, social scientists must see the world from the eyes of that individual or group. Weber called this approach *Verstehen,* which in German means "empathy." *Verstehen* implies that in conducting research social scientists must try to understand others' views of reality and the subjective aspects of their experiences, including their symbols, values, attitudes, and beliefs.

Symbolic Interactionist Theories of Social Problems

A basic premise of symbolic interactionist theories of social problems is that a condition must be defined or recognized as a social problem in order for it to be a social problem.

Based on this premise, Herbert Blumer (1971) suggested that social problems develop in stages:

- First, social problems pass through the stage of societal recognition—the process by which a social problem, for example, drunk driving, is "born."
- Second, social legitimation takes place when the social problem achieves recognition by the larger community, including media, schools, and churches. As the visibility of traffic fatalities associated with alcohol increased, so did the legitimation of drunk driving as a social problem.
- Third, the development of a social problem involves mobilization for action, which occurs when individuals and groups, such as MADD (Mothers Against Drunk Driving), become concerned about how to respond to the social condition. This mobilization leads to the development and implementation of an official plan for dealing with the problem, involving, for example, highway checkpoints, lower legal blood-alcohol levels, and tougher penalties for drunk driving.

Blumer's stage-development view of social problems is helpful in tracing the development of social problems. For example, although sexual harassment and acquaintance rape have occurred throughout the past century (at least!), these issues did not begin to receive recognition as social problems until the 1970s. Social legitimation of these problems was achieved when high schools, colleges and universities, churches, employers, and the media recognized their existence. Organized social groups mobilized to develop and implement plans to deal with these problems. For example, groups successfully lobbied for the enactment of laws against sexual harassment and the enforcement of sanctions against violators of these laws. Groups also mobilized to provide educational seminars on acquaintance rape for students and to offer support services to victims of date rape.

Some disagree with the symbolic interactionist view that social problems exist only if they are recognized. According to this view, individuals who were victims of acquaintance rape in the 1960s may be considered victims of a problem, even though acquaintance rape was not recognized at that time as a social problem.

Labelling theory, a major symbolic interactionist theory of social problems, suggests that a social condition or group is viewed as problematic if it is labelled as such. According to labelling theory, resolving social problems sometimes involves changing the meanings and definitions attributed to people and situations. For example, as long as teenagers define drinking alcohol as "cool" and "fun," they will continue to drink it illegally.

labelling theory
A symbolic interactionist theory that is concerned with how regions and communities defined as social problems are affected by being so labelled, and with the negative effects of labelling on the self-concept and behaviour of individuals, thereby contributing to the further development of identities and behaviours consistent with the label.

Feminist Theories

Feminist theory building is one practice among many in feminist action. Feminist work begins with the observation that the experiences, social relations, and locations of women's lives are missing or discounted in traditional sociology.

Harriet Martineau, perhaps the first feminist sociologist, dedicated a chapter of her 1837 study on American society to "The Political Non-Existence of Women." Feminist researchers work to move the specifics of women's lives to the centre of sociological inquiry. Just as multiple sociological perspectives developed from the discipline's earliest inception, so are there multiple feminist theories; however, as Chafetz (1997: 98) explains, in all feminist work "gender comprises a central subject matter of the theory; gender relations are viewed as a problem . . . Feminist theory seeks to understand how gender is related to social inequities . . . gender relations are not viewed as . . . immutable [and] feminist theories can . . . challenge counteract or change a status quo that disadvantages or devalues women" (ellipses in original). Many contemporary feminist thinkers also use postmodern and queer perspectives; others use more foundational views such as Marxist theory to account for a political economy of women or to understand how gender operates as a structuring institution that shapes the lives of men and women.

Dorothy Smith, who completed the bulk of her work examining institutional interactions, combined a feminist sensibility with sociological methods to produce what she has referred to as "women's standpoint" theory; that is, a view of knowledge and experience that begins from the position—or standpoint—that women occupy in larger society. This standpoint, Smith demonstrates, is a position not usually given much credence: it is marginalized. That marginalized position, she has shown, can offer critical awareness and knowledge that those who occupy positions of power cannot readily perceive, and should therefore be taken as legitimate knowledge. Smith states "[t]he women's movement has given us a sense of our right to have women's interests represented in sociology, rather than just receiving as authoritative the interests traditionally represented in a sociology put together by men" (Smith 2004: 21).

Postmodern Theories

Postmodern perspectives in the humanities and social sciences present a turn away from the positivism of earlier perspectives. They instead recognize that subjectivity and interpretation do not move in one unified direction to assess a certain, external reality. As Inglis and Hughson explain it, postmodernism resists simple categorization and rejects as overly restrictive any perspective that seeks to "create fixed categories which claim to be utterly true and objective" (2003: 140).

Among the most prominent postmodernists are Jean-François Lyotard and Jean Baudrillard. Lyotard is most well known for his charge against what he called "meta-narratives"—grand stories that aim to explain total phenomena, as Marxism, Freudian psychoanalysis, and liberalism all aim to do. Baudrillard is best known for his work on "simulacra," or the nostalgic attempt to reproduce a past history and society that, in fact, never existed. In Baudrillard's view, the spectacle of Disneyland turns history into a nostalgic commodity to be purchased again and again; reality disappears into an endless repetition of things that never occurred.

Queer Theories

Taking up the point of perpetual repetition of something that does not exist, Judith Butler criss-crosses feminism, postmodernism, and queer theory. The queer theory perspective Butler helped create refuses "the commonly assumed distinction between sex and gender, and in dismantling those allegedly causal relations that structure the difference between the two, Butler . . . foregrounds the 'instability at the very heart of sex'" (Jagose 1996: 90). Rendering clear the instability of "sex" allows sophisticated challenging of social problems that result from accepting the sex/gender model as a "natural" structure. Focusing instead on the manner in which the sex/gender structure functions to support the social problems of sexism, misogyny, and homophobia, queer theory is both an intellectual and a political perspective.

The contributions of Canadian sociologist Aaron Devor are centrally important. His work on gender and sexuality helps people understand the complexities of gender and identity in persons who do not perform gender in "traditional" ways.

Comparing Theories

Table 1.2 summarizes and compares the foundational theoretical perspectives, their criticisms, and social policy recommendations as they relate to social problems. Table 1.3 shows the comparative connections of feminist, postmodern, and queer theory. It is important to understand that the contemporary theoretical practices outlined in Table 1.3 often work together in overlapping ways and that each may draw on elements of some, or all, of the foundational theoretical work. In addition, feminist, postmodern, and queer theories are useful in a variety of disciplines outside sociology; as a result, they are very common tools in interdisciplinary discussions of the intersections between science and culture.

1.5 An Analytic Toolkit for Reading Social Problems Research

Research

The study of social problems is explained using theory, but is based on methodically collected data drawn from empirical research carried out using tools such as surveys, interviews, and participant observation. Most sociological research also requires preparing a research question by reviewing the existing literature in one's field of interest. But research without theoretical forethought and explanation afterward is nothing more than a set of lists, or descriptions—the raw data—that risks being carried out without thought or relevance. As Wilson (1983) states:

> Without theory, the empirical researcher would find it impossible to decide what to observe, how to observe it, or what to make of the observations. (p. 1)

Table 1.2 *Comparison of Foundational Theories*

	Structural-Functionalism	Conflict Theory	Symbolic Interactionism
Representative Theorists	Émile Durkheim Talcott Parsons Robert Merton	Karl Marx C. Wright Mills	George H. Mead Charles Cooley Erving Goffman
Society	Society is a set of interrelated parts; cultural consensus exists and leads to social order; natural state of society—balance and harmony.	Society is marked by power struggles over scarce resources; inequities result in conflict; social change is inevitable; natural state of society—imbalance.	Society is a network of interlocking roles; social order is constructed through interaction as individuals, through shared meaning, make sense out of their social world.
Individuals	Society's institutions socialize individuals; socialization is the process by which social control is exerted; people need society and its institutions.	People are inherently good, but are corrupted by society and its economic structure; groups with power control institutions; "order" is part of the illusion.	Humans are interpretive and interactive; they are constantly changing as their "social beings" emerge and are moulded by changing circumstances.
Cause of Social Problems?	Rapid social change: social disorganization that disrupts the harmony and balance; inadequate socialization, weak institutions, or a combination of these.	Inequality; the dominance of groups of people over other groups of people; oppression and exploitation; competition between groups.	Different interpretations of roles; labelling of individuals, groups, or behaviours as deviant; definition of an objective condition as a social problem.
Social Policy/ Solutions	Repair weak institutions; assure proper socialization; cultivate a strong collective sense of right and wrong.	Minimize competition; create an equitable system for the distribution of resources.	Reduce impact of labelling and associated stigmatization; alter definitions of what is defined as a social problem.
Criticisms	Called "sunshine sociology"; supports the maintenance of the status quo; needs to ask "functional for whom?" Does not deal with issues of power and conflict; incorrectly assumes a consensus.	Utopian model; Marxist states have failed; denies existence of cooperation and equitable exchange. Can't explain cohesion and harmony.	Concentrates on micro issues only; fails to link micro issues to macro-level concerns; too psychological in its approach; assumes label amplifies problem.

Therefore, as sociologists we usually begin by reading the theories that will help to inform our interests at the same time that we are reading in the subfields that focus on the problems that interest us.

Most students taking a course in social problems will not become researchers or conduct research on social problems. Nevertheless, we all consume research reported in the media. As consumers of research, we need to understand that our personal experiences and casual observations are less reliable than generalizations based on systematic research. One strength of social science research is that it is subjected to critical assessment by other researchers (see this chapter's *Social Problems Research Up Close* feature). The more you understand how research is done, the better able you

Table 1.3 Comparison of Contemporary Theories

	Feminist Theory	Postmodern	Queer Theory
Representative Theorists	Harriet Martineau Dorothy Smith Meg Luxton	Jean Baudrillard Jean-François Lyotard	Judith Butler Michel Foucault Aaron Devor
Society	Society has been measured without accounting for women's contributions or experiences. Women are, however, central actors and agents for change. Feminist work usually combines with other theoretical perspectives.	Rejects the view that societies progress toward their best and most rational potential. Culture is arbitrary. Focuses on internal ruptures, shifts, and perpetual strain/change in any society.	Traditional gender systems benefit a few, powerful groups of elite men and women, but can be dangerous for lesbian, gay, bisexual, and transgendered persons. The devaluation of women is central to homophobia.
Individuals	Challenges the belief in individuals as separate actors; looks at interrelations of persons within and across groups and institutions.	Individuals do not exist as autonomous units. The self is never complete, but always exists only in negotiation with social phenomena around it.	The supposedly private lives of individual persons are actually a very public fixation, governed at multiple, invasive points by law, medicine, and public policy.
Cause of Social Problems?	Separating genders in hierarchized opposition creates potentially dangerous inequalities between men and women with negative consequences across broad social institutions and groups. Women and children are especially vulnerable.	Social problems are not rooted in a single set of causes, but are subject to constantly changing power relations that are especially pervasive and dangerously obscured under globalization. There is no "truth," only claims to truth used to suppress others' agency.	Queer theory developed largely out of the late 1980s response to public panics over HIV and to medical system failures to treat with respect and adequate priority the needs of HIV+ persons, especially gay men. Now asks how sexual identity relates to various problems rooted in oppression and prejudice.
Social Policy/ Solutions	Historical desire for inclusion in liberal institutions of economy, law, and education; challenge policies and institutions that privilege male-centred values and operations.	Reject totalizing objectives; interrogate the use and abuse of knowledge; understand competing knowledge claims by assessing political motivations behind them.	Alter marriage, health, and employment law/policy to include "queer" persons. Remove tacit approval of discriminatory behaviours that threaten the rights of GLBT persons to full citizenship.
Criticisms	Has neglected women from racially, ethnically, and economically marginalized groups. Is not adequately attentive to shared oppressions of women and men in depressed or developing regions.	Is "silly" and jargon-heavy; is a conspiracy to destroy culture; is "against" truth. Even sympathizers may charge it with being overly esoteric and impractical.	Very issues-oriented; subject to internal rifts over authentic and legitimate causes. Poor critique of liberal capitalism; may neglect problems of racism, poverty, and sexism within the groups it seeks to represent.

will be to read with a purpose and with the ability to determine the strength of the validity of the research you encounter.

When we read in sociology, in addition to theoretical work we also encounter two basic categories or types of research: *qualitative research* (which uses field research and in-depth interviews to gain specific information about particular groups), and *quantitative research* (which uses surveys with attitude scales, or brief interviews with limited allowed responses in sample populations to generalize about larger implications for society as a whole).

Reading sociologically is not easy! It requires that you pay attention to the kinds of questions that have interested other researchers, and to the design that their studies have followed. Reading sociologically requires consideration of how the research process is framed, and the theoretical explanations of the research findings. But reading sociologically can be very rewarding because it invites us to think more seriously about things that interest us. Keep in mind that it is very common to read a section of text several times before understanding it fully and accurately, especially if the text is introducing readers to unfamiliar theories and/or methods.

Recent research on how we learn to read *better*—that is, in ways that make connections to the material, understand it on a deep level, and are able to apply it to other things—shows that many students do *not* read deeply. Students often do not enjoy reading, and do little more than move their eyes to "touch each word on the page," not actually taking in the meaning of what they are seeing (Roberts and Roberts 2008: 125). Roberts and Roberts (2008: 131–132) explain, citing multiple studies on student learning, that among the most effective tools for students to improve their reading is to do "reading responses" for all their assigned readings. Some professors will include reading response assignments in their courses and some will not, so we have chosen to include the five major components of the reading response assignments that have demonstrated the most benefit for students. Whether you are reading qualitative or quantitative studies, introductory or advanced materials, the following steps advised by Roberts and Roberts should help you to read more effectively, accurately, and with more purpose than if you merely allow your eyes to touch the words on the assigned pages:

1. Connect to the text by underlining *key* ideas; note five *big* ideas that emerge from the key ideas and turn those into questions; answer the five big questions that you create.
2. Summarize the readings by organizing important concepts from the reading into a graphic map, OR make a chart that shows the most important concepts.
3. When you have completed your reading, respond with a few questions (as though you were having a conversation with the author/s).
4. Study as a group: talk with your class peers about the concepts that you found to be important. At each meeting have a volunteer to note who participated and what their thoughts were about those key concepts.
5. Create a song, poem, or rap about the reading. You might want to share your creations with the rest of the class.

These tasks will satisfy all kinds of different learning styles without promoting weakness in the styles that students do not favour for themselves. Roberts and Roberts report on the success of these methods, noting that by using the reading response strategies together "students not only do the reading, they are more likely to participate in class since they have actively *processed* the reading material. They *do* something with the readings" (2008: 133).

Research Studies You Will Read in Sociology

Qualitative research assessments look for recurrent themes that emerge in the interviews, or behaviours that dominate in the observations carried out. Qualitative assessments may also spend some time on consideration of the exceptions that stand out, and pay attention to how society's members explain their own experiences. Qualitative work is often exploratory and does not aim to make large generalizations. Stakeholders such as community groups and social activist organizations may form research questions based on specific concerns in collaboration with academic researchers. Government and industry hire researchers to answer questions about policy needs and marketing interests. What kind of research—qualitative or

qualitative research
Research assessments that look for recurrent themes that emerge in the interviews or behaviours that dominate in the observations carried out.

quantitative or a mixed approach—is carried out depends on the needs of the stakeholders who work in collaboration with the researchers.

Quantitative research is carried out to survey large populations and is analyzed using statistical measures that can look for social phenomena not only as individual facts but also as correlating variables; that is, as phenomena that have a social relationship to each other. The analyses aim to determine whether the correlations are just coincidence, or whether they are causal. For example, research on the health of people in different income groups has been able to show reliably that even in Canada, where we claim to have no class distinctions, those at the low end of the income scale experience significantly worse health and have shorter life expectancies than those at middle and higher income levels. Statistical analyses of the data show that the correlations between low income and illness are not just coincidence.

The *Social Problems Research Up Close* box in this chapter introduces students to reading the design, data collection, and analysis in a large-scale survey.

quantitative research
Research that is carried out to survey large populations and is analyzed using statistical measures that can look for social phenomena not only as individual facts but as correlating variables.

Social Problems *Research Up Close*

Reading Research: Reading with a Purpose

Each chapter in this book contains a *Social Problems Research Up Close* box summarizing a research report or journal article that examines some sociologically significant topic. Some examples of the many journals in sociology are the *Canadian Journal of Sociology, Canadian Review of Sociology and Anthropology, Recherches Sociographiques, Sociologie et Sociétés,* and *Cahiers de Sociologie.* Journal articles are the primary means by which sociologists, and other academics, exchange ideas and information. Most journal articles begin with an *introduction* and *review of the literature* in which the author examines previous research on the topic, identifies specific research areas, and otherwise sets the article up for the reader.

The next major section of a standard sociological research article is entitled *sample and methods.* Here, the author describes the characteristics of the sample, if any, and the details of the type of research conducted. The type of data analysis used is also presented in this section.

The final section of a journal article includes the *findings and conclusions.* The findings of a study describe the results—that is, what the researcher found as a result of the investigation. Findings are then discussed within the context of the hypotheses and the conclusions that can be drawn. Other research results are presented in tabular form. Reading tables carefully is an important part of drawing accurate conclusions about the research hypotheses. In reading a table, you should follow these steps (see Table 1.4 on the next page):

1. *Read the title of the table and make sure that you understand what the table contains.* The title of the table indicates the unit of analysis (high school students), the dependent variable (social concerns), the independent variable (sex), and what the numbers represent (percentages).
2. *Read the information provided at the bottom of the table, including the source and any other explanatory information.* For example, the information at the bottom of this table indicates that the data are from the Project Teen Canada 2008 survey and that the sample was restricted to Canadians 15 to 19 years old in grades 10 to 12 across Canada, including CEGEP I's in Quebec.
3. *Examine the row and column headings.* This table looks at the social concerns that were identified as "very serious" by male and female teenagers in Canada.
4. *Thoroughly examine the data contained within the table, carefully looking for patterns.* As indicated in the table, there is a general tendency for far more female than male teenagers to see any "person-related" issue as serious. For example, child abuse is seen as "very serious" by 59 percent of females but just 42 percent of males. Similar large differences can be noted in relation to AIDS, violence in schools, teenage suicide, drugs, discrimination, violence against women, poverty, crime, and youth gangs. However, the differences between male and female teenagers are minor in relation to "institutional-related issues,"

(continued)

such as the environment, American influence, the economy, the threat of nuclear war, lack of Canadian unity, and Native–white and French–English relations.

5. *Use the information you have gathered in step 4 to address the hypotheses.* Clearly, young women are much more likely than young men to express concern about social issues that have a strong person-centred emphasis. When more abstract, structurally related social concerns are raised, however, male teenagers match or exceed female teenagers in their identification of the issue as "very serious."

6. *Draw conclusions consistent with the information presented.* From Table 1.4 can we conclude that a "compassion gap" exists between male and female teenagers in Canada? Can we conclude, as some have, that "[y]oung females are far more caring, sympathetic, and responsive towards people in general and the dis-privileged in particular" (Bibby and Posterski 1992: 141)? Although the data may imply it, it would be premature to reach such a conclusion. More information, from a variety of sources, is needed. The use of multiple methods and approaches to study a social phenomenon is called triangulation.

Table 1.4 *Primary Social Concerns of Canadian High School Students,* by Gender*

	% Viewing as "Very Serious"		
	Nationally	**Males**	**Females**
The environment	54%	48%	60%
Child abuse	51	42	59
Teenage suicide	46	36	55
Racial discrimination	45	38	51
Drugs	42	38	47
Violence in schools	42	33	51
Poverty	41	35	46
Violence against women	39	31	46
Crime	38	32	44
AIDS	38	34	42
Bullying	34	26	41
Unequal treatment of women	34	26	40
Youth gangs	33	30	36
Terrorism	31	29	32
American influence	24	24	24
The economy	23	24	22
Aboriginal–white relations	21	21	21
Lack of Canadian unity	19	20	18
French–English relations	16	17	15

*The Project Teen Canada 2008 sample was comprised of Canadians, 15 to 19 years old, in grades 10 to 12 across Canada, including CEGEP I's in Quebec.

SOURCE: Bibby, Reginald W. *The Project Teen Canada 2008 National Survey.* Reprinted by permission of Reginald Bibby & Associates.

Reviewing the Literature

After a research question is formulated, the researcher reviews the published material on the topic to find out the state of knowledge on the topic. Reviewing the literature also provides ideas about how to conduct research and helps investigators formulate new research questions. A literature review also allows a comparison of research findings and other sources of information, such as expert opinions, political claims, and journalistic reports.

Defining Variables

A **variable** is any measurable event, characteristic, or property that varies or is subject to change. Researchers must operationally define the variables they study. An **operational definition** specifies how to measure a variable. For example, an operational definition of the variable "religiosity" might be the number of times the respondent reports going to church or synagogue. Another operational definition of "religiosity" might be the respondent's answer to the question, "How important is religion in your life? (1 = not important, 2 = somewhat important, 3 = very important)."

Operational definitions are particularly important for defining variables that cannot be directly observed. For example, researchers cannot directly observe concepts such as "mental illness," "sexual harassment," "child neglect," "job satisfaction," and "drug abuse." Nor can researchers directly observe perceptions, values, and attitudes.

Formulating a Hypothesis

After defining the research variables, researchers formulate a **hypothesis**, which is a prediction or educated guess about how one variable is related to another variable. The **dependent variable** is the variable that the researcher wants to explain; that is, it is the variable of interest. The independent variable is the variable that is expected to explain change in the dependent variable. In formulating a hypothesis, the researcher predicts how the **independent variable** affects the dependent variable. For example, Mouw and Xie (1999) hypothesized that fluent bilingual children have higher levels of academic achievement than children who are English-only fluent; however, their analysis found "no evidence that fluent bilinguals do better than students who are fluent only in English" (p. 250). In this example, the independent variable is bilingualism and the dependent variable is school achievement. The status of a variable is not eternal. For example, in a study on quality of health in adults, school achievement may be the independent variable and quality of health will be the dependent variable, influenced by levels of education achieved.

Researchers often assess the effects of several independent variables on one or more dependent variables. For example, Jekielek (1998) examined the impact of parental conflict and marital disruption (two independent variables) on the emotional well-being of children (the dependent variable). Jekielek found that both parental conflict and marital disruption (separation or divorce) negatively affect children's emotional well-being. However, children in high-conflict intact families exhibit lower levels of well-being than children who have experienced high levels of parental conflict, but whose parents divorce or separate.

Methods of Data Collection

After identifying a research topic, reviewing the literature, and developing hypotheses, researchers decide which method of data collection to use. Alternatives include experiments, surveys, field research, and secondary data research.

variable
Any measurable event, characteristic, or property that varies or is subject to change.

operational definition
In research, a definition of a variable that specifies *how* that variable is to be measured (or was measured) in the research.

hypothesis
A prediction or educated guess about how one variable is related to another variable.

dependent variable
The variable that the researcher wants to explain.

independent variable
The variable that is expected to explain change in the dependent variable.

Experiments

experiment
A research method that involves manipulating the independent variable to determine how it affects the dependent variable.

An **experiment** involves manipulating the independent variable to determine how it affects the dependent variable. It requires one or more experimental groups exposed to the experimental treatment(s) and an unexposed **control group**. After the researcher randomly assigns participants to either an experimental or a control group, she or he measures the dependent variable. The experimental groups are exposed to the treatment, and then the researcher measures the dependent variable again. If participants have been randomly assigned to the different groups, it suggests that any difference in the dependent variable among the groups is due to the effect of the independent variable.

control group
A group that is *not exposed* to the influences or variables whose effects we want to measure on a given group.

Here is an example of a social problems experiment on poverty: providing welfare payments to one group of unemployed single mothers (experimental group) and no such payments to another group of unemployed single mothers (control group). The independent variable is welfare payments; the dependent variable is employment status. The researcher might hypothesize that mothers in the experimental group would be less likely to have a job after 12 months than mothers in the control group. An ethics review board would be needed to determine whether the risks of such a study were justifiable.

The major strength of the experimental method is that it provides evidence for causal relationships—that is, how one variable affects another. A primary weakness is that experiments are often conducted on small samples, usually in artificial laboratory settings; this may mean that the findings may not be generalizable to people in natural settings.

Surveys

survey research
A method of research that involves eliciting information from respondents through questions; includes interviews (telephone or face-to-face) and written questionnaires.

Survey research involves eliciting information from respondents through questions. An important part of survey research is selecting a sample of those to be questioned. A **sample** is a portion of the population, selected to be representative so that the information from the sample can be generalized to a larger population. For example, instead of asking all abused spouses about their experience, the researcher asks a representative sample of them and assumes that those not questioned would give similar responses. After selecting a representative sample, survey researchers either interview people, ask them to complete written questionnaires, or elicit responses to research questions via computer.

sample
In survey research, a "sample" refers to the portion of the population selected to be questioned.

1. *Interviews.* In interview research, trained interviewers ask respondents a series of questions and make written notes about or tape-record the respondents' answers. Interviews may be conducted over the telephone or face to face. One advantage of interview research is that researchers can clarify questions for the respondent and follow up on answers to particular questions. Researchers often conduct face-to-face interviews with groups of individuals who might otherwise be inaccessible. For example, research on women who work as exotic dancers can be difficult to complete because of negative stigma associated with the work. To develop a nuanced theory to explain women's experiences of their work as strippers, Chris Bruckert conducted in-depth interviews with 15 women who had worked for at least a year in the Montreal strip clubs. Her book, *Taking It Off, Putting It On,* provides a Marxist-feminist analysis of the work that she classifies as a unique "insider text" (2002: 10). An insider text does not treat subjects as a means to an end, but seeks to provide a voice for otherwise silenced groups.

   The most serious disadvantages of interview research are cost and the lack of privacy and anonymity. Respondents may feel embarrassed or threatened when asked questions that relate to personal issues such as drug use, domestic violence, and sexual behaviour. As a result, some respondents may choose not to participate in interview research on sensitive topics. Those who do participate may conceal or alter information or give socially desirable answers to the interviewer's questions. A well-trained interviewer will be able to structure interviews to minimize opportunities for successful deception.

2. *Questionnaires.* Instead of conducting personal or phone interviews, researchers may develop questionnaires that they either mail or give to a sample of respondents. Questionnaire research offers the advantages of being less expensive and time consuming than face-to-face or telephone surveys. It also provides privacy and anonymity to the research participants. This characteristic reduces the likelihood that people will feel threatened or embarrassed when asked personal questions and increases the likelihood that they will provide answers that are not intentionally inaccurate or distorted.

   The major disadvantage of mail questionnaires is that it is difficult to obtain an adequate response rate. Many people do not want to take the time or make the effort to complete and mail a questionnaire. Others may be unable to read and understand the questionnaire.

3. *"Talking" computers.* A new method of conducting survey research is to have respondents provide answers to a computer that "talks." Romer and colleagues (1997) found that respondents rated computer interviews about sexual issues more favourably than face-to-face interviews and that the former were more reliable. Such increased reliability may be particularly valuable when conducting research on drug use, stigmatized sexual behaviours, and sexual orientation.

Field Research

Field research involves observing and studying social behaviour in settings in which the behaviour occurs naturally. Two types of field research are participant observation and nonparticipant observation.

In *participant observation* research, the researcher takes part in the phenomenon being studied to obtain an insider's perspective of the people and/or behaviour being observed. John Stackhouse (1999), a middle-class, white male journalist, spent a week living on the streets of Toronto after having spent eight years living among the poor in India. Stackhouse was criticized as a dilettante, but his method, however briefly employed, allowed him greater access to understanding than simple interviews would have. In *nonparticipant observation* research, the researcher observes the phenomenon being studied without actively taking part in the group or the activity. For example, Dordick (1997) studied homelessness by observing and talking with homeless individuals in a variety of settings, but she did not live as a homeless person as part of her research.

The main advantage of field research on social problems is that it provides detailed information about the values, rituals, norms, behaviours, symbols, beliefs, and emotions of those being studied. A potential limitation is that because field research typically relies on small samples, it is less suited to generalization.

Secondary Data Research

Sometimes, researchers analyze secondary data: data already collected by other researchers or government agencies, or that exist in forms such as historical documents, police reports, school records, and official records of marriages, births, and deaths. A major advantage of using secondary data is that the data are readily

field research
Observing and studying social behaviour in settings in which the behaviour occurs naturally.

accessible, so researchers avoid the time and expense of collecting their own data. Secondary data are also often based on large representative samples. In Canada, sociologists have been able to analyze the data gathered in the national census for decades; however, recent changes to the census reveal a weakness of relying on secondary data: one is not in control of the questions asked of the surveyed population.

In 2010, the federal government in Canada discontinued the use of the long-form census, a survey that had previously been sent out to every household in Canada starting in 1971 and increasing in frequency from once per decade to once every five years in 1986. The 2011 survey marked the replacement of the mandatory long-form census with the newly created National Household Survey, a questionnaire that retained only the opening six demographic questions plus two others included on the long form. In 2006, only 20 percent of Canadian households received the full 53-question long-form survey—the one that asks for more specific information about disabilities and health, primary language in the household, place of birth, and the relationships of co-habitants to each other—and in 2011, the long-form census was dropped entirely (CBC News 2006). For social science researchers, the loss of these data has resulted in a serious dearth of information about the well-being of Canadian residents. It also means that it becomes harder for researchers to provide the most current information on trends in Canada to students, and to the populace as a whole. What this means is that it becomes more difficult to even begin the stages of assessing whether a social problem exists. Munir A. Sheikh, Chief Statistician of Canada 2008–10, has characterized the loss of the long-form census as part of a larger federal government "war on knowledge," noting that the loss of the objective data acquired with the traditional census means that governments will now be able to make policy decisions based on ideology rather than on actual evidence (Sheikh 2013). This will surely have a long-term impact on our ability to address social problems.

People can make a difference in society by the choices we make. We may choose to vote for one candidate over another, demand the right to reproductive choice or protest government policies that permit it, drive drunk or stop a friend from driving drunk, repeat a racist or sexist joke or chastise the person who tells it, and practise safe sex or risk the transmission of sexually transmitted diseases. Individuals can also make a difference by addressing social concerns in their occupational role, as well as through volunteer work.

Although individual choices have an important impact, collective social action often has a more pervasive effect. For example, in 1971, engineer Jim Bohlen, lawyer Irving Stone, and law student Paul Cote formed the Greenpeace Foundation in Vancouver to protest U.S. nuclear tests at Amchitka. In their first direct action, the 11 members of the Greenpeace Foundation set sail in a chartered trawler boat into the bomb testing range. In doing so, they attracted the interest of Canadians living downwind of the test site. The issue subsequently came before the U.S. Supreme Court; four additional tests that had been planned at Amchitka were cancelled. Since that time, Greenpeace has continued in its pursuit of "a moratorium on all those things poisoning us" and become one of the largest environmental groups in the world, with offices in several countries. As Bohlen remarked: "As individuals we are weak. Our strength is created by putting ourselves at risk" (in Nader et al. 1993: 100).

Schwalbe (1998) reminds us that we do not have to join a group or organize a protest to make positive changes in the world.

> We can change a small part of the social world single-handedly. If we treat others with more respect and compassion, if we refuse to participate in re-creating inequalities even in little ways, if we raise questions about official representation of reality, if we refuse to work in destructive industries, then we are making change. (p. 206)

1.6 Goals of the Text

This text approaches the study of social problems with several goals in mind:

1. *To provide an integrated theoretical background.* This text reflects an integrative theoretical approach to the study of social problems. More than one theoretical perspective can be used to explain a social problem because social problems usually have multiple causes.

2. *To develop an understanding that theories and methods can be extremely useful to one research project but not to another.* Many of the contemporary theories discussed in this book were developed to meet specific needs not addressed adequately by the foundational perspectives. Nonetheless, contemporary theory may borrow or develop principles from any of the foundational theories to meet the needs of the research task at hand. Knowing your research goals and needs, and developing a theoretical account rather than forcing a problem into a pre-set theory, is an important value and skill for contemporary thinkers.

3. *To encourage development of a sociological imagination.* A major insight of the sociological perspective is that various structural and cultural elements of society have far-reaching effects on individual lives and societal well-being. This insight, known as the sociological imagination, enables us to understand how social forces underlie personal misfortunes and failures, and also contribute to personal successes and achievements. Each chapter emphasizes how structural and cultural factors contribute to social problems, encouraging you to develop your sociological imagination by recognizing how structural and cultural factors influence private troubles and public issues.

4. *To provide global coverage of social problems.* The modern world is often referred to as a "global village." Understanding social problems requires an awareness of how global trends and policies affect social problems. Many social problems call for collective action involving countries around the world; efforts to end poverty, protect the environment, and reduce the spread of HIV are some of the social problems that have been addressed at the global level. Each chapter includes coverage of global aspects of social problems. We hope that this attention to the global aspects of social problems will broaden students' awareness of pressing world issues.

5. *To encourage students to take positive social action.* Individuals who understand the factors that contribute to social problems may be better able to formulate interventions to remedy those problems. Recognizing the personal pain and public costs associated with social problems encourages some to initiate social intervention.

6. *To encourage the development of critical thinking skills.* Providing students with evidence to challenge commonsense views of the social world, we provide opportunities in each chapter for students to consider where they have received knowledge about social problems, what the values are that inform that knowledge, and the reliability of the evidence that informs it. Sociologists challenge commonsense ideas not because they are "common" or because we object to knowledge that is "sensible," but because so much of the common sense that we receive is actually inaccurate, harmful, and even counterproductive to the social benefits we seek to acquire for our shared local and global society as a whole.

Understanding Social Problems

At the end of each chapter to follow we offer a section entitled *Understanding*, in which we re-emphasize the social origin of the problem being discussed, the consequences, and the alternative social solutions. It is our hope that you will end each chapter with a "sociological imagination" view of the problem and how, as a society, we might approach a solution.

Just as each chapter opens with a reflective question—*What do you already know?*—as an invitation for you to consider the knowledge you already have about a set of social problems under consideration in that chapter, we also conclude each chapter with *What do you know now?* This is an invitation to reflect critically on how you have developed, refined, or altered your knowledge about a set of social problems. By opening and ending with these questions, you can see your own development as thinkers, and can track your ability to evaluate information, apply it, and formulate your own new questions. Tracking your own development, giving credence to your own ability to think things through is not only an academic task, but also a key step to determining for yourself how you might want to get involved in working on solutions to social problems, both locally and on the global stage.

Sociologists have been studying social concerns since the Industrial Revolution in the nineteenth century. Industrialization brought about massive social changes: the influence of religion declined; families became smaller and moved from traditional, rural communities to urban settings. These and other changes have been associated with increases in crime, pollution, divorce, and juvenile delinquency. These changes and disruptions formed the initial impetus for the development of the field of sociology and continue to be a major focus of sociology.

In the spring of 2013, Prime Minister Stephen Harper accused Liberal leader Justin Trudeau of aiming to "commit sociology" after Trudeau had suggested that we need to look for the "root causes" of terrorist actions (Cohen 2013). Prime Minister Harper had admonished Trudeau for being impractical and living in an "ivory tower," and proposed that the better option was simply to use our security agencies to track terrorist organizations around the globe and at home. Harper implied that those of us who aim to think about the causes of terrorism somehow fail to condemn such violence, and diverted attention from Trudeau's—and sociological research's—actual point: that it is better to prevent terrorism than it is to have to deal with it after the fact.

There is no single agreed-upon definition of what constitutes a social problem. Most sociologists agree, however, that all social problems share two important elements: an objective social condition and a subjective interpretation of that condition. The different theoretical perspectives in sociology have their own ways to assess and explain the causes, consequences, and solutions of social problems.

Student Reflection: What Do You Know Now?

Having read the introductory chapter, consider one concern that you had at the outset. What kinds of tools do you think you might want to use to think about the social problem that you have chosen? In what ways do you see that the media, formal education, your family discussions, or religious affiliations have constructed the social concern as a problem? What kinds of claims do they make in order to draw attention to the issue as a problem? Do you agree with the validity of those claims? Do you think there could be "more to it" than the commonsense discussions indicate? We encourage you to look through the chapters and give some thought to how a sociological approach can improve our understanding of social problems. As a thought experiment, try thinking about any particular difficulty you'd normally think of as simply a personal problem or personal trouble, and try to connect it to a wider system with many variables.

Now you are using what C. Wright Mills referred to as the "sociological imagination." Congratulations! You are "committing sociology"!

What Do You Do Next?

Located at www.nelson.com/socialproblems5e

- Consolidate your knowledge with interactive and printable **Flashcards**
- Gauge your understanding with **Practice Quizzes** and **Matching Activities**
- Develop your critical thinking skills with **Self and Society** and **The Human Side** questions
- Analyze **Social Research** and **Social Problems in Global Perspective**
- Explore the implications of **Technology on Social Problems**

section 1

Problems of
Well-Being

Section 1 deals with problems frequently regarded as private rather than public issues; that is, they are viewed as internally caused or seen as a function of individual free will. People often respond to these problems by assuming that the problem is the fault of the victims—that in some way they have freely chosen their plight. In this set of problems, blame is most often attached to the individuals themselves. Thus, the physically and mentally ill (Chapter 2), the alcoholic and the drug addict (Chapter 3), the criminal and the delinquent (Chapter 4), and the divorced person and the child abuser (Chapter 5) are thought to be bad, weak, immoral, or somehow different from the average person. Consider the following scenarios:

To feed her children, a woman with a limited income decides not to fill an expensive prescription—she cannot afford both. When her condition worsens, she is blamed for failing to fill the prescription. A sociological analysis will observe that the woman did not want to be sick, but chose the least of several unfortunate alternatives. In this case, factors that make her condition worse include poverty, the privately borne costs of medication, and social norms that stress parental responsibility and sacrifice. Had she filled the prescription, she risked blame for failures as a mother.

A student drinks alcohol daily and often cuts classes. Although the public views such behaviour as a personal weakness, sociologists emphasize the role of the individual's socialization and society. For example, a disproportionate number of individuals with drinking problems were reared in homes where one or both parents drank heavily. In the general culture, media portrayals promote drinking as desirable, fun, glamorous, and a source of status. Student culture itself often emphasizes bars and drinking parties as primary sources of recreation and affiliation.

A mother comes home from work and finds her children playing and the house in disorder. She decides they must be disciplined with a beating using a wooden spoon. Repeated research shows that a history of being abused as a child is the strongest independent predictor of who will become a child abuser. Additionally, socially powerful beliefs such as acceptance of corporal punishment as "normal" and ambiguity on what constitutes appropriate discipline, laws that protect the "right" of parents to use "reasonable force" to physically punish children, and the historical and lingering belief that family matters are "private" all contribute to child abuse. To change the behaviour of abusive parenting requires that we alter societal beliefs about the punishment of children.

These examples illustrate that many behaviours result more from social factors than from individual choice. To the degree that individuals do make choices, these choices are socially constrained.

Sociologically, one's social status and enjoyment of or lack of privileges limit one's life options.

In each of the prior examples, the alternatives present for individuals are limited by the social structure of society and by the cultural and subcultural definitions of appropriate behaviour. While the sociological theories we address throughout this text take different approaches to understanding the problems identified previously, all agree that problems that first appear to be private concerns are really the result of larger social factors. Society, not the individual, is then the primary context in which problems arise and also the primary source of the solutions to those problems. In this and the following sections, we emphasize the importance of sociological analyses of sources of and solutions to social problems.

2

Illness and Health Care

Sebastien Bergeron/Vetta/Getty Images

Student Reflection: What Do You Already Know?

What have you learned about what it means to be healthy and to treat illness, and where or how did you learn it? Are you familiar with the idea that specific groups of people, or "populations," can share in health characteristics, either positive or negative? What kinds of habits, behaviours, or lifestyles have you been taught to pursue in order to be "healthy" at home, at school, or out with friends? What kinds of diseases or illnesses have you been taught to fear, or to understand as "problems" only for "other people"—maybe even hold them at fault for being sick? Even though Canada is known for our universal health care, can you think of any ways in which income and other social differences in Canada can lead to wildly different experiences of health and illness? These questions are central to the concerns we raise below.

Learning Outcomes

Through careful reading of this chapter, you should be able to:

- define the bolded key terms
- recognize the structural factors that lead to population and individual health; that is, you will be able to discern what we often assume are individual problems as social problems instead
- recognize the limits of biological explanations of health and explain ways in which social reasons can show patterns over time, across place, and within social classes
- begin to analyze a given social health problem from a variety of perspectives, including symbolic interactionism, conflict theory, feminism, critical race theory, and queer theory
- begin to analyze the role played by formal institutions such as government and medicine in constructing the meanings of health and illness in contemporary Canadian health systems and individual bodies

Over the past 150 years the world has changed in extraordinary ways. One of the most profound changes over the last century had been the increase in the average length of life. Since the end of World War II, longevity of life in most developed and developing countries has increased by almost 25 years—the greatest increase seen in the history of humankind (LaPorte 1997). For those in developed nations these life expectancy predictions have remained relatively stable into the twenty-first century.

Despite overall improvements in living conditions and medical care, health problems and health-care delivery are major concerns of individuals, families, communities, and nations. In this chapter, we review health concerns in Canada and throughout the world. The World Health Organization (1946)* defines **health** as "a state of complete physical, mental, and social well-being" (p. 3). Sociologists are concerned with how social forces affect and are affected by health and illness, why some social groups suffer more illness than others, and how illness affects individuals' sense of identity and relationships with others. Sociologists also examine health-care systems and explore how these systems can be improved.

2.1 The Global Context: Patterns of Health and Disease

The study of patterns of health and disease is called **epidemiology**, and incorporates several disciplines, including public health, medicine, biology, and sociology. An **epidemiologist** studies the social origins and distribution of poor health in a population and how patterns of health and disease vary among and within societies. In this chapter, we also look at global patterns of morbidity, longevity, mortality, and disease burden.

Patterns of Morbidity

Morbidity refers to acute and chronic illnesses and diseases and the symptoms and impairments they produce. An **acute condition** is short term; by definition, it can last no more than three months. A **chronic condition** is a long-term health problem. The rate of serious morbidity in a population provides one measure of the health of that population. Morbidity may be measured according to the incidence and prevalence of specific illnesses and diseases. **Incidence** refers to the number of new cases of a specific health problem within a given population during a specified period. **Prevalence** refers to the total number of cases of a specific health problem within a population at a given time. For example, in 2007 there were 2.5 million people newly infected with HIV worldwide—of whom 420 000 were children and roughly half were women. In the same year, the worldwide prevalence of HIV was 33.2 million, and there were 2.1 million deaths due to AIDS ("Global Summary of the HIV/AIDS Epidemic" 2007). Since HIV notification to the Public Health Agency of Canada (PHAC) began in 1985 there have been 74 174 positive cases reported (Health Canada 2011: 2); of the total, 26.7 percent of diagnoses were reported from 1979 to 2004 (Health Canada 2005a: 34) and of those 74 percent had died in the same period (p. 64). The total number of reported deaths by the year 2011 was 24 300 (Health Canada 2011: 2); however, social stigma and the absence of policy requiring the reporting of positive HIV test results and AIDS-related deaths result in data up to 2003 that do not reflect actual numbers of infections or deaths. For these reasons, Health Canada is careful to report these numbers as minimum *estimates*. We are also learning that many persons infected with HIV face co-morbidity, with higher

health
A state of complete physical, mental, and social well-being.

epidemiology
The study of the distribution of disease within a population.

epidemiologist
A scientist who studies the social origins and distribution of health problems in a population and how patterns of illness and disease vary between and within societies.

morbidity
Disease, impairment, and accidents present in a population.

acute condition
A health condition that lasts no longer than three months.

chronic condition
A long-term health problem.

incidence
The number of new cases of a specific health problem in a given population during a specified period.

prevalence
The total number of cases of a condition in a population that exist at a given time.

*Reproduced, with the permission of the publisher, from World Health Organization (1948). "WHO definition of Health," http://www.who.int/about/defintion/en/print.html.

rates of both tuberculosis and hepatitis C infections than in the general population. Indeed, in the global population of HIV-positive persons, tuberculosis is the leading cause of death (Health Canada 2007: 133). The good news is that educational and social outreach have lowered the rate of infection across Canada, while improved drug treatments for HIV have improved both quality of life and life expectancy for those with HIV (Health Canada 2011: 3). We can therefore expect that those currently infected with HIV will live longer healthier lives, thus increasing the numbers of people who are living with HIV even while new infection rates continue to fall with numbers below a range of 2250 to 4100 annually (ibid).

If we try to understand the transmission of infection and disease purely as matters of biology, we miss the key social reasons that place particular groups of people at greater risk for infection and death from infectious disease. Patterns of morbidity vary according to material social factors including social class, education, sex, and race. Morbidity patterns also vary according to a society's level of economic development and the age structure of the population. In developing nations, malnutrition, pneumonia, and parasitic and infectious diseases such as HIV/AIDS, malaria (transmitted by mosquitoes), tetanus, rabies, and measles are major health concerns. In the industrialized world, advances in sanitation, immunizations, and antibiotics have largely controlled infectious and parasitic diseases. However, the overuse of antibiotics in industrialized countries has contributed to a rise in resistant diseases, as antibiotics kill the weaker bacterial infections while allowing variants resistant to the drugs to flourish. Such antibiotic resistance, combined with sexual contact, is resulting in an increase in Canada of bacterial sexually transmitted infections, including syphilis strains resistant to antibiotic treatment (Health Canada 2002a: 22 fn14). Worldwide, the most alarming consequence of the development of drug-resistant germs is the resurgence of tuberculosis, which kills more people yearly than any other infectious disease. Tuberculosis is caused by bacilli that attack and destroy lung tissue; it is spread when infected individuals cough or sneeze. The World Health Organization estimates that one-third of the world's population is infected, although only about 10 percent of infected persons ever develop symptoms (WHO 2013a). This ratio of latent to active tuberculosis infection has remained stable since reported by Weitz (2001) on behalf of the WHO.

It is not only infectious disease that is influenced by social factors. Noninfectious diseases, such as heart disease, cancer, mental disorders, and respiratory diseases, pose the greatest health threat to the industrialized world.

The shift from a society characterized by low life expectancy and parasitic and infectious diseases to one characterized by high life expectancy and chronic and degenerative diseases is called **epidemiological transition**. As societies make the epidemiological transition, diseases that need time to develop, such as cancer, heart disease, Alzheimer's disease, arthritis, and osteoporosis, become more common, and childhood illnesses, typically caused by infectious and parasitic diseases, become less common.

Patterns of Longevity

One indicator of the health of a population is the average number of years that individuals born in a given year can expect to live, referred to as **life expectancy**.

Worldwide, life expectancy has increased dramatically over the last 50 years. However, between and within societies, wide disparities exist in life expectancy. "Japan was the first country to attain an average lifespan of over 80 years—more than double that of many less-developed countries" (Ash 2001: 57). In 2010, Japan had the longest life expectancy: 83.7 years. In the same year, life expectancy was less than or hovering just around 50 in several countries (see Table 2.1). In Canada, a female born in 2002 could expect to live 83.2 years; a male child to 76.3 years (Ash 2001: 53).

epidemiological transition
The shift from a society characterized by low life expectancy and parasitic and infectious diseases to one characterized by high life expectancy and chronic and degenerative diseases.

life expectancy
The average number of years that a person born in a given year can expect to live.

Table 2.1 *Countries with the Longest and Shortest Life Expectancies at Birth, 2010–15*

Lowest Life Expectancies		Highest Life Expectancies	
Country	Life Expectancy	Country	Life Expectancy
Sierra Leone	48.2	Japan	83.7
Guinea-Bissau	48.8	China, Hong Kong SAR	83.2
Democratic Republic of the Congo	48.9	Switzerland	82.5
Lesotho	49.1	Australia	82.1
Swaziland	49.2	Iceland	82
Afghanistan	49.3	Israel	82
Central African Republic	49.5	Italy	82
Zambia	49.6	Spain	81.8
Chad	50.1	France	81.7
Mozambique	51	Sweden	81.7

SOURCE: Adapted from United Nations, 2011. *The World Mortality Report, 2011* (Table 1.3, p. 9), http://www.un.org/en/development/desa/population/publications/pdf/mortality/worldMortalityReport2011.pdf. Reprinted by permission of The United Nations.

Patterns of Mortality

Rates of **mortality**, or death—especially those of infants, children, and women—provide sensitive indicators of a population's health. Worldwide, because of general rises in life expectancy, it is now ischemic heart disease that causes the most deaths annually, at 7 million, and this is followed closely by stroke and by lower respiratory infections, each of which kills 6.2 million people worldwide (WHO 2013b). Although HIV/AIDS still garners substantial attention, it has fallen to sixth place, with 1.6 million deaths attributed to its complications (ibid).

In Canada, the most recent data show that cancers and heart disease are the two leading causes of death, and they are far and away the most common among the top 10 that, taken together, account for 76.4 percent of all deaths in Canada each year (Statistics Canada 2009). These rates are changed somewhat from the last decade of the previous century, when over one-third of deaths (36 percent) were due to diseases of the circulatory system (e.g., ischemic heart disease and cerebrovascular diseases) while malignant neoplasms, or cancers, accounted for 28 percent of all deaths (Statistics Canada 2002).

In this chapter, we discuss how patterns of mortality are related to social factors, such as social class, sex, and education, and patterns of life expectancy. Mortality rates vary by age. For example, it is only among 15- to 19-year-olds that rates for external causes of death (e.g., suicide, motor vehicle and other types of accidents) are higher than rates for non-external causes of death (deaths arising from physiological processes). Among Canadian youth aged 15 to 19, these external factors account for three of the four most common causes of death over the last decade. Suicide remains the second leading cause of death among teenagers 15 to 19 (see Table 2.2). Cancer is the third leading cause of death, while the fourth most common cause of death is homicide.

mortality
Death.

Table 2.2 *Leading Causes of Death for Canadians Aged 15–19*

Leading Causes of Death (ICD-10)[11,12,13]	Characteristics	2005	2006	2007	2008	2009
Malignant neoplasms [C00–C97]	Rank of leading causes of death[15]	3	3	3	3	3
	Number of deaths	61	62	64	59	71
Diabetes mellitus [E10–E14]	Rank of leading causes of death[15]	9	11	7	9	12
	Number of deaths	4	4	4	8	2
Alzheimer's disease [G30]	Rank of leading causes of death[15]	23	25	24	23	22
	Number of deaths	0	0	0	0	0
Diseases of heart [I00–I09, I11, I13, I20–I51]	Rank of leading causes of death[15]	5	5	5	5	5
	Number of deaths	27	25	22	18	28
Cerebrovascular diseases [I60–I69]	Rank of leading causes of death[15]	7	7	9	8	9
	Number of deaths	8	9	5	5	4
Influenza and pneumonia [J09–J18]	Rank of leading causes of death[15]	8	9	8	7	7
	Number of deaths	6	6	7	6	12
Chronic lower respiratory diseases [J40–J47]	Rank of leading causes of death[15]	14	8	12	11	12
	Number of deaths	2	7	4	3	2
Nephritis, nephrotic syndrome and nephrosis [N00–N07, N17–N19, N25–N27]	Rank of leading causes of death[15]	12	18	13	23	22
	Number of deaths	3	1	3	0	0
Accidents (unintentional injuries) [V01–X59, Y85–Y86]	Rank of leading causes of death[15]	1	1	1	1	1
	Number of deaths	458	466	405	397	360
Intentional self-harm (suicide) [X60–X84, Y87.0]	Rank of leading causes of death[15]	2	2	2	2	2
	Number of deaths	213	152	185	205	202
Assault (homicide) [X85–Y09, Y87.1]	Rank of leading causes of death[15]	4	4	4	4	4
	Number of deaths	55	51	61	58	66

[11]The cause of death tabulated is the underlying cause of death. This is defined as (a) the disease or injury which initiated the train of events leading directly to death, or (b) the circumstances of the accident or violence which produced the fatal injury. The underlying cause is selected from the conditions listed on the medical certificate of cause of death.

[12]World Health Organization (WHO), International Statistical Classification of Diseases and Related Health Problems, 10th Revision (ICD-10).

[13]The list for ranking leading causes of death that is used in this table is based on the list that was developed and that is been used by the National Center for Health Statistics of the United States in their annual report on leading causes of death.

[14]"Other causes of death" is a residual category, which includes all causes of death that are not part of the 50 leading causes of death list.

[15]The ranking of the leading causes of death is based on the number of deaths.

SOURCE: Statistics Canada. *Table 102-0561 - Leading causes of death, total population, by age group and sex, Canada, annual*, CANSIM (database). http://www5.statcan.gc.ca/cansim/a21 (accessed: 2014-03-08)

Table 2.2 shows some modest fluctuation in natural causes of death from 2005 to 2009 but the leading four causes of death remain stable, indicating that it is overwhelmingly the case that the greatest threat to young people's health comes from external accidental trauma or deliberate violence. Indeed, the leading causes of death in the top four categories have remained stable over the course of the last decade. That two of the four leading causes of death for youth aged 15 to 19 are the result of violent assault and suicide presents a rather brutal reality and challenges the assertion that childhood is a carefree time of happiness and security.

Infant and Childhood Mortality Rates

The infant mortality rate, the number of deaths of live-born infants under one year of age per 1000 live births (in any given year), provides an important measure of the health of a population. In 2001, 24 countries had infant mortality rates over 100 (UNICEF 2003), a drop from 25 countries in 1999. These data mean that for approximately one-quarter of the world's countries, 1 in every 10 live-born babies died before reaching age one. The CIA *World Factbook* provides 2014 estimates in which only Afghanistan, Mali, and Somalia have infant mortality rates that remain so terribly high, but another 36 countries around the world have infant mortality rates exceeding 50, meaning that about 1/20 babies die prior to reaching age one (CIA 2014). By 2013, the infant mortality rate in Canada was 4.78 out of every 1000 births; for boys the rate was 5.11, while for girls it was 4.43 (ibid). These are significantly lower numbers than the more than 100 per thousand who die each year in Afghanistan, Mali, and Somalia, or the approximately 50 per thousand who die in the other 36 countries where political unrest, war, social upheaval, and a lack of health care imperil the lives of mothers and infants.

The **under-five mortality rate**, another useful measure of child health, refers to the rate of deaths of children under age five. Approximately 12 million children younger than five years of age die every year; most of these children live in developing countries. More than half of these deaths are attributed to diarrhea, acute respiratory illness, malaria, or measles, conditions that are either preventable or treatable with low-cost interventions (Rice et al. 2000). Malnutrition is associated with about half of all deaths among children (Rice et al. 2000). Mortality among infants and children declined in most developing countries from the mid-1980s through the 1990s; however, since about 2000, this decline has slowed, stopped, or reversed itself in some countries of sub-Saharan Africa, largely as a result of the rate of HIV infection among infants and children (Rustein 2000).

As much as countries among the most developed in the world enjoy generally low childhood mortality rates, the impact of income inequality inside these highly developed countries on the health and mortality of children can be dramatic. Table 2.3 shows that income distribution disparities between the highest one-fifth of earners and the lowest two-fifths of earners correlate with an increase in Canada's under-five mortality rank to 5 per 1000 as compared with Sweden's 2 per 1000. The United States, our closest geographic neighbour and a country that many of us find nearly indistinguishable from Canada, holds an even greater income disparity between the highest earners and the lowest, and an under-five mortality rate that is 40 percent higher than in Canada, at 7 per 1000. With a population 100 times larger than Canada's, the U.S. under-five mortality rate translates into thousands more children per year dying from preventable causes than in Canada.

In Table 2.3, each developed nation with the lowest mortality rate shows the least income inequality across its population. The impact of income on the health of children derives from the material access of parents to medical care, to clean and stable housing, and to a healthful diet and clean water. Meanwhile, those countries with the

under-five mortality rate
The rate of deaths among children under age five.

Table 2.3 *Childhood Mortality Rates in Developed Countries: Canada's Ranking*

	Country	Under-5 Mortality Rate (2012)		Infant Mortality Rate (under 1), 2012	Share of Household Income (%, 2007–2011*)	
		Rank	Value		Poorest 40%	Richest 20%
Countries with highest under-5 mortality rank	Sierra Leone	182	1	117	20	44
	Angola	164	2	100	15	49
	Chad	150	3	89	16x	47x
	Somalia	147	4	91	–	–
	Democratic Republic of the Congo	165	5	100	14x	51x
Countries with lowest under-5 mortality rank	Estonia	170	4	3	19x	43x
	Canada	161	5	5	20x	40x
	Australia	**161**	5	4	–	–
	Singapore	**185**	3	2	–	–
	Sweden	**185**	3	2	23	37

– Data not available.

x Data refer to years or periods other than those specified in the column heading. Such data are not included in the calculation of regional and global averages.

*Data refer to the most recent year available during the period specified in the column heading.

SOURCE: Reprinted by permission of UNICEF..

greatest disparities and attendant social upheaval show rates upward of 146 per 1000 in the under-five mortality rate. In Canada, those most at risk are families who live in rural areas that are underserviced in terms of health care and who have the least access to safe housing and clean drinking water. In Manitoba in 2003, the Kashechewan First Nation community began a boil-water advisory because of *E. coli* contamination in the water supply. Even though 2000 people had been sickened and several had died in the community from contaminated water, by 2005 no help had been offered by either the provincial or federal governments to upgrade the community's water treatment facilities. This neglect contrasts poorly with the attention paid to the community of Walkerton following the water supply crisis that sickened the Ontario town's population and caused several deaths in the spring of 2000.

Maternal Mortality Rates

maternal mortality rate
The numbers of deaths that result from complications associated with pregnancy or childbirth per 1000 pregnant women.

The **maternal mortality rate**, a measure of deaths that result from complications associated with pregnancy, childbirth, and unsafe abortion, also provides a sensitive indicator of a population's health status. The three most common causes of maternal death are hemorrhage, infection, and complications arising from unsafe abortions. The maternal mortality rate is a more sensitive indicator than any other social health measure of the disparity between the rich and the poor in a given region. Moreover, of all the health statistics monitored by the World Health Organization, maternal mortality has the largest discrepancy between developed and developing countries. For women in developed countries, the risk of dying from complications of pregnancy or childbirth is very low: of the approximately 530 000 maternal deaths that occur each year, more than 90 percent occur in developing nations (Family Care International 2007). "Safe Motherhood," the exhaustive 2007 report from Family Care International (FCI), argues that "[s]afe motherhood is fundamentally a matter of human rights; all women are entitled to good health and high-quality health services . . . Maternal deaths are linked to women's low status in society, and their lack of decision-making ability and economic power" (Family Care International 2007: 7). In other words, the dangers of pregnancy and childbirth are not inherent problems of biology but the direct consequence of social injustice. Moreover, even in the face of global economic disparity, providing women in developing nations with access to safe motherhood initiatives has been demonstrated to be highly cost-effective (ibid).

Patterns of Burden of Disease

Although infant and maternal mortality rates are sensitive indicators of population health, there is another means of measuring the health status of a population, one that combines mortality and disability. This alternative approach provides an indicator of the overall **burden of disease** on a population through a single unit of measurement: as a comprehensive unit of measurement, it combines not only the number of deaths, but also the impact of premature death and disability on a population (Murray and Lopez 1996). Called the **disability-adjusted life year (DALY)**, the measurement reflects years of life lost to premature death and years lived with a disability. However, scholars and activists inside the contemporary disability rights movement have criticized the DALY. Disability activists and scholars point out that the DALY views disability through an outmoded medical model of disease. It sees the disability itself, rather than the *social exclusion* of persons with disabilities from opportunities for economic, educational, and social well-being, as the source of the problem (Groce et al. 2000). (See also Chapter 3.)

2.2 HIV/AIDS: A Global Health Concern
HIV/AIDS Epi Update 2005

HIV, the virus that causes AIDS (acquired immunodeficiency syndrome), continues to threaten the health of populations worldwide. More than 34 million people now live with HIV/AIDS (National AIDS Trust 2011), and 97 percent live in low and middle-income countries (Kaiser Family Foundation 2010), particularly in sub-Saharan Africa where there are 23.5 million adults and children living with HIV/AIDS, and in Asia where 4.8 million live with HIV/AIDS (National AIDS Trust 2011).

Worldwide, most HIV infections are acquired through heterosexual contact, and slightly more than half of all those who live with HIV/AIDS are women (Kaiser Family Foundation 2010). HIV transmission can occur in blood-to-blood contact through sexual contact, through intravenous needle-sharing, through **perinatal transmission** from an infected mother to her newborn, through blood transfusions or other blood products, and through breast milk (Centers for Disease Control and Prevention 2010).

Worldwide, most cases of HIV infection are acquired through heterosexual contact, and slightly half of all people living with HIV/AIDS worldwide are women (Kaiser Family Foundation 2010). However, as in the United States, in Canada men who have sex with other men (MSM) are the group most at risk for acquiring HIV (46.6 percent), while intravenous drug use accounts for 13.7 percent of new transmissions, and

burden of disease
The number of deaths in a population combined with the impact of premature death and disability on that population.

disability-adjusted life year (DALY)
Years lived with illness or disability. More simply, one DALY equals one year lost of healthy life.

perinatal transmission
The transmission of infection from a mother to a fetus or newborn.

heterosexual contact for 37.2 percent of new transmissions (Government of Canada 2011b). As of 2011, just over 71 000 people were estimated to be living with HIV in Canada, about 11.4 percent more than in 2008, and of these, nearly one-quarter are women (ibid).

Since the beginning of the epidemic, AIDS has claimed more than 23 million lives (National AIDS Trust 2005). In 16 countries in sub-Saharan Africa, more than 1 in 10 persons aged 15 to 49 are HIV-infected, and 90 percent of the approximately 2 million children under age 15 who are infected with HIV live in the same sub-Saharan region (United Nations 2008: 9). Although HIV/AIDS originally emerged as an adult health problem, it has become a major killer of children under five years old, especially in developing countries (Adetunji 2000). In seven countries in southern Africa, at least 20 percent of the adult population is living with HIV.

Table 2.4 shows that the burden of HIV/AIDS is borne overwhelmingly in poor countries in sub-Saharan Africa, while North America and Europe bear relatively low levels of prevalence in both instances of infection, and of death. The HIV/AIDS epidemic creates an enormous burden for the limited health-care resources of poor countries such as these, and their economic development is thus threatened because of reductions in the available workforce in these countries, and because of the diversion of resources for development into coping with the epidemic. As of 2010, the Kaiser Family Foundation estimated that there were 16.6 million AIDS orphans in Africa, most of them in the sub-Saharan regions.

Table 2.4 **Regional HIV and AIDS Statistics, 2001 and 2009**

Regional figures on adults and children newly infected and living with HIV and AIDS-related deaths

		Adults and Children Living with HIV	Adults and Children Newly Infected	% Adult Prevalence (15–49 years)	AIDS-Related Deaths among Adults and
Sub-Saharan Africa	2009	22.5 million [20.9–24.2 million]	1.8 million [1.6–2.0 million]	5.0 [4.7–5.2]	1.3 million [1.1–1.5 million]
	2001	20.3 million [18.9–21.7 million]	2.2 million [1.9–2.4 million]	5.9 (5.6–6.1)	1.4 million [1.2–1.6 million]
Middle East and North Africa	2009	460 000 [400 000–530 000]	75 000 [61 000–92 000]	0.2 [0.2–0.3]	24 000 [20 000–27 000]
	2001	180 000 [150 000–210 000]	36 000 [32 000–42 000]	0.1 [0.1–0.1]	8300 [6300–11 000]

SOURCE: Slide 6/6 from "Regional figures on adults and children newly infected and living with HIV and AIDS-related deaths," *World Health Organization/UNAIDS, Global Report* (Table 2.2); http://www.unaids.org/documents/20101123_globalreport_slides_chapter2_em.pdf. Courtesy of UNAIDS/ONUSIDA 2014.

The high rates of HIV in developing countries, particularly sub-Saharan Africa, are societally devastating. The HIV/AIDS epidemic creates an enormous burden on the limited health-care resources of poor countries. Economic development is threatened by the HIV epidemic, which diverts national funds to health-related needs and reduces the size of a nation's workforce. Gains in life expectancy achieved in recent decades have been reversed in some countries. In Botswana, Zambia, and Zimbabwe—countries with high HIV prevalence—life expectancy at birth was lower in 2000 than it was in 1975 (Adetunji 2000).

HIV/AIDS in Canada

Between 1982, when AIDS was first diagnosed in Canada, and December 31, 2004, 19 824 AIDS cases in adults had been reported to the Centre for Infectious Disease Prevention and Control. The overwhelming majority of these cases involved men (90.9 percent). Health Canada (2005a: 5) reports, "Prior to 1994, only 6.2% of AIDS diagnoses are among adult females [over age 15], this has risen to just over 20% in the past two years . . . and is most striking in the 15-29 year age group where the proportion of AIDS diagnoses attributed to females increased from 9.9% before 1994 to 45.0% in 2004." Heterosexual contact with a high-risk partner and injection drug use are the two major risk factors for HIV infection in women (Health Canada 2002a). While the epidemiological data for Canada indicate that HIV transmission is highest among men who have sex with men, as Figure 2.1 shows, on a global scale, HIV is most prevalent among the heterosexual population.

Figure 2.1 *Estimated Exposure Category Distributions (%) among New HIV Infections in Canada by Time Period*

MSM: men who have sex with men; IDU: injecting drug users; Heterosexual: subcategories of heterosexual contact with a person at risk of HIV, origin in a country where HIV is endemic, and heterosexual as the only identified risk. A different method was used prior to 1996.

Young Canadians compose only a small proportion of the total reported cases. Of the cumulative reported AIDS cases in Canadian youth aged 10 to 19, about two of three cases were attributed to the receipt of infected blood and blood products. Among people aged 20 to 24, 51 percent of transmissions were attributed to men who have sex with men and 21 percent to heterosexual contact with a person at risk (Health Canada 2004).

HIV prevalence may be low among Canadian youth, but risk behaviour data on young Canadians suggest cause for concern. Although a 2001 national survey of Canadian teens found that 5.5 percent saw AIDS as a "very serious" issue (Bibby 2001: 43), many Canadian youth still engage in unsafe sexual practices. For example, according to the National Population Health Survey, among sexually active youth aged 15 to 19, 51 percent of females and 29 percent of males reported never or only sometimes using a condom in the past year. Among those 20 to 24 years old, the corresponding figures were 53 percent and 44 percent (Health Canada 2005b; Statistics Canada 1998a). When surveyed regarding their most recent sexual encounters, those in the 20 to 24 age group were twice as likely not to have used a condom during intercourse than those in the 15 to 17 age group (Roterman 2005: 40). Table 2.5 presents some of these data.

Table 2.5 *Non-Condom Use among Sexually Active 15- to 24-Year-Olds Who Were Single and/or Had Sex with More Than One Partner in Past Year, by Sex and Selected Characteristics, Canada, 2003*

| | Did Not Use Condom the Last Time | | | | | |
| | Total | | Males | | Females | |
	'000	%	'000	%	'000	%
Total	771.8	37.8	350.0	32.7	421.8	43.5
Age group						
15 to 17	65.4	21.5	22.3	14.8	43.1	28.0
18 to 19	146.2	32.5	58.1	25.2	88.0	40.0
20 to 24	560.3	43.6	269.5	39.1	290.7	48.8
Number of partners						
One	533.2	41.0	243.1	38.4	290.1	43.6
More than one	238.6	32.3	106.8	24.6	131.7	43.4
Two	133.4	34.0	49.3	24.2	84.1	44.4
Three	50.4	30.5	26.3	25.7	24.1	38.5
Four or more	54.8	30.3	31.2	24.2	23.5	45.5
Age at first sexual intercourse						
13 or younger	49.4	42.8	22.1	32.1	27.3	58.8
14 to 17	522.2	38.9	235.6	33.0	286.5	45.7
18 or older	200.2	34.4	92.3	32.1	108.0	36.5
Aboriginal						
Yes	41.4	42.4	16.2	41.7	25.1	42.8
No	703.2	37.5	320.9	32.3	382.3	43.5
Marital status						
Single (never married/separated/divorced/widowed)	754.8	37.5	344.1	32.5	410.7	43.0
Married/Common-law	16.0	63.3		49.2	10.3	75.3
Province/territory						
Newfoundland and Labrador	11.7	29.6	4.9	23.1	6.9	37.0
Prince Edward Island	2.5	27.5			2.0	43.3
Nova Scotia	18.2	28.6	6.8	22.9	11.4	33.5
New Brunswick	20.1	38.9	7.6	28.2	12.5	50.6
Québec	241.4	44.3	106.6	37.0	134.8	52.4
Ontario	270.5	34.9	130.5	32.0	140.0	38.1
Manitoba	26.5	36.5	12.5	33.3	14.0	39.8
Saskatchewan	19.4	33.9	7.1	24.7	12.3	43.3
Alberta	76.0	40.4	36.4	36.3	39.6	45.1
British Columbia	83.4	36.3	36.2	29.8	47.2	43.5
Territories	2.0	29.9	0.9	28.4	1.2	31.0

SOURCE: Statistics Canada. "Non-Condom Use Among Sexually Active 15- to 24-Year-Olds Who Were Single and/or Had Sex with More Than One Partner in the Past Year, by Sex and Selected Characteristics, Canada, 2003," (Health Reports), Catalogue No. 82-003, Vol. 16, No. 3, May 2005, p. 44.

Understanding HIV transmission and the impact of AIDS is greatly enhanced through the use of two theoretical lenses: these lenses focus attention on the social rather than purely biological issues involved. A **feminist** view of global trends contributes an understanding of how gender interacts with other social factors to make women and youth, especially female youth, particularly vulnerable to HIV infection. We cannot separate out the impact of "unemployment, illiteracy, gender inequalities, lack of information and services, and human rights abuses . . . factors [that] greatly increase the vulnerability of women, young people, and other marginalized groups" (Lamptey 2002: 209). Poor educational opportunities for girls, the value placed on young girls in the sex trade, and financial instability all combine to coerce young women to have unprotected sex for money. By so doing, they contribute to skyrocketing HIV transmission in the poorest nations.

2.3 Mental Illness: The Invisible Epidemic

The concepts of mental illness and mental health are not easy to define. What it means to be mentally healthy varies across and within cultures. Furthermore, mental health and mental illness may be thought of as points on a continuum. **Mental health** has nevertheless been defined as "the successful performance of mental function, resulting in productive activities, fulfilling relationships with other people, and the ability to adapt to change and to cope with adversity" (U.S. Department of Health and Human Services 1999: ix). **Mental illness** refers collectively to all mental disorders. A **mental disorder** is a health condition that is characterized by alterations in thinking, mood, and behaviour associated with distress, impaired functioning, or both. Although we all experience problems in living, in functioning, and in emotional state, such problems are not necessarily seen as mental illness—they must meet specific criteria (such as level of intensity and duration) specified in the classification manual used to diagnose mental disorders: the *Diagnostic and Statistical Manual of Mental Disorders* (DSM), now in its 5th edition (American Psychiatric Association 2013). Although a powerful management tool for use after diagnosis, the DSM, and related medicalization of mental/perceptual difference, has been criticized for its potentially damaging impact on people's day-to-day self-perception (Gergen 1994). Some examples of mental disorders are presented in Table 2.6.

Extent and Impact of Mental Illness

Canadian data indicate that in Canada, "approximately 20% of individuals will experience a mental illness during their lifetime, and the remaining 80% will be affected by an illness in family members" (CAMH 2012; Health Canada 2002b: 3). CAMH (2012) reports that 70% of all cases of mental illness show initial onset before or during adolescence, and that gender alters the expression of illness, with more men experiencing addiction and more women seeking treatment for "mood and anxiety disorders." Moreover, low income and homelessness correlate powerfully with lowered quality of mental health:

> Canadians in the lowest income group are 3 to 4 times more likely than those in the highest income group to report fair to poor mental health [and studies] in various Canadian cities indicate that between 23% and 67% of homeless people report having a mental illness. (CAMH 2012)

feminist
An umbrella term that describes both socio-political activism and academic work. The many sub-categories of feminist thought and action are united by a concern for the well-being of women. Feminists have sought for recognition that women are full human beings entitled to the same personal rights as men. In sociology, feminist work has demonstrated that gender is an important variable to be accounted for in research programs and that the well-being of women is integral to the general welfare of larger society.

mental health
The successful performance of mental function, resulting in productive activities, fulfilling relationships with other people, and the ability to adapt to change and to cope with adversity.

mental illness
A term used to refer collectively to all mental disorders.

mental disorder
A behavioural or psychological syndrome or pattern that occurs in an individual and that is associated with present distress or disability, or with a significantly increased risk of suffering, death, pain, disability, or loss of freedom.

Table 2.6 **Mental Disorders Classified by the American Psychiatric Association**

Classification	Description
Anxiety Disorders	Disorders characterized by anxiety that is manifest in phobias, panic attacks, or obsessive-compulsive disorder
Dissociative Disorders	Problems involving a splitting or dissociation of normal consciousness, such as amnesia and multiple personality
Disorders First Evident in Infancy, Childhood, or Adolescence	Including mental retardation, attention-deficit hyperactivity, and stuttering
Eating or Sleeping Disorders	Including such problems as anorexia and bulimia or insomnia and other problems associated with sleep
Impulse Control Disorders	Including the inability to control undesirable impulses, such as kleptomania, pyromania, and pathological gambling
Mood Disorders	Emotional disorders, such as major depression and bipolar (manic-depressive) disorder
Organic Mental Disorders	Psychological or behavioural disorders associated with dysfunctions of the brain caused by aging, disease, or brain damage (such as Alzheimer's disease)
Personality Disorders	Maladaptive personality traits that are generally resistant to treatment, such as paranoid and antisocial personality types
Schizophrenia and Other Psychotic Disorders	Disorders with symptoms such as delusions or hallucinations
Somatoform Disorders	Psychological problems that present themselves as symptoms of physical disease, such as hypochondria
Substance-Related Disorders	Disorders resulting from abuse of alcohol and/or drugs such as barbiturates, cocaine, or amphetamines

Worldwide, mental disorders accounted for approximately 12 percent of all disability-adjusted life years lost in 2001 (Brundtland 2000; World Health Organization 2001). Five of the leading causes of disability worldwide are mental disorders: major depression, schizophrenia, bipolar disorders, alcohol use, and obsessive-compulsive disorders (Brundtland 2000). Contrary to popular belief, children are not immune. Also, those whose parents are experiencing marital breakdown have higher levels of depression and tend to be more antisocial than children in stable homes (Statistics Canada 2005).

Causes of Mental Illnesses

Mental illnesses arise from a confluence of biological and social factors. A broad scope of research has linked many mental disorders with genetic or neurological causes involving some pathology of the brain. However, social and environmental influences, such as poverty, history of abuse, or other severe emotional trauma, also affect individuals' vulnerability to mental illness. The global increase in life expectancy has contributed to mental illnesses that affect the elderly, such as Alzheimer's disease and other forms of cognitive disorder and dementia. War within and between countries may also contribute to mental illness in such forms as post-traumatic stress disorder. In addition, "many societies and communities that customarily offered support to their needier members through family and social bonds now find it much harder to do so" (Brundtland 2000: 411). Garfinkel and Goldbloom (2000) explain that "the radical shifts in society towards technology, changes in family and societal supports and networks and the commercialization of existence . . . may account for the current epidemic of depression and other psychiatric disorders" (p. 503). In other words, mental illness is not simply an individual health problem.

2.4 Sociological Theories of Illness and Health Care

The sociological approach to the study of illness, health, and health care differs from medical, biological, and psychological approaches. Next, we discuss how sociological theories—structural-functionalism, conflict theory, feminism, symbolic interactionism, queer theory, and critical race theory—can contribute to our understanding of illness and health care.

Structural-Functionalist Perspective

A structural-functionalist approach focuses on how illness, health, and health care affect and are affected by other institutions in social life. For example, increased modernization and industrialization throughout the world have resulted in environmental pollution—a major health concern. Gender role expectations frequently encourage men to ignore their health, and social demands to delay childbearing can place both women and infants at greater risk for complications. Increasingly, patterns of health and disease are affected by **globalization**. For example, increased business travel and tourism has encouraged the global transmission of disease, such as severe acute respiratory syndrome (SARS), which surfaced in 2003 in 16 countries with a total of 1550 cases and 774 deaths, with 251 cases and 43 deaths in Canada (World Health Organization 2004).

Just as social change affects health, health concerns may lead to social change. The emergence of HIV and AIDS in the gay male population helped unite and mobilize gay rights activists in both Canada and the United States. Concerns over the hazards of using cellular phones while driving led to the 2009 legislation in Canada to outlaw the use of hand-held communication devices while driving.

A structural-functionalist approach understands health care as a social institution that functions to maintain the well-being of societal members and, consequently, of the society as a whole. Illness is dysfunctional in that it interferes with people performing needed social roles. To cope with nonfunctioning individuals and to control the negative effects of illness, society assigns a temporary and unique role to those who are ill—the sick role (Parsons 1951). This role ensures that individuals receive needed care, but at the same time, the role carries with it an expectation that the ill person will seek competent medical advice, adhere to the prescribed regimen, and return quickly to normal role obligations.

Structural-functionalists additionally explain the high salaries of physicians by arguing that society must entice the most qualified people into the demands of medical practice by offering high salaries. Without such an incentive, individuals would not be motivated to endure either the rigours of medical training or the stress of practising medicine.

globalization
The economic, political, and social interconnectedness among societies throughout the world.

Conflict Perspective

A conflict approach focuses on how wealth, status, and power, or the lack thereof, influence illness and health care. Worldwide, the have-nots not only experience the adverse health effects of poverty, but also have less access to quality medical care. In societies where women have little status and power, women's life expectancy is lower than in industrialized countries. The 2010 Human Development Report shows that gender-based inequalities that reduce women's access to education and to political representation also correspond to higher rates of maternal and infant death, with 915 maternal deaths per 100 000 live births in the 20 countries with the most gender-based inequality (United Nations 2010: 93). Consider, as well, that while public health measures, improved sanitation systems, proper housing, immunization, and antibiotics have virtually eliminated infectious diseases such as smallpox, tuberculosis, and cholera, not all Canadians have equally benefited. Largely due to crowded living conditions (i.e., housing densities on reserve are twice the national average) and poor nutrition, Aboriginal peoples are more vulnerable to TB infection than other Canadian-born persons. Though Aboriginal persons account for only 4 percent of Canada's total population, they account for 21 percent of all TB cases reported in 2008 (PHAC 2008).

Medical research agendas are also shaped by wealth, status, and power. Malaria kills twice as many people annually as does AIDS, yet in 2008 worldwide funding for the treatment and prevention of malaria totalled $358.8 million (U.S.), while funding for HIV/AIDS exceeded $5 billion (U.S.) (Congressional Research Service 2012: 9). Why? Northern developed countries, which provide most of the funding for world health–related research, experience HIV/AIDS as an immediate health crisis, while malaria, largely a disease of the global south, remains a distant problem.

The conflict perspective also focuses on how the profit motive influences health, illness, and health care. The profit motive underlies much of the illness, injury, and death that occur from hazardous working conditions and dangerous consumer products.

Feminist Perspectives

Feminist theories take gender to be a central rather than peripheral concern that influences all aspects of social life, including how one experiences health and illness, the unique health risks that women face, and the impact of broad social phenomena on women's health. This chapter has already noted why women face unique risks for HIV transmission and how a lack of control over their own reproductive health brings negative consequences for women's health and well-being. Contemporary studies in women's health demonstrate that quality of life and consequent experiences of health and illness are tied not simply or only to gender, but also to social class, to race and to ethnicity, and to age.

Grann and colleagues found that **socio-economic status (SES)** and race combined, with SES being the strongest predictor for a poor outcome, "contribute to the higher mortality rate of black women" diagnosed with breast cancer (2005: 344). To take breast and reproductive cancers as an example, where a woman lives, what her educational background is, what access she has to medical care—all these things combine to influence her risks for developing cancer, how early the cancer will be detected, the kind of treatment she will receive, and ultimately, her chances for survival. (See the discussion later in this chapter about the exploitation of our fears about cancer.) Moreover, contemporary research and theory makes clear that trying to treat risk factors as discrete and unrelated is a mistake. Markovic and colleagues

socio-economic status (SES)
Status that refers to the combination of economic and social circumstances that shape one's experiences as a member of a given class. SES addresses the likelihood that higher income and a higher place in the social hierarchy are likely to coincide, and that lower status and lower income are also likely to coincide, with attendant privileges for higher-SES groups and attendant risks for lower ones.

(2005) show that societal gender roles, domestic responsibilities, and larger socio-economic and political factors influence national health policy and combine to disadvantage women's health and well-being. For example, though we know that unsafe abortion and a lack of access to contraception are among the leading causes of maternal death in developing nations, the Canadian federal Conservative party has refused to be among the G8 countries to fund access to abortion and contraception in a shared effort to improve maternal health in developing countries (Wente 2010). A lack of knowledge about women's risk factors for conditions such as cervical cancer also works against women. For example, although vaccines to protect against infection caused by strains of human papillomavirus (HPV) promise to prevent the development of gynecological cancers, focus on the role of HPV in the development of over 90 percent of cervical cancers neglects the importance of the other factors— such as diet, smoking, access to proper nutrition, and adequate rest—that also influence the development of those cancers (which, it turns out, occur very rarely even though HPV infection is common). The easy adoption of the vaccine misses the larger health considerations that negatively influence the immune system's ability to fight off HPV infection; the vaccine does nothing to help with these other concerns, and has problematized women's sexuality in particular in order to exploit a market for vaccines whose merits remain unproven (Dias 2009). See the *Social Problems Research Up Close* feature for a detailed account of the critical research on HPV vaccines.

Social Problems *Research Up Close*

The HPV Vaccine and the Problematization of Women's Bodies

In a graduate-level major research paper completed at Wilfrid Laurier University, Canadian scholar Lisa Dias examined the manner in which women's bodies are surveilled and exploited, situated as diseased— in contrast to the taken for granted health of men's bodies—and made available to the incursions of both public health agencies and pharmaceutical companies. She argues in her master's research that at least since the production of films intended to educate the public about sexually transmitted infections (STIs), "Perceptions of women's bodies as diseased circulated in public health discourses about STTs ... [and] representations of women as 'vectors' of disease circulate" through much of the early twentieth century and its various "social purity" campaigns (Dias 2009: 4). In an extensive study detailing the manner in which campaigns to promote the HPV vaccine have been encoded, Dias demonstrates that now, in the twenty-first century, women's bodies are more aggressively surveilled and problematized than men's bodies are, and that standard cervical screening programs problematize women's sexuality in a manner that men's

sexuality is not. In her review of the extant literature on women's health care Dias finds that, while women have been a disproportionate focus of reproductive medicine, they have been largely neglected in other areas of health research, such as cardiovascular disease (CVD). Dias's research reminds us that the "common sense" acceptance of women's bodies as particularly "at risk" for reproductive and sexually transmitted diseases leaves us vulnerable to mass acceptance and implementation of vaccination programs whose long-term risks, both in terms of social cost (in the form of stigma) and health cost (in the form of complications or failures of the vaccine) are unknown.

Dias does not argue in any simple manner for rejection or acceptance of the vaccine but urges us instead to beware of the "controversy [of] competing discourses ... because these discourses speak to our current state of politics around issues of risk, gender and sexuality" (2009: 6–7). It is the meanings that people attribute to risk, "appropriate femininity," gender, and sexuality that sit at the core of Dias's analysis.

(continued)

To contextualize current debates about HPV vaccination programs, Dias turns her attention more generally to the historical treatment of TB and cancer, as well as AIDS, and finds that there is a long legacy of blaming individuals for their diseases, and holding individuals responsible for the management of their disease as *moral imperatives*. She writes, "It is apparent that the meanings [of cervical cancer] are produced in a sociocultural and historical context, that social understandings of cervical cancer are imbued with moral judgement, and that individuals are held accountable for becoming 'ill' in the first place …" (Dias 2009: 8).

Dias's research provides a symbolic and interpretive analysis of modes of dissemination of information about the HPV vaccine and about cervical cancer and the manner in which the focus on sexual danger and sexual pollution marginalizes young girls and women, setting them up as a target population that will carry the burden of managing the fears that hold sway in the cultural *zeitgeist* regarding sexuality and contagion.

Using qualitative methods, especially discourse analysis, Dias draws out the relationships among forms of power that are brought to bear on the HPV vaccine debate. Dias finds that "through medical and pharmaceutical surveillance women are encouraged to become 'responsible' for their and others' sexual and reproductive health" (p. 22). She draws particular attention to the "Tell Someone" campaign produced by Merck Frosst, the makers of Gardasil, which is the only vaccine currently available in Canada. She finds that the "someone" we are supposed to tell is presented visually and in the language of the pamphlet as exclusively female. Men are not represented as at risk for HPV infection, as carriers of HPV infection, or as persons responsible for having or disseminating knowledge about the risks of HPV infection.

Dias's objective in her research is not to promote the wholesale rejection of vaccination to protect against HPV infection; rather, she argues that "we need to be aware of the type of subject the [health] discourses of HPV and the vaccine are constructing" because the discourses personalize responsibility for health and ignore larger social factors that impede health (p. 64). Lack of access to health care for rural and marginalized women; inadequate nutrition, rest, and exercise; excessive levels of stress; and a constellation of other social hazards all combine to reduce the overall health of women, including their ability to fight off HPV infections on their own. Because many of these women lack access to the health care necessary to get the series of vaccines required to be effective in preventing HPV infection, the vaccines can be expected to have little or no impact in precisely the populations of women they would help most. Simultaneously, campaigns to "educate" women and girls about HPV unduly problematize and responsibilize women and their bodies, neglecting the role men play in the transmission of HPV.

SOURCE: Dias, Lisa V. 2009. "Burdening Women with Responsibility for Containment: A Discourse Analysis of Public Health Initiatives with Pharmaceutical Advertising for Gardasil, 'The HPV Vaccine.'" Major Research Paper, Master of Arts; Wilfrid Laurier University: Waterloo.

Symbolic Interactionist Perspective

Symbolic interactionists focus on (1) how meanings, definitions, and labels influence health, illness, and health care, and (2) how such meanings are learned through interaction with others and through media messages and portrayals. According to the symbolic interactionist perspective of illness, "there are no illnesses or diseases in nature. There are only conditions that society, or groups within it, have come to define as illness or disease" (Goldstein 1999: 31). Psychiatrist Thomas Szasz ([1961] 1970) argues that what we call "mental illness" is no more than a label conferred on those individuals who are different—that is, who don't conform to society's definitions of appropriate behaviour.

Definitions of health and illness vary over time and from society to society. In some countries, being fat is a sign of health and prosperity; in others, it is an indication of mental illness or a lack of self-control. Before medical research documented the health hazards of tobacco, our society defined cigarette smoking as fashionable. Cigarette advertisements still attempt to associate positive meanings—such as youth, sex, and romance—with smoking to entice people to smoke. A study of top-grossing American films from 1985 to 1995 revealed that 98 percent had references that supported tobacco use and 96 percent had references that supported alcohol use (Everett et al. 1998).

A growing number of behaviours and conditions are being defined as medical problems—a trend known as **medicalization**. Hyperactivity, insomnia, anxiety, and learning disabilities are examples of phenomena that some view as medical conditions in need of medical intervention. Increasingly, "normal" aspects of life, such as birth, aging, sexual development, menopause, and death, have come to be seen as medical events (Goldstein 1999).

Symbolic interactionist approaches can help us to understand why and how the latest technologies available in health care may actually do us more harm than good. In this chapter, for example, we discuss the negative impact on people's views of their own health status and experiences within health care that result from overly aggressive cancer screening.

Symbolic interactionists also focus on the stigmatizing effects of being labelled "ill." A **stigma** refers to any personal characteristic associated with social disgrace, rejection, or discrediting. (Originally, the word "stigma" referred to a mark burned into the skin of a criminal or slave.) Individuals with mental illnesses, drug addictions, physical deformities and impairments, and HIV and AIDS are particularly prone to being stigmatized. Stigmatization may lead to prejudice, discrimination, and even violence against individuals with illnesses or impairments.

Cancer Screening and the Exploitation of Fear

As a culture, we tend to place great faith in the ability of medicine to provide accurate diagnoses and to heal us of our injuries and diseases. At the same time, our general lack of direct access to and understanding of diagnostic and treatment technologies used in contemporary medicine can make us extremely suspicious about medical practice. As a result, we can have very contradictory attitudes about medical practice, and nowhere is our combination of suspicion and trust more palpable than in the diagnosis and treatment of cancers. Here, we turn our attention to two current areas of controversy in cancer screening and treatment: breast cancer and prostate cancer.

In November 2009, *The New York Times* brought to public attention a recommendation that breast cancer screening for women with no identified predisposition for the development of breast cancer be delayed from age 40 to age 50 in order to avoid overdiagnosis. In Canada, *The Globe and Mail* quickly followed suit with its own commentary on the newly released protocols, originally published in the *Annals of Internal Medicine*. Against the increasing push for blanket screening of women over the age of 40 for breast cancer, the members of the U.S. Preventive Services Task Force (USPSTF) who authored the study recommended against the use of routine mammography in women aged 40 to 49 (USPSTF 2009). The new guidelines followed up on an earlier study from 2002 that had recommended all women over age 40 be screened at least every two years for breast cancer. The new 2009 recommendations build on the conclusions of a long-term study that determined that the risk of false-positive results for the presence of cancer, the potential harms of invasive treatment, and needless exposure to the radiation from diagnostic mammography constituted harms that outweighed any potential benefits of cancer detection in the age group (Nelson 2009).

Over the last two decades, women have embraced their personal responsibility to monitor their health by using regular breast self-exam (BSE) procedures to look for

medicalization
The tendency to define negatively evaluated behaviours or conditions as medical problems in need of medical intervention.

stigma
Refers to any personal characteristic associated with social disgrace, rejection, or discrediting.

lumps that may signal a cancer developing in the breast. The process of getting women to perform BSE is a form of "responsibilization" that transfers accountability for our health from large environmental hazards and public policy and health-care services to individuals (Gray 2009). Responsibilization is a concept that refers to the movement toward demanding that individuals "become prudent subjects who must 'practice individual responsibility'" (Gray 2009: 327) to look after their own health and safety. In the context of breast cancer screening, responsibilization has required not only that women learn and perform BSE and to go for regularly scheduled clinical breast exams (CBE), even though the long-term data show that BSE has no positive influence to reduce breast cancer deaths and risks exposing women to unnecessary biopsies (Thomas et al. 2002). Furthermore, clinical breast exam carries not only the risks of invasion that we have already mentioned, but also the risk of a false sense of security when we trust clinicians to read radiologic and pathology reports correctly. Yet, recent cases in Canada demonstrate that such trust may be misplaced. In essence, if we trust the screening technology to deliver accurate information, we are missing the human component required for accurate interpretation of test results. In such cases, the problem is our faith in technology and expertise, rather than a failure of the technology itself.

In its worst manifestations, the risk of submitting to breast cancer screening has resulted in unnecessary mastectomy when test results were not properly read (CBC News 2010). Explaining the risk-benefit analysis of SBE and CBE, André Picard, MD, medical reporter for *The Globe and Mail,* writes that we have no evidence that SBE is a useful diagnostic technology and that mammography programs would have to screen 1904 women aged 39–49 for a decade to prevent a single death; in women aged 50–59, they would need to screen 1339 for 10 years to prevent one death (Picard 2009). We cannot ignore, either, that screening not only has benefits, it can cause harm. Younger, premenopausal women have denser breasts and they have far more false-positive results, leading to unnecessary biopsies that are physically painful and psychologically damaging, not to mention the additional exposure to radiation (Picard 2009).

Just as there has been an increased responsibilization of women for their own health and for identifying cancers specific to women, men have been responsibilized with regard to prostate cancer:

> For . . . men, PSA tests are . . . an essential piece of preventive medicine. . . . But a growing body of evidence shows that the PSA test [results] in a huge number of unnecessary surgeries. (Wente 2010)

However, the value of screening for prostate cancer has come under increased scrutiny in part because there are many reasons that blood PSA levels can be elevated, and in part because even when prostate cancer is diagnosed it is very often a non-aggressive form that will not lead to death even if left untreated. Conversely, the negative effects of treatment can include "erectile dysfunction, urinary incontinence, bowel dysfunction, and death. Additionally, many men who screen positive for prostate cancer face unnecessary anxiety because they may not develop symptoms within their lifetime" (Kuehn 2008).

In other words, the treatment is worse than the disease; in many cases the disease itself may never become apparent and the men will die at or beyond life expectancy from other causes.

We place our faith in medical technologies as a matter of course, yet long-term data are showing us that increased technological intervention and diagnosis can bring hazards greater than the problems the technologies seek to remedy. Responsibilization of men and women as social agents exploits our fears of death and disease and can make us vulnerable to feelings that we are not acting appropriately as citizens if we resist or refuse these interventions. Yet it may be the case that at least for certain age groups—men over 75 and women under 50—resisting medicalization and their attendant invasive procedures will protect us from a host of potential harms.

Queer Theory Perspectives

Queer theory developed largely as a response to the management and perception of HIV/AIDS in North America. The theory has drawn attention to the problems that result when HIV transmission risk is seen as something related to sexual identity. High rates of transmission for heterosexual persons proved to be a surprise to epidemiologists: they had assumed that HIV/AIDS would remain inside the gay male community. Careless assumptions about identity and behaviour that failed to note the three central contradictions of identity include these:

1. The identities we declare publicly are not necessarily the identity affiliations we maintain privately.
2. Social imperatives and assumptions about which behaviours are appropriate or unique to certain identity groups have proven to be inaccurate measures of behaviours that people actually follow.
3. The behaviours in which people engage include desires as well as practices. Both are influenced by social location, not by inherent features of biology or simplistic identity categories.

In addition to these observations, gay rights lobbyists, queer theorists, and groups such as the Gay and Lesbian Medical Association (GLMA) successfully contested the classification of homosexuality as a mental health disorder. Simultaneously, they refocused attention on how experiences of homophobia and stigma can have a negative impact on mental health for GLBT persons, or persons who are gay, lesbian, bisexual, or transgender.

Critical Race Theory and Health in Canada

Critical race theory is an important development in thinking not only about racism, but also about the very creation of the idea of "race" in the first place. Critical race theorists assess historical and contemporary evidence to show that both "race" and "ethnicity" are socially constructed ways of conceiving of people according to a hierarchized and segregated set of assumptions. Sheryl Nestel, in her research report "Colour Coded Health Care" (2012), explains the relevance of critical race theory to thinking about health-care practice in Canada:

> Scientific racism had its beginnings in Enlightenment thought, a central tenet of which was the categorization of natural phenomena, including human beings. Nineteenth- and 20th-century notions of race consequently posited that a range of immutable biological differences and race-specific diseases inhered in different population groups and that these groups could be sorted into a racial taxonomy that reflected gradations of human worth. (p. 5)

In other words, "race" was invented by scientists who sought to justify the valuation of different groups of people, but their science was founded in nothing more than already solidified beliefs about which human groups were most "evolved" and therefore most deserving of power. The scientific association of diseases with particular "races" allowed scientists and medical practitioners to ignore the social and political reasons that illnesses would develop more frequently in some groups, and led in its worst manifestation to eugenics movements of the twentieth century that sought to remove such supposedly disease-prone "races" from the human population (Fausto-Sterling 1995; Proctor 1995).

Contemporary scholarship on the health of Canadians that uses a critical race approach helps us to see that the persistent belief in the idea of distinct races has real consequences for the health of those perceived as "different" from other Canadians, and who suffer from that ascribed status as persons with a lower social value. As an example, Nestel elaborates on health-care providers' simultaneous insistence that they do not hold racist views and their practice reports that contradict that generous self-concept. In Nestel's example, the cost of their racism impacts negatively on the health of Canadian South Asian women, but applies to the treatment of other groups who are marginalized on the basis of race and/or ethnicity as well:

> [R]acist attitudes of health-care providers took three forms: essentializing explanations, culturalist explanations, and racializing explanations. The essentializing explanations . . . involved overgeneralizing about the women's culture, race, and social background. The physicians explained South Asian women's underutilization of the health-care system by their "lack of ability to follow instructions, take responsibility for their health, be proactive in their use of services and be 'good patients.' " The "culturalist explanations involved treating culture as static and frozen in time, while the racializing explanations involved "veiled references to culture, ethnicity and women's personal characteristics. . . . Among the policies that impacted negatively on South Asian women were "restrictions on the number of visitors, rigid appointments or treatment schedules, lack of translation services, and limited time spent with patients. These practices were interpreted by the South Asian women as exclusionary, while the practitioners' response was to construct the women as difficult and as a burden on the already overstretched health care system." (2012: 20)

Clearly, the social value that health-care providers ascribe to populations and the assumptions made about particular cultures can negatively impact the care that marginalized groups receive, and can negatively impact a group's willingness to seek health care.

2.5 Social Factors Associated with Health and Illness

Public health education campaigns, articles in popular magazines, postsecondary-level health courses, and health professionals emphasize that to be healthy we must adopt a healthy lifestyle. In response, many people have at least tried to quit smoking, follow a healthier diet, and include exercise in their daily or weekly routine. However, health and illness are affected by more than personal lifestyle choices. In the following section, we examine how social factors—such as social class and poverty, education, race, and gender—affect health and illness. These factors are often understood as **social determinants of health**. Dennis Raphael (2004) explains:

social determinants of health
Social factors that affect health and illness, such as social class and poverty, education, race, and gender.

> Social determinants of health determine whether individuals stay healthy or become ill . . . [and] the extent to which a person possesses the physical, social, and personal resources to identify and achieve personal aspirations, satisfy needs, and cope with the environment. . . . Since a social determinants of health approach sees mainsprings of health as being how a society organises and distributes economic and social resources, it directs attention to economic and social policies as a means of improving it. (p. 1)

We examine the experience of health keeping the social determinants approach largely at the foreground in the following sections on the health of Canadians. Health problems related to environmental problems are discussed with greater depth in Chapter 14.

Social Class and Poverty

An international group of physicians has identified poverty as the world's leading health problem ("Poverty Threatens Crisis" 1998). Poverty is associated with unsanitary living conditions, hazardous working conditions, lack of access to medical care, and inadequate nutrition (see also Chapter 10).

In Canada, socio-economic status (SES) is related to numerous aspects of health and illness (Health Canada 1999b). For example, self-rated health is strongly linked to income. According to the 1996–97 National Population Health Survey, Canadians who lived in the lowest-income households were four to seven times more likely (depending on race, ethnicity, and sex) to report fair or poor health than those who lived in the highest-income households (Figure 2.2). In addition, at each rung up the income ladder, Canadians have less sickness, longer life expectancy, and improved health. "It is estimated that if the death rates of the highest income earners applied to all Canadians, more than one-fifth of all years of life lost before age 65 could be prevented" (Health Canada 1999a: 14). Moreover, compared with those in the lowest quartile of the income distribution, Canadian men in the highest quartile can expect to live 6.3 years longer and have 14.3 more years free of disability. For women, the differences are 3 and 7.6 years, respectively (Health Canada 1999a: 26).

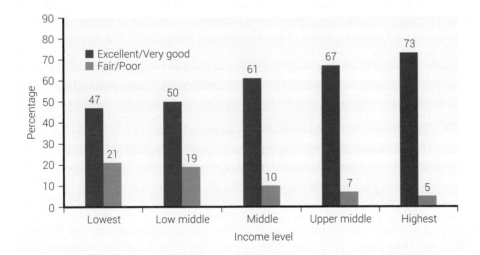

Figure 2.2 **Self-Rated Health, by Income Level,* Canadians Aged 12+, 1996–1997**

*Income levels in this figure represent total household incomes before taxes and are adjusted for family size and age-standardized.

SOURCE: Adapted from Statistics Canada. "Self-Rated Health, by Income Level, Canadians Aged 12+, 1996–1997" (Statistical Report on the Health of Canadians), Catalogue No. 82-570, 1999.

Poor persons are also more likely to report an unmet need for health care. Although in Canada access to universally insured health care remains largely unrelated to income, many low- and moderate-income Canadians have limited or no access to such health services as eye care, dentistry, mental health counselling, and prescription drugs (Health Canada 1999a).

Low socio-economic status is also associated with increased risk of a broad range of psychiatric conditions (Williams and Collins 1999). Rates of depression and substance abuse, for example, are higher in the lower socio-economic classes (Kessler et al. 1994). Why do poor people have higher rates of mental illness? One explanation suggests that individuals from lower socio-economic status groups experience greater stress as a result of their deprived and difficult living conditions. Others argue that members of the lower SES groups are simply more likely to have their behaviours identified and treated as mental illness.

Lower socio-economic groups have higher rates of mortality, in part, because they have higher rates of health risk behaviours such as smoking, drinking alcohol, being overweight, and being physically inactive. We also know that despite the widespread belief that executives are prone to stress-related heart attacks, a variety of factors place lower-SES groups at higher risk for cardiovascular disease. Even for those who move out of a low-SES group in childhood and into a higher-SES group in adulthood some significant risks can persist, resulting in increased morbidity for this group. These risks appear to be related to the instability, sense of powerlessness, and persistent stress that a low-SES child is more likely to endure. Such problems may not be remedied by advanced education and have measurable, negative impact on long-term risks for cardiovascular disease (Labonte 1992; Reid 1998). In addition, the lower class tends to experience high levels of stress while having few resources to cope with it (Cockerham 1998). Stress has been linked to a variety of physical and mental health problems, including high blood pressure, cancer, chronic fatigue, and substance abuse.

Education

In general, low levels of education are associated with higher rates of health problems and mortality (Health Canada 1999a). According to the 1996–97 National Population Health Survey, 30 percent of respondents who were university graduates rated their health as "excellent" compared with 19 percent of respondents with less than a high school education (Health Canada 1999a: 42). In addition, less educated women and men have higher rates of suicide. Low birth weight and high infant mortality are also more common among the children of less educated mothers than among children of more educated mothers. Babies of low birth weight (weighing 2500 g or less) are more likely to die in infancy, and those who do survive are more likely to suffer illness, stunted growth, and other health problems into adult life. Low birth weight has been increasing over the last three decades, from a low below 6 percent in 1979 to a national high of 6.2 percent by 2010; some of the increase is attributable to the increase in older mothers, for whom those aged 35–49 had infants with a 7.6 percent occurrence of low birth weight, and some is attributable to the marked regional disparities for mothers in the far north, where the instance of low birth weight is also 7.6 percent (Statistics Canada 2012).

One reason why lower education levels are associated with higher rates of health problems and mortality is that individuals with low levels of education are more likely to engage in health-risk behaviours such as smoking and heavy drinking. The well educated, in contrast, are less likely to smoke and drink heavily, and are more likely to exercise. Women with less education are less likely to seek prenatal care and are more likely to smoke during pregnancy. Research findings suggest that the strong association between education and income best explains differences in health outcomes and mortality rates for high and low SES groups (Lantz et al. 1998).

Gender

Gender issues affect the health of both women and men. Gender discrimination and violence against women produce adverse health effects in girls and women worldwide. Violence against women is a major public health concern: at least one in three women has been beaten, coerced into sex, or abused in some way—most often by someone she knows (United Nations Population Fund 2000). "Although neither health care workers nor the general public typically thinks of battering as a health problem, woman battering is a major cause of injury, disability and death among . . . women worldwide" (Weitz 2001: 56). In Africa, where the leading cause of death is HIV/AIDS, HIV-positive women outnumber men by 2 million; in part, that is because African women do not have the social power to refuse sexual intercourse or to demand that their male partners use condoms (United Nations Population Fund 2000). As noted earlier, women in developing countries suffer high rates of mortality and morbidity due to the high rates of complications associated with pregnancy and childbirth. The low status of women in many less developed countries results in their being nutritionally deprived and in having less access to medical care than do men. For example, in some countries in Asia and Africa, boys receive more medicine and medical treatment than girls. In Latin America and India, girls are often immunized later than boys or not at all (United Nations Population Fund 2000).

Before the twentieth century, the life expectancy of Canadian women was shorter than that of men. The cause was the high rate of mortality that resulted from complications of pregnancy and childbirth. Currently, however, Canadian women have a higher life expectancy than Canadian men (Statistics Canada 2002).

Although women tend to live longer than men do, they have higher rates of illness and disability than do men (Health Canada 1999a; Verbrugge 1999). Prevalence rates for nonfatal chronic conditions, such as arthritis, thyroid disease, and migraine headache, are typically higher for women. However, men tend to have higher rates of fatal chronic conditions, high blood pressure, heart disease, and diabetes among them. Women also tend to experience a higher incidence of acute conditions, such as colds and influenza, infections, and digestive conditions. "In sum, women live longer than men but experience more illness, whereas men experience relatively little illness but die quickly when illness strikes" (Weitz 2001: 55). As far as mental health goes, men are more likely to abuse drugs and have personality disorders, whereas women are more likely to suffer from mood disorders, such as depression and anxiety (Cockerham 1998).

Men are more prone to chronic and life-threatening diseases, such as coronary disease, because they are more likely than women to smoke, use alcohol and illegal drugs, and work under hazardous conditions. Our culture socializes men to be aggressive and competitive and to engage in risky behaviours (such as playing dangerous sports, driving fast, and being violent), which contributes to their higher risk of death from injuries and accidents. Although women are more likely to attempt suicide, men are more likely to succeed at it because they use deadlier methods. In Canada in 1999, there were 3.8 suicides among men for every suicide among women (Statistics Canada 2002). HIV infections and AIDS deaths in men outnumber those in women on every continent except sub-Saharan Africa (Joint United Nations Programme on HIV/AIDS 2000a). In part, the reason is that the socialization men receive permits and even encourages them to engage in higher-risk sexual behaviour. Men are also less likely than women to seek medical care. Boys who are brought up to believe that "real men don't get sick" often see themselves as invulnerable to illness or risk. The underuse of health services by men reflects this (Joint United Nations Programme on HIV/AIDS 2000a).

Racial and Ethnic Minority Status

In Canada, the risks to health posed by inadequate income, welfare dependency, substandard living conditions, and stresses on mental health and well-being are manifestly apparent in the lives of Aboriginal peoples (Royal Commission on Aboriginal Peoples 1996). The life expectancy of Status Indians (those whose names appear on the Indian Register maintained by the Department of Indian and Northern Affairs pursuant to the *Indian Act*) is seven to eight years shorter than for non-Aboriginal Canadians, and the infant mortality rate double that of the non-Aboriginal population. The most recent data available from Health Canada show that Aboriginal groups as a whole face heart

Chapter 2 Illness and Health Care

disease rates 1.5 times higher than the rest of Canada's population, diabetes rates that are 3 to 5 times higher (depending on region), and tuberculosis infection rates that are 8 to 10 times higher than for the rest of Canada; 15 percent of all new HIV infections occur within the Indigenous population (PHAC 2012). Vancouver Coastal Health (VCH) in the province of B.C. maintains more current data than the federally managed Health Canada publications offer, and tracks information for Aboriginal peoples not only in British Columbia but in all of Canada. VCH notes the following ongoing health challenges across Canada for Aboriginal people, who, as a population:[*]

- live on average seven fewer years
- have an infant mortality rate between two to four times higher
- have a rate of diabetes that is triple
- have double the AIDS/HIV deaths

In addition, for Aboriginal people

- alcohol-related deaths range between four and nine times higher, and drug-induced deaths are two to seven times higher
- hospitalization rate and preventable admissions are higher
- the hospitalization rate is 39 percent higher among Aboriginal men compared to non-Aboriginal men, and even higher among Aboriginal women—77 percent higher
- psychiatric hospitalization rates are 50–100 percent higher
- hospitalization rate for diabetes is 12 percent higher among Aboriginal men and 150 percent higher for Aboriginal women (Vancouver Coastal Health 2013)

Reasons for the development of diseases like diabetes and cardiovascular impairment arise from the confluence of factors that shape life for Canada's Indigenous populations. Life on reserves often means that the costs of food are significantly higher and of poorer quality—often processed foods with reduced nutritional value—than in other regions. Compare the cost of common staple foods in Figure 2.3 with the cost of the same items in your local grocery store or farmer's market.

Systemic social marginalization, and long-term effects from the traumatic abuses endemic to the residential schooling system, lead more Indigenous persons to suffer from alcohol and drug abuse as "coping measures" that can significantly impair long-term health even while dulling the pain of the trauma endured. Poverty pushes more Aboriginal women into street prostitution, where they are at greater risk for HIV infection, and crowded living conditions for Indigenous people both on and off reserve provide tuberculosis bacteria with easier means of transmission from one person to another.

In the late 1990s, in partnership with Harvard University, the First Nations Information Governance Centre (FNIGC) began tracking the health of Canada's Indigenous populations by instituting the First Nations Regional Health Survey (RHS). Phase 2 of the research began in 2008–2010, surveying 216 First Nations communities who responded with over 21 000 completed surveys of 11 043 adults aged 18 and over, 4837 youth from ages 12 to 17, and 5877 children ages 11 and under (FNIGC 2013). Because the FNIGC data collected began with premises of trust and respect for First Nations people the findings in the reports are more subtle and deliver richer information, in addition to providing the most up-to-date data available as the federal government in Canada has begun to favour releasing policy statements over new data, meaning that federally available information now is frequently a decade or more out of date.

The FNIGC Report on Phase 2 is consistent with the Vancouver Coastal Health findings on vulnerabilities to and experiences of impaired health for First Nations groups.

* Provincial Health Services Authority, 2010. *PHSA Strategic Plan 2010-2013*; http://www.phsa.ca/NR/rdonlyres/E7E981A2-26A8-4EA8-9823-491BAF714543/0/PHSAStrategicPlanFINAL2010.pdf, pp. 2-3. Reprinted with permission.

Figure 2.3 **RHS Community Survey—Cost of Food**

SOURCE: Adapted from The First Nations Regional Health Survey (RHS) Phase 2—2008/10 Selected Results, http://www.fnigc.ca/sites/default/files/RHS%20Phase%202%20 Results%20-%20HC%20presentation%20Sept %2027%202012%20FINAL%20FOR %20PUBLICATION.pdf (p. 26).

However, the FNIGC also reveals to some that the tendency to deliver only the bad news about Aboriginal health neglects to show that the individual behaviours of Indigenous people may be better than for the population as a whole. For example, while binge drinking is a larger problem for Aboriginal groups than it is for Canadians in general, with 35.3 percent of adults abstaining from all alcohol use while only 23 percent of the general adult Canadian population abstains (p. 27). The numbers for abstaining are even farther apart for youth, with 61 percent of Aboriginal youth abstaining compared to 47 percent of the general youth population—who also report binge drinking at least once a month, at 39 percent of the general population (p. 28). The FNIGC survey takes a multi-pronged approach to understanding the health status of Aboriginal people in Canada, and measures the interaction of SES along with personal relationships, health status at the time of the survey, and personal health behaviours to understand the correlations that influence the overall Aboriginal health (p. 16). Given the complexity of those interacting variables, it remains a powerful truth that even though 17.7 percent of men and 27.3 percent of the adult population held postsecondary educational attainments, by 2007, 57 percent of the population lived on household incomes of less than $30 000 per year (FNIGC 2013). Moreover, on many measures for material well-being, including the need for household repairs and availability of basic amenities in the household, the situation deteriorated markedly over the decade from 2002 to 2011 (ibid). In other words, while we have all been impacted by the economic downturn of 2008, Aboriginal groups in Canada have been among the hardest hit, and the impact on their health is predictably dire.

Racial and ethnic prejudice and discrimination may induce psychological distress that adversely affects both physical and mental health status and increases the likelihood of violence and substance abuse. Moreover, **environmental racism**, or the tendency for hazardous waste sites and polluting industries to be located near areas inhabited by those who are poor and socially marginalized, may also contribute to lower levels of health. For example, in the 1980s, the mercury poisoning of the English-Wabigoon river

environmental racism
The tendency for hazardous waste sites and polluting industries to be located in areas where the surrounding residential population is an ethnic or racial minority.

system by local pulp and paper industries led to the virtual destruction of the Grassy Narrows Indians' lifestyle and means of livelihood (Shkilnyk 1985). More recently,

> patterns of atmospheric cycling have made the North a dumping ground for industrial chemicals that . . . [are] never used there. The chemicals bioaccumulate, delivering a higher level of toxic concentration to each level up the food chain. As a result, the breast milk of Inuit mothers is 10 times as contaminated as that of southern Canadian women. In both the North and the South, mother's milk is so laden with toxic substances such as PCBs, DDT (and its breakdown product DDE) and lindane, that if it were offered for sale, it would be too contaminated to be approved as human food. (Barlow and May 2000: 184)

More recently, Beverly Jacobs 2010 detailed two ongoing research projects on Aboriginal health and environmental racism in Canada. Jacobs' work draws attention to the Kashechewan territory on James Bay, where in 2005 800 community members were sickened when their water supply was contaminated with *E. coli* bacteria. Investigation into the incident showed that the water treatment plant operator had not been properly trained, and that the delivery of proper training was the responsibility of the federal government (p. 9). The situation appears even more egregious when one understands, as Jacobs points out, that the federal government, through Health Canada, had in 2003 identified problems in the water supply and reported that "the situation in Kashechewan was a 'Walkerton-in-waiting'" (ibid). Jacobs also describes the water safety problems in Fort Chipewyan in Alberta, downstream from the infamous oil sands:

> The situation in Fort Chipewyan is quite similar to the one in Kashechewan with respect to proper water quality. With the refusal of the federal and provincial government[s] to implement any empirical studies or to take any responsibility [for] the worst water quality in Canada, it can be argued that this is environmental racism. The refusal to take action is again affecting a racialized community with high rates of cancers and deaths in the community. (Jacobs 2010: 10).

If we hope for improvements to the health of the Aboriginal population in Canada, it is clear that we have to improve such basics as the maintenance of water supplies and protection of lands, and that we need to change the commonsense attitudes of Canadians who hold prejudicial, inaccurate, and harmful views of Canada's Indigenous people.

The pathogens that made Kashechewan residents ill, that threaten the residents of Fort Chipewyan, and that cause increased rates of tuberculosis for Aboriginals across the country are biological, but the reasons the population is vulnerable to infection are social, political, and economic. We can only improve negative health outcomes determined by social factors if we work to improve those social determinants of health so that our Indigenous groups will enjoy the same beneficial social determinants as the rest of Canada.

2.6 Problems in Canadian Health Care

In 2000, the World Health Organization released its report on the first ever analysis of the world's health systems (World Health Organization 2000). The report concluded that France provides the best overall health care among major countries, followed by Italy, Spain, Oman, Austria, and Japan. After presenting a brief overview of Canadian health care, we address some of the major health-care issues in Canada.

Canadian Health Care: An Overview

Canada, like Great Britain, Sweden, Germany, and Italy, has a national health insurance system sometimes referred to as socialized medicine. Despite differences in how countries organize socialized medicine, common features are that the government

(1) directly controls the financing and organization of health services, (2) directly pays providers, (3) guarantees equal access to health care, and (4) allows some private care for individuals who are willing to pay for their medical expenses (Cockerham 1998). However, Canada's system is not truly socialized medicine in that the government does not employ medical professionals. Rather, the majority of Canada's physicians and surgeons are generally paid on a fee-for-service basis and submit their claims directly to the provincial health insurance plan for payment. Nurses are paid by the hospital and community agencies that employ them.

In 1919 William Lyon Mackenzie King first raised the idea of national, publicly funded health insurance as part of the Liberal Party platform. However, it took almost half a century before the persistent efforts of then-Saskatchewan Premier Tommy Douglas, leader of the Co-operative Commonwealth Federation (the precursor to the New Democratic Party), compelled the Canadian government to implement a universal health-care system. In 1947, Douglas's government had pioneered Canada's first universal hospital plan after testing prepaid medical insurance in the Swift Current health district and introducing a public insurance plan for hospital services. Public health-care insurance also began in Saskatchewan with coverage provided for visits to physicians and the services of physicians outside hospitals.

The role of the federal government in relation to health care is in the setting and administration of national principles for the health-care system, assisting in the financing of provincial health services through fiscal transfers, and fulfilling certain functions for which it is constitutionally responsible. The federal government is responsible for health service delivery to specific groups, including veterans, Indigenous people living on reserves, members of the military, inmates of federal penitentiaries, and the Royal Canadian Mounted Police. However, the management and delivery of health services is the responsibility of each individual province or territory, which plans, finances, and evaluates the provision of hospital care, health services, public health, and some aspects of prescription care.

To receive federal funding in the form of transfer payments, provinces must adhere to five principles in which health care must (1) be publicly administered, (2) provide comprehensive coverage for all necessary medical services and dental surgeries, (3) ensure universality to provide equal health care to all insured residents, (4) allow portability for residents to move to another province and maintain coverage from their home province for a minimum period of time, and (5) grant equal access to health-care services and providers for all insured residents. Principle 3, universal coverage, means that provincial insurance sets the fees and covers the costs of all necessary medical services; Principle 5, equal access, refers to the ability of users to gain entry to the system. Put another way, making health care accessible means that health-care providers are not allowed to prevent certain persons or groups from receiving treatment. In Canada, there is some concern that wait times for procedures prevent those in need from accessing the care they require. Prior to 2004, the only sources of information came from Statistics Canada, and from the Fraser Institute—a conservative think-tank that often favours privatization of government services, including health care. However, since 2004, the non-profit organization Canadian Institute for Health Information (CIHI) has been tracking wait-time data and their research integrity has been characterized as "the enemy of anecdote" (Yale professor Ted Marmor, quoted in CIHI 2012: x). CIHI reports that since the 2004 implementation of system-wide improvements to gather data on wait times, "by 2011, about 80% of Canadians were receiving priority procedures within benchmark timeframes" (2012: 4). Figure 2.4 gives more detailed information on patient wait times for non-elective, priority health procedures.

Concerns about how to provide universal comprehensive health care in an era of rising costs (largely due to expensive new technologies and a rapidly aging population that was living longer and, hence, using more health-care services for longer) prompted

Canada

82% Hip Replacement	
75% Knee Replacement	
79% Hip Fracture Repair	
82% Cataract*	
99% Bypass†	
97% Radiation Therapy	

	B.C.	Alta.	Sask.	Man.	Ont.	Que.	N.L.	P.E.I.	N.B.	N.S.
Hip Replacement	76%	80%	75%	59%	90%	82%	82%	71%	72%	62%
Knee Replacement	67%	70%	62%	52%	85%	78%	62%	55%	53%	44%
Hip Fracture Repair	76%	81%	84%	85%	78%	‡	87%	81%	83%	79%
Cataract	76%	59%	58%	71%	88%	88%	71%	67%	85%	65%
Bypass	99%	95%	100%	97%	100%	§	100%	**	99%	100%
Radiation Therapy	93%	98%	99%	100%	97%	98%	96%	96%	95%	83%

NOTES

*The pan-Canadian benchmark specifies cataract surgery within 16 weeks (112 days) for patients who are at high risk. There is not yet consensus on a definition of "high risk," so the benchmark is applied across all priority levels.

†The pan-Canadian benchmark specifies bypass surgery within 2 to 26 weeks (14 to 182 days), depending on how urgently care is needed. As there is a lack of comparability for urgency levels, provinces are reporting the percentage of patients treated within a 6-month time frame.

‡Quebec wait times for hip fracture repair are not included due to methodological differences in the data. For information on Quebec hip fracture wait times, see CIHI's report *Comparing Wait Times for Hip Fracture Repair in Quebec With Those in Other Jurisdictions.*

§Quebec reports the percentage of bypass patients receiving care within the benchmark for their assigned urgency level.

**P.E.I. does not offer cardiac services; patients receive care out of province.

Figure 2.4 ***Proportion of Patients Receiving Care within Benchmarks, Canada, by Province and Priority Area, April 1 to September 30, 2011***

SOURCE: CIHI, 2012. "Health Care in Canada 2012: A focus on wait times." https://secure.cihi.ca/free_products/HCIC2012-FullReport-ENweb.pdf (page 5). Ottawa: Canadian Institute for Health Information (CIHI). Reprinted with permission.

the federal government in 2001 to authorize a Royal Commission to investigate the status of health care in Canada. The resulting 2003 Romanow Report found that among other changes, the bulk of medical costs for Canadians had shifted from insured clinical care and hospital stays to home-care and prescription drugs, both of which were largely covered only under employee insurance benefits, not under universal health insurance plans (Wynne and Armstrong 2003). In other words, those who worked a number of part-time jobs, who were unemployed or had retired without benefits packages, or who were among the working poor, lacked the work-based insurance that paid for most contemporary health care. Moreover, federal funding had been dropping over the previous decade, and so clinic and hospital services had been cut back as well (Wynne and Armstrong 2003). The Romanow Report, released in 2002, made 47 sweeping recommendations to preserve and enhance the health-care system that Canadians had so come to value. Among the recommendations, the report called for "... development of a national human health resource plan, renewal and reform of primary care, expansion of coverage to home care, and development of a national pharmaceutical strategy to include public coverage for catastrophic out-of-hospital drug costs" (Kenny and Chafe 2007: 25). And yet, in spite of the general support of Canadians for the principles of our national health-care policy, and for the Romanow directives, Kenny and Chafe note that "progress on the report has stalled" (ibid). Moreover, Kenny and Chafe report that by the late 2000s, the Canadian Medical Association had begun to lobby for the system to allow doctors to work in both private services and in the public system (p. 26).

Much of doctors' ability to argue for their ability to work providing private services while still benefitting from the stability of a public system is supported by the 2005 *Chaouilli v. Quebec* court ruling that the Quebec Charter of Rights and Freedoms gave patients the right to choose to pay for private coverage in order to jump queues. However, contrary to the court's presupposition that allowing some people to pay for enhanced service would have no impact on public health-care service, there is significant evidence from other countries that when doctors work in two systems, wait lists actually get longer in the public system (Kenny and Chafe 2007: 25). In other words, the "choice and freedom" argument may appeal to all classes of people because they *imagine* themselves benefitting from more choices, but in reality, only those who can pay will benefit, and they will do so on the backs of those who will not be able to access the health care they pay for via income taxes. Moreover, without the stable public system to rely on for their income, there are not enough wealthy patrons to provide the high incomes doctors expect. Kenny and Chafe argue that popular media outlets have exploited the belief in "choice," ignoring the absence of evidence that privatization of health-care services "will help efficiency, equity, cost containment or access" (2007: 25).

Since 2001, the Canadian Medical Association (CMA) has contracted Ipsos Reid to survey a representative sample of 1200 Canadians aged 18 and over for the "National Report Card" on health and health care in Canada. Counter to media and market interests in fostering worries that our health-care system is not working, the 2012 National Report Card commissioned by the CMA showed that "74% [of Canadians] grade the overall quality of the health care services available to them in the A (39%) or B (35%) range" (Canadian Medical Association 2012: 7). Where Canadians are less satisfied is in their perception of federal and provincial government management of health care, with only 12 percent rating the federal government's handling of health care at the A level and 26 percent at the B level—and, while the poll indicates improved perceptions of care over the last 12 years, 48 percent still indicate that they believe health care in Canada is going to get worse in the future (Canadian Medical Association 2012: 6).

In addition to asking questions regarding the provision of health-care services, satisfaction with health care received, and perception of government management of health care, the Ipsos Reid survey inquires into respondents' perceptions of their own health and to barriers to their full enjoyment of good health. A national average of 34 percent of Canadians responded in 2012 that the economic downturn since 2008 had increased their stress levels significantly; for those with incomes under $30 000 per year that rate rose to 46 percent, while those with incomes of more than $60 000 per year fell below the national average to 30 percent (Canadian Medical Association 2012: 28). Furthermore, because regular dental care is not covered under the national health-care plan, the survey found that one-fifth of Canadians deferred or delayed dental care because of financial concerns, and this rate rose to almost a third of those earning below $30 000 per year (ibid). Finally, while the national data show that only 9 percent of all Canadians are getting by without prescribed medicines, that number soars to 24 percent of those in the under $30 000 annual earnings group, and plummets to just 3 percent of those making more than $60 000 per year.

What we can learn from these patterns in responses includes awareness that perceptions about health care received and health-care management do not necessarily align. In part, this lack of coherence in perception is explained by Kenny and Chafe's observations that the CMA and popular news media combined their efforts to promote the ideas of "choice" and "freedom" as linked to private delivery of health-care services. Canadians have been willing to embrace that message even if most could never hope to exercise such freedom. In addition, we can see that when people experience economic uncertainty in their personal lives, it has an income-based influence on the health habits of entire groups. Because prescription drugs are not currently covered under Canada's standard health-care plan, it is the working poor, who lack employer benefits, who sacrifice dental care and who give up their prescribed medications far more often than it is those in high-income groups.

The enjoyment of good health comes not only from being able to access health care when one needs it. Health is a product of the other things we can do to promote our own well-being. Avoiding stress, getting exercise, being involved in group or team pursuits, eating fresh, unprocessed foods and having the time to prepare and enjoy them with friends and family, and getting enough sleep are all behaviours that influence our health for the better. The Ipsos Reid 2012 report found, not surprisingly, that those in lower income groups more frequently gave up or could not afford these health promoting behaviours in the first place. The Ipsos Reid survey of 1200 Canadians assessed the difference in health promoting behaviours that Canadians are able to pursue as a national average, in income groups over $60 000 per year, and for those with incomes under $30 000 per year. The poll found that while, in general, just over one-third of Canadians felt stressed by financial problems, the frequency of poor health and stress rose to nearly half (46 percent) of those in the under $30 000 per year annual income group. Meanwhile, the report found that for those making over $60 000 per year the number experiencing stressed mental health fell to 30 percent.

Specific health-care and health-promotion activities that those in the lower income group had to give up with alarming frequency included, but are not limited to, dental visits, regular meals, and needed prescription medications (Canadian Medical Association 2012: 29) Obviously, then, health is not simply a product of a health-care system, but is a commodity that is not equally accessible to all Canadians.

Needs Assessment and Access to Health Care for Canadians

In 2010, Allin and colleagues published the results of their study on the unmet health-care needs of Canadians, explaining that they used subjective assessments of unmet needs from self-reports, rather than more traditional surveys regarding rates of health-care access and use, because

> Physicians have imperfect information about patients' health care needs so they rely on patients' communication of symptoms and history to make treatment decisions. Therefore, minority and lower socioeconomic groups may receive less effective services because of the poorer quality of communication among patients with different socioeconomic and ethnic backgrounds from their physicians. (Allin et al. 2010: 465–66)

Allin and colleagues analyzed the self-reports of 97 828 respondents to the 2003 Canada Health Survey (CCHS) regarding their answers to the question, "During the past 12 months, was there ever a time you felt you needed healthcare but you didn't receive it?", and the corresponding reasons that respondents gave for not having received care. The reasons fell into categories of personal choice, barriers to access, and wait times (pp. 468–69). Allin and colleagues analyzed the self-reported unmet needs (SUN) in relation to other variables that included highest education level attained, reported estimates of gross annual income from all sources, and self-reported quality of health. What the researchers found was that the category of reported unmet need (choice, barrier, or wait time) influenced the actual level of use of services of each SUN report:

> [T]hose who report an unmet need due to waiting are not only using more services than would be expected based on their health and socioeconomic characteristics, the difference between actual use and needs-predicted use is larger for an individual with unmet need due to waiting times than it is for an individual without an unmet need. . . . For other types of unmet needs, there is less of a clear pattern with health care utilization. Those who report unmet need due to barriers are about 10% less likely to contact a GP, but among those who had at least one [GP] visit they make 0.8 visits more than those with otherwise identical characteristics. (Allin 2010: 470)

In other words, when people see themselves as underserved they actually use *more* health care than the general, matched population. The findings of the study are not meant to be the final word, but they suggest that under Canada's national health-care policy, access to health-care services is more equitable than previous studies had thought. That is, economic barriers to health-care services did not turn out to be significant in this study, and self-perceived poor access corresponded highly with more actual use of health-care services. In common terms, it seems that it is "the squeaky wheel that gets the oil," regardless of actual health status for the respondents in the Canada Health Survey. The implication is that our health-care system is not inequitable in terms of access and care provision across SES groups in Canada.

These findings do not mean that SES is irrelevant to the health enjoyed by Canadians. Socio-economic conditions remain the greatest predictors for the enjoyment of better health and longer life expectancy, generally, for privileged SES populations, and for the more broad experience of poor health and lower life expectancy for socio-economically marginalized groups. Racialized groups in particular experience diminished health, and exclusion from our supposedly universal health-care system. As we saw in Section 2.6, in Canada it is our Indigenous populations who are placed at greatest risk for lowered general health and life expectancy, and as we noted, prejudices that medical care providers hold about certain groups can negatively impact the care they deliver to those groups.

Access to Dental Care

According to the 1996–97 National Population Health Survey, slightly more than half of all Canadians (55 percent) have dental insurance. Having dental insurance is much more common among children, youths, and working-age adults than among Canadian seniors. Among those 75 years of age and older in Canada, only 25 percent of men and 17 percent of women report having dental insurance. Income differences in relation to dental care are particularly notable: those in the highest income group are about three times as likely to have dental insurance as those in the lowest category. There are also variations in insurance coverage between provinces. Slightly more than 60 percent of residents in Ontario and Alberta have dental insurance versus lows of 40 and 43 percent in Quebec and Newfoundland, respectively. In Canada, dentists work independently of the health-care system except where in-hospital dental surgery is required.

The High Cost of Medications

Except for medication received while in institutional care, the *Canada Health Act* does not cover prescription drugs, nonprescription drugs, and over-the-counter products (e.g., cough and cold remedies, oral hygiene products, and home diagnostic kits). Instead, payers include governments through pharmacare programs, private insurance (including insurance companies, employees and employers, and unions), and patients paying directly.

At present, only four Canadian provinces provide universal drug plans. British Columbia is the only province that uses a reference-based pricing scheme. Under the scheme, the province pays for only the lowest-cost drug in each of three designated "therapeutic categories" to help reduce costs. In provinces without universal plans, Armstrong and colleagues (1998) note that "not only are many individuals left out, especially among the 'working poor,' but it is very difficult for any particular plan to control costs. At the same time, each of them faces unnecessarily high administrative costs." In consequence, the National Forum on Health has called our current drug plan situation "incompatible with Canada's vision for the health care system." It has recommended the establishment of a single-payer, publicly funded system for medicinal drugs.

Organ Replacement

Organ replacement is not a simple solution to disease; rather, it is a complex intersection of problems with resource allocation, health-care costs, and quality of life concerns. In 1996, surgeons in Canada performed 1578 transplants of kidneys, hearts, lungs, and other organs. Partly because of preventable diseases caused by lifestyle habits, and partly because primary earners have priority when organs are being allocated for transplant, men receive most transplants in general (65 percent), and most heart transplants (84 percent) in particular (Health Canada 1999b; Statistics Canada 1998a).

There is a popular perception that organ transplant "saves or dramatically improves the lives of some 1500 Canadians per year" (Baer 1997: 179). Popular appeals to sign our donor cards reinforce this, and the Canadian Medical Association promotes transplantation as a cost-saving means of treating Canadians (Baer 1997). Where transplantation can reduce suffering, few of us would refuse the right of a patient to receive one. However, studies to support the conclusion that organ transplant improves recipients' quality of life are methodologically haphazard; they also draw attention away from poor survival rates (Joralemon and Fujinaga 1996).

2.7 Strategies for Action: Improving Health and Health Care

Because poverty underlies many of the world's health problems, improving the world's health requires strategies that reduce poverty (see Chapter 10). Other chapters in this text discuss strategies to alleviate problems associated with tobacco and illegal drugs (Chapter 3), hazards in the workplace (Chapter 11), and environmental health problems (Chapter 14). Here, we discuss strategies for improving health, including improvements for maternal and infant health, HIV/AIDS prevention and alleviation, the use of computer technology in health care, and Canada's health-care reform.

Improving Maternal and Infant Health

Several factors contribute to high maternal mortality rates in less developed countries. Poor quality and inaccessible health care, malnutrition, and poor sanitation contribute to adverse health effects of pregnancy and childbirth. In developing countries, only 53 percent of all births are attended to by professionals and nearly 30 percent of women who give birth in developing countries receive no care after the birth (United Nations Population Fund 2000). Also, women in less developed countries experience higher rates of pregnancy and child-bearing and begin child-bearing at earlier ages. Thus, they face the risk of maternal death more often and before their bodies are fully developed (see also Chapter 14). Women in many countries lack access to family planning services, the support of their male partners to use contraceptive methods such as condoms, or both. Consequently, many women resort to abortion to limit their childbearing, even in countries where abortion is illegal. For more on maternal mortality rates, see Figure 2.5.

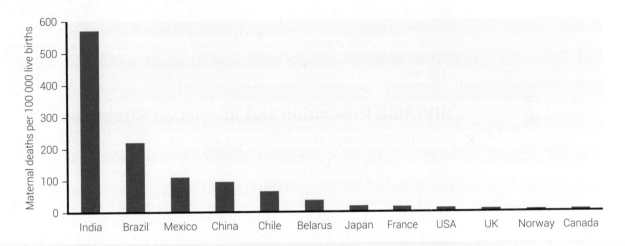

Figure 2.5 **Maternal Mortality Rates in Selected Countries, 1999 Estimates**

Illegal abortions in less developed countries have an estimated mortality risk of 100 to 1000 per 100 000 procedures (Miller and Rosenfield 1996). In contrast, the Canadian mortality risk for therapeutic abortions is very low (Health Canada 1999b). Each year, women worldwide undergo an estimated 50 million abortions, 20 million of which are unsafe, resulting in the deaths of 78 000 women (United Nations Population Fund 2000).

In 1987, the Safe Motherhood Initiative was launched. This global initiative is a partnership of governments, NGOs, agencies, donors, and women's health advocates working to protect women's health and lives, especially during pregnancy and childbirth. Improving women's health also improves the health of infants: 30 to 40 percent of infant deaths are the result of poor care during labour and delivery (Safe Motherhood Initiative 1998). The cost of ensuring that women in low-income countries get prenatal, postnatal, and perinatal health care, family planning services, and newborn care costs about $3 (U.S.) per person per year (Family Care International 1999).

The Safe Motherhood Initiative advocates improving maternal and infant health by first identifying the powerlessness that women face as an injustice countries must remedy. In many countries, men make the decisions about whether or when their wives

Chapter 2 Illness and Health Care **63**

(or partners) will have sexual relations, use contraception, or bear children. Improving and maintaining the status and power of women involves ensuring that they have the right to make decisions about their health and reproductive lives. Changes must be made in political, health, and legal systems.

The Save the Children Foundation's report "State of the World's Mothers 2004: Children Having Children" found that access to family planning and female education are the two most important determinants of the well-being of mothers and their children. Women must have access to family planning services, affordable methods of contraception, and safe abortion services. The Safe Motherhood Initiative noted that early pregnancy and birth cause the deaths of 70 000 young mothers and 1 million infants each year (Save the Children 2004: 6), and that 2 million unsafe abortions are performed every year on females aged 15 to 19 (2004: 15). The Initiative recommends reforming laws and policies to support women's reproductive health and improve access to family planning services. Doing so would mean removing legal barriers to abortion—a highly controversial issue in many countries. Promoting women's education increases the status and power of women to control their reproductive lives, exposes women to information about health issues, and also delays marriage and child-bearing.

HIV/AIDS Prevention and Alleviation Strategies

One suggested strategy to curb the spread of HIV involves encouraging individuals to get tested for HIV so they can modify their behaviour to avoid transmitting the virus to others, and so they can receive early medical intervention that can slow or prevent the onset of AIDS. Millions of HIV-infected people throughout the world are not aware that they are infected. Many are hesitant to find out if they have HIV because of the stigma associated with HIV/AIDS. HIV testing facilities are also inadequate in many developing countries. However, testing is not enough. Research suggests that individuals who have been diagnosed with HIV often continue to engage in higher-risk behaviours. One study compared behaviours in HIV-infected youth (younger than 25 years) and HIV-infected adults (25 years or older). It found that 66 percent of young women and 46 percent of adult women continued higher-risk behaviours after HIV infection; also, 28 percent of young men with HIV infection and 16 percent of infected adult men engaged in higher-risk behaviour (Diamond and Buskin 2000).

Alleviating HIV/AIDS also requires educating populations about how to protect against HIV and providing access to condoms. However, there continues to be widespread concern that sex education and access to condoms will encourage young people to become sexually active prematurely. Consequently, many sex education programs have focused solely upon abstinence. Several studies have concluded, however, that sex education programs that combine messages about abstinence and safer sex practices (e.g., condom use) may delay the initiation of sexual behaviour as well as increase preventive behaviours among young people who are already sexually active (Joint United Nations Programme on HIV/AIDS 2000c).

Alleviating HIV/AIDS requires making medical interventions accessible and affordable, especially to the poor populations in developing countries. In an effort to combat AIDS in Africa, five of the world's leading pharmaceutical companies have agreed to decrease the price of drugs used to treat HIV. But even at discounted prices, the drugs will be beyond what many Africans can afford.

There is currently no cure for HIV or AIDS. Although various prevention and alleviation strategies may help reduce the spread of HIV and AIDS deaths, the HIV pandemic "will ultimately be controlled only by immunization against HIV using a protective, cheap, simple, and widely available vaccine" (Ward 1999: 199). As of this writing, no such effective vaccine exists, although at least 29 AIDS vaccines have been clinically tested around the world without success (Gottlieb 2000).

Health Promotion

For at least 25 years, federal policy has recognized the importance of individual behaviour as a determinant of health status. In recent years, the focus has shifted from individual behaviour to the socio-economic determinants of behaviour; however, there is no doubt that health education remains an important health promotion strategy at the levels of the individual and of the broader population.

Canadian health education stresses that good nutrition, exercise, and abstention from smoking are important to good health, and it seems that many Canadians are heeding the message. For example, the 1998–99 National Population Health Survey reported that in the 12 months prior to the survey, 47 percent of the respondents had changed a facet of their behaviour to improve their health, while 54 percent recognized that some change was needed. Among the latter group, more than two-thirds (69 percent) indicated that they intended to change their behaviour in the next year. Among those who recognized a need for change, the need most commonly identified was for more exercise followed by reductions in smoking, improved nutrition, and weight loss. An absence of time and personal willpower were identified as the main barriers to making the desired lifestyle changes.

Within this survey, women were more likely than men to report having made changes in their personal behaviours in the year before the survey; women were also more likely to voice their intention to make such changes in the forthcoming year. However, differences based on gender were less notable than differences based on age. With increasing age, "[t]here was a general decline in behaviour change—whether actual, needed, or intended" (Health Canada 1999b). Individuals in Ontario were more likely to report behaviour changes in the previous year and the least likely to report any intended changes in future years. Residents of Quebec (79 percent), British Columbia (73 percent), and Alberta (61 percent) were the most likely to report intentions to change in the next year.

Programs for People with Disabilities

It would be a grave mistake to forget the necessity of ensuring the physical and social health of those who have physical or mental disabilities. People with disabilities in Canada continue to face disadvantage in areas such as work, housing, support services, transportation, and income support. Moreover, depending on the specific nature of their disability, they may or may not have access to adequate health-care and education services.

Graham (1999) has noted that "support programs and services available to persons with disabilities, which are so essential to viability within the wider community, vary enormously from one part of the country to another." He points out that in Lloydminster, which straddles the Saskatchewan-Alberta border, a person with a visual disability can obtain certain high-tech equipment on the Alberta side, but not on the Saskatchewan side: "in other words, if you live in Saskatchewan you can get a white cane—but sorry, nothing high tech." Consider as well that only two decades ago, newborns with Down syndrome often died in Canada because of physicians' recommendations that parents not correct a simple stomach blockage (Mitchell 1995: A10).

It has been suggested that a Canadian disability act is necessary to ensure that the rights and needs of people with disabilities in Canada are protected (Kerzner and Baker 1999). In the absence of such an act, organizations such as the Council of Canadians with Disabilities, the Canadian Association for Independent Living

Centres, DAWN (the DisAbled Women's Network), and the Coalition of Provincial Organizations of the Handicapped, and institutes such as the Roeher Institute, the Canadian Council on Rehabilitation and Work, the Canadian Centre on Disability Studies, and the National Aboriginal Clearing/Connecting House on Disability Issues, attempt to ensure that both the health and social needs of people with disabilities are not ignored in Canada.

Telemedicine: Computer Technology in Health Care

Computer technology offers numerous ways to reduce costs associated with health-care delivery and to improve patient care. **Telemedicine** involves using information and communication technologies to deliver a wide range of health-care services, including diagnosis, treatment, prevention, health support and information, and education of health-care workers. Telemedicine can involve the transmission of three main types of information: data, audio, and images. A patient's medical records or vital signs (such as heart rate and blood pressure) can be transmitted from one location to another. Many hospitals and clinics store their medical records electronically, allowing doctors to access information about their patients quickly and to update patient data from a distance. Specialized medical databases, such as MEDLINE, can be accessed via the Internet and offer a valuable resource for health-care practitioners and researchers. The public may also use the Internet to gain health information and support. The transmission of radiological images (such as X-ray and ultrasound) from one location to another for the purpose of interpretation or consultation has become one of the most commonly used telemedicine services. Images of tissue samples may also be transmitted to another location, where a pathologist can look at the image on a monitor and offer an interpretation.

Benefits of Telemedicine

Telemedicine has the potential to improve public health by making health care available in rural and remote areas and by providing health information to health-care workers and to the general population. In addition, "telemedicine allows the scarce resources of specialists and expensive equipment to be shared by a much greater number of patients. Doctors are no longer restricted by geographical boundaries; international specialists are able to spread their skills across continents, without leaving their own hospitals" (LaPorte 1997: 38).

Telemedicine can be used in training and educating health-care professionals and providing health-care workers with up-to-date health information. Telemedicine can also reduce health-care costs by reducing the cost of travel to major health centres or to specialists, and by reducing the length of hospitalization, since patients can be monitored at a distance.

Another benefit of telemedicine is the provision of health information and support services on the Internet. This resource helps empower individuals in managing their health concerns. According to a 2001 survey, over half of Canadians with Internet access visited a health site; 3 in 10 said they had done so at least once in the past week and another 45 percent at least once during the past month. Of those who visited a health site, half judged themselves to be more knowledgeable as a result of their efforts (Bricker and Greenspon 2001: 225). Through e-mail, bulletin boards, and chat rooms, individuals with specific health problems can network with other similarly affected individuals. This social support assists in patient recovery, reduces the number of visits to physicians and clinics, and "provides...individuals [with disabilities] with an opportunity to achieve levels of social integration that were simply not possible before" (LaPorte 1997: 33).

---

telemedicine
Using information and communication technologies to deliver a wide range of health-care services, including diagnosis, treatment, prevention, health support and information, and education of health-care workers.

In the twentieth century, advances in public health were largely due to improvements in sanitation and immunization. Advocates of telemedicine have forecast that in the twenty-first century, improvements in public health will result from the increased uses of information technology (LaPorte 1997). Telemedicine holds the promise of improving the health of individuals, families, communities, and nations. But whether or not telemedicine achieves its promise depends, in part, on whether resources are allocated to provide the technology and the training to use it.

Understanding Illness and Health Care

Human health has probably improved more over the past half century than over the previous three millennia (Feachem 2000). Yet the gap in health between rich and poor remains very wide and the very poor suffer appallingly. Health problems are affected not only by economic resources, but also by other social factors, such as aging of the population, gender, education, and race/ethnicity.

Our cultural values and beliefs emphasize the ability of individuals to control their lives through the choices they make. Thus, Westerners view health and illness as results from individual behaviour and lifestyle choices rather than as the result of social, economic, and political forces. Westerners generally agree that an individual's health is affected by the choices that person makes—choices such as whether or not to smoke, exercise, engage in sexual activity, use condoms, and wear a seatbelt. However, if the goal is to improve the health not only of individuals but also of entire populations, then the influence of social, economic, and political forces on the choices that individuals make must be taken into account. Further, by focusing on individual behaviours that affect health and illness, we often overlook both social causes and social solutions of health problems. For example, at an individual level, the public has been advised to rinse and cook meat, poultry, and eggs thoroughly and to carefully wash hands, knives, cutting boards, and so on. The goal is to avoid illness caused by *E. coli* and salmonella bacteria. Whether or not one becomes ill from contaminated meat, eggs, or poultry, though, is affected by more than individual behaviours in the kitchen. Governmental actions can also offer solutions by providing for more food inspectors and stricter regulations on food industries.

Although certain changes in medical practices and policies may help to improve world health, "the health sector should be seen as an important, but not the sole, force in the movement toward global health" (Lerer et al. 1998: 18). Improving the health of a society requires addressing diverse issues, including poverty and economic inequality, gender inequality, population growth, environmental issues, education, housing, energy, water and sanitation, agriculture, and workplace safety. Health promotion is important in the hospital, clinic, or doctor's office—but also in the various settings where people live, work, play, and learn (Antezana et al. 1998).

Perhaps the most critical public health agenda today is reducing the gap between the health of advantaged and disadvantaged populations. Feachem (2000) suggests that "addressing this problem, both between and within countries, constitutes one of the greatest challenges of the new century. Failure to do so properly will have dire consequences for the global economy, for social order and justice, and for civilization as a whole" (p. 1).

Student Reflection: What Do You Know Now?

Many "commonsense" views of health assume that private individuals can take almost complete control over their health—to promote it, or to improve it, and to avoid disease. How do you think differently about the privileges associated with the enjoyment of good health now that you have read the chapter? What kinds of changes would you recommend for health-care providers to make sure that *all* Canadian residents can access health care when they need it? What kinds of social barriers do you face in pursuing health?

What do you think about the reduction since 2003 in federally gathered and analyzed data on the health of Canadians?

Now that you know about some of the social determinants of health, how might you be able to help your own communities to have better health, and/or better access to health care?

What Do You Do Next?

Located at www.nelson.com/socialproblems5e

- Consolidate your knowledge with interactive and printable **Flashcards**
- Gauge your understanding with **Practice Quizzes** and **Matching Activities**
- Develop your critical thinking skills with **Self and Society** and **The Human Side** questions
- Analyze **Social Research** and **Social Problems in Global Perspective**
- Explore the implications of **Technology on Social Problems**

Student Reflection:
What Do You Already Know?

If you are under 25, you've probably heard the message very strongly your whole life that drinking and driving do not mix. Perhaps you've grown up in a very strict or a very permissive environment, against which you can see norms forming around teen drinking or smoking. Whatever your age, ask someone who was raised in the 1940s, 50s, or 60s how alcohol was viewed at the time, and what kinds of drugs were considered dangerous. Has Canada always had the reputation we currently have for a particularly relaxed approach to marijuana use? Is this a good thing or a bad thing? What social problems have arisen in your own street, town, or province as a result of alcohol and other drugs? What stereotypes do you see around you, at school or in your other communities? How stuck do people get in roles like the "social drinker," the "weekend binge drinker," the "pothead," or the "meth-head"? What do we do about it in terms of school policies, community services, or laws?

Learning Outcomes

Through careful reading of this chapter, you should be able to:

- define the bolded key terms
- identify the social dimensions of alcohol- and drug-related problems that affect individuals and families
- apply structural-functionalist, feminist, symbolic interactionist, and conflict theories to alcohol- and drug-related issues
- situate government and social panics about substances in a context of harm reduction efforts and medicalization of experiences
- consider intersections of class, race, gender, ethnicity, and Canadian history when understanding drug-related social problems in a given person or family's experience

3
Alcohol and Other Drugs

ranplett/Vetta/Getty Images

According to data compiled by Western University researchers on behalf of MADD (Mothers Against Drunk Driving), there were 1052 impaired driving deaths on Canada's roadways in 2009, of which 956 involved alcohol impairment. In that year there were 56 539 alcohol-related driving injuries, and almost 10 000 more injuries from generally impaired driving resulting from the use of other drugs (Solomon and Cassidy 2014: 2–3). According to the study authors these deaths and injuries are reported by the Traffic Injury Research Foundation, a database that "likely significantly understates the total number of alcohol related crash deaths and injuries" because only drivers, and not vehicle occupants, have their blood alcohol levels measured on autopsy and/or hospital admission (p. 5). What this means in practice is that vehicle occupants who exercise impaired judgment because they are drunk, and who choose as a result to get into a car driven by a drunk driver, are not recorded as deaths resulting from alcohol impairment. In addition, not all drivers in crashes involving injury and death are tested for blood toxicity (perhaps because they elude police at the scene, or because their bodies are too damaged in the crash to provide blood samples); Solomon and Cassidy explain that in such cases none of the deaths or injuries will be reported as having been related to alcohol use.

Emotionally, the loss is staggering for families, and financially, the cost to the country each year is high. MADD provides a **social cost model** that includes property damages, insurance costs, medical care, and lost income due to death or injury and states that:

> Between 1999 and 2010, traffic crashes involving alcohol and/or drugs resulted in an estimated 14,256 deaths, 841,004 injuries* and damage to 2,779,458 vehicles in property-damage only (PDO) crashes alone. It is also estimated that there were 11,880 fatal impaired driving crashes, 574,872 injury-only impaired crashes and 1,828,589 PDO impaired crashes, totalling 2,415,341 crashes. Using a social cost model, these deaths, injuries and PDO crashes cost Canadians an estimated $246.1 billion. Based on a population of 33 million people, that represents a cost of about $7,457 per Canadian. (Pitel and Solomon 2013: 5)

Substance use becomes a social problem, usually defined as *abuse*, when it interferes with the well-being of individuals and the societies in which they live—when it jeopardizes health, safety, work and academic success, family, and friends. Managing the drug problem is a difficult undertaking, though. In dealing with drugs, a society must balance individual rights and civil liberties against the personal and social harm that drugs can exacerbate: fetal exposure, suicide, impaired driving, industrial accidents, mental illness, unemployment, and youth vulnerabilities.

Although the use of alcohol is not always treated as a problem, it can become highly problematic under certain conditions. These conditions usually involve danger to others, especially when driving is involved. Therefore, under the Canadian *Criminal Code*, there are four specific types of driving offences that stem initially from drinking and driving but that extend more broadly to *impairment*:

- The first is "operating or having care or control of a motor vehicle while one's ability to drive is impaired by alcohol or a drug." The term *drug* is broadly defined here to include any substance, legal or illegal, which can cause impairment.
- The second type of offence is "[e]ngaging in impaired driving causing death or bodily harm." The 1985 introduction of this offence was intended to make the penalties for causing serious accidents while impaired harsher than those for "simply" driving while impaired. The maximum penalty for impaired driving causing bodily harm is 10 years' imprisonment and 10 years' driving prohibition; the maximum penalty for impaired driving causing death is 14 years' imprisonment and 10 years' driving prohibition.

social cost model
A way of measuring the total costs to individuals, institutions, and society as whole from the costs of premature death and of disability. Used to assess many negative social phenomena, of which impaired driving is just one, that cut short lives, create disability, and negatively impact on communities.

* MADD Canada (2013, April). "Estimating the Number and Cost of Impairment-related Traffic Crashes in Canada: 1999–2013." Reprinted with permission.

- The third type is "[o]perating or having care or control of a motor vehicle with a blood alcohol concentration (BAC) over 0.08 percent." Since May 2009, changes to Ontario laws result in drivers with a BAC level over 0.05 being considered in the "warn" range, because driving ability is significantly impaired enough at this level but below 0.08 to raise the likelihood of an accident more than sevenfold (MTO Fact Sheet: Blood Alcohol Concentration [BAC]). Even if you *could* drive safely, driving with a BAC over 0.08 is a criminal offence in Canada. The specific amount of alcohol that must be consumed to have a BAC over the specified level varies. It depends on such factors as when the individual last ate, what that person's weight and percentage of body fat are, and how quickly the alcohol was consumed. Nevertheless, BAC can be determined through an analysis of a person's blood or urine.
- The final type of offence is "[f]ailing to provide breath or blood samples for analysis without a reasonable excuse." The term *reasonable excuse* refers to an inability to comprehend the demand or to physically comply with it.

Larger questions of when to regulate, what to regulate, and who should regulate are complex social issues. Our discussion begins by looking at how drugs are used and regulated in other societies.

3.1 The Global Context: Drug Use and Abuse

Pharmacologically, a **drug** is any substance other than food that alters the structure or functioning of a living organism when it enters the bloodstream. Using this definition, everything from vitamins to Aspirin constitutes a drug. Sociologically, the term drug refers to any chemical substance that (1) has a direct effect on the user's physical, psychological, and/or intellectual functioning, (2) has the potential to be abused, and (3) has adverse consequences for the individual and/or society. Societies vary in how they define and respond to drug use. Thus, drug use is influenced by the social context of the particular society in which it occurs.

In this chapter, our concern is oriented to issues of well-being at both the macro-level of large societies and the micro-level of individuals as they are impacted by drug use, drug trafficking, and drug regulation. In other words, we are concerned primarily with the health and welfare of communities, and we treat drug use as a problem insofar as it causes harm to users and to those around them. We are also concerned, however, with the ways in which social policy and politicking related to drug use can create further problems rather than ameliorating them. We look, therefore, at some of the social factors that promote the traffic in drugs around the world, and their use-prevalence; we also examine social solutions aimed at reducing the harm caused by drug use and drug trafficking, and we interrogate drug policies that treat drug use purely as a criminal—rather than health—concern. Finally, we note that the political and economic contexts that promote the circulation of a wide variety of drugs are complex and interconnected to problems such as regional political instability, and poor employment and education opportunities.

The United Nations Office on Drugs and Crime (UNODC) tracks international data on drug use, and focuses on the need to understand both the causes and effects of illicit drug use as matters of *health:*

> The United Nations Worldwide, UNODC estimates that in 2009 between 172 million and 250 million people used illicit drugs, of whom between 18 million and 38 million were drug dependent. Drug use is one of the top 20 risk factors

drug
Any substance other than food that alters the structure and functioning of a living organism when it enters the bloodstream.

to health globally, and among the top 10 in developed countries. Drug users are at increased risk of contracting infectious diseases such as HIV, hepatitis and tuberculosis that can easily spread to the general population and add to the health care burden. (UNODC 2010: 43)

Yet, the UNODC is also clear that in spite of these disturbing numbers, the lives and situations of people around the world have improved over the last 10 years with regard to successful reductions in prevalence of drug use around the globe, and UNODC notes that a key principle in this success is to avoid treating drug use primarily as a criminal matter. UNODC observes that "Drug users can be helped, their addiction can be treated, and these individuals, once recovered, can contribute to their communities. Branding drug users as criminals is not an effective way to deal with the illicit drug problem" (ibid). Instead of treating users as criminals, the UNODC is able to point to successes where governments and aid agencies put their efforts into treatment and prevention, and argues that these efforts not only have succeeded in reducing drug use and drug dependency, but also have promoted greater social cohesion, economic development, and increased general security while simultaneously reducing health-care costs (ibid).

By contrast, we know that criminalization of illicit drug use has accomplished little beyond populating prisons with people who receive minimal or no treatment for their drug dependencies and, as a consequence, imperiling the health of prison inmates (who end up sharing needles and spread bloodborne infections such as HIV and hepatitis C, meaning that prison populations have some of the highest rates of infection). As the Canadian HIV/AIDS Legal Network (CHALN) observes, some of the prevalence of the higher rate of infection in prison populations is related to government policies that focus on punishment instead of on treatment, and they echo the UNODC recommendation from 2006 that "action to reduce prison populations and prison overcrowding should accompany . . . a comprehensive strategy to prevent HIV transmission in prisons, to improve prison health care, and to improve prison conditions" (quoted in CHALN 2008: 2). Such recommendations recognize that prisoners are likely to re-enter larger society, and that we will improve the health of all persons if we pay attention to improving the health of our most vulnerable populations, including prisoners.

Drug Use around the World

According to United Nations estimates, the prevalence of drug use around the world varies dramatically. The UN *World Drug Report* (UN-WDR) notes that there are serious methodological problems with attempting to measure drug use for any given region, including the fact that users often comprise a "hidden population," and that asking about use over a specific period of time will yield radically different results than asking about use over the course of a lifetime (UN-WDR 2009: 299). Put more simply, if asked whether they have *ever* used marijuana in their lives, for example, numbers who answer yes will be far higher than if we ask whether people have used marijuana in the last year (ibid). A constructionist approach to understanding social problems will not necessarily see a question about lifetime use providing us with a reliable indication that pot use is a social problem. To determine whether drug use *is* a social problem, we would have to determine that it is factually causative of other social harms. For a constructionist, it is more useful to understand the abuse of alcohol and other drugs as problematic only insofar as it correlates with other social problems (e.g., poverty, marginalization, poor health, negative impact on child welfare, contribution to organized crime, or directly causing harm to non-users—as in the case of impaired driving that causes death or injury).

Some differences in international drug use may result in variations in drug policies. Official government policy in the Netherlands, for example, treats the use of such drugs as marijuana, hashish, and heroin as a health issue rather than as a crime issue. Evidence now suggests that marijuana use among Dutch youth is decreasing (UN-WDR 2009).

Although lifetime-use indicators may overstate the degree to which drug use is a problem, data regarding lifetime use can still yield useful information about what kinds of vulnerabilities correlate with concentrated populations' higher usage rates. In the United Kingdom (Great Britain, Scotland, Wales, and Northern Ireland), for example, one-third of the adult population is estimated to have used drugs at some time—and, of those, 49 percent are under age 30. Statistics also indicate that when compared with non-users, drug users in the United Kingdom are more likely to be male, unemployed, and living in or around London. These numbers do not include the use of alcohol. The data indicate, then, a variety of correlations between vulnerabilities such as urban poverty, geographic location (London is a major port city), educational attainment, and increased drug use.

Great Britain has also adopted a "medical model," particularly in regard to heroin and cocaine. As early as the 1960s, English doctors prescribed opiates and cocaine for patients unlikely to quit using drugs on their own and for the treatment of withdrawal symptoms. By the 1970s, however, British laws had become more restrictive, making it difficult for either physicians or users to obtain drugs legally. Today, British government policy provides for limited distribution of drugs by licensed drug treatment specialists—that is how addicts who might otherwise resort to crime to support their habits get drugs.

In addition to using surveys to measure the prevalence of lifetime drug use, regions will also use surveys that are repeated over extended periods of time. The data so gathered can reveal trends, both upward and downward in particular regions, for specific populations and age groups. Such long-term data from Britain showed that "rave culture" correlated to unprecedented prevalence of drug use in populations not marginalized by class or race (Aldridge 2008: 189–91). However, as these so-called "children of the decade of dance" matured, drug use prevalence dropped (p. 191), and Aldridge's analysis shows that while prevalence has not dropped to its pre-1990 levels, use is well down from levels from the mid-1990s to 2000s (ibid). In short, the UK data demonstrate that population drug-use trends are not always and irretrievably upward, and are not always linked to marginalization or "deviance."

Drug Use in Canada

According to government officials and the media—both institutions with something to gain by promising to pay attention to the problem—there is a drug crisis in Canada. Canadians' concern with drugs, however, has varied over the years. In 1975, almost one in two Canadians (46 percent) identified drugs as a "very serious" problem in our country, but by 1995, this figure had declined to approximately one in three (34 percent). Similarly, while 64 percent of Canadian teens viewed drugs as a "very serious" social concern in 1992, in 2000 only 48 percent did so (Bibby 2001: 181). Currently, groups such as the Canadian Foundation for Drug Policy (CFDP) work to propose "drug laws that are effective and humane." The CFDP was formed in the early 1990s by health-care professionals and academic researchers who were concerned that the laws being enacted by the federal governments (Conservative and Liberal) were unnecessarily punitive and were doomed to fail as other prohibition legislation had done. The CFDP continues to publish research and to deliver information aimed at a broad audience, and provide most of it on their website at www.cfdp.ca.

Chapter 3 Alcohol and Other Drugs

In Canada, the use of alcohol is much more widespread than the use of illicit drugs such as marijuana and cocaine, but our response to drug use is contradictory. On the one hand, we condemn drugs such as heroin; on the other, we encourage and tolerate drugs such as alcohol. At various times in our history, many drugs that are illegal today were legal and readily available. In the 1800s and the early 1900s, opium was routinely used as a pain reliever, and morphine was taken as a treatment for dysentery and fatigue. Amphetamine-based inhalers were legally available until 1949, and cocaine was an active ingredient in Coca-Cola until 1906, when it was replaced with another drug—caffeine (Witters et al. 1992). In the 1950s, anabolic steroids were viewed as "wonder drugs" that could enhance the well-being of sick and malnourished people, promote quick weight gain in cattle, and potentially provide a cure to cancer. For a younger generation that grew up with rumours, now confirmed, about Lance Armstrong and "doping" on the professional bicycle racing circuit, it was not until 1988, when Canadian athlete Ben Johnson lost his gold medal at the Seoul Olympics for taking a performance-enhancing drug, that many Canadians become aware that the use of anabolic steroids could be problematic.

3.2 Sociological Theories of Drug Use and Abuse

Most theories of drug use and abuse concentrate on what are called psychoactive drugs. These drugs alter the functioning of the brain, affecting the moods, emotions, and perceptions of the user. Such drugs include alcohol, cocaine, heroin, and marijuana. **Drug abuse** occurs when acceptable social standards of drug use are violated, resulting in adverse physiological, psychological, and social consequences, or some combination. For example, when an individual's drug use leads to hospitalization, arrest, or divorce, such use is usually considered abusive. Drug abuse, however, does not always entail drug addiction. **Drug addiction**, or **chemical dependency**, refers to a condition in which drug use is compulsive—users are unable to stop because of their dependency. The dependency may be psychological, in that the individual needs the drug to achieve a feeling of well-being, or physical, in that withdrawal symptoms occur when the individual stops taking the drug.

Various theories provide explanations for why some people use and abuse drugs. Drug use is not simply a matter of individual choice. Theories of drug use explain how structural and cultural forces, as well as biological factors, influence drug use and society's responses to it.

Structural-Functionalist Perspective

Functionalists argue that drug abuse is a response to the weakening of norms in society. As society becomes more complex and rapid social change occurs, norms and values become unclear and ambiguous, resulting in anomie—a state of normlessness. **Anomie** may exist at the societal level, resulting in social strains and inconsistencies that lead to drug use. For example, research indicates that increased alcohol consumption in the 1830s and the 1960s was a response to rapid social change and the resulting stress (Rorabaugh 1979). Anomie produces inconsistencies in cultural norms regarding drug use. For example, while public health officials and health-care professionals warn of the dangers of alcohol and tobacco use, films still glorify the use of alcohol and tobacco, and the government subsidizes the alcohol industry. Further, such cultural traditions as giving away cigars to celebrate the birth of a child and celebrating major events with alcohol persist.

drug abuse
The violation of social standards of acceptable drug use, resulting in adverse physiological, psychological, or social consequences.

drug addiction/chemical dependency
A condition in which drug use is compulsive, and users are unable to stop because of physical or psychological dependency or both.

anomie
A state of normlessness in which norms and values are weak or unclear; results from rapid social change and is linked to many social problems, including crime, drug addiction, and violence.

Anomie may also exist at the individual level, as when a person suffers feelings of estrangement, isolation, and turmoil over appropriate and inappropriate behaviour. An adolescent whose parents are experiencing a divorce, who is separated from friends and family as a consequence of moving, or who lacks parental supervision and discipline may be more vulnerable to drug use. Thus, from a structural-functionalist perspective, drug use is a response to the absence of a perceived bond between the individual and society, and to the weakening of a consensus on what is considered acceptable. Consistent with this perspective, citing data from a larger U.S. study, Health Canada reports "a strong association between substance use problems and problematic family relationships," with 73 percent of youth with substance dependencies in the U.S. study reporting drug use to cope with dysfunctional, often abusive families (2001: 51).

Feminist Perspectives

Feminist forms of analysis are many, and employ a broad range of methods to understand social problems. No single manner of assessing substance use and dependency applies; feminist work in the area is unified by the drive to illuminate previously neglected assessment of risk factors and substance use problems unique to women. Here, we introduce two unique features of substance use facing women: (1) misuse of prescription drugs and (2) drug use during pregnancy.

In a study using data gathered from 3185 respondents, Simoni-Wastila and colleagues (2004) determined that the women's increased likelihood of being prescribed tranquillizers and other psychoactive drugs significantly increased the probability of using prescription medications for reasons other than, or in excess of, their originally intended medical purpose. The Simoni-Wastila et al. study concludes that being a woman significantly increases vulnerability to misuse of medically prescribed drugs. While theoretical explanations for this increased vulnerability vary, it is clear from other health data that because of their families' dependence on them to be in good health, women tend to pay more attention to their health, aches, and pains than men do. The increased attention puts women in more frequent contact with the health-care system, rendering them more likely recipients of prescription medications for pain, stress, and sleeplessness. In addition, role strain and role conflict may place women at increased risk for stress-related problems; they may try to deal with these by "self-medicating" through the use of alcohol, other controlled substances, and street drugs.

Drug use during pregnancy subjects women to institutional scrutiny and social blaming tactics that men do not face. Negative media attention on pregnant women who use drugs such as cocaine, heroin, and alcohol has been on the rise since the late 1980s; attention geared toward the prevention of fetal alcohol syndrome (FAS) tends to be less sensational. Broad public health campaigns in bars, restaurants, and on television aim to reduce prenatal exposure to alcohol (Figure 3.1, a poster distributed by Health Canada, provides a sample); conversely, the criminal justice system routinely prosecutes marginalized, poor women who use cocaine or heroin during pregnancy (Zivi 2000). Feminists criticize those who blame individual mothers instead of building programs that would prevent circumstances that lead to substance abuse. They argue that criminalization of these mothers "subordinate[s] women's rights and needs to those of the fetus" (Zivi 2000: 237). From a feminist perspective, the problem is not a simple act committed by an uncaring mother, but rather, a woman's response to an overwhelmingly negative social situation of poverty, racism, and victimization: it is the social situation that harms both the pregnant woman and the developing fetus. Furthermore, criminalization of this sort treats women as vehicles for breeding purposes, not as persons with the same legal rights to autonomy and agency as men.

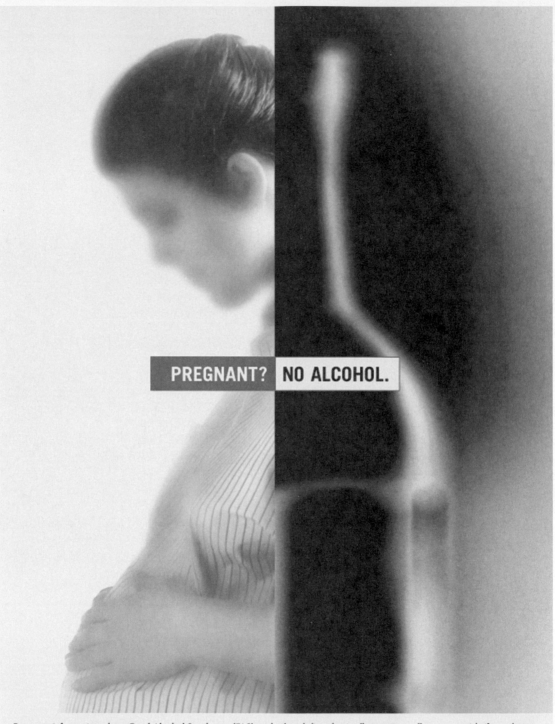

Figure 3.1 *Pregnant? No Alcohol*

Conflict Perspective

Conflict perspectives emphasize the importance of power differentials in influencing drug use behaviour and societal values concerning drug use. From a conflict perspective, drug use occurs as a response to the inequality perpetuated by a capitalist system. Alienated from work, friends, and family, as well as from larger social institutions, people may use drugs to escape the oppression and frustration that correspond to low status. Conflict theorists highlight the considerable influence of the most powerful members of society to define which drugs are illegal and to set the penalties for their production, sale, and use. Thus, alcohol, the production and sale of which benefits those with power, privilege, and influence, is legal. The sale of alcohol, for example, generates billions of dollars a year in revenues for provincial governments, as well as much federal revenue. Consider the irony: of the $39.8 billion in annual costs from substance abuse to the Canadian economy, the costs of legal drugs were the most significant, with tobacco accounting for $17 billion, alcohol $14.6 billion, and illicit drugs $8.2 billion (Rehm 2006). These numbers are calculated to include the costs of treating illness, of lost productivity, and of law enforcement, with productivity losses accounting for 61 percent of the losses. The CCSA report represents these losses on a per capita basis, as we see in Figure 3.2.

$ 1267 Total

$ 262 Illegal drugs

$ 463 Alcohol

$ 541 Tobacco

Figure 3.2 **The Costs of Substance Abuse in Canada, 2002 (in dollars per capita)**

SOURCE: Rehm, et al. (2006). "Per capita costs of substance abuse in Canada, 2002," *The Costs of Substance Abuse in Canada 2002 Highlights*. Reproduced with permission from the Canadian Centre on Substance Abuse.

In contrast to the abuse of legal substances, the consumption of "street drugs" such as cocaine and heroin is associated with the powerless and disenfranchised: the poor, minority group members, and, in particular, visible minorities. As Hackler (2000: 213) observes, "the societal demand to punish, stigmatize, and exclude users of certain substances *is not based on pharmacological evidence*" and evidence of such damage "plays a secondary role in drug policy." The use of opium by Chinese immigrants in the 1800s provides a historical example. The Chinese, who had been brought to Canada to work on the railroads, regularly smoked opium as part of their cultural tradition. However, hostility to opium use emerged in part because of a labour surplus that followed the completion of railway construction and the diminished intensity of the Gold Rush. Green (1986) notes that before this time, in the midst of a labour shortage, "the Chinese were regarded as industrious, sober, economical and law-abiding individuals" (p. 25). As jobs became scarce and the Chinese were viewed as competitors for existing positions, "earlier friendly feelings toward the Chinese changed to hostility.... There was a great demand that Chinese immigration be restricted or discontinued" (p. 24). Simultaneously, opium use, previously viewed as, at worst, "an individual medical misfortune or personal vice, free of severe moral opprobrium" (p. 25), became defined as a significant social "evil." Morgan (1978) observes:

> The first opium laws . . . were not the result of a moral crusade against the drug itself. Instead, it represented a coercive action directed against a vice that was merely an appendage of the real menace—the Chinese—and not the Chinese per se, but the labouring "Chinamen" who threatened the economic security of the white working class. (p. 59)

Criminalizing drugs such as cocaine, heroin, and marijuana exercises social control over the powerless, political opponents, and minorities. In the 1940s, marijuana was used primarily by minority group members and carried with it severe criminal penalties. However, after white middle-class students began to use marijuana in the 1970s, various lobby groups sought to reduce the penalties associated with its use. Though the nature and pharmacological properties of the drug had not changed, the population of users was now connected to power and influence. Thus, conflict theorists regard the regulation of certain drugs and drug use itself as a reflection of differences in the political, economic, and social power of various interest groups.

Symbolic Interactionist Perspective

Symbolic interactionism, emphasizing the importance of definitions and labelling, concentrates on the social meanings associated with drug use. If the initial drug use experience is defined as pleasurable it is likely to recur, and over time the individual may earn the label of "druggie." If this definition is internalized so that the individual assumes the identity, the behaviour will likely continue and may escalate.

Drug use is also learned through symbolic interaction in small groups. Friends, for example, are the most common source of drugs for teenagers (Leinwand 2000). First-time users learn not only the motivations for drug use and its techniques, but also what to experience. Becker (1966) explains how marijuana users learn to ingest the drug. A novice being coached by a regular user reports this experience:

> I was smoking like I did an ordinary cigarette. He said, "No, don't do it like that." He said, "Suck it, you know, draw in and hold it in your lungs . . . for a period of time."
> I said, "Is there any limit of time to hold it?" He said, "No, just till you feel that you want to let it out, let it out." So I did that three or four times. (p. 47)

Marijuana users not only learn *how* to smoke, but also learn to label the experience positively. When peers define certain drugs, behaviours, and experiences as not only acceptable but pleasurable, drug use is likely to continue. Interactionists also emphasize that symbols may be manipulated and used for political and economic agendas. "[A]meliorative programs which are imbued with . . . potent symbolic qualities . . . are virtually assured wide-spread public acceptance (regardless of actual effectiveness) which in turn advances the interests of political leaders who benefit from being associated with highly visible, popular symbolic programs" (Wysong et al. 1994: 461).

Symbolic interactionist research on how those with drug and alcohol dependencies structure their life histories can explain not only how users take on an identity such as "drug addict" or "alcoholic," but also how they resist such identities. A Canadian study over a period of 12 years concluding in 2004 revealed, for example, that women facing parole hearings in drug trafficking–related offences structured themselves as victims rather than as offenders, and that the members of the parole boards were inclined to facilitate these narratives: "By embracing notions of subordinate and exploited women and dominated and exploiting men, board members accept ideal types of men and women. . . . According to this perspective, women are caring persons who fall victim to male drug dealers. As a result, female drug traffickers can frequently use gender attributes of frailty and fragility to diminish their responsibility" (Silverstein 2006: 404). Silverstein does not deny that these women are vulnerable to entering drug trafficking because of pre-existing problems such as domestic violence and poverty, but demonstrates how women are made to understand and to narrate themselves only as victims if they are to convince parole boards that they ought to be released from jail. In short, the women learn to understand and portray themselves not principally as drug users, but as victims of a male drug culture.

A study of 54 people in treatment centres and hostels for persons with alcoholism carried out in Copenhagen concluded that while most people in such centres do understand themselves as alcoholics, some actively resist that identity and develop a counter narrative to explain themselves. The research in this group initially sought to understand how people became alcoholics by asking interviewees to answer questions that would illuminate a "drinking career" that had culminated in their residency in programs for people facing health and social problems related to their alcohol use (Järvinen 2001). One interviewee resisted identification as an alcoholic in a series of narrative manoeuvres that sought to establish himself as "in control":

> Whatever reason John may have had to volunteer for the interview, it cannot have been because he felt that he was an "identified alcoholic" prepared to discuss his experiences and need for alcohol treatment. Nevertheless, the line of the study led John—who explicitly declared that he had never been "interested in treatment" or in "ventilating [his] problems with each and everyone"—into a situation wherein he had to negotiate an "alcohol-related life history" for himself. The result was a compromise: John was an alcoholic but an alcoholic in perfect self-command; it was circumstances that had made him an alcoholic, not his alcoholism that had led him into troublesome circumstances. (p. 279)

Järvinen explains that resistant narratives such as the one above can be thrown into crisis when faced with a direct challenge such as the interview encounter, but that whatever internal inconsistencies appear in these narratives allow the "alcoholic" to save face. Irving Goffman explains the behaviour exhibited by the interviewee in Järvinen's account as a mode of self-protection that maintains an ideal sense of self in social interaction (p. 277).

Biological and Psychological Theories

Drug use and addiction are likely the result of a complex interplay of social, psychological, and biological forces. Biological research has primarily concentrated on the role of genetics in predisposing an individual to drug use. According to a report by the National Institute on Alcohol Abuse and Alcoholism (NIAAA 2000: xiii), "50 to 60 percent of the risk for developing alcoholism is genetic." Research also indicates that by examining inherited traits, science "can predict [in] childhood with 80 percent accuracy who is going to develop alcoholism later in life" (AAP 1998). Nonetheless, many alcoholics do not have parents who abuse alcohol, and many alcoholic parents have offspring who do not abuse alcohol.

Biological theories of drug use hypothesize that some individuals are physiologically predisposed to experience more pleasure from drugs than others and, consequently, are more likely to be drug users. According to these theories, the central nervous system processes drugs through neurotransmitters in a way that produces an unusually euphoric experience. Individuals not so physiologically inclined report less pleasant experiences and are less likely to continue use (Alcohol Alert 2000; Jarvik 1990).

Psychological explanations focus on the tendency of certain personality types to be more susceptible to drug use. Individuals who are particularly prone to anxiety may be more likely to use drugs as a way to relax, gain self-confidence, or ease tension. For example, research indicates that female adolescents who have been sexually abused or who have poor relationships with their parents are more likely to have severe drug problems (NIDA 2000a). Psychological theories of drug abuse also emphasize that drug use may be maintained by positive and negative reinforcement.

3.3 Frequently Used Legal and Illegal Drugs

Social definitions of which drugs are legal or illegal have varied over time, circumstance, and societal forces. In Canada, two of the most dangerous and widely abused drugs—alcohol and tobacco—are legal. They are also widely available, even to those who are under the legal age to be able to purchase them.

Alcohol

Canadians' attitudes toward alcohol have had a long and varied history. Although alcohol was commonly consumed in early Canada, "the moral climate in Canada after the turn of the century was one in which middle class persons with strong religious convictions were willing to believe the worst of alcohol, tobacco and other drugs. . . . The typical reaction to these perceived threats was to press for total prohibition" (Giffen et al. 1991: 150). Many have argued that the push for prohibition was a moral crusade (Gusfield 1963) against immigrant groups perceived as more likely to use alcohol. Today, Canada is experiencing a resurgence of concern about alcohol. What has been called a "new temperance" has manifested itself in increased concern about fetal alcohol syndrome and teenage drinking, and calls for strict enforcement of drinking and driving regulations.

Alcohol is the most widely used and abused drug in Canada among both adults and youths (Table 3.1). Although most people who drink alcohol do so moderately and experience few negative effects, alcoholics are psychologically and physically addicted to alcohol. Alcoholics, unlike moderate users of alcohol, both suffer from and cause various degrees of physical, economic, psychological, and personal harm as a direct result of their alcohol dependency.

Table 3.1 *Commonly Abused Drugs*.

Substances: Category and Name	Examples of Commercial and Street Names	DEA Schedule[1]/ How Administered[2]	Acute Effects/Health Risks
Tobacco			
Nicotine	Found in cigarettes, cigars, bidis, and smokeless tobacco (snuff, spit tobacco, chew)	Not scheduled/Smoked, snorted, chewed	Increased blood pressure and heart rate/Chronic lung disease; cardiovascular disease; stroke; cancers of the mouth, pharynx, larynx, esophagus, stomach, pancreas, cervix, kidney, bladder, and acute myeloid leukemia; adverse pregnancy outcomes; addiction

Table 3.1 *Commonly Abused Drugs* (continued)

Substances: Category and Name	Examples of Commercial and Street Names	DEA Schedule[1]/ How Administered[2]	Acute Effects/Health Risks
Alcohol			
Alcohol (ethyl alcohol)	Found in liquor, beer, and wine	Not scheduled/Swallowed	In low doses, euphoria, mild stimulation, relaxation, lowered inhibitions; in higher doses, drowsiness, slurred speech, nausea, emotional volatility, loss of coordination, visual distortions, impaired memory, sexual dysfunction, loss of consciousness/Increased risk of injuries, violence, fetal damage (in pregnant women); depression; neurologic deficits; hypertension; liver and heart disease; addiction; fatal overdose
Cannabinoids			
Marijuana	Blunt, dope, ganja, grass, herb, joint, bud, Mary Jane, pot, reefer, green, trees, smoke, sinsemilla, skunk, weed	I/Smoked, swallowed	Euphoria; relaxation; slowed reaction time; distorted sensory perception; impaired balance and coordination; increased heart rate and appetite; impaired learning, memory; anxiety; panic attacks; psychosis/Cough, frequent respiratory infections; possible mental health decline; addiction
Hashish	Boom, gangster, hash, hash oil, hemp	I/Smoked, swallowed	
Opioids			
Heroin	Diacetylmorphine: smack, horse, brown sugar, dope, H, junk, skag, skunk, white horse, China white; cheese (with OTC cold medicine and antihistamine)	I/Injected, smoked, snorted	Euphoria; drowsiness; impaired coordination; dizziness; confusion; nausea; sedation; feeling of heaviness in the body; slowed or arrested breathing/Constipation; endocarditis; hepatitis; HIV; addiction; fatal overdose
Opium	Laudanum, paregoric: big O, black stuff, block, gum, hop	II, III, V/Swallowed, smoked	
Stimulants			
Cocaine	Cocaine hydrochloride: blow, bump, C, candy, Charlie, coke, crack, fake, rock, snow, toot	II/Snorted, smoked, injected	Increased heart rate, blood pressure, body temperature, metabolism; feelings of exhilaration; increased energy, mental alertness; tremors; reduced appetite; irritability; anxiety; panic; paranoia; violent behavior; psychosis/Weight loss, insomnia; cardiac or cardiovascular complications; stroke; seizures; addiction

(Continued)

Table 3.1 *Commonly Abused Drugs* (continued)

Substances: Category and Name	Examples of Commercial and Street Names	DEA Schedule[1]/ How Administered[2]	Acute Effects/Health Risks
Amphetamine	Biphetamine, Dexedrine: bennies, black beauties, crosses, hearts, LA turnaround, speed, truck drivers, uppers	II/Swallowed, snorted, smoked, injected	**Also, for cocaine**—nasal damage from snorting
Methamphetamine	Desoxyn: meth, ice, crank, chalk, crystal, fre, glass, go fast, speed	II/Swallowed, snorted, smoked, injected	**Also, for methamphetamine**—severe dental problems
Club Drugs			
MDMA (methylenedioxy-methamphetamine)	Ecstasy, Adam, clarity, Eve, lover's speed, peace, uppers	I/Swallowed, snorted, injected	**MDMA**—mild hallucinogenic effects; increased tactile sensitivity; empathic feelings; lowered inhibition; anxiety; chills; sweating; teeth clenching; muscle cramping/Sleep disturbances; depression; impaired memory; hyperthermia; addiction
Flunitrazepam[3]	Rohypnol: forget-me pill, Mexican Valium, R2, roach, Roche, roofes, roofnol, rope, rophies	IV/Swallowed, snorted	**Flunitrazepam**—sedation; muscle relaxation; confusion; memory loss; dizziness; impaired coordination/Addiction
GHB[3]	Gamma-hydroxybutyrate: G, Georgia home boy, grievous bodily harm, liquid Ecstasy, soap, scoop, goop, liquid X	I/Swallowed	**GHB**—drowsiness; nausea; headache; disorientation; loss of coordination; memory loss/Unconsciousness; seizures; coma
Dissociative Drugs			
Ketamine	Ketalar SV: cat Valium, K, Special K, vitamin K	III/Injected, snorted, smoked	Feelings of being separate from one's body and environment; impaired motor function/Anxiety; tremors; numbness; memory loss; nausea
PCP and analogs	Phencyclidine: angel dust, boat, hog, love boat, peace pill	I, II/Swallowed, smoked, injected	**Also, for ketamine**—analgesia; impaired memory; delirium; respiratory depression and arrest; death
Salvia divinorum	Salvia, Shepherdess's Herb, Maria Pastora, magic mint, Sally-D	Not scheduled/Chewed, swallowed, smoked	**Also, for PCP and analogs**—analgesia; psychosis; aggression; violence; slurred speech; loss of coordination; hallucinations
Dextromethorphan (DXM)	Found in some cough and cold medications: Robotripping, Robo, Triple C	Not scheduled/Swallowed	**Also, for DXM**—euphoria; slurred speech; confusion; dizziness; distorted visual perceptions

Table 3.1 *Commonly Abused Drugs* (continued)

Substances: Category and Name	Examples of Commercial and Street Names	DEA Schedule[1]/ How Administered[2]	Acute Effects/Health Risks
Hallucinogens			
LSD	Lysergic acid diethylamide: acid, blotter, cubes, microdot yellow sunshine, blue heaven	I/Swallowed, absorbed through mouth tissues	Altered states of perception and feeling; hallucinations; nausea **Also, LSD and mescaline**—increased body temperature, heart rate, blood pressure; loss of appetite; sweating; sleeplessness; numbness, dizziness, weakness, tremors; impulsive behavior; rapid shifts in emotion
Mescaline	Buttons, cactus, mesc, peyote	I/Swallowed, smoked	
Psilocybin	Magic mushrooms, purple passion, shrooms, little smoke	I/Swallowed	**Also, for LSD**—flashbacks, hallucinogen persisting perception disorder **Also for psilocybin**—nervousness; paranoia; panic
Other Compounds			
Anabolic steroids	Anadrol, Oxandrin, Durabolin, Depo-Testosterone, Equipoise: roids, juice, gym candy, pumpers	III/Injected, swallowed, applied to skin	**Steroids**—no intoxication effects/ Hypertension; blood clotting and cholesterol changes; liver cysts; hostility and aggression; acne; in adolescents—premature stoppage of growth; in males—prostate cancer, reduced sperm production, shrunken testicles, breast enlargement; in females—menstrual irregularities, development of beard and other masculine characteristics
Inhalants	Solvents (paint thinners, gasoline, glues); gases (butane, propane, aerosol propellants, nitrous oxide); nitrites (isoamyl, isobutyl, cyclohexyl): laughing gas, poppers, snappers, whippets	Not scheduled/Inhaled through nose or mouth	**Inhalants** (varies by chemical)— stimulation; loss of inhibition; headache; nausea or vomiting; slurred speech; loss of motor coordination; wheezing/Cramps; muscle weakness; depression; memory impairment; damage to cardiovascular and nervous systems; unconsciousness; sudden death

[1]Schedule I and II drugs have a high potential for abuse. They require greater storage security and have a quota on manufacturing, among other restrictions. Schedule I drugs are available for research only and have no approved medical use; Schedule II drugs are available only by prescription (unrefillable) and require a form for ordering. Schedule III and IV drugs are available by prescription, may have five refills in six months, and may be ordered orally. Some Schedule V drugs are available over the counter.

[2]Some of the health risks are directly related to the route of drug administration. For example, injection drug use can increase the risk of infection through needle contamination with staphylococci, HIV, hepatitis, and other organisms.

[3]Associated with sexual assaults.

SOURCE: NIDA (2010).

The 2000 Project Canada youth survey found that while one in five Canadian teens drank beer, wine, or other forms of alcohol at least once a week, the weekly level for males was almost twice that of females (Bibby 2001: 97). In terms of youth-specific harms from alcohol consumption, binge drinking, defined as the consumption of five or more alcoholic beverages on at least one occasion, is a significant threat. The Ontario Ministry of Health (2009) has reported that while youth are using fewer illicit drugs for recreational purposes than they were at the end of the last century, alcohol use has been steadily climbing over the same time period, and that:

> In 2007, 25% of people in Ontario age 12-19 years reported consuming at least five or more drinks on at least one occasion in the previous 12 months. Based on 36 public health units in Ontario, the highest proportion of heavy drinkers was 65% and the lowest was 12% for people age 12-19 years who reported consuming five or more drinks on at least one occasion. (p. 39)

Risks associated with binge drinking are significant and include death (from injury or alcohol poisoning), injury, experiences of violence and of sexual assault, as well as unplanned sexual activity that can result in unplanned pregnancies and sexually transmitted infections (Ontario Ministry of Health 2009: 39). Moreover, heavy drinking over time, even if it does not become full-blown alcohol dependency, is implicated in the development of liver disease, certain cancers, and heart disease (ibid).

Although there is considerable public debate over the causes of binge drinking in youth populations, and a fair amount of blame laid at the site of families in which alcohol is openly consumed, the data on causes of alcohol abuse are more subtle with regard to family influence. This chapter's *Social Problems Research Up Close* feature draws attention to the influence of responsible alcohol use in the family home. On the whole, when we consider the research showing the relationship between educational attainment and binge drinking, and compare it to the research of alcohol use in the family home, we see that education levels correlate more strongly with problem drinking than is the open consumption of alcohol in the family.

Social Problems *Research Up Close*

Drink at Home, Make It a Family Affair

There's some debate over the relationship between onset of drinking, parents' alcohol consumption patterns, and the context in which drinking first occurs. For example, some research suggests that the more alcohol consumed in the home, the higher the likelihood that children will grow up and engage in excessive drinking behaviour. Another body of research suggests that when children use alcohol in the home, they're less likely to abuse it in the future. The following ethnography looks at the relationship between onset of drinking, parental drinking behaviour, type of alcohol consumed, and the social context in which drinking occurs.

Sample and Methods

The researchers used "anthropological ethnographic interviewing" to "understand the world as seen by the respondent within the context of the respondent's everyday life" (Strunin et al. 2010: 346). The sample was composed of 160 Italian youth and young adults—half female and half male—divided into two age groups, 16- to 18-year-olds and 25- to 30-year-olds, individuals in each age group having a variety of consumption rates.

To identify prospective subjects, an alcohol screening test was administered in two high school locations for current and former students. Further, to ensure the collection of comparable data, an interview guide was developed to make sure that all topics were covered and that the questions were asked in a specific order. A quantity–frequency index was used to measure self-reported drinking behaviour. Lastly, students were asked about their family histories, extended family members, as well as questions about their beliefs, norms, and behaviours related to alcohol use. The interviews were audiotaped, transcribed, and translated into English.

Findings and Conclusions

Youth who described drinking as part of their Italian heritage also described it in terms of being "culturally normative." For example, a young female adult described her parents' attitude toward alcohol in the following way: ". . . a simple attitude. Alcohol is a pleasure, and has to be lived as something positive, this is the type of values we have at home. A wine culture, wine at meals for the pleasure of it, no abuse because that can cause health problems."

This research points to the importance of the social context in which drinking takes place. For example, even though parents who allowed their children to drink with meals may be seen as permissive, they were also more likely to talk to their children about the dangers of alcohol, including such health issues as "addiction, liver, and heart diseases . . . and the dangers of drinking and driving."

Further, youth who were allowed to drink with meals in their homes were more likely to have their first drink within a family setting and less likely to mix types of alcohol. Alternatively, the first drink experiences of those not allowed to drink at home included drinking large amounts of more than one type of alcohol and getting drunk.

There are also differences in the likelihood of binge drinking, defined as drinking five or more drinks on one occasion, and age of getting drunk for the first time. Those who consumed alcohol with meals in the home delayed binge drinking and getting drunk when compared to respondents who were not allowed to drink in the home. Further, only those who did not drink alcohol in the home got drunk on their first occasion of drinking.

The authors conclude that, "the introduction of alcohol, typically wine, in a family setting may protect against harmful drinking including binge drinking and drunkenness" (Strunin et al. 2010: 354). The researchers also suggest that many of their findings can be generalized to other populations. For example, the United States does not have a tradition of permitting children to consume alcohol with meals and, perhaps consequently, has one of the highest adolescent consumption rates in the world. Moderate drinking at home within the context of the family setting could lower excessive drinking rates in the United States and teach healthier drinking patterns.

SOURCE: Strunin, Lee, Kirstin Lindeman, Enrico Tempesta, Pierluigi Ascani, Simona Avan, and Luca Parisi. 2010. "Familial Drinking in Italy: Harmful or Protective Factors?" *Addiction Research and Theory* 18(3): 344–358.

Of course, problem drinking does not necessarily end with youth. According to the NPHS, as education increases, so too does the likelihood that Canadians will be regular drinkers. "University graduates were most likely (61 percent) to drink at least once a month, while those with less than high school were least likely (44 percent) to do so." It additionally notes that the relationship between amount consumed and educational attainment "is similar, though less pronounced: with each successive level of education, the likelihood of having had one or more drinks weekly increased. However, university graduates were least likely to have had 14 or more drinks weekly" (Health Canada 1999: 172). This survey also found that the proportion of Canadian men and women who drank at least once per month rose steadily with increases in income, and men and women with higher incomes tended to be heavier drinkers. In other words, being able to afford to drink regularly figures directly into drinking behaviour. Demands in professional workplaces may also pressure employees into more regular social drinking, including office parties, conferences and conventions, interviews held over meals, and other meetings that take place in social venues (e.g., over golf, over drinks, etc.).

Tobacco

Tobacco was first cultivated by Indigenous people and had a central place in their religious rituals. European settlers believed that tobacco had medicinal properties and its use spread throughout Europe, assuring the economic success of the colonists in North America. Initially, people generally chewed or had tobacco in snuff. In time, smoking gained popularity even though scientific evidence that linked tobacco smoking to lung cancer existed as early as 1859 (Feagin and Feagin 1994).

Today, the health hazards of tobacco use are well documented. Smoking is associated with lung cancer, cardiovascular disease, strokes, emphysema, spontaneous abortion, premature birth, and neonatal death. In Canada, 100 people die every day from illnesses caused by smoking, and smoking accounts for more loss of life than do obesity, physical inactivity, or hypertension (Health Canada 2011b). Moreover, tobacco smoke, including exposure to second-hand smoke, kills more than 45 000 Canadians yearly—more than the combined total of all murders, alcohol-related deaths, car accidents, and suicides (see Figure 3.3).

Figure 3.3 **Estimated Deaths in Canada, 1996**

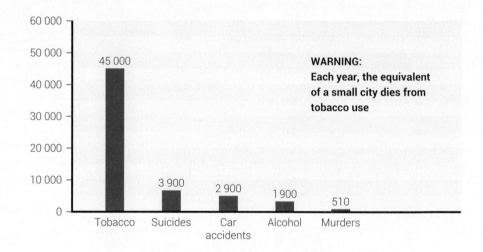

By the year 2030, tobacco-related diseases will be the number-one cause of death worldwide, killing one of every six people. In an attempt to discourage the use of tobacco by Canadians, governments have introduced various control measures, including media campaigns, public education programs, and legislated restrictions on access to cigarettes, on public smoking, and on sponsorship promotion by the tobacco industry (Health Canada 2002). In June 2002, the federal government levied a $3.50-per-carton increase in taxes on cigarettes. This increase restored federal tobacco tax rates to their pre-1994 levels. In announcing the increase, Minister of Health Anne McLellan observed: "We know that increasing taxes on tobacco directly reduces the incidence of smoking, which contributes to the overall health of Canadians" (Department of Finance Canada 2002).

Fortunately, the rate at which young people take up smoking tobacco continues to fall (see Figure 3.4), with considerable decreases in the numbers of current smokers in the middle-school-aged population since 1994:

> Prevalence of current smokers in grades 6-9 significantly decreased between 2008-09 (3%) and 2010-11 (2%). This is the lowest rate of current smokers recorded since 1994 (8%). There was no difference in the prevalence of current smokers between male and female. (Health Canada 2012)

For the population of youth in high school from grades 10–12, Health Canada reports that only 10 percent indicate they are current occasional smokers, and only 5 percent indicate they are daily current smokers (ibid). Health Canada reports that these rates continue a downward trend in youth smoking habits over the last two decades. The future health for the current generation of youth, then, has a better outlook than does the current generation of adults who took up smoking in their youth.

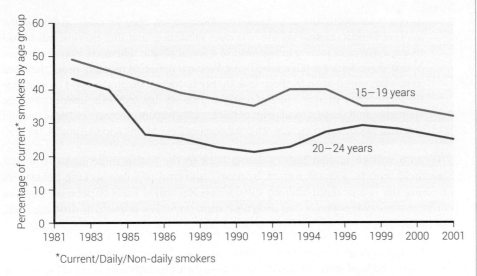

*Current/Daily/Non-daily smokers

Marijuana

Although drug abuse ranks among the top concerns of many Canadians, surveys indicate that illegal drug use of all kinds is far less common than alcohol and tobacco abuse. Marijuana remains the most commonly used and most heavily trafficked illegal drug in the world. It is estimated that more than 40 million Europeans have tried cannabis at least once and that there are 200 to 250 million marijuana users worldwide. According to the Canadian Centre on Substance Abuse, cannabis is the most widely used illicit drug in Canada with nearly 14 percent of Canadians aged 15 and over reporting use in the past year. The CCSA's survey data also showed that slightly more than 39 percent of 15- to 17-year-olds and 69.9 percent of 18- to 19-year-olds reported lifetime use, while roughly one-fifth of those who reported cannabis use in the past year indicated that they use cannabis more regularly on either a weekly (20.1%) or daily (18.1%) basis (CCSA 2009).

Marijuana's active ingredient, THC (delta-9-tetrahydrocannabinol), may act as a sedative or as a hallucinogen, depending on the amount ingested. Marijuana use dates back to 2737 B.C. in China and has a long tradition of use in India, the Middle East, and Europe. In North America, hemp, as it was then called, was used for making rope and as a folk remedy. In the 1920s, Judge Emily Murphy was the first to draw the attention of Canadians to "Marihuana—A New Menace" in her book *The Black Candle*. Although the drug was virtually unknown in Canada at the time, Murphy's book suggested that marijuana had an insidious effect on its users: it drove them insane and caused them to lose all moral sense. However, as Green (1986: 31) has noted, racism appears to have been a "critical component" in Murphy's analysis of the drug problem. According to Murphy, narcotics were part of an international conspiracy "to injure the bright-browed races of the world" and a tactic used by "aliens of colour to bring about the degeneration of the white race." However, "[a]s a result of the considerable media attention devoted to *The Black Candle* and the paucity of challenge or contradictory statements, Murphy's conception of the scourge-like effects of drug use came to dominate Canadian narcotics ideology" (Green 1986: 33).

In his research on the development of legislation around the world for controlling narcotic drugs, MacArthur Haverfield (2007) explains that in the movement of drugs from their point of discovery to the west—that is, mostly by Europeans in colonial situations—racist and ethnocentric attitudes informed both adoption of those drugs, and their regulation:

> Attempts to control the altering of consciousness are often founded on fears of the lower or foreign classes [sic] use of certain substances and that this use will spread to the majority of society in the form of a social plague. There are also similarities in that these fears are often based on a Western notion of morality or religion, and were often seized upon by those in authority to control the masses and to politicize the matter to be used in issues of power and knowledge. In North American society, opium became the first focal point of this backlash against recreational drug use and was then expanded to include other substances like cocaine and marijuana. (p. 7)

Given a written human history dating back to the fourth millennium BCE that Haverfield reports is characterized by nearly universal pleasure-seeking behaviours involving the use of mind-altering substances, Haverfield finds it peculiar that the commonsense perception is that drug regulation under law is as old as drug use itself, but he explains:

> Many people do not realize the criminalization of recreational drug use is a recent social and legal construction in North America. Canada established the first federal level anti-opium regulations less than one hundred years ago in 1908. The drug cycle is clearly evident with the passage of the 1908 *Act to Prohibit the Importation, Manufacture and Sale of Opium for other than Medical Purpose.* The historical evidence overwhelmingly supports a view of law creation based upon racial biases and . . . political opportunity . . . (p. 8).

In other words, the criminalization of drugs, including cocaine, opium and heroin, and marijuana, has been far more rooted in political agendas, racism, and ethnic bias than in any putative concern for the well-being of communities. For example, citing recent controversies over the establishment of harm reduction sites such as Vancouver's Insite safe injection facility, the CBC reported that Stephen Harper's Conservative government engaged in fear-mongering in order to gain support for Bill C-65 in 2013. Bill C-65 runs counter to the Canadian Medical Association data on the positive effect of harm reduction facilities not only in reducing deaths inside communities of drug users, but also in limiting the spread of infectious diseases from those communities into the broader public with whom they interact. In the spring of 2013, the CBC reported that in 2011 the Harper government sent out a mass mailing urging recipients to "keep heroin out of our backyards" (CBC 2013)—completely missing the point that such facilities are established only in areas where heroin and other IV drug use is already a significant health threat to a concentrated community. The letter, signed by Jenni Byrne, the 2011 Harper campaign manager, makes it sound as though supervised injection sites will mushroom out into suburban, residential communities, asking readers, "Do you want a supervised drug consumption site in your community?" and asserting that "These are facilities where drug addicts get to shoot up heroin and other illicit drugs" (Byrne 2011), suggesting that the sites will bring not only addicts but also criminal activity to ordinary citizens, and thus fuels feelings of outrage and fear that are not actually grounded in fact.

By contrast, the Canadian Medical Association's response (Eggertson 2013) reports on evidence that safe injection sites reduce crime, increase the safety of neighbourhoods where drug use is already an established problem, and promote the efforts of addicts to get off injection drugs and improve their health in other ways. Moreover, the CMA response highlights that safe injection sites improve community health and safety by lowering the rates of transmission of infections such as HIV and hepatitis C, noting that the Supreme Court had already determined in 2011 that Insite was entitled to an exemption from usual laws governing the use and supply of injectable street drugs because Insite operates in "the interests of fundamental justice" (ibid) to deliver personal security both to users and to the broader community.

Although the effects of alcohol and tobacco are, in large part, indisputable, there is less agreement about the effects of marijuana. The carcinogenic effects of marijuana are as lethal as nicotine's, but other long-term physiological effects are unknown. It appears from emergency room data that cannabis use is a significant factor in injuries and fatalities suffered in car accidents in which the driver has recently used cannabis. The CCSA 2009 paper on cannabis use and driving reports that among "drivers admitted to a regional trauma unit in Toronto, 13.9% tested positive for cannabis, [while 19.7]% of drivers killed in road crashes in Quebec were found to test positive for cannabis. An examination of fatally injured drivers in Canada between 2000 and 2006 revealed that 14.9% of those tested were positive for cannabis" (CCSA 2009: 3).

Cocaine

Cocaine is classified as a stimulant. As such, it produces feelings of excitation, alertness, and euphoria. Although such prescription stimulants as methamphetamine and dextroamphetamine are commonly abused, over the past 10 to 20 years cocaine has become the focus of societal concerns over drug abuse. Its increased use, addictive qualities, physiological effects, and worldwide distribution have fuelled the concerns. More than any other substance, cocaine has led to the present "war on drugs."

Cocaine, made from the coca plant, has been used for thousands of years, and anti-cocaine sentiment did not emerge until the early twentieth century in either the United States or Canada. In the United States, where cocaine was heavily used by urban blacks, "stereotypes about the effects of cocaine—particularly in producing 'superhuman strength, cunning and efficiency'" coincided "with a wave of repressive measures defined to ensure the subordination of blacks" (Giffen et al. 1991: 14). In Canada, it has been suggested that efforts to suppress the nonmedical use of cocaine stemmed from a highly publicized cocaine scare in Montreal and, in particular, the pioneering efforts of a probation officer of the Montreal Children's Aid Society (Giffen et al. 1991: 37, 85). In 1911, the *Opium and Drug Act* confined the legal use of cocaine and morphine to medical prescriptions; it made any other possession a criminal offence. Cocaine remains an illicit drug under the 1997 *Controlled Drugs and Substances Act* (CDSA), but its use and effects are misunderstood. For example, a 1982 *Scientific American* article suggested that cocaine was no more habit forming than potato chips (Van Dyck and Byck 1982). The percentage of Canadians reporting cocaine use is low—less than 1 percent in 2011, down from 1.9 percent reporting some use in 2004 (Health Canada 2011a).

Other Drugs

Club Drugs

These are illicit, often synthetic drugs commonly used at nightclubs or after-hours clubs, such as rave parties and speakeasies. **Club drugs** include MDMA (ecstasy), ketamine ("Special K"), LSD ("acid"), GHB ("liquid ecstasy"), and Rohypnol ("roofies"). Although popular news media have focused attention on a small number of deaths associated with ecstasy use at raves, ecstasy use is small compared with other drug

club drugs
A general term used to refer to illicit, often synthetic drugs commonly used at night clubs or all-night dances called raves.

use—less than 1 percent of the population—and its use varies with trends influencing its image and availability. Ecstasy is associated with feelings of euphoria and inner peace, yet critics argue that, as the "new cocaine," it can cause both long-term and short-term negative effects: these include permanent brain damage and hypothermia (Cloud 2000; DEA 2000).

GHB (gamma hydroxybutyrate) and Rohypnol (flunitrazepam) are often called **date-rape drugs** because of their use in rendering victims incapable of resisting sexual assaults. Rohypnol, currently illegal in both Canada and the United States, is lawfully sold in Europe and Latin America. It belongs to a class of drugs known as benzodiazepines, which also includes such common prescription drugs as Valium, Halcion, and Xanax. Rohypnol is tasteless and odourless; 1 mg of the drug can incapacitate a victim for up to 12 hours (DEA 2000; NIDA 2000b). The first major seizure of Rohypnol occurred in Canada in January 1999; 3500 doses were seized in a raid at a home in North Vancouver, British Columbia. After the raid, an RCMP spokesperson remarked: "[T]he RCMP had been under the impression, up till now, that there wasn't any Rohypnol [problem] in Canada. . . . Guess what—it's here, so we need to be concerned" (*Vancouver Sun*, January 26, 1999: A1).

Injection Drug Use

In Canada, the precise number of users who inject drugs is not known. In 1999, an estimated 34 percent of all new HIV infections stemmed from injection drug use (Auditor General 2001). Among Native peoples, the percentage of HIV infections attributable to injection drug use is especially high and has risen dramatically over time (from 29.5 percent in 1992–1996 to 52.9 percent during 1997–2001). In Canada, as in other countries, injection drug use is a major cause of the heterosexual transmission of HIV infection, hepatitis, and other infectious diseases (Health Canada 2005). The World Health Organization (2014) reports that worldwide some 16 million people are IV drug users and of those, 3 million live with HIV; moreover, the WHO reports, the IV drug use accounts for 80 percent of HIV infections in Asia and Eastern Europe. Infection prevalence such as this shows us clearly that IV drug use is not only a threat to individual users, but constitutes a larger public health problem.

Prescription Drugs

Tranquillizers and antidepressants are often used in the treatment of psychiatric disorders. For example, Prozac, Valium, and Halcion are often prescribed for the treatment of insomnia, anxiety, and depression. In Canada, women are more likely than men to use these types of drugs: 3.4 percent versus 2.0 for tranquillizers, 4.7 percent versus 2.5 percent for antidepressants, and 4.0 percent versus 2.9 percent for sleeping pills. Their use is also more common among the elderly than among the young. For example, Canadians over the age of 75 have the highest use level of sleeping pills (10.6 percent) and antidepressants (5.3 percent), while those between the ages of 65 and 74 are most likely to use tranquillizers. The divorced, separated, or widowed in Canada are also more likely to use these drugs than those who are single or married. Use of these drugs decreases as income increases (CCSA 1999). Although these drugs are most often obtained through prescription, they are frequently misused. An illegal market for them persists, and prescription misuse is common with other medications, as well.

Amphetamines are stimulants, and are legal when prescribed by a physician. Many common cold remedies contain amphetamines now used to make "crystal meth"—a street drug with skyrocketing abuse levels, especially in rural areas of Canada and the United States. Illegal use of amphetamines, made in clandestine laboratories, has been increasing. Worldwide, the production of amphetamines has increased dramatically in recent decades (World Drug Report 1997).

date-rape drugs
Drugs that are used to render victims incapable of resisting sexual assaults.

Inhalants

Common inhalants include lighter fluid, air fresheners, hair spray, glue, paint, and correction fluid. Beyond those, more than 1000 other household products are currently abused. Canadian surveys suggest that Canadians between the ages of 15 and 17 are the most likely to abuse inhalants (CCSA 1999). Regionally, solvents are used most by people in Quebec (0.2 percent), Ontario (0.1 percent), and Alberta (0.1 percent) (CCSA 1999). Solvent use is also considerably higher among Indigenous and Métis youth than among non-Indigenous populations (Gfellner and Hundelby 1995). Young people often use inhalants mistakenly believing that they are harmless or that any harm caused requires prolonged use. Inhalants are very dangerous because of their toxicity; using them may result in what is called Sudden Sniff Death Syndrome (Join Together 1998).

3.4 Societal Consequences of Drug Use and Abuse

Drugs are a social problem not only because of their adverse effects on individuals, but also as a result of the negative consequences their use has for society as a whole. Everyone is a victim of drug abuse. Drug and alcohol abuse contribute to problems within the family and to crime rates. The economic costs of drug abuse are enormous. Substance abuse and chemical dependencies also have serious consequences for the health of individuals and of populations.

Family Costs

The cost to families of drug use is incalculable. When one or both parents use or abuse drugs, needed family funds may be diverted to purchasing drugs rather than necessities. Children raised in such homes have a higher probability of neglect, behavioural disorders, and absenteeism from school; they also have lower self-concepts and face increased risk of drug abuse (AP 1999; Easley and Epstein 1991; ONDCP 2000; Tubman 1993). Drug abuse is also associated with family disintegration. For example, alcoholics are seven times more likely to separate or divorce than nonalcoholics, and as many as 40 percent of family court problems are alcohol related (Sullivan and Thompson 1994: 347).

Abuse between intimates is also linked to drug use. Research indicates that between 25 and 50 percent of men who are involved in domestic violence have substance abuse problems, and drug use contributes to 7 out of 10 cases of child maltreatment (ONDCP 2000). In a study of 320 men who were married or living with someone, twice as many reported hitting their partner only after they had been drinking, compared with those who reported the same behaviour while sober (Leonard and Blane 1992). According to Statistics Canada's Violence Against Women Survey (VAWS), a one-time survey carried out by the government of Canada in 1993, "women who are married or living with heavy drinkers are five times more likely to be assaulted by their partners than are women who live with nondrinkers" (Johnson 1996: 11). Half of all wife batterers in this survey were reported to have been drinking at the time they assaulted their wives. Women who suffered very serious abuse were approximately twice as likely to report that their spouse had been drinking at the time. The results of the VAWS indicate that "the more a man drinks the greater the likelihood that drinking will be involved in incidents of assault against his wife" (p. 1). In 2006, Statistics Canada released a new report on measurements of violence against women, and noted in the report that, along with experiences of social deprivation and/or isolation, alcohol and substance abuse remained significant contributing risk factors for violent abuse in domestic situations. These risk factors were especially apparent for Aboriginal groups, where "the breakdown of family life resulting from residential school . . . racism [and] the impact of colonialism on traditional values" (Statistics Canada 2006: 64) combined with alcohol and substance abuse to render Aboriginal women particularly vulnerable to experiencing domestic violence.

Crime and Drug Use

The relationship between crime and drug use is a complex one, and sociologists disagree as to whether drugs *cause* crime or whether criminal activity leads to drug involvement. Such a simple attribution of a causal relationship between drugs and crime may miss the point altogether; because both crime and drug use are associated with low socio-economic status, poverty may be the more powerful explanatory variable. After extensive study of the assumed drug–crime link, Gentry (1995) concludes, "the assumption that drugs and crime are causally related weakens when more representative or affluent subjects are considered" (p. 491).

In addition to the hypothesized crime–drug use link, some criminal offences are drug defined. For example, driving while intoxicated is one of the most common drug-related crimes. In 2002, Canadian police agencies reported over 82 000 incidents of impaired driving, with a death and injury rate of 7.5 per 100 000 of the population aged 16 and over (Janhevich 2003). Other criminal offences include possession, cultivation, production, and sale of controlled substances, public intoxication, and drunk and disorderly conduct. As Table 3.2 shows, in 1999, cannabis accounted for more than two-thirds of these charges and about half of the charges laid were for possession. In that year, an estimated 19 percent of offenders in the federal correctional system were serving sentences for drug offences (Auditor General 2001). In 2001, almost 92 000 drug offences were recorded by Canadian police agencies. Once again, cannabis offences were the most common, and in 2001 accounted for three out of four drug offences (Statistics Canada 2002b).

Table 3.2 **Number of Persons Charged* for Offences under the Controlled Drugs and Substances Act in Canada during 1999**

Substance	Possession	Trafficking	Importation	Cultivation	Total	Percentage
Heroin	351	800	23	–	1 174	2
Cocaine	3 375	6 990	184	–	10 549	21
Other drugs	1 797	1 561	157	–	3 515	7
Cannabis	21 381	8 112	157	4 697	34 347	70
Total	26 904	17 463	521	4 697	49 585	100
Percentage	54	35	1	10	100	

NOTE: Data report number of persons charged by most serious offence in a given incident. For example, if a person were charged with armed robbery and possession of a small quantity of drugs at the same time, the drug charge would not show up in the above figures. This policy prevents double counting of the number of persons charged.

*"Number of Persons Charged" means persons charged by police or persons whom the police recommended that charges should be laid against.

SOURCE: *Report of the Auditor General of Canada - (2001)*, Office of the Auditor General of Canada. Reproduced with the permission of the Minister of Public Works and Government Services, 2014.

The relationship between drugs, organized crime, and violence has become a major concern in Canada. Citing the conclusions of a 1998 federal government study, the Auditor General (2001: 5) notes:

> the drug trade has a significant impact on Canadians and entails substantial violence. . . . [W]ith drugs as its primary source of revenue, organized crime has intimidated police officers, judges, juries, and correctional officers. Such intimidation is a direct threat to Canada's philosophy of peace, order, and good government. Of note is that more than 150 deaths since 1994 have been attributed to "biker" wars in Quebec over control of organized crime, including the illicit drug trade.

The Auditor General's report notes that the federal Integrated Proceeds of Crime initiative, developed specifically to investigate organized crime groups, showed that 90 percent of their seizures for proceeds of criminal activity were related to the drug trade. According to the RCMP's Performance Report, the value of assets seized in 1999–2000 was $32 million (Auditor General 2001: 11).

Economic Costs

The economic costs of drug use are high. As Health Canada (1999: 184) has noted, "The 'war on drugs' currently being waged by governments around the world consumes significant government resources in an attempt to deal with drug problems." In 1996, the Canadian Centre on Substance Abuse released a study that estimated that substance abuse cost more than $18.4 billion in Canada a year, or $649 per capita. The largest economic costs of alcohol, which accounted for $7.5 billion, were for lost productivity due to sickness and premature death ($4.14 billion), followed by law enforcement ($1.36 billion) and direct health-care costs ($1.30 billion). The economic costs of tobacco amounted to more than $9.6 billion—including $6.8 billion for lost productivity and $2.68 billion for direct health-care costs. The costs of illicit drug use were estimated to be $1.4 billion, including $823 million for lost productivity due to sickness and disease and $400 million spent on the costs of law enforcement. Since then, the estimated costs of illicit drug use have gone up. For example, the RCMP estimates that the economic cost of illicit drugs alone is in the range of $8.2 billion a year in Canada and that 60 percent of all illicit drug users are between 15 and 24 years of age (RCMP 2011).

Because so much of Canada's drug strategy focuses on police attempts to curtail the supply of illicit drugs (and not to remedy the causes that push people to seek out drugs in the first place), by the end of the last century our courts were consumed by some 50 000 criminal cases related to drug offences annually, and in 1999 the courts saw some 400 000 persons appear in court in trials related to illicit drug use (Wood et al. 2003: 128). Wood and his co-authors therefore recommend that instead of focusing on criminal regulation Canada should focus on harm reduction strategies, including supervised injection sites, treatment centres for those struggling with addiction, and police efforts aimed not at sending users to jail, but directing them to harm reduction programs (p. 134).

Substance Abuse and Canada's Most Vulnerable Groups

The physical health consequences of drug use to individual users are tremendous: shortened life expectancy; higher morbidity (e.g., cirrhosis of the liver, lung cancer); exposure to HIV infection, hepatitis, and other diseases through shared needles; a weakened immune system; birth defects such as fetal alcohol syndrome; drug addiction in children; and higher death rates. Especially vulnerable are the

Aboriginal populations across Canada who have overall significantly lower levels of health than the general national population (Health Council of Canada 2006). These low levels of health correlate strongly with the presence of substance abuse in Aboriginal communities. However, substance abuse is not the cause of poor health in these populations across Canada; rather, it is part and parcel of the long-term damage to health for a group of peoples who have been subject to systemic racism, poor housing, destruction of their cultures, and systemic abuse in the institutions that had sought to "assimilate" Indigenous groups from the point of confederation to the late twentieth century. Here, we discuss the intersection of poor health, substance abuse, and policy to illuminate the unique reasons that so many Indigenous groups struggle with substance abuse and its effects in their communities.

Though popular news stories tend to focus on small communities or individuals in the Aboriginal populations as though problems with substance use were matters of personal failure, the reality is more complicated, and not a "personal trouble" at all. In particular, as research conducted by the Aboriginal Healing Association (AHA) in Canada has shown, Indigenous groups face "devastating effects [of] substance addiction, especially with regard to the impact of alcohol addiction and consequent fetal alcohol syndrome (2003: xv). But the larger point of the group's research conclusions is that **fetal alcohol syndrome** and other negative effects of alcohol on Native communities is carried across generations as a result of the harms of the residential school system rather than a result of personal weakness. The AHA explains that "the residential school system contributed to [the development of] substance abuse, but also to factors shown to be linked to alcohol abuse, such as child and adult physical, emotional and sexual abuse, mental health problems and family dysfunction" (p. xviii)

Reporting for the Canadian Centre on Substance Abuse, Dell and Lyons explain:

> The erosion of a traditional way of life has had a negative impact on Aboriginal communities, families and individuals, including multi-generational losses of homeland, traditions, language and culture. This is rooted in government legislation (including the Indian Act), systemic racism and discrimination, . . . forced relocation, placement on reserves, and the historic impact of residential schooling. These experiences have affected the health and well-being of individuals, contributing to lower social and economic status, poorer nutrition, violence, crowded living conditions and high rates of substance abuse. Although most of the information available is specific to First Nations, census data indicate that Métis share a similar socio-economic and health profile. (2007: 5)

To improve the health of these vulnerable groups of Aboriginal and Métis communities, we should be focusing not on criminal prosecution and incarceration for substance abuse (which has shown over three decades of the "war on drugs" that it is ineffective and can make matters worse) but instead on the improvement of health and harm reduction services, community cohesion, and supports for families. To do this, we need, in part, to make sure that there are better services in the rural areas where many Aboriginal and Métis people live—because, as Dell and Lyons note, when people are forced to travel long distances to get services other things are negatively impacted, such as increased costs for transportation, childcare, and lost income from missed work, as well as the absence of members from the families where, substance use problems notwithstanding, they still have responsibilities (p. 13). Dell and Lyons further note that substance use among these populations is "not the 'problem' but rather, the symptom of much broader ills faced by First Nations, Inuit and Métis in Canada" (p. 15). Solutions, they argue,

fetal alcohol syndrome (FAS)
A birth defect syndrome apparently caused by prenatal alcohol exposure. Always involves brain damage, impaired growth, and head and face anomalies.

will be most effective when they are local, respectful of traditions and cultures of Aboriginal people, non-punitive, and minimize disruption to the work and family life of people seeking treatment.

The approach that many researchers, including Dell and Lyons, are taking to the complex issues that contribute to substance abuse is referred to as an "intersectional" orientation. An intersectional approach may enhance any sociological theoretical orientation and/or method by accounting for the ways that multiple variables must be treated as co-existent features that cannot be removed from account in either the design or interpretation of a study. An intersectional orientation understands what Evelyn Simien refers to as "the simultaneity of oppression" (2007: 264), meaning that in such an orientation to how we design our studies, our methods, and our conclusions, we must account for how the features that mark people's lives—things like race, class, ethnicity, occupation, geographic situation, gender, sexuality, age, and so on—impact on the experiences they have, the choices available, and the decisions they make as a result. For Aboriginal and Métis substance abuse patterns, Dell and Lyons found that one could not expect harm reduction centres to succeed if they were not easily accessible in terms of both hours of operation and location. They also found that if a punitive model were to be imposed on mothers, threatening them with the loss of their families, then they would avoid seeking help for substance abuse problems (2007: 14). A more successful approach will allow children to accompany their mothers into treatment, perhaps even providing supports to those children (ibid).

In other words, we cannot expect women who are mothers simply to stop being mothers in order to receive treatment. Moreover, if we treat the history of state interference in family life for Aboriginal groups as though it had not destroyed the lives of thousands of children over decades of residential schooling, then we discount the legitimate fears that mothers have regarding the potential loss of their children to a system that lacks respect for Native culture and traditions, for language and family structure, and which treats all Native persons as though they were inferior to members of the so-called "founding cultures" of francophone and anglophone Canada.

Ameliorating the problems of substance abuse in Aboriginal and other marginalized populations, then, will require close and respectful collaborations that take into account the multiple oppressions that these vulnerable groups experience, and which place them at higher risk for substance abuse problems in the first place.

Substance Abuse and Mental Health

Heavy alcohol and drug use are also associated with negative consequences for an individual's mental health. Longitudinal data on both male and female adults have shown that drug users are more likely to suffer from anxiety disorders, such as phobias, depression, and antisocial personalities (White and Labouvie 1994). Other data confirm that drug users, particularly in adolescence, have a higher incidence of suicide (Bureau of Justice Statistics 1992; Cooper et al. 1992). Marijuana is also linked to short-term memory loss, learning disabilities, motivational deficits, and retarded emotional development.

The societal costs of drug-induced health concerns are also extraordinary. Health costs include the cost of disability insurance, the effects of second-hand smoke, the spread of AIDS, and the medical costs of accident and crime victims, as well as unhealthy infants and children. For example, cocaine use by pregnant women may lead to low-birth-weight babies, increased risk of miscarriage, and abnormal placental functioning (Klutt 2000).

3.5 **Treatment Alternatives**

Drug treatment reduces drug use by about 40 to 60 percent and is as effective as treating many other chronic diseases, notably diabetes and asthma (NIDA 1999: 15). Helping others to overcome chemical dependency is, however, expensive. For example, Health Canada's National Native Alcohol and Drug Abuse Program spends about $80 million annually on substance abuse treatment and prevention for on-reserve Aboriginal people, with the majority of these funds used in relation to alcohol abuse (Auditor General 2001). Persons who are interested in overcoming chemical dependency have several treatment alternatives from which to choose. Some options include hospitalization, family therapy, counselling, private and public treatment facilities, behaviour modification, pharmacotherapy (use of treatment medications), community care programs, drug maintenance programs, and employee assistance programs. Two commonly used techniques are inpatient/outpatient programs and supportive communities.

Inpatient/Outpatient Treatment

Inpatient treatment refers "to the treatment of drug dependence in a hospital and includes medical supervision of detoxification" (McCaffrey 1998: 2). Most inpatient programs last between 30 and 90 days and target individuals whose withdrawal symptoms require close monitoring (e.g., alcoholics, cocaine addicts). Some drug-dependent patients, however, can be safely treated as outpatients. Outpatient treatment allows individuals to remain in their home and work environments and is often less expensive. In outpatient treatment, the patient is under the care of a physician who evaluates the patient's progress regularly, prescribes needed medication, and watches for signs of a relapse.

The longer a patient stays in treatment, the greater the likelihood of a successful recovery. Variables that predict success include the user's motivation to change, support of family and friends, criminal justice or employer intervention, a positive relationship with therapeutic staff, and a program of recovery that addresses many of the patient's needs.

Peer Support Groups

Twelve-Step Programs

Both Alcoholics Anonymous (AA) and Narcotics Anonymous (NA) are voluntary associations whose only membership requirement is the desire to stop drinking or taking drugs. AA and NA are self-help groups in that they are operated by nonprofessionals, offer "sponsors" to each new member, and proceed along a continuum of 12 steps to recovery. Members are immediately immersed in a fellowship of caring individuals with whom they meet daily or weekly to affirm their commitment. Some have argued that AA and NA members trade their addictions for feelings of interpersonal connectedness; they bond with other group members.

Symbolic interactionists emphasize that AA and NA provide social contexts in which people develop new meanings. Abusers are surrounded by others who convey positive labels, encouragement, and social support for sobriety. Sponsors tell the new members that they can be successful in controlling alcohol and drugs "one day at a time" and provide regular interpersonal reinforcement for doing so. Although thought of as a "crutch" by some, AA members may also take medications to help prevent relapses. In a study of 222 AA members, Rychtarik and colleagues (2000) found that although over half of those surveyed thought the use of relapse-preventing medication was or might be a good idea, 29 percent reported pressures from others to stop taking the medication.

Therapeutic Communities

In **therapeutic communities**, which house between 35 and 500 people for up to 15 months, participants abstain from drugs, develop marketable skills, and receive counselling. Synanon, established in 1958, was the first therapeutic community for alcoholics and was later expanded to include other drug users. The longer a person stays at such a facility, the greater the chance of overcoming the dependency. Symbolic interactionists argue that behavioural changes appear to be a consequence of revised self-definition and the positive expectations of others.

therapeutic communities
Organizations in which 35 to 100 individuals reside for up to 15 months to abstain from drugs, develop marketable skills, and receive counselling.

In the United States, Stay'N Out, a therapeutic community for the treatment of incarcerated drug offenders, has demonstrated success in reducing recidivism. After participating in the program for at least nine months, only 23 percent of the inmates reoffended, compared with 50 percent of those not receiving treatment. The Cornerstone Program has also been successful with drug abusers in prison. Both programs include a holistic treatment approach that focuses on the social and psychological difficulties of returning to acceptable social roles (Lipton 1994: 336).

Canada, however, lacks therapeutic communities for the treatment of incarcerated drug users outside Quebec, which runs both the ECHO and STOP programs. Instead, two core substance abuse programs are offered by Corrections Canada: the Offender Substance Pre-release Program (which involves about 32 three-hour counselling sessions offered over several months) and Choices (a cognitive-behavioural modification program that calls for about 60 hours of counselling over three to four months).

3.6 Strategies for Action: Canada Responds

Drug use is a complex social issue exacerbated by the structural and cultural forces of society that contribute to its existence. While the structure of society perpetuates a system of inequality creating in some the need to escape, the culture of society, through the media and normative contradictions, sends mixed messages about the acceptability of drug use. As a result, developing programs, laws, or initiatives that are likely to end drug use may be unrealistic. Nevertheless, since 1987, Canada's Drug Strategy has emphasized the need for a "balanced" approach that combines prevention and education with law enforcement. Among its stated objectives are these: "reducing the demand for drugs; reducing drug-related mortality and morbidity by reducing high-risk behaviours, such as spreading HIV/AIDS through needle sharing; improving the effectiveness of and accessibility to substance abuse information and interventions; restricting the supply of illicit drugs; reducing the profitability of illicit trafficking; and reducing the costs of substance abuse to Canadian society" (Auditor General 2001).

Managing the illicit drug problem in Canada is inherently difficult. It requires the efforts of three levels of government—federal, provincial/territorial, and municipal—and many non-government organizations. Although integrating the efforts of three levels of government is difficult, it is essential.

Report of the Auditor General of Canada—2001

In recent years, most of the federal government's changes to legislation in relation to illicit drugs have targeted supply rather than demand. These efforts have included the amendment of the Canadian *Criminal Code* to include organized crime offences and the creation of the Financial Transactions and Reports Analysis Centre of Canada. The latter attempts to detect money laundering by monitoring financial transactions (see Table 3.3).

Table 3.3 *Addressing Illegal Drugs: The Federal Infrastructure*

Federally, 11 departments and agencies are involved in addressing illicit drug use in Canada. The major ones are:

Health Canada	Provides the leadership and coordination for Canada's Drug Strategy. It is involved directly in activities to reduce the demand for and the supply of illicit drugs. Its Office of Controlled Substances is responsible for the legislative control framework to control illicit drugs. The office administers the regulations of the *Controlled Drugs and Substances Act*, which includes processing the licensing and permit requirement for the use of controlled substances for legitimate purposes. The Office of Cannabis Medical Access deals with controls on the medical use of marijuana.
Solicitor General Canada	Plays a leadership and coordinating role in policing, security and corrections under Canada's Drug Strategy. The Department is also engaged in related activities both domestically and internationally.
RCMP	The RCMP's federal drug efforts focus on such activities as seizing drugs, investigating and arresting the upper echelon of criminal organizations involved in the drug trade, and seizing proceeds of crime. The RCMP also undertakes drug enforcement as part of the provincial and municipal policing responsibilities it performs on contract. In addition to participation in many "joint force operations" aimed at combating organized crime, the RCMP also delivers drug prevention programs. It makes some 8000 presentations annually to students, parents, employees, and community groups.
Department of Justice	Prosecutes drug cases and provides expertise to the development of legislation addressing organized crime. It has a pilot initiative, the Toronto Drug Treatment Court Program, that offers alternatives to traditional prosecution.
Canada Border Services Agency	Contributes to reducing the supply of illicit drugs in two ways. Customs intercepts illegal drugs entering Canada at our borders. For instance, it estimates that in 1999 it seized illicit drugs with a street value estimated at $351 million. Taxation audits individuals suspected of selling illicit drugs or engaging in other illegal activities and raises assessments and levies penalties where it finds unreported income. Taxation also investigates suspected tax evasion and recommends prosecution of individuals.
Correctional Services Canada	Is responsible for offenders serving criminal sentences over two years. These include individuals convicted of serious drug offences. CSC provides substance abuse and treatment programs to offenders with drug problems. It also uses security measures, including the use of sniffer dogs and urinalysis testing, to control the supply of illicit drugs in prisons.
Department of Foreign Affairs and International Trade	Collaborates with other federal departments and represents Canada in the international aspects of Canada's Drug Strategy.

SOURCE: *Report of the Auditor General of Canada - (2001)*, Office of the Auditor General of Canada. Reproduced with the permission of the Minister of Public Works and Government Services, 2014.

Government Regulations

Drawing upon Solomon (1999), we will review some of the major federal and provincial alcohol and drug laws.

In Canada, the federal government regulates the importation and exportation of alcohol products, alcohol-related excise taxes, and broadcast advertising. At present, the federal regulations prohibit broadcasting a range of messages, including those that encourage non-drinkers to consume alcohol; that direct their appeal to minors; that suggest alcohol use is positively associated with social acceptance, personal accomplishment, or success in athletic or business endeavours; or that link the consumption of alcohol with high-risk activities.

In addition, the provinces have some degree of control over the marketing and advertising of alcohol, including such market practices as price discounting, drinking contests, the use of alcohol as prizes, or the dispensing of free drinks. The majority of provincial advertising regulations target lifestyle advertising that might otherwise encourage youths to drink, drink large amounts of alcohol, or drink and drive. Each province in Canada also regulates the control and sale of alcohol within it. Currently, the legal drinking age in all Canadian provinces and territories is 19 except in Quebec, Manitoba, and Alberta where the minimum age is 18.

Harm Reduction

In September 2003, following the election of Mayor Larry Campbell, a former RCMP officer and city coroner (and the inspiration for the CBC drama *DaVinci's Inquest*), the city of Vancouver opened North America's first safe injection site (SIS). The site is popularly perceived as an endorsement and encouragement of drug use, but the reality is that site policies do not allow non-users to access safe injection sites in order to have a new experience. Instead, the goal is to have a positive impact on the reduction of disease and death related to intravenous drug use. In the years from 1992 to 1993, more than 2000 people died from overdose in Vancouver, and the director of the B.C. Centre for Excellence in HIV/AIDS notes that in the absence of such sites, "approximately 30 per cent of addicts are HIV positive and more than 90 per cent have hepatitis C virus" (in Thomson 2003). Vancouver decided to open its first SIS because data from 27 cities in Europe and Australia showed "a profound reduction in overdose deaths and the spread of diseases like HIV and hepatitis C, and a dramatic reduction in the open drug scene" (City of Vancouver 2003). SISs, then, do not promote drug use, but serve as part of a broader public health policy that recognizes the threat of drug use to the health not only of users, but of the broader community as well.

The Vancouver policy and Mayor Campbell were criticized harshly by conservative politicians in both Canada and the United States, with "top anti-drug officials in the United States [saying] Canada is going soft on the war on drugs" (*Economist* 2003). Nonetheless, B.C. Health Officer Dr. Perry Kendall reports that in each of its first two years of operation, the SIS in East Vancouver prevented close to 200 deaths by overdose (Canadian Press Service 2005). The site continues to be controversial, and subject to the vagaries of political funding models. As of 2010, the site is permitted to continue operations following a British Columbia Appeals Court ruling against the Attorney General. The B.C. decision determined that the operation of Insite is a provincial health matter and that the federal government has no interest in the operations or future structure of the service (Vancouver Coastal Health 2010).

Provincial highway traffic legislation gives police the authority to stop vehicles in a random manner to determine whether the driver has been drinking; the provinces also have the authority to issue, suspend, revoke, and reinstate driving licences. The majority of Canadian provinces have created provisions for automatic provincial licence suspensions so that a person convicted of any federal drinking and driving offence is subject to an automatic mandatory provincial licence suspension. The length of the suspension for a first, second, or subsequent conviction varies in the different provinces and territories. For example, in Manitoba, a 12-month suspension is given for a first offence and a five-year suspension for a second; in Alberta and Saskatchewan, the respective time periods are one and two years; and in Yukon, three months and a year. Moreover, with the exception of Nova Scotia and Quebec, provincial legislation authorizes police to temporarily suspend a driver's licence at roadside if, for example, a driver refuses an officer's demand to provide a breath sample or registers a BAC of 0.05 or higher. In the majority of provinces, the duration of the suspension is 24 hours. Six provinces have enacted additional legislation that authorizes police to impose 90-day administrative licence suspensions (ALS) on those who register a BAC over 0.08 percent or refuse to provide a breath or blood sample.

The provinces have also created several drinking-and-driving countermeasures. These include graduated licence programs for new drivers, which require that they abstain from drinking any alcohol prior to driving; vehicle impoundment programs to deter offenders from driving while prohibited or suspended; alcohol interlock programs, which involve the connection of a small breath-testing instrument to a vehicle that prevents it from being started or driven if the driver's BAC is over a preset limit; and mandatory remedial measures that require offenders, for example, to attend an alcohol awareness program for a first offence or, for a second or subsequent offence, undergo alcohol assessment or participate in a treatment program. The cost of participating in such programs is generally borne by the offender.

In Canada, the *Controlled Drugs and Substances Act* outlines the six federal criminal offences: possession, trafficking, possession for the purpose of trafficking, production, importing or exporting, and "prescription shopping." While the penalties for possession vary depending on the type of drug, the maximum penalties under this act for the majority of offences are severe. For example, for "Schedule I Drugs"—cocaine, heroin, opium, phencyclidine, and those drugs that, prior to May 1997, were dealt with under the *Narcotics Control Act*—the maximum penalty for trafficking, possession for the purpose of trafficking, producing, and importing and exporting is life imprisonment. Life imprisonment is also the maximum penalty for importing or exporting any amount of any form of cannabis.

Despite all the attempts to regulate the use of alcohol and drugs, some would argue that the war on drugs has done more harm than good. Duke and Gross (1994) argue that the war on drugs, much like Prohibition, has only intensified other social problems: drug-related gang violence and turf wars, the creation of syndicate-controlled black markets, unemployment, the spread of AIDS, overcrowded prisons, corrupt law enforcement officials, and the diversion of police from other serious crimes. Consistent with conflict theory, still others argue that the "war on drugs" is a war on the poor, while the drug use of the affluent goes largely ignored (Duster 1995). Herbert Gans explained the irony of institutions having vested interests in the continuation of social problems faced by the poor in his famous essay "The Uses of Poverty: The Poor Pay All." In the essay, Gans observes that for all the costs of social problems, they serve a benefit to those in power. Gans's argument rests on exposing the manner in which the poor are used as political scapegoats in order to justify a wide range of social, charity, surveillance, and penal system professions: "penology would be minuscule without the poor, as would the police. Other activities and groups that flourish because of the existence of poverty are the numbers game, the sale of heroin and cheap wines and liquors" (Gans 1971: 21). In the essay, Gans goes on to explain that, furthermore, those in socially powerful positions—including doctors, lawyers, social workers, and judges—depend on the persistence of poverty and its associated "rehabilitation" requirements for their professional and social prestige.

Deregulation or Legalization: The Debate

Deregulation is the reduction of government control over certain drugs. For example, Ontario has opened up the sale of wine to private stores. Since 1999, Canadians who require marijuana for medical purposes have been able to apply for an exemption under Section 56 of the *Controlled Drugs and Substances Act*. In 2002, more than 800 Canadians were permitted by Health Canada to possess marijuana for medical purposes. Moreover, the Marijuana Medical Access Regulations (MMAR) allow people with authorizations to possess and cultivate marijuana for medical purposes (McLellan 2002). Extending this approach, in April 1999 the board of directors of the Association of Canadian Police Chiefs recommended to the federal government that simple possession of marijuana and hashish be decriminalized—that is, that it no

deregulation
The reduction of government control of, for example, certain drugs.

longer be an offence under the *Criminal Code*. The board suggested that this strategy would clear a backlog of drug cases in the courts and allow Canadian police services to focus their resources on more serious crimes, such as drug trafficking (Fife 1999); however, the CCSA reports that even in the face of these recommendations, the number of youth charged in 2003 with possession of cannabis had tripled from the number charged in 1993, moving from 1047 to 3294 (CCSA 2007: 24). In part, the increase has to do with the increased production and availability of cannabis, but it has also to do with increased surveillance in schools. The CCSA observes:

> It is relatively common for school principals to collaborate with police forces in an attempt to curb drug use and trafficking within educational institutions. This collaboration takes many forms, but typically it means allowing police to carry out a raid to arrest some small-scale cannabis dealers or users, handing students caught by staff over to the police, or encouraging students to inform on each other. These tough responses aim first of all at sending a no-tolerance message to students and reassuring parents about the principal's attitude toward drug use. While collaboration with police generally succeeds in achieving these goals, very few dealers or users are actually arrested in this way. (2007: 25)

Decriminalization, by contrast, would promote a medical rather than criminal approach to drug use, and would encourage users to seek treatment and adopt preventive practices. Going a step further, proponents for the **legalization** of drugs affirm the right of adults to make an informed choice. They also argue that the tremendous revenues realized from drug taxes could be used to benefit all citizens, that purity and safety controls could be implemented, and that legalization would expand the number of distributors, thereby increasing competition and reducing prices. Drugs would be safer, drug-related crimes would be reduced, and production and distribution of previously controlled substances would be taken out of the hands of the underworld.

Opponents of legalization argue that it would be construed as government approval of drug use and, consequently, drug experimentation and abuse would increase. Further, although the legalization of drugs would result in substantial revenues for the government, drug trafficking and black markets would still flourish due to some drugs, notably crack, remaining illegal. Legalization would also require an extensive and costly bureaucracy to regulate the manufacture, sale, and distribution of drugs. Finally, the position that drug use is an individual's right cannot guarantee that others will not be harmed. It is illogical to assume that a greater availability of drugs will translate into a safer society.

Collective Action

Social action groups such as MADD have successfully lobbied legislators to lower maximum blood alcohol levels for drivers and to introduce zero allowable blood alcohol for young drivers. MADD, with 3.5 million members and 600 chapters in North America, has also put pressure on alcohol establishments to stop "two-for-one" offers and has pushed for laws that hold the bartenders personally liable if a served person is later involved in an alcohol-related accident. Even hosts in private homes can now be held liable if they allow someone who became impaired while drinking at their house to drive. Most important, perhaps, MADD seeks to change the meaning of alcohol use by, for example, redefining drunk driving "accidents" as violent crimes.

Sensitized to the danger of driving while impaired, some high-school principals and school boards have encouraged students to become members of SADD (Students Against Drunk Driving). Members often sign formal pledges and put emblems on their cars to signify a commitment against alcohol. "Dry grads" also encourage students

decriminalization
The removal of criminal penalties for a behaviour, as in the decriminalization of drug use.

legalization
Making prohibited behaviour legal; for example, legalizing marijuana or prostitution.

to refrain from drinking alcohol. To reduce the number of teenagers driving while drinking, local groups of parents have also organized parties at bowling alleys or school gyms as alternatives to high-school graduation parties.

Understanding Alcohol and Other Drugs

In summarizing what we know about substance abuse, drugs and their use are socially defined. As the structure of society changes, the acceptability of one drug or another changes as well. As conflict theorists assert, the status of a drug as legal or illegal is intricately linked to those who have the power to define acceptable and unacceptable drug use. There is also little doubt that rapid social change, anomie, alienation, and inequality further drug use and abuse. Symbolic interactionism plays a significant role in the process, as well—if people are labelled as "drug users" and expected to behave accordingly, drug use is likely to continue. If there is positive reinforcement of drug use or a biological predisposition to use them, the probability of drug involvement is even higher. Thus, the theories of drug use complement rather than contradict one another.

Drug use must also be conceptualized within the social context in which it occurs. In a study of high-risk youths who had become involved with drugs, Dembo and colleagues (1994) suggest that many youths in their study had been "failed by society":

> Many of them were born into economically-strained circumstances, often raised by families who neglected or abused them, or in other ways did not provide for their nurturance and wholesome development. . . . Few youths in our sample received the mental health and substance abuse treatment services they needed. (p. 25)

However, many treatment alternatives, emanating from a clinical model of drug use, assume that the origin of the problem lies within the individual rather than in the structure and culture of society. Although admittedly the problem may lie within the individual at the time treatment occurs, policies that address the social causes of drug abuse provide a better means of dealing with the drug problem in Canada.

Prevention is preferable to intervention, and given the social portrait of hard drug users—young, male, minority—prevention must entail dealing with the social conditions that foster drug use. Some data suggest that marginal youth are particularly vulnerable to drug involvement because of their lack of legitimate alternatives (Van Kammen and Loeber 1994):

> Illegal drug use may be a way to escape the strains of the severe urban conditions and dealing illegal drugs may be one of the few, if not the only, ways to provide for material needs. Intervention and treatment programs, therefore, should include efforts to find alternate ways to deal with the limiting circumstances of inner-city life, as well as create opportunities for youngsters to find more conventional ways of earning a living. (p. 22)

However, social policies dealing with drug use have been predominantly punitive rather than preventive.

In Canada and throughout the world, millions of people depend on legal drugs for the treatment of a variety of conditions, including pain, anxiety and nervousness, insomnia, depression, and fatigue. Although drugs used for these purposes are relatively harmless, the cultural message "better living through chemistry" contributes to alcohol and drug use and their consequences. These and other drugs are embedded in a political and economic context that determines who defines what drugs, in what amounts, are licit or illicit, and what programs are developed in reference to them.

Student Reflection: What Do You Know Now?

This chapter has proposed that we can consider many determinants to social problems involving alcohol, tobacco, marijuana, and other drugs. Which theories best explain drug addiction? If you were a symbolic interactionist, for example, what would it take in terms of changes to social definitions in order to "eliminate" a drug problem? Different theoretical frameworks help us to understand the role of individuals and societies in perpetuating or solving these social problems. Having considered critically a number of strategies, in what new ways can you make sense of your own social lives, your own neighbourhoods, and connections to a provincial, national, and indeed global system of meanings and effects?

What Do You Do Next?

Located at www.nelson.com/socialproblems5e

- Consolidate your knowledge with interactive and printable **Flashcards**
- Gauge your understanding with **Practice Quizzes** and **Matching Activities**
- Develop your critical thinking skills with **Self and Society** and **The Human Side** questions
- Analyze **Social Research** and **Social Problems in Global Perspective**
- Explore the implications of **Technology on Social Problems**

4

Crime and Violence

Student Reflection: What Do You Already Know?

If we are to believe news reports and government projects, it would appear that crime is on the rise, including murder. We've all heard about how a certain part of town is getting sketchier, or how dangerous it can be to walk alone both night and day. Plenty of people are taken in by the claim that we need to be tougher on crime because violence is on the rise. Are these claims borne out by the data, however? What have you observed about crime that makes you wonder about where the statistics are coming from? Many of you may have guessed by now that there is more to the question than individual failings.

Learning Outcomes

Through careful reading of this chapter, you should be able to:

- define the bolded key terms
- understand the sources of crime statistics as well as the sources of our assumptions about crime and criminals
- situate crime and violence in social contexts, such as punishments, roles, demographics, and communities
- apply sociological theories to understand and respond to crime and violence

© Pete Sherrard/iStockphoto.com

4.1 A Theory of Justice

For years, popular commentators, religious figures, and politicians have blamed various activities (dancing, listening to popular music, watching WWF wrestling) and public figures (Ludwig van Beethoven, Elvis Presley, Marilyn Manson) for the corruption of youth and dissolution of social values. Olmsted (1988) has noted that, in the past, such diverse pastimes as billiards, parachuting, surfing, pinball, attending the theatre, amateur archaeology, horse racing, butterfly collecting, motorcycling, target shooting, and ballroom dancing have all been identified as morally disreputable and socially problematic activities.

This chapter examines the criminal justice system as well as theories, types, and demographic patterns of criminal behaviour. It also addresses the conceptual problem of understanding why what counts as "crime" changes over time and place. We also examine the economic, social, and psychological costs of crime and violence. The chapter concludes with a discussion of social policies and prevention programs designed to reduce crime and violence in Canada.

Although criminal patterns and justice systems share similar attributes throughout the world, dramatic differences exist in international crime and violence rates. Though the phenomenon may have more to do with having elaborate criminal reporting systems than with actually having higher rates of problematic or harmful behaviours, in general, industrialized countries have higher rates of reported crime than do non-industrialized countries. It is easier to know for certain whether there are differences in harmful behaviours for countries with systems for reporting and dealing with criminal activity. Indeed, we see that industrialized countries have very different patterns of criminal activity.

United Nations statistics on intentional homicide, for example, show that the U.S. murder rate for 2011 is 4.7 per 100 000, compared to Canada's rate of 1.5 per 100 000, and is significantly higher than the U.K. rate, last measured in 2011, of 1.0 per 100 000. These differences are roughly consistent over the last two decades (UNODC 2011); see Figure 4.1. It is important to know that although these rates can fluctuate from year to year, the trends in one direction or another are roughly stable. The UNODC study on homicide in 58 countries offers an explanation for the patterns in rates, noting that higher murder rates correspond with higher rates of robbery reported in crime victimization surveys (UNODC 2011: 16). That we see higher rates of robbery in countries with higher levels of economic inequality in their populations is not surprising. In other words, greater economic disparities led to higher rates of violent crimes that include robbery and murder, while lower rates for both these types of crime correspond with higher levels of economic equality.

Recent data on homicide rates in Canada show that "Since 1961, ... there have been two distinct trends. Following a period of stability between 1961 and 1966, the homicide rate more than doubled over the next ten years, reaching a peak of 3.03 homicide victims per 100,000 population in 1975. Since 1975, the rate has gradually declined, with some year-to-year fluctuations. However, the 2006 rate remains higher than rates in the early 1960s" (Li 2007: 2). Moreover, it is a myth that homicide is a random act with no social determinants at work; Canadian data for 2006 continue to show that in 83 percent of cases homicide victims knew their attackers: a little more than one-third were killed by a family member, and another third were killed by an acquaintance, while an additional 12 percent were killed by someone known to them through criminal activities (Li 2007: 1). Poverty, isolation, family breakdown, and domestic violence all are distinct factors in these killings, and this chapter discusses the manner in which larger social problems such as these influence crime.

Several facts about crime are true throughout the world. First, crime is ubiquitous—there is no country without crime. Second, most countries have the same components in

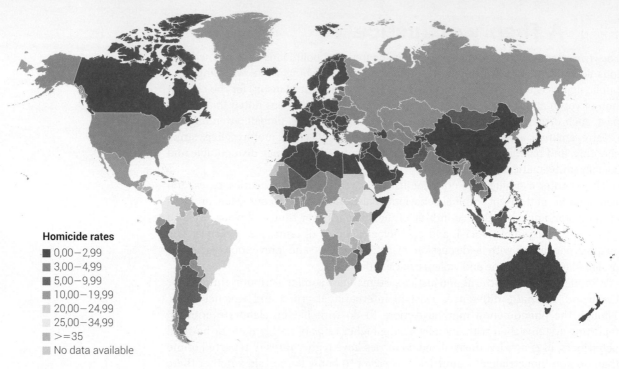

Homicide rates

- ■ 0,00–2,99
- ■ 3,00–4,99
- ■ 5,00–9,99
- ■ 10,00–19,99
- ■ 20,00–24,99
- ■ 25,00–34,99
- ■ >=35
- ■ No data available

NOTE: The boundaries and names shown and the designations used on this map do not imply official endorsement or acceptance by the United Nations.

Figure 4.1 *Homicide Rates by Select Countries, 2011*

SOURCE: Adapted from the UNODC Global Study on Homicide 2013.

their criminal justice systems: police, courts, and prisons. Third, adult males make up the largest category of crime suspects worldwide. Fourth, in all countries, theft—a property crime—is the most common crime committed, whereas violent crime is relatively rare.

Violent crime and property crimes represent only two types that occur worldwide. Although we are concerned with these types and their attendant potential for victimization, INTERPOL, the international police agency, has identified six global priority areas (INTERPOL 2011): (1) drugs and criminal organizations, including drug trafficking, (2) financial and high-tech crimes such as counterfeiting, fraud, and cybercrime, (3) trafficking of fugitives, (4) public safety and countering terrorism, (5) trafficking in human beings, and (6) fighting corruption, or, in other words, enforcing the rule of law. Each of these priority areas contains a relatively new category of crime: **transnational crime**: "organized criminal activity across one or more national borders" (U.S. Department of Justice 2003). Shelley (2007) argues that we must take transnational crime seriously:

> Transnational crime will be a defining issue of the 21st Century for policy makers—as defining the Cold War was for the 20th century and colonialism was for the 19th. Terrorists and transnational crime groups will proliferate because these crime groups are major beneficiaries of globalization. They take advantage of increased travel, trade, rapid money movements, telecommunications and computer links, and are well-positioned for growth. (p. 1)

For example, the internet has led to an explosive growth in child pornography—and easy international transmission, as shown in the recent indictment of Benjamin Levin, former deputy minister of education for Ontario from 2004–09. Levin was arrested and charged in July 2013, and his case remains in front of courts as of the writing of this

transnational crime
Criminal activity that occurs across one or more international borders. Can include movement of exploitative images and text via the internet.

edition of *Understanding Social Problems*. His arrest was precipitated by New Zealand authorities who brought some of his online activities to the attention of Canadian investigators (CBC News 2013). Levin, who is employed by the University of Toronto and holds a Canada Research Chair position there, had travelled the world working as an educational consultant, and had made several trips to New Zealand over the last several years (ibid). Levin has been charged with two counts of "distributing child pornography" and one count of "counselling to commit an indictable offence," and is also charged with "agreeing to, or arranging, a sexual offence against a child under 16" (ibid). The evidence against Levin has resulted in bail conditions awaiting trial that include not being permitted access to the internet (Rushowy 2013).

In 2005, a United Nations expert on child pornography told the UN Commission on Human Rights that governments had to act to curb the proliferation of child pornography (Klapper 2005). Increased attention to the issue has led not only to the arrest of Benjamin Levin, but also to other, larger arrests. In 2010, more than 50 people were arrested in an international pornography ring that ". . . at its peak had more than 1,000 members trading millions of sexually explicit images [of children]" (Wilson 2010: 1).

Human trafficking is another example of transnational crime. According to the Polaris Project, 12.5 million people in the world have been victims of human trafficking (Polaris Project 2011). Of that number, the U.S. Department of State (2008) estimates that 80 percent are women and girls, and that 50 percent are minors. Although the majority of those trafficked are commercially exploited in the sex trade, others are trafficked into sexual servitude, forced labour, and into use as child soldiers.

4.2 Sources of Crime Statistics

From the *National Symbol of Canada Act*, which identifies the beaver as symbolic of Canadian sovereignty, to the *Income Tax Act*, whose rules and regulations are bound in an almost 2000-page volume amended yearly, our social life is bound together by laws. Although there are 40 000 federal and provincial statutes and a broad range of municipal bylaws that define behaviour in violation of some penal law, "[u]nder the terms of the *Constitution Act*, only those offences defined by federal law can technically be called crimes" (Brantingham et al. 1995). Unlike the United States, which has many state criminal codes, Canada has a single criminal code. Most of the behaviours that we would commonly recognize as crimes (e.g., assault, kidnapping, sexual assault, murder) are contained within the federal *Criminal Code*.

A simple definition of **crime** would be "any act that violates the criminal law." For a violation to be a crime, however, the offender must have acted voluntarily and with intent and have no legally acceptable excuse or justification for the behaviour. Three major types of statistics are used to measure crime: official statistics, victimization surveys, and self-report offender surveys.

crime
The violation of norms that are written into law.

Official Statistics

Since the establishment of the first modern police force, the London Metropolitan Police Force (Scotland Yard) in 1829, police agencies have collected information about crime. Systematic national police statistics have been collected since 1857 in England and Wales, since 1920 in Canada, and since 1930 in the United States (Brantingham et al. 1995). Since 1962, Canada has used a system called the Canadian Uniform Crime Reporting Survey (UCR), developed by Statistics Canada and the Canadian Association of Chiefs of Police "to provide a measure of reliability for crime statistics through providing police agencies with a standardized set of procedures for collecting and reporting crime information" (Evans and Himelfarb 2000).

The UCR system collects information monthly from more than 400 municipal police departments, services, and agencies across Canada on 91 specific categories of crime and offences. This information is compiled and published each year with counts and calculated rates per 100 000 population presented for each province and territory, and for Canada as a whole. Within the UCR, crimes known to the police are grouped into major categories. For example, "Crimes of Violence" groups together such acts as homicide, attempted homicide, assault, abduction, sexual assault, and robbery. "Property Offences" includes such offences as breaking and entering, theft of motor vehicles, possession of stolen goods, and fraud. The UCR additionally provides information on the numbers of persons charged with different types of offences, with separate counts for adults and youths, males and females. The crimes known to police are compiled and published annually in Canada by the Canadian Centre for Justice Statistics (CCJS), the operational arm of the National Justice Statistics Initiative (NJSI).

These statistics have several shortcomings (DiIulio 1999) (see the *Social Problems Research Up Close* feature later in this chapter). Not only do many incidents of crime go unreported, but police also fail to record all the crime reports they receive. Alternatively, some rates may be exaggerated. Motivation for such distortions may come from the public (e.g., demanding that something be done) or from political or organizational pressures (e.g., budget requests). For example, a police department may "crack down" on drug-related crimes in a given year. The result is an increase in the recorded number of these offences. Such an increase reflects a change in the behaviour of law enforcement personnel, not a change in the number of drug violations. Thus, official crime statistics may be a better indicator of what police are doing than what criminals are doing.

Victimization Surveys

Victimization surveys ask people if they have been victims of crime. Although the first victimization surveys were carried out in the United States in 1966 for the President's Commission on Law Enforcement and Administration of Justice, victimization surveys in Canada have a much shorter history. As Fattah (1991) observes, "[n]o truly national victimization survey was done in Canada until the General Social Survey was carried out by Statistics Canada in 1988." For Statistics Canada's 1999 General Social Survey (GSS), 26 000 people aged 15 and older were interviewed by telephone and asked if they had been victimized by crime and, if so, where and when the crime had occurred and whether or not it had been reported to the police. Respondents were also queried on their perceptions of the level of crime in their neighbourhood, their personal fear of crime, and their views on the criminal justice system (Tufts 2000).

As we have already indicated, youth tend to be vilified in popular consciousness and in the media as increasingly dangerous and violent, even though the data on youth crime do not support this negative view. What is important and often overlooked is that youth are at risk for victimization in crimes, and understanding why requires that we look at the correlations between youth behaviours and their victimization:

> According to police-reported data, in 2003, the risk of violent victimization for children and youth increased as the child ages. Rates of violent victimization for male and female victims remain relatively similar up until the age of 8, after which male rates exceed those of females. The rate of victimization for female victims increases through the teenage years to peak at 2,463 assaults per 100,000 population at age 15. For male victims, rates increase sharply up until age 13 and peak at 2,557 at age 17. Some researchers attribute the increased rate of violent victimization of youth as a direct result of their risk-taking behaviours. (AuCoin 2005: 3)

In other words, AuCoin explains, because youth increase their use of alcohol and other drugs, and are subject to less parental supervision as they get older, they expose themselves to increased victimization risk. Risks outside the home are not the only ones that youth face, of course; youth account for 61 percent of all victims of sexual assault and 60 percent of those assaults occur at the hands of a family member. Moreover, more than half of the abductions of children are carried out not by a stranger—as the media would make it seem—but at the hands of a parent (AuCoin 2005: 1). Clearly, then, there is no simple rationale for the blanket of suspicion tossed over youth who are popularly and perennially depicted as unruly thugs (if they are boys) and hyper-sexed vixens (if they are girls). Figure 4.2 shows the increased victimization of male and female youth as age increases. Furthermore, the same data from Statistics Canada show that youth who are the witnesses to domestic violence face increased risks to their own health, and to becoming abusers themselves in adulthood. This chapter's *Social Problems Research Up Close* feature provides a nuanced analysis of the increased incidence and risk for victimization amongst street youth in Canada, and provides data that are not included in general social surveys of crime victimization.

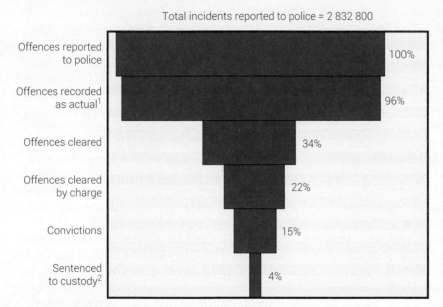

Total incidents reported to police = 2 832 800

Offences reported to police	100%
Offences recorded as actual[1]	96%
Offences cleared	34%
Offences cleared by charge	22%
Convictions	15%
Sentenced to custody[2]	4%

Percentage of police-reported offences

Figure 4.2 *Caseload within the Criminal Justice System*

SOURCE: Adapted from Statistics Canada, Canadian Centre for Justice Statistics, "Uniform Crime Reporting Survey, Adult Court Survey, and Youth Court Survey" *(Juristat)* Catalogue No.85-002-XPE, 21(11):5.

[1]An offence is considered "actual" when, following an initial investigation, the police confirm that a criminal offence has occurred. An offence is "cleared" when police are satisfied that they have identified an offender. However, it may not be possible to lay a charge against an offender because he or she is dead, under age 12, has diplomatic immunity, is already in prison, and so on. If, in the view of the police, it is possible to lay a charge against an offender, the offence is cleared by charge.

[2]Includes secure custody only for young offenders and any custodial sentence for adults.

Social Problems *Research Up Close*

Safe Streets for Whom? Homeless Youth, Social Exclusion, and Criminal Victimization

Victimization surveys tell us about the general population's experiences of crimes affecting them, but miss the elevated experiences of crimes in particularly vulnerable subcultures. Often assumed to be a threat to the general population, homeless youth, for example, are actually more frequent targets of crime than are members of the larger, general population in Canada.

(continued)

York University professor and researcher Stephen Gaetz demonstrates that it is social exclusion that places homeless youth in Canada most at risk to be victims of crime, and shows us why we should be concerned to improve the circumstances of this vulnerable group. Gaetz shows that while public discussions about crime tend to portray homeless youth as a threat to the general population, such a portrayal rests on inaccurate but "enduring notions of delinquent street urchins" (2004: 424). In fact, Gaetz's surveys with homeless youth show that they are far more often victimized by criminal activities ranging from theft and common assault to sexual assault. Social theory has explained this victimization as the result of engagement in "risky behaviours" and the "frequent[ing of] dangerous locations," but, argues Gaetz, such explanations moralize about personal choices and do not actually tell us anything about how or why youth end up in dangerous locations or participating in risky activities (p. 424).

The research carried out in Toronto, a city often thought of as very safe, demonstrates that the level of safety one enjoys on its streets is determined by social characteristics of who you are: "[a] central finding of this article is that when compared to the Canadian public, young people who are homeless experience much higher levels of criminal victimization" (p. 425). While Gaetz acknowledges that youth who are victims of crime are also somewhat more likely to engage in criminal activities themselves (including the sale of drugs, street prostitution, petty theft, and trespassing), he parts ways with theories that blame individual deviance for the experience and perpetration of these crimes. Moreover, Gaetz shows that the general public is not actually at risk of experiencing victimization at the hands of homeless youth. Homeless youth are regularly demonized in popular news reporting, and in campaigns to "clean up" the streets of any given region, but the reality is that it is homeless youth themselves who are most in danger.

To try to remedy the problems that homeless youth face, it helps, argues Gaetz, to get a better understanding of why they are in such dangerous positions in the first place. By understanding the reasons why homeless youth end up on the streets, we can, perhaps, prevent their vulnerability to homelessness. Failing that, concludes Gaetz, we need to reconceptualize homeless youth as part of the community that deserves protection and access to public safety: "Strategies that situate people who are homeless as part of the community—as persons who share rights and privileges with other citizens—have the potential to ameliorate some of the negative experiences of those whose lives are so profoundly characterized by the process of social exclusion" (p. 448).

Gaetz's conclusion is the result of a research program designed to assess the background literature on victimization and, in particular, to interrogate the popular explanations developed in an approach known as **routine activity theory**—a functionalist view that "suggests that three conditions increase the opportunity for a crime to occur: a motivated offender, a suitable target, and a lack of capable guardianship" (p. 427). Gaetz explains that this theory falls short because, although it explains the conditions that make a crime possible in the moment, it provides no good sense of how one becomes a "suitable target" in the first place, and often leaves that part of the explanation at "poor choices," asserting that "by making different choices, potential victims could lessen their risk" (p. 428). However, Gaetz argues that it is not poor choices but social exclusion that propels homeless youth into vulnerability and that "In most cases, the process of social exclusion begins before street youth become homeless, [and] it intensifies through their experience living on the streets" (p. 428).

Gaetz's interviews and surveys with 208 homeless youth showed that they hold the most dangerous jobs when they can find work at all; they often engage in dangerous methods to acquire income because more "legitimate" means are beyond their reach; they are frequently robbed because they are known to carry cash and have no one to protect them; and they are not granted the same entitlements to legal protection as other youth (pp. 430–31). In short, they are pushed into their vulnerability.

Demonstrating the kinds of social exclusion that homeless youth face, Gaetz lists off the ways in which their lives are lived very publicly, their activities policed, and their freedom of movement and security are denied:

> It is important to recognize that one of the consequences of regulating the lives of homeless people—where they can sleep, where they can sit, whether they can occupy public or semi-public places—is that they are often forcibly removed from safer spaces in the city and relegated to spaces that are potentially more dangerous and there they have less control over whom they interact with. Street youth, whether they are working, resting, or enjoying

social interactions, are continually exposed to other potential offenders. The fact that many of their peers are also homeless and more likely to adopt aggressive and violent behaviours as an adaptive strategy for life on the streets may also increase their likelihood of victimization. (p. 429)

In other words, multiple features of the everyday experiences of street youth deny them access to legitimate decision-making conditions, and push them into dangerous situations at the isolated margins of the more powerful social milieu. Thus, Gaetz explains the ways in which street youth arrive, sometimes repeatedly, in situations where they are victimized.

Among the key considerations that Gaetz encourages his readers to understand is that some of the features of the street youth population indicate that they face social exclusion *before* they actually turn to the streets.

For example, noting that "the street youth population is characterized by the over-representation of lesbian, gay, bisexual and transgendered youth" (p. 433), Gaetz reports that in his sample 29.6 percent defined themselves as "non-straight" and another 24.62 percent reported being bisexual or "bi-curious" (ibid). In addition to the prevalence of LGBT youth in the street youth population, both Aboriginal and "African Canadian" youth are overrepresented in the sample that Gaetz surveyed, at 9.1 percent and 17.7 percent, respectively. We can infer from these higher-than-typical concentrations of marginalized people within the street youth population that many were rejected by their families of origin, or faced some combination of family rejection and community isolation *before* they actually found themselves on the streets. In other words, they do not simply "choose" to be homeless.

Table 4.1 **Experiences of Criminal Victimization, Comparing Domiciled Youth in the General Public (15 to 24) with Street Youth**

	Total	Male	Female	Total	Male	Female
Assault (an attack, a face-to-face threat, or an incident with a weapon)	62.3% (186)	61.1% (108)	64.4% (73)	12.0% (3,384)	15.1%*** (1,645)	8.9%*** (1,739)
Theft (theft of personal or household property)	50.3% (186)	49.3% (108)	52.8% (73)	10.0% (3,386)	9.8% (1,646)	10.2% (1,740)
Robbery (face-to face theft in which perpetrator uses force or threat of force)	36.1% (186)	45.4%** (108)	23.3%** (73)	3.0% (3,386)	3.7%* (1,646)	2.3%* (1,740)
Sexual assault (forced sexual activity; an attempt at forced sexual activity, or unwanted sexual touching, grabbing, kissing, or fondling)	31.9% (186)	18.9%*** (106)	51.4%*** (72)	3.8% (3,384)	0.9%*** (1,645)	6.6%*** (1,739)
Vandalism (willful damage of personal property)	30.4% (186)	25.9% (108)	35.6% (73)	5.7% (3,386)	6.3% (1,646)	5.2% (1,740)
Break and enter (illegal entry of household property)	15.5% (186)	12.0% (108)	19.2% (73)	4.6% (3,386)	4.3% (1,646)	4.9% (1,740)
TOTAL reporting at least one crime incident	81.9% (186)	76.6%* (108)	91.5%* (73)	39.7% (3,421)	42.1% (1,660)	37.5% (1,761)

X^2 (significance of gender): *p < 0.05; **p < 0.01; ***p < 0.001

Statistics relating to domiciled youth are derived from Statistics Canada's General Social Survey (1999).

SOURCE: Gaetz, Stephen. 2004. Safe Streets for Whom? Homeless youth, social exclusion, and criminal victimization. *Canadian Journal of Criminology and Criminal Justice* 46:4 (423-455). Reprinted with permission from the Canadian Criminal Justice Association.

(continued)

Social Problems *Research Up Close* (continued)

Social exclusion, then, rather than poor choices, precipitates the arrival of youth into street life, and leaves them significantly more exposed to victimization from a range of crimes. Of those in Gaetz's sample population from Toronto, 81.9 percent reported having been victimized in the previous year; 79.4 percent had been victimized two or more times (p. 434). These numbers far exceed the rates for the general population, of whom only 25 percent reported being victims of crime in the previous year (ibid).

Gaetz concludes that typical discussions about public safety exclude those most at risk for experiences of criminal victimization, and urges us, at all levels of organization and government, to "consider the safety of all citizens, including those who are rightly or wrongly perceived to be dangerous, different, and 'outside' the definition of community" (p. 448) and to develop our social services and social inclusion practices accordingly.

SOURCE: Gaetz, Stephen. 2004. "Safe Streets for Whom? Homeless Youth, Social Exclusion, and Criminal Victimization," *Canadian Journal of Criminology and Criminal Justice* 46:4 (423–455).

---

routine activity theory
A view that for crimes to occur against people, certain conditions must exist. In particular, three conditions increase the opportunity for a crime to occur: a motivated offender, a suitable target, and a lack of capable guardianship of a target.

In addition to national surveys, the International Crime Victim Survey (ICVS) collected victimization data using the same questionnaire in many countries, including Canada, in 1989, 1992, 1996–97, and 2000 (Besserer 2002). This survey examines householders' experiences with crime, policing, crime prevention, and sense of safety. According to this survey, on average only 55 percent of victimization incidents are reported to police, with property crimes more likely to be reported than crimes against persons. In part, this finding reflects the general requirement by insurance companies that individuals seeking compensation for property stolen or damaged as the result of a criminal act file a police report. As Gaetz's research on homeless youth shows us, though victimization surveys provide detailed information about some crime victims, they tend to overlook the experiences of those who are too young, or too marginalized, to be reached through standard survey methods. In addition, the surveys provide less reliable data about offenders as they are able to deliver information that is based only on the perceptions of victims. The crime surveys, then, tell us about the impact of crime on some victims, but do not supply much in the way of strategies for crime prevention.

Self-Report Offender Surveys

Self-report surveys ask offenders about their criminal behaviour. The sample may consist of a population with known police records, such as a prison population, or it may include respondents from the general population, such as university students. Self-report data compensate for many of the problems associated with official statistics, but are still subject to exaggerations and concealment. Marcus Felson's research over three decades has repeatedly shown that a wide range of criminal acts never wind up in official crime reporting statistics. Among those activities indicated in self-reports but that rarely get reported to police are cannabis use, underage drinking, shoplifting, private assaults, and many small instances of fraud that add up to billions of dollars (Felson and Boba 2010: 5).

Self-report surveys reveal that virtually every adult has engaged in some type of criminal activity. Why, then, is only a fraction of the population labelled as criminal? Only a small proportion of the total population of law violators is ever convicted of a crime. For example, of 3.4 million household burglaries in the United States in 2005, only 1.9 million were reported to police, with 200 000 arrests following from those resulting in only 4000 convictions (ibid).

4.3 Sociological Theories of Crime and Violence

Some explanations of crime and violence focus on psychological aspects of offenders, such as psychopathic personalities, unhealthy relationships with parents, and mental illness. Other crime theories focus on potential biological variables, such as central nervous system malfunction, stress, hormones, vitamin or mineral deficiencies, or a presumed genetic predisposition toward aggression. Sociological theories of crime and violence emphasize the role of social factors in criminal behaviour and societal responses to it.

It is important to understand from the outset that not all perspectives approach crime and deviance in purely negative terms. The following discussion of theoretical understandings of crime and deviance shows that sometimes sociologists are interested in the positive features of crime and deviance. Structural-functionalists, for example, understand that criminal activity, such as treason or blasphemy, may encourage change in oppressive social structures and ideas in church and state treatment of persons. Conflict theorists and feminists may agree that the lack of power some individuals and groups have may necessitate breaking the law or deviating from typical behaviours in order to secure increased rights and access to privileges—like property rights or suffrage or personal autonomy. Symbolic interactionists may see in "deviance" the ability for subjects to re-vision their worlds and to make new meanings out of situations. For example, efforts over the last 20 years by various lesbian and gay rights organizations such as EGALE have resulted in recognition that same-sex partners also form families where they care for each other, care for children, and fulfil economic responsibilities. Without the efforts of organizations and persons to publicly demonstrate the place of lesbian and gay families in the larger society, we might still have partners legally unable to provide or to gain access to medical care for their partners or for the children whom they parent every day; we might still have a society that would leave gay and lesbian couples unable to benefit from insurance programs to which they had to contribute by law, and we might still have a society in which violent crimes against gays and lesbians would go unrecognized. From a variety of perspectives, then, we can see how refusing to live by the status quo can extend rights, as well as recognition, to all members of a society instead of only to the powerful.

Structural-Functionalist Perspective

According to Durkheim and other structural-functionalists, crime is functional for society. One of the functions of crime and other deviant behaviour is that it strengthens group cohesion:

> The deviant individual violates rules of conduct [that] the rest of the community holds in high respect; and when these people come together to express their outrage over the offense . . . they develop a tighter bond of solidarity than existed earlier. (Erikson 1966: 4)

Crime may also lead to social change. For example, an episode of local violence may "achieve broad improvements in city services . . . [and] be a catalyst for making public agencies more effective and responsive, for strengthening families and social institutions, and for creating public-private partnerships" (National Research Council 1994: 9–10).

While functionalism as a theoretical perspective deals directly with some aspects of crime and violence, it is not a theory of crime per se. Three major theories of crime and violence have developed from functionalism, however. The first, called **strain theory**, was developed by Robert Merton (1957), using Durkheim's concept of anomie, or normlessness. Merton argues that when legitimate means (for example, a job) of acquiring culturally defined goals (for example, money) are limited by the structure of society, the resulting strain may lead to crime.

Individuals, then, must adapt to the inconsistency between means and goals in a society that socializes everyone into wanting the same thing, but provides opportunities for only some (see Table 4.2). Conformity occurs when individuals accept the culturally defined goals and the socially legitimate means of achieving them. Merton suggests that most individuals, even those who lack easy access to the means and the goals, remain conformists. Innovation occurs when an individual accepts the goals of society, but rejects or lacks the socially legitimate means of achieving them. Innovation, the mode of adaptation most associated with criminal behaviour, explains the high rate of crime committed by uneducated and poor individuals who lack access to legitimate means of achieving the social goals of wealth and power.

Table 4.2 **Merton's Five Types of Adaptation**

	Culturally Defined Goals	Structurally Defined Means
Conformity	+	+
Innovation	+	−
Ritualism	−	+
Retreatism	−	−
Rebellion	−/+	−/+

Key: (+) = acceptance of/access to; (−) = rejection of/lack of access to; (−/+) = rejection of culturally defined goals and structurally defined means and replacement with new goals and means.

SOURCE: Reprinted with permission of Simon & Schuster, Inc., from the Free Press edition of *SOCIAL THEORY AND SOCIAL STRUCTURE* by Robert K. Merton. Copyright © 1957 by The Free Press. Copyright © renewed 1985 by Robert K. Merton. All rights reserved.

There are other ways to adapt to the inconsistency between means and goals. One is ritualism, in which the individual accepts a lifestyle of hard work, but rejects the cultural goal of monetary rewards. The ritualist goes through the motions of getting an education and working hard, yet is not committed to the goal of accumulating wealth or power. Retreatism involves rejecting both the cultural goal of success and the socially legitimate means of achieving it. The retreatist withdraws or retreats from society and may become an alcoholic, drug addict, or vagrant. Finally, rebellion occurs when an individual rejects both culturally defined goals and means and substitutes new goals and means. For example, rebels may use social or political activism to replace the goal of personal wealth with the goal of social justice and equality.

While strain theory explains criminal behaviour as a result of blocked opportunities, **subcultural theory** argues that certain groups or subcultures in society have values and attitudes that are conducive to crime and violence. Members of these groups and subcultures, as well as other individuals who interact with them, may adopt the crime-promoting attitudes and values of the group. For example, subcultural norms and values contribute to street crime. Sociologist Elijah Anderson (1994) explains that many inner-city youths live by a survival code on the streets that emphasizes gaining the respect of others through violence—the tougher you are and the more others fear you, the more respect you have in the community.

However, if blocked opportunities and subcultural values are responsible for crime, why don't all members of the affected groups become criminals? **Control theory** may answer that question. Hirschi (1969), consistent with Durkheim's emphasis on social solidarity, suggests that a strong social bond between individuals and the social order constrains some individuals from violating social norms. Hirschi identified four elements of the social bond: attachment to significant others, commitment to conventional goals, involvement in conventional activities, and belief in the moral standards of society. Several empirical tests of Hirschi's theory support the notion that the higher the attachment, commitment, involvement, and belief, the higher the social bond and the lower the probability of criminal behaviour. For example, Laub and colleagues (1998) found that a good marriage contributes to the cessation of a criminal career. Further, Warner and Rountree (1997) report that local community ties, although varying by neighbourhood and offence, decrease the probability of crimes occurring.

Conflict Perspective

Conflict theories of crime suggest that deviance is inevitable whenever two groups have differing degrees of power; in addition, the more inequality in a society, the greater the crime rate in that society. Social inequality may lead individuals to commit crimes such as armed robbery and burglary as a means of economic survival. Other individuals, who are angry and frustrated by their low position in the socio-economic hierarchy, may express their rage and frustration through crimes such as drug use, assault, and homicide. In Argentina, for example, the soaring violent crime rate is hypothesized to be "a product of the enormous imbalance in income distribution . . . between the rich and the poor" (Pertossi 2000).

According to the conflict perspective, those in power define what is criminal and what is not, and these definitions reflect the interests of the ruling class. Laws against vagrancy, for example, penalize individuals who do not contribute to the capitalist system of work and consumerism. Rather than viewing law as a mechanism that protects all members of society, conflict theorists focus on how laws are created by those in power to protect the ruling class. For example, wealthy corporations contribute money to campaigns to influence politicians to enact tax laws that serve corporate interests (Jacobs 1988), and the "criminal justice system grows increasingly punitive as labour surplus increases"— that is, as greater social control is felt to be needed (Hochstetler and Shover 1997).

Furthermore, conflict theorists argue that law enforcement is applied differentially, penalizing those without power and benefiting those with power. For example, female prostitutes are more likely to be arrested than are the men who seek their services. Unlike street criminals, corporate criminals are often punished by fines rather than by lengthy prison terms. Recent data for Canada show that in 2003–04, 51 percent of adult offenders convicted of break and enter, but just 34 percent of convicted fraud cases, resulted in a prison sentence (Thomas 2004: 12).

Societal beliefs also reflect power differentials. For example, rape myths are perpetuated by the male-dominated culture to foster the belief that women are to blame for their own victimization, thereby, in the minds of many, exonerating the offender. Such myths include the notion that when a woman says "no," she means "yes," that "good girls" don't get raped, that appearance indicates willingness, and that women secretly want to be raped. Not surprisingly, in societies where women and men have greater equality, there are fewer rapes (Sanday 1981).

Symbolic Interactionist Perspective

Two important theories of crime and violence emanate from the symbolic interactionist perspective. The first, **labelling theory**, focuses on two questions: How do

control theory
A theory that argues that a strong social bond between a person and society constrains some individuals from violating norms.

labelling theory
A symbolic interactionist theory that is concerned with the effects of labelling on the definition of a social problem (e.g., a social condition or group is viewed as problematic if it is labelled as such) and with the effects of labelling on the self-concept and behaviour of individuals (e.g., the label "juvenile delinquent" may contribute to the development of a self-concept and behaviour consistent with the label).

crime and deviance come to be defined as such, and what are the effects of being labelled as criminal or deviant? According to Howard Becker (1963):

> Social groups create deviance by making rules whose infractions constitute deviance, and by applying those rules to particular people and labelling them as outsiders. From this point of view, deviance is not a quality of the act a person commits, but rather a consequence of the application by others of rules and sanctions to an "offender." The deviant is one to whom the label has successfully been applied; deviant behaviour is behaviour that people so label. (p. 238)

primary deviance
Deviant behaviour committed before a person is caught and labelled as an offender.

Labelling theorists make a distinction between **primary deviance**, which is deviant behaviour committed before a person is caught and labelled as an offender, and **secondary deviance**, which is deviance that results from being caught and labelled. After a person violates the law and is apprehended, that person is stigmatized as a criminal. This deviant label often dominates the social identity of the person to whom it is applied. It becomes the person's "master status"; that is, the primary basis on which the person is defined by others.

secondary deviance
Deviance that results from being caught and labelled.

Being labelled as deviant often leads to further deviant behaviour because (1) the person who is labelled as deviant is often denied opportunities for engaging in non-deviant behaviour, and (2) the labelled person internalizes the deviant label, adopts a deviant self-concept, and acts accordingly. For example, the teenager who is caught selling drugs at school may be expelled and thus denied opportunities to participate in non-deviant school activities (e.g., sports, clubs) and associate with non-deviant peer groups. The labelled and stigmatized teenager may also adopt the self-concept of a "druggie" or "pusher," and continue to pursue drug-related activities and membership in the drug culture.

differential association
A theory developed by Edwin Sutherland that holds that through interaction with others, individuals learn the values, attitudes, techniques, and motives for criminal behaviour.

The assignment of meaning and definitions learned from others is also central to the second symbolic interactionist theory of crime: **differential association**. Edwin Sutherland (1939) proposed that, through interaction with others, individuals learn the values and attitudes associated with crime as well as the techniques and motivations for criminal behaviour. Individuals who are exposed to more definitions favourable to law violation than unfavourable—for example, "crime pays" versus "do the crime, you'll do the time"—are more likely to engage in criminal behaviour. Children who see their parents benefit from crime or who live in high-crime neighbourhoods where success is associated with illegal behaviour are more likely to engage in criminal behaviour.

Recent work on the influence of labelling and differential association in youth found that already-incarcerated black youth in Canada had learned early to associate their ascribed racial category with a criminal identity (Manzo and Bailey 2005). The research concludes that incarcerated black youth "articulate a view of themselves and of Black persons in general that is consistent with certain stereotypes" (p. 298). That is to say, stereotypes about black persons—for example, that all young black males are "gangstas"—have a negative impact on these youths; however, because the youths also exhibited some pride in their racial background, Manzo and Bailey believe the youths also have some "resilience" to negative stereotyping. The problem emerges, they argue quite specifically, "when the aspect [the youth] choose to embrace is inherently criminal and, quite possibly criminogenic, such as the gangsta image . . . these youth have adopted and extol" (p. 299).

Feminist Theories of Crime

Just as feminist criminology, which has been around for at least three decades, enters a more central position in sociological thinking, it faces a backlash. The backlash targets not only feminist criminology, but also other progressive justice movements, such as those against racism and poverty (Chesney-Lind 2006: 6–9). A central tenet of feminist criminology is that "to truly understand delinquency, the differences between girls' and boys' experiences and 'realities' must be examined . . . and patriarchy must be central to the study of causes of delinquency" (Belknap and Holsinger 2006: 50). Feminist criminology focuses on how the subordinate position of women in the social structure can influence the criminalization of behaviour in ways that are specifically gendered. In the following section, we offer some exemplary feminist research on how ideas about "proper behaviour" for women influence laws regarding prostitution and other aspects of the sex trade.

Sex Work and Trafficked Women

University of Ottawa criminologist Christine Bruckert has provided ground-breaking feminist analyses of the criminalization of women's bodies and behaviours through Canada's anti-prostitution laws, and—using a combination of Marxist-feminist and structuralist perspectives—of the work conditions of women strippers in Canada. Writing on contemporary debates about prostitution law in Canada in 2013, Bruckert and her co-investigator Stacey Hannem observe that:

> In Canada, the criminalized model draws on contradictory discourses that portray sex workers as both passive victims of exploitation and active agents who pose a threat to the order and safety of communities. In either case, sex workers are assumed to be incapable of acting as responsible, neo-liberal citizens, and their labour is de-legitimized and excluded from civil protections. (p. 61)

In Canada, prostitution laws are currently being reconsidered at the Supreme Court level and Bruckert and Hannem take a feminist approach to their work in order to voice their concern that Canada not reaffirm the criminality of prostitution because such a move will have the effect of removing "even the possibility of sex workers' agency" and will, instead, assert that prostitutes must be understood only as victims in need of protection (p. 62). Agency refers to the ability to make decisions and act on them, and Canada's traditional approach to sex work, especially prostitution, has been to treat it as simultaneously a deviant threat to the social order and a threat to women who, common sense assumes, cannot legitimately choose to work in sex work. But if criminalization of sex work positions women as victims, even if some of those victims are dangerous, Bruckert and Hannem also caution that completely legalized models that treat prostitution as a business are problematic because they continue to impose traditional stigmas on sex workers—who are treated as health threats—and impose mandatory health tests on such workers even though, for example, "regular testing for Hepatitis is not required in the restaurant industry" (p. 62), where, presumably, infected persons come into contact with large numbers of clients who would be vulnerable to infection. Instead, argue Bruckert and Hannem, we should be looking at the benefits of decriminalizing sex work—that is, removing it from formal regulation under the law altogether. Such a move would render sex work just another form of work that might include regulatory professional associations and standards of behaviour for both workers and clients, but would not make the very work itself subject to criminal oversight. They write that "positioning sex workers as legitimate labourers entitle[s them] to the same rights and protections as any other Canadian worker" (ibid).

Debates in Canada about sex work can be difficult to understand if one has been encouraged to think of sexual activity as something that belongs only within the confines of an intimate relationship (preferably marriage) geared toward the creation and maintenance of "family." For example, it is not uncommon to encounter a belief that "good women" do not actually enjoy sex and must, therefore, always be victims who would never willingly enter into sex work, or else be mentally ill/deviant.

Bruckert and Hannem challenge that view, but their work speaks specifically to the ability of adult women to make choices about the work that they want to do and under what conditions.

Alongside feminist views that see sex work as something that can be a legitimate profession, there are also concerns about the "traffic in women"—a form of human trafficking that moves vulnerable women from one geographic location to another (where they have no social supports or means of escape) for the purposes of compelling them to work in the sex trade. As we noted in the opening of this chapter, over 50 percent of those females who are trafficked are underage girls, and their welfare is a legitimate concern for sociologists focused on matters of social justice. However, the scale of human trafficking involving girls and women into the sex trade, explains anthropologist Elizabeth Bernstein (2010), is exaggerated in the media, and by a cooperation of conservative groups and those feminist groups that oppose the sex trade in general. Getting a clear understanding of the issues at play in the trafficking in girls and women is not an easy task, but Bernstein writes with exceptional clarity about this "dangerous manifestation of global gender inequalities" (2010: 45) and places the issue in the larger context of political and economic oppressions. Her work is, moreover, interested in how it came to be that the "strange bedfellows" of liberal media and public intellectuals alongside conservative feminists and Christian organizations were so mobilized around the relatively infrequent instance within human trafficking of trafficking girls and women into the sex trade (Bernstein 2010).

Bernstein's analysis is remarkable for providing a feminist account of problems in human trafficking that does not engage in breathless, quasi-prurient sensationalizing of the sex trade. Bernstein explains that there are two problems with much of the contemporary fixation on the relatively small portion of human trafficking that has to do with the sex trade. First, she notes that the concern over sex-trade trafficking, and human trafficking more generally, seeks to punish only the individual offenders who run the trafficking businesses or purchase sex, and neglects working on the underlying poverty, lack of education, and poor options for women that are the precursors to the traffic in human beings (p. 47). Second, Bernstein points out that human trafficking includes "sweatshop labor, agricultural work, or even corporate crime, but it has been the far less common instances of sexually trafficked women and girls that have stimulated the most concern by conservative Christians, prominent feminist activists, and the press" (p. 49).

As readers, we need to be careful to understand that Bernstein is not arguing that sexually trafficking women and girls is not a problem, but that we should question the scale of preoccupation with only the one area of human trafficking. Bernstein shows that the interest in sexually trafficked girls and women diverts attention from more common, more pervasive suffering of vulnerable persons in the neo-liberal global economy. She argues that groups who concern themselves with sex trafficking can see themselves as innocent, whereas holding them to account, or taking responsibility upon themselves, for their role as consumers of clothing and food items produced by child labourers and trafficked agricultural workers would inconvenience them and seriously compromise their view of themselves as fighters for "social justice." The near-exclusive focus on problems of sex trafficking constitutes a moral panic that does not help to improve the larger impediments to well-being that the women and girls face.

Noting that criminology has traditionally ignored women's lives and uses the same models to explain women's criminal activity as men's, feminist research explores the very different "pathways" that lead girls and women to criminal activity. Feminist pathway research shows that experiences of abuse, homophobia directed at lesbian youth, and sexual abuse all figure prominently as correlates to delinquency (D'Augelli and Dark 1994; Daly 1992; Faith 1993). The Canadian Mental Health Association (2003) observes that "68% of federally incarcerated women reported childhood physical abuse; 54% reported sexual abuse. Among aboriginal women, 90% reported physical and 61% sexual abuse." In addition to all this, a survey of girls in custody found girls were far more likely to be abandoned by their parents than boys were, even in contemporary North America (Belknap and Holsinger 2006: 58).

As demonstrated in our discussion about sex work and human trafficking into the sex trade, feminist theories of crime also note that what counts as criminal activity for women is frequently bound up with concerns to regulate women's sexuality and reproduction. Racist policy that collides with patriarchal sexism can also be a route to incarceration for delinquency. In Canada, racist policy that collides with patriarchal sexism can also be a route to incarceration for delinquency. Velma Demerson's book *Incorrigible* (2004) is an autobiographical account of her year-long incarceration for the "crime" of living with a Chinese man and being pregnant by him. The *Female Refugees Act* of 1897 defined Demerson as incorrigible; the act was not repealed until 1964. Under the act, women between the ages of 16 and 35 could be jailed for anything from "promiscuity" or pregnancy outside marriage to public drunkenness. In Demerson's case, it was her father who alerted the authorities to her cohabitation with her Chinese boyfriend.

Women not only are criminalized in very gendered ways, but also are vulnerable to neglect as victims of crime. As pointed out in our discussion about sexual assault, false beliefs about women significantly reduce the likelihood that they will report a rape; if women do report a rape, these beliefs may mean that they will not receive appropriate and diligent attention and protection through the justice system.

The "commonsense" approach to domestic violence as a recognizable social problem has itself presented a problematic and unjust view of abused women. At base, Stephanie Paterson's (2010) research shows, Canadian public policy tends to see domestic violence in patronizing terms, and as a problem best resolved by having abused women exit from their relationships—because it has no viable alternatives for women, it leaves them at risk for further abuse. Paterson explains, citing multiple studies carried out in the 1990s:

> "Protection" from harm requires removal from danger; it requires exit. Women's responses to violence are scrutinized as resistance is narrowly constructed only as exit. Women, then, either leave or stay, falsely dichotomized as either agents or victims and obscured from view are the myriad ways in which women attempt to resist abuse (Mahoney 1991, 1992, 1994). Mahoney's analysis (1992, 1306; cited in Bacchi 1999, 169) led her to characterize this dichotomization as the following: "Either you are on the playing field of liberal competition, in which case you require no protection, or you prove into a category as a victim who is being kept off the field." (p. 165)

In short, if those who set policy fail to understand the complexity of women's social relationships in terms of their social locations, then we create solutions that are too narrow to be useful, and can actually add to the risk that women face.

4.4 Types of Crime

Criminologists use the terms **conventional crime** or **street crime** to refer to "those traditional illegal behaviours that most people think of as crime" (Koenig 2000). Included here would be offences such as murder, sexual assault, assault, armed robbery, break and enter, and theft. In contrast, the term *nonconventional crime* applies to such crimes as organized crime, white-collar crime, corporate crime, and computer crime.

Most Canadians would be alarmed to hear that violent crimes accounted for 20 percent of all the crimes reported to police in 2008 (Wallace 2009). Because popular news reporting does a poor job of distinguishing between typical offences and the murders it tends to focus on, it is easy to understand why people may tend to assume that the

conventional crime (street crime)
Traditional illegal behaviour that most people think of as crime, including such offences as murder, sexual assault, assault, armed robbery, break and enter, and theft.

dramatic cases reported on the nightly news are representative of general crimes committed, but this is not the case. In 2008, only 611 of all reported violent crimes were homicides, a rate of only 1.8 homicide deaths per 100 000 population (ibid). Moreover, violent crimes in Canada constitute a minority of the total crimes reported (see Figure 4.3).

Figure 4.3 **Crime Rate Resumes Its Downward Trend Since Peaking in 1991**

SOURCE: Statistics Canada. "Police-Reported Crime Statistics in Canada, 2011." http://www.statcan.gc.ca/pub/85-002-x/2012001/article/11692-eng.htm#a1

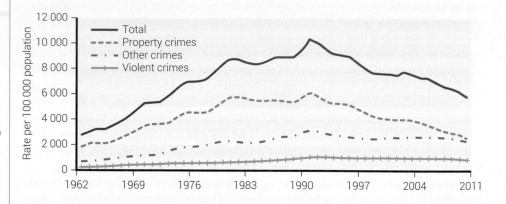

Street Crime: Violent Offences

Violent crime includes homicide, attempted murder, assault, sexual assault, other sexual offences, abduction, and robbery.

Homicide refers to the wilful killing of one human being by another individual or group of individuals. As mentioned above, although homicide is the most serious of the violent crimes, it is also the least common. When we take a longer historical view, the relative rarity of homicide remains true: Canada's homicide rate, which has been declining since the mid-1970s, remained stable at 1.8 homicides for every 100 000 people (Statistics Canada 2002); the rate declined even further through the first decade of the 2000s and rose only as high as 1.8 homicides for every 100 000 people again in 2008 (Wallace 2009). Furthermore, although homicides tend to be imagined as random crimes committed by strangers, the majority of homicides involve offenders known to their victims. Figure 4.3 shows the longitudinal, generally downward trend of crime rates in Canada since peaking in the early 1990s. Hartnagel (2012) reminds us that the rise in reported crime from the 1960s to 1990s correlates with the age of baby boomers reaching various ages of opportunity for different levels of crime—from property crimes in their youth to more sophisticated white-collar crimes as they matured, and that the drop-off since correlates with smaller successive generations. In other words, the increase or decrease in reported crimes does not necessarily tell us that Canadian social mores were declining for the years from 1962 to 1991, nor that Canadian social mores are markedly improved now.

Longitudinal analyses show, for example, that in 2001 the rate of minor assaults increased by 1 percent over the rate in 2000 and was "the key factor" in the rise in the total violent crime rate in Canada (Statistics Canada 2002). We must, however, remember that rising rates of violent crime may not result from more instances of such acts, but from the frequency of reporting and from the alteration of what counts as a criminal offence (Hackler 2005: 193–208). Hackler advises us to keep this invisible feature of crime analyses in mind: "What has changed is the manner in which we perceive and deal with violence. Many decades ago I carried a pocket knife to school. That is not acceptable today" (2005: 199).

Recent trends continue those in the historical data, showing that about two-thirds of homicide victims are men, and comprise 90 percent of adults and 86 percent of *all* those accused of homicide (Fedorowycz 1999; Wallace 2004). For both homicide and other violent crimes, the highest risk group for offending is those 16 to 34 years old (Fedorowycz 1999). The majority of homicides committed among marginal groups in North America (e.g., First Nations peoples, African-Americans) are intraracial (Hackler 2000).

Other forms of violent crime are sexual and nonsexual assaults. Both types of assault are distinguished by several categories. In relation to nonsexual assault, these categories are common assault (level 1), assault with a weapon or causing bodily harm (level 2), and aggravated assault (level 3) in which the victim is wounded, maimed, or disfigured. In addition, the *Criminal Code* outlines other types of assaults: these include but are not limited to those committed on a peace officer, an officiating member of the clergy, the Queen, and an internationally protected person.

Sexual assaults are also classified into one of three levels distinguished by the degree of physical harm to the victim: level 1 sexual assault, level 2 sexual assault (sexual assault with a weapon, threats to a third party, or causing bodily harm), and level 3 aggravated sexual assault (in which an offender, in committing a sexual assault, wounds, maims, disfigures, or endangers the life of the victim). In relation to both types of assaults, sexual and nonsexual, the least serious are the most common. According to 2009 Statistics Canada data, the likelihood of being a victim of sexual assault remained highly gendered, with more than twice as many women as men reporting sexual assaults. Meanwhile, even when men were victims of sexual assault, men were more likely to have committed those assaults (Statistics Canada 2009b). It is also important to know that while the numbers of reported sexual assaults are low, the instance of sexual assault is significantly higher. Writing for Statistics Canada, Mia Dauvergne and John Turner (2010) note that data from the General Social Survey show "less than one in ten sexual assaults were reported to police. There are many reasons given for not reporting to police, including the belief that the incident was not important enough, that it was dealt with in some other way and that it was a private matter."

In 2009, Statistics Canada released a new index to measure internal distinctions between violent and non-violent crimes reported in the Uniform Crime Reporting Survey. Figure 4.4 shows that when we create a stable baseline to help us determine whether rates of violent crime are getting generally worse, the picture is not nearly so bad as the popular media would lead us to believe. To help readers understand the index, Statistics Canada notes, "Crime severity is expressed as an index for which 2006 is the base year at 100." By 2012, the index for overall crime was 75, down from 119.1 in 1998, a significant drop of just slightly more than 37 percent over 14 years of steady drops in the rate. Figure 4.5 shows the offences most frequently heard in adult court; again, these offences are not the ones that popular news reports focus our

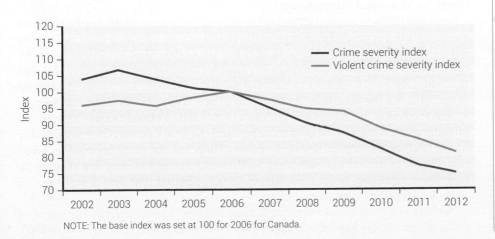

Figure 4.4 *Police-Reported Violent Crime Severity Index and Police-Reported Violent Crime Rate, 2002–2012*

SOURCE: Statistics Canada. "Police-Reported Crime Statistics in Canada, 2012." http://www.statcan.gc.ca/pub/85-002-x/2013001/article/11854-eng.htm

NOTE: The base index was set at 100 for 2006 for Canada.

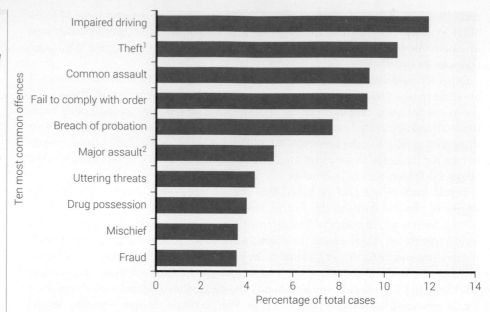

Figure 4.5 **Ten Most Common Offences for Cases Completed in Adult Criminal Court, Canada, 2010–2011**

SOURCE: Statistics Canada. 2012. Adult Criminal Court Statistics 2010/2011. Catalogue No. 85-002-X, http://www.statcan.gc.ca/pub/85-002-x/2012001/article/11646-eng.htm#a1

[1]Includes, for example, theft over and under $5 000 as well as taking a motor vehicle without consent.
[2]Includes, for example, assault with a weapon (level 2) and aggravated assault (level 3).

NOTE: A case is one or more charges against an accused person or company that were processed by the courts at the same time and received a final disposition. Cases that involve more than one charge are represented by the most serious offence. In total, data represent approximately 95% of the national adult criminal court caseload. Excludes information from superior courts in Prince Edward Island, Quebec, Ontario, Manitoba and Saskatchewan as well as municipal courts in Quebec due to the unavailability of data.

attentions on; rather, consistent with established Canadian trends, over three-quarters of cases heard in adult court for the year 2011–12 involved non-violent property crime (Dauvergne 2012a: 7). A full 12 percent of cases heard were for impaired driving. As we discussed in Chapter 3, the costs of impaired driving in terms of loss of life and injury are far from trivial, yet our collective attitude toward impaired driving is that it is a tragic mistake rather than a criminal behaviour per se, and sentencing for impaired driving remains comparatively lenient compared with other crimes that cause injury or loss of life.

Adult criminal court survey data are not reported in Manitoba, Northwest Territories, and Nunavut. In Quebec, most drug offences are recorded under residual federal statutes, resulting in an undercount of drug possession and drug trafficking cases and an overcount of residual federal statute cases.

Since the 1990s, increasing attention has been directed to **acquaintance rape**—a sexual assault committed by someone the victim knows. The term does not appear within the *Criminal Code* of Canada, and the act so described is subsumed within the three levels of sexual assault already noted. Nevertheless, it has been reported that although sexual assaults committed by acquaintances are the most likely to occur, they are the least likely to be reported and the most difficult to prosecute. Unless the sexual assault is what Williams (1984) calls a **classic rape**—that is, the offender was a stranger who used a weapon and the attack resulted in serious bodily harm—victims hesitate to report the crime. They fear not being believed. In addition, the use of "rape drugs," which render their victims unconscious (see Chapter 3), may lower reporting levels even further. It is estimated that only 1 in 10 sexual assaults is reported each year.

Robbery is distinguished from simple theft because it involves force, the threat of force, or making a victim fearful, and is, therefore, considered a violent crime. In 2003,

acquaintance rape
Rape that is committed by someone known by the victim.

classic rape
A rape committed by a stranger with the use of a weapon resulting in serious bodily injury.

the robbery rate rose for the first time in over a decade, up 5 percent over the previous year, but at levels well below where they had been in 1993 (Wallace 2004: 8). Of all the 28 000 robberies reported in 2003, close to half were committed without a weapon, 14 percent with a firearm, and 38 percent with some other weapon, usually a knife (Wallace 2004: 8). Robberies are generally committed by young people; in the late 1990s, for example, the median age of female robbers in Canada was 16; of male offenders, 21 (Kong 1999).

Street Crime: Property Offences

Property crimes involve acts committed with the intent to gain property without the use or threatened use of violence. Examples of property crime include theft, breaking and entering, motor vehicle theft, fraud, and possession of stolen property. Property crimes have declined since the early 1990s, although as of 2003–04, crimes against property still accounted for 23 percent of all crimes tried in adult court (Thomas 2004: 2). Although youth tend to be perceived as increasingly inclined toward violent assaults, the pattern of crimes committed by youth in 2006–07 continued most often to involve crimes against property (38 percent) (Thomas 2008: 3). Crimes against property include break and enter, theft, vandalism, and mischief.

Reasons why youth are more likely to engage in crimes against property can be explained by taking a variety of theoretical approaches. For example, not having access to property of their own may lead those who feel the stigma of having less to seek illegitimate means of acquiring it. Poor connections to family and to their local communities may encourage youth to seek belonging by joining others to engage in theft, break and enter, and other crimes against property. Those of us who parent youth often find ourselves replacing stolen cellphones and music players and other similar devices, and learn that these kinds of thefts are quotidian occurrences in schools and at neighbourhood parties across the country. In accounting for why these items go missing so easily, youth tend to explain that these thefts are trivial because they do not require confrontation with the victim, and that the devices themselves are toys for the rich who can afford simply to replace them.

While female offenders do commit acts of theft, their thefts are often in conjunction with the far more common offence of prostitution, which accounted for 45 percent of women's offences tried in adult court in 2003–04 while women made up only 15 percent of the total cases in adult court for the same time period (Thomas 2004: 3).

Vice Crimes

A vice crime is an illegal activity that has no complaining party; it is therefore often called a **victimless crime**. Vice crimes include the use of illegal drugs, communicating for the purposes of prostitution, and illegal gambling. Compared with crimes such as murder or robbery, less consensus exists either nationally or internationally that vice crimes should be subject to the criminal law. In the Netherlands, for example, the Prostitution Information Center in Amsterdam offers a six-day course on "prostitution as a career option," while the Australia Council of Trade Unions recently recognized women in prostitution as a labour sector (CATW 1997). In general, "prostitution is not an issue Canadians have been seeing as particularly pressing" (Bibby 1995). While one in five Canadians identified prostitution as a "very serious" social concern in 1985, a decade later it was mentioned by fewer than 1 percent.

Prostitution is not illegal in Canada; however, it is an offence to publicly communicate with another person for the purpose of buying or selling sexual services. Since 1985, the

victimless crime
An illegal activity, such as prostitution or drug use, that has no complaining party; also called "vice crime."

Chapter 4 Crime and Violence

law has clearly applied to both buyers and sellers, but it has not been evenly applied. Women charged with solicitation are far more likely than their male clients to come from socially disadvantaged positions, to have little recourse to strong legal defence, and to end up incarcerated. Meanwhile, male clients who are charged for securing the services of a prostitute will have the option to pay a fine and/or attend "John school," where for a few hours or a few days they learn in very simple terms that prostitution hurts women.

Organized crime refers to criminal activity conducted by members of a hierarchically arranged structure devoted primarily to making money through illegal means. The *Criminal Code* defines a "criminal organization" as any group, association, or other body consisting of five or more persons, whether formally or informally organized, having as one of its primary activities the commission of an indictable offence for which the maximum punishment is imprisonment for five years or more. Although often discussed under victimless crimes because of its association with prostitution, drugs, and gambling, organized crime tends to use coercive techniques. For example, organized crime groups may force legitimate businesses to pay "protection money" by threatening vandalism or violence.

The traditional notion of organized crime is the Mafia—an international band of interlocked Italian families—but members of many ethnic groups engage in organized crime. Other organized crime groups in Canada include Chinese triads, the Colombian Mafia, outlaw motorcycle gangs, the Russian Mafia, and other ethnic-based drug-trafficking groups. Their activities include drug trafficking, pimping, terrorism, extortion, serious assaults, and homicide (Stamler 2000). In addition, the Organized Crime Impact Study concluded that between $5 billion and $17 billion is laundered annually in Canada. "Money laundering is any act or attempted act to conceal or disguise the identity of illegally obtained proceeds so that they appear to have originated from legitimate sources" (Solicitor General 1999).

Organized crime also occurs at the international level, such as smuggling illegal drugs and arms. In 1999, Canada's *Extradition Act* came into force, expanding Canada's ability to extradite those who are involved in organized crime. In recognition of the borderless nature of organized crime, "Canada is . . . working in the G-8, the United Nations and the Organization of American States to develop and promote international standards to combat transnational crime, and organized crime in particular" (Solicitor General 1999).

Corporate Crime

Corporate crime includes both occupational crime, where individuals commit crimes in the course of their employment, and criminal business practices, where corporations violate the law in the interest of maximizing profit. For example, Bre-X, reputedly one of the world's largest stock frauds, cost investors $6 billion. In this case, the Calgary-based company's geologist had sought to make a worthless mining property seem valuable by salting core samples with gold. After his actions became known, the market for Bre-X stock collapsed and the company's shares became worthless (Hagan 2000). Laureen Snider's research on corporate crime in Canada demonstrates how conservative governments and businesses—those that favour "laissez-faire" capitalism—have worked in concert since the 1960s to chip away at legislation designed to protect the general public and employees from corporate abuses, including both financial and social crimes (see Table 4.3).

Occupational crime is motivated by individual gain. Employee thefts of merchandise, or pilferage, is one of the most common types of occupational crime. Other examples include embezzlement, forgery and counterfeiting, and insurance fraud. "Churning"

organized crime
Criminal activity conducted by members of a hierarchically arranged structure devoted primarily to making money through illegal means.

corporate crime
Both the fraudulent practices that may take place in the course of conducting business—for example, tax evasion and extortion—and also behaviour that is not illegal, but may be immoral and cause significant harm to society. Such business behaviours may be deliberate or may arise from indifference to the well-being of others.

Table 4.3 *Types of Corporate Crime*

Crimes against Consumers/ Financial Crimes	Crimes against Employees/Social Crimes	Crimes against the Public/Social Crimes	Crimes against the Employer
Deceptive advertising	Health and safety violations	Toxic waste disposal	Embezzlement
Antitrust violations	Wage and hour violations	Pollution violations	Pilferage
Dangerous products	Discriminatory hiring practices	Tax fraud	Misappropriation of government funds
Manufacturer kickbacks	Illegal labour practices	Security violations	Counterfeit production of goods
Physician insurance fraud	Unlawful surveillance practices	Police brutality	Business credit fraud

is one example of corporate crime, or crime that benefits the organization. As Sherrill (2000: 304) explains, churning is

> a racket in which as many as 10 million customers were sweet-talked into using the case value of their old insurance policies to pay the premiums of new, more expensive policies. They were not warned that the upgrading could be so costly that it would eat up their equity, leaving them with premiums they couldn't afford—and therefore no coverage.

Price-fixing and antitrust violations are other examples of corporate crime. Snider's research shows that declines in corporate crime rates are not the result of improved corporate practices; instead, the drops reflect government and business cooperation to approve deregulation and decriminalization agendas previously used more effectively to limit mergers, monopolies, and antitrust activities (Snider 2000: 173). The results of **neo-liberal** legislation, such as Canada's 1986 *Competition Act*, mean that even if some practices, such as false advertising, remain criminal offences, the ability and will to prosecute them has declined. Furthermore, consumer complaints from 1986 to 1996 show that business practices did not improve, but only that the public's avenues of complaint were curtailed; eventually, government budget cuts resulted in closing all the regional complaint bureaus (Snider 2000: 174).

Corporate violence, another form of corporate crime, refers to the production of unsafe products and the failure of corporations to provide safe working environments for their employees. Corporate violence is the result of negligence, the pursuit of profit at any cost, and intentional violations of health, safety, and environmental regulations. For example, in 1999, General Motors (GM) was ordered to pay $4.9 billion (U.S.) to six people who were severely burned when their car exploded in flames after a rear-end collision. In court, lawyers for the plaintiffs produced an internal GM study that acknowledged the gas tanks in the Chevrolet Malibu and El Camino, Pontiac Grand Am, and Oldsmobile Cutlass were mounted in unsafe positions—27 cm from the rear bumper. However, the GM study had also pointed out that settling lawsuits that might arise from accidents in which victims were fatally burned (calculated to be $2.40 per car produced) would be cheaper than to change where the tanks were placed (calculated to be $8.59 per car produced). Here, a profit-motivated decision was made and the placement of the gas tanks remained unaltered from 1979 to 1983. Even though the amount awarded was both the biggest product-liability award and the largest personal injury verdict in U.S. history, legal experts opined that the enormous punitive award

neo-liberal
The revival of classical liberalism that has occurred since the 1980s. Those who espouse this model for economic and political organization and policy advocate individual rights over group rights, reduction of state powers, and an increased liberalization of free-market capitalism. According to this view, when the market is free to set its own limits, then individual merit will be properly rewarded and everyone will benefit from increased growth in capital and industrial production.

corporate violence
The production of unsafe products and the failure of corporations to provide a safe working environment for their employees.

was unlikely to stand on appeal. "Even with awards in the tens of millions, it is rare for a plaintiff to actually get anything close to the jury's verdict" (White 1999). Ongoing investigation of the April 2010 BP oil-spill disaster has revealed unethical behaviours that may well have been criminal in the neglect of safety standards for deep well drilling in the sea floor. If current questions about BP's practices do reveal deliberate inattention to standards, the company may be found criminally liable not only for the considerable environmental damage to the Gulf of Mexico region but also for the deaths of the 11 rig members who died when the explosion occurred.

In Canada, some have argued that the term **corporate murder** (Swartz 1978) is an appropriate label for deaths resulting from such circumstances. Among the best-known cases are the failures of administrators within the Johns-Manville Corporation to alert workers to the serious health hazards posed by asbestos. Hagan (2000) notes that although these hazards have been recognized "since the turn of the century . . . people working with it were not informed, and the government bureaucracy and the medical community ignored the hazard." Similarly, he notes that the 1992 explosion at the Westray coal mine in Pictou County, Nova Scotia, "was not an accident, but . . . the result of conscious decisions by those responsible for the safety of the miners." Twenty-six miners were killed. An official inquiry into the disaster resulted in a report tellingly entitled *The Westray Story: A Predictable Path to Disaster*. In it, Justice Richard concludes that the managers at Westray had "displayed a certain disdain for safety and appeared to regard safety-conscious workers as the wimps in the organization" (in Hagan 2000).

corporate murder
The label for deaths as a result of unsafe consumer products.

Computer Crime

Computer crime refers to any violation of the law in which a computer is the target or the means of criminal activity. *Hacking*, or unauthorized computer intrusion, is one type of computer crime. In just one month, hackers successfully attacked the computer systems of Walt Disney World, Yahoo, eBay, and Amazon.com through "denial of service" invasions (Kong and Swartz 2000). *Identity theft*—the use of someone else's identification (e.g., social insurance number, birth date) to obtain credit—is another.

Conklin (1998) has identified other examples of computer crime:[*]

computer crime
Any violation of the law in which a computer is the target or means of criminal activity.

- Two individuals were charged with theft of 80 000 cellular phone numbers. Using a device purchased from a catalogue, the thieves picked up radio waves from passing cars, determined private cellular codes, reprogrammed computer chips with the stolen codes, and then, by inserting the new chips into their own cellular phones, charged calls to the original owners.
- A programmer made $300 a week by programming a computer to round off each employee's paycheque down to the nearest 10 (cents) and then to deposit the extra few pennies in the offender's account.
- An oil company illegally tapped into another oil company's computer to get information that allowed the offending company to underbid the other company for leasing rights.

4.5 Demographic Patterns of Crime

Although virtually everyone violates a law at some time, persons with certain demographic characteristics are disproportionately represented in the crime statistics. Victims, for example, are disproportionately young, lower-class, minority males from urban areas. Similarly, the probability of being an offender varies by gender, age, race, social class, and region.

[*]Conklin 1998; National Post (December 19): A6.

Gender and Crime

Both official statistics and self-report data indicate that males commit more crimes than females (Figure 4.6). Males are involved in more acts of crime than are females in both adult and youth age groups. The current data in Figure 4.6 repeat a long-established pattern of greater likelihood that males will commit crime. But why are males more likely? One explanation is that society views female lawbreaking as a more serious transgression of gender norms and thus places more constraints on female behaviour: "women may need a higher level of provocation before turning to crime—especially serious crime. Females who choose criminality must traverse a greater moral and psychological distance than males making the same choice" (Steffensmeier and Allan 1995: 88). Further, data suggest that males and females tend to commit different types of crimes. Men, partly because of more aggressive socialization experiences, are more likely than women are to commit violent crimes. The most recent data from Statistics Canada continue to show that women are far less likely to commit crimes than males are, and that crimes committed by women tend to be of a different type, with almost half of their crimes being those against property rather than against persons (Kong and AuCoin 2008: 3). Moreover, when women do commit crimes against persons, it tends to be common assault, rather than the more serious offences of manslaughter, murder, or sexual assault (ibid).

NOTES: Excludes incidents where the sex and/or age of the accused was unknown. Data are not nationally representative. Based on data from 122 police services representing approximately 71% of the population of Canada in 2005. Rate per 100 000 population for the geographic areas policed by the UCR2 respondents, based on populations provided by Demography Division, Statistics Canada. Populations as of July 1st: preliminary postcensal estimates for 2005.

Figure 4.6 **Females Apprehended by Police for Crimes against the Person at a Rate Five Times Lower Than Males, Selected Police Services, 2005**

SOURCE: Statistics Canada, Canadian Centre for Justice Statistics. "Female Offenders in Canada" (*Juristat*), Catalogue No. 85-002-XIE, Vol.28, No. 1, Chart 1, p. 3.

Young Offenders

Popular news media that focus for several weeks on one instance of serious crime may encourage the view that youth are increasingly dangerous and volatile. Consider the coverage of the Boxing Day shootings on Toronto's Yonge Street in 2005 or the murder of an Alberta family in 2006, a crime for which their daughter, who was 13 at the time of the murders, was found guilty. However, the long-term data are far more subtle and do not support the idea that youth are worse or more violent now than ever before.

The popular perception, though, is a powerful political motivator for those who want to prove their commitment to Canadians by getting "tough on crime" (Hogeveen 2005). The political utility of punishment over prevention is clear in the statement of Vic Toews, who, as justice minister, endorsed harsher sentencing policies for all offenders, saying, "When it comes to crime, it is the new government's firm commitment to finally respond to the concerns of police and, most importantly, of ordinary Canadians" (Deveau 2006).

According to police-reported data, the period from age 16 to 17 is the peak age of offending for both violent and property offences (Wallace 2009) and accounts for

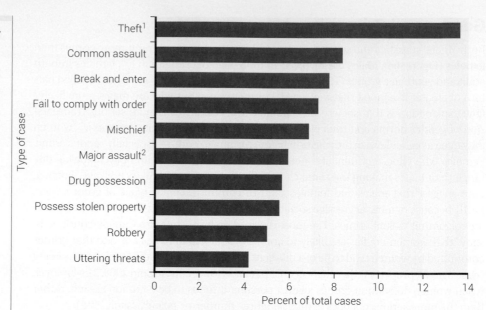

Figure 4.7 **Ten Most Common Cases Completed in Youth Court, 2011–2012**

SOURCE: Statistics Canada, 2013. Youth court statistics in Canada 2011/2012. *Juristat*. Catalogue no. 85-002-x, June 13. http://www.statcan.gc.ca/pub/85-002-x/2013001/article/11803-eng.pdf

[1]Includes, for example, theft over $5 000, theft $5 000 or under, as well as motor vehicle theft.
[2]Includes assault with a weapon (level 2) and aggravated assault (level 3).

NOTE: A case is one or more charges against an accused person or company that were processed by the courts at the same time and received a final decision. Cases that involve more than one charge are represented by the most serious offence.

55.8 percent of all crimes committed by youth. Incarceration rates for youth remain high, with just over one-fifth to just over one-quarter of all guilty findings resulting in custodial sentences for youth whose cases were resolved in the years between 2002 and 2005 (Thomas 2008: 15). The *Youth Criminal Justice Act* (YCJA) has started to correct the admitted overuse of incarceration that Brian Hogeveen's research shows to have been the herald of the *Young Offenders Act* (YOA) throughout the 1990s, when youth crime rates dropped while incarceration rates increased by 35 percent (2005: 9). Since the YCJA replaced the YOA, incarceration rates have dropped considerably, down from a high of 27 percent in 2002–03 to 17 percent in 2006–07 (Statistics Canada 2008). Figure 4.7 shows that in contrast to media reports that suggest Canadian youth are more violent and destructive than ever, the top 10 most common charges are relatively minor probation breaches and property crimes; even "common assault" refers to something as simple as throwing a punch in a bar-fight, and not to the aggravated assault charges that make news headlines. Moreover, the 2011–12 youth court statistics report a 10 percent decline in cases heard over the previous year, a "third consecutive annual decline" (Dauvergne 2012b: 3). As Dauvergne explains,

> The decrease in the total number of completed youth court cases between 2010/2011 and 2011/2012 was driven by fewer cases involving virtually every type of offence (Table 3). More specifically, decreases were seen among all types of property crime cases, including the two most common ones: theft (–17%) and break and enter (–15%). Among violent crime cases, drops included fewer major assault (–15%) and criminal harassment (–14%) cases. (p. 6)

Age and Crime

People who have not reached middle age commit most crime. Youth are the most crime prone, perhaps because this group has adult desires for goods and opportunities still out of their grasp. Why is criminal activity more prevalent among individuals in their teens and early 20s? Younger individuals are more likely to be unemployed or employed in low-wage jobs. As strain theorists argue, they have less access to legitimate means for acquiring material goods.

Various commentators have linked Canada's decreasing crime over the last decade to the country's aging population structure. Specifically, while those between the ages of 15 and 24 have a high risk of offending, this age group has decreased in size by 6 percent since 1991 (Logan 2001: 3). Unlike the 1960s, when the baby boom generation (those born between 1947 and 1966) came into their years of highest risk, the 1990s saw the products of the baby bust years (1967 to 1979). Simply put, "[t]here has been a smaller pool of people who are at the greatest risk with respect to criminal behaviour" (John Howard Society 1999: 2).

Race, Social Class, and Crime

Race is a factor in who is arrested. The overrepresentation of Aboriginal peoples in the Canadian criminal justice system has been commented on for decades by various commissions and task forces. Although Aboriginal peoples represented 2 percent of the adult population in Canada at the end of the last century, they consistently accounted for 15 to 18 percent of admissions to both provincial/territorial and federal sentenced custody over the two last decades of the century (Lonmo 2001: 8). According to recent projections and analyses offered by Calverley (2010), while Aboriginal peoples now account for 3 percent of the population they "accounted for 27 percent of all sentenced admissions to provincial custody in 2008/09, 21 percent of admissions to remand, and 18 percent of admissions to federal prisons" (Calverley, cited in Hartnagel 2012: 147). These numbers hold true in the most recent (2006) data from Correctional Service Canada, which also notes that the situation is especially bad for Aboriginal women, who represent 30 percent of those incarcerated in federal prisons.

The overrepresentation of Aboriginal persons in Canada's prisons is particularly marked in the Prairie provinces. When it comes to punishment for youth crime, those of Aboriginal background are punished far more frequently. Citing data from Statistics Canada and Correctional Service Canada, Bryan Hogeveen (2005: 82) notes, "In the prairie provinces of Manitoba and Saskatchewan, three quarters . . . of youth sentenced to custody were identified as Aboriginal, while less than 20 percent of Manitoba's youth population is identified as Native."

Possible explanations for the overrepresentation of Aboriginal people in Canada's prisons include[*]

- differential treatment by the criminal justice system—being discriminated against by the police, the courts, etc.;
- differential commission of crime and differential offence patterns—committing crimes that are more detectable—more serious or more visible—than those committed by non-Aboriginal people;
- the socio-structural deprivation of Canada's Aboriginal peoples;
- the decline of informal mechanisms of social control within Aboriginal communities; and
- systemic racism (Hartnagel 2012).

Aboriginal offenders also tend to be younger on average than others, and hence less likely to be able to access their full legal rights and to acquire good legal representation for their defence (ibid).

Although some investigators have claimed that certain races are more or less law abiding than others, such research typically fails to define "race," assumes racial purity as a given, treats crime as a unitary phenomenon, and simply presents correlational data on race and crime (Roberts and Gabor 1990). Demonstrating that a correlation exists does not, of course, prove causation.

[*]Hartnagel 2000.

There are a number of reasons why it would be inaccurate to conclude that race and crime are causally related. First, official statistics reflect the behaviours and policies of criminal justice actors. The high arrest, conviction, and incarceration rates of Aboriginal people may be due to individual and institutional bias not only against them, but also against the lower classes in general. Second, race and social class are closely related in that Aboriginal peoples are overrepresented in the lower classes. Since lower class members lack legitimate means to acquire material goods, they may turn to instrumental, or economically motivated, crimes. Further, subcultural theorists argue that, while the "haves" typically earn social respect through their socio-economic status, educational achievement, and occupational roles, the "have-nots" tend to live in communities where respect is based on physical strength and violence. Thus, what seems to be a relationship between race and crime may be, in part, a consequence of the relationship between these variables and social class.

In recent years, changes made by Parliament to the sentencing provisions of the Canadian *Criminal Code* have attempted to address the overrepresentation of Aboriginal peoples in Canada's inmate population. For example, section 718.2 specifies that "all available sanctions other than imprisonment that are reasonable in the circumstances should be considered for all offenders, *with particular attention to the circumstances of aboriginal offenders*" [emphasis added]. While being Aboriginal does not automatically result in a lesser sentence, the Supreme Court of Canada has urged judges, when sentencing an Aboriginal offender, to recognize the "broad systemic and background factors affecting Aboriginal people" (Lonmo 2001: 8). The Correctional Service of Canada also tries to assist Aboriginal people who are incarcerated by including culturally sensitive substance abuse programs, Native liaison services, and Elders' services. The Okimaw Ohci Healing Lodge for federally sentenced Aboriginal women in Maple Creek, Saskatchewan, was developed with and for the First Nations community. Sixty percent of the staff working at this facility, which places a strong emphasis on Aboriginal culture and spirituality, are of Aboriginal descent (Solicitor General 2002).

Region and Crime

In Canada, the distribution of crime varies by region. Historically, crime rates in Canada have generally increased from east to west, with Nova Scotia and Alberta providing exceptions to this general trend—Nova Scotia's crime rate has generally been higher, and Alberta's crime rate lower, than those of their neighbouring provinces (Logan 2001).

Although folk wisdom might suggest that there is more crime in larger cities than in small cities or towns, this belief would be wrong. Greater numbers of crimes occur in larger than in smaller cities, but this pattern must be set against the greater number of people living in such areas. For example, in 2001, the rate of violent crime in Toronto, Canada's largest metropolitan area, was 876 per 100 000—substantially below that of Regina (1614), Saskatoon (1663), Vancouver (1053), and Winnipeg (1309). The rate of property crime in Toronto (2932) was also lower than the property crime rate in these cities; in Regina, it was 9661 per 100 000 population; in Saskatoon, 6616; in Vancouver, 7347; and in Winnipeg, 5967. Indeed, in 2001, Toronto, along with Chicoutimi-Jonquière, Québec City, and Trois-Rivières, had the lowest crime rate among Canada's 25 census metropolitan areas (Statistics Canada 2002).

The newly developed crime severity index measures allow us to see an even more nuanced picture of crime in Canada. The index measures not simply instances of crime, but the prevalence of violent and non-violent crimes, crimes against the person, and crimes against property. Figure 4.8 shows that for 2007 the information we have just discussed holds generally true, even when we are considering regions in terms of the severity as well as the prevalence of crime. With the exception of cities in the

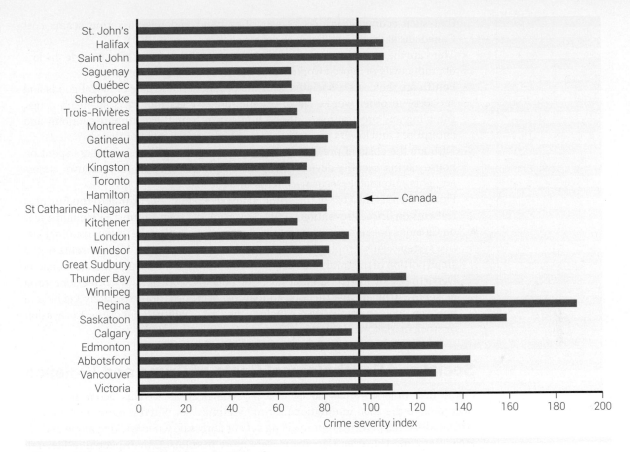

Figure 4.8 **Measuring Crime in Canada**

SOURCE: Statistics Canada, 2009. "Measuring Crime in Canada: Introducing the Crime Severity Index and Improvements to the Uniform Crime Reporting Survey." Canadian Centre for Justice Statistics. Catalogue No. 85-004-x..

western provinces, it is smaller cities that have higher severity indices, with Winnipeg, Regina, and Saskatoon having the worst results in the country.

4.6 Costs of Crime and Violence

Crime does not result only or primarily in physical injury and loss of life or property; other, less tangible costs are incurred. Although the immediate victims of criminal acts bear the costs of crime most acutely, a far broader constituency may experience the economic, social, and psychological costs of crime.

Economic Costs of Crime and Violence

Conklin (1998: 71–72) suggests that the financial costs of crime can be classified into at least six categories.

- First are direct losses from crime, such as the destruction of buildings through arson, of private property through vandalism, and of the environment by polluters.
- Second are costs associated with the transferring of property. Bank robbers, car thieves, and embezzlers have all taken property from its rightful owner at huge expense to the victim and to society. The Organized Crime Impact Study reported

CONLKIN, JOHN E. *CRIMINOLOGY*, 10th Edition © 2010, pp. 49–50. Reprinted by permission of Pearson Education, Inc., Upper Saddle River, NJ.

that such economic crimes as securities fraud and telemarketing scams cost Canadians at least $5 billion each year (Solicitor General 1999).

- Third are the major costs associated with criminal violence. These include the loss of productivity of injured workers and the medical expenses of victims.
- Fourth are the costs associated with the production and sale of illegal goods and services—in other words, illegal expenditures. When money is spent on drugs, gambling, and prostitution, it diverts funds away from the legitimate economy and enterprises, and lowers property values in high-crime neighbourhoods.
- Fifth are the costs of prevention and protection, the millions of dollars spent on house alarms, security devices, weapons for protection, bars for windows, timers for lights, automobile security systems, and the like.
- Finally, there is the cost of the criminal justice system. According to the Business Network on Crime Prevention (2001), "governments spend almost $12 billion a year on Canada's police services, courts and corrections that make up our criminal justice system." They emphasize that this figure is conservative. It "represents only a small portion of the total costs of crime." According to the 2005 data from Canada's Department of Justice, annual costs of policing, courts, and corrections total closer to $10 billion and the total annual cost of crime is approximately $46 billion; however, such estimates "do not include the cost of white-collar crime, tax evasion or stock market manipulation" (Department of Justice 2005).

Social and Psychological Costs of Crime and Violence

Crime and violence entail social and psychological, as well as economic, costs. According to the 2000 International Crime Victimization Survey, more than 8 out of 10 Canadians (83 percent) report feeling very or fairly safe when walking alone in their area after dark. However, Canadians were more pessimistic than people in Finland, Sweden, the United States, or Scotland when asked if they thought they would likely experience a break-in. The concern about crime and the prevalence of efforts to protect oneself against crime have dropped marginally from the 70 percent reported in 2002 by Besserer, but as of 2009,

> close to two-thirds of Canadians who said that they had taken at least one form of precautionary measure in their lifetime and 39 percent had done so in the 12 months preceding the survey. The most common precautionary action taken by Canadians in the 12 months preceding the survey involved changing their routine, activities or avoiding certain people or places (27%). Other common precautions included installing new locks or security bars (13%), and installing burglar alarms or motion detector lights (10%). (Brennan 2011: 9)

Reporting in 2011, Brennan's data on perceptions about crime are consistent with those from a decade ago, and show that the general perceptions of Canadians are positive; 83 percent "said that they were not at all worried when home alone in the evening . . . and 90% said they felt safe when walking alone in their neighbourhood at night" (p. 5). These very high reported levels of satisfaction with personal security in one's community dropped, however, for those who had been victimized, and furthermore varied by gender, as we see in Figure 4.9.

In various ways it is evident that the fear of crime and violence affects community life, as Brennan explains:

> Fear of crime can often act as a barrier in preventing people from participating in or performing certain activities . . . Overall, just under 6 in 10 (59%) Canadians said that they would use public transportation alone after dark more often if they felt safer from crime; while close to 4 in 10 (39%) said that they would walk alone after dark

Figure 4.9 **Self-Reported Feelings of Safety While Performing Various Activities, by Sex, 2009**

SOURCE: Statistics Canada, General Social Survey, 2009. Brennan, Shannon. 2011. "Canadians' Perceptions of Personal Safety and Crime, 2009," Component of Statistics Canada Catalogue No. 85-002-X. *Juristat*. http://www.statcan.gc.ca/pub/85-002-x/2011001/article/11577-eng.pdf (p. 8).

[†]Reference category
[*]Significantly different from reference category (p < 0.05)
[1]Includes only those who had access to public transportation in their communities.

NOTE: Data from Yukon, the Northwest Territories and Nunavut were collected using a different methodology and are therefore excluded.

more often. While fear of crime may present limitations to the lives of all Canadians, these barriers are often compounded for women . . . The 2009 GSS found that women were more likely than men (41% versus 35%) to say that they would walk alone after dark more often if they felt safer from crime. (2011: 9)

White-collar crimes also take a social and psychological toll at both the individual and the societal levels. Moore and Mills (1990) state that the effects of white-collar crime include "(a) diminished faith in a free economy and in business leaders, (b) loss of confidence in political institutions, processes and leaders, and (c) erosion of public morality" (p. 414). Crime also causes personal pain and suffering, the destruction of families, lowered self-esteem, shortened life expectancy, and disease.

4.7 **Strategies for Action: Responding to Crime and Violence**

In addition to economic policies designed to reduce unemployment and poverty, many social policies and programs have been initiated to alleviate the problem of crime and violence. These policies and programs are directed toward children at risk of being offenders, community crime prevention, criminal justice policies, and legislative action.

Youth Programs

Early intervention programs acknowledge that it is better to prevent crime than to "cure" it once it has occurred. Preschool enrichment programs, such as the Perry Preschool Project, have been successful in reducing rates of aggression in young children. After random assignment of children to either a control or experimental group, experimental group members received academically oriented interventions for one to two years, frequent home visits, and weekly parent-teacher conferences. When control and experimental groups were compared, the experimental group had better grades, higher rates of high-school graduation, lower rates of unemployment, and fewer arrests (Murray et al. 1997). Recognizing the link between youthful offenders and adult criminality, many anti-crime programs are directed toward at-risk youths. These prevention strategies include the federal government's Crime Prevention Initiative, with its focus on proactive programs for high-risk families. Other examples are youth programs such as Boys and Girls Clubs and the national Aboriginal Head Start program. These programs are designed to keep young people "off the streets," provide a safe and supportive environment, and offer activities that promote skill development and self-esteem. According to Gest and Friedman (1994), housing projects with such programs report 13 percent fewer juvenile crimes and a 25 percent decrease in the use of crack.

Community Programs

Programs such as Neighbourhood Watch, Block Parents, Crime Stoppers, and Operation Identification involve local residents in crime-prevention strategies. The objective of such programs is to reduce crime by heightening community efforts to prevent it. Neighbourhood Watch programs, developed with the help of local police departments or services, offer advice to residents on how to best protect their homes and belongings. They encourage neighbourhood members to watch out for and report any suspicious activities they see to the police.

Law Enforcement Agencies

Police policies and practices can also affect crime rates. Seagrave (1997) noted that the mission statement of every Canadian police force in the 1990s contained evidence of formal commitment to the concept of **community policing**. Community-oriented policing involves collaborative efforts among the police, the citizens of a community, and local leaders. As part of community policing efforts, officers speak to citizens' groups, consult with social agencies, and enlist the aid of corporate and political leaders in the fight against neighbourhood crime (COPS 1998; Lehrur 1999). Officers using community-policing techniques often employ "practical approaches" to crime intervention. Such solutions may include what Felson (1998) calls "situational crime prevention." Felson argues that simply minimizing the opportunity for its occurrence could prevent much crime. For example, cars could be outfitted with unbreakable glass, flush-sill lock buttons, an audible reminder to remove keys, and a high-security lock for steering columns (p. 168).

In addition, programs aimed at crime victims now exist in almost all Canadian police departments. Victim assistance programs are designed to provide crime victims with details on the progress of their case, facilitate the return of property to rightful owners, and act as referral agencies to other support groups in the local community. Often heavily dependent on volunteers, such services may signal the development of a partnership between the police and a local community agency or institution. In Ottawa, the Salvation Army works in collaboration with the Ottawa Police Department to supply victim services. In Montreal, the University of Montreal, in cooperation with the Montreal Urban Community Police, operates the Integrated Victim Assistance program (Seagrave 1997).

Criminal Justice Policy

The criminal justice system presumes that **deterrence**, or the use of harm or the threat of harm, is an effective way to prevent unwanted behaviours. It assumes that people

community policing
When police, community, and local governance structures, including politicians and religious and educational institutions, work together to prevent crime at local levels. Not intended to address large-scale concerns, but to help citizens prevent their neighbourhoods from becoming targets for crimes. Efforts range from Neighbourhood Watch programs to education about the causes of crime. Through informal networks, there can be information sharing between police and community groups.

deterrence
The use of harm or the threat of harm to prevent unwanted behaviours.

rationally choose to commit crime, weighing the rewards and consequences of their actions. Thus, the recent emphasis on "get-tough" measures holds that maximizing punishment will increase deterrence and cause crime rates to decrease. Research indicates otherwise. The effectiveness of deterrence is a function not only of the severity of the punishment, but also of the certainty and swiftness of the punishment. Further, "get-tough" policies create other criminal justice problems, including overcrowded prisons and, consequently, the need for plea bargaining and early-release programs.

Capital Punishment

With capital punishment, the state takes the life of a person as punishment for a crime. Although capital punishment has not been used in Canada since 1962 and was formally abolished in this country in 1976, the federal government retains the right to bring it back. Since the 1970s, Gallup polls have consistently noted that the majority of Canadians believe that the courts are too lenient with offenders: in the fall of 1943, Gallup reported that 80 percent of Canadians were in favour of capital punishment. In 1995, approximately 85 percent of a national random sample of Canadians maintained that the courts did not deal harshly enough with criminals, particularly young offenders, and approximately 82 percent believed that the death penalty should be exercised in some instances (Bibby 1995). Although support for the use of capital punishment has declined in recent years, data from the 2000 Project Canada survey indicate that 74 percent of Canadian adults and 59 percent of Canadian teenagers agree that "the death penalty should sometimes be used to punish criminals" (Bibby 2001: 244).

Those for and against capital punishment take different views on how to convey societal disapproval of murder. Proponents of capital punishment argue that executions of convicted murderers convey public disapproval and intolerance for such heinous crimes. Those against capital punishment believe that no one, including the state, has the right to take another person's life and that putting convicted murderers behind bars for life is a **social death** that conveys the necessary societal disapproval.

Proponents of capital punishment also argue that it deters individuals from committing murder. Critics of capital punishment hold that since most homicides are situational and unplanned, offenders do not consider the consequences of their actions before they commit the offences. Critics also point out that the United States has a much higher murder rate than Canada or Western European nations that do not practise capital punishment—and that death sentences are racially discriminatory. For example, a study on federal capital cases in the United States found that blacks were less likely than whites to have their sentences reduced through plea-bargaining (Worden 2000).

Capital punishment advocates and opponents use financial arguments, too. Advocates suggest that executing a convicted murderer relieves taxpayers of the costs involved in housing, feeding, guarding, and providing medical care for inmates. Opponents argue that the principles that decide life-and-death issues should not be determined by financial considerations. In addition, due to the lengthy and costly appeal process for capital punishment cases, taking care of convicted murderers for life may actually be less costly than sentencing them to death (Garey 1985).

Advocates and opponents of capital punishment also deal with the issue of protecting society versus the individual. Those who favour capital punishment argue that it prevents convicted individuals from committing other crimes, including the murder of another inmate or prison official. Opponents contend, however, that capital punishment may result in innocent people being sentenced to death. For example, between 1973 and 1999, 76 death-row inmates in the United States were released when new evidence supported their innocence (*Economist* 2000). Further, a report by the (U.S.) Justice Project, entitled "A Broken System," found "serious, reversible error in

social death
The removal of a person from larger society through lifetime imprisonment. By stripping the person of a meaningful position within society, lifetime imprisonment removes from that person an identity and status in the larger world. The prisoner is ejected from the relationship circles necessary for the maintenance of a personal identity.

nearly seven out of ten of the thousands of capital sentences" that were reviewed over the 23-year study period (Liebman et al. 2000). In Russia, it is reported that almost one in three (30 percent) of capital punishment cases may have had judicial errors that resulted in a wrongful execution (MacIntyre 1999). Even though 35 countries abolished the death penalty between 1985 and 1998, as of October 1, 2000, there were 3703 prisoners on death row in the United States (Ash 2001: 69; MacIntyre 1999).

The highly publicized cases of David Milgaard, Guy Paul Morin, and Donald Marshall should remind us that wrongful convictions do occur. David Milgaard served 23 years in various Canadian prisons, including the Oak Ridge institution for dangerous mentally ill offenders in Penetanguishene, Ontario, for the 1970 sex slaying of a Saskatoon nursing aide. He was finally exonerated in 1997 when DNA tests showed that he was not the killer. Donald Marshall, wrongfully convicted for the 1971 murder of a teenager who was stabbed to death in a Sydney, Nova Scotia park, spent 11 years in prison. Guy Paul Morin was wrongfully convicted in the sex slaying of a young Queensville, Ontario girl, faced two first-degree murder trials, and spent 17 months in custody. In these cases, and a handful of others, the individuals have fought for their vindication on charges of murder and received, as partial redress, financial settlements from the federal and provincial governments. In the largest settlement to date for a wrongful conviction, Milgaard received $9.25 million in compensation for his legal fees (which totalled $1.5 million), for pain and suffering, for lost income, and for out-of-pocket expenses; his mother received $750 000 for the legal and personal costs she had incurred during her long struggle to prove that her son was innocent (Bourrie 1999). There is, of course, no way of compensating those who have been wrongfully convicted and received, as a penalty, capital punishment.

Rehabilitation versus Incapacitation

An important debate focuses on the primary purpose of the criminal justice system: Is it to rehabilitate offenders or to incapacitate them through incarceration? Both **rehabilitation** and **incapacitation** are concerned with recidivism rates, or the extent to which criminals commit another crime. Advocates of rehabilitation believe that changing the criminal can reduce recidivism, whereas proponents of incapacitation think recidivism can best be reduced by placing the offender in prison so that he or she is unable to commit further crimes.

Societal fear of crime has led to a public emphasis on incapacitation, a demand for tougher mandatory sentences, and a reduction in the use of probation and parole (DiIulio 1999; Human Rights Watch 2000). Canada is, indeed, locking people up. The International Center for Prison Studies' survey data on Canada's prison population in three-year increments from 1991 to 2001 show that our incarceration rate hit a high of 131 per 100 000 population in 1994–95, and a low of 116 per 100 000 in 2001. Although we imprison fewer members of our population than the United States (724 per 100 000 population) or Russia (564) (see Figure 4.10), our incarceration rate already exceeds those of many other Western democracies. In addition, the *Youth Criminal Justice Act* of 2002–03, with its "get-tough" approach to youth, promises not only to follow a standard of high incarceration rates, but also to increase them, locking up those youth who are from the poorest and most poorly served communities in the country (Hogeveen 2005). As we discussed earlier in the chapter, our rates for youth incarceration are only marginally lower under the YCJA than under the previous YOA in Canada.

Public opinion on how to deal with youth crime is especially divided on the point of punishment. Opinion is influenced in large part by media attention and political opportunism that makes violent crime appear common rather than atypical. As a result, legislative acts must be relayed to a vacillating public with care. The message to the public has to be that no life will be ruined for the sake of punishing petty offences;

rehabilitation
A criminal justice philosophy that views the primary purpose of the criminal justice system as changing the criminal offender through such programs as education and job training, individual and group therapy, substance abuse counselling, and behaviour modification.

incapacitation
A criminal justice philosophy that views the primary purpose of the criminal justice system as preventing criminal offenders from committing further crimes against the public by putting them in prison.

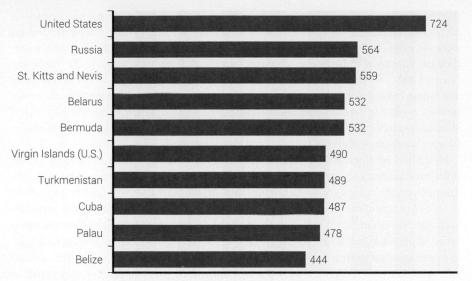

Figure 4.10 **Nations with Highest Rates of Incarceration, 2004**

SOURCE: "Ten Leading Nations in Incarceration Rates," which appeared in *New Incarceration Figures: Growth in Population Continues* (The Sentencing Project). Copyright 2005. Used with permission.

Incarceration rate (number of people in prison per 100 000 population)

however, the jailing of youth through the 1990s shows a judicial reality very different from that message to the public. While rates of incarceration for young offenders were slowly creeping toward American numbers, rates of deviance were slowly declining (Hogeveen 2005: 81). Even in the population most likely to commit crime and commonly perceived to be the most dangerous, criminal activity has been decreasing.

According to the Solicitor General of Canada (2002), approximately $2 billion is spent on Canada's adult federal and provincial correctional systems each year. The annual cost of incarceration for federal prisoners varies by gender; male prisoners cost an average of $79 555 a year and female prisoners cost an average of $169 399, for a combined annual average of $81 206 (Correctional Service Canada 2005). The CSC report on costs of incarceration explains the reason for the nearly doubled annual average for incarcerating women: there are far fewer incarcerated women, yet because they still require the same material and personnel resources for their housing and rehabilitation as men do, the costs of their incarceration are higher per capita. Unfortunately, the Office of the Solicitor General was abolished in 2005 and replaced by the Office for Public Safety, a ministerial portfolio at the federal level that has not, thus far, produced a report on the costs of incarceration, choosing instead to focus on risk assessment. We do know, however, that as of 2007 Correctional Service Canada was still holding 13 171 inmates in prisons across the country, with an annual budget of $1.8 billion (Public Safety Canada 2010: 1).

While incapacitation is clearly enhanced by longer prison sentences, rehabilitation may not be. Rehabilitation assumes that criminal behaviour is caused by sociological, psychological, biological, or a combination of these forces rather than being solely a product of free will. If such forces can be identified, the necessary change can be instituted. Rehabilitation programs include education and job training, individual and group therapy, substance abuse counselling, and behaviour modification. While the evaluation of rehabilitation programs is difficult and results are mixed, incapacitation must of necessity be a temporary measure. Unless all criminals are sentenced to life, at some point approximately 98 percent will be returned to society.

Alternatives to Incarceration

In addition to incarceration, there are other strategies that are being pursued. Offenders may be ordered by judges to provide restitution and financially compensate their victims for property loss and personal injury. Electronic monitoring requires a convicted offender to wear an electronic bracelet that is generally placed around an ankle or wrist. "If they stray too far from a receiver unit attached to a telephone, when they are supposed to be home, an alarm sounds at the monitoring centre" (Solicitor General 2002). In cases where an offender does not pose a danger to the community and where the usual jail term would be less than two years, a conditional sentence may be used, requiring the offender to seek treatment, for example. Other community-based alternatives to incarceration include a community service order requiring an offender to work a certain number of hours within the community.

Mediation services, which work in cooperation with the Crown Attorney's office, bring victimizers and their victims together in the belief that both will benefit. For example, committing a crime may require that an offender discount the consequences of his or her act on the victim or blame the victim (e.g., "she's got insurance to cover the loss," "he was asking for it"); it is thought that face-to-face meetings will encourage a sense of personal culpability and compassion for the victim. Similarly, if the *hindsight effect* encourages victims to overestimate the extent to which they could have avoided victimization (Janoff-Bulman et al. 1985), confronting one's victimizer may result in a lessened amount of self-blame. Moreover, insofar as those who have experienced criminal victimization are likely to demonstrate a heightened fear of crime, it may prove personally empowering to see their victimizers as simply other human beings.

Victim and offender mediation represents one of many programs that may flow from a framework of **restorative justice**. Restorative justice "is an approach to justice that focuses on dealing with the harmful effects of crime by engaging victims, offenders and the community in a process of reparation and healing" (Solicitor General 2002). Many Aboriginal communities have traditionally emphasized this model of justice in which[*]

- the focus is on problem solving and restoration of harmony;
- restitution and reconciliation are used as a means of restoration;
- the community acts as a facilitator in the restorative process;
- the offender is impressed with the impact of his action on the total community;
- the holistic context of an offence is taken into account including moral, social, economic, political, and religious and cosmic considerations;
- stigma of offences is removable through conformity;
- repentance and forgiveness are important factors;
- offenders take an active role in the restorative process (Bryant 1999: 21).

Unlike the traditional criminal justice process, restorative justice emphasizes individual and social healing, forgiveness, communication, and joint problem solving rather than punishment. Although the behaviour of the offender is condemned, the value of the offender as an individual is affirmed.

Legislative Action

The federal government has taken various steps to combat crime. In relation to organized crime, for example, these steps include the 1994 Anti-Smuggling Initiative, which targets smuggling and distribution networks at the border, in Canada's ports, and across the country; and the 1996 establishment of the *Witness Protection Program Act*, which established a formal, national program to protect those who assist police investigations. Legislative amendments to the *Criminal Code* in 1997 included anti-gang measures that made participation in a criminal organization an indictable offence, punishable by up to 14 years in prison. In 1998, amendments made to the *Corrections and Conditional*

restorative justice
A philosophy primarily concerned with reconciling conflict between the offender, the community, and the victim.

[*] Bryant, Marian E. 1999. "Sentencing Aboriginal Offenders." *Law Now* (October/November): 20-21. Reprinted by permission of M. Bryant.

Release Act sought to ensure that those convicted of offences related to organized crime were ineligible for accelerated parole review. In 2002, legislative changes included the introduction of three new offences that targeted those involved with criminal organizations; broader powers for law enforcement officers to seize the profits of crime and property used in a crime; and increased protection of law enforcement officers from criminal liability when they commit certain acts that would otherwise be considered illegal when investigating and infiltrating criminal organizations (Department of Justice 2002c).

Legislative efforts have also sought to curtail child sexual exploitation. For example, in 1997, amendments to the *Criminal Code* provided for the prosecution of persons who engage in child sex tourism in other countries and facilitated the apprehension and prosecution of persons who seek out the services of child victims of sexual exploitation in Canada. Bill C-15A, which came into effect on July 23, 2002, makes it illegal to use the internet to communicate with a child for the purpose of committing a sexual offence against that child, as well as to transmit, make available, export, or access child pornography. It also allows the courts to order the deletion of child pornography posted on Canadian computer systems, makes child pornography and the new internet luring offence "triggering offences" for making an application to designate a person as a dangerous offender, allows for the seizure of materials or equipment used to commit a related offence, and simplifies the process of prosecuting Canadians who sexually exploit children in other countries (Department of Justice 2002a).

In 2001, in response to the September 11, 2001, terrorist attacks in New York City and Washington, D.C., Canada's highly controversial *Anti-Terrorism Act* (Bill C-36) passed through the Senate with a vote of 45 to 21 and became law. The *Anti-Terrorism Act,* like its counterpart in the United Kingdom, defines terrorist activity as encompassing acts of violence or destruction that are intended to influence government or intimidate the public. Both definitions require proof that an offence was committed out of religious, ideological, or political motivation. Among its provisions, Canada's *Anti-Terrorism Act* allows police to exercise "preventative arrest" powers and to detain, without judicial warrant, suspected terrorists for up to 48 hours. It also extends the valid period of a wiretap and lowers the standard required to obtain a wiretap. Unlike the United States, Canada does not seek to try suspected foreign terrorists in secret military tribunals. Unlike Britain, where the law provides for a 10-year maximum penalty for simply belonging to a terrorist organization, Canada has not banned membership.

Supporters of the act have argued that, after the September 11 attacks, Canadian security had to be tightened in order to comply with Resolution 1373 of the United Nations Security Council. The resolution "called on all member countries to adopt the necessary measures to prevent any one country from becoming a haven for terrorists" (Chwialkowska 2001). Critics, however, maintain that the act's definition of terrorism is too broad, that the act contains measures that are open for abuse, and that there are only limited provisions for oversight. Moreover, some have expressed concern that **racial profiling**—the practice of targeting suspects based upon their race—will become a prominent feature of investigations conducted under this act.

Canada's *Youth Criminal Justice Act* (YCJA), which replaces the *Young Offenders Act* (1984), also represents an attempt to respond to the social problem of crime. The core principles of the YCJA are that

- protection of society is the paramount objective of the youth justice system, which is best achieved through prevention, meaningful consequences for youth crime, and rehabilitation;
- young people should be treated separately from adults under criminal law and in a separate youth justice system that emphasizes fair and proportionate accountability, keeping in mind the dependency and level of development and maturity of youth;

racial profiling
The law enforcement practice of targeting suspects based upon race.

- measures to address youth crime must hold the offender accountable; address the offending behaviour of the youth; reinforce respect for social values; encourage repair of the harm done to victims and the community; respect gender, ethnic, cultural, and linguistic differences; involve the family, community, and other agencies; and be responsive to the circumstances of youth with special requirements; and
- parents and victims have a constructive role to play in the youth justice system, and should be kept informed and encouraged to participate (Department of Justice 2002b).

Understanding Crime and Violence

What can we conclude from the information presented in this chapter? Research on crime and violence supports the contentions of both functionalists and conflict theorists. The inequality in society, along with the emphasis on material well-being and corporate profit, produces societal strains and individual frustrations. Poverty, unemployment, urban decay, and substandard schools—the symptoms of social inequality—lead, in turn, to the development of criminal subcultures and definitions favourable to law violation. Further, the continued weakening of social bonds between members of society and society as a whole, the labelling of some acts and actors as "deviant," and the differential treatment of minority groups by the criminal justice system encourage criminal behaviour. While crime and violence constitute major social problems in society, they are also symptoms of other social problems, such as poverty and economic inequality, racial discrimination, drug addiction, an overburdened educational system, and troubled families. The criminal justice system still struggles to find effective and just measures to deal with crime and criminal offenders. Many citizens and politicians have embraced the idea that society should "get tough" on crime. Get-tough measures include building more prisons and imposing lengthier mandatory prison sentences on criminal offenders. Advocates of harsher prison sentences argue that such measures make society safer. They keep criminals off the streets and deter potential criminals from committing crime. Yet, for example, an analysis of over 200 studies comparing institutionalized and non-institutionalized serious young offenders found that community-based treatment worked better than incarceration in lowering recidivism rates (Lipsey and Wilson 1998). Prison sentences not only may be ineffective in preventing crime, they may even promote it: they create an environment in which prisoners learn criminal behaviour, values, and attitudes from one another.

Rather than getting tough on crime after the fact, some advocate getting serious about prevention. Re-emphasizing the values of honesty, responsibility, and civic virtue is a basic line of prevention with which most agree. The recent move toward restorative justice, a philosophy focused on repairing the victim-offender-community relationship, is in direct response to concerns about an adversarial criminal justice system—one that encourages offenders to deny, justify, or otherwise avoid taking responsibility for their actions. As noted earlier, restorative justice holds that the justice system should be a "healing process rather than a distributor of retribution and revenge" (Siegel 2000: 278). Key components of restorative justice include restitution to the victim, remedy of the harm to the community, and mediation. At a meeting of the United Nations' Congress in Crime Prevention and Treatment of Offenders, a summary resolution, called the *Vienna Declaration,* was approved. The resolution calls for the worldwide use of restorative justice intervention.

Student Reflection: What Do You Know Now?

Canada's reputation as a place where everyone keeps the front door unlocked and people are all nice to one another is clearly a stereotype that is not borne out by numbers or experiences. We do have a number of different kinds of crimes occurring here, from corporate crime to violent crime and property damage. However, the patterns do not always line up according to our assumptions about who is involved in crime and what we should do about it. You will find that different theoretical explanations highlight different elements in the big picture of Canadian crime; none, though, recommend building more prisons and no longer reporting incarceration rates or prison costs, as the Harper government has done. Consider all the different types of crime and of justice as you reflect on your own interactions with your immediate environment or your wider community. Which theories do you find most useful to explain different categories of crime, for example white-collar crimes, violent crimes, and sex crimes? Why? Thinking ahead, and given that crime statistics are sensitive to demographic changes, suggest how the aging of the Canadian population may affect crime rates (and types of crime) as we move toward the end of the second decade of the twenty-first century. Equally interesting may be the ways in which technology, so ubiquitous in our lives already, will be deployed increasingly in the surveillance, detection, and tracking of crime.

What Do You Do Next?

Located at www.nelson.com/socialproblems5e

- Consolidate your knowledge with interactive and printable **Flashcards**
- Gauge your understanding with **Practice Quizzes** and **Matching Activities**
- Develop your critical thinking skills with **Self and Society** and **The Human Side** questions
- Analyze **Social Research** and **Social Problems in Global Perspective**
- Explore the implications of **Technology on Social Problems**

5

Family Problems

Student Reflection: What Do You Already Know?

This chapter may be more difficult than some of the others you'll read. Everyone has some relationship to families, and we are looking at some of the most negative aspects that can arise (violence and abuse). Before learning about the variety of forms "family" can take, and about the problems associated with violence, abuse, divorce, and unplanned child-bearing, consider your own assumptions about what a family is, or can be. From where do your own expectations for families and intimate relationships arise? What is your own definition of a "traditional" family, and where does it come from? What problems have you seen or experienced and how might they be addressed? If they aren't addressed, why not? To what extent have you yourself thought of such problems as individualized, and to what extent have you thought of them as having social, cultural, and political dimensions?

Learning Outcomes

Through careful reading of this chapter, you should be able to:

- define the bolded key terms
- contextualize marriage and family historically and culturally in their diversity of possible arrangements
- identify changes over time to so-called "traditional" family structures and the kinds of data collection that help make these structures visible
- apply sociological perspectives to an understanding of family structures in Canada and beyond
- challenge commonsense and traditional perspectives on family and marriage using feminist and queer approaches
- identify a range of systemic factors that inform family and intimate partner violence in their various forms and at various life stages
- consider ways of responding to violence and abuse in family and intimate relationships
- develop an understanding of the diverse issues surrounding divorce and unplanned child-bearing, including alternate views, in our changing legal, social, and cultural landscape

© AvailableLight/iStockphoto.com

Though family is generally sentimentalized and spoken about in terms that praise family above all other institutions, a sociological approach to family as a concept, structure, and institution reveals for our consideration those problems that we all know are there but tend to push aside, or to see through the lens of a "commonsense" attitude: violence and abuse in intimate and family relationships, problems of divorce, and problems associated with unplanned child-bearing. Other problems facing families are discussed in other chapters in this text. For example, families are affected by health problems (Chapter 2), substance abuse (Chapter 3), problems of youth and the elderly (Chapter 6), and problems with employment and poverty (Chapters 10 and 11). Before discussing these problems, we look briefly at the history and diversity of families worldwide, and we provide an overview of the changing patterns and structures of households and families in Canada.

5.1 The Global Context: Families of the World

Family is a central aspect of every society throughout the world, but family forms are diverse. Though we commonly think of family as something that issues forth from the bringing together of separate kinship groups through marriage, family is, in fact, a varying, historically and culturally specific organization of social relationships. It is not always or necessarily the nuclear and reproductively oriented unit so frequently conjured through the term "family." Sometimes marriage is, indeed, required as the formal sanctioning of bonds that will shape property ownership rights, inheritance and lineage laws, and—more recently—will include definitions of responsibilities of family members in the event of marital breakdown. In Canada, we also have formal legal boundaries to recognize the rights and responsibilities of persons to each other in common-law relationships. But families do not have to be defined by marriage. Because same-sex couples are still denied marriage rights throughout most of the United States, and yet clearly take on the usual relationship aspects of families (such as joint property ownership, cohabitation, business cooperation, and—increasingly often—child rearing), this text finds a compelling case to treat these and other unmarried couples, such as those in common-law relationships, as *de facto* families regardless of their legal status.

In Canada, only couples in **heterosexual monogamy** had marriage rights until 2003, when some municipalities began to grant marriage licences to same-sex couples. After years of debate that began long before the first licences were granted, on July 19, 2005 the federal Liberal government passed Bill C-38 through a Senate vote of 47 to 21 in favour (EGALE 2005) to grant equal marriage rights to same-sex couples. In 2001, the Netherlands became the first country in the world to legalize same-sex marriage. Cambodia (Kampuchea) has also extended full and equal marriage rights to homosexuals. Eight other countries, specifically Denmark (along with its dependency, Greenland), Hungary, Norway, Sweden, France, Iceland, Spain, and Germany, have enacted *registered partnership* legislation. To varying degrees, it allows same-sex couples to receive some of the legal benefits of marriage. In contrast, the United States has shown significant opposition to same-sex marriages, with 32 states passing laws forbidding it (Reidmann et al. 2003), as in the case of the "Proposition 8" vote in the 2008 California gubernatorial election that repealed same-sex marriage rights in the state. Prop 8, as it was called, was overturned in 2013 following a series of appeals; California, a state with a population larger than Canada, has finally secured marriage rights for same-sex couples.

At the global level, a pair-bond base for reproductive families is not the only model for family structures. **Polygamy**—a form of marriage in which one person may have two or more spouses—is practised in some societies. The most common form of polygamy

heterosexual monogamy
Exclusive pair-bonding between two opposite-sex persons.

polygamy
A form of marriage in which one person may have two or more spouses.

Chapter 5 Family Problems

polygyny
The concurrent marriage of one man to two or more women.

polyandry
The concurrent marriage of one woman to two or more men.

is **polygyny**—the concurrent marriage of one man with two or more women. The second form of polygamy is **polyandry**—the concurrent marriage of one woman with two or more men. Polyandry is rare, but does occur in some groups, including Tibetans and various African groups. Polgyny is relatively common in sub-Saharan Africa, but is not unheard of in more developed regions, including in locations where all forms of polygamy are illegal. For example, while it has been illegal in Canada since 1878, polygyny is practised by a fundamentalist Mormon group in Bountiful, British Columbia; the group has affiliates in Colorado and Arizona in the United States. Another historical polygynous group is the "Perfectionist" Christian sect known as the "Oneida Community." In the mid-nineteenth century, the group set up a polygynous commune in Oneida, New York, as well as the Oneida company. Though the sect dispersed at the end of the nineteenth century, the Oneida company continues to make the flatware that many typical families use to set their tables on a daily basis across North America (Edgerton 1992; Kephart 1963).

The roles and norms that structure families are highly variable across societies. For example, in Asian countries, some parents arrange marriages, selecting mates for their children. Another traditional Asian practice is for the eldest son and his wife to move in with the son's parents, where the wife takes care of her husband's parents. In some societies, it is normative for married couples to view each other as equal partners in the marriage, whereas in other societies, social values dictate that wives be subservient to husbands. The role of children also varies across societies. Some societies expect children as young as five years old to work full time to help support the family. Social acceptance of unmarried couples having children also varies widely throughout the world. Acceptance of this lifestyle ranges from 90 percent or more in parts of Western Europe to fewer than 15 percent in Singapore and India (Global Study of Family Values 1998). Finally, the ease of obtaining a divorce varies by country. Ireland did not allow divorce under any conditions until 1995, when voters took part in a public referendum, for the first time narrowly approving divorce. After the referendum, Irish legislation approved the *Family Law (Divorce) Act* in 1996 to permit divorces and remarriages in Ireland. In 2000, the Egyptian Parliament voted to allow women to file for divorce on grounds of incompatibility (Eltahawy 2000). Prior to this law, Egyptian women could file for divorce only in cases of proven physical or psychological abuse. By contrast, a man could get a divorce by simply saying "I divorce you" three times or by filing a paper with the marriage registrar—he did not even have to notify his wife. Under the new law, a woman who wants a divorce must return her husband's dowry and relinquish all financial claims, including alimony.

It is clear, then, that families take shape within specific social and cultural contexts. Neither their strengths nor their weaknesses exist in a vacuum. We need to be careful not to valorize an idealized family structure, but to consider whether a family is functioning well. As suggested by family scholars Mason et al. (2003), "the important question to ask about…families…is not how much they conform to a particular image of the family, but rather how well…they function—what kind of love, care, and nurturance do they provide?" (p. 2).

As we discuss the putative family problems addressed in this chapter—violence and abuse, divorce, and nonmarital and teenage child-bearing—we refer to social and cultural forces that contribute to these problematic events. Next, we look at changing patterns and structures of Canadian families and households.

Changing Patterns and Structures in Canadian Families and Households

The evolving Canadian census alerts us to some of the changes that have occurred in relation to thinking about the family. For example, census data show us that since the first inclusion of common-law arrangements in 1981, those including children have risen from 34 percent of all common-law families to 46 percent (Turcotte 2003: 11). The 2001 Canadian census was first to include questions recognizing same-sex partners (see Figure 5.1). Question 6 from that census also explicitly recognizes children being raised in same-sex households. To get an accurate sense of how Canada's people live, Statistics Canada alters its questions about families. To meet the changing ways that people define family for themselves, it changes its operational definition of a **census family**. On the 2006 census, a family was defined as a set of people who live together as "married, common-law, or lone-parent—generally as either a spouse, partner, parent, or child" (Milan et al. 2007), and accounted for almost 85 percent of the total population in Canada. By the time the 2006 census was carried out, the survey included a question to enumerate the number of married same-sex couples in Canada. Of the 45 300 same-sex couples enumerated in the census, about 7500 (16.5 percent) were married and 37 900 (83.5 percent) were in common-law relationships (ibid). Moreover, the 2006 count of same-sex couples had increased five times as quickly as the number of opposite-sex couples enumerated in the 2001 to 2006 census data (ibid). If the appearance of the so-called "traditional" family is changing, then, it is simultaneously clear that the majority of same-sex couples identifying themselves in the census are adopting more-or-less typical arrangements that include marriage, joint cohabitation, shared property ownership, and raising children.

census family
A now-married couple (with or without never-married sons and/or daughters of one or other spouses), a couple living common-law (again, with or without never-married sons and/or daughters of either or both parents), or a lone parent of any marital status, with at least one never-married son or daughter living in the same dwelling.

Figure 5.1
Questions 5 and 6 from the 2001 Canadian Census

SOURCE: Adapted from Statistics Canada, "2001 Canadian Census Questionaire," Questions #5 and #6, http://www.12.statscan.ca/english/census01/home/questionnaire.cfm

---

5. Is this person living with a common-law partner? Common law refers to two people of the opposite sex or of the same sex who live together as a couple but who are not legally married to each other.

☐ Yes

☐ No

6. Relationship to Person 1

For each person usually living here, describe his/her relationship to Person 1.

Mark "X" or specify one response only.

Stepchildren, adopted children and children of a common-law partner should be considered sons and daughters.

If none of the choices apply, use the "Other" box to indicate this person's relationship to Person 1. Examples of "Other" relationships to Person 1:

☐ grandparent

☐ cousin

☐ niece or nephew

☐ lodger's husband or wife

☐ room-mate's daughter or son

☐ employee

☐ husband or wife of Person 1

☐ common-law partner (opposite-sex) of Person 1

☐ common-law partner (same-sex) of Person 1

☐ son or daughter of Person 1

☐ son-in-law or daughter-in-law of Person 1

☐ grandchild of Person 1

☐ father or mother of Person 1

☐ father-in-law or mother-in-law of Person 1

☐ brother or sister of Person 1

☐ brother-in-law or sister-in-law of Person 1

☐ lodger or boarder

☐ room-mate

☐ other—Specify

_____

Raising children is remarkable, however, in that it is the one area that has declined since the previous census was carried out, with only 41.4 percent of couples with children. The decline does not necessarily mean that people no longer want to raise children, but that they are delaying child-bearing to significantly later ages:

> A growing proportion of young children aged 4 and under had a mother in her forties as more and more women delayed childbearing. In 2001, 7.8% of children aged 4 and under had a mother who was between the ages of 40 and 49. By 2006, this proportion had increased to 9.4%. (Milan et al. 2007)

The most recent Statistics Canada (2008) report on trends in fertility and birth in Canada confirms the trends revealed by Milan and her co-researchers. The data presented in Table 5.1 show both national and provincial data for maternal age and the total fertility rate in each region of the country.

In the 1950s and 1960s, the death of a spouse was the major cause of lone parenthood in Canada (with over 60 percent of all lone-parent widows or widowers); now, divorce, separation, and births outside of marriage have become the primary factors involved in the creation of lone-parent families. The 2012 Statistics Canada report "Portrait of Families and Living Arrangements in Canada" reveals that almost 20 percent of children 14 and under were living with lone parents in 2011; they report, "Of these 1,078,575 children, 82.3% lived with female lone parents. Children in lone-parent families may also receive emotional and/or financial support from a parent in another household, and with whom the child might live on a part-time basis" (p. 14).

Divorce, remarriage, and stepfamilies have also become more common in the last several decades. Projections about marital dissolution must take into account that prior to the federal divorce law of 1968 obtaining a divorce was far more difficult. Spikes in the divorce rate following the 1968 act and the 1985 amendments on improving ease of access to divorce are, then, not surprising; they cannot serve as reliable predictors of the future of marriage breakdown in Canada. Indeed, Statistics Canada observes that the annual rate for both marriage and divorce has been declining since the 1990s (Statistics Canada 2004).

For those who do divorce, remarriage remains the most common result (about 75 percent of divorced men and 65 percent of divorced women remarry); however, remarriage is on the decline. There is an increasing tendency to cohabit, particularly among younger divorced persons and among divorced men. Estimates suggest that divorced women in their 30s and 40s are now twice as likely to live common-law as to remarry (Le Bourdais et al. 2001).

Some view the trend toward diversification of family forms as a sign that marriage and family are in serious crisis. Although traditionalists may view cohabitation (both heterosexual and homosexual), divorce, and single parenthood as threats to the institution of marriage, it is unlikely that marriage will disappear. Most Canadians who cohabit eventually marry, although not necessarily to the person with whom they cohabited. Most Canadians still wish to marry, with average ages for marriage being 28 for women and 30 for men. Few adult Canadians expect to remain unmarried; only half of those who delayed marriage past age 30 expect to remain unmarried (Crompton 2005: 2).

Stable divorce rates may suggest a weakening of marriage, but we can also interpret divorce as a sign that marriage retains a very high value, such that a less-than-satisfactory marriage is unacceptable. The rate of out-of-wedlock childbirth and single parenting is also not necessarily indicative of a decline in the value of marriage; it may mean that finding a partner is more difficult. Because women who have children outside of marriage are more likely to live in poverty, they are "less attractive partners to the type of man they would consider marrying" (Crompton 2005: 3). The persistent

Table 5.1 *Crude Birth Rate, Age–Specific and Total Fertility Rates, by Geography*

Place of Residence of Mother	Age-Specific Fertility Rate[1,2]							Crude Birth Rate, Live Births	Total Fertility Rate[4]
	15 to 19 Years[3]	20 to 24 Years	25 to 29 Years	30 to 34 Years	35 to 39 Years	40 to 44 Years	45 to 49 Years	Rate per 1000 Population	Rate per 1000 Females
	Rate per 1000 Females								
Canada	14.3	53.0	102.0	107.4	50.1	8.4	0.4	11.3	1,680.8
Newfoundland and Labrador	19.4	65.2	99.6	93.2	33.2	4.0	0.1	9.7	1,577.7
Prince Edward Island	15.4	67.1	110.7	94.3	50.1	6.0	0.0	10.6	1,728.0
Nova Scotia	18.7	55.2	92.6	94.5	41.0	5.5	0.2	9.8	1,541.3
New Brunswick	20.8	70.7	104.0	86.0	31.2	4.4	0.2	9.9	1,587.9
Quebec	10.1	54.3	117.6	112.1	46.4	7.1	0.3	11.3	1,738.1
Ontario	11.1	42.5	91.2	107.8	53.6	9.4	0.5	10.9	1,584.8
Manitoba	31.3	81.8	116.2	107.8	46.5	7.5	0.2	12.8	1,959.5
Saskatchewan	36.3	91.1	131.0	105.4	40.4	6.0	0.2	13.6	2,048.5
Alberta	20.5	67.9	118.2	115.5	52.4	9.0	0.4	14.2	1,917.3
British Columbia	10.7	44.3	82.3	99.1	53.4	9.8	0.6	10.1	1,505.4
Yukon	26.3	55.3	94.4	95.4	47.3	9.2	0.0	11.3	1,637.9
Northwest Territories	31.0	105.1	101.5	106.7	58.1	13.6	0.6	16.5	2,081.8
Nunavut	117.8	203.5	134.2	88.2	42.0	11.8	0.0	25.5	2,980.9

[1] Age of mother attained at the last birthday preceding delivery.

[2] Age-specific fertility rate (ASFR) is the number of live births per 1,000 females in a specific age group. Five-year age groups were used in these tabulations (ranging from 15 to 19 years to 45 to 49 years).

[3] Live births to females under 20 years of age per 1,000 females aged 15 to 19.

[4] Total fertility rate is an estimate of the average number of live births a female can be expected to have in her lifetime, based on the age-specific fertility rates (ASFR) of a given year. The total fertility rate (TFR) = SUM of single year of age-specific fertility rates.

NOTE(S): See "Data quality, concepts and methodology—Explanatory notes for the tables."

SOURCE(S): Statistics Canada, Canadian Vital Statistics, Birth Database (CANSIM table 102-4505) and Appendix I. http://www.statcan.gc.ca/pub/84f0210x/2008000/t005-eng.htm. Date modified: 2012-12-20; Table 4. Statistics Canada, Catalogue No. 84F0210X, p. 21.

value placed on family is also evident in a national survey of Canadian teens. The survey found that almost 9 out of 10 (88 percent) expected to get married and also to stay with the same partner for life (87 percent of males and 89 percent of females) (Bibby 2001: 136).

5.2 Sociological Theories of the Family

Beyond the three major sociological theories of the family—structural-functionalism, the conflict perspective, and symbolic interactionism—in this section we see what light feminist and queer perspectives shed on various family problems.

Structural-Functionalist Perspective

The structural-functionalist perspective views the family as a social institution that performs important functions for society, including reproducing new members, regulating sexual activity and procreation, socializing the young, and providing physical and emotional care for family members. According to the structural-functionalist perspective, traditional gender roles contribute to family functioning. Thus, heterosexual two-parent families in which women perform the "expressive" role of managing household tasks and providing emotional care and nurturing to family members and men perform the "instrumental" role of earning income and making major family decisions are viewed as "normal" or "functional." Other family forms, such as single-parent families and same-sex unions, are viewed as abnormal or dysfunctional.

According to the structural-functionalist perspective, increases in divorce and lone-parent families signal a breakdown of the family. This breakdown is the result of rapid social change and social disorganization. The functionalist perspective views the breakdown of the family as one of the primary social problems in the world today—a problem of such magnitude that it leads to such secondary social problems as crime, poverty, and substance abuse.

Functionalist explanations of family problems examine how changes in other social institutions contribute to these problems. For example, a structural-functionalist view of divorce examines how changes in the economy (more dual-earner marriages) and in the legal system (such as the adoption of no-fault divorce) contribute to rising divorce rates. Changes in the economic institution, specifically falling wages among unskilled and semi-skilled men, also contribute to both intimate partner abuse and the rise in female-headed, lone-parent households (Edin 2000).

Conflict Perspective

Conflict theory focuses on how social class and power influence marriages and families. Within families, the unequal distribution of power among women and men may contribute to domestic violence. The traditional male domination of families—a system known as **patriarchy**—includes the attitude that married women are essentially the property of husbands. When wives violate or challenge the male head-of-household's authority, the male may react by "disciplining" his wife or by using anger and violence to reassert his position of power in the family. The unequal distribution of wealth between men and women, with men traditionally earning more money than women, contributes to inequities in power and fosters economic dependence of wives on husbands.

Conflict theorists also emphasize that social programs and policies that affect families are largely shaped by powerful and wealthy segments of society. The interests of corporations and businesses are often in conflict with the needs of families. Hewlett and West (1998) note that corporate interests undermine family life "by exerting

patriarchy
A tradition in which families and societies are male dominated.

enormous downward pressure on wage levels for young, child-raising adults" (p. 32). Government, influenced by corporate interests through lobbying and political financial contributions, enacts policies and laws that serve the interests of for-profit corporations, rather than families.

Symbolic Interactionist Perspective

Symbolic interactionism emphasizes that human behaviour is largely dependent on the meanings and definitions that emerge from small-group interaction. Divorce, for example, was once highly stigmatized and informally sanctioned through the criticism and rejection of divorced friends and relatives. As societal definitions of divorce became less negative, however, the divorce rate increased. The social meanings of single parenthood, cohabitation, and delayed child-bearing and marriage have changed in similar ways. As the definitions of each of these family variations became less negative, the behaviours became more common.

Symbolic interactionists also point to the effects of labelling on one's self-concept and the way the self-fulfilling prophecy can affect family members' behaviour toward one another. The **self-fulfilling prophecy** implies that we behave according to the expectations of others. For example, when a non-custodial divorced parent (usually a father) is awarded visitation rights, he may view himself as a visitor in his children's lives. The meaning attached to the visitor status can be an obstacle to the father's involvement, as the label minimizes the importance of the non-custodial parent's role and results in conflict and emotional turmoil for fathers (Pasley and Minton 2001). Fathers' rights advocates suggest replacing the term *visitation* with such terms as *parenting plan* or *time-sharing arrangement*. These latter terms do not minimize either parent's role.

The symbolic interactionist perspective is useful in understanding the dynamics of domestic violence and abuse. For example, some abusers and their victims learn to define intimate partner violence as an expression of love (Lloyd 2000). **Emotional abuse** often involves using negative labels (e.g., "stupid," "whore," "bad") to define a partner or family member. Such labels negatively affect the self-concepts of abuse victims, often convincing them that they deserve the abuse.

Feminist Perspectives

Feminist theories of family and kinship structures critique the central presupposition that family is natural and biological. Feminist thinkers find that the three foundational theories all continue to privilege a patriarchal organization of power. Feminist perspectives help us to rethink common assumptions about the basis of family to show that traditional views are based on a male model of economy and politics that "does not work for most women, who typically have childcare and other domestic responsibilities to juggle as well [as paid labour outside the home]" (Luxton 1996: 51).

Regardless of the particular differences in feminist approaches to the idea of family, all focus on sexism against women and problems with the subordination and consequent vulnerability of women and children in the family and marriage. Such problems include economic dependency, the structure of a work world at odds with child-rearing and domestic responsibilities, and sexual assault and other forms of violence within families.

Feminist work on families may also try to reimagine what families can be, what they can accomplish, and how our roles in families might change for the better. For example, just because fathers have traditionally been cast as the powerful sources of (potentially violent) discipline does not mean that they must always fulfill that role; instead, families might become sites for the exercise of gender equality wherein

self-fulfilling prophecy
A concept referring to the tendency for people to act in a manner consistent with the expectations of others.

emotional abuse
Often involves using negative labels (e.g., "stupid," "whore," "bad") to define a partner or family member. Such labels negatively affect the self-concept of abuse victims, often convincing them that they deserve the abuse.

"the raising of children [can] emphasize the qualities needed in building a culture of peace" (Gearing et al. 2001: 57). According to this view, it is not only women and children who are vulnerable in traditional family structures, but also that men lack opportunities to seek change, to pursue peaceful ways of living, and to achieve equality for themselves, their children, and their world (Gearing et al. 2001: 69). This chapter's *Social Problems Research Up Close* feature takes a feminist perspective on the demands of breastfeeding discourse and the challenges that mothers face.

Social Problems *Research Up Close*

Moral Constructions of Motherhood in Breastfeeding Discourse

Health Canada and the public health agencies in the provinces have focused their interest in maternal and child well-being with heavy promotion of breastfeeding. Breastfeeding is an advantageous strategy for public services because it is a private rather than a public initiative, and therefore a cost-effective way of downloading responsibility for population health onto individual mothers. Breastfeeding does have many advantages, but Canadian sociologist Glenda Wall (2001) demonstrates the very real problems that confront mothers in a political atmosphere that includes the "re-moralization" of pregnancy, fixation on maternal–infant bonding practices, and child-centred parenting. At the centre of the conflict that Wall's research assesses is the claim that breastfeeding is natural, and, therefore, morally preferable to bottle feeding. She argues that the need to spend enormous effort convincing people that breastfeeding is, indeed, natural and not inappropriately sexual belies that position.

Sample and Methods

The study focused on 20 widely distributed public health pamphlets from Health Canada and the province of Alberta, made available in maternity wards, doctors' offices, through public advertising, or by request to Health Canada.

The public health material was analyzed for the following features: how issues were framed, implicit assumptions, and the resulting understandings of motherhood, breastfeeding, and sexuality.

Findings and Conclusions

Wall determined that there were six specific sites of articulation in which morality, nature, and motherhood were structured in ways that overlooked serious structural and symbolic problems facing mothers on a day-to-day basis, with potentially harmful outcomes for mothers and their children.

1. *Morality and nature.* The most common feature Wall found was the moral overlap of natural mothering and claims to the naturalness of breast feeding in which the presumed naturalness of an activity is made to be the guarantee of its morality:

   . . . nature in the 1980s and 1990s, has become more commonly understood as a sacred entity, one that is pure, unsullied, ancient, wise, and deserving of respect, and that this has occurred along with increasing popular reverence for nature and natural experiences.

   The overlap between the breastfeeding discourse and cultural constructions of nature is evident, for example, in the characterization of breast milk as nature's perfect food. (p. 596)

   Wall's analysis of the complete series of publications revealed, however, that the moral purity of the milk "is only as pure as the mother who produces it" (p. 597). It is not simply that nature guarantees purity, but that mothers must adhere to the ideal standards of natural motherhood.

2. *Breastfeeding as the ultimate convenience. For whom?* Wall's research found repeated insistences that breastfeeding is far easier and more convenient than bottle feeding or formula feeding alternatives.

   Listed in almost all my sources under "benefits to breastfeeding" are the convenience of having the baby's food with you wherever you go and ready at a moment's notice and having time to relax and enjoy your baby. (p. 597)

   One of the obvious problems that this perspective misses is that if the baby's food is always with the mother, then the mother can never be separated from the baby. For however long a baby is being fed exclusively by breast, the mother has no freedom to go anywhere on her own. Wall's research showed that Health Canada publications indicate no concern for mothers as women who might want to do things as *people*, but focus instead on a notion of universal convenience in which "there is no need to sterilize or warm bottles, nor are there any bottles to take with you when you leave home with your child. The process is simple, natural, free" (Health Canada pamphlet from 1991, quoted in Wall 2001: 597).

Wall's analysis reveals that there is no recognition in the focus on convenience that mothers out in public with hungry infants may experience real limitations. The focus on convenience makes other concerns seem trivial. The inability to move freely in public because of general hostility, demands for "modesty," the physical exhaustion that breastfeeding mothers experience, and problems getting babies to nurse are all neglected, as are the problems of loss of privacy and personal identity, and of dealing with perpetually cranky babies (pp. 597–98).

3. *Contradictory views regarding the character and function of breasts.* Wall's research concludes that for all the public health insistence that breastfeeding is perfectly appropriate in any public space—surely a welcome message at a time when breastfeeding mothers were being escorted by security guards out of shopping malls or into toilets for their babies to have a midday meal in a stall—the reality is that even the public health posters and pamphlets reveal social unease about breasts, keeping the images of breastfeeding mothers "respectable and modest" with their breasts always obscured or covered. Furthermore, as Wall points out, maintaining such modest coverage in public is not easy. Fussing or distractible babies may turn away from the breast, leaving mothers suddenly and repeatedly exposed, and vulnerable to charges of immodesty. Difficulty may be especially great for new mothers trying to negotiate the public's sense of modesty, potential hostility, and their own sense of personal privacy. Yet public health advice, which only implicitly addresses public hostility, makes it all seem so simple:

A two-piece outfit with a loose top works well for breastfeeding. The top is lifted from the bottom and will keep your breasts covered. A small blanket or shawl over your shoulder can cover your breasts and your feeding baby. If you feel comfortable and confident nursing your baby, others will be at ease. (Health Canada pamphlet from 1996, quoted in Wall 2001: 598)

The real difficulties that breastfeeding mothers face when in public, Wall reports, contribute to the reasons why breastfeeding mothers end up in solitary confinement in their homes—it is not simple to nurse in public (p. 598).

4. *Moral policing of mothering.* Although the various studies on infant–mother bonding, traceable back to the mid-twentieth century work of Bowlby on infant monkeys, suggest that there is a critical and brief period in which mothers and new infants can effectively attach, Wall explains that most have been discredited within social science research. Their discrediting did not, however, result in changes to popular perception. Wall found that the 1970s conclusions on the supposedly fixed critical period for bonding were still being marshalled as evidence in late 1990s Health Canada publications. It was as though a whole world of other research had never occurred. Citing the work of Eyer, Wall explains the continuing popularity of bonding theory:

Eyer suggests that the zeal with which bonding was accepted is partly explained by the fact that it fit within a "deeply embedded ideology regarding the proper role of women" and notes that the concept has since been broadened beyond its narrow scientific definition to become deeply embedded in popular construction of motherhood. (p. 600)

The result of popular commitments to bonding theory, Wall points out, is that the lives and realities of mothers cease to be important; mothers recede and infants/children take centre stage in the discourse. Moreover, mothers who report problems with breastfeeding are cast in an especially negative light by medical discourses as being very selfish: "Disadvantages to breastfeeding are those factors perceived by the mother to be an inconvenience since there are no known disadvantages to the infant" (Lawrence, quoted in Wall 2001: 601).

5. *The self-regulating mother.* In a world in which mothers, expectant or those with infants, are romanticized "ecosystems" (p. 602), Wall argues that the women disappear as subjects with rights of their own. To be considered proper mothers, women must subordinate their needs and desires to those of the developing fetus or infant. A central feature of what is at stake is a form of quality control:

The mother here is the ecosystem within which the child's optimum food source is produced. The techniques of the self that characterize the management of

(continued)

pregnancy (eating well; avoiding smoking, alcohol and drugs) also apply here. Food guides for healthy eating and warnings that maternal consumption of alcohol, tobacco, and drugs can harm nursing babies were common in the examined material aimed at mothers. The instructions on the back of the food guide for pregnant and nursing mothers, "How to Build a Better Baby," sum up the understanding being conveyed. Here, both pregnant and breastfeeding mothers are advised to keep the chart in a prominent spot in their kitchen so that "whenever [they] think about a meal or snack, [they] can think about [their] baby too." (p. 603)

6. *The neo-liberal self-police state.* Wall finds that at the centre of breastfeeding discourse is a joining of economic and moral imperatives unique to the contemporary social and fiscal conservative movement known as neo-liberalism. Wall explains that neo-liberalism is a backlash movement that rejects the community model of social welfare and emphasizes the individual's need for "choice, self-management, and self-responsibility" (p. 603). Under neo-liberalism, it is every person to him or herself, and it's just too bad for those who can't make it on their own. For mothers, their obligation in a neo-liberal context is to produce better quality children, and to do so with maximum individual efficiency:

A healthy lifestyle has become a civic moral obligation, and breast-feeding—it is asserted—not only makes for healthier babies, but also is suggested to have lifelong health benefits. Media presentations of breastfeeding increasingly frame discussion in terms of the costs to the health care system of breastfed versus bottle-fed babies. This is true in the material examined here as well. In a fact sheet developed by Health Canada's (1998a) Canadian Perinatal Surveillance System, we find a typical reference to the fact that "the lower incidence of illness in breastfed babies reduces health care costs." In Health Canada's (1995a) poster "Breast Milk, Accept No Substitutes," it is the health benefits alone that are emphasized and the moral imperative is clear, "Your baby needs your breast milk." (p. 604)

Conclusion

The real reasons why women stop breastfeeding are completely neglected, and so the problems of social isolation, physical exhaustion, lack of child care support, demands of other children, and public hostility go unresolved.

Poor and young mothers remain most vulnerable to state intrusion into their lives and yet, because they suffer most from the structural, symbolic, and material problems listed above, they also have the lowest rates of breastfeeding in Canada.

Wall proposes, then, that what mothers need is not more social policing or trivializing and unrealistic advice, especially for poor or single mothers—to go to bed with the baby for 24 hours to rest, for example. What is needed is more attention to the feminist recommendations for better support for public child care, restructuring of work, and increased support for parenting.

SOURCE: Wall, Glenda. 2001. "Moral Constructions of Motherhood in Breastfeeding Discourse." *Gender and Society* 15(4): 592–610. © copyright 1992 by SAGE Publications. Reprinted with permission of SAGE Publications.

Queer Theory Perspectives

Large segments of the gay and lesbian population have sought marriage rights for same-sex couples, with the group EGALE providing the legal and political muscle to help secure those rights in Canada. Queer theory perspectives, however, are not equal or identical to the political movement in favour of same-sex marriage rights. Rather, the theory seeks to understand what one gains, what one loses, and what one compromises on in the search for the kind of legitimacy that the state confers when it grants people the right to marry. For example, while securing same-sex marriage rights may benefit some gay and lesbian couples with inclusion in state-sanctioned kinship arrangements, those whose personal and kinship arrangements depart more obviously from the nuclear family model will be even further marginalized and isolated (Butler 2004: 104–8).

Regardless of its position on same-sex marriage rights, queer theory and activist groups have emphasized for nearly two decades that gay, lesbian, bisexual, and transgendered (GLBT) persons are all "family." Right-wing condemnations of gay and lesbian couples as examples of moral corruption and threats to traditional families have prompted this. GLBT people are brothers, sisters, aunts, uncles, sons and daughters, and more and more frequently, parents as well. Discrimination may prevent these families from being able to gain access to or provide care in emergency situations to their partners and to the children they are parenting. Prejudice against GLBT persons may dissuade them from taking part in school activities, and many have found that once they were "out," their families' religious places of worship had no place for them. Isolation and full access to community obligations are central features that we leave out of the equation if we insist that families are defined only in reference to the nuclear, reproductive, heterosexual family.

5.3 Violence and Abuse in Intimate and Family Relationships

Although intimate and family relationships can provide stability and a sense of well-being, they can also involve physical violence, verbal and emotional abuse, sexual abuse, and neglect. It does not fit with the image we have of ourselves as Canadians, but it is nonetheless true that in Canada people are more likely to be physically assaulted, abused and neglected, sexually assaulted and molested, and killed in their own homes and by other family members than anywhere else or by anyone else. Furthermore, within those relationships marred by violence, the frequency of perpetration and the frequency of victimization are decidedly gendered, as we see in Figure 5.2.

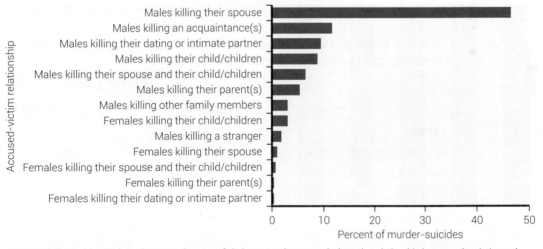

NOTE: Excludes incidents where the sex and/or age of victim was unknown and where the relationship between the victim and the accused was unknown.

Figure 5.2 **Incidents of Murder-Suicide by Accused–Victim Relationship, Canada, 2001–2011**

SOURCE: Statistics Canada. Family Violence in Canada: A Statistical Profile, 2011. *The Daily*, June 25, 2013, http://www.statcan.gc.ca/daily-quotidien/130625/t130625b001-eng.htm

Abuse in relationships can take many forms, including emotional and psychological abuse, physical violence, and sexual abuse. **Intimate partner violence** refers to actual or threatened violent crimes committed against persons by their current or former spouses, boyfriends or girlfriends, or cohabiting partners. Follingstad and Edmundsen (2010) explain that emotional abuse can take many forms including yelling

intimate partner violence
Actual or threatened violent crimes committed against persons by their current or former spouses, boyfriends, or girlfriends.

and screaming, withholding physical contact, isolating someone from family and friends, belittling or insulting behaviours, restricting a person's activities or freedom of movement, controlling their behaviour (e.g., telling them what to eat, how to dress, where they are permitted to go, and so on) and exhibiting unreasonable jealousy.

Intimate Partner Violence and Abuse

Globally, one woman in every three has been subjected to violence in an intimate relationship (United Nations Development Programme 2000). The 1999 General Social Survey (GSS) found that rates of violence reported by Canadian men and women were relatively similar (7 percent and 8 percent, respectively). According to the findings of the 2004 General Social Survey, rates of violence in spousal relationships were unchanged in the years from 1999 to 2004, with more than 650 000 women and 540 000 men experiencing some form of violence from a spouse (Statistics Canada 2005a). More recent data from Statistics Canada (2013) tell us that in 2011 violence in the family accounted for 26 percent of all reported crime, and half of those victimized were abused by current or previous partners; in other words, family abuse is most frequently committed by those who have had some form of spousal relationship, while the other half of violent acts committed is spread across other family members. In addition, of those victimized the great majority, 80 percent, are females—whether they are spouses of, children of, extended family members of, or siblings of their abusers (ibid). On the positive side, numbers of violent incidences reported fell by 6 percent between 2009 and 2011 (Statistics Canada 2013), though that timespan is too limited to tell us if we actually are in a downward trend for violence inside families. What we do know is that regions marked by extreme poverty and isolation, with the lowest levels of social cohesion, have the highest rates of family violence, as we see in Table 5.2.

Table 5.2 *Rates of Police-Reported Violent Offences against Family Members, by Province and Territory, 2011*

	Total Violent Crime	
	Number	**Rate per 100,000**
Canada	**94,839**	**279**
Newfoundland and Labrador	1,548	305
Prince Edward Island	328	227
Nova Scotia	2,309	246
New Brunswick	2,122	283
Quebec	25,887	328
Ontario	24,930	190
Manitoba	4,856	402
Saskatchewan	6,043	583
Alberta	12,108	321
British Columbia	12,306	271
Yukon	300	867
Northwest Territories	1,005	2,304
Nunavut	1,097	3,294

SOURCE: Family Violence in Canada: A Statistical Profile, 2011. *The Daily*, June 25, 2013, http://www.statcan.gc.ca/daily -quotidien/130625/t130625b001-eng.htm

Most at risk for spousal abuse are those between the ages of 15 and 24, those in common-law relationships, and those whose unions were of less than three years' duration; moreover, the forms of violence directed at women are frequently far more serious, causing greater harm (Statistics Canada 2005a). (See Figure 5.3.) Aboriginal peoples were more likely than other Canadians to report being assaulted by a spouse (about 20 percent of Aboriginal peoples compared with 7 percent of the non-Aboriginal population). "Aboriginal women in particular stand out as being at higher risk of spousal violence" (Johnson and Hotton 2001: 29). Yet, perhaps in part because mainstream feminist concerns tend to focus on issues of equal pay for equal work, childcare, and reproduction rights, argues Hillary Potter (2006), the problems of intimate partner violence, its prevention and its prosecution are overlooked (p. 109). Potter notes that because intimate partner violence is a more frequent problem in communities that suffer other forms of oppression and the stresses that ensue, it simply has not attained the central status as a serious social problem that other concerns about more privileged women's lives have garnered.

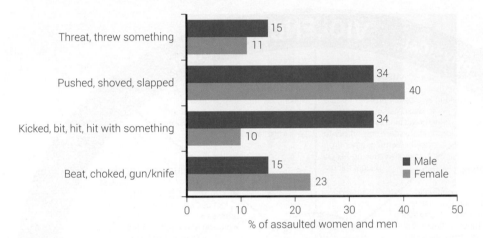

Figure 5.3 **_More Women Experience Serious Violence Than Men_**

SOURCE: Adapted from Statistics Canada. "Family Violence in Canada: A Statistical Profile 2005." *The Daily*, Catalogue No. 11-001, July 14, 2005, p. 4, www.statscan.ca/Daily/English/050714/d050714a.htm.

Data from the 1999 GSS also indicate that women are three times more likely to be injured, five times more likely to receive medical attention, and also five times more likely than men to report that they feared for their lives due to the violence they had experienced. Women were also more likely than men to report multiple incidents of spousal violence. Sixty-five percent of women who experienced spousal violence reported being assaulted on more than one occasion; for men, it was 54 percent. Twenty-six percent of women said it happened more than 10 times; for men, it was 13 percent (Bunge 2000: 14).

The 2004 GSS data show that family violence cuts across income and education levels, but also that separate factors, including youth, heavy drinking, common-law relationships of less than three years, and Aboriginal status, increase one's vulnerability. In addition, the survey found that, in general, younger people face the greatest risk of experiencing spousal violence, with the highest rates reported by young women under 25 (5 percent). Men aged 25 to 34 also reported higher rates of violence than those who were older (4 percent versus 1 percent). Furthermore, the 2004 GSS reported that the elevated risk of being a victim of spousal violence remained unchanged from the 1999 GSS, at four times higher for both men and women living in common-law unions than those in marriages. Finally, "Aboriginal people were three times more likely to be victims of spousal violence. Overall, 21% of Aboriginal people, or 24% of Aboriginal women and 18% of Aboriginal men…had suffered violence from a current or previous spouse or common-law partner in the five-year period up to 2004" (Statistics Canada 2005a).

One popular way of understanding intimate partner violence, developed in the mid-1980s by the U.S.-based Domestic Abuse Intervention Programs (DAIP), is the "Power and Control Wheel" (see Figure 5.4). The wheel focuses on the violence that occurs against women, and the DAIP explains this focus by reminding us that "…the battering of women by men continues to be a significant social problem—men commit 86 to 97 percent of all criminal assaults and women are killed 3.5 times more often than men in domestic homicides" (DAIP n.d.). What the wheel explains is intended to show batterers and abusers that not all abuse is physical, but that it can include emotional manipulation, threatening behaviour, and other forms of control, and that these different forms work in concert with each other to limit one's female partner from exercising her freedom as a person. The different parts of the wheel show how subtle forms of intimidation and violation can impinge on a victim's ability to defend herself from more obvious forms of physical and sexual abuse, and prevent her from being able to leave the situation. Most importantly, the wheel shows very clearly that the motivation behind abuse is the desire for power and control and not, as is so commonly believed, a desire for love and security. In other words, IPV is not simply a manifestation of "love"

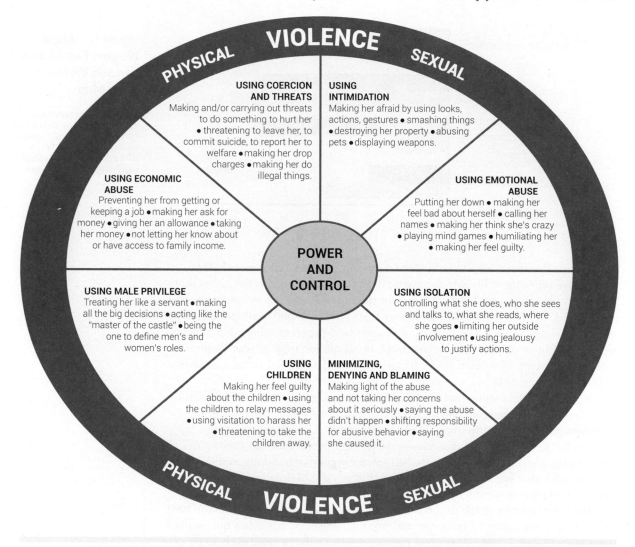

Figure 5.4 *The Power and Control Wheel*

SOURCE: The Power and Control Wheel was developed in Duluth by battered women who were attending educations groups sponsored by the local women's shelter. The wheel is used in our Creating a Process of Change for Men Who Batter curriculum, and in groups of women who are battered, to name and inspire dialogue about tactics of abuse. While we recognize that there are women who use violence against men, and that there are men and women in same-sex relationships who use violence, this wheel is meant specifically to illustrate men's abusive behaviors toward women. The Equality Wheel was developed for use with the same groups. Used with permission from Domestic Abuse Intervention Project, Home of The Duluth Model.

gone awry, but a calculated means of securing power and control. The wheel, explains the DAIP, remains specifically gendered, describing men as abusers and women as victims in order to maintain a focus on the gendered character of domestic abuse. The term "intimate partner abuse," by contrast, is gender neutral, and risks papering over the power imbalances between men and women (DAIP n.d.).

The World Health Organization has collected international data that put the prevalence of intimate partner abuse into a larger global perspective and has found that, in addition to general assault, a 10-country survey of 24 000 women revealed sexual violence against women at the hands of a partner to be common: "Between 15% and 71% of women reported physical or sexual violence by a husband or partner. Many women said that their first sexual experience was not consensual (24% in rural Peru, 28% in Tanzania, 30% in rural Bangladesh, and 40% in South Africa)" (WHO 2009). Moreover, these assaults take place overwhelmingly at the hands of intimate partners, not strangers as is so commonly imagined to be the case. A brief commentary on the study in the medical journal *The Lancet* highlights some further disturbing results of the study: in short, while men are the most frequent perpetrators of violence, women often hold attitudes that support or even endorse it:

> In several of the study sites, most women thought wife beating was justifiable under some circumstances, including refusal to have sex. These attitudes are symbolic of a general pattern of acceptance of victimisation as part of being female.[6] A culture of silence also prevails. In all countries, the interviewer was the first person many of the abused women had ever talked to about their partner's physical violence.
>
> Even in countries where resources for abused women are available, barriers such as fear, stigma, and the threat of losing their children stopped many women from seeking help.[*] (Fathalla 2005)

A multinational study carried out at McMaster University's medical school in Hamilton, Ontario and published in 2013 in *The Lancet* indicated that one in six women treated for fractures in orthopedic clinics in Canada, the United States, India, the Netherlands, and Denmark were victims of intimate partner violence. A summary of the report explains that it is even more troublesome, given this high rate of injury, that only 14 percent of women who were being treated for fractures that had resulted directly from domestic abuse were asked in any way about whether they were experiencing abuse at the hands of their domestic partners (McMaster University 2013). These findings are troubling not only because they show a failure of the medical system to take seriously the need to determine *how* their patients, particularly the women in the study, have been injured, but also because of the missed opportunity to improve the lives of those experiencing intimate partner violence. Medical professionals are often well-positioned to help those suffering from abuse to access resources that can improve their circumstances, for example social work and counselling services, safe housing, and other supports. They miss out, also, on providing services to the abuser to help prevent future abuse from occurring. After all, it may not actually be in the best interests of those involved to break up a family in which violence is occurring (especially where the abused partner is financially dependent on the abusing partner); rather, it is in the best interests of all involved to treat the causes of abuse, and to prevent it from occurring again. Thus would those most vulnerable be protected without giving up their homes, or even the partners and family members whom they may actually love.

If research such as the McMaster project reveals significant failures to protect victims of abuse in relatively wealthy countries, things can be even worse in countries where resources are more generally limited, and where the prevailing culture is even more accepting of abuse as a means of controlling wives. In other countries, resources to help women not only are more limited, but also it can be the case that women participate in the abuse of other women. In India, for example, dowry killings involve "a woman being killed by her husband or in-laws because her family is unable to meet their demands for her dowry—a payment made to a woman's in-laws upon her engagement or marriage as a gift to her new family" (UNIFEM 2007: 1). Bride burning, acid attacks, and many deaths ruled as suicides or accidents are linked to dowry disputes. Furthermore, many of these deaths take place in the kitchen of the groom's home, where the wives work closely with their mothers-in-law. The kitchen serves as a convenient location for the deaths because it is specifically the women's domain (that is, the wife is expected to be there), and because it is considered an inherently unsafe location that blends volatile cooking fuels with fire. Sometimes the mother-in-law will participate directly in setting the fire; sometimes she will agree to be called away from the kitchen so that the burning can take place. In India, courts have ruled that "customary payments" to a groom's family are not illegal (Mahapatra 2008), but in 2009 the India Supreme Court expressed outrage at such "barbaric practices" (Venkatesan 2009).

Although research on intimate violence in same-sex relationships is sparse, the few studies conducted on this issue suggest that it is quite common. More than one-third of all previous same-sex relationships and 9 percent of all current same-sex relationships include some experience of violence (Turell 2000).

Many of the dynamics reported to characterize abusive heterosexual relationships, such as alcohol and drug abuse, are also found in same-sex abusive partnerships (Halpern et al. 2004). An additional challenge for those who experience violence in same-sex relationships is that negative stigma and isolation may prevent them from seeking help and exacerbate domestic aggression (Halpern et al. 2004; Turell 2000). There is, however, an advocacy and education group based in the United States that has begun to provide support for LGBT communities and education to prevent abuse within LGBT relationships. Called the Northwest Network, and founded in 1987 by lesbian survivors, the group "…works to end abuse in our diverse lesbian, gay, bisexual and trans communities" (Northwest Network n.d.). Working with the National Resource Center on Domestic Violence, the Network released a 2007 report, "LGBT Communities and Domestic Violence." The report reveals that although domestic violence is as common and as dangerous as in heterosexual relationships, it is both poorly documented and has different dynamics at work in its instantiation (National Resource Center on Domestic Violence 2007a: 4). For example, because many people in LGBT relationships are forced by a combination of formal policies and social norms to live "in the closet," those who experience abuse have a harder time accessing support. Meanwhile, the report explains, there are "unique and specific opportunities for abusers to shape, manipulate and control their partners" (National Resource Center on Domestic Violence 2007b: 1). The report explains that various structures and features of the dominant, heteronormative world can be used to the advantage of abusers:

> An abuser can use bias in the law enforcement system to control an intimate partner with threats such as "go ahead and call the police, you'll end up in jail too and you know what they think of/do to 'us'," or "how can you turn me into the cops, you know what they think of/do to 'us'." A victim/survivor's struggle for protection from violence is further complicated by their status in the society. A compounding factor for people of color, native people, people with disabilities and other marginalized people is that oppressions endemic in the dominant culture are also endemic in LGBT communities. LGBT people from various other oppressed groups encounter additional barriers, and batterers can use these added barriers as further means to abuse their victims.[*] (p. 3)

To deal with the multiple, complex features that make LGBT persons vulnerable to abuse, and to work at prevention, various LGBT groups have created organizations to

---

[*] This material was reprinted/adapted from the publication titled *Lesbian, Gay, Bisexual and Trans (LGBT) Communities and Domestic Violence: Information and Resources (2007)* by the National Resource Center on Domestic Violence. Reprinted by permission.

provide supportive counselling from *within* LGBT communities. Such groups do not try to talk victims out of their non-heterosexual relationships; rather, they provide preventive education and support to abusers, and work to provide safe housing for LGBT persons leaving abusive relationships. In Canada, often through university organizations and community groups, intervention programs and support for LGBT members dealing with intimate partner violence are now available, and all take an approach that understands the unique dynamics that characterize violence in LGBT relationships.

Four patterns of partner violence have been identified: common couple violence, intimate terrorism, violent resistance, and mutual violent control (Johnson and Ferraro 2001). **Common couple violence** refers to occasional acts of violence arising from arguments that get out of hand. It usually does not escalate into serious or life-threatening violence. **Intimate terrorism**, violence motivated by a wish to control one's partner, involves the systematic use of not only violence, but also economic subordination, threats, isolation, verbal and emotional abuse, and other control tactics. Intimate terrorism is almost entirely perpetrated by men and is more likely to escalate over time and to involve serious injury. **Violent resistance** refers to acts of violence that are committed in self-defence. Violent resistance is almost exclusively perpetrated by women against a male partner. **Mutual violent control** is a rare pattern of abuse "that could be viewed as two intimate terrorists battling for control" (Johnson and Ferraro 2001: 169).

Among the impediments to reducing the instance of intimate partner violence, argues Nancy Berns (2004), is the nearly exclusive focus of mainstream media on those who have survived abuse rather than on those who commit it. She writes that "The victim is celebrated for having the courage to leave [...] or, conversely, blamed for staying and letting the abuse continue" (p. 3). Such a focus places the responsibility for abuse on those victimized by it and amounts to victim blaming that does nothing to prevent the occurrence of IPV. Berns proposes that our media need to take a more decidedly feminist stance that assesses the social, cultural, economic, and political forces that produce and even condone violence against women, and that, moreover, our collective efforts and media focus need to shift to assess "how individuals learn to abuse and what can be done to help them stop or to stop them [from committing abuse]" (p. 141). She offers a theory of why we do not presently provide such a focus, and argues that "it is easier to have a 'happy ending' in a story about a victim who solved her problem [than to address] the unsettling ending of a culture in need of change" (p. 159). Furthermore, research in media communications that examined the emotional responses of viewers to representations of IPV demonstrates that viewers exposed to negative messages about victim behaviours (e.g., that the victim had been drinking or having an affair) shifted "the attributions of responsibility [for being abused] toward the women" (Palazzolo and Roberto 2011: 13). In other words, our culture is very comfortable with victim blaming, and less inclined to assess the larger cultural context that tends to excuse abusers. To alter this dynamic, argue Palazzolo and Roberto, their results

> emphasize the importance of journalists framing stories in ways that focus more heavily on why the perpetrator attacked the victim, and not on what the victim may have done to provoke it. There are also a variety of other people and institutions that can help journalists frame IPV stories in productive ways. For example, spokespeople from domestic violence shelters should actively engage with reporters when IPV cases are covered. For most, this means seeking out reporters to provide contextual information, particularly from a thematic or societal perspective, rather than waiting for reporters to contact them. (p 16)

This chapter of your textbook addresses the multiple factors that families face that can precipitate abuse within the home, and so directs your attention away from stories about individual victims and survivors and toward the systemic, institutional, and political problems that place families in peril in the first place.

common couple violence
Occasional acts of violence that result from conflict that gets out of hand between persons in a relationship.

intimate terrorism
Almost entirely perpetrated by men, a form of violence that is motivated by a wish to control one's partner and involves the systemic use of not only violence, but economic subordination, threats, isolation, verbal and emotional abuse, and other control tactics. This form of violence is more likely to escalate over time and to involve serious injury.

violent resistance
Acts of violence by a partner that are committed in self-defence. Violent resistance is almost exclusively perpetrated by women against a male partner.

mutual violent control
A rare pattern of abuse when two intimate terrorists battle for control.

As we noted briefly above, intimate partner abuse also takes the form of sexual aggression, including forced sexual intercourse. **Sexual aggression** refers to sexual interaction that occurs against one's will through use of physical force, threat of force, pressure, use of alcohol or drugs, or use of position of authority. An estimated 7 to 14 percent of married women have been raped by their husbands (Monson et al. 1996). However, prior to 1983 and the introduction of Canada's sexual assault laws, it was legally impossible for a man in Canada to rape his wife because the rape law contained a marital exemption. A man could be found guilty of rape on his own wife only if he were party to someone else raping her.

Intimate violence can have devastating consequences. Many battered women are abused during pregnancy, resulting in a high rate of miscarriage and birth defects. Psychological consequences for victims of intimate partner violence can include depression, suicidal thoughts and attempts, lowered self-esteem, alcohol and other drug abuse, and post-traumatic stress disorder (National Center for Injury Prevention and Control 2000).

Battering also interferes with employment opportunities. Some abusers prohibit their partners from working. Other abusers will deliberately undermine the possibility of their partners working by "depriving them of transportation, harassing them at work, turning off alarm clocks, beating them before job interviews, and disappearing when they promise to provide child care" (Johnson and Ferraro 2001: 177). Battering also undermines employment by causing repeated absences, impairing ability to concentrate, and lowering self-esteem and aspirations.

Abuse, whether physical or emotional, is a factor in many divorces and is also a primary cause of homelessness. One study of homeless parents found that 22 percent were fleeing from abuse (National Coalition for the Homeless 1999). A second reported that half of homeless women and children were fleeing from abuse (National Coalition for the Homeless 1998). More recent "snapshots" from Statistics Canada show that the situation for women and children remains dire, with increased percentages of those in shelters fleeing from abuse: "Nearly one-third of all women who had sought temporary accommodation in a shelter for abused women on April 14, 2004 had stayed there at some time during the past.... On this date, there were 3,274 women and 2,835 children in such shelters, 82% of them were escaping abuse. The remaining women and children were there for other reasons such as housing, addictions and mental health issues. Of all women who had stayed in shelters previously, 40% had been there once in the previous year, 38% had been there two to four times, and about 1 in 10 had been to the facility five times or more during the previous year" (Statistics Canada 2005a).

According to Novac and colleagues (1996), housing status and violence are inextricably linked for women who find themselves fleeing from their homes. They observe that "homeless women with histories of family disruption and abuse distinguish being housed from being safe, so that homelessness is a problem for women, but is also a strategy for escaping violence. The relationship between violence and homelessness among women is complex, since there is also a great risk of violence when women are homeless."

The breakup of a relationship may not stop its violence. Recognition that the most dangerous time for victims was after leaving their violent relationships compelled the 1993 enactment of a law against criminal harassment, an offence for which the maximum penalty is 10 years' imprisonment. This law is directed against "stalking" behaviours that may stem from a variety of motives, including the adamant refusal of one partner to believe that the relationship has ended (Kong 1997). Criminal harassment includes repeatedly following, trying to communicate (via cards, letters, e-mails, and so on), or uttering direct or indirect threats or promises of violence or forcible intimacy. Women were the victims of over three-quarters (77 percent) of all incidents of criminal harassment reported to police in Canada in 1999. Although ex-husbands were the accused in more than one-third (36 percent) of incidents reported by women, men were more likely to report being stalked by casual acquaintances than intimate partners. In that year, ex-wives accounted for 11 percent of the perpetrators of criminal harassment incidents reported by men (Johnson and Hotton 2001: 33). The 2004 General Social Survey found that 49 percent of all restraining orders were violated, and for female victims, 52 percent of all orders were violated (AuCoin 2005). Although criminal harassment does not generally culminate in homicide, between 1994 and 2003 it remained a stable precipitating factor in 12 percent of homicides committed by male ex-partners (Beattie 2005: 50). Moreover, when criminal harassment led to homicide, it did so exclusively for female victims; stalking of men did not end in murder of male victims (Beattie 2005: 50).

Although rates for spousal homicide in Canada have been steadily declining since the mid-1990s, spousal homicides accounted for 17 percent of all solved homicides in Canada and for 46 percent of all family homicides between 1996 and 2005 (Ogrodnick 2007: 9). Further, in an analysis of data for the same time period, the rate of women killed by their spouses was five times higher than the rate for men (Dauvergne 2005a: 10). Aboriginal peoples in Canada continue to suffer disproportionately from spousal homicide; at only 3 percent of the total population in Canada, Aboriginal victims of homicide accounted for 17 percent of all victims in 2004 and 22 percent of all those accused (Dauvergne 2005b: 13).

Table 5.3 shows that domestic violence in Canada accounts for almost 18 percent, or nearly one-fifth, of all solved murders between 1998 and 2007. In other words, although

Table 5.3 *Spousal Homicide in Canada, 1998–2008*

Relationship Type[1] (Victims Killed by)	2008		2007[1]		Average 1998 to 2007	
	Number of Victims	Percent	Number of Victims	Percent	Number of Victims	Percent
Family relationship						
Spousal relationship						
Husband (legal)	22	5.2	17	4.1	23	5.1
Husband (Common-law)	10	2.4	21	5.0	21	4.5
Husband (legal, separated and divorced)[2]	9	2.1	6	1.4	15	3.3
Husband (Common-law, separated)[3]	4	0.9	5	1.2	6	1.3
Wife (legal)	6	1.4	4	1.0	3	0.7
Wife (Common-law)	10	2.4	8	1.9	10	2.1
Wife (legal, separated and divorced)[2]	0	0.0	0	0.0	2	0.3
Wife (Common-law, separated)[3]	1	0.2	0	0.0	1	0.1
Same-sex spouse (current or former)[4]	0	0.0	1	0.2	1	0.2
Total spousal	**62**	**14.7**	**62**	**14.9**	**80**	**17.7**

[1]Includes only those homicides in which there were known accused. If there were more than one accused, only the closest relationship to the victim was recorded.

[2]Includes separated common-law prior to 2005.

[3]Separated common-law husband and separated common-law wife were not introduced to the survey until 2005, therefore the average number and percentage are calculated from 2005–07.

[4]Separate variables for same-sex spouse and ex-same-sex spouse were created in 2005.

SOURCE: Adapted from Statistics Canada, Canadian Centre for Justice Statistics. "Homicide in Canada." *Juristat*, Catalogue No. 85-002-XIE2009004, Vol. 29, no. 4, p. 24.

we often imagine murders to be random occurrences, a significant portion of murders take place in the context of intimate, familial relationships. Of the murders solved that we see enumerated in Table 5.3, it is also clear that with 45 of the murders being carried out by men, the general pattern is that women are more than 2.5 times as likely to be killed by a male spouse than men are to be killed by a female spouse; this observation in no way minimizes the murders of men, but speaks purely to the frequency and level of violence that women are likely to face.

In cases of domestic violence, even if they themselves are not being directly abused, children remain vulnerable. According to the 2004 GSS, children are too frequently the observers of violence between spouses. Aboriginal children are especially vulnerable: 46 percent of non-Aboriginal women and 57 percent of Aboriginal women reported that their child(ren) had witnessed domestic violence against their mothers (Johnson and Hotton 2001: 29). Children who witness intimate violence may experience emotional, behavioural, and academic problems, and may commit violence in their own relationships later (Parker et al. 2000). Children may also commit violent acts against a parent's abusing partner.

Why do abused adults stay in abusive relationships? Reasons include love, emotional dependency, commitment to the relationship, hope that things will get better, the view that they "deserve" the violence, guilt, fear, economic dependency, and feeling stuck because of financial dependence and the need to provide food and shelter for children in the relationship. Abuse in relationships is usually not ongoing and constant, but rather occurs in cycles. The **cycle of abuse** involves a violent or abusive episode, followed by a makeup period where the abuser expresses sorrow and asks for forgiveness and "one more chance." This period may last for days, weeks, or even months; then, the next outburst of violence occurs.

Child Abuse

Child abuse refers to the "physical or mental injury, sexual abuse, negligent treatment, or maltreatment of a child under the age of 18 by a person who is responsible for the child's welfare" (Willis et al. 1992: 2). The Canadian Incidence Study of Reported Child Abuse and Neglect (CIS) was the first national study of child maltreatment investigations by child welfare services in Canada. According to the study, the most common reason for investigations was suspected neglect (Figure 5.5). Investigations by child welfare organizations substantiated 34 percent of cases involving suspected physical abuse, 38 percent of suspected sexual abuse cases, 43 percent of suspected neglect cases, and 54 percent of cases involving suspected emotional maltreatment (Trocmé and Wolfe 2001: 5). The majority (69 percent) of substantiated cases of child physical abuse involved inappropriate punishment—hitting

cycle of abuse
Involves a violent or abusive episode, followed by a makeup period where the abuser expresses sorrow and asks for forgiveness and "one more chance." The calm period may last for days, weeks, or even months; then, the next outburst of violence occurs.

child abuse
The physical or mental injury, sexual abuse, negligent treatment, or maltreatment of a child under the age of 18 by a person who is responsible for the child's welfare.

Figure 5.5 *Child Neglect Most Common Reason for Child Maltreatment Investigation*

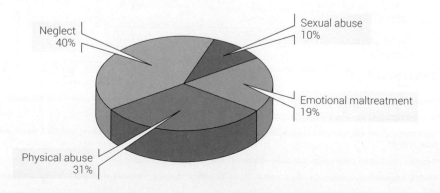

Neglect 40%

Sexual abuse 10%

Emotional maltreatment 19%

Physical abuse 31%

a child with either a hand or object that led to physical harm or put the child at substantial risk of harm. The most common form of sexual abuse within substantiated cases involved touching and fondling of the genitals (68 percent); attempted or completed sexual intercourse accounted for about a third (35 percent) of all substantiated cases. The most common form of emotional maltreatment within substantiated cases was a child's exposure to family violence followed by emotional abuse (overtly hostile, punitive treatment, or habitual or extreme verbal abuse) (Trocmé and Wolfe 2001).

Figure 5.6 shows that for all reported forms of abuse except sexual abuse, the most dangerous place for children is at home. In the home—except for sexual abuse, which occurs three times as often at the hands of biological fathers, and neglect, which occurs more than twice as often at the hands of mothers—children face similar risk at the hands of either biological parent. Sexual abuse was more likely to be perpetrated by other relatives, but is far more common among biological parents than one might expect. Although we teach children to fear strangers, Trocmé's data on child abuse show that "Other than parents, relatives [a]re the most frequently identified perpetrators" (Trocmé et al. 2001: 108).

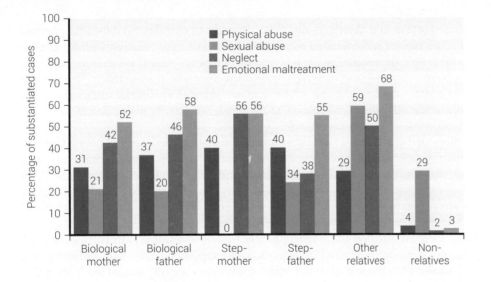

When compared to adults, children and youth are especially likely to be killed by family members (Locke et al. 2001: 15). Of the 1990 solved homicides of children and youths recorded by Canadian police agencies between 1974 and 1999, more than 6 out of 10 (63 percent) were committed by family members. As far as the frequencies for any given year, the data on homicides against children vary and show no obvious pattern (Ogrodnick 2007: 25); all we know is that parents—and especially young parents—are the most likely perpetrators, with over 70 percent of these murders being committed by parents (Dauvergne 2005b; Ogrodnick 2007). Moreover, because these killings frequently end in the suicide of the perpetrator (Ogrodnick 2007: 26), efforts to explain the motivation must encompass marital dissolution and depression as causative factors (Dauvergne 2000b: 11). (See Figure 5.7.)

Reviews of research on the effects of child abuse suggest that abused children are at higher risk for aggressive behaviour, low self-esteem, depression, and low academic achievement (Gelles and Conte 1991; Lloyd and Emery 1993). The Canadian Incidence Study (CIS) reports that in more than one-half (56 percent) of cases of substantiated physical abuse, the child was described as having some type of difficulty, with behaviour problems, negative peer involvement, depression or anxiety, violence

Figure 5.7 **Infants Are at Greatest Risk of Homicide by a Family Member, 1996–2005**

SOURCE: Statistics Canada, "Family Violence in Canada: A Statistical Profile," Catalogue no. 85-224-XIE2008000, October 2008; http://www.statcan.gc.ca/bsolc/olc-cel/olc-cel?lang=eng&catno=85-224-X.

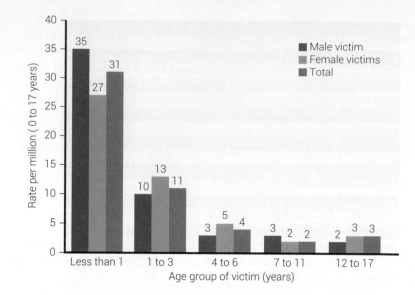

toward others, and developmental delay the most often indicated difficulties. Among child victims of substantiated sexual abuse, the five most frequently reported difficulties were depression or anxiety, age-inappropriate sexual behaviour, behaviour problems, negative peer involvement, and irregular school attendance (Trocmé and Wolfe 2001). Adolescents and adults who were abused as children are more vulnerable to low self-esteem, depression, unhappiness, anxiety, increased risk of substance abuse, criminal activity, and suicide.

Repeated studies have established strong correlations between the early abuse that children suffer and long-term negative health consequences. Like other forms of abuse, the consequences of sexual abuse of male and female children are devastating and long-term. Among females, early forced sex is associated with lower self-esteem, higher levels of depression, running away from home, alcohol and drug use, and more sexual partners (Jasinski et al. 2000; Lanz 1995; Whiffen et al. 2000). Sexually abused girls are also more likely to become pregnant as teens, have more sexual partners in adulthood, acquire sexually transmitted infections, and experience forced sex (Browning and Laumann 1997; Stock et al. 1997). Women who were sexually abused as children also report a higher frequency of post-traumatic stress disorder (Spiegel 2000) and suicide ideation (Thakkar et al. 2000). Spouses who were physically and sexually abused as children report lower marital satisfaction, higher stress, and lower family cohesion than spouses with no abuse history (Nelson and Wampler 2000). Adult males who were sexually abused as children tend to exhibit depression, substance abuse, and difficulty establishing intimate relationships (Krug 1989). Sexually abused males also have a higher risk of anxiety disorders, sleep and eating disorders, and sexual dysfunctions (Elliott and Briere 1992).

Effects of child sexual abuse are likely to be severe when the abuse is forceful, is prolonged, involves intercourse, and was perpetrated by a father or stepfather (Beitchman et al. 1992). The child not only has been violated physically, but also has lost an important social support.

Abused or neglected children may be removed from the home. Provincial child welfare laws permit abused or neglected children to be placed in out-of-home care, such as foster care; however, a preferred approach is to prevent family breakup if it can be done without jeopardizing the welfare of children in the home. **Family preservation programs** are in-home interventions for families who are at risk of having a child removed from the home due to abuse or neglect. Other abuse-prevention

family preservation program
An in-home intervention for a family who is at risk of having a child removed from the home because of abuse or neglect.

efforts focus on parent education to teach parents realistic expectations about child behaviour and methods of child discipline that do not involve corporal punishment.

Elder Abuse

Elder abuse includes physical abuse, psychological abuse, financial abuse (such as improper use of the elder's financial resources), and neglect. Elder neglect includes failure to provide basic health and hygiene needs, such as clean clothes, doctor visits, medication, and adequate nutrition. Neglect also involves unreasonable confinement, isolation of elderly family members, lack of supervision, and abandonment. (See Figure 5.8.)

The 1999 GSS asked Canadians 65 years of age or over a series of questions in relation to emotional and financial abuse by children, caregivers (individuals paid or unpaid who provide assistance or health care in the respondent's home), and spouses (including current and former spouses as well as common-law partners). It also asked questions about possible physical or sexual abuse by children, caregivers, or spouses. This survey reports very little physical or sexual violence perpetrated against older Canadians residing in a private household. "[O]nly one percent of this population of seniors indicated that they had been physically or sexually assaulted by a spouse, adult child or caregiver in the five years prior to this survey" (Bunge 2000: 27). Seven percent reported experiencing some type of emotional or financial abuse, with spouses identified as the perpetrator in the vast majority of cases. The most common form of emotional abuse reported was being verbally put down or called names (3 percent), followed by limiting contact with family or friends (2 percent). Men were more likely than women (9 percent versus 6 percent) to report being victims of emotional or financial abuse by an adult child, caregiver, or spouse. The highest rates of emotional or financial abuse were reported by older adults whose household incomes were between $30 000 and $39 000, who were divorced or separated, who lived in rural areas, and who had some postsecondary education. However, this survey did not include respondents living in institutions (e.g., retirement homes, hospitals), and so cannot provide us with information on the experiences of older Canadians who live in such settings.

According to police-reported statistics, there were 802 cases of violence committed against older adults by family members in 1999, with the most frequent assailant an adult child (43 percent), followed by a spouse (28 percent). The most common offence committed against an older adult by a family member was common assault (54 percent), followed by uttering threats (22 percent).

Factors Contributing to Intimate Partner and Family Violence and Abuse

Research suggests that cultural, community, and individual and family factors contribute to domestic violence and abuse (Willis et al. 1992).

Cultural Factors

Violence in the family stems from our society's acceptance of violence as a legitimate means of enforcing compliance and solving conflicts at personal, national, and international levels (Viano 1992). Violence and abuse in the family may be linked to cultural factors, such as violence in the media (see Chapter 4), acceptance of corporal punishment, gender inequality, and the view of women and children as property.

1. *Acceptance of corporal punishment.* **Corporal punishment** involves the use of physical force with the intention of causing a child to experience pain, but not injury, for the purpose of correction or control of a child's behaviour (Straus 2000).

elder abuse
The physical or psychological abuse, financial exploitation, or medical abuse or neglect of the elderly.

corporal punishment
The use of physical force with the intention of causing a child to experience pain, but not injury, for the purpose of correction or control of a child's behaviour.

Figure 5.8 **Facts on the Abuse of Seniors**

SOURCE: *Facts on the Abuse of Seniors*. http://www.seniors.gc.ca/end/pie/eaa/facts.pdf. Reproduced with the permission of the Minister of Employment and Social Development Canada, 2014.

Facts on the Abuse of Seniors

Elder abuse is any action by someone in a relationship of trust that results in harm or distress to an older person. Commonly recognized types of elder abuse include physical, sexual, psychological, emotional and financial as well as neglect. Often, more than one type of abuse occurs at the same time.

 Learn the signs

Learn the signs and symptoms to find out if you or a senior you know might be experiencing elder abuse or neglect.

Types of abuse

Physical and sexual abuse of seniors often includes:

- Hitting, pushing or shaking;
- Inappropriate physical and chemical restraints;
- Harm created by over or under medicating;
- Unexplained visible burns, scratches, bruises, cuts or swellings; or
- Vague or illogical explanations for injuries.

Psychological and emotional abuse of seniors may include:

- Intimidation, humiliation and harassment;
- Treating them like a child; or
- Isolating them from family, friends or regular activities.

Financial abuse of seniors can include:

- Misusing or stealing a senior's assets, property or money;
- Cashing an elderly person's cheques without authorization;
- Forging an elderly person's signature; or
- Unduly pressuring seniors to make or change a will, or to sign legal documents that they do not fully understand.

Neglect of seniors can include not providing appropriate:

- Water, food, shelter and clothing;
- Medication or medical attention; and
- Assistance with basic necessities.

 Protect yourself

Protect yourself by staying informed and knowing your rights.

Why does elder abuse happen?

Elder abuse often occurs because of the abuser's power and control over an older person. Abuse can happen when the aggressor wants to intimidate, isolate, dominate or control another person.

Who abuses seniors?

Older adults affected by abuse often know and trust the person mistreating them. Elder abuse can be caused by a family member, a friend, someone who provides assistance with basic needs or services, or health care providers in institutional settings.

Why are some older adults reluctant to talk about elder abuse?

Older adults may feel ashamed or embarrassed to tell anyone they are being abused by someone they trust. They may fear retaliation or punishment, have concerns about having to move from their home or community, or feel a sense of family loyalty.

 Reach Out

If you think you are experiencing elder abuse, ask for help. This may include support and assistance from family members or friends, caregivers, health care providers, social services, seniors' centres, police, legal professionals and/or members of faith communities.

For more information and a list of resources in your province or territory, call 1-800 O-Canada (1-800-622-6232) or visit **seniors.gc.ca.**

 Government   Gouvernement
of Canada   du Canada

Canadä

Many mental health professionals and child development specialists argue that it is ineffective and damaging to children. Children who experience corporal punishment display more antisocial behaviour and are more violent; as adults, they have an increased incidence of depression (Straus 2000). Yet, many parents accept the cultural tradition of spanking as an appropriate form of child discipline. Moreover, Canadian law specifically allows for the corporal punishment of children. Section 43 of the *Criminal Code* of Canada specifies that "[e]very schoolteacher, parent, or person standing in the place of a parent is justified in using force by way of correction toward a pupil or child, as the case may be, who is under his care, if the force does not exceed what is reasonable under the circumstances." In effect, this section allows children to be assaulted by their parents and teachers, provided that the force used in the assault is "reasonable" and for the child's "correction." Conversely, in such countries as Austria, Cyprus, Denmark, Finland, Italy, Norway, and Sweden, the use of corporal punishment in the home or school is against the law.

2. *Gender role socialization.* Traditional male gender roles have taught men to be aggressive in general and to be dominant in male–female relationships. Male abusers are likely to hold traditional attitudes toward women and male–female roles (Lloyd and Emery 2000). Anderson (1997) found that men who earn less money than their partners are more likely to be violent toward them. "Disenfranchised men then must rely on other social practices to construct a masculine image. Because it is so clearly associated with masculinity in…[our] culture, violence is a social practice that enables men to express a masculine identity" (p. 667). Traditional female gender roles have also taught women to be submissive to their male partner's control.

3. *View of women and children as property.* Before the 1978 *Family Law Reform Act* established that married women remained independent persons, wives were considered "chattel" or property of their husbands in Canada. A husband had a legal right and marital obligation to discipline and control his wife, even through the use of physical force. The historical weight of this view of women as property may contribute to men continuing to treat their wives as they wish. The view of women and children as property also explains marital rape and father–daughter incest. Historically, the penalties for rape were based on property-rights laws designed to protect a man's property—his wife or daughter—from rape by other men; a husband or father "taking" his own property was not considered rape (Russell 1990).

Community Factors

Community factors that contribute to violence and abuse in the family include social isolation and inaccessible or unaffordable health care, day care, elder care, and respite care facilities.

1. *Social isolation.* Living in social isolation from extended family and community members increases a family's risk for abuse. Isolated families are removed from material benefits, caregiving assistance, and emotional support from extended family and community members.

2. *Inaccessible or unaffordable community services.* Failure to provide medical care to children and elderly family members (a form of neglect) is sometimes due to the lack of accessible or affordable health-care services in the community. Failure to provide supervision for children and adults may result from inaccessible day care and elder care services. Without elder care and respite care facilities, socially isolated families may not have any help with the stresses of caring for elderly family members and children with special needs.

Individual and Family Factors

Individual and family factors associated with intimate partner and family violence and abuse include a family history of violence, drug and alcohol abuse, poverty, and fatherless homes.

1. *Family history of abuse.* Mothers who were sexually abused as children are more likely to physically abuse their own children (DiLillo et al. 2000). Although a history of abuse is associated with an *increased likelihood* of being abusive as an adult, *most* adults who were abused as children do not continue the pattern of abuse in their own relationships (Gelles 2000).
2. *Drug and alcohol abuse.* Alcohol use is reported as a factor in 50 to 70 percent of incidents of physical and sexual aggression in intimate relationships (Lloyd and Emery 2000). Alcohol and other drugs increase aggression in some individuals and enable the offender to avoid responsibility by blaming his or her violent behaviour on the drugs or alcohol.
3. *Poverty.* Abuse in adult relationships occurs among all socio-economic groups. However, Kaufman and Zigler (1992: 284) point to a relationship between poverty and child abuse:

   > Although most poor people do not maltreat their children, and poverty, per se, does not cause abuse and neglect, the correlates of poverty, including stress, drug abuse, and inadequate resources for food and medical care, increase the likelihood of maltreatment.

5.4 Strategies for Action: Preventing and Responding to Violence and Abuse in Intimate and Family Relationships

Strategies to prevent family violence and abuse include **primary prevention** strategies that target the general population, **secondary prevention** strategies that target groups at high risk for family violence and abuse, and **tertiary prevention** strategies that target families who have experienced abuse (Gelles 1993; Harrington and Dubowitz 1993).

Primary Prevention Strategies

Preventing violence and abuse may require broad, sweeping social changes, such as eliminating the norms that legitimize and glorify violence in society and changing society's sexist character (Gelles 2000). Specific abuse prevention strategies include public education and media campaigns that may help reduce domestic violence by conveying the criminal nature of domestic assault and offering ways to prevent abuse ("When you are angry at your child, count to 10 and call a friend . . ."). Other prevention efforts focus on parent education to teach parents realistic expectations about child behaviour and methods of child discipline that do not involve corporal punishment.

Another strategy involves reducing violence-provoking stress by reducing poverty and unemployment and providing adequate housing, child-care programs and facilities, nutrition, medical care, and educational opportunities. We also need to broaden our understanding of what a family is and to challenge misleading stereotypes about people with disabilities—their intelligence, their credibility, and their sexuality. By doing so, we can be effective in both preventing violence within families and responding to it when it occurs.

primary prevention (strategies)
Family violence prevention strategies that target the general population.

secondary prevention (strategies)
Prevention strategies that target groups that are thought to be at high risk for family violence.

tertiary prevention (strategies)
Prevention strategies that target families who have experienced family violence.

Secondary Prevention Strategies

Families at risk of experiencing violence and abuse include low-income families, parents with a history of depression or psychiatric care, single parents, teenage mothers, parents with few social and family contacts, individuals who experienced abuse in their own childhood, and parents or spouses who abuse drugs or alcohol. Secondary prevention strategies, designed to prevent abuse from occurring in high-risk families, include parent education programs, parent support groups, individual counselling, substance abuse treatment, and home visiting programs.

In response to studies that noted family violence is more prevalent in Aboriginal communities, the federal government allotted $7 million to the funding of short-term, community-based projects related to family violence in Indian and Inuit communities. These projects were part of the Family Violence and Child Sexual Abuse Initiatives. More than 180 of them, focusing on public awareness, training, community workshops, and research and program development, were funded in Native communities across Canada in the 1990s.

Care was taken to respect the strategies of intervention preferred within Aboriginal communities. Often, Aboriginal peoples view the problem of family violence as a symptom of community dysfunction. In consequence, solutions to the problem are viewed in terms of a holistic, community-wide healing process planned, developed, and implemented by Aboriginal peoples. For example, workshops dealing with issues of abuse may begin with a prayer and a sharing circle or a smudge ceremony using the local root. Communities may also use naming ceremonies and feasts to celebrate different points of healing or encourage survivors to take part in sweat lodges to ask for help for themselves and others. The Medicine Wheel, too, is favoured as a healing tool. The Wheel explains that healthy persons must use all four parts of themselves—physical, mental, emotional, and spiritual. Many versions of the Wheel are used in counselling programs.

Tertiary Prevention Strategies

What social interventions are available to families that are experiencing abuse or neglect? Abused women and children may seek relief at one of Canada's 508 shelters for abused women and their children, or "safe houses." Although shelters differ (see Table 5.4), there are residential facilities in every Canadian province and territory that provide abused women and their children with housing, food, and counselling services. *Safe houses* are private homes of individuals who volunteer to provide temporary housing to abused women who decide to leave their violent homes. Battered men are not allowed to stay at women's shelters, but many shelters help abused men by providing money for a motel room, counselling, and support services. Some communities have abuse shelters for victims of elder abuse. In August 2002, www.povnet.org/node/3728, a website providing point-and-click access to information about shelters for women and children across Canada, was launched in Toronto. A similar website, www.hotpeachpages.net, also provides abused women with helpful information on shelters (Wherry 2002). Recognizing that men also suffer from abuse, in 2008 the government of Canada produced the *Directory of Services and Programs for Abused Men in Canada*, an exhaustive 60-page booklet that contains lists organized by province and territory and printed in both official languages. The booklet is available from the Public Health Agency of Canada (PHAC). The greater number of shelters specifically designed for women and children fleeing from an abusive partner, however, reflects the fact that of those experiencing assault in the home, 83 percent of victims are women (Statistics Canada 2009).

Table 5.4 *Types of Shelters*

The term "shelter" is used broadly to refer to all residential facilities for abused women and their dependent children. The types of shelters are defined by the Transition Home Survey as:

Transition Home	Short- or moderate-term (1 day to 11 weeks) first stage emergency housing.
Second Stage Housing	Long-term (3–12 months) secure housing with support and referral services designed to assist women while they search for permanent housing.
Safe Home Network	A network of private homes in rural or remote areas where there is no full-fledged operating shelter. It offers subsidiary very short-term (1–3 days) emergency housing.
Women's Emergency Centre/Shelter	Short-term (1–21 days) respite (temporary relief) for women and their dependent children.
Emergency Shelter	Short-term (1–3 days) respite for a wide population range, not exclusively abused women. Some facilities may provide accommodation for men as well as women. This type of facility may accommodate residents who are not associated with family abuse but are without a home due to an emergency situation (e.g., eviction for non-payment of rent). Other than residential (room and board) services, these shelters offer few additional client services.
Family Resource Centre	An Ontario government initiative that serves a wide range of clients and provides clients with an extensive array of information and referrals as well as residential services.
Other	All other facilities/shelters not otherwise classified. This category may include Rural Family Violence Prevention Centres in Alberta, Interim Housing in Manitoba, and other types of emergency shelters. These services may not be exclusive to abused women.

SOURCE: Statistics Canada, "Children in shelters for abused women," *Family Violence in Canada: A Statistical Profile*, Catalogue no. 85-224-XIE2001000, June 2001; http://www.statcan.gc.ca/bsolc/olc-cel/olc-cel?catno=85-224-XIE&lang=eng#formatdisp.

Although efforts are made to keep families together, in cases where the abuser continues to be abusive and/or neglectful a court may order an abusing spouse or parent to leave the home. Abused spouses or cohabiting partners may obtain a restraining order prohibiting perpetrators. However, legal action does not always protect victims of family violence. One Canadian study that tracked 133 cases of domestic violence through the courts for an eight-month period found that almost half of the men charged with assaulting their wives broke bail conditions by harassing, stalking, or moving back in with their wives. While the return of abusive partners into the home may seem shocking, the financial dependence of women and children on male earners for family stability can compel some of the women to take back an abusive partner. The women may sincerely want their partners to change their behaviour, but not to disappear from their lives. Canadian courts have also been notably reluctant to curtail the access of abusive spouses to their children; the courts have held that a husband's commission of an assault upon his wife does not invalidate his application for child custody or the claim that he is a "good father." In situations in which a restraining order prohibits the abusive partner from establishing contact with a current or former spouse, the order itself may be unknowingly breached when the abused spouse voluntarily allows the abusive partner into the home to pick up or deliver their children.

Treatment for abusers may be voluntary or mandated by the court. It typically involves group or individual counselling or both, substance abuse counselling, and training in communication, conflict resolution, and anger management. Those who stop abusing their partners learn to take responsibility for their abusive behaviour, develop empathy for their partners' victimization by learning to see them as human beings instead of as property, reduce their dependency on their partners, and improve their communication skills (Scott and Wolfe 2000).

5.5 Divorce

Between 1968 and 1987, a time period in which family law reform introduced relaxation of legal requirements for divorce, Canada experienced a sevenfold increase in divorce (Ambert 1998: 4). However, divorce rates in Canada peaked in 1987 and have generally declined since then (see Figure 5.9); the implication is that many people had been desperate to leave marriages but had been prevented from doing so by harsh legal requirements that had defined divorce law in Canada. Suddenly able to leave their marriages, a desperate population got out in one concentrated rate-spike. However, rates for divorce have steadily fallen since, and stabilized in the *fin-de-siecle* period of the twenty to twenty-first centuries. In 1987, the crude divorce rate (the number of divorces per 100 000 population) was 362.3; in 2000, it was 231.2, and by 2003, the rate had fallen to 223.7 (Statistics Canada 2005b). Individual and relationship factors that contribute to divorce include incompatibility in values or goals, poor communication, lack of conflict resolution skills, sexual incompatibility, extramarital relationships, substance abuse, emotional or physical abuse, neglect, boredom, jealousy, and difficulty coping with change or stress related to parenting, employment, finances, in-laws, and illness. Other demographic and life course factors that are predictive of divorce include marriage order (second and subsequent marriages are more prone to divorce than first marriages), cohabitation (couples who live together before marriage are more prone to divorce), teenage marriage, premarital pregnancy, and low socio-economic status. A prime feature of divorce is that it appears to be most common in the fifth year of marriage, following the fourth anniversary. From there it declines, with 60 percent of all divorces taking place before the end of 15 years of marriage (Statistics Canada 2004).

The number of marriages has fluctuated over the past century and has been influenced by historical events. During the great Depression of the 1930s, there were fewer marriages...as people were probably less willing or able to marry during a period of higher unemployment and challenging economic circumstance. In 1939, Canada entered the Second World War and some couples may have married to reduce the likelihood of possible conscription...While low during the war years, the number of marriages rose again in 1946 at the end of the war [and remained] relatively stable throughout much of the 1950s and early 1960s before increasing during the subsequent decade...[corresponding] to...the large baby-boom cohort reaching [marriageable] ages...Despite a growing total population over time, the number of

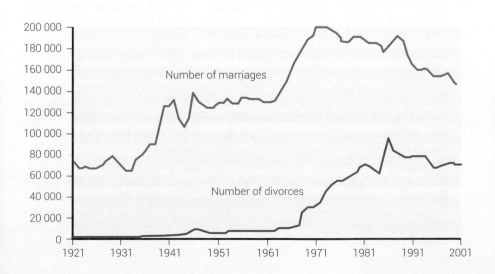

Figure 5.9 **Numbers of Marriages and Divorces in Canada, 1921–2002**

SOURCE: Statistics Canada. "Number of Marriages and Divorces in Canada, 1921–2002." *The Daily*, Catalogue No. 11-001, Tuesday, May 4, 2004, www.statscan.ca/Daily/English/040504/d040504a.htm.

people getting married has been on an overall downward trajectory for close to forty years. (Milan 2013: 10)

Statistical analyses of Canadian marriage and divorce trends demonstrate that a number of social factors contribute to the increased rate of divorce over the past four decades. These include the following structural and cultural forces:

1. *Liberalized divorce laws.* Before 1968, adultery was the only ground for divorce in Canada, except in Nova Scotia, where cruelty was sufficient grounds even before Confederation (Morrison 1987). The 1968 *Divorce Act* expanded the "fault grounds" under which a divorce could be granted. In addition to adultery, proof that one's partner had engaged in prohibited activities, such as mental or physical cruelty, gross addiction to alcohol or other drugs, sodomy, bestiality, and homosexual acts, entitled the petitioner to an immediate divorce. The 1968 *Divorce Act* also introduced what are termed **no-fault divorce** grounds that allowed couples to divorce without requiring them to stipulate their specific reason for doing so. In these cases of marital breakdown, couples were required to live apart for a three-year period before applying for a divorce and jointly consent to being divorced. In the event that one party did not wish to be divorced, the court required that five years pass from the time of separation before applying for divorce. In addition, Morton (1990: 213) notes that "[a]s an added protection for the economically dependent spouse in cases of unilateral separation, courts were given the discretion to refuse a divorce if a 'granting of the decree would be unduly harsh or unjust or would affect the making of reasonable arrangements for the maintenance [financial support] of the spouse.'"

   In 1985, a new divorce act became law. Under the current act, only one ground is available for divorce—marital breakdown—but this is defined in three ways: (1) the spouses have lived apart for one year; (2) one of the spouses has committed an act of adultery; (3) one spouse has treated the other with mental or physical cruelty. While proof of fault entitles couples to an immediate divorce, those opting for a one-year separation "may apply for a divorce any time after separation to ensure that their case is heard soon after the year is up" (Morton 1990: 214).

2. *Changing cultural values.* Our society is increasingly characterized by **individualism**—the tendency to focus on one's individual self-interests rather than on the interests of one's family and community. The rising divorce rate has been linked to the continued rise of individualism. "For many, concerns with self-fulfillment and careerism diminished their commitment to family, rendering marriage and other intimate relationships vulnerable" (Demo et al. 2000: 281). **Familism**, in contrast, refers to the view that the family unit is more important than individual interests.

   The value of marriage has also changed. The increased social acceptance of nonmarital sexuality, nonmarital child-bearing, cohabitation, and singlehood reflect the view that marriage is an option rather than an inevitability. The view of marriage as an option, rather than as an imperative, is mirrored by the view that divorce is also an acceptable option. Divorce today has less social stigma than in previous generations. "Marital dissolution, once considered to be a rare, unfortunate, and somewhat shameful deviation from normal family life" (Thompson and Amato 1999: xi), has become part of mainstream society.

3. *Increased life expectancy.* Finally, more marriages today end in divorce, in part, because people live longer than they did in previous generations. Because people live longer today than in previous generations, "'til death do us part" involves a longer commitment than it once did. Indeed, one can argue that "marriage once was as unstable as it is today, but it was cut short by death not divorce" (Emery 1999: 7).

no-fault divorce
A divorce that is granted based on the claim that there are irreconcilable differences within a marriage (as opposed to one spouse being legally at fault for the marital breakup).

individualism
A value system that stresses the importance of individual happiness.

familism
A value system that encourages family members to put their family's well-being above their individual and personal needs.

Consequences of Divorce

When parents have bitter conflict that cannot be resolved or one parent is abusing the child or the other parent, divorce may offer a solution to family problems; however, it often has negative effects for ex-spouses and their children and contributes to problems that affect society as a whole.

Health Consequences

A large number of studies have found that divorced individuals, compared to married individuals, experience lower levels of psychological well-being, including more unhappiness, depression, anxiety, and poorer self-concepts. Divorced individuals also have more health problems and a higher risk of mortality (Amato 2001). Both divorced and never-married individuals are, on average, more distressed than married people because unmarried people are more likely than married people to have low social attachment, low emotional support, and increased economic hardship (Walker 2001).

Economic Consequences

In families at the lowest income levels, divorce can improve women's income because men who earn little income can be a drain on the family's finances. However, "there is a clear pattern that the economic well-being of divorced women and their children plunges in comparison to pre-divorce levels" (Demo et al. 2000: 281). The economic costs of divorce are greater for women and children because women tend to earn less than men (see Chapter 7) and mothers devote substantially more time to household and child-care tasks than fathers do. The time that women invest in this unpaid labour restricts their educational and job opportunities as well as their income.

Men are less likely than women to be economically disadvantaged after divorce. Many men enjoy a better financial situation after divorce (Peterson 1996) as they continue to profit from earlier investments in education and career. However, men with low and unstable earnings often experience financial strain following divorce, which often underlies failure to pay child support. When custodial mothers who did not receive child support were asked why they did not receive it, 66 percent gave the reason as "father unable to pay" (Henry 1999).

Effects on Children

Although divorce, following high conflict, may improve the emotional well-being of children relative to staying in a conflicted home environment (Jekielek 1998), for many children, parental divorce has detrimental effects. With only one parent in the home, children of divorce, as well as children of never-married mothers, tend to have less adult supervision compared with children in two-parent homes. Lack of adult supervision is related to higher rates of criminality by youths, school failure, and teenage pregnancy (Popenoe 1993). A survey of 90 000 teenagers found that the mere presence of a parent in the home after school, at dinner, and at bedtime significantly reduces the risk of teenage suicide, violence, and drug use (Resnick et al. 1997). Many of the negative effects of divorce on children are related to economic hardship. Economic hardship is associated with less effective and less supportive parenting, inconsistent and harsh discipline, and emotional distress in children (Demo et al. 2000).

In a review of the literature on the effects of parental divorce on university-age students, Nielsen (1999) found that when their parents divorce and their mother remarries within a few years, most children do not suffer serious long-term consequences in terms of self-confidence, mental health, or academic achievements. However, in those cases where the mother does not remarry (about 15 percent), the consequences are more likely to be negative. Children of divorced women who do not remarry tend to experience a reduced standard of living and a lack of parental discipline. These children "fail to develop as much self-control, self-motivation, self-reliance, and self-direction as people their own age whose mothers have remarried" (Nielsen 1999: 547).

Children who live with their mothers may suffer from a damaged relationship with their nonresidential father, especially if he becomes disengaged from their lives. On the other hand, children may benefit from having more quality time with their fathers after parental divorce. Some fathers report that they became more active in the role of father after divorce. One father commented:

> In the last four and a half years, I have developed an incredibly strong and loving bond with my two sons. I am actively involved in all aspects of their lives. I have even coached their soccer and basketball teams....The time I spend with them is very quality time—if anything, the divorce has made me a better and more caring father....not to say this would not have happened if my marriage had worked out. (quoted in Pasley and Minton 2001: 248)

However, according to Canada's National Child Survey, following parental separation about one-third of children have little contact with their fathers—irregular visits or none at all. Children born of common-law unions are even less likely to see their fathers than are children born to married parents. "Since fathers who have low levels of contact with their children are least likely to pay child support, many Canadian children are at a high risk of losing both the personal and financial support of their fathers when their parents separate" (National Council of Welfare 1999: 51).

On occasion, custodial parents may actively try to alienate children from the noncustodial parent. Some of these children may develop **parental alienation syndrome (PAS)**, an emotional and psychological disturbance in which children engage in exaggerated and unjustified denigration and criticism of a parent (Gardner 1998). PAS has also been described as a form of child abuse in which one parent encourages the child to hate the other parent (Schacht 2000). Long-term effects of PAS on children can include long-term depression, inability to function, guilt, hostility, alcoholism and other drug abuse, and other symptoms of internal distress (Family Court Reform Council of America 2000).

Some noncustodial divorced fathers discontinue contact with their children as a coping strategy for managing emotional pain (Pasley and Minton 2001). Many divorced fathers are overwhelmed with feelings of failure, guilt, anger, and sadness over the separation from their children (Knox 1998). Hewlett and West (1998: 69) explain that "visiting their children only serves to remind these men of their painful loss, and they respond to this feeling by withdrawing completely."

In conclusion, we note that "while some children emerge from divorce with a strong sense of loss and feelings of anger or despair, others are capable of acknowledging that divorce has pain but also benefits for themselves and other family members" (Thompson and Amato 1999: xix). Factors that determine whether a child is scathed or strengthened by parental divorce include the quality of the child's relationship with both parents, the extent of ongoing conflict versus cooperation between the parents, and the economic circumstances of the child's household. In most circumstances, children adapt to divorce, "showing resiliency, not dysfunction" (Thompson and Amato 1999: xix).

parental alienation syndrome (PAS)
An emotional and psychological disturbance in which children engage in exaggerated and unjustified denigration and criticism of a parent.

5.6 Strategies for Action: Strengthening Postdivorce Families

Negative consequences of divorce for children may be minimized if both parents spend time with their children on a regular and consistent basis and communicate to their children that they love them and are interested in their lives. Parental conflict, in either intact families or divorced families, negatively influences the psychological well-being of children (Demo 1992). Ongoing conflict between divorced parents also tends to result in decreased involvement of non-residential parents with their children (Leite and McKenry 2000). By maintaining a civil co-parenting relationship during a separation and after divorce, parents can minimize the negative effects of divorce on their children.

What can society do to promote cooperative parenting by ex-spouses? One answer is to encourage, or even mandate, divorcing couples to participate in **divorce mediation**. In divorce mediation, divorcing couples meet with a neutral third party, a mediator, who helps them resolve issues of property division, child custody, child support, and spousal support in a way that minimizes conflict and encourages cooperation. Children of mediated divorces adjust better to the divorce than children of litigated divorces (Marlow and Sauber 1990). However, Canadian family lawyer Linda Silver Dranoff has cautioned that mediation is not always feasible and that "[s]pouses who have been bullied or dominated during the marriage may not be capable of holding their own in mediation, while rigid or abusive spouses may not be capable of the necessary flexibility and compromise" (2001: 254).

Another trend aimed at strengthening postdivorce families is the establishment of parenting programs for divorcing parents (Shapiro and Schrof 1995). For example, the B.C. Ministry of the Attorney-General began a pilot program, "Parenting after Separation," which became mandatory in 2001 for all separated couples with custody disputes over their children. Such programs emphasize the importance of cooperative co-parenting for the well-being of children. Parents are taught about children's reactions to divorce, nonconflictual co-parenting skills, and ways to avoid negative behaviour toward their ex-spouses. In some programs, children participate. Taught that they are not the cause of the divorce, children learn how to deal with grief reactions to divorce and how to talk to parents about their concerns.

divorce mediation
A process in which divorcing couples meet with a neutral third party (mediator) who assists the individuals in resolving such issues as property division, child custody, child support, and spousal support in a way that minimizes conflict and encourages cooperation.

5.7 Nonmarital and Teenage Child-Bearing

In 1975, there were approximately 31 000 Canadian children born to not-married women (9 percent of all births). In 1996, there were about 103 500 births to not-married women and their babies accounted for just under a third (31 percent) of all births (Vanier Institute of the Family 2000: 55) (see Figure 5.10). 2008 data for Canada show that the crude birth rate to unmarried women sat at 27.2 per thousand (Statistics Canada 2008: 20), a rate relatively stable with the earlier Vanier report. To understand the rise in the number of children born to not-married women, we must consider several social factors. What happens when we assess these factors is that we see that nonmarital and early child-bearing are not necessarily *problems*, though certain challenges can still arise for these families, especially where policy lags behind cultural change.

Figure 5.10 **Births to Not-Married Women**[1] **as a Percentage of Total Births (1975, 1985, and 1996)**

SOURCE: Statistics Canada. "Births," Catalogue no. 8F0210X, April 2011, p. 2.

[1]Not-married women includes single women who may be part of a common-law relationship, and women who are divorced, separated, or widowed.

Having a baby outside of marriage no longer carries the stigma it once did. For example, by the end of the twentieth century all Canadian provinces and territories (except Alberta and Nova Scotia) had enacted legislation to dispense with the distinction that used to exist in law between "legitimate" and "illegitimate" children. As a result, in terms of financial support and inheritance rights, the legal distinction between children born within marriage and those born outside of it was eliminated (Dranoff 2001).

Singlehood has also become more acceptable and more common. The dictionary once defined a *spinster* as an unmarried woman above age 30. In previous generations, being a spinster meant the fear of isolation, living alone, and being somewhat of a social outcast. Today, women are "more confident, more self-sufficient, and…no longer see marriage as a matter of survival and acceptance" (Edwards 2000: 48). The women's movement created both new opportunities for women and expectations of egalitarian relationships with men. Increasingly, university-educated women in their 30s and 40s are making "the conscious decision to have a child on their own because they haven't found Mr. Adequate, let alone Mr. Right" (Drummond 2000: 54).

Increased acceptance of cohabitation and same-sex relationships has also contributed to the rising rate of nonmarital births. The term *nonmarital* includes births to the never-marrieds as well as the separated/divorced, widowed, and cohabiting. In 1996, three-quarters of all Canadian children born to not-married women were born into common-law partnerships. In that year, the highest number of births to women who were not married (50 percent) occurred in Quebec—the province with the highest proportion of couples living common-law (24 percent) (Vanier Institute of the Family 2000: 54). As such, "[t]he large majority of children born to mothers who are not married at the time of the child's birth nonetheless begin life in a family with both their biological parents present" (ibid). In other words, though these women were not married, many were in stable common-law relationships.

A recent comparative study of teenage pregnancy in developed countries placed Canada in the "moderate" rate category (45.4 pregnancies/1000 females 15 to 19 years old) (Singh and Darroch 2000). Canada's teen pregnancy rate was about half of the high U.S. rate (83.6), but higher than the low or very low rates found in most developed European countries, such as Belgium (14.1), Denmark (22.7), Sweden (24.9), and Norway (32.3) (Singh and Darroch 2000). Nevertheless, while the pregnancy rate among every other age group of fertile women is decreasing, the teenage pregnancy rate is increasing. Although well below their all-time highs, rates of teen pregnancies have increased from 41.1 per 1000 women aged 15 to 19 in 1987 to 47.1 per 1000 in 1995 to 59.2 in 1997 (Crawford 1997; Health Canada 1999). The number of live births is not as high as these figures suggest, however, because about 40 percent of teenage pregnancies end in abortion (Figure 5.11).

Teenage pregnancy has been related to a variety of factors, including low self-esteem and hopelessness, low parental supervision, and perceived lack of future occupational

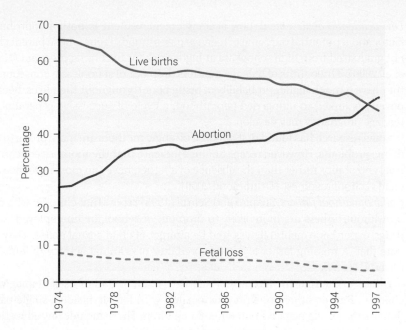

Figure 5.11 **Percentage Distribution of Outcomes of Teenage Pregnancy, Women Aged 15 to 19, Canada, 1974–1997**

SOURCE: Statistics Canada. *Table 106-9001 - Teen pregnancy, by pregnancy outcomes, females aged 15 to 19, Canada, provinces and territories, annual,* CANSIM (database) http://www5.statcan.gc.ca /cansim/a26?lang=eng&retrLang =eng&id=1069001&pattern=pregnancy&csid=

opportunities. Although lack of information about and access to contraceptives contributes to unintended teenage pregnancy, a U.S. study found that 30 to 40 percent of adolescent pregnancies are intended (Jorgensen 2000). Teenage females who do poorly in school may have little hope of success and achievement in pursuing educational and occupational goals. They may think that their only option for a meaningful role in life is to become a parent. In addition, some teenagers feel lonely and unloved and have a baby to create a sense of feeling needed and wanted.

Social Problems Related to Unplanned Child-Bearing

Many sociologists and the general public perceive teenage and unmarried childbirth to be social problems because of the adverse consequences for women and children that are associated with such births. This section outlines reasons for that perception and then presents a feminist view grounded in public health data that challenge this common perception.

1. *Poverty for single mothers and children.* Many unmarried mothers, especially teenagers, have no means of economic support or have limited earning capacity. Single mothers and their children often live in substandard housing and have inadequate nutrition and incomes. Even with public assistance, many unwed parents struggle to survive economically. The public bears some of the economic burden of supporting unmarried mothers and their children, but even with public assistance, many unwed and teenage parents often struggle to survive economically. While child poverty in Canada is not restricted to single-parent families, a far higher proportion of children living with single parents, especially lone-parent mothers, live in low-income circumstances (Reidmann et al. 2003).

2. *Poor health outcomes.* Compared with older pregnant women, pregnant teenagers are less likely to receive timely prenatal care and to gain adequate weight; they are also more likely to smoke and use alcohol and drugs during pregnancy (Jorgensen 2000; Ventura et al. 2000). As a consequence of these and other factors, infants born to teenagers are at higher risk of low birth weight, of premature birth, and of dying in the first year of life.

3. *Low academic achievement.* Low academic achievement is both a contributing factor and a potential outcome of teenage parenthood. Teens whose parents have not graduated from high school are at higher risk for becoming pregnant (Hogan et al. 2000). Three-fifths of teenage mothers drop out of school; as a consequence, they have a much higher probability of being poor throughout their lives. Because poverty is linked to unmarried parenthood, a cycle of successive generations of teenage pregnancy may develop.

   Some research has found that children of single mothers are more prone to academic problems. However, recent findings indicate that the mother's educational level and ability, rather than the absence of a father, have the most influence on a child's school readiness (Drummond 2000).

4. *Children without fathers.* Shapiro and Schrof (1995) report that children who grow up without fathers are more likely to drop out of school, be unemployed, abuse drugs, experience mental illness, and be a target of child sexual abuse. They also note that "a missing father is a better predictor of criminal activity than race or poverty" (p. 39).

   Others argue that the absence of a father is not, in and of itself, damaging to children. Rather, other conditions associated with female-headed, single-parent families may bring negative outcomes for children. These include low educational attainment of the mother, poverty, and lack of child supervision.

Challenging the Mainstream View of Teenage Child-Bearing

Arline Geronimus is a U.S.-based public health researcher. Her work on teenage mothers shows that the conclusions discussed above with regard to early child-bearing use a white, middle-class population as the benchmark against which all other lives should be assessed. Geronimus argues that delaying child-bearing at least to one's mid-20s is best understood as an adaptive strategy tied to the need to maximize the potential benefits of industrial capitalism, even while surrendering to the mechanisms of a system that render young families especially vulnerable. For those who have something to gain in a system that privileges the middle class, especially those of Euro-American background, delayed child-bearing makes sense; however, for those who have little hope of accessing those limited freedoms, an alternate adaptive strategy may be more useful: early child-bearing (2003: 882). Insofar as there is a crisis in early child-bearing, Geronimus demonstrates, it comes in the general vilification of young black mothers, who form a minority of teen mothers. However, the teen birth rate is higher for young black women than it is for young white women (p. 888).

Geronimus explains that recent welfare reform in the United States punishes young black mothers in particular because the requirement that all adult family members be working "deplete[s] the reserve of kin members available to offer childcare to the others" (p. 890). Similar changes in Canada do the same. As policy, such reforms are based on an inaccurate notion that the mothers would not have been working before. The presupposition is wrong, Geronimus concludes, because it assumes that early child-bearing will interrupt the many years of schooling required for career advancement—a future not open to the young black mothers she studies.

Moreover, Geronimus uses multivariate analyses to show that, if these same young mothers were to delay their child-bearing until their mid-20s, their risk for having babies of low birth weight would double, as would the infant mortality rate; if they delayed child-bearing until their 30s, the risk would be three times higher than for those who have their first children between the ages of 15 and 18 (1997). Current social reform to punish young women in the vulnerable groups Geronimus studies may cause further harm by removing from the mothers the extended kin and social networks available for economic, housing, and child-care support when the mothers are younger:

> Postponing childbearing increases the chance that her young children [will] compete with ailing elders for her energies and decreases the chance that their father will survive through much of their childhood. Her greatest chance of long-term labour force attachment will be if her children's pre-school years coincide with her years of peak access to social and practical support provided by relatively healthy kin. Her best chance of achieving her stated goals is by becoming a mother at a young age. (Geronimus 1997: 425)

Strategies for Action: Interventions in Teenage and Nonmarital Child-Bearing

Some interventions in teenage child-bearing aim at prevention, while other interventions attempt to minimize its negative effects. One intervention is to provide sex education and family planning programs before unwanted or unintended pregnancy occurs. However, sex education programs that emphasize abstinence and do not provide students with access to contraception are unlikely to be highly successful in preventing teenage pregnancy (Jacobs and Wolf 1995).

Other programs aim at both preventing teenage and unmarried child-bearing and minimizing its negative effects by increasing the life options of teenagers and unmarried mothers. Such programs encompass educational programs, job training, and skill building. Other programs designed to help teenage and unwed mothers and their children include public welfare prenatal programs, which help ensure the health of the mother and baby, and parenting classes for both teenage fathers and unmarried mothers.

Strategies to increase and support fathers' involvement with their children are relevant to both children of unwed mothers and children of divorce. These include promoting responsible fatherhood by improving work opportunities for low-income fathers, increasing child support collections, providing parent education training for men, and supporting access and visitation by noncustodial parents. Programs also focus on involving boys and young men in preventing teenage pregnancy and early parenting.

Because teenage parents are less likely than older parents to use positive and effective child-rearing techniques, parent education programs for teen mothers and fathers are an important component of improving the lives of young parents and their children. Geronimus's work, however, shows that conclusions about negative parenting are not as accurate as many assume them to be. Geronimus explains, citing the work of Carol Massat:

> several studies that employ more detailed multivariate analyses…fail to show teen mothers to be at increased risk of abusing or neglecting their children. No researcher of this topic has applied a research design to account for unmeasured factors…[but] the prevailing wisdom "that adolescent parents are more likely to maltreat their children than are older parents appears to be a myth entrenched in the popular culture." (1997: 413)

The harms that may come to children with young mothers are likely to be secondary to the social harms that compel young motherhood in the first place: increasingly poor health as one's population ages, poverty, lack of access to education and upwardly mobile work, and so forth. It is a research error to treat early child-bearing as the independent variable that influences all outcomes (Geronimus 1997, 2003). In short: not all teen pregnancies are unplanned, and not all unplanned child-bearing constitutes a crisis.

Understanding Family Problems

Family problems can best be understood within the context of the society and culture in which they occur. Although domestic violence, divorce, teenage pregnancy, and unmarried parenthood may appear to result from individual decisions, these decisions are influenced by myriad social and cultural forces.

The impact of family problems, including divorce, abuse, and nonmarital childbearing, is felt not only by family members, but by the larger society as well. Family members experience such life difficulties as poverty, school failure, low self-esteem, and mental and physical health problems. Each of these difficulties contributes to a cycle of family problems in the next generation. The impact on society includes public expenditures to assist single-parent families and victims of domestic violence and neglect, and to combat youth crime and lower worker productivity.

For some, the solution to family problems is rooted in encouraging marriage and discouraging other family forms, such as single parenting, cohabitation, and same-sex unions. But many family scholars argue that the fundamental issue is making sure that children are well cared for, whether or not their parents are married. Some even suggest that marriage is part of the problem, not part of the solution. According to Martha Fineman, "This obsession with marriage prevents us from looking at our social problems and addressing them....Marriage is nothing more than a piece of paper, and yet we rely on marriage to do a lot of work in this society: It becomes our family policy, our police in regard to welfare and children, the cure for poverty" (quoted in Lewin 2000: 2).

Strengthening marriage is a worthy goal because strong marriages offer many benefits to individuals and their children. However, "strengthening marriage does not have to mean a return to the patriarchal family of an earlier era....Indeed, greater marital stability will only come about when men are willing to share power, as well as housework and childcare, equally with women" (Amato 2001: 184).

Strengthening marriage does not mean that other family forms should be derided. The reality is that the family comes in many forms, each with its strengths, needs, and challenges. Given the diversity of families today, social historian Stephanie Coontz (2000: 15) suggests, "The only way forward at this point in history is to find better ways to make both marriage and its alternatives work."

Student Reflection: What Do You Know Now?

Chances are, there were parts of this chapter that you found very uncomfortable to read and review. It is very likely that you or someone you know has been affected by violence, abuse, divorce, and any number of the social and cultural factors described above. Given the new information and perspectives offered here, how will you change the way you think about your own family and relationships? How will these perspectives inform your own understanding of your gendered being in the world with others? What would equality look like to you? In what ways can you imagine your future career options intersecting with the issues raised above?

What Do You Do Next?

Located at www.nelson.com/socialproblems5e

- Consolidate your knowledge with interactive and printable **Flashcards**
- Gauge your understanding with **Practice Quizzes** and **Matching Activities**
- Develop your critical thinking skills with **Self and Society** and **The Human Side** questions
- Analyze **Social Research** and **Social Problems in Global Perspective**
- Explore the implications of **Technology on Social Problems**

section

Problems of Human Diversity

People are diverse. They vary on many dimensions, including age, gender, sexual orientation, and race and ethnicity. In most societies, including Canada, these characteristics are imbued with social significance and are used to make judgments about an individual's worth, intelligence, skills, and personality. Such labelling creates categories of people who are perceived as "different" by others as well as by themselves and, as a result, are often treated differently.

A **minority** is defined as a category of people who have unequal access to positions of power, prestige, and wealth in a society. In effect, minorities have unequal opportunities and are disadvantaged in their attempt to gain societal resources. Even though they may be a majority in terms of numbers, they may still be a minority sociologically. Because the recognition of groups or of individual people is supposed to follow principles of human rights and social justice, regardless of *how many* members of a group there are, many contemporary sociologists prefer to speak of the manner in which some groups are forced or coerced into marginal social positions; we speak, therefore, not of a minority, but of a **marginalized** group. This section of your text recognizes the persistence of the common perception of groups as "minorities," and places that perception in relation to the problems of social inequality that result from marginalization.

Because the process of marginalization involves creating and maintaining *stereotypes*, *prejudices*, and *discriminatory practices*, we consider these processes throughout each of the chapters in this section. Stereotypes are built on sets of assumptions or generalizations about the characteristics of a group of persons. Prejudices are attitudes, often negative, that prejudge individuals and groups. In the sense that we use it here, discrimination refers to the differential treatment of marginalized groups by members of the dominant

© jcarillet/iStockphoto.com

group and to the harmful effect on marginalized groups and persons. The groups we discuss in this section are all victims of stereotyping, prejudice, and discrimination.

Marginalized groups usually have certain characteristics in common. In general, members are aware of their marginal position, stay within their own group, have relatively low levels of self-esteem, are disproportionately represented in the lower socio-economic strata, and are viewed as having negative traits.

In the following chapters, we discuss categories based on age (Chapter 6), gender (Chapter 7), race and ethnicity (Chapter 8), and sexualities (Chapter 9). Although other categories of minorities exist (e.g., people with disabilities, religious minorities), we have chosen to concentrate on these four groups

because each is surrounded by issues and policies that have far-reaching social, political, and economic implications.

The cost for victims of stereotyping, prejudice, and discrimination, as well as the negative consequences for a society such as Canada, which imagines itself as a multicultural, pluralist democracy, are considered. We also consider strategies for change and encourage students to recognize problems from the perspective of those who experience them rather than from the perspective of socially dominant groups.

6

Youth and Aging

© trait2lumiere/iStockphoto.com

Student Reflection: What Do You Already Know?

As you begin this chapter, think about the ways we in Canada slice up different age categories at this point in history. What is your own definition of "youth" or "middle aged" or "elderly"? Compared to your parents' and grandparents' generations, whenever they were, how long are young people expected to be "adolescents" these days? Given that the age to vote, the age to drive, the age to which one is required to attend school, and the age to drink alcohol are often different from one another, when can youth be said to be adults? Given that some provinces have mandatory retirement and others do not, what kinds of implications might arise in either case from a social problems perspective?

Learning Outcomes

Through careful reading of this chapter, you should be able to:

- define the bolded key terms
- identify the connection between social problems and ageism
- tie the effects of labour to age categorization and expectation
- view age as a social fact and as social roles rather than as immutable biology
- understand adolescence as a cultural construction
- apply sociological perspectives to problems of youth and aging, challenging our preconceptions about life stages
- consider the variability of personhood based on age categorization, especially in terms of autonomy
- identify patterns of aging, income disparity, and social class in terms of gender, indigeneity, and labour
- link ageism and health, including caregiving, across the life stages
- act on this information to imagine ways of solving social problems and their effects on children and the aged

The young and the old are subject to different treatment in societies around the world. These differences in treatment have traditionally been associated with whether the country is more or less industrially developed. Although proportionately more elderly live in developed countries than in less developed ones, these societies have fewer statuses for the elderly to occupy. Their positions as caretakers, homeowners, employees, and producers are often assumed by those 18 to 65. Paradoxically, the less industrially developed the society, the more likely that society is to practise **senilicide**—the killing of the elderly. In some agrarian societies, the elderly are considered a burden: they are left to die or, in some cases, actively killed.

senilicide
The killing of the elderly.

6.1 The Global Context: The Young and the Old around the World

Not all societies treat the elderly as a burden. Scandinavian countries provide government support for in-home care workers for elderly who can no longer perform such tasks as cooking and cleaning. Eastern cultures, such as that of Japan, revere their elderly, in part because of their presumed proximity to honoured ancestors.

Societies also differ in the way they treat children. In less industrialized societies, children work as adults, marry at a young age, and pass from childhood directly to adulthood without a recognized period of adolescence. In contrast, in industrialized nations, children generally attend school for 12 to 16 years and thus remain financially and emotionally dependent on their families for an extended period. In other words, we can think of the extended period of childhood, and the development of adolescence as a separate life stage, *not* as objective reflections of biological stages in the life course, but as specific effects of the demands of labour specialization and labour divisions which, in industrialized and so-called "knowledge-based" societies, demand long years of increasingly specialized training. These demands prevent younger people from achieving the self-sufficiency and attendant inclusion in the larger political, economic, and policy decisions of their societies. Long years of childhood and an extended adolescence are not, then, obviously "better" ways to organize younger members of a society. After all, such a manner of organizing younger members can prevent them from exercising autonomous decision making, and extended economic vulnerability can force young people to live for a longer amount of time inside dysfunctional and, possibly, abusive families.

Because of this extended dependency, Canada treats minors differently from adults. Juveniles have a separate justice system and minimum ages for driving, drinking alcohol, joining the military, entering into a contract, marrying, dropping out of school, and voting. While we may perceive these differences in treatment as largely protective, such limitations would not be tolerated if placed on individuals on the basis of sex or race. Hence, **ageism**—the belief that age is associated with certain psychological, behavioural, or intellectual traits, at least in reference to children—is much more tolerated than sexism or racism in Canada.

It is important to remember that "childhood" is not a universally shared life-stage, defined the same way the world over, and is certainly not bounded in any simple way by age, as Virgina Morrow (2013) explains:

> …childhood is a phase in the life cycle, to be someone's child defines a relationship, variously conceptualised in differing parts of the world. The category "age" within social sciences can mean various things—not simply chronological age (which is the dominant understanding in western societies), but also functional age and relational age. (p. 151)

ageism
The belief that age is associated with certain psychological, behavioural, or intellectual traits.

What Morrow's outline means is that whether we are understood to be children or adults depends on more than just how old we are. Our social positioning as adults or as children is defined by how we interact with other members of our larger society, by the kinds of expectations placed on us, by the degree of competence that is expected of us, and by our ability to meet that level of competency. Morrow notes, citing her own fieldwork, that:

> …in Ethiopia, Andhra Pradesh in India, Peru and Vietnam…to varying degrees, children's status and roles are marked not by numerical age, but by the kinds of everyday tasks they describe doing and are expected to do. Very often, they do not know their age, or their date of birth. Birthdays are not necessarily celebrated in every country. (p. 152)

In other words, the commonsense perception of North Americans that childhood extends to at least age 10 or 12 (or the onset of puberty) and is marked by an absence of responsibilities and cares is only one worldview among many. The birthday parties that we think of as central to a childhood filled with friends and playtime make no sense to people in some other parts of the world. This does not make the Western view the correct one; after all, children in the West remain vulnerable to a variety of abuses and economic sufferings in spite of the generally sentimentalized construction of childhood so common in Western nations.

Despite this differential treatment, people in North America are fascinated with youth and being young. Not always was this the case. The elderly were once highly valued, and younger men even powdered their hair, wore wigs, and dressed in a way that made them look older. It should be remembered, however, that in 1901, only 5.05 percent of the population was 65 or older, and almost half the population (45 percent) was 19 years of age or under (Novak 1997). Being old was rare and respected; to some it signalled that God looked favourably on that individual.

Modernization theory argues that as a society becomes more technologically advanced, the position of the elderly declines (Cowgill and Holmes 1972). As land, often owned by elders, became less important, elders' knowledge and skills about land-based economies lost value. With industrialization, technological skills, training, and education became more important than land ownership.

modernization theory
A theory claiming that as society becomes more technologically advanced, the position of the elderly declines.

6.2 Youth and Aging

Age is largely socially defined. Cultural definitions of what it means to be "old" and "young" vary from society to society, from time to time, and from person to person. Where average life expectancies are very low, the old may be under age 30.

Age is also a variable with dramatic impact on a person's life. Matras (1990) identified the first four of the five points below:*

1. Age determines life experiences, since the approximate date of birth determines the historical period in which a person lives.
2. Different ages are associated with different developmental stages (physiological, psychological, and social) as well as abilities; they influence how one perceives and accesses the time period of one's age.
3. Age defines roles and expectations of behaviour. The expression "act your age" implies that some behaviours are inappropriate for people of certain ages.
4. Age influences the social groups to which one belongs. Whether one is part of a sixth grade class, a labour union, or a seniors' bridge club depends on one's age.
5. Age defines legal status. It defines when you can get a driver's licence, vote, get married without your parents' permission, and become eligible for social security benefits.

* MATRAS, JUDAH, *DEPENDENCY, OBLIGATIONS, AND ENTITLEMENTS*, 1st Edition © 1990. Adapted by permission of Pearson Education, Inc., Upper Saddle River, NJ.

Childhood, Adulthood, and Elderhood

Every society assigns different social roles to different age groups. **Age grading** is the assignment of social roles to given chronological ages (Matras 1990). Although the number of age grades varies by society, most societies make at least three distinctions: childhood, adulthood, and elderhood.

age grading
The assignment of social roles to given chronological ages.

Childhood

The period of legal infancy—meaning the period of time in which one is a legal minor requiring some form of guardian for all legal matters—in Canada is from birth through age 17 and is often subdivided into infancy, childhood, and adolescence. Infancy as a very brief life-stage has always been recognized, but the social category of childhood developed only after industrialization, urbanization, and modernization took place. Before industrialization, infant mortality was high due to the lack of adequate health care and proper nutrition. Once infants could be expected to survive infancy, the concept of childhood emerged, and society began to develop norms in reference to children. In Canada, child labour laws prohibit children from entering into the labour market, educational mandates require that children begin school by the age of six or seven and remain enrolled until they either complete secondary school or turn 18, and the sexual exploitation of children is a serious crime.

Adulthood

The period from age 18 through 64 is generally subdivided into young adulthood, adulthood, and middle age. Each status involves dramatic role changes related to entering the workforce, getting married, and having children. The concept of "middle age" developed only recently, as life expectancy has been extended. Some people in this phase belong to the **sandwich generation**, since they are often emotionally and economically responsible for both their young children and their aging parents.

There is some controversy over the creation of "adolescence" as a specific life stage that bridges the period of time from late childhood to full adulthood. For one thing, it is important to know that "adolescent" is not simply a synonym for "teenager," though there is some overlap in the popular use of these terms. For one thing, current ideas about when adolescence ends extend the arrival of adulthood well into the mid-twenties. It is an indication of how flexible our ideas about life stages are that as recently as one generation ago adolescence was generally thought to end by age 20. Book-length studies in sociology, like Canadian scholarship in Mary-Louise Adams's *The Trouble with Normal*, and British scholarship in Nancy Lesko's *Act Your Age!* show us that more than anything else, adolescence is a cultural construction that serves to focus the anxious energies of societies enduring periods of significant turmoil. Lesko explains,

> The adolescent was a trope for turn-of-the-century worries about unknown futures, about maintenance of gender and class hierarchy in changing social and cultural landscapes.... At the same time adolescence was a social fact produced through a set of practices, including emphasis on and control of sexuality, segregation of girls' and boys' curricular areas in increasing years of compulsory schooling…and unrelenting emphasis on youths' futures. (2001: 50)

Mary-Louise Adams's work shows similar conclusions for the development of the idea of adolescent youth as a problem to be managed. In her book about the development of comprehensive sex education programs in Canadian public schools Adams reveals that adolescents, and especially boys, were made out to be particularly vulnerable to corruption that would lead them away from forming heterosexual marriages,

sandwich generation
The generation that has the responsibility of simultaneously caring for their children and their aging parents.

and from contributing to the economic fabric of the larger post-war society in Canada. Adams explains that the relatively recent construction of adolescence as a specific developmental stage served the interests of a variety of professional "experts"— educators, policymakers, and physicians in particular—who, with an interest in the sexual mores of a rapidly changing era, could consolidate their power and prestige by problematizing young people who were past childhood, but not yet independently adult:

> Assumptions about the corruptibility of young people, about their need for protection from moral harm, and about their role as representatives of the future helped to set boundaries for how sexuality, in a general sense, could be understood. (p. 4)

Adams's work is important not only for the specific information about how post-war adolescents were used in the service of moral panics, but also for her more general contributions to a growing sociological awareness that our contemporary anxieties about youth are not a new social phenomenon:

> Fears about the power of mass media to divide parents from children were not unique to postwar North America. They had followed the emergence of novels in the nineteenth century, and of silent films in the 1910s and 1920s. They would re-emerge over television in the late 1950s and the 1960s. We see them today in discussions about rock videos, [video] games, and the Internet. (p. 137)

In short, while a distinct definition of when adolescence begins and ends may be elusive, it is clear that for all its shifts and variations, the idea of adolescence as a vulnerable life stage has made it easy for adults to target and complain about young people for almost 200 years. Meanwhile, young people themselves have few opportunities to offer any counter-narrative about their lives because the mass media representations and claims-making processes that present youth as a "problem" are made by and for adults who control and consume those representations.

Elderhood

At age 65, a person is likely to be considered elderly, a category often subdivided into the young-old, old, and old-old. Membership in one of these categories does not necessarily depend on chronological age. The healthy, active, independent elderly, growing in numbers, is often considered the young-old; the old-old are less healthy, less active, and more dependent. (See Table 6.1.)

Table 6.1 **Myths and Facts about the Elderly**

Health	
Myth	The elderly are always sick; most are in nursing homes.
Fact	Almost three out of four seniors aged 65 and older and living at home rate their health as good to excellent. Among seniors aged 85 and older, more than three in four rated their health as good or very good. The likelihood that an individual will live in a special-care home, such as a nursing home or hospital, increases with age; however, the 2001 census found that relatively few seniors live in such a setting (9.2 percent of senior women and 4.9 percent of senior men). Both of these proportions had declined from the time of the 1981 census (Dube 2002).
Mental Status	
Myth	The elderly are senile.
Fact	Although some of the elderly learn more slowly and forget more quickly, most remain oriented and mentally intact. Only 20 to 25 percent develop Alzheimer's disease or some other incurable form of brain disease. Senility is not inevitable as people age.

Table 6.1 **Myths and Facts about the Elderly** (continued)

Crime	
Myth	The elderly are more likely to be victims of crime than the young are.
Fact	Although older people express more fear of crime than younger people do, "studies in Britain, the United States, and Canada show that older people run less risk of victimization than any other group" (Novak 1997).
Sexuality	
Myth	Sexual satisfaction disappears with age.
Fact	Many elderly persons report sexual satisfaction. For example, in a sample of over 1300 respondents comprised of couples 75 years of age and older, over 25 percent reported having sexual intercourse once a week (Toner 1999).
Adaptability	
Myth	The elderly cannot adapt to new working conditions.
Fact	A high proportion of the elderly are flexible in accepting change in their occupations and earnings. Adaptability depends on the individual: many young are set in their ways, and many older people adapt to change readily.

SOURCES: Binstock, Robert H. 1986. "Public Policy and the Elderly." *Journal of Geriatric Psychiatry* 19: 115–43; Canadian Press, 1999; Dube, Francine. 2002. "25% of Households Have Only One Person." *National Post* (October 23): A9; Mulligan, T., and R. F. Pagluta Jr. 1991. "Sexual Interest, Activity and Satisfaction among Male Nursing Home Residents." *Archives of Sexual Behaviour* 20: 199–204; Novak, Mark. 1997. *Aging and Society: A Canadian Perspective*, 3rd ed. Scarborough, ON: Nelson; Toner, Robin. 1999. "A Majority over 45 Say Sex Lives Are Just Fine." *New York Times* (August 4): A10.

6.3 Sociological Theories of Age Inequality

Five sociological theories help explain age inequality and the continued existence of ageism in Canada. These theories—structural-functionalism, conflict theory, symbolic interactionism, feminist theory, and queer theory—are discussed in the following sections.

Structural-Functionalist Perspective

Structural-functionalism emphasizes the interdependence of society. From a functionalist perspective, the elderly must gradually relinquish their roles to younger members of society. This transition is viewed as natural and necessary to maintain the integrity of the social system. As this process continues, each new group moves up and replaces another, benefiting society and all of its members.

According to **disengagement theory**, the elderly gradually withdraw as they prepare for death, and society also withdraws from the elderly (Cummings and Henry 1961). Meanwhile, the young have learned through the educational institution how to function in the roles surrendered by the elderly. In essence, a balance in society is achieved as social actors fulfil the roles and functions of their respective age groups: the young go to school, adults fill occupational roles, and the elderly, with obsolete skills and knowledge, disengage.

However, given the increasing number of elderly who remain active and socially integrated throughout life, many sociologists now reject disengagement theory. **Activity theory** emphasizes that the elderly disengage in part because they are structurally segregated and isolated, not because of a natural tendency to do so. For those elderly who remain active, role loss may be minimal. In studying 1720 respondents who reported using a senior centre in the previous year, Miner and colleagues (1993) found

disengagement theory
A theory claiming that the elderly disengage from productive social roles to relinquish these roles to younger members of society. As this process continues, each new group moves up and replaces another, which, according to disengagement theory, benefits society and all of its members.

activity theory
A theory that emphasizes that the elderly disengage, in part, because they are structurally segregated and isolated with few opportunities to take active roles.

that those who used the centre were less disengaged and more socially active than those who did not use it.

Conflict Perspective

The conflict perspective focuses on age grading as another form of inequality—both the young and the old occupy subordinate statuses. Some conflict theorists emphasize that individuals at both ends of the age continuum are superfluous to a capitalist economy. Children are untrained, inexperienced, and neither actively producing nor consuming in an economy that requires both. Similarly, the elderly, although once working, are no longer productive and often lack required skills and levels of education. Hence, children are required to go to school in preparation for entry into a capitalist economy, and the elderly are forced to retire.

Other conflict theorists focus on how different age strata represent different interest groups that compete with one another for scarce resources. Debates about funding for public schools, child health programs, and social security largely represent the conflicting interests of the young versus the old.

In spite of popular beliefs that children have easy and secure lives, the Canadian Red Cross has identified these serious problems for Canadian children:

- 25 percent of all children experience abuse before age 16
- boys aged 4 to 7 experience three times greater incidence of sexual abuse than boys in any other age group
- 75 percent of Aboriginal girls under age 18 have been abused
- 8 percent of students experience bullying at school at least once a week
- bullying occurs every seven minutes in schools, but teachers are aware of only 4 percent of all incidents

Symbolic Interactionist Perspective

The symbolic interactionist perspective emphasizes the importance of examining the social meaning and definitions associated with age. Teenagers are often portrayed as lazy, aimless, and awkward. The elderly are also defined in stereotypical ways, contributing to a host of myths about the inevitability of physical and mental decline.

Media portrayals contribute to the negative image of the elderly. The young are typically portrayed in active, vital roles and are often overrepresented in commercials. In contrast, the elderly are portrayed as difficult, complaining, and burdensome; they are often underrepresented in commercials. A study of the elderly in popular films from the 1940s through the 1980s concluded that "older individuals of both genders were portrayed as less friendly, having less romantic activity, and enjoying fewer positive outcomes than younger characters at a movie's conclusion" (Brazzini et al. 1997: 541).

The elderly are also portrayed as childlike in terms of clothes, facial expressions, temperament, and activities—a phenomenon known as **infantilizing elders** (Arluke and Levin 1990). For example, young and old are often paired together. When Grandpa Simpson babysits Bart and his siblings, he invariably falls asleep before Bart's baby sister, Maggie. In popular film the elderly are frequently portrayed as cranky curmudgeons who can't navigate the contemporary world. Finally, the elderly are often depicted in role reversal, cared for by their adult children as in the situation comedies *Golden Girls* and *Frasier*.

Negative stereotypes and media images of the elderly engender **gerontophobia**—a shared fear or dread of the elderly. This feeling may create a self-fulfilling prophecy. In one study, seniors received one of two types of subliminal messages—those negatively stereotyping the elderly (e.g., senile) and those positively stereotyping the elderly (e.g., wise). Compared with those who received negative messages, subjects who received

infantilizing elders
The portrayal of the elderly in the media as childlike in terms of clothes, facial expression, temperament, and activities.

gerontophobia
Fear or dread of the elderly.

the positive messages scored better on memory tests and were more likely to respond that they would accept life-prolonging health interventions (Begley 2000).

Feminist Perspectives

Feminist views on aging have developed partly out of interest in gender-based power differences that can be exaggerated as women grow old, and out of interest in experiences that young girls face as they cope with mixed messages about their bodies and sexuality. One such mixed message is that a pubertal body is a sexual one, yet children must be sexually innocent. Recent work has examined how such contradictory expectations can be especially damaging to girls who experience puberty at very early ages (Liao et al. 2005). Popular, persistent messages that a young girl has somehow caused her own pubertal changes by having sexual thoughts form the backdrop for this kind of feminist analysis.

Contemporary feminist work builds on its established demonstration that women face problems of social devaluing as they move beyond their reproductive years. It goes on to examine how gender stereotyping can also have a negative impact on men—as with the insistence that "successful aging" is tied to the ability to maintain sexual virility (Calasanti and King 2005).

Feminist gerontologists challenge us to analyze how we perceive and structure what it means to be old and to examine the vulnerabilities of youth as each stage intersects with the demands of gender expectations. Scholarship in the area has been transformed by feminist insights that question the popular meanings and perceptions of the old, and recognize that for men and women, both, there is not just one way of experiencing being old (Calasanti 2004: 305). Feminist approaches combine an understanding of both structural and symbolic operations in order to understand the vulnerabilities and value of the young and the old (Biggs 2003: 45).

Queer Theory Perspectives

While popular culture promotes a youthful image of gay and lesbian people in TV programs, such as *The L Word, Queer as Folk, Will & Grace*, and *Modern Family*, and queer culture itself can be very youth-oriented in its advertising and targeted publications (e.g., *Xtra Magazine* in Canada), some theorists point out that GLBT people also grow old. (*GLBT* means gay, lesbian, bisexual, and transgendered.) Recent critical work recognizes that growing old can present serious personal and spiritual challenges for men in gay communities and that they must rethink what it means to be a man while aging in the broader gay culture (Long 2001). Studies on gay, lesbian, and bisexual persons as they age suggest that, because they have had to learn to live with negative stigmas anyway, these seniors have **crisis competence**: the ability to cope more easily with adverse social situations (Kehoe 1989); as a result, the self-reports of older gays and lesbians suggest that they do not see themselves as old until past age 70. Conversely, heterosexuals tend to see themselves as old once past age 50 (Heaphy et al. 2004: 884).

In a particularly interesting argument that refuses the commonsense placement of life stages along a progressional line that moves from infancy to "maturity," Judith Halberstam argues that

> in Western cultures, we chart the emergence of the adult from the dangerous and unruly period of adolescence as a desired process of maturation; and we create longevity as the most desirable future, applaud the pursuit of long life (under any circumstances), and pathologize modes of living that show little or no concern for longevity. Within the life cycle of the Western human subject, long periods of stability are considered to be desirable, and people who live in rapid bursts (drug addicts, for example) are characterized as immature and even dangerous. (2005: 4–5)

crisis competence
The ability of those who live facing persistent stigma to cope more easily with adverse social situations than those who have not previously encountered much prejudice.

Halberstam's view provides an important counterpoint to the normative economic and productive expectations that set constraints on "appropriate" life stages that include when we are expected to have children and how we are to organize our time, split between the productivity of work and the productivity of family. Think, for example, of the popular notion that we should, as adults, achieve a "life–work balance," a balance often held up as particularly challenging for mothers with children still at home. Halberstam explains the lack of imagination that goes into structuring our lives as a "balance" between work and family:

> The time of reproduction is ruled by…strict bourgeois rules of respectability and scheduling for married couples. Obviously, not all people who have children keep or even are able to keep reproductive time, but many and possibly most people believe that the scheduling of repro-time is natural and desirable. Family time refers to the normative scheduling of daily life (early to bed, early to rise) that accompanies the practice of child rearing. This timetable is governed by an imagined set of children's needs, and it relates to beliefs about children's health and healthful environments for child rearing. (p. 5)

To counter these constraints on the lives of women and children in particular, and which demand a certain kind of more general economic productivity that Halberstam points out serves nations and corporations first, we should perhaps think about life stages and time more queerly, less along the established "straight" line of capitalist logics of productivity that take place in turn across generations. Halberstam argues that if we remove the rigid conceptualizations and expectations of what people *should be doing* with their time in a given life stage then we can open up places for resistance against the hierarchies and power dynamics that render some groups (children, women, and queer communities most particularly) most vulnerable. In Halberstam's view, doing justice to people does not necessarily mean to make everyone blend in with the middle-class values of maximized education/health/professional status/longevity; rather, it means refusing to protect the most powerful from challenges to the status quo and it means valuing the contributions of those who live outside the normative construction of life stages shoe-horned to fit into capitalist demands for productivity.

Halberstam, then, calls for a different kind of public discourse regarding measures of success, and asks instead for "counter-publics"—those that would be concerned not with how to balance our private lives, but how to foster co-operative communities, across ages, genders, and class groups. Perhaps by refusing to segregate people according to "appropriate" productivity by age-category, Halberstam suggests, we might get to a more humane "queer time and place."

For queer youth, their experiences of neglect and of abuse are often linked to homophobia that makes them vulnerable, not only on the streets where they may be gay-bashed, but also in the home, where they may face familial hostility over their sexuality. The very use of the term *queer* as a means of self-identifying is largely a phenomenon of GLBT persons who came of age during the 1990s expansion of rights movements for GLBT persons. The phenomenon of expropriating words from their negative context and deploying them as a positive self-identification is a symbolic, linguistic strategy that Mollie Blackburn (2005) refers to as "**gaybonics**," a crisscrossing of antiracist and anti-homophobic empowerment strategies.

gaybonics
The expropriation of words from their negative context and their redeployment as positive self-identifications to combat racist and homophobic views and behaviours.

6.4 Problems of Youth in Canada

In spite of the presumed benefits of being young, numerous problems are associated with childhood. Indeed, some of our most pressing social problems can be traced to early childhood experiences and adolescent behavioural problems (Weissberg and Kuster 1997). What happens to children is increasingly defined as a social problem.

Children and the Law

Historically, children have had little control over their lives. They are forced to depend both on their parents and on the state. Beginning in the 1950s, however, increases to children's autonomy became popular and were codified in several legal decisions. In 1959, the United Nations General Assembly approved the *Declaration on the Rights of the Child*, maintaining that health care, housing, and education, and freedom from abuse, neglect, and exploitation are fundamental children's rights. Canada is a signatory to the *Convention on the Rights of the Child*, a treaty that has been described as "the most comprehensive human rights document ever adopted by the international community," and ratified by all but two countries (the United States and Somalia).

As required under Article 44 of the Convention, in 1999 the Canadian Coalition for the Rights of Children issued its first five-year nongovernmental progress report to the United Nations. Entitled *The UN Convention on the Rights of the Child: How Does Canada Measure Up?*, the report concluded that Canada meets most of its obligations under the UN Convention. It notes, for example, that children's right to education is assured in Canadian legislation, which provides for primary and secondary schooling and requires all children to attend school. It acknowledges that the *Canada Health Act* provides free universal health care for all Canadians; that refugee children are eligible for health care, education, and settlement services in Canada; and that our provincial and territorial governments have a duty to intervene to protect a child at risk from abuse or neglect. At the same time, however, the report concludes that Canada had some way to go before achieving full compliance with the Convention:*

- Canadian legislation rarely recognizes children specifically and few redress mechanisms are available to them. Thus, children's fundamental freedoms depend on the goodwill of adults. Rights education is not part of core curricula and children's Convention rights have not been widely promoted in Canada. In child welfare cases, the child's best interests are weighed against parental rights. In other areas, children's best interests are ignored or interpreted without considering children's views. The general principle of maximum survival and development is not assured for our most vulnerable children: children with disabilities, Aboriginal children, and children in the care of the state.
- Where children live often determines the degree to which their rights are met. Significant differences characterize children's programs and services in different parts of the country. Home care services for families of children with disabilities vary widely, and an effort to create standards or even to define basic services is lacking. Child welfare services are often fragmented and uncoordinated within jurisdictions, and resources are unevenly allocated. For Aboriginal children living on reserves, delivery of services is further complicated by jurisdictional disputes.
- Resources for children's programs and services are often stretched or unstable. Cutbacks to education and the closing of schools undermine access to and the quality of education, especially in special education, citizenship, social studies, and the arts. Child welfare services have been subject to budget cuts in some provinces, despite growing caseloads, chronic waiting lists, and worker burnout. Even with the high number of Aboriginal children affected by disabilities, delivery of services in Aboriginal communities is generally poor or nonexistent.
- Aboriginal children have a disability rate more than twice the national average. They are at greater risk of school failure than other Canadian children. A disproportionate number are victims of abuse and neglect compared to non-Aboriginal children. The suicide rate among Aboriginal youth is about five times the national average.

* Canadian Coalition for the Rights of Children, 2009. *Report: The UN Convention on the Rights of the Child: How Does Canada Measure Up?*, http://rightsofchildren.ca/wp-content/uploads/2009/05/un.pdf. Reprinted by permission of the Canadian Coalition for the Rights of Children.

- An estimated 535 000 children and youth under age 20 have some form of disability. Children with disabilities have varying opportunities to live "full and decent lives," yet the supports and services they need are considered only a privilege. Many families of children with disabilities lack adequate assistance. Early identification and intervention services are not universally available, and the right to appropriate education in the most enabling environment is not guaranteed.
- Our child welfare system continues to fail abused and neglected children. Inquests and inquiries into the deaths of children who were killed by their parents speak of inadequate risk assessments, insufficient training for social workers, a lack of service coordination and information sharing, a shortage of placement facilities, failed foster placements, a crisis orientation, and a lack of long-term planning for children in the care of the state.
- The refugee determination system is slow, and the long wait unduly prolongs uncertainty for children and their families. Family reunification is rarely dealt with in a positive and expeditious manner. The interests of children are ignored in decisions to deport parents. Children, even if born in Canada, do not have to be considered in deportation hearings of their parents.
- Federal and provincial legislation prohibits discrimination against people with disabilities, but people with disabilities, especially children, still experience prejudice. Young people with disabilities experience more abuse and violence than those without disabilities. In addition, dominant adult perspectives on disability issues continue to overlook children's unique needs. For example, provincial building codes include accessibility standards, but these were not designed with children in mind.
- The few complaint mechanisms that are available to children and youth tend to be difficult to access.

These issues remain salient concerns within the Canadian Coalition for the Rights of Children 2001 Report (Covell 2001). The 2001 Report emphasizes that despite unanimous support in Parliament for an all-party resolution to eliminate child poverty by 2000, "a substantial gap remained between promise and reality"—child poverty increased through the 1990s (p. 11) and remained roughly stable, with 15–16 percent of children living in poverty through the first decade of the twenty-first century (see Table 6.2). Among other identified shortcomings, the 2001 Report notes Canada's failure to repeal Section 43 of the *Criminal Code* (which provides a defence in law for those who use corporal punishment as a form of discipline) and to ensure that quality child care is both affordable and available (p. 31).

Table 6.2 *Child Poverty in Canada, 2000–2008*

Survey or program details:
Survey of Consumer Finances—3502
Survey of Labour and Income Dynamics—3889

Geography	Low Income Lines	Statistic	YEAR:								
			2000	2001	2002	2003	2004	2005	2006	2007	2008
Canada	Low income measure after tax[1]	Percentage of persons in low income under age 18 years	15.7	15.4	15.4	16.1	16.7	15.7	15.1	15.0	15.3

[1]Low income measures (LIMs), are relative measures of low income, set at 50% of adjusted median household income. These measures are categorized according to the number of persons present in the household, reflecting the economies of scale inherent in household size and composition.

SOURCE: Adapted from the Statistics Canada CANSIM database http://cansim2.statcan.gc.ca, table 202-0802, July 28, 2010.

In 2007, the United Nations International Children's Emergency Fund (UNICEF) reported that Canada ranked 12th of 22 of the world's wealthiest nations with regard to child welfare. A similar UNICEF report criticized our failure to fulfill the mandate of the 1989 resolution to eliminate child poverty by the year 2000. It noted, "Amid definitional uncertainties [over the term *poverty*], Canada's target year 2000 came and went without agreement on what the target means, or how progress towards it is to be measured, or what policies might be necessary to achieve it" (UNICEF 2005: 19). Figure 6.1 shows the effect of increasingly conservative tax and welfare policy, demonstrating that when it comes to child population welfare, Canada is among the worst of Western industrial nations. The light bars show child poverty rates based on household incomes before government taxes and transfers, while the dark bars show the rates after taxes

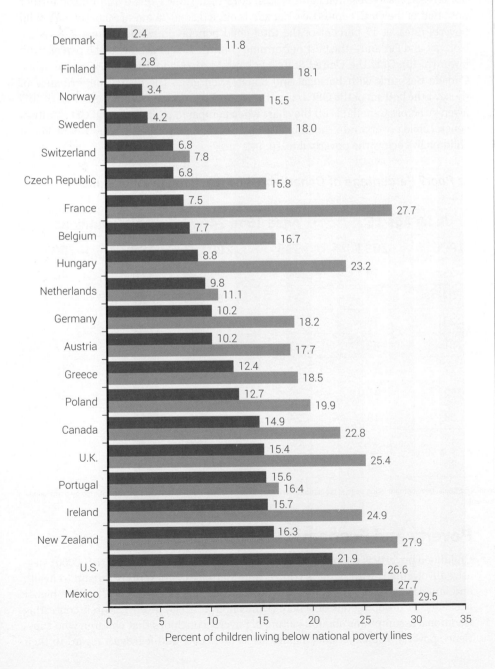

Figure 6.1 **The Impact of Taxes and Transfers**

The light bars show child poverty rates based on household incomes before government taxes and transfers, while the dark bars show the rates after taxes and transfers. The poverty line in both cases is 50 percent of median post-tax and transfer income.

SOURCE: Adapted from Figure 9 in "Child Poverty in Rich Countries—2005," *Innocenti Report Card No. 6, 2005,* UNICEF Innocenti Research Centre, Florence. Reprinted with permission.

and transfers. The poverty line in both cases is 50 percent of median post-tax and transfer income. Table 6.3 shows that in spite of governmental promises and policies, we have made no real progress in eliminating poverty for those under age 18 in Canada. Moreover, while the table shows a child poverty rate as high as 52 percent for Aboriginal children under age 15 in 1996, more recent data show that the prevalence of poverty for Aboriginal children has soared to as high as 60 percent in some areas of the country. A 2013 co-authored report from the Canadian Centre for Policy Alternatives and Save the Children Canada noted poverty rates three times higher for status First Nations children with rates over 60 percent in Manitoba and Saskatchewan. These rates reflect the terrible conditions of reserves managed under federal jurisdiction, and the report notes that the rates of poverty for Métis and Inuit and status children plummet to 27 percent when they live under provincially managed social supports but not on reserves (MacDonald and Wilson 2013: 6–12). MacDonald and Wilson further note that of the OECD countries, Canada ranks a dismal 25 out of 30 for overall child poverty rates, at 17 percent of the total child population, while Denmark, Sweden, Norway, and Finland—the best performing countries—all have rates of 5 percent and lower (p. 15). Only the United States, Poland, Mexico, and Turkey fare worse, while Canada ties rank with Portugal and Spain. Even given the dismal performance of those at the bottom of the OECD list, "the status First Nation child poverty rate of 50% [average across Canada] is off the chart when compared to any other OECD country's general child poverty rate, including that of the worst performer, Turkey, where 35% of children live below the poverty line" (p. 14).

Table 6.3 **Who Is Likely to Be Poor? Percentage of Canadians Who Are Poor, by Age Group and Select Variables**

	Under Age 15		Aged 15 to 24		All Canadians	
	1996	2001	1996	2001	1996	2001
Total population	23	19	24	20	20	16
With activity limitation	37	28	38	31	31	23
Without activity limitation	23	18	23	19	18	15
Immigrant population	51	42	41	33	28	22
Non-immigrant population	22	17	21	17	18	15
Aboriginal population	52	41	45	37	43	34
Non-Aboriginal population	23	18	24	19	19	16
Visible minority group	43	34	39	32	36	28
Non-visible minority group	20	16	22	17	18	14

SOURCE: Calculations by the Canadian Council on Social Development using special tabulations from Statistics Canada's Census, 1996 and 2001. Reprinted by permission of the Canadian Council on Social Development.

Poverty and Economic Discrimination

Childhood poverty is related to school failure (Fields and Smith 1998; NIH 2000), negative involvement with parents (Harris and Marmer 1996), serious threats to health and limited emotional development (Brooks-Gunn and Duncan 1997), and a higher likelihood of dropping out of school (Duncan et al. 1998). Even research contesting traditional assumptions about a culture of poverty concludes that children who experience poverty also experience higher levels of anxiety and fear with regard to their own sense of safety: "relative levels of privation dictates that children and youth live within a context of relatively high levels of fear and victimization and that such jeopardy may produce lifelong disadvantage" (Eisler and Schissel 2004: 371). According to the National Longitudinal Survey of Children and Youth (NLSCY), one-quarter of children aged four and five from low-income households (less than $30 000 a year) scored poorly on verbal tests that indicate readiness to learn.

Children also face discrimination in terms of employment, age restrictions, wages, and training programs. Traditionally, children worked on farms and in factories, but were displaced by the Industrial Revolution. In the 1880s, the *Factory Acts* "curbed the employment of both women and children on the grounds of protecting their health" (Krahn and Lowe 1993); by 1929, children under age 14 were legally excluded from factory and mine employment in most provinces. Designed to protect children, the law was also discriminatory in that it prohibited minors from having free access to jobs and economic independence. No such law exists for any other age group.

Without access to their own earnings, those under age 18 are principally reliant upon their families for their stability and well-being. The Canadian Council on Social Development (CCSD) has analyzed primary data from Statistics Canada's survey of Labour and Income Dynamics, and notes that while average family income in the late 1990s and early 2000s rose by 19 percent to keep pace with inflation rates in the same time period, many families remained vulnerable: "[Income] gains were greatest among the wealthiest 10% of families with children: their average pre-tax income rose by 35%…to $208,300 [while] the poorest 10% of families'…average incomes had risen by 7%, to $16,100" (CCSD 2006a: 16–17). In Table 6.4, we see the differences in pre-tax income across the income deciles in Canada, from the poorest to the wealthiest in the years from 1993 to 2003. What the table renders obvious is that children, who have no choice about the conditions in which they live, experience wildly disparate levels of wealth and poverty in Canada. Although we cannot expect to have income data for the current recession, which began after the 2006 census was completed, we can logically assume that nothing about the vulnerabilities that children face would have improved in an era of high job losses, wage freezes, and property devaluations. It is

Table 6.4 *Average Annual Family Incomes, 1993–2003*

YEAR	LOWEST	2	3	4	5	6	7	8	9	Highest	Canadian Average	Ratio of Highest to Lowest Decile
1993	$15 000	$25 600	$35 900	$44 700	$53 500	$61 800	$71 100	$82 300	$98 900	$154 100	$64 300	10.3
1995	$13 500	$24 700	$35 400	$45 000	$53 800	$64 500	$73 600	$85 000	$102 100	$159 200	$65 600	11.8
1997	$13 500	$24 000	$34 400	$43 500	$53 500	$63 400	$73 700	$85 600	$103 300	$169 500	$66 500	12.6
1999	$14 700	$27 400	$37 500	$47 400	$57 000	$66 600	$77 500	$90 900	$109 300	$186 400	$71 500	12.7
2003	$16 100	$29 500	$39 300	$49 100	$59 800	$70 200	$81 200	$95 400	$115 500	$208 300	$76 400	12.9
% increase 1993 to 2003	7.3	15.2	9.5	9.8	11.8	13.6	14.2	15.9	16.8	35.2	18.8	
$ increase 1993 to 2003	$1 100	$3 900	$3 400	$4 400	$6 300	$8 400	$10 100	$13 100	$16 600	$54 200	$12 100	

SOURCE: Calculations by the Canadian Council on Social Development using Statistics Canada's Survey of Labour and Income Dynamics. Reprinted by permission of the Canadian Council on Social Development.

depth of poverty
How far below and for
how long people live
below the low income
cut-offs (LICOs).

not just income disparity and poverty that we need to be concerned about: a further concern is **depth of poverty**, or how far below and for how long people live below the low income cut-offs (LICOs).

Research from the CCSD underscores the well-known correlations between depth of poverty and general well-being: "deep and persistent poverty has a critical effect on both the short- and long-term development and well-being of children. For example, children who live in persistent poverty are less likely to be academically prepared to start school…. They are more likely to have emotional problems, to exhibit anxiety and aggressive behaviours, and hyperactivity" (CCSD 2006a: 18).

Figure 6.2 shows that in spite of Canada's declared goal to eradicate child poverty, the depth of poverty that children under the poverty line experience remains profound.

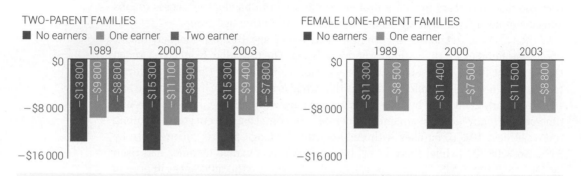

Figure 6.2 **The Depth of Child Poverty, By Family Type**

SOURCE: Calculations by the Canadian Council on Social Development using data from Statistics Canada's Income Trends in Canada, 2003. Reprinted by permission of the Canadian Council on Social Development.

Young people in Canada often find it difficult to obtain any employment. In the years from 1994 to 2004, the unemployment rate for those aged 15 to 19 ranged from 18 percent in 1994 to 13 percent in 2004 (CCSD 2006b). The high of 18 percent may be attributable to the recession of the early 1990s. The CCSD points out that those who do find work tend to hold precarious, low-skill, low-wage jobs with few benefits; such jobs serve neither to build long-term pension security nor to provide effective "ports of entry" (CCSD 2006b). In addition, those who do manage to find work "are typically employed in low paid, tedious positions, often working long hours which interfere with school attendance and academic performance" (Covell 2001: 16). Contemporary changes in the international organization of economy and work "principally affect new hires. In other words, much of the impact falls on young workers entering the job market" (CCSD 2006b: 81). Such problems may contribute to conflicts between the young and the old over resources and benefits.

Kids in Crisis

Childhood is a life stage structured by socio-cultural forces of the past and present. The old roles for children as labourers and farm helpers are disappearing, yet new, clearly defined roles have yet to emerge. While being bombarded by the media, children must face the challenges of an uncertain economic future, peer culture, popular culture, divorce, incidents of abuse, poverty, and crime. Some parents and public commentators who are worried over children's involvement in sex, drug and alcohol use, and violence even argue that childhood as a stage of life is disappearing (Adler 1994). Other theories, such as David Elkind's concept of the "hurried child," had popular appeal in the 1980s. However, Elkind's premise, which includes increased divorce rates and open emotional displays in the home undermining childhood innocence, has been called into question. Some suggest that such worries are ideologically biased accounts that fixate on negatives in a small sector of the population:

> Despite some perceptive insights…their argument falls short on several grounds. First, in their tendency to romanticize families of the past, the authors gloss over the many hardships that children endured throughout history, as well as the fact that in every historical era the way children are raised has been deemed problematic. (Lynott and Logue 1993: 486)

Although past generations of children faced hardship, contemporary threats to children's well-being should not be ignored. Table 6.5 indicates the aspirations of Canada's teens.

Table 6.5 **Expectations of Teenagers**

"Do you expect to . . ."	% indicating "Yes"		
	Nationally	**Males**	**Females**
Pursue a career	95%	94	97
Get the job you want when you graduate	87	86	87
Get married	91	89	91
Stay with the same partner for life	88	85	90
Eventually stay home and raise your children	43	40	45
Own your own home	97	96	98
Be more financially comfortable than your parents	81	82	80
Have to work overtime in order to get ahead	43	48	40
Travel extensively outside of Canada	79	74	83
Be involved in your community	68	67	70
Someday get to where you want to be in life	95	94	96

SOURCES: Bibby, Reginald W. 2009, *The Emerging Millennials*. Lethbridge: Project Canada Books, pp. 105–203; Bibby, Reginald W., *The Project Teen Canada 2008 National Survey*. Reprinted by permission of Reginald Bibby & Associates.

6.5 Demographics: The "Greying" of Canada

The population of Canada, as in many other countries around the world, is "greying," or getting older (defined here as age 65 or beyond). In 2001, the median age—the point where precisely one-half of the population is older and the other half younger—reached an all-time high of 37.6 years (see Figure 6.3) (Statistics Canada 2002). The increase in median age is one indicator of Canada's changing population structure.

The number of elderly is increasing for three reasons. First, the 10 million baby boomers born between 1947 and 1966 are aging. Second, life expectancy has increased as a result of better medical care; sanitation, nutrition, and housing improvements; and a general trend toward modernization. Finally, lowered birth rates mean fewer children and a higher percentage of the elderly. While those aged 65 or over accounted

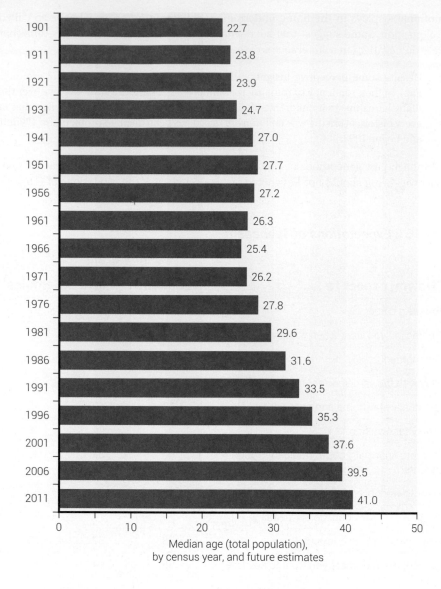

Figure 6.3 **Canada's Aging Population, 1901–2011**

SOURCE: "Canada Facing Age Crunch," by Jennifer Lewington (*The Globe and Mail*), July 17, 2002. © Copyright The Globe and Mail, Inc. All rights reserved.

Year	Value
1901	22.7
1911	23.8
1921	23.9
1931	24.7
1941	27.0
1951	27.7
1956	27.2
1961	26.3
1966	25.4
1971	26.2
1976	27.8
1981	29.6
1986	31.6
1991	33.5
1996	35.3
2001	37.6
2006	39.5
2011	41.0

Median age (total population), by census year, and future estimates

for 13 percent of the population in 2001, projections are that, if fertility rates remain low, their proportion will continue to increase in the years to come (Statistics Canada 2002).

Age Pyramids

age pyramids
Graphlike presentations that show the percentage of a population in various age groups.

Age pyramids are a way of showing in graph form the percentage of a population in various age groups. In 1901, the Canadian age pyramid looked very much like a true pyramid: the base of the pyramid was large, indicating that most people were in their younger years, and the top of the pyramid was much smaller, showing that only a small percentage of the population was elderly. However, by 2001 Canada's age pyramid scarcely resembled a pyramid at all, and reflected the aging of the Canadian population. By the time of the 2006 census, the percentage of the population over age 65 hovered just below 14 percent at 13.7 percent, while the under-15 population had fallen to a record low at 17.7 percent of the population (compare Figure 6.4 and Figure 6.5).

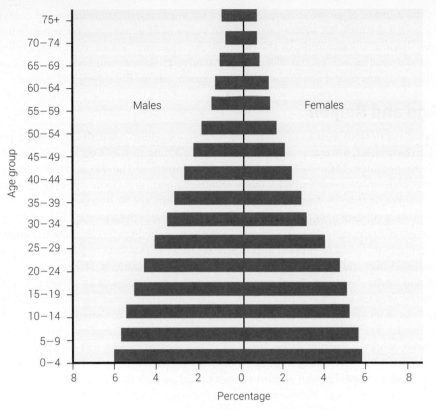

Figure 6.4 *Canadian Population Pyramid, Age and Sex, 1901*

Figure 6.5 *Age Pyramid of the Population for July 1, 1985, 1995, and 2005, Canada*

SOURCE: Statistics Canada, "Annual Demographic Statistics 2005," 91-213-XIB2005000, April 2006; http://www.statcan.gc.ca/bsolc/olc-cel/olc-cel?lang=eng&catno=91-213-X#olcinfopanel.

The number of people at various ages in a society is important because the demand for housing, education, health care, and jobs varies as different age groups, particularly baby boomers, move through the pyramid. For example, as Canada "greys," colleges and universities will recruit older students, advertisements will be directed toward older consumers, and housing and medical care needs for the elderly will increase.

Age and Region

Canada ages from west to east with one notable exception—British Columbia, a popular destination for many older Canadians. According to the 2001 census, Canada's Prairie provinces (Alberta, Saskatchewan, and Manitoba), Ontario, and the territories have relatively younger residents, while Atlantic Canada and Quebec have populations that are older than the Canadian average. Nunavut and the Northwest Territories have the lowest median ages (22.1 years and 30.1 years, respectively), with the highest proportion of their populations below age 20. Reflecting the high fertility of both Nunavut and the Northwest Territories, approximately half (47 percent) of Nunavut's population, and over one-third (35 percent) of those in the Northwest Territories, are aged 19 and under; these figures compare to the national average of 26 percent. In 2005, the last year for which population data are available, the median age for Nunavut was just shy of 23 years, and is notable for being the only region in Canada with a median age under 30 (Statistics Canada 2005: 8). In general, by 2006 Canada's urban areas had a larger working-age population between the ages of 20 and 44; this concentration of a younger workforce has primarily to do with migration out of rural areas (leaving more older people behind) and into larger urban centres (thus reducing the concentration of older people in those areas) where there are more employment opportunities (Statistics Canada 2007).

With birth rates that are higher than the Canadian average and life expectancies that are lower, Indigenous peoples as a group are younger than non-Indigenous peoples in Canada. The high fertility of the Aboriginal population also affects the age profiles of Manitoba and Saskatchewan. The older population of Canada's Atlantic region reflects two factors: low fertility in recent years and the exodus of the young to other areas of Canada. The aging of Quebec's population is largely the result of the low fertility rate in that province.

Age and Gender

The **sex ratio**—the ratio of men to women in a given society or subgroup of society—is expressed in one number: the number of males to every 100 females. The sex ratio reported for the last Canadian census was 96 males to every 100 females. In 2006, out of a total population of 31 612 895, about 51 percent were female, and their median age was 40.4. The median age of males in Canada was a little younger, at 38.6. These differences in median age grow more disparate as men and women get older. In 2006, there were only 71 percent as many men in the 75- to 84-year-old group, and roughly 45 percent as many men over age 85 as there were women.

The imbalance in the sex ratio is particularly notable at older ages. In 2006, out of the total population there were 2 448 155 women over age 65 but only 1 887 100 males. These differences in the population of elderly people have sociological significance. Men die at an earlier age than women do for both biological and sociological reasons— heart disease, stress, and occupational risk (see Chapter 2). Because of differences in death rates and a greater likelihood of widowed men remarrying, older women are more likely to be widowed and to remain widows, while men are more likely to be married up until the point of death. From an income perspective, these patterns make it more likely that elderly women will be poor (Reidmann et al. 2003: 523).

sex ratio
The ratio of men to women in a given society or subgroup of society.

Age and Social Class

Social class influences how long a person lives. In general, the higher the social class, the longer the person lives, the fewer the debilitating illnesses, the greater the number of social contacts and friends, the less likely the individual is to view him- or herself as "old," and the greater the likelihood of success in adapting to retirement. Higher social class is also related to fewer residential moves, higher life satisfaction, more leisure time, and more positively self-rated health. Functional limitations, such as problems with walking, dressing, and bathing, are also lower among higher income groups (Seeman and Adler 1998). In short, the higher one's socio-economic status, the greater the likelihood that one will enjoy a longer, happier, and healthier life.

6.6 Problems of the Elderly

The increase in the number of the elderly worldwide presents a number of institutional problems. The **dependency ratio**—the number of societal members that are under 18 or 65 and over compared with the number of people who are between 18 and 64—is increasing. By 2000, there were 62 dependants for every 100 persons between 18 and 64. Demographic statistics for Canada indicate a dependency ratio that ranges from 68 to 70 per 100 persons of working age in 2056 (Statistics Canada 2008). Some demographers propose that increases of this magnitude in the dependency ratios may lead to a shortage of workers, floundering pension plans, and declining consumer markets. It may also lead to increased taxation as governments struggle to finance elder care programs and services, and heightened intergenerational tensions as societal members compete for scarce resources (Goldberg 2000; Peterson 2000; Schieber 2000). In addition to these macro-level concerns, the elderly face challenges of their own.

dependency ratio
The number of societal members who are under 18 or 65 and over compared to the number of people who are between 18 and 64.

Work and Retirement

Retirement is a relatively recent phenomenon. Before social security, individuals continued to work into old age. Today, the proportion of retirees under age 60 is double the rate it was in the late 1970s, and one-quarter of all new retirees are between the ages of 55 and 59. In 1984, the Quebec Pension Plan reduced its minimum age requirements for retirement benefits to age 60 and, in 1987, the Canada Pension Plan followed suit. However, the desire to remain financially independent coupled with a lack of confidence in the social security system may encourage many workers to remain in the labour force past the minimum age requirements (Simon-Rusinowitz et al. 1996).

What one does (occupation), for how long (work history), and for how much (wages) are important determinants of retirement income. Employment provides the foundation for economic resources later in life. Depending upon where one lives in Canada, there are legal protections against being forced to retire. For example, on December 12, 2005, royal assent was granted to the Ontario legislature to repeal mandatory retirement; the new law allowing people to decide their own time for retirement came into effect on December 12, 2006. Some professions may still be subject to mandatory retirement, though; for example, the Supreme Court of Canada ruled in 1995 that mandatory retirement for police officers at age 60 was not discriminatory but a "bona fide occupational requirement" (Dranoff 2001: 71).

Reasons to get rid of mandatory retirement include acknowledgments that some careers cannot begin until over a decade of postsecondary education has been completed, that the task of mothering coupled with mandatory retirement means significantly reduced lifetime earnings for women, and that it makes fiscal sense for governments trying to reduce social welfare program costs to extend years in the labour force.

For the elderly who want to work, entering and remaining in the labour force may be difficult because of negative stereotypes, lower education levels, reduced geographical mobility, fewer employable skills, and discrimination. Moreover, Novak (1997: 197) notes that at least three economic forces may encourage Canadian workers to retire at age 65:

- Some workers with good pension plans may earn more money in retirement than if they keep on working. Taxes, the cost of commuting, clothes, lunches, and other work-related expenses can make working expensive.
- Most private pension plans begin to pay full benefits at age 65 ... [and] many occupational pension plans penalize a person for staying on past retirement age ...
- OAS/GIS payments start at age 65, as do the Canada and Quebec Pension Plan payments. A person who works past age 65 will still get these benefits, but will lose a large portion of them through higher taxes.

Those who wish to enter the workforce at an older age or who, because of financial necessity, find it necessary to re-enter the labour force may be stymied in their attempts. The most common reason that workers over age 45 give for ending their job search is that no work is available. Evidence for the lack of work appears in the fact that, from 1976 to 1994, the average time that unemployed 45- to 64-year-olds were out of work doubled from 17 weeks to 33 weeks. From 1999 to 2001 approximately half of older workers—twice as many as those aged 25 to 34—were in jobs with irregular hours, lower levels of income, and poor benefits; moreover, workers between ages 49 and 65 were more likely than younger workers to be in these more precarious forms of employment for longer durations (Statistics Canada 2004). Although employers cannot advertise a position by age, they can state that the position is an entry level one, or that "two to three years' experience" is required (Knoke and Kalleberg 1994).

Those who do retire may find it difficult to cope with the symbolic message that equates work with worth. A job structures one's life and provides an identity; the end of a job culturally signifies the end of one's productivity. Retirement may also involve a dramatic decrease in personal income. While 60 percent of Canadian men retire between age 55 and 64, 27 percent are living in poverty on less than $10 000 a year, and only 5 percent have an income of over $45 000 a year (Dranoff 2001: 70).

Retirement Income and Poverty

Although the elderly and children are the groups most likely to be classified as low income, this pattern is not true for elderly people living in families. In 1996, the elderly in families were the *least* likely to be low income with 8 percent of elderly persons living under the LICO; by January of 2013, this number had dropped to 6.7 percent (Conference Board of Canada 2013b). Meanwhile, partly because a low-income, sole-parent may have more than one child, those under age 18 remain the most likely to live in poverty as they outnumber the adult earners in their families. The Conference Board of Canada reports that 15.1 percent of Canadians under age 18—more than double the Nordic countries' rate of 7 percent—were living in poverty in the late 2000s (Conference Board of Canada 2013a).

In the last four decades, seniors in Canada have benefited from rising incomes. In 1951, the average senior earned slightly more than half the income of Canadians of working age; in 1995, the average senior earned $20 300, or almost $84 for every $100 earned by working-aged Canadians (Statistics Canada 1998). As we noted earlier, however, for women the risk of poverty in old age is greater than it is for men:

In 2003, the low-income rate for women aged 65 and over was 8.7% compared with 4.4% for senior men. For the past decade, however, the poverty rate of older women on their own has varied between 27% and 19% with no significant downward trend over that period. In 2003, 19% of senior women on their own compared with 15% of unattached older men were considered low income. Average incomes of women aged 65 plus who were on their own and living in poverty in 2003 were $2,300 below the poverty line. (Townson 2005)

The Public Health Agency of Canada's 2005 report "Aging and Poverty in Canada" demonstrated that for seniors living below the LICO—the level of annual income determined by Statistics Canada to be necessary to meet minimum needs—the proportions broke down such that

- 18% of women over 80 years of age
- 38% of women who were separated; 25% of divorced women
- 17% of widows; 16% of single women
- 22% of tenants
- approximately 10% of disabled seniors
- 13% of immigrants and 225 of seniors from visible minorities*

made up the 9 percent population of seniors living below Canada's low-income cutoff (PHAC 2005: 10). We see here a list of vulnerabilities that correlate with poverty, but the vulnerabilities of older women stand out in particular. Why are older women so vulnerable to poverty (ibid)?

When compared to Canadian men, Canadian women are far less likely to have access to private-sector pensions, such as those provided by employers to employees. In 1997, among Canadians 65 to 68 years of age, for example, about one in two men—but only one in four women—received some income from a private pension (Lindsay 2000: 142). "Certain groups, such as First Nations women and women with disabilities, are particularly unlikely to be covered by private pension plans, and the likelihood of poverty is particularly pronounced among elderly women with disabilities" (Nelson and Robinson 2002: 483).

The federal government encouraged Canadians to prepare for their retirement by increasing the maximum annual tax-deductible RRSP contributions to $22 000 in 2010. Even so, it is evident that not all Canadians can afford to pursue such options. Although about half of Canadians report that they are putting away money for retirement, in general, the more individuals earn, the more likely they are to save. The economic crisis that erupted in 2007 had a negative impact both on people's ability to save and on the value of their savings. Statistics Canada reported that by the end of 2008, 75 percent of private-sector employees were without a registered pension plan (RPP), and those who did have RPPs had seen the value of their plans drop in the economic crisis. Meanwhile, though our population's contributions to private pension plans had risen to 54 percent by the late 1990s, in 2008 that level had dropped back down to 50 percent. In other words, this represented a drop of 7.4 percent in those making contributions (Massoulay 2010). Perhaps showing considerable lack of faith in markets, the numbers of those contributing to RRSPs in the same time period had declined from a high of 41 percent to 34 percent by the end of 2008 (ibid). Though it may be decades before we see the impact of the declining ability of Canadians to save for their retirements, we can expect that future poverty rates for the aged will be exacerbated by the trials of the current economy. Indeed the Conference Board of Canada notes that current financial pressures are negatively affecting the well-being of elderly Canadians, and negatively influencing those of working age from being able to save efficiently for the future:

> As Canada and its peers work to encourage the growth of private pensions as a means of decreasing reliance on public pension systems, the most vulnerable among the elderly are being put at greater risk of poverty. According to The European Centre for

Social Welfare Policy and Research, "Systematic reforms have changed the nature of pension provision from defined benefit type provisions to defined contribution type provisions."[2] Defined contribution plans—in which people receive only what they put into the plan plus whatever that investment earns—can result in a greater risk of poverty in retirement for people who have earned less while working. (Conference Board of Canada 2013b)

At present, Canada's retirement income system comprises three tiers. First, governmental benefits—such as Old Age Security (OAS) and the Guaranteed Income Supplement (GIS)—are designed to forestall the likelihood of poverty by furnishing all seniors with a taxable, flat-rate benefit (adjusted every three months as the Consumer Price Index increases); these benefits are paid monthly regardless of work histories or life circumstances. Second, the government-sponsored Canada Pension Plan (CPP) and the Quebec Pension Plan (QPP) are designed to provide workers with a retirement income based on their preretirement earnings from ages 18 to 65. Third, there are private savings, which include employer-sponsored private pension plans, private investments, and RRSPs (Townson 1995). The Conference Board (2013b) reports, "Aging presents a significant challenge to the long-term sustainability of public finances through increases in demand for public pensions, health services, and long-term care in Canada…If present demographic trends continue, there will be 75 pensioners for every 100 workers in 2050." In other words, we won't have enough workers to pay for the various social services and pension needs of our elderly population.

Currently, OAS pension benefits are based on age and residency. A person qualifies for a full OAS pension after having resided in Canada for 40 years after age 18. Those who are ineligible for a full pension may receive a prorated, partial pension after a minimum of 10 years' residency in Canada. For the July–September 2002 period (amounts are adjusted quarterly), the maximum monthly OAS pension was $443.99. While OAS pension is payable at age 65, some exemptions exist. For example, in 2002, those Canadian seniors whose net incomes exceeded $56 968 yearly were required to repay some or all of their OAS benefits. The full OAS pension was clawed back when an individual's net income exceeded $92 381. More recently, Service Canada (2013), a division of the federal government, reports that federal changes to the OAS to cope with the rising proportion of elderly pensioners in Canada have increased the age of eligibility for OAS benefits from 65 to 67 for those born after 1958. The change is to begin in April 2023 and to be fully implemented by January 2029. The obvious desired outcome of this change in policy and distribution of benefits will be that those hitting age 65 in 2023 and after will delay their retirements, extending their earning years in the workforce to at least age 67. While the new policy may remove some pressures on our benefits system, such change also risks extending the years of low-level employment, underemployment, and unemployment for younger Canadian residents seeking entry into full-time, paid positions.

The GIS was introduced in 1966 to assist those seniors with little or no income other than their OAS pension. Married or common-law spouses of pensioners (opposite-sex or same-sex), as well as the conjugal survivors of deceased pensioners, may also qualify for an Old Age Allowance provided that they are between the ages of 60 and 64 and qualify under an income test. The amount given depends on the pensioner's income, conjugal relationship status, and whether the recipient's partner also receives an OAS pension or Old Age Allowance income. For example, the July–September 2006 rate for the maximum monthly GIS payment to a single pensioner, or to a married person whose spouse or partner did not receive such benefits, was $602.91, and by 2013 that amount had risen to a maximum of $747.11. It is important to remember that current levels set a maximum annual income of $16 703.99, in addition to any OAS earnings, in order to be eligible for the GIS.

While GIS and OAS benefits are unrelated to an individual's prior income history, and eligibility is currently calculated based on income at the time of reaching retirement age, CPP/QPP benefits are directly based on income earned between age 18 and the time someone claims retirement (between the ages of 60 and 70). The benefits proportionately reflect prior income patterns. Although full benefits do not begin until age 65, partial CPP/QPP payments can be received by retired persons, under certain circumstances, as early as age 60. In September 2002, the maximum pension payable at age 65 under the CPP was $788.75. By 2013, the maximum monthly payment was $1012.50 and the average was $602.86

The various social security payments for retired Canadians are not intended to ensure a middle-class level of comfort, but merely to raise the most vulnerable seniors above the LICO. Whether we will be able to continue to meet this minimum guarantee is hard to predict now, but the pressures on the system are not encouraging.

Health Issues

The biology of aging is called **senescence**. It follows a universal pattern, but does not have universal consequences. "Massive research evidence demonstrates that the aging process is neither fixed nor immutable. Biologists are now showing that many symptoms that were formerly attributed to aging—for example, certain disturbances in cardiac function or in glucose metabolism in the brain—are instead produced by disease" (Riley and Riley 1992: 221). Biological functioning is also intricately related to social variables. Altering lifestyles, activities, and social contacts affects mortality and morbidity. For example, a longitudinal study of men and women between 70 and 79 found that regular physical activity, higher numbers of ongoing positive social relationships, and a sense of self-efficacy enhanced physical and cognitive functioning (Seeman and Adler 1998).

Biological changes are consequences of either **primary aging**, caused by physiological variables such as cellular and molecular variation (e.g., grey hair), or secondary aging. **Secondary aging** entails changes attributable to poor diet, lack of exercise, increased stress, and the like. Secondary aging exacerbates and accelerates primary aging.

Although chronic ailments become more common with increased age, the most recently released Statistics Canada research on the lives of older Canadians reveals that a significant proportion—37 percent—of our elderly rate their own health as "excellent" or "very good." For those seniors who live at home, the self-reported health picture is even better, with three out of four rating their health as good to excellent (Statistics Canada 2006). The ability to remain in one's home is influenced by wealth, which also has a strong correlation with overall health, so these results are not surprising. We can expect that persons with greater wealth will more frequently have better health, and retain their independence longer into old age. A second social determinant that corresponds with the health of seniors is education. Figure 6.6 shows the correspondence of education and health with those who hold higher levels of education showing greater levels of health throughout life.

Some disturbing evidence suggests that access to health care may be decided on the basis of age in Canada. For example, in what is believed to be the first large-scale Canadian study to examine treatment for heart attacks among the elderly, the research concluded that "[t]he older you are, the less likely you are to be treated." The research, conducted by Paula Rochon of the Baycrest Centre for Geriatric Care in Toronto and the Institute for Clinical Evaluative Science, was published in the November 1999 issue of the *Canadian Medical Association Journal*. It tracked more than 15 500 heart-attack patients aged 66 and older in Ontario between April 1993 and March 1995. The findings indicated that almost half (48 percent) of Canadian seniors were not getting the life-saving drugs that greatly improve the chances of survival after a heart attack. Among the 5453 heart-attack patients deemed to be the best candidates for beta-blocker therapy, 30 percent were not provided with these drugs. Women were significantly less likely than men to receive drugs, and seniors who lived in long-term care facilities were

senescence
The biology of aging.

primary aging
Biological changes associated with aging that are due to physiological variables, such as cellular and molecular variation (e.g., grey hair).

secondary aging
Biological changes associated with aging that can be attributed to poor diet, lack of exercise, and increased stress.

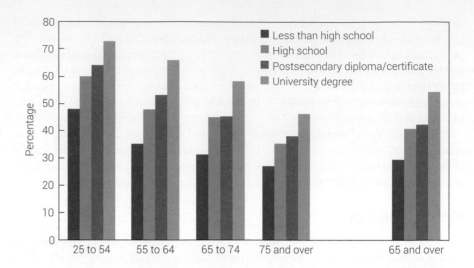

Figure 6.6
Percentage of Persons Reporting Excellent or Very Good Health by Age Group and Level of Education, 2003

SOURCE: Statistics Canada, 2006. _A Portrait of Seniors in Canada._ Catalogue No. 89-519-XIE, page 46.

twice as likely not to be treated with them. The study also reported that when compared to those seniors aged 66 to 74, older, frailer patients were three times as likely not to be treated with beta-blocker therapy. Moreover, older seniors who received the beta-blockers were often prescribed doses that were lower than what is considered medically acceptable (Arnold 1999).

In the nearly 15 years since the Rochon report was released, however, medical policy has shifted significantly toward prevention and away from treatment after the onset of a health problem. Not only does this strategy aim at reducing strain on the resources of our national health-care system—an obvious economic concern—it also aims at improving the overall quality of life enjoyed by Canada's senior population. After all, the prevention of injuries and the onset of diseases means that people will be healthier, better connected to their communities, and able to enjoy their day-to-day lives without the disruptions of poor health. The Canadian Institute for Health Information (CIHI) 2011 report on the provision of health care for seniors in Canada has observed that while those over age 65 currently represent 14 percent of the population, they consume 40 percent of all hospital services and 45 percent of all levels of government spending on health care (CIHI 2011: 28). The CIHI report observes that one of the main variables impacting the ability to access needed health-care services, in spite of a universal health-care system, is the socio-economic status of individual seniors: "despite universal access to health care in Canada, seniors with fewer personal resources, including health, wealth and social support, are also more likely to experience barriers to accessing health care" (2011: 16). The CIHI report also notes that the lowest-income groups of seniors are most likely to engage in behaviours that are "self-harming" and, therefore, most likely to suffer from negative health impacts (ibid). The report notes that the reasons for such behaviours and risks in the lowest SES groups are complex and inadequately theorized, but we know that much of such behaviour, including alcohol and other substance use, can be a stress-relieving strategy. Whether the behaviours are causative of poverty and low income and social isolation or secondary strategies varies across individuals and populations, but the report suggests that ensuring better access to community supports and to primary health-care services with a family physician can help to reduce such self-harming behaviours.

Living Arrangements

The elderly live in a variety of contexts, depending on their marital status, health, and financial status. In 2001, the elderly comprised over a third of Canada's one-person households, with women more likely than men to be divorced or widowed and living on their own. For example, for women between 75 and 84, 42.8 percent live on their own while 38.5 percent of women aged 85 and older live in one-person households (Dube 2002). In contrast, the majority of Canadian men between the ages of 50 and 89 are legally married and living with a spouse. Only among men aged 90 and over are fewer than 60 percent married and living with a partner (Reidmann et al. 2003: 483). The death of a spouse and encroaching poverty often mean that women must sell their family home and move to rental or institutional settings (National Council of Welfare 1998).

Most elderly do not want to be institutionalized, but prefer to remain in their own homes or in the homes of others, such as families and relatives. Some require elder care or assistance with daily living activities (see this chapter's *Social Problems Research Up Close* feature). However, they represent only a small proportion of the elderly population. According to the 2001 census, although the population aged 80 and older has increased 41 percent since 1996, the proportion of the population aged 15 and over which devoted some time to providing unpaid care for a senior was relatively small, at 18.2 percent. In 2001, approximately 20 percent of women and 15 percent of men reported providing care or assistance to a senior. However, less than 4 percent of women and 2 percent of men reported devoting more than 10 hours of such care in the week preceding census day (Statistics Canada 2002: 35). While well-to-do seniors may opt to live in retirement communities that offer various amenities and activities, there are many other living arrangements that span shared housing, modified independent living arrangements, and nursing homes. With shared housing, people of different ages live together in the same house or apartment; they have separate bedrooms, but share a common kitchen and dining area. In modified living arrangements, the elderly live in their own house, apartment, or condominium within a planned community where special services such as meals, transportation, and home repairs are provided. Skilled or semiskilled health-care professionals are available on the premises, and call buttons are installed so help can be summoned in case of an emergency.

Social Problems *Research Up Close*

Children and Grandchildren as Primary Caregivers

The single most significant demographic change of the next several decades will be the dramatic increase in the number of elderly worldwide. The increase in the elderly is associated with a variety of concerns, including who will care for the growing number of the old. A study by Dellman-Jenkins, Blankemeyer, and Pinkard (2000) examines a recent trend in caregiving—young adult children and grandchildren as primary caregivers.

Sample and Methods

The present research focuses on three areas: (1) characteristics of young caregivers and the assistance they provide, (2) the consequences of being a primary caregiver for the individual, and (3) caregivers' social support. Specifically, the researchers "compared the caregiving motivations, experiences and support needs of young adult grandchildren providing assistance to grandparents with those of young adult children caring for their older parents" (p. 178). Participants were recruited from a variety of sources including social service agencies, hospitals, and assisted living facilities. An open-ended interview was used in conjunction with a 65-item questionnaire. The final sample was composed of 43 caregivers—20 daughters, 2 sons, 19 granddaughters, and 2 grandsons (N=43). Eighty-one percent of the sample was white, 53 percent married, and 54 percent lived with the care-recipient; the remainder lived in a separate residence.

(continued)

Findings and Conclusions

Caregiver Role and Assistance Given. Children, compared with grandchildren, were significantly more likely to respond that they were caring for their parents because no one else would. Grandchildren were most likely to respond that they were caring for their grandparent(s) out of a sense of duty and the desire to avoid nursing home care. Grandchildren also reported volunteering to care for grandparent(s) to help their parents.

> When Alzheimer's became apparent, my parents weren't coping well with it and were mean to her (not physically). I couldn't stand it...I told them I would take her to my house. My dad told me it would be the biggest mistake I ever made. Three years later...I still disagree.

The modal category for length of caregiving for both grandchildren and children was one to five years, with approximately equal proportions of both providing around-the-clock (47 percent) versus daily assistance (53 percent). Both sets of caregivers provided transportation, companionship and emotional support, personal care, and household support (e.g., cleaning house, paying bills, making appointments).

Consequences of Role. Caretakers in general, and single caretakers in particular, reported that caretaking activities interfered with their social life. All caretakers reported spending at least three hours a day in the caretaker role. One 20-year-old granddaughter commented that, "I sometimes get mad because I think I'm doing too much for my grandpa and I don't have a life of my own—then I feel selfish for having such thoughts" (p. 184). Caretakers also reported strained family relations, particularly with spouse and children.

> I would like to go camping with my husband once in a while, but I can't just get up and go away, because

of taking care of my grandparents. Even though they have the medical alert, I'm afraid they won't use it if something goes wrong.

Further, careers were negatively affected as relocating, job performance, and achievement of long-term goals became difficult because of the demands of caregiving. Both groups also reported increases in stress, although this was significantly higher for grandchildren (81 percent) than children (59 percent). Positive outcomes were also expressed, with over 97 percent of respondents identifying some benefit or reward. Grandchildren were most likely to note maintaining a strong relationship with the care-recipient, whereas children more often listed prevention of nursing home placement as the primary benefit.

Sources of Support. All respondents reported seeking informal assistance from some source. Children most often turned to their siblings for help, whereas grandchildren most often turned to their spouse or dating partner. Formal support, although seldom sought, most often came from nursing/home health-care providers or community support groups.

The two generations of caregivers, children and grandchildren, differ little in their caregiving activities, behaviours, and strains. They do, however, differ in their motivation to assist, with grandchildren more often noting attachment rather than need or obligation as the primary reason for becoming a care-giver. Further, the authors conclude, grandchildren are "more likely to report personal rewards (e.g., greater closeness, positive memories), while children were more apt to report instrumental rewards (e.g., providing quality home-care and avoiding nursing home placement)" (p. 185).

SOURCE: Dellman-Jenkins, Mary, Maureen Blankemeyer, and Odessa Pinkard. 2000. "Young Adult Children and Grandchildren in Primary Caregiver Roles to Older Relatives and Their Service Needs." *Family Relations* 49: 177–87.

In 2001, 287 480 seniors lived in health-care institutions, including 9.2 percent of senior women and 4.9 percent of senior men (Dube 2002). Nursing home residents are not typical of the elderly—they are more likely to be widowed or quite ill or over 80, or without family to take care of them (Kinsella and Taeuber 1993). An estimated 7 percent of Canada's 3 800 000 seniors require institutional care, and 10.3 percent require some form of home care. In Canada, seniors are the "largest consumers of publicly funded home-care services"; in 1996–97, 5 percent of seniors aged 65 to 75 and 17 percent of those aged 75 and over used home-care services (Health Canada 1999: 166).

However, the demand for both publicly funded long-term care beds and home care exceeds their supply.

Victimization and Abuse

Although abuse may take place in private homes by family members, the elderly, like children, are particularly vulnerable to abuse when they are institutionalized. Pillemer and Hudson (1993) conducted interviews with a random sample of nursing home staff and found that 40 percent admitted that during the previous year, they had abused patients psychologically and 10 percent admitted to abusing them physically.

The emerging profile of the abused or neglected elderly person is of a female, 70 years or older, who has physical, mental, and/or emotional impairments and is dependent on the abuser-caregiver for both companionship and help with daily activities. Studies have found that the neglected elderly are older than elder abuse victims are, and have more physical and mental difficulties (Wittaker 1996). Most often, the abuser tends to be an adult child or spouse of the victim who misuses alcohol (Anetzberger et al. 1994). Some research suggests that the perpetrator of the abuse is more often an adult child who is financially dependent on the elderly victim (Boudreau 1993). Whether the abuser is an adult child or a spouse may simply depend on whom the elder victim lives with.

Many of the problems of the elderly are compounded by their lack of interaction with others, loneliness, and inactivity. This reality is particularly true for the old-old. The elderly are also segregated in nursing homes and retirement communities, separated from family and friends, and isolated from the flow of work and school. A cycle is perpetuated—being poor and old results in being isolated and engaging in fewer activities. Such withdrawal affects health, which makes the individual less able to establish relationships or participate in activities.

For older women who are abused, the most common place for them to receive protection is through shelter services; however, qualitative research on shelter services shows that elder abuse victims are not well served by traditional shelter services, which lack understanding of the unique needs of elderly clients:*

- Shelters may have higher noise and activity levels than is comfortable for older women.
- Some older women have difficulty fulfilling their work assignments because of their physical or mental conditions.
- The time limit on occupancy can be inadequate in terms of the complexity of some older women's problems.
- Shelter staff are usually unfamiliar with aging and the special needs of older people.
- Problems with health and mobility can hinder the use of shelters, with many lacking wheelchair accessibility.
- Most shelters are not equipped to provide the care needed by some women with health problems (e.g., assistance with bathing, eating, or other activities of daily living or dispensing medications).
- Older women may find it difficult to go to medical appointments and services, and most shelters are not set up to provide this kind of transportation and accompaniment. (Straka and Montminy 2006: 257)

While the common perception of elder abuse is that women are the most likely victims, research shows that when it comes specifically to the problem of abandonment, men are far more likely to be the victims. While only about half as many elderly men as women face physical abuse, a significant number report victimization annually

* Straka, Sylvia, and Lise Montminy. 2006. "Responding to the Needs of Older Women Experiencing Domestic Violence." *Violence against Women* 12(3): 251-67.

(Mouton et al. 2001). What is remarkable about the problem of neglect faced by so many men is that much of the problem rests on "their refusal to allow for non-family caregiving" (Mouton et al. 2001: 20) when their families are either no longer living or are unable to provide care.

Quality of Life

Although some elderly do suffer from declining mental and physical functioning, many others do not. Consider that nearly half a million Canadians aged 65 or over regularly provide temporary or ongoing child care to their grandchildren, 7 percent spend at least five hours a week helping other seniors (with some providing over 15 hours a week), about 1 in 4 works as a formal volunteer, and 6 in 10 participate in informal volunteer activities (Vanier Institute of the Family 2000: 172).

It should be evident that being old does not mean being depressed, poor, and sick. Some research indicates that the elderly may be less depressed than the young are, with several studies concluding that the elderly may have the lowest depression rates of all age groups (Health Canada 1999). Other research suggests that depression is curvilinear with age, that is, highest at the extremes of the age continuum (DeAngelis 1997). One study suggests that depression of the elderly is better treated by exercise than medication alone, or by medication and exercise combined (Livni 2000).

Among the elderly who are depressed, two social factors tend to be in operation. One is society's negative attitude toward the elderly. Words and phrases such as "old," "useless," and "a has-been" reflect cultural connotations of the aged that influence feelings of self-worth. The roles of the elderly also lose their clarity. How is a retiree supposed to feel or act? What does a retiree do? As a result, the elderly become dependent on external validation that may be weak or absent.

The second factor contributing to depression among the elderly is the process of growing old. This process carries with it a barrage of stressful life events all converging in a relatively short period. These events include health concerns, retirement, economic instability, loss of significant other(s), physical isolation, job displacement, and increased salience of the inevitability of death due to physiological decline. All of these events converge on the elderly and increase the incidence of depression and anxiety; they may also increase the decision not to prolong life.

6.7 Strategies for Action: Growing Up and Growing Old

Activism by or on behalf of children or the elderly has been increasing in recent years and, as the number of children and elderly grow, such activism is likely to escalate and to be increasingly successful. For example, global attention to the elderly led to 1999 being declared the "International Year of Older Persons" (DHHS 1998), while "the first nearly universally ratified human rights treaty in history" deals with children's rights (UNICEF 1998). Activism takes several forms, including collective action through established organizations and the exercise of political and economic power.

Collective Action

Countless organizations work on behalf of children, some of which we have already noted. Others include Aboriginal Family Services, Adoption Council of Canada, Alateen, Boys and Girls Club of Canada, Canadian Child Care Federation, Defence for Children International, Global Alliance on the Sexual Exploitation of Youth, Save the Children–Canada, and UNICEF. Many successes take place at the local level where parents, teachers, corporate officials, politicians, and citizens join together in the interests of children.

Similarly, more than a thousand organizations work toward realizing political power, economic security, and better living conditions for the elderly. These organizations include the Seniors Computer Information Project (Manitoba), Saskatchewan Seniors Mechanism, Alberta Senior Citizens Sport and Recreation Association, Council on Aging of Ottawa-Carleton, Alberta Council on Aging, Assemblée des aînés francophones du Canada, National Advisory Council on Aging, Golden Age Association (Montreal), Society for the Retired and Semi-Retired (Edmonton), and the Canadian Association of Retired Persons (CARP).

One of the earliest and most radical groups in North America was the Gray Panthers, founded in 1970 by Margaret Kuhn. The Gray Panthers in the United States were responsible for revealing the unscrupulous practices of the hearing aid industry, persuading the National Association of Broadcasters to add age to sex and race in the Television Code of Ethics statement on media images, and eliminating the mandatory retirement age. In view of these successes, it is interesting to note that the Gray Panthers, with only 50 000 to 70 000 members, is relatively small when compared with the CARP.

CARP is Canada's largest 50-plus lobby group, with more than 400 000 members. A non-profit association that does not accept funding from any government body, CARP speaks out on a wide range of issues important to those over 50. Its mandate is "to protect what we have and improve our lifestyle." Services of CARP include discounted mail-order drugs, investment opportunities, travel information, volunteer opportunities, a *Spamhunter's Resource Guide* offering practical advice for dealing with unwanted advertising offers, and news updates on issues of concern to those 50 and older. One of their most recent projects, in collaboration with the PRIME television channel, is a one-hour documentary about ageism, "What's Age Got to Do with It" (CARP 2002). There is also the Gay and Lesbian Association of Retiring Persons (GLARP), whose goal is to raise money to develop gay and lesbian retirement communities and retirement resorts (GLARP 2000).

Political and Economic Power

Children rely on others to advance their interests, while the elderly may be able to translate economic power into political. Children are unable to hold office or to vote, but child advocates have wielded much political influence in such areas as child care, education, health-care reform, and crime prevention. At the same time, because of their numbers, aging baby boomers may be particularly well situated to advance their concerns. One economist, noting that the elderly's economic power is considerable, has referred to the elderly as a "revolutionary class" (Thurow 1996). By 2030, almost half of all adults in developed countries and two-thirds of all voters will be near or at retirement age. The growing political power of the aged is already becoming evident; the Netherlands has a new political party called the Pension Party.

Understanding Youth and Aging

What can we conclude about youth and aging in Canadian society? Age is an ascribed status and, as such, is culturally defined by role expectations and implied personality traits. Society regards both the young and the old as dependent and in need of the care and protection of others. Society also defines the young and the old as physically, emotionally, and intellectually inferior. Because of these and other attributions, both age groups are sociologically a minority with limited opportunity to obtain some or all of society's resources.

Although both the young and the old are treated as minority groups, different meanings are assigned to each group. In general, the young are more highly valued than the old are. Functionalists argue that this priority on youth reflects the fact that the young are preparing to take over important statuses while the elderly are relinquishing them. Conflict theorists emphasize that in a capitalist society, both the young and the old are less valued than more productive members of society are. Conflict theorists also point out the importance of propagation, or the reproduction of workers, which may account for the greater value placed on the young than the old. Finally, symbolic interactionists describe the way that images of the young and the old intersect and are socially constructed.

The collective concern for the elderly and the significance of defining ageism as a social problem have resulted in improved economic conditions for the elderly. Currently, they are one of society's more powerful minorities. Research indicates, however, that despite their increased economic status, the elderly are still subject to discrimination in such areas as housing, employment, and medical care. They are victimized by systematic patterns of stereotyping, abuse, and prejudice.

In contrast, the position of children, while improving in some ways, remains tragic in others. Wherever there are poor families, there are poor children (see Chapters 10 and 11). Further, age-based restrictions limit their entry into certain roles, such as employee, and demand others, such as student. While most of society's members would agree that children require special protections, quality-of-life issues and rights of self-determination are only recently being debated.

Age-based decisions are potentially harmful. If budget allocations were based on indigence rather than age, more resources would be available for those truly in need. Further, age-based decisions may encourage intergenerational conflict. Government assistance should not be thought of as a zero-sum relationship—the more resources one group gets, the fewer resources another group receives. Nevertheless, some predict the emergence of a new generation gap in the next decade: one between aging boomers concerned with their pensions and personal security and their younger cohorts who will be forced to bear some of the burden for the boomers' support. This burden must be considered of especial concern within Canada due to the relatively large size of our baby boom generation and the boomers' approaching departure from the labour force. "Retiring baby boomers will have a significant impact on the size of the labour market, especially as relatively small cohorts of young people will be entering it. Boomers, those aged 37 to 55 in 2001, made up 47 percent of the labour force. Ten years later, almost half of the Boomers are 55 or over, and 18 percent are over the age of 60" (Statistics Canada 2002: 10).

Social policies that allocate resources based on need rather than on age would shift the attention of policymakers to remedying social problems rather than serving the needs of special interest groups. Age should not be used to negatively affect an individual's life any more than race, ethnicity, gender, or sexual orientation. While eliminating all age barriers or requirements is unrealistic, a movement toward assessing the needs of individuals and their abilities would be more consistent with the ideal of equal opportunity for all.

Student Reflection: What Do You Know Now?

Clearly sociological research on youth and aging gives us an alternative story to the one many of us in Canada would like to tell about ourselves (a benevolent nation with universal health care and old age security). The reasons we stay or return home to parents, the ways we treat our retirees, the realities of income disparity are all complicated by ageism. With the information you now have about children and the elderly in

Canada and around the world, which of your beliefs about age categories have been challenged, and how? The next time someone talks to you about the value of a benefits plan that includes pension contributions, or about contributing to an RRSP, what questions will arise in your mind? As you or members of your family or circle of friends have children or must deal with aging parents or grandparents, which sociological perspectives will help you to determine how to act? Why, and how?

What Do You Do Next?

Located at www.nelson.com/socialproblems5e

- Consolidate your knowledge with interactive and printable **Flashcards**
- Gauge your understanding with **Practice Quizzes** and **Matching Activities**
- Develop your critical thinking skills with **Self and Society** and The **Human Side** questions
- Analyze **Social Research** and **Social Problems in Global Perspective**
- Explore the implications of **Technology on Social Problems**

7

Gender
Inequality

Comstock/Stockbyte/Thinkstock

Student Reflection:
What Do You Already Know?

Most of you have probably debated questions about gender inequality, sexism, patriarchal oppression, and women's versus men's roles for many years already. If you've ever argued with someone about whether or not girls should play on boys' football teams, or whether Miley Cyrus is a good example or a bad example for girls, or whether only men should do society's more physically dangerous jobs, you're in the middle of gender-based and feminist debates. Some of these debates go back hundreds of years, while others are of more recent vintage. Although you may have encountered plenty of thinking in high school, college, or university classes about media influences and representations of femininity or masculinity, this chapter aims to support your thinking about gender in a more sociological way. What do you already know about income disparity, and why do you think it exists? In what ways do you see gender stratification in your own everyday life? What kinds of social problems can you already trace back to inequality between men and women? Imagine a world in which gender inequality is solved: what have you done and what might you do to make this more achievable?

Learning Outcomes

Through careful reading of this chapter, you should be able to:

- define the bolded key terms
- define sexism and identify ways in which it can account for inequality
- think structurally about gender stratification
- connect heteronormativity and sexism
- apply sociological perspectives to problems arising from gender inequality
- explain socialization and gendered ideology in relation to men's and women's different experiences of work, family, and education
- reflect on and interrogate one's own relationship to gender norms and gender inequality

In the previous chapter, we discussed the social consequences of youth and aging. This chapter looks at **sexism**—the belief that innate psychological, behavioural, and/ or intellectual differences exist between women and men and that these differences connote the superiority of one group and the inferiority of the other. As with age, such attitudes often result in prejudice and discrimination at both the individual and the institutional levels. Physicians who will not hire male nurses because they believe that women are more nurturing and empathetic and are, therefore, better nurses reflect individual discrimination. Institutional discrimination, or discrimination built into the fabric of society, is exemplified by the difficulty some women experience in finding employment; they may have no work history and few job skills as a consequence of living in traditionally defined marriage roles.

Discerning the basis for discrimination is often difficult because gender, age, sexual orientation, and race intersect. For example, First Nations people, members of visible minorities, and men and women with disabilities generally earn yearly incomes that are well below the Canadian average (Nelson and Robinson 2002). Women's earnings remain well below those of men. As of 2003, women in full-time employment still earned on average only 70.5 percent of what men did (Statistics Canada 2006: 152). Just getting to the point of having earnings can be a challenge compounded by one's race or ethnicity. Figure 7.1 shows how visible minority status can compound gender inequality in employment status. In this chapter, however, we emphasize the impact of gender inequality. **Gender** refers to the social definitions and expectations associated with being female or male and, while the concept informs our assumptions about the properties of each sex (male and female), it is distinct from the idea of **sex**, which refers to the biological distinction between males and females rather than to one's social role.

sexism
The belief that there are innate psychological, behavioural, or intellectual differences between females and males and that these differences connote the superiority of one group and the inferiority of another.

gender
The social definitions and expectations associated with being male or female.

sex
A person's biological classification as male or female.

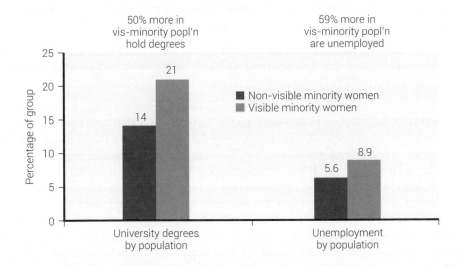

Figure 7.1 *In Spite of Higher Educational Attainments, Visible Minority Women Face Higher Unemployment*

SOURCE: Statistics Canada, 2006."Women in Canada: 5th Edition Women, A Gender-based Statistical Report. Catalogue no 89-503-XIE.

7.1 The Global Context: The Status of Women and Men

The 2005 United Nations *Human Development Report* (HDR) observes that from a global perspective, "Gender disparities are among the deepest and most pervasive of inequalities [and that disparity in developing nations results in] higher mortality rates among girls and women from birth to age 30 inverts the normal demographic gender balance" (2005a: 61). The report notes that inequality is not simply conceptual, but a concrete structural denial of health care, food, and social status. The 2013 HDR provides new and troubling data showing that in "some countries, sex-selective abortion and infanticide are artificially altering the demographic landscape, leading to a shortage of girls and women" (p. 32). The HDR points out that this violent removal of girls and women from their societies—most frequently a problem in countries in Africa, in India, and in China—is not merely an obvious problem of inequality and human rights abuses, but that it could have unintended consequences such as an increase in social violence in those areas (ibid). Reversing the trend "will involve changing many social norms, including those that affect the economic incentives of the household to have boys [and will require] ending the exploitative dowry system" (p. 33). Thus, although the most recent report lays out a number of improvements in gender disparity around the globe, we can see that some disparities are particularly imperilling to the societies where the privileging of men and boys over women and girls leads to premature death for both: males in warfare, and females through prenatal sex-selection and infanticide.

An additional United Nations report finds that, despite some progress, millions of women around the world remain victims of violence, discrimination, and abuse (Austin 2000; Leeman 2000). For example, worldwide

- over 60 million young girls, predominantly in Asia, are listed as "missing" and are likely the victims of infanticide or neglect;
- 2 million girls between the ages of 5 and 15 are forced into the sex trade each year;
- half a million women die of complications from childbirth each year, and 20 times more are seriously injured or disabled in childbirth;
- two-thirds of the world's 876 million illiterates are women;
- one in three women has been abused, beaten, or coerced into sex.

An update on similar data indicates that these problems remain throughout the developing world, especially in sub-Saharan Africa and Asia where barriers to progress include the lack of representation of women's interests in workers' organizations and low representation in basic schooling. As a result,

> women migrate to precarious and risky work situations where they are largely engaged in low-skilled occupations such as domestic work and entertainment, or worse, are trafficked in the commercial sex industry. (UN 2005b: 8)

One specific type of violence suffered by millions of women is female genital mutilation (FGM), also referred to as female genital cutting (FGC). Clitorectomy and infibulation are two forms of FGM. In a clitorectomy, the entire glans and shaft of the clitoris are amputated; the labia minora may also be excised. With infibulation, the two sides of the vulva are stitched together in infancy, leaving only a small opening for the passage of urine and menstrual blood. After marriage, the sealed opening is reopened to permit intercourse and delivery; however, the woman is often infibulated again afterward.

A World Bank report explains that FGM/C correlates with other practices. These include the refusal of condoms in some Roman Catholic communities and the prevalence of males who have sex outside of their marriages in other communities. Such practices may increase the risk for contracting infections such as HIV. The report is careful to explain, though, that practices vary widely, so FGM/C is not a reliable predictor for risk; rather, it is one of many markers for *potential* risks in behaviours specific to given communities (de Walque 2006).

Societies that practise clitorectomy and infibulation do so for a variety of economic, social, and religious reasons. Attempts to classify them in simple terms that see the roots simply as "male dominance" or as a form of cultural imprisonment do an injustice to the cultures and the women. Instead of providing reductive explanations, and targeting genital cutting practices for eradication, current wisdom argues that dealing with women's health and well-being in a holistic manner is more important. Ways of doing so include fostering "literacy, leadership skills, and social development, allowing women themselves to decide when is the right time to begin to address change in female genital cutting practices" (Gruenbaum 2005: 431). In short, women's oppression takes place in culturally complex circumstances; consequently, women require complex means of challenging and reducing those inequalities.

While it is easy to view "other" cultures in negative terms because of media fascination with practices such as female genital cutting, such a view neglects the problem of genital surgeries performed on children in North America. Across Canada, in highly specialized hospitals, children's genitals are altered to meet social gender norms regarding appearance, size, and "appropriate" masculinity or femininity. We will deal with this problem in more depth in Chapter 9.

Inequality in Canada

Although attitudes toward gender equality are increasingly liberal, Canada has a long history of gender inequality. Women have had to fight for equality: the right to vote, equal pay for comparable work, quality education, entrance into male-dominated occupations, and legal equality. Even today, most Canadians would agree that our society does not treat women and men equally. As discussed later, many national statistics support this belief: women have lower incomes; hold fewer prestigious jobs; remain concentrated in traditionally female-dominated fields of study at universities, community colleges, and trade apprenticeship programs; and are more likely than men are to live in poverty.

How much do you know about gender inequality's relationship to broad social inequality?

7.2 Sociological Theories of Gender Inequality

Both structural-functionalism and conflict theory concentrate on how the structure of society and, specifically, its institutions contribute to gender inequality. However, these two theoretical perspectives offer opposing views of the development and maintenance of gender inequality. Symbolic interactionism, on the other hand, focuses on the culture of society and how gender roles are learned through the socialization process.

Structural-Functionalist Perspective

Structural-functionalists argue that pre-industrial society required a division of labour based on gender. Women, out of biological necessity, remained in the home performing such functions as bearing, nursing, and caring for children. Men, who were physically stronger and could be away from home for long periods, were responsible for providing food, clothing, and shelter for their families. This division of labour was functional for society and, over time, became defined as both normal and natural. This perspective has been criticized by feminists, as we shall see, for taking a male-centred view of what is presumed to be beneficial for a society.

Industrialization rendered the traditional division of labour less functional, although remnants of the supporting belief system persist. Today, because of day-care facilities, lower fertility rates, and the less physically demanding and dangerous nature of jobs, the traditional division of labour is less functional.

Modern conceptions of the family, to some extent, have replaced traditional ones—families have evolved from extended to nuclear, authority is more egalitarian, more women work outside the home, and there is greater role variation in the division of labour. Functionalists argue, therefore, that as the needs of society change, the associated institutional arrangements also change.

Conflict Perspective

Many conflict theorists hold that the relationship men and women have to the production process shapes male dominance and female subordination. As society evolved to agricultural and industrial modes of production, private property developed, and men gained control of the modes of production while women remained in the home to bear and care for children. Inheritance laws ensured that ownership would remain in men's hands, furthering male domination. Laws that regarded women as property ensured that women would remain confined to the home.

As industrialization continued and the production of goods and services moved away from the home, the male–female gap continued to grow—women had less education, lower incomes, fewer occupational skills, and rarely owned property. World War II necessitated the entry of large numbers of women into the labour force, but in contrast to previous periods, many did not return home at war's end. In the final decades of the twentieth century and into the second decade of the twenty-first, women established their own place in the workforce and, facilitated by the changing nature of work and technological advances, now compete directly with men for jobs and wages (Figure 7.2). Recent data on women's employment in Canada show that, although more women are entering into what have been male-dominated fields—professional, management, and agricultural areas—their wages remain lower on the whole; they are also more likely to work in part-time positions (Statistics Canada 2006: 26).

Figure 7.2 **Employment Rate, by Gender (percent), 1976–2012**

SOURCE: Statistics Canada. Table 282-0002 - Labour force survey estimates (LFS), by sex and detailed age group, annual (persons unless otherwise noted), CANSIM (database).

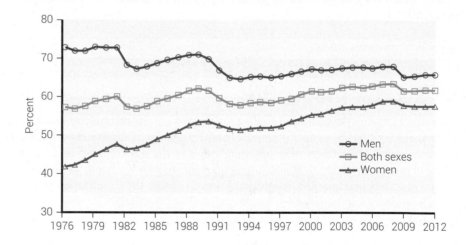

Conflict theorists also argue that continued male dominance requires a belief system supporting gender inequality. Two such beliefs are that (1) women are inferior outside the home (e.g., they are less intelligent, less reliable, and less rational), and (2) women are more valuable in the home (e.g., they have maternal instincts and are naturally nurturing). Thus, unlike functionalists, conflict theorists hold that the subordinate position of women in society is a consequence of social inducement rather than biological differences that led to the traditional division of labour.

Symbolic Interactionist Perspective

Although some scientists argue that gender differences are innate, symbolic interactionists emphasize that through the socialization process, both females and males are taught the meanings associated with being feminine and masculine. Gender assignment begins at birth, when a child is classified as either female or male. The learning of gender roles is a lifelong process, though, whereby individuals acquire society's definitions of appropriate and inappropriate gender behaviour.

We learn gender roles through family, school, and peer groups, and through popular presentations of girls and boys, and women and men. Most important, however, we learn gender roles through symbolic interaction as the messages others send us reaffirm or challenge our gender performances.

Feminist Perspectives

Feminist contributions to the study of gender have a complex history that many trace to the early contributions of Mary Wollstonecraft, who, in 1792, argued that Rousseau was wrong to have characterized girls as unworthy of education and unsuited to the demands of full citizenship. Feminist thinking is not, then, new, but developed out of and alongside the principles of Enlightenment thought: autonomy and rights for all citizens, the triumph of reason over superstition and prejudice, and the inherent value of human persons. Like other Enlightenment positions still important to contemporary social life, feminism "has an emancipatory goal. [It] is one of the social movements that—alongside the anti-war, youth, civil rights, anti-racism, and green movements—have in the last three decades reshaped modern politics" (Tepperman and Curtis 2004: 189).

What is unique about feminist thinking on gender is that, while classical structural-functionalists tended to see women's subordinate place in social structures as necessary and beneficial, and as a reflection of natural order, feminists showed that the benefits of women's subordination accrue principally to men. "Feminist scholars challenged the idea, embedded in functionalism, that **expressive** and **instrumental roles** in the family were necessarily divided along lines of gender, [and thus] disputed the idea that some family forms were more natural than others…" (Anderson 2005: 440 [boldfacing added]).

Feminism recognizes that the roles we are expected to perform as men or as women result from learning the social expectations of the worlds into which we are born. The idea that gender operates as a manifestation of social norms that vary from region to region has since been extended by the observation that everything we think about "sex" may also be an effect more of culture than of biology. As biologist Anne Fausto-Sterling (2000) has explained, as soon as we begin to talk about what the female sex or the male sex is *supposed* to do, we are talking about social imperatives; that is, we are discussing not biological truth, but social ideas. As Lorber (1998: 213) notes, building on Butler's idea of gender performance:

> Gender is so pervasive that in our society we assume it is bred into our genes. Most people find it hard to believe that gender is constantly created and re-created out of human interaction, out of social life, and is the texture and order of social life. Yet gender, like culture, is a human production that depends on everyone constantly "doing gender."

Queer Theory Perspectives

At least since the French lesbian feminist Monique Wittig argued that lesbians were not women (1992) because the term *woman* signals a gender defined by its heterosexual attachment to men, queer scholars have been contesting approaches to gender that take as obvious that there are two genders and that the two must be defined in opposition to each other.

One of the most famous contributors to the contemporary, complex understanding of how gender operates is Judith Butler (1990, 1993). Butler famously argued that gender is a form of performance, something that people have to work at in order to sustain socially meaningful positions as subjects; not something that we *have* but something that we *learn to do*, gender is a status under constant threat of dissolution because it is based in nothing concrete, but only in social mandates grounded in changeable ideological views. Butler's work set the benchmark for understanding gender as contingent, fluid, and unstable, not as a given and easy behaviour but one that has to be learned and constantly repeated if one is to maintain an identity.

expressive roles
The nurturing and emotionally supportive roles that women are generally socialized into.

instrumental roles
Task-oriented roles that males are generally socialized into.

Other scholars who have influenced sociological thinking about gender include Suzanne Kessler and Wendy McKenna (1978), who showed that our notions about gender can and should be "confronted with the possibility of other realities" (p. 164) evident in societies that actively recognize more than two, oppositional ways of being gendered.

The Australian scholar Nikki Sullivan, in her 2003 book *A Critical Introduction to Queer Theory*, explains that when we consider what we "know" about sexuality or about sex and/ or gender this ought not to be valued in terms that assume our particular historical period to be necessarily more "enlightened" or less a part of the historical period in which our knowledge understandings circulate than any of the ideas held in previous generations. Of our current era she writes, "It is very likely that fifty years from now people will cringe when they view current representations of lesbianism, or accounts of fetishism, in much the same way as we sometimes do . . ." (p. 1). There are, for example, still those—mostly working in Christian organizations—who seek to "cure" the "disease" of homosexuality using a technique they call reparative therapy (a practice we discuss in more depth in Chapter 9).

Sullivan points out that we have not entirely abandoned ideas that lesbians are "masculine," but she argues queer theory and its understanding of gender and sexuality as performative has allowed us to positively recognize that gendered identity expressions are not bound to the **heteronormative** imperative belief of "gender follows from sex, and desire follows from gender" (2003: 86). In other words, we no longer believe as they did in the early twentieth century that to be a "proper" man one had to desire a woman, and that to be a "proper" woman one had to desire a man (and motherhood).

In addition to thinking critically about heteronormativity and interrogating naturalized presuppositions about gender, in pointing out that gender is something that we have to learn to do queer theory has extended well beyond gesturing toward and contesting the violence and oppression faced by lesbian, gay, trans, and bisexual persons. As William Turner (2000) notes, the tools provided by queer theory have helped us to consider the ways in which any of us can fall victim to the oppressive demands of heteronormativity, and to ask why it is that some bodies/some persons have mattered more to us than others have. Since the feminist film theorist Teresa de Lauretis first used the term "queer" in 1991, Turner reminds us, the idea of a "queer" language has allowed feminists to think about women's lives without being constrained in "a language and conceptual framework that men had created in a political order that took little account of women, except as commodities for exchange" (p. 5).

Queer theory, then, has applications and importance for thinking not only about what it means to be lesbian, gay, bisexual, transsexual, or intersex, but, indeed, what it means to learn to perform our genders at all, what it means to be accepted as a man or as a woman, and what we can accomplish when we stretch the boundaries of what we think of as "properly" masculine or feminine.

7.3 Gender Stratification: Structural Sexism

Structural sexism, also known as "institutional sexism," refers to the ways in which the organization of society, and specifically its institutions, subordinates individuals and groups based on their sex classification. Structural sexism has resulted in gender differences in educational attainment, income levels, and occupational and political involvement.

Education and Structural Sexism

In the world's least developed countries only 70 percent as many women as men are literate, and rates for specific countries may be much lower. For example, only 31 percent as many women as men in Chad are literate; in Mali, Burkina Faso, and Yemen, only 41 percent; and in Mozambique, only 50 percent (UN 2005a). (See Table 7.1.) The

heteronormativity
The group of assumptions and demands that people fall into two opposite sexes that are reproductively oriented toward each other; as a bias, creates structures and institutions that privilege opposite-sex relations and deny full rights and freedoms and recognition to those engaged in same-sex relations.

structural sexism
The ways in which the organization of society, and specifically its institutions, subordinate individuals and groups based on their sex classification.

Table 7.1 *Gender Inequality in Education: Least Developed Nations*

Human Development Rank	Adult Literacy		Youth Literacy		Net Primary Enrolment		Net Secondary Enrolment		Gross Tertiary Enrolment	
	Female Rate (% ages 15 and above) 2003	Female Rate as % of Male Rate 2003	Female Rate (% ages 15–24) 2003	Female Rate as % of Male Rate 2003	Female Ratio (%) 2002–03	Ratio of Female to Male 2002–03	Female Ratio (%) 2002–03	Ratio of Female to Male 2002–03	Female Ratio (%) 2002–03	Ratio of Female to Male 2002–03
146 Madagascar	65.2	85	68.1	94	79	1.00	12	1.03	2	0.83
147 Swaziland	78.1	97	89.4	103	75	1.00	36	1.21	5	1.16
148 Cameroon	59.8	78	–	–	–	–	–	–	4	0.63
149 Lesotho	90.3	123	–	–	89	1.07	27	1.53	4	1.48
150 Djibouti	–	–	–	–	32	0.80	17	0.69	2	0.81
151 Yemen	28.5	41	50.9	60	59	0.71	21	0.46	5	0.28
152 Mauritania	43.4	73	55.5	82	67	0.97	14	0.77	2	0.27
153 Haiti	50.0	93	66.5	101	–	–	–	–	–	–
154 Kenya	70.2	90	80.7	101	66	1.00	24	0.98	2	0.53
155 Gambia	–	–	–	–	78	0.99	27	0.68	1	0.29
156 Guinea	–	–	–	–	58	0.80	13	0.48	–	–
157 Senegal	29.2	57	41.0	70	54	0.89	–	–	–	–
158 Nigeria	59.4	80	86.5	95	60	0.82	26	0.80	7	0.69
159 Rwanda	58.8	84	75.9	98	88	1.04	–	–	2	0.46
160 Angola	53.8	66	62.6	76	57	0.86	–	–	1	0.65
161 Eritrea	–	–	–	–	42	0.86	18	0.74	(.)	0.15
162 Benin	22.6	49	32.5	56	47	0.69	13	0.48	1	0.24
163 Côte d'Ivoire	38.2	64	51.5	74	54	0.81	15	0.57	4	0.36

(Continued)

Chapter 7 Gender Inequality **223**

Table 7.1 *Gender Inequality in Education: Least Developed Nations* (continued)

Human Development Rank	Adult Literacy		Youth Literacy		Net Primary Enrolment		Net Secondary Enrolment		Gross Tertiary Enrolment	
	Female Rate (% ages 15 and above) 2003	Female Rate as % of Male Rate 2003	Female Rate (% ages 15–24) 2003	Female Rate as % of Male Rate 2003	Female Ratio (%) 2002–03	Ratio of Female to Male 2002–03	Female Ratio (%) 2002–03	Ratio of Female to Male 2002–03	Female Ratio (%) 2002–03	Ratio of Female to Male 2002–03
164 Tanzania, U. Rep. of	62.2	80	76.2	94	81	0.98	–	–	1	0.44
165 Malawi	54.0	72	70.7	86	–	–	26	0.81	(.)	0.41
166 Zambia	59.7	78	66.1	91	68	0.98	21	0.83	2	0.46
167 Congo, Dem. Rep. of the	51.9	65	61.1	80	–	–	–	–	–	–
168 Mozambique	31.4	50	49.2	64	53	0.91	10	0.70	(.)	0.73
169 Burundi	51.9	78	69.5	92	52	0.84	8	0.78	1	0.45
170 Ethiopia	33.8	69	51.8	82	47	0.85	13	0.57	1	0.33
171 Central African Republic	33.5	52	46.8	67	–	–	–	–	1	0.19
172 Guinea-Bissau	–	–	–	–	38	0.71	6	0.55	(.)	0.18
173 Chad	12.7	31	23.1	42	51	0.68	4	0.31	(.)	0.17
174 Mali	11.9	44	16.9	52	39	0.77	–	–	–	–
175 Burkina Faso	8.1	44	14.0	55	31	0.73	7	0.67	1	0.34
176 Sierra Leone	20.5	52	29.9	64	–	–	–	–	1	0.40
177 Niger	9.4	48	14.2	54	31	0.69	5	0.67	1	0.34

SOURCE: "Gender Inequality in Education," *United Nations Human Development Report, 2005,* Table 27, s 147–177. Reprinted by permission of The United Nations.

United Nations observes that "Gender inequality is one of the most powerful brakes on human development. Women's education matters in its own right, but it is also closely associated with child mortality. The under-five mortality rate is more than twice as high for children of illiterate mothers" (UN 2005a: 31).

In Canada, the proportionate number of women with earned university education has increased noticeably over the past decades: "In 2001, 15% of women aged 15 and over had a university degree, up from just 3% in 1971" (Statistics Canada 2006: 15); however, women's representation in advanced graduate degrees remains extremely low, with only 27 percent of all completed doctorates going to women in 2001 (Statistics Canada 2006: 15) and 44 percent going to women by 2008 (Statistics Canada 2011: Table 1). Considering that women have been earning more undergraduate degrees than men in Canada for over a decade now, the drop-off in the rate of completion of advanced degrees for women should give us some pause. Additionally, while some traditionally male-dominated fields are no longer male dominated, women's participation levels in mathematics, engineering, and the physical and applied sciences remain relatively low (Table 7.2).

Table 7.2 **University Degrees, Diplomas, and Certificates Awarded by Field of Study and Gender**

	2005/2006[r]	2006/2007[r]	2007/2008[r]	2008/2009[r]	2007/2008 to 2008/2009
	Number				% Change
Total[1]	**1 050 225**	**1 066 905**	**1 072 488**	**1 112 370**	**3.7**
Male	**443 136**	**449 697**	**455 235**	**471 408**	**3.6**
Female	**606 720**	**616 953**	**617 022**	**640 674**	**3.8**
Personal improvement and leisure[1]	306	213	222	2 892	1 202.7
Male	105	93	102	1 167	1 044.1
Female	201	120	120	1 722	1 335.0
Education[1]	74 052	75 222	75 129	75 492	0.5
Male	17 694	18 018	18 105	18 051	−0.3
Female	56 325	57 171	57 000	57 405	0.7
Visual and performing arts, and communications technologies[1]	37 443	37 830	37 800	41 859	10.7
Male	12 645	12 978	12 993	14 397	10.8
Female	24 798	24 852	24 807	27 462	10.7
Humanities[1]	170 355	170 916	167 664	176 817	5.5
Male	65 910	66 000	65 307	68 436	4.8
Female	104 409	104 892	102 327	108 336	5.9
Social and behavioural sciences, and law[1]	182 010	187 770	189 996	191 016	0.5
Male	63 555	65 316	66 441	66 918	0.7
Female	118 449	122 448	123 549	124 074	0.4

(Continued)

Table 7.2 *University Degrees, Diplomas, and Certificates Awarded by Field of Study and Gender* **(continued)**

	2005/2006[r]	2006/2007[r]	2007/2008[r]	2008/2009[r]	2007/2008 to 2008/2009
		Number			% Change
Business, management and public administrations[1]	168 678	175 428	177 537	189 201	6.6
Male	79 248	82 992	84 333	89 547	6.2
Female	89 391	92 394	93 129	99 612	7.0
Physical and life sciences, and technologies[1]	90 441	92 328	93 372	94 113	0.8
Male	40 245	41 439	42 543	43 191	1.5
Female	50 190	50 880	50 820	50 916	0.2
Mathematics, computer and information sciences[1]	36 636	34 242	32 724	33 219	1.5
Male	26 682	24 912	23 844	24 135	1.2
Female	9 954	9 324	8 874	9 075	2.3
Architecture, engineering and related technologies[1]	85 533	86 313	88 470	91 890	3.9
Male	67 551	68 025	69 912	72 504	3.7
Female	17 979	18 273	18 549	19 383	4.5
Agriculture, natural resources and conservation[1]	15 252	15 708	16 032	17 091	6.6
Male	6 768	6 900	7 029	7 434	5.8
Female	8 481	8 808	9 000	9 654	7.3
Health, parks, recreation and fitness[1]	104 748	109 176	113 157	118 941	5.1
Male	29 469	30 795	32 535	34 113	4.9
Female	75 237	78 336	80 601	84 804	5.2
Personal, protective and transportation services	1 761	2 244	2 217	2 823	27.3
Male	1 038	1 287	1 299	1 554	19.6
Female	720	954	915	1 269	38.7
Other[1]	83 007				

[r]Revised

[1]Includes sex unknown

SOURCE: Statistics Canada, "University enrolment, 2008/2009", *The Daily*, 11-001-XIE, July 14, 2010; http://www.statcan.gc.ca/daily-quotidien/100714/tdq100714-eng.htm.

One explanation for why women earn fewer doctoral degrees than men do is that women are socialized to choose marriage and motherhood over long-term career preparation (Olson et al. 1990). From an early age, women are exposed to images and models of femininity that stress the importance of domestic family life. When 821 undergraduate women were asked to identify their lifestyle preference, fewer than 1 percent selected being unmarried and working full time. In contrast, 53 percent selected "graduation, full-time work, marriage, children, stop working at least until youngest child is in school, then pursue a full-time job" as their preferred lifestyle sequence (Schroeder et al. 1993: 243). Only 6 percent of 535 undergraduate men selected this same pattern. Men do not see a conflict between having children and having a demanding career because they are not expected to be the primary caregivers in the family; if they have promising professional futures, then women are still expected to step aside to provide "support" for their male partners' career development. Additionally, because many professions traditionally coded as "male" will pay more highly to those men who pursue them, individual families will decide that it makes economic sense for the woman to give up her career aspirations to care for children. Whether or not it is accurate to characterize these to be choices freely made or choices constrained by larger socio-economic forces is important for you to assess.

Structural limitations also discourage women from advancing in the educational profession. In 1996, women outnumbered men in elementary and kindergarten teaching positions by approximately four to one and were about equal in number to male teachers at the postsecondary level; however, men as university professors outnumbered them by about two to one (Statistics Canada 1998). Women seeking academic careers may also find that promotion in higher education is more difficult than it is for men. Long and colleagues (1993) examined the promotions of 556 men and 450 women with Ph.D.s in biochemistry. They found that women were less likely to be promoted to associate or full professor, were held to a higher standard than men, and were particularly disadvantaged in more prestigious departments. Throughout Canada, women remain less likely than men are to be full professors (the highest rank), and when employed as full professors women earn less on average than men who are full professors (CAUT 2006).

Income, Work, and Structural Sexism

Worldwide, on average, women earn between 25 and 50 percent of what men earn (Social Watch 2009). When data were first collected in 1967 in Canada on female-to-male earnings, the ratio stood at 58.4 percent. Since that time, it has increased notably. "Earnings have…evolved very differently by gender over the last two decades. They have been stagnant for men, increasing in 2000 for the first time since 1980. In contrast, earnings have increased steadily in each decade for women" (Statistics Canada 2003b). More women are working, and more women are working longer hours. In addition, they are more qualified; since 1980, the proportion of women workers with a university degree has almost tripled, and the proportion of women earners with a university degree now exceeds that of men. However, "[d]espite substantial gains in earnings during the past two decades, women still earn less than men" (Statistics Canada 2003b).

In general, the higher one's education level, the higher one's income. Yet, even when men and women have identical levels of educational achievement and both work full time, women, on the average, earn less than men (Table 7.3). Although women with a university degree earn substantially more than women with lower levels of education, women university graduates who were employed full time all year earned only 68.3 percent as much as their male counterparts in 2008, a drop from 74 percent as

Table 7.3 *Average Annual Earnings of Women and Men, in 2008 Constant Dollars, by Employment Status, 1976 to 2008*

Year	All Earners			Full-Time, Full-Year			Other Workers		
	Women	Men	Earnings Ratio	Women	Men	Earnings Ratio	Women	Men	Earnings Ratio
	Dollars	Dollars	Percentage	Dollars	Dollars	Percentage	Dollars	Dollars	Percentage
1976	21 100	45 100	46.8	34 100	57 300	59.4	12 200	23 400	52.2
1981	22 200	41 700	53.2	33 700	53 000	63.5	12 400	20 300	61.1
1986	23 300	40 700	57.2	34 400	52 500	65.6	13 000	17 800	72.8
1991	24 000	40 000	60.1	36 700	53 400	68.7	11 900	17 200	69.1
1996	25 400	40 000	63.6	38 600	53 000	72.8	13 000	16 800	77.1
1998	26 500	42 300	62.8	40 500	56 300	71.9	13 600	18 700	72.7
2001	27 600	44 400	62.1	40 600	58 100	69.9	15 200	19 400	78.4
2006	29 000	44 800	64.7	43 200	60 000	71.9	14 900	19 200	77.4
2007	29 900	45 500	65.7	44 100	61 700	71.4	15 400	19 300	79.7
2008	30 200	46 900	64.5	44 700	62 600	71.3	15 200	20 000	75.7

SOURCE: Statistics Canada, CANSIM table 202-0102. Statistics Canada Table 7, Average annual earnings of women and men, by employment status, in 2008 dollars, http://www.statcan.gc.ca/pub/89-503-x/2010001/article/11388/tbl/tbl007-eng.htm; Date modified: 2013-05-13.

much as their male counterparts in 1997. Moreover, while gender differences are less pronounced for younger than older women, university-educated women aged 25 to 29 who worked full time all year in 2000 earned 81 cents for every dollar earned by their male counterparts. Among those with only a high school education, women earned 77 cents to the dollar (Table 7.4).

Table 7.4 *Average Annual Earnings of Women and Men Employed Full-Year, Full-Time, by Educational Attainment, 2008*

Level of Education	Women	Men	Earnings Ratio
	Dollars		Percentage
Less than grade 9	20 800	40 400	51.5
Some secondary school	28 600	43 600	65.6
Graduated high school	35 400	50 300	70.4
Some postsecondary	36 400	50 100	72.6
Postsecondary certificate or diploma	41 100	57 700	71.2
University degree	62 800	91 800	68.3
Total	44 700	62 600	71.3

NOTE: Average annual earnings excludes Canadians with no earnings.

SOURCE: Statistics Canada, Table 9, Average annual earnings of women and men employed full-year, full-time, by educational attainment, 2008; Date modified: 2013-05-13; http://www.statcan.gc.ca/pub/89-503-x/2010001/article/11388/tbl/tbl009-eng.htm

Earnings are not the same as wages. Earnings can be increased or decreased in a given time period by working more hours or fewer. Often when we look at earnings gaps between men and women, we find that women's reduced earnings are related to women's reduced working hours. Wage gaps exist where there are actual differences in pay for men and women.

As we see in Table 7.5, the most common occupations held by young women pay less than those that men most commonly pursue, and while the wage gap narrows when women pursue occupations that are most commonly chosen by men, a gap still exists. For example, in 2000, university-educated women aged 25 to 29 who worked in the 10 most common occupations chosen by men of the same age group and qualifications earned about 89 cents for every dollar their male counterparts made (Statistics Canada 2003b). These wage ratios have remained relatively constant throughout the last decade.

The wage gap is widespread and exists in all occupational categories (Table 7.5). For example, even though women in professional and related occupations enjoy considerably higher income than women in other occupational groups, the 2000 earnings ratio for young women and men employed full time all year ranged from just over 80 percent in the sales and marketing category to near parity in elementary teaching, where women earn 98 percent of what men do. The only occupation in which women earn more than men is in social work. Moreover, it is important to keep in mind that what the table shows is that even when men work in fields dominated by women, with the exception of social work, they earn more than the women do.

Tomaskovic-Devey (1993) examined the income differences between males and females and found that the percentage of females in an occupation was the best

Table 7.5 *Average Earnings in the 10 Occupations Most Commonly Held by Those Aged 25 to 29 with a University Degree Working Full-Year, Full Time[1], by Sex, Canada, 2000*

	Number		Average Earnings		Women's Earnings as a % of Men's Earnings
	Men	Women	Men	Women	
Ten occupations most commonly held by young men					
Computer and information systems	17 710	6 450	$54 052	$45 915	84.9
Financial auditors and accountants	4 155	5 280	$42 913	$39 990	93.2
Sales marketing and advertising managers	3 125	3 320	$56 440	$46 047	81.6
Retail trade managers	2 645	2 380	$38 122	$31 596	82.9
Secondary school teachers	2 425	4 120	$36 201	$35 546	98.2
Financial and investment analysts	2 400	1 715	$52 208	$44 864	85.9
Retail salespersons and salesclerks	2 175	1 780	$33 167	$26 211	79.0
Mechanical engineers	2 155	260	$51 341	$50 668	98.7
Sales representatives, wholesale trade (non-technical)	2 000	1 425	$44 528	$41 055	92.2
Electrical and electronics engineers	1 925	325	$59 469	$53 196	89.5
Ten occupations most commonly held by young women					
Elementary school and kindergarten teachers	1 625	9 255	$36 243	$35 535	98.0
Computer and information systems	17 710	6 450	$54 052	$45 915	84.9
Financial auditors and accountants	4 155	5 280	$42 913	$39 990	93.2
Registered nurses	360	4 820	$44 688	$41 088	91.9
Secondary school teachers	2 425	4 120	$36 201	$35 546	98.2
Sales, marketing, and advertising managers	3 125	3 320	$56 440	$46 047	81.6
General office clerks	405	2 525	$30 339	$28 348	93.4
Retail trade managers	2 645	2 380	$38 122	$31 596	82.9
Social workers	430	2 285	$35 011	$36 555	104.4
Customer service information and related clerks	1 015	2 260	$32 664	$31 226	95.6

[1] Earners who worked 49 to 52 weeks during the year for 30 or more hours per week.

SOURCE: Statistics Canada, "Earnings of Canadians: Making a Living in the New Economy, 2001 Census," Analysis Series, 2001 Census, 96F0030XIE2001013, March 2003. http://www.statcan.gc.ca/bsolc/olc-cel/olc-cel?lang=eng&catno=96F0030X2001013.

predictor of an income gender gap—the higher the percentage of females, the lower the pay. Supporting this observation, a team of researchers (Kilbourne et al. 1994) analyzed data from the National Longitudinal Survey that included more than 5000 women and more than 5000 men. They concluded that occupational pay is gendered and that "occupations lose pay if they have a higher percentage of female workers or require nurturant skills" (p. 708).

Many explanations are given for why the gender pay gap exists. One is called the **devaluation hypothesis**. It argues that women are paid less because the work they perform is socially defined as less valuable than the work performed by men. Guy and Newman (2004) argued that these jobs are undervalued in part because they include a significant amount of **emotional labour**: work that involves caring, negotiating, and empathizing with people, all tasks that are rarely specified in job descriptions or performance evaluations. The other hypothesis, the **human capital hypothesis**, argues that female–male pay differences are a function of differences in women's and men's levels of education, skills, training, and work experience. Although these explanations are difficult to test, most researchers agree that there is more support for the devaluation hypothesis than for the human capital hypothesis (England and Li 2006; Padavic and Reskin 2002).

Regardless, the differences in human capital outcomes do correlate with the structural constraints that face families, and women in particular. These constraints include the absence of affordable day-care. Only the province of Quebec has a universal affordable child-care program of $9 per day per child. Ontario, by contrast, is facing scrutiny for its legislative failure to provide enough licensed child-care spots in the province, and for its failure to adopt a universal care system such as the one in Quebec. These failures have resulted in hundreds of unlicensed centres operating throughout the province, some with conditions that are hazardous to the children in them—and, as in the case of the death of 2-year-old Eva Ravikovich in the summer of 2013, they can even be deadly (Monsebratten and Ballingall 2013). Such failures combine with general societal expectations that women should be at home to produce commonly held behaviours reflecting the belief that working full-time is not appropriate for mothers. According to the Pew Research Centre (2007), only 10 percent of stay-at-home mothers felt mothers should work outside the home, and only 11 percent of working mothers felt that full-time work outside the home was "ideal" for children. Meanwhile, the same study showed that 72 percent of men with children under the age of 18 felt that working full-time outside the home was ideal, and only 20 percent of women with children under age 18 agreed that women holding full-time employment would be ideal (ibid).

Comparable worth refers to the belief that individuals in occupations, even in different occupations, should be paid equally if the job requires "comparable" levels of education, training, and responsibility. In Canada, Ontario's *Pay Equity Act* was first passed in 1988, yet by 2008 the act had still failed to address persistent failures to compensate individuals equally for work of equal value. Mary Cornish notes that "Ontario's persistent wage gap shows that many women never received the benefit of the province's legislation and others lost the gains they made initially for various reasons, including employer non-compliance, economic restructuring and inadequate government funding of pay equity adjustments and of the Pay Equity Commission and Hearings Tribunal" (2008: 22).

Even when we consider these flaws in compliance and application of pay equity legislation, things can be worse, and are: most provinces in Canada lack pay equity laws that cover both private and public sector workers; only Ontario and Quebec have pay equity laws to cover both sectors, and some provinces are completely without pay equity laws (Canadian Labour Congress 2010). Moreover, while the average wages

devaluation hypothesis
The hypothesis that argues women are paid less because the work they perform is socially defined as less valuable than the work performed by men.

emotional labour
Work traditionally performed by women in the role of providing care and concern for others, either professionally or in the home.

human capital hypothesis
The hypothesis that female–male pay differences are a function of differences in women's and men's levels of education, skills, training, and work experience.

comparable worth
Tasks and jobs that are distinct but have equal value and utility in the workplace and economy.

for women in full-time work hover around 70.5 percent of earnings for men, women of colour earn only 64 percent, with Aboriginal women earning only 46 percent of what men in full-time, year-round work earn. These increased wage disparities speak to the increased vulnerability of marginalized women in Canada (Canadian Labour Congress 2009).

Although many commonsense objections persist, insisting that women's work is "easier" than men's, and therefore less valuable, the rationale behind the development of pay equity legislation "recognizes that inequality is about more than individuals [or jobs] and their characteristics" (Armstrong 2007) and is instead rooted in "systemic discrimination" (ibid) that consistently devalues the work that women do, whatever it is that they do. Armstrong makes the point that pay equity legislation does not, in fact, provide individual women with benefits they do not deserve, but instead compares the skills, knowledge, and responsibility required to fulfill the duties of a particular job. When we remove the question of who does the job, and instead look at what the job accomplishes, then we can compensate workers appropriately for fulfilling the qualifications and responsibilities of the work itself. Once we can see the actual value of work, it is no longer feasible to pay lower wages in some sectors simply because it is work done primarily by women. For this reason, Ontario's extensive pay equity legislation, even with its imperfect application, "holds valuable lessons for jurisdictions globally" (Singh and Peng 2010: 570).

As further explanation for the persistent wage gap, a study based on data obtained from the Survey of Labour and Income Dynamics also finds that women's lower amount of work experience appears to have a significant bearing on the persistent wage gap between men and women (Statistics Canada 1998). This research reports that about 18 percent, or almost one-fifth, of the wage gap reflected the fact that women generally have less experience than their male counterparts, supervise other employees less often, and are involved in administrative decisions less frequently. Several other factors were also associated with the wage gap. These included differences in job tenure and the fact that men are more likely to graduate from programs leading to higher paying jobs and earnings. Marini and Fan (1997) also found support for the human capital hypothesis, although their research supports a third category of variables as well. They found that organizational variables (characteristics of the business, corporation, or industry) explain, in part, the gender income gap. For example, on career entry, employers channel women and men into sex-specific jobs that carry different wage rates.

In addition, the structure of women's lives in relation to their status as mothers also negatively impacts their lifetime earnings, and thusly also impacts their retirement pensions and other economic resources in a negative manner. The work of raising children, then, accounts for economic losses referred to in the literature as the "**family gap**" or the "**child penalty**." As a means of measuring women's income disparities, this earnings gap measurement assesses the incomes of women who have children against those who do not in the same educational, occupational, and age groups. Social statistician Xuelin Zhang (2009) measured these differences and found that,

> Age–earnings profiles of Canadian mothers and women without children show that women without children earned more than women with children. For example, at age 30, average hourly earnings of women with children were $15.20, compared with $18.10 for women without children (measured in 2004 dollars). On average, the earnings of women with children were 12% lower than those of women without children. And the earnings gap increased with the number of children: with one child, the gap was 9%; with two children, it was 12%; and with three or more children, 20%.

family gap/child penalty
The income losses associated with women's responsibilities for raising children. As a measure, it compares the earnings of women who have children with those who do not in the same age group, with equal educational and occupational attainments.

Work and Structural Sexism

According to the International Labour Organization, by 2008 women comprised 40.4 percent of the total global labour force (ILO 2009). Worldwide, women are overrepresented in agricultural and service sector jobs, and in vulnerable positions as unpaid labourers in family-operated endeavours. For example, as the ILO reports unpaid work on family-owned farms accounts for 85 percent of all Egyptian women's informal employment (ILO 2011a). Women are also more likely to be unemployed than are men. Increasing rates of female unemployment are, in part, a feature of the global economic crisis that began in 2008 and which persists around the world, with particularly negative impacts on women in developing countries (Social Watch 2011). For example, because women are disproportionately employed in the agricultural sector, women experience higher rates of job loss when food exports drop as global food prices rise (ITUC 2009). In short, women tend to work in jobs that have little prestige and low or no pay, where they are the facilitators for others, and where no product is produced; they are also more likely to work in positions with little or no authority, and to receive lower wages than men (WHO 2006; ILO 2009; IPC 2008). Women work 66 percent of the total number of labour hours world-wide, yet receive only 10 percent of the world's income (Foerstel 2008). Table 7.6 gives a global overview of contemporary pay gaps between men and women around the world.

Table 7.6 **Median Gender Pay Gap, 43 Countries, 2009***

	Median Gross Hourly Wage		Median Gender Pay Gap %
	Male	**Female**	
All respondents	20.0	14.8	26.3
With children	23.1	15.7	31.9
Without children	17.3	13.9	19.9
Has full-time hours	20.2	15.3	24.3
Does not have full-time hours	15.2	12.2	19.7

*There may be a slight sample bias in that younger and more educated individuals are more likely to complete an online survey.

SOURCE: ITUC, 2011. "Decisions for Work: An Examination of the Factors Influencing Women's Decisions for Work, 2010." Reprinted with permission.

No matter what the job, if a woman does it the work is likely to be valued less than if a man does it. For example, in the early nineteenth century, 90 percent of all clerks were men, and being a clerk was a prestigious profession. As the job became routine, in part because of the advent of the typewriter, the pay and prestige of the job declined and the number of female clerks increased. Today, female clerks predominate, and the position is one of relatively low pay and low prestige.

The concentration of women in certain occupations and men in other occupations is referred to as **occupational sex segregation**. In Canada, as in other countries with sex-typed work, women tend to be more highly concentrated within fewer occupations while men are more evenly distributed across a larger range of occupations (Table 7.7).

occupational sex segregation
The concentration of women in certain occupations and of men in other occupations.

Table 7.7 *Distribution of Employment by Occupations, 1987, 1999, and 2009*

Occupations[1]	1987			1999			2009		
	Women	Men	Women as a Percentage of Total Occupations	Women	Men	Women as a Percentage of Total Occupations	Women	Men	Women as a Percentage of Total Occupations
	Percentage			Percentage					
Managerial									
Senior management	0.3	0.8	21.0	0.4	0.8	28.2	0.3	0.6	31.6
Other management	5.7	9.7	30.7	6.9	10.6	35.5	6.7	10.4	37.4
Total management	6.0	10.5	30.1	7.2	11.3	35.1	7.0	11.0	37.0
Professional									
Business and finance	1.9	2.3	38.3	3.1	2.7	49.3	3.6	3.2	51.2
Natural sciences/engineering/mathematics	2.3	7.0	19.5	3.0	9.6	20.7	3.3	10.6	22.3
Social sciences/religion	4.3	2.0	61.4	5.8	2.4	67.7	7.7	2.7	72.5
Teaching	3.8	2.6	52.3	5.2	2.7	61.9	5.8	2.7	65.9
Doctors/dentists/other health	0.9	0.9	43.1	1.1	1.0	47.3	1.5	1.1	55.2
Nursing/therapy/other health related	8.3	0.9	87.1	8.1	1.1	86.3	9.1	1.2	87.1
Artistic/literary/recreational	2.7	2.1	48.4	3.4	2.4	54.1	3.7	2.9	54.4
Total professional	24.1	18.0	50.4	29.7	21.9	53.4	34.7	24.4	56.7
Clerical and administrative	29.7	7.9	73.9	24.6	6.8	75.4	23.2	6.9	75.5
Sales and services	30.0	18.4	55.2	29.4	18.6	57.3	28.9	20.1	56.9
Primary	2.3	7.2	19.7	1.9	5.9	21.6	1.3	4.9	19.5
Trades, transport and construction	2.1	28.9	5.2	2.0	26.1	6.0	2.0	26.3	6.4
Processing, manufacturing and utilities	5.8	9.1	32.4	5.2	9.3	32.2	2.9	6.3	30.1
Total occupations[1]	100.0	100.0	43.0	100.0	100.0	45.9	100.0	100.0	47.9
Total employed (thousands)	5 307.7	7 025.3	—	6 609.6	7 797.2	—	8 076.2	8 772.7	—

[1]Includes occupations that are not classified.

SOURCE: Statistics Canada, Labour Force Survey. Table 12, Distribution of employment by occupations, 1987, 1999 and 2009; http://www.statcan.gc.ca/pub/89-503-x/2010001/article/11387/tbl/tbl012-eng.htm; Date modified: 2013-05-13.

In some occupations, sex segregation has decreased in recent years. Data from the 2001 census indicate that women are "making inroads in many 'non-traditional' areas, particularly in highly skilled occupations" (Statistics Canada 2003a: 8). In the 1991–2001 period, women accounted for over one-half of the growth in high-skilled occupations (occupations that normally require a university education). Their numbers doubled in information technology occupations and more than doubled in professional occupations in business and finance. Over the last decade, the number of women managers has increased by more than 40 percent. Despite these and other changes, however, women are still heavily represented in low-prestige, low-wage, **pink-collar jobs** that offer few benefits. A **glass ceiling**—an invisible barrier that prevents women and other minorities from moving into top corporate positions—often victimizes even those women in higher paying jobs. A study of Fortune 500 companies found that women held less than 11 percent of all seats on the Fortune 500 company boards (Klein 1998). Interestingly, Cianni and Romberger's investigation (1997) of visible minority women and men in Fortune 500 companies indicates that gender has more of a role in "organizational treatment" than race.

Sex segregation in occupations continues for several reasons. First, cultural beliefs about what is an appropriate job for a man or a woman still exist. Cejka and Eagley (1999) report that the more undergraduate students believed that an occupation was male or female dominated, the more they attributed success in that occupation to masculine or feminine characteristics. Further, in an examination of gender-role orientations and attitudes toward women as managers, Burke (1994) reports that the men exhibited significantly more negative attitudes toward women as managers than did the women. (He sampled 194 Canadian undergraduate and graduate business students, 71 female and 123 male.) Burke suggests that this finding "augurs badly" for women in at least three ways. As colleagues, these men would be unlikely to endorse initiatives to develop women's careers, or they might actively endorse "backlash" strategies. They are unlikely to provide women with mentorship or sponsorship, and may act as poor role models for other men. Finally, they are unlikely to support the career aspirations of spouses or female partners.

In addition, because of gender socialization, men and women learn different skills and acquire different aspirations. Opportunity structures and expectations for men and women also vary. For example, male employers may exclude women, as may employees who fear the prestige of their profession will be lessened with the entrance of women, or who simply believe that "the ideal worker is normatively masculine" (Martin 1992: 220). Finally, since family responsibilities remain primarily with women, working mothers may feel pressure to choose professions that permit flexible hours and career paths, sometimes known as "mommy tracks." Thus, for example, women dominate the field of elementary education, which permits them to be home when their children are not in school as we see in Table 7.7.

Politics and Structural Sexism

In 1868, when the first Canadian federal general election was held, only men who owned a specified amount of property were allowed to vote; in 1885, the *Electoral Franchise Act* defined a "person" who was eligible to vote as a male who was of other than Mongolian or Chinese origin. While the 1917 *Wartime Election Act* granted wives, sisters, and mothers of servicemen the right to vote, it was not until 1918 that Canadian women won the right to vote in federal elections (Frank 1994). Women over the age of 21 were granted the right to vote in provincial elections in 1916 in Manitoba, Saskatchewan, and Alberta; in 1917 in British Columbia and Ontario; in 1918 in Nova Scotia; in 1919 in New Brunswick; in 1922 in Prince Edward Island; in

pink-collar jobs
Jobs that offer few benefits, often have low prestige, and are disproportionately held by women.

glass ceiling
An invisible, socially created barrier that prevents women and other minorities from being promoted into top corporate positions.

1925 in Newfoundland (where initially this right was limited to women over the age of 25); and in 1940 in Quebec (Whitla 1995: 320–22). These rights were first granted to white women; women from certain other ethnic groups did not receive the franchise until later. For example, Mossman (1998: 181) observes that "prior to 1960, aboriginal women (and men) in Canada were entitled to vote only if they gave up their Indian status, a status defined by the federal *Indian Act*." While an Aboriginal woman became automatically "enfranchised" if she married a white man, "it was only in the 1970s that aboriginal women's claims to equality under the *Indian Act* were tested in the Supreme Court of Canada."

Worldwide, the percentage of legislative seats held by women ranges from 30 to 40 percent in Scandinavian countries to less than 1 percent in several Middle Eastern and African countries (Kenworthy and Malami 1999). Further, women hold no more than 8 percent of ministerial positions in any developing country (World Bank 2001: 5). In response to the underrepresentation of women in the political arena, some countries have institutionalized quotas. In India, a 1993 amendment held one-third of all seats in local contests for women. The result? Eight hundred thousand women were elected. A 1996 law in Britain requires a minimum of 20 percent of each party's candidates to be women. Countries with similar policies include Finland, Germany, Mexico, South Africa, and Spain (Sheehan 2000).

There are some signs that Canada is on the road to achieving gender equality in politics. For example, in June 1993, Kim Campbell was elected Progressive Conservative Party leader and, by ascension shortly after, became Canada's first female prime minister (for an admittedly limited term of less than six months). Some years earlier, in December 1989, the election of Audrey McLaughlin as leader of the New Democratic Party (NDP) signalled the first time a Canadian woman had been elected as the leader of a national political party.

Nevertheless, in general, the more important the political office, the lower the probability a woman will hold it. Running for office requires large sums of money, the political backing of powerful individuals and interest groups, and a willingness of the voting public to elect women. Hunter and Denton (1984) note that Canadian political parties have shown a marked tendency to nominate women only after they have suffered losses at the polls or to nominate women in "lost cause" ridings where another party enjoys overwhelming voter support. It is then political party elites that hamper women "in securing nominations in the first place, and beyond this, in gaining nominations which carry a reasonable prospect of victory" (Stark 1992: 454). Minority women have even greater structural barriers to election and, not surprisingly, represent an even smaller percentage of elected officials.

Consider, for example, that while Mary Ellen Smith became, in 1918, the first woman to be elected to the Legislative Assembly in British Columbia and the first woman in the British Empire to serve as a cabinet minister, it was not until 1972 that a black woman, Rosemary Brown, won a seat in that province. Brown was the first black woman elected to any Canadian legislature. In 1991, Zanana Akande was the first black woman to be elected to the Ontario legislature. She was also the first black woman to become a cabinet minister in that province (Mandell 1995: 347).

Human Rights and Structural Sexism

The status of women in Canada was addressed by the 1970 Report of the Royal Commission on the Status of Women. The Report directed many of its recommendations to legislative reforms in the areas of the criminal law, tax and child care allowances, social assistance, immigration, and family law. The principle guiding the recommendations was that, as citizens, men and women ought to share the same rights and freedoms, have equal opportunities to exercise those rights, and be equally able to fulfill their duties as citizens. However, while advocating that men and women should be treated identically, the Report acknowledged that, on occasion, equality might demand or necessitate "special" or "different treatment" of women. For example, because women can become pregnant, the "special needs" created by pregnancy might demand acknowledgment of difference (e.g., maternity leave), or a shift from "equality of treatment" (formal equality) to "equality of outcome" (substantive equality).

In various ways, Canadian laws have not always benefited men and women in equal fashion. Consider, for example, that until 1983 most women were unable to claim pregnancy benefits under the old *Unemployment Insurance Act* (Atcheson et al. 1984: 20–21); that until 1983, husbands who raped their wives were exempt from criminal proceedings; and that before 1989, women could be fired from their jobs simply for being pregnant. Consider as well that while courts have permitted "businessmen to deduct club fees because men like to conduct business with each other over golf," have held the purchase of a Rolls-Royce "to be an incident of a professional expense" (because it enhances professional image), and have sustained claims that "making charitable contributions to enhance one's reputation in a community inheres in the business of manufacturing boxes" (Macklin 1992), Canada's *Income Tax Act* does not regard the cost of child care as a legitimate business deduction.

Attempts to "de-gender" the law have not always proven fully effective. For example, in the case of *Murdoch v. Murdoch*, Irene Murdoch claimed that, based on her contribution of money and labour during 25 years of marriage, she was entitled to half of the property owned by her husband when they divorced.

Her tasks while married had included "haying, raking, swathing, mowing, driving trucks and tractors and teams, quieting horses, taking cattle back and forth to the reserve, dehorning, vaccinating, branding, anything that was to be done…just as a man would" (Dranoff in Mossman 1998: 187). The Supreme Court of Canada's denial of Mrs. Murdoch's claim generated activism by groups concerned with women's rights. By 1980, every Canadian province, with the exception of Quebec, had enacted legislation amending the arrangements for the distribution of property between spouses at the time of separation or divorce.

Although the notion of "equal treatment" sounds fair, does treating those who are unalike the same result in equality? Mossman (1998: 187) observes, "With the benefit of hindsight, many feminists now recognize that the reform legislation in common law provinces was fundamentally flawed, since it assumed that men and women had equal access to economic self-sufficiency." In most cases, women become the custodial parents of dependent children when marriage breaks down. The constraints on full-time employment posed by the parental role, coupled with the wage gap, may continue to create substantive hardship for women upon divorce.

7.4 The Social Construction of Gender Roles: Cultural Sexism

Structural sexism is supported by a system of **cultural sexism** that perpetuates beliefs about the differences between women and men. Cultural sexism refers to the ways in which the culture of society—its norms, values, beliefs, and symbols—perpetuates the subordination of an individual or group because of the sex classification of that individual or group.

For example, the *belief* that females are less valuable than males has serious consequences. One study in Bombay, India, found that of 8000 abortions performed after amniocentesis, 7900 were of female fetuses (Anderson and Moore 1998). Cultural

cultural sexism
The ways in which the culture of society perpetuates the subordination of individuals based on their sex classification.

sexism takes place in a variety of settings, including the family, the school, and the media, as well as in everyday interactions.

Family Relations and Cultural Sexism

From birth, males and females are treated differently. For example, the toys male and female children receive convey different messages about appropriate gender roles. Toy manufacturer Mattel had to recall the Barbie doll who spoke, only to say "Math is hard!" and "Let's go shopping!" The company also faced opposition after producing a pink, flowered Barbie computer for girls and a blue Hot Wheels computer for boys. The social significance of the gender-specific computers and the public criticism arose after it was revealed that the accompanying software packages were different—the boys' package had more educational titles (Bannon 2000).

Household Division of Labour

Girls and boys work in the home in about equal amounts until the age of 18, when the female to male ratio begins to change (Robinson and Bianchi 1997: 4). In a study of household labour in 10 Western countries, Bittman and Wajcman (2000) report that "women continue to be responsible for the majority of hours of unpaid labour" ranging from a low of 70 percent in Sweden to a high of 88 percent in Italy (p. 173). The fact that women, even when working full time, contribute significantly more hours to home care than men is known as the "second shift" (Hochschild 1989). The 2001 census, the second census to include questions on unpaid work, found that women "still had the lion's share of the number of hours devoted to unpaid household work" (Statistics Canada 2003a: 17). Approximately 21 percent of women—but only 8 percent of men—devoted 30 hours or more to unpaid household work during the week prior to the census. While 13.3 percent of men reported that they did not do any hours of unpaid household work, only 7.5 percent of women reported likewise (see Table 7.8).

Table 7.8 **Percentage of Persons Aged 15 and Over, by Number of Unpaid Hours Doing Housework, Canada, 2001***

Women	
No hours	7.5
Fewer than 5 hours	17.4
5 to 14 hours	29.7
15 to 29 hours	23.9
30 or more hours	21.4
Men	
No hours	13.3
Fewer than 5 hours	30.0
5 to 14 hours	33.5
15 to 29 hours	15.4
30 or more hours	7.8

*Refers to the week preceding Census day.

SOURCE: Adapted from Statistics Canada. 2003. *2001 Census: Analysis Series.* "The Changing Profile of Canada's Labour Force." Catalogue no. 96F0030XIE2001009 (released February 11, 2003), p. 36.

Three explanations for the continued traditional division of labour emerge from the literature. The first explanation is the "time-availability approach." Consistent with the structural-functionalist perspective, this position emphasizes that role performance is a function of who has the time to accomplish certain tasks. Because women are more likely to be at home, they are more likely to perform domestic chores.

A second explanation is the "relative resources approach." This explanation, consistent with a conflict perspective, suggests that the spouse with the least power is left the most unrewarding tasks. Since men often have more education, higher incomes, and more prestigious occupations, they are less responsible for domestic labour.

"Gender role ideology," the final explanation, is consistent with a symbolic interactionist perspective. It argues that the division of labour is a consequence of traditional socialization and the accompanying attitudes and beliefs. Females and males have been socialized to perform various roles and to expect their partners to perform other complementary roles. Women typically take care of the house, men the yard. This division of labour is learned in the socialization process through the media, schools, books, and toys. A recent test of the three positions found that although all three had some support, gender role ideology was the weakest of the three in predicting work allocation (Bianchi et al. 2000). This chapter's *Social Problems Research Up Close* feature examines the influence of gender ideology on the valuation of work performed by adult family members.

Social Problems *Research Up Close*

Family, Gender Ideology, and Social Change

One of the most important questions concerning gender is the extent to which gender ideologies affect family roles. An investigation by Zuo and Tang (2000) addresses this issue by focusing on two research questions: (1) Are men less likely than women to believe in the equality of roles? and (2) Is the male "breadwinner" status predictive of beliefs about gender ideology?

Sample and Methods

Data for this investigation came from a randomly selected national U.S. sample of married persons collected by the Bureau of Sociological Research at the University of Nebraska. As part of a larger longitudinal study, respondents (N = 400 married men and 640 married women) were interviewed in 1980, 1983, and 1992. All were between the ages of 18 and 55, 95 percent were white, and 67 percent had 1992 annual incomes between $25 000 and $45 000. The proportion of a husband's income to the total family income measured the independent variable, breadwinner status. For example, a husband who provided 90 percent of the total family income received a higher score than a husband who provided 50 percent of the total family income. The

higher a respondent's score, the higher the breadwinner status and the lower the breadwinner status of their spouse. Gender ideology, the dependent variable, was measured by the extent to which a respondent agreed or disagreed with statements concerning (1) the wife's economic role (e.g., "a woman should not be employed if jobs are scarce"), (2) the provider role (e.g., "a husband should be the main breadwinner even if his wife works"), and (3) the woman's maternal role (e.g., "a woman's most important task in life is being a mother"). In combination, these three variables indicated the extent to which respondents adhered to a traditional or an egalitarian (equal partners) gender ideology.

Findings and Conclusions

The results signify that over the years studied, both men and women have shifted toward a more egalitarian gender role ideology. The shift, however, is greater for women than for men. One notable exception is in reference to beliefs about a woman's maternal role. Here, men held more egalitarian beliefs than women. The authors caution, however, that this result does not necessarily indicate that women hold more traditional

(continued)

beliefs about motherhood than men. It may be, for example, that women's stress over the lack of child-care facilities outside of the home is responsible for gender differences on this indicator.

Results also indicate that the higher a husband's breadwinner status, that is, the more he contributes to household finances, the more likely he is to hold traditional gender beliefs. Conversely, the lower a husband's breadwinner status, the more likely he is to hold egalitarian gender beliefs. Similarly, the higher a wife's breadwinner status, that is, the more she contributes to household finances, the more likely she is to hold egalitarian beliefs; the lower her breadwinner status, the more likely she is to hold traditional beliefs.

The authors conclude that the results of their study support what is called the benefits hypothesis. The benefits hypothesis holds that men whose wives earn high wages, that is, men who have lower breadwinner statuses, are likely to embrace rather than be threatened by role equality. Given the empirical support for this hypothesis, the authors predict a continued narrowing in male–female differences in gender role ideology:

> The present trend is that men's breadwinner status continues to decline; more and more individuals perform non-gendered family roles. Based on these facts, it may be predicted that the movement toward egalitarianism for both men and women will continue and a further decrease in the gender gap in gender ideology is down the road. (2000: 36)

SOURCE: Zuo, Jiping, and Shengming Tang. 2000. "Breadwinner Status and Gender Ideologies of Men and Women Regarding Family Roles." *Sociological Perspectives* 43: 29–44.

The School Experience and Cultural Sexism

Sexism is also evident in the schools. It can be found in the books students read, the curricula and tests they are exposed to, and the different ways teachers interact with students.

Textbooks

The bulk of research on gender images in textbooks and other instructional materials documents the way males and females are portrayed stereotypically. For example, Purcell and Stewart (1990) analyzed 1883 storybooks used in schools and found that they tended to depict males as clever, brave, adventurous, and income producing, and females as passive and victimized. Females were more likely to be in need of rescue and were also depicted in fewer occupational roles than males. Witt (1996), in a study of third-grade textbooks from six publishers, reports that little girls were more likely to be portrayed as having both traditionally masculine and feminine traits whereas little boys were more likely pictured as having the masculine characteristics only. These results are consistent with research that suggests that boys are much less free to explore gender differences than females, and with Purcell and Stewart's conclusion that boys are often depicted as having "to deny their feelings to show their manhood" (1990: 184). Although some evidence suggests that male and female textbook characters are increasingly portrayed as equal, portrayals largely remain stereotypical (Evans and Davies 2000).

Teacher–Student Interactions

Sexism is also reflected in the way teachers treat their students. After interviewing 800 adolescents, parents, and teachers in three school districts in Kenya, Mensch and Lloyd (1997) report that teachers were more likely to describe girls as lazy and unintelligent. "And when the girls do badly," the researchers remark, "it undoubtedly reinforces teachers' prejudices, becoming a vicious cycle." Similarly, in the United States, Sadker and Sadker (1990) observed that elementary-school and secondary-school teachers pay more attention to boys than to girls. Teachers talk to boys more, ask them more questions, listen to them more, counsel them more, give them more extended directions, and criticize and reward them more frequently. However, in *The War against Boys,* philosopher Christina Sommers (2000) argues that boys, not girls, are "on the weak side of the educational gender gap" (p. 14). Noting that boys are at a higher risk for learning disabilities and lag behind in reading and writing scores, Sommers argues that the belief about females being educationally shortchanged is untrue (see Chapter 12).

Do the differing expectations and levels of encouragement that females and males receive relate to their varying abilities, as measured by standardized tests, in such disciplines as math and science? In an experiment at the University of Waterloo, male and female university students, all of whom said they were good in math, were shown either a gender-stereotyped or a gender-neutral advertisement. When female students who had seen the female-stereotyped advertisement took a math test, they performed not only lower than women who had seen the gender-neutral advertisements, but lower than their male counterparts (Begley 2000). Research also indicates that standardized tests themselves are biased: they are almost exclusively timed, multiple-choice tests—a format that, some argue, favours males (Smolken 2000).

Media, Language, and Cultural Sexism

One concern voiced by social scientists in reference to cultural sexism is the extent to which the media portrays females and males in a limited and stereotypical fashion, and the impact of such portrayals.

Signorielli (1998) analyzed gender images presented in six media: television, movies, magazines, music videos, TV commercials, and print media advertisements. The specific items selected from each medium were those most often consumed by 12- to 17-year-old girls, for example, the 25 most-watched television shows. The results indicate the following:

- In general, media content stresses the importance of appearance and relationships for girls/women and of careers and work for boys/men.*
- Across the six media, 26 to 46 percent of women are portrayed as "thin or very thin" in contrast to 4 to 16 percent of men; 70 percent of girls wanted to look like, fix their hair like, or dress like a character on television, compared with 40 percent of boys.
- In a survey of boys and girls, both agreed that "worrying about weight, crying or whining, weakness, and flirting" are characteristics associated more with girls than with boys and that "playing sports, being a leader, and wanting to kiss or have sex" are more often characteristic of male characters.

Like media images, the words we use and the ways we use them reflect gender inequality. The term *nurse* carries the meaning of "a woman who…" and the term *engineer* suggests "a man who…." The words "broad," "old maid," and "spinster" have no male counterpart. Language is so gender stereotyped that the placement of the word "male" or "female" before titles is sometimes necessary, as in the case of "female police officer" or "male prostitute." Further, as symbolic interactionists note, the embedded meanings of words carry expectations of behaviour.

Virginia Sapiro (1994) has shown how male–female differences in communication style reflect the structure of power and authority relations between men and women. For example, women are more likely to use disclaimers ("I could be wrong but…") and self-qualifying tags ("That was a good movie, wasn't it?"). They reflect less

* Signorielli 1998

certainty about their opinions. Communication differences between women and men also reflect different socialization experiences. Women are more often passive and polite in conversation; men are less polite, interrupting more often and talking more (Tannen 1990).

7.5 Social Problems and Traditional Gender Role Socialization

Cultural sexism, transmitted through the family, school, media, and language, perpetuates traditional gender role socialization. Gender roles, however slowly, are changing. As one commentator observed (Fitzpatrick 2000: 1), "the hard lines that once helped to define masculine [and feminine] identity are blurring. Women serve in the military, play pro basketball, run corporations, and govern. Men diet, undergo cosmetic surgery, bare their souls in support groups and cook." Despite this "**gender tourism**" (Fitzpatrick 2000), most research indicates that traditional gender roles remain dominant, particularly for males who, in general, have less freedom to explore the gender continuum. Social problems that result from traditional gender socialization include the feminization of poverty, social-psychological and health costs, and conflict in relationships.

The Feminization of Poverty

Globally, the percentage of female households is increasing dramatically, with approximately 25 percent of all households in Africa, North America, the Caribbean, and parts of Europe headed by women (Population Reference Bureau 1999). Often living in poverty, many of these households are headed by young women with dependent children and older women who have outlived their spouses. More than 900 million women, worldwide, live on less than $1 a day (United Nations 2000b).

In addition to individual and institutional discrimination, traditional gender-role socialization contributes to poverty among women. Women learn to put family ahead of their education and careers. Women are expected to take primary responsibility for child care, which contributes to the alarming rate of female-headed, lone-parent families in Canada. In 1997, when compared to children in two-parent families, children in female-headed, lone-parent families were almost five times more likely to be in a low-income situation. In that year, more than half of non-elderly females (56 percent) lived below the poverty line. That means they spent more than 54.7 percent of their income on food, shelter, and clothing (Statistics Canada 1999).

Social-Psychological Costs

How shall we best understand gender differences in morbidity and mortality? Although both biological and social factors play a role, social factors may be dominant. As part of masculine gender performance, men tend to engage in more risky behaviours—heavy drinking and smoking, poor diet, lack of exercise, stress-related activities, higher drug use, and a refusal to ask for help. Men are also more likely to work in hazardous occupations than women. For example, men are more likely to be miners than women—an occupation with one of the highest mortality rates in Canada. Women's higher rates of depression are also likely to be rooted in traditional gender roles. The heavy burden of child care and household responsibilities, the gender gap and the occupation gap, and fewer socially acceptable reactions to stress—for example, it is more acceptable for males to drink alcohol than for females—contribute to gender differences in depression (Klein 1997).

gender tourism
The recent tendency for definitions of masculinity and femininity to become less clear, resulting in individual exploration of the gender continuum.

Many of the costs of traditional gender socialization are social-psychological in character. Reid and Comas-Diaz (1990) noted that the cultural subordination of women results in women having low self-esteem and being dissatisfied with their roles as spouses, homemakers or workers, mothers, and friends. In a study of self-esteem among more than 1160 students in grades 6 through 10, girls were significantly more likely to have "steadily decreasing self-esteem," whereas boys were more likely to fall into the "moderate and rising" self-esteem group (Zimmerman et al. 1997).

Not all research concludes that women have more negative self-concepts than men do. Summarizing their cross-cultural research on women and men, Williams and Best (1990) found "no evidence of an appreciable difference" in self-concepts (p. 153). They also found no consistency in the self-concepts of women and men in 14 countries: "[I]n some of the countries the men's perceived self was noticeably more favourable than the women's, whereas in others the reverse was found" (p. 152). Research shows that women are becoming more assertive and desirous of controlling their own lives rather than merely responding to the wishes of others or the limitations of the social structure (Burger and Solano 1994).

Men also suffer from traditional gender socialization. Men experience enormous cultural pressure to succeed in their work and earn high incomes. Research indicates that men with higher incomes feel more "masculine" (Rubenstein 1990). Traditional male socialization also discourages males from expressing emotion—part of what Pollock (2000a) calls the "boy code."

On the average, men in Canada die earlier than women, although gender differences in life expectancy have been shrinking (Statistics Canada 2001). Traditional male gender socialization is linked to males' higher rates of heart disease, cirrhosis of the liver, most cancers, AIDS, homicide, drug- and alcohol-induced deaths, suicide, and firearm and motor vehicle accidents (Wilkins 1996). Females, however, after the age of 15, are twice as likely to suffer from depression as males (Kalb 2000) and much more likely to suffer from anorexia or bulimia. Seven million women and girls suffer from eating disorders (Wilmot 1999).

Conflict in Relationships

Gender inequality also has an impact on relationships. For example, negotiating work and home life can be a source of relationship problems. While men in traditional versus dual-income relationships are more likely to report being satisfied with household task arrangements, women in dual-income families are the most likely to be dissatisfied with household task arrangements (Baker et al. 1996). Further, the belief that one's partner is not doing a fair amount of the housework is associated with a perception of lower spousal social support (Van Willigen and Drentea 1997).

We must consider the practical difficulties of raising families, having careers, and maintaining a happy and healthy relationship with a partner. Successfully balancing work, marriage, and children may require a number of strategies, including a mutually satisfying distribution of household labour, rejection of such stereotypical roles as "supermom" and "breadwinner dad," seeking outside help from others (e.g., child care givers, domestic workers), and a strong commitment to the family unit.

Finally, violence in intimate relationships is gendered (see Chapters 4 and 5). Although men are more likely to be victims of violent crime, women are more likely to be victims of sexual assault and domestic violence that results in physical harm. Violence against women reflects male socialization that emphasizes aggression and dominance over women. Male violence is a consequence of gender socialization and a definition of masculinity which holds that "as long as nobody is seriously hurt, no lethal weapons are employed, and especially within the framework of sports and games—football, soccer, boxing, wrestling—aggression and violence are widely accepted and even encouraged in boys" (Pollock 2000b: 40).

7.6 Strategies for Action: Toward Gender Equality

Efforts to achieve gender equality have been largely fuelled by the feminist movement. Despite a conservative backlash, feminists, and to a lesser extent men's activist groups, have made some gains in reducing structural and cultural sexism in the workplace and in the political arena.

Grassroots Developments

Feminism

Feminism is the belief that women and men should have equal rights and responsibilities. However, in its early incarnation, the suffrage movement in Canada, or the "first wave" of feminism, "was less a 'woman's movement' than an attempt on the part of particular men and women, predominantly urban professionals and entrepreneurs, to supervise [the moral development of] society" (Bacchi 1983: 13). First at the local level, and later at the national and provincial levels, thousands of upper- and middle-class women sought to ameliorate a host of social ills. They became active in the temperance movement; in campaigns for religious instruction, better workplace conditions, improvements in public health and child welfare; and in the development of living facilities for single women. Women's early activism in these areas was often linked to "women's auxiliaries, institutes and missionary societies to spread the word of God" (Errington 1993: 73). Established by Christian churches, these groups advanced as the philanthropic extension of women's "natural" expertise as wives, mothers, and "guardians" of moral virtue.

In 1876, Dr. Emily Howard Stowe founded the Toronto Women's Literary Club, an organization that "in 1883 ... took a name more revealing of its politics: the Toronto Women's Suffrage Association" (Adamson et al. 1988: 33). Stowe's organization launched a campaign to demand the franchise for women at every political level and for women's rights to education and entrance into the prestigious occupations. However, when compared to their counterparts in the United States and England, early Canadian feminists were more likely to engage in a war of words than in firebrand tactics.

In the decades between the first and second waves of the feminist movement, the position of women did improve in Canadian society. Moreover, as Wine and Ristock (1991: 1) have suggested, "[p]erhaps the most impressive impact of the [women's] movement is the massive shift in the consciousness of the Canadian public in terms of affirmation of women's right to equality, including reproductive freedom, equal treatment in the workplace, and freedom from violence." However, it has been acknowledged that the second wave of the women's movement did not always or consistently recognize, include, or champion the needs of all Canadian women equally. For example, women with disabilities often found their needs excluded or marginalized (Driedger 1993). Similarly, Wine and Ristock (1991: 13) have observed that "though women's organizations provided some support,... [t]he activist work of Native women to change section 12(b) of the *Indian Act*, and its denial of treaty rights to Native women who married non-Native men...[was a] battle fought almost entirely by Native women." As Cassidy and colleagues (1998: 26) acknowledge in their discussion of "silenced and forgotten women"—First Nations women, black women, immigrant women, women with disabilities, and poor women—only recently has the second wave of the women's movement "begun to address criticisms that white, middle-class feminists have denied, dismissed, and denigrated the experiences of differently raced, abled, and classed women."

The Men's Movement

As a consequence of the women's rights movement, men began to re-evaluate their own gender status. In *Unlocking the Iron Cage*, Michael Schwalbe (1996) examines the men's movement as both participant and researcher. For three years, he attended meetings and interviewed active members. His research indicates that participants, in general, are white middle-class men who feel they have little emotional support, who question relationships with their fathers and sons, and who are overburdened by responsibilities, unsatisfactory careers, and what is perceived as an overly competitive society.

As with any grassroots movement, several factions co-exist in the men's movement. Some men's organizations advocate gender equality; others developed to oppose "feminism" and what was perceived as male bashing. For example, the Promise Keepers are part of a Christian men's movement that has often been criticized as racially intolerant, patriarchal, and antifeminist. However, one female researcher and author who attended meetings incognito as a man reports: "I'm struck with how close it all sounds like feminism" (Leo 1997).

Today, issues of custody and fathers' rights headline the men's rights movement and have led to increased visibility (Goldberg 1997). Many members of such groups argue that society portrays men as disposable, and that as fathers and husbands, workers and soldiers, they feel that they can be replaced by other men willing to do what they do. They also hold that there is nothing male affirming in society and that the social reforms of the last 30 years have "been the deliberate degradation and disempowerment of men economically, legally and socially" (NCFM 1998: 7). Still other men's advocates focus less on men's rights and more on personal growth, advocating "the restoration of earlier versions of masculinity" (Cohen 2001: 393).

Public Policy

The introduction of policy changes and programs designed to eliminate gender inequality has not been without controversy. Here, we direct attention to sexual harassment and employment equity and note some of the debates these issues have inspired in recent years.

Sexual Harassment

Canadian case law has recognized that sexual harassment is a multifaceted phenomenon that may include sexual assault; unwanted touching or patting; leering and sexually suggestive gestures; demands for sexual favours; derogatory or degrading remarks; repeated and unwelcome sexual flirtations, advances, or propositions; the use of sexually degrading words to describe a person; sexist jokes that cause embarrassment; and displaying sexually offensive material. The Law Society of Canada notes that "[w]hether a particular type of conduct constitutes sexual harassment is sometimes difficult to determine" and that although "the severity of the conduct may be the most conclusive factor…what is determinative is a combination of frequency, severity and persistence" (in Mossman 1997: 244). In 1998, complaints of sexual harassment accounted for one-fifth of new complaints brought to the Canadian Human Rights Commission (Dranoff 2001: 73).

There are two types of **sexual harassment**: (1) *quid pro quo*, in which an employer requires sexual favours in exchange for a promotion, salary increase, or any other

sexual harassment
When an employer requires sexual favours in exchange for a promotion, salary increase, or any other employee benefit, or the existence of a hostile environment that unreasonably interferes with job performance, as in the case of sexually explicit remarks or insults being made to an employee.

employee benefit, and (2) the existence of a hostile environment that unreasonably interferes with job performance, as in the case of sexually explicit comments or insults being made to an employee. Sexual harassment occurs at all occupational levels, and some research suggests that the number of incidents of sexual harassment is inversely proportional to the number of women in an occupational category (Fitzgerald and Shullman 1993). Female doctors (Schneider and Phillips 1997) and lawyers (Rosenberg et al. 1997) report high rates of sexual harassment, in the first case by male patients and in the second by male colleagues. Sexual harassment is also a worldwide phenomenon. For example, 70 percent of female government employees in Japan report being sexually harassed at work (Yamaguchi 2000). Finally, sexual harassment is not exclusively a "women's problem." Research suggests that approximately 15 percent of men are subject to it (Henslin and Nelson 1997).

Employment Equity

employment equity
An attempt to ensure that there is a proportional number of designated target groups (e.g., women, visible minorities, Aboriginal peoples, and people with disabilities) throughout all income and occupational levels at ratios that are consistent with the proportion of these groups within the local or regional workforce.

The passage of the *Canadian Human Rights Act* in 1977 provided the legal foundation for **employment equity**. Section 16(1) of the *Canadian Human Rights Act* asserts that it is not a discriminatory practice to adopt or carry out a special program, plan, or arrangement designed to prevent, eliminate, or reduce disadvantages suffered by persons or groups because of race, national or ethnic origin, skin colour, religion, age, sex, family status, marital status, or disability by improving their opportunities in respect to goods, services, facilities, accommodations, or employment. Thus, the act implicitly asserts that employment equity does not constitute reverse discrimination. Rather, under the terms of reference of the Canadian Human Rights Commission, charged with administering the act, an employment equity program may be required as part of the settlement of a complaint of discrimination, as a strategic attempt to forestall the future recurrence of discriminatory practices.

The federal *Employment Equity Act* (1985) required the federal public service, federally regulated companies (e.g., banks and Crown corporations), and all private-sector employers with 100 or more employees that did over $200 000 worth of business with the federal government to have employment equity plans and to ensure that their procedures for hiring, firing, promotion, and training were equitable to all groups. The goal was to redress discrimination against women, visible minorities, people with disabilities, and First Nations people. However, the only penalties that could be imposed were for the organization's failure to file yearly progress reports. In 1996, legislative changes to the act made it practically potent. For example, the disadvantaged groups to be protected under this legislation were more precisely defined. Employers were required to identify and eliminate barriers to employment, implement positive policies and practices, prepare a plan defining short-term (under three years) and long-term goals, and establish a timetable for the implementation of these plans. The act is now enforced by the Canadian Human Rights Commission. The Commission has the authority to conduct compliance audits to ensure that "numerical goals (not quotas) are met, to hold tribunals and to levy fines of up to $50 000 for noncompliance with the law" (Dranoff 2001: 57).

Opponents of employment equity argue that, despite the good intentions of its creators, employment equity will not quell discrimination, may well lead us back to the degrading colour/racial/gender consciousness of the past, and may latently function to create resentment of and hostility toward those groups that it seeks to help. Consider, for example, that in August 1999, academics from across Canada wrote letters to officials at Wilfrid Laurier University to protest a job posting for a psychology professor: the posting specified that only women would be considered. "Obviously, at Laurier the commitment to...fairness and the pursuit of academic excellence takes a back seat to social goals like achieving a gender balance in departments. This bodes...ill for your institution, which has gone down in my estimation, as I'm sure it has in that of many academics," read one letter received by the institution. The gender-specific job posting was described by the chairperson of the psychology department at Laurier as an attempt to "address a gender imbalance" in the psychology department at that university; at the time of the posting, in the department 18 professors were men and only 4 were women.

Academics protesting the job posting also submitted numerous queries to the Ontario Human Rights Commission, questioning the university's use of section 14 of the *Ontario Human Rights Code*. The Code stipulates that a special program may be implemented as long as it does not infringe on other rights—such as freedom from discrimination—and "is designed to relieve hardship or economic disadvantage." Although they conceded that women have suffered job discrimination at universities in the past, critics of the gender-specific posting argued that women academics were "hardly a disadvantaged group" (*National Post* 1999: A4).

International Efforts

The Convention to Eliminate All Forms of Discrimination Against Women (CEDAW), also known as the International Women's Bill of Rights, was adopted by the United Nations in 1979. CEDAW establishes rights for women not previously recognized internationally in a variety of areas, including education, politics, work, law, and family life. Over 166 countries have ratified the treaty, including every country in the Western Hemisphere and every industrialized nation in the world but for Switzerland and the United States (Rabin 2000; United Nations 2000a).

In addition to many other global efforts, individual countries have instituted programs or policies designed to combat sexism and gender inequality. For example, Japan has implemented the Basic Law for a Gender-Equal Society, a "blueprint for gender equality in the home and workplace" (Yumiko 2000: 41). The South African Bill of Rights prohibits discrimination on the basis of, among other things, gender, pregnancy, and marital status (IWRP 2000), and China has established a Programme for the Development of Chinese Women, which focuses on empowering women in the areas of education, human rights, health, child care, employment, and political power (*WIN News* 2000).

Understanding Gender Inequality

Gender roles and the social inequality they create are ingrained in our social and cultural ideologies and institutions, and are, therefore, difficult to alter. For example, in almost all societies, women are primarily responsible for child care and men for military service and national defence (World Bank 2001). Nevertheless, as we have seen in this chapter, growing attention to gender issues in social life has spurred some change. Women, traditionally expected to give domestic life first priority, are now finding it acceptable to be more ambitious in seeking a career outside the home. Men, traditionally expected to be aggressive and task oriented, are now expected to be more caring and nurturing. Women seem to value gender equality more than men do, however, perhaps because women have more to gain. For instance, 84 percent of 600 adult women said that the ideal man is caring and nurturing; only 52 percent of 601 adult men said that the ideal woman is ambitious (Rubenstein 1990: 160).

Men also have much to gain by gender equality, though. Eliminating gender stereotypes and redefining gender in terms of equality does not mean liberating only women, but liberating men and our society as well. "What we have been talking about is allowing people to be more fully human and creating a society that will reflect that humanity. Surely that is a goal worth striving for" (Basow 1992: 359). Regardless of whether traditional gender roles emerged out of biological necessity, as the functionalists argue, or out of economic oppression, as the conflict theorists hold, or both, it is clear today that gender inequality carries a high price: poverty, loss of human capital, feelings of worthlessness, violence, physical and mental illness, and death. Surely, the costs are too high to keep paying.

Student Reflection: What Do You Know Now?

As a measure of your own changed—or reinforced—thinking, consider again the final question posed at the beginning of the chapter in "What do you already know?" Imagine a world in which gender inequality is solved: what have you done and what might you do to make this more achievable? Given the different perspectives you've just encountered on gender-based oppression and its relationship to larger problems of inequality globally, is your answer any different? Now think about your own cultural background. To what extent do cultural factors and structural factors intertwine when you consider a question like "why is it more acceptable for women to do traditionally male work roles than for men to take on traditionally female work roles?"

What Do You Do Next?

Located at www.nelson.com/socialproblems5e

- Consolidate your knowledge with interactive and printable **Flashcards**
- Gauge your understanding with **Practice Quizzes** and **Matching Activities**
- Develop your critical thinking skills with **Self and Society** and **The Human Side** questions
- Analyze **Social Research** and **Social Problems in Global Perspective**
- Explore the implications of **Technology on Social Problems**

Student Reflection:
What Do You Already Know?

If you or someone you know is aware of the 1970s initiatives in Canada to see ourselves quite differently from the United States in terms of cultural diversity, you'll perhaps recall the assertion that while the United States takes a "melting pot" approach to difference, Canada is a "multicultural mosaic." Official multiculturalism plays out in many arenas, including in the school you may be studying at right now. Not all is always straightforward, though, in this fairly optimistic view of Canada. Perhaps you already know this because you yourself have experienced some form of racism or ethnocentrism. Sociological thinking can help us to think critically about the various types of oppressive structures in Canadian society and culture.

Learning Outcomes

Through careful reading of this chapter, you should be able to:

- define the bolded key terms
- clarify the relationship between U.S. and Canadian approaches to immigration and diversity
- understand the symbolic and material constructions of ethnicity in Canada's political positions over time, including the commitment to "multiculturalism" and the role of the census in analyzing socio-economic data
- consider the historical context in which definitions of race emerge as apparently natural categories, and their contemporary social and political implications
- explain Aboriginality and charter groups in Canadian discussions of institutionalized identities
- contextualize forms of oppression based on population, ethnicity, and power
- apply the various sociological perspectives to an analysis of racialized groups
- respond intersectionally to prejudice, racism, and discrimination in Canadian and global contexts

8

Critical Studies in Race and Ethnicity

Galina Barskaya/Shutterstock.com

NEL

249

Canada is increasingly diversified in the racial and ethnic composition of its population. Consider that whereas in 1901 there were only 25 different ethnic groups of ancestry record, Canadians identified more than 200 ethnic groups in answering the 2006 census question on ethnic ancestry (Statistics Canada 2008a). In that year, more than 5 million individuals, or 16.2 percent of the population, identified themselves as visible minorities (ibid). Many Canadians might be startled to realize that, amid such diversity, some individuals in Canada would espouse the killing of another human being simply because of skin colour or ethnicity; many others would not be surprised.

In this chapter, we discuss the character and foundations of prejudice to uncover the operations of discrimination and its consequences for both racial and ethnic minorities. We also discuss strategies designed to reduce prejudice and discrimination. We begin by examining racial and ethnic diversity worldwide and in Canada, emphasizing first that the concept of race is based on social rather than biological definitions.

8.1 The Global Context: Diversity Worldwide

From a perspective focused on how human societies and relationships are structured— largely organized into groups with unequal access to power and resources—"race" refers not to biological differences, but to categories people occupy based on ascribed characteristics, such as skin colour. No biological basis for categorizing persons according to race exists; however, sociologists recognize that such categories create important distinctions in how people experience the social world and their place in it. Whatever our internal similarities may be, the process of organizing people into racialized categories focuses people into groups defined by difference and inequality. Since those differences have been largely defined by conflict, they have important social implications for outcomes related to health and well-being. As well meaning as it may be to insist that people are all the same "on the inside," such a stance risks ignoring the specific differences that people experience because of their racialized statuses in societies defined by inequality.

This chapter explores the problems and privileges that arise in social relations structured through race and ethnicity.

The Social Construction of Race

The concept of **race** refers to a category of people believed to share distinct physical characteristics deemed socially significant. Racial groups are sometimes distinguished based on such physical characteristics as skin colour, hair texture, facial features, and body shape and size. Some physical variations among people are the result of living for thousands of years in different geographical regions (Molnar 1983). For example, humans living in regions with hotter climates developed darker skin from a natural skin pigment, melanin, which protects the skin from the sun's rays. In regions with moderate or colder climates, people had little need for protection from the sun and developed lighter skin.

Cultural definitions of race have taught us to view race as a scientific categorization of people based on biological differences between groups of individuals. Yet, racial categories are based more on social definitions than on biological differences. Anthropologist Mark Cohen (1998) explains that distinctions among human

race

A category of people who are believed to share distinct physical characteristics that are deemed socially significant.

populations are graded, not abrupt. Skin colour is not black or white, but rather ranges from dark to light with many gradations of shades. Noses are not either broad or narrow, but come in a range of shapes. Physical traits such as these, as well as hair colour and other both visible and invisible characteristics, come in an infinite number of combinations. For example, a person with dark skin can have any blood type and can have a broad nose (a common combination in West Africa), a narrow nose (a common trait in East Africa), or even blond hair (a combination found in Australia and Papua New Guinea).

The science of genetics also challenges the notion of race. Geneticists have discovered that "the genes of black and white . . . [North Americans] probably are 99.9 percent alike" (Cohen 1998: B4). Furthermore, genetic studies indicate that genetic variation is greater within racially classified populations than between racial groups (Keita and Kittles 1997). Classifying people into different races fails to recognize that over the course of human history migration and intermarriage have resulted in the blending of genetically transmitted traits. For example, if you traced your ancestry back as far as the Norman Conquest of 1066, you would find yourself claiming 41 million ancestors (Fitzhugh 1991: 290). With the passage of time, fewer if any individuals can claim that their racial or ethnic ancestry is "pure." Thus, there are no "pure" races; people in virtually all societies have genetically mixed backgrounds. Even analyses that have developed out of the human genome project, which have been able to use genetic markers to determine the locations from which an individual's ancestors originated, are clear to point out that "the connection [between race and biology] is generally quite blurry because of multiple other nongenetic connotation of race, the lack of defined boundaries between populations and the fact that many individuals have ancestors from multiple regions of the world" (Collins 2004: S13). It is for these kinds of reasons that the American Anthropological Association has passed a resolution stating that "differentiating species into biologically defined 'race' has proven meaningless and unscientific" (Etzioni 1997: 39). Scientists who reject the race concept now speak of **populations** when referring to groups that most people would call races (Zack 1998).

Clear evidence that race is a social concept is that different societies construct different systems of racial classification and these systems change over time (Niemonen 1999). Leggon (1999) explains, "The major significance of race is not biological but social and political, insofar as race is used as the primary line of demarcation separating 'we' from 'they' and, consequently, becomes a basis for distinctive treatment of a group by another" (p. 382). However, the social significance of "race" remains evident throughout the world.

Understanding that there is no such biological thing as "race" and that the concept is a social construction with political uses does not tell us exactly what "racism" is. To understand racism, explain Robert Miles and Malcolm Brown (2003), we must think of it not as a set of particular acts or attitudes but as an ideology that is used in the service of separating "us" from "them" in the building of nation states and the creation of corollary nationalist ideologies (p. 7). Defending their assertion that racism is an ideology, Miles and Brown continue in the second edition of *Racism* to explain that as an ideology, racism is any conceptualization, activity, or representation of human beings that forms a distorted view both of human beings and of their social relations (p. 9). As an ideology, then, racism cleaves to the ideologies of nationalism as they explain:

> . . . the 'nation' will inevitably identify itself with the 'race', because historical, cultural, political, and other distinguishing factors of a 'nation' are ultimately subsumed under the idea of 'race'. This inevitably leads to a nationalistic purism, and ideology that 'we' must not be contaminated by 'them' (whether 'they' are German Jews in

populations
The word that scientists who reject the race concept now use when referring to groups that most people would call races.

the 1930s, Bosnian Muslims in the 1990s, or asylum seekers in early twenty-first century Europe) . . . At the same time, the ideology of nationalism, under the influence of racism, develops into an ethnocentric conception of humanity and, where the national unit is powerful enough, [it develops into] a programme of cultural imperialism. (Miles and Brown 2003: 7)

As an ideology, Miles and Brown argue, "some articulations of racism are morally worse than others" (2003: 12). For example, that racism is the result of an intellectual error (as there is actually no such thing as "race" at a biological level) is not so morally problematic as the political and practical uses that the intellectual error is put to, such as the purposeful distortion of the conditions of people's lives and the "anti-egalitarian, socially unjust" laws and policies that may be born from and served by the intellectual error (p. 12). Citing the earlier work of Martin Luther King, Miles and Brown argue that racist ideologies are wrong not simply because they are errors, but because they fuel oppressive and sometimes violent relations between groups, and because as such it damages and distorts the whole of humanity: "Injustice anywhere is a threat to justice everywhere. We are caught in [a] . . . network of mutuality, tied in a single garment of destiny. Whatever affects one directly, affects all indirectly" (King, quoted in Miles and Brown 2003: 12).

Patterns of Racial and Ethnic Group Interaction

When two or more racial or ethnic groups come into contact, one of several patterns of interaction may occur, including genocide, expulsion or population transfer, slavery, colonialism, segregation, acculturation, assimilation, pluralism, and amalgamation. These patterns of interaction may occur when two or more groups exist in the same society or when different groups from different societies come into contact. Although not all patterns of interaction between racial and ethnic groups are destructive, author and Mayan shaman Martin Prechtel reminds us that "Every human on this earth, whether from Africa, Asia, Europe, or the Americas, has ancestors whose stories, rituals, ingenuity, language, and life ways were taken away, enslaved, banned, exploited, twisted, or destroyed" (quoted in Jensen 2001: 13).

- **Genocide** refers to the deliberate, systematic annihilation of an entire nation or people. The European invasion of the Americas, beginning in the sixteenth century, resulted in the decimation of most of the original inhabitants of North and South America. For example, labelling Aboriginal peoples as "savages" allowed early settlers and visiting fishermen to commit "atrocities of a most barbaric kind" upon the Beothuk of Newfoundland (Rowe 1977: 146). Indeed, some scholars have claimed that the eventual extinction of the Beothuk resulted from the "sport of Indian hunting": murder committed "for fun" (Horwood 1969) and for the payment of a bounty for each Beothuk killed (Such 1978: 62). Although some Native groups were intentionally killed, others fell victim to diseases brought by the Europeans. In the twentieth century, Adolf Hitler led the Nazi extermination of more than 12 million people, including more than 6 million Jews. More recently, ethnic Serbs have attempted to eliminate Muslims from parts of Bosnia—a process they call "ethnic cleansing."
- **Expulsion** or **population transfer** occurs when a dominant group forces a subordinate group to leave the country or to live only in designated areas of the country. During World War II, about 22 000 Japanese-Canadians lost their rights, had their homes, property, and businesses confiscated, and were confined to internment camps. In addition, the "Deemed Suspect"—refugees from Germany and Austria—were deported from England to Canada and interned here as "enemy

genocide
The systematic annihilation of one racial or ethnic group by another.

expulsion (population transfer)
When a dominant group forces a subordinate group to leave the country or to live only in designated areas of the country.

aliens." Between 1940 and 1943, 2300 individuals "deemed suspect" were interned in Canada within eight camps (Columbo 1986).

- **Slavery** exists when one group treats another group as property to exploit for financial gain. The dominant group forces the enslaved group to live a life of servitude, without the basic rights and privileges enjoyed by the dominant group. In early American history, slavery was tolerated and legal for three centuries. In what is now Canada, slavery was practised by several Indian tribes on the Northwest Coast, and by Europeans beginning in 1500 in Newfoundland. By 1608, the French brought black slaves to Canada and the first slave transported directly from Africa sold in 1629. In New France, there were 3604 recorded slaves by 1759, 1132 of whom were black, the remainder of whom were "panis" (Indians). The "right" of Canadians to own and sell Native people as slaves was declared on May 29, 1733. Canada prohibited the importation of slaves in 1793; that same year, an act of the Upper Canada legislature ruled that all children in its jurisdiction born to slaves after that year were to be free upon reaching age 25 and proposed the gradual emancipation of slaves. Although the last slave auction in Canada was held in 1797 in Montreal, slavery remained technically legal in most of Canada until 1834 when it was abolished for the entire British Empire (Winks 1999).

- **Colonialism** occurs when a racial or ethnic group from one society takes over and dominates the racial or ethnic group(s) of another society. The European invasion of North America, the British occupation of India, and the Dutch presence in South Africa before the end of apartheid are examples of outsiders taking over a country and controlling the native population. As a territory of the United States, Puerto Rico is essentially a colony whose residents are U.S. citizens, but who cannot vote in presidential elections unless they move to the mainland.

- **Segregation** refers to the physical separation of two groups in residence, workplace, and social functions. Segregation may be **de jure** (Latin meaning "by law") or **de facto** ("in fact"). For example, blacks across Canada were treated as inferior from the time they began to settle here. They were prohibited from entering restaurants, hotels, and recreational facilities, and barred from most professions. In Nova Scotia and Ontario, where blacks were most concentrated, blacks were often forced into segregated schools. The last segregated school in southwestern Ontario closed in 1956; however, Windsor, Ontario, did not desegregate its public facilities until 1975—it was the last municipality to do so (Henry and Tator 1985: 321–22). In like fashion, because of a range of discriminatory legislation in British Columbia, "where anti-Asian sentiment was endemic from the 1850s to the 1950s . . . Chinese, Japanese and South Asians could not vote, practise law or pharmacy, be elected to public office, serve on juries or work in public works, education or the civil service" (Driedger 1999: 1889). Consider as well that in the 1920s and 1930s, Jews were automatically excluded from employment in major institutions, such as banks and the police, and were barred from elite social clubs, beaches, and holiday resorts in Montreal, Toronto, and Winnipeg. Universities set limits on Jewish enrolment (Henry et al. 1995).

- **Acculturation** refers to the loss of the culture in which a person was originally raised to a culture imposed either by immigration or colonization. Acculturation may involve learning the dominant language, adopting new values and behaviours, and changing the spelling of the family name. In some instances, acculturation may be forced. For example, the 1977 passage of the French Language Charter (Bill 101) established French as the official language of Quebec and made French the legal language of work and the public sector. It also resulted in a situation in which educational instruction takes place almost exclusively in French, with English granted "secondary language status." Similarly, the Canadian government's policy

slavery
A condition in which one social group treats another group as property to exploit for financial gain.

colonialism
When a racial or ethnic group from one society takes over and dominates the racial or ethnic group(s) of another society.

segregation
The physical and social separation of categories of individuals, such as racial or ethnic groups.

de jure segregation
Segregation that is required by law.

de facto segregation
Segregation that is not required by law, but exists "in fact," often as a result of housing and socio-economic patterns.

acculturation
Learning the culture of a group different from the one in which a person was originally raised.

assimilation
The process by which minority groups gradually adopt the cultural patterns of the dominant majority group.

secondary assimilation
The integration of different groups in public areas and in social institutions, such as in government, neighbourhoods, schools, and the workplace.

primary assimilation
The integration of different groups in personal, intimate associations such as friends, family, and spouses.

amalgamation
The physical blending of different racial or ethnic groups, resulting in a new and distinct genetic and cultural population; results from the intermarriage of racial and ethnic groups over generations.

marital assimilation
Assimilation that occurs when different ethnic or racial groups become married or pair-bonded and produce children.

endogamy
The social norm that influences people to marry within their social group and discourages interracial and interethnic marriages.

of "aggressive civilization" was designed to destroy all aspects of Aboriginal culture. It was imposed throughout the Native residential schools.

- **Assimilation** is the process by which formerly distinct and separate groups merge and become integrated as one. There are two types of assimilation: secondary and primary. **Secondary assimilation** occurs when different groups become integrated in public areas and in social institutions, such as neighbourhoods, schools, the workplace, and in government. **Primary assimilation** occurs when members of different groups are integrated in personal, intimate associations, such as friends, family, and spouses. The degree of acculturation and assimilation that occurs between majority and minority groups depends in part on (1) whether minority group members have voluntary or involuntary contact with the majority group and (2) whether majority group members accept or reject newcomers or minority group members. Groups that voluntarily immigrate and that are accepted by "host" society members will experience an easier time acculturating and assimilating than those that are forced through slavery, frontier expansion, or military conquest into contact with the majority group and are rejected by them.

- **Amalgamation**, also known as **marital assimilation**, occurs when members of different ethnic or racial groups form families and produce children. Although in most societies the norm of **endogamy** influences individuals to marry within their social group, interracial marriages have become more acceptable in Canada in the past few decades. This higher level of acceptance is markedly different from a relatively recent past in which women could be criminalized for marrying "outside" their race. The Project Canada national surveys of adults, which have examined attitudes in this country since 1975, report increases in the percentages of those expressing approval toward racial intermarriage (Bibby 2007; Table 8.1). In 2001, there were 217 500 mixed unions (marriages and common-law unions) involving either persons from two different visible minority groups or one person from a visible minority group and one who is not. Table 8.2 lays out patterns of marriage between persons in mixed unions. Drawn from the 2006 census, Table 8.2 belongs to a larger report that explains that those who are in mixed unions are likely to have been born in Canada, noting that "56% had a partner or spouse who was either a non-visible minority or was a member of a different visible minority group compared to 12% for those who were foreign-born" (Milan et al. 2010: 71). The report explains the increased likelihood of marrying someone with different ancestry for those visible minorities born in Canada by reminding us that those who immigrate usually do so as adults, and have already married in their countries of origin (ibid).

Table 8.1 *Approval of Intergroup Marriage, 1975–2007*

	1975	1990	2005	2007
White and Aboriginals	73%	84	93	95
White and Asians	64	82	93	95
White and East Indians/Pakistanis	56	76	91	95
White and Blacks	55	78	92	95**

**NOTE: Bibby states approval levels have *almost* reached 95% between whites and Aboriginals, Asians, East Indians/Pakistanis, and blacks (2007).

SOURCE: Bibby, Reginald W. 2006. *The Boomer Factor*. Toronto: Bastian Books, p. 9. Reprinted by permission of Reginald Bibby & Associates.

Table 8.2 *Outgroup Pairing by Visible Minority Group, 2006*

	Couples		
	Total Number	Mixed Union Percentage	Same Visible Minority Group
Visible Minority Group			
All visible minority groups[1]	1 214 400	23.8	76.2
Japanese	29 700	74.7	25.3
Latin American	85 200	47.0	53.0
Black	136 000	40.6	59.4
Filipino	107 400	33.1	66.9
Southeast Asian	58 100	31.1	68.9
Arab/West Asian	105 700	25.0	74.9
Korean	34 800	19.5	80.5
Chinese	321 700	17.4	82.6
South Asian	327 200	12.7	87.3
Multiple groups or n.i.e.[2]	50 400	58.4	41.6

[1] The number of couples by specific visible minority group does not sum to the total because if the two persons in a couple belong to two different visible minority groups, these couples are counted in each group.

[2] Belonging to multiple visible minority groups means that respondents reported more than one visible minority group by checking two or more mark-in circles, e.g., Black and South Asian. Less common visible minority groups are reported in the visible minority n.i.e. (not included elsewhere) category. This category includes respondents who reported a write-in response such as Guyanese, West Indian, Kurd, Tibetan, Polynesian and Pacific Islander.

SOURCE: Statistics Canada, "A portrait of couples in mixed unions", *Canadian Social Trends*, Cat. 11-008-XIE2010001, No. 89, April 2010; http://www.statcan.gc.ca/bsolc/olc-cel/olc-cel?lang=eng&catno=11-008-X.

8.2 Multiculturalism in Canada

Pluralism refers to a state in which racial and ethnic groups maintain their distinctness, but respect each other and have equal access to social resources. In Switzerland, for example, four ethnic groups—French, Italian, German, and Romansch—maintain their distinct cultural heritages and group identities in an atmosphere of mutual respect and social equality. Similarly, a policy of cultural pluralism, or **multiculturalism**, is evidenced in the description of Canada as a "mosaic" of peoples, which dates back at the very least to the 1926 publication of Ken Foster's *Our Canadian Mosaic*. Government documents such as *Multiculturalism: Being Canadian* (1987) have—straining their credibility—extended the claim for multiculturalism all the way back to the sixteenth-century "joining" of Europeans with the Aboriginal peoples already in Canada (Day 1998: 42). Richard Day argues that it is an ongoing and deliberate effort of those who build Canadian social policy to deal with the *problem* of diversity by reframing it as a "national jewel" in which "Diversity is present, but only in the context of a perfectly structured (integrated) whole. And, if this unity is to be maintained, the individual elements of the mosaic must be preserved, prevented from exceeding their boundaries" (p. 60). In other words, the perceived threat of multiple racial and ethnic differences must be defused by creating a regularized

pluralism
A state in which racial or ethnic groups maintain their distinctness, but respect each other and have equal access to social resources.

multiculturalism
A philosophy that argues that the culture of a society should represent and embrace all racial and ethnic groups in that society.

order out of what would otherwise explode the unity of Canadian culture. Canada encourages the expression of ethnic and other differences; however, Canada's official policy advocating multiculturalism, not in effect until 1971, was born out of a rather more complex political context than many remember or realize. In his speech to the House of Commons on October 8, 1971, Prime Minister Pierre Trudeau committed his government to "a policy of multiculturalism within a bilingual framework . . . as the most suitable means of assuring the cultural freedom of Canadians" (in Columbo 1986: 353). When launching its policy in 1971, the Canadian government confirmed its commitment to an ideal acknowledging that Canada, while officially bilingual, had no "official" culture—that is, that none of the distinguishable cultures took precedence over the others.

Writing in 1965 on the issue of the power structure of class and ethnicity in Canada, John Porter debunked the popularly held belief that Canada was a "classless" society (or alternately, that almost all Canadians are "middle class"). His book *The Vertical Mosaic* argues that "in a society . . . made up of many cultural groups there is usually some relationship between a person's membership in these groups and his class position, and, consequently, his chances of reaching positions of power [are also affected]" (Porter 1965: xii). A central concern in Porter's work is the relationship between the lower economic power and status enjoyed in Canada by those ethnic groups that are not part of the two founding, charter groups (the British and the French). In essence, the legacy of racist ideologies that existed at the founding of Canada in the nineteenth century, and in the heaviest years of immigration into Canada in the early decades of the twentieth century, led to the concentration of already existing wealth and power that were seen as the natural right of the presumed-to-be superior British and French charter groups, while the various ethnic groups that arrived as immigrants were vertically stratified on income and prestige levels that Porter explains thus:

> In social processes of this kind, there gradually develops a reciprocal relationship between ethnicity and social class. A given ethnic group appropriates particular roles and designates other ethnic groups for the less preferred ones. Often the low status group accepts its inferior position. Through time, the relative status positions, reinforced by stereotypes and social images—the Irish policeman and the Irish maid, for example—harden and become perpetuated over a very long time. In the general scheme of class and status that evolves with economic growth and immigration, there exists an "entrance status" to be assumed by the less preferred ethnic groups. Entrance status implies lower level occupational roles and subjection to processes of assimilation laid down and judged by the charter group. (1965: 63–64)

When Porter originally produced *The Vertical Mosaic* in 1965, it appeared that the Chinese in Canada would occupy a permanent position on the bottom of the economic ladder, and his comments about Irish policemen and Irish maids gesture toward the dominant beliefs of the ruling groups that the Irish had more natural ties to criminality, with the police having to work closely with thieves, and perception that Irish housemaids were likely working in prostitution at least some of the time. For example, the song "Molly Malone," about a poor Dublin girl who dies in the street from a fever, was written by an Englishman, James Yorkston, and the fever in the song likely refers to the syphilis that the fictional Molly Malone would have contracted while working in the streets of Dublin as a prostitute (Kilfeather 2005: 6). In other words, in British-dominated nineteenth- and twentieth-century Canada, the stereotype of both the Irish maid and the Irish policeman had covert meanings that were extremely disparaging.

The development of the policy was neither a gesture of beneficence nor a measure intended to right previous wrongs; it was a response to tensions that arose in communities, especially among Ukrainians, not recognized by Trudeau's effort to settle French and English as Canada's official languages. The Royal Commission on Bilingualism and Biculturalism, struck in 1969, revealed that for the bilingual policy to have a hope of succeeding, other official measures would have to be taken to recognize the substantial contributions of non-English and non-French cultures to the creation of Canada as a nation. Wood and Gilbert (2005) found that the popular perception of multiculturalism as a policy rooted in social justice concerns arises from the policy's transmission through schools to those who came of age in the Trudeau years 1969–1982; however, this perception does not accurately reflect "the view of Trudeau and his government that language and culture were to be regarded as separable" (p. 681). In effect, multicultural policy was the most effective way to sell official bilingualism without insisting on official biculturalism.

Since its institutionalization in 1971 Liberal policy, and its revision under the Progressive Conservative government in 1988, multiculturalism has come to mean that as a society Canadians value diversity and plurality. In July 1988, the Progressive Conservative government passed a bill to introduce the *Canadian Multiculturalism Act*, setting forth the multiculturalism policy: to wit, "to recognize all Canadians as full and equal participants in Canadian society." Since 1972 there has been a minister responsible for multiculturalism, and since 1973 a Canadian Multiculturalism Council and a Multiculturalism Directorate within the Department of the Secretary of State. In 1991, a Department of Multiculturalism and Citizenship was established to emphasize that multiculturalism empowers minorities to pursue the dual goals of ethnicity and equality.

Canada's multicultural program, based on the goals of the multicultural policy and the *Canadian Multicultural Act*, has three fundamental goals: (1) identity—fostering a society that recognizes, respects, and reflects a diversity of cultures such that people of all backgrounds feel a sense of belonging and attachment to Canada; (2) civic participation—developing active citizens with both the opportunity and the capacity to help shape the future of Canada and its communities; and (3) social justice—building a society that ensures fair and equitable treatment and that respects the dignity of peoples of all origins and accommodates them. Contemporary critical assessments of official multiculturalism point out, however, that multicultural policy has done little to alleviate the negative influence of racism and ethnocentrism on the life chances of ethnically and racially marked groups in Canada. Some argue that multiculturalism has created only a shallow tolerance of "diversity," attractive only insofar as "this 'food and festivals' brand of aestheticized difference—premised largely on the exotic pleasure of 'visible' and 'edible' ethnicity—emerges from enterprises of more recent vintage: more or less neoliberal schemes engineered to 'sell diversity' and consolidate 'competitive city' status [on cities seeking 'world class' status]" (Goonewardena and Kipfer 2005: 672).

In the following sections, we critically assess the promise and the limitations of official multiculturalism when it comes to meeting its mandate to value and recognize equally all the groups who contribute to the national identity and society that is Canada.

Visible Minorities in Canada

Before 1996, the Canadian census derived indirect information on the numbers and characteristics of persons who were visible minorities from responses to questions on ethnic or cultural origin. However, as of 1996, the Canadian census introduced a new question that asked respondents directly if they were members of one of the population groups defined by the *Employment Equity Act* as "visible minorities," or "persons, other than Aboriginal peoples, who are non-Caucasian in race or non-White in colour." Included under this definition are Chinese, South Asians, Blacks, Arabs and West Asians, Filipinos, Southeast Asians, Latin Americans, Japanese, Koreans, and Pacific Islanders. Census respondents were asked to indicate their population group by checking one or more of 10 mark-in categories. While Canadian scholars generally prefer to speak of the process of "racialization" because it points to the power dynamics and inequalities that place some groups into marginalized groups, and does not assume that "race" is simply a fact that we can all "see," the Canadian government continues to use the term "visible minority" in their data and policy documents. In this textbook, we use the term "visible minority" only where it reflects the language of government documents.

Since 1981, there has been a threefold increase in Canada's visible minority population and, based on current trends, it is expected that by 2016 visible minorities will account for one-fifth of Canada's population (Statistics Canada 2003a). According to Statistics Canada information from the 2006 census, "Between 2001 and 2006, the visible minority population increased at a much faster pace than the total population. Its rate of growth was 27.2%, five times faster than the 5.4% increase for the population as a whole" (Statistics Canada 2008a).

To maintain population growth Canada relies on immigration for about two-thirds of our current growth (Chui et al. 2007: 6), and the highly skilled immigrants that Canada encourages to immigrate are no longer likely to be of European descent (Table 8.3). Those who do emigrate from Europe tend to arrive from Eastern Europe, and account

Table 8.3 *Top 10 Countries of Birth of Recent Immigrants, 1981–2006*

Order	2006 Census	2001 Census	1996 Census	1991 Census	1981 Census
1	People's Republic of China	People's Republic of China	Hong Kong	Hong Kong	United Kingdom
2	India	India	People's Republic of China	Poland	Viet Nam
3	Philippines	Philippines	India	People's Republic of China	United States of America
4	Pakistan	Pakistan	Philippines	India	India
5	United States of America	Hong Kong	Sri Lanka	Philippines	Philippines
6	South Korea	Iran	Poland	United Kingdom	Jamaica
7	Romania	Taiwan	Taiwan	Viet Nam	Hong Kong
8	Iran	United States of America	Viet Nam	United States of America	Portugal
9	United Kingdom	South Korea	United States of America	Lebanon	Taiwan
10	Colombia	Sri Lanka	United Kingdom	Portugal	People's Republic of China

NOTE: "Recent immigrants" refers to landed immigrants who arrived in Canada within five years prior to a given census.

SOURCE: Statistics Canada, "Immigration in Canada: A portrait of the Foreign born population, 2006 Census", Cat. 97-557-XIE2006001, December 2007; http://www.statcan.gc.ca/bsolc/olc-cel/olc-cel?lang=eng&catno=97-557-X2006001.

for 16.1 percent of all immigrants who arrived in Canada between 2001 and 2006 (Chui et al. 2007: 10). The changes in immigration patterns over the past 25 years have to do with political shifts both in and outside Canada. Chui and colleagues explain that "changes in Canada's immigration programs to build on social, humanitarian and economic goals, and international events affecting the movements of migrants and refugees" (p. 9) are at the heart of shifts in immigration patterns.

In 2002, Canada's federal immigration policy was changed from the 1976 *Immigration Act* to the *Immigration and Refugee Protection Act* (IRPA). The IRPA classifies immigrants to Canada into "three basic categories of permanent residents, which correspond to major programme initiatives: reuniting families, contributing to economic development and protecting refugees" (CIC 2012: 1). In the decade between 2002 and 2012, immigrants in each year accounted for 0.7 to 0.8 percent of Canada's permanent population, and ranged from a low of 221 349 arrivals to Canada in 2003 to a high of 280 689 arrivals in 2010 (CIC 2012: 3). The federal office of Citizenship and Immigration Canada released long-term data in 2012 showing the patterns of immigration to Canada since 1860, just prior to Confederation, right up to 2012. While popular opinion—often expressed in Canadian news media—seems concerned that there is too much immigration into Canada now, and that the jobs of Canadians already here are threatened by these new arrivals, the reality is that immigration to Canada hit its highest point in terms of percentages and the actual numbers of arrivals in the first decades of the twentieth century. In 1913, 400 000 immigrants arrived in Canada and accounted for 5.5 percent of the total population in that year (CIC 2012: 2–3).

Although commonsense attitudes regarding immigration can focus on the presumed negative impact of a perceived "flood" of refugee arrivals to Canada, the reality of Canada's immigration policies means that the vast majority of those who have arrived in Canada since 1988, peaking in the later years of the twenty-first century's first decade, came as "economic immigrants" (see Figure 8.1). Economic immigrants are those whose entry to Canada is secured by their ability to contribute to contemporary needs in Canada's business and labour force, as Immigration Canada explains:

> Economic immigrants are people selected for their skills and ability to contribute to Canada's economy, including skilled workers, business immigrants, provincial and territorial nominees, and live-in caregivers. The skilled worker component includes immigrants who are able to demonstrate their ability to enter the labour market and successfully establish in Canada by meeting selection criteria that assess factors such as education, English or French language abilities, and work experience. The business immigrant component includes those who invest their money in an approved venture, those who intend to run their own business, or those who intend to be self-employed. . . . Live-in caregivers are temporary foreign workers who are granted permanent residence after their participation in the Live-in Caregiver

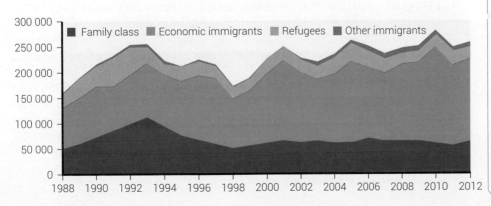

Figure 8.1 **Canada, Permanent Residents by Category, 1988–2012**

SOURCE: Facts and Figures 2012—Immigration Overview Permanent and Temporary Residents. http://www.cic.gc.ca/english/resources/statistics/facts2012/index.asp. Reprinted with permission.

Program. Initially, live-in caregivers must be qualified to provide care for children, sick or elderly people, or persons with a disability. Successful candidates are granted temporary resident status and a work permit and, after two years, are eligible to apply for permanent resident status.* (CIC 2012: 1)

Considerable variation exists in the proportion of visible minorities within Canada's provinces and territories. Ontario and British Columbia, which contain half the country's total population, account for almost three-quarters of the visible minority population. In 2006 visible minorities accounted for 24.8 percent of the population in British Columbia, 22.8 percent in Ontario, and 13.9 percent in Alberta—but just 1.1 percent in Newfoundland and Labrador, while Prince Edward Island has a visible minority population of 1.4 percent, and Nova Scotia has a visible minority population of 4.2 percent. Because many of those in the visible minority population have arrived as well-trained, highly educated immigrants, it is not surprising that the majority of visible minorities live in one of Canada's 25 census metropolitan areas (CMAs). A CMA is an urban area whose principal or central city has a population of at least 100 000. Furthermore, CMAs offer established communities for visible minority immigrants to settle in, making larger urban areas more attractive than rural communities.

Aboriginality

The *Constitution Act, 1982,* defines "aboriginal peoples of Canada" as belonging to four major groups:

1. *Status Indians.* Persons whose names appear on the Indian Register maintained by the Department of Indian and Northern Affairs Canada under the *Indian Act* and who are registered as Indians for the purpose of special entitlements.
2. *Nonstatus Indians.* Those whose Indian status has been extinguished for a variety of reasons and whose names do not appear on the Indian Register. Previously, Indians gave up their official status when they wanted to vote, to drink alcohol off the reserve, or (if they were women) to marry a non-Indian. In 1985, the federal government introduced Bill C-31, which enabled Indian women to regain their legal status if they had lost it by marrying men who did not possess Indian status. The bill also allowed all first-generation children of such marriages and any Indian who had been disenfranchised to regain their legal status as Indian. In consequence, the number of nonstatus Indians has dwindled.
3. *Métis.* The descendants of Indian and non-Indian unions (principally between Indians and Europeans and, prior to Confederation, between Indians and the French). Previously regarded as "half-breeds," the Métis have sought to establish their status within Canadian society, past and present. For example, they have suggested that Louis Riel be regarded as the "Father of Confederation" for the Métis and argued that Riel "intuitively sensed the future for Canada and wanted to guarantee a place for Métis people in that future" (Kilgour 1988: 48).
4. *The Inuit.* This term, meaning "the people," replaced "Eskimos," an Algonquian word meaning "eaters of raw flesh" that is now considered derogatory. The Inuit became the first Aboriginal group in Canada to achieve at least partial self-determination with the creation of Nunavut (Inuktitut for "our land"). First proposed in 1976 as an Inuit homeland by the Inuit Tapirisat (an association of Inuit leaders) and established by the *Nunavut Act* of June 1993, Nunavut became a constitutional entity on April 1, 1999. About 80 percent of Nunavut's total population (about 27 000) is Inuit (Craufurd-Lewis 1999: 1686).

*Facts and Figures 2012—Immigration Overview Permanent and Temporary Residents. http://www.cic.gc.ca/english/resources/statistics/facts2012/index.asp. Reprinted with permission.

In 1996, a question about ancestry and identity of Native persons appeared on the census for the first time: "Is this person an Aboriginal person, that is, North American Indian, Métis, or Inuit (Eskimo)?" The 2001 and 2006 census questionnaires have continued to include this question. In the following section we summarize information from the 2001 and 2006 census reports on Canada's Aboriginal peoples.

By 2001, 976 300 individuals said they were members of at least one of three Aboriginal groups: North American Indian, Métis, or Inuit (Figure 8.2). By 2006, over 1.1 million identified as belonging to one of the three Aboriginal groups in Canada. The increase in the Aboriginal population stems from a high birth rate, an increased tendency of people to identify themselves as Aboriginal, and fewer incompletely enumerated reserves. In 2006, almost one-half (48 percent) of the Aboriginal population was under age 25, and the median age for the total population was 22; for the Métis fully one-quarter of the population is aged 14 and under. Compared to these high percentages of young people, seniors account for only 5 percent of the Aboriginal population. To some extent these percentages reflect a high birth rate for the three Aboriginal groups, but the percentages also reflect the reduced life expectancy for North American Indian, Métis, and Inuit people.

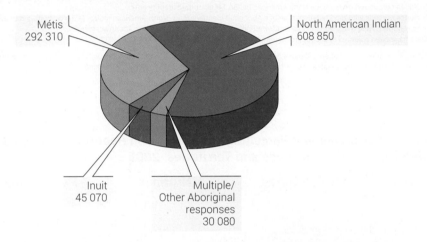

Métis
292 310

North American Indian
608 850

Inuit
45 070

Multiple/
Other Aboriginal
responses
30 080

Figure 8.2 **Aboriginal Makeup, 2001**

SOURCE: Adapted from Statistics Canada, 2003. "Census of Population: Immigration, Birthplace and Birthplace of Parents, Citizenship, Ethnic Origin, Visible Minorities and Aboriginal Peoples." *The Daily*, January 21.

The status of Canada's Native peoples reflects the strains of almost 400 years of cultural domination, exploitation, and exclusion. The consequences are not surprising. Native people suffer the lowest levels of education, income, health, and employment in Canada. Social conditions on many Native reserves—the lands set aside for the exclusive use of status Indians—reflect the historical and political neglect that Canada has shown toward its Indigenous peoples. On many reserves, housing fails to meet the most basic structural standards. Less than half of on-reserve homes have sewer or water hook-ups and half can best be described as overcrowded (Frideres 1993). Native men on reserves die, on average, seven years sooner than other Canadians, and the life expectancy for Native women remains six years lower than the national norm (Health Canada 1999). It has been estimated that the suicide rate among the Aboriginal population averages two to seven times that of the Canadian population as a whole (Health Canada 1999).

Table 8.4 gives us a demographic view of Aboriginal groups in Canada, and Table 8.5 provides us with information about Native peoples who self-identify on census reports. Native people do not view themselves as simply part of multicultural Canada; rather, they seek recognition of their sovereign status as the ancestral occupants of Canada. In support of this position, the main conclusion of the 1996 Royal Commission on Aboriginal Peoples "was the need for a complete restructuring of the relationship

Table 8.4 **Size and Growth of the Population by Aboriginal Identity, Canada 1996 and 2006**

Aboriginal Identity	2006	Percentage Change from 1996 to 2006[3]
Total population	31 241 030	9
Aboriginal identity population	1 172 790	45
First Nations people[1]	698 025	29
Metis[1]	389 785	91
Inuit[1]	50 485	26
Multiple and other Aboriginal responses[2]	34 500	34
Non-Aboriginal population	30 068 240	8

NOTES:

[1]Includes persons who reported a North American Indian, Métis or Inuit identity only.
[2]Includes persons who reported more than one Aboriginal identity group (North American Indian, Métis or Inuit) and those who reported being a Registered Indian and/or Band member without reporting an Aboriginal identity.
[3]Data have been adjusted to account for incompletely enumerated reserves in 1996 and 2006.

SOURCE: Adapted from Statistics Canada, "Aboriginal Peoples in Canada in 2006, 2006 Census," Cat. 97-558-XIE2006001, January 2008; http://www.statcan.gc.ca/bsolc/olc-cel/olc-cel?lang=eng&catno=97-558-X2006001.

Table 8.5 **Number and Percentage of Population Reporting Aboriginal Identity, Canada, Provinces and Territories, 2006**

Provinces and Territories	Number	Percentage
Canada	1 172 790	100
Newfoundland and Labrador	23 450	2
Prince Edward Island	1 730	0.1
Nova Scotia	24 175	2
New Brunswick	17 655	2
Quebec	108 430	9
Ontario	242 495	21
Manitoba	175 395	15
Saskatchewan	141 890	12
Alberta	188 365	16
British Columbia	196 075	17
Yukon Territory	7 580	0.6
Northwest Territories	20 635	2
Nunavut	24 920	2

SOURCE: Statistics Canada, "Aboriginal Peoples in Canada in 2006, 2006 Census," Cat. 97-558-XIE2006001, January 2008; http://www.statcan.gc.ca/bsolc/olc-cel/olc-cel?lang=eng&catno=97-558-X2006001.

between aboriginal and non-aboriginal peoples in Canada." Doerr (1999: 3) notes that the recommendations included

> Governmental commitment to a new set of ethical principles . . . acknowledg[ing] and respect[ing] aboriginal cultures and values, the origins of aboriginal nationhood and the inherent right to aboriginal self-determination.
>
> That the further development of aboriginal governments should focus on aboriginal nations rather than single communities . . . [and] the establishment of an aboriginal parliament which would comprise aboriginal representatives and advise Parliament on matters affecting aboriginal peoples.
>
> The need to significantly increase land holdings for First Nations in southern Canada . . . [and] a recommendation for an independent lands and treaties tribunal to oversee negotiations among federal, provincial and aboriginal governments on land issues.
>
> Adoption of aboriginal health and healing strategies, an aboriginal peoples international university, educational programs to support aboriginal self-government and public education initiatives to promote cultural sensitivity and understanding among non-aboriginals.

However, in its response to the Report, the federal government limited itself to pursuing four objectives: "renewing partnerships; strengthening aboriginal governance; developing a new fiscal relationship; and supporting strong communities, people and economies" (Doerr 1999: 4). The federal government also issued a Statement of Reconciliation, which expressed regret for past errors and a determination to learn from these errors. It committed $350 million to support community-based healing.

Ethnic Diversity in Canada

Ethnicity refers to a shared cultural heritage or nationality. Ethnic groups may be distinguished based on language, forms of family structures and roles of family members, religious beliefs and practices, dietary customs, forms of artistic expression such as music and dance, and national origin.

Canadians come from a variety of ethnic backgrounds, though "racial" backgrounds may be shared. "Ethnic origin," as defined in the 2001 Canadian census, refers to ethnic or cultural ancestry; it should not be confused with place of birth, citizenship, or nationality. Before 1996, the census question "To which ethnic or cultural group(s) did this person's ancestors belong?" was accompanied by a list of the 15 most frequent ethnic origins. Respondents were asked to mark as many from this list as applicable and were provided with two blank spaces in which they could indicate ethnic origins not included on the list. However, as of the 1996 census, the format of the ethnic origin question was modified. Rather than providing respondents with a list of answer categories, respondents are given four blank spaces to indicate single or multiple ethnic origins. "Canadian" was the fifth most frequently reported ethnic origin in the 1991 census. In recognition of that fact, for the first time in 1996 "Canadian" was included among the examples given of how this question might be answered.

The inclusion of this example "resulted in a major change in the way ethnic origins were reported" (Statistics Canada 1998). In 2001, 6.7 million people (23 percent of Canada's total population) reported their ethnic origin as "Canadian." By 2006, the number reporting "Canadian" as their ethnic origin had risen to just over 10 million, or nearly one-third of the total population. The census allowed respondents to choose more than one origin, as did 4.3 million of those who chose "Canadian" as one of their origins. Statistics Canada accounts for the enormous changes in the reporting of ancestry noting that it is more common now to have mixed unions, and to see individuals with far greater awareness about their family histories and heritage. They do note a distinction between

ethnicity
A shared cultural heritage or national origin.

Table 8.6 **Top 10 Ethnic Origins by Generational Status for People Aged 15 Years and Over, Canada, 2006**

First Generation			Second Generation			Third Generation or More		
Ethnic Origin	**Number**	**%**	**Ethnic Origin**	**Number**	**%**	**Ethnic Origin**	**Number**	**%**
Total population	6 124 560	100.0	Total population	4 006 420	100.0	Total population	15 533 240	100.0
Chinese	916 845	15.0	English	1 035 145	25.8	Canadian	7 236 370	46.6
East Indian	612 460	10.0	Scottish	635 600	15.9	English	3 794 250	24.4
English	547 865	8.9	Canadian	613 445	15.3	French	3 530 505	22.7
Italian	366 205	6.0	German	524 645	13.1	Scottish	2 865 800	18.4
German	352 805	5.8	Irish	496 990	12.4	Irish	2 755 420	17.7
Filipino	288 515	4.7	Italian	439 275	11.0	German	1 604 225	10.3
Scottish	271 545	4.4	French	284 900	7.1	North American Indian	813 405	5.2
Irish	230 975	3.8	Dutch (Netherlands)	253 325	6.3	Ukrainian	642 955	4.1
Polish	213 715	3.5	Ukrainian	212 860	5.3	Dutch (Netherlands)	376 555	2.4
Portuguese	195 480	3.2	Polish	203 725	5.1	Polish	364 980	2.3

NOTE:

[1]Table shows total responses. Because some respondents reported more than one ethnic origin, the sum of the total for all categories does not equal 100.

SOURCE: Statistics Canada, "Canada's Ethnocultural Mosaic, 2006 Census," Cat. 97-562-XWE2006001, April 2008; http://www.statcan.gc.ca/bsolc/olc-cel/olc-cel?catno=97-562-XWE&lang=eng.

those respondents born in Canada and those born elsewhere: 47.6 percent of Canadian-born respondents listed multiple ancestry, while only 17.2 percent of the foreign-born population noted more than one ethnic ancestry (Statistics Canada 2008c: 10).

Table 8.6 provides us with a generational view of how Canada's population identifies its ethnic background(s). Statistics Canada's decision to include the ethnic category of "Canadian" has not been without controversy. According to Jack Jedwab, the head of the Association for Canadian Studies, injecting nationalism into the census only frustrates the work of researchers. "The sheer number of people who identify themselves as Canadians makes it difficult to determine how many people are not indicating their ethnic background" (*National Post* 1999a: A1). More recently, there has been considerable debate over whether the ethnicity question ought to be deleted from the Canadian census. However, questions regarding ethnicity can help census researchers to assess correlations between health measures, employment, housing, and ethnicity. In refusing to ask the question, we would risk not having the data we need to identify and serve better those populations that are vulnerable to the effects of socio-political prejudice. As of the most recent 2011 census, questions about ethnicity were still included on both the short forms sent to 80 percent of households and on the long forms sent to 20 percent of households.

The Québécois

In Canada, we have traditionally spoken of the English and French as "**charter groups**," to reflect the historical importance of these groups in Canada. Although the *British North America Act* of 1867 acknowledged and enshrined the rights and privileges of the French and the British as the founding or charter groups of Canadian

charter groups
A term that has been traditionally used in Canada to refer to the English and French and that reflects the historical importance of these groups in Canada's history.

society, "the history of English-French relations in Canada is one of competition between two collectivities engaged in constructing and maintaining a society" (Breton 1988: 557). Indeed, Lord Durham's 1839 description of this relationship as "two nations warring in the bosom of a single state" may still strike some as apt. As Behiels (1999: 909) has commented, views similar to Durham's constitute a gross simplification of the character of francophone-anglophone relations, which have "ebbed and flowed in response to changing socioeconomic, political and ideological factors as well as to the commitment of Canada's majority and minority francophone communities to survival and equality."

During the period between Confederation and World War II, the building of institutions in Canada largely favoured the English. The development of the Canadian collective identity, Breton (1988) has argued, was not modelled on something uniquely Canadian, but rather on something decidedly "British" and "Protestant." Although in the English collectivity immigration was pursued as the central means for ensuring the growth of the English-speaking population, in Quebec the concern that French Roman Catholics would be drowned in a British Protestant sea found expression in a policy that encouraged child-bearing. Nevertheless, with the influx of English-speaking merchants and settlers into Quebec, the English, although a statistical minority, gradually assumed power. Over time, the English in Quebec became an elite that dominated in the areas of finance, transportation, and staples. English-speaking groups came to dominate the Quebec economy and the politico-bureaucratic groups that strongly influenced the federal government.

Urban migration, a postwar industrial expansion, and reforms made during the 1960s in Quebec encouraged a strong rise in Quebec nationalism. Under the leadership of Jean Lesage, the provincial government initiated a broad range of structural and ideological reforms that increased the role of the state and reduced the power and primacy of the Roman Catholic Church. Francophones in Quebec responded to a steeply declining birth rate and an increase in the number of non-francophone immigrants (many of whom chose to use English at work and for the schooling of their children). Many of them believed that for Quebec to survive as a French-speaking society, the French language would have to be aggressively promoted. More and more, francophones tended to equate their collective identity with the empowerment of Quebec itself. Those who had formerly referred to themselves as "canadien" or "canadien-français" increasingly began to use the term "Québécois" and to assert their belief that Quebec was capable of directing and controlling its own future.

The victory of the Parti Québécois, a political party dedicated to Quebec's achievement of independent nationhood, in the 1976 Quebec election notified Canadians of both the strength of French nationalism within that province and the depth of Québécois dissatisfaction. Neither the 1969 passage of Canada's *Official Languages Act*, nor the passage in 1977 of the French Language Charter (Bill 101) in Quebec, extinguished the perceived threat of assimilation. (Bill 101 established French as the only official language of education, work, and the public sector in that province.)

Since then, "French Canada's attempt to redefine its role within Canada has produced vigorous public debate and considerable political turmoil" (Behiels 1999: 911). The desire to create a French homeland that is predominantly French in character is not, strictly speaking, a "new" idea, but one that has circulated since at least the time of Confederation. However, it gained a sense of immediacy in the early 1990s when Lucien Bouchard's secessionist Bloc Québécois won 54 of the province's 75 federal seats. In 1994, then Parti Québécois leader Jacques Parizeau announced a referendum on the concept of sovereignty-partnership for 1995. The Parti Québécois maintained that should Canada refuse "to negotiate an economic association with an independent Quebec following a majority vote . . . Quebec would unilaterally declare its independence from Canada" (p. 912).

With polls leading up to the referendum suggesting that the decision would be based on a very close vote, Prime Minister Jean Chrétien promised the Québécois a veto over all major constitutional changes and recognition of Quebec as a distinct society (Balthazar 1997: 8). When the referendum vote was held, 51 percent voted "No" to sovereignty and 49 percent voted "Yes"—a wafer-thin rejection of sovereignty that Parizeau blamed on "money and the ethnic vote." A poll conducted in 1995 reported that one in three Canadians and one in two Quebecers believed that "the country . . . [would] cease to exist by the end of the decade" (*Maclean's* 1999: 28).

In the aftermath of the referendum, on December 11, 1995, the federal government passed a resolution supporting the concept of Quebec as a distinct society, and on February 2, 1996, Bill C-110—which granted all five regions of Canada, including Quebec, a veto over future constitutional changes—received royal assent and passed into law.

The federal government referred the question of whether or not Quebec had the right to secede unilaterally from Canada to the Supreme Court of Canada. The Supreme Court of Canada later issued the unanimous ruling that Quebec did not have this right either under Canadian constitutional law or under international law. However, the Supreme Court also held the view that

> if Quebec voters demonstrated a clear, and not just a simple, majority on a straight-forward question on outright secession, then Ottawa and the other provinces would have an obligation to enter into negotiations with the government of Quebec. They also pointed out that there was no guarantee that such negotiations would succeed or that the territory of the province of Quebec would remain intact if the negotiations succeeded since the rights of the majority had to respect those of the various minorities. (Behiels 1999: 912)

However, the Supreme Court failed to define what it meant by "clear" or "substantial." In November 1999, Prime Minister Jean Chrétien announced that his cabinet had agreed that the federal government would have to act to ensure that these terms were clearly defined. The government tabled the Clarity Bill, which set out the conditions under which Ottawa would negotiate the separation of a province following a referendum win by Yes forces. Although the draft bill declared that a simple majority of 50 percent plus one would not be enough to trigger separation, it did not specify what percentage would.

In response to this move by the federal government, Joseph Facal, Quebec's intergovernmental affairs minister, announced that only Quebec's National Assembly could decide the wording of the referendum and the terms for leaving Canada. According to Facal, "Ottawa, inspired by a Soviet-style law, is trying to impose a real straitjacket on Quebec's political future. It's an assault without precedent on the democratic rights of the people of Quebec to choose the political future it wants to choose" (*National Post* 1999b: A11). For their part, the Bloc Québécois labelled the move "a crime against history," and Quebec premier Lucien Bouchard called Ottawa's move "a strain on Canada's democratic reputation in the eyes of the international community" (*Maclean's* 1999: 83).

An Angus Reid survey of Quebec residents, released on December 14, 1999, found that 80 percent of those polled agreed that a clear referendum question was needed and 59 percent said that a clear majority—more than 50 percent plus one—was needed before Quebec could negotiate separation.

A second poll, conducted by Ekos Research Associates in December 1999, found that only 30 percent of Quebecers would vote for outright independence in a referendum; 64 percent favoured the status quo. Only 17 percent of Quebecers stated that they expected that Quebec would be a country in five years' time—the lowest level ever reported in a survey (*National Post* 1999c: A7). In the 2014 provincial election, under Pauline Marois, the Parti Quebecois lost its leadership position in Quebec, partly because of changes to the Quebec charter proposed by the PQ that the public largely agreed were racist and xenophobic.

8.3 Canadian Immigration

Immigration is, arguably, the area of public policy that has had the greatest impact on Canada's history, economy, multicultural identity, and regional diversity. The growing racial and ethnic diversity of Canada is largely attributable to immigration.

The history of Canada's immigration policies is far from exemplary, though. In the 1870s and 1880s, the active effort to recruit immigrants to Canada for labour-intensive industries was accompanied by regulations that sought to preserve Canada's "English stock" by restricting or denying entry to certain groups. These regulations reflected the sentiment that, while useful as labourers, certain groups were "undesirable" as permanent residents of Canada. For example, hostility toward Asians and a fear of the "yellow peril" is clear in the statement by Sir John A. Macdonald, Canada's first prime minister, that "a Mongolian or Chinese population in our country . . . would not be a wholesome element" (in Sher 1983: 33). Canada's 1910 *Immigration Act* gave the government the formal power to "prohibit for a stated period, or permanently, the landing in Canada . . . of immigrants belonging to any race unsuited to the climate or requirements of Canada." Laws to prohibit anyone who did not come directly to Canada from their country of origin from landing effectively eliminated the entry of people from India, "who had no choice but to book passages on ships through a third country because no direct routes existed to Vancouver" (Bricker and Greenspon 2001: 287). In 1919, regulations explicitly prohibited Doukhobors, Mennonites, and Hutterites.

In 1923, Canada's *Chinese Immigration Act* barred the Chinese entry, and Chinese persons already in Canada were not allowed to sponsor family or relatives. In the same year, the federal government listed Poland, Yugoslavia, Hungary, and Romania as "non-preferred" countries for the purposes of immigration. Abella and Troper (1998: 108) emphasize that Canada's refusal to accept Jewish refugees from Hitler's Europe reflected the pervasive anti-Semitism of pre-war Canada. They note that when a senior Canadian official was asked by journalists how many Jewish refugees would be admitted after the war, the official responded, "None is too many." "It is perhaps no surprise therefore that Canada had by far the worst record of any Western country for providing sanctuary to the Jews of Europe in the 1930s and 1940s" (Abella 1999: 90).

In 1947, Prime Minister William Lyon Mackenzie King pledged to remove "objectionable discrimination" from the *Immigration Act*. Certain blatantly discriminatory features of the Act were removed, but Canada's immigration policy still included "selective restriction." Preferred candidates were British, Irish, French, or American. The Ministry of Citizenship and Immigration was to determine the suitability of other would-be immigrants in light of "the climate, educational, social, industrial, labour, and other requirements in Canada." A person applying to immigrate to Canada could be declared "undesirable" because of "his peculiar customs, habits, modes of life, methods of holding property or his general inability to assimilate."

In the 1950s, the Canadian government, under pressure from other countries of the Commonwealth, began to relax its immigration policies. However, not until the White Paper of 1966 and the Regulations of 1967 was there a call for the abolishment of discrimination based on race, colour, religion, national origin, or gender (not until 1978 was homosexuality officially removed as a prohibited category). Immigration was to respond to Canada's need for workers, and cultural enrichment was added as part of Canada's immigration objectives.

As of "May 15, 2001, 5.4 million people, or 18.4 percent of the total population, were born outside of Canada" (Statistics Canada 2003b). Only in Australia is the proportion of the population born outside of the country higher than it is in Canada (Statistics Canada 2003a: 5). Of those immigrating to Canada in the 1990s, 58 percent were born in Asia (including the Middle East), 20 percent in Europe, 11 percent in the Caribbean and Central and South America, 8 percent in Africa, and 3 percent in the United States. Among those who immigrated to Canada during the 1990s, the leading country of birth was the People's Republic of China (Statistics Canada 2003a).

Quebec is also being transformed by immigration. "Immigrants make up about 10 percent of the population of Quebec, less than many other provinces, but the fastest growing segment of the population nonetheless" (Bricker and Greenspon 2001: 294).

Canada currently divides its immigration intake into three categories: (1) economic immigrants, who accounted for about 153 000 of those who arrived in 2001; (2) family-status immigrants (a parent, child, spouse, and so on of a Canadian resident), who comprised 66 000 new immigrants; and (3) refugees, who numbered 27 800. Recent changes to our immigration law emphasize the desirability of attracting skilled workers with the selection system placing considerable weight on an applicant's education or trade skills, language proficiency, and "adaptability" (which includes the education of an applicant's spouse) (Janigan 2002).

Canada is a signatory to the 1951 United Nations Convention Relating to the Status of Refugees. The *Immigration Act, 1976,* and the 1992 amendments introduced by Bill C-86 additionally provide for the admission of "designated classes" on humanitarian grounds. A UN Convention refugee is defined as a person who "owing to a well-founded fear of being prosecuted for reasons of race, religion, nationality, membership in a particular social group or political opinion, is outside the country of his nationality and is unable, or owing to such fear, is unwilling to avail himself of the protection of that country." The term *designated classes* is used to refer to "a variety of refugee-like situations including mass outflows . . . disproportionate punishment for violation of strict exit controls (self-exiles) and, for specific countries, the internally displaced (political prisoners and oppressed people)" (Boyd 2000: 84).

Some notable differences are apparent between the immigrant population and the Canadian-born population. While 44 percent of those who arrived in 2001 spoke neither English nor French, almost 60 percent of those who were adults had a postsecondary degree (compared with 43 percent of the existing population) (Janigan 2002). Compared to those who are Canadian born, recent immigrants, regardless of their country of birth, tend to be in better health—a tendency that reflects the demands of our immigration requirements (Health Canada 1999).

In other ways, however, recent immigrants are less fortunate than Canadian-born residents. For example, although the 2006 census found that males who had immigrated to Canada within the last five years were better educated than their Canadian counterparts (58.2 percent of immigrants held a university degree, while only 19.9 percent of Canadian-born men had achieved a university degree), the immigrant males earned only 63 cents on the dollar compared to the Canadian-born (Statistics Canada 2009: 21). The situation for women was similar, with average earnings of 56 cents for every dollar earned by their Canadian-born counterparts (ibid). In both cases, these low earnings and higher levels of education represent significant deterioration in opportunity and earning power for recent immigrants, who had earned significantly *more* in 1980 than recent immigrants to Canada were earning in the first decade of the 2000s. Using constant dollars, the Statistics Canada data show that average earnings for the recently immigrated have fallen 21.1 percent since 1980 (Statistics Canada

2009: 40). In addition, "[t]he earnings gain associated with immigrant skills, among them language and university education, has fallen" (Statistics Canada 2003c).

Reactions toward immigration are mixed. For example, while data from a 1999 survey indicate that 6 out of 10 Canadians feel that cultural diversity enhances Canadian identity, "[o]nly 14 percent . . . [said] they would like to see more immigration in future versus 43 percent who like the current levels and 41 percent who would like us to scale down" (Bricker and Greenspon 2001: 297). A poll conducted in the wake of the terrorist attacks on the United States on September 11, 2001, suggests a hardening of attitudes toward both immigrants and refugees (Figure 8.3). For example, this survey found that almost one in two Canadians (49 percent) supported restricting immigration from Muslim countries (*Maclean's* 2001/2002). A second survey, conducted shortly before the first anniversary of the tragedy of 9/11, found that over a third of respondents (35 percent) wanted our immigration laws and quotas tightened greatly, while 34 percent wanted them tightened somewhat; only 3 percent wanted immigration rules relaxed (Granastein 2002). An explanation for the shift in attitudes cannot be attributed only to the events of 9/11; we must also account for people's emotional and psychological responses to the *multiple* uncertainties that 9/11 signals:

> attitudes toward immigration that have become increasingly favorable in recent years are likely to become substantially more negative as a result of the September 11, 2001 "Attack on America." This prediction is based on psychological theorizing and research on the consequences of the direct realistic and symbolic threats that the Attack has engendered, as well as on the impact of the more indirect consequences of the Attack, which include economic and social uncertainty. As a result of this confluence of effects, it is likely that in the next few years, policy makers in the United States and Canada will be faced with a difficult task. (Esses et al. 2002: 79–80)

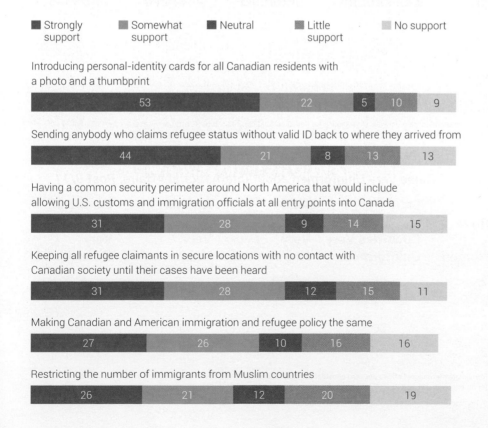

■ Strongly support   ■ Somewhat support   ■ Neutral   ■ Little support   ■ No support

Introducing personal-identity cards for all Canadian residents with a photo and a thumbprint

| 53 | 22 | 5 | 10 | 9 |

Sending anybody who claims refugee status without valid ID back to where they arrived from

| 44 | 21 | 8 | 13 | 13 |

Having a common security perimeter around North America that would include allowing U.S. customs and immigration officials at all entry points into Canada

| 31 | 28 | 9 | 14 | 15 |

Keeping all refugee claimants in secure locations with no contact with Canadian society until their cases have been heard

| 31 | 28 | 12 | 15 | 11 |

Making Canadian and American immigration and refugee policy the same

| 27 | 26 | 10 | 16 | 16 |

Restricting the number of immigrants from Muslim countries

| 26 | 21 | 12 | 20 | 19 |

Figure 8.3 *A Hardening of Attitudes toward Immigrants and Refugees*

SOURCE: *Maclean's*. "Since Sept. 11: The Responses Show how Terrorism and War have Left their Mark." December 31 2001:39. Reprinted by permission of the publisher.

An Environics poll in August 2002 showed, however, that increased hostility toward immigrants, especially those from Arab countries, correlated strongly with the level of knowledge respondents had about international affairs; in short, the greater the knowledge, the less hostile respondents were. (See Table 8.7 and Table 8.8.) Nonetheless, in both groups, many of the survey's respondents felt there were "too many" immigrants from Asian, Latin American, and African countries. In other words, the events of 9/11 appear to have disturbed what may have been a tenuous form of tolerance among non-immigrant Canadians, a population whose attitudes toward immigrants hardly appear to be positive, based on their responses in the Environics data.

Managing Canada's increasing diversity has also become a challenge for the federal government and municipal governments, for school boards, and for businesses. According to research conducted by the Privy Council Office, federal efforts will be required to fill an expanding gap in providing English training for the young and to match the skills of new immigrants to job openings. At the municipal level, there will be a challenge to deliver services to a multilingual population. The problem of figuring out who needs what is also essential. For example, while 47 percent of new immigrants fall into a low-income bracket, those from Mexico and Central America suffer from unusually high rates of unemployment, and those from Vietnam have marked difficulty with the school system.

Table 8.7 *Immigration Views of Those Very Well Informed about International Affairs, Post 9/11*

	Arab Countries Very Well Informed	Latin American Countries Very Well Informed	Asian Countries Very Well Informed	African Countries Very Well Informed	European Countries Very Well Informed
Too many	39	19	35	27	10
Too few	11	24	14	26	43
Right number	40	45	45	35	40
DK/NA	9	12	6	12	7

SOURCE: "The Impact of September 11th on Immigration," by Jack Jedwab, (Association for Canadian Studies), 2002, Table 6. http//www.acs-aec.ca/Polls/Poll12.pdf. Reprinted with permission.

Table 8.8 *Immigration Views of Those Very Uninformed about International Affairs, Post 9/11*

	Arab Countries Very Uninformed	Latin American Countries Very Uninformed	Asian Countries Very Uninformed	African Countries Very Uninformed	European Countries Very Uninformed
Too many	52	35	53	31	31
Too few	6	14	8	16	17
Right number	29	35	27	38	38
DK/NA	13	17	13	15	13

Those who consider themselves very uninformed on international affairs possess considerably greater degrees in the view that there are too many immigrants from Arab and Asian countries and for that matter from other countries as well.

SOURCE: "The Impact of September 11th on Immigration," by Jack Jedwab, (Association for Canadian Studies), 2002, Table 7. http//www.acs-aec.ca/Polls/Poll12.pdf. Reprinted with permission.

8.4 Sociological Theories of Race and Ethnicity

Some theories of race and ethnicity suggest that individuals with certain personality types are more likely to be prejudiced against or to direct hostility toward minority group members. Sociologists, however, concentrate on the impact of the structure and culture of society on race and ethnicity. The major sociological theories lend insight into the continued subordination of minorities.

Structural-Functionalist Perspective

Functionalists emphasize that each component of society contributes to the stability of the whole. In the past, inequality between majority and minority groups was functional for some groups in society. For example, in the United States, the belief in the superiority of one group over another provided moral justification for slavery, supplying the South with the means to develop an agricultural economy based on cotton. Further, southern whites perpetuated the belief that emancipation would be detrimental for blacks, who were highly dependent upon their "white masters" for survival (Nash 1962).

Functionalists recognize, however, that racial and ethnic inequality is also dysfunctional for society (Schaefer 1998; Williams and Morris 1993). A society that practises discrimination fails to develop and utilize the resources of minority members. Prejudice and discrimination aggravate social problems, such as crime and violence, war, poverty, health problems, unemployment, and drug use—problems that cause human suffering and financial burdens for individuals and society.

Conflict Perspective

Conflict theorists emphasize the role of economic competition in creating and maintaining racial and ethnic group tensions. Majority group subordination of racial and ethnic minorities reflects perceived or real economic threats by the minority. For example, although 15 000 Chinese were allowed to enter Canada as a pool of inexpensive labour for the building of the transcontinental railway, on its completion, they were treated as unwelcome guests. In 1885, the infamous "head tax" was imposed on every Chinese immigrant to Canada. Initially set at $50, the head tax was increased to $100 in 1900, and three years later to $500—an astronomical amount at that time—in an obvious attempt to restrict the entrance of Chinese and other Asians to Canada.

Further, conflict theorists suggest that capitalists profit by maintaining a surplus labour force; that is, having more workers than are needed. A surplus labour force ensures that wages remain low, because someone is always available to take a disgruntled worker's place. Minorities who are disproportionately unemployed serve the interests of the business owners by providing surplus labour, keeping wages low, and, consequently, enabling the owners to maximize profits.

Conflict theorists also argue that the wealthy and powerful elites foster negative attitudes toward minorities to maintain racial and ethnic tensions among workers. As long as workers are divided along racial and ethnic lines, they are less likely to join forces to advance their own interests at the expense of the capitalists. In addition, the "haves" perpetuate racial and ethnic tensions among the "have nots" to deflect attention away from their own greed and exploitation of workers.

Struggles over political power also affect interactions between groups organized by race and ethnicity. When the first free elections were held in South Africa, the Black

African National Congress (ANC), led by Nelson Mandela, campaigned on a platform that promised several plans of affirmative action—these would reverse the four decades of apartheid that barred black South Africans from political participation and denied them many basic human rights. The White Nation Party, trying to maintain the position of political power it had held during apartheid, also promised affirmative action in the 1994 election campaign, but it did not announce this change in platform until two months before the election, when polls began to predict a landslide victory for the African National Congress (Guillebeau 1999).

Symbolic Interactionist Perspective

The symbolic interactionist perspective focuses on how meanings and definitions contribute to the subordinate position of certain racial and ethnic groups. The different connotations of the colours white and black are a case in point. The white knight is good, and the black knight is evil; angel food cake is white, devil's food cake is black. Other negative terms associated with black include black sheep, black plague, black magic, black mass, blackballed, and blacklisted. The continued use of such derogatory labels as Jap, Gook, Spic, Frog, Kraut, Coon, Chink, Wop, and Mick also confirms the power of language in perpetuating negative attitudes toward minority group members.

For example, research by Donakowski and Esses (1996) concludes that the labels used to refer to minority groups play a role in the attitudes that are expressed toward them. In their research, 108 Canadian university students responded to a questionnaire that assessed attitudes toward Native peoples, as well as three components of attitudes: stereotypes (characteristics attributed to the group), symbolic beliefs (beliefs that the group promotes or threatens cherished values, customs, and traditions), and emotions. Five different labels were used for the group: Aboriginal peoples, First Nations people, Native Canadians, Native Indians, and Native peoples. Among non-Native students, the term *Aboriginal peoples* was associated with the most positive attitude, followed by Native peoples, Native Indians, First Nations people, and Native Canadians.

Noting that attitudes toward Native peoples were less favourable when the labels Native Canadians and First Nations were used, the researchers conclude that this stemmed, in part, from the symbolic beliefs that came to mind in response to these labels. When labelled Native Canadians or First Nations people, Native peoples were viewed as more likely to threaten national unity than when the three other labels were used. The researchers conclude, "it is possible that when the label First Nations People is used, individuals may be more likely to base their attitudes toward the group on beliefs about the political role of Natives in Canada. A Native activist organization in Canada goes by a similar name: 'Assembly of First Nations' . . . [and the label may] remind people that Natives are now working within Canadian society toward more autonomy and political power" (p. 90).

The labelling perspective directs us to consider the role that negative stereotypes play in race and ethnicity. **Stereotypes** are exaggerations or generalizations about the characteristics and behaviour of a particular group. Negative stereotyping of minorities leads to a self-fulfilling prophecy. As Schaefer (1998: 17) explains:

> Self-fulfilling prophecies can be devastating for minority groups. Such groups often find that they are allowed to hold only low-paying jobs with little prestige or opportunity for advancement. The rationale of the dominant society is that these minority individuals lack the ability to perform in more important and lucrative positions. Training to become scientists, executives, or physicians is denied to many subordinate group individuals, who are then locked into society's inferior jobs. As a result, the

stereotypes
Oversimplified or exaggerated generalizations about a category of individuals. Stereotypes are either untrue or are gross distortions of reality.

false definition becomes real. The subordinate group has become inferior because it was defined at the start as inferior and was therefore prevented from achieving the levels attained by the majority.

Feminist Perspectives

Students are often surprised to find that feminists and women from racially and ethnically marginalized groups do not necessarily share an easy alliance. The reason for tensions between women seeking social justice *as women* and women seeking social justice from social locations also marked by race and ethnicity is that "general" feminist approaches to social justice have taken whiteness for granted and have assumed that being a woman was both an essential and universal trait. Feminist historical roots in Eurocentric, bourgeois values from Mary Wollstonecraft to Betty Friedan have tended to neglect the specific concerns of women from non-dominant groups.

In Canada, for example, the National Action Committee on the Status of Women (NAC), founded in 1971, was for 22 years largely the domain only of professional, white women. In 1993, for the first time, NAC elected a woman of colour, Sunera Thobani, as its leader. While the organization had finally begun to actively support women of colour, reserving spaces for members-at-large for women from marginalized groups, some powerful white women complained that they had thus lost their representation.

Showing particular rancour was Liberal member of Parliament Mary Clancy, then the Liberal Women's Issues critic. Of Thobani's victory, Clancy claimed: "They [NAC] have taken on the interests of doubly or triply disadvantaged women—and left mainstream women feeling alienated. Of course, disadvantaged women need help. But being a woman in this country is a disadvantage in itself" (quoted in Bergman 1993: 16).

Clancy, and others like her, failed to comprehend that their vision of NAC represented the interests of liberal feminists seeking formal equality before the law, career opportunities, and wage parity with men; women who lacked access to such privileges could not expect to benefit from such limited, formal gains.

Feminist organization and feminist thinking in Canada have changed a great deal since Clancy's outburst. Contemporary antiracist feminism, influenced by postcolonial and postmodern theory, provides simultaneous, critical interrogations of race, class, and gender, throwing into question "the everyday world of common social relations, values, and practices of cultural and power" (Bannerji 2000: 544).

Becky Thompson (2001) reminds us of the contributions of antiracist feminists to feminism since the **second wave feminism** of the latter half of the twentieth century. She writes:

> I want young women to know the rich, complicated, contentious, and visionary history of multiracial feminism and to know the nuanced controversies with Second Wave feminism. I want them to know that Shirley Chisholm ran for president in 1972; that Celestine Ware wrote a Black radical feminist text in the 1970s which offered an inspiring conception of revolution with a deep sense of humanity; that before Mab Segrest went to work for an organization against the Klan in North Carolina, she and others published an independent lesbian journal . . . that included some of the most important and compelling race-conscious writing by white women and women of color to date. (p. 350)

Because of the development of awareness that "race," class, ethnicity, dis/ability, and social location all work together to shape the ways the women live and experience the everyday worlds of work, family, leisure, and so forth, there has within feminist thought and political movements over the last five decades been a view that we must include all these facets of women's backgrounds in our assessments and theorizations about women's lives. This approach is called "intersectional," and it aims to account for the discrete but intersecting characteristics—such as race and class and gender—that cannot be

second wave feminism
Twentieth-century resurgence of feminist thought, sometimes attributed to the establishment of suffrage in Canada, to the publication of de Beauvoir's *Second Sex* in France, or to the publication of Betty Friedan's *The Feminine Mystique.*

disentangled as variables that impact on women's lives. It is important to remember that the appreciation that gender is not the only site of oppression for women did not come out of traditional second wave feminist work typical of the 1970s, but instead developed because racialized women challenged the second wave "focus on gender. Their critiques . . . led to a better understanding of the intersection of oppressions and to the specific forms in which they are manifested in groups of women" (Agnew 2009).

Queer Theory Perspectives

Katherine Snider, from the University of Toronto, demonstrates in her work on multiculturalism, education, and sexuality that multicultural initiatives have been inadequate to youth populations simultaneously marginalized because of their sexuality *and* race and/or ethnicity. Taking a largely structural approach, Snider explains that the popular understanding of multiculturalism as a benign force fails to comprehend that as a policy, it operates to manage troublesome populations. Such a position does not have to interrogate its own values or systems for delivering them, thereby "avoiding the more difficult task of examining the structure of education and the curriculum, and the embedded racism on which these were built" (1996: 295). Snider directs her attention specifically to the Toronto District School Board's 1995 creation of the Triangle School, a facility set up to manage youth who risk dropping out because of their experiences of homophobia. The trouble, Snider points out, is that to enroll in the Triangle School, young people must be "out" in the *public* world, prepared to abandon the private world of family if the family cannot accept their queer sexuality. The emphasis on being "out" as a requirement for entry into the school may place in peril students who cannot divorce their sexuality from their race and/or ethnicity. Snider explains: "there is a conspicuous analytical failure to see gender and race (if you are male and white) as mitigating factors in the process of revealing sexual orientation. . . . the coming out discourse categorically under-estimates the beneficial influence and support that the private sphere provides to many youth which, by coming out, they risk losing" (p. 296). In other words, the school's policy fails to understand the complex intersecting oppressions that students can face.

In addition to these problems, institutions like the Triangle School, while they may provide refuge, fail to enforce the multiculturalist mandate to value people's differences. Instead, they remove difference from the regular system and do not demand that homophobic students, teachers, or administrators change their behaviours.

Work like Snider's represents a new and underexplored area in Canada, but it is crucial if we are to think seriously about the specific needs, challenges, and contributions of people who experience marginalization at the place where sexuality, race, and ethnicity meet.

Perspectives in Critical Race Theory

While it is true that in many ways things have improved for people in racialized groups in Canada, the research and thinking contributed by critical race theorists demonstrate clearly that it would be a mistake to believe the usual liberalist story that racism is no longer a problem, and that we have moved beyond the need to consider how the perception of "race" influences the treatment and privileges that people experience or cannot access. Critical race theory (often abbreviated as CRT), explains Margaret Zamudio and colleagues, is especially useful for thinking about how race intersects with educational opportunities, because CRT "offers [a] race conscious approach to understanding educational inequality [and] offers educators and students alike . . . effective solutions to the challenges that students of colour face in school" (Zamudio et al. 2011: 3). If, for example, history courses and books suggest that a group has neither an important place in Canada nor a significant history on the world stage—as is so often the case for the way that black culture is misrepresented, if it is presented at all—then it is not surprising that black students would "tune out" of such socio-historical classes.

CRT can also help us to understand why liberal declarations that presume the universal equality of all Canadians to be a matter of fact prevent us from solving the long-term problems of the residential school system that was imposed on Indigenous persons in Canada well into the last third of the twentieth century. CRT looks at the manifest functions that institutions sought to fulfill, but also uses tools derived from feminist activism and thinking and from post-structuralist scholarship as well. In other words, CRT is a polyvalent perspective that combines tools from other traditions and views in order to challenge dominant stories that would otherwise make it impossible for us to see clearly how racism operates in a world that claims to be "post-race."

Although CRT has been a powerful tool for evaluating and ameliorating problems of race-based social injustice in schools, it was actually developed originally by legal scholars (Ford and Airhihenbuwa 2010: s30) who sought to improve the ability of racialized groups in Canada to access the rights they had been promised under, for example, the human rights code. But just as CRT has expanded into application in educational settings, it also has considerable practical and scholarly importance for health studies. Ford and Airhihenbuwa observe that "Critical Race Theory offers the field of public health a new paradigm for investigating the root causes of health disparities. Based on race equity and social justice principles, Critical Race Theory encourages the development of solutions that bridge gaps in health, housing, employment, and other factors that condition living" (ibid).

In Canada, the work of George Dei (OISE) and Jasmin Zine (WLU) stands out for their CRT contributions to critical studies in education. Writing for the Wellesley Institute in Toronto, Sheryl Nestel has employed CRT to great effect in her report "Colour Coded Health Care" released in 2012. Citing larger empirical studies completed by Nancy Krieger, Nestel identifies six ways* in which racialized groups are placed at significant risk for the development of poorer health than dominant groups:

1. economic and social deprivation
2. exposure to toxic materials and hazardous conditions
3. socially inflicted trauma
4. targeted marketing of commodities that harm health
5. inadequate or degrading health care
6. degradation of ecosystems for indigenous populations. (Nestel 2012)

Throughout this textbook, we address problems that racialized groups face at a greater frequency and/or intensity precisely because we have not moved beyond the problems of racism. Often the data that we present have been developed by those who take a CRT approach in their work.

8.5 Prejudice and Racism

Prejudice refers to an attitude or judgment, usually negative, about an entire category of people. Prejudice may be directed toward individuals of a particular religion, sexual orientation, political affiliation, age, social class, sex, race, or ethnicity. **Racism** is a belief system, or ideology, that includes three basic ideas (Marger 2000):

1. Humans are divided naturally into different physical types.
2. The physical traits associated with each human type are innately related to the culture, personality, and intelligence of each type.
3. On the basis of their genetic inheritance, some groups are innately superior to others.

*Krieger, N. (2011). *Epidemiology and the people's health*. Oxford, England, and New York, NY: Oxford University Press, p. 223. By permission of Oxford University Press, USA.

prejudice
An attitude or judgment, usually negative, about an entire category of people based on their group membership.

racism
The belief that certain groups of people are innately inferior to other groups of people based on their racial classification. Racism serves to justify discrimination against groups that are perceived as inferior.

The perception that certain groups have inferior traits serves to justify subordination and mistreatment of those groups.

Aversive and Modern Racism

Compared with traditional, "old-fashioned" prejudice, which is blatant, direct, and conscious, contemporary forms of prejudice are often subtle, indirect, and unconscious. Two variants of these more subtle forms of prejudice include aversive racism and modern racism.

Aversive Racism

Aversive racism represents a subtle, often unintentional form of prejudice exhibited by many well-intentioned people who possess strong egalitarian values and who view themselves as nonprejudiced. The negative feelings that aversive racists have toward minority groups are not feelings of hostility or hate, but rather feelings of discomfort, uneasiness, disgust, and sometimes fear (Gaertner and Dovidio 2000). Aversive racists may not be fully aware that they harbour these negative racial feelings; indeed, they disapprove of individuals who are prejudiced and would feel falsely accused if they were labelled as prejudiced. "Aversive racists find Blacks 'aversive,' while at the same time find any suggestion that they might be prejudiced 'aversive' as well" (Gaertner and Dovidio 2000: 14).

Another aspect of aversive racism is the presence of "pro-white" attitudes—as opposed to, for example, "anti-black" attitudes. In several studies, respondents did not indicate that blacks were worse than whites, only that whites were better than blacks (Gaertner and Dovidio 2000). For example, blacks were not rated as being lazier than whites, but whites were rated as being more ambitious than blacks. Gaertner and Dovidio (2000) explain that "aversive racists would not characterize Blacks more negatively than whites because that response could readily be interpreted by others or oneself, to reflect racial prejudice" (p. 27). Compared with anti-black attitudes, pro-white attitudes reflect a more subtle prejudice that, although less overtly negative, is still racial bias.

Modern Racism

Like aversive racism, **modern racism** involves the rejection of traditional racist beliefs, but a modern racist displaces negative racial feelings onto more abstract social and political issues. The modern racist believes that serious discrimination in Canada no longer exists, that any continuing racial inequality is the fault of minority group members, and that demands for employment equity for minorities are unfair and unjustified. "Modern racism tends to 'blame the victim' and place the responsibility for change and improvements on the minority groups, not on the larger society" (Healey 1997: 55). Like aversive racists, modern racists tend to be unaware of their negative racial feelings and do not view themselves as prejudiced.

Learning to Be Prejudiced: The Role of Socialization, Stereotypes, and the Media

Psychological theories of prejudice focus on forces within the individual that give rise to prejudice. For example, the **frustration-aggression theory** of prejudice (also known as the **scapegoating theory**) suggests that prejudice is a form of hostility that results from frustration. According to this theory, minority groups serve as convenient targets of displaced aggression. The **authoritarian-personality theory**

---

aversive racism
A subtle, often unintentional form of prejudice exhibited by many individuals who possess strong egalitarian values and who view themselves as non-prejudiced.

modern racism
A subtle and complex form of racism in which individuals are not explicitly racist, but tend to hold negative views of racial minorities and blame minorities for their social disadvantages.

frustration-aggression theory (scapegoating theory)
A psychological theory of prejudice that suggests prejudice is a form of hostility resulting from frustration. According to this theory, minority groups serve as convenient targets of displaced aggression.

authoritarian-personality theory
A psychological theory of prejudice that suggests prejudice arises in people with a certain personality type. According to this theory, people with an authoritarian personality, who are highly conformist, intolerant, cynical, and preoccupied with power, are prone to prejudice.

of prejudice suggests that prejudice arises in people with a certain personality type. According to this theory, people with an authoritarian personality—who are highly conformist, intolerant, cynical, and preoccupied with power—are prone to being prejudiced.

Rather than focus on the individual, sociologists focus on social forces that contribute to prejudice. Earlier we explained how intergroup conflict over wealth, power, and prestige gives rise to negative feelings and attitudes that serve to protect and enhance dominant group interests. In the following discussion, we explain how prejudice is learned through socialization, stereotypes, and the media.

Learning Prejudice through Socialization

In the socialization process, individuals adopt the values, beliefs, and perceptions of their family, peers, culture, and social groups. Prejudice is taught and learned through socialization, although it need not be taught directly and intentionally. Parents who may teach their children to not be prejudiced yet live in an all-white neighbourhood, attend an all-white church, and have only white friends may be indirectly teaching negative racial attitudes to their children. Socialization may also be direct, as in the case of a parent who uses racial slurs in the presence of her children, or forbids her children to play with children from a certain racial or ethnic background. Children may also learn prejudicial attitudes from their peers. The telling of racial and ethnic jokes among friends, for example, perpetuates stereotypes that foster negative racial and ethnic attitudes.

Stereotypes

Prejudicial attitudes toward racial and ethnic groups are based on false or inadequate group images known as stereotypes. Consider, in this context, Toronto mayor Mel Lastman's "joke" about travelling to Africa: "What the hell do I want to go to a place like Mombasa? . . . I just see myself in a pot of boiling water with all these natives dancing around me" (Deziel and Cameron 2001/2002: 21). As noted earlier, stereotypes are exaggerations or generalizations about the characteristics and behaviour of a particular group.

Prejudice and the Media

The media contribute to prejudice by portraying minorities in negative and stereotypical ways, or by not portraying them at all. For example, Mosher (1998) notes that the racialization of crime has a long history in Canada, with the Canadian news media displaying an increasing tendency to attribute the social problem of crime to blacks and Asians. Research by Claxton-Oldfield and Keefe (1999) on stereotypes about the Innu of Davis Inlet, Labrador, also suggests the potency of the media in shaping public opinion about different racial and ethnic groups. In the first part of their research, a sample of 22 male and 56 female Newfoundland college students (aged 18 to 23) were asked to list the characteristics that came to mind about the Innu and to indicate where these impressions came from. At least 20 percent of the students described the Innu as being uneducated, alcoholic, poor, and isolated, and called them gas-sniffers. The two most important sources for the students' impressions of the Innu were television and newspapers. In the second phase of their investigation, the researchers examined the image of the Innu in a daily Newfoundland newspaper for one year (January to December 1996). Headline analysis revealed that conflict and deviance words (e.g., gas-sniffing, sexual abuse, protest) appeared in 44 percent of the headlines of newspaper items about the Innu. The researchers conclude that stereotypes of the Innu mirror the images portrayed of them in the media.

8.6 Discrimination Against Racial and Ethnic Minorities

Whereas prejudice refers to attitudes, **discrimination** refers to actions or practices that result in differential treatment of categories of individuals. Although prejudicial attitudes often accompany discriminatory behaviour or practices, one may be evident without the other.

Individual versus Institutional Discrimination

Individual discrimination occurs when individuals treat persons unfairly or unequally because of their group membership. Individual discrimination may be overt or adaptive. In **overt discrimination**, the individual discriminates because of his or her own prejudicial attitudes. For example, a white landlord may refuse to rent to a First Nations family because of her own prejudice against Aboriginal peoples.

Suppose a Vietnamese-Canadian family wants to rent an apartment in a predominantly white neighbourhood. If the landlord is prejudiced against the Vietnamese and does not allow the family to rent the apartment, that landlord has engaged in overt discrimination. However, what if the landlord is not prejudiced against the Vietnamese, but still refuses to rent to a Vietnamese family? Perhaps that landlord is engaging in **adaptive discrimination**, or discrimination that is based on the prejudice of others. In this example, the landlord may fear that if he rents to a Vietnamese-Canadian family, other renters who are prejudiced against the Vietnamese may move out of the building or neighbourhood and leave the landlord with unrented apartments. Overt and adaptive individual discrimination may coexist. For example, a landlord may not rent an apartment to a Vietnamese family because of her own prejudices *and* the fear that other tenants may move out.

Institutional discrimination occurs when normal operations and procedures of social institutions result in unequal treatment of minorities. Institutional discrimination is covert and insidious and maintains the subordinate position of minorities in society. As conflict theorists emphasize, majority group members make rules that favour their own group.

Although discrimination may have become more subtle and less overt, racial and ethnic minorities continue to experience discrimination and its effects in almost every sphere of social life (Noh and Belser 1999; Stodolska and Jackson 1998). For example, Kunz and colleagues (2000)* find that

- foreign-born visible minorities experience greater discrepancies between education and occupation than other groups (fewer than half of those with a university education have high-skill-level jobs);
- even with postsecondary education, unemployment rates are higher for racial minorities, especially foreign-born visible minorities (12 percent) and Aboriginal peoples (23 percent) compared to whites (7 percent) and Canadian-born visible minorities (8 percent);
- given the same level of education, whites, whether foreign or Canadian-born, are three times as likely as Aboriginal peoples and about twice as likely as foreign-born visible minorities to be in the highest income quintile;
- Canadian-born visible minorities are still less likely than whites (Canadian and foreign-born) to be in the top 20 percent of the income distribution (Weiner 2001).

Next, we look at the extent and brutality of hate crimes against minorities.

*Unequal Access: A Canadian Profile of Racial Differences in Education Employment and Income. Canadian Race Relations Foundation, http://www.crr.ca/en/component/content/article/292-english/policies-and-research/23538-unequal-access-a-canadian-profile-of-racial-differences-in-education-employment-and-income. Reprinted with permission.

---

discrimination
Differential treatment of individuals based on their group membership.

individual discrimination
Discriminatory acts by individuals that are based on prejudicial attitudes.

overt discrimination
Discrimination that occurs because of an individual's own prejudicial attitudes.

adaptive discrimination
Discrimination that is based on the prejudice of others.

institutional discrimination
Discrimination in which the normal operations and procedures of social institutions result in unequal treatment of minorities.

Hate Crime Victimization

A **hate crime**, or **bias-motivated crime**, is an act of violence motivated by prejudice or bias against racial, ethnic, religious, and sexual-orientation groups. Examples include intimidation (e.g., threats), destruction or damage of property, physical assault, and murder. Section 718.2 of the *Criminal Code* provides that "evidence that [an offence] was motivated by bias, prejudice or hate based on race, national or ethnic origin, colour, religion, sex, age, mental or physical disability, sexual orientation or any other similar factor" is to be considered an aggravating circumstance in sentencing convicted offenders. For example, in the case of *R. v. Ingram and Grimsdale* (1977), it was held that "an assault which is racially motivated renders the offence more heinous. Such assaults, unfortunately, invite imitation and repetition by others and incite retaliation. The danger is even greater in a multicultural, pluralistic urban society." In addition, section 319 of the *Criminal Code* defines wilfully promoting hatred against any identifiable group—"any section of the public distinguished by colour, race, religion, or ethnic group"—and advocating genocide as criminal offences, punishable by up to two years' imprisonment. Perhaps the best-known prosecution under the latter section of the Code is that of James Keegstra, a former Alberta high-school teacher who was accused of fomenting hatred against the Jews in his classroom lectures. Keegstra was subsequently charged under the subsection of Canada's *Criminal Code* that prohibits hate propaganda other than in private conversations. The case was later appealed to the Supreme Court of Canada. In 1996, the Supreme Court ruled that although hate propaganda "formed part of protected freedom of expression pursuant to subsection 2(b) of the Canadian Charter of Rights and Freedoms" its prohibition was reasonable and "supported by international documents to which Canada is a party and sections 15 (equality) and 27 (multiculturalism) of the Charter" (Beaudoin 1999: 1237).

In other cases, the attempt to curtail the spread of hate propaganda has been less successful. Ernst Zundel published a brochure entitled "Did Six Million Really Die?" His brochure claimed that the Holocaust was a myth propagated by a worldwide Jewish conspiracy. He was subsequently charged under section 181 of the *Criminal Code*, which makes the wilful dissemination of false news a criminal offence. The Supreme Court of Canada ruled that this section of the Code denied Zundel the right to freedom of expression, as guaranteed under the *Canadian Charter of Rights and Freedoms*, and that section 181 was not justified in a free and democratic society.

Canada's 1999 General Social Survey produced, for the first time, estimates of self-reported hate crime victimization at the national level. It concluded that there were 272 000 crimes where the victim felt that hate was the motive, with over 4 of 10 (43 percent) believing that hatred of race or ethnicity was involved (Blackwell 2002). However, while the United States has systematically compiled statistics on hate crimes since the 1990 passage of the *Hate Crimes Statistics Act*, Canada lacks a national system for collecting hate-crime statistics. "There has been little systematic research in Canada upon the nature and incidence of hate crimes" (Roberts 1995). There is also considerable variation in Canada in the definitions of "hate crimes" employed by various Canadian police departments. Some police services, such as Montreal's, do not gather any information on hate crimes at all.

The Canadian Arab Federation, the Canadian chapter of the Council on American Islamic Relations, the Canadian Jewish Congress, and B'nai Brith Canada all report a surge in hate crimes since the September 11, 2001, terrorist attacks. For example, B'nai Brith Canada, which compiles an annual audit of anti-Semitic incidents, reports that by June 2002 there had been over 180 such offences, ranging from the burning of synagogues to bomb threats and assaults, compared to 286 in all of 2001 (Blackwell 2002). Six months after the tragedy of September 11, a report prepared by the Council

hate crime (bias-motivated crime)
An act of violence motivated by prejudice.

on American-Islamic Relations noted 120 anti-Muslim incidents across Canada, including 10 death threats, 13 cases of physical violence, and 12 attacks on mosques and Islamic centres (Ray 2002). The 2001 annual report of the hate crimes unit of the Toronto Police Services reports 338 incidents in 2001 (up from 204 the previous year) and suggests that approximately "90 percent of the increase can be linked to the terrorist attacks . . . with Muslims being the group most frequently targeted" (*KW Record* 2002).

Levin and McDevitt (1995) found that the motivations for hate crimes were of three distinct types: thrill, defensive, and mission. Thrill hate crimes are committed by offenders who are looking for excitement and attack victims for the "fun of it." Defensive hate crimes involve offenders who view their attacks as necessary to protect their community, workplace, or campus from "outsiders." Perpetrators of defensive hate crimes are trying to send a message that their victims do not belong in a particular community, workplace, or campus and that anyone in the victim's group who dares to "intrude" could be the next victim. Mission hate crimes are perpetrated by offenders who have dedicated their lives to bigotry. In Levin and McDevitt's study of hate crimes in Boston, the most common type of hate crime was thrill hate crime (58 percent) followed by defensive hate crime (41 percent).

The least common but most violent type of hate crime is the mission hate crime. First described and identified by Jack Levin and Jack McDevitt in 1993, and refined in 2002, missionaries typically identify "with a specific leader or higher power[;] these offenders seek to rid the world of evil by disposing of the members of an identified and despised group" (Momen 2008: 17). Those who follow charismatic leaders of racist groups tend to see themselves as being on a mission, and Momen adds to Levin and McDevitt's typology for this group with the observation that "Mission hate offenders do not attack in response to any real threat or event, rather their intention is to eliminate all members of an outgroup who they feel is responsible for their misfortunes. Perpetrators of mission hate crimes often have severe mental disorders and exhibit conspiratorial thoughts" (Momen 2008: 15).

While our criminal code identifies hate crimes as detrimental activities that enact or are meant to incite hatred against an entire group, there is no specific court prohibition on what we have come to refer to in popular media and some scholarly circles as **racial profiling**.

In practice, racial profiling targets particular groups for heightened surveillance based on the idea that supposed/presumed higher historical rates of criminal activity in a given group are an objective fact rather than the consequence of higher rates of surveillance of that group, and can only be prevented by subjecting that group to more police activity. In other words, we may never know if young white males in affluent suburbs commit as many petty crimes, including acts of vandalism and theft, as do young black males from poor neighbourhoods.

The kinds of policing activities that may be involved in racial profiling include more frequent roadside stops or other random stop-and-search procedures carried out against persons who are not suspected of committing any particular crime, but are considered suspicious because they belong to a particular racialized group. Those most vulnerable to these stop-and-search procedures are young black men, and black communities in Canada are most likely to see racial profiling as a problem while whites and Asian groups "are more likely to believe that profiling is a useful crime-fighting tool" (Wortly and Owusu-Bempah 2011: 395).

Returning to our discussion in Chapter 1 of Spector and Kitsuse's demonstration that social problems are not simple, objective facts that already exist and merely await our notice, it is worth noting here that sociologists are not necessarily in agreement regarding how to assess or how best to remedy racial profiling. To determine both what

racial profiling
The practice, usually if not exclusively carried out in law enforcement or border crossing, that subjects some groups to increased surveillance or scrutiny based on racial or ethnic factors rather than any specific reason for suspicion.

the act is and whether that act is racist requires serious consideration of both the practices that police carry out, and how those practices are perceived or interpreted by all the stakeholders involved (community members and police alike). A well-known debate broke out between highly respected sociologists whose work shares a focus on the perception and treatment of race, as well as the creation and maintenance on the inequalities that are associated with both institutional and individual racism in Canada. The debate was principally between McMaster University sociologists Vic Satzewich and William Shaffir on the one hand, and Frances Henry and Carol Tator at York University on the other hand. The debate was set off with the 2009 publication "Racism versus Professionalism: Claims and Counter-Claims" by Satzewich and Shaffir, and was carried through in a series of responses and observations in rejoinder articles by Henry and Tator (2011), as well as by Ronald-Frans Melchers (2011), all in the *Canadian Journal of Criminology and Criminal Justice*. At issue was Satzewich and Shaffir's attempt to understand how the police view their own work, and what the implications of those views are for the elimination of the problems of institutional racism. They concluded that we cannot understand racial profiling and put an end to it if we insist on seeing it as a set of individual racist acts and intentions.

In their initial article, Satzewich and Shaffir detail their findings from interviews carried out with 18 members of the Hamilton Police Force. The interviewees were from all ranks and positions in the force, and spanned a range of years on the force from being relatively new recruits to being very senior members. Half of the interviewees were white, and half were from visible minority groups; two were women and the remainder were men (2009: 206). Satzewich and Shaffir rely on some of the conceptual work that had been previously completed by Henry and Tator in 2006, as well as by the noted criminologist Janet Chan. In particular, they note that these scholars explain that the everyday culture of policing differs from the perceptions and policies set out by management (Satzewich and Shaffir 2009: 213), but what Satzewich and Shaffir found in their own work was the two levels of policing (management and everyday work) actually shared the same declared values regarding the obvious need to value diversity in the Hamilton community. Satzewich and Shaffir are careful to explain, however, the declared valuing of diversity did not prevent the force from maintaining three specific, symbolic strategies for deflecting responsibility and attention on their profiling practices *away* from the police and *toward* those who experience profiling. The three strategies that Satzewich and Shaffir identify in their article are (1) the claim not to tolerate intolerance; (2) a discourse that values multiculturalism; and (3) a discourse that blames the victim. In other words, Satzewich and Shaffir did not conclude that the force never carried out activities that might count as racial profiling; rather, they concluded that as newer recruits are socialized into police work, they learn how to recast profiling so that "the well socialized member of this subculture [the police force] is able to emphasize the distinction between criminal profiling and racial profiling" (p. 219).

Where the controversy erupted was in the recommendation from Satzewich and Shaffir that "if we want to seek an appropriate solution to the problem of racial profiling, we need to have a clear assessment of the source of the problem" (p. 220). In other words, for Satzewich and Shaffir it is not enough simply to label a practice as racial profiling, because that will not make it stop. Instead, they argue, we need to understand that while scholars like Henry and Tator have cast any act that results in unequal treatment of a racialized group as racist, police tend to think not about the results of their actions but about their motives for acting in the first place. Satzewich and Shaffir write, "From the perspective of the police, while groups [who cry foul] may garner attention, this is hardly the outcome of racialized police practices; they engage in criminal profiling, not racial profiling" (ibid).

Henry and Tator (2011) took issue with Satzewich and Shaffir's analysis, arguing that:

> in analysing the strategies of deflection and rationalization commonly used by the police and drawn from their subculture, Satzewich and Shaffir [do not develop] another theory to explain the presence of racial profiling but merely [show] how the police themselves ... admit to racial profiling because they believe that this practice is a natural part of their work as police officers and managers. ... Satzewich and Shaffir appear to dismiss the significant body of research that demonstrates the nature and extent of how minorized groups and individuals are criminalised through a series of processes including racialization and culturalization. (2011: 69)

However, writing in the same 2011 volume of the journal, University of Ottawa criminologist Ronald-Frans Melchers found that Henry and Tator mischaracterize Satzewich and Shaffir's work. In short, it is not that Satzewich and Shaffir refuse the existence of racial profiling, or reject its general sociological definition as Henry and Tator charge. Rather, corrects Melchers, Satzewich and Shaffir show us that the police reframe racial profiling as "criminal profiling," and so officers and forces recast public scrutiny of police activities staking claims "that it is police critics who mistakenly conclude that blacks are singled out for differential treatment" (Melchers 2011: 106). Finally, in the same 2011 issue, Janet Chan argues that we need to pay attention to the lessons from Satzewich and Shaffir's analysis because the hazards of racial profiling present a wider negative impact "lead[ing] both to a feeling of being harassed and to a sense of alienation from the legal system and the wider society. For victims ... the intention of the policing agent is not an issue; the sense of injustice and insecurity is what stays with them" (2011: 75). For Chan, the important point that emerges from Satzewich and Shaffir is not, as Henry and Tator suggest, that we should assert that there is no racial profiling where the police officers declare no personal intent, but rather that we must deal with and change the "race-based deployment [of racial profiling as] an organizational or local practice" (2011: 76). In other words, we cannot solve the issue by targeting individual officers' acts or intentions, but must change institutional and organizational practices.

8.7 Strategies for Action: Responding to Prejudice, Racism, and Discrimination

Next, we look at various strategies that address problems of prejudice, racism, and discrimination. These include multicultural education, diversity training in the workplace, and political strategies.

Multicultural Education in Schools and Communities

multicultural education
Education that includes all racial and ethnic groups in the school curriculum and promotes awareness and appreciation for cultural diversity.

In schools across the nation, **multicultural education**, which encompasses a broad range of programs and strategies, works to dispel myths, stereotypes, and ignorance about minorities, promotes tolerance and appreciation of diversity, and includes minority groups in the school curriculum (see also Chapter 12). With multicultural education, the school curriculum reflects the diversity of Canadian society and fosters an awareness and appreciation of the contributions of different racial and ethnic groups to Canadian culture. The proclaimed goals of multicultural education are not, however, effectively realized in schools. That is because they remain at the margins of a curriculum that continues to place Euro-American culture at the centre, as the benchmark against which all other things are assessed. Critical education researcher and critical race theorist Jasmin Zine observes, for example, that schools in Canada*

- Have special festival days that "reduce the wealth of your knowledge and experience to 'saris, samosa and steel bands' (and yet you know you didn't learn about Canadian history through bagpipes and meat pies)"
- Continue to be run principally by white administrators who serve as "a constant reminder of the glass ceilings that limit your chances to achieve positions of power because of your race, class and gender . . ."
- Have students "perform" their cultural heritage, which turns them into "a tourist spectacle, [whose] Anglo-Canadian classmates are never asked to do the same. (Cindy, could you wear a traditional costume of your British ancestors to school for Canada Day?)" (2002: 37)

Colleges and universities, perhaps because they have greater freedom to set their own curricula, have developed courses and degree programs in critical race and ethnic studies, and provide support for multicultural, student-run organizations. Evidence suggests a number of positive outcomes for both minority and majority students who take such programs, including increased racial understanding and cultural awareness, increased social interaction with students who have backgrounds different from their own, improved cognitive development, increased support for efforts to achieve educational equity, and greater satisfaction with their experience of higher education (Humphreys 1999). This chapter's *Social Problems Research Up Close* feature presents a study that identifies various factors that influence first-year students' openness to diversity.

*From J. Zine, 2002. *Inclusive Schooling in a Pluralist Society*, p. 37. Toronto: Canadian Education Association. Reprinted by permission of the Canadian Education Association.

Social Problems *Research Up Close*

What Influences Students' Openness to Diversity?

A study by Pascarella and colleagues (1996) sought to determine how students' openness to diversity is influenced by four different sets of factors: student background characteristics, environmental emphases of the institution attended, measures of the students' academic experience, and measures of students' social involvement.

Sample and Methods

The researchers collected data from 2290 first-year students at 18 colleges and universities. The dependent variable was a scale designed to measure openness to diversity (see scale). This scale not only assesses an individual's openness to cultural, racial, and value diversity; it also measures the extent to which an individual enjoys being challenged by different ideas, values, and perspectives.

Openness to Diversity/Challenge Scale

(Scored on a Likert-type scale: 5 = strongly agree to 1 = strongly disagree)

1. I enjoy having discussions with people whose ideas and values are different from my own.
2. The real value of a college/university education lies in being introduced to different values.
3. I enjoy talking with people who have values different from mine because it helps me understand myself and my values better.
4. Learning about people from different cultures is a very important part of my university/college education.
5. I enjoy taking courses that challenge my beliefs and values.
6. The courses I enjoy the most are those that make me think about things from a different perspective.

(continued)

7. Contact with individuals whose background (e.g., race, national origin, sexual orientation) is different from my own is an essential part of my college/university education.
8. I enjoy courses that are intellectually challenging.

Four sets of independent variables were developed, each of which consisted of numerous measures: (1) precollege/preuniversity variables (including a measure of precollege/preuniversity openness to diversity and precollege/preuniversity academic ability), (2) environmental emphasis of the college/university (including a measure of the degree of racial discrimination at the institution), (3) student academic experiences (including number of social science courses taken and self-reported number of hours spent studying per week), and (4) student social/nonacademic experiences (including involvement in clubs and organizations and assessment of students' peer interactions and topics of conversation).

Findings

The precollege/preuniversity measure of openness to diversity/challenge had the strongest effect on openness to diversity/challenge after the first year of attendance. Women and non-white students had higher levels of openness to diversity/challenge than men and white students.

The extent to which students perceived their institution as having a nondiscriminatory racial environment had a positive impact on openness to diversity. Hours spent studying had a small positive effect, while the number of mathematics courses taken during the first year of college had a small negative impact.

Living on campus, participating in a racial or cultural awareness workshop, and hours worked per week had positive effects on openness to diversity/challenge, while joining a fraternity or sorority had a negative effect. In addition, "the more students interact with diverse peers and the greater the extent to which such interactions focus on controversial or value-laden issues that may engender a change in perspective or opinion, the greater one's development of openness to diversity and challenge" (p. 188).

The findings of this study suggest that colleges and universities that offer racial or cultural awareness workshops can foster students' appreciation and acceptance of cultural, racial, and value diversity. Encouraging openness to diversity may also be achieved by the institution establishing policies and programs that sensitize students and personnel to racial discrimination and demonstrate that such discrimination is not acceptable. Colleges and universities may also consider interventions to counteract the negative influence of membership in fraternities or sororities on openness to diversity.

Finally, the fact that precollege/preuniversity openness to diversity had the largest effect on openness to diversity among first-year students points to the need to foster openness to diversity in the elementary-school and secondary-school grades. Multicultural programs, educational approaches, and school policies that discourage and sanction prejudice and discrimination will help achieve this.

SOURCES: Based on Pascarella, Ernest T., Marcia Edison, Amaury Nora, Linda Serra Hagedorn, and Patrick T. Terenzini. 1996. "Influences on Students' Openness to Diversity and Challenge in the First Year of College." *Journal of Higher Education* 67(2): 174–93. © 1996 The Ohio State University. Reproduced with permission.

Efforts to recruit and admit historically disadvantaged groups in institutions of higher education have also been found to foster positive relationships among diverse groups and enrich the educational experience of all students. Gurin (1999) found that students with the most exposure to diverse populations during university had the most cross-racial interactions five years after leaving university. A poll of law students at two universities also found that nearly 90 percent of the students said that diversity in the classroom provided them with a better educational experience. About 9 in 10 students also said that the contact they had with students of different racial or ethnic backgrounds influenced them to change their view on some aspect of human rights (*Race Relations Reporter* 1999).

Diversity Training in the Workplace

Increasingly, corporations have begun to implement efforts to reduce prejudice and discrimination in the workplace through an educational approach known as **diversity training**. Broadly defined, diversity training involves "raising personal awareness about individual 'differences' in the workplace and how those differences inhibit or enhance the way people work together and get work done" (Wheeler 1994: 10). Diversity training may address such issues as stereotyping and cross-cultural insensitivity, as well as provide workers with specific information on cultural norms of different groups and how these norms affect work behaviour and social interactions.

Political Strategies

Various political strategies have been implemented or suggested to reduce prejudice and discrimination. However, although it is readily apparent that strategies such as employment equity (see Chapter 7) can prevent or reduce discriminatory practices, their effects are complex. For example, legal policies that prohibit discrimination can increase modern forms of prejudice, as in the case of individuals who conclude that because laws and policies prohibit discrimination, any social disadvantages of minorities must be their own fault. On the other hand, any improvements in the socio-economic status of minorities that result from legal/political policies may help to replace negative images of minorities with positive ones. For example, it has been suggested that employment equity provides minority role models. "Nonwhites in educational and professional positions where they were previously not present function as models for other, especially younger, members of their racial group who can identify with them and form realistic goals to occupy the same roles themselves" (Zack 1998: 51).

Understanding Race and Ethnicity

After considering the material presented in this chapter, what understanding about race and ethnicity are we left with? First, we have seen that racial categories are socially constructed with no scientific validity. Racial and ethnic categories are largely arbitrary, imprecise, and misleading. Although some scholars suggest that we abandon racial and ethnic labels, others advocate adding new categories—multiracial and multiethnic—to reflect the identities of a growing segment of the Canadian population.

Conflict theorists and functionalists agree that prejudice, discrimination, and racism have benefited certain groups in society. But racial and ethnic disharmony has created tensions that disrupt social equilibrium. Symbolic interactionists note that negative labelling of minority group members, which is learned through interaction with others, contributes to the subordinate position of minorities.

Prejudice, racism, and discrimination are debilitating forces in the lives of minorities. In spite of these negative forces, many minority group members succeed in living productive, meaningful, and prosperous lives; however, many others cannot overcome the social disadvantages associated with their minority status—they become victims of a cycle of poverty (see Chapter 10). Alterations in the structure of society are needed. Increasing opportunities for minorities—in education, employment and income, and political participation—is crucial to achieving racial and ethnic equality. In addition, policymakers concerned with racial and ethnic equality must find ways to reduce the racial/ethnic wealth gap and foster wealth accumulation among minorities (Conley 1999). As noted earlier, access to wealth affects many dimensions of well-being.

Human rights activist Lani Guinier (1998) suggests that "the real challenge is to . . . use race as a window on issues of class, issues of gender, and issues of fundamental

diversity training
Workplace training programs designed to increase employees' awareness of cultural differences in the workplace and how these differences may affect job performance.

fairness, not just to talk about race as if it's a question of individual bigotry or individual prejudice. The issue is more than about making friends—it's about making change." But, as Shipler (1998) argues, making change requires that members of society recognize that change is necessary, that a problem that needs rectifying:

> One has to perceive the problem to embrace the solutions. If you think that racism isn't harmful unless it wears sheets or burns crosses or bars blacks from motels and restaurants, you will support only the crudest anti-discrimination laws and not the more refined methods. . . . (p. 2)

Finally, it is important to consider the role of class in the casting of concerns related to race and ethnicity. bell hooks (2000) warns that focusing on issues of race and gender can deflect attention away from the larger issue of class division that increasingly separates the "haves" from the "have nots." Addressing class inequality must, suggests hooks, be part of any meaningful strategy to reduce inequalities suffered by minority groups.

Student Reflection: What Do You Know Now?

This chapter begins in part by challenging the very existence of the category "race" as a biological fact. This is not to deny its existence for people as an experienced identity: it is of course a social fact, revived and reconsolidated every day by all our actions and beliefs. How have definitions, stereotypes, and other elements of racialized and ethnic identity played out in your own schools and communities over time? Has it been the case that you've lived in neighbourhoods or gone to schools "known" for certain cultural backgrounds? What are some of the biases that emerged? Have you ever been asked to "perform" your own cultural background in elementary or secondary school settings? Consider as well the demographics of your current school if you are studying formally right now. What research questions might arise if you want to find out about certain inequalities?

What Do You Do Next?

Located at www.nelson.com/socialproblems5e

- Consolidate your knowledge with interactive and printable **Flashcards**
- Gauge your understanding with **Practice Quizzes** and **Matching Activities**
- Develop your critical thinking skills with **Self and Society** and **The Human Side** questions
- Analyze **Social Research** and **Social Problems in Global Perspective**
- Explore the implications of **Technology on Social Problems**

9
Sexualities

Student Reflection:
What Do You Already Know?

In Kitchener, Ontario, a policy decision recently was reversed permitting community groups—including the local Pride group—to fly flags on specific poles outside city hall that previously could fly only government flags. This action was hailed by many as a step forward given that most other communities already allowed emblems like the Rainbow Flag to fly (much of the controversy came on the heels of the flying of pride flags in other cities around the time of the Sochi Olympics, in solidarity with gay and lesbian athletes). To what extent is it important to have visible, publicly supported statements through such symbolic displays? This chapter is one way into such questions. It is likely that as someone studying in a Canadian institution, you'll be quite aware of efforts to be inclusive in terms of sexuality and gender identity. Increasingly, trans issues are raised in media and around campuses, for example. No matter what your own personal identity, it is helpful for us all to consider these forms of diversity as seriously as we do the others with which they intersect in relation to social problems.

Learning Outcomes

Through careful reading of this chapter, you should be able to:

- define the bolded key terms
- explain the historical and contemporary concepts of sexual and gender identities, including outlining the controversy about biological and social determinants
- understand the workings of heterosexism, homophobia, biphobia, transphobia, and discrimination based on sexual and gender identity, including their effects on people
- apply sociological theories of sexual orientation to historical and contemporary lived experiences
- respond to sexual and gender identity based prejudice and discrimination in the context of historical and contemporary policy, law, and activism

© efenzi/iStockphoto.com

9.1 The Canadian Context

On November 17, 2001, 42-year-old Aaron Webster was beaten to death in a vicious attack in a parking lot in Stanley Park, Vancouver, in what is believed to have been British Columbia's first lethal incident of "gay bashing." Webster had been bludgeoned with either a baseball bat or a pool cue by a group of three to four men and left to die. At a memorial service for Webster that drew more than 1500 participants, Vancouver Police Inspector Dave Jones referred to Webster as the victim of a "hate crime, pure and simple" and promised that his department would "do everything in our power" to find the perpetrators and "bring them to justice" (Associated Press 2001; Nagle 2001).

Of the many issues raised by Aaron Webster's death, one was the adequacy of the definition of a "hate crime" under Canada's *Criminal Code* (Bush and Sainz 2001). According to the *Criminal Code* of the time, crimes committed against sexual orientation minorities were not, technically speaking, "hate crimes" (Wetzel 2001). In 1999, Justice Minister Anne McLellan had announced that she would introduce amendments to the Code to protect lesbians and gays from hate crimes, but by 2001 that had not happened (EGALE 2001).

Arising out of Aaron Webster's death, Bill C-250 was tabled in the House of Commons in 2003. The bill extended Canada's already existing hate crimes law to include as an "identifiable group" those who experience hate crimes as a result of their perceived sexual orientation—one need not *be* lesbian, transgendered, bisexual, or gay to experience a hate crime. In 2004, on April 29, Bill C-250 was granted Royal Assent and became part of Canada's criminal legal code. Introduced to the House of Commons as a private member's bill by British Columbia MP Svend Robinson, Bill C-250 was initially passed by the House of Commons on September 13, 2003, and adds "sexual orientation" to the text of subsection 318(4) so that gays and lesbians would be included in the "identifiable group" category that had previously included recognition only for colour, race, religion, and ethnic origin.

Thus, sexual minority groups were included in the ethnic model of multiculturalism that lay the foundations for the rationale of the initial law against hate crimes. Viewing crimes against those perceived to be sexual minorities as hate crimes instead of criminal assaults recognizes that the motivational aspect of prejudice heightens the threat to the general good of Canada's people. In principle, our hate crimes law is intended to protect not only specific groups, but also our national value system of *multiculturalism*. The law sends the message that prejudice is no excuse and that the courts and nation do not agree that some people "deserve a beating" (or worse) because of their skin colour, race, ethnicity, religion, or sexuality. At its foundation, hate crimes are specifically identified as distinct from other forms of crime because they inflict a "**disproportionate harm**" on the victims. Citing the work of Garafolo and Martin (1991) in a report for Canada's Department of Justice, Julian Roberts (1995) notes three distinct characteristics that separate hate crimes from other crimes. First, hate crimes attack a core feature of the victim's identity, with the implication being that there is nothing the victim can do to prevent being the target of an attack; better locks and avoiding walking alone at night do not solve the problem of prejudice. Second, hate crimes negatively impact entire communities by making other members of a vulnerable group fear for their safety and security:

> Hate crimes convey a message of fear to all members of the community to which the specific individual belongs. The seriousness of a hate crime cannot be fully understood without taking this additional element into consideration. The harm lies in the atmosphere of fear and apprehension to which all hate crimes contribute. (Roberts 1995: 3)

disproportionate harm
Exceeds harm inflicted on individuals; has as its goal to intimidate and/or injure an entire community.

Finally, research on the extent of injury in other regions that track hate crimes shows that where a crime is motivated by hate, the injuries and damage inflicted on victims are more severe than in cases of crimes not motivated by particular hatred (Roberts 1995: 4). Following from the passage of Bill C-250, parliamentarians have undertaken during two separate sittings of the legislature to pick up where C-250 had left off and add to the recognition of crimes carried out against the "identifiable group" covered in C-250 by recognizing that gender expression and identity should be added along with sexual identity to the list of uniquely vulnerable groups in need of particular recognition and protections under our hate crimes laws.

First, lobby groups and activists worked to see Bill C-389 passed into law. The bill, introduced by NDP MP Bill Siksay, sought to include both **gender identity** and **gender expression** as prohibited grounds for discrimination, and to make targeted crimes based on gender identity and/or gender expression subject to punishment under Canada's hate crimes law. The bill passed the report stage on December 8, 2010 at the House of Commons level, with 143 votes in favour and 131 against (EGALE 2010). And yet, the bill did not go forward, and was not passed into law. Instead, it had to be reintroduced in a later session of parliament. We discuss the current state of the bill in further detail later in the chapter in its reintroduced state, brought forward again as a private member's bill and now known as Bill C-279, currently awaiting third reading in Parliament.

In this chapter we examine prejudice and discrimination toward those who engage in same-sex activity whether male or female, and those who identify as lesbian, gay, transexual, or bisexual. We also address problems of homophobia and transphobia.

It is beyond the scope of this chapter, though, to explore how sexual diversity and its cultural meanings vary throughout the world. Rather, our focus is on Western conceptions of sexual diversity. Sexuality has often been thought of in terms of "**sexual orientation**," whereby individuals are classified as heterosexual, bisexual, or homosexual, based on their emotional and sexual attractions, relationships, and self-identification. However, current scholarship and activism in the field note that the concept of orientation, while sometimes useful—as in the hate crimes law—does not allow room to think about the ways in which desires, attractions, and practices can vary over our lifetimes; furthermore, it encourages the assumption that all people in a given identity category share identical and unchanging desires and practices. Biologist Anne Fausto-Sterling (2001) has taken her own life history as an example of the shifts and complexities for which a simple use of "orientation" simply cannot account:

> This young girl didn't like dolls, kept pet snakes and frogs, and grew up first with heterosexual interests and later developed homosexual ones. How are we to interpret her life, or any life? Speculating about genes for analytic personalities or homosexuality may make for good party chitchat or provide solace for those eager to explain why someone turned out "that way." But partitioning genes from environment, nature from nurture, is a scientific dead end, a bad way of thinking about human development. Instead, I suggest we heed the words of the philosophers John Dewey and Arthur Bentley, who half a century ago "asserted the right to see together…much that is talked about conventionally as if it were composed of irreconcilable fears." (pp. 234–35)

While some advocate using the term **transgender** to include lesbians, gays, and bisexuals—those whose bodies do not fit neatly into either the male or female category, or whose behaviour is incongruous with the roles and expectations for their sex in the society in which they live (Bornstein 1994; Bullough 2000; Gilbert 2000; Herdt 2001)—others observe that such a conceptualization risks collapsing very real political and personal experiences into one falsely homogenized image (Hines 2006; Roen 2001; Sullivan 2003; Valentine 2007). In common usage, transgender can include transexuals (individuals who have undergone hormone treatment and sex reassignment surgery to

gender identity
The gender that a person feels him- or herself to be. Sometimes gender identity is concordant with one's assigned sex at birth, and sometimes one's gender identity is more fluid, or can be "opposite" to one's sex of rearing.

gender expression
How we express our gender (as masculine, feminine, tomboy, or androgynous, as "butch," "straight," etc.).

sexual orientation
The identification of individuals as heterosexual, bisexual, or homosexual based on their emotional and sexual attractions, relationships, self-identity, and lifestyle.

transgender
Persons who do not fit neatly into either the male or female category, or whose behaviour is not congruent with the rules and expectations for their sex in the society in which they live.

achieve a new identity as a member of the biologically opposite sex) and those who choose to assert and claim their non-adherence to standard gender roles.

There is some controversy over how people categorize transgender and transsexual persons, and what distinguishes the concepts. In his critical ethnography, David Valentine (2007) seeks to map the manner in which these terms arose, what they describe, who gets to use them, and for what purposes. Valentine explains that the terms "transgender" and "transsexual" are politicized categories that have largely been imposed from the outside by juridical interests, social scientists, and health workers. Very importantly, Valentine also situates the distinct conceptualization of transgender, transex/uality, and homosexual/ity as the effect of the twentieth-century medical system, which did the work of separating the previously enmeshed concepts of gender and sexuality. Valentine's account helps to explain why some people who identify as transexual have not had—and do not necessarily wish to have—surgery to effect a movement from one sex to the other; for these people the separation of gender and sexuality as imposed from the outside does not reflect their lives as they experience them. Valentine's analysis reveals that the adoption of transgender and transex has occurred mostly in circles of socio-economic privilege where people are able to use concepts in order to gain access to health benefits, or to political rights lobbying, but that many people who are gender variant find that the subtle overlapping of their experiences of sexuality, gender, class, and race cannot be captured by either term.

Much of the current scholarship and social activism regarding the treatment and political and social agendas of **lesbigays** also includes trans-identified persons; hence, the term **GLBT** is often used to refer collectively to gays, lesbians, bisexuals, and transgendered individuals (Craig 2002; Goldie 2001).

We begin by summarizing the legal status of lesbians and gay men around the world. Then, we review biological and environmental explanations for different sexualities, and apply sociological theories to better understand the social mechanisms that shape the way people understand and respond to various sexualities. The chapter ends with a discussion of strategies to reduce homophobia and discrimination against those who are gender variant. Because the label "homosexual" developed in the nineteenth century as a medical diagnosis of disease (Krafft-Ebing 1965), and tends to refer more to men than to women, we have chosen to use the term same-sex to refer to sexual practices and relationships that take place between persons of the same sex. This choice does not get around the problematic assumption that males and females are somehow "opposite," but it does avoid the language of pathology. We reserve the term homosexual only for historical accuracy when discussing legal and biomedical thinking on same-sex behaviour.

Because contemporary Western societies are largely heteronormative, few people who view themselves as heterosexual ever have to confront their own assumptions about why they are heterosexual. Instead, many heterosexuals pose questions to gay, lesbian, and bisexual people that begin with the premise that homosexuality is a problem. The "Heterosexual Questionnaire," featured as Table 9.1, first appeared in 1982 in *Changing Men*. It confronts readers with their own assumptions, forcing them to consider their ideas more carefully. Though the questionnaire is now over 30 years old, the questions it asks remain relevant because even when people "accept" homosexuality, they often assume that there is some unique "cause" for a person not to develop according to the unquestioned, heterosexual template for human beings. Read the questionnaire for yourself. What do you think about having to provide an explanation for your own desires, whether for the same sex or the "opposite" sex? Have you ever posed these kinds of questions, or heard them posed, to people you have learned were gay, lesbian, or bisexual?

Throughout this chapter, we consider heteronormative assumptions more carefully and encourage questioning of the idea that people are "naturally" heterosexual and will remain that way unless something "goes wrong."

lesbigays
A collective term sometimes used to refer to lesbians, gays, and bisexuals.

GLBT
A term used to refer collectively to gays, lesbians, bisexuals, and transgendered individuals.

Table 9.1 *The Heterosexual Questionnaire*

1. What do you think caused your heterosexuality?

2. When and how did you decide you were a heterosexual?

3. Is it possible that your heterosexuality is just a phase you may grow out of?

4. Is it possible that your heterosexuality stems from a neurotic fear of others of the same sex?

5. If you have never slept with a person of the same sex, is it possible that all you need is a good gay lover?

6. Do your parents know that you are straight? Do your friends and/or roommate(s) know? How did they react?

7. Why do you insist on flaunting your heterosexuality? Can't you just be who you are and keep it quiet?

8. Why do heterosexuals place so much emphasis on sex?

9. Why do heterosexuals feel compelled to seduce others into their lifestyle?

10. A disproportionate majority of child molesters are heterosexual. Do you consider it safe to expose children to heterosexual teachers?

11. Just what do men and women do in bed together? How can they truly know how to please each other, being so anatomically different?

12. With all the societal support marriage receives, the divorce rate is spiralling. Why are there so few stable relationships among heterosexuals?

13. Statistics show that lesbians have the lowest incidence of sexually transmitted diseases. Is it really safe for a woman to maintain a heterosexual lifestyle and run the risk of disease and pregnancy?

14. How can you become a whole person if you limit yourself to compulsive, exclusive heterosexuality?

15. Considering the menace of overpopulation, how could the human race survive if everyone were heterosexual?

16. Could you trust a heterosexual therapist to be objective? Don't you feel she or he might be inclined to influence you in the direction of his or her own leanings?

17. There seem to be very few happy heterosexuals. Techniques have been developed that might enable you to change if you really want to. Have you considered trying aversion therapy?

18. Would you want your child to be heterosexual, knowing the problems that she or he would face?

SOURCE: Rochlin, M. 1982. "The Heterosexual Questionnaire." *Changing Men* (Spring).

9.2 The Global Context: A World View of Laws Pertaining to Same-Sex Activity

Same-sex behaviour and love relationships have existed throughout human history and in most, perhaps all, human societies (Kirkpatrick 2000). Legal penalties for violating laws that prohibit same-sex sexual acts vary. In 10 countries, individuals found guilty of engaging in same-sex sexual behaviour may receive the death penalty. For example, a

Somali lesbian couple were sentenced to death for "exercising unnatural behaviour" ("Jail, Death Sentences in Africa" 2001). Although executions in this region are performed by firing squads, religious tradition dictates that those convicted of homosexuality should either have a wall pushed over onto them or be thrown off a roof or other high place.

In general, countries throughout the world are moving toward increased legal protection of sexual-orientation minorities. Between 1984 and 1995, 86 countries changed their policies regarding sex between men, sex between women, or both, and nearly every change was toward increased liberalization of policies on same-sex sexual behaviour (Frank and McEneaney 1999). According to the International Gay and Lesbian Human Rights Commission (IGLHRC), 86 countries still have laws to prohibit sexual acts carried out in private between consenting adults (IGLHRC 2003). In 1996 South Africa became the first country in the world to include in its constitution a clause banning discrimination based on sexual orientation. Canada, Fiji, and Ecuador also have constitutions that ban discrimination based on sexual orientation ("Constitutional Protection" 1999). In the *Lawrence v. Texas* case, the U.S. Supreme Court settled that state laws prohibiting "homosexual sodomy" were unconstitutional and, therefore, unenforceable; it also ruled that such laws fundamentally violated the right to privacy. In Canada, meanwhile, same-sex sexual activity between consenting adults has been protected as a private matter since the passing of the 1969 Omnibus bill of Pierre Trudeau, who quipped, "The state has no business in the bedrooms of the nation." How law enforcement agencies have interpreted what counts as a private venue has still rendered the GLBT community vulnerable to persecution on occasion— with, for example, the infamous Toronto Bathhouse Raids of 1983 and the 2000 raid on a lesbian club, The Pussy Palace, in Toronto.

Around the globe, attitudes and laws regarding same-sex relationships vary widely, from the recognitions we see in Canada to severely oppressive governments in other areas. As this edition of your textbook is being authored, for example, the world is preparing for the 2014 Olympic games in Sochi, Russia. However, Russia's current government under president Vladimir Putin has cracked down on the rights of LGBT persons in Russia. Although same-sex relations were decriminalized in Russia in 1993, after the fall of the Soviet Union in 1991, the current government has been increasing restrictions and passed a law in 2013 to ban any form of "propaganda" to minors regarding "non-traditional sexual relations" (Russian LGBT Network 2013). The punishments—which can include fines up to 1 million rubles, the arrest and detainment for up to 15 days of visitors to the country, and deportation from Russia—are so severe that the International Lesbian Gay Association (ILGA) Europe branch now ranks Russia last among 49 countries in Europe for rights protections for LGBT persons (Figure 9.1). There are concerns that foreign visitors to Russia who want to attend the 2014 Olympics will not be safe if they are suspected of being lesbian, gay, trans, or bisexual. And for those who live in Russia things are much more unsettled now, as Russian-American journalist Masha Gessen, herself a lesbian and a mother, explains:

> One of the pernicious things about what's going on in Russia is that there are few people who are as publicly out as I was, but [LGBT people] are generally comfortable, or have been comfortable until recently. So they don't have a closet to hide in, especially if they have kids. Often their pediatrician knows, their schoolteachers know, their neighbors know. What are they supposed to do? How are they supposed to suddenly un-come out and prevent social services from coming after their kids? (National Public Radio 2014)

In Brazil, a gay, lesbian, bisexual, or transgendered individual is murdered, on average, every two days. However, the brutal gay-bashing murder of Edson Neris da Silva by a gang of about 30 people resulted in what some believe is Brazil's first trial and

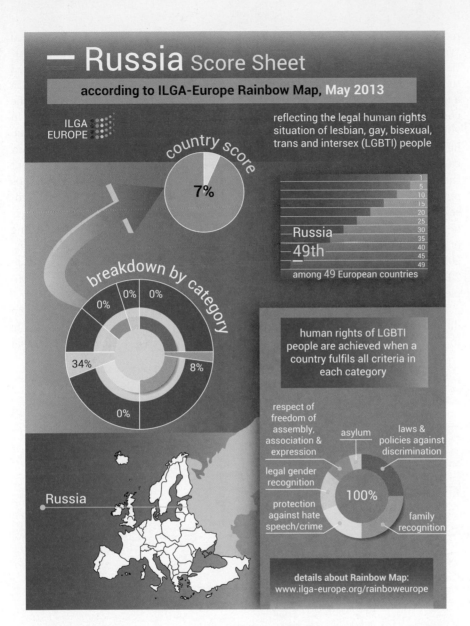

Figure 9.1 **Russia Score Sheet**

SOURCE: Courtesy of ILGA Europe.

convictions in an antigay hate crime ("Brazilian Killers Sentenced" 2001). The first two gang members tried for this murder were sentenced to 21 years in prison.

In June 2000, Canada enacted a bill that extends to same-sex couples and unmarried heterosexual couples who have lived together for at least a year all the benefits and obligations of married couples (*LAWbriefs* 2000). (More recent changes are discussed later in this chapter.) In the same month, Brazil extended to same-sex couples the right to inherit each other's pension and social security benefits. The law represents the first time a Latin American country has legally recognized gay relationships (*LAWbriefs* 2000). Also in 2000, the Netherlands enacted a law allowing same-sex marriages. Just after the stroke of midnight on the day the Dutch law went into effect (April 1, 2001), the world's first fully legal same-sex civil marriages took place in Amsterdam (Drinkwater 2001).

Closer to home, a referendum on the issue of "gay marriage" was part of the 2004 federal election in the United States. All 11 states that included the question voted to ban gay marriage (National Conference of State Legislatures 2004). In the years since, California's Proposition 8—which banned same-sex marriages and refused to recognize those that the state had already granted—was repealed (February 2012), and Washington, New Jersey, Maryland, and North Carolina all legalized same-sex marriage (in 2012). Meanwhile, the Conservative minority government in Canada proposed to reopen the issue of marriages for same-sex couples in the House of Commons with a free vote; in December 2006 the issue did go to a free vote over whether to revisit the constitutionality of same-sex marriage, but was defeated with 175 nays to 123 yeas. In 2012 Canada began to examine how to grant divorces for non-residents of Canada who had travelled to Canada in order to marry. When such couples want to divorce, they cannot do so in their home countries if same-sex marriages are not recognized, but they still face legal concerns about how to divide assets, care for children, and perhaps remarry—just as divorcing couples in heterosexual marriages do. However, heterosexual couples who marry in Canada but return to live elsewhere can divorce in their home countries where their marriages are recognized. Bill C-32, allowing the granting of a Canadian divorce to non-residents who were married in Canada, passed in June 2013 and received Royal Assent in the summer of that year (Government of Canada 2013). At least until their home countries or states recognize same-sex marriages, couples who marry in Canada will have to file for divorce in Canada.

As you will see later in this chapter, the road to equal marriage rights has been difficult to travel, with powerful groups intervening to stop the advance of civil rights to same-sex couples along the way. Figure 9.2 provides an at-a-glance view of global

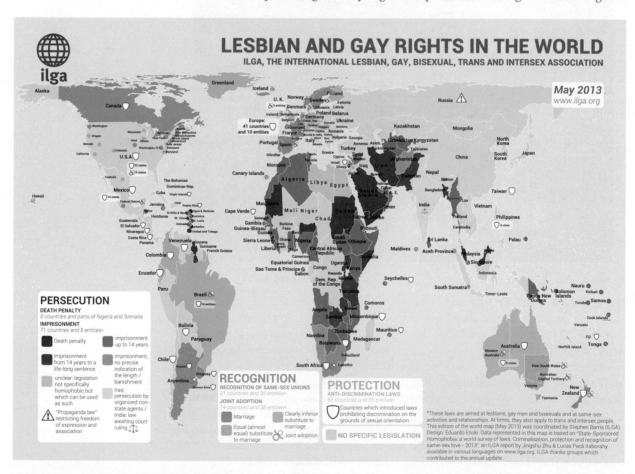

Figure 9.2 **Global Attitudes to Same-Sex Relations, 2013: Lesbian and Gay Rights in the World**

SOURCE: Courtesy of ILGA.

attitudes toward same-sex relations, including legal protections, recognitions, and regions with legal persecution and violent repression of same-sex relations.

Clearly, public legitimation of same-sex relations is occurring in the global society. Human rights treaties and transnational social movement organizations have increasingly asserted the rights of persons to engage in same-sex relations. International organizations, such as Amnesty International, which resolved in 1991 to defend those imprisoned for homosexuality, the International Lesbian and Gay Association (founded in 1978), and the International Gay and Lesbian Human Rights Commission (founded in 1990), continue to fight prejudice and discrimination against lesbians and gays. Despite the worldwide movement toward increased acceptance and protection of homosexual individuals, the status and rights of lesbians and gays in Canada continues to be one of the most divisive issues in Canadian society. Shifts in government demonstrate that rights secured through law may also be rescinded through law. In response, many queer theorists and activists question the wisdom of spending effort on legal recognition of gay marriage; they argue that it may be more practical simply to reject marriage rights.

9.3 Homosexuality and Bisexuality: Prevalence and Explanations

In their exhaustive research on sexual behaviour, Kinsey and colleagues (1953) found that a substantial proportion of respondents reported having had same-sex sexual experiences. The data revealed that 37 percent of men and 13 percent of women had at least one homosexual experience since adolescence. Yet, very few of the individuals in Kinsey's research reported exclusive homosexual behaviour. These data led Kinsey to conclude that most people are not exclusively heterosexual or homosexual. Rather, Kinsey suggested an individual's sexuality may have both heterosexual and homosexual elements, and that exclusive heterosexuality and homosexuality represent two ends of a continuum. He felt that most individuals fall somewhere within the continuum. Kinsey's early sex research demonstrated the difficulty of classifying individuals as heterosexual, homosexual, or bisexual, demonstrating the poor grounds for creating such medicalized types.

More recent data bear out Kinsey's findings. They suggest that changes in norms, negative sanctions, and restrictions, combined with more positive sensibilities about what it means to be involved in same-sex relationships, may correlate positively with increases in the percentage of women and men reporting same-sex sexual partnering in the past five years—the percentage increased from 0.2 in 1988 to 2.8 in 1998 (Butler 2000). This research also notes the following:

> These estimates of same-gender sex partnering should not be taken as estimates of the proportion of the population that is gay or lesbian. Some people may engage in same-gender sexual activity and yet identify as heterosexual, whereas other people may identify as gay or lesbian but may not have been sexually active in recent years. (p. 342)

Origins of Sexual-Orientation Diversity: Nature or Nurture?

One of the prevailing questions about homosexuality and bisexuality centres on origin or "cause." Because heterosexuality is considered normative and "natural," causes of heterosexuality are rarely considered. Many researchers now believe that an interaction of biological and environmental forces affects the development of one's sexual orientation (De Cecco and Parker 1995).

Environmental Explanations of Sexual Orientation

According to Doell (1995: 352), "we all probably develop, from infancy, the capacity to have heterosexual, homosexual, or bisexual relationships." Environmental theories propose that such factors as availability of sexual partners, early sexual experiences, and sexual reinforcement influence subsequent sexual orientation. The degree to which early sexual experiences have been negative or positive has been hypothesized as influencing sexual orientation. Having pleasurable same-sex experiences would likely increase the probability of a homosexual orientation. By the same token, it has been suggested that early traumatic sexual experiences may cause fear of heterosexual activity. However, a study that compared sexual histories of lesbian and heterosexual women found no differences in the incidence of traumatic experiences with men (Brannock and Chapman 1990).

Biological Origins of Sexual Orientation

Biological explanations of sexual orientation diversity usually focus on genetic or hormonal differences between heterosexuals and homosexuals. In an overview of genetics research on homosexual and heterosexual orientations, Pillard and Bailey (1998) conclude that genes account for at least half of the variance in sexual orientation. Their review of family, twin, and adoptee studies indicates that homosexuality (and thus heterosexuality) runs in families. However, the empirical research on isolating a biological-cause basis for sexuality is less than convincing in its findings.

For example, science has yet to identify a "homosexuality" gene despite the assertion of some researchers, such as Hamer and colleagues (1993), who claim to have discovered *statistical* evidence for its existence. In their examination of 40 pairs of gay brothers, Hamer and colleagues note that a significantly higher number than expected of the pairs (33 out of 40 versus 20 out of 40) shared matching DNA in a region called Xq28 at the tip of the X chromosome, a chromosome males inherit from their biological mothers. The researchers focused on this chromosome after noting in previous research that more gay male relatives appear to be found on the mother's side of the family.

Hamer and his research team did not isolate a specific gene, or even a specific set of genes, existing within that chromosomal region; they only provided the statistics-based suggestion that such genes must be there. Nor do they specifically account for the homosexuality of those brothers who do not possess the matching DNA. Furthermore, they have not examined heterosexual brothers for the existence or nonexistence of matching DNA in the Xq28 region to determine whether heterosexual brothers are similar to or different from homosexual brothers (Peele and DeGrandpre 1995). Consider, as well, the results of a Canadian study (Rice et al. 1999) based on 62 gay male sibling pairs. When the microsatellite markers at position Xq28 were analyzed, Hamer's suggestion of an X-linked gene underlying homosexuality was not supported.

Among the serious methodological problems confronting such research is determining what counts as "homosexuality"; the definitions vary from one study to another and what subjects mean when they say they are homosexual may not be the same from one subject to the next. Is it an issue of desire? of activity? of identity? Nevertheless, researchers continue in the quest to isolate a biological cause for human sexuality. This chapter's *Social Problems Research Up Close* feature highlights one such recent effort.

Can Homosexuals Change Their Sexual Orientation?

Although "homosexuality" was removed from the *Diagnostic and Statistical Manual* in 1974, some conservative, often Christian organizations claim to be able to "cure" homosexuality through **reparative therapy** or conversion therapy. Some religious organizations, like the U.S.-based Exodus, sponsor ex-gay ministries, which claim to

reparative therapy
Various therapies that are aimed at changing homosexuals' sexual attraction.

"cure" homosexuals and transform them into heterosexuals through prayer and other forms of "therapy." Critics of ex-gay ministries take a different approach:

> The cure for unhappiness is not the "ex-gay" ministries—but coming out with dignity and self-respect. It is not gay men and lesbians who need to change...but negative attitudes and discrimination against gay people that need to be abolished. (Besen 2000: 7)

Social Problems *Research Up Close*

Youth Speak Up about Homophobia and Transphobia*

This report discusses the results of a national survey of Canadian high school students undertaken in order to identify the forms and extent of their experiences of homophobic and transphobic incidents at school and the efficacy of measures being taken by schools to combat these common forms of bullying.

Phase One of the study involved surveying almost 1700 students from across Canada through two methods: individual online participation and in-school sessions conducted in four school boards. This report analyzes the data from individual online participation.

Educators and researchers have long been aware that students experience homophobic incidents ranging from hearing "gay" used as a synonym for "stupid" or "worthless" to being insulted or assaulted because of their actual or perceived sexual or transgender identity. However, the lack of a solid Canadian evidence base has been a major impediment faced by educators who need to understand the situation of lesbian, gay, bisexual, transgender, queer, and questioning (LGBTQ) students in order to respond appropriately and to assure the school community that homophobic and transphobic bullying are neither rare nor harmless but major problems that schools need to address.

Summary of Methods for Data Gathering and Analysis

The survey itself was a 54-item questionnaire made available online and in print, and consisting mostly of multiple-choice questions of three kinds: demographic (e.g., age, province, gender identity, sexual identity), experiences (e.g., hearing the word gay used as an insult, being verbally harassed), and institutional responses (e.g., staff intervention, inclusive safe-school policies). Quantitative data were tested for statistical significance through bivariate analyses that compared the responses of various groups of students (e.g., LGBTQ and non-LGBTQ, LGB and transgender, current versus past).

Key Findings: Unsafe Spaces

Homophobic comments:

- Current students were even more likely than past students to hear expressions such as "that's so gay" in school.
- Current students were also more likely than past students to hear homophobic comments from other students every day in school.

One sign of progress:

- Current students were significantly less likely than past students to report that school staff never intervened.

Impacts

- Three-quarters of LGBTQ students and 95 percent of trans-gender students felt unsafe at school, compared to one-fifth of straight students.
- Over a quarter of LGBTQ students and almost half of transgender students had skipped school because they felt unsafe, compared to fewer than a tenth of non-LGBTQ.
- Many LGBTQ students would not be comfortable talking to their teachers (four in ten), their principal (six in ten), or their coach (seven in ten) about LGBTQ issues.
- Only one in five LGBTQ students could talk to a parent very comfortably about LGBTQ issues. Three-quarters could talk to a close friend about these issues.
- Over half of LGBTQ students did not feel accepted at school, and almost half felt they could not be themselves at school, compared to one-fifth of straight students.
- Transgender students (over a third) were twice as likely as LGB students to strongly agree that they sometimes feel very depressed about their school and that they do not belong at their school, and four times as likely as straight students.

*Taylor, Catherine, et al. 2009 "Executive Summary," *Youth Speak Up About Homophobia and Transphobia*. EGALE Canada: Winnipeg. Reprinted by permission of Egale Canadian Human Rights Trust.

(continued)

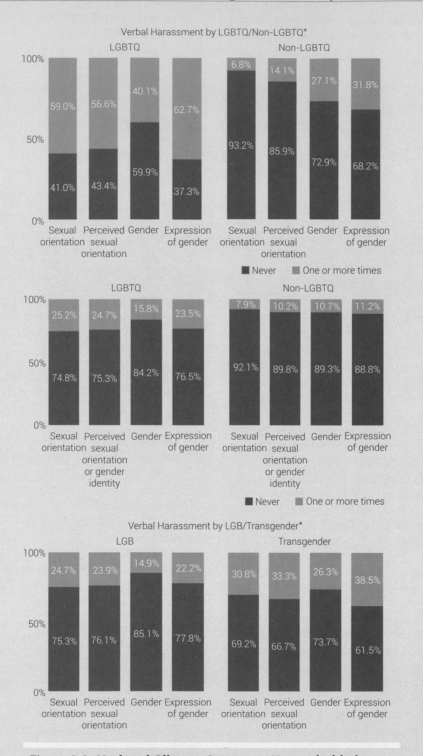

Figure 9.3 **National Climate Survey on Homophobia in Canadian Schools**

*Taylor, Catherine, et al. 2009 "Executive Summary," *Youth Speak Up About Homophobia and Transphobia*. EGALE Canada: Winnipeg. Reprinted by permission of Egale Canadian Human Rights Trust.

Institutional responses:

- Fewer than half of participants knew whether their school had a policy for reporting homophobic incidents.
- Of those participants who did know, only one-third believed there was such a policy.

LGBTQ students who believed their schools have anti-homophobia policies were much more likely than other LGBTQ students …

- to feel their school community was supportive (one-half compared to fewer than one-fifth),
- to feel comfortable talking to a counsellor (one-half compared to fewer than one-third), and to feel comfortable talking to classmates (over one-third compared to one-fifth),
- to believe their school was becoming less homophobic,
- to hear fewer homophobic comments and to say that staff intervene more often,
- to report homophobic incidents to staff and their parents, and
- to feel attached to their school.

LGBTQ students who believed their schools have anti-homophobia policies were much less likely than other LGBTQ students…

- to have had lies and rumours spread about them at school or on the internet,
- to have had property stolen or intentionally damaged,
- to feel unsafe at school, and
- to have been verbally or physically harassed.

The results were similar for students who believed that their school districts had such policies.

Conclusions and Recommendations

This survey confirms what LGBTQ students and their allies have known for some time: that despite Canada's leadership on human rights for LGBTQ people, a great deal of verbal and physical homophobic and transphobic harassment goes on in Canadian schools, that LGBTQ students are more likely to be aware of it than are other students who are not its main targets, and that the institutional response to harassment has more often than not been inadequate.

The survey also shows, however, that the situation is much improved where schools and school divisions have developed safe-schools policies and procedures that explicitly address homophobia and have informed students of their existence. In such schools, LGBTQ students are less likely to hear homophobic comments or to be targeted by verbal or physical harassment, they are more likely to report it to staff and parents when

they are, and staff are more likely to intervene. In these schools, LGBTQ students feel safer, more accepted, and more attached to their school.

Developing inclusive safe schools policies and making them known to students is not a complete solution. However, this survey has identified significant differences between schools with and schools without inclusive policies.

Recommendations

1. That schools develop and implement anti-homophobia and anti-transphobia policies and make these policies well known to students, parents, administration, and all staff as a positive part of their commitment to making schools safe.
2. That schools strongly support the efforts of students to start Gay-Straight Alliances (GSAs).
3. That in schools where students have not come forward, administration should ask teachers to offer to work with students to start a GSA. It is not safe to assume that LGBTQ students would prefer to go through high school isolated from their peers and teachers.
4. That school divisions develop anti-homophobia and anti-transphobia policies to provide leadership for schools. Although our analysis showed that students are less likely to know about division-level policies, it would be helpful for principals to know that their school-level efforts have strong divisional endorsement in the form of official policy at that level.
5. That provincial Ministries of Education advocate the inclusion of anti-homophobia and anti-transphobia measures in safe schools policies and programs, including those of Catholic schools, along with steps for the implementation of these policies, in order to provide institutional support and motivation to divisional and school staff.
6. That individuals and organizations with expertise in anti-homophobia and anti-transphobia education be consulted in the above developments.

What students have told us in the First National Climate Survey on Homophobia in Canadian Schools is that speaking up works, and that they want the adults in their lives to do their part, too. These students are weary of seeing teachers and principals look the other way. And they are grateful to the many dedicated school staff who have worked to make schools safer for everyone in their care—not everyone but them.

The Canadian Psychiatric Association, the Canadian Psychological Association, and the Canadian Medical Association agree that sexual orientation cannot be changed, and that efforts to change sexual orientation do not work and may be harmful (Human Rights Campaign 2000a). In addition, close scrutiny of reports of "successful" reparative therapy reveal that (1) many claims come from organizations with an ideological perspective on sexual orientation, rather than from unbiased researchers; (2) the treatments and their outcomes are poorly documented; and (3) the length of time that clients are followed after treatment is too short to evaluate their success or failure (Human Rights Campaign 2000a). In addition, at least 13 ministries of one reparative therapy group, Exodus, have closed because their directors reverted to homosexuality (Fone 2000).

9.4 Sociological Theories of Sexual Orientation

Sociological theories do not explain the origin or "cause" of sexual orientation, but help explain societal reactions to and contexts for sexual diversity. The sociology of sexuality can provide insight into shifting meanings in sexual identity and provide critical insight on the overlap of institutions and ideologies (like marriage, sexism, and heterosexism) and the costs of those overlaps as expressed in the form of prejudice, harm, and bias. Sociological inquiry brings a decidedly *social* understanding of the intersection of gender ideologies and sexualities.

Structural-Functionalist Perspective

Structural-functionalists, focusing on the operations fulfilled through institutions, emphasize the importance of monogamous heterosexual relationships for the reproduction, nurturance, and socialization of children. From a functionalist perspective, sexual relations are defined as "deviant" when they do not fulfill the family institution's main function of producing and rearing children. Clearly, this argument is less salient in a society in which (1) other institutions, most notably schools, have supplemented the traditional functions of the family; (2) a societal goal is to reduce population; and (3) same-sex couples can and do raise children.

Some functionalists argue that antagonisms between heterosexuals and homosexuals may disrupt social equilibrium. Durkheim, however, recognized that deviation from society's norms "may be useful as a prelude to reforms which daily become more necessary" ([1938] 1993: 66). Specifically, the gay rights movement has motivated many people to re-examine their treatment of sexual-orientation minorities; it has also produced a sense of cohesion and solidarity among members of the gay population (although bisexuals and the transgendered have often been excluded from gay and lesbian communities and organizations). Bringing benefit to society as a whole, gay activism has been instrumental in advocating for more research on HIV and AIDS, more and better health services for HIV and AIDS patients, protection of the rights of HIV-infected individuals, and HIV/AIDS public education.

Finally, the structural-functionalist focus on the interconnectedness of society fosters an understanding that urbanization has contributed to the formation of strong social networks of gays and bisexuals. Cities "acted as magnets, drawing in gay migrants who felt isolated and threatened in smaller towns and rural areas" (Button et al. 1997: 15; Goldie 2001). Given the formation of gay communities in large cities, it is not surprising that the gay rights movement first emerged in large urban centres.

Other research has demonstrated that the worldwide rise in liberalized national policies on same-sex relations and the lesbian and gay rights social movement has been influenced by three cultural changes: (1) the rise of individualism that values personal satisfaction, (2) increasing gender equality, and (3) the emergence of a global society in which nations are influenced by international pressures (Frank and McEneaney 1999). Whereas once sex was approved strictly for the purpose of family reproduction, sex increasingly serves to pleasure individualized men and women in society. Individualism "appears to loosen the tie between sex and procreation, allowing more personal modes of sexual expression" (p. 930).

Gender equality involves the breakdown of sharply differentiated sex roles, thereby supporting the varied expressions of male and female sexuality. Globalization permits the international community to influence individual nations. For example, when Zimbabwe President Robert Mugabe pursued antihomosexual policies in 1995, many international organizations and human rights associations joined to protest his actions and to ask that he halt his campaign. The pressure of international opinion led Zimbabwe's Supreme Court to rule in favour of lesbian and gay groups' right to organize.

Conflict Perspective

Conflict theorists, particularly those who do not emphasize a purely economic perspective, note that the antagonisms between "straight" and GLBT communities represent a basic division in society between those with power and those without power. When one group has control of society's institutions and resources, as in the case of heterosexuals, it has the authority to dominate other groups. Current battles over gay rights form one example of the political struggle between those with power and those without it.

A classic example of the power struggle between gays and "straights" took place in 1973. At that time, the American Psychiatric Association (APA) met to revise its classification scheme of mental disorders. Homosexual activists had been appealing to the APA for years to remove homosexuality from its list of mental illnesses, but with little success. However, in 1973, the APA's board of directors voted to remove homosexuality from its official list of mental disorders. The board's move encountered much resistance from conservative APA members. The issue was put to a referendum, which reaffirmed the board's decision (Bayer 1987).

In recent years, many organizations have recognized that implementing antidiscrimination policies that include sexual orientation is good for the bottom line. Over half (51 percent) of Fortune 500 companies and 82 percent of Fortune 1000 companies have included sexual orientation in their nondiscrimination policies, and employers are increasingly offering benefits to domestic partners of GLBT employees (Human Rights Campaign 2000b). Gay-friendly workplaces help employers maintain a competitive edge in recruiting and a talented and productive workforce.

In some settings, however, the changes have been hard won. Gay rights activists have turned to Canadian courtrooms and human rights tribunals, successfully employing the equality provision of the *Canadian Charter of Rights and Freedoms*. As a result of their activities, some Canadian workplaces have been transformed as "[g]overnments have changed legislation and policies either because courts have ordered them to do so or because of threats of court cases" (Dranoff 2001: 133).

In summary, conflict theory frames the gay rights movement and the opposition to it as a struggle over power, prestige, and economic resources. Recent trends toward increased social acceptance of homosexuality may, in part, reflect the corporate world's competition over the gay and lesbian consumer dollar.

Symbolic Interactionist Perspective

Symbolic interactionism focuses on the meanings of heterosexuality, homosexuality, and bisexuality and how these meanings are socially constructed. The meanings we associate with same-sex relations are learned from society—from family, peers, religion, and the media. Freedman and D'Emilio (1990: 485) observed: "sexual meanings are subject to the forces of culture. Human beings learn how to express themselves sexually, and the content and outcome of that learning vary widely across cultures and across time."

Historical and cross-cultural research reveals the socially constructed nature of sexuality and its meanings. Although many North Americans assume that same-sex romantic relationships have always been taboo, during the nineteenth century, "romantic friendships" between women were encouraged and regarded as preparation for a successful marriage. President Grover Cleveland's sister Rose, for example, wrote to her friend Evangeline Whipple in 1890: "It makes me heavy with emotion...all my whole being leans out to you.... I dare not think of your arms" (Goode and Wagner 1993: 49).

The symbolic interactionist perspective also points to the effects of labelling on individuals. Once individuals become identified or labelled as lesbian, gay, or bisexual, that label tends to become their **master status**. In other words, the dominant heterosexual community tends to view "gay," "lesbian," and "bisexual" as the most socially significant statuses of individuals identified as such. Esterberg (1997: 377) notes that "unlike heterosexuals, who are defined by their family structures, communities, occupations, or other aspects of their lives, lesbians, gay men, and bisexuals are often defined primarily by what they do in bed. Many lesbians, gay men, and bisexuals, however, view their identity as social and political as well as sexual."

Feminist Perspectives

Feminist work on sexuality is diverse, a result of highly variable concerns that arise in the attempt to understand sexuality. A foundational point, however, is the clear observation that issues related to sexuality are central to women's lives, not marginal or frivolous. Clearly, for example, women's ability to acquire education and to achieve a measure of financial independence—both very important in a capitalist context—depends on women's ability to control their reproduction, a matter tied in part to sexuality.

Feminist work has also revealed that beliefs about women's sexuality have made them extremely vulnerable to a variety of oppressive forces. Among these is the tendency to "pedestalize" some women for their ability to act appropriately as good mothers and wives, adornments for men of privileged classes; meanwhile, women from marginalized groups may be simultaneously eroticized and vilified as "excessively sexual." This oppositional pairing of women as good and bad is popularly known as the "Madonna/whore dichotomy." Feminists have pointed out that in such a symbolic and structural ordering no woman is free—a problem we take up further throughout this chapter.

It is important to remember that feminist work does not have to be done by women, though it often is. For example, Sander Gilman's historical assessment of racism and sexism in medicine revealed that nineteenth-century "experts" claimed that African women, Jewish women, and European prostitutes and lesbians all shared similarly deviant and *excessively large* genitalia (Gilman 1985).

What makes a work on sexuality feminist if it is not the body of the researcher? A central answer to that question arrives in the principle of **anti-essentialism** developed within feminist scholarship since the 1980s. Anti-essentialist work observes that nothing is guaranteed by the body, most particularly by the sex, of a person. Instead,

---

master status
The status that is considered the most significant in a person's social identity.

anti-essentialism
The refusal of simplistic biological explanations for complex social relations, motivations, behaviours, and identifications.

our social and cultural contexts shape who we are. It is through this **constructionist** position that much contemporary feminist work on sexuality operates. A constructionist approach understands, for example, that "how we classify individuals according to sex [as a matter of law] is a matter of interpretation.... Moreover, what we take sex itself to be [as a biological phenomenon] ... is also a question of interpretation" (Warnke 2005: 113). "Sex" then is a matter of perception and a vehicle for controlling how bodies are organized into categories. As Gayle Rubin observed in "The Traffic in Women" (1975), sex and sexuality are the central mechanisms through which societies organize their kinship systems, with those labelled as women bearing the burden of structural inequality that guarantees men the bulk of power.

Finally, feminist scholarship observes that what counts as sexuality and how sex is organized varies around the world; it is not universally identical, even though every society has a sex-based system for organizing its members.

Queer Theory Perspectives

The most prominent contributors to the sociological application of queer theory to the understanding of sexualities are Michel Foucault and Judith Butler. Their conceptual work has largely shaped the tools and approach we use to critically assess powerful and normative institutions.

Foucault's exhaustive three-volume work on sexuality (1990a, 1990b, 1990c) makes the point that bodies and sexualities came to have meaning only as a result of a variety of interventions and invasions: these label us by sex, by practice, and by general state-of-health assessments that teach us how to see ourselves and to understand our practices and desires by the tools of science, law, and medicine that Foucault labelled as a form of "gaze." A *gaze* is a view that imposes meaning rather than being simply a passive way of looking; it is, instead, a look that can pass judgment, mete out punishments, make assessments, and tell us who we are as much as demand it. For Foucault, the gaze structures the meanings of sexuality, for example, through claims to genetic foundations for predispositions, orientations, desires, and practices. The gaze can structure meanings through the admittance of some forms of marriage but not others, thereby conferring or refusing legitimacy; finally, the gaze requires that we also look back at it to confirm that we accept its conclusions as truths, for example, in popular media claims that overstate the conclusions of biomedicine with regard to what "causes" same-sex desire.

Butler, who began writing on gender and sexuality in the late 1980s, made the powerful observation that as the symbolic basis upon which a variety of social and sexual demands are fixed, gender is not a natural expression of our sex, but a means of conveying and of securing a socially legitimated place for ourselves—a place from which we can be recognized as male or female, and out of which a variety of norms regarding sex(uality) are expressed. In her 1990 book *Gender Trouble*, Butler argued that gender was a performance, something that was unstable, and that all of us have to work at it every day, to make ourselves knowable and recognizable to others. Many people took her statement to suggest that we could simply decide on our gender and then act it out. However, Butler later argued in *Bodies That Matter* (1993) that this was a misreading: our performance could not be freely and individually willed, but was compelled by those around us; those who do not "fit in" to the performance demands are placed at grave risk in a heteronormative and homophobic society.

For the social study of sexualities, the combined observations of feminist and queer theories help us to understand that the way things are is not the way things have to be, that oppressive functions can be challenged, and that claims to "the naturalness" of one form of sexuality operate to the benefit of only a tiny minority of the population, providing neither an accurate description nor an adequate understanding of sex and

constructionist
The belief that social context provides the mode and meaning for both sexuality and gendered behaviours, roles, and relationships.

sexuality. Moreover, such claims place many people, including most women and those who are in some way "queer," in highly vulnerable positions.

9.5 Heterosexism, Homophobia, and Biphobia

Heterosexism refers to "an ideological system that denies, denigrates, and stigmatizes any nonheterosexual form of behaviour, identity, relationship, or community" (Herek 1990: 316). Heterosexism is based on the belief that heterosexuality is "natural" and, therefore, "normal," that it is superior to homosexuality, and that homosexuality is what happens when something disrupts a presupposed "natural order." Heterosexism lays the foundation for prejudice and discrimination against GLBT persons. Prejudice refers to negative attitudes, whereas discrimination refers to behaviour that denies individuals or groups equality of treatment.

Homophobia

The term **homophobia** is commonly used to refer to negative attitudes and emotions toward homosexuality and those who engage in it. Other terms that refer to negative attitudes and emotions toward homosexuality include *homonegativity* and *antigay bias.*

Prevailing attitudes can, however, shift; as with most social phenomena, change is always possible. We can identify some of the features that have correlated with large shifts in popular attitudes and perception. People who are younger, more educated, never married, living in the West, living in heavily populated urban areas, and Jewish are least likely to have antigay attitudes (Klassen et al. 1989). Also, positive contact with GLBT people is associated with less homophobia (Simon 1995). The development of attitudes is, however, complex. Sociological studies reveal that issues of class, of education, of family history, of one's gender, and so forth are all influential forces in attitude development.

In a study of undergraduates (101 men, 98 women) attending a Canadian university where most students were of working-class or middle-class families of European descent, Schellenberg and colleagues (1999) found that attitudes toward gay men were more negative than toward lesbians. When compared to science or business students, students in the faculties of arts and social sciences had more positive attitudes toward gay men, and women were more positive than men were. Attitudes toward gay men improved with time spent at university, but only for male students. Although attitudes toward lesbians also improved with time at university, this trend was not associated with students' gender or faculty of enrolment. Schellenberg and colleagues conclude that university education may encourage a reduction in antihomosexual prejudice among young people, particularly among young men. In an effort to reduce homophobia and its consequences, campuses across Canada have set up "Positive Space" programs. These let people know that homophobic and hateful behaviour will not be tolerated, and that GLBT students can find a safe place to think, learn, and live on the campus.

Cultural Origins of Homophobia

Why is homosexuality viewed so negatively in North America? Antigay bias has its roots in various aspects of our culture.

1. *Religion.* Most individuals who view homosexuality as unacceptable say they object on religious grounds (Rosin and Morin 1999). Although some religious groups accept homosexuality, many religions teach that homosexuality is sinful and prohibited

heterosexism
The belief that heterosexuality is the superior sexual orientation; it results in prejudice and discrimination against homosexuals and bisexuals.

homophobia
Negative attitudes toward homosexuality.

by God. The Roman Catholic Church rejects all homosexual expression and resists any attempt to validate or sanction the homosexual orientation. Some fundamentalist churches have endorsed the death penalty for homosexual people and teach the view that AIDS is God's punishment for engaging in homosexual sex (Nugent and Gramick 1989). In June 1999, a U.S. Baptist preacher from Topeka, Kansas, announced that he and a group of his followers would be leading a demonstration on the steps of the Supreme Court of Canada to protest its decision to extend the definition of "spouse" to same-sex couples. Mr. Phelps, who on previous occasions had picketed gay funerals, same-sex unions, and even Girl Scout meetings brandishing signs that read "AIDS cures fags," had announced, "We're coming to spread the gospel to you sinners." Phelps referred to Canada as the "sperm bank of Satan" and vowed that he and his supporters would burn Canadian flags in protest. In the end, Mr. Phelps did not appear and his group blamed the unwillingness of Canadian police, "who are as blackhearted as the perverts," to provide him with the level of protection he sought as the reason for the group's absence (Anderssen 1999).

Some religious groups, such as the Quakers, accept homosexuality, and other groups have made reforms toward increased acceptance of lesbians and gays. In the United States, some Episcopal priests perform "ceremonies of union" between same-sex couples; some Reform Jewish groups sponsor gay synagogues, and the United Church of Christ ordains gay men and women (Fone 2000). The United Church of Canada has ignited conflict by declaring that "all persons, regardless of their sexual orientation, are welcome to become full members of the church and are eligible for ordination as ministers" (in Dawson 1993: 323).

2. *Marital and procreative bias.* Many societies have traditionally condoned sex only when it occurs in a marital context that provides for the possibility of producing and rearing children. However, science continues to challenge the necessity of opposite-sex parents. "Under cell nuclear replacement, scientists replace the nucleus from the egg of a female donor with the nucleus from a sperm cell. The resulting 'male egg,' containing only male DNA, is then fertilized in vitro by sperm from another man" (Honore 2000). Even though already-available assisted reproductive technologies make it possible for gay individuals and couples to have children, many people believe that only heterosexual married couples should use these advances (Franklin 1993).

3. *Concern about HIV and AIDS.* Although transmission rates vary upward and downward for different groups over time and most cases of HIV and AIDS worldwide are attributed to heterosexual transmission, HIV and AIDS in Canada is more prevalent among gay and bisexual men than among other groups. Because of this, many people associate HIV and AIDS with homosexuality and bisexuality. Lesbians, incidentally, have a very low risk for sexually transmitted HIV—a lower risk than heterosexual women do.

4. *Threat to the power of the majority.* Like other minority groups, the gay minority threatens the power of the majority. Fearing loss of power, the majority group stigmatizes gays and lesbians and transgender people as a way of limiting their power.

5. *Rigid gender roles.* Antigay sentiments also stem from rigid gender roles. When Cooper Thompson (1995) was asked to give a guest presentation on male roles at a suburban high school, male students told him that the most humiliating insult was being called a "fag." The boys in this school gave Thompson the impression that they were expected to conform to rigid, narrow standards of masculinity to avoid being labelled in this way.

From a conflict perspective, heterosexual men's subordination and devaluation of gay men reinforces gender inequality. "By devaluing gay men… heterosexual men devalue the feminine and anything associated with it" (Price and Dalecki 1998: 155–56). Negative views toward lesbians also reinforce the patriarchal system of male dominance. Social disapproval of lesbians is a form of punishment for women who relinquish traditional female sexual and economic dependence on men. Not surprisingly, research findings suggest that individuals with traditional gender role attitudes tend to hold more negative views toward homosexuality (Louderback and Whitley 1997).

6. *Psychiatric labelling.* As noted earlier, before 1973 the APA (American Psychiatric Association) defined homosexuality as a mental disorder, and "treatment" included lobotomies, aversive conditioning, and, in some cases, castration. The APA definition contributed to negative reactions to gays and also created feelings of guilt, low self-esteem, anger, and depression for many gays and lesbians. The psychiatric care system is now busily treating the very conditions it, in part, created.

7. *Myths and negative stereotypes.* Prejudice toward gays and lesbians may also stem from some of the unsupported beliefs and negative stereotypes regarding same-sex sexuality. One such belief is that gays and lesbians lack "family values," such as monogamy and commitment to relationships. While some do engage in casual sex, as do some heterosexuals, many gay and lesbian couples develop and maintain long-term committed relationships.

Another myth is that, as groups, gay men and lesbians (to a lesser extent perhaps because of the common assumption that women are less sexual than men) are child molesters. Yet, the ratio of heterosexual to gay male child molesters is approximately 11 to 1 (Moser 1992). When a father sexually assaults his daughter, the media do not report that something is wrong with heterosexuality or with traditional families, but when a homosexual is reported to have molested a child, it is viewed as confirmation of "the way homosexuals are" (Mohr 1995: 404).

Biphobia

Just as the term *homophobia* refers to negative attitudes toward gay men and lesbians, **biphobia** refers to "the parallel set of negative beliefs about and stigmatization of bisexuality and those identified as bisexual" (Paul 1996: 449). Although heterosexuals often reject both homosexual- and bisexual-identified individuals, bisexual-identified women and men also face rejection from many homosexual individuals. Thus, bisexuals experience "double discrimination."

Biphobia includes negative stereotyping of bisexuals; the exclusion of bisexuals from social and political organizations of lesbians and gay men; and fear and distrust of, as well as anger and hostility toward, people who identify themselves as bisexual (Firestein 1996). Individuals who are biphobic often believe that bisexuals are really homosexuals afraid to acknowledge their real identity or homosexuals maintaining heterosexual relationships to avoid rejection by the heterosexual mainstream. Bisexual individuals are sometimes viewed as heterosexuals who are looking for exotic sexual experiences.

Negative attitudes regarding bisexuality and people who identify as bisexual are not the exclusive domain of heterosexual homophobes. Lesbian philosopher Elizabeth Grosz suggested in a conference paper that "bisexuality was a luxury, that bisexuals want to have their cake and eat it" (Angelides 1995: 27). Steven Angelides (1995) holds out this summary of Grosz's position as a statement that exemplifies a not uncommon mistrust of bisexuals by gays and lesbians, but argues that attitudes such as Grosz's rest on ideas about identity that reinforce the notion that someone who is not oppressed based on a given trait (like race, ethnicity, or sexuality) cannot fully commit to anti-oppressive politics. Angelides argues that biphobia discounts the productive and rich political value of bisexuality and avers that our ethical commitments are built on awareness, not identity, and that our political commitments do not have to be bounded and bordered by our personal desires.

Effects of Homophobia and Heterosexism on Heterosexuals

The homophobic and heterosexist social climate of our society is often viewed in terms of how it victimizes the gay population. However, heterosexuals are also victimized by homophobia and heterosexism. "Hatred, fear, and ignorance are bad for the bigot as well as the victim" (*Homophobia 101* 2000).

Due to the antigay climate, heterosexuals, especially males, are hindered in their own self-expression and intimacy in same-sex friendships. "The threat of victimization (i.e., antigay violence) probably also causes many heterosexuals to conform to gender roles and to restrict their expressions of (nonsexual) physical affection for members of their own sex" (Garnets et al. 1990: 380). Homophobic epithets frighten youth who do not conform to gender role expectations, leading some youth to avoid activities that they might otherwise enjoy and benefit from (arts for boys, athletics for girls, for example) (*Homophobia 101* 2000).

Some sexual assaults are related to homophobia and compulsory heterosexuality. For example, some men who participate in gang rape entice others into the act "by implying that those who do not participate are unmanly or homosexual" (Sanday 1995: 399). Homonegativity also encourages early sexual activity among adolescent men. Adolescent male virgins are often teased by their peers, who say things like "You mean you don't do it with girls yet? What are you, a fag or something?" Not wanting to be labelled and stigmatized as a "fag," some adolescent boys "prove" their heterosexuality by having sex with girls.

Antigay cultural attitudes also affect family members and friends of homosexuals, who often fear that their lesbian or gay friend or family member will be victimized by antigay prejudice and discrimination. Youth with gay and lesbian family members are often taunted by their peers.

As we have already noted, extreme homophobia can lead to instances of physical violence against homosexuals. But "gay bashings" are crimes of perception because victims of antigay violence may not be homosexual, only perceived as being homosexual. Many heterosexuals have been victims of antigay physical violence because the attacker(s) perceived them to be gay. Antigay harassment has also been a factor in some cases of school violence. One study concluded, "For boys, no other type of harassment provoked as strong a reaction on average; boys in this study would be less upset about physical abuse than they would be if someone called them gay" (Dozetos 2001).

9.6 Discrimination against Sexual-Orientation Minorities

Like other minority groups in Canada, GLBT persons have experienced and continue to experience various forms of discrimination. From 1952 to 1977, immigration laws prohibited homosexuals from entering Canada and subjected homosexuals to the threat of deportation if their sexual orientation became known. From 1892 to 1969, Canadian criminal law made certain forms of sexual conduct engaged in by gay men illegal and rendered gay men vulnerable to indefinite incarceration as "dangerous sexual offenders."

Next, we look at sexual-orientation discrimination in the workplace, in family matters, and in violent expressions of hate.

Discrimination in the Workplace

In recent years, the percentage of Canadians who express approval of equal employment rights for homosexuals has increased. Nevertheless, many Canadians still feel that homosexuals should not be entitled to the same rights and privileges as others.

While support levels for gays working in a variety of different occupations increased between 1988 and 2001, certain occupations are still considered "more suitable" than others. For example, the vast majority of Canadians find it acceptable for gays to work as salespersons (94 percent vs. 72 percent in 1988), members of Parliament (86 percent vs. 62 percent in 1988), members of the Canadian Forces (82 percent vs. 60 percent in 1988), physicians (82 percent vs. 52 percent in 1988), or prison officers (75 percent vs. 44 percent in 1988). However, there is less support for gays working as junior-school teachers (67 percent vs. 45 percent in 1988) or members of the clergy (63 percent vs. 44 percent in 1988) (Bricker and Greenspon 2001: 267–68).

Only a few decades ago, there were few legal protections for gay and lesbian individuals who experienced employment discrimination. In the 1960s, hostility toward gays in the workplace led to more than 8000 gay men being investigated by the RCMP; as a result, approximately 150 gay federal civil servants resigned or were dismissed from their employment positions without just cause. It was only in 1992 that the Canadian armed forces, facing a court challenge, agreed to stop discrimination against gays. At the time of writing, discrimination on the basis of sexual orientation was prohibited everywhere in Canada except for the Northwest Territories and Nunavut. While Alberta's legislation does not state this prohibition specifically, the Supreme Court of Canada declared in the 1998 case of *Vriend v. Alberta* that Alberta's human rights legislation "would be interpreted to include sexual orientation as a prohibited ground—whether or not it is specified in the legislation…. This marked the first time the Supreme Court of Canada amended legislation on constitutional grounds by reading into law new rights that elected politicians had expressly refused to grant" (Dranoff 2001: 134).

Discrimination in Family Relationships

In addition to discrimination in the workplace, sexual-orientation minorities in Canada have also experienced discrimination in policies on marriage, child custody and visitation, and adoption.

Same-Sex Marriage

In June of 1999, the Canadian House of Commons voted overwhelmingly in favour of a motion, introduced by Eric Lowther, the Reform Party critic on "Children and Families," opposing same-sex marriages. The motion, which signalled the first time same-sex marriage was the subject of a vote in the House of Commons, affirmed the exclusion of gays and lesbians from the institution of marriage; it also committed Parliament to "take all necessary steps" to preserve legal marriage as an opposite-sex institution. Although passing the motion had no immediate legal impact, it might be presumed that as an official declaration of Parliament's position on the matter, the "necessary steps" could include invoking the "notwithstanding" clause within the Constitution. This clause allows governments to opt out of the *Charter of Rights and Freedoms* and to deny equality to some of their citizens—in this case, lesbians and gay men. In total, 216 members of Parliament (MPs) from all parties voted in favour of the motion, including the overwhelming majority of the Liberal caucus (all but 11), all Reform Party MPs, and a number of those from the New Democratic Party, Bloc Québécois, and Progressive Conservative Party. Only 55 MPs voted against the motion. Although a "free vote"— with MPs able to "vote their conscience" rather than follow a party line—had been expected, in the end the Liberal government adopted a government position that supported the Reform Party (EGALE 1999). By 2005, though, the then minority Liberal government passed legislation to permit same-sex marriages.

In that year, various provincial governments also grappled with the issues presented by same-sex marriages. In May 1999, the Supreme Court of Ontario ruled that an

Ontario law that excluded gays and lesbians from a definition of common-law couples was unconstitutional. Shortly after, the Ontario government passed an omnibus bill that amended 67 of its laws to include same-sex couples.

Although the Supreme Court's ruling was binding only on the Ontario government, several other provinces quickly announced plans to make similar changes. For example, in June of that year, when the Quebec National Assembly unanimously passed Bill 32, Quebec became the first Canadian province to ensure that same-sex couples would receive all the benefits and responsibilities of opposite-sex couples. Bill 32 changed the definition of "spouse" within that province and committed the Quebec government to making changes in 39 provincial laws and regulations. A month later, the British Columbia government introduced the "Definition of Spouse Amendment," which expanded the definition of "spouse" in that province to include "a person who has lived and cohabited with another person, for a period of at least two years immediately before the other person's death, in a 'marriage-like' relationship, including a marriagelike relationship between persons of the same gender." In that province, same-sex couples who meet this definition have the same spousal rights and responsibilities as heterosexual couples, including a right to contract into property and pensions, and to inherit from their partner as a spouse if the partner dies without a will.

In 2000, legislation in Nova Scotia revised the definition of "spouse" to include both opposite and same-sex couples who have lived together in a conjugal relationship for at least one year. In that year, "for the first time in the seven years it had been asking the question, less than half of Canadians [48 percent] opposed same-sex marriage" (Bricker and Greenspon 2001: 267).

Advocates of same-sex marriage maintain that as long as same-sex couples cannot be legally married, they will not be viewed as legitimate families by the larger society and will face undue stress as a result. On the other hand, opponents of same-sex marriage do not want their children to learn that homosexuality is an accepted and acceptable life. Many of them view homosexuality as unnatural, sick, and/or immoral.

The most common argument against same-sex marriage is that it subverts the stability and integrity of the heterosexual family. Sullivan (1997), though, points out that gays and lesbians are already part of heterosexual families:

> [Homosexuals] are sons and daughters, brothers and sisters, even mothers and fathers, of heterosexuals. The distinction between "families" and "homosexuals" is, to begin with, empirically false; and the stability of existing families is closely linked to how homosexuals are treated within them. (p. 147)

According to the 2001 Canadian census, 13 percent of female same-sex couples have children living with them and 3 percent of same-sex male couples are also parenting children (Arnold 2002).

Child Custody, Visitation, and Reproductive Rights

Another milestone for gay activists was attained in 2001 when, for the first time, a Canadian survey reported majority support for gay adoption (Bricker and Greenspon 2001: 267). In 1995, an Ontario provincial judge ruled that gay and lesbian couples have the right to apply to adopt a child under that province's *Child and Family Services Act*. In 1998, British Columbia passed amendments to its *Adoption Act* and *Family Relations Act* that provided same-sex couples who cohabit continuously for two years with the same right to apply to adopt a child. In 1999, Alberta joined with these provinces in permitting same-sex couples to adopt.

Little was known until relatively recently about the nature of gay and lesbian family life. Many published accounts were non-empirical and saturated with a heterosexist bias that framed gay and lesbian families as "deviant" and "pathological." Even though research on gay and lesbian families expanded dramatically in the 1990s (e.g., Arnup 1995; Benkov 1994; Stone 1990; Weston 1991), generalizable information still remains sparse due to nonrandom sampling, limited sample sizes, and the diversities of these families occasioned by ethnicity, class, age of parents and offspring, and circumstances leading to family formation. However, in a review of research on family relationships of lesbians and gay men, Patterson (2001) concludes that "the greater majority of children with lesbian or gay parents grow up to identify themselves as heterosexual" and that "concerns about possible difficulties in personal development among children of lesbian and gay parents have not been sustained by the results of research" (p. 279). Patterson (2001) additionally notes that the "home environments provided by lesbian and gay parents are just as likely as those provided by heterosexual parents to enable psychosocial growth among family members" (p. 283).

At least in theory, custody and access orders in Canada are equally available to members of same-sex unions and opposite-sex unions, with decisions made in "the best interests of the child." However, while "[n]othing in Canadian law stops a homosexual parent from applying for custody, the courts will often take judicial notice of the fact that some harm might arise from living with a homosexual parent" (Yogis et al. 1996: 56). Yogis and colleagues note that Canadian case law suggests that "custody is awarded to discreet, non-militant homosexual parents who do not flaunt their sexual orientation" (p. 56).

Hate Crimes against Sexual-Orientation Minorities

In eighteenth-century North America, where laws against same-sex sexual activity often included the death penalty, violence against gays and lesbians was widespread, and included beatings, burnings, various kinds of torture, and execution (Button et al. 1997). Although such treatment of sexual-orientation minorities is no longer legally condoned, gays, lesbians, and bisexuals continue to be victimized by hate crimes. Surveys indicate that as many as one-fourth of lesbians and gay men report having been victims of physical attacks because of their sexual orientation (Herek 1989). A survey of more than 3000 high-school students found that students who reported having engaged in same-sex relations were more than three times as likely to report not going to school because they felt unsafe and more than twice as likely to report having been threatened or injured with a weapon at school (Faulkner and Cranston 1998). These students were also significantly more likely to report that their property was deliberately damaged or stolen at school.

Hate-motivated violence toward sexual-orientation minorities can be brutal. The following example is given in *Reaching Out: A Report on Lesbian, Gay, and Bisexual Youth Issues in Canada*, prepared for the United Church of Canada by John Fisher (1999), then-executive director of Equality for Gays and Lesbians Everywhere (EGALE):

> When Christian Hernandez was 14 and a Grade 9 student at Notre Dame College High School in Niagara Falls, Ontario, he screwed up his courage and told his best friend that he was gay. That was his first mistake. "He told me he couldn't accept it," recalls Hernandez. "And he began to spread it around." Over the next two years, Hernandez was teased and harassed almost daily. One day, a group of boys waited for him after school. Their leader had a knife, and, says Hernandez, "He told me he didn't accept faggots, that we brought AIDS into the world." The boy then cut Hernandez on the neck, putting him in the hospital for a week. When Hernandez told his parents about the attack, his father, who has since moved back to his native El Salvador, said he would "rather have a dead son than a queer son."*

*Fisher, 1999. *A Report on Lesbian, Gay and Bisexual Youth Issues in Canada*. Ottawa: EGALE. Reprinted by permission of Egale Canadian Human Rights Trust.

Next, we highlight some of the strategies for reducing and responding to prejudice and discrimination toward sexual-orientation minorities.

9.7 Strategies for Action: Reducing Antigay Prejudice and Discrimination

Many of the efforts to change policies and attitudes regarding sexual-orientation minorities have been spearheaded by organizations. These include the above-mentioned EGALE, Canada's only national equal rights organization advocating for lesbians, gays, and bisexuals, with members in every province and territory; Parents, Family, and Friends of Lesbians and Gays (PFLAG); Victoria Youth Pride Society; Pink Triangle Services Youth Group in Ottawa; Lesbian and Gay Health Services in Saskatoon; and the British Columbia Civil Liberties Association. The gay rights movement continues to be active in promoting HIV/AIDS research, adequate health care for AIDS victims, securing housing for HIV+ persons, and maintaining the rights of HIV-infected individuals.

These organizations are also politically active in their efforts to achieve equal rights for gays, lesbians, and bisexuals and trans persons. EGALE was formed principally to secure the legal right for same-sex couples to marry in Canada, but since achieving that goal in 2003, EGALE has continued to work to secure the rights and recognitions of all sexual minority groups. For example, EGALE is currently working to have Bill C-279, the so-called "Gender Identity Bill," passed by Parliament and secured with Royal Assent. The bill, which would alter the *Human Rights Act* to include gender identity as a "prohibited ground of discrimination," would require that the law take gender identity into consideration "as an aggravating circumstance" in crimes against persons, and be cognizant of its protected status when sentencing perpetrators of crimes carried out on persons because of their perceived gender identity (http://openparliament.ca/bills/41-1/C-279).

In addition, demonstrative and cultural expressions of gay activism, such as "gay pride" celebrations, marches, demonstrations, or other cultural activities promoting gay rights, are important in organizing gay activists. However, it has been noted that

> Too many people have seen the cultural activity as a substitute for democratic political participation. In too many cases over the past decades we have left the political arena to our most dedicated opponents [of gay rights], whose letter writing, phone calling, and lobbying have easily triumphed over our marching, demonstrating, and dancing. The most important lesson…is that politics—conventional, boring, but essential politics—will ultimately have a major impact on the extent to which we can rid our lives of prejudice. (Frank 1997: xi)

In Canada, the various political parties have shown different levels of support for gay rights issues. For example, despite its caucus dominance from 1993 to 2005, no Liberal member of Parliament identified himself or herself as gay, lesbian, or bisexual and some, such as Roseanne Stoke and Tom Wappel, consistently referred to homosexuality as "unnatural," "immoral," and a "perversion." In the context of Parliamentary debate over Bill C-279, Conservative MP Rob Anders from Calgary West delivered a petition against C-279, which he referred to not as the "gender identity bill" but as the "bathroom bill," arguing that if it were to pass "it would give transgendered men access to women's public washroom facilities" and that, by extension, children might be exposed to dangerous men in women's bathrooms (http://openparliament.ca/bills/41-1/C-279/). That Minister Anders had not even bothered to use the appropriate terminology to refer to a trans person in such a scenario (transwoman) and instead chose to refer to "transgendered men" reveals disrespect and refusal to understand where actual vulnerabilities lie. After all, as EGALE reports:

> 20% of trans people reported being the victim of a physical or sexual assault because they are trans. A further 34% have been verbally harassed or threatened because of their gender identity. Furthermore, a study by Egale Canada Human Rights Trust found that 74% of trans youth reported being verbally harassed and 37% reported being physically harassed or assaulted in school because of their gender identity. And yet there has not been a single case in which the hate crime sentencing provisions of the Criminal Code have ever been applied to such heinous crimes. (EGALE 2012)*

Although in the late 1990s Winnipeg elected its first openly gay mayor, Glen Murray, it would seem presumptuous to suppose that the issue of a candidate's sexual orientation is not considered relevant by at least some voters. It seems undeniable that the Christian right, religious and church groups, conservative family groups, and other conservative organizations and their political allies will continue to crusade against gay rights, and will continue to distort the concerns of those who are most vulnerable to experiences of violence and discrimination, trying to make them seem instead to be the most likely to perpetrate odious behaviours as we see MP Rob Anders try to do in his rhetoric cited above. The Rainbow Health Coalition has been archived by the federal government, and its pages, which had offered up-to-date information regarding health care for LGBTQI people across Canada, are no longer live; the coalition is no longer supported under Health Canada (Health Canada 2014). Nevertheless, opposition groups are up against an increasingly powerful pro–gay rights movement, and progress is ongoing. For example, Ontario now allows trans persons to change their sex on legal identification papers without requiring them to have undergone sex reassignment surgery (SRS). And initiatives such as the Triangle School offer safe places that were unthinkable for queer youth in previous generations. Meanwhile, some provinces have developed their own networks, such as Rainbow Health Ontario, for LGBTQI communities to access health information. In British Columbia, Vancouver Coastal Health operates a transgender health program that helps to inform clinicians and care providers about best practices, and provides trans persons with answers to their specific health questions (http://transhealth.vch.ca), including the "standards of care" for British Columbia as of 2013. Nova Scotia, Ontario, Alberta, British Columbia, Quebec, and Saskatchewan all provide complete coverage for SRS, though Saskatchewan residents are required to be diagnosed with "Gender Identity Disorder" through CAMH in Ontario, and must have their surgery in Montreal where the fees for SRS exceed the amounts determined in Saskatchewan. Manitoba provides partial coverage for SRS but does not include breast augmentation procedures. Manitobans seeking SRS must also be recommended by CAMH in Toronto. In the Maritimes there is no formal policy to provide coverage for SRS but EGALE reports that "in most Atlantic provinces … in practice SRS is paid for on a case-by-case basis" (EGALE 2004).

Educational Strategies: Policies and Programs in the Schools

A survey of youths' risk behaviour found that 30 percent of gay teens attempted suicide in the previous year, compared with 7 percent of their straight peers (reported in Platt 2001). Forty percent of gay youth report schoolwork being negatively affected by conflicts around sexual orientation, and over one-quarter of gay youth drop out of

*Egale Canada Human Rights Trust, 2012. "Human Rights Day a Call for Consensus on Gender Identity Bill," http://egale.ca/all/human-rights-day-a-call-for-consensus-on-gender-identity-bill/. Reprinted with permission of Egale Canada Human Rights Trust.

school (Chase 2000; *Homophobia 101* 2000). Research conducted in Calgary reports that gay and bisexual males were "almost 14 times more likely to have made a serious suicide attempt at some point in their lives than their heterosexually oriented counterparts" and that lesbian, gay, and bisexual youth of colour were dramatically over-represented in attempted suicide statistics. According to one of the authors of this research, Pierre Tremblay, "This is the fallout of living with no guidance and no support. It's a problem every teacher knows about, but too often the attitude is, 'we would like to help, but we don't want to promote homosexuality.' It is a total abdication" (in Fisher 1999). All of these findings suggest that if schools are to promote the health and well-being of all students, they must address the needs of gay, lesbian, and bisexual youth and promote acceptance of sexual-orientation diversity within the school setting (Flowers and Buston 2001; Murphy 2001). One strategy for promoting tolerance for diversity among students involves establishing and enforcing a school policy prohibiting antigay behaviour. Another strategy for addressing the needs of homosexual and bisexual youth is having school-based support groups. Such groups can help students increase self-esteem, overcome their sense of isolation, provide information and resources, and provide a resource for parents. In-service training for teachers and other staff is also important and may include examining the effects of antigay bias, dispelling myths about homosexuality, and brainstorming ways to create a more inclusive environment (Mathison 1998). Most public schools, though, offer little support and education regarding sexual-orientation diversity. Most schools lack support groups or special counselling services for gay and lesbian youth, and the majority of schools do not have any policies prohibiting antigay harassment (Button et al. 1997).

Nevertheless, some progress is being made. In Toronto, the Triangle Program offers gays who have been harassed at school an alternative place to study for up to 18 months and a curriculum that emphasizes the contributions of gays and lesbians in various fields, though as our chapter on education notes, this program is not without limitations. Various Canadian school boards and teaching institutes have adopted policies or initiatives that promote the equal treatment of gays and lesbians. For example, the Vancouver School Board's Statement of Mission and Beliefs states, "We believe in equitable treatment for all individuals, regardless of race, culture, gender, religion, socio economic status, sexual orientation or physical or mental ability." In addition, the federal government has launched a national initiative, the "Safe Spaces Project," funded by the federal Department of Health, to help produce educational materials for both heterosexual and lesbian and gay youth on lesbian, gay, and bisexual issues, and to create safe spaces for lesbian, gay, and bisexual youth.

Campus Policies Regarding Homosexuality

Student groups have been active in the gay liberation movement since the 1960s. Numerous gay student groups are organized in community colleges and universities across Canada.

D'Emilio (1990) suggests that colleges and universities have the ability and the responsibility to promote gay rights and social acceptance of homosexual people:

> For reasons that I cannot quite fathom, I still expect the academy to embrace higher standards of civility, decency, and justice than the society around it. Having been granted the extraordinary privilege of thinking critically as a way of life, we should be astute enough to recognize when a group of people is being systematically mistreated. We have the intelligence to devise solutions to problems that appear in our community. I expect us also to have the courage to lead rather than follow. (p. 18)

In addition to including sexual orientation in discrimination policies, colleges and universities have also taken more proactive measures to support the lesbigay student population. Such measures have included offering gay and lesbian studies programs, social centres, and support groups, and sponsoring events and activities that celebrate diversity. "These programs serve as both a refuge for lesbians and gay men on campus, and common ground from which to launch educational projects that foster respect for difference" (Lambda Legal Defense and Education Fund 2000: 10).

Strategies for reducing antigay prejudice and discrimination are influenced largely by politicians, religious leaders, courts, and educators, who will continue to make decisions that either promote the well-being of sexual-orientation minorities or hinder it. Ultimately, however, each individual must decide to embrace either an inclusive or an exclusive ideology; collectively, those individual decisions will determine the future treatment of sexual-orientation minorities.

In addition, lesbigay individuals must find their own strategies for living in a homophobic and biphobic society. They may find encouragement in the following:

> If you dream of a world in which you can put your partner's picture on your desk, then put his picture on your desk...and you will live in such a world.
>
> If you dream of a world in which there are more openly gay elected officials, then run for office...and you will live in such a world.
>
> And if you dream of a world in which you can take your partner to the office party...then take her to the party. I do, and now I live in such a world.
>
> Remember, there are two things that keep us oppressed—them and us. We are half of the equation. (Baldwin 2000)

Understanding Sexualities

As both functionalists and conflict theorists note, "alternatives" to heterosexuality are threatening to traditionalists because they require new understandings and arrangements of family, child-rearing, and gender roles. The conflict is expressed in economic, social, and legal discrimination by the majority. GLBT individuals are also victimized by hate crimes, and in some countries, same-sex activity is punished with sanctions ranging from fines to imprisonment and even death.

Evidence suggests that sexuality, like handedness, may have a biological component. The debate between biological and social explanations is commonly referred to as the "nature versus nurture" debate. Research indicates that both forces affect sexual orientation, although debate over which is dominant continues. Sociologists are interested in society's response to sexual-orientation diversity and how that response affects the quality of life of society's members. Because individuals' views toward sexuality are related to their beliefs about what "causes" any deviation from sexual norms, the question of the origins of sexual-orientation diversity has sociological significance.

Prejudice and discrimination toward sexual-orientation minorities are rooted in various aspects of culture, such as religious views, rigid gender roles, and negative myths and stereotypes. Hate crimes against homosexuals and bisexuals are blatant examples of the discrimination that sexual-orientation minorities continue to experience.

Attitudes toward lesbians and gays have become more accepting. One explanation for these changing attitudes is that awareness of personal contact with openly gay individuals has increased in recent years as more people come out to family and friends. "This is likely to increase support for gay and lesbian equality because contacts with openly gay individuals reduce negative stereotypes and ignorance" (Wilcox and

Wolpert 2000: 414). Another explanation for changing attitudes toward homosexuality is the positive depiction of gays and lesbians in the popular media. In 1992 *Roseanne* and *Melrose Place* had gay and lesbian characters, in 1998 Ellen DeGeneres came out on her sitcom *Ellen*, and by the 2000s, central gay and lesbian characters appeared in many television shows, including *Dawson's Creek, Will & Grace, Buffy the Vampire Slayer, Friends, ER, Spin City,* and *Normal, Ohio* (Deziel 2000). To these we can add the cable-television series *Six Feet Under* and *The L Word*.

But, as one scholar expressed: "the new confidence and social visibility of homosexuals…have by no means conquered homophobia. Indeed it stands as the last acceptable prejudice" (Fone 2000: 411). Although the gay rights movement has made significant gains in the last few decades, it has also suffered losses and defeat due to opposition groups and politicians. Many strategies for promoting gay rights have been successful and the Canadian public is becoming increasingly supportive of gay rights. But, as Yang (1999) points out, as the antigay minority diminishes in size, "it often becomes more dedicated and impassioned" (p. ii). For those who believe that all Canadians, regardless of sexual orientation, should be treated equally,

> Our task in the coming years is to get…[those] who support our cause to feel as passionately outraged by the injustices we face and to be as strongly motivated to act in support of our rights as our adversaries are in their opposition to our rights. (p. iii)

Student Reflection: What Do You Know Now?

As in the case of race, there is a powerful argument out there that sexuality and gender identity are biologically inevitable. Is it possible to restate these categories as, like race, a social fact? Lady Gaga would need to change the lyrics to "Born This Way," for one thing. But what are the costs and benefits of sticking to a genetic or otherwise internal reason for identity? What claims are made possible on systems (health care, marriage institutions, insurance, legal decision making, and so on) when an identity category is configured as NOT a choice but a biological fact? Does thinking of it in terms of ethnicity help—as part of multiculturalism in Canada, for example? In what ways might activists in one area benefit from working on struggles for equality with activists in another, even if they disagree about what is foundational to identity in each case? Reflect on your own response to media portrayals of GLBT individuals and to events in your own locale that are salient.

What Do You Do Next?

Located at www.nelson.com/socialproblems5e

- Consolidate your knowledge with interactive and printable **Flashcards**
- Gauge your understanding with **Practice Quizzes** and **Matching Activities**
- Develop your critical thinking skills with **Self and Society** and **The Human Side** questions
- Analyze **Social Research** and **Social Problems in Global Perspective**
- Explore the implications of **Technology on Social Problems**

section 3

Problems of Inequality and Power

The 2004 Disney movie *The* Incredibles speaks to the problem of living in a world in which everyone is "special." In such a world, no differences in ability are tolerated and exceptional talents are punished. Perpetually disciplined to suppress his superhero talents in order to avoid standing out, young Dash Parr says to his former-superhero mother, "If everyone is special, doesn't that mean that no one is?" Dash's inquisitive observation hit a nerve with audiences and became a hot conversation topic at the time of the film's release.

Differences between people in and of themselves are *not* what is meant by inequality as a social problem. Few would want to live in a society where everyone was the same. Where some fear that the erasure of difference means the denial of talent, when sociologists turn attention to problems of difference we aim to remove the arbitrary barriers that prevent people from expressing talent and from having access to a healthy and stable quality of life. Problems of inequality and power concern inequities in the quality of life—as we see with problems of poverty in Canada and around the world (Chapter 10). As we will see in Chapter 11, structural inequality affects opportunities to work and prosper, and we address the negative impact of low socio-economic status in completing higher education in Chapter 12.

The highly interrelated chapters in Section 3—"Poverty: National and International Issues," "Work and Unemployment," and "Problems in Education"—speak to the need for examining both the cultural and the structural underpinnings of the social problems described.

NEL

10

Poverty: National and International Issues

© Blue_Cutler/iStockphoto.com

Student Reflection: What Do You Already Know?

As a general rule, your Canadian author's sociology students over time have had difficulty seeing class-based oppression in Canada. While they are aware that income levels vary, most self-identify, when asked, as middle-class. One suspects that Canadians like the idea of a nation full of middle-class families. However, the income levels within that middle class vary strikingly, and one of the major insights from sociological thinking ought to include the effects of income disparity—the gap between the richest and the poorest. We also invite you to think about class along lines other than pure income levels. Social inequality arises in part due to different "social capital" and tends to reproduce itself over generations. You very likely think of Canada as a nation that is more benevolent, socially, than some. To be sure, we have a history of health care and other social programs designed to support the poorest among us as well as the middle earners. Is it working?

Learning Outcomes

Through careful reading of this chapter, you should be able to:

- define the bolded key terms
- compare what can be studied, changed, and improved by using various measures of poverty, including multidimensional measures
- apply sociological theories of social inequality to the problem of poverty in Canada
- uncover and challenge assumptions about poverty in relation to age, gender, educational attainment, disability, ethnicity, and work patterns
- identify various consequences of poverty in terms of educational, family, and housing outcomes
- situate poverty's consequences over time for individuals, families, and societies (in Canada and globally) in the larger context of inequality and power
- explain government's role in addressing poverty historically and in the contemporary context federally and provincially through tax benefits, minimum wage, and pay equity initiatives, as well as on the global stage through debt relief, investment, and support for charity
- critically examine the cost of poverty and its potential elimination

10.1 The Global Context: Poverty and Economic Inequality around the World

Who are the poor? Are rates of world poverty increasing, decreasing, or remaining stable? The answers depend on how we define and measure poverty.

Defining and Measuring Poverty

Traditionally, **poverty** has been defined as the lack of resources necessary for material well-being—especially food and water, but also housing, land, and health care. This lack of resources that leads to hunger and physical deprivation is known as **absolute poverty**. **Relative poverty** refers to a deficiency in material and economic resources compared with some other population. Consider, for example, that while many Canadians are poor, they still have resources and a level of material well-being of which the millions living in absolute poverty can only dream.

Governments, researchers, and organizations use various measures of poverty. Next, we describe international and Canadian measures of poverty.

International Measures of Poverty

The World Bank sets a "poverty threshold" of $1.25 per day in constant dollars based on a 2005 benchmark. Using this threshold the World Bank reports that in 2010, 1.22 billion of the world's people (21 percent of those in developing countries) still lived at or below the poverty threshold for developing regions. While the drop to roughly one-fifth of the developing world living in poverty marks significant progress, the number that the World Bank reports is more than half of what it was in 1990 when 43 percent lived at or below the poverty line in the developing world. The World Bank has set a target of having fewer than 3 percent of the developing world living at or below poverty by 2030 (World Bank 2014). The World Bank is interested not only in the very poorest, but also in improving the lives of those who are merely "'less well-off' (the bottom 40 percent)," and is measuring increases in the standard of living for this group in five-year increments. Reducing the number of persons living in poverty around the globe and improving the lives of the bottom 40 percent are goals that the World Bank reports some significant progress in achieving; however, the organization also notes that challenges persist in meeting those goals: "A country's efforts to reduce poverty can be hampered by a lack of jobs, weak safety nets, poor infrastructure, low productivity or other challenges. . . . despite progress, differences in access to education, health services, basic infrastructure and job opportunities are still an urgent development challenge" (World Bank 2014).

While Credit Suisse prefers to write about levels of "household wealth" around the globe, they have produced a map of global wealth distribution that shows very clearly it is only Europe, North America, Australia, New Zealand, and Japan that enjoy the highest standard of living, while most countries in Africa, all of India, most of South America, and portions of Asia and the boundary between Europe and Russia—in Belarus, Ukraine, and Moldova—live in marked poverty. See Figure 10.1, which examines world wealth levels.

Even given these broad patterns in global wealth and poverty, the Credit Suisse data note that there can be gross income inequality in the poorest regions of the world where there are, nonetheless, significant numbers of "super rich" who enjoy lavish standards of living. For the year 2012, the Credit Suisse "estimate[s] that more than six million residents in both Japan and China joined the top global decile, along with around half a million new members in Chile, Colombia and Hong Kong" (Davies et al. 2012: 14). Another

poverty
Lacking resources for an "adequate" standard of living.

absolute poverty
The chronic absence of the basic necessities of life, including food, clean water, and housing.

relative poverty
A deficiency in material and economic resources compared with some other population.

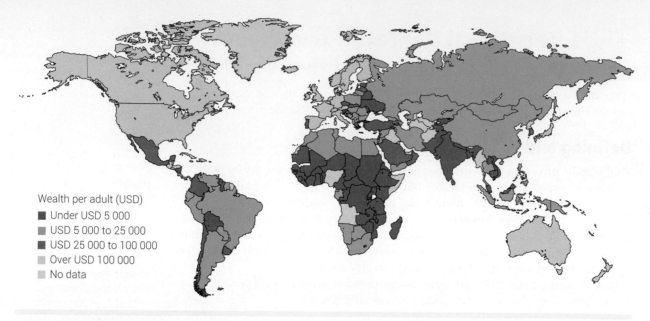

Figure 10.1 **World Wealth Levels, 2012**

Wealth per adult (USD)
- ■ Under USD 5 000
- ■ USD 5 000 to 25 000
- ■ USD 25 000 to 100 000
- ■ Over USD 100 000
- ■ No data

SOURCE: Credit Suisse, 2013. *Global Wealth Data Book 2013*, page 19. Reprinted by permission of Credit Suisse.

Human Poverty Index (HPI)

A composite measure of poverty based on three measures of deprivation: (1) deprivation of life, which is measured by the percentage of people expected to die before age 40; (2) deprivation of knowledge, which is measured by the percentage of adults who are illiterate; and (3) deprivation in living standards, which is measured as a composite of three variables—the percentage of people without access to health services, the percentage of people without access to safe water, and the percentage of malnourished children under five.

poverty measure used by the World Health Organization (WHO) is based on a household's ability to meet the minimum calorie requirements of its members. According to this poverty measure, a household is considered poor if it cannot meet 80 percent of the minimum caloric requirements (established by WHO), even when using 80 percent of its income to buy food.

In industrial countries, national poverty lines are sometimes based on the median household income of a country's population. According to this relative poverty measure, members of a household are considered poor if their household income is less than 50 percent of the median household income in that country.

Research on poverty concludes that poverty is multidimensional and includes such dimensions as food insecurity; poor housing; unemployment; psychological distress; powerlessness; hopelessness; lack of access to health care, education, and transportation; and vulnerability (Narayan 2000). To capture the multidimensional nature of poverty, the United Nations Development Programme (1997) developed a composite measure of poverty: the **Human Poverty Index (HPI)**. Rather than measure poverty by income, three measures of deprivation are combined to yield the HPI: (1) deprivation of a long, healthy life, (2) deprivation of knowledge, and (3) deprivation of decent living standards. As shown in Table 10.1, the HPI for developing countries is measured differently than for industrialized countries (HPI-2). For the assessment of some OECD countries, the UN Human Development Report for 2007/2008 added a fourth dimension, social exclusion, in HPI-2. The perspective taken by the United Nations HPI is that poverty is not a singular problem but rather one with multiple dimensions, and multiple impacts. The UN Human Development Report (2010) explains the inclusion of these four measures of deprivation, noting that "Money based measures are obviously important, but deprivations in other dimensions and their overlap need to be considered . . . because households facing multiple deprivations are likely to be in worse situations than income poverty measures suggest" (Klugman 2010: 94). In addition, the multidimensional approach to

Table 10.1 *Measures of Human Poverty in Developing and Industrialized Countries*

	Longevity	Knowledge	Decent Standard of Living	Social Exclusion (for selected OECD countries)
For developing countries	Probability at birth of not surviving to age 40	Adult illiteracy	A composite measure based on the following: Percentage of people without access to safe water Percentage of people without access to health services Percentage of children under age five who are underweight	
For industrialized countries	Probability at birth of not surviving to age 60	Adult functional illiteracy rate	Percentage of people living below the income poverty line, which is set at 50 percent of median disposable income	**Social Exclusion** Measured by the rate of long-term unemployment (greater than 12 months)

SOURCE: Adapted from the United Nations Development Programme. 2000. *Human Development Report 2000* (page 16, table 1). New York: Oxford University Press; "Calculating the Human Development Indices, HPI-2," Technical Note, *Human Development Report 2007/2008*. New York: Palgrave-Macmillan.

measuring poverty allows us to assess what kinds of community participation we can promote in impoverished areas in order to ameliorate the negative privations to which the poor are vulnerable. The Index is a useful complement to income measures of poverty and "will serve as a strong reminder that eradicating poverty will always require more than increasing the income of the poorest" (United Nations Development Programme 1997: 19).

Among the 17 industrialized countries for which the HPI-2 was calculated in 2001, Sweden had the lowest level of human poverty (6.8 percent), followed by Norway (7.5 percent) and the Netherlands (8.5 percent). By 2010, at the 20-year mark for the annual report, the Human Development Index could demonstrate some significant movement upward for some countries, especially those that were most vulnerable in 1990, when the first data report was issued. The 2010 report explains the nuances of improvement thusly: "Someone born in The Gambia in 1970 could expect to live to age 41—some 33 years fewer than someone born in Norway. By 2010 life expectancy in The Gambia had increased by 16 years (to 57) but in Norway by only 7 years. Thus, while the gap in life expectancy between Norway and The Gambia is still huge (24 years), it has shrunk by more than a fourth" (Klugman 2010: 29). In other words, the negative impacts of global inequalities remain staggering, even when significant improvements are made in vulnerable populations. In addition, the 2010 report shows that not all movement across the HDI is markedly upward; one-quarter of all the countries surveyed had a development increase of less than one-fifth over 1990 levels, and 10 countries surveyed saw no overall improvement at all (Klugman 2010: 30).

Measures of poverty tell us how many (or what percentage of) people are living in poverty in a given year. Another way to assess poverty is to note the degree to which those who are poor stay in poverty from year to year. This assessment can be done by calculating the average annual poverty exit rate—the share of the poor in one year who have left poverty by the following year. One study followed the same families over a five-year period in six countries—Canada, Germany, Netherlands, Sweden, the United Kingdom, and the United States (reported in Mishel et al. 2001). The results indicated that, with the exception of the Netherlands, the poor in Canada were more likely than the poor elsewhere to leave poverty from one year to the next. According to this research, 44 percent of the poor in the Netherlands and 42 percent of the poor in Canada escape poverty each year, compared with 28.6 percent of the poor in the United States, 29.1 percent in the United Kingdom, 36 percent in Sweden, and 37 percent in Germany. We can extrapolate from these data that although the same proportion of people in Canada are poor every year, those who are poor are not *the same* people year after year. This observation leads in turn to another: that if the same proportion of people remains poor year after year, there must be reasons beyond individual characteristics to explain the persistence of poverty.

Canadian Measures of Poverty

Statistics Canada developed the **low income cut-offs (LICOs)** as a measure of poverty in 1968. Estimating that poor families or individuals spent approximately 34.7 percent or more of their pre-tax income on such basic needs as food, shelter, and clothing, the agency then added 20 percentage points to determine the cut-off. In consequence, it was arbitrarily established as a standard that families or individuals who spent 54.7 percent of their pre-tax income on food, clothing, and shelter would be in financial difficulty. Recognizing that the minimum income level necessary to avoid financial hardship varies with changes in the cost of living, family size, and place of residence, Statistics Canada calculates different low income cut-offs for different communities and for families of varying sizes within these communities. For example, in 2004, the low income cut-off for a family of four living in an urban area with a population of half a million or more was $37 791. For a family of four living in a rural area, it was $26 015.

The Daily Bread Food Bank in Toronto has been at the fore of developing and reporting on Canadian measures of deprivation levels. The Daily Bread report from 2009 takes specific notice that not just individuals are vulnerable to the deprivations of poverty but that entire communities are at risk, and therefore uses a "community-based poverty measure" to assess the deprivations experienced by the poor (Matern et al. 2009). The kinds of things that the report asked about included assessing whether people who used the food bank had the kitchens, tools, and appliances required to prepare healthy foods, whether they could keep their homes "adequately" warm, whether food bank users had a savings of $20 per month for emergencies or long-term use, and whether people had any money at all to spend on themselves (2009: 9). The results showed that for food bank users, 41 percent had no vacuum, 29 percent had no microwave oven, and 30 percent had no telephone; 21 percent could not afford to keep the home adequately warm; 68 percent were unable to save $20 a month; and 61 percent had no money to spend on themselves each week (2009: 11). The Daily Bread used this initial survey of food bank users to develop a more refined set of questions and commissioned Ipsos Reid to assess the Ontario population across income levels. The results of the Ipsos Reid poll provide a "deprivation score" for Ontario residents who live at or below the low-income measure (LIM), and are displayed in Table 10.2. Higher deprivation scores indicate the largest correspondence between the degree to which the item is out of reach for respondents, and the degree to which all respondents felt the item was necessary.

Another way of measuring poverty is to employ the **market basket measure (MBM)**, which is based on the concept of "necessaries" as defined by the eighteenth-century economist Adam Smith: "Whatever the custom of the country

---

low income cut-offs (LICOs)
Developed by Statistics Canada as a measure of poverty. Estimating that poor families or individuals spend approximately 34.7 percent or more of their pre-tax income on such basic needs as food, shelter, and clothing, 20 percentage points were added to this figure to determine the cut-off. This standard suggests that individuals or families who spent 54.7 percent of their pre-tax income on food, clothing, and shelter would experience financial difficulty. Different low income cut-off lines are established by Statistics Canada for different communities as well as for families of varying sizes within these communities.

market basket measure (MBM)
An assessment of the minimum level of income required to provide for the basic needs that a given society would find it "indecent" to be without.

Table 10.2 *Final List of 10 Deprivation Indicators*

Item	L = % Under LIM Who Cannot Afford	H = % Over LIM Who Cannot Afford	Under LIM Minus Over LIM A − B	P = % Who Feel Item Is Necessary	Deprivation Score = [(L − H) × P]
Dental Care	32	8	24	91	2 184
Savings	43	14	29	74	0
Replace/repair broken electrical goods	35	9	26	71	1 846
Replace/repair furniture	46	15	31	57	0
Small amount of money	38	12	26	65	0
Presents	25	5	20	65	1 300
Clothes for job interviews	21	4	17	70	1 190
Friends or family over for a meal	29	8	21	50	1 050
Fresh fruits and vegetables	16	3	13	80	1 040
Transportation	12	2	10	88	880
Hobby	21	7	14	55	770
Meat, fish or vegetarian equivalent	11	2	9	82	738
Pest free home	11	3	8	90	720
Prescriptions	9	3	6	88	528
Two pairs of shoes	8	2	6	84	504
Cable television	16	4	12	34	408
Warm coat	5	1	4	93	372
Vacuum cleaner	7	1	6	60	360
Personal care items	4	0	4	83	332
Warm home	5	2	3	92	276
Stereo	15	4	11	24	264
Telephone	2	0	2	89	178
Internet access at home	4	1	3	55	165
DVD player	9	2	7	23	161
Microwave	5	1	4	39	156

SOURCE: *Developing a Deprivation Index: The Research Process*, by Richard Matern, Michael Mendelson and Michael Oliphant, p. 23. Published December 2009 by Daily Bread Food Bank and the Caledon Institute of Social Policy.

renders it indecent for creditable people, even of the lowest order, to be without." While provinces use the market basket concept to set welfare rates, defining what, exactly, are "necessaries" is not easy. The concept as used by Smith implies that necessaries are broader than what is needed for mere subsistence; yet, as we discuss later, some necessary items simply do not count in the MBM.

Another way of defining low income or the "poverty line" is to employ the **low-income measure (LIM)**. Using the LIM, Statistics Canada has established a figure for the needs of one adult and proceeded on the assumption that family needs increase in proportion to family size, with each additional adult increasing the family's needs by 40 percent of the first adult and each additional child increasing the family's needs by 30 percent. To calculate how many Canadians, individuals, or family members lack sufficient income to cover their basic needs for food, clothing, shelter, and other necessities, Statistics Canada compares these income figures with the actual family and individual incomes. Table 10.3 shows after-tax income needed as of 2010 to avoid the serious depth of poverty of the low income cut-offs in Canada. In addition to giving us a long view of increased need in after-tax income by using 1992 as the base year, the table helps us to see that the size of community in which one lives influences both the cost of living and earnings. The table also shows us that the minimum wage in Canada will take those who live in semi-urban and urban areas only marginally over the poverty line, and only if they have deductible costs to their income in excess of the first $11 038 amount, which is not taxable in Canada.

low-income measure (LIM)

For the purposes of assessing low income using this measure, Statistics Canada has established a figure for the needs of one adult and proceeded on the assumption that family needs increase in proportion to the size of the family, with each additional adult increasing the family needs by 40 percent of the first adult and each additional child increasing the family's needs by 30 percent.

Table 10.3 *Low Income Cut-Offs, After Tax, 1992–2010 (1992 base)*

Size of Family Unit	Community Size				
		Census Agglomeration (CA)		Census Metropolitan Area (CMA)	
	Rural Areas Outside CMA or CA[1]	Less than 30 000 Inhabitants[2]	Between 30 000 and 99 999 Inhabitants	Between 100 000 and 499 999 Inhabitants	500 000 Inhabitants or More
	Current Dollars				
1992					
1 person	8 848	10 126	11 296	11 439	13 526
2 persons	10 769	12 325	13 749	13 922	16 462
3 persons	13 410	15 346	17 120	17 336	20 499
4 persons	16 729	19 146	21 359	21 628	25 574
5 persons	19 050	21 802	24 322	24 628	29 121
6 persons	21 127	24 179	26 974	27 313	32 296
7 or more persons	23 204	26 556	29 625	29 998	35 471

Table 10.3 *Low Income Cut-Offs, After Tax, 1992–2010 (1992 base)* **(continued)**

Size of Family Unit	Rural Areas Outside CMA or CA[1]	Census Agglomeration (CA)		Census Metropolitan Area (CMA)	
		Less than 30 000 Inhabitants[2]	Between 30 000 and 99 999 Inhabitants	Between 100 000 and 499 999 Inhabitants	500 000 Inhabitants or More
		Current Dollars			
1993					
1 person	9 017	10 319	11 511	11 657	13 784
2 persons	10 974	12 560	14 011	14 187	16 776
3 persons	13 665	15 638	17 446	17 666	20 889
4 persons	17 048	19 511	21 766	22 040	26 061
5 persons	19 413	22 217	24 785	25 097	29 676
6 persons	21 529	24 640	27 488	27 833	32 911
7 or more persons	23 646	27 062	30 189	30 569	36 147
1994					
1 person	9 027	10 331	11 525	11 671	13 800
2 persons	10 987	12 574	14 027	14 204	16 795
3 persons	13 681	15 657	17 466	17 687	20 914
4 persons	17 068	19 533	21 791	22 066	26 092
5 persons	19 436	22 243	24 814	25 126	29 710
6 persons	21 555	24 668	27 520	27 866	32 950
7 or more persons	23 674	27 093	30 225	30 605	36 189
1995					
1 person	9 227	10 560	11 780	11 929	14 106
2 persons	11 231	12 853	14 338	14 519	17 168
3 persons	13 985	16 004	17 854	18 079	21 378
4 persons	17 446	19 967	22 274	22 555	26 670
5 persons	19 866	22 736	25 364	25 683	30 369
6 persons	22 032	25 215	28 130	28 484	33 680
7 or more persons	24 198	27 694	30 895	31 284	36 991

(Continued)

Size of Family Unit	Community Size				
		Census Agglomeration (CA)		Census Metropolitan Area (CMA)	
	Rural Areas Outside CMA or CA[1]	Less than 30 000 Inhabitants[2]	Between 30 000 and 99 999 Inhabitants	Between 100 000 and 499 999 Inhabitants	500 000 Inhabitants or More
	Current Dollars				
1996					
1 person	9 364	10 717	11 955	12 106	14 315
2 persons	11 397	13 044	14 551	14 734	17 422
3 persons	14 192	16 241	18 119	18 347	21 695
4 persons	17 705	20 263	22 605	22 890	27 066
5 persons	20 161	23 074	25 741	26 065	30 820
6 persons	22 359	25 589	28 547	28 906	34 180
7 or more persons	24 558	28 105	31 353	31 748	37 540
1997					
1 person	9 522	10 898	12 157	12 311	14 557
2 persons	11 589	13 264	14 797	14 983	17 716
3 persons	14 432	16 515	18 424	18 657	22 061
4 persons	18 004	20 605	22 986	23 276	27 522
5 persons	20 501	23 463	26 175	26 504	31 340
6 persons	22 737	26 021	29 029	29 394	34 757
7 or more persons	24 972	28 579	31 882	32 284	38 174
1998					
1 person	9 617	11 006	12 278	12 433	14 701
2 persons	11 705	13 396	14 944	15 132	17 893
3 persons	14 575	16 680	18 608	18 843	22 280
4 persons	18 183	20 810	23 215	23 508	27 797
5 persons	20 706	23 697	26 436	26 768	31 652
6 persons	22 963	26 280	29 318	29 687	35 103
7 or more persons	25 221	28 864	32 200	32 605	38 554

Table 10.3 **Low Income Cut-Offs, After Tax, 1992–2010 (1992 base)** (continued)

Size of Family Unit	Rural Areas Outside CMA or CA[1]	Census Agglomeration (CA)		Census Metropolitan Area (CMA)	
		Less than 30 000 Inhabitants[2]	Between 30 000 and 99 999 Inhabitants	Between 100 000 and 499 999 Inhabitants	500 000 Inhabitants or More
		Current Dollars			
1999					
1 person	9 785	11 199	12 493	12 651	14 959
2 persons	11 910	13 631	15 206	15 397	18 206
3 persons	14 831	16 972	18 934	19 173	22 671
4 persons	18 501	21 175	23 622	23 920	28 284
5 persons	21 068	24 112	26 899	27 237	32 206
6 persons	23 365	26 741	29 832	30 207	35 718
7 or more persons	25 663	29 370	32 764	33 176	39 229
2000					
1 person	10 049	11 500	12 829	12 991	15 362
2 persons	12 231	13 998	15 615	15 811	18 696
3 persons	15 230	17 429	19 443	19 689	23 281
4 persons	18 999	21 744	24 258	24 563	29 045
5 persons	21 635	24 761	27 623	27 970	33 073
6 persons	23 994	27 460	30 635	31 020	36 679
7 or more persons	26 353	30 160	33 646	34 069	40 285
2001					
1 person	10 302	11 790	13 152	13 318	15 748
2 persons	12 538	14 350	16 008	16 209	19 166
3 persons	15 613	17 867	19 933	20 184	23 867
4 persons	19 477	22 291	24 868	25 181	29 775
5 persons	22 180	25 384	28 318	28 674	33 905
6 persons	24 598	28 151	31 405	31 800	37 602
7 or more persons	27 016	30 919	34 492	34 926	41 298

(Continued)

Table 10.3 **Low Income Cut-Offs, After Tax, 1992–2010 (1992 base)** (continued)

Size of Family Unit		Community Size			
			Census Agglomeration (CA)	Census Metropolitan Area (CMA)	
	Rural Areas Outside CMA or CA[1]	Less than 30 000 Inhabitants[2]	Between 30 000 and 99 999 Inhabitants	Between 100 000 and 499 999 Inhabitants	500 000 Inhabitants or More
		Current Dollars			
2002					
1 person	10 533	12 055	13 448	13 618	16 102
2 persons	12 820	14 673	16 368	16 574	19 598
3 persons	15 964	18 269	20 381	20 638	24 404
4 persons	19 915	22 793	25 427	25 748	30 445
5 persons	22 679	25 955	28 955	29 319	34 668
6 persons	25 151	28 785	32 112	32 515	38 448
7 or more persons	27 624	31 614	35 268	35 712	42 227
2003					
1 person	10 828	12 392	13 824	13 999	16 553
2 persons	13 179	15 083	16 826	17 038	20 146
3 persons	16 411	18 781	20 952	21 216	25 087
4 persons	20 473	23 431	26 139	26 469	31 298
5 persons	23 314	26 681	29 765	30 140	35 639
6 persons	25 855	29 590	33 011	33 426	39 524
7 or more persons	28 397	32 499	36 255	36 712	43 410
2004					
1 person	11 028	12 621	14 080	14 258	16 859
2 persons	13 423	15 362	17 137	17 353	20 519
3 persons	16 715	19 128	21 339	21 608	25 551
4 persons	20 852	23 864	26 622	26 958	31 876
5 persons	23 744	27 175	30 316	30 697	36 297
6 persons	26 333	30 137	33 621	34 044	40 255
7 or more persons	28 922	33 100	36 925	37 390	44 212

Table 10.3 *Low Income Cut-Offs, After Tax, 1992–2010 (1992 base)* **(continued)**

Size of Family Unit	Rural Areas Outside CMA or CA[1]	Census Agglomeration (CA)		Census Metropolitan Area (CMA)	
		Less than 30 000 Inhabitants[2]	Between 30 000 and 99 999 Inhabitants	Between 100 000 and 499 999 Inhabitants	500 000 Inhabitants or More
	Current Dollars				
2005					
1 person	11 271	12 899	14 389	14 571	17 230
2 persons	13 718	15 700	17 514	17 734	20 969
3 persons	17 082	19 548	21 808	22 083	26 112
4 persons	21 310	24 388	27 207	27 550	32 576
5 persons	24 266	27 772	30 982	31 371	37 095
6 persons	26 912	30 799	34 360	34 792	41 139
7 or more persons	29 557	33 827	37 737	38 212	45 183
2006					
1 person	11 492	13 152	14 671	14 857	17 568
2 persons	13 987	16 008	17 857	18 082	21 381
3 persons	17 417	19 932	22 236	22 516	26 624
4 persons	21 728	24 867	27 741	28 091	33 216
5 persons	24 742	28 317	31 590	31 987	37 823
6 persons	27 440	31 404	35 034	35 474	41 946
7 or more persons	30 138	34 491	38 477	38 962	46 070
2007					
1 person	11 745	13 441	14 994	15 184	17 954
2 persons	14 295	16 360	18 250	18 480	21 851
3 persons	17 800	20 370	22 725	23 011	27 210
4 persons	22 206	25 414	28 352	28 709	33 946
5 persons	25 287	28 940	32 285	32 691	38 655
6 persons	28 044	32 095	35 805	36 255	42 869
7 or more persons	30 801	35 250	39 324	39 819	47 084

(Continued)

Size of Family Unit	Community Size				
		Census Agglomeration (CA)		Census Metropolitan Area (CMA)	
	Rural Areas Outside CMA or CA[1]	Less than 30 000 Inhabitants[2]	Between 30 000 and 99 999 Inhabitants	Between 100 000 and 499 999 Inhabitants	500 000 Inhabitants or More
		Current Dollars			
2008					
1 person	12 019	13 754	15 344	15 538	18 373
2 persons	14 628	16 741	18 676	18 911	22 361
3 persons	18 215	20 845	23 255	23 548	27 844
4 persons	22 724	26 007	29 013	29 378	34 738
5 persons	25 876	29 614	33 037	33 453	39 556
6 persons	28 698	32 843	36 640	37 100	43 869
7 or more persons	31 519	36 072	40 241	40 747	48 181
2009					
1 person	12 050	13 791	15 384	15 579	18 421
2 persons	14 666	16 785	18 725	18 960	22 420
3 persons	18 263	20 900	23 316	23 610	27 918
4 persons	22 783	26 075	29 089	29 455	34 829
5 persons	25 944	29 692	33 124	33 541	39 660
6 persons	28 773	32 929	36 736	37 198	43 984
7 or more persons	31 602	36 167	40 346	40 854	48 308
2010					
1 person	12 271	14 044	15 666	15 865	18 759
2 persons	14 936	17 094	19 069	19 308	22 831
3 persons	18 598	21 283	23 744	24 043	28 430
4 persons	23 202	26 554	29 623	29 996	35 469
5 persons	26 421	30 237	33 732	34 157	40 388
6 persons	29 301	33 534	37 410	37 881	44 791
7 or more persons	32 182	36 831	41 087	41 604	49 195

[1]Can include some small population centres.

[2]Includes population centres with less than 10 000 inhabitants.

SOURCE: Statistics Canada, Table 1, Low income cut-offs (1992 base) after tax, http://www.statcan.gc.ca/pub/75f0002m/2011002/tbl/tbl01-eng.htm; Date modified: 2011-08-23.

Clearly, estimating the numbers of Canadians who are poor is no simple task. The writings of Christopher Sarlo (1992; 1996) have repeatedly drawn attention to what he perceives to be the inadequacies of employing the LICO as a measure of poverty in Canada. For example, he notes that the LICO does not include benefits in kind, or capital gains, or, of course, unreported income. Sarlo claims that "of all households below the LICO in 1990, almost one in five owned their homes, mortgage free . . . 97 percent had colour television . . . 53 percent owned a car—the same rate as for those above the poverty line" (in Coyne 1997).

According to Sarlo, "poverty, as it has been traditionally understood, has been virtually eliminated" (1992: 2). And in 2013, writing for the conservative policy think-tank the Fraser Institute, Sarlo reasserted his position: "Poverty is a condition of serious deprivation. What we need, and what I make a renewed case for in this paper, is a measure that allows us to track the number of Canadians who are unable to acquire all of the basic necessities" (2013: 1). For Sarlo, though, this claim is based on the assumptions that non-nutritious consumables such as coffee, ketchup, and jam are unnecessary, that $636 a year is enough to provide an individual with a year's supply of clothing and footwear, and that personal care costs (things like soap, shampoo, razors, haircuts, and other personal hygiene items) should be met at $144.50 per person (2013: 10). For those who experience toothaches or trouble with their vision, Sarlo "assumes that dental societies will provide free dental services to low-income families and that Lions Clubs will provide free eyeglasses" (Krahn 1994: 2.8). Sarlo argues that his critics oppose his measures in "quite emotional terms" that fail to understand the necessity of holding a "stringent" line on what counts as poverty (2013: 13), and he maintains that relative measures such as a line set at "half of the median income" (2013: 2) are not serious enough about "poverty." To put the notion of "serious deprivation" into practical terms, Sarlo's definition means that only those who live in conditions like the Attawapiskat First Nation, which lacks access to clean potable water, secure housing, and nutritious food, count as "impoverished." Those who live below the median income level, by contrast, might struggle or experience occasional food insecurity, or have to choose between medicine and heat, but do not meet Sarlo's poverty definition.

However, scholars have long argued that taking low income seriously is not equal to making emotional claims about poverty. For example, Ross and colleagues (1994) emphasize that in employing the LICOs "Statistics Canada does not claim to measure poverty; rather, it defines a set of income cutoffs below which people may be said to live in strained circumstances."

Writing for the Centre for Policy Alternatives in 2013, economist David Macdonald and former foreign diplomat Daniel Wilson argue that we must be very careful to make sure that our low-income measures are not leaving out certain sectors of the population. In particular, they are concerned that Aboriginal children—those from First Nations, Métis, and Inuit groups—are left out of some official measures such as the census Survey of Labour and Income Dynamics (SLID). Macdonald and Wilson explain that because the SLID does not apply to those living on reserve, it cannot measure the presence or depth of child poverty amongst Aboriginal groups in Canada. They further explain the consequences of measures that exclude certain regions, and the use of averages in census reports:

> Based on data from the 2006 census, . . . the average child poverty rate for all children in Canada is 17%, while the average child poverty rate for all Indigenous children is more than twice that figure, at 40%. In fact, even among children living in poverty in Canada, three distinct tiers exist. The first tier, with a poverty rate of 12%, excludes Indigenous, racialized and immigrant children. This is three to four times the rate of the best-performing OECD countries. The second tier of child poverty includes racialized children who suffer a poverty rate of 22%, immigrant children whose poverty rate is 33%, and Métis, Inuit and non-status First Nations children at 27%. Most

shocking, however, is that fully half—50%—of status First Nations children live below the poverty line. This number grows to 62% in Manitoba and 64% in Saskatchewan. (Macdonald and Wilson, 2013: 6)

As we have noted, the ways that we think about what constitutes a minimum standard of living, whether that is a hard "poverty" threshold or a low-income measure, has practical consequences—it determines who will receive help and who will not and what types of social policies and programs are thought necessary. Wilson and Macdonald note that "For status First Nations children living on reserves, the federal government [funds] social services, health care, education and income supports. Transfer payments for these social services on reserve have increased by a mere 2% per year since 1996, unadjusted for population growth or need." In other words, the transfer payments that are intended as a form of payment for the ongoing use of Aboriginal land ceded in various treaties have not kept pace with the value extracted from the land, nor with the needs of Aboriginal peoples. The larger population and federal government continue to profit, and the original people continue to suffer.

The Extent of Global Poverty and Economic Inequality

The *Global Poverty Report* (2000) found that globally the proportion of people living on less than $1 per day fell from 29 percent in 1987 to 26 percent in 1998. But World Bank measures show general stagnation since then, with about one-quarter of the world population living on less than $2 a day in current dollars (World Bank 2007). For the developing world, the 2010 World Bank data using 2005 constant dollars estimate that one-fifth of the population lives at or below poverty levels. Social indicators have seen some improvement over the last three decades, but the situation has not improved consistently for all populations. And, as we discuss later in this chapter in the section on poverty and racialization, the Aboriginal populations of Canada—of which those at greatest risk are Registered Indians and Inuit—remain largely excluded from the nation's general prosperity. The 2005 United Nations *Report on the World Social Situation* notes that "monetary poverty has gradually worsened in many parts of the world."

Data from the *Report on the World Social Situation* show us that in terms of household wealth:

- The richest 1 percent of adults in the world own 40 percent of global household wealth; the richest 2 percent of adults own more than half of global wealth; and the richest 10 percent of adults owns 85 percent of total global wealth.
- The poorest half of the world population owns barely 1 percent of global wealth.
- Households with per adult assets of $2200 are in the top half of the world wealth distribution; assets of $61 000 per adult places a household in the top 10 percent, and assets of more than $500·000 per adult places a household in the richest 1 percent of the world population.
- Although North America has only 6 percent of the world's adult population, it accounts for 34 percent of all household wealth worldwide.

"As the seriousness of the problem has grown more evident, poverty and poverty reduction strategies have become increasingly prominent in development discourse" (United Nations 2005: 54). Clearly, the strategies have not served well many of the world's poorest:

In Europe and Central Asia the total number of people living on less than US$1 a day grew by more than 14 million between 1981 and 2001. In excess worsening poverty in Eastern Europe and the commonwealth independent states (CIS) has contributed substantially to the trend towards increased poverty in Europe and Central Asia since 1993. . . . In Tajikistan, a 14 percent increase in the country's population was accompanied by 64 percent decline in GDP and escalating poverty levels. In Azerbaijan, sound macroeconomic policies have ensured economic stability and highly real GDP growth; however, these economic successes have not been reflected in the lives of people, 49 percent of whom live in poverty. (United Nations 2005: 56)

In spite of some improvements around the globe, economic inequality remains a serious problem, with 1.4 billion of the world's population living in extreme poverty (United Nations 2008). According to economic impact studies carried out by the United Nations, reductions in global poverty have been aided by debt write-offs for the poorest nations, by improving access to clean drinking water and to basic medical care (vaccination, and maternal health care), and by improving access to primary education; however, rising costs associated with food distribution combined with the lasting impact of the 2008 economic meltdown will have a "disproportionate impact" on the world's poorest people (ibid). Consider that in 1998, the combined wealth of the world's 200 richest people was $1 trillion. In the same year, the combined income of the 582 million people living in the 43 least developed countries was $146 billion (United Nations Development Programme 2000).

As these past trends continue, global economic inequality remains a persistent problem. Pro-globalization lobbyists and economists may argue that these disparities are a feature of transition or of incomplete entry into a global economy; on the other hand, Ray Kiely argues that such claims "that the poorest countries are poor because they are 'insufficiently globalized'" deliberately obscure the hierarchical and domination-oriented structure of neo-liberal economics, blaming the poor for their poverty on a global scale (2005: 910). Moreover, developed nations have seen their wealth drastically deteriorate in the years since the onset of the 2008 economic crisis. Iceland's national wealth fell by 30 percent between 2008 and 2010 (Keating et al. 2010), and the losses for Ireland, Greece, Spain, and Portugal have been similarly devastating. Armed with this critical perspective, we can challenge the idea that the solution to global poverty is to surrender more deeply to global capitalism.

10.2 Sociological Theories of Poverty and Economic Inequality

The different theoretical perspectives have distinct ways of assessing economic inequality. For example, structural-functionalists have argued that inequalities serve a functional purpose by providing a labour force to do undesirable work, and conflict theorists have argued that inequalities benefit only those who profit from the alienation and labour of others. Feminist theorists have drawn our attention to the manner in which economic inequality is gendered and what the impact of impaired access to economic resources means for women and children around the world. In this section, we examine these and other sociological perspectives on poverty and economic inequality.

Structural-Functionalist Perspective

According to the structural-functionalist perspective, social stratification serves several positive functions. Decades ago, Davis and Moore (1945) argued that because the various occupational roles in society require different levels of ability, expertise, and knowledge, an unequal economic reward system helps to ensure that the person who performs a particular role is the most qualified. As people acquire certain levels of expertise and academic accreditation, they are progressively rewarded. Such a system, argued Davis and Moore, motivates people to achieve by offering higher rewards for higher achievements. If physicians were not offered high salaries, for example, who would want to endure the arduous years of medical training and long, stressful hours at a hospital?

The structural-functionalist view of poverty suggests that a certain amount of poverty has positive functions for dominant groups. Although poor people are often viewed as a burden to society, having a pool of low-paid, impoverished workers ensures that there will be people willing to do dirty, dangerous, and difficult work that others refuse to do. Poverty also provides employment for those who work in the "poverty industry" (such as welfare workers) and supplies a market for inferior goods, such as older, dilapidated homes and automobiles (Gans 1972).

Contemporary sociologists have directed much criticism at the structural-functionalist view of poverty and economic inequality. They point out that many important occupations (such as child-care work) are poorly paid, whereas many non-essential occupations (such as professional sports and entertainment) garner astronomical sums. Functionalism also accepts poverty as unavoidable and ignores the role of inheritance in the distribution of rewards.

Public Ideas about Poverty

Using randomly selected populations from Edmonton and Toronto, Linda Reutter from the University of Alberta, along with a group of co-investigators from Ontario and Alberta, used survey and interview methods to measure public attributions for poverty in Canada.

Within a larger set of survey questions, the investigators asked six questions on the respondents' exposure to poverty and five questions on what participants perceived to be the causes of poverty. Finding out what people think causes poverty and what kinds of perceptions they base those beliefs on is important, as Reutter and her colleagues point out. Beliefs about the causes of poverty influence ideas about who deserves help and who does not, can contribute to inclusive or exclusive behaviours—even in institutional settings, and can influence social policy (2006: 6).

The research begins with a structural view that social exclusion is a purposeful process that marginalizes some persons and groups through the implementation of formal and informal practices that include social policies, programs, institutions, and actors (Reutter et al. 2006: 2). As Reutter and her co-investigators explain,

> Framing poverty in terms of social exclusion represents a shift from viewing deprivation in terms of individual attributes to the social relations, mechanisms and institutions responsible for deprivation, thereby situating debates more explicitly within the context of power and inequality. (2006: 2)

The findings in this study are subtle, but two features emerge from the data. The first is that Canadians on the whole show a relatively high level of appreciation for the structural, rather than presumed individual reasons for poverty; the second is that greater education on poverty issues still correlated strongly with elevated understanding of structural causes for poverty (Reutter et al. 2006: 19).

Conflict Perspective

proletariat
Workers who were often exploited by the bourgeoisie.

bourgeoisie
The owners of the means of production.

Conflict theorists, who work principally in a Marxist framework, think that economic inequality results from domination over the **proletariat** (workers) by the **bourgeoisie** (owners of the means of production). The bourgeoisie accumulate wealth as they profit from the labour of the proletariat, who earn wages far below the earnings of the bourgeoisie. As Marx and Engels explained in *The Communist Manifesto*, the proletariat is "the class of modern wage-labourers, who, having no means of production of their own, are reduced to selling their labour power in order to live" (1967: 79). In our contemporary economy, anyone who works for an employer, even if well paid, depends on the employer to provide wages and conditions of work. If the owners decide to downsize or relocate, then even highly paid workers can find themselves in perilous conditions. However, unlike those in trades, the new professional class is more likely to be able to find new employment and to have other resources to provide stability. Skilled and unskilled workers are more vulnerable to alterations in how corporations will secure profits. They are likely to have more difficulty securing employment if their trades are moved away. In all scenarios, however, employees exchange labour for wages, and "profit" is what employers can extract above the cost of production. Marx explained that profit is "**surplus value**" and its benefits always go to the owner of the means of production rather than to the producer of the work.

Conflict theorists understand and analyze the manner in which various social institutions serve the interests of the dominant class. The educational institution furthers the ideals of capitalism by perpetuating the belief in equal opportunity and the value of the work ethic. The proletariat, dependent on the capitalistic system, learns to identify with capitalist values instead of identifying their own needs. Members continue to be exploited and to accept the belief that poverty results from personal failure rather than from a flawed economic structure.

Conflict theorists note how laws and policies benefit the wealthy at the expense of larger societies. Laws and policies that favour the rich—sometimes referred to as **wealthfare** or **corporate welfare**—include special subsidies and tax breaks to corporations, and other laws and policies that benefit corporations and the wealthy. Between 1994 and 1999, federal handouts to businesses topped $14 billion (Canadian Centre for Policy Alternatives Monitor [CCPAM] 1999). Ed Finn (2006), a policy analyst with CCPAM, argues that corporate welfare lies behind the "broken promises by Canadian governments to eradicate poverty, notably the all-party pledge in Parliament in 1989 to eliminate child poverty by 2000." Corporate "tax breaks" or "loopholes" are the "result of an economic system that glorifies greed and bars a more equitable distribution of income" (Finn 2006: n.p.). They cost the Canadian treasury billions. "Businesses are still permitted to deduct from the money they owe in taxes 20 percent of their expenses for meals and entertainment—such as luxury boxes at the Sky-Dome and escort services—from their taxable income" (Barlow and Campbell 1995: 174–75). In addition, "generous tax subsidies to oil and gas companies for their exploration and development costs" (ibid) divert half a billion a year from Canada's treasury. Indeed,

> So many tax loopholes are available to corporations that each year tens of thousands of profitable companies pay not a penny in income taxes.... Canada has the second worst record in the industrialized world (after Australia) for taxing wealth, making it a tax haven for wealthy individuals. (pp. 175–76)

Throughout the world, "free market" economic reform policies have been hailed as a solution to poverty. Yet, while such economic reform has benefited many wealthy corporations and investors, it has also resulted in increasing levels of global poverty. As companies relocate to countries with abundant supplies of cheap labour, wages decline. Lower wages lead to decreased consumer spending, which leads to more industries closing plants, bankruptcies, and downsizing. The results include higher unemployment rates and a surplus of workers, pushing employers to lower wages even more. Chossudovsky (1998) suggests that "this new international economic order feeds on human poverty and cheap labour" (p. 299).

Symbolic Interactionist Perspective

Symbolic interactionism focuses on how meanings, labels, and definitions affect and are affected by social life. This view calls attention to ways in which wealth and

surplus value
A concept developed by Marx; refers to the difference in the amount people will pay for a service or consumer good compared to the cost of its production—surplus value produces the profit from exploited labour.

wealthfare
Governmental policies and regulations that economically favour the wealthy.

corporate welfare
Laws and policies that favour corporations, such as low-interest government loans to failing businesses and special subsidies and tax breaks to corporations.

poverty are defined and the consequences of being labelled as "poor." Individuals who are viewed as poor—especially those receiving public assistance, or welfare—are often stigmatized as lazy, irresponsible, and lacking in abilities, motivation, and moral values. Indeed, the phrase "poor but honest" implicitly suggests that we view honesty and low income as an unlikely combination and must single out those who are poor and honest as exceptions to the rule. Wealthy individuals, on the other hand, tend to be viewed as capable, motivated, hard working, and deserving of their wealth.

The symbolic interaction perspective also focuses on the meanings of being poor. A qualitative study of over 40 000 poor women and men in 50 countries around the world explored the meanings of poverty from the perspective of those who live in poverty (Narayan 2000). Among the study's findings is that the experience of poverty involves psychological dimensions, such as powerlessness, voicelessness, dependency, shame, and humiliation.

Meanings and definitions of wealth and poverty vary across societies and across time. For example, the Dinka are the largest ethnic group in the sub-Saharan African country of Sudan. By global standards, the Dinka are among the poorest of the poor, being among the least modernized peoples of the world. In the Dinka culture, wealth is measured in large part according to how many cattle a person owns. But to the Dinka, cattle have a social, moral, and spiritual value as well as an economic value. In Dinka culture, a man pays an average "bridewealth" of 50 cows to the family of his bride. Thus, men use cattle to obtain wives to beget children, especially sons, to ensure the continuity of their ancestral lineage and, according to Dinka religious beliefs, their linkage with God. Although modernized populations might label the Dinka as poor, the Dinka do not.

Definitions of poverty also vary within societies. For example, in Ghana men associate poverty with a lack of material assets, whereas for women, poverty is defined as food insecurity (Narayan 2000).

Lewis (1966) accounted for the persistence of poverty, arguing that, over time, the poor develop norms, values, beliefs, and self-concepts that contribute to their own plight. According to Lewis, the **culture of poverty** is characterized by female-centred households, an emphasis on gratification in the present rather than in the future, and a relative lack of participation in society's major institutions. "The people in the culture of poverty have a strong feeling of marginality, of helplessness, of dependency, of not belonging…. Along with this feeling of powerlessness is a widespread feeling of inferiority, of personal unworthiness" (Lewis 1998: 7). The culture of poverty view emphasizes that the behaviours, values, and attitudes exhibited by the chronically poor are transmitted from one generation to the next, perpetuating the cycle of poverty experienced by the **underclass**—people living in persistent poverty. Critics of the culture of poverty approach point out that behaviours, values, and attitudes of the underclass emerge from the constraints and blocked opportunities that have resulted largely from the disappearance of work (Van Kempen 1997; Wilson 1996) (see also Chapter 8).

Feminist Perspectives

Feminist perspectives on economic inequality begin with the observation that poverty is a gendered phenomenon. This is not to say that there are not poor men or that the working class is not oppressed as a group; however, when we look closely at poverty, we can see that it affects women more frequently than men. Using a **gender-based analysis**, feminist policy analysts hold gender to be a key feature for understanding vulnerability to poverty and to the differential effects of poverty on, for example, the children one would be parenting. Gender-based analysis works to understand the

culture of poverty
The set of norms, values, and beliefs and self-concepts that contribute to the persistence of poverty among the underclass.

underclass
A persistently poor and socially disadvantaged group that disproportionately experiences joblessness, welfare dependency, involvement in criminal activity, dysfunctional families, and low educational attainment.

gender-based analysis
Feminist policy analysis that understands gender to be a key factor in vulnerability to poverty and the differential effects of poverty; it uses gender as a central grounding point for analysis.

structures that contribute to women's poverty, seeking to understand why, for example, of those who are over age 18 and living in poverty 54 percent are women (NAPO 2006). The Canadian Research Institute for the Advancement of Women (CRIAW), however, has adopted a more complex method of assessing poverty among women, called intersectional feminist frameworks (IFFs). A framework

> involves analysis of how processes of occupation, nation building, slavery, labour migration, employment regulation, and disenfranchisement of racialised groups, among others, contribute to the depth of poverty experienced by indigenous and racialised women. (CRIAW 2006: 16)

Feminist work on poverty also uses unique methods, such as **narrative analysis**, combining a feminist focus on women's experiences with a symbolic approach to data interpretation. For example, a group of researchers from Ontario used narrative analysis to understand how young women speak about how their experiences of poverty can intersect with negative health and housing problems. Using narrative analysis for the study revealed that poverty and homelessness are not discrete problems, but permeate all aspects of these young homeless women's lives, including experiences of violence and discrimination that contribute to lower overall health and well-being (Reid, Burman, and Forchuk 2005: 252–53).

Feminist analysis of poverty can shed light on the routes to poverty for women, making the point that disability and illness can be powerful forces that move women from being "working poor" to impoverished as they lose their jobs, their stability, perhaps their children, and their homes (Neal 2004). Work such as Neal's can also make clear what the experience of homelessness can mean when apprehended through a gender-aware lens. For example, Neal observes that "both men and women who are homeless are caught in a gender crisis. Men who are homeless are 'failed men' because they cannot support themselves [while] women who are homeless fit the gender stereotype of the feminine woman—dependent and needy" (p. 28). Normative expectations that successful men are providers and successful women are wives to successful men diminish even further those who live in poverty.

Queer Theory Perspectives

Although a tendency to treat socio-economic status as independent of concerns about sexuality exists, studies on GLBT groups reveal that sexuality is an important variable influencing economic and other measures of social well-being. Yali and Revinson (2004) note in their work on mental health and coping with crisis that people live their lives at the intersection of many different contexts: race, class, gender, ethnicity, and, of course, sexuality.

A challenge of complex intersectionality is that determining the needs of the GLBT population can be an elusive task. Carroll and Ratner (2001), in their research on GLBT social movements supported through a Vancouver community centre, point out that "pluralisation of identity and weakening of the singular collective identity have given rise to a continuing crisis. The centre's constituency is culturally and socioeconomically quite mixed, and the scope of sexuality politics is too narrow to support a broad project of moral-intellectual reform that could serve as a political basis of impunity" (p. 612). In other words, while some members of the GLBT community have moved from political vulnerability in the 1970s in Vancouver to contemporary prosperity, some still face economic challenges and social isolation that hinge partly on sexual identity. Members of the GLBT community were more able to rely on government service agencies to provide basic health care and other social support services, leaving the community centre to serve mostly as a social connection support (p. 613). The obvious

narrative analysis
A feminist practice that combines a symbolic approach with the collection of women's life histories as legitimate sources of knowledge and information.

problem is that when government services separate issues of social connection from issues of economic well-being, they miss the intersections of sexuality with the experience of well-being. Meanwhile, the centre's social connection focus tends to neglect the needs of those who are less prosperous in the GLBT community.

For example, transphobia exists not only in the heterosexual world but sometimes also in gay and lesbian circles. Among the most vulnerable to poverty as a correlate of sexuality are transgender persons who, as a result of transphobia, may have a harder time finding and securing employment and housing. Lesbians, who contend with sexism as well as with homophobia, may face similarly multi-layered obstacles to socio-economic stability.

Outside Canada, work on sexual minorities around the world gives insight to the perils that sexually non-normative people may face:

> These may include men who were denied the right to love other men by the legislation left in place by the British Empire. . . . They may include sex workers who are routinely abused by the police, denied access to services and stayed with ties as "prostitutes," only come to the attention of development agencies when they migrate for sex work, and become the "victims" of trafficking . . . [and] lesbians may find it impossible to hide their sexuality in the workplace facing the prospect of losing their jobs or insuring low wages and working conditions. (Institute of Development Studies 2006: 1)

In the United States, the transgender writer and social justice activist Leslie Feinberg (1993) provides a narrative of growing up poor and transgender, suffering economically as a result of transphobia in workplace and personal life. It is one of the few such detailed insights into the effects of discrimination on socio-economic status and well-being for transgendered persons.

10.3 Wealth, Economic Inequality, and Poverty in Canada

Canada is a nation of tremendous economic variation ranging from the very rich to the very poor. Signs of this disparity are visible everywhere, from opulent mansions to squalid rooming houses, from those who drive or are driven in luxury cars to those who cannot afford the price of a monthly bus pass.

Wealth in Canada

wealth
The total assets of an individual or household minus liabilities.

Wealth refers to the total assets of an individual or household, minus liabilities (mortgages, loans, and debts). Wealth includes the value of a home; investment real estate; cars; an unincorporated business; life insurance (cash value); stocks, bonds, mutual funds, and trusts; chequing and savings accounts; retirement savings plans; and valuable collectibles. A 2001 Statistics Canada study reveals that Canada is an "increasingly polarized country, with the top 20 percent of families gaining a whopping 39 percent in accumulated wealth since 1984, while the average wealth of the bottom 20 percent actually shrunk" (Centre for Social Justice 2001). As of 2012, the Thomson family, owners of one of the most powerful and diverse publishing businesses, comprised the richest Canadian family, with a net worth of over $26 billion (see Table 10.4). The holdings of those on "The Rich List" show just how great the division is between the richest and even "high income" families, as well as how marked is the concentration of wealth in very few hands in Canada.

Table 10.4 *"The Rich List"*

1. Thomson Family (Thomson Reuters)	$26.10 billion
2. Galen Weston (George Weston Ltd., Loblaw Cos. Ltd., Holt Renfrew)	$10.38 billion
3. J. K. and John Irving (Irving Oil)	$7.86 billion
4. Rogers Family (Rogers Communications)	$7.60 billion
5. James Pattison (Jim Pattison Group)	$7.39 billion
6. Saputo Family (Saputo Inc.)	$5.24 billion
7. Paul Desmarais Sr. Estate (Power Corporation Financial)	$4.93 billion
8. Jeffrey S. Skoll (eBay)	$4.92 billion
9. Richardson Family (Richardson GMP)	$4.45 billion
10. Carlo Fidani (Orlando Group)	$4.1 billion

SOURCE: Adapted from "The Rich List," *Canadian Business Magazine*. http://www.canadianbusiness.com/list-and-rankings/rich-100-the-full-2014-ranking/. Used with permission.

Economic Inequality in Canada

The three decades after the end of World War II were a time of unprecedented economic prosperity in Canada. Throughout the 1950s and 1960s, unemployment and inflation were low and a steady increase in personal incomes financed the growth of the social safety net, including universal health care, the Canada Pension Plan, unemployment insurance, and inexpensive postsecondary education. By the 1970s, however, there were increases in both consumer prices and unemployment levels, and a halt in the growth of real income. Because of economic downturns, economic inequality—the gap between the wealthy and the poor—grew significantly. Much has changed since, beginning with government introduction of various fiscally conservative tax measures and policy decisions, such as deregulation, privatization, free trade, and monetarism. These measures, which reflected a "corporate agenda," have most obviously benefited corporations and those whom economist John Kenneth Galbraith dubbed the "contented classes."

Barlow and Campbell (1995: 76) point out that income inequality in Canada not only has been growing in the past decades, "but it has been picking up speed." High-income families have reaped benefits from very high interest rates on their savings, and tax breaks, lower income tax rates, and an increase in both the numbers of those employed within professional and managerial groups and the level of executive earnings; others have fared poorly. Declines in family income and median real wages, rising unemployment, increases in part-time, temporary, and low-paying jobs, and the accelerated pace of social cuts (designed to make Canada's system of social security more "affordable" and to level the free-trade playing field) have had a huge impact on Canada's poor. According to research conducted by the Toronto Centre for Social Justice, the average incomes of the top 10 percent of families with children in 1973 were 8.5 times those of the bottom 10 percent; by 1996, the ratio was to 10.2 to 1 (Yalnizyan 1998). To get a sense of just how marked the disparities are between the lowest and highest earners, it may help to use the model developed by the Dutch economist Jan Pen in *The Economist*:

> The first passers-by, the owners of loss-making businesses, are invisible: their heads are below ground. Then come the jobless and the working poor, who are midgets. After half an hour the strollers are still only waist-high, since America's median income is only half the mean. It takes nearly 45 minutes before normal-sized people appear. But then, in the final minutes, giants thunder by. With six minutes to go they

are 12 feet tall. When the 400 highest earners walk by, right at the end, each is more than two miles tall. (Pen 2011)

The gap between the richest and poorest families increased after 1995, when the federal government made drastic cuts in social program spending, and the cuts have hit poorest families the hardest (Bricker and Greenspon 2001; Daub and Young 1999; National Council of Welfare 2000). While in 1989 the top quintile of families with the highest incomes received 41.9 percent of total market income, this proportion rose to 45.2 percent in 1998. In contrast, the share of the market income going to the 20 percent of families with the lowest incomes decreased from 3.8 percent to 3.1 percent over the same time period. Moreover, "[d]espite the equalizing role played by transfers and taxes, the gap between the two ends of the income scale widened slightly during the 1990s, even on an after-tax basis" (Statistics Canada 2000).

Patterns of Poverty in Canada

Poverty is not as widespread or severe in Canada as in many less developed countries, but nevertheless represents a significant social problem. According to the National Council of Welfare (2000), "[i]n 1999, there were 1 025 000 families and 1 677 000 unattached individuals living in poverty in Canada." However, poverty is not equally distributed. Poverty rates vary according to age, education, gender, family structure, disability, race/ethnicity, and labour force participation.

Age and Poverty

Despite a political landscape rich in rhetoric about children, Canada has had little success in reducing child poverty (see Chapter 6). In 1989, when the House of Commons passed a unanimous resolution to eliminate child poverty in Canada by the year 2000, the child poverty rate was 15.2 percent—representing about one million poor children. While the child poverty rate in Canada peaked in 1996 (at 21.6 percent) and has declined since, the child poverty rate in 1999 was 18.7 percent (about 1.3 million children). The child poverty rate in Canada remained higher than the average poverty rate (16.2 percent). Moreover, in 1999, "most Canadian poor families with children needed, on average, more than $8000 before taxes and more than $5000 after taxes just to meet the poverty line" (National Council of Welfare 2000). During the period 1993 to 1998, children under six were the most likely of all age groups to have lived in poverty for all six years. The National Council of Welfare (2004: 52) further notes that some measures of poverty, for instance the market basket measure (MBM), do not include costs associated with child care in their assessment of what families require to live; however, because child care is a necessity for working parents with young children, it is a basic expense. Poor families with working parents may often be living far below MBM estimates for low income.

Government programs and policies (see Chapter 6) have led to an improvement in the poverty rate among Canada's seniors. Between 1980 and 1999, the poverty rate for Canada's seniors was almost halved, from 34 percent in 1980 to 17.7 percent in 1999 (National Council of Welfare 2000). However, while the poverty rate among senior couples is low (4.7 percent in 1999), unattached seniors experience high rates of poverty. Moreover, while the poverty rate of senior unattached men decreased from 35.1 percent in 1998 to 31.9 percent in 1999, the poverty rate of unattached senior women rose from the already high rate of 47.9 percent in 1998 to an even higher rate of 48.5 percent in 1999.

Education and Poverty

In general, the higher a person's level of educational attainment, the less likely that person is to be poor (see also Chapter 12). For example, in 1999, Canadian families in which the principal income earner had at least a university degree had a poverty rate of 6 percent. In contrast, single-parent mothers with less than a high school diploma had a poverty rate of 82.3 percent. However, "[a]lthough level of education and poverty rates are somewhat inversely related, education is not always a guarantee against poverty" (National Council of Welfare 2000: 7). More than half (52 percent) of the 1 667 000 poor unattached individuals in 1999 had at least a high school diploma.

Gender and Poverty

Women are more likely than men are to live below the poverty line—a phenomenon referred to as the **feminization of poverty**. As discussed in Chapter 7, women are less likely than men are to pursue advanced educational degrees in nontraditional areas of study. They also tend to be more heavily concentrated in a narrower range of jobs than men are and within lower paying jobs, such as service and clerical work (Statistics Canada 2002). Women who are minorities or who are single mothers are at increased risk of being poor. Table 10.5 gives us a decade-long view of earnings stagnation for women as a proportion of average earnings of men for the same period.

feminization of poverty
The disproportionate distribution of poverty among women

Table 10.5 *Average Earnings by Sex and Work Pattern, 2002–2011 (all earners)*

	Women	Men	Earnings Ratio
	$ constant 2011		%
2002	29 300	46 700	62.8
2003	29 000	46 000	62.9
2004	29 400	46 200	63.5
2005	30 000	46 900	64.0
2006	30 500	47 100	64.7
2007	31 300	47 800	65.5
2008	31 700	49 300	64.3
2009	32 600	47 400	68.6
2010	32 600	47 800	68.1
2011	32 100	48 100	66.7

NOTE: Data before 1996 are drawn from Survey of Consumer Finances (SCF) and data since 1996 are taken from the Survey of Labour and Income Dynamics (SLID). The surveys use different definitions, and as a result the number of people working full-year full-time in the SLID is smaller than in the SCF.

SOURCE: Statistics Canada, CANSIM, table 202-0102. Last modified: 2013-06-27. http://www.statcan.gc.ca/tables-tableaux/sum-som/l01/cst01/labor01a-eng.htm

Family Structure and Poverty

Poverty is much more prevalent among female-headed single-parent households than among other types of family structures. The relationship between family structure and poverty helps to explain why women and children have higher poverty rates than men (see also Chapter 5). While the poverty rate for families headed by single-parent families fluctuated between 51.8 percent and 61.8 percent between 1980 and 1999, in 1999, "single-mother families were the only family type with a majority of its members still living below the poverty line" (National Council of Welfare 2000: 15). In comparison, the poverty rate in 1999 for families headed by single-parent fathers was 18 percent (down from 25.4 percent in 1980).

Disability and Poverty

According to data compiled by the Canadian Council on Social Development (Fawcett 1999), disability is a strong indicator of poverty. Across Canada, single persons with a disability receiving social assistance have benefits equal to only 41 to 53 percent of the LICO for their regions (National Council of Welfare 2003: 27). In 1995, 36.2 percent of women with disabilities versus 18.5 percent of Canadians without disabilities aged 15 to 64 were poor. Because of structural sexism, significant differences exist in the poverty rates between men with disabilities and women with disabilities, particularly those women who have full-time, full-year employment. However, a substantial proportion of people with disabilities do not participate in the paid labour force at all. For those whose primary source of income comes in the form of disability pension, monthly rent alone would consume between 82 and 98 percent of income in three Canadian cities sampled: Ottawa, Vancouver, and Halifax (Neal 2004: 39).

Obtaining employment and remaining employed often pose significant difficulty to persons with disabilities, regardless of gender. First, employment discontinuities are common due to the cyclical nature of some disabilities and a tendency for those with disabilities to be the "last hired and the first fired." In addition, while many income support programs, including social assistance and disability pensions, provide support for disability-related expenses (e.g., medication and transportation), such supports disappear when individuals with disabilities become employed. Accordingly, if one's employment income does not cover such expenses, one cannot "afford to work." As Fawcett (1999) points out, "persons with disabilities who look for work face a dilemma: in their attempts to convince potential employers that they are capable of working, they may disqualify themselves from the social assistance and disability supports they need in order to survive." Table 10.6 gives a sense of the consequences of poverty for those with disabilities relative to the larger population's risk.

Table 10.6 *Food Insecurity among Persons with and without Disabilities, by Age and Gender*

	15–34	35–49	50–64	Aged 65+
Persons with Disabilities				
Men	25.0%	20.3%	14.3%	6.4%
Women	24.4%	24.1%	19.5%	7.0%
Persons without Disabilities				
Men	10.6%	7.7%	4.1%	2.4%
Women	12.0%	8.9%	4.9%	2.5%

SOURCE: Canadian Council on Social Development, 2003. Table 4. "CCSD's Disability information Sheet." No. 10.

Compared to those without disabilities, both women and men with disabilities are more likely to be the sole providers of family income. However, the situation is particularly bleak among women with disabilities because they are more likely than other groups to live as lone parents. In 1996, almost 1 in 10 (9.7 percent) women with a disability was a lone parent (compared with 7.6 percent of women without disabilities, 2.8 percent of men with disabilities, and 1.1 percent of men without disabilities). Women with disabilities who obtain full-time, full-year employment typically earn less than either women without disabilities or men with disabilities. Figure 10.2 shows the disparity in incomes according to gender.

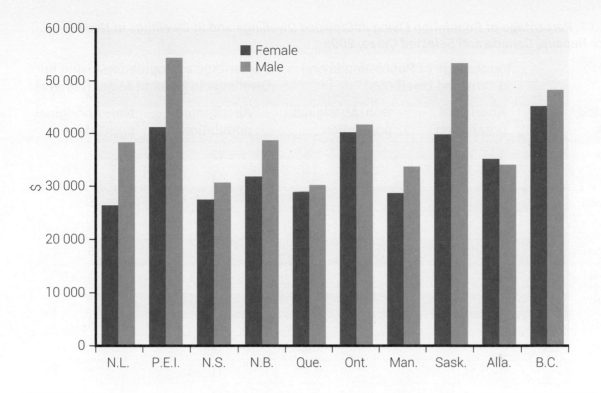

Figure 10.2 **Average Earnings of Full-Year, Full-Time Earners, 2001**

SOURCE: Statistics Canada, The Canada e-Book, 11-404-XIE; hosted at Library and Archives http://epe.lac-bac.gc.ca/100/205/301/statcan/canada_e-book-ef/05-01-21/142.206.72.67/r002_e.htm

Race and Ethnicity and Poverty

Based on the findings of the 2006 Canadian census, the negative impact of low income is high among visible minorities in Canada and especially among its Aboriginal people (Table 10.7), who live over 3.5 times more frequently in homes that require major repairs, with regionally specific disparities often being even greater. The 2006 census data also show that Canada's Aboriginal population is far more likely to live in homes with overcrowding problems. Overcrowding can exacerbate health problems and increase stress as people try to negotiate multiple, complex relationships in tight spaces.

Canada's recent immigrant population tends also to be a visible minority population, and because of the overlap of these statuses remains vulnerable to below-average employment incomes (Palameta 2005). Palameta's analysis of income data used multiple regressions to determine the influence of immigration, education, and visible minority status, and found that:

- women, unmarried persons, those with no high school diploma, and those living in a province other than Ontario were most likely to experience low income for at least one year. However, in each case, the likelihood for recent immigrants was two to three times more than for the Canadian-born
- those with university degrees [had earnings that] were about the same as non-immigrants with no high school diploma
- visible minority immigrants were significantly more likely than other immigrants to be in low income, regardless of time in Canada. (Palameta 2005: 14)

Palameta's detailed analysis demonstrates that the longer-term patterns for income disparity between visible minority immigrants to Canada and those born in Canada

Table 10.7 *Percentage of Population Living in Crowded Dwellings and in Dwellings in Need of Major Repairs, Canada and Selected Cities, 2006*

Selected Cities	Percentage of Population Living in Crowded Dwellings[1]		Percentage of Population Living in Dwellings in Need of Major Repairs[2]	
	Aboriginal population	Non-Aboriginal population	Aboriginal population	Non-Aboriginal population
Canada	11	3	23	7
Prince Albert	11	1	14	7
Saskatoon	9	1	12	5
Regina	9	1	14	7
Edmonton	8	2	14	5
Winnipeg	5	3	16	3
Vancouver	4	5	15	6
Toronto	3	7	12	6
Montréal	2	3	14	8
Calgary	2	2	11	5
Ottawa-Gatineau	1	2	14	5

NOTES:

[1]"Crowding" is defined as more than one person per room. Not counted as rooms are bathrooms, halls, vestibules, and rooms used solely for business purposes.

[2]Dwellings in need of major repairs are those that, in the judgement of the respondent, require major repairs to such things as defective plumbing or electrical wiring, and/or structural repairs to walls, floors, or ceilings, etc.

SOURCE: Statistics Canada. "Aboriginal Peoples in Canada in 2006: Inuit, Métis and First Nations, 2006 Census." *Aboriginal Peoples 2006 Census*, Catalogue No. 97-558-XIE,

remain stable (ibid). Between 1993 and 1998, approximately 42.5 percent of Canada's immigrant visible minorities lived in poverty for at least one year; that compared to 29.5 percent of the total population. In addition, "15.6 percent of immigrant visible minorities lived in poverty for all six years, compared with five percent of persons who are not visible minorities" (National Council of Welfare 2002b: 6).

Poor housing conditions are generally secondary to low earnings and low levels of relative wealth. Aboriginal people, who are vulnerable to poor housing conditions, experience heightened risk of poverty (see also Chapters 2 and 8). Excluding the Aboriginal population who lived on reserves, in Yukon, or Northwest Territories (where income is generally lower than for the Aboriginal population living off reserve), Statistics Canada found that in 1995, 44 percent of the Aboriginal population was below its low income cut-offs. Among those who identified themselves as North American Indians, almost half (48 percent) were in a low-income situation. Among the Métis (the second largest group), almost 4 in 10 (39 percent) were in a low-income situation. In that year, three out of five Aboriginal children under the age of six were in low-income families. Among those aged 6 to 14, the incidence of low income was 48 percent, or more than twice the national rate of 22 percent (Statistics Canada 1998b). Between 1993 and 1999, 49.4 percent of Aboriginal persons living off reserve lived in poverty in at least one of the six years; an estimated 12.6 percent lived in long-term poverty during this six-year period (National Council of Welfare 2002b: 6). More recent secondary analysis of the income data from 1996, 2001, and 2006 census data shows that the gains for Aboriginal populations have been so slow that "If the rate of diminishment of the income gap between

1996 and 2006 continues, it will take 63 years for the Aboriginal population to catch up to the rest of Canada" (Wilson and Macdonald 2010: 8).

An analysis of the economic performance of racialized group members and other Canadians over the period 1996–98 (Galabuzi 2001) also finds evidence of "economic apartheid," or the economic segregation and social marginalization of racialized groups, particularly in urban areas. Among Galabuzi's findings were these:

- There is a persistent and sizeable (double digit) gap between the economic performance of racialized group members and other Canadians. . . . In 1998 there was a 24 percent gap in average before-tax income and a 20 percent gap in after-tax income.
- A racialized labour market is an endemic feature of the Canadian economy. Charactcristic of the racial and gender labour market segmentation is the over-representation of racialized (particularly women) members in low paid, low-end occupations and low income sectors, and also temporary work. They arc especially overrepresented in low-end service sector jobs and precarious and unregulated temporary or contingent work.
- Income inequalities are a significant contributor to racialized group members' persistent above-average poverty rates across the nation, and particularly in urban areas where they are concentrated. The patterns suggest that a process of racialization of poverty is underway.

Labour Force Participation and Poverty

A common image of the poor is that they are jobless and unable or unwilling to work. Although the Canadian poor are primarily children and adults not in the labour force, many poor are classified as "**working poor**." Consider that in 1999, over 40 percent of the more than one million Canadian families who lived in poverty were headed by persons who were employed. "Single-parent mothers working full-time, full-year still had a poverty rate of 19.7 percent" (National Council of Welfare 2002b: 7).

Labour force attachment does, to be sure, offer a buffer against poverty. In 1999, the poverty rate for unattached individuals under 65 and for their families decreased as their weeks of paid employment increased. Specifically, among unattached individuals, the poverty rate for persons with no paid work was 80.1 percent versus 18.4 percent for those who worked 49 to 52 weeks. For families, the poverty rate for those with no paid work was 56 percent versus 3 percent among families with 103 or more weeks of paid work (that is, two full-year workers).

working poor
Individuals who work in the labour force, but who nevertheless live in poverty.

10.4 Consequences of Poverty and Economic Inequality

Poverty is associated with health problems, problems in education, problems in families and parenting, and housing problems. These various problems are interrelated and contribute to the perpetuation of poverty across generations, feeding a cycle of intergenerational poverty. In addition, poverty and economic inequality breed social conflict and war.

Health Problems and Poverty

In Chapter 2, we noted that poverty has been identified as the world's leading health problem. Persistent poverty is associated with higher rates of infant mortality and childhood deaths and lower life expectancies among adults. Although access to universally insured health care remains largely unrelated to income in Canada, many low-income and moderate-income Canadians have limited or no access to such health services as eye care, dentistry, mental health counselling, and prescription drugs (Health Canada 1999).

Economic inequality also affects psychological and physical health. "[P]erceptions of inequality translate into psychological feelings of lack of security, lower self-esteem, envy and unhappiness, which, either directly or through their effects on life-styles, cause illness" (Streeten 1998: 5). People who live in areas with the greatest gap between the rich and the poor are much more likely to rate their own health as poor or fair than people who live in areas where income is more equitably distributed (Kennedy et al. 1998).

Educational Problems and Poverty

Research indicates that children living in poverty are more likely to suffer academically than are children who are not poor. "Overall, poor children receive lower grades, receive lower scores on standardized tests, are less likely to finish high school, and are less likely to attend or graduate from university than are nonpoor youth" (Seccombe 2001: 323). The various health problems associated with childhood poverty contribute to poor academic performance (see Chapter 12). In addition, because poor parents have less schooling, on average, than do nonpoor parents, they may be less able to encourage and help their children succeed in school. However, research suggests that family income is a stronger predictor of ability and achievement outcomes than are measures of parental schooling or family structure (Duncan and Brooks-Gunn 1997). Poor parents have fewer resources to provide educational experiences (such as travel), private tutoring, books, and computers for their children. Not surprisingly, parental wealth strongly influences university enrolment (Conley 2001).

Poverty also presents obstacles to educational advancement among poor adults. Women and men who want to further their education in order to escape poverty may have to work while attending school or may be unable to attend school because of unaffordable child care, transportation, tuition, fees, books, or a combination of things.

Family and Parenting Problems Associated with Poverty

Family problems and poverty can aggravate each other. In some cases, family problems contribute to poverty. For example, domestic violence causes some women to flee from their homes and live in poverty without the economic support of their husbands. Poverty also contributes to family problems. The stresses associated with poverty contribute to substance abuse, domestic violence, child abuse, divorce, and questionable parenting practices. For example, poor parents unable to afford child-care expenses are more likely to leave children home without adult supervision. Poor parents are more likely than other parents are to use harsh disciplinary techniques, such as physical punishment; they are also more likely to value obedience and less likely to be supportive of their children (Mayer 1997; Seccombe 2001).

The National Longitudinal Survey of Children and Youth reports that the capacity of parents to care for children and their children's developmental outcomes are better at each step up the income ladder. Low social support, family dysfunction, and parental depression, all of which have significant negative effects on children, are all more common in low-income households. According to this study, 18 percent of children living in low-income households (versus 8 percent of children in middle-income households and 5 percent of children in higher income families) lived with parents who had many symptoms of depression (National Council of Welfare 1999c).

A significant body of research in social problems takes as obvious that early mothering is deleterious and then seeks to explain that young women from low income backgrounds are more likely to become mothers at significantly younger ages than the general population around them. For example, Luker (1996) uses a symbolic approach to understand teen mothering in North America and argues that "the high rate of early childbearing is a measure of how bleak life is for young people who are living in poor communities and who have no obvious arenas for success" (p. 189). For poor young women, who have few employment opportunities and are disillusioned with education, "child-bearing ... is one of the few ways ... such women feel they can make a change in their lives" (p. 182). Given that many studies have asserted that early child-bearing is associated with numerous problems, such as increased risk of premature or low-birth-weight babies, dropping out of school, and lower future earning potential due to lack of academic achievement, the lack of choice that Luker asserts seems especially troublesome.

As we noted in Chapter 5, citing the extensive research of Arline Geronimus, the actual outcomes for young mothers can be more positive for women from populations in which health deteriorates rapidly through one's late 20s and 30s than for those who delay child-bearing in the same community. More current thinking on young mothering is more nuanced, and does not look only at "poor" teens, thus avoiding the perhaps cynical exploitation of young women's choices to become mothers as research cases that advance their own academic careers. Recent research in public health demonstrates that the middle-class biases of traditional research on young mothering has delivered a skewed vision of young mothering, and that we should not assume that all young mothers come from disadvantaged backgrounds. SmithBattle's research (2007), for example, demonstrates that not all young mothers come from impoverished backgrounds, and that the outcomes for children of teen mothers depends on the class background from which the mothers hailed. SmithBattle explains that when there are negative outcomes for children of young mothers, it is the impact of socio-economic disadvantage and not the age of the mother that corresponds to greater challenges and problems for young mothers. Using a structuralist approach instead of a symbolic one SmithBattle writes,

> Early research overstated the negative outcomes of teen mothering by overlooking structural inequalities in education, residential patterns, and employment that predispose teen mothering in the first place. . . . The findings reported here reveal that teen mothers embark on mothering with vastly different constraints, possibilities, and contradictions that are located in the social world[s] they inherited as children. (2007: 418)

Instead of focusing on the negative, symbolic "push factors" that lead poor young women to have children while they are young, SmithBattle urges public health nurses—who are frontline service providers to young and new mothers—to "advocate for programs and policies that address the cumulative impact of disadvantage and racial prejudice on young families" and to recognize the "growing evidence that unfavourable outcomes for teen mothers and their children are primarily due to the structural conditions of poverty, and not maternal age" (2007: 418).

That it is poverty, and not age, that presents the challenges SmithBattle sees some young mothers and not others facing, presents a serious rebuke to those sociologists, health-care workers, and social service providers who treat *age* of the mother as the primary problem. Put another way, negative outcomes for children are more likely in any case that involves economic deprivation, regardless of the marital status or age of the mother. Young middle-class mothers have life courses and trajectories for their children that are concordant with their general class group because their socio-economic advantages have a generally protective effect on their children (2007: 417).

Housing and Homelessness

According to the National Council of Welfare (1998: 53), finding decent and affordable housing that is suitable to a family's needs "is one of the biggest financial burdens for people on welfare and for low-income people in general." The provision of housing for lower-income Canadians has been an area of continuing governmental concern since the first Canadian social-housing legislation, the 1938 *National Housing Act*, made provision for the construction of low-rent housing.

The majority of low-income families and unattached individuals are renters rather than homeowners. For example, as of March 1997, 68.2 percent of all those living on welfare lived in rental housing; only a small proportion lived in their own homes (6.9 percent) or in subsidized housing (6.8 percent). Among couples with children, 71.3 percent were renters, 16.2 percent were homeowners, 8.2 percent lived in subsidized housing, and 4.2 percent lived in other forms of housing, including boarding or living with relatives. Among single-parent families, 76.6 percent were renters, 6.3 percent lived in their own homes, 11 percent lived in subsidized housing, and 6.1 percent lived in other forms of housing. In general, single parents on welfare made proportionately more use of subsidized housing and were far less likely to board or to live with relatives.

Poor individuals are more likely than their nonpoor counterparts are to have spartan accommodations in high-crime neighbourhoods (Mayer 1997); yet, even substandard housing would be a blessing to many people who live without conventional housing—the homeless.

Homelessness is a growing problem in Canada. It is estimated that as many as 200 000 Canadians are homeless, including increasing numbers of women and children, Aboriginal people, adolescents, and people with mental illnesses (Health Canada 1999). Some homeless individuals have been forced out of their houses or apartments by rising rents or the inability to pay the mortgage. The homeless population also includes runaway or "throw away" youths, and individuals who have been released from mental hospitals because of the movement to deinstitutionalize individuals with psychiatric disorders.

Intergenerational Poverty

As we have seen, problems associated with poverty, such as health and educational problems, create a cycle of poverty from one generation to the next. Poverty that is transmitted from one generation to the next is called **intergenerational poverty**.

intergenerational poverty
Poverty that is transmitted from one generation to the next.

Intergenerational poverty creates a persistently poor and socially disadvantaged population sometimes referred to as the underclass. The term *underclass* usually refers to impoverished individuals who have low educational attainment, have criminal records, are unmarried mothers on welfare, or are ghetto residents. Although the underclass is stereotyped as being composed of minorities living in inner-city ghetto communities, the underclass is a far more heterogeneous population than that (Alex-Assensoh 1995).

Mead (1992) argues that intergenerational poverty may be caused by welfare dependency. According to Mead, when poor adults rely on welfare, the stigma of welfare fades, and welfare recipients develop poor work ethics that are passed on to their children. William Julius Wilson attributes intergenerational poverty and the underclass to a variety of social factors, including the decline in well-paid jobs and their movement out of urban areas, the resultant decline in the availability of marriageable males able to support a family, declining marriage rates and an increase in out-of-wedlock births, the migration of the middle class to the suburbs, and the impact of deteriorating neighbourhoods on children and youth (Wilson 1987; 1996).

Using income tax information reported by a cohort of approximately 285 000 men and women aged 28 to 31 in 1994, Corak (1998) related the total market income of these young adults to the incomes of their fathers and mothers in 1982 (when his participants were 16 to 19 years of age and still living at home). Among his findings: the adult sons and daughters of very low-income fathers—those in the bottom 10 percent of income earners—were overrepresented in the lowest income decile. A detailed description of Corak's findings is contained within this chapter's *Social Problems Research Up Close*.

Social Problems *Research Up Close*

Family Income and Postsecondary Education Participation in Canada

Regardless of their own backgrounds or income levels, parents in Canada hope for their children to be able to participate in some form of postsecondary education. In their 2003 study carried out for the Family and Labour Studies Division of Statistics Canada, Corak, Lipps, and Zhao explain the mix of high expectations and effective income barriers that leave many families' hopes unfulfilled:

> On the one hand about 85% of Canadian parents hope their children will pursue post-secondary studies. This aspiration is shared across the income distribution, with 80% of those parents with less than $30 000 of income also holding this expectation[...]. On the other hand the climate surrounding the financing of post-secondary education has changed significantly, with the 1990s witnessing notably sharp increases in university tuition fees. In this climate lower income families may not be as well positioned as higher income families to realize their expectations. (2003: 1)

Citing Statistics Canada research on university participation rates, Corak, Lipps, and Zhao report that while fewer than 20 percent of families with incomes of less than $30 000 in 2001 were able to save for postsecondary education costs, roughly 66 percent of those with incomes of $80 000 were able to save for their children to attend some form of postsecondary schooling (ibid). What Corak and his co-authors sought to do in their study was to analyze and explain the relationship of family income to the participation rates of young people in postsecondary education, and cast their main question as one of whether "higher education [is] increasingly the purview of the well-to-do" (2003: 1).

To answer their question, Corak, Lipps, and Zhao provide a history of government funding for university education in Canada, summarized from the original report in Figures 10.3 and 10.4.

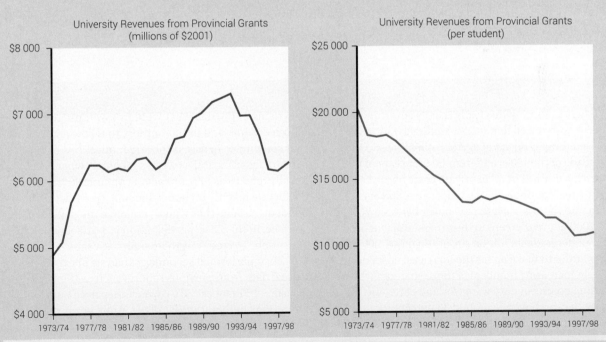

Figure 10.3 *University Revenues from Provincial Grants*

SOURCE: Corak, M., Garth Lipps, and John Zhao. 2003. *Family Income and Participation in Post-secondary Education.* Family and Labour Studies Division, Statistics Canada. Catalogue 11F0019MIE No. 210.

(continued)

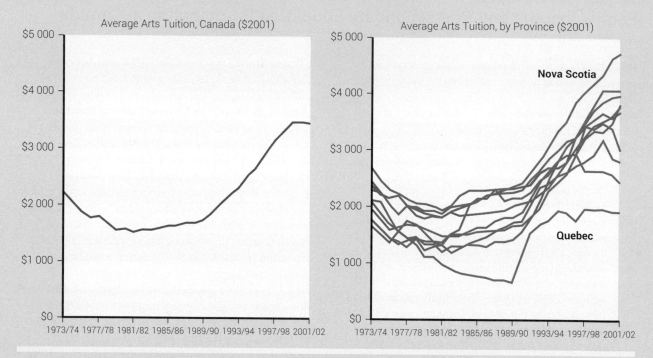

Figure 10.4 *Average Arts Tuition Fees, Canada and Provinces 1972–2002*

SOURCE: Corak, M., Garth Lipps, and John Zhao. 2003. *Family Income and Participation in Post-secondary Education.* Family and Labour Studies Division, Statistics Canada. Catalogue 11F0019MIE No. 210.

The figures show quite clearly that as government trends show reduced funding for students tuitions increased roughly apace, at skyrocketing levels in the last decade of the 1900s and into the first years of the 2000s. This upward trend in private costs borne by students has continued in the years since, and average tuition rates across Canada now hover between $6000 and $7000 per year except in the province of Quebec, where undergraduate tuition sits at roughly $2200 per year. In order to make up for the increased costs borne privately, increasing numbers of those students who *were* attending postsecondary were working part-time by 2001, with rates hovering around 35 percent for university students and around 45 percent for college students; by contrast, in 1979 just over 20 percent of university students and just over 25 percent of college students were working part-time (p. 29, Figure 5). Meanwhile, their data reveal that students enjoy less independence from their families, as more and more of them remain at home to defray living expenses while they are in postsecondary studies (p. 32, Figure 8).

Arriving at the data that would show these trends required Corak and his co-authors to follow a method that sought not to assess the larger questions of cultural or social capital as well as income—what we usually refer to as SES, or socio-economic status—but to "focus explicitly on family income" (p. 7) as the independent variable that would influence the dependent variable, in this case, participation in postsecondary education. To carry out their analyses, Corak, Lipps, and Zhao performed secondary analysis of existing statistical data from previous reports such as the Survey of Consumer Finances (SCF), which they note has some limitations in that it measures only one given year of a family's income and so "may not reflect at any point in time the true financial resources parents may have to support their children's education. The use of annual income rather than a measure of permanent income will lead the correlation between family income and post-secondary participation to be understated" (p. 9). Because of these limitations in the available data in the SCF, the researchers also analyzed data from the

General Social Survey (GSS) in three different years: 1986, 1994, and 2001 (p. 10). Their analysis of GSS showed that if the SCF understated the relationship of family income to postsecondary participation, the GSS overstated the influence of income on educational attainment. The researchers, therefore, combined the two in order to set upper and lower limits on the correlation of income to participation in postsecondary education (p. 10).

The conclusion of the study notes that while Canadian families tend to value higher education, partly because they see it—perhaps mistakenly—as a "pathway to higher earnings" (p. 13), not all families are equally able to save for its increasing costs. Interestingly, given that analysis, the data did not, however, show a downward trend for lower-income families to send their children into postsecondary education. Corak and his co-authors write:

> At the most general level . . . post-secondary education at the end of the 1990s was no more the domain of the relatively better off than it was during the 1980s. It is certainly the case that children from higher income families are more likely to attend university, but this has not changed dramatically . . . with the introduction of higher tuition fees.
>
> . . . That said, the costs of higher education have certainly increased and in part these costs have been shifted onto students, as reflected in much higher levels of borrowing and the decline in university participation rates [and increase in lower-cost college programmes] of those from middle income families. (pp. 13–14)

The general findings of the study, then, were not that those in lower-income families would participate any less in the opening years of the twenty-first century than in the closing decades of the twentieth, but that students from lower-income families would have to bear increasing cost burdens, take out more loans (and thus pay more in the end for their educations than those who can afford the sticker price upfront), and work more often while registered as full-time students. They also found that for young men the choice of areas to study would lean more toward vocational programs at the college level, with more definite employment outcomes (p. 14). Thus, when the type of institution is taken into account—that is, whether university or college—the researchers find "There is a clear positive correlation between parental income and university attendance, and this correlation . . . became stronger during the early to mid 1990s when tuition fees began increasing significantly" (p. 14).

Regarding those questions that the research did not address because of the tight controls on the variables studied, Corak, Lipps, and Zhao suggest that future work might consider the influence of rising standards for admission into particular programs, effectively keeping out those students who are less likely to hold the cultural capital to fulfill admissions requirements (p. 15), and they also suggest that further research into earlier childhood experiences that "place them in the fortunate situation of choosing to continue their education (sic) after high school graduation" (p. 15) could reveal worthwhile information about positive or protective influences across income groups.

SOURCE: Corak, M., Garth Lipps, and John Zhao. 2003. *Family Income and Participation in Post-secondary Education.* Family and Labour Studies Division, Statistics Canada. Catalogue 11F0019MIE No. 210.

War and Social Conflict

Poverty is often the root cause of conflict and war within and between nations as "the desperation of the poor is never quiet for long" (Speth 1998: 281). Not only does poverty breed conflict and war, but also war contributes to poverty. For example, war contributes to homelessness as individuals and families are forced to flee from their homes. Military and weapons spending associated with war diverts resources away from economic development and social spending on health and education.

Briggs (1998) suggests that the widening economic inequalities present a threat to social order. He asks how long a country can maintain social order "when increasing numbers of persons are left out of the banquet while a few are allowed to gorge?" (p. 474). Although Karl Marx predicted that the proletariat would revolt against the capitalists, Briggs does not foresee a revival of Marxism: "the means of surveillance and the methods of suppression by the governments of industrialized states are far too great to offer any prospect of success for such endeavors" (p. 476). Instead, Briggs predicts that capitalism and its resulting economic inequalities will lead to social anarchy—a state of political disorder and weakening of political authority.

10.5 Strategies for Action: Antipoverty Programs, Policies, and Proposals

In Canada, federal, provincial, and local governments have devoted considerable attention and resources to antipoverty programs since the 1960s. In 1964, "the United States launched its 'war against poverty' and Canada began a more quiet campaign of study and legislation in an effort to understand better the causes of and remedies for poverty" (Ross and Lochhead 1999: 1881).

The 1960s and 1970s saw the introduction of several significant pieces of antipoverty legislation in Canada. Recognition that the private pension system failed to provide adequate support for retired low-income workers and their families led to the introduction of the Canada and Quebec pension plans and to the Guaranteed Income Supplement program for those elderly individuals with little or no income other than Old Age Security. In 1966, the Canada Assistance Plan (CAP) was introduced. The CAP replaced the "many piecemeal cost-shared programs that the federal and provincial governments had begun entering into as far back as 1927" with a comprehensive social-assistance program that provided a major source of funds for people with disabilities who were unemployed, offered assistance to others in low-income circumstances, and brought a wide array of social services (e.g., daycare, family counselling, homemaker and child-welfare services) under federal cost sharing (Ross and Lochhead 1999: 1888). At least in theory, the CAP was designed not only to respond to the problem of poverty, but also to prevent it. In 1968, the *Medical Care Act* (medicare) provided free access to basic health care for all Canadians. The *Unemployment Insurance Act* (1940), which ushered in Canada's first national social-insurance program, was amended in 1971 to provide greater coverage to the unemployed as well as to the sick.

In this section, we describe some national and international responses to poverty and note the role of charity and the nonprofit sector in the alleviation of poverty.

Government Public Assistance and Welfare Programs in Canada

Under the *Constitution Act,* social and welfare services are the responsibility of the provincial and territorial governments. However, the federal government is also involved in the provision of these services through its cost-sharing agreements with the provinces and territories. Before April 1996, the federal government provided financial support for social services to the provinces and territories through a 50–50 cost-sharing scheme called the Canada Assistance Plan. The CAP aimed at improving standards of provincial social-assistance programs and introduced national standards into public welfare for the first time. In place of "a confusing mix of program categories based on the poor law practice of separating the 'worthy' [e.g., people with disabilities] from the 'unworthy' poor ... one program [was to be established by each province and territory in exchange for federal funding] to meet financial need—provincial social assistance" (Guest 1999a: 2203). Despite this intent, welfare remains inadequate for handling the needs of the poor in Canada. The National Council of Welfare observes that current rhetoric and policies regarding welfare remain punitive; it notes, too, that social assistance is far below poverty lines across the nation, especially for single persons whose allowable benefits may be only 20 to 44 percent of the poverty line (2003: 25, 74).

However, beginning in the 1970s and in response to rising unemployment and inflation, claims were made that Canada's economic prosperity was best assured by decreasing government expenditures, particularly for social programs.

Since that time, Moscovitch (1999: 2496) notes that both the federal and the provincial governments have used the following methods to control social expenditures: "changing eligibility and benefits, particularly under unemployment insurance and social assistance; 'privatizing' provincial social programs by contracting out responsibility for social services (particularly those relating to children and the aged); provincial attempts to raise revenues through Medicare premiums and user fees; decreasing social-program budgets relatively if not absolutely; imposing an eroding level of assistance benefits; and termination of some social programs." In an attempt to reduce expenditures on social programs, between 1984 and 1993 the federal Progressive Conservative governments further reduced old-age security benefits at middle-income levels and above, decreased the range of workers who were covered by Unemployment Insurance and the benefits available to them, and imposed spending limits on Canada's three richest provinces— Ontario, British Columbia, and Alberta—effectively forcing these provinces to absorb up to 70 percent of the costs. In its 1997 report, *Another Look at Welfare Reform*, the National Council of Welfare noted that provincial and territorial governments also implemented cuts to most welfare programs, with the most extreme example occurring in Ontario in 1995, with a 21.6 percent cut to welfare recipients. The depth of this cut, the report emphasizes, "was completely arbitrary, with no assessment of how people who depended on welfare would be able to afford adequate food, clothing and shelter, let alone the impact of these cuts on young children and their families." While those with disabilities were exempted from the cuts, families with children were not.

In February 1995, the federal budget introduced the *Canada Health and Social Transfer* (CHST) (which became effective in April 1996) and eliminated two federal transfer programs: Established Programs Financing, which provided for the consolidation of hospital, medicare, and postsecondary education funding, and the Canada Assistance Plan. The CHST combined federal transfer payments for social assistance (previously under the CAP) with those for medicare and postsecondary education into a single "block" transfer made up of cash payments and tax points. As a result, Canada's social safety net was fundamentally altered. Among the changes: "the new arrangement included a significant cut in federal support for these programs and a significant change in the way the provinces and territories account for the money they receive" (National Council of Welfare 1999b: 79).

Under the CHST, the provinces now have greater discretion in deciding how to apportion their share of the reduced federal transfer. At least theoretically, provincial and territorial governments could elect to use all of the federal money they receive for medicare and devote none to the other areas. Guest (1999a: 2203) points out that "Some have already made the decision to cut social-assistance programs to Canada's poorest families and individuals—Ontario and Alberta—while British Columbia has imposed a residence requirement of three months on all new applications for social assistance." It is also evident that not all groups affected by spending cuts are equally vocal nor are all voices equally heard. As Guest reports, "One concern by welfare advocates is that money will be siphoned from welfare to cool the anger of health and higher education supporters" (p. 2203).

Family Allowance and Child Benefits

Canada's first universal welfare program, introduced in 1945, was **family allowance**, a monthly allowance paid to families with children. The term *universal* here refers to

family allowance
Canada's first universal welfare program, introduced in 1945, which promised a monthly allowance paid to families with children. The term *universal* here refers to the fact that the benefit flowed from the principle of entitlement and was available without reference to a recipient's income or assets.

the fact that such benefits flowed from the principle of entitlement and were available without reference to a recipient's income or assets. In contrast, when benefits are directed at particular groups within the population, the funds are called **demogrants**.

Following a failed attempt in 1972 to replace the universality of family allowances with selectivity related to income, the federal government introduced a new *Family Allowance Act* that made family allowances taxable. In 1978, further restructuring occurred. The government established a Refundable Child Tax Credit, which offered $200 per year for families with incomes under $18 000 and taxed away benefits entirely for those whose incomes reached $26 000. The tax credit was financed through scaling back the amount of monthly family allowance payments (from an average of $28 per month to $20) and through the reduction or elimination of other tax exemptions for children. Beginning in 1985, family benefits were further restructured with the partial indexing of family allowances and child tax credits. As well, the number of families qualifying for the tax credit was reduced when the maximum income for receipt of the credit was decreased from $26 300 to $23 500. Guest (1999b: 815) reports that by 1991, these changes "represented a spending cut in family benefits [of] $550 million . . . with only a token increase" in the net family benefits received by Canada's poorest families.

In 1989, the universality of family allowances disappeared, with the federal government requiring parents with upper incomes to repay all of their benefits at the time they paid their yearly taxes. In 1991, family allowances, the Refundable Child Tax Credit, and a nonrefundable child tax credit were consolidated into a new **Canada Child Tax Benefit (CCTB)**. The CCTB is a tax-free monthly payment made to eligible families to help them with the cost of raising children under the age of 18. Benefits are calculated for a 12-month period based on the number of children in a family and their ages, the applicant's province or territory of residence, the family's net income, and the applicant's (or his or her spouse's) deduction for child-care expenses. Except in Alberta, the basic benefit in 2002 was $95.91 a month for each child under age 18 plus $6.66 a month for a third or additional child, plus $19.00 for each child under 7. In Alberta, the basic monthly benefit rate was $87.91 for children under 7, $93.83 for children aged 7 to 11, $105.00 for children aged 12 to 15 and $111.25 for children aged 16 to 17 (Canada Customs and Revenue Agency 2002). The CCTB is based on net family income reported on the tax return of the previous year and is gradually reduced as family income reaches an "income ceiling" ($32 960 in 2002).

The federal government increased the Canada Child Tax Benefit in July of 1998 for low-income families by adding a **National Child Benefit Supplement (NCBS)**. This tax-free monthly benefit for low-income families with children under age 18 is the federal government's contribution to the **National Child Benefit (NCB)**. In 2002, the NCBS amounts were $1293 a year for a one-child family and $2380 for a two-child family. Families with three or more children receive $2380 for the first two children plus $1009 a year for the third or each additional child. The maximum NCBS is paid only to those families with a net income of under $22 397 (Canada Customs and Revenue Agency 2002). It is reduced by a percentage amount (which depends on the number of children within a family) when the family net income exceeds this amount. In most of Canada's provinces and territories, the NCBS is considered income and will affect the amount of social assistance that families are eligible to receive.

The NCB is a joint initiative of federal, provincial, and territorial governments designed to help prevent and reduce the depth of child poverty and to promote parental attachment to the workforce by improving available benefits and services. According to the *National Child Benefit Progress Report 1999*, "key to the NCB is the effort to move child benefits out of the welfare system so that when parents leave social assistance for work, these benefits go with them, helping to ensure their children's well-being during this transition" (Government of Canada 1999).

Employment Insurance Benefits

In January 1997, the *Employment Insurance Act* was implemented in Canada, replacing the former Unemployment Insurance (UI) Program. Individuals may receive regular benefits if they lose a job through no fault of their own and cannot find work. Those who quit their job without just cause or who are fired for misconduct are ineligible to receive Employment Insurance (EI) benefits. Similarly, those affected by a strike, lockout, or other forms of labour dispute are ineligible unless they are not taking part in the dispute, are not giving money to support the dispute, and are not directly interested in the dispute (that is, their wages or working conditions are not affected by the dispute's outcome).

To be eligible for EI benefits, individuals must apply; have paid into the EI account; have been without work and pay for at least seven consecutive days; have worked for the required number of hours based on where they live and the unemployment rate in their area; be available for work but unable to find it; and be in Canada. The current system is based on hours of paid work and responds to variations in work situations, such as part time, extended hours, or compressed weeks. Whether a person works full time, part time, or on a seasonal basis, the hours worked for pay are accumulated toward eligibility for EI benefits. These hours include overtime (which is calculated on an hour-for-hour rate) and paid leave (which is insured for the number of hours that normally would be worked in that period).

To qualify for EI, most individuals will need to have worked between 420 and 700 hours during the last 52 weeks or since the start of their last claim, whichever is shorter. The specific number of hours of insurable employment in the past 52 weeks needed to qualify for EI depends on the unemployment rate in the region where each person lives. For example, in an area where the regional rate of unemployment is 0 percent to 6 percent, 700 hours of insurable employment are necessary; in an area with a regional unemployment rate of 9.1 percent to 10 percent, 560 hours are needed. In an area with a regional unemployment rate of 13.1 percent or higher, 420 hours are needed. In some instances, however, individuals will need a great number of insurable work hours in the past 52 weeks to qualify. For example, among those who are in the workforce for the first time, a minimum of 910 hours of insurable work in the past 52 weeks is required. Those who apply for sickness, maternity, or parental benefits will need 700 hours of insurable work. Those who have previously committed EI violations may also face increases in the number of hours they are required to possess before qualifying for EI benefits.

The length of time for which benefits can be received depends on the regional unemployment rate and how long an individual has worked in the last 52 weeks or since their last claim (whichever is shorter). Depending on the amount of insurable hours, benefits can be received from 14 to a maximum of 45 weeks. The basic benefit rate is 55 percent of average insured earnings up to a maximum payment of $413 per week. However, those who have drawn regular benefits in the past may have their benefits adjusted and reduced under the "intensity rule." Under this rule, benefit rates are reduced by 1 percent for every 20 weeks of regular benefits claimed since June 30, 1996, to a maximum of 5 percent if that person has more than 100 weeks of benefits over that five-year period.

Individuals receiving regular benefits can earn up to 25 percent of their weekly benefits or $50 (whichever is higher) without changing the weekly amount they receive. However, all earnings above this limit are deducted dollar for dollar from their weekly benefits. Other sources of money that can affect the amount of EI benefits include Canada Pension Plan or Quebec Pension Plan retirement income, self-employment earnings, or monies received in damages for wrongful dismissal. (Payments from private RRSPs, disability pensions, survivor's pensions, or

Family Supplement
Those families with children in a low-income situation (i.e., having a family net income under $25 921 a year) and who receive the Canada Child Tax Benefit automatically receive the Family Supplement with a rate based on family net income and the number and ages of children in the family.

Dominion-Provincial Student Aid Program (DSAP)
An act passed by the federal government in 1939. Under DSAP, the federal government contributed to each participating province and the province was expected to provide an equal amount of assistance to students.

Canada Student Loans Program (CSLP)
A plan that permits eligible Canadian citizens and permanent residents to finance their postsecondary education with government-sponsored loans. Full-time students, enrolled in a program that lasts for at least 12 weeks, may qualify for a loan based on the costs of their program and on the financial resources available to them.

Canada Student Financial Assistance Act (CSFA Act)
The *CSFA Act* of 1994 revised the Canada Student Loans Plan and increased the amounts of the maximum loans available for full-time and part-time students.

dependent's pensions do not affect the calculation of EI payments.) Depending on net income and past claim history, all or some of the EI benefits received may have to be repaid at income tax time.

Families with children in a low-income situation—that is, with a family net income under $25 921 a year, and who receive the Canada Child Tax Benefit (CCTB)—automatically receive the **Family Supplement**, with a rate based on family net income and the number and ages of children in the family. If both spouses claim EI at the same time, only one can receive the Family Supplement.

Over time, the percentage of unemployed Canadians who are eligible for UI or EI benefits has fallen. Since the 1970s, the federal government has also steadily trimmed away the benefits available to unemployed workers. For example, while in the early 1970s weekly benefits were as high as 75 percent of a person's maximum weekly insurable earnings while employed, they are now, as earlier noted, 55 percent. Similarly, while in the early 1970s the maximum length available for regular benefits was 51 weeks, it is now 45 weeks. Although some of those who are unemployed are able to locate and obtain employment quickly, for others their unemployment will last far longer than the benefit coverage that EI provides.

Guest (1999a: 2203) emphasizes that we should be concerned about the separation of claimants into "normal" and "frequent user" categories. He observes that frequent users "may suffer benefit reductions and possibly be subject to an income test, and receipt of benefit might be contingent on the claimant's willingness to take part in community work projects or training programs." As a result, he argues, "This is no longer social insurance but a form of 'workfare.'"

Educational Assistance

In Canada, public education is free until the end of secondary school (or "high school"). However, the costs associated with higher education have long been recognized to pose special problems to those of low income. Until 1939 and the federal government's passage of the **Dominion-Provincial Student Aid Program (DSAP)**, economic assistance for low-income persons wanting to attend postsecondary institutions was limited to those high scholastic achievers who could obtain privately funded assistance from universities and colleges. The encroachment of the federal government into the area of education (which, under the *Constitution Act, 1867*, is the exclusive domain of provincial legislatures) was legitimated with reference to economic growth, labour training, and labour mobility—areas that fell under federal jurisdiction. From this vantage point, the DSAP was simply a subset of the *Youth Training Act* or another part of national economic policy. By 1944, all of Canada's provinces had joined the plan; however, in 1954, Quebec opted out of the arrangement, "citing constitutional reasons of provincial primacy and autonomy in higher education" (Orlikow 1999: 2265). DSAP was discontinued in 1967.

In 1964, the **Canada Student Loans Program (CSLP)** was established. Under this plan, the federal government guarantees loans to all full-time students demonstrating financial need to a provincial or territorial government. These loans must be repaid over a period that does not exceed 9.5 years at a rate of interest that is set annually. Students are not required to begin making payments until six months after they have ceased to be full-time students, but interest on the monies owed begins to accrue as soon as they leave full-time studies. In 1994, the ***Canada Student Financial Assistance Act (CSFA Act)*** revised the CSLP, increasing the amounts of the maximum loans available to full-time and part-time students; establishing a national program of grants for students with permanent disabilities, part-time students with high financial need, students with dependants, and women in doctoral programs in certain fields; and expanding interest relief for unemployed borrowers and those of low income. In 1998, the government also introduced new measures to assist students in loan repayment.

Most recently, the introduction of Registered Education Saving Plans (RESPs) represents an attempt to assist families who can afford to set monies aside for the future costs of their children's education. Family members can contribute up to $4000 a year (up to a maximum of $20 000) into RESPs on behalf of a particular beneficiary. The Canada Education Savings Grant (CESG) is added to the monies invested. The CESG is a federal government grant, paid directly into a beneficiary's RESP, that provides 20 percent to the first $2000 in contributions made into an RESP per eligible beneficiary on an annual basis. RESPs grow tax free until such time as the beneficiary is ready to attend any eligible postsecondary educational institution (Human Resources Development Canada 2001).

Nevertheless, the rising cost of tuition (up 115 percent since 1980) will continue to make the costs of postsecondary education difficult for many and prohibitive for some (see also Chapter 12).

Maternal and Parental Benefits

In Canada, maternity and parental leave is part of our federal employment insurance system. Under Canada's current EI rules, new mothers receive a maximum of 15 weeks of pregnancy benefits (the first two of which are nonpayable) *only* if they have worked at least 600 hours in the 52 weeks prior, and then they receive only 55 percent of their normal weekly pay to a maximum of $413 a week. Employment Insurance additionally provides for a maximum of 35 weeks of parental leave (to either a natural or adoptive parent) that is payable up to one year after the birth of an infant or the placement of an adopted child.

Under provincial and territorial legislation, all Canadian provinces and territories provide either 17 or 18 weeks of unpaid maternity leave. "In every jurisdiction, the laws guarantee an employee reinstatement after the leave period to at least a comparable job with the same or similar wages and benefits, without loss of seniority" (Dranoff 2001: 44). However, not all employees (e.g., domestics) are protected under most employment standards legislation.

Child Support Enforcement

In February 1997, Bill C-41 received royal assent and became law in May of that year. This legislation included amendments to the *Divorce Act* to establish a framework for the use of child support guidelines; amendments to the *Family Orders and Agreements Enforcement Assistance Act* (FOAEA) that added Canada Revenue Agency to the list of federal departments whose databanks can be searched to locate persons who have breached family support orders; new provisions in the FOAEA Act to establish a federal licence denial scheme that will also authorize the suspension of passports and certain federal transport licences when a payer of child support has persistently breached support obligations; amendments to the *Garnishment, Attachment and Pension Diversion Act* to expand access to federal public service employee pension benefits to satisfy support arrears, and amendments to the *Shipping Act* to allow the wages of a person working at sea to be garnished to support a family obligation. All Canadian provinces now have their own programs to protect against the nonpayment of child support.

Under the *Divorce Act*, either spouse or former spouse may be ordered to pay child support. Child support is neither taxable for the parent who receives the support nor is it deductible for the parent who pays the support on agreements made after May 1,

1997. (Child support agreements made before this date are not affected by this ruling.) Child support is also completely protected against bankruptcy claims.

Welfare in Canada: Myths and Realities

Public attitudes toward welfare assistance and welfare recipients are generally negative. Rather than view poverty as the problem, many Canadians view welfare as the problem. What are some of the common myths about welfare that perpetuate negative images of welfare and welfare recipients?

MYTH 1

People receiving welfare are lazy and have no work ethic.

Reality

First, single parents on welfare already do work—they do the work of parenting. Albelda and Tilly (1997: 111) emphasize that "raising children is work. It requires time, skills, and commitment. While we as a society do not place a monetary value on it, it is work that is invaluable—and indeed, essential to the survival of our society." Single parents and people with disabilities tend to have longer spells on welfare and those who are *able to work* tend to have shorter spells. Second, it should be evident that not all persons who would prefer to work are able to find jobs, particularly those in low-skill job categories. For example, Newfoundland has long had very high rates of unemployment, a fact that helps to explain why its welfare caseload is heavily laden with long-term welfare recipients. The National Council of Welfare (1999b: 17) notes that "Canada has seen a decline in the number of secure, full-time, well-paying jobs and an increase in the number of short-term, part-time jobs with low wages, few benefits and little or no security." As the Council emphasizes, "For those individuals with low levels of education, 'bad' jobs are often the only real possibilities of employment, yet they cannot eliminate child and family poverty, no matter how hard a parent works. When lay-offs come, parents fall still further behind." Some provinces, such as Ontario, have incorporated "workfare" into the welfare system, which requires able-bodied people to do specific jobs as a condition of welfare. However, most of the workfare jobs are menial jobs that are unlikely to lead to permanent employment.

Rather than disparage the work ethic of those on welfare, the National Council of Welfare (1998: 62) emphasizes that it might be well to recognize that "everyone is at risk of falling on welfare at some point in their lives. The numbers speak for themselves: an estimated 1 910 900 people in Canada were on welfare as of March 31, 2001" (National Council of Welfare 2002a). As the Council observes, "Losing a job, losing a spouse, and losing good health are some of the reasons that people go on welfare. The biggest myth of all would be to assume that most of us are immune to any of these personal tragedies or the many other misfortunes that can lead to reliance on welfare."

MYTH 2

Welfare benefits are granted to many people who are not eligible to receive them and welfare fraud is rampant.

Reality

Although some people obtain welfare benefits through fraudulent means, it is much more common for people who are eligible to receive welfare to not receive benefits. A main reason for not receiving benefits is lack of information—people do not know they are eligible. Some people who are eligible for public assistance do not apply for it because they do not want to be stigmatized as lazy people who just want a "free ride" at the taxpayers' expense—their sense of personal pride prevents them from receiving public assistance. Others want to avoid the administrative hassles involved in obtaining it.

Nevertheless, the impression that welfare fraud is widespread is undoubtedly suggested by government statistics on welfare "fraud and misuse." For example, in December 1999, Ontario's Community and Social Service Minister John Baird boasted that $35 million in "fraud savings" had occurred because of increased government vigilance in policing welfare recipients. However, what the ministry figures show is not truly welfare "fraud" on the part of claimants at all, but rather overpayments resulting from administrative errors as well as a notable vigour in relation to the disqualification of vulnerable individuals from receiving assistance. While in 1997–98, 61 653 cases were investigated for "welfare fraud," in fewer than one in four cases (23.9 percent) did the Ministry reduce the amount of the benefit or terminate the benefit altogether; only 1.2 percent (or 1100) of the cases investigated resulted in a criminal conviction for fraud. In addition, in more than 90 percent of the 14 771 cases in which the Ministry reduced the amount of the benefit or terminated benefits altogether, such actions were the result of an administrative error, not fraud. Reductions in benefits or termination of benefits can occur in the absence of any wrongdoing on the part of welfare recipients. For example, should the Consolidated Verification Project (CVP) investigation reveal that a document is missing from a welfare recipient's file, the recipient is required to provide the necessary paperwork (whether it is two days or 20 years old) or face termination of benefits.

MYTH 3

Most welfare parents are teenagers.

Reality

According to the National Council of Welfare (1998), teenage single parents accounted for only 3 percent of single parents on welfare in March 1997. Parents in their 20s to 40s accounted for 87 percent of couples with children on welfare and 91 percent of single parents on welfare.

MYTH 4

Most welfare mothers have large families with many children.

Reality

Mothers receiving welfare have no more children, on average, than mothers in the general population.

MYTH 5

Unmarried women have children so they can receive benefits. If single mothers already receive benefits, they have more children to receive increased benefits.

Reality

Research consistently shows that receiving welfare does not significantly increase out-of-wedlock births (Albelda and Tilly 1997).

MYTH 6

Most people on welfare also have income from part-time work or Employment Insurance or government pensions.

Reality

According to the National Council of Welfare (1998), only 29 percent of welfare cases in March 1997 had outside income from work, government pensions, support payments, Employment Insurance, or other sources. Among couples with children, wages were the most common form of outside income; among single parents with children, child support or alimony was the most common source of outside income, with wages a close second. While transfer payments and wages were the main sources of outside income both for couples without children and for unattached persons, the percentage of unattached persons receiving either form of outside income was extremely low.

MYTH 7

Almost all the people on welfare are adults.

Reality

According to the National Council of Welfare (1998: 31), in March 1997, dependent children accounted for nearly 1.1 million of the people on welfare in Canada.

Despite the public perception that welfare benefits are too generous, cash and other forms of assistance to the poor do not meet the basic needs for many individuals and families who receive such benefits.

Minimum Wage Increase

As noted earlier, many families that leave welfare for work are still living in poverty because of involuntary part-time work and low wages. One strategy for improving the standard of living for low-income individuals and families is to increase the minimum wage (Schenk 2001). As the National Council of Welfare (1999b: 18) has noted, "Nowhere in Canada are minimum wages high enough to allow even full-time workers to escape poverty. . . . [and] [t]he situation is much worse when a minimum wage worker has children to support."

In British Columbia, where the minimum wage will increase from $10 an hour to $10.25 per hour in October 2014, the hourly rate is significantly below the 2014 Ontario minimum wage of $11 per hour even though Vancouver has the highest housing costs in the country. Meanwhile, the Ontario government under Premier Kathleen Wynne has recently been criticized for a policy that links increases in the minimum wage to increases in the Consumer Price Index (CPI). Critics argue that as the current minimum wage in Ontario falls well below a living wage, increases tied to the CPI will mean that the minimum wage continues to lag behind the minimum needs of workers. Writing in the *Toronto Star*, Carol Goar observes that "Had [Wynne's advisory panel] taken a hard look at the CPI, they would have realized that hundreds of the goods and services in the 'fixed basket of commodities' Statistics Canada uses to track price movements are irrelevant to people struggling to pay their rent, buy groceries, and keep the lights on" (Goar 2014). Clearly, minimum wages come nowhere near to covering the costs of living. The map in Figure 10.5 shows the minimum wages in provinces and territories across Canada current as of February 2014.

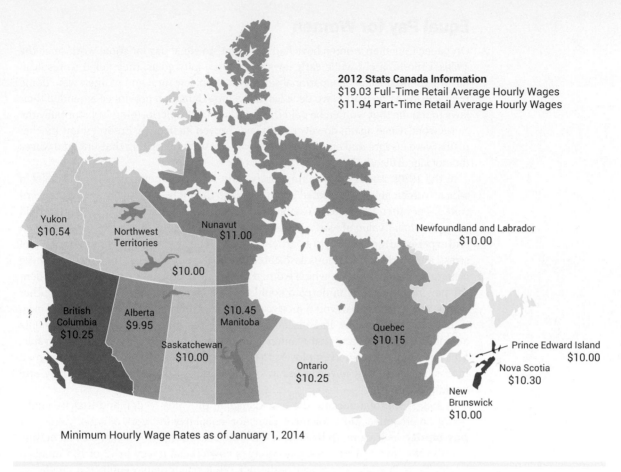

2012 Stats Canada Information
$19.03 Full-Time Retail Average Hourly Wages
$11.94 Part-Time Retail Average Hourly Wages

Yukon
$10.54

Northwest
Territories

Nunavut
$11.00

$10.00

British
Columbia
$10.25

Alberta
$9.95

$10.45
Manitoba

Saskatchewan
$10.00

Ontario
$10.25

Quebec
$10.15

Newfoundland and Labrador
$10.00

Prince Edward Island
$10.00

Nova Scotia
$10.30

New
Brunswick
$10.00

Minimum Hourly Wage Rates as of January 1, 2014

Figure 10.5 *Minimum Wage across Canada*

SOURCE: Statistics Canada. Hourly Minimum Wages in Canada for Adult Workers. Labour Program. http://srv116.services.gc.ca/dimt-wid/sm-mw/rpt2.aspx?lang=eng&dec=5

Those opposed to increasing the minimum wage argue that such an increase would result in higher unemployment and fewer benefits for low-wage workers. However, research has failed to find any systematic significant job loss associated with minimum wage increases (Economic Policy Institute 2000).

The National Council of Welfare has made these recommendations:

- The federal government must provide wage supplements to parents in the labour force to cover the additional costs of raising children.
- Governments must provide job training that prepares workers for new jobs.
- Governments must ensure that postsecondary educational opportunities are open to everyone, not just students who are lucky enough to have families able to afford to pay their tuition fees and living expenses.
- Governments must ensure that legislation governing unpaid maternity and parental leave in their jurisdictions adequately covers the time that parents are required to care for young children. Existing parental leaves cover the first months of children's lives, but parents also need time to care for sick children and take them to medical appointments when their children are much older.
- Governments must ensure that employment and pay equity laws are strengthened and enforced.

Equal Pay for Women

On paper, Canadian women have had the "right" to equal pay for equal work since the 1950s. Unfortunately, while early laws enunciated lofty goals, they failed to result in fair wages. Because of occupational sex segregation, few men and women were doing precisely the same work. Two decades later, some Canadian provinces amended their laws to require that women be paid the same as men for performing "substantially the same work." Once again, however, such laws proved ineffective. Enforcement mechanisms were meagre and employers found various ways of arguing that unequal wages did not signal discrimination on the basis of sex.

In the 1980s, researchers found women earn less than men partly because jobs in which women are concentrated are valued less than jobs in which men are concentrated. They therefore tried to establish gender-neutral standards by which they could judge the dollar value of work. These standards include such factors as the education and experience required to do a particular job and the level of responsibility, amount of stress, and working conditions associated with it. Researchers felt that, by using these criteria to compare jobs in which women and men are concentrated, they could identify pay inequities. The underpaid could then be compensated accordingly. In other words, women and men would receive equal pay for jobs of "comparable worth," even if they did different jobs. In consequence, during the mid-1980s, some governments amended the law to state that women should be paid equally for work of equal value. This amendment required employers to compare the rates of pay for women and men in dissimilar jobs that nevertheless involved the same skill, effort, responsibility, and working conditions.

In 1985, Manitoba became the first Canadian province to demand that its public sector be proactive and implement plans for "equal pay for work of equal value"—or **pay equity**, as it came to be called. With the exceptions of Alberta, Saskatchewan, and the Northwest Territories, pay equity is now official policy in 10 of 13 Canadian jurisdictions. Provisions vary widely, though. While policy on pay equity is a significant step toward achieving gender equality, inequity remains, as evidenced by both the persistence of the wage gap between working men and women and women's heightened susceptibility to poverty.

Charity, Nonprofit Organizations, and Nongovernmental Organizations

Various types of aid to the poor are provided through individual and corporate donations to charities and nonprofit organizations. In 1996, the average charitable donation declared by tax filers was $730. Four billion dollars in donations was declared in that year. Canadians residing in the richer provinces were not more likely to donate to charities and were not the most generous donors. Rather, those residing in Manitoba and Prince Edward Island were the most likely to donate, and residents of Newfoundland, the province with the lowest total median income, made the highest median donation. Corporations also donate to charitable causes. In 1982, they contributed some $200 million; in 1995, they contributed $500 million to charities (Statistics Canada 1998a).

Charity involves giving not only money, but also time and effort in the form of volunteering. In Canada, those who reside in the Prairie provinces and the well educated are particularly likely to be volunteers. Women are slightly more likely than men are to be volunteers, and rural and small-town residents are more likely than city dwellers to serve as volunteers. Nevertheless, high rates of volunteerism are found in cities such as Saskatoon (44 percent), Calgary (38 percent), and Edmonton (Statistics Canada 1998a).

pay equity
Also known as "equal pay for work of equal value"; requires equal pay for women who perform jobs of equal value to men in the same establishment. Employers are required to compare women's and men's jobs on the basis of skill, effort, responsibility, and working conditions to determine their value.

Nongovernmental organizations (NGOs) address many issues related to human rights, social justice, and environmental concerns. The number of international NGOs grew from fewer than 400 in 1900 to 26 000 in the year 2000—more than four times as many as existed just 10 years earlier (Knickerbocker 2000; Paul 2000). At the Millennium Forum meeting in 2000, representatives from more than 1000 NGOs called for a UN Global Poverty Eradication Fund to ensure that poor people have access to credit (Deen 2000). The NGOs declared that poverty is the most widespread violation of human rights and called upon governments around the world to make the alleviation of poverty a priority.

International Responses to Poverty

Alleviating worldwide poverty continues to be a major concern for developing and developed countries. Approaches to poverty reduction include promoting economic growth and investing in "human capital." Conflict resolution and the promotion of peace are also important for reducing poverty worldwide.

Promoting Economic Growth

Economic growth, over the long term, generally reduces poverty (United Nations Development Programme 1997). An expanding economy creates new employment opportunities and more goods and services. In 1998, 150 million of the world's workers were unemployed (United Nations Development Programme 2000). As employment prospects improve, individuals are able to buy more goods and services. The increased demand for goods and services, in turn, stimulates economic growth. As emphasized in Chapter 14, economic development requires controlling population growth and protecting the environment and natural resources—often destroyed and depleted in the process of economic growth.

However, economic growth does not always reduce poverty; in some cases, it increases it. For example, growth resulting from technological progress may reduce demand for unskilled workers. Growth does not help poverty reduction when public spending is diverted away from meeting the needs of the poor and instead is used to pay international debt, finance military operations, and support corporations that do not pay workers fair wages. The World Bank loans about $30 billion a year to developing nations to pay primarily for roads, bridges, and industrialized agriculture that mostly benefit corporations. "Relatively little attention or money has been given to developing basic social services, building schools and clinics, and building decent public sanitation and clean water systems in some of the world's poorest countries" (Mann 2000: 2). Thus, "economic growth, though essential for poverty reduction, is not enough. Growth must be pro-poor, expanding the opportunities and life choices of poor people" (United Nations Development Programme 1997: 72–73). Because three-fourths of poor people in most developing countries depend on agriculture for their livelihoods, economic growth to reduce poverty must include raising the productivity of small-scale agriculture. Not only does improving the productivity of small-scale agriculture create employment, it also reduces food prices. The poor benefit the most because about 70 percent of their income is spent on food (United Nations Development Programme 1997).

Investing in Human Capital

Promoting economic development in a society requires having a productive workforce. Yet, in many poor countries, large segments of the population are illiterate and without job skills, or are malnourished and in poor health. A key feature of poverty reduction strategies involves investing in human capital. The term **human capital** refers to the skills, knowledge, and capabilities of the individual. Investments in human capital involve programs and policies that enhance individuals' health, skills, knowledge, and capabilities. Among such programs and policies are those that provide adequate nutrition, sanitation, housing, health care (including reproductive health care and family planning), and educational and job training. Nobel Laureate Gary Becker has concluded, "the case is overwhelming that investments in human capital are one of the most effective ways to raise the poor to decent levels of income and health" (reported in Hill 1998: 279).

Poor health is both a consequence and cause of poverty; improving the health status of a population is a significant step toward breaking the cycle of poverty. Increasing the educational levels of a population better prepares individuals for paid employment and for participation in political affairs that affect poverty and other economic and political issues. Improving the educational level and overall status of women in developing countries is also associated with lower birth rates, which in turn fosters economic development.

One way to help poor countries invest in human capital and reduce poverty is to provide debt relief. If African countries were relieved of their national debts, they would have funds that would save the lives of millions of children and provide basic education to millions of girls and women. Providing debt relief to the 20 worst affected countries would cost between $5.5 billion and $7.7 billion—roughly the cost of building the Euro-Disney theme park in France (United Nations Development Programme 1997).

Understanding Poverty: National and International Issues

As we have seen in this chapter, economic prosperity has not been evenly distributed: the rich have become richer, while the poor have become poorer. Meanwhile, Canada has implemented measures that essentially weaken the safety net for the most impoverished segment of the population, to a large extent, children. The decrease in assistance to the poor is a major reason poverty rates have remained high, despite the economic prosperity of the country. Many families leaving welfare report struggling to get food, shelter, medical care, child care, and transportation. The effects of poverty on children perpetuate the cycle of poverty. Larin (1998) notes that "while it always has been possible for individuals to move up the economic ladder, the odds against it are high for individuals who suffer from the ill effects of poverty during childhood" (p. 26). Given the association between poverty and poor health and low educational attainment, poor children often grow up to be poor adults who are unable to escape poverty.

Canadians commonly believe that the rich are deserving and the poor are failures. Blaming poverty on individuals rather than on structural and cultural factors implies not only that poor individuals are responsible for their plight, but also that they are responsible for improving their condition. If we hold individuals accountable for their poverty, we fail to make society accountable for making investments in human capital that are necessary to alleviate poverty. Such human capital investments include providing health care, adequate food and housing, education, child care, and job training. Economist Lewis Hill (1998) believes that "the fundamental cause of perpetual poverty is the failure of…people to invest adequately in the human capital represented by impoverished children" (p. 299). Blaming the poor for their plight also fails to recognize that there are not enough jobs for those who want to work and that many jobs fail to pay wages that enable families to escape poverty. Finally, blaming the poor for their condition diverts attention away from the recognition that the wealthy—individuals and corporations—receive far more benefits in the form of wealthfare or corporate welfare, without the stigma of welfare.

Ending or reducing poverty begins with the recognition that doing so is a worthy ideal and an attainable goal. Imagine a world where everyone had comfortable shelter, plentiful food, adequate medical care, and education. If this imaginary world were achieved, and absolute poverty were effectively eliminated, what would the effects be on such social problems as crime, drug abuse, family problems (such as domestic violence, child abuse, and divorce), health problems, prejudice and racism, and international conflict?

It would be too costly to eliminate poverty—or would it? According to one source, the cost of eradicating poverty worldwide would be only about 1 percent of global income—and no more than 2 to 3 percent of national income in all but the poorest countries (United Nations Development Programme 1997). Certainly, the costs of allowing poverty to continue are much greater than that.

Student Reflection: What Do You Know Now?

Reflecting on your own situation and your family history with regard to income levels, class background, ethnicity, educational attainment, and so on, identify assumptions of yours that may have been challenged by information in this chapter. What are some stereotypes or assumptions that you have reconsidered as a result of thinking sociologically? Does your current province of residence take a particular position with regard to helping to alleviate the effects of poverty? Which particular government party seems to be on the side of social assistance? Thinking more locally, how accessible are services that are meant to help those in need? If you could present a solution to your local council for an initiative that would address the consequences of poverty, what would that solution look like?

What Do You Do Next?

Located at www.nelson.com/socialproblems5e

- Consolidate your knowledge with interactive and printable **Flashcards**
- Gauge your understanding with **Practice Quizzes** and **Matching Activities**
- Develop your critical thinking skills with **Self and Society** and **The Human Side** questions
- Analyze **Social Research** and **Social Problems in Global Perspective**
- Explore the implications of **Technology on Social Problems**

Work and Unemployment

© AlpamayoPhoto/iStockphoto.com

Student Reflection: What Do You Already Know?

One reason why you might be reading this textbook right now is that you are enrolled in a formal program that you hope will lead to some kind of work. Most of us plan to contribute in some way our labour in exchange for wages. Thinking about your work history and work future in the context of changes in employment patterns, technological advances, families and aging, and so on may already have been part of your decision about higher education pursuits. This chapter is one way of seeing that bigger picture in more critically reflective terms.

Learning Outcomes

Through careful reading of this chapter, you should be able to:

- define the bolded key terms
- understand the historical and contemporary processes of industrialization, postindustrial economies, multinational corporate entities, and state-business interactions as they relate to social problems
- differentiate among primary, secondary, and tertiary work sectors and their changing ratios over time in Canada
- evaluate the pros and cons of new forms of work and connectivity enabled by technological innovations
- apply the central sociological theories as well as feminist and queer theories of work to historical and contemporary phenomena
- discuss work-related social problems such as child labour, health and safety, dissatisfaction and alienation, unemployment and underemployment, and struggles for workers' rights
- reflect on the special case of industrial agriculture and migrant farm workers as an intersection of labour, economics, corporate power, social problems, and the environment
- consider strategies like better childcare, flextime, job sharing, benefits, and others to improve conditions for workers locally and internationally

11.1 The Global Context: The Economy in the Twenty-First Century

In recent decades, innovations in communication and information technology have spawned the emergence of a **global economy**—an interconnected network of economic activity that transcends national borders and spans the world. The globalization of economic activity means that, more and more, our jobs, the products and services we buy, and our nation's political policies and agendas influence and are influenced by economic activities occurring around the world. After summarizing the two main economic systems in the world—capitalism and socialism—we look at the emergence of corporate multinationalism. We then describe how industrialization and postindustrialization have changed the nature of work.

In 1999, 11 of the 15 European Union nations began making the transition from their national currency to a new common currency—the euro—that has locked them together financially. The adoption of the euro reflects the increasing globalization of economic institutions. The term **economic institution** refers to the structure and means by which a society produces, distributes, and consumes goods and services. While the first years of the euro zone brought increased power to nations that had previously had weak currencies, the interdependency of the European Union (EU) has also brought significant difficulty to the people of the EU. The recent financial crises in euro zone countries have combined with debt management problems across the EU, but where the major news media tend to report these as problems of individual state governments, sociological work on the economic problems of the EU notes that it is the financial industry's ability to offload its problems onto state governments that we need to pay attention to (Deutschmann 2011: 17–20). When states rather than industries are held accountable for financial collapse, it is the citizens who end up paying the price. Deutschmann explains that the problems of Greece, Ireland, Spain, Italy, and Belgium are related to the private financial industry crisis that emerged in the United States in 2007–08:

> the American subprime crisis [was] the prelude of a global crisis, resulting from a long term over-accumulation of private financial assets [...] A tremendous volume of uncovered titles had been piled up which due to its dimensions and inherent "systemic risks" could not simply be written off. Therefore the crisis became a political issue. The US and European Governments intervened by voluminous parcels of credit, credit guarantees, subsidies and public expenditures [...] to prevent a deepening of the collapse. [...] On the one hand that helped to bring about an immediate stabilization, on the other hand, public debts exploded [...] The increase of public debt had been even more marked in the US and in Britain than in Euroland. As a result, the financial markets became suspicious about the credit worthiness of the very agency that saved them from collapse, the national states. This means that the financial industry has managed to externalize her [sic] own problem and to transform it into a problem of the states. (2011: 17)

Deutschmann suggests that those nations most targeted as financially weak would not now be in such large-scale difficulty if they had maintained their own currencies (2011: 18), though Peter North argues in the same issue of *Economic Sociology* that the use of individual currencies for nations provides no guarantee of nation-state stability. Instead, North suggests that nations in the EU might do better with regional currencies that would operate alongside the euro (2011: 25). These smaller, regional currencies—such as the *Roland*, used in Bremen, and the *Chiemgauer*, used in Bavaria—benefit local communities for the trade of locally produced goods, food, and services. These

global economy
An interconnected network of economic activity that transcends national borders.

economic institution
The structure and means by which a society produces, distributes, and consumes goods and services.

micro-currencies exist alongside the euro but are backed by local banks and co-operatives, which allows for a high level of user adoption and robust use in regional trade operations (ibid).

The reason that people in the EU may want to adopt local currencies for use alongside the euro is that it restores local economic power to workers, merchants, and regional services, making people less vulnerable to the exploitation of a financial industry that takes big risks and then offloads its failures onto states to manage. Local currencies can help protect regions against negative consequences of national debt ratios that suddenly balloon because of fallout from financial industry crises. If local currencies prove to be helpful and viable we may see similar monetary strategies adopted outside the EU.

Capitalism and Socialism

The principal economic systems in the world are capitalism and socialism. Under **capitalism**, private individuals or groups invest capital (money, technology, machines) to produce goods and services to sell for a profit in a competitive market. Capitalism is characterized by economic motivation through profit, the determination of prices and wages primarily through supply and demand, and the absence of governmental intervention in the economy. More people are working today in a capitalist economy than ever before in history (Went 2000). Critics of capitalism argue that it creates too many social evils, including alienated workers, poor working conditions, near-poverty wages, unemployment, a polluted and depleted environment, and world conflict over resources.

Pure capitalism (known as "hands off" capitalism) exists only when market forces can operate without interference from the government. However, in Canada, many restraints to the laissez-faire model have traditionally existed. *State capitalism* is a form of capitalism in which private citizens own the means of production and pursue profits, but do so within a vast system of laws designed to protect the welfare of the population. In Canada, state capitalism also refers to public or state investment in sectors of the economy that could be private. Canada's economy was once described as "a strange mix of interventionism and free-market policies" (Hallsworth 1993: 445); however, since the 1980s, the state has begun to withdraw from the private sector by selling off public assets (e.g., Petro-Canada, Air Canada) and through an ongoing process of deregulation (e.g., the North American Free Trade Agreement, the reduction of interprovincial trade barriers, and the "open skies" agreement with the United States).

Socialism emphasizes public rather than private ownership. Theoretically, goods and services are equitably distributed according to the needs of the citizens. Whereas capitalism emphasizes individual freedom, socialism emphasizes social equality.

Advocates for capitalism and socialism claim that the one they support results in economic well-being for society and for its members. In reality, both capitalist and socialist countries have been unable to fulfill their promises. Although the overall standard of living is higher in capitalist countries, so is economic inequality. Some theorists suggest that capitalist countries will adopt elements of socialism and socialist countries will adopt elements of capitalism. This idea, known as the **convergence hypothesis**, is reflected in the economies of Germany, France, and Sweden, which are sometimes called "integrated economies" because they have elements of both capitalism and socialism.

Corporate Multinationalism

Corporate multinationalism is the practice of corporations having a home base in one country and branches, or affiliates, in other countries. Corporate multinationalism allows businesses to avoid import tariffs and costs associated with transporting

capitalism
An economic system in which private individuals or groups invest capital to produce goods and services, for a profit, in a competitive market.

socialism
An economic ideology that emphasizes public rather than private ownership. Theoretically, goods and services are equitably distributed according to the needs of the citizens.

convergence hypothesis
The argument that capitalist countries will adopt elements of socialism and socialist countries will adopt elements of capitalism; that is, they will converge.

corporate multinationalism
The practice of corporations having their home base in one country and branches, or affiliates, in other countries.

goods to another country. Access to raw materials, cheap foreign labour, and avoidance of government regulations and labour laws also drive corporate multinationalism. "By moving production plants abroad, business managers may be able to work foreign employees for long hours under dangerous conditions at low pay, pollute the environment with impunity, and pretty much have their way with local communities. Then the business may be able to ship its goods back to its home country at lower costs and bigger profits" (Caston 1998: 274–75).

Although multinationalization provides jobs for managers, secures profits for investors, and helps Canada compete in the global economy, it also has "far-reaching and detrimental consequences" (Epstein et al. 1993: 206). Corporate multinationalization must take its share of the blame for an array of social problems, such as poverty resulting from fewer jobs, urban decline resulting from factories moving away, and racial and ethnic tensions resulting from competition for jobs. In addition, as Maule (1999: 1536) points out, "[l]ess developed countries argue that they have traded political independence for economic and cultural dependence. Politically, there remains concern over the extent to which multinational corporations are used as instruments of foreign policy by the governments of countries where parent companies are located. Culturally, the concern is over the loss of national identity." Noting that the rapid increase of foreign ownership in the Canadian economy after World War I was linked to the rise of multinational corporations, economic nationalists have expressed concern over "the special problems created by this type of investment, particularly the stunted and distorted pattern of economic development" and the broader impact of multinationals on Canadian society, identity, and sovereignty (Rotstein 1999: 717). For example, Bellan (1999) points out that

> Huge and increasing amounts of money have to be remitted to U.S. owners in the form of dividends on their investment and contributions by branch plants toward head office costs of administration, research, product development and advertising.
>
> A large proportion of these payments must be made in U.S. dollars … The consequence is that a very large fraction of the U.S. dollars that Canada earns by its exports must be used to make interest and dividend payments and branch plant remittances to U.S. firms. (pp. 884–85)

Second, Bellan charges that multinational corporations have "carried on their Canadian operations to serve their own best interests, not those of Canada," with industrial research and development that are "essential to industrial innovation and growth" generally conducted in their U.S. facilities rather than at their Canadian branch plants. Third, he notes that multinationals show no particular loyalty to Canada when the demand for their products falls or a cheaper source of supplies or labour is found in another country.

Industrialization, Postindustrialization, and the Changing Nature of Work

The nature of work has been shaped by the **Industrial Revolution**, the period between the mid–eighteenth century and the early nineteenth century when the factory system was introduced in England. Industrialization dramatically altered the nature of work: machines replaced hand tools; and steam, gasoline, and electric power replaced human or animal power. Industrialization also led to the development of mass-production assembly lines and an increased division of labour. Factories contributed to the emergence of large cities, where earlier informal social interactions dominated by primary relationships were replaced by formal interactions centred on secondary groups. Instead of the family-centred economy characteristic of an agricultural society, people began to work outside the home for wages.

Industrial Revolution
The period between the mid-eighteenth and the early nineteenth centuries when machines and factories became the primary means for producing goods.

Postindustrialization refers to the shift from an industrial economy dominated by manufacturing jobs to an economy dominated by service-oriented, information-intensive occupations. Postindustrialization is characterized by a highly educated workforce, automated and computerized production methods, increased government involvement in economic issues, and a higher standard of living (Bell 1973). Like industrialization before it, postindustrialization has transformed the nature of work.

The three fundamental work sectors (primary, secondary, and tertiary) reflect the major economic transformation in society—the Industrial Revolution and the Postindustrial Revolution. The **primary work sector** involves the production of raw materials and food goods. In developing countries with little industrialization, about 60 percent of the labour force works in agricultural activities; in Canada less than 3 percent of the workforce is in farming (Bracey 1995; *Report on the World Social Situation* 1997; Statistics Canada 1998). The **secondary work sector** involves the production of manufactured goods from raw materials (e.g., paper from wood). The **tertiary work sector** includes professional, managerial, technical-support, and service jobs. The transition to a postindustrial society is marked by a decrease in manufacturing jobs and an increase in service and information-technology jobs in the tertiary work sector. For example, even though the high-tech sector was struggling on several fronts in 2000, the demand for computer specialists led the growth in the Canadian labour force during the 1990s, most notably in the latter half of the decade (Statistics Canada 2003: 8). Between 1991 and 2001, almost one-half of the growth in the Canadian labour force "occurred in highly skilled occupations that normally require university qualifications, while low skilled occupations requiring high-school or less accounted for only a quarter of the increase" (Statistics Canada 2003: 5). Consider as well that, in 2001, the "top 10 disappearing jobs" in Canada were, in order: typist; typesetter; watch/clock repairer; statistical clerk; fisher; bank teller; telephone operator; tool and die maker; farmer; and locomotive operator. In that year, the "top 10 growth careers" in Canada were, in order: in-home nurse; nurse practitioner; physician; teacher, special education; pharmacist; programmer; psychiatrist; radiology technician; registered nurse; and physiotherapist (Ash 2001: 194).

As Andrew Jackson notes, paid labour (rather than investment income or inherited wealth) is integral to family income and well-being in Canada, and yet, while he reports that roughly two-thirds of all income for Canadians comes from paid labour, and 80 percent of women with employed spouses are now also working and contributing to family income, we are simultaneously delaying entry into full-time paid work as years of schooling required for entry mean that many young adults do not have full-time employment (2010: 5). Meanwhile, Jackson observes, pressures on pension plans and reductions in income support for older Canadians mean that dreams of retiring before age 65 are "receding" (ibid). Jackson sums up our situation thus:

> …the fundamental reality is that we live in a market or capitalist society. We must work to live, and our income from work centrally determines our standard of living. […] The kinds of jobs we hold and the wages we earn largely determine the kinds of homes and neighbourhoods in which we live, the extent to which we can buy the goods and services we want, the extent to which we can provide our children with opportunities and our ability to balance work with family and community life and opportunities for leisure (2010: 5).

In a postindustrial society, highly skilled and technological personnel are needed, but Canada struggles to find personnel within its domestic population. Data from the 2001 census indicate that Canada has increasingly looked to immigration as a source of skills and knowledge. The 2001 census "showed a dramatic increase in the proportion of recent immigrants working in high skilled occupations—those that normally require a university education" (Statistics Canada 2003: 13). While immigrants who arrived between 1986 and 1990 accounted for 13 percent of the workforce in highly skilled occupations in 1991, in 2001, recent immigrants aged 25 to 64 who arrived during the 1990s represented almost one-quarter (24 percent) of the workforce in highly skilled occupations.

Recent immigrants have played an important role in the growth of highly skilled occupations in Canada over the 1990s, particularly in computer-related occupations and accounting. The proportion of new immigrants aged 25 to 44 who worked in information technology occupations rose from about 3 percent in 1991 to 12 percent in 2001. New immigrants were also overrepresented in engineering and natural sciences occupations. "In 2001, three percent of recent immigrants aged 25 to 44 in the labour force were in engineering compared to only one percent of the Canadian born. Similarly, 1.2 percent of recent immigrants were in natural sciences occupations compared to 0.6 percent of the Canadian born" (Statistics Canada 2003: 14). In developing countries, many individuals with the highest level of skill and education leave the country in search of work abroad, leading to the phenomenon known as the **brain drain** (see also Chapter 12). Although employers in developed countries benefit, developing countries lose valuable labour.

The Age of Information Technology

The idea that we live in an "information age" has become popular, with news stories frequently devoting attention to the new conditions of work and ever-changing means of managing and relaying information. For example, the Waterloo-based corporation BlackBerry (formerly Research In Motion) is still lauded as a domestic contributor with a powerful position in the world market for wireless communication.

However, popular attention is also paid to the kinds of problems that workers outfitted with the BlackBerry and similar devices may face because "the gadget takes the workplace anywhere the worker goes" (NPR 2005). The resulting tendency for employees to become obsessive about answering the emails and calls that come through on their BlackBerry devices has led to the creation of the term "crackberry," referring to the inability to shut off the connection to work.

Clinical psychiatrist Edward Hallowell remarks that workers with mobile devices such as the BlackBerry are increasingly burdened, to the point of collapse, under mountains of data and overwhelming employer expectations that they be perpetually "on call" (NPR 2005).

Companies regard telework and other flexible work arrangements as important in recruiting and maintaining good employees. Telework can also lower turnover and thus save companies expenses associated with hiring and training replacement employees. However, Bowles (2000) reports that companies are beginning to express dissatisfaction with telework "because they believe that it causes resentment among office-bound colleagues and weakens corporate loyalty" (p. 2). Telework eliminates offices that teleworkers don't need, allows employers to consolidate others, and reduces related overhead costs (Lovelace 2000). Several studies of managers and employees at large companies conclude that telework increases worker productivity (Lovelace 2000).

Some studies have shown that employee satisfaction among teleworkers is higher than for their non-teleworking counterparts (Lovelace 2000). Much of the job satisfaction among telecommuters is related to the job flexibility that enables them to balance work and family demands. Telework can provide flexibility to working parents and

brain drain
The phenomenon whereby many individuals with the highest level of skill and education leave the country in search of work abroad.

adults caring for aging parents, thus reducing role conflict and strengthening family life. One father of three children described his being home when his children came back from school as being "the most significant impact" of his telecommuting (Riley, Mandavilli, and Heino 2000: 5). He also took time during the day to take his children to school, to the doctor's office, and to run errands (ibid). However, a study of children whose parents work at home found that older children (grades 7 to 12) were more likely to agree that "my father does not have the energy to do things with me because of his job" and "my father has not been in a good mood with me because of his job" than the children of fathers who work in an office (Galinsky and Kim 2000). The effects of telework on parent–child relationships seem to depend then on how each parent interacts with his or her children, and on the perceptions of the child as well. One author of this textbook found, for example, that when her child was little, he experienced her working at home on a book to be a case of having to say "good-bye" to mommy several times a day, whereas his young friends either had mothers who were "stay-at-home moms" who could devote undivided attention to their children, or left for work in the morning and said "good-bye" only once. The child with the telecommuting parent, then—as we see in Galinsky and Kim (2000)—may experience an ironic sense that their parent is less available to them than is the parent who actually leaves the house to go to work.

Telework may expand job opportunities for rural job seekers who lack local employment opportunities, and for low-income urban job seekers who lack access to suburban jobs (Kukreja and Neely 2000). Telework can also bring work opportunities to individuals with disabilities. Some of the technologies that have been developed for individuals with serious disabilities include "Eye Gaze" (a communication system that allows people to operate a computer with their eyes); "Magic Wand Keyboard" (for people with limited or no hand movement); and "Switched Adapted Mouse and Trackball" (that allows clicking the mouse with other parts of the body) (Bowles 2000).

Telework also allows individuals to reduce or eliminate daily commutes. Consider that eliminating a 50-minute daily commute allows an individual to gain almost five weeks per year in time (Lovelace 2000).

Whatever the benefits of avoiding commuter-stress, those professions and work environments defined by information relay find that workers may suffer from "**technostress**," which arises from having too many tasks to perform simultaneously, while also keeping up with perpetually changing demands to operate new and emerging technologies with ease (Clark and Kalin 1996: 30). Though writing before the advent of portable communication devices for receiving wireless email and data, Clark and Kalin observed librarians at a national conference "who would never dream of having their phone calls or postal mail forwarded to the conference now feel compelled to stand in long lines to check their e-mail—even though the very people with whom they regularly communicate are likely attending that conference!" As workplaces go, postsecondary institutions have long maintained vague distinctions between workplace and home, with many professors and college instructors frequently working from home, and with some schools traditionally having faculty dons and college deans who live on campus. The world of IT (information technology) extends that tradition, bringing new problems and benefits to postsecondary education. Internet connections to libraries and use of communication technologies can move research and teaching into the home as more and more institutions offer distance education, and increase research demands on faculty. Being able to work from home may positively influence faculty life by allowing high productivity while maintaining connection to home-life and family; however, it comes with a downside, a demand for rapid responses from students accustomed to a "culture of instant information and instant response. The learner's sense of the 'rolling present' can make faculty feel pressured to spend large amounts of time

technostress
Stress that arises specifically from having too many tasks to perform simultaneously, while keeping up with perpetually changing demands to operate new and emerging technologies with ease.

interacting with … students who frequently perceive … education as 'always open' …" (McLean 2006). It is not unusual for faculty to report receiving several emails in a single day from a single student who, with increasing incivility, demands to know why the initial email has not yet been answered.

In addition to the problems of stress related to technology-saturated work environments, constant change in the technologies can result in three basic problems in the workplace: first, it requires workers to alter their skill sets constantly; second, the skills workers learn tend to be in the area of specific applications rather than in problem solving and decision making, so are not transferable; and third, those workers in higher level professional and managerial positions tend to receive more training and more skill upgrading than those in the lower ranks, which exaggerates the division in skill sets over time (Krahn and Lowe 2002: 297).

The use of new technologies in the production and manufacturing sector can promote the deskilling of jobs as skilled labourers are replaced with automated machines. Krahn and Lowe (2002: 296) note that automated machinery has not only replaced skilled workers in specific trades but where "[p]reviously, a group of workers with a broad range of skills relieved others, one at a time, from their various positions on the line. With the new technology every one took breaks of the same time, so that the multiskilled relief workers were no longer needed."

Finally, even those professional workers who are highly paid find that their conditions of work are extremely competitive and highly unstable, with frequent changes of both employer and career. The IT worker becomes a "free-floating individual, connected on-line to a variety of task-performing organizations, ever competing for resources and personal support, and assuming limited responsibilities towards a limited people for limited time" (Carnoy and Castells 1997: 35). Carnoy and Castells characterize such work conditions as a case of perpetual and progressive deterioration against which old methods of organizing under industrialization no longer work. To cope with this new reality, IT workers are more and more frequently turning to an older means of organizing, one that predates industrialism and trade unions: professional guilds. Although guilds have no ability to secure workers' rights through collective bargaining, Benner (2003) finds that guilds can foster a protective and developmental community in which workers compete together, rather than against one another:

> contemporary guilds have improved their members' career opportunities, through improving skill development, facilitating access to new job opportunities, and organizing advocacy efforts. Thus, given the factors that have given rise to these new occupational communities are unlikely to change, efforts to build a collective action through occupational solidarity can be an important component of broader strategies aimed at building security for workers in the information economy. (p. 182)

11.2 Sociological Theories of Work and the Economy

Numerous theories in economics, political science, and history address the nature of work and the economy. In sociology, structural-functionalism, conflict theory, and symbolic interactionism serve as theoretical lenses through which we may better understand work and economic issues and activities. In addition to the central theoretical perspectives traditionally applied to issues in work and economic systems, this edition of the text adds the increasingly important observations and critical tools provided by feminist and queer theory perspectives. Feminist and queer theory perspectives take a position focused on the unique challenges for GLBT persons and women who, as workers and economic contributors, contend with economic and work structures founded on a heterosexist division of labour.

Structural-Functionalist Perspective

The structural-functionalist perspective holds that the economic institution is one of the most important social institutions, providing fundamental necessities common to all human societies, including food, clothing, and shelter, and thus contributing to social stability. After the basic survival needs of a society are met, surplus materials and wealth may be allocated to other social uses, such as maintaining military protection from enemies, supporting political and religious leaders, providing formal education, supporting an expanding population, and providing entertainment and recreational activities. Societal development is dependent on an economic surplus in a society (Lenski and Lenski 1987).

Although the economic institution is functional for society, elements of it may be dysfunctional. For example, before industrialization, agrarian societies had a low division of labour in that few work roles were available to members of society. Limited work roles meant that society's members shared similar roles and thus developed similar norms and values (Durkheim [1893] 1966). In contrast, industrial societies are characterized by many work roles, or a high division of labour, and cohesion is based not on the similarity of people and their roles but on their interdependence. People in industrial societies need the skills and services that others provide. The lack of common norms and values in industrialized societies may result in **anomie**—a state of normlessness—which is linked to a variety of social problems, crime, drug addiction, and violence among them (see Chapters 3 and 4).

Conflict Perspective

According to Karl Marx, capitalism is responsible for the inequality and conflict within and between societies. The ruling class controls the economic system for its own benefit and exploits and oppresses the working masses. While structural-functionalism views the economic institution as benefiting society as a whole, conflict theory holds that capitalism benefits an elite class that controls not only the economy, but other aspects of society as well—the media, politics and law, education, and religion.

For example, corporate power is reflected in the policies of the International Monetary Fund (IMF) and the World Bank, which pressure developing countries to open their economies to foreign corporations, promoting export production at the expense of local consumption, encouraging the exploitation of labour as a means of attracting foreign investment, and hastening the degradation of natural resources as countries sell their forests and minerals to earn money to pay back loans (see Chapter 10). Ambrose (1998) asserts that "for some time now, the IMF has been the chief architect of the global economy, using debt leverage to force governments around the world to give big corporations and billionaires everything they want—low taxes, cheap labour, loose regulations—so they will locate in their countries" (p. 5).

Treaties such as the North American Free Trade Agreement (NAFTA) and the General Agreement on Tariffs and Trade (GATT) also benefit corporations. They provide corporations with greater access to foreign markets, many say, at the expense of workers. "These laws increasingly allow corporations to go anywhere and do anything they like, and prohibit workers and the governments that supposedly represent them from doing much about it" (Danaher 1998: 1).

According to the conflict perspective, work trends that benefit employees, such as worksite health promotion programs and work–family policies (discussed later in this chapter) are not the result of altruistic or humanitarian concern for workers' well-being.

anomie
A state of normlessness in which norms and values are weak or unclear; results from rapid social change and is linked to many social problems, including crime, drug addiction, and violence.

Rather, corporate leaders recognize that these programs and policies result in higher job productivity and lower health-care costs. They are thus good for the bottom line.

Symbolic Interactionist Perspective

According to symbolic interactionism, the work role is a central part of a person's identity. For example, identifying a person as a truck driver provides a different social meaning than identifying someone as a physician. The title of a person's work status also gives meaning and self-worth to the individual. A job is one of an individual's most important statuses; for many, it is the master, or the most significant, status.

In this model, distribution of economic compensation may become a primary measure of self-worth obtained through another's recognition of one's value. Heidegren (2004: 367) explains that "within a capitalist society ... struggles for recognition mainly relate to the principle of achievement: the experience of disrespect for their achievements leads social groups to struggle for greater social esteem for raising claims to an economic redistribution in their advantage."

As symbolic interactionists note, definitions and meanings influence behaviour. Meanings and definitions of child labour (discussed later) contribute to its perpetuation. In some countries, children learn to regard working as a necessary and important responsibility and rite of passage, rather than as an abuse of human rights. Some children look forward to becoming bonded to a master "in the same way that ... children [in our society] look forward to a communion or getting a driver's license" (Silvers 1996: 83).

Symbolic interactionism emphasizes that attitudes and behaviours are influenced by interaction with others. The applications of symbolic interactionism in the workplace are numerous—employers and managers are concerned with using interpersonal interaction techniques that achieve the attitudes and behaviours they want from their employees; union organizers are concerned with using interpersonal interaction techniques that persuade workers to unionize; and job-training programs are concerned with using interpersonal interaction techniques to motivate participants.

Feminist Perspectives

Because ideology structures the institutions of economy and family as a continuing distinction between a public and male sphere and a private and female sphere, many feminists concentrate on the challenges faced by women who operate in both worlds. Liberal feminists tend to focus on policy initiatives ensuring equal pay for equal work, family–work balance, and child-labour concerns. Though there have been some hard-won successes, the goal has been thwarted by determining what counts as "equal," by persistent devaluation of home life, and by contradictory stances on child labour (all discussed in this chapter).

Feminist work illuminates the constraints of gender-role divisions between the public and private worlds of paid employment and domestic work. Feminists observe that the distinction is very much based on classist presuppositions about what men and women are *supposed to do* in their gender roles. That is, to accept the idea that women do not work—or that they *should* not work—is to forget that some women *must* work for pay outside the home. This is not to say that we should ignore economist Marilyn Waring's (1988) detailed analysis on the significant value of domestic labour; rather, it is to acknowledge that entry into paid labour may not be a matter of choice but of necessity for women—just as much as it is for men.

Providing a sense of how we came to such a contradictory present, Jane Errington (1993) illuminates the subtle historical shifts in sensibilities about work, gender, and the needs of a changing Canada in the years around Confederation:

> the transition from pioneering communities to a stratified Victorian society was largely complete. All women were expected to remain within the private sphere of the

home and those who could not were allowed to pursue only those endeavors … considered natural extensions of a true woman's place—teaching, nursing, and domestic service. … Ironically, as the ideology of dynasty city became increasingly entrenched, the industrialized nation of British North America was simultaneously encouraging the complete division of public and private spheres and forcing a growing number of unskilled women into the factories as poorly paid wage labourers. (p. 68)

Aware that gender roles constrain the lives of men as well as women, some feminists assess problems that men can face in a world that defines "proper" masculinity in contradictory terms of fatherhood and worker/economic provider. Susan Halford (2006: 385) argues that the worlds of fatherhood and work no longer have to compete and that whatever challenges new information technologies pose (discussed later in this chapter), they may also hold the promise of breaking the divide between work and home, allowing workers to maintain greater contact with their families without impairing their work productivity.

Christina Hughes (2004) reminds readers that class background, cultural capital, and ethnicity may remain as persistent causes of self-limiting behaviours, of not wanting to trespass "a step too far" (p. 539). An example is how women from marginalized groups are likely to see all the ways that they "do not belong" in a given sector or workplace. Hughes also notes, however, that women can use their recognition of their class origins to remain grounded in principles that matter to them (p. 542). Avoiding the "step too far" is about retaining honesty and integrity; it's about not "selling out."

Issues regarding employment status, class, immigration, child labour, racism, and other forms of discrimination are also important feminist concerns.

Queer Theory Perspectives

Among the many important contributions of queer theory to the understanding of work and economy is a corrective to the traditional view that the home sphere is heterosexual. Even in a current context where most families require two incomes to get by, the division of family and work, based as it is on a gendered division of labour, makes the normative assumption that women work by choice, not out of necessity, and that all women have male "breadwinners" to support them. More generally, it is now well established that GLBT persons have to maintain constant awareness, called **discrimination management**, about how safe it is to reveal their sexuality in workplaces, where it is generally assumed that everyone is heterosexual (Adams et al. 2005: 215). In short, while their co-workers can freely discuss upcoming weddings, births, breakups, and so forth, GLBT workers face worries about homophobia in the workplace that limit expression and discussion of their lives and identities.

Current scholarship on GLBT workers also reveals unique problems when class-based vulnerability intersects with homophobia at work. Elizabeth McDermott's (2006) research shows that lesbians face not only sexism, but also homophobia in the workplace; she notes as well that working-class lesbians tend to work in environments where "being women does not make sense [to their co-workers] except in a heterosexual relationship" so they "masquerade" as heterosexual just to survive (p. 204). McDermott finds that working-class lesbians face greater stress on their psychological well-being than other lesbians do, or than straight women do as a result of sexism (p. 205).

Queer work and activism focused on work and the economy not only is concerned with GLBT people as workers, but also argues that as a marginalized group, the queer community is uniquely placed to offer serious social justice–oriented critiques of capitalism. Canadian sociologist Alan Sears, for example, cautions against getting too excited about marketing ploys that structure the GLBT community as an affluent

discrimination management
Individual efforts to prevent being targeted for discriminatory behaviours in the workplace.

"niche market" in which "our real diversity is obscured by the dominance of homoge-neous images [of buff, young, affluent, consumers]" (2005: 109). Instead, Sears argues that the queer community should retain and foster "the best of the liberationist poli-tics that emerged after Stonewall: the militancy, the breadth of vision and the transfor-mative commitments" (p. 109).

11.3 Problems of Work and Unemployment

Next, we examine unemployment and other problems associated with work. Problems of discrimination in the workplace based on gender, age, race and ethnicity, and sexual orientation appear in other chapters. Here, we discuss problems concerning child labour, health and safety hazards in the workplace, job dissatisfaction and alienation, work–family concerns, unemployment and underemployment, and labour unions and their struggles for workers' rights.

Child Labour: A Global Problem

Child labour involves children performing work that is hazardous, that interferes with a child's education, or that harms a child's health or physical, mental, spiritual, or moral development (U.S. Department of Labor 1995). In spring 2006, the B.C. leg-islature ruled that children could enter into paid labour at age 12, while in the rest of Canada the entry age remains set at 14. Even though virtually every country in the world has laws that limit or prohibit the extent to which children can be employed, child labour persists worldwide.

An estimated 250 million children between 5 and 14 work for a living (Human Rights Watch 2001). Child labourers work in factories, workshops, construction sites, mines, quarries, and fields, on deep-sea fishing boats, at home, and on the street. In Egypt, over one million children aged 7 to 12 work each year in cotton pest management. When they are perceived to be slowing down, they endure routine beatings with wooded switches by their supervisors. They face exposure to heat and pesticides ("Underage and Unprotected" 2001). Children typically earn the equivalent of $1 per day and work from 7:00 a.m. to 6:00 p.m. with one midday break, seven days a week.

Children as young as five or six also work in domestic service. In one Latin American country, an estimated 22 percent of all working children are employed as servants (International Labour Organization 2000). This form of child labour is difficult to mon-itor because of the hidden nature of the practice.

Children additionally number among the millions of people worldwide who work in **sweatshops**—work environments characterized by less-than-minimum wage pay, excessively long hours of work (often without overtime pay), unsafe or inhumane working conditions, abusive treatment of workers by employers, and the lack of worker organizations. Sweatshop conditions occur in a wide variety of industries, including garment production, manufacturing, mining, and agriculture. The dangerous condi-tions of sweatshops result in high rates of illness, injury, and death. The International Labour Organization (ILO) estimates 1.4 million workers worldwide die on the job or from occupational disease each year (*Multinational Monitor* 2000). In one tragic example of death resulting from sweatshop conditions, at least 53 workers, including 10 children, were burned to death in a fire at a Sagar Chowdury garment factory in Bangladesh (Hargis 2001). The fire, caused by an electrical short circuit, engulfed the entire factory with 900 workers who were *locked inside*. Local residents and fire-fighters broke open the locked gates of the building and rescued survivors.

child labour
Children performing work that is hazardous, that interferes with their education, or that harms their health or physical, mental, spiritual, or moral development.

sweatshops
Work environments characterized by less than minimum wage pay, excessively long hours of work often without overtime pay, unsafe or inhumane working conditions, abusive treatment of workers by employers, or the lack of worker organizations aimed at negotiating better work conditions.

Although Canada supports the ILO's International Programme for the Elimination of Child Labour (International Labour Organization 2006: 224), Alberta and British Columbia have both lowered the minimum age of employment to include young people aged 12 to 14 in sectors previously closed to people so young. The Saskatchewan Federation of Labour (2006: 2) notes that these changes "contravene the International Labour Organization (ILO's) Minimum Age Convention, 1973 (No. 138), which states that 'The minimum age … shall not be less than the age of completion of compulsory schooling and, in any case, shall not be less than 15 years.'"

Bonded labour—an extreme form of child labour—refers to the repayment of a debt through labour. Typically, an employer loans money to parents, who then give the employer their children as labourers to repay the debt. Sometimes the child is taken far away from the family to work; other times the child works in the same village and continues to live at home. The children are unable to work off the debt because of high interest rates, low wages, and wage deductions for meals, lodging, and mistakes made at work (U.S. Department of Labor 1995). Bonded labour is like slavery; a bonded worker is not free to leave the workplace. Between 10 and 20 million children in the world are forced to work as bonded labourers (Parker 1998). Bonded labour is most common in India, Nepal, Bangladesh, and Pakistan.

bonded labour
The repayment of a debt through labour.

Causes of Child Labour

Poverty, economic exploitation, social values, and lack of access to education are factors contributing to the persistence of child labour. One mother in Bangladesh whose 12-year-old daughter works up to 14 hours a day in a garment sweatshop explained: "Children shouldn't have to work. . . . But if she didn't, we'd go hungry" (Parker 1998: 47). The economic advantages to industries that profit from child labour perpetuate the practice. Traditional social values have also contributed to child labour. In the words of one employer in Pakistan who uses child labour, "Child labour is a tradition the West cannot understand and must not attempt to change" (Silvers 1996: 86). Finally, child labour results from failure to provide education to all children. The education system in Pakistan, for example, can accommodate about one-third of the country's school-aged children, leaving the remainder to join the child labour pool.

Child Prostitution and Trafficking

One of the worst forms of child labour is child prostitution and child trafficking. Although it is impossible to identify how prevalent child prostitution is, research estimates suggest that the problem is widespread. For example, surveys have identified 3000 child prostitutes in Montreal, 2930 in Athens, and up to 300 000 in the United States (Dorman 2001). Child prostitution, which occurs throughout the world, is particularly prevalent in Asia and Central and South America. In poor countries, families often sell the sexual services of their children in an attempt to get money. Some children are kidnapped or lured by traffickers with promises of employment—employment that in itself would constitute a form of human trafficking and illegal child labour—but end up in a brothel. An estimated one-quarter of all visitors using child prostitutes in Asia are North American businessmen or military personnel (Kennedy 1996).

A 2013 report from child labour specialist Mary E. Miller for the Washington State Department of Labour and Industries explains that the root causes of child labour, exploitation, and trafficking are manifold, but can be attributed principally to poverty caused by globalization, to inadequate wages for adults (meaning children have to make up the shortfall to cover family requirements), to the cheap labour demanded by desire for cheap consumer goods, to civil unrest and health crises that lead to large populations of orphaned children, to inadequate education, and to a lack of political interest in improving children's lives (Miller 2013).

Some critical work on the well-being of children takes a rather subtler approach to understanding trafficking and argues that trafficking has captured popular interest at the expense of other significant and even more pervasive forms of child suffering around the world. Julia O'Connell Davidson has argued, for example, that because the UN definitions of "trafficking" are so broad, they are capacious enough to allow outrage from both far right and far left ends of the political spectrum:

> Those whose interest in the phenomenon stems from a concern with human rights lobby to extend its application to all migrants who end up in forced labour and slavery-like situations 'no matter how people arrive in these conditions'[...] while those whose primary concern is to control and restrict immigration and/or limit governments' humanitarian obligations to migrants make a distinction between 'innocent' and 'deserving' victims of trafficking (VoTs) who exercised absolutely no choice or agency at any stage of the process, and 'undeserving' migrants deemed to have brought suffering upon themselves through their own actions and choices…(2011: 457)

For O'Connell Davidson, the vagueness of the UN Protocol, because it relies on adult notions of agency and choice, has no relevant application for children, who by definition have no capacity to consent to their movement (ibid). In other words, the policies we have do nothing for children; yet secondary to highly successful claims-making on the part of international lobbyists and activist organizations, "child trafficking" has become an uncontested, apparently agreed-upon moral problem. O'Connell Davidson explains that as a result it is almost unthinkable to challenge the idea of "child trafficking":

> To think of millions of children torn from their homes, then raped, beaten, brutalized and sexualized is emotionally moving. It can and does excite people to act on their behalf. Huge amounts of money, time and energy have been expended by governments, international agencies, child rights agencies and NGOs on combating child trafficking' politicians from across the political spectrum publicly condemn it [...] large companies and A-list celebrities lend their backing to campaigns against it; ordinary people donate money to help fight it. (p. 460)

And yet, O'Connell Davidson reminds us that in our outrage, our attention is diverted from the larger problems that children face in fleeing as "illegal" migrants—often with their families—from civil unrest, from economic turmoil, and from political and religious oppression in their home countries. She notes that immigration policies regularly place at risk those children who migrate in a state of flight and "can be exposed to many of the same risks and dangers that anti-'child-trafficking' campaigners identify as the harms of 'trafficking'—violence; sexual abuse; HIV infection; forcible separation from their family; incarceration in appalling conditions" (p. 462). In other words, she argues, immigration laws expose migrant children to all the same hazards that trafficking can do, and yet it is only trafficking that is the object of outrage, and government policy is overlooked as a root cause of children's suffering (ibid).

O'Connell Davidson explains that anti-trafficking discourses constitute the trafficked child as a "*real* child" that has been abused, and are "not about migration or immigration" (p. 463)—a view that O'Connell Davidson rejects. She holds UNICEF up for particular criticism for its 2004 statement that trafficking is much different and much worse than the illegal movement of people, often smuggled, across borders. Of the UNICEF position, O'Connell Davidson writes, "That an organization whose mission is to ensure 'special protection for the most disadvantaged children—victims of war, disasters, extreme poverty' [...] would engage in this kind of moral ranking of misery is extraordinary" (p. 464).

We have spent some significant time on this critical approach to thinking about the claims made about child trafficking not to discourage concern about the harms and abuses inflicted on children, but to encourage our students to avoid falling into the same trap of ranking the miseries that children can face when they live and work in inherently dangerous and unstable conditions, when their families are forced to flee from economic, political, and religious oppression, or when civil war throws their lives into disarray.

To try to understand child labour or child trafficking as separate from the political and economic conditions that are the precursors to these problems, or to highlight one form of suffering at the expense of another, is to fail these children on a level that is, quite literally, global.

Consequences of Child Labour

Child labourers are at risk for a variety of health problems, such as injuries, stunted growth, and many diseases. Child carpet weavers develop gnarled fingers from the repetitive work, and their spines are curved from sitting at looms all day. Young brick-workers breathe in dust from the dry bricks and sand, causing scarring of the lungs and early death. Child farmworkers are exposed to harmful pesticides. In rural areas, more child workers in agriculture die from pesticide poisonings than from all of the most common childhood diseases put together (UNICEF 2000). Child prostitutes are often physically abused by their pimps and customers, are at high risk for acquiring HIV and other sexually transmitted infections, and suffer the emotional scars of their exploitation. Child labourers are fed inadequate diets and endure harsh punishment from their employers. One girl who was forced into prostitution in Bangkok said: "One time I refused to sleep with a man and they slapped me, hit me with a cane and bashed my head against the wall. One of my friends tried to run away but unfortunately she was caught and very badly beaten" (Parker 1998: 42).

Child labour also increases poverty by depressing already low wages. Parker (1998: 48) explains:

> For every child who works, there may be an adult who cannot find a job. Children are usually paid less than adult workers—sometimes only one-third of what adults earn. As a result, adult workers' wages stay low or go down. When parents cannot find jobs, they are more likely to send their children to work. They have more children in the hope of increasing their income. Each generation of poor, uneducated child workers becomes the next generation of poor parents who must send their kids to work. Then the cycle of poverty and illiteracy continues.

Health and Safety Hazards in the Workplace

Accidents at work and hazardous working conditions contribute to illnesses, injuries, and deaths. Globally, an estimated 1.4 million workers die on the job or from occupational diseases every year (*Multinational Monitor* 2000). Some occupational health and safety hazards are attributed to wilful disregard of information and guidelines concerning worker safety. For example, the dangers of asbestos were known as early as 1918, when insurance companies stopped selling life insurance policies to asbestos workers. Nevertheless, the asbestos industry took little action until the 1960s. Of the half-million workers exposed to "significant doses of asbestos," 100 000 will die from lung cancer, 35 000 from mesothelioma, and 35 000 from asbestosis (Coleman 1994: 79).

In 1999, the Ontario Federation of Labour (OFL) launched a campaign to push the government for stricter limits on the exposure to toxic substances in workplaces and to demand that enough inspectors be put in place to ensure those limits are adhered to in all companies. In support of these demands, the OFL produced documents, obtained by the Canadian Auto Workers union through Freedom of Information requests, that showed a blatant disregard for the health and well-being of workers. For example, even though company and government officials knew that workers at the Holmes Insulation plant in Sarnia were being poisoned and exposed to amounts of asbestos that were far beyond the allowable limits, no one did anything to stop it. The OFL has compiled a top 12 dangerous workplace materials list: asbestos, benzene, cadmium, diesel exhaust emissions, fibreglass, formaldehyde, lead, metalworking fluids (used in coolants and lubricants in cutting, drilling, and machining metal), nickel, silica, styrene, and vinyl chloride (Simone 1999). Occupations related to insulating remain classified as the seventh most dangerous in Canada because of the dangers associated with long-term exposure to asbestos (Statistics Canada 1998).

In an average year in the 1970s, approximately 11 workers for every 100 000 workers died in the course of, or because of, their employment. In the 1990s, the fatality rate fell to seven deaths for every 100 000 workers. The three most dangerous occupations in Canada are, in order, the cutting and loading of rock, general mine labouring, and operating small engines (Statistics Canada 1998).

Workplace Illnesses and Injuries

Although the rate of workplace injuries that result in loss of activity and time-loss from work has been declining steadily over the last two decades, from 49 per 1000 workers in 1987 to 28 per 1000 workers in 1996, workplace injuries remain a significant hazard for Canadians. According to the most recently analyzed data on workplace injuries in Canada, approximately 630 000 Canadians were seriously injured on the job, having serious injuries that resulted in a limitation of their activities, including cognitive function (Wilkins and MacKenzie 2007: 1). In addition, an average of 465 on-the-job deaths occurred in each of the years from 2002 to 2004, with significantly greater risk for workers in the trades, workers who are male, and workers with annual income below $60 000 (ibid). According to the data gathered by Wilkins and MacKenzie, those who work as cooks and those who work as machinists are at significantly greater risk of sustaining a serious workplace injury than for any other occupation. As Figure 11.1 shows, even with significant improvements and failing rates of injury across the board—due largely to improvements in workplace safety regulations and practices—since 1994

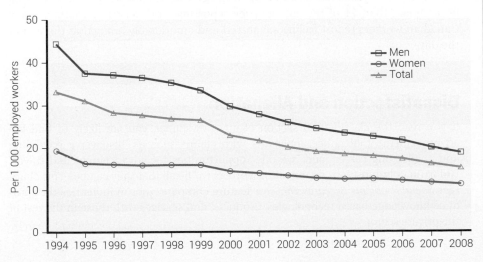

Figure 11.1 **Work-Related Injuries, by Gender, per 1000 Employed Workers, 1994–2008**

SOURCE: Statistics Canada. "Indicators of Well-being in Canada: Work and Work Related Injuries." 2011. http://www4.hrsdc.gc.ca/.3ndic.1t.4r@-eng.jsp?iid=20

Chapter 11 Work and Unemployment

the rate of workplace injury for men has remained at roughly double the rate for women whether in the white-collar or trades sectors. The 2011 Statistics Canada workplace safety report notes that as of "2008, men experienced a higher rate of injury (18.8 cases per 1,000 employed men) than did women (11.2 cases per 1,000 employed women)."

The most common types of workplace illnesses that develop in white-collar workers are associated with repeated trauma, such as carpal tunnel syndrome (a wrist disorder that can cause numbness, tingling, and severe pain), tendonitis (inflammation of the tendons), lower-back injury, and noise-induced hearing loss. Such disorders—referred to by a number of terms, including **cumulative trauma disorders**, **repetitive strain disorders**, and **repeated trauma disorders**—are muscle, tendon, vascular, and nerve injuries that result from repeated or sustained actions or exertions of different body parts. Cumulative trauma disorders are classified as illnesses, not as injuries, because they are not sudden, instantaneous traumatic events.

Shift work, in which workers change from one of three sets of eight-hour shifts to another on a rotating basis, holds significantly higher risk for injury than does work in which employees work a regular daytime schedule (Wilkins and MacKenzie, 2007: 10). Shift work tends to be very hard on workers' cardiovascular health, contributes to the development of obesity secondary to disrupted eating patterns, and has been associated with a greater risk of on-the-job injury due to tiredness. Overtime work also significantly increases the risk of injury to workers who are regularly asked to work beyond their regular shifts (ibid).

Job Stress and Chronic Fatigue

Another work-related health hazard is job stress and chronic fatigue. To measure work stress, the 1996–97 National Population Health Survey used a scale composed of 12 questions describing working conditions that were answered on a five-point scale of agree or disagree. The minimum score on the scale was 0 and the maximum was 45; "high stress" was defined as a score of 30 or higher. Using this scale, the survey found that more women reported high work stress levels than men did in every age category, with women aged 20 to 24 almost three times as likely to report high work stress as the average Canadian worker. Notable differences in high work stress also existed among persons in different types of households. Single parents were twice as likely as Canadians in couple relationships without children to report high work stress (Health Canada 1999). Although Canadian workers report working fewer hours than 21 of the 25 countries reporting workweek information, many Canadian workers report feeling exhausted and emotionally drained at the end of the day.

Dissatisfaction and Alienation

If you read the classified ad section of any newspaper, you are likely to find job advertisements that entice applicants with claims such as "discover a rewarding and challenging career" and "we offer opportunities for advancement and travel." Unfortunately, most jobs do not allow workers to "be all that they can be." This chapter's *Social Problems Research Up Close* feature compares jobs in industries that produce knowledge-based technologies, products, and services with those in the rest of the private sector.

cumulative trauma disorders
The most common type of workplace injury; it includes muscle, tendon, vascular, and nerve injuries that result from repeated or sustained actions or exertions of different body parts. Jobs that are associated with high rates of upper body cumulative stress disorders include computer programming, manufacturing, meat packing, poultry processing, and clerical or office work.

repetitive strain disorders (repeated trauma disorders)
The most common types of workplace illnesses include muscle, tendon, vascular, and nerve injuries that result from repeated or sustained actions or exertions of different body parts. Jobs that are associated with high rates of upper body repeated trauma disorders include computer programming, manufacturing, meat packaging, poultry processing, and clerical/office work.

shift work
The use of a 24-hour schedule to create workdays of three eight-hour shifts. Some workers have "split shifts" in which their eight hours are interrupted by unpaid periods of over an hour, effectively extending the workers' days to 10 hours or more. Split shifts are common in the hospitality sector.

Social Problems *Research Up Close*

Workplace and Employee Survey: Better Jobs in the New Economy?

Sample and Methods

The 1999 Workplace and Employee Survey (WES), conducted by Statistics Canada, compared jobs in industries that produce knowledge-based technologies, products, and services with those in the rest of the private sector. The WES covers the private sector (i.e., all industries with the exception of farming, fishing, hunting, trapping and public administration). Within this study, the term "knowledge-based industries" refers to "industries that spend a relatively large amount of resources on research and development and have professionals, such as scientists and engineers, as a substantial proportion of their workforce" (Statistics Canada 2002). In addition, it is limited to jobs in research and development-based firms that produce knowledge-based technologies, products, and services. Included here would be most, although not all, industries within the information and communication technology sector, including telecommunications, data processing, and computer systems design, as well as the pharmaceutical and chemical manufacturing industries.

Within this study, industries were classified into five mutually exclusive groups: (1) knowledge-based in the goods sector; (2) knowledge-based in the service sector; (3) other goods producing; (4) retail trade and consumer services; and (5) other professional and other services. The study examined job characteristics such as work hours, hourly wages, pension coverage, stock options, personal and family support programs, teamwork, performance appraisal, grievance systems, and job satisfaction.

Findings and Conclusions

Workers in knowledge-based industries receive relatively high wages, have good fringe benefits, and often profit from fitness and recreation services as well as employee assistance programs. However, many work fairly long hours, and those employed in the service sector rarely have access to a formal grievance system in their workplace …

1. *Workers in knowledge-based industries receive relatively high wages.* On average, employees in knowledge-based industries earned $24.09 per hour in 1999, 32 percent more than the $18.19 received by employees in other industries. The wage gap between knowledge-based industries and other industries was 14 percent for university graduates, compared with 31 percent for other workers with some postsecondary education. Employees in knowledge-based workplaces earn relatively high wages for a number of reasons. They are generally better educated than other workers and tend to be employed in larger establishments, which generally pay higher wages. They may also receive higher wages to compensate for the relatively high costs of living in larger areas, where such workplaces tend to be located. Many of these employees are in high-paying professional occupations such as engineering and science. Lastly, some, such as university graduates, could receive higher wages as compensation for relatively long hours …

2. *Workers often have stock options.* Employees in knowledge-based industries were not necessarily better covered by a registered pension plan than other workers. For instance, 40 percent of employees in service-producing, knowledge-based workplaces had a pension plan in 1999, compared with 48 percent of their counterparts in professional and other services. However, 31 percent of employees in service-producing knowledge-based workplaces received stock options, five times the proportion (6 percent) in professional and other services. On average, employees in knowledge-based industries were more likely to be covered by life or disability insurance, supplemental medical insurance, and dental plans. They were also more likely to have profit-sharing plans …

3. *Employees often benefit from fitness services and assistance programs.* Roughly 25 percent of employees in knowledge-based industries were in workplaces that provided fitness and recreation services (on- or off-site). The corresponding numbers for other goods-producing industries, professional and other services, and retail trade and consumer services were 15 percent, 17 percent and 5 percent, respectively. In addition, 40 percent of workers in knowledge-based workplaces were offered employee assistance programs (counselling, substance abuse control, financial assistance, legal aid). Such

(continued)

programs were available to 35 percent, 29 percent and 8 percent of employees in professional and other services, other goods-producing industries, and retail trade and consumer services, respectively …

4. *University graduates in knowledge-based industries work fairly long hours.* Compared to their counterparts in the rest of the economy, university graduates employed full time in knowledge-based industries worked either longer hours or more hours of unpaid overtime. Their total workweek, including unpaid overtime, averaged 46.6 hours per week. This was at least two hours more than in professional and other services (44.3) or in retail trade and consumer services (44.4) …

5. *In the service sector, few have access to a formal grievance system.* In 1999, 20 percent of employees in knowledge-based industries were unionized. This compares with 13 percent in consumer services and retail trade, and 33 percent in professional and other services or in other goods-producing industries. However, there were substantial differences within the knowledge-based sector. About 14 percent of employees in service-producing workplaces were unionized, compared with

25 percent in goods-producing workplaces. As a result, only 18 percent of workers in service-producing, knowledge-based industries reported having access to a formal grievance system such as a labour-management committee or an outside arbitrator. In contrast, access to such a system was reported by 46 percent of those in goods-producing, knowledge-based industries, 41 percent in professional and other services, and 38 percent in other goods-producing industries …

6. *Performance appraisal is more frequent in knowledge-based industries.* At least 65 percent of employees in knowledge-based industries had their job performance evaluated through a standard process, compared with only 45 percent to 58 percent of workers in other industries. Furthermore, employees in knowledge-based industries were almost twice as likely to have their level of pay or benefits directly affected by job evaluation results. Thus, work evaluation was more systematic in the knowledge-based sector than in other industries.

SOURCE: Adapted from Statistics Canada. "Workplace and Employee Survey: Better jobs in the new economy?" 1999, Catalogue 11-001, July 18, 2002, http://www .statcan.gc.ca/daily-quotidien/020718/dq020718b-eng.htm

alienation
The concept used by Karl Marx to describe the condition when workers feel powerlessness and meaninglessness as a result of performing repetitive, isolated work tasks. Alienation involves becoming estranged from one's work, the products one creates, other human beings, or one's self; it also refers to powerlessness and meaninglessness experienced by students in traditional, restrictive educational institutions.

Factors that contribute to job satisfaction include income, prestige, a feeling of accomplishment, autonomy, a sense of being challenged by the job, opportunities to be creative, congenial co-workers, the feeling that one is making a contribution, fair rewards (pay and benefits), promotion opportunities, and job security (Bavendam 2000; Robie et al. 1998). These factors often overlap—for example, high-paying jobs tend to have more prestige, be more autonomous, provide more benefits, and permit greater creativity. However, many jobs lack these qualities, leaving workers dissatisfied. Moreover, many Canadians are worried that they may lose their jobs in the next few years. In 2001, 20 percent of Canadians told pollsters that they were concerned that someone in their household would lose a job (Bricker and Greenspon 2001: 18).

One form of job dissatisfaction is a feeling of **alienation**. A high division of labour and specialization of work roles characterize work in industrialized societies. As a result, workers' tasks are repetitive and monotonous, involving little or no creativity. Limited to specific tasks by their work roles, workers are unable to express and utilize their full potential—intellectual, emotional, and physical. According to Marx, when workers are merely cogs in a machine they become estranged from their work, the product they create, other human beings, and themselves. Marx called this estrangement "alienation."

Alienation usually has four components: powerlessness, meaninglessness, normlessness, and self-estrangement. Powerlessness results from working in an environment in which workers have little or no control over the decisions that affect their work. Meaninglessness results when workers do not find fulfillment in their work. Workers may experience normlessness if workplace norms are unclear or conflicting.

For example, many companies that have family leave policies informally discourage workers from using them, or workplaces that officially promote nondiscrimination in reality practise discrimination. Finally, a feeling of self-estrangement stems from the workers' inability to realize their full human potential in their work roles and from a lack of connections to others. In general, traditional "women's work" is more alienating than "men's work" (Ross and Wright 1998). "Homemaking exposes women to routine, unfulfilling, isolated work; and part-time employment exposes them to routine, unfulfilling work, with little decision-making autonomy" (p. 343).

Work–Family Concerns

As a result of a combination of social forces including economic pressures, changing gender ideologies, improved contraception, increased life expectancy, and the marked trend toward smaller families, the dual-earner family has become the "new norm" in Canada (Table 11.1). Families in which there are two earners raising children have significantly higher earnings than those not raising children. There is an obvious reason for the differences in earnings between couples not raising children and those with children for whom they are financially responsible. First, the age group with dependent children tends to be at the height of their earning potential, while those without children are likely to be younger and not yet ready to have kids, or much older and finished raising children. Both the younger and older cohorts have lower average earnings, either because they are at entry stages of their careers, or have reduced their household revenues to retirement sources of income and/or part-time work. It is important to note here that families with dependent children have significantly higher costs than those who have not yet had children or have finished raising them. Moreover, the quality of life for dual-earner families with dependent children can be much more stressful than for childless families. Understandably, for many employed parents, balancing work and family demands is a daily challenge. When Hochschild (1997) asked a sample of employed parents, "Overall, how well do you feel you can balance the demands of your work and family?" only 9 percent said, "very well" (pp. 199–200). (Work–family concerns are also discussed in Chapters 5, 7, and 10.)

Table 11.1 *Average Income after Tax by Economic Family Types, 2007–2011*

	2007	2008	2009	2010	2011
	\$ constant 2011				
Economic families[1], two people or more	77 500	78 500	78 700	78 800	79 600
Elderly families[2]	58 700	58 400	58 000	57 900	57 700
Married couples only	57 100	56 100	56 600	57 500	56 500
All other elderly families	64 200	67 200	63 500	59 100	62 300
Non-elderly families[3]	80 900	82 100	82 700	83 000	84 000
Married couples only	75 500	75 600	76 200	75 300	76 100
No earner	38 000	33 900	44 800	41 000	44 000
One earner	60 800	59 900	61 100	60 900	64 100
Two earners	83 600	84 800	83 900	82 800	83 300

(*Continued*)

Table 11.1 *Average Income after Tax by Economic Family Types, 2007–2011* (continued)

	2007	2008	2009	2010	2011
	$ constant 2011				
Two parent families with children[4]	88 300	89 000	89 000	91 400	93 700
No earner	31 300	29 600	33 100	52 900[E]	36 700
One earner	63 300	62 900	63 900	63 800	71 100
Two earners	87 600	89 100	89 800	92 300	94 100
Three or more earners	110 200	111 900	109 600	111 800	114 300
Married couples with other relatives	109 000	114 500	115 800	113 800	114 600
Lone-parent families[4]	45 000	46 000	48 000	48 200	45 100
Male lone-parent families	56 200	56 900	58 500	58 600	55 100
Female lone-parent families	42 500	43 500	45 800	46 100	43 000
No earner	19 300	21 900	21 100	22 900	21 000
One earner	42 300	41 100	45 000	46 600	41 400
Two or more earners	58 100	61 000	65 600	62 800	60 000
All other non-elderly families	67 300	69 900	68 400	66 100	67 200
Unattached individuals	32 000	32 500	32 900	33 000	31 400
Elderly male	33 400	34 500	34 000	34 800	34 400
Non-earner	29 700	32 000	31 600	30 500	29 100
Earner	46 000	44 100	45 100	48 600	49 500
Elderly female	27 700	28 200	29 800	29 300	29 700
Non-earner	26 600	27 100	28 200	27 000	27 700
Earner	36 500	35 900	41 000	43 300	40 300
Non-elderly male	35 100	36 100	35 000	36 300	33 500
Non-earner	14 400	14 000	12 700	12 700	12 800
Earner	39 000	40 400	39 600	41 100	38 100
Non-elderly female	29 700	29 600	31 400	30 200	28 600
Non-earner	14 600	15 000	16 700	15 100	15 000
Earner	33 700	33 800	35 000	34 600	32 900

[E]use with caution.

NOTE: Average income after tax is total income, which includes government transfers, less income tax.

[1]An economic family is a group of individuals sharing a common dwelling unit who are related by blood, marriage (including common-law relationships) or adoption.

[2]Families in which the major income earner is 65 years of age and over.

[3]Families in which the major income earner is less than 65 years of age.

[4]With children less than 18 years of age.

SOURCE: Statistics Canada. "Average income after tax by economic family types (2007 to 2011)." CANISM Table 202-0603. Catalogue no. 75-202X. http://www.statcan.gc.ca/tables-tableaux/sum-som/l01/cst01/famil21a-eng.htm

Unemployment and Underemployment

The International Labour Organization (2001) reports that one-third of the world's workforce is unemployed or underemployed. Poor countries tend to suffer high rates of unemployment. For example, recent unemployment rates in South Africa and Lesotho (a southern African country) were 23 percent and 42 percent, respectively (International Labour Organization 2001).

Measures of **unemployment** consider an individual to be unemployed if he or she is currently without employment, is actively seeking employment, and is available for employment. Unemployment figures do not include "discouraged workers," who have given up on finding a job. **Underemployment** is a broader term that includes discouraged workers, and those working part time but who wish to work full time. For example, although the overall size of the Canadian labour force has grown significantly in the past three decades, much of the growth has been in part-time and self employment, neither of which provides benefits or pensions. In 1998, about 30 percent of adult women working part-time were doing so involuntarily because they could not obtain full-time employment (Statistics Canada 1999). By 2009 the number of women in part-time work who wished to work full time had improved somewhat, dropping to 25.9 percent, but because women tend to take on higher child-care burdens and often receive less financial support from family to go to school, women still represent 70 percent of the part-time workforce, often paying significantly into their education costs (Ferrao 2010: 13).

Types and Causes of Unemployment

Unemployment can be either discriminatory or structural. **Discriminatory unemployment** involves high rates of unemployment among particular social groups, such as racial and ethnic minorities and women (see Chapters 7 and 8). **Structural unemployment** exists when there are not enough jobs available for those who want them. Structural unemployment is the result of social factors rather than personal inadequacies of the unemployed or discrimination.

For example, unemployment can result from **corporate downsizing**—the corporate practice of discharging large numbers of employees. Simply put, the term *downsizing* is a euphemism for mass firing of employees (Caston 1998). Another cause of unemployment is **job exportation**, the relocation of Canadian jobs to other countries where products can be produced more cheaply. Job exportation has had a particularly profound effect on garment workers and the Canadian garment industry over the past decade (Yanz and Jeffcott 1997). **Automation**, or the replacement of human labour with machinery and equipment, is another feature of the work landscape that contributes to unemployment. For example, recorded phone trees, automated teller machines (ATMs), automatic car washes, and assembly-line robots do jobs that otherwise would be performed by workers.

Because of the changing nature of work, displaced workers may find themselves unable to obtain adequate employment. Consider, for example, that since 1989 the number of employed clerical workers in Canada has dropped from 2.2 million to 1.9 million while the number of manufacturing jobs has declined from 1.8 million to 1.7 million. Between 2004 and 2008, the manufacturing sector saw another 322 000 job losses—and, because of the recession, workers laid off from their manufacturing jobs were likely to struggle to find employment elsewhere (Bernard 2009: 1).

Industrial Food Production and Agricultural Workers

One of the few places in North America in which industrial manufacturing and processing remains a powerful employer is in food production; however, even there, it

unemployment
The unemployed are those who want and are able to work, but who have no work at present. For statistical purposes, Statistics Canada defines the unemployed in these ways: (1) as people who did not work in the labour market during the survey reference week (but may have done housework, etc.); (2) as people who were available for work and actively looked for it in the past four weeks; (3) as people laid off for 26 weeks or fewer and expecting to be recalled by their employer; or (4) as people who were waiting for new jobs to begin within four weeks.

underemployment
Employment in a job that is underpaid; is not commensurate with one's skills, experience, or education; or involves working fewer hours than desired.

discriminatory unemployment
High rates of unemployment among particular social groups, such as racial and ethnic minorities and women.

structural unemployment
Exists when there are not enough jobs available for those who want them; unemployment that results from structural variables, such as government and business downsizing, job exportation, automation, a reduction in the number of new and existing businesses, an increase in the number of people looking for jobs, and a recessionary economy where fewer goods are purchased and, therefore, fewer employees are needed.

corporate downsizing
The corporate practice of discharging large numbers of employees. Simply put, the term *downsizing* is a euphemism for mass firing of employees.

job exportation
The relocation of jobs to other countries where products can be produced more cheaply.

automation
A type of technology in which self-operated machines accomplish tasks formerly done by workers; develops as a society moves toward industrialization and becomes more concerned with the mass production of goods.

is mostly the mega-corporations in industrial farming and meat packing that benefit, while the well-being of small farmers and of workers in food processing plants is imperiled.

In "The Chain Never Stops," an essay originally published in 2001 and reprinted in 2013 because of its continued importance, Eric Schlosser notes that the meat processing industry is the most dangerous in America:

> The meatpacking industry not only has the highest injury rate, but also has the highest rate of serious injury—more than 5 times the national average, as measured in lost workdays. ...about 40 000 meatpacking workers are injured on the job every year. But the actual number is probably higher. The meatpacking industry has a well-documented history of discouraging injury reports, falsifying injury data, and putting injured workers back on the job quickly to minimize the reporting of lost workdays. (2013: 486)

Reporting on working in environments that are saturated in blood, where workers move animals that weigh several hundred pounds on swift chain-conveyors, and in which the primary tools of the workers include chainsaws and stun-hammers to kill the cattle, it is no surprise that Schlosser reports injuries such as entirely lost limbs (to grinders and chainsaws) or deaths caused by slipping into the strike zone of the stun-hammers. On top of all this, however, Schlosser reminds us that workers are often not English-speaking, and are inclined to accept terribly low hourly wages of $9.50 per hour because in their home country of Mexico their wages would have hovered around $7 per day (p. 487). In other words, the workers are highly vulnerable to dangerous and poorly compensated labour conditions: "They tend to be poor, vulnerable and fearful. From the industry's point of view, they are ideal workers: cheap, largely interchangeable, and disposable" (ibid).

In Canada, major U.S. meatpackers like Cargill are moving in. Cargill has two plants in Canada, one in High River, Alberta, where they process 4500 head of cattle every day, and one in Guelph, Ontario, where they process 1500 head of cattle every day. The two plants account for 55 percent of all the beef processed in Canada (www .cargill.ca).

Much of the danger, and the environmental threat, of the meatpacking industry could, however, be removed if consumers were willing to pay more for their meats. Switching to vegetarianism might be a solution, except that it requires the use of chemical fertilizers if we are not going to grow food in conjunction with ranching and animal husbandry. Therefore, if what we want is a complete ecosystem, not dependent on chemical fertilizers or the hazards of industrial food production, we should start finding ways to support our small ranchers, organic farmers, and small butchers. In these local ways, we can offer safe and clean environments for animals, for soil protection, and we can support farmers when we buy directly from them through community supported agriculture (CSAs), food co-ops, and farmers' markets. Wages go up for food producers, and work conditions are made safer when we buy from smaller producers who retain autonomy in their work.

In Canada, we can also improve the lives of agricultural food production workers if we follow the recommendations from the organization Justice for Migrant Workers (J4MW), developed in the aftermath of a horrific late-winter crash that killed 11 Peruvian migrant workers who had come to southwestern Ontario to work in a poultry processing facility. J4MW has set up four main demands for migrant workers: to have "the right to Employment Insurance, the right to apply for citizenship in Canada, the right to be treated with respect and dignity, and the right to appeal" (quoted in McKarney 2013). Though the first of J4MW's demands is based on false information, if the workers who died in the crash had, for example, had the right to be treated with respect and dignity, they may have refused to be transported to and from work in an unsafe vehicle and might therefore still be alive today.

That said, McKarney, an anthropologist from the University of Western Ontario, was careful to distinguish between individual farmers, who may treat workers very well, and a system that does not value or adequately protect migrant farm workers, and argues that a media and activist focus on "bad farmers" does a serious disservice to those more typical farmers who treat workers well and may even become a close friend and part of a larger social support network to those workers, as in the case cited in McKarney's field notes from a 2012 interview:

> One story was with Donald's brother in law's church. One of the workers attended the church, and one of his brother's workers had died and something happened a year later with his house back in Jamaica. So the church raised money and his brother in law went down in the off-season to Jamaica and helped rebuild a house for the worker's wife, who was now by herself. (p. 59)

For McKarney, then, the media fascination with catastrophic events, and the demands of an activist organization like J4MW (which inaccurately suggests migrant workers who arrive to Canada under the Seasonal Agricultural Worker Program do not receive employment insurance) make things worse "by making growers reluctant to talk, isolating them further and perpetuating a status quo in which key players have tuned out and turned inward in the face of constant, arguably oversimplified criticism" (pp. 57–58). In other words, while we should definitely be mindful of the challenges that migrant farm workers face, we can do better by them when we engage with them and with their employers respectfully, without oversimplifying the conditions of their work, or our role as consumers in those conditions.

Effects of Unemployment and Underemployment

The personal consequences of unemployment (and in some cases, underemployment) include anxiety, depression, alcohol abuse, and lowered self-esteem and confidence (Feather 1990; Liem and Liem 1990; Tremblay et al. 2002). Unemployment has consequences for families and communities as well, and has been linked to increased family violence (Reidmann et al. 2003). Unemployment may also mean losing supplemental health-care benefits for workers and their families, and underemployed individuals rarely get health-care benefits from their employers. Unemployment and underemployment result in a decline in an individual's standard of living.

11.4 Strategies for Action: Responses to Workers' Concerns

Government, private business, human rights organizations, and labour organizations play important roles in responding to the concerns of workers. Next, we look at responses to child labour, efforts to strengthen labour, workforce development and job-creation programs, responses to worker health and safety concerns, work–family policies and programs, public child-care assistance for working families, the workplace and family life, and challenges to corporate power and globalization.

Responses to Child Labour

The International Programme on the Elimination of Child Labour has been working to remove child labourers from oppressive work conditions, provide them with education, and provide their parents with jobs or income. From its beginning in 1992, the program grew from six participating countries to more than 200 participating countries in 2000 (Human Rights Watch 2001).

In 1999, 174 nations adopted the Convention on the Worst Forms of Child Labour, and by September 2000, 37 countries had ratified the convention (Human Rights Watch 2001). This move represents a global consensus to end the most severe forms of child labour, and the convention requires nations to take immediate measures to abolish child slavery, trafficking, debt bondage, child prostitution and pornography, and forced labour.

Human rights organizations, such as the International Labour Organization, UNICEF, and the Child Labour Coalition, are also active in the campaign against child labour. Another organization, the Bonded Labour Liberation Front (BLLF), has led the fight against bonded and child labour in Pakistan, freeing 30 000 adults and children from brick kilns, carpet factories, and farms, and placing 11 000 children in its own primary school system (Silvers 1996). However, employers in Pakistan have threatened workers with violence if they talk with "the abolitionists" or possess "illegal communist propaganda." Human rights activists campaigning against child labour have also been victims of threats and violence.

The United Nations International Children's Emergency Fund recommends that national and international corporations adopt codes of conduct guaranteeing that neither they nor their subcontractors will employ children in conditions that violate their rights (UNICEF 1997). Some industries, including rug and clothing manufacturers, use labels and logos to indicate that child labourers do not make their products. The Fair Labor Association (FLA) involves six leading apparel and footwear companies. These companies voluntarily take part in a monitoring system to inspect their overseas factories and require them to meet minimum labour standards, such as not requiring workers to work more than 60 hours a week. However, critics point out a number of problems with the FLA, including (1) standards are too low (allows below-poverty wages and excessive overtime); (2) only 10 percent of companies' factories must be monitored yearly; (3) companies can influence which factories are inspected and who does the inspection; and (4) the FLA does not uphold workers' right to organize (Benjamin 1998). Critics charge that companies use their participation in FLA as a marketing tool. Once "certified" by FLA, companies can sew a label into their products saying they were made under fair working conditions.

Pressure from students and other opponents of child and sweatshop labour along with consumer boycotts of products made by child and sweatshop labour have resulted in some improvements. Factories that make goods for companies such as Nike and Gap have cut back on child labour, use less dangerous chemicals, and require fewer employees to work 80-hour weeks (Greenhouse 2000; Klein 2000). At many factories, supervisors have stopped hitting employees, have improved ventilation, and have stopped requiring workers to obtain permission to use the toilet. But improvements are not widespread and oppressive forms of labour continue throughout the world. According to the National Labour Committee, two areas where "progress seems to grind to a halt" are efforts to form unions and efforts to achieve wage increases (Greenhouse 2000).

Efforts to eliminate child labour cannot succeed unless the impoverished conditions that contribute to its practice are alleviated. A living minimum wage must be established for adult workers so they will not need to send their children to work. We should also keep in mind that until relatively recently in Canada, it was common for children to work to contribute to the family income. Summer "holidays" are a holdover from the need to dismiss children to work on their family farms in the growing and harvest season; prior to the mid-twentieth century many children did not attend school beyond the ninth grade because they needed to help contribute to their family income.

We need also to consider our own role in the global market's reliance on cheap goods imported from faraway places. From a conflict perspective, our own interest in getting a "bargain" is sustained from a position of power in which our own children are protected against early and dangerous labour while the children of distant countries make cheap commodities for us. Often, these commodities are toys we give to our own children. Structural-functionalists, meanwhile, may argue that child labour serves a positive purpose now in developing areas in the same way that it served a positive purpose for Canadian families from our founding to the mid-twentieth century: providing income and a better standard of living to families. In thinking about these views, we should consider whether the threat to the well-being of child labourers is adequately set off by the gains for their families (often, the answer is no), and whether we really need all those cheap goods that we would be loath to see our own children labouring to manufacture.

Efforts to Strengthen Labour

International norms established by the United Nations and the International Labour Organization declare the right of workers to organize, negotiate with management, and strike (Human Rights Watch 2000). In European countries, labour unions are generally strong (Mishel et al. 2001). However, in many less developed countries and countries undergoing economic transition, workers and labour unions struggle to have a voice. A survey of 113 countries by the International Confederation of Free Trade Unions (ICFTU) found that both corporations and governments repressed union efforts ("Global Labor Repression" 2000). Among the survey's findings are these:

- in 1999, Colombia was the most dangerous place for trade unionists with 76 of 140 trade unionists who were victims of targeted killings, or were "disappeared,"
- nearly 3000 people were arrested for attempting to organize workers' unions,
- 1500 were injured, beaten, or tortured,
- at least 5800 were harassed for being involved in trade union activities,
- another 700 trade unionists received death threats,
- about 12 000 active trade union members were unfairly dismissed or refused reinstatement, in their workplaces, and,
- governments successfully repressed at least 140 strikes or demonstrations, sometimes with the aid of employers.

In spite of these repressive actions, labour unions have played an important role in fighting for fair wages and benefits, healthy and safe work environments, and other forms of worker advocacy. In Canada, about 3.7 million paid workers belonged to unions during the first half of 2000, with workers in Newfoundland the most likely to be union members (with just under 40 percent of all paid employees union members). In that year, the average hourly earnings of unionized workers exceeded those of nonunionized workers for both full-time and part-time workers (Statistics Canada 2002). Almost all of Canada's nurses and teachers, about one-third of Canada's white-collar workers, half of Canada's professional and managerial workers, and 4 in 10 blue-collar workers were union members (Statistics Canada 1998; Statistics Canada 2002). Although union representation of workers has remained relatively high at about one-third of all workers in Canada over the last decade, union representation is nonetheless in slow, steady decline, as we see in Figure 11.2. Data acquired since the modest spike in union membership in 2010 indicate that total union coverage in Canada continues to hover around 30 percent, and we do not expect to see coverage rates like those of the twentieth century again.

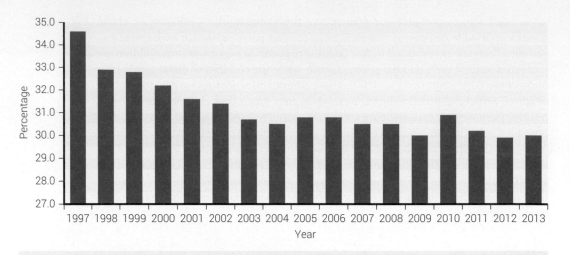

Figure 11.2 *Union Coverage Rate in Canada, 1997–2013*

SOURCE: *Union Coverage in Canada, 2013*, http://www.labour.gc.ca/eng/resources/info/publications/unon_coverage/union_coverage.shtml. Employment and Social Development Canada, 2014. Reproduced with the permission of the Minister of Employment and Social Development Canada, 2014.

Canadian women workers were less likely than their male counterparts to be unionized, but unionization among women has risen since 1997, while union membership for men has dropped significantly in the same time period. By 2012, just under 33 percent of women workers were unionized, while men's membership in unions now hovers around 30 percent. In 1999, women accounted for 46 percent of all union members in Canada (Ghalam 2000: 106). The growth in unionization among women stems from several factors, including "most notably, their growing presence in the heavily unionized public sector" (Ghalam 2000: 106). Work traditionally done by men in the manufacturing sector has, by contrast, been in decline for the same time period. As more men enter into work in areas not traditionally unionized, we see their union membership numbers decline. Trades generally work through guilds that help to protect individual contractors and small business owners, and professional work outside the public sector is rarely unionized.

Workforce Development and Job-Creation Programs

The International Labour Organization estimated in 2001 that over 500 million new jobs were needed by 2010 to accommodate new entrants to the workforce and to reduce current unemployment levels by half. Developing a workforce and creating jobs involves far-reaching efforts, including those designed to improve health and health care, alleviate poverty and malnutrition, develop infrastructures, and provide universal education.

In Canada, workforce development programs have provided a variety of services, including assessment to evaluate skills and needs, career counselling, job search assistance, basic education, occupational training (classroom and on-the-job), public employment, job placement, and stipends or other support services for child care and transportation assistance (Levitan et al. 1998). Numerous studies have looked at the effectiveness of workforce development programs. In general, "evaluations indicate that employment and training programs enhance the earnings and employment of participants, although the effects vary by service population, are often modest because of brief training durations and the inherent difficulty of alleviating long-term deficiencies, and are not always cost effective" (Levitan et al. 1998: 199). However, funding for federal job training programs is insufficient to reach more than a small fraction of the workforce, and even those who complete training and retraining programs do not always find new jobs at comparable wages.

Efforts to prepare high school students for work include the establishment of technical and vocational high schools and school-to-work programs. School-to-work programs involve partnerships between business, labour, government, education, and community organizations that help prepare high school students for jobs (Leonard 1996). Although the programs vary, in general they allow high school students to explore different careers and provide job skill training and work-based learning experiences, often with pay (Bassi and Ludwig 2000). Nevertheless, for many young Canadians employment continues to be elusive, with "McJobs"—dead-end jobs in the service industry—the only option.

Regardless of the ebbs and flows in government efforts to create jobs, we must consider where the jobs are being created. The Canadian economy can be described as a **split labour market** (or dual economy) because it is made up of two labour markets. The *primary labour market* refers to jobs that are stable, economically rewarding, and associated with benefits. These jobs are usually occupied by the most educated and trained individuals (e.g., a corporate attorney, teacher, or accountant). The *secondary labour market* refers to jobs that involve low pay, no security, few benefits, and little chance for advancement. These workers often lack a union to protect them and are more likely to be dissatisfied with their jobs than workers in the primary labour market.

Responses to Worker Health and Safety Concerns

Over the past few decades, health and safety conditions in the workplace have improved because of media attention, regulations, demands by unions for change, and more white-collar jobs. Canadian governments have expanded workplace protection through human rights laws, which prohibit discrimination in hiring, promotion, and working conditions, and workers' compensation programs, which pay partial lost wages to sick or injured workers. Although corporations may complain that there is too much interference and regulation of the workplace, the state has a long history in Canada of exercising its interest in promoting better health for its population through improved working conditions. Krahn and Lowe explain that it is to laws developed in the late nineteenth century that we owe the protection of children against dangerous labour when they are underage, but the same laws, which grouped women and children together, had the effect of removing women from paid labour in factories (2002: 311).

The *Canada Labour Code*, in 1986, established the right of workers to be told about the potential hazards of workplace materials, with this "right to know" buttressed by the national Workplace Hazardous Materials Information System. Worker health and safety committees are also a standard feature of companies in many industrialized countries and are mandatory in most of Europe. These committees are authorized to inspect workplaces and cite employers for violations of health and safety regulations. Krahn and Lowe (2002: 311) remind us that "all of these approaches to dealing with health and safety issues—standard setting and enforcement by the state, collective bargaining between unions and employers, and the no-fault compensation system— offer little room for direct involvement on the part of workers who are most directly affected by unsafe and unhealthy working conditions."

Maximizing the health and safety of workers involves more than implementing, monitoring, and enforcing regulations. Increasingly, businesses and corporations are promoting workers' health (and corporate profits) by offering work-site health programs of health education, screening, and interventions designed to achieve better health among workers. Programs range from single interventions (such as screening for high blood pressure) to comprehensive health and fitness programs, aerobic

split labour market
The existence of primary and secondary labour markets. A primary labour market refers to jobs that are stable and economically rewarding and have many benefits; a secondary labour market refers to jobs that offer little pay, no security, few benefits, and little chance for advancement.

exercise and fitness, nutrition and weight control, stress management, smoking cessation, cancer-risk screening, drug and alcohol abuse prevention, accident prevention, and health information (Conrad 1999). Some workplaces have nap rooms, allowing workers to take naps (Bettelheim 1998). Many companies have employee assistance programs to help employees and their families with substance abuse, family discord, depression, and other mental health problems.

At the same time, one highly controversial health and safety strategy used by business management is behavioural-based safety programs. Instead of examining how work processes and conditions compromise health and safety on the job, **behaviour-based safety programs** direct attention to workers themselves as the problem. Behaviour-based safety programs claim that 80 to 96 percent of job injuries and illnesses are caused by workers' own carelessness and unsafe acts (Frederick and Lessin 2000).

Critics contend that behaviour-based safety programs divert attention away from employers' failures to provide safe working conditions. For example, when a worker slipped and fell on the ice in the parking lot of a tire manufacturing company,

> the official accident report ... stated, "Worker's eyes not on path," as the cause of the injury. The report did not mention the need to have ice and snow removed from the parking lot. It did not mention that the sidewalk had not been cleared of snow and ice for several weeks, even though workers were required to use the sidewalk periodically. (Frederick and Lessin 2000)

Critics also say that the real goal of behaviour-based safety programs is to discourage workers from reporting illness and injuries. Workers whose employers have implemented behaviour-based safety programs describe an atmosphere of fear in the workplace, such that workers are reluctant to report injuries and illnesses for fear of being labelled an "unsafe worker" (Frederick and Lessin 2000).

Work–Family Policies and Programs

The influx of women into the workplace has been accompanied by an increase in government and company policies designed to help women and men balance their work and family roles. As of this writing, Canada's employment insurance program permits parents of newborns or of adoptees to take 35 weeks of paid parental leave in which either parent may take the total allowable leave, or the parents may share it. Because pregnancy and birth can be especially taxing, birth mothers may receive up to an additional 15 weeks of maternity leave and can start their claims up to 8 weeks prior to the expected birth. To make the claim for parental leave, the person receiving the benefit must have worked at least 600 hours during the previous year (HRDC 2006). These benefits provide 55 percent of their normal weekly pay to a maximum weekly gross amount of $413 (HRDC 2006). While women who claim maternity benefits are prohibited from employment, those who receive parental benefits are allowed to work part time and earn 25 percent of their wage up to a set minimum.

Results from the longitudinal Survey of Labour and Income Dynamics (SLID) indicate self-employment and the absence of maternity leave correlate with quick returns to paid work. "The odds of the mother's returning to work by the end of the first month [following a child's birth] were almost six times higher when she did *not* receive maternity leave benefits. Also, the odds of returning early were almost eight times higher for the self-employed than for employees" (Marshall 1999: 22). In general, however, mothers evidenced a strong attachment to participation in the paid labour force: only 7 percent of all Canadian women who gave birth in the early 1990s had not returned to paid work after two years. Non-returnees were more likely to have been employed in part-time

behaviour-based safety programs
A controversial health and safety strategy used by business management in which health and safety problems in the workplace are attributed to workers' behaviour rather than to work processes and conditions.

work and less likely to have held, prior to giving birth, a unionized job or a professional job. In addition, non-returnees had, on average, spent less time at their last job than those who returned and earned lower median salaries ($16 700 versus $25 000).

Women in Canada today are less likely to interrupt their paid work and, when interruptions do occur, return to gainful employment more quickly than women did in the past. Despite the common assumption that mothers do not work outside the home, Table 11.2 and Figure 11.3 show that most mothers in Canada, even those with very young children, are in paid employment. Yet, not all Canadian provinces and territories have shown equal commitment to providing Canada's workers with access to safe, affordable, and accessible child care.

Table 11.2 *Employment of Mothers, by Age of Youngest Child and Family Status, 1976–2009*

	Female Lone Parents				Women with Partners			
	Youngest Child Less Than 3	Youngest Child Aged 3 to 5	Youngest Child Aged 6 to 15	Youngest Child Less Than 16	Youngest Child Less Than 3	Youngest Child Aged 3 to 5	Youngest Child Aged 6 to 15	Youngest Child Less Than 16
Year	Percentage							
1976	27.6	45.1	54.0	48.3	27.6	36.0	45.5	38.3
1981	32.5	51.8	61.5	54.5	39.7	46.0	55.4	48.7
1986	29.8	47.2	60.1	51.7	51.1	55.6	62.2	57.4
1991	30.9	47.5	62.3	52.1	57.0	62.3	70.3	64.5
1996	32.9	46.2	62.6	53.1	61.0	63.3	71.5	66.6
2001	45.5	61.0	73.7	66.5	63.2	68.3	75.7	70.9
2006	46.3	66.2	76.6	69.9	66.5	70.1	78.6	73.6
2007	49.8	68.1	76.9	70.8	67.0	73.5	80.0	75.0
2008	49.1	65.6	77.9	70.6	66.3	71.2	80.5	74.5
2009	45.9	66.0	75.7	68.9	66.5	70.5	79.2	73.8

SOURCE: Statistics Canada, 2011. "Employment of Mothers, by Age of Youngest Child and Family Status, 1976 – 2009 ," *Women in Canada: A Gender-based Statistical Report, 2011*, Catalogue No. 89-503 X, released July 2011, p. 117.

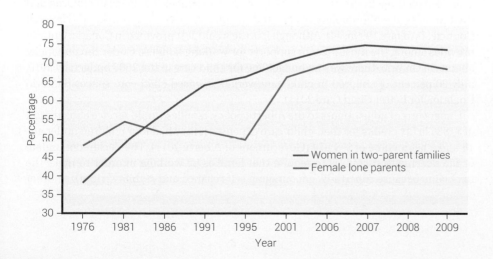

Figure 11.3
Employment of Women with Children, by Family Status, 1976–2009

SOURCE: Statistics Canada, 2011. "Percentage of Employed Women with Children, by Family Status, 1976 to 2009," *Women in Canada: A Gender-based Statistical Report, 2011*. Catalogue no. 89-503 X, released July 2011, p. 118.

Chapter 11 Work and Unemployment

Public Child-Care Assistance for Working Families

The lack of affordable, quality child care is one stressor that many Canadian parents confront. Although "[c]hild care is a fact of life for Canadian children and their families very little regulated child care even exists in Canada" (National Council of Welfare 1999b: 17). While the costs of child care in general, and for preschoolers in particular, are high and rising, the federal, provincial, and territorial governments have cut funding for social programs, cut or frozen subsidies to low-income families, and made eligibility criteria for subsidies more restrictive. In addition, parents of children with special needs and parents who work irregular hours or shift work may find it impossible to obtain child care. Even for those provinces that have introduced full-day kindergarten, families in shift work cannot benefit from that form of child care.

In 1997, Quebec introduced a comprehensive family policy aimed at integrating family benefits, paid parental level, child care, and kindergarten. Its child-care component heralded universally available, affordable child care in that province. The aim was to make every child in Quebec, by 2001, able to receive child care for $5 a day (and for as little as $2 a day for certain low-income families). This nominal fee was to entitle a child to a maximum of 10 hours a day of child care, one meal, two snacks, and use of all educational materials. In September all 5-year-olds in Quebec whose families desired it became entitled to receive full-time kindergarten, with $5-a-day after-school care organized by the educational authorities; the government offered similar benefits for junior kindergarten and early intervention programs for families on welfare. In September all 3-year-olds became eligible for $5-a-day child care. In 2000, Quebec launched 10 pilot projects offering evening, weekend, and even overnight child care—all available at the same $5-a-day rate (Doherty 2001). While the costs of providing such a comprehensive system are significant, Quebec's policy has been lauded as "a pioneering approach to family supports in North America" (National Council of Welfare 1999a: 44).

In March 2000, the province of British Columbia became the second jurisdiction in North America to move toward publicly funded child care for all families "rich, poor, and the large majority in between" (Canadian Council on Social Development 2001: 6). Since January 1, 2001, families in British Columbia who seek before- and after-school care for their children became able to access licensed spaces on and off school sites at a cost to parents of $7 a day during the school year and $14 a day during school holidays.

However, elsewhere in Canada, the provision of child care remains "severely compromised on three fronts: the availability of spaces to meet the needs of children and their families, the affordability of care and the quality of services provided" (National Council of Welfare 1999b: 44). Although it is the wealthiest province in Canada, Ontario provides among the most meagre supports for working families. Under the provincial liberals in Ontario, there was no budget line for child care in the 2008 budget; by 2010, only 20 percent of children in child care were in licensed child-care spaces (Ontario Coalition for Better Child Care 2011).

Under current adjustments to the Alberta policy, families would receive a maximum of $1836 in tax credits for their child-care expenses if they had four children under age 18 and a net income of $79 874 (Government of Alberta 2011). The declared mandate of the tax-credit program is to require that families be working in order to make the tax claim, because Alberta is "encouraging self-reliance and stability" (ibid). Another way of understanding the Alberta policy is that whereas provinces are dependent on the successful care and education of children, who are the next generation of human resources (i.e., future resources for the provincial GDP), the province seeks to minimize its investment in the development of that resource.

Under the Conservative government, as of July 1, 2006, all families in Canada with children under the age of six were entitled to payments of $100 per month per child under the Universal Child Care Benefit. Families that can claim the Canada Child Tax Benefit automatically receive the monthly disbursements, but others must apply and meet certain citizenship and immigration requirements to qualify (Canada Revenue Agency 2006). Like the Ontario and Alberta plans, the program claims a commitment to universal child care, but its ability to deliver universal child care is limited by meagre funding levels. Moreover, because each province and territory sets its own regulations about sources of allowable employment income for those receiving social assistance, some families will find that receipt of the child-care supplement means a partial or equal deduction in their social assistance benefits. In other words, there will be no change in parental ability to find work outside the home.

While some provinces, notably Ontario and the Maritimes, now provide full-day kindergarten as a mode of child-care delivery that blends care with formal education, the policy has not been extended across the country. And yet a 2012 graduate research paper completed in economics at the University of Ottawa uses a multi-method analysis of labour force participation and shows that labour participation for previously unemployed mothers of young children increases, as does the ability to enjoy leisure time when their income levels increase, especially for women who had not been able to enter the workforce because of the problems with having only half-day kindergarten in a 9–5 world:

> When Kindergarten is introduced, it is as if the mother receives a subsidy that pays for the entirety of childcare for a fixed number of hours a day. This provision ... changes the budget available to the mother, and thus influences the mother's employment decisions. ... The mother has greater motivation to work because she gains a higher wage with the subsidization of childcare increasing her net wage ... (Wilson 2012: 19)

As social policy, then, full-day kindergarten and other forms of subsidized child care improve labour-force participation rates, increase family well-being, and provide opportunities for families to have more leisure activities together, and yet our governments across the country still do not provide adequate subsidies for preschool-aged children, and provide full-day care at the kindergarten level in only some regions. Conservative attitudes about where women "belong," and fiscal policies that treat children as a "private" issue instead of a public concern, are the major impediments to the creation of universally subsidized care in Canada. As a result, fewer women participate full-time in the labour force, and our GDP is negatively impacted as a result. For families at the low end of waged labour, it means opportunities to improve their family income levels are denied.

The Workplace and Family Life

Offering employees greater flexibility in their work hours could also help parents to balance their work and family demands. Flexible work arrangements, which benefit childfree workers as well as employed parents, include flextime, job sharing, a compressed workweek, and telecommuting. **Flextime** allows employees to begin and end the workday at different times, as long as 40 hours per week are maintained. With

flextime
An option in work scheduling that allows employees to begin and end the workday at different times as long as they perform a given number of hours of work per week.

job sharing
A work option in which two people share and are paid for one job.

compressed workweek
Workplace option in which employees work a full week, full time, but in four rather than five days.

telecommuting
A work option in which workers complete all or part of their work at home with the use of information technology.

job sharing, two workers share the responsibility of one job. In Canada, job-sharers are most likely to be well-educated individuals. About half have a college or university education, and about 4 of 10 are professionals; nurses and teachers are most likely to participate in job sharing (Statistics Canada 1998).

A **compressed workweek** allows employees to condense their work into fewer days (e.g., four 10-hour days each week). **Telecommuting** allows employees to work part time or full time at home or at a satellite office. A study of U.S. companies found that the more women and minorities a company has in managerial positions, the more likely that company is to offer flexible work options (Galinsky and Bond 1998).

Fran Rodgers, president of Work/Family Directions, explains the need for work–family policies:

> For over 20 years we at Work/Family Directions have asked employees in all industries what it would take for them to contribute more at work. Every study found the same thing: They need aid with their dependent care, more flexibility and control over the hours and conditions of work, and a corporate culture in which they are not punished because they have families. These are fundamental needs of our society and of every worker. (Galinsky et al. 1993: 51)

Challenges to Corporate Power and Globalization

Challenges to corporate power have also taken root in Canada and throughout the world. Anti-globalization activists have targeted the World Trade Organization (WTO), the International Monetary Fund (IMF), and the World Bank as forces that advance corporate-led globalization at the expense of social goals such as justice, community, national sovereignty, cultural diversity, ecological sustainability, and workers' rights.

In 1999, 50 000 street protesters and Third World delegates demonstrated in opposition to the policies of the WTO that promoted corporate-led globalization. Another confrontation between pro- and anti-globalization forces occurred at the 2000 meeting of the IMF and the World Bank in Washington, and later at the 2002 meetings of the G-8 leaders in Kananaskis, Alberta. Media attention to such protests contributes to the growing worldwide awareness of the forces of corporate globalization and its social, environmental, and economic effects. However, governments that want to get business matters tended to with a minimum of interference from the people that governments putatively serve are treating resisters and demonstrators more and more aggressively. In summer 2010 the fourth meeting of the G-20 was held in Toronto, and the city was barricaded in its central core, with steel fences that restricted the movement of Toronto's residents. The 2011 CBC documentary "You Should Have Stayed at Home," presented by *The Fifth Estate*, exposed some of the most egregious violations of the civil rights of peaceful protesters and bystanders at the summit, including the violent beatings of persons "guilty" of nothing more than being within striking distance of the 10 000 police on the streets. Roughly 1150 people were arrested and detained on the weekend of the G-20 summit, held without charge. Precise numbers in publicly available reports vary, but the CBC indicated that of the 1150 held only 300 were ever charged, and by mid-October 2010 charges against 159 of those had been dropped (CBC News 2010). As of the writing of this edition of the text, 18 people remain charged as "anarchist" conspirators but it could be years before they have their cases heard at trial (Krauss 2010).

Understanding Work and Unemployment

On December 10, 1948, the General Assembly of the United Nations adopted and proclaimed the Universal Declaration of Human Rights, some of which appears below.

> Article 23. Everyone has the right to work, to free choice of employment, to just and favourable conditions of work and to protection against unemployment.
>
> Everyone, without any discrimination, has the right to equal pay for equal work.
>
> Everyone who works has the right to just and favourable remuneration ensuring for himself [sic] and his [sic] family an existence worthy of human dignity, and supplemented, if necessary, by other means of social protection.
>
> Everyone has the right to form and to join trade unions for the protection of his [sic] interests.
>
> Article 24. Everyone has the right to rest and leisure, including reasonable limitation of working hours and periodic holidays with pay.*

More than half a century later, workers around the world are still fighting for these basic rights as proclaimed in the Universal Declaration of Human Rights.

To understand social problems associated with work and unemployment, we must first recognize the power and influence of governments and corporations on the workplace. We must also be aware of the role that technological developments and postindustrialization have on what we produce, how we produce it, where we produce it, and who does the producing. Canada is moving away from producing manufactured goods toward producing services. The labour-intensive blue-collar assembly line is declining in importance, and information-intensive white-collar occupations are increasing. Because of increasing corporate multinationalization, Canadian jobs are moving to foreign countries where labour is cheap, regulations are lax, and raw materials are available. Finally, the workforce is becoming more diverse in terms of gender and racial and ethnic background and is including more contingent workers than in the past.

Decisions made by Canadian corporations about what and where to invest influence the quantity and quality of jobs available in Canada. As conflict theorists argue, such investment decisions are motivated by profit, which is part of a capitalist system. Profit is also a driving factor in deciding how and when technological devices will be used to replace workers and increase productivity, but if goods and services are produced too efficiently, workers are laid off and high unemployment results. When people lack money to buy products, sales slump, a recession ensues, and social welfare programs are needed to support the unemployed. When the government increases spending to pay for its social programs, it expands the deficit and increases the national debt. Deficit spending and a large national debt make it difficult to recover from the recession, and the cycle continues.

Those adhering to the classic view of capitalism argue for limited government intervention on the premise that business will regulate itself via an "invisible hand" or "market forces." For example, if corporations produce a desired product at a low price, people will buy it, which means workers will be hired to produce the product, and so on.

Ironically, those who support limited government intervention also sometimes advocate government intervention to bail out failed banks and troubled businesses (or hockey teams). Such government help benefits the powerful segments of our

---

*Universal Declaration of Human Rights, General Assembly, United Nations. http://www.un.org/en/documents/udhr. Reprinted by permission of the United Nations.

society. Yet, when economic policies hurt less powerful groups, such as minorities, there has been a collective hesitance to support or provide social welfare programs. It is also ironic that such bailout programs, which contradict the ideals of capitalism, are needed because of capitalism. For example, the profit motive leads to multinationalization, which leads to unemployment, which leads to the need for government programs. The various forces transforming our economy are interrelated—technology, globalization, capital flight through multinationalization, and the movement toward a service economy (Eitzen and Zinn 1990). For the individual worker, the concepts of work, job, and career have changed forever.

Student Reflection: What Do You Know Now?

It's very likely that, wherever you are from, there have been changes in the primary, secondary, and tertiary work sectors in your hometown between the 1990s and today. Using one or more sociological theories, analyze the social consequences. Can you think of any labour-related solutions?

Look up occupational disease fatality data in your home province. What do these data tell you about the impact of working in dangerous occupations on the elderly and middle-aged? Can you extrapolate what kinds of social problems within families are addressed by compensation claims? Reflect on the role of government, government regulation, and social welfare in health and aging related to workplaces.

Many popular media stories suggest that millennials, as they enter the workforce, have higher expectations of work–life balance and less loyalty to a single company. What do earnings, injury, and sector analyses tell you about the kinds of careers that might work best in this sense, if it is indeed true that the newer generation is different from previous ones (rather than workplaces simply having changed)? Who will continue to do the jobs that have less flexibility?

What Do You Do Next?

Located at www.nelson.com/socialproblems5e

- Consolidate your knowledge with interactive and printable **Flashcards**
- Gauge your understanding with **Practice Quizzes** and **Matching Activities**
- Develop your critical thinking skills with **Self and Society** and **The Human Side** questions
- Analyze **Social Research** and **Social Problems in Global Perspective**
- Explore the implications of **Technology on Social Problems**

Student Reflection:
What Do You Already Know?

Education is something that all of us, technically, are supposed to have gone through to a certain age if we grew up in Canada. Reporting on it and understanding it more deeply is complex because of its local, provincial, and national levels. It seems obvious that going on to postsecondary school will lead to better outcomes for self and family over time—that is, more money! So many current debates exist (perhaps even within your own family) about what the right diploma or degree is to succeed, and for how long people should stay in school versus join the workforce. Perhaps in your history you have seen family members do very well without a high school education, and yet now the stigma attached to dropping out is very tangible. This chapter should help to make sense of what actually drives socially positive outcomes (it isn't always the obvious) and give context for richer discussions about the social problems associated with the institution of education.

Learning Outcomes

Through careful reading of this chapter, you should be able to:

- define the bolded key terms
- explain the uniquely Canadian aspects of the education sector based on religion, language, federal-provincial funding models, and educational attainment levels historically and in the present
- identify both the liberating and oppressive cultural practices of acculturation, socialization, and hierarchy in formal schooling
- apply sociological and critical perspectives to education as an institution both historically and currently
- explain the links between social problems and education, and question assumed links
- compare educational success and attainment levels based on gender, socio-economic status, aboriginal status, and citizenship status
- contrast various implications of standardized tests and outcomes
- situate school violence in its border context of educational and social issues
- reflect on the social cost, economic cost, and the social good of education both generally and in determining one's own pathway through such a system

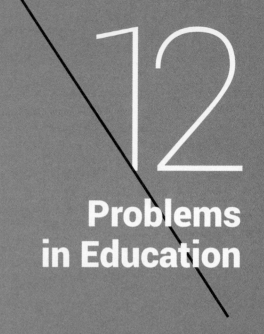

12
Problems in Education

hxdbzxy/iStock/Thinkstock

Education is often claimed as a panacea—the cure-all for poverty and prejudice, drugs and violence, war and hatred—yet daily, it seems, we are reminded of problems that exist in Canada's educational system. Some have charged that our educational system is encumbered by seniority and indifference to absolute educational outcomes, which hamper Canada's ability to compete. Others direct attention to the ravages of budget cuts, increasing tuition costs, and staggering levels of student debt. Others highlight funding "reforms" that have triggered dramatic cuts to **special education** programs and the allied services of speech pathologists and psychologists (Schofield 1999). In this chapter we look at these concerns but we also address problems that are a built-in feature of an institution that grants enormous power over the day-to-day lives of children, and over their futures as well. Though common sense views education as an obvious social good, in this chapter we also look at some of the very negative objectives that educational policy and institutions have pursued in Canada.

Can one institution, riddled with obstacles, be a solution for other social problems? In this chapter, we focus on this question, starting with the global context.

special education
Remedial education designed to help children and adults who are exceptional in some way, including but not limited to intellectual developmental delays, visual or auditory disabilities, and emotional or specific learning difficulties.

12.1 The Global Context: Cross-Cultural Variation in Education

Looking only at the Canadian educational system might lead to the conclusion that most societies have developed some method of formal instruction for their members. After all, there are over 5 million students enrolled in public school at the elementary and secondary levels in Canada, more than 100 universities and degree-granting colleges, and nearly 140 community colleges offering diploma programs in trades and polytechnic programs. These institutions employ over 41 000 full-time professors at the university level (Statistics Canada 2012) and educate nearly 2 million students, of whom just over 730 000 are enrolled in college programs (Statistics Canada 2013a). In reality, many societies have no formal mechanism for educating the masses. As a result, 20 percent of adults around the world—776 million people—cannot read or write; two-thirds of them are women (UNESCO 2012).

Education at a Glance, a research publication from the OECD, reports on educational trends and achievements using statistical measures for over 35 countries. The 2013 report reveals some interesting trends. First, in the decades of OECD reportage the majority of OECD countries have increased the average level of educational attainments of their populations, and tertiary—university and college level—education has grown significantly. Completion of advanced years of secondary school "has become the most common level attained by young people" (OECD 2013: 26). Even with this change, and even with higher attainment levels for young women compared to young men at the tertiary level, more men than women still complete upper secondary levels (p. 27). What these data suggest is that young men still profit more from completion of secondary school than do young women, and so they enter the workforce at that point; those young women, by contrast, who manage to complete secondary school more frequently, proceed to postsecondary education in university and vocational schools. Even with increases in average levels of educational attainment, the OECD report tells us that less than 35 percent of adults attain a postsecondary education (p. 27).

A second trend shows the link between education and income (though it is not always clear that higher educational attainment is the cause rather the consequence of wealth). The positive correspondence between employment status and education is clearer, with much higher unemployment rates across the board for those with lower educational attainment levels (p. 89).

Third, notes the OECD 2011 report on educational spending, the average expense per student per year for every year from the start of elementary school to the start of secondary school is equal to $9860 (U.S.), and each year of secondary school garners an average expenditure of $8852 (U.S.) per student. The highest level of contribution occurs at the university and college level, where the average expenditure is $18 258 (U.S.) per student each year. These expenses include both public and private funding contributions combined. In Figure 12.1, the lighter blue colour shows the portion of public funds contributed, the orange represents the private funding contributed, and the darker blue shows the portion of private funding that has received some public subsidy (for example, subsidized private housing for students, or reductions in public transportation fees).

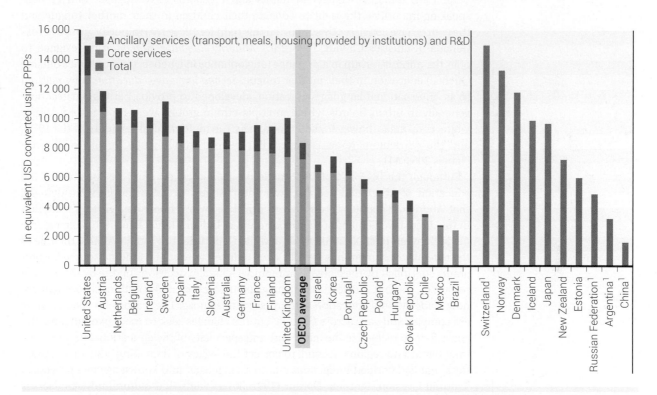

Figure 12.1 *Annual Expenditure per Student by Educational Institutions from Primary through Tertiary Education, by Type of Service, 2008*

1. Public institutions only.
Countries are ranked in descending order of expenditure per student by educational institutions for core services.

SOURCE: OECD (2011). *Education at a Glance 2011: OECD Indicators*. OECD Publishing. http://dx.doi.org/10.1787/eag-2011-en.

Canada continues to operate public education according to the terms of the *British North America Act*, which identified education as a provincial responsibility and gave each province the constitutional authority to develop its own educational organization. Although education in Yukon, the Northwest Territories, and Nunavut is funded by the federal government, it is governed by ordinances of the assemblies of these regions. In consequence, Canada has 13 unique school systems that fund and administer public, private, denominational, and linguistic schools somewhat differently.

The issues of religion and language are two of the differences that exist within our system of education.

Consider, for example, that our Constitution, unlike that of the United States, protects denominational, or "separate," schools. However, "[a]s each province joined Confederation, it brought its own approach to religious schools and Canadians are still dealing with the legacy of this process" (Statistics Canada 1998: 146). In Canada, free public education in a nondenominational public school system is available for all Canadians. So long as denominational schools operated by the Roman Catholic Church agree to admit non-Roman Catholic students, they receive public funding in Ontario (James 2004: 45). Alberta, Saskatchewan, Yukon, and the Northwest Territories also provide public funding for Roman Catholic schools. Elsewhere, any separate schools are privately funded. Until 1997, Newfoundland had an entirely denominational system of education; however, in that year, a public vote abolished its 277-year-old system of church-run schools.

"In 1982, Canada's Charter of Rights and Freedoms gave English- and French-speaking minorities the right to educate their children in their mother tongue and the courts have consistently supported this right for these two minority groups across Canada" (Statistics Canada 1998: 146). *Minority language education* is designed to offer the minority group in a province (anglophones in Quebec, francophones outside Quebec) education in their mother tongue. *Second language education*, now referred to as "international language education," developed to provide heritage instruction, generally in urban boards where multiple ethnic groups were represented; largely white, rural areas, however, did little to meet the multicultural mandate of the 1970s and the curriculum remains largely Eurocentric throughout Canada to this day (James 2004: 44).

Although the BNA Act of 1867 made the federal government responsible for the education of Aboriginal peoples, over the past few decades the growing demand that Aboriginal peoples be allowed to run their own schools has led to a reduction in the direct involvement of the Department of Indian Affairs. Because of agreements made between First Nations bands and the Department of Indian Affairs, the role of the federal government has steadily been reduced to that of a funding source for programs controlled by the Native community. Generally, decisions on the distribution of resources, staffing, curriculum, language of instruction, and length of school year are now made by band education authorities in most areas. The reasons for such changes are complex and vary across Canada, but the changes seek to meet two fundamental goals: first, to recognize the autonomy and specificity of the educational needs of distinct bands and regions; second, to correct the legacy of damaging educational practices that had derided Indigenous cultures, languages, and knowledge in a process of "cultural invasion." Antonia Dardur (1991: 36) explains that cultural invasion "serves the sustained social, political and economic oppression of subordinate groups" largely by teaching the subordinate groups to see their own languages and cultures as inferior.

For all of the problems in education, Canadians hold a strong belief in its importance—and with good reason. Consider that in 2001, Statistics Canada reported that while the average family headed by a high school graduate enjoyed a net worth of approximately $65 000, this figure rose to $120 000 for a family headed by a university graduate and about $320 000 for those with a professional degree in law, medicine, dentistry, and the like (Bricker and Greenspon 2001: 158). At the same time, however, Canadians are increasingly likely to raise questions about the quality of education in this country. One survey reported that "a staggering 82 percent of parents worried about the quality of education received by their children," while a second found that over one in three Canadians (37 percent) thought that education was in worse shape than 25 years earlier (Bricker and Greenspon 2001: 156, 162). Many perceive that there is considerable room—and need—for improvement.

12.2 Sociological Theories of Education

The three major sociological perspectives—structural-functionalism, conflict theory, and symbolic interactionism—are important in explaining different aspects of Canadian education. This chapter also provides critical perspectives that include feminist, queer, and antiracist interventions into the institution, practice, and purpose of education.

Structural-Functionalist Perspective

According to structural-functionalism, the educational institution accomplishes important tasks for society, including instruction, socialization, the sorting of individuals into various statuses, and the provision of custodial care. Many social problems, such as unemployment, crime and delinquency, and poverty, may be linked to the failure of the educational institution to fulfill these basic functions (see Chapters 4, 10, and 11). Structural-functionalists also examine the reciprocal influences of the educational institution and other social institutions, including the family, the political institution, and the economic institution.

Instruction

A major function of education is to teach students the knowledge and skills necessary for future occupational roles, self-development, and social functioning. Although some parents teach their children basic knowledge and skills at home, most parents rely on schools to teach their children to read, spell, write, tell time, count money, and use computers. The failure of schools to instruct students in basic knowledge and skills both causes and results from many other social problems.

Socialization

The socialization function of education involves teaching students to respect authority—behaviour that is essential for social organization (Merton 1968). Students learn to respond to authority by asking permission to leave the classroom, sitting quietly at their desks, and raising their hands before asking a question. Students who do not learn to respect and obey teachers may later disrespect and disobey employers, police officers, and judges.

The educational institution also socializes youth into the dominant culture. Schools attempt to instill and maintain the norms, values, traditions, and symbols of the culture in a variety of ways, such as celebrating holidays (Remembrance Day, Thanksgiving); requiring students to speak and write in English and French; displaying the Canadian flag; and discouraging violence, drug use, and cheating.

Whether schools function well in Canada may be a matter of vantage point. As the number and size of racial and ethnic minority groups have increased, Canadian schools have had to account for practices that directly contradict official policy on multiculturalism in Canada and for practices that trivialize non-dominant cultures. For example, Canadian sociologist Jasmin Zine (2002) argues that a variety of racist and Eurocentric practices still serve dominant groups while marginalizing particular groups in schools across the country. Among the commonplace, but problematic practices that Zine draws attention to are the following:

- A narration of history that focuses almost exclusively on Europe, as with "Medieval Times" curricula that entirely neglect flourishing civilizations from the time in China, Africa, and Spain.
- Calling upon ethnically and/or racially "other" students to perform their culture for their classmates while Anglo-Canadian children are not called upon to perform their British heritage.

- Having all the complexity of your heritage and culture reduced to "saris, samosa and steel bands" trotted out for school festivals, while simultaneously knowing that we don't learn Canadian history via bagpipes and meat pies. (Zine 2002: 37)*

Practices such as these, which developed alongside multicultural policy in the 1970s, Zine argues, are incredibly damaging for minoritized students: they learn in unequivocal terms that their cultures don't count, that their richness does not have to be acknowledged. Instead of perpetuating Eurocentric curricula and attitudes, Zine proposes a multi-centric approach, one in which diversity operates not as an "add on," but as "a starting point for knowledge integration, in which the historical achievements of all societies are examined, validated and respected" (p. 38).

Sorting Individuals into Statuses

Schools sort individuals into statuses by providing credentials for individuals who achieve various levels of education at various schools within the system. These credentials sort people into different statuses—for example, "high school graduate," "Rhodes scholar," and "Ph.D." Further, schools sort individuals into professional statuses by awarding degrees in such fields as medicine, nursing, and law. The significance of such statuses lies in their association with occupational prestige and income—in general, the higher one's education, the higher one's income (Ghalam 2000). Table 12.1 shows the correspondence between education levels and income over 25 years from 1980 to 2005.

Table 12.1 **Median Earnings, in 2005 Constant Dollars, of Male and Female Recent Immigrant Earners and Canadian-Born Earners Aged 25 to 54, with or without a University Degree, Canada, 1980–2005**

| | Recent Immigrant Earners[1] | | | | Canadian-Born Earners[1] | | | | Recent Immigrant to Canadian-Born Earnings Ratio | | | |
| | With a University Degree | | With No University Degree | | With a University Degree | | With No University Degree | | With a University Degree | | With No University Degree | |
	Males	Females	Males	Females	Males	Females	Males	Females	Males	Females	Males	Females
Year	**2005 Constant Dollars**								**Ratio**			
1980	48 541	24 317	36 467	18 548	63 040	41 241	43 641	21 463	0.77	0.59	0.84	0.86
1990	38 351	25 959	27 301	17 931	61 332	41 245	40 757	23 267	0.63	0.63	0.67	0.77
2000	35 816	22 511	25 951	16 794	61 505	43 637	39 902	25 622	0.58	0.52	0.65	0.66
2005	30 332	18 969	24 470	14 233	62 566	44 545	40 235	25 590	0.48	0.43	0.61	0.56

NOTE: The numbers refer to all earners, whether or not they worked on a full-time basis for a full year. Individuals with self-employment income are included while those living in institutions are excluded.

SOURCE: Statistics Canada, *Earnings and Incomes of Canadian over the Past Quarter Century, 2006 Census,* Cat. 97-563-XIE2006001, May 2008; http://www.statcan.gc.ca/bsolc/olc-cel/olc-cel?catno=97-563-XIE2006001&lang=eng#formatdisp.

Custodial Care

The educational system also provides custodial care (Merton 1968), which is particularly valuable to single-parent and dual-earner families, and the likely reason for the increase in enrolments of 3- and 4-year-olds. The school system provides free

*From J. Zine, 2002. *Inclusive Schooling in a Pluralist Society*, p. 37. Toronto: Canadian Education Association. Reprinted by permission of the Canadian Education Association.

supervision and care for children and adolescents until they complete secondary, or "high," school—almost 13 000 hours per pupil. Some school districts are experimenting with offering classes on a 12-month basis, on Saturdays, and as part of longer school days. Working parents, the hope that increased supervision will reduce delinquency rates, and higher educational standards that require more hours of study are some of the motivations behind the "more time" movement (Wilgoren 2001).

Conflict Perspective

Conflict theorists emphasize that the educational institution solidifies the class positions of groups and allows the elite to control the masses. Although the official goal of education in society is to provide a universal mechanism for achievement, educational opportunities and the quality of education are not equally distributed.

Conflict theorists point out that the socialization function of education is really indoctrination into a capitalist ideology. In essence, students are socialized to value the interests of the state and to function to sustain it. Such indoctrination begins in kindergarten. Rosabeth Moss Kanter (1972) coined the term *the organization child* to refer to the child in nursery school who is most comfortable with supervision, guidance, and adult control. Teachers cultivate the organization child by providing daily routines and rewarding those who conform. In essence, teachers train future workers to be obedient to authority.

Further, to conflict theorists, education serves as a mechanism for **cultural imperialism**, or the indoctrination into the dominant culture of a society. When cultural imperialism exists, the norms, values, traditions, and languages of minorities are systematically ignored. For example, in his analysis of the development of the educational system in Ontario in the mid-1800s, Neil McDonald emphasized how education was seen as crucial for maintaining dominant ideologies. He notes that the chief architect of the Ontario school system, Egerton Ryerson, purposefully set out to create a system in which "young people would remain loyal to the Crown ... never participate in the kind of rebellion which had been put down in Upper Canada in 1837, and ... cooperate with one another, regardless of their social class backgrounds." Through education, the working class were to be persuaded that "their interests were also those of the middle and upper classes and that, as a collectivity, there was a 'common' or 'public good' towards which all must work" (McDonald, as cited in Curtis and Lambert 1994: 12). As Curtis and Lambert (1994: 12) remark, "In short, Ryerson's objective was social control, and he charged the schools with the responsibility of inculcating the beliefs and attitudes of mind that would accomplish it."

Traditionally, the school curriculum has not given voice to the perspective of minority groups, including women. Moreover, the cultural genocide promoted within the residential schools for Canada's Indigenous peoples must be recognized as one of the bleakest notes in the history of Canadian education. As only one example, Native students who dared to speak their own language were routinely punished by having a sewing needle pushed through their tongue. This practice was known as the "needle torture."

In her 1993 book *Resistance and Renewal: Surviving the Indian Residential School*, Celia Haig-Brown provides a historical overview of the goals of pre-Confederation Canada, and the colonial view that European culture was superior to that of the Native groups already established in Canada. Haig-Brown reports that the province of Canada in 1847 published a report that set the directions in policy for Indian Education. Clearly expressed in the report is a perceived-as-obvious need "to raise [aboriginal people] to the level of the whites" (Province of Canada report quoted in Haig-Brown 1993: 29). Haig-Brown summarizes the general recommendations of the report that Indians were to be held under jurisdiction of the Crown rather than of colonial provinces, that efforts to convert Native peoples to Christianity continue to be asserted, and that schools were to be established under the guidance of missionaries.

cultural imperialism
The indoctrination into the dominant culture of a society; when cultural imperialism exists, the norms, values, traditions, and languages of minorities are systematically ignored.

In essence, cultural genocide was written in educational policy. Within the discussion of the recommendations is the following comment:

> Their education must consist not merely of the training of the mind, but of a weaning from the habits and feelings of their ancestors, and the acquirements of the language, arts and customs of civilized life. (Haig-Brown 1993: 29)

These goals, initially set by the colonial province of Canada with the specific and targeted objective of the acculturation of Indigenous people, remained in operation until the last residential schools in Canada closed in 1996 in Saskatchewan, where they were still operating as the last holdouts of colonialist education programs aimed at erasing Indigenous culture and language in Canada. In other words, although the popular, shared memory in dominant Canadian circles usually imagines residential schools as a thing of the distant past, a large population of young adult Native people in Canada are contemporary survivors of the genocidal aims of the residential school system.

Finally, the conflict perspective focuses on what Kozol (1991) calls the "savage inequalities" in education that perpetuate racial inequality. Change must come in classroom practices that recognize cultural variability. As sociologist Pierre Bourdieu explains, every child arrives in the classroom with his or her own very rich **cultural capital**, which includes language, artistic tastes, specific knowledge, and links to community and to resources outside the school (Brooks and Thompson 2005). However, the cultural capital of all students is not equally valued; it is a matter not of student shortcomings, but of highly constraining curricula that do not value what children from marginalized groups have to offer the classroom. Brooks and Thompson (2005: 49) explain:

> Focusing on the academic curriculum to the exclusion of the social curriculum constricts learning for all students. But it does the most harm to students of low socio-economic status, who may depend on teachers to bridge the gap between their own cultural capital and the mainstream…

Although we are faced with increasingly tight curricula and testing measures, Brooks and Thompson argue that we can still incorporate considerations about social justice. We can invite and include student contributions on, for example, the important people and occupations in their communities, even if those positions are not accorded "high status" in the mainstream view.

Symbolic Interactionist Perspective

Whereas structural-functionalism and conflict theory focus on macro-level issues, such as institutional influences and power relations, symbolic interactionism examines education from a micro perspective. This perspective is concerned with individual and small-group issues, such as teacher-student interactions, the students' self-esteem, and the self-fulfilling prophecy.

Teacher-Student Interactions

Symbolic interactionists have examined the ways in which students and teachers view and relate to one another. For example, children from economically advantaged homes may be more likely to bring social and verbal skills into the classroom that elicit approval from teachers. From the teachers' point of view, middle-class children are easy and fun to teach: they grasp the material quickly, do their homework, and are more likely to "value" the educational process. Children from economically disadvantaged homes often bring fewer social and verbal skills to those same

cultural capital
Refers to the symbolic and material aspects of cultural heritage and understanding. To have high cultural capital is to possess and understand elite forms of art, language use and speech, dress and comportment, architecture and other aesthetic movements. Those with low cultural capital have either less access to and understanding of elite forms, or a culture unrecognized by those in power.

middle-class teachers, who may, inadvertently, hold up social mirrors of disapproval. Teacher disapproval contributes to the lower self-esteem among disadvantaged youth.

Self-Fulfilling Prophecy

The **self-fulfilling prophecy** occurs when people act in a manner consistent with the expectations of others. For example, a teacher who defines a student as a slow learner may be less likely to call on that student or to encourage the student to pursue difficult subjects. As a consequence of the teacher's behaviour, the student is more likely to perform at a lower level.

A now-classic study by Rosenthal and Jacobson (1968) provided empirical evidence of the self-fulfilling prophecy in the public school system. Five elementary school students were selected at random and identified for their teachers as "spurters." Such a label implied that they had superior intelligence and academic ability. In reality, they were no different from the other students in their classes. At the end of the school year, however, these five students scored higher on their intelligence quotient (IQ) tests and made higher grades than their classmates who were not labelled as spurters. In addition, the teachers rated the spurters more likely to succeed than the "nonspurters." Because the teachers expected the spurters to do well, they treated the students in a way that encouraged better school performance.

self-fulfilling prophecy
A concept referring to the tendency for people to act in a manner consistent with the expectations of others.

Critical Theories of Education

Louis Althusser was neither simply a Marxist nor only a structuralist, but a thinker who combined both views to account for how states operate and hold power. Althusser (1919–1990) observed that education belonged to a group of structures—including, among others, family and religion—that served state-sponsored views, or ideologies. Althusser (1971) termed these structures "Ideological State Apparatuses" (ISAs). He applied his view to unpack the main goals of education, which he saw as twofold: children learn how to do the things the state will require of them as workers and to observe the rules of their culture.

> [Children] go varying distances in their studies, but at any rate they learn to read, to write and to add—i.e. a number of techniques, and a number of other things as well, including elements (which may be rudimentary or on the contrary thorough-going) of "scientific" or "literary culture," which are directly useful in the different jobs in production (one instruction for manual workers, another for technicians, a third for engineers, a final one for higher management, etc.). Thus they learn know-how.
>
> But besides these techniques and knowledges ... children at school also learn the "rules" of good behaviour, i.e. the attitude that should be observed by every agent in the division of labour, according to the job he is "destined" for: rules of morality, civic and professional conscience, which actually means rules of respect for the socio-technical division of labour and ultimately the rules of the order established by class domination. They also learn to "speak proper French," to "handle" the workers correctly, i.e. actually (for the future capitalists and their servants) to "order them about" properly, i.e. (ideally) to "speak to them" in the right way, etc. (Althusser 1971: 132)

In Althusser's view, the state and the dominant class profit most from the educational institution. The state profits from teaching pupils to value that particular state over all others, and the dominant class profits most from having a reliable institution to produce generation after generation of workers to carry out its will and uphold its values.

Feminist Perspectives

In Canada, it was not until the 1880s, several decades after the 1827 establishment of the nation's first university, the University of Toronto, that women were admitted as students for university education. Further, it was not until the 1970s that women could enrol in Canada's military colleges. Today, representation of women as faculty remains inequitable across disciplines even though women now far outnumber men as undergraduates.

In the 1970s, women faculty began to organize individual courses with a focus on women's contributions and issues. They recognized that women's history, experience, thinking, and contributions to culture and to the academy were largely absent from university courses that focused almost exclusively on men's accomplishments and men's lives. There is a debate over who launched "the first" Women's Studies program in Canada, but the first courses appeared in 1970–71 as initiatives of individual professors and activist collectives (PAR-L n.d.).

At the high-school level, curricula continue to reflect the values and accomplishments of the dominant groups, and this pattern extends beyond the issue of class and race to gender as well. However, in Ontario in 2005, an energetic and committed group of young women undergraduates launched the Miss G Project. They took their name from the 1873 medical attribution of the death of a patient identified only as "Miss G____" to the supposed overexertion of her brain in the pursuit of learning (Clarke 1873). The Miss G Collective seeks to promote equity in education by including gender-based content at the high-school level:

> Equity in education is a policy commitment of the Ontario Secondary School Curriculum, but without recognizing gender and its implications, the curriculum fails to meet this commitment. […] In high school, we never encountered a fair and appropriate introduction to the very real contributions and histories of women and feminisms. (Miss G Collective 2005)

Whether feminists have sought to build an education for themselves, simply by means of access, or viewed their efforts as an endeavour to share with others, the goal has been to provide the benefits of information, of increased educational attainment, and of access to a world that one can understand and interpret for oneself.

Feminist perspectives also provide a critical assessment of educational traditions. They struggle to navigate the need for the power that comes with increased education while resisting the seductions of the hierarchical structure of the institution (Humble et al. 2006).

Feminists may also critique aspects of education that can thwart the educational goals of women. For example, a critique of latent functions presents this idea: "Being perceived as (hetero)sexually attractive and having a 'high-status' boyfriend elevated a young woman's standing among her classmates, which meant that schoolwork and friendship [are] pushed to the side" (Gilmartin 2005: 610).

12.3 Who Succeeds? The Inequality of Educational Attainment

The 1996 census was the first Canadian census to record a higher number of university graduates than of people reporting less than a Grade 9 education. Among the 29 countries surveyed by the Organisation for Economic Co-operation and Development in 2000, only three countries had higher proportions of their working-age population with a university degree—the United States (28 percent), Norway

(26 percent), and the Netherlands (21 percent) (Statistics Canada 2003a: 10). However, "[i]f university and college are combined, no other OECD nation had a higher proportion than Canada" in that year (Statistics Canada 2003a: 10). By 2006, Canada still had the world's highest proportion of adults with postsecondary levels of educational attainment (university or college). When ranked for university attainment only, Canada currently ranks at third place, behind Korea and Japan, out of 37 OECD nations surveyed for the population from age 24–65 (Figure 12.2).

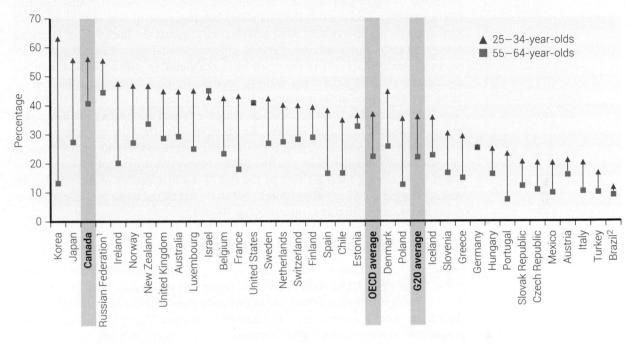

1. Year of reference 2002.
2. Year of reference 2009.
Countries are ranked in descending order of the percentage of 25–34 year-olds who have attained tertiary education.

Figure 12.2 **Population That Has Tertiary Education, Percentage by Age Group, 2010**

SOURCE: OECD (2012). *Education at a Glance 2012: OECD Indicators*. OECD Publishing. http://dx.doi.org/10.1787/eag-2012-en

Regardless of our admirable showing in the OECD rankings, it is important to keep in mind that not all Canadian residents enjoy equal opportunity to achieve higher levels of education. As noted earlier, conflict theory focuses on inequalities in the educational system. Educational inequality is based on social class and family background, race and ethnicity, and gender. Each of these factors influences who succeeds in school.

Comparisons in 1996 and 2001 among self-identified Aboriginal individuals aged 25 to 64 suggest that progress has occurred. According to the 2006 census, the share of Aboriginal respondents with postsecondary qualifications increased to 44 percent, and those whose education was limited to a high-school diploma had fallen to 21 percent. In consequence, the gap between the educational profile of the Aboriginal and non-Aboriginal populations has narrowed somewhat, particularly in relation to the proportions with a trade certificate (16 percent of the working-age Aboriginal population and 13 percent of the working-age non-Aboriginal population) or college qualifications (15 percent among Aboriginal people and 18 percent among non-Aboriginal people). "However, the gap in university graduates remained wide. In 1996, 6 percent of

Chapter 12 Problems in Education

Aboriginal people aged 25 to 64 had a university education. This increased to 8 percent in 2001" (Statistics Canada 2003a: 16). By 2006, this percentage remained unchanged at 8 percent, and the share of adult Aboriginal persons without a high school diploma was 34 percent (Statistics Canada 2008: 19).

It remains to be seen whether the Ontario Ministry of Training Colleges and Universities (MTCU) Policy Framework Document of 2011 will effect the kinds of changes in attitude suggested by Brooks and Thompson; the document aims in particular to repair past educational injustices imposed on Native groups. Lorenzo Cherubini (2012) explains that the 2011 policy "situates, to some degree, the challenges and obstacles encountered by Aboriginal learners against the backdrop of changing demographics, community consultations, and institutional capacities that will better represent Aboriginal learners' identities and worldviews" (p. 45); however, Cherubini also cautions that we need to assess the policy with a critical awareness of the limits of using statistical frequencies to measure educational attainments, and how attainment "gaps" can be closed without actually improving the lives of prospective Aboriginal students (pp. 46–47). Cherubini explains, for example, that while the raw numbers and frequencies of postsecondary educational attainments have risen for Native students in a number of Canadian cities, the frequencies for non-Native persons has increased much more quickly, meaning that by the end of the first decade of the twenty-first century the gap between Native educational attainments and those of Non-native students had widened from 1981 measures (pp. 48–49).

Social Class and Family Background

One of the best predictors of educational success and attainment is socio-economic status (Lam 1997). Children in middle and upper socio-economic brackets are more likely to perform better in school and to complete more years of education than children from lower socio-economic brackets. For example, Muller and Schiller (2000) report that students from higher socio-economic backgrounds are more likely to enrol in advanced mathematics course credits and to graduate from high school— two indicators of future educational and occupational success. Canadian data on educational attainment released by Statistics Canada showed that young people from high-income families were 1.5 times more likely than those from low-income families to have been enrolled in a postsecondary institution (71.0/48.8 = 1.5) and about 2.5 times more likely to have gone to university in 1998 (39.6/16.3 = 2.4). Clearly, class correlates strongly with whether one gets a postsecondary education in Canada, and it correlates even more strongly with whether one will get a university education. This strong correlation is long established and got worse rather than better over the nearly two decades from 1979 to 1997. For some income groups, in fact, the disparity in participation rates has remained roughly even as more students enrol in postsecondary education (Statistics Canada 2003b).

While noting that "[p]oor children are not always disadvantaged and disadvantaged children are not always poor" (Health Canada 1999: 73), the 1996–1997 National Longitudinal Survey of Children and Youth (NLSCY) found that household income was clearly associated with school readiness—an important indicator of developmental maturity and future success at school (Doherty 1997). Figure 12.3 shows the relationship between university participation and parents' income measured over eight years. Problems of poor health, hyperactivity, and delayed vocabulary development are higher among children in low-income families than among children from more privileged families (Ross 1998). Children who score low on school readiness are also more likely to have mothers with low levels of education and to live in neighbourhoods that their mothers characterize as unsafe or as lacking in social cohesiveness (Health Canada 1999: 79).

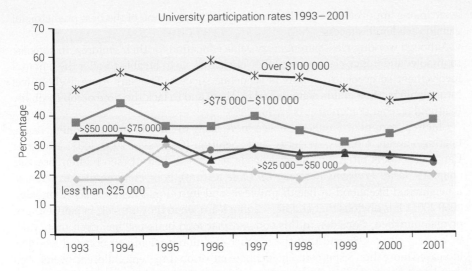

University participation rates 1993–2001

Over $100 000

>$75 000–$100 000

>$50 000–$75 000

>$25 000–$50 000

less than $25 000

Figure 12.3
University Participation Rates for Youth, 1993–2001

SOURCE: Statistics Canada, February 2005. "Participation in Post-Secondary Education: Has the Role of Parental Income and Education Changed over the 1990's?" Analytical Studies Branch Research Paper Series, Catalogue No. 11F0019MIE —No. 243, p. 12.

A report released in 2005 through Statistics Canada (Drolet 2005: 26) confirms the importance of family income to educational attainment and entry into university:

> Although university participation rates generally rise as family incomes increase, there is little difference in participation rates among youths from modest-income (below $75,000) and low-income families. Overall, the correlation between university participation and family income changed very little between 1993 and 2001.

A subtle but important point emerges in Drolet's observation above: It is not only that entry into university is prohibitively expensive for low-income families, but also that it is beyond the reach of families with incomes that hover in the modest "middle income bracket."

In a country with widely available public education, why do we see differences in educational attainment based on income? Lower-income families have less money to buy books and computers, to hire tutors, and to provide lessons in activities such as dance and music; also, parents are less likely to take their children to museums and zoos. For example, in 1998, the majority of Canadian parents who owned a home computer reported buying it for educational purposes; 90 percent said that having a computer had positively affected their children's learning ability and 79 percent claimed that it had improved the quality of their child's homework. However, in that year, three out of four households (74 percent) in the highest income group had computers, compared with fewer than one in five households (18 percent) in the lowest income group (Canadian Council on Social Development 2001).

Parents in low-income brackets are also less likely to expect their children to go to college or university, and their behaviour may lead to a self-fulfilling prophecy. "Only half of children aged 12 and 13 in families with incomes of less than $20 000 per year hoped to go to university. The figure was 71 percent for children from families with incomes over $80 000" (Canadian Council on Social Development 2001). As we have noted, a disproportionate number of children from low-income families do not go on to institutions of higher learning (Levinson 2000).

Because low-income parents often have low academic attainments, they often possess only limited language and academic skills. Children learn the limited language skills of their parents, which restricts their academic ability. Low-income parents may be unable to help their children with homework because they themselves lack the academic skills to understand the criteria. Call and colleagues (1997) report that even among impoverished youths, parental education is one of the best predictors of a child's academic success.

Although working-class parents may value education for their children, in contrast to middle- and upper-class parents they are less likely to be able to offer the parental involvement so crucial to children's academic success. They are more likely to feel intimidated by their child's schools and teachers and to lack the time or job flexibility to attend teacher conferences (Lareau 1989).

Children from poor families are also more likely to have lower functioning vision, hearing, speech, mobility, dexterity, and cognition (Campaign 2000 2001). However, Canada's schools often lack special needs services to help these children (see this chapter's *Social Problems Research Up Close* feature). Poor children also experience a heightened likelihood of health problems and nutritional deficiencies (Campaign 2000 2001). It is obvious that children cannot learn when they are sick, in pain, hungry, or malnourished. Consider, in this context, that food bank use has risen more than 92 percent since 1989 and that the number of children relying on donated food has increased more than 85 percent. "Inadequate nutrition threatens children's overall well being as it has been linked to a variety of physical, cognitive, social and emotional problems" (Covell 2001: 25).

Social Problems *Research Up Close*

Special Education

Special education is designed to help children who require special educational help due to "low intelligence, visual or auditory impairment, or emotional or specific learning difficulties, disabilities or problems" (Brown 1999: 741). Special education is a critical community resource, too often absent in our schools.

Sample and Methods

In order to investigate the educational resources available for children with special needs in Canada, Angela Kierstead and Louise Harvey (2001) conducted key informant interviews in each province with experts in the field of special education. During the summer of 2000, 17 experts from across Canada in the field of special education were interviewed. The survey was divided into three main sections: general context of special education services; assessment of how well children's needs are met; and special education resources.

Findings and Conclusions

An overwhelming majority of respondents (88 percent) reported that their educational systems have gone through major restructuring over the last five years. However, when asked if the educational system in their province was meeting the needs of children with special needs, only 19 percent said "yes." When asked if their

educational system was able to identify all those children who would benefit from special education, about six in ten said, "yes."

The majority of respondents believed that there was substantial inequality in the delivery of services to children in rural and urban areas, with children in urban centres far more likely to receive a better level of service. When asked if the need for special education services had increased, decreased, or remained constant in recent years, 94 percent of respondents reported an increase. When asked to account for why the dramatic increase had occurred, respondents attributed at least part of the increase to growing parental awareness of learning disabilities. In addition, they noted that some provinces, such as Newfoundland, have systems in place to determine what the needs of a child are and whether or not the child requires supplemental special education services.

Respondents in this survey believed that children with physical disabilities were the group most likely to receive an acceptable level of service, regardless of whether they lived in an urban or rural area. Children with hearing impairments were felt to receive very different levels of service, depending on where they lived. While 71 percent of respondents believed that children with hearing impairments who lived in cities were completely or adequately served, only 28 percent felt that this group of children in rural areas received adequate levels of service. The services provided to children with attention deficit disorder (ADD) or attention deficit hyperactivity disorder (ADHD) were generally viewed as poor, regardless of where children lived: "87 percent of respondents reported that the needs of children with ADD/ADHD living in urban areas were being met only somewhat or not at all; for children ... in rural areas, an overwhelming 93 percent of respondents stated that students' needs were met only somewhat or inadequately" (p. 3).

Respondents identified the lack of qualified personnel to provide such services as a key factor in explaining the inadequacy of services for ADD/ADHD children. They noted that, in many provinces, classroom teachers are not required to take courses in special education. In addition, the majority (88 percent) believed that there were not enough special education teachers available; over half (53 percent) believed that the number of special education teachers had decreased over the past five years. Finally, when asked about the level of funding for special education in their province or territory, 82 percent felt that it was inadequate. Complexities in provincial funding formulas, stringent guidelines, and an increase in the paperwork required of teachers in completing special education claims forms were all identified as factors that negatively affected the provision of services to children with special needs.

SOURCE: Kierstead, Angela, and Louise Harvey. 2001. "Special Education in Canada." *Perception* 25(2), Fall.

Early developmental programs may decrease the chances of developmental problems in children and enhance their performance within schools. For example, **Head Start** programs are based on the belief that to assist children, the entire family must be helped (Fact Sheet 2000). Evaluations of Head Start programs in Canada and the United States report such benefits as "more students completing school and with better grades; fewer young people needing mental health services; fewer parents abusing alcohol with concurrent reductions of alcohol's impact on children; a reduction in family violence; [and] fewer students with preventable disabilities and reduced demand for medical services" (Government of Canada 2001; Summary Report 2001). In Edmonton, for example, Head Start programs have existed for 25 years.

Head Start programs have been identified as particularly important in increasing the educational success of Aboriginal students. Canada introduced the Aboriginal Head Start Program in 1995 and the First Nations Head Start in 1998. In 1998, the federal government announced that it would provide permanent funding for the Aboriginal Head Start programs that already existed in Canada as well as additional funds for the establishment of new Head Start programs on reserves. It is estimated, though, that existing programs reach only about 5 percent of the Aboriginal children who could potentially benefit from their availability (George 1998). The costs of providing early childhood intervention programs are significant. Nevertheless, investments in the critical early years of a child's life benefit not only Canada's children, but our economy as well. Indeed, one Canadian study reports, "every dollar spent in early intervention can save seven dollars in future expenditures in health and social spending" (Health Canada 1999: 88).

Head Start
A U.S. project begun to help preschool children from disadvantaged families.

Racial and Ethnic Minorities

Socio-economic status interacts with race and ethnicity. Because race and ethnicity are so closely tied to socio-economic status, it appears that race or ethnicity alone can determine school success. Although race and ethnicity also have independent effects on educational achievement (Bankston and Caldas 1997; Jencks and Phillips 1998), their relationship to school success is largely due to their association with socio-economic status.

One reason why some minority students have academic difficulty is that they did not learn English as their first language. As previously noted, growing numbers of immigrant children of school age do not speak either of Canada's official languages upon arrival. Another factor that may have a negative impact upon both immigrant and minority students is the use of tests to assess academic achievement and ability that are biased against minorities. For example, questions on standardized tests often require students to have knowledge that is specific to the white middle-class majority culture, and cultural bias built into the IQ tests used in schools further privileges children from already advantaged backgrounds.

In addition, minority students may be disadvantaged by overt racism and discrimination. It has been noted, for example, that "[m]any visible minorities, such as native people and blacks, continue to have much greater school dropout rates" (Livingstone 1999: 743). Moreover, while research conducted by the Toronto Board of Education (1993) suggests that immigrant children, in general, do well at school after a period of acclimatization, a notable exception exists with respect to Afro-Canadian children. These children "experience lower rates of integration into the educational system and have lower levels of educational attainment."

Table 12.2 shows participation rates in postsecondary education for students from traditionally underrepresented and "minority" groups. Derived from the Canadian

Table 12.2 *Rates of Access to College and University for Underrepresented and Minority Groups*
YITS Cohort A, Cycle 4[1]

	All Provinces		
	College	University	Any
		Percent	
All	**33.0**	**41.7**	**74.7**
Family income			
Income below $50 000	34.8	31.4	66.2
Income greater than $50 000	32.1	46.9	79.0
Parental education			
No post secondary	36.6	24.3	60.9
At least some post secondary	31.5	49.2	80.7
Community type			
Rural	35.5	31.5	67.0
Population centre	32.3	44.7	77.0
Family type			
Single parent	35.5	33.0	68.5
Two-parent family	32.5	43.5	76.0
Immigrant status			
First-generation immigrant	29.6	57.0	86.6
Second-generation immigrant	30.0	53.0	83.0
Non-Immigrant	34.2	37.0	71.2
Aboriginal status			
Aboriginal	28.0	23.1	51.1
Non-Aboriginal	33.2	42.2	75.4

[1]YITS Cycle A consists of youth who were 15 years old in 2000. The students were surveyed again in 2002, 2004, 2006, 2008 and 2010 (cycles 2, 3, 4, 5 and 6). The analysis is based on the respondents' postsecondary education status in 2006 (Cycle 4) when they were age 21. Source: Statistics Canada. Youth in Transition Survey. Cohort A. Cycle 4.

In contrast, first-and second-generation children of immigrants had higher rates of participation in postsecondary education than non-immigrant youth. This was driven largely by the former's university participation rates, which were 20.0 percentage points higher for first-generation children of immigrants and 16.0 percentage points higher for second-generation children of immigrants compared to non-immigrant youth.

SOURCE: Statistics Canada. "Education Matters: Insights on Education, Learning, and Training in Canada." Catalogue no. 81-004X, Vol. 8, no. 4. http://www.statcan.gc.ca/pub/81-004-x/2011004/article/11595-eng.htm#a

Youth in Transition Survey (YITS), what the table shows us is that a number of independent variables—including immigration status, family income, parental educational attainment, and Aboriginal status—are at play in predicting the likelihood of entry into postsecondary education for given groups of youth. Powerful predictors for lowered participation rates include family income lower than $50 000 per year, and Aboriginal status. Quite interestingly, and possibly because parents may immigrate specifically in order to provide greater opportunities for their children, first generation children of immigrants are more likely to proceed to university and college than are non-immigrant youth in Canada.

An ongoing debate in Canada is whether or not students, at all levels, are better served by a faculty whose composition is less singular and reflects the diversity of our population. It has been noted that while the composition of Canada's student population is becoming increasingly multicultural, this is less true of Canada's teachers now and in the foreseeable future (Canadian Council on Social Development 1999). Moreover, as the number and size of racial and ethnic minority groups increase, some have suggested the need for more inclusive curricula to promote multicultural education. Edmonton, for example, already offers children such alternatives to French as Arabic, German, Ukrainian, and Mandarin; in 2001, the number of students enrolled in these programs (2250) exceeded the number enrolled in French immersion (1895). School boards in both Calgary and Edmonton have also launched publicly funded Spanish bilingualism programs (Bricker and Greenspon 2001: 284).

In addition, it has been argued that **multicultural education**, education that includes all racial and ethnic groups in the school curriculum, is necessary to promote awareness and appreciation for cultural diversity (Conciatore 2000; Henry et al. 2000). Some recommend that "the experiences of women (and of First Nations people, working-class people, visible minorities and other disadvantaged groups) must be incorporated into the curriculum ... The purpose of schooling must be to 'empower' ... them, to give them the ability to participate fully in struggles, large and small, to gain respect, dignity and power."

Not all, however, agree. For example, Thomas Sowell (1994), a prolific African-American scholar and darling of those who oppose "affirmative action" initiatives, maintains that the limited amount of class time available makes it impossible for educators to include the experiences of non-dominant groups. He says that to try to add such experiences is foolish and unnecessary.

Canadian education specialists, such as George Dei (2001) and Jasmin Zine (2002), however, argue that positions such as Sowell's misinterpret what inclusive curricula look like. Inclusive curricula do not simply try to cover more in less time, adding more information to an already crammed curriculum; rather, inclusive and antiracist education pays critical attention to Eurocentric curricula, decentring its assumptions and its reproduction of racist attitudes about what counts as "knowledge" (Dei 2001). In other words, education should not be limited to input of facts, but of teaching different ways to consider "the facts."

Such opposing viewpoints reflect the "culture wars" that surround education today. However, as John Wilson (in Whitehead 1994: 13) has suggested, these debates may well provide educators with a unique opportunity to contemplate and reassess "the questions of what should be taught and how we ought to teach."

multicultural education Education that includes all racial and ethnic groups in the school curriculum and promotes awareness and appreciation for cultural diversity.

Gender

Worldwide, women receive less education than men. Two-thirds of the world's 920 million illiterate people are women (United Nations Population Fund 1999).

Historically, schools have discriminated against women. When Martha Humm Lewis gained entrance to a training school for teachers in New Brunswick in 1849, the principal of the school cautioned her to "enter the classroom ten minutes before the male students, sit alone at the back of the room, always wear a veil, leave the classroom five minutes before the end of the lesson and leave the building without speaking to any of the young men" (MacLellan 1972, in Schaefer et al. 1996: 282). Although Canadian schools are not typically segregated by sex any longer, a look at the elementary schools that were built prior to 1960 will likely yield a large number with the designations "Girls" and "Boys" over separate entrances, reflecting past attempts to keep the sexes apart.

Since the 1960s, the women's movement has sought to end sexism in education. For example, the 1970 Canadian Royal Commission on the Status of Women made the following recommendations: "adoption of textbooks that portray both sexes in diversified roles and occupations; provision of career information about the broad field of occupational choice for girls; improved availability of sport programs for both sexes; development of educational programs to meet the special needs of rural and immigrant women and of Indian and Inuit girls and young women; and the continuing education of women with family responsibilities" (as cited in Mackie 1991: 158). Three decades later, textbooks using gender-neutral language and images are increasingly being adopted and there has been a trend toward a more integrated curriculum in which boys and girls learn, for example, both auto mechanics and cooking.

Traditional gender roles account for many of the differences in educational achievement and attainment between women and men. As noted in Chapter 7, schools, teachers, and educational materials reinforce traditional gender roles in several ways. Some evidence suggests, for example, that teachers provide less attention and encouragement to girls than to boys and that textbooks tend to stereotype females and males in traditional roles (Evans and Davies 2000).

Most of the research on gender inequality in the school focuses on how female students are disadvantaged in the educational system. But what about male students? As discussed in Chapter 7, the argument that girls have been educationally shortchanged has recently come under attack—some academicians charge that it is boys, not girls, who have been left behind (Sommers 2000).

The problems that boys bring to school may require schools to devote more resources and attention to them. More than 70 percent of students with learning disabilities such as dyslexia are male, as are 75 percent of students identified as having serious emotional problems. Boys are also more likely than girls to have speech impairments, to be labelled as mentally retarded, to exhibit discipline problems, to drop out of school, and to feel alienated from the learning process (Bushweller 1995; Goldberg 1999; Sommers 2000).

Some educational reformers have suggested a return to single-sex schools for both males and females. For males, the argument is that boys could benefit from the masculine environment provided by all-male academies where male teachers serve as positive role models. For females, the argument is that same-sex schools minimize the stereotyping, harassment, and discrimination that can exist in mixed-sex classrooms. However, researcher Maggie Ford concludes that the evidence indicates "that separating by sex is not the solution to gender inequity in education. When elements of good education are present, girls and boys succeed" (AAUW 1998).

12.4 Problems in the Canadian Educational System

Let us examine some of the major problems that have been identified within Canadian education today—and several potential solutions.

Low Levels of Academic Achievement

Worrisome evidence that suggested the inferiority of the Canadian school system appeared throughout the 1990s. For some social commentators, such evidence proved the inadequacy of our educational system and, in particular, the aftermath of **grade inflation** (the awarding of A's to students whose work warrants lower grades) and **social promotion** (the practice of passing students from one grade to the next even though they have not mastered the necessary grade-level skills). Canadian schools, critics charged, churned out **functional illiterates**: people who cannot "read basic signs or maps, complete simple forms, or carry on many of the tasks required of an adult" (Literacy 2000: 1).

In response to the disappointing performance of Canadian students on international tests, many Canadians clamoured for the administration of provincewide standardized tests for both students and teachers. Such tests, it was argued, would allow school performance to be independently and objectively assessed. Indeed, a May 2000 poll reported that more than 8 in 10 of those surveyed supported provincewide tests for students. A similar proportion believed that high school students should be required to pass both a compulsory literacy test and a standardized, provincewide knowledge test prior to graduation (Bricker and Greenspon 2001: 165–66).

However, some analysts emphasized that the results of international tests are misleading for various reasons (Barlow and Robertson 1994; Bracey 1998; Schrag 1997). First, most countries that participated in the study did not follow sampling guidelines. Specifically, many excluded those students whom educational administrators thought would perform badly on the exam. As a result, these countries artificially inflated their scores. Second, different countries have different kinds of secondary school systems. For instance, some keep students in school for 14 years, while others, like Canada, have 12-year systems. Some countries have higher dropout rates than Canada has and/or siphon off poor academic performers to trades schools and job-training programs before they complete high school. As a result, only the top performers remain by the last year of high school. In contrast, Canada attempts to ensure that as many students as possible graduate from high school since it is hoped that high rates of completion of secondary education will enhance the quality of democracy, increase social cohesion in a culturally diverse society, and improve economic performance.

Despite the limitations of international comparisons, many Canadians still felt buoyed when the results of the most recent international tests in reading, math, and science were released in 2001. Among 32 countries, Canada ranked second overall in reading and fifth in math and science. When provincial results were analyzed separately, students in Alberta, Quebec, and British Columbia ranked among the best in the world. Indeed, Alberta students obtained the highest scores in the world in reading and placed third in both science and math. Quebec came second in math with scores that rivalled those of students in Japan. Other provinces, however, most notably those in the Atlantic region, did not fare as well (Sokoloff 2001).

George Dei reminds us that measures such as these are highly politicized and sit at the centre of manufactured anxieties about global markets and Canada's ability to compete. Commenting on increased testing and restrictive curriculum changes throughout the 1990s in Ontario, Dei (1999) remarks:

> The intent of these initiatives was to insert Ontario into the global marketplace, thereby ensuring that schools would be able to produce a cheap and compliant labor force. However, in order for these reforms to be pushed through without a serious public backlash, it was necessary to create a "crisis in schooling." By undermining the reputation of public education, the Conservatives manufactured a province wide concern over "the declining quality of Ontario education." . . . Within months of the

grade inflation
Higher grades given than the work warrants; a general increase in student grades without a corresponding increase in learning.

social promotion
The passing of students from grade to grade even if they are failing.

functional illiterates
High-school graduates who have difficulty with basic reading and math skills.

Conservative accession, schools across the province found that many of the programs that had worked toward equity and social justice were either cut back severely or were terminated altogether.

School Dropouts

According to the latest available figures, Canada ranks in the middle of OECD nations with an overall dropout rate of 10.9 percent (Bowlby 2008). However, even though the stereotype of the dropout is that of a poorly motivated underachiever who prefers to live on social assistance and use drugs, a Statistics Canada report presents a different picture: "The reasons behind the decision to drop out of high school reported by 20-year-olds in the Youth in Transition Survey differed somewhat between males and females. Young men were less likely to be engaged in school than young women and were more likely to report wanting to work/earn money as a reason for dropping out of high school" (ibid). Female school leavers, by contrast, were more likely to have had children to raise, with 15.9 percent leaving due to pregnancy (ibid). The greater likelihood that young women are caring for their young children than young men are does not mean that early child-bearing is the main reason young women leave school; young mothers are a significant minority of female school leavers. In addition, the rate of young men dropping out of school—12.2 percent—is significantly greater than the rate of young women leaving school—7.2 percent (ibid).

Contrary to popular stereotypes, Sid Gilbert and Bruce Orok (1993: 3) report that many school leavers come from intact, two-parent homes, were doing well at school, and were either not working or working only moderate hours prior to leaving school. Upon leaving school, school leavers were generally employed, worked long hours, and planned to continue with further education or job training. "Among male school leavers aged 18-20, the two most important reasons for leaving were that they preferred work to school (28 percent) and boredom (19 percent).... Female leavers aged 18-20 cited boredom (22 percent) and problems with schoolwork (13 percent) as the top two reasons for leaving school." Nine percent of male respondents mentioned the need to work for financial reasons, while 8 percent mentioned problems with teachers. A subtle point that should not be overlooked is that many of the respondents intended to return to school—and that is, indeed, what we find in long-term surveys of those who leave high school before completing their diplomas. Long-term surveys of youth in Canada show that by their late twenties only 6 percent of those who had left school early remained without a high school diploma or equivalent; furthermore, of those who had left school early but later returned a total of 43 percent had gone on to postsecondary education (Statistics Canada 2010). In other words, a high school diploma is not necessarily the limit in educational attainment for those who leave school early. Indeed, of the 43 percent who had gone on to postsecondary education, one-fifth did so without ever completing high school equivalency. The negative "dropout" label, which sounds so *permanent,* does not capture the full picture or long-term outcomes for school leavers, or do justice to their own educational aspirations.

Long-term improvements notwithstanding, the economic and social consequences of dropping out of school are significant. Dropouts are more likely than those who complete high school to be unemployed and to earn less when they are employed (*Digest of Educational Statistics* 2001). According to recent reports from Statistics Canada, the unemployment rate for those aged 20 to 24 without a high-school diploma or equivalent in 2004–05 was 19.4 percent, double the rate for all 20- to 24-year-olds (Bowlby 2008). There are, however, some hopeful signs:

The substantial decline in the dropout rate over the past decade suggests that many of the programs that have been put in place to encourage young people to stay in school until they graduate are meeting with success. Programs have also been put in place to afford high school drop-outs a second chance, by offering the opportunity to return to school to complete the requirements for high school graduation. One can expect that take up of 'second-chance' programs is influenced in part by the early labour-market experiences of young drop-outs who find they face real difficulties in securing stable, long-term employment that actually pays a decent wage. (ibid)

Student Violence

On April 28, 1999, a 15-year-old boy in Taber, Alberta, gunned down one teen and wounded another in a school hallway. In February 2000, three Toronto teenagers were wounded in a gun battle in a high school parking lot; the same day, at another Toronto high school, a 13-year-old boy was charged with choking and sexually assaulting a 17-year-old girl. Concealed in his inside jacket pocket at the time was a bored-out starter's pistol, loaded with .22 calibre bullets and ready to fire (Appleby 2000). In the fall of 2006, Kimveer Gill entered Dawson College CEGEP in Montreal and shot 19 people, killing one and seriously injuring the others before killing himself with a shotgun blast to his head.

While we might prefer to think of aggression and violence in school as exceptional, evidence suggests that they are not (Table 12.3). The table, initially reported in the 2008 report *The Road to Health* produced by the School Community Safety Advisory Panel, shows that contemporary schools in Toronto are anything but "safe." The report underscores that while the media discussion of violence in schools tends to concentrate on notorious neighbourhoods,

> the anonymous surveys at Westview Centennial (870 of the 1200 students responded) indicated that 23% of students reported that they know someone who had brought a gun to school in the past two years. 22.5% reported that they have seen a gun in the past two years. 6.1% reported that they knew four or more people who brought guns to school in the past two years. *Far from being a "Jane/Finch" issue, the problem is city-wide…* [emphasis added] (p. 3).*

In other words, the problems are spread across the city of Toronto, as they are in other cities in Canada, and are not isolated in "troublesome" neighbourhoods. These observations bear out with broader trends over the last 15 years in Canada.

A 1999 survey of 2000 Alberta students in Grades 7 to 12 reports that violence was highest among students in Grades 8 and 9. Approximately 16 percent of students in this survey acknowledged bringing weapons to school, with illegal knives and replica

Table 12.3 **Table of Violent Incidents**

Category	On School Property	Off School Property	NW2
Gun incidents—actual/replicas/pellet/reported	54	26	3
Weapons incidents—knives and tasers only—could be in possession/threatening	30	5	0
Robberies	10	5	0
Sexual assaults	31	16	2

SOURCE: Excerpted from Julian Falconer (2008). "The Road to Health: A Final Report on School Safety." Reprinted by permission of Julian Falconer.

*Excerpted from Julian Falconer (2008). "The Road to Health: A Final Report on School Safety." Reprinted by permission of Julian Falconer.

weapons the most common (Canadian Press 2000). The 2000 Project Canada Survey on teens finds that one in two Canadian teens views violence in schools as a "very serious" problem. Female teenagers were especially likely to view violence in schools in that way (59 percent of female teens versus 40 percent of males) (Bibby 2001: 81). About one in three teenagers (32 percent) reported having a close friend who had been physically attacked at school. Male teens were especially likely to report having a friend who experienced physical violence while at school (39 percent of males versus 25 percent of females) (Bibby 2001: 82). In addition, it should be noted that aggressive acts by students do not always entail physical violence. In 2002, in a landmark case that was reputedly the first to hold schoolyard bullies to account, a 16-year-old girl was found guilty of criminal harassment for her role in bullying a Grade 9 Abbotsford, B.C., student, Dawn-Marie Wesley. Wesley was so tormented that she committed suicide in November 2000 (*Maclean's* 2002).

Various attempts have been made to redress the problem of violence, bullying, and harassment in schools. "In what is believed to be the first measure of its kind in Canada," the city of Edmonton passed a bylaw in March 2003 that bans harassment of people under 18 (Mahoney 2003: A8). The bylaw, which took effect in May 2003, defines *bullying* as "repeated intimidation of others" including "real or threatened infliction of various types of abuse, including physical, verbal, emotional, or written," and covers bullying in public places. Those who bully can be given a $250 ticket—and it's anticipated that the use of this bylaw will be heaviest in schools. Some schools have installed security systems, hired security guards, shortened school days to eliminate free time, and expelled troublemakers.

Other schools, however, advocate a different approach to the problem of antisocial and aggressive behaviour in schools. For example, after experiencing several incidents of racially charged violence, Cole Harbour High School in Nova Scotia introduced a "Student of the Week" program, designed to encourage students to learn respect for the cultures of others, and implemented a system of peer mediators. Peer mediators are students who are given special training in mediation techniques under the supervision of a staff person, in order to work at the front line in conflict between small numbers of students. The Cole Harbour school mandate encourages students to develop "a sense of responsibility for the condition of their school; they feel they have control over events in the school; and the program creates an environment where a minor conflict can be handled without the principal's intervention." Alberta's Safe and Caring Schools project advocates that the problem of school violence is best dealt with through community-wide efforts to encourage responsible behaviour. According to the Safe and Caring Schools project, early intervention and prevention are needed.

Consistent with this approach, Dan Offord, former head of child psychiatry at McMaster University, has argued that attempts to reduce violent behaviour in schools must begin with screening programs directed at children in early grades who display antisocial behaviour. His argument suggests that as many as 20 percent of school-aged children and teens suffer "from some type of emotional disorder" and that "at least 12 percent" could benefit from individual attention. Moreover, he maintains that while many find a "get tough" approach appealing, "there has to be a place for everyone in schools... you can't just push kids out of the school system. Where do they go?" (as cited in Crane 1999: A2). Among the problems with the various "get tough" approaches and "zero tolerance" policies is that they are disproportionately targeting racially and ethnically minorized children and youth in public schools. Where these children already have their academic needs neglected, and where they are already disproportionately held out of programs that help more privileged children to stay in the academic stream, black, Muslim, and South Asian students are more frequently pushed out of the school system using a series of increasingly alienating and punitive policies (Bhattacharjee, 2003: 50–52).

The High Costs of Education

Canada compares favourably to many other countries in terms of various indicators of education. For example, compared to most other Western countries, we tend to spend a higher proportion of our GDP (gross domestic product) on education. Moreover, unlike the majority of countries worldwide, we encourage those who are imprisoned in Canada's penitentiaries to enrol in secondary, vocational, and postsecondary courses on site or through correspondence. At the same time, however, problems exist.

Reduced funding for public and postsecondary education and an increased reliance at the college and university level on student fees has led, in turn, to soaring increases in tuition costs for Canadian postsecondary students, demands for postsecondary institutions to accept more students (without additional funding), less academic hiring, rising student–faculty ratios, and dwindling resources. Private families across the country are experiencing an increasing burden on their private contributions to schooling at the same time that government use of public funding has been diverted away from schools, colleges, and universities. Whether in the form of an increased share of the total cost of tuition for postsecondary education, or in increased out-of-pocket expenses for school programs, library acquisitions, and field trips in public schools, families pay increasing amounts out of pocket for education. Yet these ostensibly "public" institutions are actually seeing declining budgets that result in reductions in full-time staff, and cut-backs in available funds for things like library holdings and other supports for academic resources. The negative consequences outlined by Johnston—shrinking numbers of lab assistants, outdated lab equipment, reductions to library budgets, and crumbling buildings (1999: 51)—have only gotten worse and more obvious in the 15 years since. Would-be and current postsecondary students and their families are increasingly forced to confront the financial burdens posed by higher education—and the costs are considerable. Table 12.4 and Figure 12.4 provide at-a-glance views of the financial burdens that students face in the pursuit of a tertiary education.

Table 12.4 *Average Undergraduate Tuition Fees for Canadian Full-Time Students, by Province*

	2012/2013[r]	2013/2014[p]	2012/2013 to 2013/2014
	Current Dollars		% Change
Canada	**5 586**	**5 772**	**3.3**
Newfoundland and Labrador	2 644	2 644	0.0
Prince Edward Island	5 474	5 696	4.1
Nova Scotia	5 977	6 185	3.5
New Brunswick	5 940	6 133	3.2
Quebec	2 565	2 653	3.4
Ontario	6 975	7 259	4.1
Manitoba	3 720	3 779	1.6
Saskatchewan	6 106	6 394	4.7
Alberta	5 670	5 670	0.0
British Columbia	4 931	5 029	2.0

[r]revised
[p]preliminary

SOURCE: Statistics Canada. "University Tuition Fee's 2013/2014." *The Daily*. September 12, 2013. http://www.statcan.gc.ca/daily-quotidien/130912/t130912b001-eng.htm

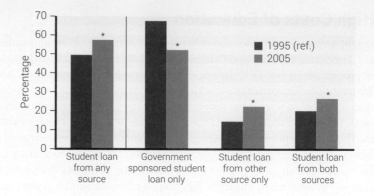

Figure 12.4 Student Loan Sources

SOURCE: Statistics Canada, "The Financial Impact of Student Loans," *Perspectives on Labour and Income*, Cat. 75-001-XIE2010101, vol. 11 no. 1, January 2010; http://www.statcan.gc.ca/bsolc/olc-cel/olc-cel?lang=eng&catno=75-001 -X.

Although the cost of postsecondary education in Canada "has always been a responsibility shared by society through tax dollars, and by parents and children through personal savings," soaring tuitions (up 115 percent since 1980) contrast sharply with the 1 percent rise in average family income (after adjusting for inflation) (Clark 1999: 24). Using data from the National Graduates Survey of 1995, Clark (1999) examined the extent of student debt and the impact of high debt on postsecondary graduates who had used government loans to finance their studies. He reports that both college and bachelor's degree graduates were most likely to finance their education through employment earnings (59 percent college, 69 percent bachelor's) and student loans (41 percent college, 42 percent bachelor's). While parents ranked third for those who acquired bachelor's degrees, neither college nor university students identified scholarships, fellowships, prizes, grants, or bursaries as a significant source of funding. Students from families with lower parental education (those whose fathers had not completed high school) were more likely to use student loans than those students with higher parental education. As well, students in their late 20s were more likely to borrow from government student loan programs and to borrow the most.

By the mid-2000s the patterns we see above only grew, further attenuating the already perilous position of students from middle and lower income groups:

> In constant dollars, university tuition fees in 2002 were the highest they had ever been at any time in the past century. Measured against the buying power of a middle income tradesman, university tuition fees in 2002 were more expensive than at anytime in the preceding 130 years, with the exception of the beginning of the Second World War. (Fisher et al. 2006: 58)

It is not surprising, perhaps, that those who borrowed from student loan programs often faced difficulty in paying back the monies they had received. Clark reports that "during the two years following graduation, one-sixth of 1995 college and bachelor's borrowers indicated they were already having difficulty making payments on their government student loans." Women with bachelor's degrees were more likely than men with bachelor's degrees were to have difficulty paying off their loans; however, among college graduates, there were only marginal differences in repayment difficulties between women and men. Fisher et al. explain that these problems with repayment stem from a federal policy that moved the Canada Student Loan Program into the hands of private lenders (i.e., banks) and away from the government's books (2006: 54–55). The move increased the levels and pace of repayment that students would have to undertake on graduation, and where students had previously been able to take student loans regardless of previous financial difficulties, new restrictions meant that credit history could result in students having their loan applications denied (ibid). In effect, those who had the least financial privilege as youth had the most significant cost barriers to the completion of postsecondary education. Furthermore,

Fisher et al. calculated increases in tuition and note that, "When measured against after-tax family income, university tuition fees increased from 6 per cent in 1990–91 to 9 per cent in 1998–99 for families in the middle income quintile, and jumped from 14 per cent to 23 per cent for families in the lowest income quintile" (2006: 58).

For those who pursue professional degrees, the burden may be even more oppressive. Consider, for example, that since 1998, when the Ontario government deregulated tuition fees for professional and graduate programs, allowing institutions to set tuition fee levels, tuition fees have soared. Law school tuition fees rose 217 percent between 1990 and 2003 (CAUT 2005: 1). For the year 2005–06, annual tuition fees for dentistry programs in Canada averaged $12 942; for medicine programs, annual fees averaged $10 349. Finally, graduate tuition fees in Canada averaged $5699 per year compared to $4214 for undergraduate education (Statistics Canada 2005). Statistics Canada (2005) notes that these increases in fees far outstripped increases in the Consumer Price Index.

Inadequate School Facilities and Persons with Disabilities

We have previously noted that special education programs for children with learning disabilities are unavailable for many of those who could benefit from them. More broadly, however, since the early 1990s, the Canadian school system has experienced budget cuts and the message to "do more with less." With the proclaimed intent of improving school standards, provincial governments have often removed resources from the educational system, centralized control of schools by imposing standardized testing and new curricula, and reduced the power of school boards. In theory, these measures allow provincial governments to balance their budgets, stimulate economic growth, and offer taxpayers tax cuts.

Decreasing educational resources obviously reduces the number of jobs available for principals, teachers, and support staff and increases educational inequality. With fewer teachers, a pared back curriculum, and increasing costs being shouldered by families rather than the state, the prospects of children from lower socio-economic strata may be grim. As we have seen, the Canadian educational system has generally acted to reproduce the country's stratification system. Since the early 1990s, however, it has acted to help increase the degree of social stratification in Canadian society (Johnston 2001).

According to Michael Fullan ([1982] 2001; Hammonds 2002), we must reinvest and reinvent our system of education. He argues that education must become a "meaningful learning community," a setting in which all participants engage in education because it brings them substantial moral benefits. He maintains that students learn best when engaged in achieving mastery of subjects that they deem relevant to their needs and backgrounds. Similarly, he argues that teachers teach best when they feel empowered by having the autonomy, resources, peer support, and professional development they require.

12.5 Strategies for Action: Trends and Innovations in Canadian Education

Canadians rank improving education as one of their top priorities. In 2000, when an Angus Reid Group survey asked Canadians to volunteer their "top-of-mind" priority issues, education was mentioned by 29 percent of respondents as a national priority, surpassed only by health care (Bricker and Greenspon 2001: 150). In addition, it is evident that education plays a critical role in Canadian society. Education has been referred to "as the one truly proactive public investment we make. It is not designed to address a problem, but rather to build the society we want for the future by investing in the creation of human and social capacity" (Canadian Council on Social Development 1999). Yet, at the same time, our educational system must be reactive, responsive to Canada's changing demography—changes in the age composition of our population, its ethno-racial mix, and family structures—as well as to trends in the labour market, the economy, and the development of information and communications technology. There is no shortage of suggestions on how we can improve our educational system. Here we review but a few.

Moral and Interpersonal Education

Most school curricula neglect the human side of education—the moral and interpersonal aspects of developing as an individual and as a member of society. Proponents of character education argue that students should "be engaged in a general education that guides them in caring for self, intimate others, global others, plants, animals, the environment, objects and instruments, and ideas" (Noddings 1995: 369). For example, service learning programs are community-based initiatives in which students volunteer in the community and receive academic credit for doing so. Studies on student outcomes have linked service learning to enhanced civic responsibility and moral reasoning, increased tolerance of diversity and promotion of racial equality, and a strong commitment to volunteerism (Aberle-Grasse 2000; Waterman 1997; Zlotkowski 1996). Character education also occurs to some extent in schools that have peer mediation and conflict resolution programs. Such programs teach the values of nonviolence, collaboration, and helping others, as well as skills in interpersonal communication and conflict resolution.

Computer Technology in Education

Computers in the classroom allow students to access large amounts of information. The proliferation of computers both in school and at home may mean that teachers will become facilitators and coaches rather than sole providers of information. Not only do computers enable students to access enormous amounts of information, including that from the World Wide Web, but they also allow students to progress at their own pace.

Canada was one of the first countries to link its student body to the information superhighway. By 1997, almost all Canadian schools had internet access through the SchoolNet electronic network. In that year, Industry Canada's "Computers in the Schools" program had placed more than 20 000 computers and 40 000 pieces of software in Canadian schools and libraries (Canadian Council on Social Development 1999). The attempt to make educational settings inclusive also suggests the benefits of computer technology in education. Software that reads aloud what is on the screen, large-screen monitors, voice-input software, and scanners are among the technologies used by differently abled students in Canada (Fichten et al. 1999).

However, computer technology is not equally accessible to all students, and varies dramatically by levels of parental education, income and race, and/or ethnic background. Complicating somewhat the view that the presence of a computer in the home is a strong predictor for school success, Vigdor and Ladd (2010) found that the presence of a computer in the home could actually decrease math and reading proficiency. The reason for the potential negative impact of computers in homes has to do principally with how the computer is most frequently used. If, for example, the home computer is used mostly for gaming or for online socializing, it can be a powerful distractor from the more concentrated work required to develop strong reading comprehension and logic skills.

In addition, while there was strong enthusiasm for the development of massive open online courses (MOOC) designed to provide learning programs that reflected the curricula at elite schools such as MIT and Stanford, the experiment in delivering these online courses to several thousand "self-directed" students has proven less effective than initially promised. According to a summative report on a series of MOOC failures (Lewin 2013), while MOOCs had been developed with the specific goal of bringing higher education to those who could not usually afford it, particularly students in poor countries. those 80 percent who successfully completed a MOOC were already holders of some form of university degree. Moreover, the specific experiment in Oakland, California charter schools that partnered with Udacity, an online "open" system that promised to bring elite education to the masses, failed massively:

> Despite access to the Udacity mentors, the online students last spring—including many from a charter high school in Oakland—did worse than those who took the classes on campus. In the algebra class, fewer than a quarter of the students—and only 12 percent of the high school students—earned a passing grade. (Lewin 2013)

These failures do not necessarily mean that online learning on a grand scale is over, explains Lewin, but that it needs to be rethought, redesigned, and perhaps focused on more practical endeavours that pair online learners with apprenticing opportunities in their own communities. Certainly we know that students who enrol in typical online courses miss out on the chance to discuss ideas in face-to-face settings with their peers and professors, and we know also that it requires considerable self-motivation and discipline to complete work when there is no "real" person to keep one on track.

In spite of these failures and limitations, the lure of online learning retains a strong popular appeal, in part because it allows students to remain at home, and to engage in their studies with a flexible time-frame that can accommodate more rigid work schedules. For reasons such as these, the current Liberal government in Ontario, under Premier Wynne, is pushing for more colleges and universities to offer online courses organized through a "central hub" to be built at a cost of $42 million and expected to start operating some time in 2015 (Bradshaw 2014). The plan promises that courses will be more "portable" across the Ontario university and college system, but that portability is of little importance if students are less likely to complete online courses than more traditional classes held on campus.

Alternative School Choices

Traditionally, children have gone to school in the district where they live. However, alternative schools, home schooling, and private schools provide parents with alternative school choices for their children. **Alternative schools** began in Canada in the 1970s. According to Chernos (1998: 13), "Perhaps the one element that unifies alternative schools is their diversity. Each operates within school board and education ministry guidelines, yet maintains a unique character."

For example, in London, Ontario, Richmond Centre and Dundas Centre Schools "are intended as an interim measure for students experiencing social, emotional, psychological, behavioral or academic troubles" (Chernos 1998: 15). The London board also maintains other alternative schools for Native youth, Annishnabe and Wiingashk, both of which incorporate Native culture and traditions within a core curriculum of basic Grade 9 to 12 subjects. In Toronto, the focus of Horizon Alternative Senior School "is on creating a caring community" and on balancing "core subjects . . . with an outward world-view that emphasizes self-expression, debate, role playing dialogue and conflict resolution" (Chernos 1998: 13). In Ontario alone, there are several dozen elementary and secondary schools that bill themselves as alternative schools.

alternative schools
Alternative schools began in Canada in the 1970s. Each operates within school board and education ministry guidelines, but is unique in its character.

Alternative schools typically offer a variety of innovative and experimental programs. They generally have low student populations ranging from 70 to 250, with small, informal classes; they place emphasis on close interaction between students and teachers. In many alternative high schools, student representatives join teachers, parents, and, sometimes, community members on the school's board of directors. According to Levin (1999: 732), alternative schools can be distinguished by "the sense of ownership, autonomy and control that teachers, parents, and students feel towards their school even as governments and school boards move to assert and maintain stronger administrative control" upon them. Indeed, he suggests that "alternative schools may be forerunners of a more decentralized, pluralistic, community-based education system." Although there has been enough popular skepticism regarding their less regulated organization of student learning, and of the self-directed nature of the learning students can pursue in them, that alternative schools in Canada have never threatened to become the mode of the mainstream, these schools, with their tiny populations, often boast a higher concentration of high-profile alumni than mainstream schools do. SEED Alternative school in Toronto, for example, counts among its alumni Cory Doctorow, the founder of Boing Boing (an internet news aggregator); Edward Waitzer, former TSE head and corporate lawyer; Melissa Franklin, Department Chair at Harvard's physics department; Lee Kline, an industrial and architectural designer and owner of IMG Interior Manufacturing; and Morgan Holmes, one of the authors of this textbook, who attended SEED in the mid-1980s.

However, not all boards in Canada operate alternative schools, or if they do, those schools are segregated sites designed specifically for students who have been compelled to leave the regular system because they have come into conflict with the law. For example, in the Waterloo Region District School Board (WRDSB), covering Kitchener, Waterloo, and Cambridge, the only alternative school (other than traditional night school, summer school, and programs for institutionalized learners) is "U-Turn," with sites in Cambridge and Waterloo. Previously for students aged 16–18 who have been forced to leave the regular system because they have substance abuse or behavioural problems, sometimes serious enough to have brought them into contact with the youth criminal justice system, the program was modified in 2013–2014 to target "disengaged" students aged 15–17 as an early intervention program. U-Turn's goal remains, according to the WRDSB, to transition students "back to home-school programming" (WRDSB 2014).

The Toronto and Waterloo board approaches to alternative schooling represent very different commitments, one quite broad, and the other quite narrow. While the Toronto alternative system also includes schools for "at risk" youth who have come into conflict with the law, the mandate to provide alternative systems that include Afrocentric schools and schools for exceptionally talented students is very different from the Waterloo delivery of "gifted" programming exclusively within mainstream schools, and alternative campuses that deal only with "troubled" youth.

Across the country, those who can afford to opt out of publicly funded schooling and who seek alternative schooling for their children may send them to the popular Waldorf and Montessori schools with their impressive records for student achievement. It is, however, unclear whether those student achievements are effected most powerfully by the Waldorf and Montessori systems, or by the financial privileges their families can bestow on them. It is likely some combination of socio-economic privilege and the curricular design of these schools that contributes to student successes.

Some parents are choosing not to send their children to school at all but to teach them at home. For some parents, **home schooling** is part of a fundamentalist

home schooling
The education of children at home instead of in a public or private school; often part of a fundamentalist movement to protect children from perceived non-Christian values in the public schools.

movement to protect children from perceived non-Christian values in the public schools. Other parents are concerned about the quality of their children's education and their safety.

How does being schooled at home instead of attending public school affect children? Some evidence suggests that home-schooled children perform as well as or better than their institutionally schooled counterparts (Webb 1989; Winters 2000).

Another choice parents may make is to send their children to a private school. The primary reason parents send their children to private schools is for religious instruction. The second most frequent reason is the belief that private schools are superior to public schools in terms of academic achievement. Research suggests, however, that when controlling for parents' education and income, there are few differences in private and public school educational outcomes (Ascher et al. 1997; Cohen 1998; Shanker 1996). Parents also choose private schools for their children in order to have greater control over school policy or to obtain a specific course of instruction, such as dance or music.

Understanding Problems in Education

What can we conclude about the state of the educational system in Canada? Any criticism of education must take into account that over a century ago, many children did not receive even a primary school education. Instead, they worked in factories and on farms to help support their families. Whatever education they received came from the family or the religious institution. It is evident that Canada has come a long way since that time. From humble beginnings, education in Canada has grown into a massive industry with total expenditures now exceeding $61 billion a year (Girvan 2000: 82).

At the same time, it is evident that problems exist. While public schools are supposed to provide all Canadian children with the academic and social foundations necessary to participate in society in a productive and meaningful way, some students remain marginalized and do not enjoy their benefits as much as others. As conflict theorists note, the educational institution can perpetuate a downward cycle of failure, alienation, and hopelessness. Breaking the cycle requires providing adequate funding for teachers, school buildings, equipment, and educational materials. In addition, jobs must be provided for those who successfully complete their education. Students with little hope of job success will continue to experience low motivation as long as job prospects are bleak and earnings in available jobs are low. Ray and Mickelson (1993: 14–15) explain:

> School reforms of any kind are unlikely to succeed if… students cannot anticipate opportunity structures that reward diligent efforts in school. Employers are not apt to find highly disciplined and motivated young employees for jobs that are unstable and low paying.

Finally, "if we are to improve the skills and attitudes of future generations of workers, we must also focus attention and resources on the quality of the lives children lead outside the school" (Murnane 1994: 290). We must provide support to families so children grow up in healthy, safe, and nurturing environments. Children are the future of our nation and of the world. Whatever resources we provide to improve the lives and education of children are sure to be wise investments in our collective future.

Student Reflection: What Do You Know Now?

If you or someone you know plans to become a teacher, how would you explain the relevance of this chapter to the actual classroom? How much sociology should teachers need to study in order to understand social problems, including problems associated with non-middle class, non-dominant groups? Which parts of the chapter would a teacher need to know more about to succeed in making change? What about people in roles other than teacher, but with frontline contact with various publics?

Can you think of a way in which school could encourage unruliness, open-endedness, and difference rather than compliance, rigidity, and sameness? Should it?

Consider your own relationship to schooling and your future plans for work; has your reading of this chapter prompted any critical reflection on your current course or courses, your program, your identity as a learner, your future plans?

What Do You Do Next?

Located at www.nelson.com/socialproblems5e

- Consolidate your knowledge with interactive and printable **Flashcards**
- Gauge your understanding with **Practice Quizzes** and **Matching Activities**
- Develop your critical thinking skills with **Self and Society** and **The Human Side** questions
- Analyze **Social Research** and **Social Problems in Global Perspective**
- Explore the implications of **Technology on Social Problems**

13

Environmental Problems

Student Reflection: What Do You Already Know?

As this textbook goes to press, 40- to 100-watt incandescent light bulbs will no longer be permitted to be imported into Canada. This is one example of a regulation meant to have a positive impact on global greenhouse gas emissions, and is part of a larger movement to make better decisions for the planet we share with all other life forms as well as land, air, and sea. The interconnectedness of social and physical location has meant that we are faced with "wicked" problems—problems for which the solutions lead to other problems—and knowing what will affect something else, and when and where, is nearly impossible. A young adult having come through Canadian schooling could be forgiven for feeling overwhelmed by the scale of environmental problems; it's the responsibility of parents, families, and children to monitor the kinds of paper, plastic, metal, and glass that go into our blue recycling boxes, and we're made to feel guilty if we mis-sort our garbage. Yet the local focus needs a broader context. This chapter provides sociological ways of thinking about actions, policies, resource use, and their various effects on social groups and systems, in Canada and globally.

Learning Outcomes

Through careful reading of this chapter, you should be able to:

- define the bolded key terms
- apply sociological theories and ecofeminism to the global context for environmental problems
- clarify the various types of human–environment interaction in relation to social problems
- identify complex relationships among wind, water, air, plants and animals, and human activity over time
- raise your own awareness of Canada's role in these relationships, not only from water to oil sands to radioactive waste to the Kyoto agreement and science funding, but also in terms of a history of settler colonialism
- identify social causes of environmental damage and social costs of that damage on various populations
- differentiate effects on social groups using the concept of environmental racism
- consider the impact of changing food waste habits as one way to contribute to positive change
- move from ingrained ideas of personal, individual change to demanding corporate and systemic change
- weigh the consequences of acting differently in one area on the other related areas of environmental concern

© Jacobtl/iStockphoto.com

13.1 The Global Context: Globalization and the Environment

In 1992, leaders from across the globe met at the first Earth Summit in Rio de Janeiro to forge agreements to protect the planet's environment and at the same time alleviate world poverty. When world leaders met a decade later for the second Earth Summit, held in Johannesburg, South Africa, the overall state of the environment had deteriorated and poverty had deepened. How is it that the combined efforts of leaders who met at the first Earth Summit were so ineffectual? A large part of the answer lies in the increasing globalization of the last two decades. Three aspects of globalization have affected the environment: (1) the permeability of international borders to pollution and environmental problems, (2) cultural and social integration spurred by communication and information technology, and (3) growth of free trade and transnational corporations.

Permeability of International Borders

Environmental problems such as global warming and destruction of the ozone layer (discussed later in this chapter) demonstrate that environmental problems extend far beyond their source to affect the entire planet and its inhabitants. A striking example of the permeability of international borders to pollution is the spread of toxic chemicals (such as PCBs) from the southern hemisphere into the Arctic. In as little as five days, chemicals from the tropics can evaporate from the soil, ride the winds thousands of kilometres north, condense in the cold air, and fall on the Arctic in the form of toxic snow or rain (French 2000). This phenomenon was discovered in the mid-1980s, when scientists found high levels of PCBs in the breast milk of Inuit women in the Canadian Arctic.

Another environmental problem involving permeability of borders is **bioinvasion**: the emergence of organisms in regions where they are not native. Bioinvasion is largely a product of the growth of global trade and tourism (Chafe 2005). Exotic species travel in the ballast water of ships (water taken in to stabilize empty vessels as they cross waterways), in packing material, in shipments of crops and other goods, and in many other ways. Invasive species may compete with native species for food, start an epidemic, or prey on natives, threatening not only their immediate victims but also the entire ecosystem in which the victims live.

Red fire ants are an example of a bioinvasion. In 1957, they travelled from Paraguay and Brazil on shiploads of lumber to Mobile, Alabama, and have since spread throughout the southern states, causing damage to gardens and yards, invading the food supplies (seeds, young plants, and insects) of other animals, and harming humans with their painful sting (Hilgenkamp 2005). You might be surprised to learn that the domestic cat is considered among the world's 100 worst invasive species. Cats, native to northeast Africa, have spread to every part of the world and are responsible for the decline and extinction of many species of birds (Global Invasive Species Database 2006).

Cultural and Social Integration

As mass media infiltrate the world, people across the globe aspire to consume the products and mimic the materially saturated lifestyles portrayed in movies, television, and advertising. As patterns of consumption in developing countries increasingly follow those in wealthier Western nations, so do the problems associated with overconsumption: depletion of natural resources, pollution, and global warming.

bioinvasion
The emergence of organisms in regions where they are not native.

Conversely, the internet and other forms of mass communication have helped to integrate the efforts of diverse environmental groups, creating new opportunities for environmental groups to join forces, share information, and educate the public.

The Growth of Transnational Corporations and Free Trade Agreements

The world's economy is dominated by transnational corporations, many of which have established factories and other operations in developing countries where labour and environmental laws are lax. Transnational corporations have been implicated in environmentally destructive activities—from mining and cutting timber to dumping toxic waste.

The World Trade Organization (WTO) and free trade agreements such as NAFTA (North American Free Trade Agreement) and the FTAA (Free Trade Area of the Americas) allow transnational corporations to pursue profits, expand markets, use natural resources, and exploit cheap labour in developing countries; at the same time, the ability of governments to protect natural resources or to implement environmental legislation is weakened. Transnational corporations have influenced the world's most powerful nations to institutionalize an international system of governance that values commercialism, corporate rights, and "free" trade over the environment, human rights, worker rights, and human health (Bruno and Karliner 2002). Under NAFTA's Chapter 11 provisions, corporations can challenge local and provincial/state environmental policies; federal regulations, including those for controlled substances; and court rulings, if such regulatory measures and government actions negatively affect profits.

Any country that decides, for example, to ban the export of raw logs as a means of conserving its forests—or, as another example, to ban the use of carcinogenic pesticides—can be charged under the WTO by member states on behalf of their corporations for obstructing the free flow of trade and investment. A secret tribunal of trade officials would then decide whether these laws were "trade restrictive" under the WTO rules and should therefore be struck down. Once the secret tribunal issues its edict, no appeal is possible. The convicted country is obligated to change its laws or face the prospect of perpetual trade sanctions (Clarke 2002: 44). As of early 2005, 42 cases had been filed by corporate interests and investors, 11 of which had been finalized. Five corporations that won their claims received $35 million paid by taxpayers in Canada and Mexico. For example, in the late 1990s, Ethyl, a U.S. chemical company, used NAFTA rules to challenge Canadian environmental regulation of the toxic gasoline additive MMT. Ethyl won the suit, and Canada paid $13 million in damages and legal fees to Ethyl and reversed the ban on MMT (Public Citizen 2005). Although the United States has not, as of this writing, lost a case, it is only a matter of time before a corporation based in Mexico or Canada wins a NAFTA case against the United States (Public Citizen 2005).

13.2 Sociological Theories of Environmental Problems

Each of the three main sociological theories—structural-functionalism, conflict theory, and symbolic interactionism—as well as ecofeminist theory provide insights into social causes of and responses to environmental problems.

Structural-Functionalist Perspective

Structural-functionalism emphasizes the interdependence between human beings and the natural environment. From this perspective, human actions, social patterns, and cultural values affect the environment, and, in turn, the environment affects social life. Structural-functionalism also helps us to understand how changes in one aspect of the social system affect other aspects of society. For example, agriculture, forestry, and fishing provide 50 percent of all jobs worldwide and 70 percent of jobs in sub-Saharan Africa, East Asia, and the Pacific (World Resources Institute 2000). As croplands become scarce or degraded, as forests shrink, and as marine life dwindles, millions of people who make their living from these natural resources must find alternative livelihoods. Globally, there are an estimated 30 million environmental refugees—individuals who have migrated because they can no longer secure a livelihood as a result of environmental problems (Margesson 2005). As individuals lose their source of income, so do nations. In one-fourth of the world's nations, crops, timber, and fish contribute more to the nation's economy than industrial goods do (World Resources Institute 2000).

The environmental impact of different regions and cultural uses of the land and its resources can be measured through an **environmental footprint**—determined by the patterns of production and consumption in that person's culture. The environmental footprint of an average person in a high-income country is about six times bigger than that of someone in a low-income country and many more times larger than in the least developed nations (United Nations Population Fund 2004).

Structural-functionalism also helps us to understand and assess how changes in one aspect of the social system affect other aspects of society. For example, in the two years after the terrorist attacks of September 11, 2001, public concern about most environmental problems declined sharply, most likely as a result of increasing worry about the economy and terrorism over the same period (Saad 2002). The effect of oil prices on the economy provides another illustration of how a change in one aspect of the social system affects other aspects of society. When the price of oil skyrocketed after Hurricane Katrina in 2005, businesses suffered and consumers struggled to pay higher prices for food and other goods. Because so much of our economy depends on oil, an oil shortage or price spike affects virtually every aspect of our economy.

The structural-functionalist perspective raises our awareness of latent dysfunctions—negative consequences of social actions that are unintended and not widely recognized. For example, consider the more than 840 000 dams worldwide. The dams provide water to irrigate farmlands and supply 17 percent of the world's electricity, yet dam building has had unintended negative consequences for the environment, including the loss of wetlands and wildlife habitat, the emission of methane (a gas that contributes to global warming) from rotting vegetation trapped in reservoirs, and the alteration of river flows downstream, which kills plant and animal life ("A Prescription" 2001). Dams have also displaced millions of people from their homes. As philosopher Kathleen Moore points out, "Sometimes in maximizing the benefits in one place, you create a greater harm somewhere else.... While it might sometimes seem that small acts of cruelty or destruction are justified because they create a greater good, we need to be aware of the hidden systematic costs" (Jensen 2001: 11). Being aware of latent dysfunctions means paying attention to the unintended and often hidden environmental consequences of human activities.

Conflict Perspective

The conflict perspective focuses on how wealth, power, and the pursuit of profit underlie many environmental problems. Wealth is related to consumption patterns that cause environmental problems. Wealthy nations have higher per capita consumption of petroleum, wood, metals, cement, and other commodities that deplete Earth's resources, emit pollutants, and generate large volumes of waste. The wealthiest 20 percent of the world's population is responsible for 86 percent of total private consumption (Bright 2003). Moreover, the capitalist pursuit of profit encourages making money from industry regardless of the damage done to the environment. McDaniel (2005: 22–23) notes that

environmental footprint
The environmental impact of building, farming, consuming, etc. The footprint is measured in terms of loss of arable land, use of water resources, fuel depletion, and carbon emissions.

"our culture tolerates environmentalism only so long as it has minimal impact on big business.... In an economically centered culture, jobs come first, not the health of people or the environment." In short, wealthy nations exploit less developed nations for raw materials, labour, and as a market to sell goods to (Barbosa 2009).

To maximize growth, manufacturers design products intended to become obsolete. As a result of this **planned obsolescence**, consumers continually throw away functional products and purchase replacements. Industry profits at the expense of the environment, which is subject to the constant production of goods and must absorb ever-increasing amounts of waste.

Industries also use their power and wealth to influence politicians' environmental and energy policies as well as the public's beliefs about environmental issues. ExxonMobil, the world's largest oil company, has spent millions of dollars on lobbying and has funded numerous organizations that have tried to discredit scientific findings that link fossil fuel burning to global climate change (Mooney 2005). Despite the agreement of hundreds of scientists from around the world that global warming is occurring and is largely due to "greenhouse gases" released by fossil fuel burning, the Bush administration pulled out of the Kyoto Protocol—an international agreement to reduce greenhouse gas emissions—citing "incomplete" science as the reason.

In 2006, the federal government in Canada, under Prime Minister Stephen Harper, announced its commitment to the principles of the Kyoto accord (Palmer 2006); however, it also made clear that Canada was unlikely to meet its targets for reductions in greenhouse gas emissions promised at the time the accord came into effect on February 15, 2005. Finally, in 2011, the Harper Conservatives formally withdrew from the Kyoto accord, arguing that Canada would face $14 billion in international penalties for not meeting the 2012 targets. Then Environment Minister Peter Kent made the claim that Canada was withdrawing because, "To meet the target under 2012 would be the equivalent of either removing every car, truck, ATV, tractor, ambulance, police car and vehicle of every kind from Canadian roads, or closing down the entire farming and agricultural sector and cutting heat to every home, office, hospital, factory and building in Canada" (quoted in Kennedy 2011). For these assertions Kent was sometimes criticized for fear mongering, and Canada was also criticized more generally for being the first nation to remove itself from the accord (Black 2011).

However, BBC correspondent Richard Black noted that it was actually not a surprise that Canada withdrew from the accord under the Conservatives. Canada's withdrawal from the Kyoto accord may have been a fairly silent affair on the domestic political scene; however, news outlets around the world took notice, and reporters from such respected and relatively "conservative" organizations as the BBC World Service noted that Canada's withdrawal was symptomatic not only of our failure to meet Kyoto's 2020 targets, but also of Canada's kowtowing to American policy and trade demands (Black 2011).

International scholarship on the matter has focused on how Canada's federal government managed to avoid condemnation from its citizenry over the decision to abandon the Kyoto accord. In particular, Young and Coutinho (2013) note that the unwillingness of Canada's general population to question the government decision is secondary to claims-making activities of the Harper government that promoted both public ignorance on the issue of climate change in general and of the Kyoto provisions in particular. They demonstrate the government's purposeful focus on the economic priorities of the country, and a move away from Harper's more personal denial of climate change as a mere "hypothesis" (Young and Coutinho 2013: 96). In sum, the government succeeded in redirecting Canadian attention to pragmatic matters of jobs and the economy by controlling the message on research regarding climate change, and in particular have supported research that favours the fossil-fuel industry forming much of Canada's primary industry: the extraction of natural resources. Moreover,

planned obsolescence
The manufacturing of products that are intended to become inoperative or outdated in a fairly short time.

"the Harper government eliminated or scaled back funding for several national networks for climate science, including the Canadian Climate Impacts and Adaptations Research Network, which was closed and its website emptied of all reports and publications" (Young and Coutinho 2013: 101).

While these claims-making strategies may have successfully distracted attention away from environmental concern within Canada over our departure from the Kyoto accord, external assessors have taken notice. For example, McEvoy (2013) writes that, "Canada … was in clear violation of their commitments under the Kyoto Protocol …" (p. 484, fn 7). McEvoy is clear that Canada's failure on Kyoto was, in part, a result of the failure of international bodies to create "enforcement mechanisms … that sustained more cooperation" (p. 484). In short, without incentives that encourage effort to reduce global carbon emissions, countries around the globe, including Canada, will continue to prioritize short-term economic and political goals over more long-term environmental protection goals.

Meanwhile, even fiscally conservative newspapers in Canada such as *The Economist* have been critical of the rhetoric used by Environment Minister Peter Kent to justify Canada's withdrawal, noting the claims that meeting Kyoto targets would require the removal of every vehicle from Canadian roads and closing down infrastructure was a gross exaggeration made by a government with an established "loathing" (Anonymous 2011) of the Kyoto Accord. The anonymous author in *The Economist* article further notes that the decision to withdraw from the accord destroyed our reputation for being a "good global citizen … [and could] make tar-sands oil harder to sell abroad" (ibid). In other words, withdrawal might actually threaten the very economic interests that the Harper government regularly touted in its claims-making activities to justify Canada's departure from the Kyoto accord.

That governments can claim to adhere to the spirit of the accord and simultaneously back away from keeping promises speaks to the limitations of the accord's language, couched as it is in terms of goal setting. One can endlessly defer the goal while still claiming to be adhering to the principles of the pact.

Ecofeminist Perspective

ecofeminism
A synthesis of feminism, environmentalism, and anti-militarism.

Ecological feminism, or **ecofeminism**, began in 1974 when French feminist Françoise d'Eaubonn coined the term *ecological feminisme* to call attention to women's potential to energize an ecological revolution (Warren 2000). Ecofeminists view environmental problems as resulting from human domination of the environment and see connections between the domination of women, people of colour, children, and the poor and the domination of nature. Throughout the world and in developing countries in particular, men are dominant in deciding how natural resources are used. Men are dominant in positions of government and corporate leadership and own most of the land. By some estimates, women around the world hold title to less than 2 percent of the land that is owned (MacDonald and Nierenberg 2003). In contrast to a male-oriented view of natural resources as a means to an end—a means to profit and power—ecofeminists often embrace a spiritual approach to addressing environmental problems, drawing on pagan, Native, New Age, and Eastern religious traditions that emphasize the close connection between women and nature (Mother Earth) (Schaeffer 2003).

Symbolic Interactionist Perspective

The symbolic interactionist perspective focuses on how meanings, labels, and definitions learned through interaction and through the media affect environmental problems. Whether an individual recycles, drives an SUV, or joins an environmental activist group is influenced by the meanings and definitions of these behaviours that the individual learns through interaction with others.

Large corporations and industries commonly use marketing and public relations strategies to construct favourable meanings of their corporation or industry. The term **greenwashing** refers to the way in which environmentally and socially damaging companies portray their corporate image and products as being "environmentally friendly" or socially responsible. Greenwashing is commonly used by public relations firms that specialize in damage control for clients whose reputations and profits have been hurt by poor environmental practices. Walmart, for example, has paid millions of dollars in fines and settlements for a number of environmental violations, including excessive storm runoff at construction sites, petroleum storage violations, and *Clean Air Act* violations (Wal-Mart Watch 2005). When Walmart announced in 2005 that it would donate $35 million (less than 1 percent of its 2004 profits) to the National Fish and Wildlife Foundation over a 10-year period to purchase one acre of conservation land for every acre of land developed by Walmart, many environmentalists accused Walmart of greenwashing. Just before Earth Day (April 22) in 2005, Walmart bought full-page ads in at least 20 newspapers touting its new program, Acres for America (Associated Press 2005). Such publicity suggests that Walmart's Acres for America program is designed to improve Walmart's public image. The comments of Eric Olson of the Sierra Club reflect the skepticism that many environmentalists have toward corporate greenwashing: "Wal-Mart thinks it can paint over its record with a nice shade of green, but that won't hide its true colors" (quoted by Associated Press 2005).

Ford Motor Company was accused of greenwashing in 2004 when it advertised its Escape Hybrid sport utility vehicle as an example of Ford's commitment to the environment when, for the fifth consecutive year, Ford's vehicles had the worst overall fuel economy of all major automakers. In fact, Ford's fleetwide fuel economy was worse in 2004 than it was in 1984! And hybrids accounted for less than 1 percent of Ford's annual sales (Johnson 2004).

Greenwashing also occurs in the political arena when political leaders attempt to portray an environmentally damaging policy or program as environmentally friendly. Consider, for example, U.S. President George Bush's Clear Skies Initiative. The initiative allows five times more mercury emissions, one and a half times more sulphur dioxide emissions, and hundreds of thousands more tonnes of smog-forming nitrogen oxide emissions than those allowed under the 1970 *Clean Air Act* (Clarren 2005). Naming it the Clear Skies Initiative is a blatant example of greenwashing.

Although greenwashing involves manipulation of public perception to maximize profits, many corporations make genuine and legitimate efforts to improve their operations, packaging, or overall sense of corporate responsibility toward the environment. For example, in 1990 McDonald's announced that it was phasing out foam packaging and switching to a new, paper-based packaging that is partially degradable. But many environmentalists are not satisfied with what they see as token environmentalism, or as Peter Dykstra of Greenpeace calls it, 5 percent of environmental virtue to mask 95 percent of environmental vice (Hager and Burton 2000).

Greenwashing can cause controversy and divisions among environmentalists. Consider Earth Day, which has brought environmentalists together to celebrate Earth and to increase public awareness of environmental issues every April 22 since 1970. In recent years, Earth Day events have been sponsored by corporations such as Office Depot, Texas Instruments, Raytheon Missile Systems, and Waste Management (a Houston-based company responsible for numerous hazardous waste sites). Some environmentalists, including Earth Day's founder, former senator Gaylord Nelson, consider the participation of corporations in Earth Day evidence of the celebration's success; other environmentalists oppose corporate sponsorship of Earth Day events, accusing corporations of using their financial support of Earth Day as a public relations greenwashing strategy. John Stauber, a critic of corporations that hide their damaging environmental practices behind green advertising and marketing, says that "Waste

greenwashing
The corporate practice of displaying a sense of corporate responsibility for the environment. For example, many companies publicly emphasize the steps they have taken to help the environment. Another greenwashing strategy is to retool, repackage, or relabel a company's product.

Management sponsoring Earth Day is similar to Enron sponsoring a seminar on corporate responsibility" (quoted by Cappiello 2003). In recent years, environmentalists have withdrawn from and protested Earth Day events in cities across the country because the events were sponsored by corporations.

13.3 Environmental Problems: An Overview

Over the past 50 years humans have altered **ecosystems**—the complex and dynamic relationships between forms of life and the environments they inhabit—more rapidly and extensively than in any other comparable period in history (Millennium Ecosystem Assessment 2005). As a result, humans have created environmental problems, including depletion of natural resources; air, land, and water pollution; global warming; environmental illness; environmental injustice; threats to biodiversity; and disappearing livelihoods. Because many of these environmental problems are related to the ways that humans produce and consume energy, we begin this section with an overview of global energy use.

Energy Use Worldwide: An Overview

Being mindful of environmental problems means seeing the connections between energy use and our daily lives.

Everything we consume or use—our homes, their contents, our cars and the roads we travel, the clothes we wear, and the food we eat—requires energy to produce and package, to distribute to shops or front doors, to operate, and then to get rid of. We rarely consider where this energy comes from or how much of it we use—or how much we truly need (Sawin 2004: 25).

Most of the world's energy use—nearly 82 percent—comes from fossil fuels, which include oil, coal and peat, and natural gas. As Figure 13.1 shows, our global reliance on

ecosystems
Complex environments that support a variety of interdependent life forms.

1973 and 2011 Fuel Shares of TPES

1973 — 6 109 Mtoe
Biofuels and waste 10.6%
Other** 0.1%
Hydro 1.8%
Coal/peat 24.6%
Nuclear 0.9%
Natural gas 16.0%
Oil 46.0%

2011 — 13 113 Mtoe
Biofuels and waste 10.0%
Other** 1.0%
Hydro 2.3%
Coal/peat 28.8%
Nuclear 5.1%
Natural gas 21.3%
Oil 31.5%

*World includes international aviation and international marine bunkers.
**Other includes geothermal, solar, wind, heat, etc.

Figure 13.1 *World Energy Production by Source, 2011*

SOURCE: International Energy Agency, 2013 "Key World Energy Statistics," p. 6.

nuclear energy has increased five times since 1973, reducing our reliance on fossil fuels only marginally. Later in this chapter, we discuss the promise and problems associated with nuclear energy production. As you continue reading this chapter, notice that the world's major environmental problems—air, land, and water pollution, destruction of habitats, biodiversity loss, global warming, and environmental illness—are linked to the production and use of fossil fuels.

Hydroelectric power accounts for only 2.3 percent of our global energy use, and involves generating electricity from moving water. As water passes through a dam into a river below, energy is produced by a turbine in the dam. Although hydroelectric power is nonpolluting and inexpensive, it is criticized for affecting natural habitats. For example, dams make certain fish unable to swim upstream to reproduce. Canada produces more hydroelectric power than any other country, followed by Brazil, China, and the United States (Energy Information Administration 2005).

Nuclear power, accounting for 5.1 percent of world energy production, and the only source for the products and technologies central to the practice of nuclear medicine (used mostly for diagnosing and treating an array of cancers), is associated with a number of problems related to radioactive nuclear waste—problems that are discussed later in this chapter. Only 1 percent of the world's energy comes from clean renewable resources, which include geothermal power (from the heat of the earth), solar power, wind power, and biomass (e.g., fuel wood, crops, and animal wastes), which are primarily used by poor populations in developing countries. One-fourth of the world's population—1.6 billion people—lack access to electricity in their homes and use biomass for heating and cooking (Flavin and Aeck 2005).

Depletion of Natural Resources

Population growth, combined with consumption patterns, is depleting natural resources such as forests, water, minerals, and fossil fuels.

Water supplies around the world are dwindling while the demand for water continues to increase because of industrialization, rising living standards, and changing diets that include more food products that require larger amounts of water to produce, such as milk, eggs, chicken, and beef. Currently, 50 countries are facing moderate or severe water stress; by the year 2030, nearly half the world's population will be living in areas of high water stress (WWF 2008; World Water Assessment Program 2009). With 70 percent of freshwater use going to agriculture, water shortages threaten food production and supply.

The world's forests are also being depleted. The demand for new land, fuel, and raw materials has resulted in **deforestation**—the conversion of forestland to nonforest land (Intergovernmental Panel on Climate Change 2001a). Global forest cover has been reduced by half of what it was 8000 years ago (Gardner 2005). Between the 1960s and the 1990s, one-fifth of the world's tropical forests were cut or burned (Youth 2003). The major causes of deforestation are the expansion of agricultural land, human settlements, wood harvesting, and road building. We currently lose 13 million hectares of forest every year as the trees are cut down and the land converted for human use (UNEP 2008).

Deforestation has serious negative effects. It displaces people and wild species from their habitats; soil erosion caused by deforestation can cause severe flooding; and, as we explain later in this chapter, deforestation contributes to global warming.

Deforestation also contributes to **desertification**—the degradation of semi-arid land, which results in the expansion of desert land unusable for agriculture. Overgrazing by cattle and other herd animals also contributes to desertification. As more land turns into desert, populations can no longer sustain a livelihood on the land, so they migrate to urban areas or other countries, contributing to social and political

deforestation
The destruction of Earth's rainforests.

desertification
The expansion of deserts and the loss of usable land due to the overuse of semi-arid land on the desert margins for animal grazing and obtaining firewood.

instability. The problem of desertification is most severe in Africa (Reese 2001). As more land turns into desert, populations can no longer sustain a livelihood on the land, and so they migrate to urban areas or other countries, contributing to social and political instability.

The demands that humanity makes on Earth's natural resources is known as the environmental footprint. A person's environmental footprint is determined by the patterns of production and consumption in that person's culture. Environmental footprints are a measure of how much of Earth people require to provide the natural resources they consume, and are often expressed in terms of global hectares per person (1 hectare equals about 2.47 acres). Collectively, human demand on the world's natural resources exceeds Earth's capacity by nearly a third; 77 percent of us are living in ecological debt, using more natural resources than Earth can sustain. If we continue current patterns of consumption, we would need the equivalent of two planets to support us by 2030 (WWF 2008).

Air Pollution

Transportation vehicles, fuel combustion, industrial processes (such as the burning of coal and the processing of minerals from mining), and solid waste disposal have contributed to the growing levels of air pollutants, including carbon monoxide, sulphur dioxide, nitrogen dioxide, mercury, and lead. Air pollution levels are highest in areas with both heavy industry and traffic congestion, such as Los Angeles, New Delhi, Jakarta, Bangkok, Tehran, Beijing, and Mexico City. Air pollution, which is linked to heart disease, lung cancer, emphysema, chronic bronchitis, and asthma, kills about 3 million people a year (Pimentel et al. 2007). Figure 13.2 shows the per capita contributions to air pollution by region.

Figure 13.2 *CO$_2$ Emissions per Capita by Region, 2014*

SOURCE: Adapted from International Energy Agency, 2013. "Key World Energy Statistics: Selected Indicators for 2011," pp. 48–49.

CO$_2$ Emissions (metric tons per capita)		
Arab World	4.6	2010
Caribbean small states	9.9	2010
East Asia & Pacific	4.9	2010
Euro area	7.4	2010
European Union	7.3	2010
Europe & Central Asia	5.3	2010
Latin America & Caribbean	2.7	2010
Least developed countries: UN classification	0.3	2010
Middle East & North Africa	3.9	2010
OECD members	10.1	2010
Other small states	1.5	2010
Pacific Island small states	1.1	2010
Small states	3.5	2010
South Asia	1.4	2010
Sub-Saharan Africa	0.8	2010
World	4.9	2010

In Canada, the popularity among boomers of minivans, SUVs, and other light trucks has alarmed environmentalists. These vehicles, when compared with the standard passenger car, not only guzzle one-third more gas, but also spew one-third more pollution out their tailpipes (as cited in Speirs 2000: A24). While the David Suzuki Foundation has remarked that "[t]his light truck category is a moving disaster" (Speirs 2000: A24), sales of light trucks have accounted for more than 50 percent of the passenger vehicle market in recent years. Only the high price of oil, rather than concern for the environment, is cutting into the sales of large vehicles, which suggests that if gas prices should drop again, fuel-efficient, small cars will lose their appeal.

Indoor Air Pollution

When we hear the phrase *air pollution*, we typically think of industrial smokestacks and vehicle exhausts pouring grey streams of chemical matter into the air. But indoor air pollution is also a major problem, especially in poor countries.

About half the world's population and up to 90 percent of rural households in developing countries rely on wood and unprocessed biomass (dung and crop residues) for cooking and heating fuel (Bruce et al. 2000). These fuels are typically burned indoors in open fires or in poorly functioning stoves, producing hazardous emissions such as soot particles, carbon monoxide, nitrous oxides, sulphur oxides, and formaldehyde. Long-term exposure to the smoke contributes to respiratory illness, lung cancer, tuberculosis, and blindness; an estimated two million deaths in developing countries each year result from exposure to indoor air pollution. According to the World Health Organization, indoor air pollution ranks fifth as a risk factor for ill health worldwide—behind malnutrition, AIDS, tobacco use, and poor water and sanitation (Bruce et al. 2000; Mishra et al. 2002).

Even in affluent countries much air pollution, invisible to the eye, exists where we least expect it—in our homes, schools, workplaces, and public buildings. Sources of indoor air pollution include lead dust (from old lead-based paint); secondhand tobacco smoke; by-products of combustion (e.g., carbon monoxide) from stoves, furnaces, fireplaces, heaters, and dryers; and other common household, personal, and commercial products (American Lung Association 2005).

Some of the most common indoor pollutants include carpeting (which emits more than a dozen toxic chemicals); mattresses, sofas, and pillows (which emit formaldehyde and fire retardants); pressed wood found in kitchen cabinets and furniture (which emits formaldehyde); and wool blankets and dry-cleaned clothing (which emit trichloroethylene). Air fresheners, deodorizers, and disinfectants emit the pesticide paradichlorobenzene. Potentially harmful organic solvents are present in numerous office supplies, including glue, correction fluid, printing ink, carbonless paper, and felt-tip markers. Many homes today contain a cocktail of toxic chemicals: "Styrene (from plastics), benzene (from plastics and rubber), toluene and xylene, trichloroethylene, dichloromethane, trimethylbenzene, hexanes, phenols, pentanes and much more outgas from our everyday furnishings, construction materials, and appliances" (Rogers 2002).

Destruction of the Ozone Layer

The ozone layer of Earth's atmosphere absorbs most of the harmful ultraviolet-B radiation from the sun and completely screens out lethal ultraviolet-C radiation. The ozone layer is thus essential to life on Earth. Yet the use of certain chemicals has weakened the ozone layer. The depletion of the ozone layer allows hazardous levels of ultraviolet rays to reach Earth's surface. It is linked to increases in skin cancer and cataracts, weakened immune systems, reduced crop yields, damage to ocean ecosystems and reduced fishing yields, and adverse effects on animals.

Destructive Water and Land Use in Canada

In Alberta, largely in the Athabasca region with intended pipeline to run all the way to Kitimat, B.C., covering roughly 1200 kilometres, Enbridge Inc. (a major energy supply company in Canada) plans to supply some 525 000 barrels of oil to Asian-Pacific consumers by 2030 (Preston 2013; Schindler 2010). The oil that Enbridge intends to run in the pipeline is to be synthesized from bitumen, an asphalt-like substance found in the "oil sand" northern regions of Alberta and Edmonton. Among the problems with this form of oil extraction is that the process requires enormous quantities of water; generally three to four barrels of water are required to produce one barrel of oil, and as Huseman and Short (2012) explain, the result is that "… 480 million gallons of contaminated waste water are [already] dumped daily" (p. 221). The water is required because bitumen cannot otherwise be extracted from the sands, and so "… must be made to flow into wells by 'in situ' techniques, which reduce the viscosity by injecting steam, solvents, and/or hot air into the sands" (ibid). Moreover, as David Schindler, writing in the premier science journal *Nature* (2010) explains,

> The extraction of oil from the sands is energy intensive: the energy cost per barrel is higher than for conventional crude oil, although it is difficult to quantify the life-cycle emission differences. Emissions of carbon dioxide are expected to reach 108 megatonnes by 2020—a fifth of Canada's current [total] national emissions. (p. 300)

The extraction of bitumen for the purposes of delivering oil to foreign markets is, then, a process structured by market competitions, and informed by Canada's long and traditional reliance on the exploitation of natural resources for trade. This legacy goes back as far as the initial fur-trade established under the Hudson's Bay Corporation in the seventeenth century and has *always* been couched in the structural approach of **settler colonialism** to the land. The process is an environmental hazard, but also a social problem because of the human communities that it threatens.

First among the threatened communities, in addition to all those located along the proposed pipeline corridor, are the Indigenous people of northern Alberta and Saskatchewan—and they have, not surprisingly, moved to try to oppose the potentially disastrous growth of the oil fracking industry in Canada. As Jen Preston (2013) notes, among the instantiating reasons for the development of the Idle No More resistance movement among Indigenous groups in Canada is the environmental destruction of land and water resources on Indigenous lands. Yet, instead of listening to the concerns of the Idle No More movement, the current Conservative government, under Prime Minister Stephen Harper,

> established a new RCMP-led anti-terrorism unit in June 2012—the K Division Integrated National Security Enforcement Team (INSET). According to Assistant Commissioner Gilles Michaud of National Security Criminal Investigations, the counter-terrorism unit is designed to 'gather intelligence to prevent attacks before they happen' and to protect the energy industry from 'attacks by extremists'. (Preston 2013: 43)

In other words, political resistance movements aimed at protecting vulnerable groups and territories have been criminalized, and government resources are being concentrated on protecting the ability of corporations to pollute vast tracts of land and to destroy freshwater ecosystems.

As Schindler notes, the mine pits and the tailings ponds, where the polluted water is dumped after fracking is completed, already cover a territory four times larger than it was in 1992, for a total of 650 square kilometres, or about one-tenth the surface area of Alberta (p. 300). Considering the projected growth in fracking over the next few decades, it really should not be only Indigenous groups who are concerned enough to try to curtail that growth.

settler colonialism
Refers to a means of structuring land use in ways that eliminate Native/Indigenous populations from the land; ruptures the cultural ties of Indigenous peoples to the land, and so commits cultural genocide as well.

The oil sands are not the only threat to the freshwater supply in Canada, nor the only threat to Northern Indigenous peoples. Victor Martinez and his colleagues from the British Columbia Cancer Agency (BCCA) inform us that arsenic-contaminated water is a serious threat coming to Yellowknife and other regions in Canada:

> More than a quarter of a million tons of arsenic generated over 50 years during the operation of the Giant Mine in Yellowknife reside underground and in piles aboveground. Because cleanup is deemed too great a health risk, the arsenic will be frozen in the ground, at a cost of nearly one billion Canadian dollars. In almost every province, arsenic-contaminated drinking water is a growing health concern…(2013: 559)

Data and political relationships such as these surely challenge the popular image of Canada as a largely unspoiled land without internal conflicts between groups of people, and the solutions require more than simply turning out the lights for Earth Hour, picking up litter on Earth Day, or recycling our post-consumer packaging waste. Although all of us can certainly make decisions—for example, to walk more, cycle more, use public transit and drive less or not at all; to live in smaller homes or apartments in city centres instead of paving over farmland for suburban developments; to try to eat locally as much as possible, all decisions that reduce our collective dependency on oil—we also need effective strategies to prevent corporate exploitation of the land and water systems. But what do those strategies look like? The advocacy group Keepers of the Athabasca* and main researcher Helene Walsh have authored a major policy manual that proposes a pause, or temporary stop to all oil sands development in Canada, and call for the 13 objectives to be met before any consideration of oil sand development starts up again. Among the objectives are the following:

- Develop and implement a regional strategic plan that includes long-term management objectives and a process for achieving these objectives.
- Restore the environmental condition of the area and honour the treaty rights of Aboriginal people.
- Establish independent monitoring of environmental effects to increase public confidence in results.
- Restore caribou habitat and the habitat of other wildlife species.
- Develop the technology to eliminate tailings ponds and the harmful effects of tailings wet or dry and eliminate the need for end pit lakes. (Walsh 2012: 33–34)

Many of the other strategies listed by the Keepers of the Athabasca assume that useful technologies can be developed over time to eliminate the deleterious practices of fracking, and the group embraces technologies with environmentally protective potential; they are not calling for everyone to give up on the modern world. At base, the group seeks accountability for and responsibility to upholding processes that put treaty rights, habitats, and ecosystems first, and that's not difficult to accomplish; it is merely a matter of political will.

Acid Rain

Air pollutants, such as sulphur dioxide and nitrogen oxide, mix with precipitation to form **acid rain**. Polluted rain, snow, and fog contaminate crops, forests, lakes, and rivers. Acid rain is a particular threat in Ontario, New Brunswick, Nova Scotia, and Quebec because these provinces are directly in the path of much of the continent's SO_2 and NO_x emissions, and the nonporous granite that composes most of the Canadian Shield is less able to absorb acid rain. Roughly 40 percent of Canada's total land area (about four million square kilometres) is extremely sensitive to acid rain (Statistics Canada 1998). Moreover, because pollutants in the air are carried by the

*Courtesy of Helene Walsh.

acid rain
The mixture of precipitation with air pollutants, such as sulphur dioxide and nitrogen oxide.

wind, industrial pollution in the midwest United States falls back to Earth as acid rain on southeast Canada and the northeast New England states. Acid rain is not just a problem in North America, though; it decimates plant and animal species around the globe. "The Parthenon, Taj Mahal, and Michelangelo's statues are dissolving under the onslaught of the acid pouring out of the skies" (Blatt 2005: 161).

Global Warming and Climate Change

In 2005, scientists reported that the Ilulissat glacier in Greenland, considered one of the wonders of the world, had shrunk by more than 9.6 kilometres in two or three years (Bohan 2005). In the same year, Russian researchers discovered that the world's largest frozen peat bog, located in Siberia, is melting, turning this once frozen area the size of Germany and France combined into a mass of shallow lakes (Pearce 2005). The melting of Greenland's Ilulissat glacier and Siberia's peat bog contributes to growing evidence of **global warming**.

Globally, the 1990s was the warmest decade on record since record keeping began in the late 1800s. The hottest year on record was 1998, followed by 2002 and 2003. The year 2004 rated as the fourth warmest year on record (National Oceanic and Atmospheric Administration 2005). Average global air temperature rose by 0.68 degrees Celsius over the twentieth century; between 1990 and 2100, this temperature is expected to rise by as much as 5.88 degrees Celsius (Intergovernmental Panel on Climate Change 2001b).

Consumer habits play a large part in the emission of greenhouse gases. Especially important is not only how far and how often we drive, but also how hot or cool we keep our homes in winter and summer, how often we use appliances, and whether our homes are properly insulated or not, as well as whether we purchase more local produce or more produce trucked from distant locations. Despite the impact of consumer habits, the federal Conservative government withdrew support of the "One Tonne Challenge," an initiative intended to encourage greater energy conservation by average Canadians. On why the federal government withdrew its support we can only speculate, but an obvious effect of greater conservation would be a reduction in consumption, a potentially serious problem for Canada's economic growth.

Causes of Global Warming

Although the cause of global warming remains a disputed topic, the prevailing scientific view is that **greenhouse gases**—primarily carbon dioxide, methane, and nitrous oxide—accumulate in the atmosphere and act like the glass in a greenhouse, holding heat from the sun close to Earth. Since 1750, atmospheric concentrations of carbon dioxide, the main greenhouse gas, have increased by 31 percent, methane by 151 percent, and nitrous oxide by 17 percent (Intergovernmental Panel on Climate Change 2001b).

The primary source of carbon dioxide emissions is fossil fuel burning. Total world carbon dioxide emissions from fossil fuels were 25.2 billion tonnes in 2003, an increase of 17.1 percent from 1993.

Deforestation also contributes to increasing levels of carbon dioxide in the atmosphere. Trees and other plant life use carbon dioxide and release oxygen into the air. As forests are cut down, fewer trees are available to absorb the carbon dioxide.

In Canada, more than a third of emissions "come directly from the energy industry, a byproduct of oil, gas, coal, and electricity production. The remaining two-thirds is released by industries and activities that subsequently use that energy. Transportation accounts for 25 percent of all emissions" (Stanford 2002: 12). Due to the heavy pollution caused by oil and gas operations, Alberta is "far and away Canada's leading greenhouse gas polluter, releasing more emissions than Ontario (which has four times the population) ... [or] in per capita terms, more than three times the Canadian average"

global warming
The increasing average global air temperature, caused mainly by the accumulation of various gases that collect in the atmosphere.

greenhouse gases
The collection of increasing amounts of chlorofluorocarbons (CFCs), carbon dioxide, methane, and other gases in the atmosphere, where they act like the glass in a greenhouse, holding heat from the sun close to Earth and preventing the heat from rising back into space.

(Stanford 2002: 12). As Figure 13.3 shows us, the most economically powerful and central provinces—Quebec, Ontario, and Alberta—literally fuel the rest of the country, and the well-being and quality of life that many Canadians enjoy across the country is currently dependent on the continued exploitation of these natural resources. Yet there are practical strategies that we can consider as ordinary people to reduce our reliance on these polluting and exploitative practices.

Figure 13.3
Greenhouse Gas Emissions by Province and Territory, 1990, 2005 and 2012

SOURCE: © Her Majesty The Queen in Right of Canada, Environment Canada, 2013. Reproduced with the permission of the Minister of Public Works and Government Services Canada.

NOTE: Emission levels for some previous years have been revised in light of improvements to estimation methods and availability of new data.

One of the most wasteful areas for any Canadian individual or family relates to our food habits. Food that ends up going to rot in stores and in refrigerators across the nation accounts for $27 billion in economic losses every year. More than 50 percent of those losses are the result of individual consumer habits that include buying more than we need, cooking and preparing portions that are too large, and not eating leftovers in time (Gooch et al. 2010: 4). Somewhat surprisingly, Gooch and his co-researchers have found that only one-fifth of the food we throw away in our homes is actually "waste"— things like cores, bones, and peelings—and that everything else that becomes "garbage" is simply the result of poor planning and poor use of what we have. If consumer habits were to improve, we would cut down on this unnecessary waste, and also reduce the other problems associated with overproduction of foods that only end up being thrown away: soil degradation, water depletion, and pollution secondary to transport and packaging.

In their extensive analysis of food waste in Canada, Gooch, Felfel, and Marenick (2010) show that 51 percent of waste occurs in family homes. Consumers regularly purchase far more food than they need; among the implications of this is that, rather than having a food production shortage, developed nations produce and import much more food than our populations require. Gooch and his co-researchers demonstrate that if consumers were more careful other areas of waste would also improve in response, as demand for so much excess food would diminish production needs from the field to the retail stores. Among the things we can do as consumers to improve our habits include having much smaller refrigerators in our homes, growing our own gardens—whether on balconies, in community gardens, or in our backyards—and purchasing food in smaller amounts more frequently. Standing orders for set amounts of food from a local **community supported agriculture (CSA)** organization and from a small butcher can significantly reduce household food waste, and save families money too.

community supported agriculture (CSA)
CSAs are family farms that sell "shares" to community members. A family purchases a share of the farm's yield for each season and then picks up a weekly order that always contains the same weight in seasonal produce. Some CSAs also provide meats that have been raised on pastures instead of feedlots.

Effects of Global Warming and Climate Change

After Hurricane Katrina devastated the U.S. Gulf Coast, increased attention was given to the role that global warming and climate change play in weather events. "While not all extreme weather events can be attributed directly to climate change, the intensity of such events is likely to increase as a result of global warming" (UNEP 2005: 2).

Global warming and climate change are projected to affect regions in different ways. As temperature increases, some areas will experience heavier rain, whereas other regions will get drier. Some regions will experience increased water availability and crop yields, but other regions, particularly tropical and subtropical regions, are expected to experience decreased water availability and a reduction in crop yields. Global warming results in shifts of plant and animal habitats and the increased risk of extinction of some species. Regions that experience increased rainfall as a result of increasing temperatures may face increases in waterborne diseases and diseases transmitted by insects. Over time, climate change may produce opposite effects on the same resource. For example, in the short term forest productivity is likely to increase in response to higher levels of carbon dioxide in the air, but over the long term forest productivity is likely to decrease because of drought, fire, insects, and disease.

As global warming melts glaciers and permafrost, the sea level will continue to rise. Global average sea levels rose 0.1 m–0.2 m during the twentieth century and are expected to rise by 0.09 m–0.88 m from 1990 to 2100. As sea levels rise, some island countries, as well as some barrier islands, are likely to disappear and low-lying coastal areas will be increasingly vulnerable to storm surges and flooding. If global warming continues, Greenland's ice cap could melt within a few hundred years, raising the level of Earth's oceans by more than 6 m and threatening the lives of the 21.2 billion people who live within 32 km of the coastline (Bohan 2005).

In urban areas, flooding can be a problem where storm drains and waste management systems are inadequate. Increased flooding associated with global warming is expected to result in increases in drownings and in diarrheal and respiratory diseases. Increases in the number of people exposed to insect- and water-related diseases, such as malaria and cholera, are also expected. Even if greenhouse gases are stabilized, global air temperature and sea level are expected to continue to rise for hundreds of years.

Another effect of global warming is that it contributes to further warming of the planet—a process known as a *positive feedback loop*. For example, the melting of Siberia's frozen peat bog—a result of global warming—could release billions of tons of methane, a potent greenhouse gas, into the atmosphere (Pearce 2005). And the melting of ice and snow—another result of global warming—exposes more land and ocean area, which absorbs more heat than ice and snow, further warming the planet.

Land Pollution

About 30 percent of the world's surface is land, which provides soil to grow the food we eat. Increasingly, humans are polluting the land with nuclear waste, solid waste, and pesticides.

Nuclear and Radioactive Waste

Nuclear waste, resulting from both nuclear weapons production and nuclear reactors or power plants, contains radioactive plutonium, a substance linked to cancer and genetic defects. Radioactive plutonium has a half-life of 24 000 years, meaning that it takes 24 000 years for the radioactivity to be reduced by half (Mead 1998). Thus, nuclear waste in the environment remains potentially harmful to human and other life for thousands of years.

In Canada, radioactive waste has been produced since the early 1930s, when the first uranium mine began operating in the Northwest Territories at Port Radium (see Figure 13.4). Radium was refined for medical use and uranium was later processed at Port Hope, Ontario. In the 1940s, research and development on the application of nuclear energy to produce electricity began at the Chalk River Laboratories of Atomic Energy of Canada Limited (AECL). Currently, radioactive waste is produced from uranium mining, milling, refining and conversion; nuclear fuel fabrication; nuclear reactor operations; and nuclear research and radioisotope manufacture and use. Under Canada's Radioactive Waste Policy Framework, producers and owners of radioactive waste are responsible for the funding, organization, management, and operation of disposal and other facilities required for their waste.

Figure 13.4 **Radioactive Waste Sites in Canada as of December 31, 2010**

NOTE: These locations relate to the peaceful applications of nuclear energy; national defence–related sites are not included.

SOURCE: The Inventory of Radioactive Waste in Canada (Low Level Radioactive Waste Management Office).

Nuclear plants are home to many hazards. They have about 47 000 tonnes of radioactive spent fuel, with about 9100 tonnes of that amount sealed in casks (Vedantam 2005). Poor management of the generation and storage processes can end catastrophically. Accidents at nuclear power plants, such as the 1986 accident at Chernobyl, and the potential for nuclear reactors to be targeted by terrorists add to the actual and potential dangers of nuclear power plants.

Recognizing the hazards of nuclear power plants and their waste, Germany became the first country to order all of its 19 nuclear power plants shut down by 2020 ("Nukes Rebuked" 2000). But other countries are building or planning to build new reactors. In spring 2006, in Canada, Ontario Premier Dalton McGuinty announced a $40 billion increase for the development of nuclear power generation in his province, citing arguments that alternatives to nuclear power are "too dirty" (Howlett 2006). The decision was taken despite McGuinty's own dissatisfaction with it.

On March 11, 2011, a massive earthquake and tsunami hit Japan, setting off a partial meltdown at the Fukushima nuclear plant; the effects of this event are still unfolding. The degree of meltdown and levels of radiation being released at the plant are not known in definite terms. Although the disaster is nowhere near the scale of the 1986 Chernobyl complete meltdown, the events have once again underscored the vulnerabilities of nuclear power generation. The long-term effects of the breaches in containment at Fukushima are not possible to predict at this time; however, Wade Allison (2011), a nuclear and medical physicist at Oxford, has argued that fears regarding the effects of radiation are greatly exaggerated, that acceptable limits on annual exposure to radiation are far too conservative, and that the routine use of radiation therapy to treat cancers is equal to 20 000 years' worth of "acceptable levels" as stated by public policies set around the globe following the Chernobyl disaster. Allison reminds us to keep the dangers of radiation in perspective, and to be mindful of more significant dangers of climate change, chemical spills (such as the disaster in Bhopal, India), and what would happen if we had no electric power for the millions of people who rely on nuclear power generation. Since then, Allison has cautioned us to remember that in addition to the vast physical destruction they wrought, the Japanese tsunami and earthquake were the direct cause of over 18 000 deaths, while the partial meltdown at Fukishima has produced soil contamination and displacement of over 1000 people and no deaths, and none attributable to the meltdown are expected by nuclear scientists to occur in the future (Allison 2013).

Solid Waste

In Canada, the waste generated by Canadians is on the rise. Although our recycling habits are showing proportional increases, our production of unrecyclable waste is also on the rise. According to a federal report from 2005, each Canadian produces about 383 kg of solid waste per year, or about 30 green garbage bags full (Statistics Canada 2005). Of the total waste generated for the period studied, more than 9.5 million tonnes went into landfill sites or was incinerated, and about 2.5 million tonnes went into recycling (Statistics Canada 2005). Figures such as these do not include mining, agricultural, and industrial waste; demolition and construction wastes; junked autos; or obsolete equipment wastes of which more than half is taken to landfills. The availability of landfill space is limited, however.

Pesticides

Pesticides are used worldwide for crops and gardens; outdoor mosquito control; the care of lawns, parks, and golf courses; and indoor pest control. Pesticides contaminate food, water, and air and can be absorbed through the skin, swallowed, or inhaled. At least 53 carcinogenic pesticides are applied to major U.S. food crops (Blatt 2005) and find their way onto Canadian dining tables every day. Many common pesticides are considered potential carcinogens and neurotoxins. In an analysis of 1260 domestic and 4252 imported food samples, pesticide residues were detected in 31.2 percent of the domestic samples and 33.4 percent of the imported samples (Food and Drug Administration 2008). Pesticides also contaminate our groundwater supplies.

Water Pollution

Around the world, water is being polluted by harmful substances, including pesticides, vehicle exhaust, acid rain, oil spills, and industrial, military, and agricultural waste.

Water pollution is most severe in developing countries, where more than one billion people lack access to clean water. In developing nations, more than 80 percent of untreated sewage is dumped directly into rivers, lakes, and seas that are also used for drinking and bathing (World Water Assessment Program 2009). Mining operations, located primarily in developing countries, are notoriously damaging to the environment. Modern gold-mining techniques use cyanide to extract gold from low-grade ore. In 2000, a dam holding cyanide-laced waste at a Romanian gold mine broke, dumping 22 million gallons of cyanide-laced waste into the Tisza River, which flowed into Hungary and Serbia. Some have called this event the worst environmental disaster since the 1986 Chernobyl nuclear explosion. In West Papua, Indonesia, a U.S.-owned gold mine still dumps 109 000 tonnes of cyanide-laced waste into local rivers every day (Ayres 2004). Most gold is used to make jewellery, hardly a necessity. About 270 000 tonnes of waste are generated for every tonne of marketable gold—which translates roughly into 3 tonnes of waste per gold wedding ring (Sampat 2003).

Canadians tend to take fresh water for granted, as they water lawns and clean their cars, take long showers, and leave the water running while they brush their teeth, but Canada's own water supply is in danger. An Environment Canada report explains:

> Although the overall extent of the problem across Canada is unknown, many individual cases of contamination have been investigated such as Ville Mercier in Quebec; the highway de-icing salt problem in Nova Scotia; industrial effluents in Elmira, Ontario; various pesticides in the Prairie provinces; industrial contamination in Vancouver, British Columbia; and so on.... Contamination problems are increasing in Canada primarily because of the large and growing number of toxic compounds used in industry and agriculture. (Environment Canada 2006)

Groundwater pollution in Canada includes—but is not limited to—flame retardants and insecticides in marine and freshwater supplies in British Columbia (Elliott et al. 2006) and in Ville Mercier, Quebec, where dumping waste into an old gravel pit rendered the water unsafe for use or consumption (Environment Canada 2006).

Chemicals, Carcinogens, and Health Problems

Although Canada's *Environmental Protection Act* sets the laws intended to protect our environment, there are serious indications that our laws are falling dangerously short of being effective. In 2005, 11 Canadians from across Canada had their blood tested for the presence of toxic chemicals and heavy metals such as lead and mercury; on average, the people tested had 44 of the 60 chemical compounds the blood tests were designed to identify, including Teflon, DDT, flame retardants, and PCBs (ENS 2005). Those who volunteered for the study were chosen from locations across the country, and although they all had what they considered to be "healthy lifestyles," all had suffered contamination as a result of day-to-day living in an industrialized nation. Similar conclusions were reached when the lead levels of Inuit women were tested and showed concentrations significantly higher than for the general population (Levesque et al. 2003). The Levesque study determined that the replacement of traditional hunting practices with the use of "modern" lead-shot shotguns presented a new danger in traditional food sources for the Inuit. Meanwhile, for Canadians everywhere, flame retardants and stain repellents are entering our bloodstreams—consumer items that fill average households pose serious hazards, as the chemicals from clothes, furniture, and cooking and storage utensils leech into our bodies through ingestion and skin contact day in and day out.

In addition to their carcinogenic (cancer-causing) potential, many chemicals found in common household, personal, and commercial products can result in temporary acute symptoms, such as drowsiness, disorientation, headache, dizziness, nausea, fatigue, shortness of breath, cramps, diarrhea, and irritation of the eyes, nose, throat, and lungs. Long-term exposure can affect the nervous system, reproductive system, liver, kidneys, heart, and blood. Fragrances, which are found in many consumer products, may produce sensory irritation, pulmonary irritation, decreases in expiratory airflow velocity, and possible neurotoxic effects (Fisher 1998). Fragrance products can cause skin sensitivity, rashes, headache, sneezing, watery eyes, sinus problems, nausea, wheezing, shortness of breath, inability to concentrate, dizziness, sore throat, cough, hyperactivity, fatigue, and drowsiness (DesJardins 1997). More and more businesses are voluntarily limiting or banning fragrances in the workplace to accommodate employees who experience ill effects from exposure to scented products. This chapter's *Social Problems Research Up Close* feature describes the Third National Report on Human Exposure to Environmental Chemicals (Centers for Disease Control and Prevention 2005).

Vulnerability of Children

The World Health Organization estimates that 5500 children die each day from diseases linked to polluted water, air, and food (Mastny 2003). It is estimated that in the United States, 1 in 200 children suffers developmental or neurological deficits as a result of exposure to toxic substances during pregnancy or after birth (UNEP 2002). Asthma, the number one childhood illness in the United States, is linked to air pollution.

Children are more vulnerable than adults to the harmful effects of most pollutants for a number of reasons. For instance, children drink more fluids, eat more food, and inhale more air per unit of body weight than do adults; in addition, crawling and a tendency to put their hands and other things in their mouths provide more opportunities to ingest chemical or heavy metal residues.

Social Problems *Research Up Close*

Human Exposure to Environmental Chemicals

In 2001, the Centers for Disease Control and Prevention published a landmark study that reported measures of human exposure to 27 environmental chemicals, 24 of which had never been measured before in a nationally representative sample of the U.S. population. The Second National Report on Human Exposure to Environmental Chemicals and the Third National Report on Human Exposure to Environmental Chemicals (Centers for Disease Control and Prevention 2003, 2005) are continuations of the ongoing assessment of the U.S. population's exposure to environmental chemicals. For the Second Report, human exposure to 116 chemicals was tested. A key finding of

the Second Report was that phthalates—compounds found in such products as soap, shampoo, hair spray, many types of nail polish, and flexible plastics—are absorbed by humans. For the Third Report, exposure to 148 chemicals was tested.

Methods and Sample

The Third National Report on Human Exposure to Environmental Chemicals is based on 2001-2002 data from the National Health and Nutrition Examination Survey (NHANES) conducted by the National Center for Health Statistics.

The NHANES is a series of surveys designed to collect data on the health and nutritional status of the U.S. population.

The NHANES is based on a representative sample of the noninstitutionalized, civilian U.S. population, with an oversampling of African Americans, Mexican Americans, adolescents (ages 12-19 years), older Americans (age 60 years and older), and pregnant women to produce more reliable estimates for these groups. The samples did not specifically target people who were believed to have high or unusual exposures to environmental chemicals.

Assessing research participants' exposure to environmental chemicals involved measuring the chemicals or their metabolites (breakdown products) in the participants' blood or urine—a method known as bio-monitoring. Blood was obtained by venipuncture for participants one year and older, and urine specimens were collected for people six years and older.

The chemicals measured in the research participants' blood and urine were grouped into the following categories:

1. Metals (including barium, cobalt, lead, mercury, uranium, and others)
2. Cotinine (tracks human exposure to tobacco and tobacco smoke)
3. Organophosphate, organochlorine, and other pesticides
4. Phthalates (chemicals commonly used in such consumer products as soap, shampoo, hair spray, nail polish, and flexible plastics)
5. Polycyclic aromatic hydrocarbons (PAHs)
6. Dioxins, furans, and polychlorinated biphenyls (PCBs)
7. Phytoestrogens
8. Herbicides
9. Pyrethroid, carbamate, and other pesticides

How did the Centers for Disease Control and Prevention (CDC) determine which chemicals to test? In 2002, the CDC solicited nominations from the public for candidate chemicals or categories of chemicals for possible inclusion in future reports and received nominations for hundreds of chemicals. The CDC selected the chemicals to be tested on the basis of several factors, including (1) scientific data that suggested exposure in the U.S. population, (2) the seriousness of health effects known or suspected to result from exposure, (3) the need to assess public health efforts to reduce exposure to a chemical, and (4) the cost of analysis for the chemical.

The researchers conducting the study for the CDC had several objectives, including these:

- to determine which selected environmental chemicals are getting into the bodies of Americans and at what concentrations;
- for chemicals that have a known toxicity level, to determine the prevalence of people in the U.S. population with levels above those toxicity levels;
- to establish reference ranges that can be used by physicians and scientists to determine whether a person or group has an unusually high level of exposure;
- to assess the effectiveness of public health efforts to reduce the exposure of Americans to specific environmental chemicals;
- to track, over time, trends in the levels of exposure of the U.S. population to environmental chemicals; and
- to determine whether exposure levels are higher among minorities, children, women of child-bearing age, or other potentially vulnerable groups.

Key Findings and Conclusions

Selected findings from the Third National Report on Human Exposure to Environmental Chemicals (Centers for Disease Control and Prevention 2005) include the following:

- *New Measures for Some Widely Used Insecticides.* The Third Report presents first-time exposure information for five commonly used pyrethroid insecticides. The findings suggest widespread exposure to pyrethroid insecticides in the U.S. population.
- *Establishment of Reference Ranges.* The levels of chemicals found in the blood and urine of the research participants provide reference ranges (also known as background exposure levels) for all the environmental chemicals for which participants were tested. Physicians, researchers, and public health officials use the reference ranges to determine whether individuals or groups are experiencing levels of exposure that are unusually high compared to the level of exposure experienced by the rest of the population. The Third Report established reference ranges for 38 of the 148 chemicals tested (reference ranges for the remaining 110 chemicals were established in earlier reports).
- *Reduced Exposure of the U.S. Population to Environmental Tobacco Smoke.* Cotinine is a metabolite of nicotine that tracks exposure to environmental tobacco smoke (ETS) among nonsmokers; higher cotinine levels reflect more exposure to ETS. Results from the Third Report show that from 1988-1991 to 1999-2002, median levels in nonsmokers decreased by about 69 percent in children

(continued)

and adolescents and by about 75 percent in adults. Levels in blacks were more than twice the levels in Mexican Americans and non-Hispanic whites. Although efforts to reduce ETS exposure show significant progress, ETS exposure remains a major public health concern.

- *Continued Progress in Reducing Blood-Lead Levels among Children.* For the period 1999-2002, 1.6 percent of children aged 1-5 had elevated blood-lead levels, a decrease from 4.4 percent in the early 1990s. This significant decrease reflects the success of public health efforts to lower the exposure of children to lead—this exposure could come from living in homes containing lead-based paint or lead-contaminated dust. Nevertheless, children at high risk for lead exposure remain a major public health concern.

Because the presence of an environmental chemical in a person's blood or urine does not necessarily mean that the chemical will cause disease, more studies are needed to determine which levels of these chemicals in people result in disease. Research has already documented adverse health effects of lead and environmental tobacco smoke. However, for many environmental chemicals, few studies are available, and more research is needed to assess health risks associated with different blood or urine levels of these chemicals. Future CDC reports, expected to be released every two years, will include more chemicals and will also address the following questions:

1. Are chemical exposure levels increasing or decreasing over time?
2. Are public health efforts to reduce chemical exposure effective?
3. Do certain groups of people have higher levels of chemical exposure than other groups?

---

multiple chemical sensitivity (MCS)
A controversial health condition in which, after one or more acute or traumatic exposures to a chemical or group of chemicals, people experience adverse effects from low levels of chemical exposure that do not produce symptoms in the general public.

environmental injustice
The tendency for socially and politically marginalized groups to bear the brunt of environmental ills.

environmental racism
The tendency for hazardous waste sites and polluting industries to be located in areas where the surrounding residential population is an ethnic or racial minority.

Multiple Chemical Sensitivity Disorder

Multiple chemical sensitivity (MCS), also known as environmental illness, is a condition whereby individuals experience adverse reactions when exposed to low levels of chemicals found in everyday substances—vehicle exhaust, fresh paint, housecleaning products, perfume and other fragrances, synthetic building materials, and numerous other petrochemical-based products. Symptoms of MCS include headache, burning eyes, difficulty in breathing, stomach distress or nausea, loss of mental concentration, and dizziness. The onset of MCS is often linked to acute exposure to a high level of chemicals or to chronic long-term exposure. Sufferers of MCS often avoid public places or wear protective breathing filters to avoid inhaling the many chemical substances in the environment. Some individuals with MCS build houses made from materials that do not contain the chemicals that are typically found in building materials. Although estimates of the prevalence of chemical sensitivity vary, one study reported that in the Atlanta, Georgia, metropolitan area, 12.6 percent of a population sample reported an unusual sensitivity to common chemicals, and 3.1 percent had been diagnosed as having MCS or environmental illness (Caress et al. 2002).

Environmental Injustice

Although environmental pollution and degradation and depletion of natural resources affect us all, some groups are more affected than others. **Environmental injustice**, also referred to as **environmental racism**, refers to the tendency for socially and politically marginalized groups to bear the brunt of environmental ills.

Environmental Injustice in Canada and North America

Although often sold to tourists and perceived by citizens as a pristine land of wide open spaces, Canada faces worsening environmental problems related to day-to-day pollution and overconsumption and, occasionally, catastrophic crises. An ongoing and largely unacknowledged problem, urban air pollution in southern Ontario is the attributable cause of approximately 1800 premature deaths every year in the province (Krajnc 2000: 111). Meanwhile, in the spring of 2000, on the Victoria Day weekend, the Ontario town of Walkerton was hit with a water-contamination crisis that killed 7 residents and made 2800 others sick (Snider 2004: 270). Although many perceive the failures of the public utilities employees Stan and Frank Koebel as responsible for the water contamination, environmental disasters such as Walkerton are rarely the result of the actions of only a few people. Snider explains that the lack of care the Koebel brothers showed to their duties was encouraged by Progressive Conservative government rhetoric of the time, which included an all-out attack on the Ministry of Environment policies developed under the previous NDP (New Democratic Party) leadership; thus, what previously had been law had become only a set of guidelines as the Harris government sought to do away with "onerous reporting requirements"—requirements that, had they been in place when flooding between May 8 and 12 caused a local farm's manure spread to contaminate town wells, would have resulted in an immediate "boil water advisory," preventing the health catastrophe that followed. Walkerton, then, was the disastrous culmination of industrial farming practices, bad weather, and abdication of responsibility at both individual and governmental levels.

But Walkerton was not the last water crisis that Ontario would see. In October 2005, nearly 500 First Nations residents from the Kashechewan reserve north of Timmins had to be evacuated because of *E. coli* contamination of their water. By the first days of November, over 850 people had been evacuated. The situation ultimately revealed to the rest of the nation that, unlike the town of Walkerton's singular crisis point, the Kashechewan reserve had faced many years of water problems, partly because the reserve had been placed in an area subject to flooding (CBC News 2005).

Other regions in Canada, largely populated by Aboriginal peoples, show the negative effects of environmental problems associated with industrial development in regions far away. Pollution in the Far North is so concentrated that the food supply is contaminated, and new mothers fear the dangers of breastfeeding their infants (Johansen 2002).

The discovery that the Inuit in Canada were suffering most from industrial pollution created many thousands of kilometres away came by accident in the mid-1980s. Bioscientist Eric Dewailly sought Inuit women as a control group for a test on PCB contamination of breast milk in Quebec women. Instead of finding that the Inuit women comprised a pristine population, however, Dewailly found that the Inuit women's milk contained levels many times higher than women in southern regions for various chemical compounds, including pesticides, PCBs, and other industrial chemicals (cited in Johansen 2002). In more recent research, Dewailly (1996) and his co-researchers found that in addition to PCBs, compounds related to the insecticide DDT were found in high concentrations in the breast milk of Inuit women. Dewailly's experiment methods were able to use the milk as a reliable predictor of the chemical compounds in the mothers' bodies; that is, not just in the milk. Based on what is already known about the effects of DDT and PCBs, Dewailly concludes that the population of Northern women is at increased risk for diseases such as breast cancer, resulting from chemical fallout from industrial practices over which the population has no control, and in which members have little if any vested interest (Dewailly 1996: 1245).

An area between New Orleans and Baton Rouge, Louisiana—known as Cancer Alley because of its high rates of cancer—has about 140 chemical plants. The people who live and work in Cancer Alley are disproportionately poor and black. One resident of Norco, Louisiana, who lived next to a Shell Oil refinery and chemical plant, reported that nearly everyone in the community suffered from health problems caused by industry pollution (Bullard 2000). When nearly all the chemical plants in Cancer Alley were damaged by Hurricane Katrina in 2005, residents and their homes were exposed to the toxic poisons released from these plants into floodwaters.

These examples show us that race and ethnicity, as well as region, correlate with other features of socio-economic status to make some groups far more vulnerable than others to the dangers of environmental problems.

Environmental Injustice around the World

Although environmental pollution and degradation and depletion of natural resources affects us all, some groups are more affected than others. Marginalized groups, including Indigenous peoples, and other vulnerable and impoverished communities, such as peasants and nomadic tribes, are often powerless to fight against government and corporate powers that maintain environmentally damaging industries. At the Second International Indigenous Youth Conference in Vancouver, a delegate from the Igorot tribal people of the Philippines explained, "Indigenous people are no longer able to plant fruits or vegetables because the…mercury poisoning, produced from massive logging and mining operations, inhibits the growth of any plant life" (Sterritt 2005: n.p.). Indigenous groups in Nigeria, such as the Urhobo, Isoko, Kalabare, and Ogoni, are facing environmental threats caused by oil production operations run by transnational corporations. Oil spills, natural gas fires, and leaks from toxic waste pits have polluted the soil, water, and air, and have compromised the health of various local tribes. "Formerly lush agricultural land is now covered by oil slicks, and much vegetation and wildlife has been destroyed. Many Ogoni suffer from respiratory diseases and cancer, and birth defects are frequent" (Renner 1996: 57). The environmental injustices experienced by the Ogoni and the Igorot represent only a very few of those that have occurred. Renner (1996) warns that "minority populations and indigenous peoples around the globe are facing massive degradation of their environments that threatens to irreversibly alter, indeed destroy, their ways of life and cultures" (p. 59).

In the United States, polluting industries, industrial and waste facilities, and transportation arteries (that generate vehicle emissions pollution) are often located in minority communities (Bullard 2000). More than half (56 percent) of people living within 3 km of a commercial hazardous waste site are people of colour (Bullard et al. 2007). Rates of poverty are also higher among households located near hazardous waste facilities. However, "racial disparities are more prevalent and extensive than socioeconomic disparities, suggesting that race has more to do with the current distribution of the nation's hazardous waste facilities than poverty" (Bullard et al. 2007: 60).

Threats to Biodiversity

About 1.9 million species of life have been identified on Earth (Baillie et al. 2004). However, there may be 10 times that number and perhaps many times more if we include microbial diversity (Chivian and Bernstein 2004). This enormous diversity of life, known as **biodiversity**, provides food, medicines, fibres, and fuel; purifies air and fresh water; pollinates crops and vegetation; and makes soils fertile.

In recent decades, we have witnessed mass extinction rates of diverse life forms. On average, one species of plant or animal life becomes extinct every 20 minutes (Levin and Levin 2002). Unlike the extinction of the dinosaurs millions of years ago, species

biodiversity
The variability of living organisms on Earth.

are disappearing today due to human causes (Hunter 2001). Biologists expect that at least half of the 1.9 million species alive today will become extinct over the next few centuries as a result of habitat loss caused by deforestation and urban sprawl, overharvesting, and global warming (Cincotta and Engelman 2000). Another threat to biodiversity is overexploitation of species for their meat, hides, horns, or medicinal or entertainment value. A poacher, for example, can earn several hundred dollars for a single rhinoceros horn—equivalent to a year's salary in many African countries. That same horn, ground up and used as a medicinal product, can sell for half a million dollars in Asia (Schmidt 2004). The International Fund for Animal Welfare (2005) checked the internet for one week and found more than 9000 wild animal products and specimens and live wild animals for sale—predominantly from species protected by law—a figure that represents "only the tip of the iceberg" (p. ii).

As shown in Table 13.1, 22 103 species worldwide are threatened with extinction; this is a more than two-fold increase from 1996, when the IUCN reported 10 533 species threatened. Most extinctions today result from habitat loss caused by deforestation and urban sprawl, overharvesting, global warming, and bioinvasion—environmental problems caused by human activity (Cincotta and Engelman 2000; Leahy 2009).

Light Pollution

Light pollution refers to artificial lighting that is annoying, unnecessary, and/or harmful to life forms on Earth. Canada, like much of the rest of the world, has become increasingly "lit up" with artificial light. Almost all people in developed societies use artificial light, reducing the natural period of darkness at night. Yet, "darkness is as essential to our biological welfare, to our internal clockwork, as light itself" (Klinkenborg 2008: 109). Some research suggests that exposure to artificial light at night contributes to sleep disorders, depression, and other mood disorders. Other studies have found a link between exposure to artificial light at night and breast cancer (Chepesiuk 2009).

Light pollution also has adverse effects on the migration, feeding, and reproductive patterns of many animal species (Chepesiuk 2009; Klinkenborg 2008). For example, frogs have been found to inhibit their mating calls, and bats alter their feeding behaviour when they are exposed to artificial light at night. Sea turtles, which have a natural predisposition to nest on dark beaches, find fewer of them to nest on. When sea turtle eggs hatch, the babies instinctually go toward the brighter, reflective sea horizon, but are confused by artificial lighting near the beach and may wander off toward the artificially lit beach development.

Environmental Problems and Disappearing Livelihoods

Environmental problems threaten the ability of Earth to sustain its growing population. Agriculture, forestry, and fishing provide 50 percent of all jobs worldwide and 70 percent of jobs in sub-Saharan Africa, East Asia, and the Pacific (World Resources Institute 2000). As croplands become scarce or degraded, as forests shrink, and as marine life dwindles, millions of people who make their living from these natural resources must find alternative livelihoods. In Canada's Maritime provinces, collapse of the cod fishing industry in the 1990s from overfishing left 30 000 fishers dependent on government welfare payments and decimated the economies of hundreds of communities (World Resources Institute 2000).

Globally, there are an estimated 30 million **environmental refugees**—individuals who have migrated because they can no longer secure a livelihood as a result of deforestation, desertification, soil erosion, and other environmental problems (Margesson 2005).

environmental refugees
People forced to move because of environmental destruction.

Table 13.1 *Threatened Species Worldwide, 2014*

	Estimated Number of Described Species[1]	Number of Threatened Species[2] in 2014 (IUCN red list version 2014.1)	Species Evaluated in 2014, as % of Species Described[2,3]	Lower Estimate of % Threatened Species in 2014 (number threatened as % of extant evaluated species)[2,3,4]	Best Estimate of % Threatened Species in 2014 (number threatened as % of extant data sufficient evaluated species)[2,3,4]	Upper Estimate of % Threatened Species in 2014 (number threatened + DD as % of extant evaluated species)[2,3,4]
Vertebrates						
Mammals[5]	5 514	1194	100%	22%	26%	37%
Birds	10 065	1308	100%	13.17%	13.25%	14%
Reptiles	9 952	902	43%		Insufficient coverage	
Amphibians	7 259	1961	88%	31%	41%	56%
Fishes	32 800	2172	35%		Insufficient coverage	
Subtotal	**65 590**	**7537**	**57%**			
Invertebrates						
Insects	1 000 000	950	0.5%		Insufficient coverage	
Molluscs	85 000	1929	8%		Insufficient coverage	
Crustaceans[6]	47 000	725	7%		Insufficient coverage	
Corals	2 175	235	39%		Insufficient coverage	
Arachnids	102 248	157	0.20%		Insufficient coverage	
Velvet Worms	165	9	7%		Insufficient coverage	
Horseshoe Crabs	4	0	100%	0%	0%	75%
Others	68 658	65	0.66%		Insufficient coverage	
Subtotal	**1 305 250**	**4070**	**1%**			
Plants[7]						
Mosses[8]	16 236	76	0.6%		Insufficient coverage	
Ferns and Allies[9]	12 000	194	3%		Insufficient coverage	

	Described species	No. threatened 2012	% threatened			
Gymnosperms	1 052	400	96%	40%	40%	42%
Flowering Plants	268 000	9808	7%	Insufficient coverage	Insufficient coverage	Insufficient coverage
Green Algae[10]	4 242	0	0.3%	Insufficient coverage	Insufficient coverage	
Red Algae[10]	6 144	9	0.9%	Insufficient coverage	Insufficient coverage	
Subtotal	**307 674**	**10 487**	**6%**			
Fungi & Protists						
Lichens	17 000	2	0.01%	Insufficient coverage		
Mushrooms	31 496	1	0.003%	Insufficient coverage		
Brown Algae[10]	3 127	6	0.5%	Insufficient coverage		
Subtotal	**51 623**	**9**	**0.03%**			
Total	**1 730 137**	**22 103**	**4%**			

Threatened species include those classified as critically endangered, endangered, and vulnerable.

NOTES (for rows and columns as indicated by the superscripted numbers):

[1] The sources used for the numbers of described species in each taxonomic group are listed below.

[2] Threatened species are those listed as Critically Endangered (CR), Endangered (EN) or Vulnerable (VU).

[3] Where <80% of species within a group have been evaluated, figures for % threatened species are not provided because there is insufficient coverage for these groups. It is only possible to provide reliable figures for % threatened species for those groups that are completely or almost completely evaluated (>90% of species evaluated), but the actual number of threatened species is often uncertain because it is not known whether Data Deficient (DD) species are actually threatened or not.

[4] The percentage of threatened species can be calculated for those groups that are completely or almost completely evaluated (>90% of species evaluated), but the actual number of threatened species is often uncertain because it is not known whether Data Deficient (DD) species are actually threatened or not. Therefore, a range of percentages is provided: lower estimate = % threatened extant species (if all DD species are not threatened); best estimate = % threatened extant species (if DD species are equally threatened as data sufficient species); upper estimate = % threatened extant species (if all DD species are threatened). If a single figure is required for reporting purposes, the best estimate figure should be used.

[5] The number of described and evaluated mammals excludes domesticated species like sheep (Ovis aries), goats (Capra hircus), Dromedary (Camelus dromedarius), etc.

[6] Crustaceans include six classes: Malacostraca (crabs, lobsters, shrimp, woodlice, etc.); Branchiopoda (fairy shrimp, clam shrimp, etc.); Cephalocarida (horseshoe shrimp); Ostracoda (seed shrimp); Maxillopoda (barnacles, copepods, etc.); and Remipedia (remipedes).

[7] The plant numbers DO NOT include species from the 1997 IUCN Red List of Threatened Plants (Walter and Gillett 1998) as those were all assessed using the pre-1994 IUCN system of threat categorization. Hence the numbers of threatened plants are very much lower when compared to the 1997 results. The results from this Red List and the 1997 Plants Red List should be combined together when reporting on threatened plants.

[8] Mosses include the true mosses (Bryophyta), the hornworts (Anthocerotophyta), and liverworts (Marchantiophyta).

[9] The ferns and allies include club mosses and spike mosses (Lycopodiopsida), quillworts (Isoetopsida), horsetails (Equisetopsida) and ferns (Marattiopsida, Polypodiopsida and Psilotopsida).

[10] Seaweeds are included in the green algae (Chlorophyta, Charophyta), red algae (Rhodophyta), and brown algae (Ochrophyta or Heterokontophyta).

SOURCE: Adapted from International Union for Conservation of Nature, "Changes in numbers of species in the threatened categories (CR, EN, VU) from 1996 to 2013." http://www.iucnredlist.org/about/summary-statistics. Reprinted by permission of the International Union for Conservation of Nature.

As individuals lose their source of income, so do nations. In one-fourth of the world's nations, crops, timber, and fish contribute more to the nation's economy than industrial goods do (World Resources Institute 2000).

13.4 Social Causes of Environmental Problems

Various structural and cultural factors have contributed to environmental problems. These include population growth, industrialization and economic development, and cultural values and attitudes, such as individualism, materialism, and militarism.

Population Growth

The world's population doubled to 6 billion in 1999 from 3 billion in 1960, and it is projected to reach more than 9 billion by 2050. Population growth places increased demands on natural resources and results in increased waste. As Hunter (2001) explains:

> Global population size is inherently connected to land, air, and water environments because each and every individual uses environmental resources and contributes to environmental pollution. While the scale of resource use and the level of wastes produced vary across individuals and across cultural contexts, the fact remains that land, water, and air are necessary for human survival. (p. 12)

However, curbing population growth is not as critical as addressing the ways in which populations produce, distribute, and consume goods and services. Wealthy, industrialized countries have the slowest rates of population growth, yet these countries consume the most natural resources and contribute most to pollution, global warming, and other environmental problems.

Industrialization and Economic Development

Many of the environmental problems confronting the world, including global warming and the depletion of the ozone layer, are associated with industrialization and economic development. Industrialized countries, for example, consume more energy and natural resources and contribute more pollution to the environment than poor countries.

The relationship between level of economic development and environmental pollution is curvilinear rather than linear. For example, industrial emissions are minimal in regions with low levels of economic development and are high in the middle-development range as developing countries move through the early stages of industrialization. At more advanced industrial stages, though, industrial emissions ease because heavy-polluting manufacturing industries decline and "cleaner" service industries increase, and because rising incomes are associated with a greater demand for environmental quality and cleaner technologies. However, a positive linear correlation has been demonstrated between per capita income and national carbon dioxide emissions (Hunter 2001).

In less developed countries, environmental problems are largely the result of poverty and the priority of economic survival over environmental concerns. Vajpeyi (1995) explains:

> Policymakers in the Third World are often in conflict with the ever-increasing demands to satisfy basic human needs—clean air, water, adequate food, shelter, education—and to safeguard the environmental quality. Given the scarce economic

and technical resources at their disposal, most of these policymakers have ignored long-range environmental concerns and opted for short-range economic and political gains. (p. 24)

A major environmental concern today is the growing economy of China—the most populated country in the world. The income of China's 1.3 billion people has been growing at a rapid rate, and along with that rising income, Chinese consumers are increasingly able to spend money on cars, travel, meat, and other goods and services that use fossil fuels. If China were to increase its fuel consumption to that typical of North Americans, China would use more than the current world production of 2.5 billion tons per year. In addition, if the Chinese were to use oil at the same rate as North Americans, by 2031 China would need 99 million barrels of oil a day—more than the current world production of 79 million barrels per day (Aslam 2005).

In considering the effects of economic development on the environment, note that the ways we measure economic development and the "health" of economies also influence environmental outcomes. Two primary measures of economic development and the health of economies are gross domestic product (GDP) and consumer spending. But these measures overlook the social and environmental costs of the production and consumption of goods and services. Until definitions and measurements of "economic development" and "economic health" reflect these costs, the pursuit of economic development will continue to contribute to environmental problems.

Cultural Values and Attitudes

Cultural values and attitudes that contribute to environmental problems include individualism, materialism, and militarism.

Individualism

Individualism, a way of thinking central to capitalist economies, puts individual interests over collective welfare. Although recycling may benefit the collective environment, many individuals do not recycle because of the personal inconvenience involved in washing and sorting recyclable items. Similarly, individuals often indulge in countless behaviours that provide enjoyment and convenience at the expense of the environment: taking long showers, using dishwashing machines, doing recreational boating, eating meat frequently, using air conditioning, and driving gas-powered cars to run short errands instead of walking.

Materialism

Materialism, or the emphasis on worldly possessions, encourages individuals to continually purchase new items and throw away old ones. The media bombard us daily with advertisements that tell us life will be better if we purchase a particular product. After the terrorist attacks of September 11, 2001, U.S. President George Bush advised Americans that it was their patriotic duty to go to the malls and spend money. Many Canadians followed suit. Materialism contributes to pollution and environmental degradation by supporting polluting and resource-depleting industries and by contributing to waste.

Militarism

The cultural value of militarism also contributes to environmental degradation. "It is generally agreed that the number one polluter in the United States is the American military. It is responsible each year for the generation of more than one-third of the nation's toxic waste ... an amount greater than the five largest international chemical companies combined" (Blatt 2005: 25). Toxic substances from military vehicles, weapons materials, and munitions pollute the air, land, and groundwater in and around military bases and training areas. The Pentagon has asked Congress to loosen environmental laws for the military, so that training exercises can occur unimpeded (Janofsky 2005). In addition, the Environmental Protection Agency is forbidden to investigate or sue the military (Blatt 2005).

13.5 Strategies for Action: Responding to Environmental Problems

One strategy for alleviating environmental problems is to lower fertility rates and slow population growth. Responses to environmental problems also include environmental activism, environmental education, the use of "green" energy, modifications in consumer products and behaviour, and government regulations and legislation. Sustainable economic development and international cooperation and assistance also play important roles in alleviating environmental problems.

Environmental Activism and Industry Resistance

Environmentalist groups exert pressure on the government to initiate or intensify actions related to environmental protection. They also design and implement their own projects and disseminate information to the public about environmental issues.

In North America, environmentalist groups date back to 1892, with the establishment of the Sierra Club, followed by the Audubon Society in 1905. Other environmental groups include, but are not limited to, the Canadian Environmental Law Association, Canadian Environmental Defence Fund, Canadian Environmental Network, Great Lakes United, Common Frontiers, Greenpeace, Environmental Action, Natural Resources Defense Council, World Watch Institute, National Recycling Coalition, Campaign for Nuclear Phase-Out, and the New Brunswick Environmental Network. In Ontario, the Ontario Environment Network joins together the efforts of 187 member groups, and as a network provides affiliation to the Canadian Environmental Network. This national group encourages public participation in the development of environmental protection policy.

Industries, major contributors to environmental problems, often fight against environmental efforts that threaten their products, but not always. Some industries are joining the environmental movement for a variety of reasons, including pressure from consumers and environmental groups, the desire to improve their public image, and genuine concern for the environment. For example, in 1997, British Petroleum (BP) publicly acknowledged that global warming is a threat to human and environmental health and began working with the environmental organization Environmental Defense to develop ways to reduce its greenhouse gas emissions ("Global Corporations Join Us" 2000). This initiative led to the development of the Partnership for Climate Action—a collaboration between Environmental Defense and seven of the world's largest corporations (including companies in the petroleum, aluminum, chemical, and electric power sectors) to take action against global warming. Participating companies have committed to report their emissions publicly, and each has a firm target for emissions reductions. Environmental Defense is working with each company to devise ways to improve energy efficiency, use renewable energy sources, and improve manufacturing processes.

BP, along with several other industries, has also withdrawn from membership in the Global Climate Coalition—an industry group that denies global warming and the role that industries play in the emission of greenhouse gases. Other industries that have quit the Global Climate Coalition include Ford, Shell Oil, Dow Chemical, General Motors, and Daimler-Chrysler (Associated Press 2000).

Canadian sociologist Glenda Wall (2000) cautions, however, that when we focus on altering individual behaviours—for example with regard to consumption, recycling, and limiting family sizes—we risk being seriously distracted from the industrial practices that continue, often largely unchecked, to threaten the environment. Wall provides a critical analysis of the historical shift away from a sense of "consumerism" that in the 1970s focused on critical assessment of, and active movement to find alternatives to, capitalism. This perspective involved "thinking and talking about pollution and other environmental issues *as social issues*" [emphasis added] (p. 205). Wall argues that as we moved toward a view of consumerism as individual behaviours related to overconsumption of goods, we lost sight of the need to demand more environmentally sound industrial practices.

Ecoterrorism

An extreme form of environmental activism, sometimes referred to as **ecoterrorism**, involves the use of criminal or violent actions in an effort to protect wildlife or the environment (Denson 2000). The best-known ecoterrorist groups are the Earth Liberation Front (ELF) and the Animal Liberation Front (ALF). ELF and ALF are international underground movements consisting of autonomous individuals and small groups who engage in "direct action" to (1) inflict economic damage on those profiting from the destruction and exploitation of the natural environment, (2) save animals from places of abuse (e.g., laboratories, factory farms, fur farms), and (3) reveal information and educate the public on atrocities committed against Earth and all the species that populate it. Direct actions of ELF and ALF have included setting fire to a golf club in Guelph, Ontario; setting fire to gas-guzzling Hummers and other SUVs at car dealerships; vandalizing SUVs parked on streets and in driveways; setting fire to construction sites (in opposition to the development); and smashing windows at the homes of fur retailers. Because the direct actions of ELF and ALF are illegal, activists work anonymously and without any centralized organization or coordination. Although critics of ecoterrorism cite the damage done by such tactics, members and supporters of ecoterrorist groups claim that the real terrorists are corporations that plunder the Earth. While we may not condone ecoterrorism, the very real environmental destruction associated with suburban sprawl requires attention and ought to encourage us to rethink how we should organize our daily living habits, how we should think about what makes a community a "desirable" place to live, and for whom it may be deleterious.

ecoterrorism
Any violent crime intended to coerce, intimidate, or change public policy on behalf of the natural world.

The Role of Corporations in the Environmental Movement

Corporations are major contributors to environmental problems and often fight against environmental efforts that threaten their profits. Some corporations, however, are joining the environmental movement for a variety of reasons, including pressure from consumers and environmental groups, the desire to improve their public image, genuine concern for the environment, and concern for maximizing current or future profits.

In 1994, out of concern for public and environmental health, Interface, with Ray Anderson as the chief executive officer, set a goal of being a sustainable company by 2020—"a company that will grow by cleaning up the world, not by polluting or degrading it" (McDaniel 2005: 33). Anderson envisioned recycling all the materials used, not releasing any toxins into the environment, and using solar energy to power all production. The company has made significant progress toward these goals.

Car manufacturers can play a role in the environmental movement by developing fuel-efficient and alternative-fuel vehicles. In collaboration with the environmental organization Environmental Defense, FedEx has developed a hybrid electric delivery truck that cuts smog-forming pollution by 65 percent, reduces soot by 96 percent, and goes 57 percent farther on a gallon of fuel (Environmental Defense 2004). In 2004, Daimler-Chrysler introduced its Smart Car in Canada; the car had already been available in Europe for several years. The Smart Car carries only two passengers and is designed for city driving, but promises far greater fuel efficiency and lower greenhouse-gas emissions than typical passenger cars. It uses just 4.2 L of diesel fuel to travel 100 km.

Environmental Education

One goal of environmental organizations and activists is to educate the public about environmental issues and the seriousness of environmental problems. Some Americans underestimate the seriousness of environmental concerns because they lack accurate information about environmental issues. In a national survey of U.S. adults, most (69 percent) rated themselves as having either "a lot" (10 percent) or "a fair amount" (59 percent) of knowledge about environmental issues and problems (National Environmental Education 1999). Yet, on 7 of 10 questions asked about emerging environmental issues, more Americans gave incorrect answers than correct ones. The average was 3.2 correct answers out of 10 questions. Even those who rated themselves as having "a lot" of environmental knowledge, as well as those with a college degree, scored only 4 of 10 items correctly. The authors of the study concluded:

> Increased knowledge is the key to changing attitudes and behaviors on issues critical to our environmental future. If Americans can answer an average of only 3 of 10 simple knowledge questions, there is a clear need to provide environmental information in a form that the American public can easily digest and act upon. (National Environmental Education 1999: 41)

For most North Americans, a main source of information about environmental issues is the media. However, because the media are owned by corporations and wealthy individuals with corporate ties, unbiased information about environmental impacts of corporate activities may not readily be found in mainstream media channels. Indeed, the public must consider the source in interpreting information about environmental issues. Propaganda by corporations sometimes comes packaged as "environmental education." Hager and Burton (2000: 107) explain: "Corporate interests realize the value of getting their spin into the classrooms of future consumers and voters." However, Canadian publications, such as *Adbusters*, continue to offer alternative news, information, and analyses independent from corporate interests or financing, and in direct opposition to values of individualist materialism.

"Green" Energy

As noted earlier, many of the environmental problems facing the world today are linked to energy use, particularly the use of fossil fuels. Increasing the use of "green" energy—energy that is renewable and nonpolluting—can help alleviate environmental problems associated with fossil fuels. Also known as clean energy, green energy sources include solar power, wind power, biofuel, and hydrogen. Although clean energy represents less than 1 percent of world energy production, it is expected to increase.

Solar Power

The world's fastest developing clean energy is photovoltaic cells—a form of solar power that converts sunlight to electricity (Sawin 2005). Japan, which produces half of all photovoltaic cells, aims for photovoltaic cells to generate 10 percent of Japan's electricity by 2030. Driven by government incentive programs, Germany and other European countries are also increasing their use of solar cells to provide electricity. In the United States, California leads the nation in photovoltaic cell use.

Another form of solar power is the use of solar thermal collectors, which capture the sun's warmth to heat building space and water. China is the world's leader in solar thermal production and use, followed by Japan, Europe, and Turkey (Sawin 2005). The United States was once the world leader in solar thermal production, but has fallen far behind because of low natural gas prices and the lack of government incentives. Another form of solar power comes from "concentrating solar power plants," which use the sun's heat to make steam to turn electricity-producing turbines.

Wind Power

Wind power is the world's second fastest-growing energy source, after solar power. Wind turbines, which turn wind energy into electricity, are operating in more than 65 countries, although nearly three-fourths of wind power is produced in Europe. In Germany, the leading country in wind power, wind energy meets 6.6 percent of electricity needs. As of April 2006, Canada had operational turbines sufficient to power over 280 000 homes (Natural Resources Canada 2006).

One disadvantage of wind power is that birds have been known to fly into the turbines and die. However, this problem has been mitigated in recent years through the use of painted blades, slower rotational speeds, and careful wind turbine placement.

Biofuel

Biofuels are derived from agricultural crops. They burn cleaner than fossil fuels, are renewable, and can create agricultural jobs and revenues for countries while reducing dependence on imported oil.

Two types of biofuels are ethanol and biodiesel. Ethanol is an alcohol-based fuel that is produced by fermenting and distilling sugar obtained from agricultural crops such as corn, beets, sugar cane, barley, and wheat. Ethanol is blended with gasoline to create E85 (85 percent ethanol, 15 percent gasoline). Vehicles that run on E85, called flexible fuel vehicles, have been used by government and in private fleets for years. They have just recently become available to consumers. However, only a small fraction of passenger vehicles are flexible fuel vehicles, and many owners of these vehicles do not know that their vehicle can operate with E85 and/or do not have access to a gas station that sells E85 (Price 2006).

Another problem associated with ethanol fuel is that increased demand for corn, which is used to make most ethanol in the United States, has driven up the price of corn, resulting in higher food prices (many processed food items contain corn, and animal feed is largely corn). And as corn prices rise, so too do those of rice and wheat because the crops compete for land. Rising food prices threaten the survival of the world's poorest 2 billion people, who depend on grain to survive. The grain it takes to fill a 25-gallon tank with ethanol would feed one person for an entire year (Brown 2007).

Increased corn and/or sugar cane production to meet the demand for ethanol also has adverse environmental effects, including increased use and runoff of fertilizers, pesticides, and herbicides; depletion of water resources; and soil erosion. In addition, tropical forests are being clear-cut to make room for "energy crops," leaving less land for conservation and wildlife (Price 2006); biofuel refineries commonly run on coal and natural gas (which emit greenhouse gases); farm equipment and fertilizer production require fossil fuels; and the use of ethanol involves emissions of several pollutants. Finally, even if 100 percent of the U.S. corn crop were used to produce ethanol, it would only displace less than 15 percent of U.S. gasoline use (Food and Water Watch 2007).

Biodiesel fuel is a cleaner-burning diesel fuel made from vegetable oils and animal fats, including recycled cooking oil. Some individuals who make their own biodiesel fuel obtain used cooking oil from restaurants at no charge. The European Union, the leading manufacturer of biodiesel, hopes that biofuels will supply 20 percent of the fuel market in 2020 (Aeck 2005). More than 60 companies in Canada are now working to develop and improve biofuel technologies (Government of Canada 2006).

Hydrogen Power

Hydrogen, the most plentiful element on Earth, is a clean-burning fuel that can be used for electricity production, heating, cooling, and transportation. Many see a movement to a hydrogen economy as a long-term solution to the environmental and political problems associated with fossil fuels. Further research is needed, however, to develop nonpolluting and cost-effective ways to extract and transport hydrogen. In the meantime, all the major auto manufacturers are developing hydrogen fuel cell technology. In 2004, California Governor Arnold Schwarzenegger issued an executive order calling for the development of a Hydrogen Highway Network Blueprint Plan to make hydrogen a viable alternative transportation fuel in his state.

Modifications in Consumer Behaviour

In industrialized countries, consumers are making "green" choices in their behaviour and in their purchases that reflect concern for the environment. In some cases, these choices cost more; for example, paying more for organically grown food or for clothing made from organic cotton. In many cases, however, consumers are motivated to make green choices in their purchasing behaviour because doing so saves money. For example, after gas prices topped $1 per litre in 2005, sales of gas-guzzling SUVs dropped, and sales of fuel-efficient cars, such as hybrids, increased. According to Dan Becker, director of the Sierra Club's global warming program, switching to fuel-efficient vehicles such as hybrids is the single biggest step to reducing dependency on foreign oil (Gartner 2005).

Consumers often consider their utility bill when they choose energy-efficient appliances and electrical equipment. To assist consumers in choosing energy-efficient products, in 1992 the U.S. Environmental Protection Agency (EPA) introduced the Energy Star label for products that meet EPA energy-efficiency standards. Globally, 37 countries use an energy-efficient labelling system for appliances and electronic equipment (Makower et al. 2005). Canada now uses the Energy Star labelling system as well.

Green energy sources, such as wind turbines and solar conversion panels, are available across Canada, but it is often up to consumers to purchase their own alternative power sources and then sell back to the utility companies any excess energy they produce. Thus, the local grid that delivers electricity combines all power—green or not. The amount of clean power available to average consumers is generated on their behalf and added to the larger pool of electricity (Vartan 2005). To check availability of green energy in their region, consumers should call their utility company and ask.

Green Building

Green building practices incorporate design elements to maximize efficient use of energy while minimizing the impact of buildings on local and global environments.

The Canada Green Building Council (CGBC) has organized to ensure that buildings seeking green designation meet certain environmentally sound standards. Buildings achieve ratings on the Leadership in Energy and Environmental Design (LEED-Canada) standards scale developed to assess how environmentally friendly a given site is in the following areas: water efficiency, energy and atmospheric impact, materials and resource use, and indoor environmental quality. Ratings range through the categories certified, silver, gold, and platinum, and are derived from a points-based assessment of how well a building meets the standards.

Some outstanding examples of green architecture in Canada can be found at the Canada Green Building Council (CGBC) website. These include the Nose Creek Recreation and Library facility in Calgary, the Vancouver Port Authority head office, and the Pavillons Lassonde at l'École Polytechnique in Montreal (CGBC 2006).

Government Policies, Regulations, and Funding

Worldwide, governments spend about $1 trillion (U.S. dollars) per year in subsidies that allow the prices of fuel, timber, metals, and minerals (and products using these materials) to be much lower than they otherwise would be, encouraging greater consumption (Renner 2004). In that way, government policies can worsen environmental problems. But government policies, regulations, and funding can also play a role in protecting and restoring the environment. At the local, provincial/state, regional, and federal levels, governments have implemented policies and regulations affecting the production and use of pollutants, the preservation of natural resources and biodiversity, and the use of renewable energy.

For example, in 2003 the European Union drafted legislation known as REACH (Registration, Evaluation, and Authorization of CHemicals), which requires chemical companies to conduct safety and environmental tests to prove that the chemicals they are producing are safe. If they cannot prove that a chemical is safe, it will be banned from the market (Rifkin 2004). The European Union has become a world leader in environmental stewardship by placing the "precautionary principle" at the centre of its regulatory policy. The precautionary principle requires industry to prove that their products are safe.

Government policies and regulations also affect energy use. In 2004, more than 20 countries committed to specific targets for the renewable share of total energy use (UNEP 2005). Some environmentalists propose that governments use taxes to discourage environmentally damaging practices and products (Brown and Mitchell 1998). In the 1990s, several European governments increased taxes on environmentally harmful activities and products (such as gasoline, diesel, and motor vehicles) and decreased taxes on income and labour (Renner 2004).

Sustainable Economic Development

Achieving global cooperation on environmental issues is difficult, in part, because developed countries (primarily in the northern hemisphere) have different economic agendas than those of developing countries (primarily in the southern hemisphere). The northern agenda emphasizes preserving wealth and affluent lifestyles, whereas the southern agenda focuses on overcoming mass poverty and achieving a higher quality of life (Koenig 1995). Southern countries are concerned that northern industrialized countries—having already achieved economic wealth—will impose international environmental policies that restrict their economic growth just as they are beginning to industrialize. Global strategies to preserve the environment must address both wasteful lifestyles in some nations and the need to overcome overpopulation and widespread poverty in others.

Development encompasses more than economic growth; it involves sustainability—the long-term environmental, social, and economic health of societies. **Sustainable development** involves meeting the needs of the present world without endangering the ability of future generations to meet their own needs. "The aim here is for those alive today to meet their own needs without making it impossible for future generations to meet theirs.... This in turn calls for an economic structure within which we consume only as much as the natural environment can produce, and make only as much waste as it can absorb" (McMichael et al. 2000: 1067).

Sustainable development requires the use of clean, renewable energy. Renewable energy projects in developing countries have demonstrated that providing affordable access to green energy, such as solar, wind, and biofuels, helps to alleviate poverty. The projects provide energy for creating businesses and jobs, and provide power for refrigerating medicine, sterilizing medical equipment, and supplying freshwater and sewer services needed to reduce infectious disease and improve health (Flavin and Aeck 2005).

International Cooperation and Assistance

Global environmental concerns—global warming, destruction of the ozone layer, and loss of biodiversity among them—call for global solutions forged through international cooperation and assistance. For example, the 1987 Montreal Protocol on Substances That Deplete the Ozone Layer forged an agreement made by 70 nations to curb the production of CFCs (which contribute to ozone depletion and global warming). The 1992 Earth Summit in Rio de Janeiro brought together heads of state, delegates from more than 170 nations and nongovernmental organizations, and participants to discuss an international agenda for both economic development and the environment. The 1992 Earth Summit resulted in the Rio Declaration—"a nonbinding statement of broad principles to guide environmental policy, vaguely committing its signatories not to damage the environment of other nations by activities within their borders and to acknowledge environmental protection as an integral part of development" (Koenig 1995: 15).

In 1997, delegates from 160 nations met in Kyoto, Japan, and forged the **Kyoto Protocol**—the first international agreement to place legally binding limits on greenhouse gas emissions from developed countries. The United States, which produces one-fourth of the world's greenhouse-gas emissions, rejected Kyoto in 2001, and in 2006, Canada announced that it would be unable to meet its Kyoto targets. In 2004, the Russian Federation joined more than 120 other countries in ratifying the treaty, which came into force in early 2005.

One major criticism of the Kyoto accord is that it allows countries with high greenhouse-gas emission levels to use credit transfers to trade their levels with low-producing countries, thus balancing out the emissions declared on paper. In short, industrialized nations would not have to alter their practices much, and developing nations risk being compelled by economic and political considerations to assume the burden of other countries' emissions, something that would inhibit the development of their own industrialization.

In another global environmental treaty, the Stockholm Convention, representatives from 122 countries drafted an agreement to phase out a group of dangerous chemicals known as persistent organic pollutants. More recently, Germany hosted a major intergovernmental conference, Renewables 2004. The conference resulted in the adoption of the International Action Programme on Renewables, which supports more than 200 ongoing or planned policies and projects in over 150 countries (UNEP 2005). In December 2009, the Climate Conference in Copenhagen sought to make progress where the Kyoto accord had failed. Unfortunately, the conference failed to reach any international agreements. The failure of the conference is attributed to a variety of political and social factors, key among them that, unlike E.U. leaders, the U.S. president cannot make a decision without the approval of Congress; that the weather at the time was frigid and snowy and thus undermined people's *belief* in the seriousness of climate change; that delegates from participating countries did not have equal recognition of their concerns at the table; and that a "24-hour news culture" impaired the ability to deliver analysis and evaluation from those with the scientific ability to do so and favoured delivery of sound bites from lobbyists instead (BBC News 2009).

Some countries do not have the technical or economic resources to implement the requirements of environmental treaties. Wealthy industrialized countries can help less-developed countries address environmental concerns through economic aid. Because industrialized countries have more economic and technological resources, they bear primary responsibility for leading the nations of the world toward environmental cooperation. Jan (1995) emphasizes the importance of international environmental cooperation and the role of developed countries in this endeavour:

> Advanced countries must be willing to sacrifice their own economic well-being to help improve the environment of the poor, developing countries. Failing to do this will lead to irreparable damage to our global environment. Environmental protection is no longer the affair of any one country. It has become an urgent global issue. Environmental pollution recognizes no national boundaries. No country, especially a poor country, can solve this problem alone. (pp. 82–83)

Understanding Environmental Problems

Environmental problems are linked to a number of interrelated features of social life, including corporate globalization, rapid and dramatic population growth, expanding world industrialization, patterns of excessive consumption, and reliance on fossil fuels for energy. Growing evidence of the irreversible effects of global warming and loss of biodiversity, increased concerns about the link between global warming and extreme weather events such as Hurricane Katrina, and adverse health effects of toxic waste and other forms of pollution suggest that we cannot ignore environmental problems.

Many North Americans believe in a "technological fix" for the environment—that science and technology will solve environmental problems. Paradoxically, the same environmental problems that have been caused by technology may be solved by technological innovations designed to clean up pollution, preserve natural resources and habitats, and provide clean forms of energy. Leaders of government and industry, though, must have the will to finance, develop, and use technologies that do not pollute or deplete the environment. When asked how companies can produce products without polluting the environment, corporate attorney Robert Hinkley suggested that, first, it must become a goal to do so:

> I don't have the technological answers for how it can be done, but neither did President John F. Kennedy when he announced a national goal to land a man on the moon by the end of the 1960s. The point is that, to eliminate pollution, we first have to make it our goal. Once we've done that, we will devote the resources necessary to make it happen. We will develop technologies that we never thought possible. But if

we don't make it our goal, then we will never devote the resources, never develop the technology, and never solve the problem. (quoted by Cooper 2004: 11)

But the direction of technological innovation is largely under the control of transnational corporations that place profits over environmental protection.

Unless the global community challenges the power of transnational corporations to pursue profits at the expense of environmental and human health, corporate behaviour will continue to take a heavy toll on the health of the planet and its inhabitants. Political and military conflicts centred in the Middle East are likely to continue as long as oil plays the lead role in providing the world's energy.

Global cooperation is also vital to resolving environmental concerns, but is difficult to achieve because rich and poor countries have different economic development agendas: developing poor countries struggle to survive and provide for the basic needs of their citizens; developed wealthy countries struggle to maintain their wealth and relatively high standard of living. Can both agendas be achieved without further pollution and destruction of the environment? Is sustainable economic development an attainable goal? With mounting concern about climate change, the impacts of air pollution on health, rising oil prices, and the need to ensure energy access to all, governments worldwide have strengthened their commitment to sustainable, renewable energy policies and projects (UNEP 2005).

Since September 11, 2001, world leaders, the media, and citizens in countries across the world have been preoccupied with terrorism. Lester Brown, of the Earth Policy Institute, warns against the environmental dangers of such preoccupation:

> Terrorism is certainly a matter of concern, but if it diverts us from the environmental trends that are undermining our future until it is too late to reverse them, Osama bin Laden and his followers will have achieved their goal of bringing down Western civilization in a way they could not have imagined. (Brown 2003: 5)

In 2004, the Nobel Peace Prize was given to Wangari Maathai for leading a grassroots environmental campaign to plant 30 million trees across Kenya. For the first time ever, the Nobel Peace Prize was awarded to someone for accomplishments in restoring the environment. In her acceptance speech, Maathai explained, "A degraded environment leads to a scramble for scarce resources and may culminate in poverty and even conflict" (quoted by Little 2005: 2). With ongoing conflict around the world, it is time for leaders to recognize the importance of a healthy environment for world peace and to prioritize environmental protection in their political agendas.

Student Reflection: What Do You Know Now?

Having read this chapter, look around your immediate environment—whether it is a classroom in an institutional building, or a private space where you are accessing a virtual course. What options are there for recycling, and what materials? Is there composting available? How would you recycle electronics if you needed to in this place? What objects around your person and around the space are connected to global environmental impact, and how? How much food will be thrown away this week or month in your living space?

Again on a local level, reflect critically on environmental efforts. Who sponsors your local Earth Day? Who sponsored it in elementary school (if you went to school in a place that held it)? Would you boycott Earth Day if certain corporations were involved? Which ones, and why?

On a broader level, consider what an effective carbon trading or carbon offset program—one that's not greenwashing—would look like. What would convince you that the program was legitimate and not greenwashing? How, if at all, would you include social capital and social problems in calculating carbon offset points?

What Do You Do Next?

Located at http://www.nelson.com/socialproblems5e

- Consolidate your knowledge with interactive and printable **Flashcards**
- Gauge your understanding with **Practice Quizzes** and **Matching Activities**
- Develop your critical thinking skills with **Self and Society** and **The Human Side** questions
- Analyze **Social Research** and **Social Problems in Global Perspective**
- Explore the implications of **Technology on Social Problems**

14

Armed Conflict in Global Perspective

Student Reflection: What Do You Already Know?

If you grew up in a Canadian school system, it is likely you learned that we are a peacekeeping nation, advising other nations on how best to run a democracy and acting when called upon by allies. If you grew up outside Canada, was this also your view? What is your own history or family history in terms of awareness of armed forces and involvement in armed conflict? For many Canadians, the World Wars still figure prominently in our responses to social and political problems. Annual remembrances, school visits by veterans, and talks by more recent ex-military commanders figure prominently in our self-definition as a country. To think sociologically about armed conflict is to move away from, or challenge, such straightforward messages. This chapter addresses the impact of armed conflict across institutions, on individuals and groups, and on the environment.

Learning Outcomes

Through careful reading of this chapter, you should be able to:

- define the bolded key terms
- connect the history of armed conflict and industrialization in social change terms
- explain the social costs of military spending and military action, and the social benefits that might accrue after war
- interrogate the traditional Canadian identity as a "peacekeeper" nation
- analyze the role of imagery in posters and films in the construction of war and identity
- apply the classic sociological theories and feminism to the question of war and society, at the international systemic level and in individual lives
- explain social problems associated with armed conflict and its aftermath, including death and disability, rape and forced prostitution, displacement of women and children, social-psychological costs, diversion of economic resources, and environmental destruction
- consider local, national, and international actions that could contribute to global peace

© Chapin31/iStockphoto.com

Armed conflict (of which officially declared wars are only one manifestation) is one of the great paradoxes of human history. It is used to protect, but also to annihilate, and can sometimes even threaten the welfare and safety of those it aims to serve—as in the case of the use of nuclear weapons. Armed conflicts have created and defended nations but have also destroyed them. The scars of civil wars can remain for decades or centuries, even if they are resolved with the nation intact, as happened with the U.S. civil war. War, the most violent form of conflict, refers to organized armed violence aimed at a social group in pursuit of an objective. Wars have existed throughout human history and continue in the contemporary world. Whether war is just or unjust, defensive or offensive, it involves the most horrendous atrocities known to humankind. This is especially true in the twenty-first century, when nearly all wars are fought in populated areas rather than on remote battlefields. War is often conducted within the routine of daily life—and this can have deadly consequences. Thus, war is not only a social problem in and of itself; it contributes to a host of other social problems—death, disease, and disability, crime and immorality, psychological terror, loss of economic resources, and environmental devastation. In this chapter, we discuss each of these issues within the context of conflict, war, and terrorism, the most threatening of all social problems.

14.1 The Global Context: Conflict in a Changing World

Canada's Changing Role

Though many readers will be aware that Canada initially deployed troops in Afghanistan in 2002 and withdrew officially in 2013, Canada's Department of National Defence last released public information in 2011 regarding a total of 13 other locations around the world where troops were actively deployed and, in addition, of three separate missions in Afghanistan (National Defence 2010; Minister of Public Works/Government of Canada 2011). The locations outside Afghanistan included three active deployments in Africa, one in Saudi Arabia, one in Haiti, and one in Russia. While not all of these deployments have involved armed military personnel on the ground, Canada's mission in Afghanistan in particular raises the issue of why we have chosen in this chapter to talk about "armed conflict" as something distinct from "war."

We may see the casualties and other damage in Afghanistan and know intuitively that it is "a war," but the language of international diplomacy splits hairs on the point. The Canadian Department of National Defence avoids the language of conflict, explaining that we "are there because the Afghan government asked for our help ... to rebuild their nation as a stable, democratic, self-sufficient society" (National Defence 2010). By this account, then, the Canadian mission in Afghanistan is not an act of war, but neither is it an effort at peacekeeping: "Afghanistan is not a peacekeeping mission. There are no ceasefire arrangements to enforce or negotiated peace settlements to respect" (ibid). The National Defence explanation is certainly a narrative meant to appease a public confused about why we are there. After all, some of us remember quite clearly committing our military forces specifically to aid U.S. retaliation following the 9/11 attack by Al Qaeda in what Art Eggleton, then Minister of Defence, characterized as a "campaign against terrorism" (Eggleton 2001), but which Southam Publications labelled as the "war on terrorism" in creating the title that ran with the article.

Whether we characterize the entry of the Canadian military into Afghanistan as a "campaign" or a "war" against terror, Canada entered into 2011 with 2830 troops— nearly three times as many as were sent in 2001—still actively deployed in three areas in Afghanistan (National Defence 2010); it is clear that ours has not been the "short-term stabilization" effort that Eggleton asserted it would be. Indeed, although *The Globe and Mail* asserted in early 2008 that the Afghan mission was winding down (Curry and LeBlanc 2008), federal spending increases in the defence budget continue, suggesting that Canada's future will include more military support work in war zones rather than peacekeeping in post-conflict territories. In 2008, David Perry, formerly a director of the Dalhousie University Centre for Foreign Policy Studies, estimated that by the time all the costs of Canada's missions in Afghanistan were tallied, including those of caring for injured and traumatized veterans, the war would cost Canada $22 billion in current dollars (Pugliese 2008). Perry's estimates were verified by retired Commodore Eric Lehre (ibid). In addition, for every year between 1993 and 2007, the last year for which the Canadian government released data, base projected expenditures exceeded a "low" of $9.38 billion projected and actual expenses of $10.26 billion in 1998/99 (National Defence 2010). By 2006/07 the projected budget reached $14.8 billion for "national defence" and actual expenditures were $15.7 billion (ibid).

War and Social Change

The very act that now threatens modern civilization—war—is largely responsible for creating the advanced civilization in which we live. Before large political states existed, people lived in small groups and villages. War broke the barriers of autonomy between local groups and permitted small villages to be incorporated into larger political units known as chiefdoms. Centuries of warfare between chiefdoms culminated in the development of the state. The state is "an apparatus of power, a set of institutions—the central government, the armed forces, the regulatory and police agencies—whose most important functions involve the use of force, the control of territory, and the maintenance of internal order" (Porter 1994: 5–6). The creation of the state in turn led to other profound social and cultural changes:

> And once the state emerged, the gates were flung open to enormous cultural advances, advances undreamed of during—and impossible under—a regimen of small autonomous villages. ... Only in large political units, far removed in structure from the small autonomous communities from which they sprang, was it possible for great advances to be made in the arts and sciences, in economics and technology, and indeed in every field of culture central to the great industrial civilizations of the world. (Carneiro 1994: 14–15)

Industrialization and technology could not have developed in the small social groups that existed before military action consolidated them into larger states. Thus, war contributed indirectly to the industrialization and technological sophistication that characterize the modern world. Industrialization, in turn, has had two major influences on war. Cohen (1986) calculated the number of wars fought per decade in industrial and preindustrial nations and concluded that "as societies become more industrialized, their proneness to warfare decreases" (p. 265). Thus, for example, in 2008 there were 16 major armed conflicts, the majority of which were in less developed countries in Africa and Asia (SIPRI 2009a).

Although industrialization may decrease a society's propensity to war, it also increases the potential destruction of war. With industrialization, military technology became more sophisticated and more lethal. Rifles and cannons replaced the clubs, arrows, and swords used in more primitive warfare and, in turn, were replaced by tanks, bombers, and nuclear warheads. Today, the use of new technologies such as high-performance sensors, information processors, directed energy technologies, precision-guided munitions, and computer worms and viruses have changed the very nature of conflict, war, and terrorism. For example, according to one defence analyst, "the U.S. military alone fields 7,000 unmanned drones in the air, like the Predators that fire missiles into Pakistan—and roughly another 12,000 on the ground, like the Packbots that hunt for roadside bombs in Iraq" (Singer 2009: 1).

In the postindustrial information age, computer technology not only has revolutionized the nature of warfare but also has made societies more vulnerable to external attacks. For example, in 2009, North Korea attacked computer systems in the United States and in South Korea, resulting in brief disruptions to government and major commercial networks (Sang-Hun and Markoff 2009). Information technologies are also forcing governments to become more accountable with regard to foreign policy, intelligence gathering and dissemination, and diplomatic relations. The highly controversial website WikiLeaks, for example, has prompted excoriating criticism from world leaders and analysts who have characterized the leaks as irresponsible and purposeless—or even as dangerous to the safety of deployed troops around the world (ABC News 2010). In response to these characterizations, WikiLeaks founder Julian Assange has defended the right of the public to know the horrors, both intended and collateral, of the armed conflict in regions such as Iraq. WikiLeaks' July 2010 release of more than 90 000 documents related to the Afghan war revealed, for example, that "all these people [were] killed in the small events that we haven't heard about which numerically eclipse the big events … It's the boy killed by a shell that missed the target. It's villagers that have gone to hospital as a result of a missed air strike" (Assange, quoted in ABC News 2010). It is not clear yet to what degree new public awareness of the costs of war will influence the pursuit of new means of creating positive social change, but the hope of those who defend the release of the information seek at the very least not to achieve social change on the backs of vulnerable citizens.

14.2 Sociological Theories of Armed Conflict and War

Sociological perspectives can help us understand various aspects of armed conflict, especially as it manifests in the formality of "war." In this section, we describe how structural-functionalism, conflict theory, symbolic interactionism, and feminist thought can be applied to the study of war.

Structural-Functionalist Perspective

Structural-functionalism focuses on the functions that war serves and suggests that war would not exist unless it had positive outcomes for society. We have already noted that war has served to consolidate small autonomous social groups into larger political states. An estimated 600 000 autonomous political units existed in the world at about 1000 B.C. Today, that number has dwindled to fewer than 200.

Another major function of war is that it produces social cohesion and unity among societal members by giving them both a "common cause" and a common enemy. Unless a war is extremely unpopular, military conflict also promotes economic and political cooperation. Internal domestic conflicts between political parties, minority groups, and special interest groups often dissolve as they unite to fight the common enemy. During World War II, Canadian and British troops consolidated under British military organizational structures to defeat Germany and the Axis Powers (Italy, Japan, Hungary, Bulgaria, and Romania). More recently, in the years since the American invasion into Afghanistan, Canada has demonstrated its social support for the United States by supplying troops to "police" the Kandahar. However, under the Chretien government Canada refused to enter the war against Iraq and urged instead that the

Bush government continue to exert pressure on Iraq through United Nations channels. Although Canada's refusal to enter the war has been vindicated in the long run by the absence of evidence for the development of "weapons of mass destruction" (WMD), at the time American Ambassador Paul Cellucci asserted that Canada's refusal undermined our claims of support for the U.S. people (Barry 2005: abstract). Just because the demonstration of allegiance can serve claims for social cohesion and solidarity does not mean that entry into war is always an appropriate cost of that cohesion.

Canada's role post 9/11 in relations with the United States has brought to the fore other questionable costs associated with forming allegiances. For example, Canada has faced pointed criticism for the manner in which one of our own citizens, Omar Khadr, a child, was—at least by some accounts—abandoned by Canada and allowed to languish in the Guantanamo prison. Khadr was captured in Afghanistan in 2002 when he was 15, and imprisoned in Guantanamo for allegedly having killed an American soldier; he remained in Guantanamo until 2010 without facing a specific charge or having a trial. As explained in the recently published *Omar Khadr, Oh Canada* (Williamson 2012), there is photographic evidence to indicate that Khadr was coerced at the point of his capture and that he did not, in fact, throw the grenade that killed the American soldier (pp. xviii–xix). And yet Khadr languished in Guantanamo until 2010, with successive Canadian governments doing nothing to repatriate him to Canada. Khadr was detained for eight years in a system that was determined in 2006 to violate the Geneva Conventions regarding the constitution of war crimes tribunals (p. xvii). In short, Canada turned its back on a child who appears to have been forced, while he was still very young, by a domineering father to act as a soldier. Furthermore, while Canadians have organized to set up charities like War Child to rescue child soldiers, our governments have allowed a child to grow up in a prison that has been deemed illegal, and to be held there without proper legal representation, and, perhaps worst of all, with the wilful refusal of Canadian government officials to step in to advocate for Khadr's release.

Writing an explanation for the vilification of Muslim men and the exploitation of Muslim women as victims, Concordia university professor Yasmin Jiwani observes that Canadian spectators on the Khadr case, and the larger structuring of our role in the Afghanistan occupation, are encouraged to see Muslim men and women through the "… ever-reaching fibriles of the carceral net [that] have been reinforced and fortified by the rationalizations of the 'war on terror.' Terrifying and terrorizing, the visual discourses and practices of the war ensnare subjects through heightened surveillance mechanisms enhancing their visibility [as irredeemable Others]" (Jiwani 2011: 25). In other words, our media and our politicians have stripped people like Omar Khadr of their personhood and have exploited them in order to foster support for Canada's role in the "war on terror," and have done this in a manner that is inconsistent with international law, inconsistent with our own policy toward the protection of our citizens, and in violation of the UN agreement on the rights of children.

In the short term, war may also increase employment and stimulate the economy. The increased production needed to fight World War II helped pull Canada, Britain, and the United States out of the Great Depression. The investments in the manufacturing sector during World War II also had a long-term impact on the U.S. economy. Hooks and Bloomquist (1992) studied the effect of the war on the U.S. economy between 1947 and 1972, and concluded that the U.S. government "directed, and in large measure, paid for a 65 percent expansion of the total investment in plant and equipment" (p. 304). War can also have the opposite effect, however. In a 2005 restructuring of the military, the Pentagon, seeking a "meaner, leaner fighting machine," recommended shutting down or reconfiguring nearly 180 military installations, "ranging from tiny Army reserve centers to sprawling Air Force bases that have been the economic anchors of their communities for generations" (Schmitt 2005), at a cost of thousands of civilian jobs.

Wars also function to inspire scientific and technological developments that are useful to civilians. For example, innovations in battlefield surgery during World War II and the Korean War resulted in instruments and procedures that later became common practice in civilian hospital emergency wards (Zoroya 2006). Research on laser-based defence systems led to laser surgery; research in nuclear fission and fusion facilitated the development of nuclear power; and the internet was created by the Pentagon for military purposes. In the U.S. airline industry, which owes much of its technology to the development of air power by the Department of Defense, the distinction between military and civilian technology is important because different government agencies regulate its export. The Department of Commerce regulates the export of parts produced for use on commercial airlines, whereas the Department of State imposes stricter controls on parts produced for military aircraft to prevent sales to countries at odds with U.S. foreign policy objectives (Millman 2008). Other **dual-use technologies**, a term referring to defence-funded innovations that have commercial and civilian applications, include SLICE, a high-speed twin-hull water vessel originally made for the Office of Naval Research. SLICE has a variety of commercial applications, "including its use as a tour or sport fishing boat, oceanographic research vessel, oil spill response ship, and high-speed ferry" (State of Hawaii 2000).

War also serves to encourage social reform. After a major war, members of society have a sense of shared sacrifice and a desire to heal wounds and rebuild normal patterns of life. They put political pressure on the state to care for war victims, improve social and political conditions, and reward those who have sacrificed lives, family members, and property in battle. As Porter (1994) explained, "Since … the lower economic strata usually contribute more of their blood in battle than the wealthier classes, war often gives impetus to social welfare reforms" (p. 19).

Finally, the U.S. military has historically provided an alternative for the advancement of poor or disadvantaged groups who otherwise face discrimination or limited opportunities in the formal economy. The military's specialized training, tuition assistance programs for a college education, and preferential hiring practices improve the prospects of veterans to find a decent job or career after their service (Military 2007).

Conflict Perspective

Conflict theorists emphasize that the roots of war are often antagonisms that emerge whenever two or more ethnic groups (e.g., Bosnians and Serbs), countries (United States and Vietnam), or regions within countries (the U.S. North and South) struggle for control of resources or have different political, economic, or religious ideologies. In addition, conflict theory suggests that war benefits the corporate, military, and political elites. Corporate elites benefit because war often results in the victor taking control of the raw materials of the losing nations, thereby creating a bigger supply of raw materials for its own industries. Indeed, many corporations profit from defence spending. Under the Pentagon's bid-and-proposal program, for example, corporations can charge the cost of preparing proposals for new weapons as overhead on their Department of Defense contracts. Also, Pentagon contracts often guarantee a profit to the developing corporations. Even if the project's cost exceeds initial estimates, called a cost overrun, the corporation still receives the agreed-on profit. In the late 1950s, President Dwight D. Eisenhower referred to this close association between the military and the defence industry as the **military-industrial complex**.

Contemporary examples of the military-industrial complex include the Bush administration's direct link to defence spending. Even as the U.S. government was deciding

dual-use technologies
Defence-funded innovations that have commercial and civilian applications.

military-industrial complex
The close association between the military and the defence industry.

Chapter 14 Armed Conflict in Global Perspective

on the war in Iraq, "many former Republican officials and political associates of the Bush administration [were] associated with the Carlyle Group, an equity investment firm with billions of dollars in military and aerospace assets" (Knickerbocker 2002: 2). Further, news media have come to rely heavily on retired military professionals with ties to the defence establishment and military contractors for interpretation of the Iraq and Afghanistan wars. This close "intersection of network news and wartime commerce" blurs the line between security policy and private commercial interests (Barstow 2008: 1).

The military elite benefit because war and the preparations for it provide prestige and employment for military officials. For example, Military Professional Resources Inc. (MPRI), an organization staffed by former military, defence, law enforcement, and other professionals, serves "the national security needs of the U.S. government, selected foreign governments, international organizations, and the private sector" and lists capabilities such as war gaming, force development and management, and democracy transition assistance (Military Professional Resources Inc. 2007: 1). MPRI is one of four U.S. firms that are under a $300 million contract from the Department of Defense to produce public service announcements, news, and entertainment for the Iraqi media. The three-year project (2009 to 2011) supports Iraqi and U.S. political goals such as promoting reconciliation and nonsectarian nationalism, as well as pro-military, pro-police, and pro-U.S. attitudes (DeYoung and Pincus 2009).

According to some estimates, private contractors such as MPRI and many others contributed more than 180 000 civilians to the occupation of Iraq, about 20 000 more than the U.S. military and government employees deployed in country (Miller 2007). Private security companies—for-profit organizations contracted by the U.S. government to perform security functions that the military formerly provided—account for a significant portion of the U.S. forces. According to estimates from Congressional Research Service, 50 private security companies employ more than 30 000 personnel in Iraq. Twenty of these companies and at least 10 000 of their employees are under contract with the U.S. government, costing between $3 billion and $6 billion from 2003 to 2007 (CRS 2008).

War also benefits the political elite by giving government officials more power. Porter (1994) observed that "throughout modern history, war has been the level by which ... governments have imposed increasingly larger tax burdens on increasingly broader segments of society, thus enabling ever-higher levels of spending to be sustained, even in peacetime" (p. 14). Political leaders who lead their country to a military victory also benefit from the prestige and hero status conferred on them.

Feminist Perspectives

Feminists and many other analysts often note the overwhelming association between war and gender. By and large, men have historically carried out active combat. Nature-based arguments about gender—that is, that men are innately aggressive or violent and women inherently peaceful—are not generally supported by social science research and do not adequately explain why men are more likely to kill than women. Feminists emphasize the social construction of aggressive masculine identities and their manipulation by elites as important reasons for the association between masculinity and militarized violence (Alexander and Hawkesworth 2008). In this section we discuss the controversy regarding gendered participation in armed conflict, and also address the historical participation of Canadian women in military service (see Figure 14.1). In this chapter's *Social Problems Research Up Close* feature we discuss the negative effect of war on young women and girls in Northern Uganda.

Canadian Women's Roles in the Armed Forces

Often, people assume that women have participated very little in war efforts until quite recently; however, the inability to enlist for active duty did not mean that women did not participate in the larger "war effort" in each of the World Wars, both of which had Canadian soldiers subsumed into the larger British armed forces. The Queen's University Archives on Canadian Women's participation in World War I, for example, note that

> Over 2000 women enlisted as nursing sisters in the Canadian Expeditionary Force during WWI. The role of women at the front was very limited because of army rules and social constraints. The women of Canada started an organization called, "The

TO THE WOMEN OF CANADA

1. You have read what the Germans have done in Belgium. Have you thought what they would do if they invaded this Country ?

2. Do you realize that the safety of your home and children depends on our getting more men NOW ?

3. Do you realize that the one word "GO" from you may send another man to fight for our King and Country ?

4. When the War is over and someone asks your husband or your son what he did in the great War, is he to hang his head because you would not let him go ?

WON'T YOU HELP AND SEND A MAN TO ENLIST TO-DAY ?

Figure 14.1 *To the Women of Canada*

SOURCE: Queen's University Archives, V043.

Social Problems *Research Up Close*

The Effect of War on Young Women and Girls in Northern Uganda

In January 2006, Olara Otunnu, a former United Nations advocate for child victims of war, described Uganda as "the worst place in the world to be a child" (Large 2006). For 20 years, starting in 1986, northern Uganda has experienced a guerrilla war that has displaced nearly two million people and caused widespread poverty. For much of the war, the two main combatants were the government of Uganda and the Lord's Resistance Army (LRA), a rebel group led by Joseph Kony, a ruthless and unstable commander who fought to restore his ethnic group to power. Tens of thousands of Ugandan children were forcibly conscripted into the government's army or abducted by the LRA where they were sexually abused and forced into combat. Many thousands more were killed or wounded.

When the fighting subsided in 2006, more than 800 000 Ugandans were living in government-run camps (Large 2006). In view of the dependence on international aid groups such as the United Nations World Food Programme, UNICEF, and Médecins

Sans Frontières for food and medical care, other international groups intervened in the most war-torn areas to develop additional support projects. Among the most important of these projects were those designed to reintegrate child soldiers into the local communities.

Annan et al. (2008), in conducting the Survey of War Affected Youth (SWAY), wanted to provide information to the United Nations and other international agencies to help them develop and improve youth-related social services. Focusing, in part, on the impact of the war on young women and girls, SWAY provides reliable data about this population through a systematic random sample of households in the most affected areas.

Sample and Methods

Between October 2006 and August 2007, the SWAY team employed two methods of data collection. First, they administered a large-scale quantitative survey

(continued)

to young women and girls in two districts of Uganda. Relying on lists used by the World Food Programme for food distribution, 1100 households were randomly selected. Household members were interviewed and asked to identify all youth living in the household in 1996. From this retrospective sample, Annan and colleagues identified 857 female youth between the ages of 14 and 35 in 2006 (who were between the ages of 4 and 25 in 1996, as the worst violence of the war began). The researchers then identified, located, and interviewed 619 respondents from this sample. Second, Annan et al. (2008) drew a nonrandom subsample of 30 girls from these respondents and conducted in-depth, qualitative interviews with them.

The data the researchers collected focused on the women's and girls' experiences during and after the war including their experiences with abduction, as "forced wives" assigned to LRA commanders, and with their families, communities, and nongovernmental organizations (NGO) upon returning home. In addition, the SWAY team collected data about the well-being of women and girls in the study, including their recent economic activity, education, physical and mental health, and community participation, among many other variables.

Findings and Conclusions

The data that SWAY researchers collected detailed the extent of violence and identified some important and surprising results. Because Annan and her colleagues had randomly sampled the population, they could use their data to estimate the total amount of violence that young women and girls experienced. They concluded that about 66 000 (20 percent) of all women and girls between the ages of 14 and 30 in 2006 had been abducted by the LRA during the previous 10 years. The researchers report that, "The average age for females at first abduction is approximately 16 years of age, with the majority of females experiencing abduction between the ages of 10 to 18 years of age" (p. 46). Forty percent of abductees were held in captivity for less than 14 days, 25 percent between two weeks and one year, and 19 percent for over a year. Five percent never returned home and are presumed dead. Twenty-five percent were given to LRA members as "forced wives," and of that number, half gave birth to at least one child as a result of their captivity.

Many of the abducted young women and girls witnessed horrendous acts of violence during their captivity, at rates well above what non-abductees experienced. They witnessed (1) the beating and torture of others (83 percent); (2) the violent death of a family member or friend (53 percent); (3) occupied houses being set on fire (42 percent); (4) multiple, simultaneous killings (38 percent); and (5) injuries from combat or a land mine (24 percent).

The abductees were also forced to commit a variety of brutal acts. Seventeen percent said they were forced to kill an opposing soldier; 21 percent were forced to kill an unknown civilian; and 5 percent were forced to kill a family member or friend. In addition, 21 percent were forced to beat or cut a civilian, and 25 percent were made to step on or otherwise abuse a corpse. In each of these categories, less than 1 percent of non-abducted girls and youth committed such acts.

The LRA commanders distributed the young women and girls as "forced wives," partly on the basis of seniority. Half of the senior commanders took five or more wives, whereas low-ranking commanders took, on the average, two wives. When many young women and girls were abducted at the same time, they were distributed randomly among the rebels, as this account from a woman forcibly married after her abduction at 17 illustrates:

> After reaching the LRA camp, I was grouped with other females who were recently abducted. [The commander] gave the orders to his escorts to distribute the wives. Clothes were placed in bags and put into a pile. The men who wanted wives stood nearby and watched as girls were told to pick a bag of clothing. Whoever owned the clothing then became the man to that girl. The clothes I picked belonged to a 35-year-old fighter. (p. 40)

Other forced wives reported that commanders chose wives on the basis of their appearance and their educational level. As one abductee remembered: "The prettiest, more educated girls were the first to be chosen and commanders always chose before fighters. … [Commanders] preferred girls with education because they needed them to write down numbers when radio codes were coming in" (p. 43).

Most of the young women and girls (68 percent) who were held for more than two weeks escaped on their own. Of the remainder, the LRA captors released 27 percent and the Ugandan Army rescued 5 percent. Forced wives were more carefully guarded by their captors than other detainees—83 percent escaped, 10 percent were rescued by the Ugandan military, and only seven percent were released by the LRA.

Surprisingly, only a small percentage of female abductees reported severe psychological distress. Forced wives exhibited a slightly higher rate of distress than other abductees. Problems were most pronounced when the captives returned home to their families, but generally lessened over time. In fact, 83 percent of abductees reported positive relationships with their families and communities. According to Annan et al. (2008), "resilience and acceptance rather than rejection or trauma" was the norm in most families. Despite the violence they were forced to commit in captivity, former abductees were no more likely to commit violence, engage in fights, or report hostility after their release than non-abductees.

The SWAY team used this and other data they created to help aid agencies identify sub-groups within the population of abductees who were especially in need of assistance as they returned home. One of these groups was forced wives who gave birth during their abduction: "Girls who return from captivity with children are three times less likely to return to school than those who do not conceive children in captivity and 10 times less likely

to return to school than girls who were never abducted" (p. 43). Also, because about one-third of female abductees returned home at the age of 18 or older, the researchers advised that age-based social service programs that targeted children under 18 were missing a significant percentage of the population in need.

Finally, NGO and government aid programs used categories like "abducted" and "forced wives" to determine categories of people requiring the most assistance. Based on the data, the research team concluded that these were "crude and poor predictors of vulnerability" among young women and girls affected by the war. In fact, regardless of whether they had been abducted or not, female youth who came from poor households, were unemployed, estranged from their families, suffered injuries or illness, and exhibited the highest levels of stress were ironically the least likely to receive assistance. By using rigorous methods of sampling and data collection, the Survey of War Affected Youth helped support groups revise their category-based approach in targeting the population to one based on "real needs" among those who suffered most from the devastation brought on by the war.

SOURCE: Annan, J. & Blattman, C. 2008. The Reintegration of Child and Youth Combatants in Northern Uganda: Myth and Reality. In Muggah, R. (Ed.) *Securing Protection: Dealing with Fighters in the Aftermath of War*. New York, NY Routledge Press.

Canadian Women's Hospital Ship Fund". They raised money by organizing concerts, tag days, teas, card parties, lectures, and bazaars. Women also raised money for the Red Cross, Belgian Relief, and Canadian Patriotic Fund. (Queen's University 2010)*

In the midst of World War II, following several years of effort to incorporate women into military service, Carolyn Gossage (2001) notes that the Canadian Women's Army Corps (CWAC) was established. Although the service stopped short of permitting women to enter into combat roles, many women were eager for such inclusion. The years of persistent arguments made by women that they had more to offer to the war effort than just to work in mess halls and clerical positions finally resulted in CWAC members performing more active roles, including driving transport vehicles, running messages, and operating phones; the rationale was that adding these kinds of jobs to those already done by women during World War II would relieve male soldiers for combat service (Gossage 2001: 41–42). Other historical accounts give a sense of just how many women ended up serving following the 1941 creation of the CWAC: "In 1941, the Canadian government recruited over 45,000 women volunteers for fulltime military service other than nursing. Women worked as mechanics, parachute riggers and heavy mobile equipment drivers" (CBC News 2006). Canadian women's contributions to military service have been expanding ever since, and women have served in active combat roles since 1989 (ibid).

*Queen's University Archives

Women's participation in these and other "war efforts" has been encouraged with a variety of patriotic messages that invoke women's unique duty, but the reasons for women's participation is more complex than simply responding to the call for patriotism. Women's participation in military service has been, in part, an effort for women not to be indebted to men for their freedom and inclusion as citizens.

Although some feminists view women's participation in the military as a matter of equal rights, others object because they see war as an extension of patriarchy and the subordination of women in male-dominated societies. Ironically, because protection of women is perceived as a feature of masculine identity, feminists also point out that war and other conflicts are often justified using "the language of feminism" (Viner 2002). For example, President Bush used respect for women's rights and protection of women subjugated under the Taliban as a partial justification for the attack on Afghanistan in 2001 (Viner 2002). As we discuss below, there has been considerable feminist resistance to this justification tactic, and other similar ones.

To a large extent, says Marian Eide, "if rights were won for women through war work, then combat eligibility, while an ambivalent privilege, must have more than symbolic meaning for women's full citizenship" (Eide 2008: 49). In other words, many of the day-to-day privileges of citizenship that women enjoy are the result of wars waged to create the nations that are capable of conferring citizenship and granting the rights and protections that go along with citizenship. However, the historical fact of the creation of nations and citizens, argues Eide, can be used in dangerous ways to mobilize support for wars that we suspect may not be just. For example, military strategists and journalists seized on the idea that the current war in Afghanistan was a just war rather than an unjust invasion because

> occupation and regime change would … provide the occasion for the transformation of an extreme patriarchal culture imposed by the Taliban in which women were forced to live in conditions akin to slavery. Feminist discourse and its cosmopolitan allegiances were conscripted in this war effort. … When Allied forces entered Kabul in 2001, Western journalists fed the need for activist intervention in Afghani women's plight; they "gathered with the specific intent of broadcasting images of women abandoning their burqas." (p. 57)

What Eide's essay and the critical work of other feminist scholars interested in these justifications for war argue is that the "liberation" of Afghani women leaves them in a similar predicament of having their citizenship rely on a war in which they have no say, and, moreover, which has done away with the religious traditions that they have understood as part of their spiritual and physical "home."

Danielle Poe's work uses the idea of an ethical position based in women's sexual difference from men to question the very concept of justifiable war—such as one that, it is claimed, will liberate the vulnerable and transform an oppressive regime into a free society. Thus, Poe goes further than critiquing claims such as those that Eide brings to our attention, and makes the point that "of the many flaws with just war theorizing, perhaps the most damning is that just war doctrine tends to justify wars … at a time when we ought to be thinking about ways to eliminate wars" (Poe 2008: 33). Poe's argument favours a view of human connectedness as a horizontal rather than hierarchical set of relations grounded in the values of kindness, compassion, and hospitality (p. 40). According to this view, one does not have to take an absolute stand against all wars, but should act in ways that preserve and protect the interests and safety of others—as Poe argues is exemplified in the actions of Carlos Mejia, who "was deployed to Iraq in April 2003, and after a two week leave, filed to be a conscientious objector; he refused to return to Iraq to participate in an unjust war. His application was denied, and he served a one-year jail sentence for desertion. … Mejia does not support abolition of war; he maintains that the Iraq war is unjust and he has a moral obligation not to participate" (p. 43).

Symbolic Interactionist Perspective

The symbolic interactionist perspective focuses on how meanings and definitions influence attitudes and behaviours regarding conflict and war. The development of attitudes and behaviours that support war begins in childhood. Movies romanticize war, children play war games with toy weapons, and various video and computer games glorify heroes conquering villains.

Symbolic interactionism helps to explain how military recruits and civilians develop a mindset for war by defining war and its consequences as acceptable and necessary. Through its use in various phrases, the word "war" has achieved a positive connotation of actively working to combat a given problem, as in the examples of the war on drugs, the war on poverty, and the war on crime. Positive labels and favourable definitions of military personnel facilitate military recruitment and public support of armed forces.

McGill University in Montreal houses an extensive collection of war posters that were used from World War I onward to rally support for the wars, to encourage the enlistment of young men into the armed forces, and to enlist the support of women who were expected willingly to deliver their sons into combat. A symbolic approach to understanding the motivations and perceptions of young enlistees can help us to understand how soldiers cope with the mismatch between the realities of combat and the romanticization of the war in enlistment propaganda.

Douglas Kellner argues that in terms of popular messages, Hollywood cinema has maintained a tradition of "following the trajectory of U.S. foreign policy at least since the end of the Second World War" (1995: 83) and of fostering enlistments. For a current generation of students, Hollywood separates the world into "good guys" and "bad guys," and casts soldiers on "our side" as heroes who have no doubts about the clarity of their missions.

Indeed, films that came out around the time of the 9/11 attacks—such as *Rules of Engagement*—chastise viewers who think that an Arab population could be anything other than evil. Indeed, a military leader who visited the Wilfrid Laurier University campus in the fall of 2002 underscored the very same message about Arab people, stating at a campus lecture that "It's impossible for us as rational human beings to figure out their irrational minds. They're not really of this world" (Stogran 2002). Stogran's comments were intended to recruit students into considering a military career without any moral conundrum. But if young people succumb to recruiting posters like the one in Figure 14.2, or to films and lectures, this does not mean that they remain forever singularly committed to the romanticized patriotism that drew them into military service in the first place.

The sketches in Figure 14.3 and Figure 14.4 appear in their original format on a single sheet of double-sided paper; they were messages sent home in 1942 by an 18-year-old enlistee, Nicholas Cowan, who had gone to war hoping to become the kind of hero

Figure 14.2 *Fly and Fight with the RCAF Recruiting Poster*

SOURCE: Courtesy of Rare Books and Special Collections, McGill University Library

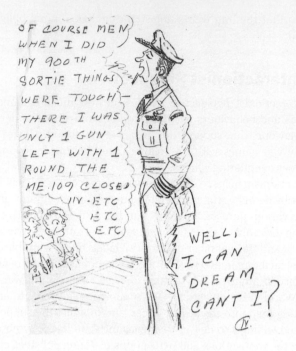

Figure 14.3 **"Well, I can dream can't I?"**

SOURCE: Personal archive of M. Morgan Holmes. Nicholas E. Cowan circa 1944

Figure 14.4 **"Commando? Who the Hell said that??"**

SOURCE: Personal archive of M. Morgan Holmes. Nicholas E. Cowan circa 1944

he envisioned in Figure 14.3, but who recognized that his actual experiences in the war were destroying him (and those around him), as he shows in the unflattering self-portrait in Figure 14.4. The final, simple facts of his narrative are these: Nicholas Cowan and his crew went missing in action on or about the night of June 28, 1944. On this particular night, RAF Six Group out of Tholthorpe lost 22 crews, each with five boys, its largest losses to that point in the war. At the time that the crews were lost there were more than 230 bombers in the air, making it very likely that the lost crews were hit by their own flak. His mother was compensated for her loss with the silver cross, a pendant awarded to mothers and widows of soldiers killed in service. Unlike the mother in Figure 14.1, Kay never got to see her eldest son, a gifted classics student, return from the war. Like the mothers of 22 456 airmen and women whose bodies were never recovered, the best Kay could do to remember her child would be to visit the Air Forces Memorial in Surrey, England (Figure 14.5).

Figure 14.5 *Air Forces Memorial in Surrey, England*

SOURCE: Chrislofoto/Shutterstock.com

As with any other official record, Nicky's enlistment records indicate his date of enlistment, height, eye colour, rank, general health, level of education, and religion. All the vital statistics are noted, but the record provides very little that is useful for developing an understanding of what is lost in a war.

It is partly because the official records are so spare that a symbolic interactionist approach can be so helpful for enhancing our understandings. The drawings that Nicky sent home during the war were deeply conflicted. Figure 14.3 and Figure 14.4, as exemplars of a larger collection, present two opposing self-images. On the one hand we see a projected self, well decorated for various and wildly spectacular feats—including 900 sorties, whereas the highest number of missions actually completed by any single RAF soldier in the Second World War was 222. The image is clearly a fantasy with an audience of civilians and soldiers looking on with rapt attention while Nicky appears confident almost to the point of being arrogant. His hands are thrust in his pockets and a cigarette dangles nonchalantly from his lips, evoking highly recognizable versions of masculinity drawn from Hollywood cinema at the time.

That masculine trope of the conquering hero is not simply an artifact of the distant past. In the fall of 2002, When Lt. Col Pat Stogran was giving his public lecture at Wilfrid Laurier University, he stepped up to the microphone to speak and took up a posture similar to the stance we see in Figure 14.3. Lt. Col. Stogran opened his address by saying, "In my next lifetime I could hope for nothing better than to come back and tell war stories all day long" (Stogran 2002). Obviously, the hero telling tales of adventure is a persistent trope that, knowingly or not, works with other forms of propaganda feeding heroic dreams. However, that young people, men especially, are seduced by such narratives does not mean that they never develop other, more critical views. In Figure 14.4 we see a less glamorous depiction of life at Tholthorpe. In this single frame, Nicky rejects the British notion of the commando as a member of the military elite and shows himself as hungover, possibly ill, and definitely unfit for battle—perhaps because few soldiers actually have the stomach to do what they were recruited to do. The drawings that Nicky sent home, with the exception of ones like Figure 14.4, were always about life on the ground, on leave, in the barracks. He never sent home letters or drawings about his missions. What is speakable in the collection is a variety of ways of being young and male (from dashing and heroic to slovenly and hungover, from invincible to irascible). What is unspeakable is the actual act of war.

As an illustrative case, the meanings that one young boy/man gives to himself illuminate the particular areas of vulnerability that young men can inhabit and experience. Sometimes the experiences register in a manner that seems fully self-aware, and sometimes with little or no critical reflection at all. What is clear for us as readers is that recruiting propaganda is extremely effective in making its appeals, and that awareness that armed conflicts are horrific rather than heroic comes too late for soldiers on all sides of a conflict.

Governments may use propaganda and appeals to patriotism to generate support for war efforts and to motivate individuals to join armed forces. Salladay (2003), for example, notes that those in favour of the war on Iraq have commandeered the language of patriotism, making it difficult but necessary for peace activists to use the same symbols or phrases. In their study of the U.S. peace movement, Woehrle et al. (2008) observed that the government and supporters of U.S. wars often framed the issue as "supporting our boys" or "supporting the troops." This made public discussion about whether a particular war is effective or justifiable appear to be a betrayal of soldiers. A similar framework and imperative operate in Canada, where it is not at all unusual to encounter bumper stickers that command us to "support the troops." By analyzing public statements from leading peace movement groups that opposed the first Gulf War (1991) and the Iraq war, the researchers documented how opponents of these wars developed a counternarrative that "peace is patriotic" and reframed the issue around how war itself endangered the troops, how government policies failed to provide for the welfare of troops, and how the well-being of civilians was negatively affected by war.

To legitimize war, the act of killing in war is not regarded as "murder." Deaths that result from war are referred to as casualties. Bombing military and civilian targets appears more acceptable when nuclear missiles are "peacekeepers" that are equipped with multiple "peace heads." Killing the enemy is more acceptable when derogatory, racist, and dehumanizing labels convey the attitude that the enemy is less than human.

Such labels are socially constructed as images, often through the media, and are presented to the public. Social constructionists, like symbolic interactionists in general, emphasize the social aspects of "knowing." Thus, Li and Izard (2003) used content analysis to analyze newspaper and television coverage of the World Trade Center and Pentagon attacks on September 11. The researchers examined the first eight hours of coverage of the attacks presented on CNN, ABC, CBS, NBC, and Fox, as well as in eight major U.S. newspapers (including the *Los Angeles Times*, the *New York Times*, and the *Washington Post*). Results of the analysis indicated that newspaper articles tended to have a "human interest" emphasis, whereas television coverage was more often "guiding and consoling." Other results suggested that both media relied most heavily on government sources, that newspapers and the networks were equally factual, and that networks were more homogeneous in their presentation than newspapers. One indication of the importance of the media lies in former President George W. Bush's creation of the Office of Global Communications—"a huge production company, issuing daily scripts on the Iraq war to U.S. spokesmen around the world, auditioning generals to give media briefings, and booking administration stars on foreign news shows" (Kemper 2003: 1).

14.3 **Roots of Armed Conflict**

The causes of war and armed conflict are numerous and complex. Most armed conflicts involve more than one cause. The immediate cause of a war may be a border dispute, for example, but religious tensions that have existed between the two combatant countries for decades may also contribute to the war. The following section reviews various causes of war.

Conflict over Land and Other Natural Resources

Nations often go to war in an attempt to acquire or maintain control over natural resources, such as land, water, and oil. Michael Klare, author of *Resource Wars: The New Landscape of Global Conflict* (2001), predicted that wars will increasingly be fought over resources as supplies of the most needed resources diminish. Disputed borders have been common motives for war. Conflicts are most likely to arise when borders are physically easy to cross and are not clearly delineated by natural boundaries such as major rivers, oceans, or mountain ranges.

Water is another valuable resource that has led to wars. Unlike other resources, water is universally required for survival. At various times, the empires of Egypt, Mesopotamia, India, and China all went to war over irrigation rights. In 1998, five years after Eritrea gained independence from Ethiopia, forces clashed over control of the port city Assab and, with it, access to the Red Sea.

Not only do the oil-rich countries in the Middle East present a tempting target in themselves, but war in the region can also threaten other nations that are dependent on Middle Eastern oil. Thus, when Iraq seized Kuwait and threatened the supply of oil from the Persian Gulf, the United States and many other nations reacted militarily in the Gulf War. In a document prepared for the Center for Strategic and International Studies, Starr and Stoll (1989) warned that soon water, not oil, will be the dominant resource issue of the Middle East. According to Worldwatch Institute, "despite modern technology and feats of engineering, a secure water future for much of the world remains elusive." The prognosis for Egypt, Jordan, Israel, the West Bank, the Gaza Strip, Syria, and Iraq is especially alarming. If present consumption patterns continue, emerging water shortages, combined with a deterioration in water quality, will lead to more competition and conflict (2003: 1).

Despite such predictions, tensions in the Middle East have erupted into fighting repeatedly in recent years—but not over water. In July 2006, Israel and Lebanon fought a border war that killed a thousand people and displaced a million Lebanese. Civil war erupted in the Palestinian territories between rival parties when Hamas seized control of the Gaza Strip in response to Fatah's refusal to hand over the government after Hamas won legislative elections (BBC 2007a). Further, in the summer of 2007, hundreds were killed when Lebanese security forces attacked Palestinian militants based in Lebanon's refugee camps (BBC 2007b). In December 2008, the Israeli military launched air strikes against Gaza to prepare the way for its January 2009 ground invasion that lasted 22 days. Israeli authorities claimed the campaign was intended to stop Hamas's rocket attacks against civilians in southern Israel (BBC 2009).

Conflict over Values and Ideologies

Many countries initiate war not over resources but over beliefs. World War II was largely a war over differing political ideologies: democracy versus fascism. The Cold War involved the clash of opposing economic ideologies: capitalism versus communism.

Conflicts over values or ideologies are not easily resolved. They are less likely to end in compromise or negotiation because they are fuelled by people's convictions. For example, when a representative sample of American Jews were asked, "Do you agree or disagree with the following statement? 'The goal of Arabs is not the return of occupied territories but rather the destruction of Israel,'" 81 percent agreed, 13 percent disagreed, and 6 percent were unsure (American Jewish Committee 2007).

If ideological differences can contribute to war, do ideological similarities discourage war? The answer seems to be yes; in general, countries with similar ideologies are less likely to engage in war with each other than countries with differing ideological values (Dixon 1994). Democratic nations are particularly disinclined to wage war against one another (Brown et al. 1996; Rasler and Thompson 2005).

Racial, Ethnic, and Religious Hostilities

Racial, ethnic, and religious groups vary in their cultural beliefs, values, and traditions. Thus, conflicts between racial, ethnic, and religious groups often stem from conflicting values and ideologies. Such hostilities are also fuelled by competition over land and other scarce natural and economic resources. Gioseffi (1993) noted that "experts agree that the depleted world economy, wasted on war efforts, is in great measure the reason for renewed ethnic and religious strife. 'Haves' fight with 'have-nots' for the smaller piece of the pie that must go around" (p. xviii). Racial, ethnic, and religious hostilities are sometimes perpetuated by a wealthy minority to divert attention away from their exploitations, and to maintain their own position of power. Such **constructivist explanations** of ethnic conflict—those that emphasize the role of leaders of ethnic groups in stirring up inter-communal hostility—differ sharply from **primordial explanations**, or those that emphasize the existence of "ancient hatreds" rooted in deep psychological or cultural differences between ethnic groups.

As described by Paul (1998), sociologist Daniel Chirot argued that the recent worldwide increase in ethnic hostilities is a consequence of "retribalization"—that is, the tendency for groups, lost in a globalized culture, to seek solace in the "extended family of an ethnic group" (p. 56). Chirot identified five levels of ethnic conflict: (1) multiethnic societies without serious conflict (e.g., Switzerland), (2) multiethnic societies with controlled conflict (e.g., United States and Canada), (3) societies with ethnic conflict that has been resolved (e.g., South Africa), (4) societies with serious ethnic conflict leading to warfare (e.g., Sri Lanka), and (5) societies with genocidal ethnic conflict, including "ethnic cleansing" (e.g., Darfur). Religious differences as a source of conflict have recently come to the forefront. An Islamic jihad, or holy war, has been blamed for the September 11 attacks on the World Trade Center and Pentagon as well as for bombings in Kashmir, Sudan, the Philippines, Indonesia, Kenya, Tanzania, Saudi Arabia, Spain, and Great Britain. Some claim that Islamic beliefs in and of themselves have led to recent conflicts (Feder 2003). Others contend that religious fanatics, not the religion itself, are responsible for violent confrontations.

Defence Against Hostile Attacks

The threat or fear of being attacked may cause the leaders of a country to declare war on the nation that poses the threat. This is an example of what experts in international relations refer to as the security dilemma: "actions to increase one's security may only decrease the security of others and lead them to respond in ways that decrease one's own security" (Levy 2001: 7). Such situations may lead to war inadvertently. The threat may come from a foreign country or from a group within the country. After Germany invaded Poland in 1939, Britain and France declared war on Germany out of fear that they would be Germany's next victims. Germany attacked Russia in World War I, in part out of fear that Russia had entered the arms race and would use its weapons against Germany. Japan bombed Pearl Harbor hoping to avoid a later confrontation with the U.S. Pacific fleet, which posed a threat to the Japanese military. In 2001, a United States-led coalition bombed Afghanistan in response to the September 11 terrorist attacks. Moreover, in March 2003, the United States, Great Britain, and a loosely coupled "coalition of the willing" invaded Iraq in response to perceived threats of weapons of mass destruction and the reported failure of Saddam Hussein to cooperate with United Nations weapons inspectors. Yet, in 2005, a presidential

constructivist explanations
Emphasize the role of leaders of ethnic groups in stirring up inter-communal hostility.

primordial explanations
Those explanations that emphasize the existence of "ancient hatreds" rooted in deep psychological or cultural differences between ethnic groups, often involving a history of grievance and victimization, real or imagined, by the enemy group.

commission concluded that the attack on Iraq was based on faulty intelligence and that, in fact, "America's spy agencies were 'dead wrong' in most of their judgments about Iraq's weapons of mass destruction" (Shrader 2005: 1). As a result, by 2007, many Americans—more than 60 percent—favoured a partial or complete withdrawal from Iraq (CNN/Opinion Research Corporation Poll 2007). Many believe that the public's desire for withdrawal from Iraq was a key factor in the outcome of the 2008 U.S. presidential election. The Obama administration withdrew the last remaining combat brigade from Iraq in August of 2010.

Revolutions and Civil Wars

Revolutions and civil wars involve citizens warring against their own government and often result in significant political, economic, and social change. The difference between a revolution and a civil war is not always easy to determine. Scholars generally agree that revolutions involve sweeping changes that fundamentally alter the distribution of power in society (Skocpol 1994). The American Revolution resulted from colonists revolting against British control. Eventually, they succeeded and established a republic where none existed before. The Russian Revolution involved a revolt against a corrupt, autocratic, and out-of-touch ruler, Czar Nicholas II. Among other changes, the revolution led to wide-scale seizure of land by peasants who formerly were economically dependent on large landowners.

Civil wars may result in a different government or a new set of leaders but do not necessarily lead to such large-scale social change. Because the distinction between a revolution and a civil war depends upon the outcome of the struggle, it may take many years after the fighting before observers agree on how to classify it. Revolutions and civil wars are more likely to occur when a government is weak or divided, when it is not responsive to the concerns and demands of its citizens, and when strong leaders are willing to mount opposition to the government (Barkan and Snowden 2001; Renner 2000).

One of the world's longest running civil wars came to an end in May 2009. Since 1983, the government of Sri Lanka fought an insurgency led by the Liberation Tigers of Tamil Eelam (LTTE). Also known as the Tamil Tigers, the LTTE were separatist militants who sought to carve an independent state out of the northern and eastern portions of this island country. The war resulted in more than 68 000 deaths (Gardner 2007). The Sri Lankan Army defeated the last remnants of the LTTE and killed their leader in May 2009 (Buncombe 2009). Like many civil wars, the war in Sri Lanka was also a struggle between a majority community (in this case, Sinhalese Buddhists) and a relatively poor and disadvantaged minority community (Hindu Tamils). Despite the end of the war, a political settlement with the minority community has not been achieved. Civil wars have also erupted in newly independent republics created by the collapse of communism in eastern Europe, as well as in Rwanda, Sierra Leone, Chile, Uganda, Liberia, and Sudan.

The civil war in Syria has quickly become one of the deadliest in recent decades. Protests against government corruption and the arrests of political dissenters in March 2011 met with a police crackdown that left several protestors dead. Continued protests spurred the Syrian government, led by President Bashar Al-Assad, to deploy military force against the protestors. As military and government officials began to defect from the regime and join the side of the rebels under the banner of the Free Syrian Army, the conflict moved from one of political dissent to full-scale civil war between two military forces fighting for control of the government. In the summer of 2012 the United Nations formally accused the Assad regime of war crimes, and one year later the United States pledged military aid to the Free Syrian Army after evidence emerged that the Assad regime was using chemical weapons against civilians (Kaphle 2013).

At the time of writing this edition of *Understanding Social Problems*, Crimea, a territory claimed by both the Ukraine and by Russia, but which has been globally recognized as an autonomous republic since 1991, is the site of a civil war and also of invasion and annexation by Russia. However, the political history and relations between ethnic language groups in the Ukraine are so significantly complicated that the journalist and author Marina Lewycka, writing for the British newspaper *The Guardian* in March 2014, argues that instead of seeking simple stories about good guys and bad guys:

> ... the leaders of the US and EU would do well to spend a few minutes swotting up on the history of this volatile region. They would learn that Crimea has a long history of conflict between its Ukrainian, Russian and Tartar communities, and has been ping-ponging back and forth between Ottoman, Russian and Ukrainian jurisdiction for years. The last time the British got involved was in 1853–6, and that, too, was a shambles. This time, the west's intervention has been foolish and inept, and its hypocrisy is shameful. (Lewycka 2014)

Nationalism

Some countries engage in war in an effort to maintain or restore national pride. For example, Scheff (1994) argued that "Hitler's rise to power was laid by the treatment Germany received at the end of World War I at the hands of the victors" (p. 121). Excluded from the League of Nations, punished by the Treaty of Versailles, and ostracized by the world community, Germany turned to Nationalism as a reaction to material and symbolic exclusion.

In the late 1970s, Iranian militants seized the U.S. embassy in Tehran and held its occupants hostage for more than a year. President Carter's attempt to use military forces to free the hostages was not successful. The failure intensified doubts about the United States' ability to use military power effectively to achieve its goals. The hostages in Iran were eventually released but doubts about the strength and efficacy of the U.S. military called into question the country's status as a world power. Subsequently, the U.S. military invaded the small island of Grenada because the government of Grenada was building an airfield large enough to accommodate major military armaments. U.S. officials feared the airfield would be used for hostile attacks on the United States, but the U.S. invasion of Grenada also served to restore faith in the power and effectiveness of the U.S. military.

14.4 Social Problems Associated with Armed Conflict

Social problems associated with armed conflict include death and disability; rape, forced prostitution, and displacement of women and children; social-psychological costs; diversion of economic resources; and environmental destruction.

Death and Disability

Many Canadian lives have been lost in wars, including 64 944 in World War I and 42 042 in World War II (Common Wealth War Graves Commission). Since entering Afghanistan in 2001, 154 Canadian soldiers have been killed (Brewster and Rennie 2010). The CBC maintains a Web-based archive of in-depth coverage of the Afghanistan conflict, and includes photographs, rank and unit information, the province of residence, and date of death for each soldier killed. Many civilians and enemy combatants also die or are injured in war. For example, based on a survey by the World Health Organization, an estimated 151 000 Iraqi civilians and insurgents died from war-related injuries between March 2003 and

June 2006 (Wilson 2008). Despite thousands of Iraqi deaths, many North Americans are unaware of this tremendous loss of life. In a program the Pentagon developed, American reporters were "embedded" into U.S. military units to provide "journalists with a detailed understanding of military culture and life on the frontlines" (Lindner 2009: 21). One of the byproducts of this program, however, was that 90 percent of the stories by embedded journalists were written from the perspective of the American soldier, focusing "on the horrors facing the troops, rather than upon the thousands of Iraqis who died" (p. 45). With so much U.S.-based broadcast news being available to Canadians, and with the reliance on agencies such as A.P. Reuters, the impact of bias in U.S. news reporting on the perceptions of Canadian news consumers should not be underestimated.

The impact of war and terrorism extends far beyond those who are killed. Many of those who survive war incur disabling injuries or contract diseases. For example, one million people worldwide have been killed or disabled by land mines—a continuing problem in the aftermath of the 2003 war with Iraq (Renner 2005). In 1997, the Mine Ban Treaty, which requires that governments destroy stockpiles within four years and clear land mine fields within 10 years, became international law. To date, 156 countries have signed the agreement; 39 countries remain, including China, India, Israel, Russia, and the United States (ICBL 2009). War-related deaths and disabilities also deplete the labour force, create orphans and single-parent families, and burden taxpayers who must pay for the care of orphans and disabled war veterans (see Chapter 2 for a discussion of military health care).

The killing of unarmed civilians is also likely to undermine the credibility of armed forces and make their goals more difficult to defend. In Iraq, for example, the events in Haditha, a city in western Iraq, became international news, outraged Iraqis, and led to intense condemnation of the U.S. mission. In November 2005, after a roadside bomb killed one Marine and wounded two others, "Marines shot five Iraqis standing by a car and went house to house looking for insurgents, using grenades and machine guns to clear houses" (Watkins 2007: 1). Twenty-four Iraqis were killed, many of them women and children, "shot in the chest and head from close range" (McGirk 2006: 3). After *TIME* magazine broke the story in March 2006 (McGirk 2006), the military investigated and reversed its claim that the civilians died as a result of the roadside bomb. Eight marines were accused of wrongdoing during the incident; charges against six of them were dismissed, one was cleared of all charges, and one awaits court martial proceedings (Puckett and Faraj 2009; Reuters 2008).

Rape, Forced Prostitution, and Displacement of Women and Children

Half a century ago, the Geneva Convention prohibited rape and forced prostitution in war. Nevertheless, both continue to occur in modern conflicts.

Before and during World War II, the Japanese military forced 100 000 to 200 000 women and teenage girls into prostitution as military "comfort women." These women were forced to have sex with dozens of soldiers every day in "comfort stations." Many of the women died as a result of untreated sexually transmitted diseases, harsh punishment, or indiscriminate acts of torture.

Since 1998, Congolese government forces have fought Ugandan and Rwandan rebels. Women have paid a high price for this civil war, in which gang rape is "so violent, so systematic, so common … that thousands of women are suffering from vaginal fistula, leaving them unable to control bodily functions and enduring ostracism and the threat of debilitating health problems" (Wax 2003: 1). Though much less common than violence against women, aid workers also see increasing incidents of rape and sexual violence against men as "yet another way for armed groups to humiliate and demoralize Congolese communities into submission" (Gettleman 2009: 1). United Nations officials call the situation in Congo "the worst sexual violence in the world" (Gettleman 2008: 1).

Feminist analyses of wartime rape emphasize that the practice reflects not only a military strategy but also ethnic and gender dominance. For example, Refugees International, a humanitarian aid group, reports that rape is "a systematic weapon of ethnic cleansing" against Darfuris and is "linked to the destruction of their communities" (Boustany 2007: 9). Under Darfur's traditional law, prosecution of rapists is nearly impossible: Four male witnesses are required to accuse a rapist in court and single women risk severe corporal punishment for having sex outside of marriage. In addition to the political power of feminist analysis of rape as a form of military strategy, international courts have determined that rape during war constitutes a crime against humanity, and yet rape and sexual violence persist around the world in various conflict sites.

Focusing attention on the use of rape and other sexual violence in the Democratic Republic of Congo (DCR), Stacy Banwell (2014) argues that current globalization policies mix with hegemonic masculinity to reproduce instances of sexual violence and rape in the DCR. However, Banwell is clear that standard international law shows that "… rape and sexual violence during war are no longer just considered the inevitable by-products of warfare" (p. 56), and that feminist analyses of gender-based violence around the globe can help to end the use of sexual violence and rape in the military, in colonization efforts, and in efforts to recuperate masculinity from the subordinating effects of war (ibid); she notes that seeing the influence of invasive globalization is "key to ending this type of violence against civilian women. State-corporate crimes are being committed through global markets and global trade that are both directly and indirectly related to the gender-based violence … being committed in the Congo" (p. 55). Because victims in the DCR do not have safe recourse to the courts to make complaints that international courts would recognize, it is up to a larger community to prevent gender-based sexual violence, rather than try to prosecute cases after the fact.

War and terrorism also force women and children to flee to other countries or other regions of their homeland. For example, since 1990, at least 17 million children have been forced to leave their homeland because of armed conflict (Save the Children 2005). Refugee women and female children are particularly vulnerable to sexual abuse and exploitation by locals, members of security forces, border guards, or other refugees. In refugee camps, women and children may also be subjected to sexual violation. A 2003 report by Save the Children examined the treatment of women and children in 40 conflict zones. The use of child soldiers was reported in 70 percent of the zones, and trafficking of women and girls was reported in 85 percent of the zones. Wars are particularly dangerous for the very young—"Nine out of ten countries with the highest under-5 mortality rates are experiencing, or emerging from, armed conflict." These include Sierra Leone, Angola, Afghanistan, Niger, Liberia, Somalia, Mali, Chad, and the Democratic Republic of the Congo (Save the Children 2007: 13). Save the Children also estimated that, worldwide, 40 million children of primary school age—nearly one in three of all children in war zones—are prevented from attending school because of armed conflict (Save the Children 2009).

Social-Psychological Costs

Living with or under the threat of war disrupts social-psychological well-being and family functioning. For example, Myers-Brown et al. (2000) report that Yugoslavian children suffer from depression, anxiety, and fear as a response to conflicts in that region, emotional responses not unlike those Americans experienced after the events of 9/11 (NASP 2003). More recently, as a result of the war, there is evidence that many Iraqi children suffer from everything from "nightmares and bedwetting to withdrawal, muteness, panic attacks and violence towards other children, sometimes even to their own parents" (Howard 2007: 1). Further, a study of children in postwar Sierra Leone found that over 70 percent of boys and girls whose parents had been killed were at "serious risk" of suicide (Morgan and Behrendt 2009).

Guerrilla warfare is particularly costly in terms of its psychological toll on soldiers. In Iraq, soldiers were repeatedly traumatized as "guerrilla insurgents attack[cd] with impunity," and death was as likely to come from "hand grenades thrown by children, [as] earth-rattling bombs in suicide trucks, or snipers hid hidden in bombed out buildings (Waters 2005: 1).

Military personnel who engage in combat and civilians who are victimized by war may experience a form of psychological distress known as **posttraumatic stress disorder (PTSD)**, a clinical term referring to a set of symptoms that can result from any traumatic experience, including crime victimization, rape, or war. Symptoms of PTSD include sleep disturbances, recurring nightmares, flashbacks, and poor concentration (NCPSD 2007). For example, Canadian Lieutenant General Romeo Dallaire, head of the United Nations peacekeeping mission in Rwanda, witnessed horrific acts of genocide. Four years after his return, he continued to have images of "being in a valley at sunset, waist deep in bodies, covered in blood" (quoted in Rosenberg 2000: 14). PTSD is also associated with other personal problems, such as alcoholism, family violence, divorce, and suicide. Estimates of PTSD vary widely, although are consistently higher among combat versus noncombat veterans. In a telephone study of 1965 military personnel who had been deployed to Iraq and Afghanistan, 14 percent reported current symptoms of PTSD, 14 percent reported current symptoms of major depression, and 9 percent reported symptoms consistent with both conditions (Tanielian et al. 2008). If these estimates are correct, the researchers calculate that, as of April 2008, 303 000 Iraq and Afghanistan veterans were suffering from PTSD or major depression. However, the rate of PTSD among soldiers is difficult to measure for several reasons. First, there is a lag, often of several years, between the time of exposure to trauma and the manifestation of symptoms. Second, soldiers are generally reluctant to report symptoms or to seek help (Wein 2009).

posttraumatic stress disorder (PTSD)
A clinical term referring to a set of symptoms that can result from any traumatic experience, including crime victimization, rape, or war.

Diversion of Economic Resources

As discussed earlier, maintaining the military and engaging in warfare require enormous financial capital and human support. In 2008, worldwide military expenditures totalled more than $1.46 trillion (SIPRI 2009b). This amount exceeds the combined government research expenditures on developing new energy technologies, improving human health, raising agricultural productivity, and controlling pollution.

Money that is spent for military purposes could be allocated to social programs. In Canada, however, even as social programs including health, education, environmental protection, and social assistance are subject to continual budget reductions, our military spending has risen to levels that exceed those of the Cold War era, surpassing that amount by 2.3 percent annually in adjusted dollars (Staples and Robinson 2007). Yet the popular perception is that we do not spend *enough* on our military. Bill Robinson (2009) explains that politicians and pundits like to promote the idea that Canada is a miserly spender when it comes to military expenses, and yet:

> Canada will spend $21.185 billion on its military forces in fiscal year (FY) 2009–10, 9.6% more than it did last year (FY 2008–09) and about 15% more than it did in its peak spending year during the Cold War (FY 1952–53). Our military spending will be 22% higher than it was in the year the Berlin Wall came down, FY 1989–90, and 56% higher than it was in FY 1998–99, the year Canadian spending reached its post–Cold War minimum (all figures adjusted for inflation). It is twenty times the size of federal Environment Department spending ($1.064 billion). (n.p.)

Writing for the *Edmonton Journal*, Elinor Sloan, a Carleton University professor of international relations, demonstrates the verity of Robinson's assertions in her claim that "Some 58 per cent [of Canadians] think we should spend what the military needs to sustain the Canadian Forces' ability to fight terrorism in places like Afghanistan, support humanitarian missions, such as what we saw in Haiti, and defend Canada's homeland, for example in the North" (2010: A16). These attitudes likely developed in an era of military budget cutbacks in the late twentieth century, after the end of the Cold War—when, in the 1990s, Canada cut military spending by $29 billion over the previous decade (Feiler 2003). The cuts "led to calls for increased spending by a diverse group of critics, including increasingly vocal Canadian defense-oriented think tanks, veterans organizations, Liberal members of Parliament and, from Washington, President Bush" (ibid).

Environmental Destruction

The environmental damage that occurs during war devastates human populations long after war ends. As the casings for land mines erode, poisonous substances—often carcinogenic—leak into the ground (United Nations Association of the United States of America 2003). In 1991, during the Gulf War, Iraqi troops set 650 oil wells on fire (Figure 14.6), releasing oil that covers the surface of the Kuwaiti desert and continues to seep into the ground, threatening underground water supplies. The smoke from the fires that hung over the Gulf region for eight months contained soot, sulphur dioxide, and nitrogen oxides—the major components of acid rain—and a variety of toxic and potentially carcinogenic chemicals and heavy metals. The U.S. Environmental Protection Agency estimates that, in March 1991, about 10 times as much air pollution was being emitted in Kuwait as by all U.S. industrial and power-generating plants combined (Environmental Media Services 2002; Funke 1994; Renner 1993).

Figure 14.6 ***Oil Wells on Fire, Kuwaiti Desert***

Oil smoke from the 650 burning oil wells left in the wake of the Gulf War contains soot, sulphur dioxide, and nitrogen oxides, the major components of acid rain, along with a variety of toxic and potentially carcinogenic chemicals and heavy metals.

SOURCE: © Michel Lipschitz/Associated Press.

Combatants often intentionally exploit natural resources to fuel their efforts. The local elephant population was heavily depleted during the civil war in southern Angola. The rebel group UNITA killed the animals to trade ivory for money to buy weapons. In addition, many were killed or fatally crippled by land mines planted by the guerrillas, though scientists report that, remarkably, the animals seemed to have learned to avoid mined areas (Marshall 2007). Between 1992 and 1997, UNITA also earned $3.7 billion to support its fighting from the sale of "conflict" or "blood" diamonds (GreenKarat 2007). Depending upon the location of diamonds, mining can be highly destructive to riverbed ecosystems or to areas surrounding open-pit mines.

The ultimate environmental catastrophe facing the planet is a massive exchange thermonuclear war. Aside from the immediate human casualties, poisoned air, poisoned crops, and radioactive rain, many scientists agree that the dust storms and concentrations of particles would block vital sunlight and lower temperatures in the northern hemisphere, creating a nuclear winter. In the event of large-scale nuclear war, most living things on Earth would die. For example, a nuclear blast and the resulting blast wave create overpressure—the amount of pressure in excess of ordinary atmospheric levels as measured by pounds per inch (psi). As described in a report sponsored by the U.S. Air Force:

- At 20 of overpressure, even reinforced-concrete buildings are destroyed
- Most factories and commercial buildings, as well as wood-frame and brick houses
- Most houses and lightly constructed commercial and industrial structures
- Suffices to blow away the walls of steel-frame buildings
- Even 1 will produce flying glass and debris sufficient to injure large numbers of people. (Ochmanek and Schwartz 2008: 6)

The fear of nuclear war has greatly contributed to the military and arms buildup, which, ironically, also causes environmental destruction even in times of peace. For example, in practising military manoeuvres, the armed forces demolish natural vegetation, disturb wildlife habitats, erode soil, silt up streams, and cause flooding. Bombs exploded during peacetime leak radiation into the atmosphere and groundwater. From 1945 to 1990, 1908 bombs were tested—that is, exploded—at more than 35 sites around the world. Although underground testing has reduced radiation, some radioactive material still escapes into the atmosphere and is suspected of seeping into groundwater.

Finally, although arms control and disarmament treaties of the last decade have called for the disposal of huge stockpiles of weapons, no completely safe means of disposing of weapons and ammunition exist. Many activist groups have called for placing weapons in storage until safe disposal methods are found. Unfortunately, the longer the weapons are stored, the more they deteriorate, increasing the likelihood of dangerous leakage. In 2003, a federal judge gave permission, despite objections by environmentalists, to incinerate 2000 tons of nerve agents and mustard gas left from the Cold War era. Although the army says that it is safe to dispose of the weapons, they have issued protective gear in case of an "accident" to the nearly 20 000 residents who live nearby (CNN 2003).

14.5 Strategies for Action: In Search of Global Peace

Various strategies and policies are aimed at creating and maintaining global peace. These include the redistribution of economic resources, peacekeeping activities of the United Nations, mediation and arbitration, and arms control and disarmament.

Redistribution of Economic Resources

Inequality in economic resources contributes to conflict and war because the increasing disparity in wealth and resources between rich and poor nations fuels hostilities and resentment. Therefore, any measures that result in a more equal distribution of economic resources are likely to prevent conflict. John J. Shanahan (1995), retired U.S. Navy vice admiral and former director of the Center for Defense

Information, suggested that wealthy nations can help reduce the social and economic roots of conflict by providing economic assistance to poorer countries. Nevertheless, U.S. military expenditures for national defence far outweigh U.S. economic assistance to foreign countries. For instance, the Obama administration's 2010 budget request for foreign affairs (including all nonmilitary foreign aid, the U.S. Department of State, the Peace Corps, and scholarly exchange programs) was $51.7 billion, or about 4 percent of the entire federal budget and 7.7 percent of the total request for the Department of Defense, the wars in Afghanistan and Iraq, and the global war on terrorism (Office of Management and Budget 2009).

Strategies that reduce population growth are likely to result in higher levels of economic well-being. Funke (1994) explained that "rapidly increasing populations in poorer countries will lead to environmental overload and resource depletion in the next century, which will most likely result in political upheaval and violence as well as mass starvation" (p. 326). Although achieving worldwide economic well-being is important for minimizing global conflict, it is important that economic development does not occur at the expense of the environment.

Finally, former United Nations Secretary General Kofi Annan, in an address to the United Nations, observed that it is not poverty per se that leads to conflict but rather the "inequality among domestic social groups" (Deen 2000). Referencing a research report completed by the Tokyo-based United Nations University, Annan argued that "inequality … based on ethnicity, religion, national identity, or economic class … tends to be reflected in unequal access to political power that too often forecloses paths to peaceful change" (Deen 2000).

Peacekeeping Activities of the United Nations

Founded in 1945 after the devastation of World War II, the United Nations (UN) today includes 192 member states and is the principal organ of world governance. In its early years, the UN's main mission was the elimination of war from society.

In fact, the UN charter begins, "We the people of the United Nations—Determined to save succeeding generations from the scourge of war." During the past 65 years, the UN has developed major institutions and initiatives in support of international law, economic development, human rights, education, health, and other forms of social progress. The Security Council is the most powerful branch of the United Nations. Comprised of 15 member states, it has the power to impose economic sanctions against states that violate international law. It can also use force, when necessary, to restore international peace and security.

The United Nations has engaged in more than 60 peacekeeping operations since 1948 (United Nations 2009). United Nations peacekeepers—military personnel in their distinctive blue helmets or blue berets, civilian police, and a range of other civilians—help implement peace agreements, monitor ceasefires, create buffer zones, or support complex military and civilian functions essential to maintain peace and begin reconstruction and institution building in societies devastated by war (United Nations 2003: 1). Recently, the UN has been involved in overseeing multinational peacekeeping forces in Bosnia, East Timor, Sudan, Burundi, Haiti, Liberia, and Ethiopia (United Nations 2009).

In the last few years, the UN has come under heavy criticism. First, in recent missions, developing nations have supplied more than 75 percent of the troops while developed countries—United States, Japan, and Europe—have contributed 85 percent of the finances. As one UN official commented, "You can't have a situation where some nations contribute blood and others only money" (quoted by Vesely 2001: 8). Second, a review of UN peacekeeping operations noted several failed missions, including an intervention in Somalia in which 44 U.S. marines were killed (Lamont 2001). Third, as typified by the debate over the disarming of Iraq, the UN cannot take sides but must wait for a consensus of its members that, if not forthcoming, undermines the strength of the organization (Goure 2003). The consequences of delays can be staggering. For example, under the Genocide Convention of 1948, the UN is obligated to prevent instances of genocide, defined as "acts committed with the intent to destroy, in whole or in part, a national, racial, ethnical or religious group" (United Nations 1948). In 2000, the UN Security Council formally acknowledged its failure to prevent the 1994 genocide in Rwanda (BBC 2000). After the death of 10 Belgian soldiers in the days leading up to the genocide, and without a consensus for action among the members, the Security Council ignored warnings from the mission's commander about impending disaster and withdrew its 2500 peacekeepers.

Finally, the concept of the UN is that its members represent individual nations, not a region or the world. And because nations tend to act in their own best economic and security interests, UN actions performed in the name of world peace may be motivated by nations acting in their own interests.

As a result of such criticisms, outgoing UN Secretary General Kofi Annan called on the 191 members of the UN to approve the most far-reaching changes in the 60-year history of the organization (Lederer 2005). One of the most controversial recommendations concerns the composition of the Security Council, the most important decision-making body of the organization. Annan's recommendation that the 15 members of the Security Council—a body dominated by the United States, Great Britain, France, Russia, and China—be changed to include a more representative number of nations could, if approved, shift the global balance of power. Ban Ki-moon, former foreign minister of South Korea, was elected as the eighth Secretary General in October 2006 (MacAskill et al. 2006), after campaigning for the position on a platform that included support for the UN reforms. So far, the United Nations has not been able to reach agreement about whether and how to expand the membership of the Security Council.

Mediation and Arbitration

Most conflicts are resolved through nonviolent means (Worldwatch Institute 2003). Mediation and arbitration are just two of the nonviolent strategies used to resolve conflicts and to stop or prevent war. In **mediation**, a neutral third party intervenes and facilitates negotiation between representatives or leaders of conflicting groups. Good mediators do not impose solutions but rather help disputing parties generate options for resolving the conflict (Conflict Research Consortium 2003). Ideally, a mediated resolution to a conflict meets at least some of the concerns and interests of each party to the conflict. In other words, mediation attempts to find "win-win" solutions in which each side is satisfied with the solution.

Although mediation is used to resolve conflict between individuals, it is also a valuable tool for resolving international conflicts. For example, former U.S. Senator George Mitchell successfully mediated talks between parties to the conflict in Northern Ireland in 1998. The resulting political agreement continues to hold today. President Obama appointed Senator Mitchell as special envoy to the Middle East in order to pursue a negotiated political settlement. Also, in May 2008, the government of Qatar mediated talks between Lebanon's political parties that resulted in an agreement that averted civil war after an 18-month political crisis. Using mediation as a means of resolving international conflict is often difficult, given the complexity of the issues. However, research by Bercovitch (2003) shows that there are more mediators available and more instances of mediation in international affairs than ever before. For example, Bercovitch identified more than 250 separate mediation attempts during the Balkan wars of the early and mid-1990s.

mediation
A nonviolent strategy used to resolve conflicts and to stop or prevent war where a neutral third party intervenes and facilitates negotiation between representatives or leaders of conflicting groups.

Arbitration also involves a neutral third party who listens to evidence and arguments presented by conflicting groups. Unlike mediation, however, the neutral third party in arbitration arrives at a decision that the two conflicting parties agree in advance to accept. For instance, the Permanent Court of Arbitration—an intergovernmental organization based in The Hague since 1899—arbitrates disputes about territory, treaty compliance, human rights, commerce, and investment among any of its 107 member states who signed and ratified either of its two founding legal conventions. Recent cases include a dispute between France, Britain, and Northern Ireland about the Eurotunnel, a boundary dispute between Eritrea and Ethiopia, and a boundary dispute between the government of Sudan and the Sudan People's Liberation Army (Permanent Court of Arbitration 2009).

Arms Control and Disarmament

In the 1960s, the United States and the Soviet Union led the world in a nuclear arms race, with each competing to build a larger and more destructive arsenal of nuclear weapons than its adversary. If either superpower were to initiate a full-scale war, the retaliatory powers of the other nation would result in the destruction of both nations as well as much of the planet. Thus, the principle of mutually assured destruction (MAD) that developed from nuclear weapons capabilities transformed war from a win-lose proposition to a lose-lose scenario. If both sides would lose in a war, the theory suggested, neither side would initiate war. At its peak year in 1966, the U.S. stockpile of nuclear weapons included more than 32 000 warheads and bombs.

As their arsenals continued to grow at an astronomical cost, both sides recognized the necessity for nuclear arms control including the reduction of defence spending, weapons production and deployment, and armed forces. Throughout the Cold War and even today, much of the behaviour of the United States and the Soviet Union has been governed by major arms control initiatives. These initiatives include:

- The Limited Test Ban Treaty that prohibited testing of nuclear weapons in the atmosphere, underwater, and in outer space
- The Strategic Arms Limitation Treaties (SALT I and II) that limited the development of nuclear missiles and defensive antiballistic missiles
- The Strategic Arms Reduction Treaties (START I and II) that significantly reduced the number of nuclear missiles, warheads, and bombers
- The Strategic Offensive Reduction Treaty (SORT) that requires that the United States and the Russian Federation (i.e., the remaining countries of the former Soviet Union) each reduce their number of strategic nuclear warheads to between 1,700 and 2,200 by 2012. (Atomic Archive 2009)

In 2009, the United States and the Russian Federation announced plans to negotiate further cuts in their nuclear stockpiles, reducing them to between 1500 and 1675 strategic nuclear warheads each (Baker and Cooper 2009).

With the end of the Cold War came the growing realization that, even as Russia and the United States greatly reduced their arsenals, other countries were poised to acquire nuclear weapons or expand their existing arsenals. Thus, the focus on arms control shifted toward the issue of nuclear proliferation—that is, the spread of nuclear technology to nonnuclear states.

Nuclear Nonproliferation Treaty

The Nuclear Nonproliferation Treaty (NPT) was signed in 1970, and was the first treaty governing the spread of nuclear weapons technology from the original nuclear weapons states (i.e., the United States, the Soviet Union, the United Kingdom, France, and China) to nonnuclear countries. The NPT was renewed in 2000, and adopted by 187 countries. The NPT holds that countries without nuclear weapons will not try to get them; in exchange, the countries with nuclear weapons agree that they will not provide nuclear weapons to countries that do not have them. Signatory states without nuclear weapons also agree to allow the International Atomic Energy Agency to verify compliance with the treaty through on-site inspections (Atomic Archive 2009). Only India, Israel, and Pakistan have not signed the agreement, although each of these states is known to possess a nuclear arsenal. Further, many experts suspect that Iran and Syria—both signatories to the NPT—are developing nuclear weapons programs. Both countries claim that their nuclear reactors are for peaceful purposes (e.g., domestic power consumption), not to develop a nuclear weapons arsenal. However, a recent report by the International Atomic Energy Agency tentatively concluded that Iran has "sufficient information to be able to design and produce a workable" atomic bomb (Broad and Sanger 2009: 1).

In January 2003, North Korea, under suspicion of secretly producing nuclear weapons, announced that it was withdrawing from the treaty, effective immediately (Arms Control Association 2003). In July 2005, after "more than a year of stalemate, North Korea agreed ... to return to disarmament talks ... and pledged to discuss eliminating its nuclear-weapons program" (Brinkley and Sanger 2005: 1). However, in May 2009, shortly after testing a long-range missile over Japan, North Korea detonated a nuclear device underground, heightening fears that it would launch a nuclear attack against South Korea, China, or Japan (NTI 2009).

Even if military superpowers honour agreements to limit arms, the availability of black-market nuclear weapons and materials presents a threat to global security. One of the most successful nuclear weapons brokers was Pakistan's Abdul Qadeer Khan. Khan, the "father" of Pakistan's nuclear weapons program, sold the technology and equipment required to make nuclear weapons to rogue states such as Iran and North Korea. He is also suspected of selling nuclear weapons to Al Qaeda (Powell and McGirk 2005).

In 2003, the United States accused Iran of operating a covert nuclear weapons program. Although Iranian officials responded that their nuclear program was solely for the purpose of generating electricity, concerns escalated with Iran's successful test of a 1200-mile-range missile in 2009 (Dareini 2009). Hostile public statements about Israel by Iran's president Mahmoud Ahmadinejad deepen already grave concerns about Iran's possible acquisition of nuclear weapons. Analysts fear the development of nuclear weapons by Iran would spur a nuclear competition with Israel, the only other state in the Middle East to possess nuclear weapons, and provoke other states in the region to acquire them (Salem 2007). Nonetheless, analysts disagree about whether there is evidence that Iran, despite the capability, is designing a nuclear warhead (Broad et al. 2009).

Many observers consider South Asia the world's most dangerous nuclear rivalry. India and Pakistan are the only two nuclear powers that share a border and have repeatedly fired upon each other's armies while in possession of nuclear weapons (Stimson Center 2007). India first detonated nuclear weapons in 1974. Pakistan detonated six weapons in 1998, a few weeks after India's second round of nuclear tests. Although precise figures are hard to come by, experts estimate that India has about 50 nuclear bombs, and Pakistan has between 40 and 70 nuclear bombs (Center for Defense Information 2007). Pakistan, however, is aggressively expanding its nuclear weapons program (Shanker and Sanger 2009).

Many fear that a conventional military confrontation between these two countries may someday escalate to an exchange of nuclear weapons. In addition, widespread social unrest in Pakistan coupled with clashes in 2009 between Taliban forces and

Pakistan's army 60 miles from the capital, Islamabad, have heightened fears about the security of Pakistan's nuclear arsenal and its vulnerability to seizure by extremist forces (Kerr and Nikitin 2009).

As states that want to obtain nuclear weapons are quick to point out, nuclear states that advocate for nonproliferation possess well over 25 000 weapons, a huge reduction in the world's arsenal from Cold War days but still a massive potential threat to Earth. "Do as I say not as I do" is a weak bargaining position. Recognizing this situation, and with concern about the possibility of new arms races, many high-level experts have begun to advocate a more comprehensive approach to banning nuclear weapons—with the United States leading the nuclear powers toward complete nuclear disarmament. In January 2007, three former U.S. Secretaries of State (George Schultz, William Perry, and Henry Kissinger) and former chairman of the Senate Armed Services Committee Sam Nunn published an editorial in the *Wall Street Journal* advocating that the United States "take the world to the next stage" of disarmament to "a world free of nuclear weapons" (Schultz et al. 2007). As a start, their proposal advocated the elimination of all short-range nuclear missiles, a complete halt in the production of weapons-grade uranium, and continued reduction of nuclear forces. President Barack Obama visited Russia in July 2009 to sign an agreement that reduced the strategic nuclear arsenals of the United States and the Russian Federation by about 25 percent. This was reportedly "a first step in a broader effort intended to reduce the threat of such weapons drastically and to prevent their further spread to unstable regions" (Levy and Baker 2009).

The Problem of Small Arms

Although the devastation caused by even one nuclear war could affect millions, the availability of conventional weapons fuels many active wars around the world. Small arms and light weapons include handguns, submachine guns and automatic weapons, grenades, mortars, land mines, and light missiles. The Small Arms Survey estimated that, in 2006, 639 million firearms were in circulation, with about 59 percent of them being owned legally (Geneva Graduate Institute for International Studies 2006). Civilians purchased 80 percent of these weapons and were the victims of 90 percent of the casualties caused by them. Half a million people die each year as a result of small arms use, 200 000 in homicides and suicides and the rest during wars and other armed conflicts.

Unlike control of weapons of mass destruction such as chemical and biological weapons, controlling the flow of small arms is not easy because they have many legitimate uses by the military, by law enforcement officials, and for recreational or sporting activities (Schroeder 2007). Small arms are easy to afford, to use, to conceal, and to transport illegally. The small arms trade is also lucrative. Between 2000 and 2006, the top five exporters of military small arms were the United States ($228.5 million), Belgium ($27.1 million), France ($22.6 million), Germany ($16.2 million), and the United Kingdom ($13.6 million). The United States accounted for 54 percent of small arms exports during this time period (Small Arms Survey 2009).

The U.S. State Department's Office of Weapons Removal and Abatement (WRA) administers a program that has supported the destruction of 1.3 million weapons and 50 000 tons of ammunition in 33 countries since its founding in 2001 (Office of Weapons Removal and Abatement 2009). The availability of these weapons fuels terrorist groups and undermines efforts to promote peace after wars have formally concluded. "If not expeditiously destroyed or secured, stocks of arms and ammunition left over after the cessation of hostilities frequently recirculate into neighboring regions, exacerbating conflict and crime" (U.S. Department of State 2007: 1). Operating on a budget of $16.1 million in 2007, the Bush administration increased the WRA budget to $44.3 million in 2008 (Office of Weapons Removal and Abatement 2009).

Understanding Armed Conflict and War

Each of the theoretical positions discussed in this chapter reflects the realities of global conflict. As structural-functionalists argue, war offers societal benefits—social cohesion, economic prosperity, scientific and technological developments, and social change. Furthermore, as conflict theorists contend, wars often occur for economic reasons because corporate elites and political leaders benefit from the spoils of war—land and water resources and raw materials. The symbolic interactionist perspective emphasizes the role that meanings, labels, and definitions play in creating conflict and contributing to acts of war. Feminist approaches use gender-based analyses to consider the impact of armed conflict and political instability on women and children, but also offer corrective history of women's participation in various war efforts.

The September 11 attacks on the World Trade Center and the Pentagon and the aftermath—the battle against terrorism, the bombing of Afghanistan, and the war with Iraq—changed the world we live in. For some theorists, these events were inevitable. Political scientist Samuel P. Huntington argued that such conflict represents a clash of civilizations. In *The Clash of Civilizations and the Remaking of World Order* (1996), Huntington argued that in the new world order

> the most pervasive, important and dangerous conflicts will not be between social classes, rich and poor, or economically defined groups, but between people belonging to different cultural entities … the most dangerous cultural conflicts are those along the fault lines between civilizations … the line separating peoples of Western Christianity, on the one hand, from Muslim and Orthodox peoples on the other. (p. 28)

Although not without critics, the clash-of-civilizations hypothesis has some support. In an interview of almost 10 000 people from nine Muslim states representing half of all Muslims worldwide, only 22 percent had favourable opinions toward the United States (CNN 2003). Even more significantly, 67 percent saw the September 11 attacks as "morally justified," and the majority of respondents found the United States to be overly materialistic and secular and having a corrupting influence on other nations. Moreover, according to a poll of world public opinion taken every year since 2002, positive attitudes about the United States are consistently lowest in predominantly Muslim countries (Pew Research Center 2009). Although favourable views of the United States increased dramatically in a small number of Muslim countries after the election of President Obama, the 2009 poll found that only small minorities continued to see the United States favourably in most predominantly Muslim counties (for example, 14 percent in Turkey, 15 percent in Palestinian territories, 16 percent in Pakistan, 25 percent in Jordan, and 27 percent in Egypt).

Ultimately, we are all members of one community—Earth—and have a vested interest in staying alive and protecting the resources of our environment for our own and future generations. But, as we have seen, conflict between groups is a feature of social life, and human existence, that is not likely to disappear. What is at stake—human lives and the ability of our planet to sustain life—merits serious attention. World leaders have traditionally followed the advice of philosopher Karl von Clausewitz: "If you want peace, prepare for war." Thus, nations have sought to protect themselves by maintaining large military forces and massive weapons systems. These strategies are associated with serious costs, particularly in hard economic times. In diverting resources away from other social concerns, defence spending undermines a society's ability to improve the overall security and well-being of its citizens. Conversely, defence-spending cutbacks, although unlikely in the present climate, could potentially free up resources for other social agendas, including lowering taxes, reducing the national debt, addressing environmental concerns, eradicating hunger and poverty, improving health care, upgrading educational services, and improving housing and transportation. Therein lies the promise of a "peace dividend." The hope is that future dialogue on the problems of war and terrorism will redefine national and international security to encompass social, economic, and environmental well-being.

Student Reflection: What Do You Know Now?

Having finished this chapter, the last in the textbook if you read them in order, we encourage you to consider specific questions about armed conflict but also to think across the other chapters in the section and the textbook as a whole. We leave you with a series of questions.

What kind of position do you now hold about Canada as peacekeeping nation? If your view has changed, what changed it?

Consider the advertising campaigns sponsored by our government (e.g., "heritage moments"), as well as filmic representations of war, recruiting activities by armed forces, and so on. To what extent can you uncover certain meanings about nation, identity, masculinity, society?

What social costs can you predict in terms of family displacement, education, health care, and so forth as we see unfolding various military coups, terroristic attacks, and other actions around the globe? For example, as this edition is being prepared, the governments of Ukraine and Thailand have fallen; hundreds of girls have been kidnapped from a school in Nigeria; Canada's forces are involved in operations on many continents and have been involved domestically as well over the years. Find out more about our role, and reflect on how local feelings of "being Canadian" are or are not tempered by the information you discover. To what extent does justifiable and very public outrage over Nigerian kidnappings of girls at the same time redirect our attention away from the hundreds of Aboriginal women missing in Canada as of 2014?

Should women fight on the front lines of armed conflicts as part of a formal military? What are the arguments for and against, and which arguments are feminist ones?

If the military-industrial complex provides us with new technologies that improve life for many social groups, can this be justified given the high economic and social costs in other areas?

What Do You Do Next?

Located at www.nelson.com/socialproblems5e

- Consolidate your knowledge with interactive and printable **Flashcards**
- Gauge your understanding with **Practice Quizzes** and **Matching Activities**
- Develop your critical thinking skills with **Self and Society** and **The Human Side** questions
- Analyze **Social Research** and **Social Problems in Global Perspective**
- Explore the implications of **Technology on Social Problems**

REFERENCES

Preface

Anderson, Lorin W. and David R. Krathwohl (eds.). 2001. *A Taxonomy for Learning, Teaching, and Assessing: A Revision of Bloom's Taxonomy of Educational Objectives.* New York: Longman.

Safransky, Sy. 1990. *Sunbeams: A Book of Quotations.* Berkeley, CA: North Atlantic Books.

Chapter 1

Benoit, Cecilia, Dena Carroll, and Munaza Chaudry. 2003. "In Search of a Healing Place: Aboriginal Women in Vancouver's Eastside." *Social Science and Medicine* 56: 821–33.

Bibby, Reginald W. 1995. *The Bibby Report: Social Trends Canadian Style.* Toronto: Stoddart.

———. 2001. *Canada's Teens: Today, Yesterday, and Tomorrow.* Toronto: Stoddart.

Bibby, Reginald W. and Donald C. Posterski. 1992. *Teen Trends: A Nation in Motion.* Toronto: Stoddart.

Blumer, Herbert. 1971. "Social Problems as Collective Behavior." *Social Problems* 8(3): 298–306.

Bruckert, Chris. 2002. *Taking It Off, Putting It On.* Toronto: Women's Press.

CBC News. 2006. *Census FAQs.* Canadian Broadcasting Corporation, May 2006.

Chafetz, Janet S. 1997. "Feminist Theory and Sociology: Underutilized Contributions to Mainstream Theory." *Annual Review of Sociology* 23: 97–120.

Cohen, Tobi. 2013. "String of Terror Incidents No Reason to 'Commit Sociology': Stephen Harper." *National Post*, April 25.

Dordick, Gwendolyn A. 1997. *Something Left to Lose: Personal Relations and Survival among New York's Homeless.* Philadelphia: Temple University Press.

Eitzen, Stanley and Maxine Baca Zinn. 2000. *Social Problems.* Boston: Allyn and Bacon.

Hewlett, Sylvia Ann. 1992. *When the Bough Breaks: The Cost of Neglecting Our Children.* New York: Harper Perennial.

Hills, Stuart L. (ed.). 1987. *Corporate Violence: Injury and Death for Profit.* Lanham, MN: Rowman and Littlefield.

Human Dev. Report. 2010. *Human Developmental Report: 20th Anniversary Edition.* United Nations Development Programme. New York: Palgrave Macmillan.

Inglis, David and John Hughson. 2003. *Confronting Culture: Sociological Vistas.* Oxford: Polity Press.

Jagose, Annamarie. 1996. *Queer Theory: An Introduction.* New York: NYU Press.

Jekielek, Susan M. 1998. "Parental Conflict, Marital Disruption and Children's Emotional Well-Being." *Social Forces* 76: 905–35.

Krahn, Harvey. 2004. "Choose Your Parents Carefully." Pp. 187–203 in *Social Inequality in Canada,* 4th ed., edited by Edward Grabb, James Curtis, and Neil Guppy. Toronto: Prentice Hall.

Krahn, Harvey and Graham S. Lowe. 2002. *Work, Industry, and Canadian Society,* 4th ed. Scarborough, ON: Thomson Nelson.

Leach, Belinda. 2005. "Agency and the Gendered Imagination: Women's Actions and Local Culture in Steelworker Families." *Identities: Global Studies in Culture and Power* 12(1): 1–22.

Marshall, Joan and Natalie Foster. 2002. "'Between Belonging': Habitus and the Migration Experience." *The Canadian Geographer* 46: 63–83.

Merton, Robert K. 1968. *Social Theory and Social Structure.* New York: Free Press.

Miki, Roy. 2000. "Altered States: Global Currents, the Spectral Nation, and the Production of 'Asian Canadian.'" *Canadian Studies* 35(3): 43–72.

Mills, C. Wright. 1959. *The Sociological Imagination.* London: Oxford University Press.

Mouw, Ted and Yu Xie. 1999. "Bilingualism and Academic Achievement of Asian Immigrants." *American Sociological Review* 64: 232–52.

Nader, Ralph, Nadia Milleron, and Duff Conacher. 1993. *Canada Firsts.* Toronto: McClelland & Stewart Inc.

Roberts, Judith C. and Keith A. Roberts. 2008. "Deep Reading, Cost/Benefit, and the Construction of Meaning: Enhancing Reading Comprehension and Deep Learning in Sociology Courses." *Teaching Sociology* (*American Sociological Association*) 36(2): 125–40.

Romer, D., R. Hornik, B. Stanton, M. Black, X. Li, I. Ricardo, and S. Feigelman. 1997. "'Talking Computers': A Reliable and Private Method to Conduct Interviews on Sensitive Topics with Children." *Journal of Sex Research* 34: 3–9.

Schwalbe, Michael. 1998. *The Sociologically Examined Life: Pieces of the Conversation.* Mountain View, CA: Mayfield Publishing Company.

Sheikh, Munir A. 2013. "Good Government and Statistics Canada: The Need for True Independence." *Academic Matters,* May 2013. Available at http://www.academicmatters.ca/2013/05/good-government-and-statistics-canada-the-need-for-true-independence/

Smith, Dorothy. 2004. "Women's Perspective as a Radical Critique of Sociology." Pp. 21–34 in *The Feminist Standpoint Theory Reader,* edited by Sandra Harding. New York: Routledge.

Spector, Malcolm and John I. Kitsuse. 2001. *Constructing Social Problems.* New Brunswick, NJ: Transaction Publishers.

Stackhouse, John. 1999. "My Life without a Home." *The Globe and Mail* (December 18): A17.

Thomas, W. I. [1931] 1966. "The Relation of Research to the Social Process." Pp. 289–305 in *W. I. Thomas on Social Organization and Social Personality,* edited by Morris Janowitz. Chicago: University of Chicago Press.

Wilson, John. 1983. *Social Theory.* Englewood Cliffs, NJ: Prentice-Hall.

Chapter 2

Adetunji, Jacob. 2000. "Trends in Under-5 Mortality Rates and the HIV/AIDS Epidemic." *Bulletin of the World Health Organization* 78(10): 1200–06.

Allin, Sarah, Michel Grignon, and Julian le Grande. 2010. "Subjective Unmet Need and Utilization of Health Care Services in Canada: What Are the Equity Implications?" *Social Science and Medicine* 70(3): 465–472.

American Psychiatric Association. 2013. *Diagnostic and Statistical Manual of Mental Disorders,* 5th ed. Washington, DC: American Psychiatric Association.

Antezana, Fernando S., Claire M. Chollat-Traquet, and Derik Yach. 1998. "Health for All in the 21st Century." *World Health Statistics Quarterly* 51: 3–6.

Armstrong, Pat, Hugh Armstrong, and Claudia Fegan. 1998. *Universal Health Care: What the United States Can Learn from the Canadian Experience.* New York: The New Press.

Ash, Russell. 2001. *The Top 10 of Everything: Canadian Edition 2002.* Toronto: Dorling Kindersley Limited.

Baer, Nicole. 1997. "Canada's Organ Shortage Is Severe and Getting Worse." *Canadian Medical Association Journal* 157: 179–82.

Barlow, Maude and Elizabeth May. 2000. *Frederick Street: Life and Death on Canada's Love Canal.* Toronto: HarperCollins.

Bibby, Reginald W. 2001. *Canada's Teens: Today, Yesterday, and Tomorrow.* Toronto: Stoddart.

Bricker, Darrell and Edward Greenspon. 2001. *Searching for Certainty: Inside the New Canadian Mindset.* Toronto: Doubleday Canada.

Brundtland, Gro Harlem. 2000. "Mental Health in the 21st Century." *Bulletin of the World Health Organization* 78(4): 411.

CAMH. 2012. "Mental Health and Addiction Statistics." http://www.camh.ca/en/hospital/about_camh/newsroom/for_reporters/Pages/addictionmentalhealthstatistics.aspx

Canadian Medical Association (CMA). 2012. Canadian Medical Association 2012 National Report Card. Prepared by Ipsos Reid. Ottawa: August 2012.

CBC News. 2010. "Misdiagnosed: Anatomy of Newfoundland's Cancer Testing Scandal." http://www.cbc.ca/news/background/cancer/misdiagnosed.html

Centers for Disease Control and Prevention. 2010. HIV Transmission. http://www.cdc.gov

Chaouilli v. Quebec (Attorney General), no. 29272, Sup Ct. of Canada 130 C.R.R. (2d) 99:2005 C.R.R. LEXIS 76.

CIA. 2014. *World Factbook.* https://www.cia.gov/library/publications/the-world-factbook/rankorder/2091rank.html

CIHI (Canadian Institute for Health Information). 2012. Health Care in Canada, 2010: A Focus on Wait Times. Ottawa, ON.

Cockerham, William C. 1998. *Medical Sociology,* 7th ed. Upper Saddle River, NJ: Prentice Hall.

Congressional Research Service. 2012. The President's Emergency Plan for AIDS Relief (PEPFAR): Funding Issues after a Decade of Implementation, FY2004-FY2013.

Diamond, Catherine and Susan Buskin. 2000. "Continued Risky Behavior in HIV-Infected Youth." *American Journal of Public Health* 90(1): 115–18.

Dias, Lisa V. 2009. "Burdening Women with Responsibility for Containment: A Discourse Analysis of Public Health Initiatives and Pharmaceutical Advertising for Gardasil, 'The HPV Vaccine.'" Major Research Paper, Master of Arts. Wilfrid Laurier University: Waterloo.

Everett, Sherry A., Rae L. Schnuth, and Joanne L. Tribble. 1998. "Tobacco and Alcohol Use in Top-Grossing American Films." *Journal of Community Health* 23: 317–24.

Family Care International. 1999. "Safe Motherhood." http://www.safemotherhood.org/init_facts.htm

———. 2007. "Safe Motherhood: A Review." http://www.familycareintl.org/UserFiles/File/SM%20A%20Review_%20Full_Report_FINAL.pdf

Fausto-Sterling, Anne. 1995. "Gender, Race, and Nation: The Comparative Anatomy of 'Hottentot' Women in Europe, 1815–1817." Pp. 19–45 in *Deviant Bodies,* edited by Jennifer Terry and Jacqueline Urla. Bloomington, IN: Indiana University Press.

Feachem, Richard G. A. 2000. "Poverty and Inequality: A Proper Focus for the New Century." *The International Journal of Public Health* (Bulletin of the World Health Organization) 78: 1–2.

FNIGC (First Nations Information Governance Centre). 2013. "First Nations Regional Health Survey (RHS), Phase 2—2008/10 Selected Results," Ottawa: http://www.fnigc.ca

Garfinkel, P. E. and D. Goldbloom. 2000. "Mental Health—Getting Beyond Stigma and Categories." *Bulletin of the World Health Organization* 78(4): 503–5.

Gergen, Kenneth J. 1994. *Realities and Relationships: Soundings in Social Construction.* Cambridge, MA: Harvard University Press.

"Global Summary of the HIV/AIDS Epidemic, 2007." http://www.unaids.org

Goldstein, Michael S. 1999. "The Origins of the Health Movement." Pp. 31–41 in *Health, Illness, and Healing: Society, Social Context, and Self,* edited by Kathy Charmaz and Debora A. Paterniti. Los Angeles: Roxbury Publishing Co.

Gottlieb, Scott. 2000. "Oral AIDS Vaccine to Be Tested in the Republic of Uganda." *Bulletin of the World Health Organization* 78(7): 946–56.

Government of canada. 2011b. Healthy Canadians. http://healthycanadians.gc.ca/health-sante/disease-maladie/hiv-vih-eng.php

Graham, Mel. 1999. "Budget 2000 and People with Disabilities." *Abilities: Canadian Lifestyle Magazine for People with Disabilities* 41 (Winter): 48.

Grann, Victor, et al. 2005. "Regional and Racial Disparities in Breast Cancer-Specific Mortality." *Social Science and Medicine* 62: 337–47.

Gray, Gary. 2009. "The Responsibilization Strategy of Health and Safety." *British Journal of Criminology* 49: 326–42.

Groce, N. E., M. Chamie, and A. Me. 2000. "Measuring the Quality of Life: Rethinking the World Bank's Disability Adjusted Life Years." *Disability World* 3 (June-July). http://www.disabilityworld.org/June-July2000/International/DALY.html

Health Canada. 1999a. *Toward a Healthy Future: Second Report on the Health of Canadians.*

Prepared by the Federal, Provincial, and Territorial Advisory Committee on Population Health for the Meeting of Ministers of Health, Charlottetown, PEI, September.

———. 1999b. *Statistical Report on the Health of Canadians.* December 25. http://www.hc-sc.gc.ca/hppb/phdd/report/state/eng/over.html

———. 2002a. "HIV and AIDS among Women in Canada." *HIV/AIDS Epi Update,* April. http://www.hc-sc.gc.ca/pphb-dgspsp/publicat/epiu-aepi/hiv-vih/women_e.html

———. 2002b. "A Report on Mental Illness in Canada." Catalogue no. 0-6623817-5.

———. 2004. "HIV and AIDS among Youth in Canada." *HIV/AIDS Epi Update,* May.

———. 2005a. *HIV/AIDS in Canada: Surveillance Report to December 31, 2004.* Ottawa: Public Health Agency of Canada.

———. 2005b. *HIV/AIDS Epi Updates.* Ottawa: Public Health Agency of Canada.

———. 2007. *HIV/AIDS Epi Updates.* Ottawa: Public Health Agency of Canada.

———. 2011. *Summary: Estimates of HIV Prevalence and Incidence in Canada, 2011.* Prepared by Surveillance and Epidemiology Division, Professional Guidelines and Public Health Practice Division, Centre for Communicable Disease and Infection Control, and Public Health Agency of Canada, Ottawa.

Jacobs, Beverly. 2010. "Environmental Racism on Indigenous Lands." Canadian Political Science Association. http://www.cpsa-acsp.ca/papers-2010/Jacobs.pdf

Joint United Nations Programme on HIV/AIDS. 2000a. "AIDS: Men Make a Difference: World AIDS Campaign." http://www.unaids.org

———. 2000c. "Innovative Approaches to HIV Prevention." http://www.unaids.org

Joralemon, Donald and Kim Fujinaga. 1996. "Studying Quality of Life after Organ Transplantation: Research Problems and Solutions." *Social Science and Medicine* 44(9): 1259–69.

Kaiser Family Foundation. 2010. "The Global HIV/AIDS Epidemic Fact Sheet." http://www.kff.org

Kenny, Nuala and Roger Chafe. 2007. "Pushing Right Against the Evidence: Turbulent Times for Canadian Healthcare." *Hastings Center Report,* 37(5): 24–25.

Kerzner, Lana and David Baker. 1999. *A Canadians with Disability Act?* May 14. http://www.hc-sc.gc.ca

Kessler, Ronald C., Katherine A. McGonagle, Shanyang Zhao, Christopher B. Nelson, Michael Hughes, Suzann Eshleman, Hans-Ulrich Wittchen, and Kenneth S. Kendler. 1994. "Lifetime and 12-Month Prevalence of DSM-III-R Psychiatric Disorders in the United States." *Archives of General Psychiatry* 51: 8–19.

Kuehn, Bridget M. 2008. "Prostate Cancer Screening." *The Journal of the American Medical Association* 300(12): 1403.

Labonte, Ronald. 1992. "Heart Health Inequalities in Canada: Models, Theory and Planning." *Health Promotion International* 72(2): 119–28.

Lamptey, Peter. 2002. "Reducing Heterosexual Transmission of HIV in Poor Countries." *British Medical Journal* 342 (January): 207–11.

Lantz, Paula M., James S. House, James M. Lepkowski, David R. Williams, Richard P. Mero, and Jieming Chen. 1998. "Socioeconomic Factors, Health Behaviors, and Mortality: Results from a Nationally Representative Prospective Study of U.S. Adults." *Journal of the American Medical Association* 279: 1703–8.

LaPorte, Ronald E. 1997. "Improving Public Health via the Information Superhighway." June 8, 1998. http://www.the-scientist.library.upenn.edu/yr1997/august/opin_97018.html

Lerer, Leonard B., Alan D. Lopez, Tord Kjellstrom, and Derek Yach. 1998. "Health for All: Analyzing Health Status and Determinants." *World Health Statistics Quarterly* 51: 7–20.

Markovic, Milica, Vesna Kesic, Lidija Topic, and Bojana Matejic. 2005. "Barriers to Cervical Cancer Screening: A Qualitative Study with Women in Serbia." *Social Science and Medicine* 61: 2528–35.

Miller, K. and A. Rosenfield. 1996. "Population and Women's Reproductive Health: An International Perspective." *Annual Review of Public Health* 17: 359–82.

Mitchell, Alana. 1995. "Down's Transplant Bid Poses Dilemma." *The Globe and Mail* (April 28): A1, A10.

Murray, C. and A. Lopez (eds.). 1996. *The Global Burden of Disease*. Boston: Harvard University Press.

National AIDS Trust. 2005. *Fact Sheet 3: Global Impact*. London: National AIDS Trust.

———. 2011. "International Statistics." http://www.nat.org.uk/HIV-Facts/Statistics/International-statistics.aspx

Nelson, Heidi. 2009. "Screening for Breast Cancer: An Update for the U.S. Preventive Services Task Force." *Annals of Internal Medicine* 151(100): 727–37.

Nestel, Sheryl. 2012. "Colour Coded Health Care: The Impacts of Race and Racism on Canadians' Health." Produced by Wellesley Institute. http://www.wellesleyinstitute.com/wp-content/uploads/2012/02/Colour-Coded-Health-Care.pdf

Parsons, Talcott. 1951. *The Social System*. New York: The Free Press.

PHAC (Public Health Agency of Canada). 2008. "Tuberculosis in Canada, 2008."

http://www.phac-aspc.gc.ca/tbpc-latb/pubs/tbcan08/tbcan08-es-eng.php

———. 2012. "First Nations and Inuit Health." http://www.hc-sc.gc.ca/fniah-spnia/diseases-maladies/index-eng.php

Picard, Andre. 2009. "Base Breast-Screening on Reason, Not Passion." *The Globe and Mail*, Nov. 19, 2009.

"Poverty Threatens Crisis." 1998. *Popline* 20 (May-June): 3.

Proctor, N. Robert. 1995. "The Destruction of 'Lives Not Worth Living.'" Pp. 170–196 in *Deviant Bodies*, edited by Jennifer Terry and Jacqueline Urla. Bloomington, IN: Indiana University Press.

Raphael, D. 2004. "Introduction." Pp. 1–18 in *Social Determinants of Health*, edited by D. Raphael. Toronto: Canadian Scholars Press.

Reid, Robert. 1998. Canadian Cardiovascular Society 1998: Consensus Conference on the Prevention of Cardiovascular Diseases: The Role of the Cardiovascular Specialist.

Rice, Amy L., Lisa Sacco, Adnan Hyder, and Robert E. Black. 2000. "Malnutrition as an Underlying Cause of Childhood Deaths Associated with Infectious Diseases in Developing Countries." *Bulletin of the World Health Organization* 78(10): 1207–21.

Roterman, Michelle. 2005. "Sex, Condoms, and STDs among Young People." *Health Reports* 16: 39–42.

Royal Commission on Aboriginal Peoples. 1996. *Looking Forward, Looking Back: Report of the Royal Commission on Aboriginal Peoples*, vol. 1. Ottawa: Supply and Services Canada.

Rustein, Shea O. 2000. "Factors Associated with Trends in Infant and Child Mortality in Developing Countries During the 1990s." *Bulletin of the World Health Organization* 78(10): 1256–70.

Safe Motherhood Initiative. 1998. "Fact and Figures." September 24. http://www.safemotherhood.org/init_facts.htm

Save the Children Foundation. 2004. *State of the World's Mothers 2004: Children Having Children*. Washington, DC: Save the Children Foundation. http://www.savethechildren.org/publications

Shkilnyk, Anastasia. 1985. *A Poison Stronger Than Love*. New Haven, CT: Yale University Press.

Statistics Canada. 1998a. *Canada Yearbook 1999*. Ottawa: Ministry of Industry.

———. 2002. "Deaths, 1999." *The Daily*, May 7. http://www.statcan.ca/Daily/English/020507/d020507b.htm

———. 2005. "Divorce and the Mental Health of Children." *The Daily*, December 13.

———. 2009. "Leading Causes of Death in Canada, 2009." http://www.statcan.gc.ca/

pub/84-215-x/2012001/table-tableau/tbl001-eng.htm

———. 2012. "Health—Low Birth Weight." Accessed July 4, 2013. http://www4.hrsdc.gc.ca/.3ndic.1t.4r@-eng.jsp?iid=4

Szasz, Thomas. [1961] 1970. *The Myth of Mental Illness: Foundations of a Theory of Personal Conduct*. New York: Harper and Row.

Thomas et al. 2002. "Randomized Trial of Breast Self-Examination in Shanghai: Final Results." *Journal of the National Cancer Institute* 94(19): 1445–1457.

UNICEF (United Nations International Children's Emergency Fund). 2003. *The State of the World's Children, 2003*. New York: UNICEF. http://www.unicef.org/sowc03/contents/pdf/SOWC03-eng.pdf

United Nations. 2008. "Report on the Global AIDS Epidemic, 2008." Joint United Nations Programme on HIV/AIDS (UNAIDS).

United Nations. 2010. *Human Development Report 2010: 20th Anniversary Edition*. New York: UN Development Programme.

United Nations Population Fund. 2000. *The State of World Population Report 2000*. http://www.unfpa.org/SWP/2000/english/index.

U.S. Department of Health and Human Services. 1999. *Mental Health: A Report of the Surgeon General: Executive Summary*. Rockville, MD: U.S Government Printing Office.

USPSTF. 2009. "Screening for Breast Cancer: U.S. Preventive Services Task Force Recommendation Statement." *Annals of Internal Medicine* 151(100): 716–26.

Vancouver Coastal Health. 2013. "Aboriginal Health Facts." Accessed July 5, 2013. http://aboriginalhealth.vch.ca/facts.htm

Verbrugge, Lois M. 1999. "Pathways of Health and Death." Pp. 377–94 in *Health, Illness, and Healing: Society, Social Context, and Self*, edited by Kathy Charmaz and Debora A. Paterniti. Los Angeles: Roxbury Publishing Co.

Ward, Darrell E. 1999. *The AmFAR AIDS Handbook*. New York: W. W. Norton & Company.

Weitz, Rose. 2001. *The Sociology of Health, Illness, and Health Care: A Critical Approach*, 2nd ed. Belmont, CA: Wadsworth Publishing Co.

Wente, Margaret. 2010. "Prostate Cancer Dilemma." *The Globe and Mail*, Feb. 8, 2010.

Williams, David R. and Chiquita Collins. 1999. "U.S. Socioeconomic and Racial Differences in Health: Patterns, and Explanations." Pp. 349–76 in *Health, Illness, and Healing: Society, Social Context, and Self*, edited by Kathy Charmaz and Debora A. Paterniti. Los Angeles: Roxbury Publishing Co.

World Health Organization (WHO). 1946. "Constitution of the World Health Organization." New York: World Health Organization Interim Commission.

———. 2000. *The World Health Report 2000*. http://www.who.int

———. 2001. *The World Health Report 2001*. http://www.who.int

———. 2004. Summary of Probable SARS Cases with Onset of Illness from 1 November 2002 to 31 July 2003.

World Health Organization (WHO). 2013a. "Tuberculosis." http://www.who.int/mediacentre/factsheets/fs104/en

———. 2013b. "Top 10 Causes of Death." http://who.int/mediacentre/factsheets/fs310/en/#

Wynne, Michael and Wendy Armstrong. 2003, March. "Building on Values: The Future of Health Care in Canada." *Health Issues* 74: 9–13.

Chapter 3

AAP (Australian Associated Press). 1998. "Genetics of Alcoholism." *Institute of Alcohol Studies Update*. London: IAS Publications.

Aboriginal Healing Association. 2003. Fetal Alcohol Syndrome among Aboriginal People in Canada: Review and Analysis of the Intergenerational Links to Residential Schools. Prepared by: Caroline L. Tait, Aboriginal Mental Health Research Team, National Network of Aboriginal Mental Health Research, Cultural and Mental Health Research Unit, Sir Mortimer B. Davis-Jewish General Hospital, Ottawa.

Alcohol Alert. 2000. "Mechanisms of Addiction." *National Institute on Alcohol Abuse and Alcoholism* 46 (April): 2.

Aldridge, Judith. 2008. "Decline But No Fall? New Millennium Trends in Young People's Use of Illegal and Illicit Drugs in Britain." *Health Education* 108(3): 189–206.

AP (Associated Press). 1999. "Alcoholism Touches Millions." December 30. http://abcnews.go.com

Auditor General (of Canada). 2001. *2001 Report of the Auditor General of Canada*. http://www.oag-bvg.gc.ca/domino/reports.nsf/html/0111xe06.html

Becker, H. S. 1966. *Outsiders: Studies in the Sociology of Deviance*. New York: Free Press.

Bibby, Reginald W. 2001. *Canada's Teens: Today, Yesterday, and Tomorrow*. Toronto: Stoddart.

Bureau of Justice Statistics. 1992. "Drugs, Crime, and the Justice System: A National Report from the Bureau of Justice Statistics." U.S. Department of Justice, Office of Justice Programs. Washington, DC: U.S.

Government Printing Office, Superintendent of Documents.

Byrne, Jenni. 2011. "Keep Heroin Out of Our Backyards." http://www.conservative.ca/?page_id=3190

Canadian Press Service. 2005. "Officials Say Safe Injection Site a Success." CTV.ca, "Health." December 30, 2005. http://www.ctv.ca/servlet/ArticleNews/story/CTVNews/1126834518603_80/?hub=Health

CBC. 2013. "AIDS Calgary Slams Safe Injection Rules Set Out by Ottawa." June 7. Accessed August 27, 2014. http://www.cbc.ca/news/calgary/aids-calgary-slams-safe-injection-rules-set-out-by-ottawa-1.1403384

CCSA (Canadian Centre on Substance Abuse). 1999. *Canadian Profile, 1999: Alcohol, Tobacco, and Other Drugs*. Ottawa: Canadian Centre on Substance Abuse and Centre for Addiction and Mental Health.

———. 2007. "Substance Abuse in Canada: Youth in Focus." http://www.ccsa.ca/Eng/KnowledgeCentre/Our Publications/Pages/SubstanceAbuseinCanada.aspx

———. 2009. "Clearing the Smoke on Cannabis: Cannabis Use and Driving." CCSA: Ottawa. http://www.ccsa.ca/2009 CCSA Documents/ccsa-11789-2009.pdf

CHALN. 2008. "HIV and Hepatitis C in Prisons: The Facts." Report. Accessed August 27, 2014. http://www.aidslaw.ca/publications/interfaces/downloadFile.php?ref=1309

City of Vancouver. 2003. "Supervised Injection Sites: Frequently Asked Questions." Pamphlet. Vancouver: City of Vancouver.

Cloud, John. 2000. "The Lure of Ecstasy." *Time* (June 5): 63–72.

Cooper, M., R. Corrado, A. M. Karlberg, and L. P. Adams. 1992. "Aboriginal Suicide in British Columbia: An Overview." *Canada's Mental Health* (September): 19–23.

DEA (Drug Enforcement Administration). 2000. "An Overview of Club Drugs." *Drug Intelligence Brief*, February. 1-10. Washington, DC: U.S. Department of Justice.

Dell, Colleen and Tara Lyons. 2007. Harm Reduction Policies and Programs for Persons of Aboriginal Descent. Canadian Centre on Substance Abuse: Ottawa. http://www.ccsa.ca/2007%20CCSA%20Documents/ccsa-011515-2007.pdf

Dembo, Richard, Linda Williams, Jeffrey Fagan, and James Schmeidler. 1994. "Development and Assessment of a Classification of High Risk Youths." *Journal of Drug Issues* 24: 25–53.

Department of Finance Canada. 2002. "Government Announces Tobacco Tax Increases to Discourage Smoking." June 17. http://www.fin.gc.ca/news/02/02-052e.html

Duke, Steven and Albert C. Gross. 1994. *America's Longest War: Rethinking Our Tragic Crusade against Drugs*. New York: G. P. Putnam and Sons.

Duster, Troy. 1995. "The New Crisis of Legitimacy in Controls, Prisons, and Legal Structures." *American Sociologist* 26: 20–29.

Easley, Margaret and Norman Epstein. 1991. "Coping with Stress in a Family with an Alcoholic Parent." *Family Relations* 40: 218–24.

Economist, The. 2003. "The Americas: Needling the Neighbours; Canadian Drug Policy." (September 20): 68.

Eggertson, Laura. 2013. "Legislation Ignores Benefits of Safe Injection Sites, Say Doctors." *Canadian Medical Association Journal*. June 28. http://www.cmaj.ca/content/early/2013/07/02/cmaj.109-4536

Feagin, Joe R. and C. B. Feagin. 1994. *Social Problems*. Englewood Cliffs, NJ: Prentice-Hall.

Fife, R. 1999. "Police Chiefs Get through to the Top." *National Post*, April 22.

Gans, Herbert J. 1971. "The Uses of Poverty: The Poor Pay All." *Social Policy* July/August: 20–24.

Gentry, Cynthia. 1995. "Crime Control through Drug Control." Pp. 477–93 in *Criminology*, 2nd ed., edited by Joseph F. Sheley. Belmont, CA: Wadsworth.

Gfellner, B. M. and J. D. Hundelby. 1995. "Patterns of Drug Use among Native and White Adolescents: 1990–1993." *Canadian Journal of Public Health* 86: 95–97.

Giffen, P. J., S. Endicott, and S. Lambert. 1991. *Panic and Indifference: The Politics of Canada's Drug Laws*. Ottawa: Canadian Centre on Substance Abuse.

Green, Melvyn. 1986. "The History of Canadian Narcotics Control: The Formative Years." Pp. 24–40 in *The Social Dimensions of Law*, edited by Neil Boyd. Scarborough, ON: Prentice Hall.

Gusfield, Joseph. 1963. *Contested Meanings: The Construction of Alcohol Problems*. Madison: University of Wisconsin Press.

Hackler, James C. 2000. *Canadian Criminology: Strategies and Perspectives*, 2nd ed. Scarborough, ON: Prentice Hall Allyn and Bacon Canada.

Haverfield, MacArthur L. 2007. "The Genesis of Global Narcotics Control: An Analytical Examination of the Process of Prohibition." M.A. Thesis: Simon Fraser University, 2007. Accessed August 27, 2014. summit.sfu.ca/system/files/iritems1/8092/etd2974.pdf

Health Canada. 1999. *Statistical Report on the Health of Canadians*. December 25. http://www.hc-sc.gc.ca/hppb/phdd/report/stat/eng/over.html

———. 2001. "Research Results for First Half of 2001—February to June 2001." http://www.hc-sc.gc.ca/hl-vs/tobac-tabac/research-recherche/stat/ctums-esutc/2001/rfh-rppma-2001_e.html

———. 2002. *The Scoop on Smoking—Health Canada for Youth.* http://www.hc-sc.gc.ca/hecs-sesc/tobacco/youth/scoop.html

———. 2005. *HIV and AIDS in Canada: Surveillance Report to December 31, 2004.* Ottawa: Public Health Agency of Canada.

——. 2011a. "Major Findings from the Canadian Alcohol and Drug Use Survey." http://www.hc-sc.gc.ca/hc-ps/drugs-drogues/stat/_2011/summary-sommaire-eng.php

———. 2011b. "Smoking and Mortality." Accessed August 2, 2013. http://www.hc-sc.gc.ca/hc-ps/tobac-tabac/legislation/label-etiquette/mortal-eng.php

———. 2012. "Summary of the Results of the 2010–11 Youth Smoking Survey." Accessed August 2, 2013. http://www.hc-sc.gc.ca/hc-ps/tobac-tabac/research-recherche/stat/_survey-sondage_2010-2011/result-eng.php

Health Council of Canada. 2006. *Health Care Renewal in Canada: Clearing the Road to Quality.* Toronto, February.

Janhevich, Derek, et al. 2003. "Impaired Driving and Other Traffic Offences, 2002." *Juristat* 23(9).

Jarvik, M. 1990. "The Drug Dilemma: Manipulating the Demand." *Science* 250: 387–92.

Jarvinen, Margaretha. 2001. "Accounting for Trouble: Identity Negotiations in Qualitative Interviews with Alcoholics." *Symbolic Interaction* 24(3): 263–284.

Johnson, Holly. 1996. *Dangerous Domains: Violence against Women in Canada.* Scarborough, ON: Nelson.

Join Together. 1998 (July 11). "Inhalant Abuse." *Hot Issues.* http://www.jointogether.org/sa/issues/hot_issues/inhalants/default.html

Klutt, Edward C. 2000. "Pathology of Drug Abuse." http://www.medlib-utah.edu/WebPath

Leinwand, Donna. 2000. "20% Say They Used Drugs with Their Mom or Dad . . ." *USA Today* (August 24): 1A.

Leonard, K. E. and H. T. Blane. 1992. "Alcohol and Marital Aggression in a National Sample of Young Men." *Journal of Interpersonal Violence* 7: 19–30.

Lipton, Douglas S. 1994. "The Correctional Opportunity: Pathways to Drug Treatment for Offenders." *Journal of Drug Issues* 24: 331–48.

McCaffrey, Barry. 1998. "Remarks by Barry McCaffrey, Director, Office of National Drug Control Policy, to the United Nations General Assembly: Special Session on Drugs." Office of National Drug Control Policy. http://www.whitehousedrugpolicy.gov/news/speeches

McLellan, Anne. 2002. "Medical Marijuana." *National Post* (August 29): A19.

Morgan, Patricia A. 1978. "The Legislation of Drug Law: Economic Crisis and Social Control." *Journal of Drug Issues* 8: 53–62.

Murphy, Judge Emily. 1922. *The Black Candle.* Toronto: Thomas Allen.

NIAAA (National Institute on Alcohol Abuse and Alcoholism). 2000. "Tenth Special Report on Alcohol and Health to the U.S. Congress." Washington, DC.

NIDA (National Institute on Drug Abuse). 1999. "Principles of Effective Treatment." NIDA. National Institute of Health. Publication No. 99-4180.Washington, DC.

———. 2000a. "Researcher Announces Latest Study on Drug Dependence and Abuse." News Releases. http://www.nida.nih.gov

———. 2000b. "Club Drugs." Community Alert Bulletin. http://www.nida.nih.gov/ClubAlert/Clubdrugalert.html

ONDCP (Office of National Drug Control Policy). 2000. "The Link between Drugs and Crime." Chapter II. *The National Drug Control Strategy 2000 Annual Report.* http://whitehousedrugpolicy.gov

Ontario Ministry of Health and Long-Term Care (MOHLTC). 2009. Initial Report on Public Health: August 2009. Accessed August 5, 2013. http://www.health.gov.on.ca/en/public/publications/pubhealth/init_report/index.html

RCMP (Royal Canadian Mounted Police). 2011. Untitled Report: "Did you Know?" Accessed August 1, 2013. http://www.rcmp-grc.gc.ca/de-pd/index-eng.htm

Rehm, J. et al. 2006. "The Costs of Substance Abuse in Canada 2002." Figure 2. Canadian Centre on Substance Abuse. http://www.ccsa.ca

Rorabaugh, W. J. 1979. *The Alcoholic Republic: An American Tradition.* New York: Oxford University Press.

Rychtarik, Robert G., Gerald J. Connors, Kurt H. Dermen, and Paul Stasiewicz. 2000. "Alcoholics Anonymous and the Use of Medications to Prevent Relapse." *Journal of Studies on Alcohol* 61: 134–41.

Silverstein, Martin. 2006. "Justice in Genderland: Through a Parole Looking Glass." *Symbolic Interaction* 29(3): 393–410.

Simien, Evelyn M. 2007. "Doing Intersectionality Research: From Conceptual Issues to Practical Examples." *Politics & Gender* 3(2): 264–271.

Simoni-Wastila, Linda, et al. 2004. "Gender and Other Factors Associated with the Non-Medical Use of Abusable Prescription Drugs." *Substance Use and Misuse* 39(1): 1–23.

Solomon, R. and M. Cassidy. 2014. Estimated Number and Percentage of Alcohol and Impairment-Related Crash Fatalities and Injuries, by Jurisdiction, Age and Population: Canada, 2009. Oakville, ON: MADD Canada.

Solomon, Robert. 1999. "Alcohol and Drug Law." Pp. 295–315 in *Canadian Profile, 1999: Alcohol, Tobacco and Other Drugs,* edited by Canadian Centre on Substance Abuse. Ottawa: Canadian Centre on Substance Abuse and Centre for Addiction and Mental Health.

Statistics Canada. 2002b. "Crime Statistics, 2001." *The Daily,* July 17. http://www.statcan.ca/Daily/English/020717/d020717b.htm

———. 2006. Measuring Violence against Women: Statistical Trends 2006. Minister of Industry: Ottawa. Catalogue no. 85-570-XIE

Sullivan, Thomas and Kenrick S. Thompson. 1994. *Social Problems.* New York: Macmillan.

Thomson, Hilary. 2003. "Vancouver Ready for Safe Injection Sites, Say UBC Experts." *UBC Reports* 49(1).

Tubman, J. 1993. "Family Risk Factors, Parental Alcohol Use, and Problem Behaviors among School-Aged Children." *Family Relations* 42: 81–86.

UNODC (United Nations Office on Drugs and Crime). 2010. *Report: Cutting the Threads of Drugs, Crime and Terrorism.* http://www.unodc.org/documents/frontpage/UNODC_Annual_Report_2010_LowRes.pdf

UN-WDR (United Nations World Drug Report). 2009. *World Drug Report.* United Nations Office on Drugs and Crime. http://www.unodc.org/unodc/en/data-and-analysis/WDR-2009.html

Van Dyck, C. and R. Byck. 1982. "Cocaine." *Scientific American* 246: 128–41.

Van Kammen, Welmoet B. and Rolf Loeber. 1994. "Are Fluctuations in Delinquent Activities Related to the Onset and Offset in Juvenile Illegal Drug Use and Drug Dealing?" *Journal of Drug Issues* 24: 9–24.

Vancouver Coastal Health. 2010. "Supervised Injection: Legal Status." http://supervisedinjection.vch.ca/legal_status

White, Helene Raskin and Erich W. Labouvie. 1994. "Generality versus Specificity of Problem Behavior: Psychological and Functional Differences." *Journal of Drug Issues* 24: 55–74.

Witters, Weldon, Peter Venturelli, and Glen Hanson. 1992. *Drugs and Society,* 3rd ed. Boston: Jones and Bartlett.

Wood, E., Thomas Kerr, Patricia M. Spittal, Mark W. Tyndall, Micheal V. O'Shaughnessy, and Martin Schechter. 2003. "The Health Care and Fiscal Costs of the Illicit Drug Use Epidemic: The Impact of Conventional Drug Control Strategies." *BC Medical Journal* 45(3): 128–134.

World Drug Report. 1997. "Report Highlights." United Nations International Drug Control Program. New York: United Nations.

World Health Organization. 2014. HIV Injecting Drug Use. http://www.who.int/hiv/topics/idu/en

Wysong, Earl, Richard Aniskiewicz, and David Wright. 1994. "Truth and Dare: Tracking Drug Education to Graduation and as Symbolic Politics." *Social Problems* 41: 448–68.

Zivi, Karen. 2000. "Who Is the Guilty Party? Rights, Motherhood, and the Problem of Prenatal Drug Exposure." *Law and Society Review* 34(1): 237–58.

Chapter 4

Anderson, Elijah. 1994. "The Code of the Streets: Sociology of Urban Violence." *Atlantic* 273(5): 80–91.

Ash, Russell. 2001. *The Top 10 of Everything: Canadian Edition 2002.* Toronto: Dorling Kindersley Limited.

AuCoin, Kathy. 2005. "Children and Youth as Victims of Violent Crime." *Juristat* 25(1). Catalogue no. 85-002-XIE. Ottawa.

Becker, Howard S. 1963. *Outsiders: Studies in the Sociology of Deviance.* New York: Free Press.

Belknap, Joanne, and Kristi Holsinger. 2006. "The Gendered Nature of Risk Factors for Delinquency." *Feminist Criminology* 1(1): 48–71.

Bernstein, Elizabeth. 2010. "Militarized Humanitarianism Meets Carceral Feminism: The Politics of Sex, Rights, and Freedom in Contemporary Antitrafficking Campaigns." *Signs* 36(1): 45–71.

Besserer, Sandra. 2002. "Criminal Victimization: An International Perspective: Results of the 2000 International Crime Victimization Survey." Ottawa: Canadian Centre for Justice Statistics. 17 pages. Issued as *Juristat* 22(4). Catalogue no. 85-002-XPE.

Bibby, Reginald W. 1995. *The Bibby Report: Social Trends Canadian Style.* Toronto: Stoddart.

———. 2001. *Canada's Teens: Today, Yesterday, and Tomorrow.* Toronto: Stoddart.

Bourrie, Mark. 1999. "Compensating the Innocent." *Canadian Lawyer* (November/December): 29–32.

Brantingham, Paul J., Shihong Mu, and Arvind Verma. 1995. "Patterns in Canadian Crime." Pp. 187–246 in *Canadian Criminology: Perspectives on Crime and Criminality,* 2nd ed., edited by Margaret A. Jackson and Curt T. Griffiths. Toronto: Harcourt Brace and Company.

Brennan, Shannon. 2011. "Canadians' Perceptions of Personal Safety and Crime, 2009." *Juristat* 1 (December) Catalogue no. 85-002-X.

Bruckert, Chris and Stacey Hannem. 2013. "Rethinking the Prostitution Debates: Transcending Structural Stigma in Systemic Responses to Sex Work." *Canadian Journal of Law and Society* 28(1): 43–63.

Bryant, Marian E. 1999. "Sentencing Aboriginal Offenders." *Law Now* (October/November): 20–21.

Business Network on Crime Prevention. 2001. "The Cost of Crime." http://www.crime-prevention.org/english/publications/economic/invest/cost_e.html

Calverley, Donna. 2010. "Adult Correctional Services in Canada, 2008/09." *Juristat* 30(3).

Canadian Mental Health Association. 2003. "Women's Mental Health." *Special Populations.* January 14, 2006. http://www.ontario.cmha.ca/content/about_mental_illness/women.asp?cID=3974

CATW (Coalition Against Trafficking in Women). 1997. "Promoting Sex Work in the Netherlands." *Coalition Report* 4(1). http://www.uri.edu/artsci/wms/hughes/catw

CBC News. 2013. "Child Porn Charges for Toronto Prof, Ex-Adviser to Ont. Premier." July 8. Accessed August 18, 2013. http://www.cbc.ca/news/canada/toronto/story/2013/07/08/toronto-police-benjamin-levin-london-new-zealand.html

Chesney-Lind, Meda. 2006. "Patriarchy, Crime, and Justice." *Feminist Criminology* 1(1): 6–26.

Chwialkowska, Luiza. 2001. "Anti-Terrorism Bill Becomes Law." *National Post* (December 19): A6.

Conklin, John E. 1998. *Criminology,* 6th ed. Boston: Allyn and Bacon.

COPS. 1998. "About the Office of Community Oriented Policing Services (COPS)." http://communitypolicing.org/copspage.html

Correctional Service Canada. 2005. "Basic Facts about the Correctional Service of Canada". Catalogue No. HS 82-17/2005 (p.9).

———. 2006. "Basic Facts about the Correctional Service of Canada." Catalogue no. HS 82-17/2005 (p. 9).

Daly, K. 1992. "Women's Pathways to Felony Court." *Review of Law and Women's Studies* 2: 11–52.

D'Augelli, A. R. and L. J. Dark. 1994. "Lesbian, Gay, and Bisexual Youths." Pp. 177–96 in *Reason to Hope: A Psychological Perspective on Violence and Youth,* edited by L. D. Enron et al. Washington, DC: American Psychological Association.

Dauvergne, Mia. 2012a. "Adult Criminal Court Statistics in Canada, 2010/2011." *Juristat.* Statistics Canada Catalogue no. 85-002-X.

———. 2012b. "Youth Court Statistics in Canada, 2011/2012." *Juristat.* Statistics Canada Catalogue no. 85-002-X.

Dauvergne, Mia and John Turner. 2010. "Police-Reported Crime Statistics in Canada, 2009." *Juristat,* Summer 2010. http://www.statcan.gc.ca/pub/85-002-x/2010002/article/11292-eng.htm#a

Demerson, Velma. 2004. *Incorrigible.* Waterloo, ON: Wilfrid Laurier University Press.

Department of Justice (Canada). 2002a. "Highlights of Anti-Terrorism Act." http://www.canada.justice.gc.ca/en/news/nr/2001/doc_27787.html

———. 2002b. "Canada's Youth Criminal Justice Act: A New Law—A New Approach." http://www.canada.justice.gc.ca/en/dept/pub/ycja/youth_html

———. 2002c. "Organized Crime Legislation Comes into Force." http://www.canada.justice.gc.ca/en/news/nr/2002/doc_29525.html

———. 2005. "The National Strategy on Community Safety and Crime Prevention." Department of Justice.

Deveau, Scott. 2006. "Crime Bill Sets Mandatory Minimum Sentences." *The Globe and Mail Update,* national ed., May 4. http://www.theglobeandmail.com/servlet/story/RTGAM.20060504.wcrime0505/PPVStory/?DENIED=1

DiIulio, John. 1999. "Federal Crime Policy: Time for a Moratorium." *Brookings Review* 17(1): 17.

Economist, The. 2000. "Dead Man Walking Out." (June 10): 21–23.

Erikson, Kai T. 1966. *Wayward Puritans.* New York: John Wiley and Sons.

Evans, John and Alexander Himelfarb. 2000. "Counting Crime." Pp. 60–93 in *Criminology: A Canadian Perspective,* 4th ed., edited by Rick Linden. Toronto: Harcourt Brace and Company.

Faith, K. 1993. *Unruly Women: The Politics of Confinement and Resistance.* Vancouver: Press Gang.

Fattah, Ezzat A. 1991. *Understanding Criminal Victimization: An Introduction to Theoretical Victimology.* Scarborough, ON: Prentice Hall.

Fedorowycz, Orest. 1999. "Homicide in Canada, 1998." *Juristat* 19 (October). Catalogue no. 85-002-XIE.

Felson, Marcus. 1998. *Crime and Everyday Life,* 2nd ed. Thousand Oaks, CA: Pine Forge Press.

Felson, Marcus and Rachel Boba. 2010. *Crime and Everyday Life.* Thousand Oaks, CA: Sage.

Garey, M. 1985. "The Cost of Taking a Life: Dollars and Sense of the Death Penalty." *U.C. Davis Law Review* 18: 1221–73.

Gest, Ted and Dorian Friedman. 1994. "The New Crime Wave." *U.S. News and World Report* (August 29): 26–28.

Hackler, James C. 2000. *Canadian Criminology: Strategies and Perspectives.* Scarborough, ON: Prentice Hall Allyn and Bacon Canada.

———. 2005. *Canadian Criminology: Strategies and Perspectives,* 2nd ed. Scarborough, ON: Prentice Hall Allyn and Bacon Canada.

Hagan, John. 2000. "White-Collar and Corporate Crime." Pp. 459–82 in *Criminology: A Canadian Perspective,* 4th ed., edited by Rick Linden. Toronto: Harcourt Brace and Company.

Hartnagel, Timothy F. 2012. "Correlates of Criminal Behaviour." Pp. 132–178 in *Criminology: A Canadian Perspective*, 7th ed., edited by Rick Linden. Toronto: Nelson Educational Publishing.

Hirschi, Travis. 1969. *Causes of Delinquency.* Berkeley: University of California Press.

Hochstetler, Andrew and Neal Shover. 1997. "Street Crime, Labor Surplus, and Criminal Punishment, 1980/1990." *Social Problems* 44(3): 358–67.

Hogeveen, Brian R. 2005. "If We Are Tough on Crime, If We Punish Crime, Then People Get the Message." *Punishment and Society* 7(1): 73–89.

Human Rights Watch. 2000. *Human Rights Watch World Report 2000.United States.* http://www.hrw.org/wr2k/us.html

INTERPOL. 2011. Annual Report. Page 41. http://www.interpol.int/en/News-and-media/publications/Annual-reports/2011

Jacobs, David. 1988. "Corporate Economic Power and the State: A Longitudinal Assessment of Two Explanations." *American Journal of Sociology* 93: 852–81.

Janoff-Bulman, Ronnie, C. Timko, and L. Carli. 1985. "Cognitive Biases in Blaming the Victim." *Journal of Experimental Social Psychology* 23: 161–77.

John Howard Society. 1999. *Check & Balance: The Facts about Facts.* Toronto: The John Howard Society of Ontario.

Klapper, Bradley. 2005. "UN Told Governments Must Combat Internet Child Pornography." Associated Press (April 14). http://informationweek.com

Koenig, Daniel J. 2000. "Conventional or 'Street' Crime." Pp. 396–429 in *Criminology: A Canadian Perspective*, 4th ed., edited by Rick Linden. Toronto: Harcourt Brace and Company.

Kong, Deborah and Jon Swartz. 2000. "Experts See Rash of Hack Attacks Coming . . ." *USA Today* (September 27): 1B.

Kong, Rebecca. 1999. "Canadian Crime Statistics, 1997." Pp. 117–37 in *The Juristat Reader: A Statistical Overview of the Canadian Justice System,* edited by Canadian Centre for Justice Statistics. Toronto: Thompson Educational Publishing.

Kong, Rebecca and Kathy AuCoin. 2008. "Female Offenders in Canada." *Juristat* 28(1). Catalogue no. 85-002-XIE.

Laub, John, Daniel S. Nagan, and Robert Sampson. 1998. "Trajectories of Change in Criminal Offending: Good Marriages and the Desistance Process." *American Sociological Review* 63 (April): 22–38.

Lehrur, Eli. 1999. "Communities and Cops Join Forces." *Insight on the News* 15 (January 25): 16.

Li, Geoffrey. 2007. "Homicide in Canada: 2006." *Juristat.* Catalogue no. 85-002-XPE, Ottawa.

Liebman, James S., Jeffery Fagan, and Valerie West. 2000. "A Broken System: Error Rates in Capital Cases, 1973–1995." http://justice.policy.net/jpreport

Lipsey, M. W. and D. B. Wilson. 1998. "Effective Intervention for Serious Juvenile Offenders: A Synthesis of Research." In *Serious and Violent Offenders*, edited by R. Loeber and David Farrington. Thousand Oaks, CA: Sage Publications.

Logan, Ron. 2001. "Crime Statistics in Canada, 2000." *Juristat* 21 (July). Catalogue no. 85-002-XPE.

Lonmo, Charlene. 2001. "Adult Correctional Services in Canada, 1999–2000." *Juristat* 21 (July). Catalogue no. 85-002-XPE.

MacIntyre, John. 1999. ". . . and Counting." *Canadian Lawyer* (November/December): 6.

Manzo, John F. and Monetta M. Bailey. 2005. "On the Assimilation of Racial Stereotypes and Black Canadian Young Offenders." *Canadian Review of Sociology and Anthropology* 42(3): 283–300.

Merton, Robert. 1957. "Social Structure and Anomie." In *Social Theory and Social Structure.* Glencoe, IL: Free Press.

Moore, Elizabeth and Michael Mills. 1990. "The Neglected Victims and Unexamined Costs of White Collar Crime." *Crime and Delinquency* 36: 408–18.

Murray, Mary E., Nancy Guerra, and Kirk Williams. 1997. "Violence Prevention for the Twenty-First Century." Pp. 105–28 in *Enhancing Children's Awareness*, edited by Roger P. Weissberg, Thomas Gullota, Robert L. Hampton, Bruce Ryan, and Gerald Adams. Thousand Oaks, CA: Sage Publications.

National Research Council. 1994. *Violence in Urban America: Mobilizing a Response.* Washington, DC: National Academy Press.

Olmsted, A. D. 1988. "Morally Controversial Leisure." *Symbolic Interaction* 11: 277–87.

Paterson, Stephanie. 2010. "'Resistors,' 'Helpless Victims,' and 'Willing Participants': The Construction of Women's Resistance in Canadian Anti-Violence Policy." *Social Policy* 17(2): 159–184.

Pertossi, Mayra. 2000. "ANALYSIS—Argentine Crime Rate Soars." September 27. http://news.excite.com

Polaris Project. 2011. "International Trafficking" Available at http://www.polarisproject.org

Public Safety Canada. 2010. "Corrections and Conditional Release in Canada: A General Primer 2010." Catalogue no. PS4-64/2010E-PDF. http://www.publicsafety.gc.ca/res/cor/rep/2010-03-nt-bkgr-eng.aspx

Roberts, Julian and Thomas Gabor. 1990. "Race and Crime: A Critique." *Canadian Journal of Criminology* 92 (April): 291–313.

Rushowy, Kristin. 2013. "U of T Professor Charged with Child Porn 'Ceases' All Duties." *Toronto Star* (July 22). Accessed August 18, 2013. http://www.thestar.com/news/gta/2013/07/22/toronto_professor_charged_with_child_porn_ceases_all_duties_at_u_of_t.html

Sanday, P. R. 1981. "The Sociocultural Context of Rape: A Cross-Cultural Study." *Journal of Social Issues* 37: 5–27.

Seagrave, J. 1997. *Introduction to Policing in Canada.* Scarborough, ON: Prentice Hall.

Shelley, Louise. 2007. "Terrorism, Transnational Crime and Corruption Center." American University. http://www.american.edu/traccc

Sherrill, Robert. 2000. "A Year in Corporate Crime." Pp. 302–8 in *Social Problems in the Modern World*, edited by Frances Moulder. Belmont, CA: Wadsworth.

Siegel, Larry. 2000. *Criminology.* Belmont, CA: Wadsworth.

Snider, Laureen. 2000. "The Sociology of Corporate Crime: An Obituary (Or: Whose Knowledge Claims Have Legs?)." *Theoretical Criminology* 4(2): 169–206.

Solicitor General. 1999. "Organized Crime." http://www.sgc.gc.ca/EFact/eorgcrime.htm

———. 2002. "Factsheets." http://www.sgc.ca/Efact/emyths.htm

———. 2008: "Youth Court Statistics, 2006/2007" Juristat Vol 28: 4. Catalog no. 85-002-X.

Stamler, Rodney T. 2000. "Organized Crime." Pp. 429–58 In *Criminology: A Canadian Perspective*, 4th ed., edited by Rick Linden. Toronto: Harcourt Brace and Company.

Statistics Canada. 2002. "Crime Statistics, 2001." *The Daily*, July 17. http://www.statcan.ca/Daily/English/020717/d020717b.htm

———. 2008: "Youth Court Statistics, 2006/2007" Juristat Vol 28: 4. Catalog no. 85-002-X.

———. 2009b. "Security—Victims of Violent Crime." http://www4.hrsdc.gc.ca/.3ndic.1t.4r@-eng.jsp?iid=61

Steffensmeier, Darrell and Emilie Allan. 1995. "Criminal Behavior: Gender and Age." Pp. 83–113 in *Criminology: A Contemporary Handbook*, 2nd ed., edited by Joseph F. Sheley. Belmont, CA: Wadsworth.

Sutherland, Edwin H. 1939. *Criminology.* Philadelphia: Lippincott.

Swartz, Joel. 1978. "Silent Killers at Work." Pp. 114–28 in *Corporate and Governmental Deviance*, edited by M. David Ermann and Richard Lundman. New York: Oxford University Press.

Thomas, Jennifer. 2008. "Youth Court Statistics, 2003/04." *Juristat* 25(4). Catalogue no. 85-002-XPE.

Thomas, Mikhail. 2004. "Adult Criminal Court Statistics 2003/04." *Juristat* 24(12). Catalogue no.85-002-XPE.

Tufts, Jennifer. 2000. "Public Attitudes toward the Criminal Justice System." *Juristat* 20(12). Catalogue no. 85-002-XPE.

UNODC (United Nations Office on Drugs and Crime). 2011. "2011 Global Study on Homi-

cide: Trends, Contexts, Data." http://www
.unodc.org/documents/data-and-analysis/
statistics/Homicide/Globa_study_on
_homicide_2011_web.pdf

U.S. Department of Justice. 2003. "Global Crime
Issues." In *International Center Global Crimes
Issues,* National Center of Justice. Washington,
DC: U.S. Government Printing Office.

U.S. Department of State. 2008 (June 4).
"Trafficking in Persons Report." http"//
www.state.gov

Wallace, Marnie. 2004. "Crime Statistics in
Canada." *Juristat* 24(6).Catalogue no. 85-
002-IXE.

Wallace, Marnie. 2009. "Police-Reported
Crime Statistics in Canada, 2008." *Juristat*
29(3). Catalogue no.85-002-X.

Warner, Barbara and Pamela Wilcox Rountree. 1997. "Local Social Ties in a Community and Crime Model." *Social Problems*
4(4): 520–36.

White, Michael. 1999. "GM Ordered to Pay
Accident Victims $49B." *National Post* (July
10): A1.

Williams, Linda. 1984. "The Classic Rape:
When Do Victims Report?" *Social Problems*
31: 459–67.

Wilson, Charles. 2010. "Indiana Child Porn
Ring: Feds Bust International Online
Operation, More Than 50 Arrested." *The
Huffington Post,* May 26.

Worden, Amy. 2000. "More Whites Than Blacks
Evade Death Penalty." http://www.apb news
.com/newscenter/breaking-news/2000/
07/24deathpleas0/24_01.html

Chapter 5

Amato, Paul R. 2001. "The Consequences
of Divorce for Adult and Children."
Pp. 488–506 in *Understanding Families into
the New Millennium: A Decade in Review,*
edited by Robert M. Milardo. Minneapolis:
National Council on Family Relations.

Ambert, Anne-Marie. 1998. "Divorce: Facts,
Figures and Consequences." Vanier Institute of the Family. http://www.vifamily.ca/
cft/divorce/divorce.htm

Anderson, Kristin L. 1997. "Gender, Status,
and Domestic Violence: An Integration of
Feminist and Family Violence Approaches."
Journal of Marriage and the Family 59: 655–59.

AuCoin, Kathy. 2005. "Talking—Criminal
Harassment." *Family Violence in Canada: A
Statistical Profile 2005.* Statistics Canada.
Catalogue no. 85-224-XIE: 33–37.

Beattie, Karen. 2005. *Spousal Homicides.* Ottawa: Statistics Canada, Canadian Centre for
Justice Statistics.

Beitchman, J. H., K. J. Zuker, J. E. Hood, G. A.
daCosta, D. Akman, and E. Cassavia. 1992.
"A Review of the Long-Term Effects of Child
Sexual Abuse." *Child Abuse and Neglect* 16:
101–19.

Berns, Nancy. 2004. *Framing the Victim: Domestic Violence, Media, and Social Problems.*
New York: Aldine de Gruyter.

Bibby, Reginald W. 2001. *Canada's Teens:
Today, Yesterday, and Tomorrow.* Toronto:
Stoddart.

Browning, Christopher R. and Edward O.
Laumann. 1997. "Sexual Contact between
Children and Adults: A Life Course Perspective." *American Sociological Review* 62:
540–60.

Bunge, Valerie Pottie. 2000. "Spousal Violence."
Pp. 11–21 in *Family Violence in Canada: A
Statistical Profile 2000,* edited by Statistics
Canada. Catalogue no. 85-224-XIE. Ottawa:
Minister of Industry.

Butler, Judith. 2004. *Undoing Gender.* London
and New York: Routledge.

Coontz, Stephanie. 2000. "Marriage: Then and
Now." *Phi Kappa Phi Journal* 80: 10–15.

Crawford, Trish. 1997. "Sexual Health
Programs Are at Risk." *Toronto Star*
(August 23): M1.

Crompton, Susan. 2005. "Always a Bridesmaid."
Canadian Social Trends 77 (Summer): 2–8.

Dauvergne, Mia. 2005a. "Spousal Homicide
Rate in Canada, 2004." *Juristat* 25(6). Catalogue no. 85-002-XPE.

———. 2005b. "Homicide in Canada,
2004." *Juristat* 26(6). Catalogue no. 85-002-
XPE.

Demo, David H. 1992. "Parent-Child Relations:
Assessing Recent Changes." *Journal of
Marriage and the Family* 54: 104–17.

Demo, David H., Mark A. Fine, and Lawrence
H. Ganong. 2000. "Divorce as a Family
Stressor." Pp. 279–302 in *Families & Change:
Coping with Stressful Events and Transi-
tions,* 2nd ed., edited by P. C. McKenry
and S. J. Price. Thousand Oaks, CA: Sage
Publications.

DiLillo, D., G. C. Tremblay, and L. Peterson.
2000. "Linking Childhood Sexual Abuse and
Abusive Parenting: The Mediating Role of
Maternal Anger." *Child Abuse and Neglect*
24: 767–79.

Dranoff, Linda Silver. 2001. *Everyone's Guide to
the Law.* Toronto: HarperCollins Publishers
Ltd.

Drummond, Tammerlin. 2000. "Mom on Her
Own." *Time* (August 28): 54–55.

Edgerton, Robert B. 1992. *Sick Societies: Challenging the Myth of Primitive Harmony.* New
York: The Free Press.

Edin, Kathryn. 2000. "What Do Low-Income
Single Mothers Say about Marriage?" *Social
Problems* 47(1): 112–33.

Edwards, Tamala M. 2000. "Flying Solo." *Time*
(August 28): 49–53.

EGALE. 2005. "We Won!" *Info-Egale* 2(5).

Elliott, D. M. and J. Briere. 1992. "The Sexually
Abused Boy: Problems in Manhood." *Medical Aspects of Human Sexuality* 26: 68–71.

Eltahawy, Mona. 2000. "Giving Wives a Way Out."
U.S. News & World Report 128 (March 6): 35.

Emery, Robert E. 1999. "Postdivorce Family
Life for Children: An Overview of Research
and Some Implications for Policy." Pp. 3–27
in *The Postdivorce Family: Children, Parenting, and Society,* edited by R. A. Thompson
and P. R. Amato. Thousand Oaks, CA: Sage
Publications.

Family Court Reform Council of America.
2000. "Parental Alienation Syndrome."
31441 Santa Margarita Parkway, Suite A184.
Rancho Santa Margarita, CA 92688.

Fathalla, Mahmoud F. 2005. "Comment: When
Home Is No Longer Safe: Intimate-Partner
Violence." *Lancet* 366: 1909–10.

Follingstad, D. R. and M. Edmundsen. 2010. "Is
Psychological Abuse Reciprocal in Intimate
Relationships? Data from a National Sam-
ple of American Adults." *Journal of Family
Violence* (25)5: 495–508.

Gardner, Richard A. 1998. *The Parental
Alienation Syndrome,* 2nd ed. Cresskill, NJ:
Creative Therapeutics, Inc.

Gearing, Robin, Niloo Zand, and Geordie
Colvin. 2001. "Engaging Fathers: A Point
of Entry in Promoting a Culture of Peace."
*Journal of the Association for Research on
Mothering* 3(2): 57–73.

Gelles, Richard J. 1993. "Family Violence."
Pp. 1–24 in *Family Violence: Prevention
and Treatment,* edited by Robert L.
Hampton, Thomas P. Gullotta, Gerald
R. Adams, Earl H. Potter III, and Roger
P. Weissberg. Newbury Park, CA: Sage
Publications.

———. 2000. "Violence, Abuse, and Neglect in
Families." Pp. 183–207 in *Families & Change:
Coping with Stressful Events and Transi-
tions,* 2nd ed., edited by P. C. McKenry
and S. J. Price. Thousand Oaks, CA: Sage
Publications.

Gelles, Richard J. and Jon R. Conte. 1991. "Domestic Violence and Sexual Abuse of Children: A Review of Research in the Eighties."
Pp. 327–40 in *Contemporary Families:
Looking Forward, Looking Back,* edited by
Alan Booth. Minneapolis: National Council
on Family Relations.

Geronimus, Arline. 1997. "Teenage Child-
bearing and Personal Responsibility:
An Alternative View." *Political Science
Quarterly* 112(3): 405–30.

———. 2003. "Damned If You Do: Culture,
Identity, Privilege, and Childbearing in the
United States." *Social Science and Medicine*
57: 881–93.

Global Study of Family Values. 1998.
The Gallup Organization. April 13.
http://198.175.140.8/Special_ Reports/
family.htm

Halpern, Carolyn Tucker, et al. 2004. "Prevalence of Partner Violence in Same-Sex

Romantic and Sexual Relationships in a National Sample of Adolescents." *Journal of Adolescent Health* 35: 124–31.

Harrington, Donna and Howard Dubowitz. 1993. "What Can Be Done to Prevent Child Maltreatment?" Pp. 258–80 in *Family Violence: Prevention and Treatment*, edited by Robert L. Hampton, Thomas P. Gullotta, Gerald R. Adams, Earl H. Potter III, and Roger P. Weissberg. Newbury Park, CA: Sage Publications.

Health Canada. 1999. *Statistical Report on the Health of Canadians.* December 25. http://www.hc-sc. gc.ca/hppb/phdd/report/state/eng/over.html

Henry, Ronald K. 1999. "Child Support at a Crossroads: When the Real World Intrudes upon Academics and Advocates." *Family Law Quarterly* 33 (Spring): 235–64.

Hewlett, Sylvia Ann and Cornel West. 1998. *The War against Parents: What We Can Do for Beleaguered Moms and Dads.* Boston: Houghton Mifflin Company.

Hogan, D. P., R. Sun, and G. T. Cornwell. 2000. "Sexual and Fertility Behaviors of American Females Aged 15–19 Years: 1985, 1990, and 1995. *American Journal of Public Health* 90: 1421–25.

Jacobs, C. D. and E. M. Wolf. 1995. "School Sexuality Education and Adolescent Risk-Taking Behavior." *Journal of School Health* 65: 91–5.

Jasinski, J. L., L. M. Williams, and J. Siegel. 2000. "Childhood Physical and Sexual Abuse as Risk Factors for Heavy Drinking among African-American Women: A Prospective Study." *Child Abuse and Neglect* 24: 1061–71.

Jekielek, Susan M. 1998. "Parental Conflict, Marital Disruption and Children's Emotional Well-Being." *Social Forces* 76: 905–35.

Johnson, Holly and Tina Hotton. 2001. "Spousal Violence." Pp. 26–41 in *Family Violence in Canada: A Statistical Profile 2001*, edited by Statistics Canada. July. Catalogue no. 85-224-XIE. Ottawa: Minister of Industry.

Johnson, Michael P. and Kathleen Ferraro. 2001. "Research on Domestic Violence in the 1990s: Making Distinctions." Pp. 167–182 in *Understanding Families Into the New Millennium: A Decade in Review*, edited by Robert M. Milardo. Minneapolis: National Council on Family Relations.

Jorgensen, Stephen R. 2000. "Adolescent Pregnancy Prevention: Prospects for 2000 and Beyond." Presidential Address at the National Council on Family Relations 62nd Annual Conference, November 11. Minneapolis, MN.

Kaufman, Joan and Edward Zigler. 1992. "The Prevention of Child Maltreatment: Programming, Research, and Policy." Pp. 269–95

in *Prevention of Child Maltreatment: Developmental and Ecological Perspectives*, edited by Diane J. Willis, E. Wayne Holden, and Mindy Rosenberg. New York: John Wiley & Sons.

Kephart, William. 1963. "Experimental Family Organization: An Historico-Cultural Report on the Oneida Community." *Marriage and Family Living* 25(3): 261–71.

Knox, David (with Kermit Leggett). 1998. *The Divorced Dad's Survival Book: How to Stay Connected with Your Kids.* New York: Insight Books.

Kong, R. 1997. "Criminal Harassment in Canada." *Canadian Social Trends* 45 (Autumn): 29–33.

Krug, Ronald S. 1989. "Adult Male Report of Childhood Sexual Abuse by Mothers: Case Description, Motivations, and Long-Term Consequences." *Child Abuse and Neglect* 13: 111–19.

Lanz, Jean B. 1995. "Psychological, Behavioral, and Social Characteristics Associated with Early Forced Sexual Intercourse among Pregnant Adolescents." *Journal of Interpersonal Violence* 10: 188–200.

Le Bourdais, Celine, Neill Ghislaine, and Pierre Turcotte. 2001. "The Changing Face of Conjugal Relationships." *Canadian School Trends* (Spring): 14–17.

Leite, Randy W. and Patrick C. McKenry. 2000. "Aspects of Father Status and Post-Divorce Father Involvement with Children." Poster session at the National Council on Family Relations 62nd Annual Conference, November 10–13. Minneapolis, MN.

Lewin, Tamar. 2000. "Fears for Children's Well-Being Complicates a Debate over Marriage." *The New York Times on the Web*, November 4. http://www.nytimes .com/2000/11/04/arts/04MARR.html

Lloyd, Sally A. 2000. "Intimate Violence: Paradoxes of Romance, Conflict, and Control." *National Forum* 80(4): 19–22.

Lloyd, S. A. and B. C. Emery. 1993. "Abuse in the Family: An Ecological, Life-Cycle Perspective." Pp. 129–52 in *Family Relations: Challenges for the Future*, edited by T. H. Brubaker. Newbury Park, CA: Sage Publications.

———. 2000. *The Dark Side of Courtship: Physical and Sexual Aggression.* Thousand Oaks, CA: Sage Publications.

Locke, Daisy, Sara Beattie, and Sean Miller. 2001. "Homicide of Children and Youth." Pp. 15–18 in *Family Violence in Canada: A Statistical Profile 2001.* Statistics Canada, July. Catalogue no. 85-224-XIE. Ottawa: Minister of Industry.

Luxton, Meg. 1996. "Conceptualizing 'Families': Theoretical Frameworks and Family Research." In *Families: Changing Trends in Canada*, 3rd ed., edited by Maureen Baker. Toronto: McGraw-Hill Ryerson.

Mahapatra, Dhananjay. 2008 (February). "Customary Payments, Gifts Not Dowry: SC." *The Times of India.* http://timesofindia .indiatimes.com

Marlow, L. and S. R. Sauber. 1990. *The Handbook of Divorce Mediation.* New York: Plenum.

Mason, Mary, A. Skolnik, and S. D. Sugarman. 2003. "Introduction." Pp. 1–13 in *All Our Families*, 2nd ed., edited by Mary Mason, Arlene Skolnick, and Stephen D. Sugarman. New York: Oxford University Press.

McMaster University. 2013. "1 in 6 women at Fracture Clinics Report Domestic Violence." June 11. Accessed September 10, 2013. http://fhs.mcmaster.ca/main/news/news_2013/praise_study.html

Milan, Anne. 2013. "Marital Status: Overview, 2011." Statistics Canada. Component of Catalogue no. 91-209-X, Report on the Demographic Situation in Canada.

Milan, Anne, Mireille Vezina, and Carrie Wells. 2007. "Family Portrait: Continuity and Change in Canadian Families and Households in 2006: 2006 Census." Statistics Canada. Catalogue no. 97-553-X.

Monson, C. M., G. R. Byrd, and J. Langhinrichsen-Rohling. 1996. "To Have and to Hold: Perceptions of Marital Rape." *Journal of Interpersonal Violence* 11: 410–24.

Morrison, N. 1987. "Separation and Divorce." Pp. 125–43 in *The Canadian Woman's Legal Guide*, edited by M. J. Dymond. Toronto: Doubleday.

Morton, M. 1990. "Controversies within Family Law." Pp. 211–40 in *Families: Changing Trends in Canada*, edited by M. Baker. Toronto: McGraw-Hill Ryerson.

National Center for Injury Prevention and Control. 2000. "Intimate Partner Violence Fact Sheet." Atlanta, GA: National Center for Injury Prevention and Control.

National Coalition for the Homeless. 1998. "Domestic Violence and Homelessness." *NCH Fact Sheet No. 8.* National Coalition for the Homeless.

———. 1999. NCH Fact Sheet #1. "Why Are People Homeless?" http://www .nationalhomeless.org/causes.html

National Council of Welfare. 1999. *Children First: A Pre-Budget Report by the National Council of Welfare.* Autumn. http://www.ncwcnbes.net.htmdocument/reportchildfirst.htm

National Resource Center on Domestic Violence. 2007a. "LGBT Communities and Domestic Violence: Overview." NRCDV: Harrisburg: Pennsylvania. http://nwnetwork .org/wp-content/uploads/2011/11/National -Resource-Center_LGBTDV-Full.pdf

———. 2007b. "Key Issue: Dynamics of Domestic Violence." NRCDV: Harrisburg: Pennsylvania. http://nwnetwork.org/

wp-content/uploads/2011/11/National
-Resource-Center_LGBTDV-Full.pdf

Nelson, B. S. and K. S. Wampler. 2000. "Systemic Effects of Trauma in Clinic Couples: An Exploratory Study of Secondary Trauma Resulting from Childhood Abuse." *Journal of Marriage and Family Counseling* 26: 171–84.

Nielsen, L. 1999. "College Aged Students with Divorced Parents: Facts and Fiction." *College Student Journal* 33: 543–72.

Northwest Network. nwnetwork.org/who -we-are

Novac, S., J. Brown, and C. Bourbonnais. 1996. *No Room of Her Own: A Literature Review on Women and Homelessness.* Canadian Mortgage and Housing Corporation. May 1, 2000. http://www.cmhc-schl.gc.ca/cmhc.html

Ogrodnick, Lucie. 2007. "Family Violence in Canada: A Statistical Profile: 2007." Statistics Canada. Catalogue no. 85-224-XIE.

Palazzolo, Kellie E. and Anthony J. Roberto. 2011. "Media Representations of Intimate Partner Violence and Punishment Preferences: Exploring the Role of Attributions and Emotions." *Journal of Applied Communication Research* (39)1: 1–18.

Parker, Marcie, R. Edward Bergmark, Mark Attridge, and Jude Miller-Burke. 2000. "Domestic Violence and Its Effect on Children." *National Council on Family Relations Report* 45(4): F6–F7.

Pasley, Kay and Carmelle Minton. 2001. "Generative Fathering after Divorce and Remarriage: Beyond the 'Disappearing Dad.'" Pp. 239–48 in *Men and Masculinity: A Text Reader*, edited by T. F. Cohen. Belmont, CA: Wadsworth.

Peterson, Richard R. 1996. "A Re-evaluation of the Economic Consequences of Divorce." *American Sociological Review* 61: 528–36.

Popenoe, David. 1993. "Point of View: Scholars Should Worry about the Disintegration of the American Family." *Chronicle of Higher Education* (April 14): A48.

Potter, Hillary. 2006. "An Argument for Black Feminist Criminology." *Feminist Criminology* 1(2): 106–124.

Resnick, Michael, Peter S. Bearman, Robert W. Blum, Karl E. Bauman, Kathleen M. Harris, Jo Jones, Joyce Tabor, Trish Beubring, Renee E. Sieving, Marcia Shew, Marjore Ireland, Linda H. Berringer, and J. Richard Udry. 1997. "Protecting Adolescents from Harm." *Journal of the American Medical Association* 278 (September 10): 823–32.

Riedmann, Agnes, Mary Ann Lamanna, and Adie Nelson. 2003. *Marriages and Families: Making Choices in a Diverse Society,* 1st Canadian ed. Toronto: Thomson Nelson.

Russell, D. E. 1990. *Rape in Marriage.* Bloomington, IN: Indiana University Press.

Schacht, Thomas E. 2000. "Protection Strategies to Protect Professionals and Families Involved in High-Conflict Divorce." *UALR Law Review* 22(3): 565–92.

Scott, K. L. and D. A. Wolfe. 2000. "Change among Batterers: Examining Men's Success Stories." *Journal of Interpersonal Violence* 15: 827–42.

Shapiro, Joseph P. and Joannie M. Schrof. 1995. "Honor Thy Children." *U.S. News and World Report* (February 27): 39–49.

Singh, Susheela and Jacqueline E. Darroch. 2000. "Adolescent Pregnancy and Childbearing: Levels and Trends in Developed Countries." *Family Planning Perspectives* 32(1): 14–23.

Spiegel, D. 2000. "Suffer the Children: Long-Term Effects of Sexual Abuse." *Society* 37: 18–20.

Statistics Canada. 2004. "Divorces." *The Daily,* May 4.

———. 2005a. "Family Violence in Canada: A Statistical Profile." *The Daily,* July 14.

———. 2005b. "Divorces." *The Daily,* March 9.

———. 2008. "Births." Catalogue no. 84F0210x.

———. 2009. "Family Violence in Canada: A Statistical Profile." Catalogue no. 85-224-XHYPERLINK "http://www.uregina.ca/resolve/PDFs/Family Violence in Canada A Statistical Profile 2009.pdf" http://www.uregina.ca/resolve/PDFs/Family%20Violence%20in%20Canada%20A%20Statistical%20Profile%20%202009.pdf

———. 2012. "Portrait of Families and Living Arrangements in Canada: Families, Households and Marital Status 2011 Census Population." 2011 Census: Analysis Series. Catalogue no. 98-312-X201101.

———. 2013. *The Daily,* June 25. http://www .statcan.gc.ca/daily-quotidien/130625/dq130625b-eng.htm

Stock, J. L., M. A. Bell, D. K. Boyer, and F. A. Connell. 1997. "Adolescent Pregnancy and Sexual Risk-Taking among Sexually Abused Girls." *Family Planning Perspectives* 29: 200–203.

Straus, Murray. 2000. "Corporal Punishment and Primary Prevention of Physical Abuse." *Child Abuse and Neglect* 24: 1109–14.

Thakkar, R. R., P. M. Gutierrez, C. L. Kuczen, and T. R. McCanne. 2000. "History of Physical and/or Sexual Abuse, and Current Suicidality in College Women." *Child Abuse and Neglect* 24: 1345–54.

Thompson, Ross A., and Paul R. Amato. 1999. "The Postdivorce Family: An Introduction to the Issues." Pp. xi–xxiii in *The Postdivorce Family: Children, Parenting, and Society,* edited by R. A. Thompson and P. R. Amato. Thousand Oaks, CA: Sage Publications.

Trocmé, Nico and David Wolfe. 2001. "The Canadian Incidence Study of Reported Child Abuse and Neglect." Pp. 4–14 in *Family Violence in Canada: A Statistical Profile*

2001. Statistics Canada, July. Catalogue no. 85-224-XIE. Ottawa: Minister of Industry.

Trocmé, Nico, et al. 2001. *Canadian Incidence Study of Reported Child Abuse and Neglect: Final Report.* Health Canada. Catalogue no. H49-151/2000E. Ottawa: Minister of Public Works and Government Services.

Turcotte, Pierre. 2003. "Update on Families." *Canadian Social Trends.* pp. 11–15. Catalogue no. 11-008.

Turell, Susan. 2000. "A Descriptive Analysis of Same-Sex Relationship Violence for a Diverse Sample." *Journal of Family Violence* 15(3): 281–93.

UNIFEM (United Nations Development Fund for Women). 2007. http://www.unifem.org/campaigns/trust_fund_10th_anniversary/facts_figures.php?page=4

United Nations Development Programme. 2000. *Human Development Report 2000.* Cary, NC: Oxford University Press.

Vanier Institute of the Family. 2000. *Profiling Canada's Families II.* Nepean, ON: Vanier Institute of the Family.

Venkatesan, J. 2009. "Supreme Court Anguish over Dowry Deaths." *The Hindu.* June 2. http://www.hindu.com/2009/06/02/stories/2009060260980100.htm

Ventura, Stephanie J., Sally C. Curtain, and T. J. Matthews. 2000. "Variations in Teenage Birth Rates, 1991–1998." *National Vital Statistics Reports* 48 (April 24).

Viano, C. Emilio. 1992. "Violence among Intimates: Major Issues and Approaches." Pp. 3–12 in *Intimate Violence: Interdisciplinary Perspectives,* edited by C. E. Viano. Washington, DC: Hemisphere.

Walker, Alexis J. 2001. "Refracted Knowledge: Viewing Families through the Prism of Social Science." Pp. 52–65 in *Understanding Families into the New Millennium: A Decade in Review,* edited by Robert M. Milardo. Minneapolis: National Council on Family Relations.

Wall, Glenda. 2001. "Moral Constructions of Motherhood in Breastfeeding Discourse." *Gender and Society* 15(4): 592–610.

Wherry, Aaron. 2002. "Shelternet.ca Aims to Reach Women across the Country." *The Globe and Mail* (August 13): A18.

Whiffen, V. E., J. M. Thompson, and J. A. Aube. 2000. "Mediators of the Link between Childhood Sexual Abuse and Adult Depressive Symptoms." *Journal of Interpersonal Violence* 15: 1100–20.

WHO (World Health Organization). 2009 (Nov.). Fact Sheet No. 239.

Willis, Diane J., E. Wayne Holden, and Mindy Rosenberg. 1992. "Child Maltreatment Prevention: Introduction and Historical Overview." Pp. 1–14 in *Prevention of Child Maltreatment: Developmental and Ecological Perspectives,* edited by Diane J. Willis,

E. Wayne Holden, and Mindy Rosenberg. New York: John Wiley and Sons.

Chapter 6

Adams, Mary-Louise. 2003 (1997). *The Trouble with Normal: Postwar Youth and the Making of Heterosexuality.* Toronto: University of Toronto Press.

Adler, Jerry. 1994. "Kids Growing Up Scared." *Newsweek* (January 10): 43–50.

Anetzberger, Georgia J., Jill E. Korbin, and Craig Austin. 1994. "Alcoholism and Elder Abuse." *Journal of Interpersonal Violence* 9: 184–93.

Arluke, Arnold, and Jack Levin. 1990. "'Second Childhood': Old Age in Popular Culture." Pp. 261–65 in *Readings on Social Problems,* edited by W. Feigelman. Fort Worth, TX: Holt, Rinehart and Winston.

Arnold, Tom. 1999. "Older Heart-Attack Patients Less Likely to Get Vital Drugs." *National Post* (November 30): A5.

Begley, Sharon. 2000. "The Stereotype Trap." *Newsweek* (November 6): 66–68.

Biggs, Simon. 2003. "Age, Gender, Narratives and Masquerades." *Journal of Aging Studies* 18: 45–58.

Blackburn, Mollie. 2005. "Agency in Borderland Discourses: Examining Language Use in a Community Center with Black Queer Youth." *Teachers College Record* 107(1): 89–103.

Boudreau, François A. 1993. "Elder Abuse." Pp. 142–58 in *Family Violence: Prevention and Treatment,* edited by R. L. Hampton, T. P. Gullota, G. R. Adams, E. H. Potter III, and R. P. Weissberg. Newbury Park, CA: Sage Publications.

Brazzini, D. G., W. D. McIntosh, S. M. Smith, S. Cook, and C. Harris. 1997. "The Aging Woman in Popular Film: Underrepresented, Unattractive, Unfriendly, and Unintelligent." *Sex Roles* 36: 531–43.

Brooks-Gunn, Jeanne and Greg Duncan. 1997. "The Effects of Poverty on Children." *Future of Children* 7(2): 55–70.

Calasanti, Toni. 2004. "Feminist Gerontology and Old Men." *Journal of Gerontology* 59(6): 305–14.

Calasanti, Toni and Neal King. 2005. "Firming the Floppy Penis: Age, Class and Gender Relations in the Lives of Old Men." *Men and Masculinities* 8(1): 3–23.

Canadian Red Cross. 2006. "The Prevalence of Abuse, Harassment and Assault in Young Lives." Accessed June 10, 2006. http://www.redcross.ca/article.asp?id=011147&tid=001

CARP (Canadian Association of Retired Persons). 2002. http://www.fifty-plus.net

CCSD (Canada Council on Social Development). 2006. "Economic Security." *The Progress of Canada's Children and Youth, 2006:* 16–22.

———. 2006b. "Labour Force Profile of Youth." *The Progress of Canada's Children and Youth, 2006:* 77–83.

CIHI (Canadian Institute for Health Information). 2011. *Health Care in Canada, 2011: A Focus on Seniors and Aging.* http://www.cihi.ca/CIHI-ext-portal/internet/EN/document/health+system+performance/quality+of+care+and+outcomes/release_01dec11

Conference Board of Canada. 2013a. "Child Poverty." In *How Canada Performs.* http://www.conferenceboard.ca/hcp/details/society/child-poverty.aspx

———. 2013b. "Elderly Poverty." In *How Canada Performs.* http://www.conferenceboard.ca/hcp/details/society/elderly-poverty.aspx

Covell, Katherine. 2001. *Canada's Nongovernmental Organizations Report.* Submitted for the United Nations General Assembly Special Session September 19–21, 2001 (on behalf of the Canadian Coalition for the Rights of Children), February 2001.

Cowgill, Donald and Lowell Holmes. 1972. *Aging and Modernization.* New York: Appleton-Century-Crofts.

Cummings, Elaine and William Henry. 1961. *Growing Old: The Process of Disengagement.* New York: Basic Books.

DeAngelis, Tori. 1997. "Elderly May Be Less Depressed Than the Young." *APA Monitor* (October). http://www.apa.org/monitor/oct97/elderly.html

DHHS (Department of Health and Human Services). 1998. "Statement of Jeanette Takamura." U.S. Department of Health and Human Services, Administration on Aging. June 8. http://www.aoa.dhhs.gov/pr/graying.html

Dranoff, Linda Silver. 2001. *Everyone's Guide to the Law.* Toronto: HarperCollins Publishers Ltd.

Dube, Francine. 2002. "25% of Households Have Only One Person." *National Post* (October 23): A9.

Duncan, Greg, W. Jean Yeung, Jeanne Brooks-Gunn, and Judith Smith. 1998. "How Much Does Childhood Poverty Affect the Life Chance of Children?" *American Sociological Review* 63: 402–23.

Eisler, Lauren, and Bernard Schissel. 2004. "Privation and Vulnerability to Victimization for Canadian Youth." *Youth Violence and Juvenile Justice* 2(4): 359–73.

Fields, Jason and Kristin Smith. 1998. "Poverty, Family Structure, and Child Well-Being." Population Division. Washington, DC: U.S. Bureau of the Census.

GLARP (Gay and Lesbian Association of Retiring Persons). 2000. http://www.gaylesbianretiring.org/about.htm

Goldberg, Beverly. 2000. *Age Works.* New York: Free Press.

Halberstam, Judith. 2005. *In a Queer Time and Place.* New York: New York University Press.

Harris, Kathleen and Jeremy Marmer. 1996. "Poverty, Paternal Involvement and Adolescent Well-Being." *Journal of Family Issues* 17(5): 614–40.

Health Canada. 1999. *Statistical Report on the Health of Canadians.* December 25. http://www.hc-sc.gc.ca/hppb/phdd/report/state/eng/over.html

Heaphy, Brian, Andrew Yip, and Debbie Thompson. 2004. "Ageing in a Non-Heterosexual Context." *Ageing & Society* 24(6): 881–902.

Kehoe, M. 1989. *Lesbians over 60 Speak for Themselves.* New York: Haworth Press.

Kinsella, K. and C. M. Taeuber. 1993. *An Aging World.* Washington, DC: U.S. Bureau of the Census.

Knoke, David and Arne L. Kalleberg. 1994. "Job Training in U.S. Organizations." *American Sociological Review* 59: 537–46.

Krahn, H. K. and G. S. Lowe. 1993. *Work, Industry, and Canadian Society,* 2nd ed. Scarborough, ON: Nelson.

Lesko, Nancy. 2001. *Act Your Age! A Cultural Construction of Adolescence.* London: Taylor & Francis (Routledge Falmer).

Liao, L. M., et al. 2005. "Experience of Early Pubertal Development: A Preliminary Analysis." *Journal of Reproductive and Infant Psychology* 23(3): 219–33.

Lindsay, Colin. 2000. "Income." Pp. 135–54 in *Women in Canada: A Gender-Based Statistical Report.* Catalogue no. 89-503-XPE. Ottawa: Statistics Canada.

Livni, Ephrat. 2000 (September 21). "Exercise, the Anti-Drug." http://abcnews.go.com/sections/living/Daily/News/depression_elderly000921.htm

Long, Ron. 2001. "Becoming the Men We're Ceasing to Be: A Gay Agenda for Aging in a Youth Culture." *Theology and Sexuality* 15: 94–113.

Lynott, Patricia and Barbara Logue. 1993. "The 'Hurried Child': The Myth of Lost Childhood in Contemporary American Society." *Sociological Forum* 8(3): 471–91.

MacDonald, David and D. Wilson. 2013. *Poverty or Prosperity: Indigenous Children in Canada.* Canadian Centre for Policy Alternatives: Ottawa. Available from https://www.policyalternatives.ca/sites/default/files/uploads/publications/National%20Office/2013/06/Poverty_or_Prosperity_Indigenous_Children.pdf

Massoulay, Karim. 2010. "Participation in Private Retirement Savings Plans, 1997 to 2008." Statistics Canada. Catalogue no. 13F0026M, no. 1.

Matras, Judah. 1990. *Dependency, Obligations, and Entitlements: A New Sociology of Aging, the Life Course, and the Elderly.* Englewood Cliffs, NJ: Prentice-Hall.

Miner, Sonia, John Logan, and Glenna Spitze. 1993. "Predicting Frequency of Senior Center Attendance." *Gerontologist* 33: 650–57.

Morrow, Virginia. 2013. "What's in a Number? Unsettling the Boundaries of Age." *Childhood* 20(2): 151–155

Mouton, Charles, et al. 2001. "Abuse and Neglect in Older Men." *Clinical Gerontologist* 24(3/4): 15–26.

National Council of Welfare. 1998. *Profiles of Welfare: Myths and Realities: A Report by the National Council of Welfare.* Spring. http://www.ncwcnbes.net/htmdocument/reportprowelfare.repprowelfare.htm

Nelson, Adie and Barrie W. Robinson. 2002. *Gender in Canada,* 2nd ed. Toronto: Prentice Hall.

NIH (National Institute of Health). 2000. "Nation's Children Gain Many Areas." NIH news release, July 13. http://www.nih.gov/news/pr/jul2000

Novak, Mark. 1997. *Aging and Society: A Canadian Perspective,* 3rd ed. Scarborough, ON: Nelson.

Peterson, Peter. 2000. "Gray Dawn." Pp. 126–133 in *Social Problems of the Modern World,* edited by Frances Moulder. Belmont, CA: Wadsworth.

PHAC. 2005. "Seniors on the Margins: Aging in Poverty in Canada." Minister of Public Works and Government Services Canada. Catalogue no. H88-5/3-2005.

Pillemer, Karl and Beth Hudson. 1993. "A Model Abuse Prevention Program for Nursing Assistants." *Gerontologist* 33(1): 128–31.

Riedmann, Agnes, Mary Ann Lamanna, and Adie Nelson. 2003. *Marriages and Families.* Toronto: Thomson Nelson.

Riley, Matilda W. and John W. Riley. 1992. "The Lives of Older People and Changing Social Roles." Pp. 220–31 in *Issues in Society,* edited by Hugh Lena, William Helmreich, and William McCord. New York: McGraw-Hill.

Schieber, Sylvester. 2000. "The Global Aging Crisis." *Electric Perspectives* 25: 18–28.

Seeman, Teresa E. and Nancy Adler. 1998. "Older Americans: Who Will They Be?" *National Forum* (Spring): 22–5.

Service Canada. 2013. Old Age Security Pension. http://www.servicecanada.gc.ca/eng/services/pensions/oas/pension/index.shtml

Simon-Rusinowitz, Lori, Constance Krach, Lori Marks, Diane Piktialis, and Laura Wilson. 1996. "Grandparents in the Workplace: the Effects of Economic and Labor Trends." *Generations* 20(1): 41–44.

Statistics Canada. 1998. *Canada Yearbook.* Ottawa: Ministry of Industry.

———. 2002. "2001 Census: Canada." http://www12.statcan.ca/english/census01/products/analytic/companion/age/canada.cf

———. 2004. "Study: Duration of Non-Standard Employment." *The Daily,* December 15.

———. 2005. "Projections of the Aboriginal Populations, Canada, Provinces and Territories 2001 to 2017." Catalogue no. 91-547-XIE. Ottawa.

———. 2006. "A Portrait of Seniors in Canada." Catalogue no. 89-519-XIE: 46.

———. 2007. "Portrait of the Canadian Population in 2006, by Age and Sex, 2006 Census." Catalogue no. 97-551-XIE. Ottawa.

———. 2008. "Canadian Demographics at a Glance." Catalogue no. 91-003-X: 25.

Straka, Sylvia and Lise Montminy. 2006. "Responding to the Needs of Older Women Experiencing Domestic Violence." *Violence against Women* 12(3): 251–67.

Thurow, Lester C. 1996. "The Birth of a Revolutionary Class." *New York Times Magazine* (May 19): 46–47.

Townson, Monica. 1995. *Financial Futures: Mid-Life Prospects for a Secure Retirement.* Ottawa: Canadian Advisory Council on the Status of Women.

———. 2005. "Poverty Issues for Canadian Women." *Gender Equality Consultation.* http://www.swc-cfc. gc.ca/resources/consultations/ges09-2005/poverty_e.html#_ednref17

UNICEF (United Nations International Children's Emergency Fund). 1998. "The First Nearly Universally Ratified Human Rights Treaty in History." *Status.* Washington, DC: UNICEF. http://www.unicef.org/crc/status.html

———. 2005. *Canada: Children Still Waiting.* Florence: Innocenti Research Centre.

Vanier Institute of the Family. 2000. *Profiling Canada's Families II.* Nepean, ON: Vanier Institute of the Family.

Weissberg, Roger P. and Carol Kuster. 1997. "Introduction and Overview: Let's Make Healthy Children 2010 a National Priority." Pp. 1–16 in *Enhancing Children's Well-Being,* edited by Roger Weissberg, Thomas Gullotta, Robert Hampton, Bruce Ryan, and Gerald Adams. Thousand Oaks, CA: Sage Publications.

Wittaker, Terri. 1996. "Violence, Gender and Elder Abuse." Pp. 147–60 in *Violence and Gender Relations: Theories and Interventions,* edited by Brid Featherstone. Thousand Oaks, CA: Sage Publications Inc.

Chapter 7

Adamson, N., L. Briskin, and M. McPhail. 1988. *Feminists Organizing for Change: The Contemporary Women's Movement in Canada.* Don Mills, ON: Oxford University Press.

Anderson, John and Molly Moore. 1998. "The Burden of Womanhood." Pp. 170–75 in *Global Issues 98/99,* edited by Robert Jackson. Guilford, CT: Dushkin/McGraw-Hill.

Anderson, Margaret. 2005. "Thinking about Women." *Gender and Society* 19(4): 437–55.

Armstrong, Pat. 2007. "Back to Basics: Seeking Pay Equity for Women in Canada." *Labour and Industry* 18(2): 11–32.

Atcheson, E., M. Eberts, E. Symes, and J. Stoddart. 1984. *Women and Legal Action.* Ottawa: Canadian Advisory Council on the Status of Women.

Austin, Jonathan D. 2000. "U.N. Report: Women's Unequal Treatment Hurts Economies." CNN.com, September 20. http://www.cnn.com/2000/world/europe/09/20.un.population.report

Bacchi, C. L. 1983. *Liberation Deferred? The Ideas of the English-Canadian Suffragists, 1877–1918.* Toronto: University of Toronto Press.

Baker, Robin, Gary Kriger, and Pamela Riley. 1996. "Time, Dirt and Money: The Effects of Gender, Gender Ideology, and Type of Earner Marriage on Time, Household Task, and Economic Satisfaction among Couples with Children." *Journal of Social Behavior and Personality* 11: 161–77.

Bannon, Lisa. 2000. "Why Girls and Boys Get Different Toys." *The Wall Street Journal,* February 14: B1.

Basow, Susan A. 1992. *Gender: Stereotypes and Roles,* 3rd ed. Pacific Grove, CA: Brooks/Cole.

Begley, Sharon. 2000. "The Stereotype Trap." *Newsweek* (November 6): 66–68.

Bianchi, Susanne M., Melissa A. Milkie, Liana C. Sayer, and John Robinson. 2000. "Is Anyone Doing the Housework? Trends in the Gender Division of Household Labor." *Social Forces* 79: 191–228.

Bittman, Michael and Judy Wajcman. 2000. "The Rush Hour: The Character of Leisure Time and Gender Equity." *Social Forces* 79: 165–89.

Burger, Jerry M. and Cecilia H. Solano. 1994. "Changes in Desire for Control over Time: Gender Differences in a Ten-Year Longitudinal Study." *Sex Roles* 31: 465–72.

Burke, R. J. 1994. "Canadian Business Students' Attitudes towards Women as Managers." *Psychological Reports* 75: 1123–29.

Butler, Judith. 1990. *Gender Trouble.* New York: Routledge.

———. 1993. *Bodies That Matter: On the Discursive Limits of Sex.* New York: Routledge.

Canadian Labour Congress. 2009. "Women's Economic Equality Fact Sheets." Available at http://www.canadianlabour.ca/news-room/publications/womens-economic-equality-fact-sheets

———. 2010. "A Quick Education in Pay Equity—Women's Economic Equality." http://www.canadianlabour.ca/news-room/publications/quick-education-pay-equity-womens-economic-equality

Cassidy, B., R. Lord, and N. Mandell. 1998. "Silenced and Forgotten Women: Race, Poverty, and Disability." Pp. 26–54 in *Feminist*

Issues: Race, Class and Sexuality, 2nd ed., edited by N. Mandell. Scarborough, ON: Prentice Hall Allyn and Bacon Canada.

CAUT (Canadian Association of University Teachers). 2006. "CAUT Survey Shows P.S.E. Gender Inequity Widespread." *Bulletin.* http://www.caut.ca/en/bulletin/issues/2006_apr/news_pse_gender.asp

Cejka, Mary Ann and Alice Eagley. 1999. "Gender Stereotypic Images of Occupations Correspond to the Sex Segregation of Employment." *Personality and Social Psychology Bulletin* 25: 413–23.

Cianni, Mary and Beverly Romberger. 1997. "Life in the Corporation: A Multi-Method Study of the Experiences of Male and Female Asian, Black, Hispanic and White Employees." *Gender, Work and Organization* 4: 116–29.

Cohen, Theodore. 2001. *Men and Masculinity.* Belmont, CA: Wadsworth.

Cornish, M. 2008. "Please Act to End Ontario's Violation of United Nations Human Rights Standards." Open Letter to Premier Dalton McGuinty. Toronto: Equal Pay Coalition: 3.

De Walque, Damien. 2006. *Who Gets AIDS and How?* World Bank Report.

Dranoff, Linda Silver. 2001. *Everyone's Guide to the Law.* Toronto: HarperCollins Publishers Ltd.

Driedger, D. 1993. "Discovering Disabled Women's History." Pp. 173–88 in *And Still We Rise,* edited by L. Carty. Toronto: Women's Press.

England, Paula and Su Li. 2006. "Desegregation Stalled: The Changing Gender Composition of College Majors, 1971–2002." *Gender & Society* 20: 657–677.

Errington, J. 1993. "Pioneers and Suffragists." Pp. 59–91 in *Changing Patterns: Women in Canada,* 2nd ed., edited by S. Burt, L. Code, and L. Dorney. Toronto: McClelland & Stewart Inc.

Evans, Lorraine and Kimberly Davies. 2000. "No Sissy Boys Here." *Sex Roles* (February): 255–71.

Fausto-Sterling, Anne. 2000. *Sexing the Body.* New York: Basic Books.

Fitzgerald, Louise F. and Sandra L. Shullman. 1993. "Sexual Harassment: A Research Analysis and Agenda for the '90s." *Journal of Vocational Behavior* 40: 5–27.

Fitzpatrick, Catherine. 2000. "Modern Image of Masculinity Changes with Rise of New Celebrities." *Detroit News,* June 24. http://detnews.com/2000/religion/0006/24

Foerstel, Karen. 2008. "Women's Rights: Are Violence and Discrimination against Women Declining?" *Global Researcher* 2(5): 115–147.

Frank, J. 1994. "Voting and Contributing: Political Participation in Canada." Pp. 333–57 in *Canadian Social Trends: A Canadian Studies Reader* 2. Toronto: Thompson Educational Publishing.

Goldberg, Stephanie. 1997. "Making Room for Daddy." *American Bar Association Journal* 83: 48–52.

Gruenbaum, Ellen. 2005. "Socio-Cultural Dynamics of Female Genital Cutting: Research Findings, Gaps and Directions." *Culture, Health and Sexuality* 7(5): 429–41.

Guy M. E. and M. A. Newman. 2004. "Women's Jobs, Men's Jobs: Sex Segregation and Emotional Labor." *Public Administration Review* 64(3): 289–298.

Henslin, J. and A. Nelson. 1997. *Essentials of Sociology.* Scarborough, ON: Allyn and Bacon.

Hochschild, Arlie. 1989. *The Second Shift: Working Patterns and the Revolution at Home.* New York: Viking Penguin.

Hunter, A. and M. Denton. 1984. "Do Female Candidates 'Lose' Votes?" *Canadian Review of Sociology and Anthropology* 2: 395–406.

International Labour Organization. 2009 (March). *Global Employment Trends for Women.* Available at http://www.ilo.org

———. 2011a. *Equality at Work: The Continuing Challenge.* Available at http://www.ilo.org

———. 2011b. *Global Unemployment Trends 2011.* Available at http://www.ilo.org

IPC. 2008. "Gender, Labour, Markets and Poverty: an overview." Poverty in Focus. Vol 13. January 2008. Available from www.amherst.edu/system/files/media/0100/IPCPovertyInFocus13.pdf

ITUC (International Trade Union Commission). 2009. *Gender (In)Equality in the Labour Market: An Overview of Global Trends and Development.* Available at http://ituc-csi.org

IWRP (International Women's Right's Project). 2000. "The First CEDAW Impact Study." http://www.yorku.ca/iwrp/cedawReport

Kalb, Claudia. 2000. "What Boys Really Want." *Newsweek,* July 2. http://www.msnbc.com/news/428301.asp

Kenworthy, Lane and Melissa Malami. 1999. "Gender Inequality in Political Representation: A Worldwide Comparative Analysis." *Social Forces* 78: 235–69.

Kessler, Suzanne and Wendy McKenna. 1978. *Gender: An Ethnomethodological Approach.* Chicago: University of Chicago Press.

Kilbourne, Barbara S., George Farkas, Kurt Beron, Dorothea Weir, and Paula England. 1994. "Returns to Skill, Compensating Differentials, and Gender Bias: Effects of Occupational Characteristics on the Wages of White Women and Men." *American Journal of Sociology* 100: 689–719.

Klein, Matthew. 1997. "Blue Jeans." *American Demographics* (August): 23.

———. 1998. "Women's Trip to the Top." *American Demographics* (February): 22.

Leeman, Sue. 2000 (September 20). "The More Things Change . . ." ABC News.

Leo, John. 1997. "Fairness? Promises, Promises." *U.S. News and World Report* 123(4): 18.

Long, J. Scott, Paul D. Allison, and Robert McGinnis. 1993. "Rank Advancement in Academic Careers: Sex Differences and the Effects of Productivity." *American Sociological Review* 58: 703–22.

Lorber, Judith. 1998. "Night to His Day." Pp. 213–20 in *Reading between the Lines,* edited by Amanda Konradi and Martha Schmidt. Mountain View, CA: Mayfield Publishing.

Macklin, A. 1992. "*Symes v. M.N.R.:* Where Sex Meets Class." *Canadian Journal of Women and the Law* 5: 498.

Mandell, N. 1995. "Introduction." Pp. vii–xxi in *Feminist Issues: Race, Class and Sexuality.* Scarborough, ON: Prentice Hall Allyn and Bacon Canada.

Marini, Margaret Mooney and Pi-Ling Fan. 1997. "The Gender Gap in Earnings at Career Entry." *American Sociological Review* 62: 588–604.

Martin, Patricia Yancey. 1992. "Gender, Interaction, and Inequality in Organizations." Pp. 20–31 in *Gender, Interaction, and Inequality,* edited by Cecilia Ridgeway. New York: Springer-Verlag.

Mensch, Barbara and Cynthia Lloyd. 1997. "Gender Differences in the Schooling of Adolescents in Low-Income Countries: The Case of Kenya." *Policy Research Working Paper no. 95.* New York: Population Council.

Monsebratten, Laurie and Alex Ballingall. 2013. "Daycare Crisis: Ontario Inspections Reveal Numerous Violations." *Toronto Star* (November 23). Available at http://www.thestar.com/news/gta/2013/11/23/day-care_crisis_ontario_inspections_reveal_numerous_violations.html

Mossman, Mary Jane. 1997. *Readings on Law, Gender, Equality.* Materials prepared for the study use of students at Osgoode Hall School of Law of York University.

———. 1998. "The Paradox of Feminist Engagement with Law." Pp. 180–207 in *Feminist Issues: Race, Class, and Sexuality,* edited by N. Mandell. Scarborough, ON: Prentice Hall Allyn and Bacon Canada.

National Post. 1999. "Job Ad Seeking Only Women Draws Criticism." (August 6): A4.

NCFM (National Coalition of Free Men). 1998. "Historical." Manhasset, NY: NCFM. http://ncfm.org

Nelson, Adie and Barrie W. Robinson. 2002. *Gender in Canada,* 2nd ed. Toronto: Pearson Education Canada.

Olson, Josephine E., Irene H. Frieze, and Ellen G. Detlefsen. 1990. "Having It All? Combining Work and Family in a Male and a Female Profession." *Sex Roles* 23: 515–34.

Padavic, Irene and Barbara Reskin. 2002. *Women and Men at Work,* 2nd ed. Thousand Oaks, CA: Pine Forge Press.

Pew Research Centre. 2007. "Fewer Mothers Prefer Full Time Work." Available at: http://www.pewsocialtrends.org/files/2010/10/WomenWorking.pdf

Pollock, William. 2000a. *Real Boys' Voices.* New York: Random House.

———. 2000b. "The Columbine Syndrome." *National Forum* 80: 39–42.

Population Reference Bureau. 1999. "World Population: More Than Just Numbers." Washington, DC. http://www.prb.org

Purcell, Piper and Lara Stewart. 1990. "Dick and Jane in 1989." *Sex Roles* 22: 177–85.

Rabin, Sarah. 2000. "Feminists Take CEDAW into Our Own Hands." National Organization for Women. http://63111.42.146/cgs/gs_article.asp?ArticleD=1863

Reid, Pamela T. and Lillian Comas-Diaz. 1990. "Gender and Ethnicity: Perspectives on Dual Status." *Sex Roles* 22: 397–408.

Robinson, John P. and Suzanne Bianchi. 1997. "The Children's Hours." *American Demographics* (December): 1–6.

Rosenberg, Janet, Harry Perlstadt, and William Phillips. 1997. "Now That We Are Here: Discrimination, Disparagement, and Harassment at Work and the Experience of Women Lawyers." Pp. 247–59 in *Workplace/Women's Place,* edited by Dana Dunn. Los Angeles: Roxbury.

Rubenstein, Carin. 1990. "A Brave New World." *New Woman* 20(10): 158–64.

Sadker, Myra and David Sadker. 1990. "Confronting Sexism in the College Classroom." Pp. 176–87 in *Gender in the Classroom: Power and Pedagogy,* edited by S. L. Gabriel and I. Smithson. Chicago: University of Illinois Press.

Sapiro, Virginia. 1994. *Women in American Society.* Mountain View, CA: Mayfield.

Schneider, Margaret and Susan Phillips. 1997. "A Qualitative Study of Sexual Harassment of Female Doctors by Patients." *Social Science and Medicine* 45: 669–76.

Schroeder, K. A., L. L. Blood, and D. Maluso. 1993. "Gender Differences and Similarities between Male and Female Undergraduate Students Regarding Expectations for Career and Family Roles." *College Student Journal* 27: 237–49.

Schwalbe, Michael. 1996. *Unlocking the Iron Cage: The Men's Movement, Gender Politics, and American Culture.* New York: Oxford University Press.

Sheehan, Molly. 2000. "Women Slowly Gain Ground in Politics." Pp. 152–53 in *Vital Signs: The Environmental Trends That Are Shaping Our Future,* edited by Linda Starke. New York: W. W. Norton Company.

Signorielli, Nancy. 1998. "Reflections of Girls in the Media: A Content Analysis across Six Media." *Overview.* http://childrennow.org/media/mc97/ReflectSummary.html

Singh, Parbudyai and Ping Peng. 2010. "Canada's Bold Experiment with Pay Equity." *Women in Management* 25(7): 570–585.

Smolken, Rachael. 2000. "Girls SAT Scores Still Lag Boys." *Post Gazette.* http://www.post-gazette.com/headlines/20000830sat2.asp

Social Watch. 2009. "Gender: 20th Century Debts, 21st Century Shame." *Social Watch Report 2009.* Available at http://www.socialwatch.org

———. 2011. *Social Watch Report 2010: After the Fall.* Available at http://www.socialwatch.org

Sommers, Christina Hoff. 2000. *The War against Boys: How Misguided Feminism Is Harming Young Men.* New York: Simon and Schuster.

Stark, R. 1992. *Sociology,* 4th ed. Belmont, CA: Wadsworth.

Statistics Canada. 1998. "1996 Census: Labour Force Activity, Occupation and Industry, Place of Work, Mode of Transportation to Work, Unpaid Work." *The Daily,* March 17. http://www.statcan.ca/Daily/English/980317/d980317.htm

———. 1999. *The Daily,* April 14. http://www.statcan.ca/Daily/English/990417/d990417.htm

———. 2001. "Impact of Smoking on Life Expectancy and Disability." *The Daily,* June 22. http://www.statcan.ca/Daily/English/010622/d010622a.htm

———. 2003a. "The Changing Profile of Canada's Labour Force." *2001 Census: Analysis Series.* Catalogue no. 96F0030XIE2001009 (released February 11, 2003), p. 36.

———. 2003b. "Earnings of Canadians: Making a Living in New Economy." Catalogue no. 96F0030XIE2001013. http://www12.statcan.ca/english/census01/Products/Analytic/companion/earn/charts/menwom.cfm

———. 2006. *Women in Canada, 5th Edition: A Gender-Based Statistical Report.* Catalogue no. 0010589-503- XIE.

———. 2011. "Education Indicators in Canada: Doctoral Students and University Teaching Staff." Catalogue no. 81-599-X (006): 4.

Sullivan, Nikki. 2003. *A Critical Introduction to Queer Theory.* New York: New York University Press.

Tannen, Deborah. 1990. *You Just Don't Understand: Women and Men in Conversation.* New York: Ballantine Books.

Tepperman, Lorne and Jim Curtis. 2004. *Social Problems: A Canadian Perspective.* Toronto: Oxford.

Tomaskovic-Devey, Donald. 1993. "The Gender and Race Composition of Jobs and the Male/Female, White/Black Pay Gap." *Social Forces* 72(1): 45–76.

Turner, William. 2000. *A Genealogy of Queer Theory.* Philadelphia: Temple University Press.

United Nations. 2000a. "Convention on the Elimination of All Forms of Discrimination against Women." http://un.org/womenwatch/daw/cedaw

———. 2000b. "Strengthening Women's Economic Capacity." United Nations Development Fund for Women. http://www.unifem. undp.org/economic.htm

———. 2005a. *Human Development Report 2005.* New York: UN Development Programme.

———. 2005b. *Progress towards the Millennium Development Goals.* New York: UN Development Programme.

———. 2013. *Human Development Report 2013.* New York: UN Development Programme.

Van Willigen, Marieke and Patricia Drentea. 1997. "Benefits of Equitable Relationships: The Impact of Sense of Failure, Household Division of Labor, and Decision-Making Power on Social Support." Presented at the Meeting of the American Sociological Association, Toronto, August.

Whitla, W. 1995. "A Chronology of Women in Canada." Pp. 315–53 in *Feminist Issues: Race, Class and Sexuality,* edited by N. Mandell. Scarborough, ON: Prentice Hall Canada.

WHO (World Health Organization). 2006. *Gender and Women's Mental Health.* Available at http://www.who.int/mental_health

Wilkins, K. 1996. "Causes of Death: How the Sexes Differ." *Canadian Social Trends* 41: 11–17.

Williams, John E. and Deborah L. Best. 1990. *Measuring Sex Stereotypes: A Multination Study.* London: Sage Publications.

Wilmot, Alyssa. 1999. "First National Love Your Body Day a Big Success." Press release. *National Organization for Women Newsletter* (Winter). http://www.now.org

Wine, J. D. and J. L. Ristock (eds.). 1991. "Introduction: Feminist Activism in Canada." Pp. 1–18 in *Women and Social Change: Feminist Activism in Canada.* Toronto: James Lorimer.

WIN (Women's International Network) News. 2000. "Reports from around the World." (Autumn): 50–58.

Witt, S. D. 1996. "Traditional or Androgynous: An Analysis to Determine Gender Role Orientation of Basal Readers." *Child Study Journal* 26: 303–18.

Wittig, Monique. 1992. *The Straight Mind.* New York: Beacon Press.

World Bank. 2001. "Engendering Development." World Bank Policy Research Report.

http://www.worldbank.org/gender/pur/newsummary.htm

Yamaguchi, Mari. 2000. "Female Government Workers Face Harassment." http://news.excite.com/news/ap/001227/05/int.Japan

Yumiko, Ehara. 2000. "Feminism's Growing Pains." *Japan Quarterly* 47: 41–48.

Zhang, Xuelin. 2009. "Earnings of Women with and Without Children," *Perspectives on Labour and Income* (10)3: March. Statistics Canada Catalogue no. 75-001-XIE.

Zimmerman, Marc A., Laurel Copeland, Jean Shope, and T. E. Dielman. 1997. "A Longitudinal Study of Self-Esteem: Implications for Adolescent Development." *Journal of Youth and Adolescence* 26(2): 117–41.

Chapter 8

Abella, Irving. 1999. "Anti-Semitism." P. 90 in *The Canadian Encyclopedia: Year 2000 Edition*, edited by James H. Marsh. Toronto: McClelland & Stewart Inc.

Abella, Irving and H. Troper. 1998. *None Is Too Many: Canada and the Jews of Europe, 1933–1948*. Toronto: Lester Publishing.

Agnew, Vijay. 2007. "The Conundrum of Inclusion: Racialized Women in Public Policy Reports." In *Racialized Migrant Women in Canada: Essays on Health, Violence and Equity*, edited by Vijay Agnew. Toronto: University of Toronto Press.

Balthazar, Louis. 1997. "Quebec and the Idea of Federalism." An Occasional Paper. Montreal: McGill Institute for the Study of Canada, pp. 1–8.

Bannerji, Himani. 2000. "The Paradox of Diversity: The Construction of a Multicultural Canada and 'Women of Colour.'" *Women's Studies International Forum* 23(5): 537–60.

Beaudoin, Gerald A. 1999. "Keegstra Case." Pp. 1237 in *The Canadian Encyclopedia: Year 2000 Edition*, edited by James H. Marsh. Toronto: McClelland & Stewart Inc.

Behiels, M. D. 1999. "Francophone-Anglophone Relations." Pp. 909–13 in *The Canadian Encyclopedia: Year 2000 Edition*, edited by James H. Marsh. Toronto: McClelland & Stewart Inc.

Bergman, Brian. 1993. "A Break with Custom." *Maclean's* 106(34): 16.

Bibby, Reginald W. 2007 (August 29). Racial Intermarriage: Canada and the U.S. *Canada Press Release*, University of Lethbridge. http://www.reginaldbibby.com/datahighlights.html

Blackwell, Tom. 2002. "Racial Tension Peaked after Sept. 11 Attacks." *National Post* (July 16): A7.

Boyd, Monica. 2000. "Canada's Refugees Flows: Gender Inequality." *Canadian Social Trends* 3: 84–87. Toronto: Thompson Educational Publishing.

Breton, R. 1988. "French-English Relations." Pp. 557–85 in *Understanding Canadian Society*, edited by J. E. Curtis and L. Tepperman. Toronto: McGraw-Hill Ryerson Limited.

Bricker, Darrell and Edward Greenspon. 2001. *Searching for Certainty: Inside the New Canadian Mindset*. Toronto: Doubleday Canada.

Chan, Janet. 2011. "Racial Profiling and Police Subculture." *Criminology and Criminal Justice* 53(1): 75–78.

Chui, T., Kelly Tran, and Helene Maheux. 2007. "Immigration in Canada: A Portrait of the Foreign-Born Population: 2006 Census." Statistics Canada. Catalogue no.97-557-X: 37.

CIC (Citizenship and Immigration Canada). 2012. *Canada Facts and Figures: Immigration Overview Permanent and Temporary Residents*. Produced by Research and Evaluation Branch and Citizenship and Immigration Canada. Ottawa. http://www.cic.gc.ca/english/resources/statistics/menu-fact.asp

Claxton-Oldfield, Stephen and Sheila M. Keefe. 1999. "Assessing Stereotypes about the Innu of Davis Inlet, Labrador." *Canadian Journal of Behavioural Sciences* 31(2): 86–91.

Cohen, Mark Nathan. 1998. "Culture, Not Race, Explains Human Diversity." *Chronicle of Higher Education* 44(32): B4–B5.

Collins, F. S. 2004. "What We Do and Don't Know about 'Race,' 'Ethnicity,' Genetics and Health at the Dawn of the Genome Era." *Nature Genetics Supplement* 36(11): s13–s15.

Columbo, J. R. 1986. *1001 Questions about Canada*. Toronto: Doubleday.

Conley, Dalton. 1999. *Being Black, Living in the Red: Race, Wealth, and Social Policy in America*. Berkeley: University of California Press.

Craufurd-Lewis, M. 1999. "Nunavut." P. 1686 in *The Canadian Encyclopedia: Year 2000 Edition*, edited by James H. Marsh. Toronto: McClelland & Stewart Inc.

Day, R. 1998. "Constructing the Official Canadian: A Genealogy of the Mosaic Metaphor in State Policy Discourse." *Topia* 2: 42–66.

Deziel, Shanda and Amy Cameron. 2001/2002. "Overbites." *Maclean's* (December 31-January 7): 11.

Doerr, A. 1999. "Royal Commission on Aboriginal Peoples." Pp. 3–4 in *The Canadian Encyclopedia: Year 2000 Edition*, edited by James H. Marsh. Toronto: McClelland & Stewart Inc.

Donakowski, D. W. and V. M. Esses. 1996. "Native Canadians, First Nations, or Aboriginals: The Effects of Labels on Attitudes toward Native Peoples." *Canadian Journal of Behavioural Science* 28: 86–91.

Driedger, L. 1999. "Prejudice and Discrimination." Pp. 1888–92 in *The Canadian Encyclopedia: Year 2000 Edition*, edited by James H. Marsh. Toronto: McClelland & Stewart Inc.

Esses, Victoria, et al. 2002. "Public Attitudes toward Immigration in the United States and Canada in Response to the September 11, 2001 'Attack of America.'" *Analyses of Social Issues and Public Policy* 2(1): 69–85.

Etzioni, Amitai. 1997. "New Issues: Rethinking Race." *Public Perspective* (June-July): 39–40. May 11, 1998. http://www.ropercenter.unconn.edu/pubper/pdf/!84b.htm

Fitzhugh, T. V. 1991. *The Dictionary of Genealogy*, 3rd ed. London: A. and C. Black.

Ford, Chandra and Collins O. Airhihenbuwa. 2010. "Critical Race Theory, Race Equity, and Public Health: Toward Antiracism Praxis." *American Journal of Public Health* 100(S1): s30–s35.

Frideres, J. S. 1993. "Health Promotion and Indian Communities: Social Support or Social Disorganization." Pp. 269–95 in *Racial Minorities, Medicine and Health*, edited by B. Singh Bolaria and R. Bolaria. Halifax: Fernwood.

Gaertner, Samuel L. and John F. Dovidio. 2000. *Reducing Intergroup Bias: The Common Ingroup Identity Model*. Philadelphia: Taylor & Francis Group.

Goonewardena, Kanishka and Stefan Kipfer. 2005. "Spaces of Difference: Reflections from Toronto on Multiculturalism, Bourgeois Urbanism and the Possibility of a Radical Urban Politics." *International Journal of Urban and Regional Research* 29(3): 670–78.

Granastein, Ron. 2002. "Al-Qaida's Here." *Toronto Sun* (September 6): 4.

Guillebeau, Christopher. 1999. "Affirmative Action in a Global Perspective: The Cases of South Africa and Brazil." *Sociological Spectrum* 19(4): 443–65.

Guinier, Lani. 1998. Interview with Paula Zahn. *CBS Evening News*, July 18.

Gurin, Patricia. 1999. "New Research on the Benefits of Diversity in College and Beyond: An Empirical Analysis." *Diversity Digest* (Spring): 5–15.

Healey, Joseph F. 1997. *Race, Ethnicity, and Gender in the United States: Inequality, Group Conflict, and Power*. Thousand Oaks, CA: Pine Forge Press.

Health Canada. 1999. *Toward a Healthy Future: Second Report on the Health of Canadians*. Prepared by the Federal, Provincial, and Territorial Advisory Committee of Population Health for the Meeting of Ministers of Health, Charlottetown, PEI, September.

Henry, Frances and Carol Tator. 1985. "Racism in Canada: Social Myths and Strategies for Change." Pp. 321–35 in *Ethnicity and Ethnic Relations in Canada*, 2nd ed., edited by Rita M. Bienvenue and Jay E.Goldstein. Toronto: Butterworths.

———. 2011. "Rejoinder to Satzewich and Shaffir on 'Racism versus Professionalism: Claims and Counter Claims about Racial Profiling.'" *Canadian Journal of Criminology and Criminal Justice* 53(1): 65–74.

Henry, Frances, Carol Tator, Winston Mattis, and Tim Rees. 1995. *The Colour of Democracy.* Toronto: Harcourt Brace.

hooks, bell. 2000. *Where We Stand: Class Matters.* New York: Routledge.

Horwood, Harold. 1969. *Newfoundland.* Toronto: Macmillan.

Humphreys, Debra. 1999. "Diversity and the College Curriculum: How Colleges & Universities Are Preparing Students for a Changing World." *DiversityWeb.* http://www.inform.umd.edu/EdRes/Topic/Di...Leadersguide/CT/curriculum_briefing.html

Janigan, Mary. 2002. "Immigrants." *Maclean's* (December 16): 10–25.

Jensen, Derrick. 2001. "Saving the Indigenous Soul: An Interview with Martin Prechtel." *The Sun* 304 (April): 4–15.

Keita, S. O. Y. and Rick A. Kittles. 1997. "The Persistence of Racial Thinking and the Myth of Racial Divergence." *American Anthropologist* 99(3): 534–44.

Kilfeather, Siobhán Marie. 2005. *Dublin: A Cultural History.* London and New York: Oxford University Press.

Kilgour, David. 1988. *Uneasy Patriots: Western Canadians in Confederation.* Edmonton: Lone Pine Press.

Kunz, Jean Lock, Anne Milan, and Sylvain Schetagne. 2000. *Unequal Access: A Canadian Profile of Racial Differences in Education, Employment & Income.* Toronto: Canadian Race Relations Foundation. http://www.crr.ca

KW Record. 2002. "Feeling the Backlash." *Kitchener-Waterloo Record* (September 3): C11.

Leggon, Cheryl B. 1999. "Introduction: Race and Ethnicity—A Global Perspective." *Sociological Spectrum* 19(4): 381–85.

Levin, Jack and Jack McDevitt. 1995. "Landmark Study Reveals Hate Crimes Vary Significantly by Offender Motivation." *Klanwatch Intelligence Report* (August): 7–9.

Maclean's. 1999. "What Makes a Canadian?" (December 20): 45–48.

———. 2001/2002. "Since Sept. 11: The Responses Show How Terrorism and War Have Left Their Mark." (December 31-January 7): 38–39.

Marger, Martin N. 2000. *Race and Ethnic Relations: American and Global Perspectives,* 5th ed. Belmont, CA: Wadsworth.

Melchers, Ron. 2011. "Comment on the Rejoinder of Henry and Tator to Satzevich and Shaffir." *Canadian Journal of Criminology and Criminal Justice* 53(1): 105–111.

Milan, A., Helene Maheux, and Tina Chui. 2010 (April 20). "A Portrait of Couples in Mixed Unions." Statistics Canada. Ottawa. *Canadian Social Trends:* 70–80.

Miles, Robert, and Malcolm Brown. 2003. *Racism,* 2nd ed. New York: Routledge Press.

Molnar, Stephen. 1983. *Human Variation: Races, Types, and Ethnic Groups,* 2nd ed. Englewood Cliffs, NJ: Prentice-Hall.

Momen, Rayna A. 2008. "Empirical Study of Hate Crimes in the United States: A Systematic Test of Levin and McDevitt's Typology of Offenders." Unpublished Master's Thesis, West Virginia University. UMI no.1458752.

Mosher, Clayton J. 1998. *Discrimination and Denial: Systemic Racism in Ontario's Legal and Criminal Justice System, 1892–1961.* Toronto: University of Toronto Press.

Nash, Manning. 1962. "Race and the Ideology of Race." *Current Anthropology* 3: 258–88.

National Post. 1999a. "StatsCan Debates: How Canadian Are We?" (November 30): A1.

———. 1999b. "Conditions Curtail Quebec's Right to Self-Determination." (December 11): A11.

———. 1999c. "Clarity Act Fails to Arouse Separatist Sentiments." (December 15): A7.

Nestel, Sheryl. 2012. "Colour Coded Healthcare: The Impacts of Race and Racism on Canadians' Health." Produced by Wellesley Institute. Available at http://www.wellesleyinstitute.com/wp-content/uploads/2012/02/Colour-Coded-Health-Care.pdf

Niemonen, Jack. 1999. "Deconstructing Cultural Pluralism." *Sociological Spectrum* 19(4): 401–19.

Noh, S. and M. Belser. 1999. "Perceived Racial Discrimination, Depression, and Coping: A Study of Southeast Asian Refugees in Canada." *Journal of Health and Social Behavior* 40(3): 193–207.

Porter, John. 1965. *The Vertical Mosaic: An Analysis of Social Class and Power in Canada.* Toronto: University of Toronto Press.

Race Relations Reporter. 1999. Volume VII (8), October 15. New York: CH II Publishers, Inc. 200 West 57th St., New York, NY 10019.

Ray, Peter. 2002. "Arabs, Muslims Still Live in Fear of Attacks." *Toronto Star* (March 23): A20.

Roberts, J. 1995. "Disproportionate Harm: Hate Crime in Canada." http://ftp.nizkor.org/hweb/orgs/Canadian/canada/justice/disproportionate-harm

Rowe, Frederick W. 1977. *Extinction: The Beothuks of Newfoundland.* Toronto: McGraw-Hill Ryerson.

Satzewich, Vic and William Shaffir. 2009. "Racism versus Professionalism: Claims and Counter-claims about Racial Profiling." *Canadian Journal of Criminology and Criminal Justice* 51(2): 199–226.

Schaefer, Richard T. 1998. *Racial and Ethnic Groups,* 7th ed. New York: HarperCollins.

Sher, J. 1983. *White Hoods: Canada's Ku Klux Klan.* Vancouver: New Star Books.

Shipler, David K. 1998. "Subtle vs. Overt Racism." *Washington Spectator* 24 (March 15): 1–3.

Snider, Katherine. 1996. "Race and Sexual Orientation: The (Im)Possibility of These Intersections on Educational Policy." *Harvard Educational Review* 66(2): 294–302.

Statistics Canada. 1998. "1996 Census: Ethnic Origin, Visible Minorities." *The Daily,* February 17. http://www.statcan.ca/Daily/English/980217/d980217/d980217.htm

———. 2003a. "Canada's Ethnocultural Portrait: The Changing Mosaic." 2001 Census: Analysis Series. Catalogue no. 96F0030X-IE2001008.

———. 2003b. "Census of a Population: Immigration, Birthplace, Birthplace of Parents, Citizenship, Ethnic Origin, Visible Minorities and Aboriginal Peoples." *The Daily,* January 21. http://www.statcan.ca/Daily/English/030121/d030121.htm

———. 2003c. "Earnings of Canadians: Making a Living in the New Economy." Catalogue no. 96F0030XIE2001013. http://www12.statcan.ca/english/census01/Products/Analytic/companion/earn/charts/menwom.cfm

———. 2008a. "2006 Census: Ethnic Origin, Visible Minorities, Place of Work and Mode of Transportation." *The Daily,* April 2. http://www.statcan.gc.ca/daily-quotidien/080402/dq080402a-eng.htm

———. 2008c. "Canada's Ethnocultural Mosaic: 2006 Census," Census Year 2006. Ottawa. Catalogue no. 97-562-X.

———. 2009. "Earnings and Incomes of Canadians over the Past Quarter Century: 2006 Census: Earnings." Ottawa. Catalogue 97-563-X.

Stodolska, M. and E. L. Jackson. 1998. "Discrimination in Leisure and Work Experience by a White Ethnic Minority Group." *Journal of Leisure Research* 30(1): 23–41

Such, P. 1978. *The Vanished People: The Beothuk People of Newfoundland.* Toronto: NC Press.

Thompson, Becky. 2001. *A Promise and a Way of Life: White Antiracist Activism.* Minneapolis: University of Minnesota Press.

Weiner, Nan. 2001. "Employment Barriers Still Block Aboriginals & Visible Minorities." *CAUT Bulletin* (April): A9, A10.

Wheeler, Michael L. 1994. *Diversity Training: A Research Report.* New York: The Conference Board.

Williams, Eddie N. and Milton D. Morris. 1993. "Racism and Our Future." Pp. 417–24 in *Race in America: The Struggle for Equality,* edited by Herbert Hill and James E. Jones Jr. Madison: University of Wisconsin Press.

Winks, Robin W. 1999. "Slavery." P. 2174 in *The Canadian Encyclopedia Year 2000 Edition,* edited by James H. Marsh. Toronto: McClelland & Stewart Inc.

Wood, Patricia and Liette Gilbert. 2005. "Multiculturalism in Canada: Accidental Discourse, Alternative Vision, Urban Practice." *International Journal of Urban and Regional Research* 29(3): 679–91.

Wortly, S. and Akwasi Owusu-Bempah. 2011. "The Usual Suspects: Police Stop and Search Practices in Canada." *Policing & Society* 21(4): 395–407.

Zack, Naomi. 1998. *Thinking about Race.* Belmont, CA: Wadsworth Publishing Co.

Zamudio, Margaret, Caskey Russell, Francisco Rios, and Jacquelyn L. Bridgeman, eds. 2011. *Critical Race Theory Matters: Education and Ideology.* New York: Routledge.

Zine, Jasmin. 2002. "Inclusive Schooling in a Plural Society: Removing the Margins." *Education Canada* 42(3): 36–39.

Chapter 9

Anderssen, Erin. 1999. "Gay-Bashing Preacher Calls Off Protest." *The Globe and Mail,* June 29. http://www.egale.ca/archives/press/9906299gm.htm

Angelides, S. 1995. "Rethinking the Political: Poststructuralism and the Economy of (Hetero)Sexuality." *Critical Inqueeries* 1(1): 27–46.

Arnold, Tom. 2002. "Common-Law Families on the Rise." *National Post* (October 23): A9.

Arnup, Katherine (ed.). 1995. *Lesbian Parenting: Living with Pride and Prejudice.* Charlottetown, PEI: gynergy books.

Associated Press. 2001. "Vancouver Gay Man Beaten to Death: Police Suspect Hate Crime." http://www.planetqnews.com/0812/11.shtml

Baldwin, Tammy. 2000. "Never Doubt." Speech delivered at Millennium March, Washington, DC, April 2000.

Bayer, Ronald. 1987. *Homosexuality and American Psychiatry: The Politics of Diagnosis,* 2nd ed. Princeton, NJ: Princeton University Press.

Benkov, Laura. 1994. *Reinventing the Family: The Emerging Story of Gay and Lesbian Parents.* New York: Crown Publishers.

Besen, Wayne. 2000. "Introduction." In Human Rights Campaign, *Feeling Free: Personal Stories: How Love and Self-Acceptance Saved Us from "Ex-Gay" Ministries,* p. 7. Washington, DC: Human Rights Campaign Foundation.

Bornstein, Kate. 1994. *Gender Outlaw: On Men, Women, and the Rest of Us.* New York: Routledge.

Brannock, J. C. and B. E. Chapman. 1990. "Negative Sexual Experiences with Men among Heterosexual Women and Lesbians." *Journal of Homosexuality* 19: 105–10.

"Brazilian Killers Sentenced." 2001. PlanetOut.com, February 15. http://www.planetout.com/news/article-print.html?2001/02/15/1

Bricker, Darrell and Edward Greenspon. 2001. *Searching for Certainty: Inside the New Canadian Mindset.* Toronto: Doubleday Canada.

Bullough, Vern L. 2000. "Transgenderism and the Concept of Gender." *International Journal of Transgenderism.* Special issue 4 (July-September).

Bush, Irene R. and Anthony Sainz. 2001. "Competencies at the Intersection of Difference, Tolerance, and Prevention of Hate Crimes." Pp. 205–24 in *From Hate Crimes to Human Rights: A Tribute to Matthew Shepard,* edited by Mary E. Swigonski and Robin S. Mama. New York: Haworth Press.

Butler, Amy C. 2000. "Trends in Same-Gender Sexual Partnering, 1988–1998." *The Journal of Sex Research* 37(4): 333–43.

Butler, Judith. 1990. *Gender Trouble.* New York: Routledge.

———. 1993. *Bodies That Matter: On the Discursive Limits of 'Sex.'* New York: Routledge.

Button, James W., Barbara A. Rienzo, and Kenneth D. Wald. 1997. *Private Lives, Public Conflicts: Battles over Gay Rights in American Communities.* Washington, DC: CQ Press.

Chase, Bob. 2000. "NEA President Bob Chase's Historic Speech from 2000 GLSEN Conference." http://www.glsen.org/templates/resources/record.html?section=14&record=255

"Constitutional Protection." 1999. GayLawNet, February 14. http://www.nexus.net.au/~dba/news.html#top

Craig, Kellina M. 2002. "Examining Hate-Motivated Aggression: A Review of the Social Psychological Literature on Hate Crimes as a Distinct Form of Aggression." *Aggression & Violent Behavior* 7 (January-February): 85–101.

Dawson, Lorne. 1993. "Religion and Legitimacy." Pp. 311–27 in *Contemporary Sociology: Critical Perspectives,* edited by Peter S. Li and B. Singh Bolaria. Toronto: Copp Clark Pitman.

De Cecco, John P. and D. A. Parker. 1995. "The Biology of Homosexuality: Sexual Orientation or Sexual Preference?" *Journal of Homosexuality* 28: 1–28.

D'Emilio, John. 1990. "The Campus Environment for Gay and Lesbian Life." *Academe* 76(1): 16–9.

Deziel, Shanda. 2000. "Gaily Prime Time." *Maclean's* (October 30): 54.

Doell, R. G. 1995. "Sexuality in the Brain." *Journal of Homosexuality* 28: 345–56.

Dozetos, Barbara. 2001. "School Shooter Taunted as 'Gay.'" PlanetOut.com, March 7. http://www.planetout.com/news/article-print.html?2001/03/07/1

Dranoff, Linda Silver. 2001. *Everyone's Guide to the Law.* Toronto: HarperCollins Publishers Ltd.

Drinkwater, Gregg. 2001. "Netherlands to Celebrate First Gay Marriages." PlanetOut.com, March 30. http://www.planetout.com/news/article-print.html?2001/03/2

Durkheim, Emile. 1993. "The Normal and the Pathological." Originally published in *The Rules of Sociological Method, 1938.* Pp. 33–63 in *Social Deviance,* edited by Henry N. Pontell. Englewood Cliffs, NJ: Prentice-Hall.

EGALE. 1999. "Press Release." June 7. http://www.egale.ca/politics.motion.htm

———. 2001. "Svend Robinson Introduces Bill, EGALE Renews Call for Hate Crimes Protection in Wake of Murder of Gay Man in Vancouver." Press release, November 22. http://www.egale.ca/pressrel/011122.htm

———. 2004, October. "Sex Reassignment Surgery (SRS) Backgrounder." http://egale.ca/all/sex-reassignment-surgery-srs-backgrounder

———. 2010. "Update on Bill C-389." http://trans.egale.ca/2010/12/update-on-bill-c-389

———. 2012. "Human Rights Day a Call for Consensus on Gender Identity Bill." Research and Policy, December 10. http://egale.ca/all/human-rights-day-a-call-for-consensus-on-gender-identity-bill

Esterberg, K. 1997. *Lesbian and Bisexual Identities: Constructing Communities, Constructing Selves.* Philadelphia: Temple University Press.

Faulkner, Anne H. and Kevin Cranston. 1998. "Correlates of Same-Sex Sexual Behavior in a Random Sample of Massachusetts High School Students." *Journal of Public Health* 88 (February): 262–66.

Fausto-Sterling, Anne. 2001. *Sexing the Body.* New York: Basic Books.

Firestein, B. A. 1996. "Bisexuality as Paradigm Shift: Transforming Our Disciplines." Pp. 263–91 in *Bisexuality: The Psychology and Politics of an Invisible Minority,* edited by B. A. Firestein. Thousand Oaks, CA: Sage.

Fisher, John. 1999. *A Report on Lesbian, Gay and Bisexual Youth Issues in Canada.* Ottawa: EGALE.

Flowers, Paul and Katie Buston. 2001. "'I Was Terrified of Being Different': Exploring Gay Men's Accounts of Growing Up in a Heterosexist Society." *Journal of Adolescence. Special Issue: Gay, Lesbian, and Bisexual Youth* 24 (February): 51–65.

Fone, Byrne. 2000. *Homophobia: A History.* New York: Henry Holt and Company.

Foucault, Michel. 1990a. *The History of Sexuality, Volume One: An Introduction.* Trans. Robert Hurley. New York: Vintage.

———. 1990b. *The History of Sexuality, Volume Two: The Use of Pleasure.* Trans. Robert Hurley. New York: Vintage.

———. 1990c. *The History of Sexuality, Volume Three: The Care of the Self.* Trans. Robert Hurley. New York: Vintage.

Frank, Barney. 1997. Foreword. In *Private Lives, Public Conflicts: Battles over Gay Rights in American Communities,* edited by J. W. Button, B. A. Rienzo, and K. D. Wald. Washington, DC: CQ Press.

Frank, David John and Elizabeth H. McEneaney. 1999. "The Individualization of Society and the Liberalization of State Policies on Same-Sex Relations, 1984–1995." *Social Forces* 77(3): 911–44.

Franklin, Sarah. 1993. "Essentialism, Which Essentialism? Some Implications of Reproductive and Genetic Techno-Science." *Journal of Homosexuality* 24: 27–39.

Freedman, Estelle B. and John D'Emilio. 1990. "Problems Encountered in Writing the History of Sexuality: Sources, Theory, and Interpretation." *Journal of Sex Research* 27: 481–95.

Garnets, L., G. M. Herek, and B. Levy. 1990. "Violence and Victimization of Lesbians and Gay Men: Mental Health Consequences." *Journal of Interpersonal Violence* 5: 366–83.

Gilbert, Michael. 2000. "The Transgendered Philosopher." *International Journal of Transgenderism.* Special issue 4 (July-September).

Gilman, Sander. 1985. *Difference and Pathology: Stereotypes of Sexuality, Race and Madness.* Ithaca: Cornell University Press.

Goldie, Terry. 2001. *In a Queer Country: Gay & Lesbian Studies in the Canadian Context.* Vancouver: Arsenal Pulp Press.

Goode, Erica E. and Betsy Wagner. 1993. "Intimate Friendships." *U.S. News and World Report* (July 5): 49–52.

Government of Canada. 2013. Bill C-32 (Historical) Civil Marriage of Non-residents Act An Act to amend the Civil Marriage Act. http://openparliament.ca/bills/41-1/C-32

Hamer, D., P. F. Copeland, S. Hu, V. L. Magnuson, N. Hu, and A. M. L. Pattatucci. 1993. "A Linkage between DNA Markers on the X Chromosome and Male Sexual Orientation." *Science* 261: 321–27.

Health Canada. 2014. Archived: Primary Health Transition Fund. http://www .apps.hc-sc.gc.ca/hcs-sss/phctf-fassp .nsf/WebProject/0025?OpenDocument &lang=eng&

Herdt, Gilbert. 2001. "Social Change, Sexual Diversity, and Tolerance for Bisexuality in the United States." Pp. 267–83 in *Lesbian, Gay, and Bisexual Identities and Youth: Psychological Perspectives,* edited by Anthony R. D'Augelli and Charlotte J. Patterson. New York: Oxford University Press.

Herek, Gregory M. 1989. "Hate Crimes against Lesbians and Gay Men." *American Psychologist* 44: 948–55.

———. 1990. "The Context of Anti-Gay Violence: Notes on Cultural and Psychological Heterosexism." *Journal of Interpersonal Violence* 5: 316–33.

Hines, S. 2006. "Intimate Transitions: Transgender Practices of Partnering and Parenting." *Sociology* 40(2): 353–71.

Homophobia 101: Teaching Respect for All. 2000. The Gay, Lesbian, and Straight Education Network. http://www.glsen.org

Honore, Carl. 2000. "'Male Egg' Could Enable Two Men to Conceive a Child." *National Post* (September 26): A1, A12.

Human Rights Campaign. 2000a. *Feeling Free: Personal Stories: How Love and Self-Acceptance Saved Us from "Ex-Gay" Ministries.* Washington, DC: Human Rights Campaign.

———. 2000b. *The State of the Workplace for Lesbian, Gay, Bisexual and Transgendered Americans, 2000.* Washington, DC: Human Rights Campaign Foundation.

International Gay and Lesbian Human Rights Commission (IGLHRC). 2003. "Where Having Sex Is a Crime: Criminalization and Decriminalization of Homosexual Acts." http://www.iglhrc.org/site/iglhrc/ content.php?type=1&id=77

"Jail, Death Sentences in Africa." 2001. PlanetOut.com, February 21. http:// www.planetout.com/news/articleprint .html?2001/02/21/2

Kinsey, A. C., W. B. Pomeroy, C. E. Martin, and P. H. Gebhard. 1953. *Sexual Behavior in the Human Female.* Philadelphia: W. B. Saunders.

Kirkpatrick, R. C. 2000. "The Evolution of Human Sexual Behavior." *Current Anthropology* 41(3): 385.

Klassen, Albert D., Colin J. Williams, and Eugene E. Levitt. 1989. *Sex and Morality in the United States.* Middletown, CT: Wesleyan University Press.

Krafft-Ebing, Richard von. 1965. *Psychopathia Sexualis.* Introd. by Franklin S. Klaf. London: Staples Press.

Lambda Legal Defense and Education Fund. 2000. *Student Advocacy for University Anti-Bias Policies That Include Sexual Orientation.* Publications, July 6. http://www .lambdalegal.org

LAWbriefs. 2000. "Recent Developments in Sexual Orientation and Gender Identity Law." *LAWbriefs* 3 (Fall).

Louderback, L. A. and B. E. Whitley. 1997. "Perceived Erotic Value of Homosexuality and Sex-Role Attitudes as Mediators of Sex Differences in Heterosexual College Students' Attitudes toward Lesbians and Gay Men." *Journal of Sex Research* 34: 175–82.

Mathison, Carla. 1998. "The Invisible Minority: Preparing Teachers to Meet the Needs of Gay and Lesbian Youth." *Journal of Teacher Education* 49: 151–55.

Mohr, Richard D. 1995. "Anti-Gay Stereotypes." Pp. 402–8 in *Race, Class, and Gender in the United States,* 3rd ed., edited by P. S. Rothenberg. New York: St. Martin's Press.

Moser, Charles. 1992. "Lust, Lack of Desire, and Paraphilias: Some Thoughts and Possible Connections." *Journal of Sex and Marital Therapy* 18: 65–69.

Murphy, Timothy F. 2001. "Commentary: Lesbian, Gay, Bisexual, and Transgender Medical Students and Their Ethical Conflicts." *Journal of the Gay & Lesbian Medical Association.* Special issue 5 (March): 31–35.

Nagle, Matt. 2001. "Gay Man Murdered in Vancouver's Stanley Park." *Seattle Gay News,* November 23. http://www.sgn .org/2001/11/23

National Conference of State Legislatures. 2004. "Voters Decide High-Profile Issues on State Ballots Same Sex Marriage Bans Pass, Mixed Results for Tort Reform." http://www.ncsl. org/programs/legman/statevote/ir2004.htm

National Public Radio. 2014. Fresh Air Interview with Masha Gessen. Original Broadcast Date: January 8, 2014. Accessed January 18, 2014. http://www.npr.org/ 2014/01/08/260746432/the-pussy -riot-arrests-and-the-crackdown-that -followed

Nugent, Robert and Jeannine Gramick. 1989. "Homosexuality: Protestant, Catholic, and Jewish Issues: A Fishbone Tale." *Journal of Homosexuality* 18: 7–46.

Patterson, Charlotte J. 2001. "Family Relationships of Lesbians and Gay Men." Pp. 271–88 in *Understanding Families into the New Millennium: A Decade in Review,* edited by Robert M. Milardo. Minneapolis, MN: National Council on Family Relations.

Paul, J. P. 1996. "Bisexuality: Exploring/Exploding the Boundaries." Pp. 436–61 in *The Lives of Lesbians, Gays, and Bisexuals: Children to Adults,* edited by R. Savin-Williams and K. M. Cohen. Fort Worth, TX: Harcourt Brace.

Peele, S. and R. DeGrandpre. 1995. "My Genes Made Me Do It." *Psychology Today* 28 (July/ August): 50–53.

Pillard, Richard C. and J. Michael Bailey. 1998. "Human Sexuality Has a Heritable Component." *Human Biology* 70 (April): 347–65.

Platt, Leah. 2001. "Not Your Father's High School Club." *The American Prospect* 12(1): A37–A39.

Price, Jammie and Michael G. Dalecki. 1998. "The Social Basis of Homophobia: An Empirical Illustration." *Sociological Spectrum* 18: 143–59.

Rice, G., C. Anderson, N. Risch, and G. Ebers. 1999. "Male Homosexuality: Absence of

Linkage to Micro-satellite Markets at Xq28." *Science* 284 (April 23): 665–67.

Roberts, J. V. 1995. "Disproportionate Harm: Hate Crime in Canada." Ottawa, Department of Justice Canada. WD1995-11e.

Roen, Katrina. 2001. "Transgender Theory and Embodiment: The Risk of Racial Marginalisation." *Journal of Gender Studies* 10(3): 253–63.

Rosin, Hanna and Richard Morin. 1999. "In One Area, Americans Still Draw a Line on Acceptability." *Washington Post*, national weekly edition, 16 (January 11): 8.

Rubin, Gayle. 1975. "The Traffic in Women: Notes on the Political Economy of Sex." Pp. 157–210 in *Toward an Anthropology of Women*, edited by Rayna R. Reiter. New York: Monthly Review Press.

Russian LGBT Network. 2013. "The State Duma Passed the Bill on 'Non-Traditional Sexual Relations.'" Available at http://www.lgbtnet.ru/en/content/state-duma-passed-bill-non-traditional-sexual-relations

Sanday, Peggy R. 1995. "Pulling Train." Pp. 396–402 in *Race, Class, and Gender in the United States*, 3rd ed., edited by P. S. Rothenberg. New York: St. Martin's Press.

Schellenberg, E. Glenn, Jessie Hirt, and Alan Sears. 1999. "Attitudes toward Homosexuals among Students at a Canadian University." *Sex Roles* 40(1/2): 139–52.

Simon, A. 1995. "Some Correlates of Individuals' Attitudes toward Lesbians." *Journal of Homosexuality* 29: 89–103.

Stone, Sharon D. (ed.). 1990. "Lesbian Mothers: Organizing." Pp. 191–205. in *Lesbians in Canada*. Toronto: Between the Lines.

Sullivan, A. 1997. "The Conservative Case." Pp. 146–54 in *Same-Sex Marriage: Pro and Con*, edited by A. Sullivan. New York: Vintage Books.

Sullivan, Nikki. 2003. *A Critical Introduction to Queer Theory*. New York: New York University Press.

Thompson, Cooper. 1995. "A New Vision of Masculinity." Pp. 475–81 in *Race, Class, and Gender in the United States*, 3rd ed., edited by P. S. Rothenberg. New York: St. Martin's Press.

Valentine, D. 2007. *Imagining Transgender*. Durham and London: Duke University Press.

Warnke, Georgia. 2005. "Race, Gender, and Antiessentialist Politics." *Signs* 31(1): 93–116.

Weston, Kath. 1991. *Families We Choose: Lesbians, Gays, Kinship*. New York: Columbia University Press.

Wetzel, Janice Wood. 2001. "Human Rights in the 20th Century: Weren't Gays and Lesbians Human?" Pp. 15–31 in *From Hate Crimes to Human Rights: A Tribute to Matthew Shep-*

ard, edited by Mary E. Swigonski and Robin S. Mama. New York: Haworth Press.

Wilcox, Clyde and Robin Wolpert. 2000. "Gay Rights in the Public Sphere: Public Opinion on Gay and Lesbian Equality." Pp. 409–32 in *The Politics of Gay Rights*, edited by Craig A. Rimmerman, Kenneth D. Wald, and Clyde Wilcox. Chicago: University of Chicago Press.

Yang, Alan. 1999. *From Wrongs to Rights 1973 to 1999: Public Opinion on Gay and Lesbian Americans Moves toward Equality*. New York: The Policy Institute of the National Gay and Lesbian Task Force.

Yogis, J. A., R. R. Duplak, and J. R. Trainor. 1996. *Sexual Orientation and Canadian Law: An Assessment of the Law Affecting Lesbian and Gay Persons*. Toronto: Emond Montgomery Publications Limited.

Chapter 10

Albelda, Randy and Chris Tilly. 1997. *Glass Ceilings and Bottomless Pits: Women's Work, Women's Poverty*. Boston, MA: South End Press.

Alex-Assensoh, Yvette. 1995. "Myths about Race and the Underclass." *Urban Affairs Review* 31: 3–19.

Barlow, Maude and Bruce Campbell. 1995. *Straight through the Heart*. Toronto: Harper-Collins Publishers Ltd.

Bricker, Darrell and Edward Greenspon. 2001. *Searching for Certainty: Inside the New Canadian Mindset*. Toronto: Doubleday Canada.

Briggs, Vernon M. Jr. 1998. "American-Style Capitalism and Income Disparity: The Challenge of Social Anarchy." *Journal of Economic Issues* 32(2): 473–81.

Canada Customs and Revenue Agency. 2002. "About the Canada Child Tax Benefit (CCTB)." http://www.ccra-adrc.gc.ca/benefits/faq_about-e.html

Canadian Centre for Policy Alternatives Monitor. 1999. September. http://www.policyalternatives.ca

Canadian Research Institute for the Advancement of Women (CRIAW). 2006. "Intersectional Feminist Frameworks: An Emerging Vision." Ottawa: CRIAW.

Carroll, William and R. S. Ratner. 2001. "Sustaining Oppositional Cultures in 'Post-Socialist' Times: A Comparative Study of Three Social Movement Organisations." *Sociology* 35(3): 605–29.

Centre for Social Justice. 2001. "Wealth of the Top 20% of Families Surges 39% since 1984, while the Bottom Sinks." March 15. http://www.socialjustice.org/media/releas/wealthgap.html

Chossudovsky, Michel. 1998. "Global Poverty in the Late Twentieth Century." *Journal of International Affairs* 52(1): 293–303.

Conley, Dalton. 2001. "Capital for College: Parental Assets and Postsecondary School-

ing." *Sociology of Education* 74 (January): 59–72.

Corak, Miles. 1998. "Getting Ahead in Life: Does Your Parents' Income Count?" *Canadian Social Trends* 49 (Summer): 6–15.

Corak, M., Garth Lipps, and John Zhao. 2003. *Family Income and Participation in Post-Secondary Education*. Family and Labour Studies Division: Analytic Studies Branch research paper series, Statistics Canada. Catalogue no. 11F0019MIE No. 210

Coyne, Andrew. 1997. "Poverty Study Raises Questions." *Kitchener-Waterloo Record* (July 17): A7.

Daub, Shannon and Margaret Young. 1999. "Families Need More Than Tax Fairness." http://www.policyalternatives.ca

Davies, James, Rodrigo Lluberas, and Anthony Sharrocks. 2012. Credit Suisse Global Wealth Division. "World Wealth Levels, 2012." http://www.international-adviser.com/ia/media/Media/Credit-Suisse-Global-Wealth-Databook-2013.pdf

Davis, Kingsley and Wilbert Moore. 1945. "Some Principles of Stratification." *American Sociological Review* 10: 242–49.

Deen, Thalif. 2000. "NGOs Call for UN Poverty Eradication Fund." Global Policy Forum. http://www.globalpolicy.org/msummit/millenni/millfor3.htm

Dranoff, Linda Silver. 2001. *Everyone's Guide to the Law*. Toronto: HarperCollins Publishers Ltd.

Duncan, Greg J. and Jeanne Brooks-Gunn. 1997. "Income Effects across the Life Span: Integration and Interpretation." Pp. 596–610 in *Consequences of Growing Up Poor*, edited by Greg J. Duncan and Jeanne Brooks-Gunn. New York: Russell Sage Foundation.

Economic Policy Institute. 2000. "Issue Guide to the Minimum Wage." http://www.epinet.org/Issuesguides/minwage/minwagefaq.html

Fawcett, Gail. 1999. "Disability in the Labour Market: Barriers and Solutions." *Perception* 23 (December). Canadian Council on Social Development. http://www.ccsd.ca/perception/233/disab.htm

Feinberg, Leslie. 1993. *Stone Butch Blues*. New York: Firebrand Books.

Finn, Ed. 2006. "December 2005: The 'Big Business Bang' Theory: Social, Economic, Environmental Ills All Have the Same Cause." Ottawa: Canadian Centre for Policy Alternatives. June 10. http://www.policy-alternatives.ca/MonitorIssues/2005/12/MonitorIssue1274/index.cfm?pa=DDC3F905

Galabuzi, Grace Edward. 2001. *Canada's Creeping Economic Apartheid: The Economic Segregation and Social Marginalisation of*

Racialised Groups, 2nd ed. Toronto: CSJ Foundation for Research and Education.

Gans, Herbert J. 1972. "The Positive Functions of Poverty." *American Journal of Sociology* 78 (September): 275–388.

Global Poverty Report. 2000. G8 Okinawa Summit, July 2000.

Goar, Carol. 2014. "Ontario's Minimum Wage Plan Locks Many into Poverty." *Toronto Star.* February 4. 2014.

Government of Canada. 1999. *National Child Benefit Progress Report 1999.* http://www .socialunion.gc.ca/NCB-99/html

Guest, Dennis. 1999a. "Social Security." Pp. 2200–2204 in *The Canadian Encyclopedia: Year 2000 Edition,* edited by James H. Marsh. Toronto: McClelland & Stewart Inc.

———. 1999b. "Family Allowance." Pp. 1815–16 in *The Canadian Encyclopedia: Year 2000 Edition,* edited by James H. Marsh. Toronto: McClelland & Stewart Inc.

Health Canada. 1999. *Toward a Healthy Future: Second Report on the Health of Canadians.* Prepared by the Federal, Provincial, and Territorial Advisory Committee on Population Health for the Meeting of Ministers of Health, Charlottetown, PEI, September 1999.

Hill, Lewis E. 1998. "The Institutional Economics of Poverty: An Inquiry into the Causes and Effects of Poverty." *Journal of Economic Issues* 32(2): 279–86.

Human Resources Development Canada. 2001. "What Is the CESG?" http://www .hrdc-drhc.gc.ca/brib/learnlit/cesg/013/ 001_e.shtml

Institute of Development Studies. 2006. *Realising Sexual Rights.* U.K.: Institute of Development Studies.

Keating, G., Michael O'Sullivan, Anthony Shorrocks, James B. Davies, and Rodrigo Lluberas. 2010. *Global Wealth Report.* Zurich: Credit Suisse.

Kennedy, Bruce P., Ichiro Kawachi, Roberta Glass, and Deborah Prothrow-Stith. 1998. "Income Distribution, Socioeconomic Status, and Self-Rated Health in the U.S.: Multilevel Analysis." *British Medical Journal* 317(7163): 917–22.

Kiely, Ray. 2005. "Globalization and Poverty, and the Poverty of Globalization Theory." *Current Sociology* 53(6): 895–914.

Klugman, J. 2010. *Human Development Report 2010: The Real Wealth of Nations—Pathways to Human Development.* New York: United Nations Development Programme.

Knickerbocker, Brad. 2000. "Nongovernmental Organizations Are Fighting and Winning Social, Political Battles." Global Policy Forum. http://www.globalpolicy.org/ ngos/00role.htm

Krahn, Harvey. 1994. "Social Stratification." Pp. 2.1–2.31 in *New Society Brief Edition: Sociology for the Twenty-First Century,*

edited by Robert Brym. Toronto: Harcourt Brace Jovanovich.

Larin, Kathryn. 1998. "Should We Be Worried about the Widening Gap between the Rich and the Poor?" *Insight on the News* 14(5): 24–28.

Lewis, Oscar. 1966. "The Culture of Poverty." *Scientific American* 2(5): 19–25.

———. 1998. "The Culture of Poverty: Resolving Common Social Problems." *Society* 35(2): 7–10.

Luker, Kristin. 1996. *Dubious Conceptions: The Politics of Teenage Pregnancy.* Cambridge, MA: Harvard University Press.

Macdonald, David and Daniel Wilson. 2013. "Poverty or Prosperity." Canadian Centre for Policy Alternatives. Available at http:// www.policyalternatives.ca

Mann, Judy. 2000. "Demonstrators at the Barricades Aren't Very Subtle, But They Sometimes Win." *The Washington Spectator* 26 (May 15): 1–3.

Marx, Karl and Friedrich Engels. 1967[1888]. *The Communist Manifesto.* New York: Penguin.

Matern, Richard, Michael Mendelson, and Michael Oliphant. 2009. "Developing a Deprivation Index: The Research Process." Daily Bread Food Bank and Caledon Institute of Social Policy.

Mayer, Susan E. 1997. *What Money Can't Buy: Family Income and Children's Life Chances.* Cambridge, MA: Harvard University Press.

Mead, L. 1992. *The New Politics of Poverty: The Non-Working Poor in America.* New York: Basic Books.

Mishel, Lawrence, Jared Bernstein, and John Schmitt. 2001. *The State of Working America 2000/2001.* Ithaca, NY: Cornell University Press.

Moscovitch, Allan. 1999. "Welfare State." Pp. 2493–96 in *The Canadian Encyclopedia: Year 2000 Edition,* edited by James H. Marsh. Toronto: McClelland & Stewart Inc.

Narayan, Deepa. 2000. *Voices of the Poor: Can Anyone Hear Us?* New York: Oxford University Press.

NAPO (National Anti-Poverty Organization). 2006. "The Face of Poverty in Canada: An Overview." Ottawa: National Anti-Poverty Organization.

National Council of Welfare. 1997. "Canada Welfare Incomes." http://csf.colorado.edu/ lists/psn/dec97/0071.html

———. 1998. *Profiles of Welfare: Myths and Realities: A Report by the National Council of Welfare.* Spring. http://www.ncwcnbes .net/htmdocument/reportprowelfare .repprowelfare.htm

———. 1999a. *Children First: A Pre-Budget Report by the National Council of Welfare.* Autumn. http://www.ncwcnbes.net/ htmdocument/reportchildfirst/ repchildfirst.htm

———. 1999b. "No Such Thing as a 'Typical' Welfare Case, Says National Council of Welfare Report." http://www.ncwcnbes .net/htmdocument/reportprowelfare/ PRESSPROWELFARE.htm

———. 1999c. *Preschool Children: Promises to Keep.* Spring. http://www.ncwcnbes.net/ htmdocument/reportpromise/firstpag.htm

———. 2000. *Poverty Profile 1998.* Ottawa: Ministry of Public Works.

———. 2002a. "Fact Sheet: Welfare Recipients." http://www.ncwcnbes.net/htmdocument/ principales/numberwelfare.htm

———. 2002b. *Poverty Profile 1999.* http:// www.ncwcnbes.net/htmdocument/ reportpovertypro000/Introduction.html

———. 2003. *Welfare Incomes 2003.* Ottawa: National Council of Welfare.

———. 2004. *Income for Living?* Ottawa: National Council of Welfare.

Neal, Rusty. 2004. *Voices: Women, Poverty and Homelessness in Canada.* Ottawa: National Anti-Poverty Association.

Orlikow, Lionel. 1999. "Students, Financial Aid." Pp. 2264–65 in *The Canadian Encyclopedia: Year 2000 Edition,* edited by James H. Marsh. Toronto: McClelland & Stewart Inc.

Palameta, B. 2005. "Low Income among Immigrants and Visible Minorities: Perspectives." Statistics Canada. Catalogue no. 75-001-XIE. Ottawa.

Paul, James A. 2000. "NGOs and Global Policy-Making." Global Policy Forum. http:// www.globalpolicy.org/ngos/analysis/ anal00htm

Pen, Jan. 2011 (Jan. 20). "The Rise and Fall of the Cognitive Elite." *The Economist.* London: The Economist Newspaper Limited.

Reid, Shyanne, Helen Burman, and Cheryl Forchuk. 2005. "Living on the Streets in Canada: A Feminist Narrative Study of Girls and Young Women." *Issues in Comprehensive Pediatric Nursing* 28: 237–56.

Reutter, Linda, et al. 2006. "Public Attributions for Poverty in Canada." *Canadian Review of Sociology and Anthropology* 43(1): 1–22.

Ross, David P. and Clarence Lochhead. 1999. "Poverty." Pp. 1880–82 in *The Canadian Encyclopedia: Year 2000 Edition,* edited by James H. Marsh. Toronto: McClelland & Stewart Inc.

Ross, David P., E. Richard Shillington, and Clarence Lochhead. 1994. *The Canadian Fact Book on Poverty.* Ottawa: Canadian Council on Social Development.

Sarlo, Christopher. 1992. *Poverty in Canada.* Vancouver: The Fraser Institute.

———. 1996. *Poverty in Canada.* Vancouver: The Fraser Institute.

———. 2013. "Poverty: Where Do We Draw the Line?" Fraser Institute (November). Available at: http://ssrn.com/abstract =2354442

Schenk, Christopher. 2001. *From Poverty Wages to a Living Wage.* Toronto: CJS Foundation for Research and Education.

Seccombe, Karen. 2001. "Families in Poverty in the 1990s: Trends, Causes, Consequences, and Lessons Learned." Pp. 313–32 in *Understanding Families into the New Millennium: A Decade in Review,* edited by Robert M. Milardo. Minneapolis, MN: National Council on Family Relations.

SmithBattle, L. 2007. "Legacies of Advantage and Disadvantage: The Case of Teen Mothers." *Public Health Nursing* 25(5): 409–420.

Speth, James Gustave. 1998. "Poverty: A Denial of Human Rights." *Journal of International Affairs* 52(1): 277–86.

Statistics Canada. 1998a. *Canada Yearbook 1999.* Ottawa: Minister of Industry.

———. 1998b. *The Daily,* May 12. http://www.statscan.ca:80/Daily/English/980512/d980512.htm

———. 2000. "Family Income 1998." *The Daily,* June 12. http://www.statcan.ca/Daily/English/000612/d000612a.htm

———. 2002. "Gender Pay Differentials: Impact of the Workplace." *The Daily,* June 19. http://www.statcan.ca/Daily/English/020619/d020619b.htm

Streeten, Paul. 1998. "Beyond the Six Veils: Conceptualizing and Measuring Poverty." *Journal of International Affairs* 52(1): 1–8.

United Nations. 2005. *Report on the World Social Situation, 2005.* New York: United Nations.

———. 2008. "More People Living in Extreme Poverty Than Previously Thought—World Bank." http://www.un.org/apps/news/story.asp?NewsID=27842&Cr=poverty&Cr1=world%20bank

United Nations Development Programme (UNDP). 1997. *Human Development Report 1997.* New York: Oxford University Press.

———. 2000. *Human Development Report 2000.* New York: Oxford University Press.

———. 2010. *Human Developmental Report: 20th Anniversary Edition.* New York: Palgrave Macmillan.

Van Kempen, Eva T. 1997. "Poverty Pockets and Life Chances: On the Role of Place in Shaping Social Inequality." *American Behavioural Scientist* 41(3): 430–50.

Wilson, D. and David Macdonald. 2010. *The Income Gap between Aboriginal Peoples and the Rest of Canada.* Ottawa: Canadian Centre for Policy Alternatives.

Wilson, William J. 1987. *The Truly Disadvantaged: The Inner City, the Underclass, and Public Policy.* Chicago: University of Chicago Press.

———. 1996. *When Work Disappears: The World of the New Urban Poor.* New York: Knopf.

World Bank. 2007. "Understanding Poverty." http://www.worldbank.org

———. 2014. "Poverty Overview." Accessed January 29, 2014. http://www.worldbank.org/en/topic/poverty/overview

Yali, Ann Marie and Tracey Revinson. 2004. "How Changes in Population Demographics Will Impact Health Psychology: Incorporating a Broader Notion of Cultural Competence into the Field." *Health Psychology* 23(2): 147–55.

Yalnizyan, A. 1998. *The Growing Gap.* Toronto: Centre for Social Justice.

Chapter 11

Adams, Eve, Betsy Cahill, and Stacy Ackerland. 2005. "A Qualitative Study of Latino Lesbian and Gay Youths' Experiences with Discrimination and the Career Development Process." *Journal of Vocational Behaviour* 66: 199–218.

Ambrose, Soren. 1998. "The Case against the IMF." Campaign for Human Rights Newsletter 12, December 8. http://www.summersault.co . . . wsletter/news12.html

Ash, Russell. 2001. *The Top 10 of Everything: Canadian Edition 2002.* Toronto: Dorling Kindersley Limited.

Bassi, Laurie J. and Jens Ludwig. 2000. "School-to-Work Programs in the United States: A Multi-Firm Case Study of Training, Benefits, and Costs." *Industrial and Labor Relations Review* 53 (January): 219.

Bavendam, James. 2000. "Managing Job Satisfaction." Special Reports 6: 1–2. Bavendam Research Incorporated. http://www.bavendam.com

Bell, Daniel. 1973. *The Coming of Post-Industrial Society.* New York: Basic Books.

Bellan, Ruben C. 1999. "Foreign Investment." Pp. 884–85 in *The Canadian Encyclopedia: Year 2000 Edition,* edited by James H. Marsh. Toronto: McClelland & Stewart Inc.

Benjamin, Medea. 1998. "What's Fair about Fair Labor Association (FLA)?" Sweatshop Watch. http://www.sweatshopwatch.org/swatch/headlines/1998/org/swatch/headlines/1998/gex_fla.html

Benner, Chris. 2003. "'Computers in the Wild': Guilds, and Next-Generation Union Is Center in the Information Revolution." *IRSH* 48: 181–204.

Bernard, A. 2009. "Job Stability and Unemployment Duration in Manufacturing." Ottawa: Statistics Canada. Catalogue no. 75-001-X.

Bettelheim, Adriel. 1998. "Sleep Deprivation." *CQ Researcher* 8(24): 553–76.

Bowles, Diane O. 2000. "Growth in Telework." Paper presented at the symposium *Telework and the New Workplace of the 21st Century.* Xavier University, New Orleans, October 16.

Bracey, Gerald W. 1995. "The Fifth Bracey Report on the Condition of Public Education." *Phi Delta Kappan* (October): 149–62.

Bricker, Darrell and Edward Greenspon. 2001. *Searching for Certainty: Inside the New Canadian Mindset.* Toronto: Doubleday Canada.

Canada Revenue Agency. 2006. "Universal Child Care Benefit." http://www.cra-arc.gc.ca/benefits/uccb/faq-e.html#q2

Canadian Council on Social Development. 2001. The Progress of Canada's Children 2001—Highlights. March. http://www.ccsd.ca/pubs/2001/pcc2001.hl.htm

Carnoy, Martin and Manuel Castells. 1997. *Sustainable Flexibility: A Prospective Study on Work, Family and Society in the Information Age.* Paris: Organisation for Economic Development.

Caston, Richard J. 1998. *Life in a Business-Oriented Society: A Sociological Perspective.* Boston: Allyn and Bacon.

CBC News. 2010. "Dozens of G20 Accused Have Charges Dropped." October 14. http://www.cbc.ca/news/canada/toronto/story/2010/10/14/g20-charges-dropped685.html

CBC News (Gillian Findlay). 2011. "You Should Have Stayed at Home." *The Fifth Estate.* T. Weinstein. Canada, CBC: 45 min.

Clark, Katie and Sally Kalin. 1996. "Technostressed Out? How to Cope in the Digital Age." *Library Journal* (August): 30–32.

Coleman, James. 1994. *The Criminal Elite: The Sociology of White Collar Crime,* 3rd ed. New York: St. Martin's Press.

Conrad, Peter. 1999. "Wellness in the Work Place: Potentials and Pitfalls of Work-Site Health Promotion." Pp. 263–75 in *Health, Illness, and Healing: Society, Social Context, and Self,* edited by K. Charmaz and D. A. Paterniti. Los Angeles: Roxbury Publishing Company.

Danaher, Kevin. 1998. "Are Workers Waking Up?" Global Exchange: Education for Action. December 17. http://www.globalexchange.org/education/economy/laborday.html

Deutschmann, C. 2011. "The Euro Trouble and the Global Financial Crisis." *Economic Sociology: The European Electronic Newsletter* 12: 17–21.

Doherty, Gillian. 2001. "Moving towards Achieving Quality Child Care." Pp. 126–41 in *Our Children's Future: Child Care Policy in Canada,* edited by Gordon Cleveland and Michael Krashinsky. Toronto: University of Toronto Press.

Dorman, Peter. 2001. "Child Labour in the Developed Economies." Geneva: International Labour Office.

Durkheim, Emile. [1893] 1966. *On the Division of Labor in Society,* trans. G. Simpson. New York: Free Press.

Eitzen, Stanley and Maxine Baca Zinn (eds.). 1990. *The Reshaping of America: Social Consequences of the Changing Economy.* Englewood Cliffs, NJ: Prentice-Hall.

Epstein, Gerald, Julie Graham, and Jessica Nembhard (eds.). 1993. "Third World Socialism and the Demise of COMECON." Pp. 405–20 in *Creating a New World Economy: Forces of Change and Plans of Action*. Philadelphia: Temple University Press.

Errington, Jane. 1993. "Pioneers and Suffragists." Pp. 59–91 in *Changing Patterns: Women in Canada*, 2nd ed., edited by Lorraine Code, Lindsay Dorney, and Sandra Burt. Toronto: McClelland & Stewart Inc.

Feather, Norman T. 1990. *The Psychological Impact of Unemployment*. New York: Springer-Verlag.

Ferrao, Vincent. 2010. "'Paid Work' Series: Women in Canada: A Gender-Based Statistical Report." Statistics Canada. Catalogue no.89-503-X.

Frederick, James and Nancy Lessin. 2000. "Blame the Worker: The Rise of Behavioral-Based Safety Programs." *Multinational Monitor* 21 (November). http://www.essential.org/monitor/mm2000/00november/toc.html

Galinsky, Ellen and James T. Bond. 1998. *The 1998 Business Work-Life Study*. New York: Families and Work Institute.

Galinsky, Ellen and Stacy S. Kim. 2000. "Navigating Work and Parenting by Working at Home: Perspectives of Workers and Children Whose Parents Work at Home." Paper presented at the symposium *Telework and the New Workplace of the 21st Century*. Xavier University, New Orleans, October 16.

Ghalam, Nancy Zukewich. 2000. "Paid and Unpaid Work." Pp. 97–134 in *Women in Canada 2000: A Gender-Based Statistical Report*. Ottawa: Statistics Canada.

"Global Labor Repression." 2000. Behind the Lines. *Multinational Monitor* 21 (November). http://www.essential.org/monitor/mm2000/00november/toc.html

Government of Alberta. 2011. "Alberta Family Employment Tax Credit." http://www.finance.alberta.ca/business/tax_rebates/alberta_family_employment_taxcredit.html

Greenhouse, Steven. 2000. "Anti-Sweatshop Movement Is Achieving Gains Overseas." *The New York Times on the Web*. http://nytimes.com

Halford, Susan. 2006. "Collapsing the Boundaries? Fatherhood, Organization and Home-Working." *Gender, Work and Organization* 13(4): 383–402.

Hallsworth, Alan. 1993. "The External Trade of Canada." Pp. 432–39 in *The U.S.A. and Canada*. London: Europa Publications.

Hargis, Michael J. 2001. "Bangladesh: Garment Workers Burned to Death." *Industrial Worker* #1630, 98 (January/February). http://parsons.ww.org/~iw/jan2001/stories/intl.html

Health Canada. 1999. Statistical Report on the Health of Canadians. December 25. http://www.hc-sc.gc.ca/hppb/phdd/report/state/eng/over.html

Heidegren, Carl-Goran. 2004. "Recognition and Social Theory." *Acta Sociologica* 47(4): 365–73.

Hochschild, Arlie Russell. 1997. *The Time Bind: When Work Becomes Home and Home Becomes Work*. New York: Henry Holt and Company.

Hughes, Christina. 2004. "Class and Other Identifications in Managerial Careers: The Case of the Lemon Dress." *Work and Organization* 11(5): 526–43.

Human Resources and Development Canada (HRDC). 2006. "Employment Insurance (EI) and Maternity, Parental and Sickness Benefits." Ottawa: HRDC. Accessed June 10, 2006. http://www.hrsdc.gc.ca/asp/gateway.asp?hr=en/ei/types/special.shtml&hs=aed#Who

Human Rights Watch. 2000. "Unfair Advantage: Workers' Freedom of Association in the United States under International Human Rights Standards." http://www.hrw.org/reports/2000/uslabor

———. 2001. *World Report 2001*. http://www.hrw.org

International Labour Organization. 2000. "Statistics: Revealing a Hidden Tragedy." http://www.ilo.org/public...ish/standards/idec/simpoc/stats/4stt.htm

———. 2001. *World Employment Report 2001: Life at Work in the Information Economy*. Geneva: International Labour Organization.

———. 2006. *Review of Annual Reports under the Follow-up to the International Labour Organization Declaration of Fundamental Principles and Rights at Work*. Geneva: International Labour Organization.

Jackson, Andrew. 2010. *Work and Labour: Critical Issues*, 2nd ed. Toronto: Canadian Scholar's Press.

Kennedy, Joseph II. 1996. "Keynote Address." Pp. 1–6 in *Forced Labor: The Prostitution of Children*. Washington, DC: U.S. Department of Labor, Bureau of International Labor Affairs.

Klein, Naomi. 2000. *No Logo: Taking Aim at the Brand Name Bullies*. Toronto: Vintage Canada.

Krahn, Harvey and Graham Lowe. 2002. *Work, Industry and Canadian Society*. Toronto: Thomson Nelson.

Krauss, K. 2010. "G8/G20 Communique: G20 News and Legal Fall Out." Rabble.ca: News for the Rest of Us. http://www.rabble.ca/blogs/bloggers/statica/2010/09/g8g20-communiqu%C3%A9-g20-news-and-legal-fall-out

Kukreja, Anil and George M. Neely, Sr. 2000. "Strategies for Preventing the Digital Divide." Paper presented at the symposium *Telework and the New Workplace of the 21st Century*. Xavier University, New Orleans, October 16.

Lenski, Gerard and J. Lenski. 1987. *Human Societies: An Introduction to Macrosociology*, 5th ed. New York: McGraw-Hill.

Leonard, Bill. 1996. "From School to Work: Partnerships Smooth the Transition." *HR Magazine* (Society for Human Resource Management). December 8, 1998. http://www.shrm.org/hrmag...articles/0796cov.htm

Levitan, Sar A., Garth L. Mangum, and Stephen L. Mangum. 1998. *Programs in Aid of the Poor*, 7th ed. Baltimore: Johns Hopkins University Press.

Liem, Joan H. and G. Ramsey Liem. 1990. "Understanding the Individual and Family Effects of Unemployment." Pp. 175–204 in *Stress between Work and Family*, edited by J. Eckenrode and S. Gore. New York: Plenum Press.

Lovelace, Glenn. 2000. "The Nuts and Bolts of Telework." Paper presented at the symposium *Telework and the New Workplace of the 21st Century*. Xavier University, New Orleans, October 16.

Marshall, Katherine. 1999. "Employment after Childbirth." *Perspectives on Labour and Income* (Autumn): 15–25. Catalogue no.75-001-XPE.

Maule, C. J. 1999. "Multinational Corporation." Pp. 1536 in *The Canadian Encyclopedia: Year 2000 Edition*, edited by James H. Marsh. Toronto: McClelland & Stewart Inc.

McDermott, Elizabeth. 2006. "Surviving in Dangerous Places: Lesbian Identity Performances in the Workplace." *Feminism and Psychology* 16: 193–211.

McKarney, Matthew. 2013. "In Defense of a Livelihood: Ontario Growers and the Seasonal Agricultural Workers Program Debate." Unpublished Master of Arts Thesis, University of Western Ontario, London.

McLean, Jennifer. 2006. "Forgotten Faculty: Stress and Job Satisfaction among Distance Educators." *Online Journal of Distance Learning and Education* 9(2). http://www.westga.edu/~distance/ojdla/summer92/mclean92.html

Miller, Mary E. 2013. "Child Labor Issues and Human Trafficking." Presentation delivered to University of Washington, January 11, 2013. http://www.law.washington.edu/AsianLaw/HumanTrafficking/Miller-ChildLabor.pdf

Mishel, Lawrence, Jared Bernstein, and John Schmitt. 2001. *The State of Working America, 2000–2001*. Economic Policy Institute Series. Ithaca, NY: Cornell University Press.

Multinational Monitor. 2000. "Editorial: What Is Society Willing to Spend on Human

Beings?" *Multinational Monitor* 21 (November). http://www.essential.org/monitor/mm2000/00november

National Council of Welfare. 1999a. *Children First: A Pre-Budget Report by the National Council of Welfare.* http://www.ncwcnbes.net/htmdocument/reportchildrenfirst.htm

———. 1999b. *Preschool Children: Promises to Keep.* http://www.ncwcnbes.net/htmdocument/reportpromise/firstpag.html

National Public Radio (NPR). 2005. "Blackberry or Crackberry?" The Morning Edition, originally broadcast January 12, 2005. Available at http://www.npr.org/templates/story/story.php?storyId=4279486

North, P. 2011. "Should Crisis-Hit Countries Leave the Eurozone?" *Economic Sociology: The European Electronic Newsletter* 12: 21–26.

O'Connell Davidson, Julia. 2011. "Moving Children? Child Trafficking, Child Migration, and Child Rights." *Critical Social Policy* 31(3): 454–477.

Ontario Coalition for Better Childcare. 2011. "Child Care: Ontario Can't Work without It." http://www.childcareontario.org/?p=4205

Parker, David L. (with Lee Engfer and Robert Conrow). 1998. *Stolen Dreams: Portraits of Working Children.* Minneapolis: Lerner Publications Company.

Reidmann, Agnes, Mary Ann Lamanna, and Adie Nelson. 2003. *Marriages and Families.* Toronto: Thomson Nelson.

Report on the World Social Situation. 1997. New York: United Nations.

Riley, Patricia, Anu Mandavilli, and Rebecca Heino. 2000. "Observing the Impact of Communication and Information Technology on 'Network.'" Paper presented at the symposium *Telework and the New Workplace of the 21st Century.* Xavier University, New Orleans, October 16.

Robie, Chet, Ann Marie Ryan, Robert A. Schmieder, Luis Fernando Parra, and Patricia C. Smith. 1998. "The Relation between Job Level and Job Satisfaction." *Group and Organizational Management* 23(4): 470–86.

Ross, Catherine E. and Marylyn P. Wright. 1998. "Women's Work, Men's Work, and the Sense of Control." *Work and Occupations* 25(3): 333–55.

Rotstein, Abraham. 1999. "Economic Nationalism." Pp. 716–17 in *The Canadian Encyclopedia Year 2000 Edition,* edited by James H. Marsh. Toronto: McClelland & Stewart Inc.

Saskatchewan Federation of Labour. 2006. Brief to the Saskatchewan Minimum Wage Board on Minimum Age of Employment and Employer-Provided Transportation Home.

Schlosser, Eric. 2013. (2001). "The Chain Never Stops." In *Food and Culture: A Reader,* 3rd ed., edited by Carole Counihan and Penny Van Estrick. London and New York: Routledge.

Sears, Alan. 2005. "Queer Anti-Capitalism: What's Left of Lesbian and Gay Liberation." *Science and Society* 69(1): 92–112.

Silvers, Jonathan. 1996. "Child Labor in Pakistan." *Atlantic Monthly* 277(2): 79–92.

Simone, Rose. 1999. "Couple Speak Out about Dangers of Toxic Substances in Workplace." *Kitchener-Waterloo Record* (November 10): B7.

Statistics Canada. 1998. Canadian Profile 2000. Ottawa: Ministry of Industry.

———. 1999. "Labour Force Update: An Overview of the Labour Market." *The Daily,* January 27.

———. 2002. "Unionization." *The Daily,* August 24. http://www.statcan.ca/Daily/English/000824/d000824d.htm

———. 2003. "Earnings of Canadians: Making a Living in the New Economy." *The Daily,* March 11. http://www12.statcan.ca/english/census01/Products/Analytic/companion/earn/contents.cfm

———. 2011. "Indicators of Well-being in Canada: Work and Work Related Injuries." http://www4.hrsdc.gc.ca/.3ndic.1t.4r@-eng.jsp?iid=20

Tremblay, Stephane, Nancy A. Ross, and Jean-Marie Berthelot. 2002. "Regional Socio-Economic Context and Health." Supplement to Health Reports 13. Catalogue no. 92-003. Ottawa: Statistics Canada.

"Underage and Unprotected: Child Labor in Egypt's Cotton Fields." 2001. *Human Rights Watch* 13 (January).

UNICEF (United Nations International Children's Emergency Fund). 1997. *State of the World's Children, 1997.* New York: United Nations.

———. 2000. *The Progress of Nations 2000.* New York: United Nations.

U.S. Department of Labor. 1995. "By the Sweat and Toil of Children." The Use of Child Labor in U.S. Agricultural Imports and Forced and Bonded Child Labor, Vol. 2. Washington, DC: U.S. Department of Labor, Bureau of International Labor Affairs.

Waring, Marilyn. 1988. *If Women Counted.* Toronto: Macmillan.

Went, Robert. 2000. *Globalization: Neoliberal Challenge, Radical Responses.* Sterling, VA: Pluto Press.

Wilkins, K. and S. G. Mackenzie. 2007. "Work Injuries." *Health Reports.* Statistics Canada. Catalogue no. 82-003: 18.

Wilson, Tara. 2012. Did Full-Day Kindergarten Policy Changes in the Maritime Provinces in the 1990s Change Maternal Labour Force Participation? Unpublished Major Research Paper, Department of Economics, University of Ottawa.

Yanz, Lynda and Bob Jeffcott. 1997. "Fighting Sweatshops/Building Solidarity: Exposing the Gap." *Canadian Dimensions* 31 (October): 25–29.

Chapter 12

AAUW (American Association of University Women). 1998. "Report Finds Separating by Sex Not the Solution to Gender Inequity in School." Press release (2300). http://aauw.org

Aberle-Grasse, Melissa. 2000. "The Washington Study Service-Learning Year of Eastern Mennonite University: Reflections on 23 Years of Service Learning." *American Behavioral Scientist* 43: 848–57.

Althusser, Louis. 1971. "Ideology and Ideological State Apparatuses." Trans. Ben Brewster. Pp. 127–86 in *Lenin and Philosophy and Other Essays.* New York: Monthly Review Press.

Appleby, Timothy. 2000. "Weapons Turn Up More Often at Schools: Police." *The Globe and Mail* (February 18): A18.

Ascher, Carol, Norm Fruchter, and Robert Berne. 1997. *Hard Lessons: Public Schools and Privatization.* New York: Twentieth Century Fund.

Bankston, Carl and Stephen Caldas. 1997. "The American School Dilemma: Race and Scholastic Performance." *Sociological Quarterly* 38(3): 423–29.

Barlow, Maude and Heather-Jane Robertson. 1994. *Class Warfare: The Assault on Canada's Schools.* Toronto: Key Porter Books.

Bhattacharjee, K. 2003. *The Ontario Safe Schools Act: School Discipline and Discrimination.* Toronto: Ontario Human Rights Commission. http://www.ohrc.on.ca/en/resources/discussion_consultation/SafeSchoolsConsultRepENG?page=SafeSchoolsConsult RepENG-V_.html

Bibby, Reginald W. 2001. *Canada's Teens: Today, Yesterday, and Tomorrow.* Toronto: Stoddart.

Bowlby, G. 2008. "Provincial Drop-Out Rates." *Labour Force Survey.* Ottawa: Statistics Canada. http://www.statcan.gc.ca/pub/81-004-x/2005004/8984-eng.htm

Bracey, Gerald W. 1998. "Are U.S. Students Behind?" *The American Prospect* 37 (March-April): 54–70. http://www.prospect.org/archives/37/37bracfs.html

Bradshaw, James. 2014. "Ontario to Launch $42-Million Central Hub for Online Postsecondary Classes." *The Globe and Mail* (January 13). Accessed March 1, 2014. http://www.theglobeandmail.com/news/politics/ontario-to-launch-central-hub-for-online-postsecondary-classes/article16299333/

Bricker, Darrell and Edward Greenspon. 2001. *Searching for Certainty: Inside the New Canadian Mindset.* Toronto: Doubleday Canada.

Brooks, Jacqueline and E. G. Thompson. 2005. "Social Justice in the Classroom." *Educational Leadership* 63(1): 48–52.

Bushweller, Kevin. 1995. "Turning Our Backs on Boys." *Education Digest* (January): 9–12.

Call, Kathleen, Lorie Grabowski, Jeylan Mortimer, Katherine Nash, and Chaimun Lee. 1997. "Impoverished Youth and the Attainment Process." Presented at the annual meeting of the American Sociological Association, Toronto, Canada, August.

Campaign 2000. 2001. "Child Poverty in Canada: Report Card 2000." Toronto Campaign 2000.

Canadian Council on Social Development. 1999. *Thinking Ahead: Trends Affecting Public Education in the Future.* Ottawa: Canadian Council on Social Development.

———. 2001. *The Progress of Canada's Children 2001—Highlights.* http://www.ccsd.ca/pubs/2-1/pcc2001.hl.htm

Canadian Press. 2000. "School Violence: Read All about It." *The Globe and Mail* (May 6): A15.

CAUT. 2005. "University Tuition Fees in Canada, 2003." *Education Review* 5(1): 1–4.

Chernos, Saul. 1998. "Alternative Route." *Education Today* 10 (Winter): 12–15.

Cherubini, Lorenzo. 2012. "Post-secondary Aboriginal Educational Policy in Ontario: Policy and Practical Implications." *Aboriginal Policy Studies* 2(1): 42–55.

Clark, Warren. 1999. "Paying off Student Loans." *Canadian Social Trends* 51 (Winter): 24–28.

Clarke, Edward H. 1873. *Sex in Education; or, a Fair Chance for the Girls.* Boston: J. R. Osgood and Co.

Cohen, Warren. 1998. "Vouchers for Good and Ill." *U.S. News and World Report* (April 27): 46.

Conciatore, Jacqueline. 2000. "Study Shows That More than Half of American Colleges Now Have Diversity Requirements." *Black Issues in Higher Education* 17: 22.

Covell, Katherine. 2001. *Canada's NonGovernmental Organizations Report.* Submitted for the United Nations General Assembly Special Session, September 19–21 (on behalf of the Canadian Coalition for the Rights of Children), February 2001.

Crane, Jennifer. 1999. "Help Troublemakers, Schools Told: Expelling Kids Breeds Violence, Psychiatrist Says." *Toronto Star* (May 24): A2.

Curtis, James E. and Ronald D. Lambert. 1994. "Ideology and Social Change." Pp. 710–58 in *The Social World,* 3rd ed., edited by Lorne Tepperman, James E. Curtis, and R. Jack Richardson. Toronto: McGraw-Hill.

Dardur, Antonia. 1991. *Culture and Power in the Classroom: A Critical Foundation for Bicultural Education.* New York: Bergin and Garvey.

Dei, George. 1999. "School Reforms in Ontario: The Marketization of Education and the Resulting Silence on Equity." *Alberta Journal of Educational Research* 45(2): 111.

———. 2001. "Rescuing the Theory: Anti-Racism and Inclusive Education." *Race, Gender and Class* 8(1): 139.

Digest of Educational Statistics. 2001. Chapters 1-6. National Center for Educational Statistics. http://nces.ed.gov/pubs2001/digest

Doherty, G. 1997. *Zero to Six: The Basis for School Readiness.* Ottawa: Applied Research Branch, Human Resources Development Canada (#R-97-8E).

Drolet, M. 2005. "Participation in Post-Secondary Education in Canada: Has the Role of Parental Income and Education Changed over the 1990s?" Ottawa: Statistics Canada. 11F0019MIE No. 243.

Evans, Lorraine and Kimberly Davies. 2000. "No Sissy Boys Here." *Sex Roles* (February): 255–71.

Fact Sheet. 2000. "2000 Head Start Fact Sheet." Research and Statistics. Washington, DC: Department of Health and Human Services.

Fichten, Catherine S., Maria Barile, and Evelyn Reid. 1999. "Computer Technologies and Women with Disabilities: Is There Common Ground?" *1999 SWC Supplement:* 5, 10. Ottawa: CAUT.

Fisher, Donald, et al. 2006. *Canadian Federal Policy and Postsecondary Education.* University of British Columbia: The Centre for Policy Studies in Higher Education and Training: Faculty of Education. http://www.chet.educ.ubc.ca

Fullan, Michael. [1982] 2001. *The New Meaning of Educational Change,* 3rd ed. New York: Teachers College Press.

George, Jane. 1998. "Kuujjuaq Daycare Thrives on Federal Head Start Program." *Nunatsiaq News,* October 29.

Ghalam, Nancy Z. 2000. "Paid and Unpaid Work." In *Women in Canada 2000: A Gender-Based Report,* pp. 97–134. Ottawa: Statistics Canada.

Gilbert, Sid and Bruce Orok. 1993. "School Leavers." *Canadian Social Trends* (Winter): 2–7.

Gilmartin, Shannon. 2005. "The Centrality and Costs of Heterosexual Romantic Love among First-Year College Women." *The Journal of Higher Education* 76(6): 609–33.

Girvan, Susan (ed.). 2000. *Canadian Global Almanac.* Toronto: Macmillan Canada.

Goldberg, Carey. 1999. "After Girls Get Attention, Focus is on Boys' Woes." P. 6 in *Themes of the Times: New York Times,* Upper Saddle River, NJ: Prentice-Hall.

Government of Canada. 2001. "Early Intervention Programs." http://www.hrdc-drhc.gc.ca

Haig-Brown, Celia. 1993. *Resistance and Renewal: Surviving the Indian Residential School.* Vancouver: Arsenal Pulp Press.

Hammonds, Bruce. 2002. "The Latest Ideas on School Reform by Michael Fullan." *Leading and Learning for the 21st Century* (June 29): 1, 3. http://www.leading-learning.co.nz/newsletters/vol101-no03-2002.html

Health Canada. 1999. *Statistical Report on the Health of Canadians.* December 25. http://www.hc-sc.gc.ca/hppb/phdd/report/state/eng/over.html

Henry, Frances, Carol Tator, Winston Mattis, and Tim Rees. 2000. *The Colour of Democracy: Racism in Canadian Society,* 2nd ed. Toronto: Harcourt Brace Canada.

Humble, Aine, Catherine Richards Solomon, Katherine Allen, Karen Blaisure, and Michael Johnson. 2006. "Feminism and Mentoring of Graduate Students." *Family Relations* 55: 2–15.

James, Carl. 2004. "Assimilation to Accommodation: Immigrants and Changing Patterns of Schooling." *Education Canada* 44(4): 43–45.

Jencks, Christopher, and Meredith Phillips. 1998. "America's Next Achievement Test: Closing the Black-White Test Score Gap." *The American Prospect* (September/October): 44–53.

Johnston, Ann Dowsett. 1999. *Maclean's* (November 15): 31.

———. 2001. "Survival of the Fittest." *Maclean's* (April 23). http://www.macleans.ca

Kanter, Rosabeth Moss. 1972. "The Organization Child: Experience Management in a Nursery School." *Sociology of Education* 45: 186–211.

Kozol, Jonathan. 1991. *Savage Inequalities: Children in America's Schools.* New York: Crown Publishers.

Lam, Julia. 1997. "The Employment Activity of Chinese-American High-School Students and Its Relationship to Academic Achievement." Presented at the Annual Meeting of the American Sociological Association, Toronto, August.

Lareau, Annette. 1989. *Home Advantage: Social Class and Parental Intervention in Elementary Education.* Philadelphia: Falmer Press.

Levin, Malcolm. 1999. "Alternative Education." P. 732 in *The Canadian Encyclopedia: Year 2000 Edition,* edited by James H. Marsh. Toronto: McClelland & Stewart Inc.

Levinson, Arlene. 2000. "Study Evaluates Higher Education." Excite.News. http://www.excite.com/news/ap/00130/08/grading

Lewin, Tamar. 2013. "After Setbacks, Online Courses are Rethought." *New York Times* (December 10). Accessed March 1, 2014. http://www.nytimes.com/2013/12/11/us/after-setbacks-online-courses-are-rethought.html

Literacy. 2000. "Basic Literacy." Literacy Volunteers of America. http://www.literacyvolunteers.org/about/basic

Livingstone, D. N. 1999. "Educational Opportunity." Pp. 743–44 in *The Canadian Encyclopedia: Year 2000 Edition*, edited by James H. Marsh. Toronto: McClelland & Stewart Inc.

Mackie, Marlene. 1991. *Gender Explorations in Canada: Further Explorations*. Toronto: Butterworths.

Maclean's. 2002. "Ruling against Bullying." (April 8): 14.

Mahoney, Jill. 2003. "New Edmonton Bylaw Aims to Fight Bullying." *The Globe and Mail* (March 12): A8.

Merton, Robert K. 1968. *Social Theory and Social Structure*. New York: Free Press.

Miss G Collective. 2005. "The Miss G Project." Accessed July 1, 2006. http://www.themissgproject.org

Muller, Chandra, and Katherine Schiller. 2000. "Leveling the Playing Field?" *Sociology of Education* 73: 196–218.

Murnane, Richard J. 1994. "Education and the Well-Being of the Next Generation." Pp. 289–307 in *Confronting Poverty: Prescriptions for Change*, edited by Sheldon H. Danziger, Gary D. Sandefur, and Daniel H. Weinberg. New York: Russell Sage Foundation.

Noddings, Nel. 1995. "A Morally Defensible Mission for Schools in the Twenty-first Century." *Phi Delta Kappan* (January): 365–68.

OECD. 2013. *Education at a Glance 2013: OECD Indicators*. OECD Publishing. http://dx.doi.org/10.1787/eag-2013-en

PAR-L. n.d. "A Chronology of the Development of Women's Studies in Canada: The 1970's." Accessed June 27, 2006. http://www.unb.ca/PAR-L/chronology1.htm

Ray, Carol A. and Roslyn A. Mickelson. 1993. "Restructuring Students for Restructured Work: The Economy, School Reform, and Non-College-Bound Youths." *Sociology of Education* 66: 1–20.

Rosenthal, Robert and Lenore Jacobson. 1968. *Pygmalion in the Classroom: Teacher Expectations and Pupils' Intellectual Development*. New York: Holt, Rinehart and Winston.

Ross, David. 1998. "Rethinking Child Poverty." *Insight, Perception* 22(1): 9–11.

Schaefer, Richard T., Robert P. Lamm, Penny Biles, and Susannah J. Wilson. 1996. *Sociology: An Introduction*. Toronto: McGraw-Hill Ryerson.

Schofield, John. 1999. "Learning on the Front Lines." *Maclean's* (January 15): 90–94.

Schrag, Peter. 1997. "The New Myth of Our Failing Schools." *The Atlantic Monthly* (October). http://www.theatlantic.com/issues/97oct/fail.htm

School Community Safety Advisory Panel. 2008. *The Road to Health: A Final Report on School Safety*.

Shanker, Albert. 1996. "Mythical Choice and Real Standards." Pp. 154–72 in *Reducing Poverty in America*, edited by Michael Darby. Thousand Oaks, CA: Sage.

Sokoloff, Heather. 2001. "OECD Shows Alberta No. 1 in Reading Skills." *National Post* (December 5): A1, A17.

Sommers, Christina Hoff. 2000. *The War against Boys: How Misguided Feminism Is Harming Young Men*. New York: Simon and Schuster.

Sowell, Thomas. 1994. "Multicultural Education Is Harmful." Pp. 104–8 in *Culture Wars: Opposing Viewpoints*, edited by David Bender and Bruno Leone. San Diego, CA: Greenhaven Press, Inc.

Statistics Canada. 1998. *Canada Yearbook 1999*. Ottawa: Minister of Industry.

———. 2003a. "Education in Canada: Raising the Standard." Catalogue no. 96F0030X-IE2001012. http://www12.statcan.ca/english/census01/products/Analytic/companion/educ/contents.cfm

———. 2003b. "Family Income and Participation in Postsecondary Education." Catalogue no.11F0019MIE No. 210.

———. 2005. "University Tuition Fees." *The Daily*, September 1.

———. 2008. "Educational Portrait of Canada, 2006 Census." Ottawa: Minister of Industry. Catalogue no. 97-560-X.

———. 2010. "Education Indicators in Canada: Interrupting High School and Returning to Education." Catalogue no. 81-599-X (005).

———. 2012. CANSIM table 477-0017, Number of full-time teaching staff at Canadian universities, by rank, sex, Canada and provinces, annual (number) [Table]. CANISM (database). Last modified: 2012-05-03.

———. 2013a. CANSIM table 477-0019, Postsecondary enrolments by registration status, Pan-Canadian Standard Classification of Education, Classification of Instructional Programs, Primary Grouping, sex and immigration status, annual (number) [Table]. CANISM (database). Last modified: 2013-11-27.

Toronto Board of Education. 1993. *The 1991 Every Secondary Student Survey, Part II: Detailed Profiles of Toronto's Secondary School Students*. Toronto: Toronto Board of Education Research Services.

UNESCO (United Nations Educational, Scientific, and Cultural Organization). 2012. "EFA Global Monitoring Report." Available at http://www.unesco.org

United Nations Population Fund. 1999. "Campaign Issues: Facing the Facts." Face to Face. http://www.facecampaign.org

Vigdor, Jacob L. and Helen F. Ladd. 2010. "Scaling the Digital Divide: Home Computer Technology and Student Achievement." NBER Working Paper No. 16078, Issued June 2010.

Waterman, Alan. S. (ed.). 1997. *Service-Learning: Applications from the Research*. Mahwah, NJ: Lawrence Erlbaum Associates Publishers.

Webb, Julie. 1989. "The Outcomes of Home-Based Education: Employment and Other Issues." *Educational Review* 41: 121–33.

Whitehead, Fred (ed.). 1994. *Culture Wars: Opposing Viewpoints*. San Diego, CA: Greenhaven Press, Inc.

Wilgoren, Jodi. 2001. "Calls for Change in the Scheduling of the School Day." *The New York Times on the Web*, January 10. http://www.nytimes.com/2001/01/10/nyregion/10scho.html

Winters, Rebecca. 2000. "From Home to Harvard." *Time*, September 11. http://www.time.com/time/magazine/articles

WRDSB. 2014. Year End Review—Board Improvement Plan for Student Achievement. Prepared by John Bryant, Director, Waterloo District School Board, 51 Ardelt Avenue, Kitchener Ontario. http://www.wrdsb.ca/board-meetings/wp-content/uploads/sites/25/YREndRev_AppJune23-14.pdf

Zine, Jasmin. 2002. "Inclusive Schooling in a Plural Society: Removing the Margins." *Education Canada* 42(3): 36–39.

Zlotkowski, E. 1996. "Opportunity for All: Linking Service-Learning and Business Education." *Journal of Business Ethics* 1: 5–19.

Chapter 13

Aeck, Molly. 2005. "Biofuel Use Growing Rapidly." Pp. 38–39 in *Vital Signs 2005*, edited by Linda Starke. New York: W. W. Norton.

Allison, Wade. 2011. "Viewpoint: We Should Stop Running Away from Radiation." BBC News: World Edition. http://www.bbc.co.uk/news/world-12860842

———. 2013. "Why Fear of Radiation Is Wrong Personally, Scientifically, Socio-Economically, Environmentally." Oxford University, Public Lecture, July 2, 2013. http://www.radiationandreason.com/uploads//enc_WhyFearofRadiationisWrong-.pdf

American Lung Association. 2005. *Lung Disease Data in Culturally Diverse Communities: 2005*. Available at http://www.lungusa.org

Anonymous 2011. "Kyoto and Out." *The Economist*. December 17, 2011. Accessed May 4, 2014. http://www.economist.com/node/21541849

Aslam, Abid. 2005 (October 9). "Planet Faces Nightmare Forecasts as Chinese Consumption Grows and Grows." Common Dreams News Center. Available at http://www.commondreams.org

Associated Press. 2000 (January 7). "Daimler-Chrysler Corporation Quits Global Climate Coalition." *Environmental News Network.* http://www.enn.com/news/

———. 2005 (April 13). "Wal-Mart Pledges $35 Million for Wildlife." MSNBC.com. Available at http://www.msnbc.msn.com

Ayres, Ed. 2004. "The Hidden Shame of the Global Industrial Economy." *World Watch Magazine* (January- February): 18–29.

Baillie, J. E. M., C. Hilton-Taylor, and S. N. Stuart (eds.). 2004. *2004 IUCN Red List of Threatened Species: A Global Species Assessment.* Cambridge, England: International Union for Conservation of Nature and Natural Resources.

Barbosa, L. C. 2009. "Change by Necessity: Ecological Limits to Capitalism, Climate Change, and Obstacles to Transition to an Environmentally Sustainable Economy." SSRN. http://ssrn.com/abstract=1458114

BBC News. 2009. "Why Did Copenhagen Fail to Deliver a Climate Deal?" http://news.bbc.co.uk/2/hi/8426835.stm

Black, R. 2011. "Canada Under Fire over Kyoto Protocol Exit." BBC News: US & Canada. December 13, 2011. Accessed April 21, 2014. http://www.bbc.com/news/world-us-canada-16165033

Blatt, Harvey. 2005. *America's Environmental Report Card: Are We Making the Grade?* Cambridge, MA: MIT Press.

Bohan, Caren. 2005 (August 23). "The Illulissat Glacier, a Wonder of the World Melting Away." Common Dreams News Center. Available at http://www.commondreams.org

Bright, Chris. 2003. "A History of Our Future." Pp. 3–13 in *State of the World 2003,* edited by Linda Starke. New York: W. W. Norton.

Brown, Lester R. 2003. *Plan B: Rescuing a Planet under Stress and a Civilization in Trouble.* New York: W. W. Norton.

———. 2007 (Jan. 4). "Distillery Demand for Grain to Fuel Cars Vastly Understated: World May Be Facing Highest Grain Prices in History." *Earth Policy News.* http://www.earthpolicy.org

Brown, Lester R. and Jennifer Mitchell. 1998. "Building a New Economy." Pp. 168–87 in *State of the World 1998,* edited by Lester R. Brown, Christopher Flavin, and Hilary French. New York: W. W. Norton.

Bruce, Nigel, Rogelio Perez-Padilla, and Rachel Albalak. 2000. "Indoor Air Pollution in Developing Countries: A Major Environmental and Public Health Challenge." *Bulletin of the World Health Organization* 78(9): 1078–92.

Bruno, Kenny and Joshua Karliner. 2002. *Earthsummit.biz: The Corporate Takeover of Sustainable Development.* CorpWatch and Food First Books. Available at http://www.corpwatch.org

Bullard, Robert D. 2000. *Dumping in Dixie: Race, Class, and Environmental Quality,* 3rd ed. Boulder, CO: Westview Press.

Bullard, Robert D., et al. 2007. *Toxic Wastes and Race at Twenty 1987–2007.* Cleveland: United Church of Christ.

Cappiello, Dina. 2003. "Corporations Co-opt Earth Day." *Houston Chronicle,* April 22. Available at http://www.houstonchronicle.com

Caress, Stanley, Anne C. Steinemann, and Caitlin Waddick. 2002. "Symptomatology and Etiology of Multiple Chemical Sensitivities in the Southeastern United States." *Archives of Environmental Health* 57(5): 429–436.

CBC News. 2005 (October 30). "McGuinty Visits Kashechewan Evacuees." CBC News Online. http://www.cbc.ca/story/canada/national/2005/10/30/kashechewan051030.html

Centers for Disease Control and Prevention, National Center for Environmental Health. 2003. *Second National Report on Human Exposure to Environmental Chemicals.* Atlanta, GA: Centers for Disease Control and Prevention.

———. 2005. *Third National Report on Human Exposure to Environmental Chemicals.* Atlanta, GA: Centers for Disease Control and Prevention.

CGBC (Canada Green Building Council). 2006. "Leed Certified Buildings." http://www.cagbc.org/green_building_projects/leed_certified_buildings.php

Chafe, Zoe. 2005. "Bioinvasions." Pp. 60–61 in *State of the World 2005,* edited by Linda Starke. New York: W. W. Norton.

Chepesiuk, R. 2009. "Missing the Dark: Health Effects of Light Pollution." *Environmental Health Perspectives* 117: A20–A27.

Chivian, Eric and Aaron S. Bernstein. 2004. "Embedded in Nature: Human Health and Biodiversity." *Environmental Health Perspectives* 112(1). Available at http://ehp.niehs.nih.gov

Cincotta, Richard P. and Robert Engelman. 2000. *Human Population and the Future of Biological Diversity.* Washington, DC: Population Action International.

Clarke, Tony. 2002. "Twilight of the Corporation." Pp. 41–45 in *Social Problems, Annual Editions 02/03,* 30th ed., edited by Kurt Finster-Busch. Guilford, CT: McGraw-Hill/Dushkin.

Clarren, Rebecca. 2005. "Dirty Politics, Foul Air." *The Nation* (March 14): 6, 8.

Cooper, Arnie. 2004. "Twenty-Eight Words That Could Change the World: Robert Hinkley's Plan to Tame Corporate Power." *The Sun* 345 (September): 4–11.

Denson, Bryan. 2000. "Shadowy Saboteurs." *The IRE Journal* (Investigative Reports and Editors, Inc.) 23 (May/June): 12–14.

DesJardins, Andrea. 1997. "Sweet Poison: What Your Nose Can't Tell You about the Dangers of Perfume." January 20, 1999. http://members.aol.com/enviroknow/perfume/sweet_poison.htm

Dewailly, Eric, et al. 1996. "Polychlorinated Biphenyl (Pcb) and Dichlorodiphenyl Dichloroethylene (Dde) Concentration in the Breast Milk of Women in Quebec." *American Journal of Public Health* 86(9): 1241–46.

Elliott, John E., et al. 2006. "Brominated Flame Retardants and Halogenated Phenolic Compounds in North American West Coast Bald Eaglet." *Environmental Science and Technology* 40(20): 6275–81.

Energy Information Administration. 2005. *International Energy Annual 2003.* U.S. Department of Energy. Available at http://www.eia.doe.gov

ENS (Environmental News Service). 2005 (November 15). "Lab Tests Find 60 Toxic Chemicals in Canadians' Blood." http://www.ens-newswire.com/ens/nov2005/2005-11-15.asp

Environment Canada. 2006. "Clean Energy Canada." http://www.cleanenergy.gc.ca/canada/companies_e.asp?item=179

Environmental Defense. 2004. *2004 Annual Report.* Available at http://www.environmentaldefense.org

Fisher, Brandy E. 1998. "Scents and Sensitivity." *Environmental Health Perspectives* 106(12). February 1, 1999. http://ehpnet1.niehs.nih.gov/docs/1998/106-12/focus-abs.html

Flavin, Chris and Molly Hull Aeck. 2005 (September 15). "Cleaner, Greener, and Richer." *TomPaine.com.* Available at http://wu.oneworld.net

Food and Drug Administration. 2008. "Pesticide Residue Monitoring Program Results and Discussion FY 2006." http://www.fda.gov/Food/FoodSafety/FoodContaminantsAdulteration/Pesticides/ResidueMonitoringReports/ucm125187.htm

Food and Water Watch and Network for New Energy Choices. 2007. *The Rush to Ethanol: Not All Biofuels Are Created Equal.* http://www.newenergychoices.org

French, Hilary. 2000. "Environmental Treaties Gain Ground." Pp. 134–35 in *Vital Signs 2000,* edited by Lester R. Brown, Michael Renner, and Brian Halwell. New York: W. W. Norton & Co.

Gardner, Gary. 2005. "Forest Loss Continues." Pp. 92–93 in *Vital Signs 2005,* edited by Linda Starke. New York: W. W. Norton.

Gartner, John. 2005 (September 13). "Sierra Club Gets Behind the Wheel." *Wired News.* Available at http://www.wired.com/news

"Global Corporations Join Us to Reduce Greenhouse Gas Emissions." 2000. *Environmental Defense* 31 (November): 5.

Global Invasive Species Database. 2006. *100 of the World's Worst Invasive Alien Species.* Auckland, NZ: Invasive Species Specialist Group, University of Auckland.

Gooch, Martin, Abdek Felfel, and Nicole Marenick. 2010. Food Waste in Canada: Opportunities to Increase the Competitiveness of Canada's Agri-Food Sector, While Simultaneously Improving the Environment. George Morris Centre. Accessed May 4, 2014. Available at http://vcm-international.com/wp-content/uploads/2013/04/Food-Waste-in-Canada-112410.pdf

Government of Canada. 2006. "Innovation Roadmap on Bio-based Feedstocks, Fuels and Industrial Products." *Technology Roadmaps,* June 6. http://strategis.ic.gc.ca/epic/internet/intrm-crt.nsf/en/rm00115e.html

Hager, Nicky and Bob Burton. 2000. *Secrets and Lies: The Anatomy of an Anti-Environmental PR Campaign.* Monroe, ME: Common Courage Press.

Hilgenkamp, K. 2005. *Environmental Health: Ecological Perspectives.* London and Mississauga: Jones and Bartlett.

Howlett, Karen. 2006. "I Don't Like Nuclear Energy." *Globe and Mail* (June 26): A5.

Hunter, Lori M. 2001. *The Environmental Implications of Population Dynamics.* Santa Monica, CA: Rand Corporation.

Huseman, J. and D. Short. 2012. "A Slow Industrial Genocide': Oil Sands and the Indigenous Peoples of Northern Alberta," *International Journal of Human Rights* 16(1): 216–237.

Intergovernmental Panel on Climate Change. 2001a. *Climate Change 2001: The Scientific Basis.* United Nations Environmental Programme and the World Meteorological Organization. http://www.ipcc.ch

———. 2001b. *Climate Change 2001: Impacts, Adaptation, and Vulnerability.* United Nations Environmental Programme and the World Meteorological Organization. http://www.ipcc.ch

International Fund for Animal Welfare. 2005. *Caught in the Web: Wildlife Trade on the Internet.* Available at http://www.ifaw.org

Jan, George P. 1995. "Environmental Protection in China." Pp. 71–84 in *Environmental Policies in the Third World: A Comparative Analysis,* edited by O. P. Dwivedi and Dhirendra K. Vajpeyi. Westport, CT: Greenwood Press.

Janofsky, Michael. 2005. "Pentagon Is Asking Congress to Loosen Environmental Laws." *New York Times,* May 11. Available at http://www.nytimes.com

Jensen, Derrick. 2001. "A Weakened World Cannot Forgive Us: An Interview with Kathleen Dean Moore." *The Sun* 303 (March): 4–13.

Johansen, Bruce E. 2002. "The Inuit's Struggle with Dioxins and Other Organic Pollutants." *American Indian Quarterly* 26(3): 479–90.

Johnson, Geoffrey. 2004 (April). *Don't Be Fooled: America's Ten Worst Greenwashers.* The Green Life. Available at http://www.thegreenlife.org

Kennedy, Mark. 2011. "Canada Formally Withdrawing from Kyoto Protocol." *National Post,* December 12, 2011. Accessed April 20, 2013. http://news.nationalpost.com/2011/12/12/canada-formally-withdrawig-from-kyoto-protocol

Klinkenborg, V. 2008. "Our Vanishing Night." *National Geographic* 214(5).

Koenig, Dieter. 1995. "Sustainable Development: Linking Global Environmental Change to Technology Cooperation." Pp. 1–21 in *Environmental Policies in the Third World: A Comparative Analysis,* edited by O. P. Dwivedi, and Dhirendra K. Vajpeyi. Westport, CT: Greenwood Press.

Krajnc, Anita. 2000. "Whither Ontario's Environment? Neo-Conservatism and the Decline of the Environment Ministry." *Canadian Public Policy* 26(1): 111–27.

Leahy, S. 2009. *Tight Controls Could Save Global Fisheries.* Inter Press Service. http://ipsnews.net/news.asp?idnews=47912

Levesque, B., et al. 2003. "Monitoring of Umbilical Cord Blood Lead Levels and Sources Assessment among the Inuit." *Occupational and Environmental Medicine* 60: 693–95.

Levin, Phillip S. and Donald A. Levin. 2002. "The Real Biodiversity Crisis." *American Scientist* 90(1): 6.

Little, Amanda Griscom. 2005. "Maathai on the Prize: An Interview with Nobel Peace Prize Winner Wangari Maathai." *Grist Magazine,* February 15. Available at http://www.grist.org

MacDonald, Mia and Danielle Nierenberg. 2003. "Linking Population, Women, and Biodiversity." Pp. 38–61 in *State of the World 2003,* edited by Linda Starke. New York: W. W. Norton.

Makower, Joel, Ron Pernick, and Clint Wilder. 2005. *Clean Energy Trends 2005.* Clean Edge. Available at http://www.cleanedge.com

Margesson, Rhoda. 2005. "Environmental Refugees." Pp. 40–41 in *State of the World 2005,* edited by Linda Starke. New York: W. W. Norton.

Martinez, Victor D., et al. 2013. "Emerging Arsenic Threat in Canada." *Science* 342(Nov.): 559.

Mastny, Lisa. 2003. "State of the World: A Year in Review." Pp. xix–xxiii in *State of the World 2003,* edited by Linda Starke. New York: W. W. Norton.

McDaniel, Carl N. 2005. *Wisdom for a Livable Planet.* San Antonio: Trinity University Press.

McEvoy, David M. 2013. "Enforcing Compliance with International Environmental Agreements Using a Deposit-Refund System." *International Environmental Agreements* 13: 481–496.

McMichael, Anthony J., Kirk R. Smith, and Carlos F. Corvalan. 2000. "The Sustainability Transition: A New Challenge." *Bulletin of the World Health Organization* 78(9): 1067.

Mead, Leila. 1998. "Radioactive Wastelands." *The Green Guide* 53 (April 14): 1–3.

Millennium Ecosystem Assessment. 2005. *Ecosystems and Human Well-Being: Synthesis.* Washington, DC: Island Press.

Mishra, Vinod, Robert D. Retherford, and Kirk R. Smith. 2002. "Indoor Air Pollution: The Quiet Killer." *Asia Pacific Issues* 63: 1–8.

Mooney, Chris. 2005. "Some Like It Hot." *Mother Jones* (May-June). Available at http://www.MotherJones.com

National Environmental Education and Training Foundation, and Roper Starch Worldwide. 1999. *NEETF/Roper Report Card.* Washington, DC: National Environmental Education and Training Foundation.

National Oceanic and Atmospheric Administration. 2005 (January 13). *Climate of 2004 Annual Review.* Available at http://www.ncdc.noaa.gov

Natural Resources Canada. 2006. "About Wind Energy." http://www.canren.gc.ca/tech_appl/index.asp?CaId=6&PgId=232

"Nukes Rebuked." 2000 (July 1). *Washington Spectator* 26(13): 4.

Palmer, Randall. 2006 (July 14). "Canada Stresses Commitment to Kyoto Climate Pact." Reuters Canada. http://ca.today.reuters.com/news/newsArticle.aspx?type=domesticNews&storyID=2006-07 14T154612Z_01_L14904845_RTRIDST_0_CANADA-GROUP-BRITAIN-CANADA-COL.XML

Pearce, Fred. 2005. "Climate Warming as Siberia Melts." *New Scientist,* August 11. Available at http://www.NewScientist.com

Pimentel, D. S. 2007. "Ecology of Increasing Diseases: Population Growth and Environmental Degradation." *Human Ecology* 35(6): 653–668.

"A Prescription for Reducing the Damage Caused by Dams." 2001. *Environmental Defense* 32 (March).

Preston, Jen. 2013. "Neoliberal Settler Colonialism, Canada and the Tar Sands," *Race Class* 55(2): 42–59.

Price, T. 2006. "The New Environmentalism." *QC Researcher* 16(42): 987–1007.

Public Citizen. 2005 (February). *NAFTA Chapter 11 Investor-State Cases: Lessons for the Central*

America Free Trade Agreement. Public Citizens Global Trade Watch Publication E9014. Available at http://www.citizen.org

Reese, April. 2001 (February). *Africa's Struggle with Desertification*. Population Reference Bureau. Available at http://www.prb.org/regions/africa/africadesertification.html

Renner, Michael. 1996. *Fighting for Survival: Environmental Decline, Social Conflict, and the New Age of Insecurity*. New York: W. W. Norton.

———. 2004. "Moving toward a Less Consumptive Economy." Pp. 96–119 in *State of the World 2004*, edited by Linda Starke. New York: W. W. Norton.

Rifkin, Jeremy. 2004. *The European Dream: How Europe's Vision of the Future Is Quietly Eclipsing the American Dream*. New York: Tarcher/Penguin.

Rogers, Sherry A. 2002. *Detoxify or Die*. Sarasota, FL: Sand Key.

Saad, Lydia. 2002. *Americans Sharply Divided on Seriousness of Global Warming*. Gallup News Service. Available at http://www.gallup.org

Sampat, Payal. 2003. "Scrapping Mining Dependence." Pp. 110–129 in *State of the World 2003*, edited by Linda Starke. New York: W. W. Norton.

Sawin, Janet L. 2004. "Making Better Energy Choices." Pp. 24–43 in *State of the World 2004*, edited by Linda Starke. New York: W. W. Norton.

———. 2005. "Solar Energy Markets Booming." Pp. 36–37 in *Vital Signs 2005*, edited by Linda Starke. New York: W. W. Norton.

Schaeffer, Robert K. 2003.*Understanding Globalization: The Social Consequences of Political, Economic, and Environmental Change*, 2nd ed. Lanham, MD: Rowman & Littlefield.

Schindler, Mark. 2010. "Tar Sands Need Solid Science." *Nature* 468: 499–501.

Schmidt, Charles W. 2004. "Environmental Crimes: Prompting at the Earth's Expense." *Environmental Health Perspectives* 112(2): A96–A103.

Snider, Laureen. 2004. "Resisting Neo-Liberalism: The Poisoned Water Disaster in Walkerton, Ontario." *Social and Legal Studies* 13(2): 265–89.

Speirs, Rosemary. 2000. "For Boomers, Minivans Are Still a Big Gas." *Toronto Star* (March 11): A24.

Stanford, Jim. 2002. "Hot Air over Kyoto." *THIS magazine* (July/August): 12–13.

Statistics Canada. 1998. *Canada Year Book 2000*. Ottawa: Ministry of Industry.

———. 2005. "Human Activity and the Environment: Solid Waste." *The Daily*, December 2.

Sterritt, Angela. 2005. "Indigenous Youth Challenge Corporate Mining." *Cultural Survival,*

Weekly Indigenous News, July 15. Available at http://www.cs.org/publications/win/win-article.cfm?id=2699& highlight= Angela%20Sterritt

UNEP (United Nations Environment Programme). 2002. *North America's Environment: A Thirty-Year State of the Environment and Policy Retrospectives*. Available at http://www.na.unep.net

———. 2005. *GEO Yearbook 2004/5*. http://www.unep.org

———. 2008. *Yearbook 2007: An Overview of Our Changing Environment*. http://www.unep.org

United Nations Population Fund. 2004. *The State of World Population 2004*. New York: United Nations.

Vajpeyi, Dhirendra K. 1995. "External Factors Influencing Environmental Policy-Making: Role of Multilateral Development Aid Agencies." Pp. 24–45 in *Environmental Policies in the Third World: A Comparative Analysis*, edited by O. P. Dwivedi and Dhirendra K. Vajpeyi. Westport, CT: Greenwood Press.

Vartan, Starre. 2005. "Money Matters: Buying Cleaner Energy." *E Magazine* 16(5). Available at http://www.emagazine.com

Vedantam, Shankar. 2005. "Storage Plan Approved for Nuclear Waste." *Washington Post*, September 10. Available at http://www.washingtonpost.com

Wall, Glenda. 2000. "Recent Representations in Popular Environmental Discourse: Individualism, Wastefulness and the Global Economy." *Canadian Review of Sociology and Anthropology* 37(3): 249–65.

Wal-Mart Watch. 2005. *Wal-Mart Watch*. Press release, April 6. Available at http://walmartwatch.com

Walsh, Helene. 2012. "Alberta's Oil Sands Development Is Not Responsible—Moratorium Needed." Report for Keepers of the Athabasca. Accessed September 24, 2014. http://www.keepersofthewater.ca/files/cumulativeeffects2012.pdf

Warren, Karen J. 2000. *Ecofeminist Philosophy: A Western Perspective on What It Is and Why It Matters*. Lanham, MD: Rowman & Littlefield.

World Resources Institute. 2000. "Why Care about Ecosystems?" In *World Resources 2000–2001: People and Ecosystems—The Fraying Web of Life*. Washington, DC: World Resources Institute.

World Water Assessment Program. 2009. "Water in a Changing World." United Nations World Water Development Report 3, UNESCO.

WWF. 2008. "Infrastructure Problems: River Navigation Schemes." www.panda.org/about_wwf/what_we_do/freshwater/problems/infrastructure/river_navigation/index.cfm

Young, Nathan and Aline Coutinho. 2013. "Government, Anti-Reflexivity, and the Construction of Public Ignorance about Climate Change: Australia and Canada Compared." *Global Environmental Politics* 13(2): 89–108.

Youth, Howard. 2003. "Watching Birds Disappear." Pp. 85–109 in *State of the World 2003*, edited by Linda Starke. New York: W. W. Norton.

Chapter 14

ABC News. 2010 (Oct. 26). "Defence Says Most WikiLeaks Material Already Public." ABC News Australia. http://www.abc.net.au/news/stories/2010/10/26/3048922.htm

Alexander, Karen and Mary E. Hawkesworth, eds. 2008. *War and Terror: Feminist Perspectives*. Chicago: University of Chicago Press.

American Jewish Committee. 2007. *2006 Annual Survey of American Jewish Opinion*. Available at http://www.ajc.org

Annan, Jeannie, Christopher Blattman, Khristopher Carlson, and Dyan Mazurana. 2008. "Findings from the Survey of War-Affected Youth (SWAY) Phase II." Available at https://wikis.uit.tufts.edu/confluence/display

Arms Control Association. 2003 (May). *The Nuclear Proliferation Treaty at a Glance*. Available at http://www.armscontrol.org/factsheets

Atomic Archive. 2009. *Arms Control Treaties*. Available at http://www.atomicarchive.com

Baker, Peter and Helene Cooper. 2009. "U.S. and Russia to Consider Reductions of Nuclear Arsenals in Talks for New Treaty." *New York Times*, March 31. Available at http://www.nytimes.com

Banwell, Stacy. 2014. "Rape and Sexual Violence in the Democratic Republic of Congo: A Case Study of Gender-Based Violence." *Journal of Gender Studies* 23(1): 45–58.

Barkan, Steven and Lynne Snowden. 2001. *Collective Violence*. Boston: Allyn and Bacon.

Barry, Donald. 2005. "Chretien, Bush and the War in Iraq." *American Review of Canadian Studies* 35(2): 215–246.

Barstow, David. 2008. "One Man's Military-Industrial-Media Complex." *New York Times*, November 29. Available at http://www.nytimes.com

BBC. 2000. "UN Admits Rwanda Genocide Failure." BBC News, April 15. Available at http://news.bbc.co.uk

———. 2007a. "Hamas Takes Full Control of Gaza." BBC News, June 15. Available at http://news.bbc.co.uk

———. 2007b. "Fresh Clashes Engulf Lebanon Camp." BBC News, June 1. Available at http://news.bbc.co.uk

———. 2009. "Gaza Crisis: Key Maps & Time-lines." BBC News, January 18. Available at http://news.bbc.co.uk

Bercovitch, Jacob, ed. 2003. *Studies in International Mediation: Advances in Foreign Policy Analysis.* New York: Palgrave Macmillan.

Boustany, Nora. 2007. "Janjaweed Using Rape as 'Integral' Weapon in Darfur, Aid Group Says." *Washington Post,* July 3. Available at http://www.washingtonpost.com

Brewster, Murray and Steve Rennie. 2010. "Canadian Soldier Killed in Roadside Bomb." *The Globe and Mail.* Accessed December 20, 2010. http://www.theglobeandmail.com/news/world/asia-pacific/canadian-soldier-killed-in-a-roadside-bomb-in-afghanistan/article1843714

Brinkley, Joel and David E. Sanger. 2005. "North Koreans Agree to Resume Nuclear Talks." *New York Times,* July 10. Available at http://www.nytimes.com

Broad, William J., Mark Mazzetti, and David E. Sanger. 2009. "A Nuclear Debate: Is Iran Designing Warheads?" *The New York Times,* September 28. Available at http://www.nytimes.com

Broad, William J. and David E. Sanger. 2009 (October 3). "Report Says Iran Has Data to Make a Nuclear Bomb." Available at http://www.nytimes.com

Brown, Michael E., Sean M. Lynn-Jones, and Steven E. Miller, eds. 1996. *Debating the Democratic Peace.* Cambridge, MA: MIT Press.

Buncombe, Andrew. 2009. "End of Sri Lanka's Civil War Brings Back Tourists." *The Independent,* August 16. Available at http://www.independent.co.uk

Carneiro, Robert L. 1994. "War and Peace: Alternating Realities in Human History." Pp. 3–27 in *Studying War: Anthropological Perspectives,* edited by S. P. Reyna and R. E. Downs. Langhorne, PA: Gordon & Breach.

CBC News. 2006 (May 30). "Canada's Military Women in the Canadian Military." Accessed December 14, 2010. http://www.cbc.ca/news/background/cdnmilitary/women-cdnmilitary.html

Center for Defense Information. 2007 (April 30). *The World's Nuclear Arsenals.* Available at http://www.cdi.org

CNN. 2003 (February 26). *Poll: Muslims Call U.S. Ruthless, Arrogant.* Available at http://www.cnn.com

CNN/Opinion Research Corporation Poll. 2007 (June 22-24). *Iraq.* Available at http://www.pollingreport.com/iraq3.htm

Cohen, Ronald. 1986. "War and Peace Proneness in Pre- and Post-industrial States." Pp. 253–267 in *Peace and War: Cross-Cultural Perspectives,* edited by M. L. Foster and R. A. Rubinstein. New Brunswick, NJ: Transaction Books.

Conflict Research Consortium. 2003. *Mediation.* Available at http://www.colorado.edu/conflict/peace

CRS (Congressional Research Service). 2008 (August 25). *Private Security Contractors in Iraq: Background, Legal Status, and Other Issues.* Available at http://www.opencrs.com

Curry, Bill and Daniel LeBlanc. 2008 (Feb. 23). "Defence Priorities Subject to Tough Budget Decisions." *The Globe and Mail.*

Dareini, Ali Akbar. 2009. "Iran Missile Test: Ahmadinejad Says It's Within Israel's Range." *Huffington Post,* May 20. Available at http://www.huffingtonpost.com

Deen, Thalif. 2000 (September 9). *Inequality Primary Cause of Wars, Says Annan.* Available at http://www.hartford-hwp.com/archives

DeYoung, Karen and Walter Pincus. 2009 (October 3). *Iraq: U.S. to Fund Pro-American Publicity in Iraqi Media.* Available at http://www.corpwatch.org

Dixon, William J. 1994. "Democracy and the Peaceful Settlement of International Conflict." *American Political Science Review* 88(1): 14–32.

Eggleton, Art. 2001 (Nov. 30). "Canada a Full Partner in War on Terrorism, Insists Eggleton." *Edmonton Journal:* A17.

Eide, Marian. 2008. "'The Stigma of Nation': Feminist Just War, Privilege and Responsibility." *Hypatia* 23(2): 48–60.

Environmental Media Services. 2002 (October 7). *Environmental Impacts of War.* Available at http://www.ems.org

Feder, Don. 2003. "Islamic Beliefs Led to the Attack on America." Pp. 20–23 in *The Terrorist Attack on America,* edited by Mary E. Williams. Farmington Hills, MA: Greenhaven Press.

Feiler, Jeremy. 2003 (Aug. 7). "Canada Prepares for Major Defense Review with Transformation in Mind." *Inside the Pentagon.* Reprinted: http://www.forces.gc.ca/site/focus/canada-us-canada-eu/pentagon1-eng.asp

Funke, Odelia. 1994. "National Security and the Environment." Pp. 323–345 in *Environmental Policy in the 1990s: Toward a New Agenda,* 2nd ed., edited by Norman J. Vig and Michael E. Kraft. Washington, DC: Congressional Quarterly.

Gardner, Simon. 2007 (February 22). *Sri Lanka Says Sinks Rebel Boats on Truce Anniversary.* Available at http://www.reuters.com

Geneva Graduate Institute for International Studies. 2006. *Small Arms Survey, 2006.* New York: Oxford University Press.

Gettleman, Jeffrey. 2008. "Rape Victims' Words Help Jolt Congo into Change." *New York Times,* October 18. Available at http://www.nytimes.com

———. 2009. "Symbol of Unhealed Congo—Male Rape Victims." *New York Times,*

August 4. Available at http://www.nytimes.com

Gioseffi, Daniela. 1993. "Introduction." Pp. xi–l in *On Prejudice: A Global Perspective,* edited by Daniela Gioseffi. New York: Anchor Books, Doubleday.

Gossage, Carolyn. 2001. *Greatcoats and Glamour Boots.* Revised ed. Toronto: Dundurn Press.

Goure, Don. 2003. *First Casualties? NATO, the U.N.* MSNBC News, March 20. Available at http://www.msnbc.com/news

GreenKarat. 2007. *Mining for Gems.* Available at http://www.greenkarat.com

Hooks, Gregory and Leonard E. Bloomquist. 1992. "The Legacy of World War II for Regional Growth and Decline: The Effects of Wartime Investments on U.S. Manufacturing, 1947–72." *Social Forces* 71(2): 303–337.

Howard, Michael. 2007. "Children of War: The Generation Traumatised by Violence in Iraq." *The Guardian,* February 6. Available at http://www.guardian.co.uk

Huntington, Samuel. 1996. *The Clash of Civilizations and the Remaking of World Order.* New York: Simon and Schuster.

ICBL (International Campaign to Ban Landmines). 2009. *Making the Treaties Universal.* Available at http://www.icbl.org

Jiwani, Yasmin. 2011. "Trapped in the Carceral Net: Race, Gender, and the "War on Terror."" *Global Media Journal—Canadian Edition* 4(2): 13–31.

Kaphle, Anup. 2013. "Timeline: Unrest in Syria." *The Washington Post.* June 13. Available at apps.washingtonpost.com

Kellner, Douglas. 1995. *Media Culture.* New York and London: Routledge.

Kemper, Bob. 2003. "Agency Wages Media Battle." *Chicago Tribune,* April 7. Available at http://www.chicagotribune.com

Kerr, Paul K. and Mary Beth Nikitin. 2009. *Pakistan's Nuclear Weapons: Proliferation and Security Issues.* Congressional Research Service, June 12. Available at http://www.opencrs.com

Klare, Michael. 2001. *Resource Wars: The New Landscape of Global Conflict.* New York: Metropolitan Books.

Knickerbocker, Brad. 2002. "Return of the Military-Industrial Complex?" *Christian Science Monitor,* February 13. Available at http://www.csmonitor.com

Lamont, Beth. 2001. "The New Mandate for UN Peacekeeping." *The Humanist* 61: 39–41.

Large, Tim. 2006. *Crisis Profile: What's Going On in Northern Uganda?* Thomas Reuters Foundation. Available at http://www.alertnet.org

Lederer, Edith. 2005 (May 20). "Annan Lays Out Sweeping Changes to U.N." Associated Press. Available at http://www.apnews.com

Levy, Clifford J. and Peter Baker. 2009. "U.S. Russian Nuclear Agreement Is First Step in Broad Effort." *The Washington Post,* July 6. Available at http://www.washingtonpost.com

Levy, Jack S. 2001. "Theories of Interstate and Intrastate War: A Levels of Analysis Approach." Pp. 3–27 in *Turbulent Peace: The Challenges of Managing International Conflict,* edited by Chester A. Crocker, Fen Osler Hampson, and Pamela Aall. Washington, DC: U.S. Institute of Peace.

Lewycka, Marina. 2014. "Ukraine and the West: Hot Air and Hypocrisy." *The Guardian.* March 10, 2014. http://www.theguardian.com/world/2014/mar/10/ukraine-and-west-hot-air-hypocrisy-crimea-russia

Li, Xigen and Ralph Izard. 2003. "Media in a Crisis Situation Involving National Interest: A Content Analysis of Major U.S. Newspapers' and TV Networks' Coverage of the 9/11 Tragedy." *Newspaper Research Journal* 24: 1–16.

Lindner, Andrew M. 2009. "Among the Troops: Seeing the Iraq War through Three Journalistic Vantage Points." *Social Problems* 56(1): 21–48.

MacAskill, Ewen, Ed Pilkington, and Jon Watts. 2006. "Despair at UN over Selection of 'Faceless' Ban Ki-moon as General Secretary." *The Guardian,* October 7. Available at http://www.guardian.co.uk

Marshall, Leon. 2007 (July 16). *Elephants "Learn" to Avoid Land Mines in War-Torn Angola.* National Geographic News. Available at http://www.nationalgeographic.com

McGirk, Tim. 2006. "Collateral Damage or Civilian Massacre in Haditha?" *TIME,* March 19. Available at http://www.time.com

Military. 2007. *Tuition Assistance (TA) Program Overview.* Available at http://education.military.com

Military Professional Resources Inc. 2007. *About MPRI.* Available at http://www.mpri.com

Miller, T. Christian. 2007. "Private Contractors Outnumber U.S. Troops in Iraq." *Los Angeles Times,* July 4. Available at http://www.latimes.com

Millman, Jason. 2008. "Industry Applauds New Dual-Use Rule." *Hartford Business Journal,* September 29. Available at http://www.hartfordbusiness.com

Minister of Public Works/Government of Canada 2011. "Operations" http://www.forces.gc.ca/en/operations/past.page

Morgan, Jenny and Alice Behrendt. 2009. *Silent Suffering: The Psychological Impact of War, HIV, and Other High-Risk Situations on Girls and Boys in West and Central Africa.* Woking: Plan. Available at http://plan-international.org

Myers-Brown, Karen, Kathleen Walker, and Judith A. Myers-Walls. 2000. "Children's Reactions to International Conflict: A Cross-Cultural Analysis." Paper presented at the National Council of Family Relations, Minneapolis, November 20.

NASP (National Association of School Psychologists). 2003. *Children and Fear of War and Terrorism.* Available at http://www.nasponline.org

National Defence. 2010 (April 27). "Canadian Expeditionary Force Command." Accessed December 12, 2010. http://www.cefcom.forces.gc.ca/pa-ap/ops/fs-fr/afg-eng.asp

NCPSD (National Center for Posttraumatic Stress Disorder). 2007. *What Is Post Traumatic Stress Disorder?* Available at http://www.ncptsd.va.gov

NTI (Nuclear Threat Initiative). 2009. *North Korea Profile.* Available at http://www.nti.org

Office of Management and Budget. 2009. Table S-7: Funding Levels for Appropriated ("Discretionary") Programs by Agency. Available at http://www.whitehouse.gov

Office of Weapons Removal and Abatement. 2009. *To Walk the Earth in Safety: The United States' Commitment to Humanitarian Mine Action and Conventional Weapons Destruction.* Available at http://www.state.gov

Ochmanek, David and Lowell H. Schwartz. 2008. "The Challenge of Nuclear-Armed Regional Adversaries." Rand Project Air Force. Available at http://www.rand.org

Paul, Annie Murphy. 1998. "Psychology's Own Peace Corps." *Psychology Today* 31: 56–60.

Permanent Court of Arbitration. 2009. *About Us* and *Cases.* Available at http://www.pca-cpa.org

Pew Research Center. 2009 (July 23). *Confidence in Obama Lifts U.S. Image Around the World: Most Muslim Publics Not So Easily Moved.* Pew Global Attitudes Project. Available at http://www.pewglobal.org

Poe, Danielle. 2008. "Replacing Just War Theory with an Ethics of Sexual Difference." *Hypatia* 23(2): 33–47.

Porter, Bruce D. 1994. *War and the Rise of the State: The Military Foundations of Modern Politics.* New York: Free Press.

Powell, Bill and Tim McGirk. 2005. "The Man Who Sold the Bomb." *Time,* February 14, pp. 22–31.

Puckett, Neal and Haytham Faraj. 2009 (June 25). *Navy-Marine Corps Court Hears Appeal in Wuterich v. U.S.* Available at http://www.puckettfaraj.com

Pugliese, David. 2008 (Sept. 18). "Afghan War Costs $22b, So Far." *Ottawa Citizen:* A18.

Queen's University. 2010. "An Archival Look at World War I: Women and the War." http://archives.queensu.ca/Exhibits/archres/wwi-intro/women.html

Rasler, Karen and William R. Thompson. 2005. *Puzzles of the Democratic Peace: Theory, Geopolitics, and the Transformation of World Politics.* New York: Palgrave Macmillan.

Renner, Michael. 1993. "Environmental Dimensions of Disarmament and Conversion." Pp. 88–132 in *Real Security: Converting the Defense Economy and Building Peace,* edited by Karl Cassady and Gregory A. Bischak. Albany: State University of New York Press.

———. 2000. "Number of Wars on Upswing." Pp. 110–111 in *Vital Signs: The Environmental Trends That Are Shaping Our Future,* edited by Linda Starke. New York: W. W. Norton.

———. 2005. "Disarming Postwar Societies." Pp. 122–123 in *State of the World: 2005,* edited by Linda Starke. New York: W. W. Norton.

Reuters. 2008. "Case Dropped Against Officer Accused in Iraq Killings." *New York Times,* June 18. Available at http://www.nytimes.com

Robinson, Bill. 2009. "Canadian Military Spending 2009." Canadian Centre for Policy Alternatives. http://www.policyalternatives.ca.remote.libproxy.wlu.ca/sites/default/files/uploads/publications/reports/docs/Canadian%20Military%20Spending%202009.pdf

Rosenberg, Tina. 2000. "The Unbearable Memories of a U.N. Peacekeeper." *New York Times,* October 8, pp. 4, 14.

Salem, Paul. 2007. "Dealing with Iran's Rapid Rise in Regional Influence." *The Japan Times,* February 22. Available at http://www.carnegieendowment.org

Salladay, Robert. 2003 (April 7). Anti-War Patriots Find They Need to Reclaim Words, Symbols, Even U.S. Flag from Conservatives. Available at http://www.commondreams.org

Sang-Hun, Choe and John Markoff. 2009. "Cyberattacks Jam Government and Commercial Web Sites in U.S. and South Korea." *The New York Times,* July 8. Available at http://www.nytimes.com

Save the Children. 2005. One World, One Wish: The Campaign to Help Children and Women Affected by War. Available at http://www.savethechildren.org

———. 2007. *State of the World's Mothers: Saving the Lives of Children Under Five.* Available at http://www.savethechildren.org

———. 2009. *Last in Line, Last in School 2009.* Available at http://www.savethechildren.org

Scheff, Thomas. 1994. *Bloody Revenge.* Boulder, CO: Westview Press.

Schmitt, Eric. 2005. "Pentagon Seeks to Shut Down Bases Across Nation." *New York Times,* May 14. Available at http://www.nytimes.com

Schroeder, Matt. 2007. "The Illicit Arms Trade." Washington, DC: Federation of American Scientists. Available at http://www.fas.org

Schultz, George P., William J. Perry, Henry A. Kissinger, and Sam Nunn. 2007. "A World Free of Nuclear Weapons." *Wall Street Journal,* January 4. Available at http://www.wsj.com

Shanahan, John J. 1995. "Director's Letter." *Defense Monitor* 24(6): 8.

Shanker, Thom and David E. Sanger. 2009. "Pakistan Is Rapidly Adding Nuclear Arms, U.S. Says." *New York Times,* May 17. Available at http://www.nytimes.com

Shrader, Katherine. 2005. "WMD Commission Releases Scathing Report." *Washington Post,* March 31. Available at http://www.washingtonpost.com

Singer, Peter W. 2009. "Attack of the Military Drones." *The National,* June 29. Available at http://www.brookings.edu

SIPRI (Stockholm International Peace Research Institute). 2009a. *SIPRI Yearbook 2009: Armaments, Disarmament, and International Security.* Oxford, UK: Oxford University Press.

———. 2009b. *Recent Trends in Military Expenditure.* Available at http://www.sipri.org

Skocpol, Theda. 1994. *Social Revolutions in the Modern World.* Cambridge, UK: Cambridge University Press.

Sloan, Elinor. 2010 (Mar. 11). "Government Missing Mark in Plan to Cut Back Military Spending: Poll Shows Canadians Like Idea of Strong, Well-Equipped Armed Forces." *Edmonton Journal:* A16.

Small Arms Survey. 2009. *Shadows of War.* Available at http://www.smallarmssurvey.org

Staples, Steven and Bill Robinson. 2007. "More Than the Cold War: Canada's Military Spending 2007–2008." Canadian Centre for Policy Alternatives: http://www.policyalternatives.ca.remote.libproxy.wlu.ca/documents/National_Office_Pubs/2007/More_Than_the_Cold_War.pdf

Starr, J. R. and D. C. Stoll. 1989. *U.S. Foreign Policy on Water Resources in the Middle East.* Washington, DC: Center for Strategic and International Studies.

State of Hawaii. 2000. *Dual-Use Technologies.* Available at http://www.state.hi.us

Stimson Center. 2007. *Reducing Nuclear Dangers in South Asia.* Available at http://www.stimson.org

Stogran, P. 2002 (Nov. 29). Public Lecture at Wilfrid Laurier University, Waterloo, ON.

Tanielian, Terri, Lisa H. Jaycox, Terry L. Schell, Grant N. Marshall, Audrey Burnam, Christine Eibner, Benjamin R. Karney, Lisa S. Meredith, Jeanne S. Ringe, Mary E. Vaiana, and the Invisible Wounds Study Team. 2008. "Invisible Wounds of War: Summary and Recommendations for Addressing Psychological and Cognitive Injuries." Available at http://www.rand.org

United Nations. 1948. Convention on the Prevention and Punishment of the Crime of Genocide. Available at http://www.un.org

———. 2003. *Some Questions and Answers.* Available at http://www.unicef.org

———. 2009. *United Nations Peacekeeping Operations.* Available at http://www.un.org/Depts/dpko/dpko/bnote.htm

United Nations Association of the United States of America. 2003. *The Problem: Impact of Landmines.* Available at http://www.landmines.org

U.S. Department of State. 2007. *Small Arms/Light Weapons Destruction.* Available at http://www.state.gov

Vesely, Milan. 2001. "UN Peacekeepers: Warriors or Victims?" *African Business* 261: 8–10.

Viner, Katharine. 2002. "Feminism as Imperialism." *The Guardian,* September 21. Available at http://www/guardian.co.uk

Waters, Rob. 2005. "The Psychic Costs of War." *Psychotherapy Networker,* March-April, pp. 1–3.

Watkins, Thomas. 2007. *Haditha Hearings Enter Fourth Day. Time,* May 11. Available at http://www.time.com

Wax, Emily. 2003. "War Horror: Rape Ruining Women's Health." *Miami Herald,* November 3. Available at http://www.miami.com

Wein, Lawrence. 2009. "Counting the Walking Wounded." *New York Times,* January 25. Available at http://www.nytimes.com

Williamson, Janice. 2012. *Omar Khadr, Oh Canada.* McGill-Queen's University Press: Montreal and Kingston.

Wilson, Brenda. 2008. "WHO Estimates Iraqi Death Toll at 151,000." January 9. Available at http://www.npr.org

Woehrle, Lynne M., Patrick G. Coy, and Gregory M. Maney. 2008. *Contesting Patriotism: Culture, Power, and Strategy in the Peace Movement.* Lanham, MD: Rowman & Littlefield Publishers, Inc.

Worldwatch Institute. 2003. *Vital Signs: The Trends That Are Shaping Our Future.* New York: W. W. Norton.

Zoroya, Gregg. 2006. "Lifesaving Knowledge, Innovation Emerge in War Clinic." *USA Today,* March 27. Available at http://www.usatoday.com

GLOSSARY

absolute poverty The chronic absence of the basic necessities of life, including food, clean water, and housing.

acculturation Learning the culture of a group different from the one in which a person was originally raised.

achieved status A status assigned on the basis of some characteristic or behaviour over which the individual has some control.

acid rain The mixture of precipitation with air pollutants, such as sulphur dioxide and nitrogen oxide.

acquaintance rape Rape that is committed by someone known by the victim.

activity theory A theory that emphasizes that the elderly disengage, in part, because they are structurally segregated and isolated with few opportunities to take active roles.

acute condition A health condition that lasts no longer than three months.

adaptive discrimination Discrimination that is based on the prejudice of others.

age grading The assignment of social roles to given chronological ages.

age pyramids Graphlike presentations that show the percentage of a population in various age groups.

ageism The belief that age is associated with certain psychological, behavioural, or intellectual traits.

alienation The concept used by Karl Marx to describe the condition when workers feel powerlessness and meaninglessness as a result of performing repetitive, isolated work tasks. Alienation involves becoming estranged from one's work and/or education, the products one creates, other human beings, or one's self.

alternative schools Alternative schools began in Canada in the 1970s. Each operates within school board and education ministry guidelines, but is unique in its character.

amalgamation The physical blending of different racial or ethnic groups, resulting in a new and distinct genetic and cultural population; results from the intermarriage of racial and ethnic groups over generations.

anomie A state of normlessness in which norms and values are weak or unclear; results from rapid social change and is linked to many social problems, including crime, drug addiction, and violence.

anti-essentialism The refusal of simplistic biological explanations for complex social relations, motivations, behaviours, and identifications.

arbitration A nonviolent strategy used to resolve conflicts and to stop or prevent war where a neutral third party in arbitration arrives at a decision that the two conflicting parties agree in advance to accept.

ascribed status A status that society assigns to an individual on the basis of factors over which the individual has no control.

assimilation The process by which minority groups gradually adopt the cultural patterns of the dominant majority group.

authoritarian-personality theory A psychological theory of prejudice that suggests prejudice arises in people with a certain personality type. According to this theory, people with an authoritarian personality, who are highly conformist, intolerant, cynical, and preoccupied with power, are prone to prejudice.

automation A type of technology in which self-operated machines accomplish tasks formerly done by workers; develops as a society moves toward industrialization and becomes more concerned with the mass production of goods.

aversive racism A subtle, often unintentional form of prejudice exhibited by many individuals who possess strong egalitarian values and who view themselves as non-prejudiced.

behaviour-based safety programs A controversial health and safety strategy used by business management in which health and safety problems in the workplace are attributed to workers' behaviour rather than to work processes and conditions.

beliefs Definitions and explanations about what is assumed to be true.

biodiversity The variability of living organisms on Earth.

bioinvasion The emergence of organisms in regions where they are not native.

biphobia Negative attitudes toward bisexuality and people who identify as bisexual.

bonded labour The repayment of a debt through labour.

bourgeoisie The owners of the means of production.

brain drain The phenomenon whereby many individuals with the highest level of skill and education leave the country in search of work abroad.

burden of disease The number of deaths in a population combined with the impact of premature death and disability on that population.

Canada Child Tax Benefit (CCTB) A tax-free monthly payment made to eligible families to help them with the cost of raising children under the age of 18. Benefits are calculated for a 12-month period based on the number of children in a family and their ages, the applicant's province or territory of residence, the family's net income, and the applicant's (or the applicant's spouse's) deduction for child care expenses.

Canada Student Financial Assistance Act (CSFA Act) The *CSFA Act* of 1994 revised the Canada Student Loans Plan and increased the amounts of the maximum loans available for full-time and part-time students.

Canada Student Loans Program (CSLP) A plan that permits eligible Canadian citizens and permanent residents to finance their postsecondary education with government-sponsored loans. Full-time students, enrolled in a program that lasts for at least 12 weeks, may qualify for a loan based on the costs of their program and on the financial resources available to them.

capitalism An economic system in which private individuals or groups invest capital to produce goods and services, for a profit, in a competitive market.

census family A now-married couple (with or without never-married sons and/or daughters of one or other spouses), a couple living common-law (again, with or without never-married sons and/or daughters of either or both parents), or a lone parent of any marital status, with at least one never-married son or daughter living in the same dwelling.

charter groups A term that has been traditionally used in Canada to refer to the English and French and that reflects the historical importance of these groups in Canada's history.

child abuse The physical or mental injury, sexual abuse, negligent treatment, or maltreatment of a child under the age of 18 by a person who is responsible for the child's welfare.

child labour Children performing work that is hazardous, that interferes with their education, or that harms their health or physical, mental, spiritual, or moral development.

chronic condition A long-term health problem.

claims-making activities The strategies and actions that individuals or groups undertake to define social conditions as social problems that require remedy.

classic rape A rape committed by a stranger with the use of a weapon resulting in serious bodily injury.

club drugs A general term used to refer to illicit, often synthetic drugs commonly used at night clubs or all-night dances called raves.

colonialism When a racial or ethnic group from one society takes over and dominates the racial or ethnic group(s) of another society.

common couple violence Occasional acts of violence that result from conflict that gets out of hand between persons in a relationship.

community policing When police, community, and local governance structures, including politicians, and religious and educational institutions, work together to prevent crime at local levels. Not intended to address large-scale concerns, but to help citizens prevent their neighbourhoods from becoming targets for crimes. Efforts range from Neighbourhood Watch programs to education about the causes of crime. Through informal networks, there can be information sharing between police and community groups.

community supported agriculture (CSA) CSAs are family farms that sell "shares" to community members. A family purchases a share of the farm's yield for each season and then picks up a weekly order that always contains the same weight in seasonal produce. Some CSAs also provide meats that have been raised on pastures instead of feedlots.

comparable worth Tasks and jobs that are distinct but have equal value and utility in the workplace and economy.

compressed workweek Workplace option in which employees work a full week, full time, but in four rather than five days.

computer crime Any violation of the law in which a computer is the target or means of criminal activity.

conflict theory The theoretical framework that understands material inequalities to be a driving force behind many social problems. Some sociologists prefer to use "Marxist theory" to name this approach to thinking about social inequalities.

constructionist The belief that social context provides the mode and meaning for both sexuality and gendered behaviours, roles, and relationships.

constructivist explanations Emphasize the role of leaders of ethnic groups in stirring up inter-communal hostility.

control group A group that is *not exposed* to the influences or variables whose effects we want to measure on a given group.

control theory A theory that argues that a strong social bond between a person and society constrains some individuals from violating norms.

conventional crime (street crime) Traditional illegal behaviour that most people think of as crime, including such offences as murder, sexual assault, assault, armed robbery, break and enter, and theft.

convergence hypothesis The argument that capitalist countries will adopt elements of socialism and socialist countries will adopt elements of capitalism; that is, they will converge.

corporal punishment The use of physical force with the intention of causing a child to experience pain, but not injury, for the purpose of correction or control of a child's behaviour.

corporate crime Both the fraudulent practices that may take place in the course of conducting business—for example, tax evasion and extortion—and also behaviour that is not illegal, but may be immoral and cause significant harm to society. Such business behaviours may be deliberate or may arise from indifference to the well-being of others.

corporate downsizing The corporate practice of discharging large numbers of employees. Simply put, the term *downsizing* is a euphemism for mass firing of employees.

corporate multinationalism The practice of corporations having their home base in one country and branches, or affiliates, in other countries.

corporate murder The label for deaths as a result of unsafe consumer products.

corporate violence The production of unsafe products and the failure of corporations to provide a safe working environment for their employees.

corporate welfare Laws and policies that favour corporations, such as low-interest government loans to failing businesses and special subsidies and tax breaks to corporations.

crime The violation of norms that are written into law.

crisis competence The ability of those who live facing persistent stigma to cope more easily with adverse social situations than those who have not previously encountered much prejudice.

cultural capital Refers to the symbolic and material aspects of cultural heritage and understanding. To have high cultural capital is to possess and understand elite forms of art, language use and speech, dress and comportment, architecture and other aesthetic movements. Those with low cultural capital have either less access to and understanding of elite forms, or a culture unrecognized by those in power.

cultural imperialism The indoctrination into the dominant culture of a society; when cultural imperialism exists, the norms, values, traditions, and languages of minorities are systematically ignored.

cultural sexism The ways in which the culture of society perpetuates the subordination of individuals based on their sex classification.

culture of poverty The set of norms, values, and beliefs and self-concepts that contribute to the persistence of poverty among the underclass.

cumulative trauma disorders The most common type of workplace injury; it includes muscle, tendon, vascular, and nerve injuries that result from repeated or sustained actions or exertions of different body parts. Jobs that are associated with high rates of upper body cumulative stress disorders include computer programming, manufacturing, meat packing, poultry processing, and clerical or office work.

cycle of abuse Involves a violent or abusive episode, followed by a makeup period where the abuser expresses sorrow and asks for forgiveness and "one more chance." The calm period may last for days, weeks, or even months; then, the next outburst of violence occurs.

date-rape drugs Drugs that are used to render victims incapable of resisting sexual assaults.

de facto segregation Segregation that is not required by law, but exists "in fact," often as a result of housing and socio-economic patterns.

de jure segregation Segregation that is required by law.

decriminalization The removal of criminal penalties for a behaviour, as in the decriminalization of drug use.

deforestation The destruction of Earth's rainforests.

demogrant A benefit directed at a particular group within the population.

dependency ratio The number of societal members who are under 18 or 65 and over compared to the number of people who are between 18 and 64.

dependent variable The variable that the researcher wants to explain.

depth of poverty How far below and for how long people live below the low income cut-offs (LICOs).

deregulation The reduction of government control of, for example, certain drugs.

desertification The expansion of deserts and the loss of usable land due to the overuse of semi-arid land on the desert margins for animal grazing and obtaining firewood.

deterrence The use of harm or the threat of harm to prevent unwanted behaviours.

devaluation hypothesis The hypothesis that argues that women are paid less because the work they perform is socially defined as less valuable than the work performed by men.

differential association A theory developed by Edwin Sutherland that holds that through interaction with others, individuals learn the values, attitudes, techniques, and motives for criminal behaviour.

disability-adjusted life year (DALY) Years lived with illness or disability. More simply, one DALY equals one year lost of healthy life.

discrimination Differential treatment of individuals based on their group membership.

discrimination management Individual efforts to prevent being targeted for discriminatory behaviours in the workplace.

discriminatory unemployment High rates of unemployment among particular social groups, such as racial and ethnic minorities and women.

disengagement theory A theory claiming that the elderly disengage from productive social roles to relinquish these roles to younger members of society. As this process continues, each new group moves up and replaces another, which, according to disengagement theory, benefits society and all of its members.

disproportionate harm Exceeds harm inflicted on individuals; has as its goal to intimidate and/or injure an entire community.

diversity training Workplace training programs designed to increase employees' awareness of cultural differences in the workplace and how these differences may affect job performance.

divorce mediation A process in which divorcing couples meet with a neutral third party (mediator) who assists the individuals

in resolving such issues as property division, child custody, child support, and spousal support in a way that minimizes conflict and encourages cooperation.

Dominion-Provincial Student Aid Program (DSAP) An act passed by the federal government in 1939. Under DSAP, the federal government contributed to each participating province and the province was expected to provide an equal amount of assistance to students.

drug Any substance other than food that alters the structure and functioning of a living organism when it enters the bloodstream.

drug abuse The violation of social standards of acceptable drug use, resulting in adverse physiological, psychological, or social consequences.

drug addiction/chemical dependency A condition in which drug use is compulsive, and users are unable to stop because of physical or psychological dependency or both.

dual-use technologies Defence-funded innovations that have commercial and civilian applications.

ecofeminism A synthesis of feminism, environmentalism, and anti-militarism.

economic institution The structure and means by which a society produces, distributes, and consumes goods and services.

ecosystems Complex environments that support a variety of interdependent life forms.

ecoterrorism Any violent crime intended to coerce, intimidate, or change public policy on behalf of the natural world.

elder abuse The physical or psychological abuse, financial exploitation, or medical abuse or neglect of the elderly.

emotional abuse Often involves using negative labels (e.g., "stupid," "whore," "bad") to define a partner or family member. Such labels negatively affect the self-concept of abuse victims, often convincing them that they deserve the abuse.

emotional labour Work traditionally performed by women in the role of providing care and concern for others, either professionally or in the home.

employment equity An attempt to ensure that there is a proportional number of designated target groups (e.g., women, visible minorities, Aboriginal peoples, and people with disabilities) throughout all income and occupational levels at ratios that are consistent with the proportion of these groups within the local or regional workforce.

endogamy The social norm that influences people to marry within their social group and discourages interracial and interethnic marriages.

environmental footprint The environmental impact of building, farming, consuming, etc. The footprint is measured in terms of loss of arable land, use of water resources, fuel depletion, and carbon emissions.

environmental injustice The tendency for socially and politically marginalized groups to bear the brunt of environmental ills.

environmental racism The tendency for hazardous waste sites and polluting industries to be located in areas where the surrounding residential population is an ethnic or racial minority.

environmental refugees People forced to move because of environmental destruction.

epidemiological transition The shift from a society characterized by low life expectancy and parasitic and infectious diseases to one characterized by high life expectancy and chronic and degenerative diseases.

epidemiologist A scientist who studies the social origins and distribution of health problems in a population and how patterns of illness and disease vary between and within societies.

epidemiology The study of the distribution of disease within a population.

ethnicity A shared cultural heritage or national origin.

experiment A research method that involves manipulating the independent variable to determine how it affects the dependent variable.

expressive roles The nurturing and emotionally supportive roles that women are generally socialized into.

expulsion (population transfer) When a dominant group forces a subordinate group to leave the country or to live only in designated areas of the country.

familism A value system that encourages family members to put their family's well-being above their individual and personal needs.

family allowance Canada's first universal welfare program, introduced in 1945, which promised a monthly allowance paid to families with children. The term *universal* here refers to the fact that the benefit flowed from the principle of entitlement and was available without reference to a recipient's income or assets.

family gap/child penalty The income losses associated with women's responsibilities for raising children. As a measure, it compares the earnings of women who have children with those who do not in the same age group, with equal educational and occupational attainments.

family preservation program An in-home intervention for a family who is at risk of having a child removed from the home because of abuse or neglect.

Family Supplement Those families with children in a low-income situation (i.e., having a family net income under $25 921 a year) and who receive the Canada Child Tax Benefit automatically receive the Family Supplement with a rate based on family net income and the number and ages of children in the family.

feminist An umbrella term that describes both socio-political activism and academic work. The many sub-categories of feminist thought and action are united by a concern for the well-being of women. Feminists have sought for recognition that women are full human beings entitled to the same personal rights as men. In sociology, feminist work has demonstrated that gender is an important variable to be accounted for in research programs and that the well-being of women is integral to the general welfare of larger society.

feminist theory A set of diverse perspectives joined by the focus on sex and gender as defining and important categories of oppression.

feminization of poverty The disproportionate distribution of poverty among women.

fetal alcohol syndrome (FAS) A birth defect syndrome apparently caused by prenatal alcohol exposure. Always involves brain damage, impaired growth, and head and face anomalies.

field research Observing and studying social behaviour in settings in which the behaviour occurs naturally.

flextime An option in work scheduling that allows employees to begin and end the workday at different times as long as they perform a given number of hours of work per week.

folkways The customs and manners of society.

frustration-aggression theory (scapegoating theory) A psychological theory of prejudice that suggests prejudice is a form of hostility resulting from frustration. According to this theory, minority groups serve as convenient targets of displaced aggression.

functional illiterates High-school graduates who have difficulty with basic reading and math skills.

gaybonics The expropriation of words from their negative context and their redeployment as positive self-identifications to combat racist and homophobic views and behaviours.

gender The social definitions and expectations associated with being male or female.

gender expression How we express our gender (as masculine, feminine, tomboys or androgynous, as "butch," "straight," etc.).

gender identity The gender that a person feels him or herself to be. Sometimes gender identity is concordant with one's assigned sex at birth, and sometimes one's gender identity is more fluid, or can be "opposite" to one's sex of rearing.

gender tourism The recent tendency for definitions of masculinity and femininity to become less clear, resulting in individual exploration of the gender continuum.

gender-based analysis Feminist policy analysis that understands gender to be a key factor in vulnerability to poverty and the differential effects of poverty; it uses gender as a central grounding point for analysis.

genocide The systematic annihilation of one racial or ethnic group by another.

gerontophobia Fear or dread of the elderly.

glass ceiling An invisible, socially created barrier that prevents women and other minorities from being promoted into top corporate positions.

GLBT A term used to refer collectively to gays, lesbians, bisexuals, and transgendered individuals.

global economy An interconnected network of economic activity that transcends national borders.

global warming The increasing average global air temperature, caused mainly by the accumulation of various gases that collect in the atmosphere.

globalization The economic, political, and social interconnectedness among societies throughout the world.

grade inflation Higher grades given than the work warrants; a general increase in student grades without a corresponding increase in learning.

greenhouse gases The collection of increasing amounts of chlorofluorocarbons (CFCs), carbon dioxide, methane, and other gases in the atmosphere, where they act like the glass in a greenhouse, holding heat from the sun close to the earth and preventing the heat from rising back into space.

greenwashing The corporate practice of displaying a sense of corporate responsibility for the environment. For example, many companies publicly emphasize the steps they have taken to help the environment. Another greenwashing strategy is to retool, repackage, or relabel a company's product.

hate crime (bias-motivated crime) An act of violence motivated by prejudice.

Head Start A U.S. project begun to help preschool children from disadvantaged families.

health A state of complete physical, mental, and social well-being.

heteronormativity The group of assumptions and demands that people fall into two opposite sexes that are reproductively oriented toward each other; as a bias, creates structures and institutions that privilege opposite-sex relations and deny full rights and freedoms and recognition to those engaged in same-sex relations.

heterosexism The belief that heterosexuality is the superior sexual orientation; it results in prejudice and discrimination against homosexuals and bisexuals.

heterosexual monogamy Exclusive pair-bonding between two opposite-sex persons.

home schooling The education of children at home instead of in a public or private school; often part of a fundamentalist movement to protect children from perceived non-Christian values in the public schools.

homophobia Negative attitudes toward homosexuality.

human capital The skills, knowledge, and capabilities of the individual.

human capital hypothesis The hypothesis that female–male pay differences are a function of differences in women's and men's levels of education, skills, training, and work experience.

Human Poverty Index (HPI) A composite measure of poverty based on three measures of deprivation: (1) deprivation of life, which is measured by the percentage of people expected to die before age 40; (2) deprivation of knowledge, which is measured by the percentage of adults who are illiterate; and (3) deprivation in living standards, which is measured as a composite of three variables—the percentage of people without access to health services, the percentage of people without access to safe water, and the percentage of malnourished children under five.

hypothesis A prediction or educated guess about how one variable is related to another variable.

incapacitation A criminal justice philosophy that views the primary purpose of the criminal justice system as preventing criminal offenders from committing further crimes against the public by putting them in prison.

incidence The number of new cases of a specific health problem in a given population during a specified period.

independent variable The variable that is expected to explain change in the dependent variable.

individual discrimination Discriminatory acts by individuals that are based on prejudicial attitudes.

individualism A value system that stresses the importance of individual happiness.

Industrial Revolution The period between the mid-eighteenth and the early nineteenth centuries when machines and factories became the primary means for producing goods.

infantilizing elders The portrayal of the elderly in the media as childlike in terms of clothes, facial expression, temperament, and activities.

institution An established and enduring pattern of social relationships. The five traditional social institutions are family, religion, politics, economics, and education. Institutions are the largest elements of social structure.

institutional discrimination Discrimination in which the normal operations and procedures of social institutions result in unequal treatment of minorities.

instrumental roles Task-oriented roles that males are generally socialized into.

intergenerational poverty Poverty that is transmitted from one generation to the next.

intimate partner violence Actual or threatened violent crimes committed against persons by their current or former spouses, boyfriends, or girlfriends.

intimate terrorism Almost entirely perpetrated by men, a form of violence that is motivated by a wish to control one's partner and involves the systemic use of not only violence, but economic subordination, threats, isolation, verbal and emotional abuse, and other control tactics. This form of violence is more likely to escalate over time and to involve serious injury.

job exportation The relocation of jobs to other countries where products can be produced more cheaply.

job sharing A work option in which two people share and are paid for one job.

Kyoto Protocol Developed by the United Nations Framework Convention on Climate Change, the protocol aims to have signatories make efforts to reduce greenhouse gas emissions. As of 2010, 191 countries had ratified the protocol.

labelling theory A symbolic interactionist theory that is concerned with how regions and communities defined as social problems are affected by being so labelled, and with the negative effects of labelling on the self-concept and behaviour of individuals, thereby contributing to the further development of identities and behaviours consistent with the label.

latent function Consequence that is unintended and often hidden or unrecognized; for example, a latent function of education is to provide schools that function as babysitters for employed parents.

laws Norms that are formalized and backed by political authority.

legalization Making prohibited behaviour legal; for example, legalizing marijuana or prostitution.

lesbigays A collective term sometimes used to refer to lesbians, gays, and bisexuals.

life expectancy The average number of years that a person born in a given year can expect to live.

low income cut-offs (LICOs) Developed by Statistics Canada as a measure of poverty. Estimating that poor families or individuals spend approximately 34.7 percent or more of their pre-tax income on such basic needs as food, shelter, and clothing, 20 percentage points were added to this figure to determine the cut-off. This standard suggests that individuals or families who spent 54.7 percent of their pre-tax income on food, clothing, and shelter would experience financial difficulty. Different low income cut-off lines are established by Statistics Canada for different communities as well as for families of varying sizes within these communities.

low-income measure (LIM) For the purposes of assessing low income using this measure, Statistics Canada has established a figure for the needs of one adult and proceeded on the assumption that family needs increase in proportion to the size of the family, with each additional adult increasing the family needs by 40 percent of the first adult and each additional child increasing the family's needs by 30 percent.

macro-sociology The study of large aspects of society, such as institutions and large social groups.

manifest function A consequence that is intended and commonly recognized; for example, a manifest function of education is to transmit knowledge and skills to youth.

marital assimilation Assimilation that occurs when different ethnic or racial groups become married or pair-bonded and produce children.

market basket measure (MBM) An assessment of the minimum level of income required to provide for the basic needs that a given society would find it "indecent" to be without.

master status The status that is considered the most significant in a person's social identity.

maternal mortality rate The numbers of deaths that result from complications associated with pregnancy or childbirth per 1000 pregnant women.

mediation A nonviolent strategy used to resolve conflicts and to stop or prevent war where a neutral third party intervenes and facilitates negotiation between representatives or leaders of conflicting groups.

medicalization The tendency to define negatively evaluated behaviours or conditions as medical problems in need of medical intervention.

mental disorder A behavioural or psychological syndrome or pattern that occurs in an individual and that is associated with present distress or disability, or with a significantly increased risk of suffering, death, pain, disability, or loss of freedom.

mental health The successful performance of mental function, resulting in productive activities, fulfilling relationships with other people, and the ability to adapt to change and to cope with adversity.

mental illness A term used to refer collectively to all mental disorders.

micro-sociology The study of the social psychological dynamics of individuals interacting in small groups.

military-industrial complex The close association between the military and the defence industry.

modern racism A subtle and complex form of racism in which individuals are not explicitly racist, but tend to hold negative views of racial minorities and blame minorities for their social disadvantages.

modernization theory A theory claiming that as society becomes more technologically advanced, the position of the elderly declines.

morbidity Disease, impairment, and accidents present in a population.

mores Norms that have a moral basis.

mortality Death.

multicultural education Education that includes all racial and ethnic groups in the school curriculum and promotes awareness and appreciation for cultural diversity.

multiculturalism A philosophy that argues that the culture of a society should represent and embrace all racial and ethnic groups in that society.

multiple chemical sensitivity (MCS) A controversial health condition in which, after one or more acute or traumatic exposures to a chemical or group of chemicals, people experience adverse effects from low levels of chemical exposure that do not produce symptoms in the general public.

mutual violent control A rare pattern of abuse when two intimate terrorists battle for control.

narrative analysis A feminist practice that combines a symbolic approach with the collection of women's life histories as legitimate sources of knowledge and information.

National Child Benefit (NCB) Introduced in July 1998, NCB is a joint initiative of federal, provincial, and territorial governments designed to help prevent and reduce the depth of child poverty and to promote parental attachment to the workforce.

National Child Benefit Supplement (NCBS) A monthly benefit for low-income families with children that is the federal government's contribution to the National Child Benefit (NCB).

neo-liberal The revival of classical liberalism that has occurred since the 1980s. Those who espouse this model for economic and political organization and policy advocate individual rights over group rights, reduction of state powers, and an increased liberalization of free-market capitalism. According to this view, when the market is free to set its own limits, then individual merit will be properly rewarded and everyone will benefit from increased growth in capital and industrial production.

no-fault divorce A divorce that is granted based on the claim that there are irreconcilable differences within a marriage (as opposed to one spouse being legally at fault for the marital breakup).

norms Socially defined rules of behaviour, including folkways, mores, and laws.

objective element (of a social problem) Awareness of social conditions through one's own life experience and through reports in the media.

occupational sex segregation The concentration of women in certain occupations and of men in other occupations.

operational definition In research, a definition of a variable that specifies *how* that variable is to be measured (or was measured) in the research.

organized crime Criminal activity conducted by members of a hierarchically arranged structure devoted primarily to making money through illegal means.

overt discrimination Discrimination that occurs because of an individual's own prejudicial attitudes.

parental alienation syndrome (PAS) An emotional and psychological disturbance in which children engage in exaggerated and unjustified denigration and criticism of a parent.

patriarchy A tradition in which families and societies are male dominated.

pay equity Also known as "equal pay for work of equal value"; requires equal pay for women who perform jobs of equal value to men in the same establishment. Employers are required to compare women's and men's jobs on the basis of skill, effort, responsibility, and working conditions to determine their value.

perinatal transmission The transmission of infection from a mother to a fetus or newborn.

pink-collar jobs Jobs that offer few benefits, often have low prestige, and are disproportionately held by women.

planned obsolescence The manufacturing of products that are intended to become inoperative or outdated in a fairly short time.

pluralism A state in which racial or ethnic groups maintain their distinctness, but respect each other and have equal access to social resources.

polyandry The concurrent marriage of one woman to two or more men.

polygamy A form of marriage in which one person may have two or more spouses.

polygyny The concurrent marriage of one man to two or more women.

populations The word that scientists who reject the race concept now use when referring to groups that most people would call races.

postindustrialization The shift from an industrial economy dominated by manufacturing jobs to an economy dominated by service-oriented, information-intensive occupations.

postmodern theory A theory that rejects the positivist notion that societies are completely rational and that a single truth about social worlds can be identified. The theory takes account of the competing realities according to and through which people live their lives.

posttraumatic stress disorder (PTSD) A clinical term referring to a set of symptoms that can result from any traumatic experience, including crime victimization, rape, or war.

poverty Lacking resources for an "adequate" standard of living.

prejudice An attitude or judgment, usually negative, about an entire category of people based on their group membership.

prevalence The total number of cases of a condition in a population that exist at a given time.

primary aging Biological changes associated with aging that are due to physiological variables, such as cellular and molecular variation (e.g., grey hair).

primary assimilation The integration of different groups in personal, intimate associations such as friends, family, and spouses.

primary deviance Deviant behaviour committed before a person is caught and labelled as an offender.

primary group A small group characterized by intimate and informal interaction.

primary prevention (strategies) Family violence prevention strategies that target the general population.

primordial explanations Those explanations that emphasize the existence of "ancient hatreds" rooted in deep psychological or cultural differences between ethnic groups, often involving a history of grievance and victimization, real or imagined, by the enemy group.

proletariat Workers who were often exploited by the bourgeoisie.

qualitative research Research assessments that look for recurrent themes that emerge in the interviews or behaviours that dominate in the observations carried out.

quantitative research Research that is carried out to survey large populations and is analyzed using statistical measures that can look for social phenomena not only as individual facts but as correlating variables.

queer theory A theory that developed largely out of the late 1980s response to public panics over HIV and to medical system failures to treat with respect and adequate priority the needs of HIV+ persons, especially gay men. Queer theory now asks how sexual identity relates to various problems rooted in oppression and prejudice. It provides an important analytic tool to understand the oppressive treatment of gay, lesbian, bisexual, and transgender persons in societal structures and in cultural representation.

race A category of people who are believed to share distinct physical characteristics that are deemed socially significant.

racial profiling The law enforcement practice of targeting suspects based upon race.

racism The belief that certain groups of people are innately inferior to other groups of people based on their racial classification. Racism serves to justify discrimination against groups that are perceived as inferior.

rehabilitation A criminal justice philosophy that views the primary purpose of the criminal justice system as changing the criminal offender through such programs as education and job training, individual and group therapy, substance abuse counselling, and behaviour modification.

relative poverty A deficiency in material and economic resources compared with some other population.

reparative therapy Various therapies that are aimed at changing homosexuals' sexual attraction.

repetitive strain disorders (repeated trauma disorders) The most common types of workplace illnesses include muscle, tendon, vascular, and nerve injuries that result from repeated or sustained actions or exertions of different body parts. Jobs that are associated with high rates of upper body repeated trauma disorders include computer programming, manufacturing, meat packaging, poultry processing, and clerical/office work.

restorative justice A philosophy primarily concerned with reconciling conflict between the offender, the community, and the victim.

role A set of rights, obligations, and expectations associated with a status.

routine activity theory A view that for crimes to occur against people, certain conditions must exist. In particular, three conditions increase the opportunity for a crime to occur: a motivated offender, a suitable target, and a lack of capable guardianship of a target.

sample In survey research, a "sample" refers to the portion of the population selected to be questioned.

sanctions Social consequences for conforming to or violating norms. Types of sanctions include positive, negative, formal, and informal.

sandwich generation The generation that has the responsibility of simultaneously caring for their children and their aging parents.

second wave feminism Twentieth-century resurgence of feminist thought, sometimes attributed to the establishment of suffrage in Canada, to the publication of de Beauvoir's *Second Sex* in France, or to the publication of Betty Friedan's *The Feminine Mystique*.

secondary aging Biological changes associated with aging that can be attributed to poor diet, lack of exercise, and increased stress.

secondary assimilation The integration of different groups in public areas and in social institutions, such as in government, neighbourhoods, schools, and the workplace.

secondary deviance Deviance that results from being caught and labelled.

secondary group A group characterized by impersonal and formal interaction.

secondary prevention (strategies) Prevention strategies that target groups that are thought to be at high risk for family violence.

segregation The physical and social separation of categories of individuals, such as racial or ethnic groups.

self-fulfilling prophecy A concept referring to the tendency for people to act in a manner consistent with the expectations of others.

senescence The biology of aging.

senilicide The killing of the elderly.

settler colonialism Refers to a means of structuring land use in ways that eliminate Native/Indigenous populations from the land; ruptures the cultural ties of Indigenous peoples to the land, and so commits cultural genocide as well.

sex A person's biological classification as male or female.

sex ratio The ratio of men to women in a given society or subgroup of society.

sexism The belief that there are innate psychological, behavioural, or intellectual differences between females and males and that these differences connote the superiority of one group and the inferiority of another.

sexual aggression Sexual interaction that occurs against one's will through the use of physical force, pressure, use of alcohol/drugs, or use of position of authority.

sexual harassment When an employer requires sexual favours in exchange for a promotion, salary increase, or any other employee benefit, or the existence of a hostile environment that unreasonably interferes with job performance, as in the case of sexually explicit remarks or insults being made to an employee.

sexual orientation The identification of individuals as heterosexual, bisexual, or homosexual based on their emotional and sexual attractions, relationships, self-identity, and lifestyle.

shift work The use of a 24-hour schedule to create workdays of three eight-hour shifts.

Some workers have "split shifts" in which their eight hours are interrupted by unpaid periods of over an hour, effectively extending the workers' days to 10 hours or more. Split shifts are common in the hospitality sector.

slavery A condition in which one social group treats another group as property to exploit for financial gain.

social cost model A way of measuring the total costs to individuals, institutions, and society as a whole from the costs of premature death and of disability. Used to assess many negative social phenomena, of which impaired driving is just one, that cut short lives, create disability, and negatively impact on communities.

social death The removal of a person from larger society through lifetime imprisonment. By stripping the person of a meaningful position within society, lifetime imprisonment removes from that person an identity and status in the larger world. The prisoner is ejected from the relationship circles necessary for the maintenance of a personal identity.

social determinants of health Social factors that affect health and illness, such as social class and poverty, education, race, and gender.

social facts Émile Durkheim refers to the phenomena that occur in the world as objectively identifiable facts. If the phenomena arise as a result of structural organization and functional needs, or dysfunctional problems, then those facts are not merely idiosyncrasies, but the result of social structures—they are part of the function of the society under consideration. Employment rates, morbidity, and mortality, as well as rates of population growth or decline, are all examples of "social facts."

social group Two or more people who have a common identity and who interact and form a social relationship; institutions are made up of social groups.

social problem A social condition that a segment of society views as harmful to members of society and in need of remedy.

social promotion The passing of students from grade to grade even if they are failing.

socialism An economic ideology that emphasizes public rather than private ownership. Theoretically, goods and services are equitably distributed according to the needs of the citizens.

socio-economic status (SES) Status that refers to the combination of economic and social circumstances that shape one's experiences as a member of a given class. SES addresses the likelihood that higher income and a higher place in the social hierarchy are likely to coincide, and that lower status and lower income are also likely to coincide, with attendant privileges for higher-SES groups and attendant risks for lower ones.

sociological imagination A term coined by C. Wright Mills to refer to the ability to see the connections between our personal lives and the social world in which we live.

special education Remedial education designed to help children and adults who are exceptional in some way, including but not limited to, intellectual developmental delays, visual or auditory disabilities, and emotional or specific learning difficulties.

split labour market The existence of primary and secondary labour markets. A primary labour market refers to jobs that are stable and economically rewarding and have many benefits; a secondary labour market refers to jobs that offer little pay, no security, few benefits, and little chance for advancement.

status A position a person occupies within a social group.

stereotypes Oversimplified or exaggerated generalizations about a category of individuals. Stereotypes are either untrue or are gross distortions of reality.

stigma Refers to any personal characteristic associated with social disgrace, rejection, or discrediting.

strain theory A theory that argues that when legitimate means of acquiring culturally defined goals are limited by the structure of society, the resulting strain may lead to crime or other deviance.

structural sexism The ways in which the organization of society, and specifically its institutions, subordinate individuals and groups based on their sex classification.

structural unemployment Exists when there are not enough jobs available for those who want them; unemployment that results from structural variables, such as government and business downsizing, job exportation, automation, a reduction in the number of new and existing businesses, an increase in the number of people looking for jobs, and a recessionary economy where fewer goods are purchased and, therefore, fewer employees are needed.

structural-functionalism A sociological perspective that views society as a system of interconnected parts that work together in harmony to maintain a state of balance and social equilibrium for the whole; focuses on how each part of society influences and is influenced by other parts.

subcultural theory A theory that argues that certain groups or subcultures in society have values and attitudes that are conducive to crime and violence.

subjective element (of a social problem) The belief that a particular social condition is harmful to society, or to a segment of society, and that it should and can be changed.

surplus value A concept developed by Marx; refers to the difference in the amount people will pay for a service or consumer good compared to the cost of its production—surplus value produces the profit from exploited labour.

survey research A method of research that involves eliciting information from respondents through questions; includes interviews (telephone or face-to-face) and written questionnaires.

sustainable development Societal development that meets the needs of current generations without threatening the future of subsequent generations.

sweatshops Work environments characterized by less than minimum wage pay, excessively long hours of work often without overtime pay, unsafe or inhumane working conditions, abusive treatment of workers by employers, or the lack of worker organizations aimed at negotiating better work conditions.

symbol Something that represents something else.

symbolic interactionism A sociological perspective that emphasizes that human behaviour is influenced by definitions and meanings that are created and maintained through symbolic interaction with others.

technostress Stress that arises specifically from having too many tasks to perform simultaneously, while keeping up with perpetually changing demands to operate new and emerging technologies with ease.

telecommuting A work option in which workers complete all or part of their work at home with the use of information technology.

telemedicine Using information and communication technologies to deliver a wide range of health-care services, including diagnosis, treatment, prevention, health support and information, and education of health-care workers.

tertiary prevention (strategies) Prevention strategies that target families who have experienced family violence.

therapeutic communities Organizations in which 35 to 100 individuals reside for up to 15 months to abstain from drugs, develop marketable skills, and receive counselling.

transgendered individuals Persons who do not fit neatly into either the male or female category, or whose behaviour is not congruent with the rules and expectations for their sex in the society in which they live.

transnational crime Criminal activity that occurs across one or more international borders. Can include movement of exploitative images and text via the internet.

underclass A persistently poor and socially disadvantaged group that disproportionately experiences joblessness, welfare dependency, involvement in criminal activity, dysfunctional families, and low educational attainment.

underemployment Employment in a job that is underpaid; is not commensurate with one's skills, experience, or education; or involves working fewer hours than desired.

under-five mortality rate The rate of deaths among children under age five.

unemployment The unemployed are those who want and are able to work, but who have no work at present. For statistical purposes, Statistics Canada defines the unemployed in these ways: (1) as people who did not work in the labour market during the survey reference week (but may have done housework, etc.); (2) as people who were available for work and actively looked for it in the past four weeks; (3) as people laid off for 26 weeks or fewer and expecting to be recalled by their employer; or (4) as people who were waiting for new jobs to begin within four weeks.

values Social agreements about what is considered good and bad, right and wrong, desirable and undesirable.

variable Any measurable event, characteristic, or property that varies or is subject to change.

victimless crime An illegal activity, such as prostitution or drug use, that has no complaining party; also called "vice crime."

violent resistance Acts of violence by a partner that are committed in self-defence. Violent resistance is almost exclusively perpetrated by women against a male partner.

wealth The total assets of an individual or household minus liabilities

wealthfare Governmental policies and regulations that economically favour the wealthy.

work sectors (primary, secondary, tertiary) The division of the labour force into distinct categories (primary, secondary, and tertiary) based on the types of goods or services produced.

working poor Individuals who work in the labour force, but who nevertheless live in poverty.

NAME INDEX

SUBJECT INDEX

feminist perspective on, 375–376

future perspectives on, 399–400

global context of, 367

international promotion of, 363

queer theory perspective, 376–377

redistribution of resources for, 494–495

sociological theories of, 373–377

structural-functionalist perspective, 373–374

sustainable development and, 465–466

symbolic interactionist perspective, 375

work and unemployment problems, 377–389

Economic inequality, poverty and, 339–340

Economic institution, definition of, 367

Ecosystems, 438

Ecoterrorism, 461

Education, 282–284, 402–429

academic achievement levels, 419–420

alternative schools, 427–429

assistance for, 356–357

Canadian education system, 418–425

computer technology in, 426–427

conflict perspective, 407–408

critical theories of, 409

cross-cultural variations in, 402–404

cultural imperialism and, 407–408

as custodial care, 406–407

for disabled persons, 425

distance learning, 427

drinking patterns and, 85

dropout rates, 420–421

economic costs of, 403f, 423–425, 423f, 424f

educational inequality survey, 416t

environmental, 462

facilities problems, 425

feminist perspectives on, 410

future perspectives on, 429

gay youth policies and programs and, 312–314

gender issues in, 418

health and illness and, 52

home schooling, 428–429

income and, 222–227, 223t–226t

inequality of attainment in, 410–418

instruction in, 405

minority language education, 404

moral and interpersonal education, 426

multicultural education and, 416–417

nonmarital and teenage childbearing and impact on, 178

poverty and, 340–341, 346

for racial and ethnic minorities, 415–417

school experience and cultural sexism and, 240–241

self-fulfilling prophecy in, 409

social class and family background and, 412–414

socialization and, 405–406

sociological theories of, 405–410

special education, 402, 414–415

status-oriented classification in, 406, 406t

structural sexism and, 222–227, 223t–226t

structural-functionalist perspectives on, 405–407, 406t

student violence, 421–422, 421t

symbolic interactionist perspective, 408–409

teacher-student interactions, 408–409

trends and innovations in, 425–429

university participation rates, 413f

EGALE, 310–311

Egypt, marriage and family law in, 144

Elderly

abuse of, 165–166, 166f, 211–212

action policies for, 212–215

caregivers for, 209–210

crisis competence and, 191

demographics of, 199–203

health issues among, 207–208, 208f

Infantilization of, 190

living arrangements for, 208–210

myths and facts about, 188–189, 188t–189t

quality of life for, 212

retirement income and poverty of, 204–207

social problems of, 203–212

sociological theories concerning, 188–189

work and retirement for, 203–207

Electoral Franchise Act, 235

Emotional abuse, 149

child abuse, 162–164, 162f–163f

Emotional labour, 231

Empathy (*Verstehen*), symbolic interactionism and, 13

Employment equity, 246–247

Employment Equity Act, 246, 258

Employment insurance benefits, 355–356

Endogamy, 254, 254f, 255f

Energy consumption, 438, 438f

Environment

actions and strategies for improving, 460–462

activism and industry resistance, 460–462

air pollution and, 440–441, 440f

armed conflict and destruction of, 492–493

biodiversity and, 454–458, 456t–457t

border permeability and, 432

chemicals, carcinogens, and health problems, 449–452

conflict perspective on, 434–436

consumer behaviour modification and, 464

corporate role and, 461–462

cultural and social integration and, 432–433

cultural values and, 459–460

depletion of natural resources and, 439–440

disappearing livelihoods and, 455–458

ecofeminist perspective on, 436

ecosystems overview, 438–439

ecoterrorism, 461

education concerning, 462

energy use and, 438–439, 438f

environmental injustice and, 452–454

future perspectives on, 467–477

global warming and climate change, 444–446, 445f

globalization and, 432, 438–439, 438f

government policies and regulations, 465

"green" technology and, 462–465

industrialization and economic development and, 458–460

international cooperation and assistance, 466–467

land pollution, 446–448

light pollution, 455

nuclear and radioactive waste, 446–448, 447f

pesticides and, 448

populations growth and, 458

social causes of, 458–460

sociological theories on, 433–438

solid waste, 448

structural-functionalist perspectives on, 433–434

sustainability initiatives and, 465–466

symbolic interactionist perspective on, 436–438

transnational corporations and free trade agreements, 433

water pollution, 449

Environmental activism, 460–462

Environmental footprint, 434, 440

Environmental injustice, 452–454

Environmental racism, 452–454

illness and health care and, 55–56

Environmental refugees, 455

Epidemiological transition, 32

Epidemiologist, 31

Epidemiology, 31

Ethnic minorities

armed conflict and role of, 486

educational attainment among, 415–417

illness and health care among, 53–56

poverty and, 343–345, 344t

racial profiling of, 139

Ethnicity, 263–264

conflict perspective on, 271–272

crime and, 129–130

discrimination and, 278–282

diversity training on, 285

feminist perspective on, 273–274

future perspectives on, 285–286

global diversity and, 250–255

illness and health care and, 53–56

immigration and, 267–273

multicultural education concerning, 282–284

multiculturalism in Canada and, 255–267

patterns of group interaction, 252–255, 255f

political strategies concerning, 285

prejudice and racism and, 276–280

queer theory and, 274

social construction of, 250–252

sociological theories on, 271–275

UNICEF, 195–196, 390
Uniform Crime Reporting Survey, 106–107, 121–122, 121f
Unionization rates, 391–392, 392f
United Nations
  labour reforms and, 391–392
  peacekeeping activities of, 494–495
Universal Child Care Benefit, 397
Universal health care in Canada, 57–62
Unlocking the Iron Cage (Schwalbe), 245
"Uses of Poverty: The Poor Pay All, The" (Gans), 100

V

Values
  conflict over, 485–486
  culture and, 7
Variables, 21
Vice crimes, 123–124
Victim assistance programs, 134
Victimization
  of elderly, 211–212
  hate crimes, 279–280
  surveys on crime, 108–109
Victimless crime, 123–124
Violence
  action against, 133–140
  common couple violence, 159
  community factors in family violence, 168
  costs of, 131–133
  demographic patterns of, 126–131
  drug abuse and, 91–93
  against elderly, 211–212
  future perspectives on, 140
  gender inequality and, 244–245
  intimate partner violence and abuse, 154–158, 155f, 161t
  racial, ethnic and minority status and, 55
  social costs of, 132–133
  sociological theories of, 113–119
  statistical sources on, 108–112
  strategies for action against, 133–140

student violence, 421–422, 421t
  theory of justice and, 105–107
  against women, 121–122
  youth-related mortality patterns and, 33–35, 34t
Violence Against Women Survey (VAWS), 91–92
Violent offenses, 120–123, 120f, 121f
Violent resistance, 159
Visitation rights, 149
  homosexuality and, 309–310
Voting rights, gender issues and, 235–236

W

Wage gap, gender inequality and, 227–230, 233t
Wal-Mart, 437
War. *See also* Armed conflict
  images of, 481–483
  poverty and, 351–352
  social change and, 472–473
Wartime Election Act, 235
Water, armed conflict over, 485
Water pollution, 449
Wealth, 338–339, 339t
  environmental problems and, 435
  health care and illness and, 44
  poverty and, 338–345, 339t
  redistribution of, 494
Wealthfare, 335
Welfare
  government public assistance, 352–360
  myths and realities in Canada about, 358–360
  nonmarital and teenage childbearing and reform of, 178–179
Well-being, problems of, overview, 28, 30
Westrat Story: A Predictable Path to Disaster, The (Richard), 126
WikiLeaks, 473
Wind power, 463
Witness Protection Program Act, 138

Women
  age demographics among, 202
  armed conflict and fate of, 489–490
  in Canadian Armed Forces, 477
  crime and, 127, 127f
  with disabilities, violence against, 166
  education for, 410
  family structure and role of, 149–150
  global inequality status of, 217–219, 217f
  human rights for, 236–237
  intimate partner violence and abuse and, 154–158, 155f, 161t
  pay equity for, 362
  poverty levels of elderly women, 204–207
  property crime by, 127
  structural sexism and, 222–237
  union membership of, 392, 392f
  violence against, 121–122, 211–212
  in workforce, 385–386, 385t–386t, 394–398, 395f
Work. *See also* Labour
  action strategies for improvement of, 389–398
  age of information technology and, 371–373
  child labour and, 197–199, 377–380, 389–391
  dissatisfaction and alienation at, 382–385
  diversity training and, 285
  elderly and, 203–204
  employee survey concerning, 383–384
  employment equity and, 246–247
  families and impact of, 385–386, 385t–386t, 394–398, 395f
  future perspectives on, 399–400
  health and safety hazards of, 380–382, 381t, 393–394

homosexual discrimination and, 307–308
industrialization and postindustrialization and nature of, 369–371
marital division of, 242–244
poverty and, 345
primary, secondary, and tertiary sectors, 370–371
structural sexism and, 233–235, 234t
underemployment and, 387
unemployment problems and, 387–389
unionization and, 391–392, 392f
workforce development and job-creation programs, 392–393
Working poor, 345
Workplace and Employee Survey (WES), 383–384
Workplace Hazardous Materials Information System, 393–394
World Bank, 374
World Health Organization, poverty measurements, 320
World Trade Organization (WTO), 398, 433

Y

"You Should Have Stayed at Home" (documentary), 398
Young Offenders Act, 139
Youth
  crime and, 127–128, 128f, 133–134
  global context of, 185–186
  homophobia and transphobia among, 297–299
  legal issues for, 193–196, 195f
  poverty in Canada, 194t
  problems in Canada of, 193–199
  programs for, 133–134
  university participation rates for, 412–414, 416–417, 416t
Youth Criminal Justice Act, 128, 136–137, 139